When should I travel to get the best airfare?
Where do I go for answers to my travel questions?
What's the best and easiest way to plan and book my trip?

frommers.travelocity.com

Frommer's, the travel guide leader, has teamed up with **Travelocity.com**, the leader in online travel, to bring you an in-depth, easy-to-use resource designed to help you plan and book your trip online.

At **frommers.travelocity.com**, you'll find free online updates about your destination from the experts at Frommer's plus the outstanding travel planning and purchasing features of Travelocity.com. Travelocity.com provides reservations capabilities for 95 percent of all airline seats sold, more than 47,000 hotels, and over 50 car rental companies. In addition, Travelocity.com offers more than 2,000 exciting vacation and cruise packages. Travelocity.com puts you in complete control of your travel planning with these and other great features:

Expert travel guidance from Frommer's - over 150 writers reporting from around the world!

Best Fare Finder - an interactive calendar tells you when to travel to get the best airfare

Fare Watcher - we'll track airfare changes to your favorite destinations

Dream Maps - a mapping feature that suggests travel opportunities based on your budget

Shop Safe Guarantee - 24 hours a day / 7 days a week live customer service, and more!

Whether traveling on a tight budget, looking for a quick weekend getaway, or planning the trip of a lifetime, Frommer's guides and Travelocity.com will make your travel dreams a reality. You've bought the book, now book the trip!

Travelocity.com
A Sabre Company

Frommer's®

Other Great Guides for Your Trip:

Frommer's Italy

Frommer's Rome

Frommer's Tuscany & Umbria

Frommer's Northern Italy

Frommer's Portable Venice

Frommer's Portable Florence

Italy For Dummies

Frommer's Europe

Frommer's Europe from $70 a Day

Frommer's Gay & Lesbian Europe

Here's what the critics say about Frommer's:

"Amazingly easy to use. Very portable, very complete."
—*Booklist*

♦

"The only mainstream guide to list specific prices. The Walter Cronkite of guidebooks—with all that implies."
—*Travel & Leisure*

♦

"Complete, concise, and filled wih useful information."
—*New York Daily News*

♦

"Hotel information is close to encyclopedic."
—*Des Moines Sunday Register*

♦

"The best series for travelers who want one easy-to-use guide-book."
—*US Airways Magazine*

ITALY
FROM $70 A DAY
3RD EDITION

by Reid Bramblett & Lynn A. Levine

HUNGRY MINDS, INC.

New York, NY • Cleveland, OH • Indianapolis, IN

ABOUT THE AUTHORS

Reid Bramblett is the author of *Frommer's Tuscany & Umbria,* the upcoming *Frommer's Northern Italy* and *Portable Florence,* and *Europe For Dummies,* as well as a contributor to *Frommer's Europe from $70 a Day.* He also helped found guidebookwriters.com. When not on the road, he splits his time between his native Philadelphia and Columbia, Missouri.

Driven by the uncontrollable urge to tell people where to go, **Lynn A. Levine** has found an eminently rewarding niche writing travel guides. She's the author of the first edition of *Frommer's Turkey,* a contributor to *Frommer's Southeast Asia,* and a writer for several online travel sites. When not on airplanes, she splits her time among Florence, Italy; Manhattan; and the New Jersey 'burbs.

Published by:

HUNGRY MINDS, INC.

909 Third Ave.
New York, NY 10022

Find us online at **www.frommers.com**

ISBN 0-7645-6291-6
ISSN 1091-9430

Editor: Ron Boudreau
Special thanks to Lorraine Festa and Alexis Flippin
Production Editor: M. Faunette Johnston
Photo Editor: Richard Fox
Design by Michele Laseau
Cartographer: Elizabeth Puhl
Page creation by Hungry Minds Indianapolis Production Services

Front cover photo: Rome's Colosseum illuminated at night

SPECIAL SALES

For general information on Hungry Minds' products and services please call our Customer Care department at 800-762-2974. For reseller information, including discounts, bulk sales, customized editions, and premium sales, please call our Customer Care department at 800-434-3422.

Manufactured in the United States of America.

5   4   3   2   1

Contents

v

4 Florence: Birthplace of the Renaissance 166

by Reid Bramblett

5 Tuscany & Umbria 227

by Reid Bramblett

6 Bologna & Emilia-Romagna 306

by Reid Bramblett

List of Maps

AN INVITATION TO THE READER

In researching this book, we discovered many wonderful places—hotels, restaurants, shops, and more. We're sure you'll find others. Please tell us about them, so we can share the information with your fellow travelers in upcoming editions. If you were disappointed with a recommendation, we'd love to know that too. Please write to:

Frommer's Italy from $70 a Day, 3rd Edition
Hungry Minds, Inc.
909 Third Avenue
New York, NY 10022

AN ADDITIONAL NOTE

Please be advised that travel information is subject to change at any time—and this is especially true of prices. We therefore suggest that you write or call ahead for confirmation when making your travel plans. The authors, editors, and publisher cannot be held responsible for the experiences of readers while traveling. Your safety is important to us, however, so we encourage you to stay alert and be aware of your surroundings. Keep a close eye on cameras, purses, and wallets, all favorite targets of thieves and pickpockets.

WHAT THE SYMBOLS MEAN

✪ Frommer's Favorites

Our favorite places and experiences—outstanding for quality, value, or both.

The following abbreviations are used for credit cards:

AE	American Express	DISC	Discover
CB	Carte Blanche	MC	MasterCard
DC	Diners Club	V	Visa

FIND FROMMER'S ONLINE

www.frommers.com offers up-to-the-minute listings on almost 200 cities around the globe—including the latest bargains and candid, personal articles updated daily by Arthur Frommer himself. No other Web site offers such comprehensive and timely coverage of the world of travel.

The Best of Italy from $70 a Day

by Reid Bramblett & Lynn A. Levine

Two authors. One country. A myriad of experiences. Deciding what to see and do in Italy is not easy. Especially on a budget. Here, we've put our heads together and come up with the best of what this diverse country has to offer.

1 The Best Travel Experiences for Free (or Almost)

- **Enjoying Rome's Best Nighttime Panorama:** After a leisurely 3-hour dinner at a tiny trattoria in Rome's working-class neighborhood of Trastevere, stroll the cobblestone alleyways, then climb the Gianicolo hill for a moonlit panorama of the Eternal City. See chapter 3.

- **Listening to the Vespers in San Miniato** (Florence): This is one of the few places left in Italy where Gregorian chant is still sung. Here, in one of Florence's oldest churches, late-afternoon vespers transport you back to the lost centuries of the hilltop Romanesque church's 11th-century origins. See chapter 4.

- **Biking Through the Town and on the Walls of Ferrara:** For spectacular views, bike along the wide paths on Ferrara's medieval walls, which encircle the city with an aerie of greenery. Many hotels offer guests free use of bicycles. See chapter 6.

- **Taking a *Vaporetto* Ride on the Grand Canal** (Venice): For a fraction of the cost of a gondola ride, the no. 1 *vaporetto* **(motor launch)** plies the Grand Canal, past hundreds of Gothic and Byzantine palazzi redolent of the days when Venice was a powerful and wealthy maritime republic. Angle for a seat on the open-air deck up front. See chapter 7.

- **Cruising Lake Como** (Lake District): Board a lake steamer for the pleasant trip from Bellagio to other picturesque small villages on the section of the lake known as the Centro Lago. To the north, the lake is backed by snowcapped Alps, while the shorelines are lush with verdant gardens. As the steamer heads from one port to another, ochre- and pastel-colored villages will beckon you to disembark and explore their ancient streets and piazze—a good reason to purchase a day pass. See chapter 9.

- **Climbing Up the Flanks of the Matterhorn in the Valle d'Aosta:** An excellent trail leads from Cervina-Breuil up the flank of this impressive mountain. A moderately strenuous uphill trek of 90 minutes will get you to the breathtaking Lac du Goillet, and from there, it's another 90 minutes to the Colle Superiore delle Cime Bianche, a plateau with heart-stopping views. See chapter 10.

- **Walking in the Cinque Terre** (Italian Riviera): While away your time in the Cinque Terre by strolling from one lovely village to another along the Mediterranean on trails with views that'll take your breath away. See chapter 11.
- **Exploring the Land of the *Trulli*** (Apulia): The Valle d'Itria is a lush, surreal landscape carpeted with vineyards and speckled with one of Europe's oddest forms of vernacular architecture: the *trulli,* pointy whitewashed houses constructed without mortar and roofed by a cone of dark stones stacked in concentric circles. The capital of the region is Alberobello, a UNESCO World Heritage town made up of over 1,000 *trulli*—you can even spend the night in one (see "The Best Hotel Deals," below). See chapter 12.
- **Driving the Magnificent Amalfi Coast *Once:*** The 30-mile ride down the Amalfi Drive is one of the most awe-inspiring, character-building, and hair-raising experiences on record. This two-lane road clings sometimes hundreds of feet up the cliff side, twisting and plunging past verdant gorges, tiny fishing villages, posh resort towns, and sparkling isolated beaches washed by bright azure waters. SITA buses make the winding and wonderful journey from Sorrento to Amalfi for a mere two bucks. See chapter 12.
- **Sailing the Amalfi Coast Through the Eyes of Anthony Minghella** (Ischia): In *The Talented Mr. Ripley,* Ischia's Castello Aragonese and the magnificent waters served as a backdrop for the unspoiled Italian coastal experience of a bygone era. For $15 per person, the island's cooperative water taxi will take you on a tour that circles this stunning island. When you're done, a dip in a thermal pool awaits. See chapter 12.
- **Taking a Sunset Picnic to the Valley of the Temples** (Agrigento, Sicily): The setting is humbling, the view inspiring, and, propped up against an ancient column, the experience is unparalleled. The setting sun bathes the temples in a mystical warm glow, then, in succession, the floodlights illuminate the valley's temples. Entrance to the archaeological site is free. See chapter 13.

2 The Best Bargain Destinations

- **Florence:** Meander in and out of the centuries of the Middle Ages and Renaissance when Florence was one of the richest, most vibrant and aesthetic cities in Western civilization. If you secure your modestly priced hotel in advance, you'll find that one of Italy's most expensive cities needn't break your budget. Choose your trattorie carefully, avoid the shopping temptations (or bargain hard in Italy's best outdoor leather market), wander its streets, and savor a priceless vacation that can be orchestrated for not a lot of lire. See chapter 4.
- **Chianti** (Tuscany): The very heartland of Tuscany stretches between Florence and Siena. Here the serendipity of lazy vineyard-hopping drives and spontaneous wine-tasting stops is heightened by the region's visually stunning landscape. Staring is free on the old Chiantigiana road, which links a string of picturesque wine towns that dot a history-rich area of forested hills, castles, stone farmhouses–turned–B&Bs, and wine-producing estates. See chapter 5.
- **Ferrara** (Emilia-Romagna): This elegant city of rose-colored brick is much less expensive than nearby Bologna or Parma. You can take in all the Renaissance art and architecture with a pass that provides discount admission to some of the best

museums in town. It's not expensive to get around either—some hotels provide free bicycles, or you can rent one for $6 a day. See chapter 6.

- **Venice:** A magnificent, and never-ending stage set, Venice is one of Italy's most expensive destinations, *unless* you go in the off-season when it's reclaimed by the Venetians during its empty winter months, or pick one of our recommended budget gems. Off season, even the pricier hotels can cost half as much, the local residents are less harried, and the fog-cloaked corners of Venice promise mystery and mystique and million-dollar memories, even for the frugal traveler. See chapter 7.

- **Piemonte Wine Country:** Getting and tasting Asti Spumante, Barbaresco, and Barolo wines at at-the-source prices is reason enough to call this area a bargain destination. Strolling through the medieval and Renaissance towns that rise from the vineyards, and finding low-country accommodations doesn't hurt either. See chapter 10.

- **Cinque Terre** (Italian Riviera): You won't find a more beautiful coastline than the Cinque Terre, lined with olive groves, vineyards, villages set above the sea, and hidden coves. The best part is that you can find low-cost accommodations (doubles run about $40 a night), excellent, inexpensive food, beaches, and free walking trails. See chapter 11.

- **Lecce** (Apulia): Intrepid travelers who make it all the way down into the stiletto tip of the heel on Italy's boot are often surprised to discover such a thriving city, and a stage set for some of Italy's prettiest and most unique baroque architecture. Lecce's cafes serve delectable pastries, its artisan studios carry on the city's wonderful papier-mâché tradition, and since it's so out-of-the-way, prices remain rock bottom. See chapter 12.

- **Ischia** (Campania): Capri's sibling island demurely stands alone. Rather than the soaring cliffs of Capri, Ischia rises out of the Bay of Naples with slightly less drama, but plenty of charm. As yet undiscovered by the tourist hordes, Ischia's prices are still appealing, and the island's beaches and thermal "gardens" remain unspoiled by the march of advancement. See chapter 12.

- **Ostuni** (Apulia): Whitewashed in a fresh coat of paint yearly, Ostuni, also known as the "White City," is a marvelous medieval city that supports daily local life without compromising the history within the ancient walls. Built on the crest of a hill, away from its alluring coastline—the primary attraction for weekenders— the treasures of the old city remain and prices stay much lower than anywhere else along the coastline that connects Bari with Brindisi. See chapter 12.

- **Cefalù** (Sicily): A Sicilian resort without the high price tag, Cefalù makes up for a lack of sightseeing options in characteristic Saracen alleys and a glorious sunset vista of the portside houses. Cefalù has a sweeping bay ideal for beachgoers and boasts a handful of cheap and charming fringe hotels with access to private rocky coves hidden behind stunning *faraglioni* (cliffs). See chapter 13.

3 The Best Small Towns

- **Lucca** (Tuscany): Protected from the new millennium within its remarkable swath of Renaissance ramparts (said to be among the best preserved in Europe), Lucca evokes the charm of an elegant small town. Within these historic parameters, local matrons tool around on bicycles (everyone does—Lucca is like a quaint hill town without the hill), young mothers with strollers walk the rampart's promenade beneath the shade of centuries-old plane trees, and exuberant examples of Pisan-Romanesque architecture draw visitors to the Duomo and

San Michele in Foro. Hometown boy Puccini would have no problem recognizing the city he always held close to his music-filled heart. See chapter 5.

- **Gubbio** (Umbria): This proud, austere, no-nonsense mountain town has only recently figured on the maps of the intrepid off-the-beaten-path trekkers. Blessedly hard to get to, Gubbio has slumbered through the centuries and today offers one of the country's best-preserved scenarios of medieval architecture and ambience. Built into the side of the forest-clad Monte Igino, a funicular up to the Basilica of its beloved patron, St. Ubaldo, provides stunning panorama and a chance to consider the centuries-old serenity of the time-locked outpost that poet Gabriele D'Annunzio called the "City of Silence." See chapter 5.

- **Brixen** (South Tyrol): It's hard to believe that this quaint town was the center of a large ecclesiastical principality for almost 800 years. It is rich in history and natural beauty, and you can explore vineyards, mountains, and impressive museums and monuments, as well as amble through the town's pastel-colored houses and narrow cobblestone streets. See chapter 8.

- **Bellagio** (Lake District): The prettiest of all the towns in Italy's lake country, Bellagio was peaceful enough for Franz Liszt to use it as a retreat, and since it hasn't been inundated with throngs of tourists since, it could work for you, too. See chapter 9.

- **Ravello** (Campania): The Amalfi Coast could be described as a parody of itself, particularly in August, but only 3 miles up in the hills is a lush retreat worlds away from the tourist crush below. Perched at the lip of the verdant Valley of the Dragon, the quiet beauty and sculpted gardens of Ravello provide the perfect venue for public concerts throughout the year, tempting newcomers to explore the scenery that inspired Wagner's *Parsifal*. See chapter 12.

- **Alberobello** (Apulia): The de-facto capital of the "Land of the *Trulli*"—those cone-topped houses that dot the entire Itria Valley—this fairytale town has even been declared a national monument. But far from becoming slaves to the inevitable tourist trade, the citizens of this quiet town are remarkable for their warmth and hospitality. Ten minutes in this town and you'll probably be booked through your stay for dinners in several private homes. See chapter 12.

- **Ostuni** (Salento, Apulia): It's easy for the uninformed to bypass this enchanting little town on the way through to the "major" stops in Apulia. So be informed: Ostuni is so much more than a day at the beach—an afternoon spent walking through the whitewashed medieval alleyways of the "White City" makes for serious poetry. See chapter 12.

- **Erice** (Sicily): Sitting on a clifftop that soars well above the cloud line, Erice is a medieval town that frequently meets thick tufts of fog that engulf the cobbled streets in a mysterious and romantic mist. This sacred city was established as a religious center in honor of the Earth goddess centuries before the Greeks and later the Romans showed up and renamed her Venus. See chapter 13.

4 The Best Cathedrals

- **Basilica di San Pietro** (Rome): A monument not only to Christendom but to the Renaissance and Baroque eras, this cathedral was designed by Bramante, decorated by Bernini, and crowned with a dome by Michelangelo. Within its walls are some of the world's most renowned treasures: *St. Peter* by Arnolfo di Cambio and Michelangelo's haunting *Pietà*, a masterpiece representation in marble of Christ in the arms of Mary at the deposition, carved when the artist was only 19 years old. If that's not humbling, then a glimpse of the pope will be. See chapter 3.

- **Pantheon** (Rome): This consecrated church is more like a cathedral to architecture, with its perfect hemispheric dome and flawless proportions. Expertly engineered by Emperor Hadrian in the A.D. 2nd century, the Pantheon survived the test of time, until Pope Urban VIII had the bronze tiles of the portico melted down to make the baldicchino for St. Peter's and 80 cannons. Today, you can pay your respects to genius, as well as to Raphael, whose tomb resides within. See chapter 3.
- **Duomo (Cathedral of Santa Maria del Fiore)** (Florence): The red-tiled dome of Florence's magnificent Duomo has dominated the skyline for 5 centuries. In its day, it was the largest unsupported dome in the world, dwarfing the structures of ancient Greece and Rome. In true Renaissance style, it was and still is considered a major architectural feat and was the high point of architect Filippo Brunelleschi's illustrious career. In 1996, an extensive and elaborate 15-year restoration was finally completed on the colorful 16th-century frescoes covering the inside of the cupola and depicting the world's largest painting of the *Last Judgment*. See chapter 4.
- **Duomo** (Siena, Tuscany): Begun in 1196, this black-and-white marble striped cathedral sits atop Siena's highest hill, and is one of the most beautiful and ambitious Gothic churches in Italy. Its exterior's extravagant zebra-striped marble bands borrowed from Pisan-Lucchese architecture continue indoors. Masterpieces here include a priceless pavement of masterful mosaics, 56 etched and inlaid marble panels created by more than 40 artisans; the octagonal pulpit, carved by master Tuscan sculptor Nicola Pisano; and the lavish Libreria Piccolomini, frescoed by Pinturicchio in the late 15th century with the life of the Siena-born Pope Pius II, quintessential Renaissance man and humanist, and still housed with that Pope's important illuminated manuscript collection. See chapter 5.
- **Duomo** (Orvieto, Umbria): Begun in 1290, and with a bold, beautiful, and intricately ornamented facade that stands out among Italy's Gothic masterpieces, Orvieto's Duomo is also known for one of the greatest fresco cycles of the Renaissance in its Chapel of San Brizio. The cycle, begun by Fra Angelico and completed by Luca Signorelli, depicts in vivid detail the *Last Judgment,* one that was said to have influenced Michelangelo in his own interpretation for the Sistine Chapel. See chapter 5.
- **Duomo** (Parma): Built in the 12th century, Parma's Duomo is one of the great achievements of Italian Romanesque architecture. The true star of the show however is Correggio's great masterpiece, his dramatic *Assumption of the Virgin,* which adorns the octagonal cupola. See chapter 6.
- **Basilica di San Marco** (Venice): Surely the most exotic and Eastern of the Western world's Christian churches, the onion-domed and mosaic-covered San Marco took much of its inspiration from ancient Constantinople's Hagia Sophia. Somewhere inside the mysterious candlelit cavern of the 1,000-year-old church, which began as the private chapel of the governing doges, are the remains of St. Mark, revered patron saint of Venice's ancient maritime republic. His "mascot," the winged lion, is linked to the city as closely as the "quadriga," the four ancient magnificent chariot horses that decorate the open loggia of St. Mark's Basilica overlooking one of the world's great squares. See chapter 7.
- **Duomo** (Milan, Lombardy): It took 5 centuries to build this magnificent Gothic cathedral—the fourth largest church in the world. It's marked by 135 marble spires, a stunning triangular facade, and some 3,400 statues flanking the massive but airy, almost fanciful exterior. The interior, lit by brilliant stained-glass

windows, is more serene. Lord Tennyson rapturously wrote about the view of the Alps from the roof. See chapter 9.

- **Cattedrale di Monreale** (Sicily): Nothing short of jaw-dropping, this awesome church stands as a testament to the craftsmanship of imported Greek artisans from Byzantium, who carpeted the interior with 68,472 square feet of glittering mosaics. In the cathedral's serene cloisters, you can while away the hours contemplating the hundreds of one-of-a kind, twisted and inlaid minicolumns. If you see anything in Sicily, make it Monreale. See chapter 13.

5 The Best Museums

- **Musei Vaticani** (Rome): Centuries of collections and "indulgences" had to come to something: one of the wealthiest collections of art and historic artifacts in the world. The Vatican Museum's origins are humble, beginning in 1503 with Pope Julius II della Rovere's placement of a statue of Apollo in the courtyard of the Belvedere Palace and culminating in a showpiece of 12 galleries and papal apartments filled with a veritable catalogue of civilization. There's everything from the Raphael Rooms, with their *School of Athens* fresco to Michelangelo's incomparable Sistine Chapel, with its fingers-almost-touching depiction of *God Creating Adam.* In between, you'll find that statue of Apollo, plus a surfeit of Greek and Roman statues, medieval tapestries, illuminated manuscripts, ancient Egyptian and Chinese art, Etruscan artifacts, and a painting gallery covering everyone from Giotto and Leonardo to Caravaggio's *Deposition* and Raphael's final work, the magnificent *Transfiguration.* See chapter 3.
- **Galleria Borghese** (Rome): Never has such a small space packed such an amazing punch: Reopened after a 14-year restoration, the Galleria Borghese elicits an audible "wow" at every step. The Pinacoteca is a shrine to Renaissance painting, with works by Andrea del Sarto, Girlandaio, Pinturicchio, Fra' Bartolomeo, and Lorenzo di Credi. Raphael makes an entrance with his *Deposition,* and Botticelli is represented by his *Madonna col Bambino e San Giovannino,* while Caravaggio's works simply provide a tease for his tour de force in the Sculpture Gallery. Here, along with some of Caravaggio's most poignant works, is a collection of marble masterpieces by Gianlorenzo Bernini, including the *Rape of Persephone, Apollo and Daphne,* and the lifelike *Pauline Bonaparte as Venus.* See chapter 3.
- **Villa Giulia** (Rome): This is the single greatest museum devoted to the ancient, pre-Roman Etruscan culture. These guys left behind painted vases and some beautiful funerary art, including a terra-cotta sarcophagus lid bearing life-sized— and remarkably lifelike—full-body portraits of a husband and wife, smiling enigmatically and wearing their finest togas, sitting back to enjoy one final, eternal feast together. See chapter 3.
- **Museo Nazionale Romano** (Rome): After languishing behind the closed doors of the Baths of Diocletian for years, the most extensive and comprehensive collections of Roman art anywhere in the world are finally open to public viewing, housed in four of the city's top museums: Palazzo Altemps, Palazzo Massimo alle Terme, the Aula Ottagona, and the restored Baths of Diocletian. This reorganization of exhibitions allows you to appreciate not only an astounding collection of sculpture, mosaics, coinage and jewelry, and never-before-seen frescoes, but also the glorious spaces, ancient and modern, in which they reside. See chapter 3.
- **Galleria degli Uffizi** (Florence): When the Medici were the affluent men about town, this was the headquarters of the Duchy of Tuscany. For today's visitor, it is the riverside repository of the greatest collection of Renaissance paintings in the

world—Giotto's *Maestà,* Botticelli's *Birth of Venus* and *Allegory of Spring,* Michelangelo's *Holy Family*—bequeathed to Florence with the understanding that it would never leave the city of the Medici, nor these hallowed walls. The peculiar "Stendhal's Syndrome," the malaise of vertigo from the sheer overload of unparalleled culture, most likely was first experienced here. See chapter 4.

- **Museo Nazionale del Bargello** (Florence): The harsh, fortresslike Bargello, incarnated as the constable's headquarters and local prison among other things, is to Renaissance sculpture what the Uffizi is to Renaissance painting. Within this cavernous medieval shell lies a handsomely displayed collection without equal in Italy, with early works by Michelangelo and magnificent pieces by the early Renaissance master Donatello. See chapter 4.

- **Galleria dell'Accademia** (Florence): Michelangelo's *David,* one of the world's most recognized statues, looms in stark perfection beneath the rotunda of the main room built exclusively for its display when it was moved here from the Piazza Signoria for safekeeping. After standing in awe before its magnificence, many visitors leave, drained, without seeing the museum's other Michelangelos, particularly four never-finished *Prisoners* (or *Slaves*) struggling magnificently to free themselves from within. See chapter 4.

- **Palazzo Pitti's Galleria Palatina** (Florence): The former residence of the Medici, the enormous Palazzo Pitti is home to seven museums, the largest collection of galleries in Florence under one roof. The Galleria Palatina section, 26 art-filled rooms on the first floor of the palace, is the star attraction, home to one of the finest collections of Italian Renaissance and Baroque masters in Europe, and is the most important in Florence after the Uffizi's. The art of the 16th century is the forte of the Palatina, in particular that of Raphael and his many Madonnas. The museum's treasures also include a large collection of works by Andrea del Sarto, Fra' Bartolomeo, some superb works by Rubens, canvases by Tintoretto, Veronese, Caravaggio, and a number of stunning portraits by Titian. See chapter 4.

- **Galleria dell'Accademia** (Venice): The glory that was Venice lives on in the Accademia, the definitive treasure house of Venetian painting and one of Europe's great museums. Exhibited chronologically from the 13th through the 18th centuries, there is said to be no one hallmark masterpiece in this collection; rather, this is an outstanding and comprehensive showcase of works by all the great master painters of Venice—Veronese, Tintoretto, Titian—the largest such collection in the world. Most of all, though, the works open a window onto the Venice of 500 years ago. Indeed, you'll see in the canvases how little Venice, perhaps least of any city in Europe, has changed over the centuries. See chapter 7.

- **Collezione Peggy Guggenheim** (Venice): Considered to be one of the most comprehensive and important collections of modern art in the world, this collection of painting and sculpture was assembled by eccentric and eclectic American expatriate Peggy Guggenheim in her own home. She did an excellent job of it with particular strengths in Cubism, European Abstraction, Surrealism, and Abstract Expressionism since about 1910. See chapter 7.

- **Museo Archeologico** (Naples): If you've come all this way just to pass through Naples on your way to Pompeii, you're missing half the show. Anything that hadn't already been carted off from the ruins by looters is housed here, including a special exhibit of erotic art in the *Gabinetto Segreto,* or Secret Chamber. Not to be overshadowed is an extensive collection of ancient sculptural masterpieces, including the *Farnese Bull,* a 13-foot-high ancient narration carved out of one gargantuan block of marble. See chapter 12.

6   The Best Ancient Ruins

- **Foro Romano** (Rome): This poetic collection of architectural detritus marks the spot where an empire ruled the ancient civilized world. You can explore the Roman Forum in an hour or two, but whether or not you pack a picnic lunch or simply gaze down over the zone from street level, the Forum's allure will call you back. See chapter 3.

- **Colosseo** (Rome): A well-known symbol of the Eternal City, the Colosseum for many *is* Rome. That's a heavy responsibility to bear, but this broken yet enduring structure succeeds admirably. Built over Nero's private lake (see Domus Aurea, below), the arena accommodated up to 50,000 Romans who came for bloody gladiator matches and wild beast massacres. Practically speaking, it's the largest amphitheater in the world, and a study for the classical orders of architecture. See chapter 3.

- **Domus Aurea** (Rome): After 20 years of study and excavations, The Domus Aurea, or "Golden House," is finally open to the public, revealing frequently mind-blowing testament to how the richer half lived. No expense was spared in the construction of this 150-room palace that surveyed four of Rome's hills and included Nero's private lake, hunting grounds, pastures, and vineyard. Completely swathed in gold, jewels, and works of art, Domus Aurea is a brilliant masterwork of megalomania in ancient Rome. See chapter 3.

- **Arena di Verona** (Verona): One of the best preserved Roman amphitheaters in the world and the best known in Italy after Rome's Colosseum, the elliptical Arena was built of a slightly pinkish marble around the year A.D. 100 and stands in the middle of town in the Piazza Brà. Its perfect acoustics have survived the millennia and make it one of the wonders of the ancient world and one of the most fascinating venues today for live moonlit performances (opera here is fantastic), conducted without microphones. See chapter 8.

- **Pompeii and Herculaneum** (Campania): One of the most tragic events in recorded history occurred in A.D. 79, when Mt. Vesuvius blew its top 12 miles into the air, claimed the lives of thousands, and annihilated two thriving and prosperous cities. In Pompeii, it was a high speed tidal wave of volcanic ash and superheated gases that violently hurled itself upon the city; in Herculaneum, it was a steady flow of scalding mud that scorched the victims' bodies down to the bone. The quick, devastating burials, however, did preserve two ancient cities, with villas, shops, public baths, and brothels uncovered much as they were almost 2,000 years ago. See chapter 12.

- **Greek Temples at Paestum** (Campania): Who'd expect to see such awesome ancient Greek temples in the middle of mozzarella country? Only an hour south of Naples stands the 9th-century B.C. Greek colony of Paestum, founded when *Magna Graecia* extended into Southern Italy. Actually, Paestum has something even Greece can't claim: the only known examples of ancient Greek fresco in the world. See chapter 12.

- **Greek Temples of Sicily** (Segesta, Selinunte, and Agrigento): These shockingly poignant remnants left by Greek colonies in the age of *Magna Graecia,* or the "Greater Greece," reside in some of the most spectacular settings in Sicily. The temple of **Segesta** glows in tones of warm gold, sitting on the edge of a deep ravine surrounded by rolling hills covered with jasmine and aloe. **Selinunte** retains much of its original mystery with an anonymous jumble of re-erected temples, stretched out over two hills that flow gracefully into the Mediterranean. Settled along a manmade ridge below the modern city of **Agrigento** is the Valley of the Temples, a string of Doric temples awash in olive groves and pink almond blossoms in spring. One of these buildings, the exquisite Temple of Concord, ranks as one of the two best-preserved Greek temples on earth. See chapter 13.

- **Villa Romana del Casale at Piazza Armerina** (Sicily): In the little hamlet of Casale outside of the town of Piazza Armerina lies the most extensive, intact, and colorful ancient mosaics in all of the Roman world. The grounds of the villa, probably built as a hunting lodge for Emperor Maximus, include a peristyled main house, a triclinium, a bath complex, and a vast number of rooms for entertaining and regurgitating. With the stables and kitchen yet to be excavated, the 37,800 square feet of mosaics is just the tip of the iceberg. See chapter 13.

7 The Best Wine-Tasting Experiences

- **Montalcino and Montepulciano** (southern Tuscany): This less-trod area south of Siena is sacred ground to wine connoisseurs for its unsurpassed **Brunello di Montalcino** and **Vino Nobile di Montepulciano.** Both of the picturesque hill towns have enotecas and cantinas right in town; Montalcino's mighty Medici fortress has been reincarnated as a rustic wine bar. Those with a rental car can head out into the highly scenic countryside outside of Montalcino to the Fattoria Barbi, one of the area's most respected wine-producing estates, for a tasting and country-style dinner, even an overnight stay. See chapter 5.
- **Enoteca Italiana Permanente** (Siena, Tuscany): Siena sits to the south of the Chianti-designated area, so there could be no better setting to showcase Italy's timeless wine culture. Set within the massive military fortress built by Cosimo dei Medici in 1560, this wine-tasting bar provides a wide selection. The emphasis is on Tuscan wines—many made in the fabled Chianti area of Siena's backyard—but this enoteca is a national concern owned and operated by the government to support the Italian wine tradition. See chapter 5.
- **Torgiano** (Umbria): Ten miles to Perugia's southeast lies the small town of Torgiano, whose unique wine museum (and wonderful retail enoteca and osteria next door) is a must-do pilgrimage for serious oenophiles. With twenty well-organized, well-lit rooms that trace every aspect of viticulture, this is the only museum of its kind—unexpectedly interesting and certainly the most attractive—in Italy. The museum is owned by the Lungarotti family, Umbria's most noted wine producers and one of the most celebrated in the Italian wine scene. See chapter 5.
- **Verona** (Veneto): The epicenter of the region's important viticulture (Veneto produces more DOC wine than any other region in Italy), Verona hosts the annual VinItaly wine fair held every April, a highly prestigious event in the global wine world. A number of authentic old-time wine bars still populate the medieval back streets of the fair city of Romeo and Juliet fame. First opened in 1890, the **Bottega del Vino** boasts a wine cellar holding an unmatched 80,000-bottle selection. Belly up to the old oak bar and sample from five dozen good-to-excellent wines for sale by the glass, particularly the Veronese trio of bardolino and valpolicello (reds) and soave (white). **Masi** is one of the most respected producers, one of many in the Verona hills, whose cantinas are open to the public for wine-tasting visits. See chapter 8.
- **Barolo** (Piemonte Wine Country): This romantic town is full of shops selling the village's rich red wines, held by many to be the most complex, powerful reds in Italy. The highlight is the **Castello di Barolo,** which houses a wine museum and enoteca in its cavernous cellars. See chapter 10.

- **Monterosso** (Italian Riviera): At the **Enoteca Internazionale** in this small, charming town in the Cinque Terre, you can taste local wines from the vineyards that cling to the nearby cliffs. See chapter 11.

8 The Best Festivals

- **Rome's Festa de' Noiantri:** Rome's archetypal working-class neighborhood of Trastevere—across the Tiber River from the rest of the city, with its own dialect and proud folk and literary traditions—celebrates its uniqueness in mid-July in the "Feast of We Others," a week of communal banqueting at long tables set on the cobblestones of its alleyways, concerts and plays in the piazza, and a street fair on the main drag. See chapter 3.
- **Easter and Holy Week:** In **Rome,** the pope leads a stations-of-the-cross procession around the Colosseum on Good Friday, and tosses a blessing out his Vatican window on Easter Sunday to everyone in Piazza San Pietro below. Throughout **southern Italy and Sicily,** Easter Week brings out Spanish-influenced processions of hooded confraternity members walking before floats of both Passion scenes and of the Madonna dressed in rich robes and trailing streamers of pinned-together 10,000L bills. There are especially fine processions in **Taranto,** Apulia, and **Trapani,** Sicily. See chapters 3, 12, and 13.
- **Carnevale, Venice** (Veneto) **and Viareggio** (Tuscany): Venice's Carnevale is the best known of Italy's pre-Lenten celebrations. All of Venice becomes a stage and everyone is on it. A salute to the final years of the Serene Republic when unbridled gambling and gamboling went on for months before Shrove Tuesday, it is now confined to two event-packed weeks when the piazzas and streets are jammed with historical costumes and theatrical getups that are nothing short of astounding. Music concerts from Baroque to salsa fill every imaginable venue in town, most of them free-of-charge, with a wild crescendo of private masked balls and a night of brilliant fireworks illuminating the Grand Canal.

    Tuscany's seaside resort of **Viareggio** hosts the runner-up to Venice, with enormous floats of mostly political figures of the moment that parade through the crowds for the four Sundays of Lent. If anyone is in costume, they're usually under 10 and of the Zorro and cowboy set. See chapters 5 and 7.
- **Il Palio** (Siena): In July and August, this bareback, breakneck horse race between the ancient divisions of Siena's 17 *contrade* (neighborhoods) turns the dirt-packed Piazza del Campo into an emotional sea of local fans and bewildered tourists who can't believe what they're seeing. The costumed pageantry before the two annual Palios and the victory and consolation feasts that take place afterward are just as entrancing. Tickets for the grandstands are pretty much impossible to get, but join the 100,000 crazies who fill the middle of the Campo for an experience you'll never forget. See chapter 5.
- **Giostra del Saracino** (Arezzo, Tuscany): The quirkily lopsided Piazza Grande is the timeless backdrop for the most entertaining of Italy's many jousting festivals in August and September. Here, the target for the medieval tilting tournament is an "infidel" automaton that, when hit by a lance, hits back. The influence of Tuscan-born Franco Zeffirelli can be seen in the fascinating costumes of the elaborate procession that wends through the town's evocative medieval streets. See chapter 5.
- **Spoleto Festival** (Umbria): Formerly known as the Festival of Two Worlds, this annual June event is a world-class bash celebrating music, dance, and theater. It has long enticed major names, troupes, and orchestras from all corners of the

globe, with an arts-savvy audience to match. The ancient hill town offers a few unique venues such as an ancient Roman amphitheater and its extremely picturesque Piazza del Duomo. See chapter 5.

- **Corso dei Ceri** (Gubbio, Umbria): On May 15, three huge wooden towers called *ceri* (candles), weighing 880 pounds each, are raced around town by changing teams of burly young men in a fevered atmosphere akin to Pamplona's Running of the Bulls. This unique holiday is one of Italy's most ancient celebrations, loaded with pagan implications. Each tower is topped by the small statue of a saint, one of them the town's beloved 12th-century patron, St. Ubaldo, who always wins. See chapter 5.
- **Miracolo di San Gennaro** (Naples): St. Janarius was beheaded in the 4th century, but his followers preserved the head and two vials of his blood. Now, whenever those glass vials are brought near the skull, the coagulated blood in them liquefies and begins to boil in a standing miracle renowned the world over—even in New York City, southern Italian immigrants honor San Gennaro in their biggest annual street festival. Back home in Naples, the liquefaction miracle is repeated several times throughout the year for the benefit of the devout, who attend the Byzantine masses held in the saint's honor in order to line up and kiss the vials for good luck. They honor the saint thusly on the first Saturday of May, September 19, and December 16. See chapter 12.

9 The Best Hotel Deals

- **Coronet** (Rome; ☎ **06-679-0653**): Taking up a portion of the Doria Pamphili family's aristocratic palazzo, the Coronet's got antiques, high ceilings, and the baronial atmosphere of forgotten centuries. Doubles run as low as $80. See chapter 3.
- **Navona** (Rome; ☎ **06-6821-1391**): It's always a safe bet to stay in a hotel in the immediate wake of renovations, but when the owner is the architect overseeing the project, you'd better get on the phone right now and make your reservations. The rooms at the Navona are not only pristine, tasteful, and decorated with limited-edition artworks, they are located a stone's throw from the Baroque wonders of Piazza Navona and right in the center of the historic quarter. Doubles begin at $95. See chapter 3.
- **Firenze** (Florence; ☎ **055-268-301**): A former student crash pad, and today a renovated two-star choice that appeals to all age levels, the Firenze is ideally situated between the Duomo and the Piazza della Signoria. A fresh overall look, great bathrooms for this price range, and an address that beats the best put this hotel on every insider's short list. But don't expect a staff that's too professional or accommodating or you'll leave disappointed. Starting at $75 for a double with bathroom, this is one of *centro storico's* best values. See chapter 4.
- **Piccolo Hotel Puccini** (Lucca, Tuscany; ☎ **0583-55-421**): If you're planning a stay in Lucca, Giacomo Puccini's hometown, look no further than this charming three-star hotel in a 15th-century palazzo in front of the building where the great composer was born. Some of the hotel rooms overlook the small piazza and its bronze statue of Puccini. Paolo and Raffaella, the young and enthusiastic couple who run the place, have lightened and brightened it up and do everything to make this a perfect choice for those who appreciate tasteful attention and discreet professionalism. Piazza San Michele, one of Lucca's loveliest squares, is two steps away. Doubles start at $73. See chapter 5.

- **Piccolo Hotel Etruria** (Siena, Tuscany; ☎ **0577-288-088**): This recently refurbished hotel is lovely enough to be your base in Tuscany—at $65 for a double, it's too great a find to be used as a mere one-night stop. The proud Fattorini family oversaw every painstaking detail in its recent renovation, and the taste and quality level is something one usually finds in hotels at thrice the cost. See chapter 5.
- **B&B Locanda Borgonuovo** (Ferrara, Emilia-Romagna; ☎ **0532-211-100**): Outstanding hospitality and charm is the name of the game here. Starting at $80, you can stay on a medieval palazzo in guest rooms decorated with an eclectic mix of antiques. The breakfasts served in the garden are feasts. See chapter 6.
- **Cappello** (Ravenna, Emilia-Romagna; ☎ **0544-219-813**): This hotel is a true deal considering what you get for $100 per double. The best rooms have been carved out of grand salons and are enormous; the bathrooms are clad in marble or highly polished hardwoods, with luxurious stall showers and tubs, and, like the bedrooms, lit with Venetian glass fixtures. See chapter 6.
- **La Cascina del Monastero** (La Morra, Piedmont Wine Country; ☎ **0173-509-245**): What better way to spend your time in the wine country than to stay at a bed and breakfast at a farm that bottles wine and harvests fruit? Housed in a converted old and charismatic farm building, the rooms have exposed timbers and brass beds. Doubles run for about $60 to $70. See chapter 10.
- **Da Cecio** (Cinque Terre, Italian Riviera; ☎ **0187-812-138**): After walking through the Cinque Terre, relax in your room at this old stone house in the countryside as you gaze out at the ocean, olive groves, and the nearby hilltop town of Corniglia. Doubles cost $45 to $50. See chapter 11.
- **Bella Capri** (Naples; ☎ **081-552-9494**): With the paint still fresh on the walls, Bella Capri is a clean, simple budget hotel ideally located for exploring in Naples. With a warm welcome from Alfredo and Gerardo, your touring plans will be a snap because they've gone out of their way to see that everything you could possibly get at the tourist information office is right here at the reception desk. You can also take breakfast on a private terrace overlooking the docks, all for as low as $60 a double. See chapter 12.
- **Il Moresco Grand Hotel Terme** (Ischia, Campania; ☎ **081-981-366**): Five-star luxury, personalized attention, a thermal spring-fed spa, and meals served by a white-gloved staff, all for the cost of a haircut in Manhattan. Doubles begin at $125, at this slice of paradise, but you may want to splurge for a superior room or a suite, or even put your money to better use in the talented hands of Leonardo, the expert masseur. See chapter 12.
- **Trullidea** (Alberobello, Apulia; ☎ **080-432-3860**): Some hotels are clearly a destination in themselves, especially when they've been declared a national monument by UNESCO. Trullidea, a series of independent efficiencies under the conical stone roofs of the ancient *trulli,* truly offers a peek into the lifestyles of the Alberobellese, without requiring us to sacrifice even a whit of comfort. When the tour buses clear out, there's nothing left but you, a chatty neighbor, and an infinite cluster of twinkling stars. Doubles cost about $60. See chapter 12.
- **Lo Spagnulo** (Ostuni, Apulia; ☎ **0831-350-209**): Hidden in miles and miles of olive groves is the former residence of the Reverend Don Saverio Lopez y Royo of Pamplona, Spain. This rural manor house offers the Italian farmer's version of an American dude ranch, but with loads more panache, from the pavilion dining room to the arched rose garden. Very little, if any, English is spoken here, but for $23 per person (all meals and transfers included) maybe you should consider picking up those language tapes you've been talking about for years. See chapter 12.

- **Gardenia** (Palermo, Sicily; ☎ **091-322-761**): The transformation is complete, and completely miraculous. This former run-down budget option is now one of Palermo's best buys, a pleasing three-star pension in one of the more convenient neighborhoods. Expect parquet floors, fresh grouting in the bath, and lovely upholstery, down to the last "G" embroidered on your pillowcase. Doubles cost $70. See chapter 13.
- **La Pinetta** (Erice, Sicily; ☎ **0923-869-783**): On this clifftop oasis not known for its bargain prices, there's still a swatch of wooded serenity costing as little as $80 for a double. Sensitively constructed in a forest of pine trees, La Pinetta provides a bit more solitude and romance than the alternatives in Erice's center, and it's just a few minutes walk to the upper cobbled streets of this amazing medieval town. See chapter 13.
- **Gran Bretagna** (Siracusa, Sicily; ☎ **0931-68-765**): Closed for renovations in 2000, we can only try to imagine what improvements are in store in what was already a charming best buy on Siracusa's historic Ortigia Island. Imagine rooms better than those with a personal touch, some frescoed, some unusually spacious, and all charming. Call to confirm opening. See chapter 13.
- **Gallodoro** (Taormina, Sicily; ☎ **0942-23-860**): For the best price-to-quality ratio in Taormina, the Gallodoro wins, with doubles for $55. Granted, you'll miss out on the élan of staying in a terraced villa with arched-Saracen windows peeking out through insistent blossoms, but here, at the bottom of the cable car line, you're at the beach. See chapter 13.

10 The Best Rooms with a View

- **Abruzzi** (Rome; ☎ **06-679-2021**): Short of sleeping under the oculus of its dome, this is as close as you'll get to the Pantheon. For a meager $75, you can fling open your shutters onto this stunning architectural masterpiece, and contemplate the engineering techniques available 2000 years ago. And you don't even have to go outside to join the party. See chapter 3.
- **Torre Guelfa** (Florence; ☎ **055-239-6338**). The breathtaking 360° view from the medieval tower that gives the hotel its name justifies beyond reasonable doubt the pricey rates. But the riveting view from the tallest privately owned tower in Florence's *centro storico* is only one of many reasons to stay in this tastefully renovated, Renaissance-style landmark hotel. You can revel in a slightly less awesome view from your huge, private terrace if you're lucky enough to check into room no. 15. It's a splurge at $150 a night, but the views are worth it. See chapter 4.
- **Ai do Mori** (Venice; ☎ **041-520-4817**): The more accessible lower floors (there is no elevator and the hotel begins on the second floor with most rooms above) are slightly larger and offer interesting rooftop views, but the somewhat smaller top-floor rooms of this centrally sited hotel boast wonderful views that embrace San Marco's many domes and the nearby Torre dell'Orologio (Clock Tower) whose two bronze Moors ring the bells every hour. The atticlike top-floor Artist's Room is cozy and charming, with its own private terrace and views that for $80 (for a double) beat anything offered by neighboring five-star hotels. See chapter 7.
- **Montana** (Cortina d'Ampezzo, Dolomites; ☎ **0436-862-126**). You can see a generous swath of mountain peaks from most of the cozy, paneled rooms at this pleasant Alpine-style hotel right in the center of town. Surprising in this often overpriced resort, rates start at $74 for a double (in off-season) and include a generous breakfast. See chapter 8.

- **Milano** (Varenna, Lake District; ☎ **0341-830-298**): The main point of coming to the Italian Lakes is to enjoy the moody and romantic expanses of water backed by mountains and gardens, and the homey, attractive Milano offers vistas like this from all of its rooms, some of them have large terraces hanging over the water as well. While a room with a view can come with a high price tag at the many lakeside hotels, commodious, comfortable accommodations at the Milano are a bargain at $100. See chapter 9.
- **Al Castello da Diego** (Novello, Piedmont Wine Country; ☎ **0173-744-011**): This Victorian castle is perched on the precipice of a summit with stunning views of the rolling vineyards and villages below. Plus, the large rooms are a delight, decorated with antiques of the claw-footed variety and equipped with baths that are tucked into turrets. Many rooms have terraces, and with rates starting at $75 for a double, are very reasonably priced. See chapter 10.
- **Il Monastero** (Ischia, Campania; ☎ **081-992-435**): Remember that gorgeous island in the background of *The Talented Mr. Ripley's* fictitious Mongibello? Well, for one, it's not an island; it's attached to Ischia by a narrow causeway. See the majestic fortress walls? That's the imposing Castello Aragonese, whose ramparts and ruined basilicas dominate the entire northeast corner of the island. At the center of the castle is Il Monastero, a simple budget pensione taking up the rooms of the ex-Convent di Clausura. All of the rooms open onto the communal panoramic terrace, with sweeping and wonderful views of the mountainous island and sea far beyond the ramparts. Doubles cost $83. See chapter 12.
- **Villa Athena** (Agrigento, Sicily; ☎ **0922-596-288**): Set within the confines of the archaeological zone of the "Valley of the Temples," almost every room in this converted 18th-century villa enjoys a view of the perfectly preserved Temple of Concord, framed by olive groves and bougainvillea. Your cost is a mere $125 for a double, a small price to pay for 5th-century B.C. romance and floodlit Doric columns as seen from your own private balcony. See chapter 13.

11 The Best Affordable Hideaways by the Sea

- **Capo** (Bordighera, Italian Riviera; ☎ **0184-261-558**): Location, location, location. The only hotel in the old city of Bordighera is stunningly located on a hilltop with views over the lower town and sea below. There always seems to be a cooling breeze here. From the balconies off the rooms, which run $40 to $65 per double, you can look up and down the coast as far as the eye can see. See chapter 11.
- **La Camogliese** (Camogli, the Riviera Levante; ☎ **0185-771-402**): Call this a hideaway by the seas. Not only is the popular hotel near a beach, but the owner will direct you to more hideaways along the nearby coast. This is especially convenient because this attractive hotel is also near the train station, and double rooms cost only $45 to $55. See chapter 11.
- **Villa Rosa** (Positano; ☎ **089-811-955**): The large, echoing accommodations of this former *affittacamere* (rooming house) are still being converted into hotel rooms, so the furnishings are spanking new. Aside from the great prices and kindly family management, the real attraction here is the view from your own bougainvillea-arbored sitting terrace across the inlet to a postcard-perfect shot of Positano's most photogenic quarter, the whitewashed and pastel cube houses climbing up the headland in a jumble of balconies and flowers. The best part is realizing that you're only paying about $95 for your double but are getting a better view than the famous Hotel Sireneuse across the street for less than one-fifth the price. See chapter 12.

- **Villa Eva** (Anacapri; ☎ **081-837-1549**): Located in the hills above Anacapri and nowhere near Capri center, Villa Eva is the Isle of Capri's slice of paradise—a lush, exotic jungle thick with flowering vines and vegetation. If you don't stay here, you'll be sorry, even if the sea is a 20-minute walk away, just close enough for that pre-twilight swim in the Blue Grotto. Doubles begin at $65. See chapter 12.
- **La Tonnarella** (Sorrento; ☎ **081-878-1153**): Terraced below the quiet road leading out of town, La Tonnarella enjoys a stunning position high above the Bay of Sorrento, with views of the Sorrento headlands from almost every corner. Access to the beach at the base of the cliff is by elevator, or via a lovely wooded path, and the grounds feature pine-shaded terraces and gardens for wandering about or enjoying a quiet meal. The hotel retains a 19th-century feel with oriental runners, loads of wood, and plenty of ceramic tile that give even the humblest of hotels a crisp elegance. Doubles begin at $100. See chapter 12.
- **Il Moresco Grand Hotel Terme** (Ischia, Campania; ☎ **081-981-366**): Il Moresco may lack its own private beach, but a few steps across the narrow leafy road you can settle into a beachside lounge at their five-star sister hotel. You may not even make it to the beach, though, preferring instead to slip into a thermal pool (indoors or out), sweat in the sauna, steep in the Turkish bath, or indulge in any number of spa treatments. The restorative environment of this lush and mountainous hideaway, still for the most part a secret, is yours for about $125 a night for a double. See chapter 12.
- **Arathena Rocks Hotel** (Giardini Naxos-Taormina, Sicily; ☎ **0942-51-349**): The Arathena Rocks Hotel, set dramatically on the extreme tip of Punto Schisò, is comfortably removed from the resort crowds of Giardini-Naxos, enjoying its private and jagged lava "beach." The terrace pool, set in a traditional sculpted Italian garden, provides an alternative to the rugged lava stones. It's only a 20-minute bus ride up to the colorful gardens and medieval streets of hilltop Taormina, where a hotelier would balk at the $55 per person you're paying for such luxury, dinner included. See chapter 13.
- **Villa Nettuno** (Taormina, Sicily; ☎ **0942-23-797**): One of the last family-owned gems remaining in overdeveloped Taormina, Villa Nettuno retains its small, genteel 19th-century character. The kindly Sciglio family is able to keep prices down—doubles are easy to take at $60—because they refuse to work with agencies, and thus avoid commissions. The private and overgrown gardens climb the terraced hillside up to an isolated stone gazebo, with its perfect panorama and savory solitude. With the cable car across the street, it's a quick and easy descent to the beaches of Mazzarò and Isola Bella. See chapter 13.

12 The Best Affordable Restaurants

- **Fiaschetteria Beltramme** (Rome; no phone): If you can find an empty table at this ultra-traditional seven-table bistro, it won't take long for you to become a parody of the 1950s caricature on the wall—the one of the rotund man pronouncing in Italian, "I can't believe I ate all that!" The recipes are hallowed, the service is consistent, and the decor is humble. See chapter 3.
- **Ditirambo** (Rome; ☎ **06-687-1626**): Run by a group of affable and handsome entrepreneurs, Ditirambo deviates from the nuts and bolts of traditional Roman cuisine, opening its palate to innovative and outstanding dishes representative of Italy's regional cooking. Reservations are essential. See chapter 3.

- **Il Latini** (Florence; ☎ **055-210-916**): Il Latini works hard to keep the air of archetypical trattoria—long, shared tables, hammocks hanging from the beamed ceiling—even if it has expanded to multiple rooms and tourists now know to flock here to join the local regulars in line for a table. While there's no official set-priced menu, the waiters are inclined simply to serve you as much as you can eat and drink of their delicious crostini, thick soups and pastas, platters of varied roast meats, desserts, bottomless wine and mineral water, even after-dinner grappa, and then just charge everyone at the table $28 a head, which is an amazing price for a meal that will leave you stuffed for days and filled with fond memories for years. See Chapter 4.
- **Da Giulio** (Lucca, Tuscany; ☎ **0583-55-948**): Delighted foreigners and locals of uncompromising allegiance agree that this big, airy, and forever busy trattoria is one of Tuscany's undisputed stars. Although casual, this is not the place to occupy a much-coveted table for just a pasta and salad. Save up your appetite and come for a full-blown homestyle feast of *la cucina toscana,* trying all of Giulio's traditional rustic specialties. Waiters know not to recommend certain local delicacies to non-Italian diners, unless you look like the type who enjoys tripe, *tartara di cavallo* (horse meat tartare), or veal snout. See chapter 5.
- **Osteria le Logge** (Siena, Tuscany; ☎ **0577-48-013**): This convivial and highly recommended Sienese trattoria is two steps off the gorgeous Piazza del Campo and a well-known destination for locals and well-informed visitors who join the standing-room-only scenario of those who keep this place packed. Its delicious *pasta fresca* (fresh homemade pasta) launches each memorable meal, with entrees that are all about the simple perfection of grilled meats. The excellent choice of extra-virgin olive oil is enough to confirm the affable owner's seriousness, seconded by a small but discerning wine list that is topped by his own limited production of Rosso and Brunello di Montepulciano. See chapter 5.
- **Olindo Faccioli** (Bologna; ☎ **051-223-171**): This intimate, inconspicuous restaurant has a limited, but delightful menu. The specials lean toward a light, vegetarian cuisine, but the starter of tuna carpaccio will satisfy fish-eaters as well. You can linger here as you decide which of the 400 vintages of wine will go best with your meal. See chapter 6.
- **Al Brindisi** (Ferrara; ☎ **0532-209-142**): This just may be the oldest wine bar in the world—it's been around since 1435. The two timbered dining rooms are stacked to the ceiling with wine bottles and for $1.50 and up, you can choose a glass from this overwhelming selection. Have some appetizers, sausage, or pumpkin ravioli with your wine; or go for the whole shebang with one of the many tourist and tasting menus, which include a feast of appetizers, a special main course of the day, dessert, and a carafe of wine, all for $9 to $40. See chapter 6.
- **Osteria dal Duca** (Verona; ☎ **045-594-474**): There are no written records to confirm that this 13th-century palazzo was once owned by the Montecchi (Montagues) family and, thankfully, the discreet management never considered calling this place the "Ristorante Romeo." But here you are in "fair Verona," nonetheless, dining in what is believed to be Romeo's house, a characteristic medieval palazzo, and enjoying one of the nicest meals in town in a spirited and friendly neighborhood ambience fueled by the amiable family that keeps this place always abuzz. It will be simple, it will be delicious, you'll probably make friends with the people sitting next to you, and you'll always remember your meal at Romeo's restaurant. See chapter 8.

- **Cantine Sanremese** (San Remo, Italian Riveria; ☎ **0184-572-063**): Old habits die hard at the Cantine Sanremese, so come here to sample traditional, home-made Ligurian cuisine. Instead of ordering main dishes, sample the *sardemaira* (the local foccacia-like bread), *torte verde* (a quiche of fresh green vegetables), or any of their delicious soups, including minestrone thick with fresh vegetables and garnished with pesto. See chapter 11.
- **De Mananan** (Corniglia, Italian Riveria; ☎ **0187-821-166**): In this intimate restaurant, which is carved into an ancient stone cellar, the owners/chefs use only the finest ingredients to prepare homemade specialties such as pesto or *funghi porcini* (wild mushrooms), mussels, grilled fish, fresh anchovies stuffed with herbs, or *coniglio nostrano,* rabbit roasted in a white sauce. See chapter 11.
- **Cucina Casareccia** (Lecce, Apulia; ☎ **0832-245-178**): Dining at this tiny trat-toria makes you feel as if you should have brought a bottle of wine: Concetta Cantoro treats customers as if they were guests in her own home, husband Mar-cello is a fine host. Leave the menu selection to the experts and sit back and enjoy. See chapter 12.
- **Antica Focacceria San Francesco** (Palermo, Sicily; ☎ **091-320-264**) "Slum-ming it" has never been so fun. This over-lit, high-ceilinged joint resembles a wait-ing room more than a restaurant, and serves up some of the heaviest, greasiest, finger-lickingest food I've ever eaten (though I'll probably pass on the spleen next time). You won't get much more authentic Palermitano then this. See chapter 13.
- **La Forchetta** (Agrigento, Sicily; ☎ **0922-596-266**): Every inch the traditional neighborhood trattoria, La Forchetta has true Sicilian character and excellent home cooking. Matriarch Mamma Giuseppa is a genuine blast, haranguing the wait staff (often her sons) one minute and graciously greeting you the next. See chapter 13.

13 The Best Cafes

- **Caffè Sant'Eustachio** (Rome): Famed for their froth, Sant'Eustachio is consis-tently packed at least three deep at the bar, everyone clamoring for a shot of their special blend. But it's no wonder nobody ever leaves: There's so little coffee beneath all that foam that you have to keep getting refills to get a decent amount of coffee! While you wait, the shop obliges with a tiny glass-case display of delec-table coffee paraphernalia, all reasonably priced. See chapter 3.
- **Caffè Rivoire** (Florence): The pudding-rich hot chocolate of Florence's premier historical cafe is second to the real reason for a visit: its dead-on view of the city's greatest piazza and a front-row seat for people-watching. The ambience is old world inside and out: The stately Palazzo Vecchio looms in front of outdoor tables and the piazza's most celebrated statue, a copy of Michelangelo's fabled *David.* Inside, it's cozy and elegant, and no one raises an eyebrow if you nurse a tea for several hours. See chapter 4.
- **Bar Giuseppe** (Bologna): When you're tired of outdoor cafes, head underground to the Bar Giuseppe, which stretches for at least a block beneath historical arcades. The gelato here—more than 40 flavors—is pretty darn good, too. See chapter 6.
- **Historic Cafes of Piazza San Marco** (Venice): The nostalgic 18th-century **Caffè Florian** is the best known of this stunning piazza, and the most famous. But the truth is, if the weather is lovely, and the other three cafes have moved their hundreds of tables outdoors, the piazza becomes one big bellini-sipping

people-watching stage with St. Mark's Basilica as its singular backdrop. Around the corner, just in front of the Palazzo Ducale, is the **Caffè Chioggia,** the only cafe with a view of the water and the Clock Tower (whose bronze Moors began striking the hour in 1999 again after a 5-year renovation). Each of the piazza cafes has its own three- or four-piece **orchestrina,** but the music at the Chioggia is held to be the best and least commercial (no "New York, New York" here). See chapter 7.

- **Antico Caffè Dante** (Verona): The interior of Verona's oldest cafe is rather formal (and expensive), but set up camp here at an outdoor table in Verona's loveliest piazza, named for the early Renaissance man of letters whose statue commemorates his love for the city and the ruling Scalageri family who hosted him during his years of exile. If you're lucky enough to hold tickets for the opera in the city's 2,000-year-old Arena amphitheater, this is the traditional spot for an after-opera drink to complete, and contemplate, the evening's magic. See chapter 8.

- **Antica Pasticceria Gelateria Klainguti** (Genoa): Verdi enjoyed Genoa's oldest and best bakery. You probably will, too, for its *Falstaff* (a sweet brioche) and a stupefying selection of pastries and chocolates. See chapter 11.

- **Gran Caffé Gambrinus** (Naples): This courtly 19th-century bastion of Neapolitan society recaptures the golden age of Naples. Enjoy your creamy cappuccino and flaky *sfogliatella* pastry at one of the indoor tables surrounded by deluxe decor, or at an outside table in the shadows of the Royal Palace and the Umberto I Opera House, and watch the manic traffic race by. See chapter 12.

Planning Your Trip: The Basics

2

by Reid Bramblett

The days when Italy was a dirt-cheap idyllic destination of good food and countless treasures are a myth of the past, but there are still a myriad of inexpensive ways to enjoy its remarkable wonders and the incomparability of its *dolce vita*. With some flexibility and advance planning, a moderate budget can go a long way. This chapter shows you how to organize and get your trip together and on the road.

1 Fifty Money-Saving Tips

This chapter is full of money-saving hints, insider information, contacts, and expertise accumulated over the authors' innumerable fact-finding trips. You'll enjoy your trip even more knowing you're getting the biggest bang for your buck, easily keeping your costs for accommodation (let's say breakfast is included), lunch, and dinner to as little as $70 per day. (We assume that two adults are traveling together and that between the two of you, you have $140 to spend. Traveling alone has other pluses and drawbacks but usually turns out to be slightly more expensive, mostly due to the hotel factor.) The costs of transportation, activities, sightseeing, and entertainment are extra, but we have plenty of insider tips to save you money on those activities as well.

It's hard to go wrong in Italy and so easy to go right if you give some heed to the following tips.

WHEN TO GO

1. So the weather isn't always a perfect 75°F and the skies aren't always cloud-free. But **off-season Italy** promises the biggest cuts in airfare, the beauty of popping up at small hotels (more discounted rates) without needing a reservation confirmed three months in advance, the blessed absence of lines at the museums, and finding the local people less harried and more accommodating. For more details on high- versus low-season travel, see "When to Go," later in this chapter.

PACKAGE DEALS, INTERNATIONAL & DOMESTIC TRAVEL

2. An enjoyable, affordable trip begins long before leaving home. Do your cyber homework: Surf the Internet and save. There are lots and lots of Web pages and online services designed to clue

Cyber Deals for Net Surfers

It's possible to get some great deals on airfare, hotels, and car rentals via the Internet. The Web sites we've highlighted below are worth checking out, especially since all services are free.

Now incorporating Preview Travel, ✪ **Travelocity** (www.travelocity.com; www.previewtravel.com; www.frommers.travelocity.com) is Frommer's online travel-planning/booking partner. Travelocity uses the SABRE system to offer reservations and tickets for more than 400 airlines, plus reservations and purchase capabilities for more than 45,000 hotels and 50 car-rental companies. An exclusive feature of this system is its **Low Fare Search Engine,** which automatically searches for the three lowest-priced itineraries based on a traveler's criteria. Last-minute deals and consolidator fares are included in the search. If you book with Travelocity, you can select specific seats for your flights with online seat maps and also view diagrams of the most popular commercial aircraft. The **Hotel Finder** provides street-level location maps and photos of selected hotels. With the **Fare Watcher** e-mail feature, you can select up to five routes and receive e-mail notices when the fare changes by $25 or more. Travelocity's **Destination Guide** includes updated information on some 260 destinations worldwide—supplied by Frommer's.

Expedia (www.expedia.com) is Travelocity's major competitor. It offers several ways of obtaining the best possible fares: **Flight Price Matcher** service allows your preferred airline to match an available fare with a competitor; a comprehensive **Fare Compare** area shows the differences in fare categories and airlines; and **Fare Calendar** helps you plan your trip around the best possible fares. Its main limitation is that like many online databases, Expedia focuses on the major airlines and hotel chains, so don't expect to find too many budget airlines or one-of-a-kind B&Bs here.

TRIP.com began as a site geared toward business travelers, but its innovative features and highly personalized approach have broadened its appeal to leisure travelers as well. It is the leading travel site for those using mobile devices to access Internet travel information. TRIP.com includes a trip-planning function that provides the average and lowest fare for the route requested, in addition to the current available fare. An on-site **newsstand** features breaking news on airfare sales and other travel specials. Among its most popular features are **Flight TRACKER** and **intelliTRIP.** Flight TRACKER allows users to track any commercial flight en route to its destination anywhere in the United States, while accessing real-time FAA-based flight monitoring data. intelliTRIP is a travel search tool that allows users to identify the best airline, hotel, and rental-car rates in less than 90 seconds. In addition, the site offers e-mail notification of flight delays, plus city resource guides, currency converters, and a weekly e-mail newsletter of fare updates, travel tips, and traveler forums.

you in on discounted airfares, accommodations, and car rentals. See "Cyber Deals for Net Surfers," above for some sites that offer real deals.

3. **No computer? No problem.** Visit a travel agent and see what bargains or deals they offer you that you wouldn't have access to independently. It doesn't cost you

Yahoo! (www.travel.yahoo.com) is currently the most popular of the Internet information portals, and its travel site is a comprehensive mix of online booking, daily travel news, and destination information. The **Best Fares** area offers what it promises, plus provides feedback on refining your search if you have flexibility in travel dates or times. There is also an active section of **message boards** for discussions on travel in general and specific destinations.

At **Priceline.com**, you decide what you want to pay for your airline ticket or hotel room. Input desired travel dates and destination, the price you want to pay, and your credit card number. Priceline then does a search to determine if any supplier will accept the price; if the price is accepted, the ticket is immediately bought and charged to your credit card. The Web site offers a similar deal for hotel rooms, rental cars, and more.

Operated by the ETN (European Travel Network), **Discount Tickets** (www.discount-tickets.com) offers discounts on airfares between the United States and other countries, plus accommodations, car rentals, and tours. A bargain-hunter's dream, **Moment's Notice** (www.moments-notice.com) is updated each morning, and many of the deals offered are snapped up by the end of the day. A drawback is that many of these vacations require you to drop everything and go almost immediately.

Most major airlines offer a free e-mail service known as **E-Savers**, from which you'll receive the best bargain airfares on a weekly basis. Here's how it works: Once a week (usually Wednesday), subscribers receive a list of discounted flights to and from various destinations, both international and domestic. Now here's the catch: These fares are only available if you leave the very next Saturday (or sometimes Friday night) and return on the following Monday or Tuesday. It's really a service for the spontaneously inclined and travelers looking for a quick getaway (better a few days in Italy than none at all). But the fares are cheap, so it's worth taking a look. If you have a preference for certain airlines (in other words, the ones you fly most frequently), sign up with them first. Another caveat: You'll get frequent-flyer miles if you purchase one of these fares, but you can't use miles to buy the ticket.

Here's a list of airlines and their Web addresses, where you can not only get on the e-mailing lists but also book flights directly:

- **American Airlines:** www.aa.com
- **Continental Airlines:** www. continental.com
- **TWA:** www.twa.com
- **Northwest Airlines:** www.nwa.com
- **US Airways:** www.usairways.com

Concierge.com, another good travel site, allows you to sign up for almost all of these airline e-mail lists at once.

a thing, and there's no obligation to buy. It never hurts to ask. See "Organized Tours, Package Tours & Tour Operators," later in this chapter, for a list of agencies that specialize in trips to Italy.

4. When calling the airlines directly, always ask for the lowest possible fare. Be flexible in your schedule—flying on weekdays versus weekends, or even at a different time of day, can make a difference. Find out the exact dates of the seasonal rates; these differ from airline to airline even though the destination stays the same. Some flights into or out of Rome versus Milan may differ in price. Don't forget to ask about discounts for seniors, students, or children.

5. Buy your ticket well in advance. Most airlines discount tickets purchased 7, 14, or 21 days before the departure dates.

6. Or buy your ticket at the last minute—something best recommended if you have a flexible schedule and are traveling off-season when availability is more probable.

7. Be an educated traveler. Read the travel section of your local newspaper (especially weekend editions) for special promotional fares and discounts and know who's offering what and for how much.

8. Check your newspaper for consolidators or wholesalers, once more frequently known as "bucket shops." These companies operate by alleviating blocks of unsold tickets from the major international airlines. It's still not a bad idea to check their records first with the Better Business Bureau, but most operate firmly aboveboard and offer substantial savings, particularly off-season: See those we list in the section "Getting There Without Going Broke," later in this chapter.

9. Check package deals and escorted trips—even if you're not a groupie. You may find the air and hotel savings alone make them worth considering; many trips are unstructured enough to let you split from the group and do your own thing. You might even wind up preferring the companionship of the others on board and the luxury of having every day's bothersome details prearranged. Air/hotel packages (often offered by the airlines themselves) also offer great savings, though hotels are sometimes on the outskirts of towns (hence the big discounts); check their locations first if this is important to you.

10. Domestic or one-way flights within Italy (or Europe) can be killers. The most distant flights within Italy (Venice to Palermo, for example) might be a contender for air travel, but opt for the train at a fraction of the cost, breaking up your travel times with overnight stops planned along the way. There is never a shortage of sights between any two points.

    All major airports have rail or bus service to get you to and from downtown—Rome and Pisa's ultraconvenient trains pull right into the airport itself. Taxis are expensive though tempting to jet-lagged travelers laden with luggage.

11. Which reminds me: Travel lightly! You'll never wear or need half of the stuff you're convinced you can't live without. The inconvenience you'll find at every turn is what you'll remember long after your trip! What you'll save on cabs, porters, and energy can be considerable. Never take more than you can carry single-handedly when running for a bus or train.

12. Train travel in Italy has improved immeasurably since the 1970s and 1980s. The newer **"InterCity"** trains are clean and efficient enough to make second-class travel a near first-class experience. The fancy, fast-paced **EuroStar** trains can cut speed, but is a 1-hour (or less) difference worth the extra cost?

13. Map out your strategy before leaving to see if a **Eurail pass** will save you or cost you money. On long international stretches of train travel, the former is usually true. Within Italy, buying second-class point-to-point tickets as you go may save you money. The Eurail pass is cheapest when purchased at home before leaving.

14. Use public transportation in cities rather than taxis. It also offers a peek into the daily lifestyles of the local residents. Most concentrated historical districts make

sightseeing most enjoyable when done on foot; in the large cities like Rome or Milan, consider daily or weekly passes for unlimited travel on buses or subways.

CAR RENTALS

15. Call around to all the major car-rental agencies; promotional rates sometimes make the big boys the best. Make a reservation before leaving home, but make one last inquiry before getting on the plane to see if any new lower rates have been introduced in the meantime. Making your reservation before leaving for Italy is almost always a guaranteed money saver.

16. Ask questions about waivers and insurance suggested and required by the rental agency and then check with your **credit card company** to see what they offer before booking. Don't wind up paying for the same coverage twice, or getting charged for extraneous coverage that is recommended but not obligatory.

17. Aim for the least expensive economy car category (unless you'll be making long *autostrada* stretches when it will seem you're standing still as virtually every other vehicle zips by). If you're told they're unavailable in an attempt to have you book the next most expensive model, call elsewhere. Know in advance that almost all rental cars in Italy are stick shift; to book an automatic transmission—if any are available—will hike the price considerably. Air-conditioning will also cost extra, so consider the weather you'll be encountering.

18. Book the weekly rates to save. To book a car for just a day or two for a tool in the country is an expensive venture. However, to book for a longer period, only to have the car sit in an expensive parking lot (almost all historic centers now ban car traffic entirely) doesn't make sense either. Have a loose idea of what your vacation's schedule will be, and work around that.

19. Parking is a nightmare in Italy and the police are serious about enforcing tow-away zones. Don't try to conserve parking-lot costs by parking on the streets if you're not sure what the streets signs say (a red slashed circle filled in with blue means no parking; spaces painted with blue lines means you have to pay, either at a meter or to a parking official; yellow lines mean handicapped parking; white lines mean you need a local permit, which, only if you're lucky, can your hotel supply). The cost of retrieving a towed car is only half as bad as the hassle of trying to find it and getting it back without the incident ruining your entire trip.

20. If you decide to rent once you're already in Italy, check out the prices and then call a friend back home and ask them to book for you from there if the rates are less; they almost always are.

21. Always return your rental car full of gas, or the rental agency will charge you for it, usually at top lire. Don't have heart failure at the cost of gas (*benzina*) in Italy: It is some of Europe's most expensive. The cars get excellent mileage, however, and you won't have to fill up often.

22. The largest cities may have car-rental offices at both the airport and downtown. There is often an extra charge to pick up at one and drop off at another; using downtown branches is almost always cheaper. To pick up and drop off in two different cities is even worse. In two different countries—better take the train.

ACCOMMODATIONS

23. If you're traveling during high season (roughly Easter through September or October), book early. You won't get any discounts, but you won't be forced to spend more by upgrading just to find a vacancy in town.

24. If the idea doesn't faze you, consider a less expensive room with a shared bathroom instead of an en suite private bathroom. Ask how many rooms will be

sharing the bathroom—sometimes it is as few as two; if the other room is vacant, the bathroom will be yours alone.

25. Many of the hotels listed in this book don't advertise seasonal rates, but there's usually some discount offered during the slow periods. Always ask. The more nights you stay, the more you're likely to get a discount. The way you approach the subject is very important: A smile and a pretty-please upon check-in is always more successful than a hard-nosed demand. If it's a slow month and late afternoon, the advantage is yours.

26. Don't underestimate the power of Frommer's. Mention of this book in your faxed request or a flash of the book upon check-in will notify the hotel from whence you come. Most of the worthier hotels we list year after year are very appreciative of the volume and quality of travelers (that's you) that we bring to their establishment and they're apt to do their best to accommodate you when and if possible.

27. Is your room so dismal you could just cry? Keep cool and polite, but voice your disappointment and ask if you might be shown another room. Be specific about what bothers you—the soft mattress or lack of light might not be something found in all rooms. You might even get upgraded at no extra cost. Don't resort to drama and histrionics.

28. Single rooms in Italy can be downright miniscule. If you're traveling alone and it's off-season, ask if the management might be so kind to offer you a double room at a single occupancy rate. Many of them will if the rooms are available; always ask.

29. Before arranging your own parking, check first with your hotel. Hotels often have a standing deal with a nearby parking facility. In Venice, hotels will give you a voucher to present at the parking lots on the outskirts of town.

30. Breakfast. Is it included or not? Always ask, and ask if it is continental or buffet. If they expect you to pay $5 per person (for example) for a prepackaged month-old *cornetto* (croissant) and cup of mediocre coffee, check out the charming outdoor cafe down the block instead. If the self-service, all-you-can-eat buffet of cold cuts, fresh rolls, juice, yogurt, and—well, you get the drift—is offered in a *simpatico* setting and will keep you going till dinner, dig in, enjoy yourself, and grab an apple for the road.

31. Never make telephone calls from your room if you can avoid it, especially long-distance ones. The service charge and taxes tagged on to the briefest call home will ruin the moment of enjoyment it brought. Use calling cards at public phones or arrange to have your family call you at designated hours.

32. The "frigo bar" (minibar) is a mixed blessing. That Diet Coke (*Coca Lite*) and Toblerone candy bar can set you back an easy $10. Check the price list before giving in to hunger pangs, and know what you're about to eat—it might not taste that good.

33. Each hotel's policy regarding children is different, so be specific regarding the children's ages when booking: Generally speaking, children under 12 (sometimes 10) stay for free in the parents' room. Remember: There's no fudging the children's age with the obligatory presentation of the passport upon check-in.

EATING

34. Take advantage of Italy's cornucopia of excellent bakeries and food stores and make every lunch a picnic. Yes, you'll save more to spend on dinner, but you'll also wind up enjoying a million-dollar lunch in an opera-set piazza.

35. It's lunchtime and it's rainy or cold, or you just need to sit indoors for a while, but an expensive meal is out of your budget. Italy is slowly leaning toward the affordable quick lunch. Bars and cafes are serving informal lunches of pastas and salads as much to local merchants and workers as to cost-conscious travelers, usually for $6 to $7 or less.

36. If you're running over your day's budget (couldn't resist the calfskin attaché case?), remember that this is the country that gave us pizza and wine. Find a pizzeria with outdoor seating, order a carafe of the house wine (***vino della casa***), and eat like a king (spend like a poor man). Save your three-course trattoria meal for a more solvent day.

37. Tourist menus (***menù turistico***) or fixed-price menus (***menu a prezzo fisso***) sound like a good deal, and often are. But portions may be smaller, choices less varied or uninspired (expect the ubiquitous spaghetti with tomato sauce and roast chicken). Menus are usually posted in the window, so peruse your choices before entering and ordering.

38. If you aren't accustomed to eating so much but want to taste it all, order a ***mezza porzione*** (**half portion**) of pasta for your first course, so you have room left for your second course—and be charged accordingly. Most restaurants will gladly oblige.

39. The rule of thumb in this cafe society: Always expect to pay more at a table than at the bar, more at an outdoor table (consider it your cover charge for the free piazza-life entertainment). That said, don't expect to be rushed: For the cost of an iced-tea or mineral water, you can sit and write postcards for hours and you'll never overstay your welcome.

40. If you've been snacking all day and would be happy with just a good plate of pasta and not a full-blown repast, make sure you choose your restaurant well. You might anger some establishments if you occupy a table for a single course dinner and not the full nine yards. Casual, informal neighborhood joints won't give a second thought to you lingering over a simple pasta, salad, and glass of wine.

    House wines can be surprisingly good and inexpensive. Enjoying a good bottled wine will bring your bill up a notch but hey, that's probably what you're visiting Italy for anyway. Stick with wines of the region, and experiment with some of the small-time, lesser-known (but not necessarily less sophisticated) wine producers of the area. For the wallet-challenged, go with the mineral water, and stop off at a wine bar after dinner and choose one very special cru by-the-glass in a convivial *ambiente*.

SIGHTSEEING

41. Make a beeline for the **Tourist Information Office** to check out special events, free concerts, arts festivals, and so on, to maximize your (always too brief) stay in town. Some museums offer one evening a week free; outdoor evening or church concerts are free, not infrequent, and lovely. Sometimes your hotel staff can be twice as helpful and informed than the tourism people.

42. To get the most on always increasing museum admissions, see if you can buy tickets in advance to eliminate waiting in line. Always ask about senior and student discounts. Extended hours for summer months are often confirmed at the last minute (therefore not reflected in guidebooks) and are not widely publicized: If you're in-the-know, you might have Florence's Uffizi Galleries to yourself at 10 o'clock in the evening—put a price on that!

43. More and more cities are offering joint tickets or passes for both major and minor museums. You might be able to get admission to as many as 10 museums

over an open period of time. But study which museums are included—they are often obscure and esoteric collections that are of little interest or inconveniently located for the tourist on a tight schedule.

44. Free, do-it-yourself walking tours are a viable substitute for the expensive, escorted tours. But the latter are worth your while if your time in town is extremely limited and the sites are many. Before signing up for a half or full day tour, see exactly which sites will be visited so you don't miss those of most interest to you.

45. Don't shortchange yourself on people-watching in Italy, the single great pastime that has been perfected here as an art form, and the best free entertainment you're bound to see anywhere. Pull up a cafe chair and settle in; to avoid any charge at all, a piazza bench will do fine.

SHOPPING

46. Before splurging on that fragile glassware from Venice or hand-painted ceramic platter from Deruta, consider the cost of shipping, which can double an otherwise respectable price. Do you really want to carry a package around for the rest of your trip? Some stores don't offer shipping and doing the job yourself (buying packing supplies and so on) is troublesome and time consuming. Insurance hikes the cost even further.

47. Pay by credit card as often as possible: The fewer transaction fees (incurred by ATMs or changing traveler's checks to cash) needed, the more saved.

48. Alas, **bargaining** in Italy, once a theatrical and generally enjoyable part of every purchase, is fast becoming a dying animal. But if you're buying more than one item, paying by cash or traveler's checks, are in an open-air market, and/or have struck up a friendly banter with the merchant, give it a shot. The best time to test your talents is during the slow months, when the market or shop looks like it's hungry for business.

49. Don't forget to cash in on your **value-added tax (VAT)** if you qualify. Millions of dollars of unclaimed refunds are the result of forgetful or uninformed tourists.

50. By now the world is a village. Be realistic about what you can and cannot find back home of the legion made-in-Italy souvenirs you're dying to snatch up. Do you really want to spend a precious afternoon in Florence tracking down a pair of black leather gloves that are a dime a dozen at home, when it could be time far better spent gazing upon the wonder of Michelangelo's *David?*

2 The Regions in Brief

Italy as we know it was united only in the 1860s, and people still tend to identify themselves more as, say, Romans, Tuscans, or Sicilians than as Italians. Regional dialects are so diverse and strong that for a Neapolitan to converse with a Milanese, he has to resort to the common "textbook Italian" learned in school.

Here's a quick rundown of the regions covered in this guide to help you understand the country and aid you in deciding where you want to visit.

ROME & LAZIO

Lazio (Latium) and its capital, **Rome (Roma)**, are at the center of Italy and, some say, of the Western world. Rome is where the philosophy and traditions of the ancient Greek east met the pragmatism and robust west to form one of the world's greatest empires. Rome is an intricate layering of ancient, medieval, Renaissance, baroque, and

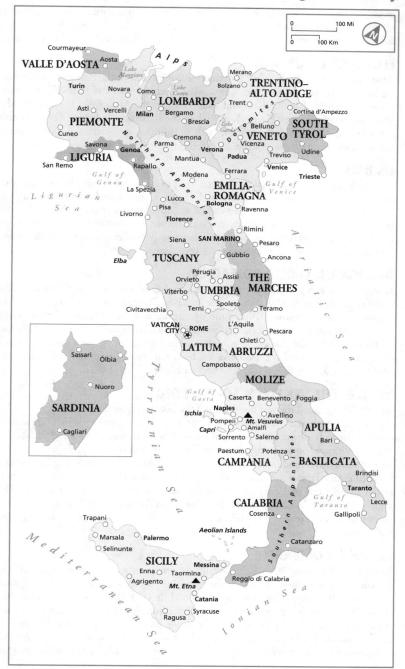

The Regions of Italy

modern cities. You can scramble about the Colosseum and Forum, explore churches filled with baroque paintings by Caravaggio, gawk at Michelangelo's Sistine ceiling frescoes, or simply enjoy a gelato under the shade of a Bernini-designed fountain.

FLORENCE & TUSCANY

Beautiful, magically lit **Tuscany (Toscana)** was the cradle of the Renaissance, producing such artistic geniuses as Giotto, Leonardo, Michelangelo, and Botticelli. From the rolling vineyards of the Chianti and wide valley of the Arno River rise one wonder after another: **Florence (Firenze),** capital of the Renaissance; **Siena,** city of Gothic painters and medieval palaces; **Pisa,** with its Romanesque cathedral and famously leaning tower; and dozens of other art-filled hill towns.

UMBRIA

St. Francis was born in **Umbria,** the green heart of Italy, and perhaps his gentle nature derived from the region's serene hills and valleys, a sun-blessed landscape similar to that of its neighbor, Tuscany. The capital city of **Perugia** strikes a happy balance between medieval hill town, Renaissance art center, and bustling modern university city. Other Umbrian towns include such marvelously medieval centers as **Gubbio** and **Spoleto,** as well as that early Renaissance gem **Assisi.**

BOLOGNA & EMILIA-ROMAGNA

History has left its mark on the central region of **Emilia-Romagna,** riding along the north of the Appenine Mountains to the Po Valley. **Ravenna** was the last capital of the empire and later the stronghold of the Byzantines and the Visigoths. **Ferrara** was a center of Renaissance art and culture, while **Parma,** one of the most powerful duchies in Europe under the Farnese family, is a famed producer of parmigiano reggiano cheese and prosciutto ham. **Bologna** has been renowned for its university since the Middle Ages, and its fine cuisine throughout history.

VENICE, THE VENETO & SOUTH TYROL

The Po River created the vast floodplain of the **Veneto** under the brow of pre-Venetian Alps to the north and the Dolomites in the west. What draws visitors to these agricultural flatlands are the art treasures of **Padua (Padova),** the Renaissance villas of Palladio in **Vicenza,** and—rising on pilings from a lagoon on the Adriatic coast—that year-round carnival and most serene city of canals, **Venice (Venezia).** The **Dolomites,** bordering Austria, cap the eastern stretches of the **South Tyrol** region with sharp pinnacles straight out of a fairy tale, while the peaks of the Alps crown the west. This region is home to legendary resorts like **Cortina d'Ampezzo** and **Merano,** as well as cities like **Trent (Trento)** and **Bolzano** that lie at the crossroads of the German and Italian worlds.

MILAN & LOMBARDY

Lombardy (Lombardia) is Italy's wealthiest province, an industrial, financial, and agricultural powerhouse named for the Lombards, a Germanic people who migrated south over the Alps in the Dark Ages. Beyond its Po Valley factories and cities, the scenic diversity of this prosperous region ranges from legendary lakes like **Como** and **Maggiore** backed by Alpine peaks to the fertile plains of the Po River. The region's capital, **Milan (Milano)**—hotbed of high fashion, high finance, and avant-garde design—is a city of great art and architecture as well (Leonardo's *The Last Supper* is but the beginning), and the region's Renaissance past is still much in evidence in **Cremona, Mantua,** and the other cities of the Lombard plains.

PIEMONTE & THE VALLE D'AOSTA

Piemonte (Piedmont) means "foot of the mountains," and the Alps are in sight from almost every parcel of Italy's northernmost province, which borders Switzerland and France. The flat plains of the Po River rise into rolling hills clad with orchards and vineyards. North of **Turin**—the historic, baroque capital of the region and, with its auto factories, a cornerstone of Italy's "economic miracle"—the plains meet the Alps head-on in the **Valle d'Aosta,** with its craggy mountains, craggy mountain folks, and year-round skiing.

LIGURIA & THE ITALIAN RIVIERA

The **Italian Riviera** follows the Ligurian Sea along a narrow coastal band backed by mountains. At the center of the rocky coast of **Liguria** is **Genoa (Genova),** the country's first port and still its most important—a fascinating city that greets visitors with a remarkable assemblage of Renaissance art and architecture. Some of Italy's most famous seaside retreats flank Genoa on either side: from the tony resort of **San Remo** on France's doorstep all the way down to the picturesque string of fishing villages known as the **Cinque Terre** that line the coast just above Tuscany.

CAMPANIA

Welcome to the good life: **Campania** has been a refuge for the world-weary for over 2,000 years, from imperial Roman villas to modern resort towns. Campania wraps around **Naples (Napoli)**—that chaotic but beautiful city often overlooked on the grand tour—and is rimmed by the gorgeous **Amalfi Coast** with its necklace of comely villages: ravishing **Ravello,** historic **Amalfi,** and posh **Positano.** The seductive isles of **Capri** and **Ischia** lie just offshore. In A.D. 79, Campania's menacing volcano Mt. Vesuvius rained tons of ash on the Roman port of **Pompeii,** preserving it as an evocative ghost town offering a unique glimpse into ancient civilization.

APULIA

This is the very sole of Italy, the bottom of the boot. **Apulia (Pulia),** running the length of the boot heel, puts the lie to the "poor south" reputation of southern Italy—10% of the world's supply of olive oil comes from here, and its ports are some of the Mediterranean's busiest. The region's austerely beautiful scenery, whitewashed buildings, and serene beaches have begun attracting visitors in much larger numbers.

SICILY

A mountainous triangle at the crossroads of the Mediterranean (and its largest island), **Sicily (Sicilia)** sits just a few miles off the tip of Italy's toe—and only a few dozen from Tunisia, swept by both the cold *tramontana* winds from the north and the parched, sandy *scirocco* winds off the Sahara. A landscape at once fertile and foreboding, lush and harsh, Sicily has hosted every Mediterranean civilization from the Greeks and Islamic North Africans through the Spanish Bourbons to today's Italians (with the Romans, Normans, Austrians, and, yes, the Mafia, in between). The past 3,000 years have imparted upon this island of lemons, olives, and almonds a rich heritage to enjoy, from Greek temples to mosaic-filled Norman cathedrals, Moorish palaces to tony seaside resorts.

3 Visitor Information, Entry Requirements & Customs

VISITOR INFORMATION

TOURIST OFFICES   For information before you go, contact the **Italian National Tourist Office (Ente Nazionale Italiano per il Turismo,** or **ENIT).** The Web address is **www.italiantourism.com**. You can also write directly (in English or Italian) to the provincial or local tourist boards of areas you plan to visit, but don't expect Swiss efficiency with a return response. These provincial tourist boards, **Ente Provinciale per il Turismo (E.P.T.),** operate in the principal towns of the provinces. The local tourist boards, occasionally referred to as **Azienda Autonoma Soggiorno** or more simply **Ufficio di Informazione,** operate in all places of tourist interest, and you can get a list from the Italian government tourist offices. When trying to contact the offices themselves, be aware that readers have complained the office isn't as helpful as it could be. Here are the foreign branches:

- **United States**   630 Fifth Ave., Suite 1565, New York, NY 10111 (☎ **212/245-4822;** fax 212/586-9249); 500 N. Michigan Ave., Suite 2240, Chicago, IL 60611 (☎ **312/644-0996;** fax 312/644-3019); 12400 Wilshire Blvd., Suite 550, Los Angeles, CA 90025 (☎ **310/820-2977;** fax 310/820-6357).
- **Canada**   175 Bloor St. East, Suite 907, South Tower, Toronto (Ontario) M4W 3R8 Canada (☎ **416/925-4882;** fax 416/925-4799).
- **United Kingdom**   1 Princes St., London W1R 8AY (☎ **020/7408-1254;** fax 0171/493-6695).

INTERNET RESOURCES   Major Internet sites like Yahoo! (**www.yahoo.com**), Excite (**www.excite.com**), Lycos (**www.lycos.com**), and Infoseek (**www.infoseek. com**) contain subcategories on travel, country/regional information, and culture—search these for links to Web sites specializing in Italy.

General Information   One of the best resources for general travel and destination-specific information is Excite's City.Net (**travel.excite.com/show/?loc=2290**). Other good general sites are Travel Italy (**www.travel.it**), which includes updated tourist information as well as details about hotels and house rentals, spas, transportation services, tour operators, and more; In Italy On-line (**www.initaly.com**), with details on accommodations, tours, festivals, shopping, and more; Hello Italy (**www. gatourism.it**), a hotel reservations service; the Italian Tourist Web Guide (**www. itwg.com**), with on-line hotel reservations and information on art and history; Italy in a Flash (**www.italyflash.com**), offering hotel information, railway and airline schedules, latest exchange rates, weather, and current news; and Let's Roam Italy (**library.thinkquest.org/2838**), a great site for students and younger travelers, with travel tips, information about Italian culture and history, and a list of e-mail addresses for English-speaking students in Italy so you can find an e-mail pal who can tell you more about the country.

Rome   Rome boasts the most sites of any Italian city (no surprise). One of the best is run by Travelocity (**www.travelocity.com**). From the home page, click on the "Destinations & Interests" button, then navigate your way to "Rome and Environs." It has hundreds of listings—full-fledged write-ups in most cases—for everything from sights, hotels, and restaurants to shopping, nightlife, tour companies, and an excellent festivals and events calendar. Roma 2000 (**www.roma2000.it**) is very graphics-heavy with a wealth of information on sightseeing, including some walking tours. It also lists dozens of hotels, restaurants, and shops, but mostly gives just the addresses and phone

The Best of Budget Travel from the King of Budget Travel

Forget the usual travel magazines: They generally focus on high-end vacations, and even when they boast about "deals," the savings they claim are really negligible. However, now there's the bimonthly *Arthur Frommer's Budget Travel,* available for $14.95 per year. This full-color magazine is filled with all the details concerning "vacations for real people." You can find individual issues on the shelves, or order a subscription by calling ☎ **800/829-9121** or by checking out Arthur Frommer's Web site at **www.frommers.com**.

numbers. Try Nerone: The Insider's Guide to Rome (**www.nerone.cc/index.htm**), with visitor as well as cultural and sightseeing information. You can search for general info at **www.romeguide.it** or download the latest issue of *Time Out Rome* at **www.timeout.com**. For an unrelentingly religious site with a wonderful armchair photo tour of the Vatican and its art treasures, head to Christus Rex (**www.christusrex.org**).

Florence   Welcome to the Incredible City of Florence, Italy (**www/tiac.net/users/pendini/hotel.html**), includes details on hotels, museums, music, "hidden corners," and lots more; at Your Way to Florence (**www.arca.net/florence.htm**), you'll find info about art, history, museums and monuments, churches, hotels, and theaters.

Venice   Venice Today (**www.iuav.unive.it/~juli/ventoday.htm**), provides weekly updated details on the city and its events, news, and tourism, plus links to other Venice sites. There's more on Venice at **www.doge.it**, where you'll find everything from the latest happenings to the most affordable hotel rooms.

ENTRY REQUIREMENTS

Citizens of the United States, Canada, Great Britain, Ireland, Australia, and New Zealand with a **valid passport** do not need a visa to enter Italy if they don't expect to stay more than 90 days and don't expect to work there. Those who want to stay longer can apply for a permit for an additional stay of 90 days, which, as a rule, is granted immediately. Applicants for such an extension should bring their passport to the nearest police headquarters (*questura*) or inquire at their home country's consulate or embassy.

CUSTOMS

HEADING THERE   Overseas visitors can bring along most items for personal use duty-free, including fishing tackle, a sporting gun and 200 cartridges, a pair of skis, two tennis racquets, a baby carriage, two hand cameras with 10 rolls of film (though they really don't care how much film you bring; I've had over 100 rolls before), and 400 cigarettes (two cartons) or a quantity of cigars or pipe tobacco not exceeding 500 grams (1.1 lbs.). There are strict limits on importing alcoholic beverages. However, limits are much more liberal for alcohol bought tax-paid in other countries of the European Union.

COMING HOME   **For U.S. Citizens**   You may bring home $400 worth of goods duty free, providing you've been out of the country at least 48 hours and haven't used the exemption in the past 30 days. This includes one liter of an alcohol beverage (you must, of course, be over 21), 200 cigarettes, and 100 cigars. Antiques over 100 years old and works of art are exempt from the $400 limit, as is anything you mail home. You may mail up to $200 worth of goods to yourself (marked "for personal use") and up to $100 to others (marked "unsolicited gift") once each day, so long as the package does not include alcohol or tobacco products.

Do not try to take any meat products, not even cured, vacuum-packed prosciutto or salami, back to the United States. Your goods will be confiscated at U.S. Customs, no matter what the shopkeeper in Italy says. Any fresh food—meats, fruits, vegetables, or breads—are also strictly forbidden to enter the United States from foreign soil. On the other hand, any cheese too hard to be spreadable is usually allowed (don't try it on anything runnier than a brie).

For more specific guidance, contact the **U.S. Customs Service,** P.O. Box 7407, Washington, DC 20044 (☎ **202/927-6724**), to request the free pamphlet *Know Before You Go*. You can download it from the Internet at **www.customs. ustreas.gov/travel/know.htm**. If you make purchases in Italy, it's important to keep your receipts. For refunds of the value-added tax (IVA in Italy), see "Getting the VAT (IVA) Back," later in this chapter

For EU Citizens   As Italy is an EU member, you can take back to any other EU country as much as you'll probably need of traditionally taxed goods without paying additional duties. The customs office does issue theoretical guidelines for the maximum amounts allowed: 800 cigarettes, 10 liters each of fortified wines and spirits, 90 liters of wine (of which 60 can be sparkling), and a mere 110 liters of beer (you must, of course, be over 17 to bring in alcohol or tobacco products). Remember, **duty free** no longer exists if you're moving within the EU, only when you're leaving an EU country for a non-EU one. For details, get in touch with **Her Majesty's Customs and Excise Office,** New King's Beam House, 22 Upper Ground, London, SE1 9PJ (☎ **020/7620-1313**), for more information.

4 Money

There are no restrictions on how much foreign currency you can bring into Italy, though if it's substantial, you should declare the amount brought in so that, if there's a question, you can prove to the Italian Customs office on leaving that the currency came from outside the country. Italian currency taken into or out of Italy may not exceed 200,000L in denominations of 50,000L or lower.

CURRENCY

The basic unit of Italian currency is the **lira** (plural: **lire**), abbreviated as **L** in this book. Coins are issued in denominations of 50L, 100L, 200L, 500L, and 1,000L (with ancient 10s and 20s rarely found), and bills come in denominations of 1,000L, 2,000L, 5,000L, 10,000L, 50,000L, 100,000L, and 500,000L. Coins for 50L and 100L come in two sizes each, the newer ones both around the size of a nickel (which can't yet be used in any coin-accepting machines or public phones).

With the arrival of the euro fast upon us (see below), things will change considerably. Until then, interbank rates are established daily and listed in most international newspapers. To get a transaction as close to this rate as possible, pay for as much as possible with credit cards. ATMs and bank cards offer close to the same rate, plus an added-on fee for cash transactions.

Currency Converter

All the prices in this book were calculated at the rate of 2,000L to $1. However, the exchange rate constantly fluctuates. If you have access to the Web, you can get an instant exchange rate by logging onto **www.x-rates.com/calculator.html**.

The Debut of the Euro

The adoption of a single European currency, called the **euro** (€), is a contentious move within Europe. Even though most of Western Europe has been closely interconnected as an economic and trade unit for years, the official merger of its national currencies and economies is another matter. Up until the last minute, all the countries involved jockeyed for the best deal for their own nation before the final papers were signed, and even now that the euro is an official currency, they're still fighting over the details of how it will be phased in, and the currency has steadily slipped against the dollar ever since its debut (good news for American travelers; bad for Europeans).

In January 1999, the 12 countries that chose to adopt the euro—Austria, Belgium, Finland, France, Germany, Ireland, Italy, Luxembourg, the Netherlands, Portugal, and Spain, later joined by Greece—officially locked their exchange rates together and switched most business transactions and computer and credit-card banking over to the new single currency—which, seeming to have partly stabilized its downward slide (especially after the international banking community intervened to shore it up), currently hovers at a rate of $1 = € 0.87, £1 = € 0.60, and 1,000L = € 0.52. Several countries have opted out from switching over for the time being, including Britain, Denmark, and Sweden (though Denmark and Sweden seem to be moving closer to voting it in); Switzerland is not part of the EU.

But for those 12 euro countries, things changed immediately. Everything from stocks and bonds to hotel rooms and canned peas began being stickered with two prices: the rate in the local currency and that in euros (even some countries not using the euro have started doing it). Not every little shopkeep and greengrocer has started double pricing yet, but the euro is gradually seeping into every nook and cranny of Europe. In many establishments, you can even choose to charge items on your credit card at the euro price rather than the price in Italian lire. Both prices will translate to the exact same dollar amount, of course, but since now you'll be able to see the flat euro price for hotel rooms in Paris, Berlin, and Rome, you can better comparison shop without juggling any complicated conversions in your head.

But don't get too excited. The euro as physical banknotes and coins currency won't be issued until January 1, 2002, and the various national currencies won't be fully withdrawn until 2 months later (recently cut down from the original 6 months). Since you'll still be juggling lire in the thousands until then, prices in this book are quoted in lire. For more information on the euro, check out **www.europa.eu.int/euro**.

Although exchange rates are more favorable at the point of arrival, it is often helpful to exchange at least some money before going abroad (standing in line upon your arrival at the Milan or Rome airport's *cambio* may make you miss the next bus leaving for downtown). Check with the major banks (which charge the smallest fee) or your local American Express or Thomas Cook offices. You can order Italian lire in advance from the following: American Express (cardholders only) (☎ **800/553-6782**), Thomas Cook (☎ **800/287-7362**), Chase Manhattan Bank (☎ **800/935-9935**), or International Currency Express (☎ **888/842-0880** or 888/287-6628).

When exchanging money in Italy, it's best to exchange currency or traveler's checks at a bank, not a *cambio* (exchange bureau), hotel, or shop. Currency and traveler's checks (for which you'll receive a better rate than cash) can be changed at all principal airports and some travel agencies, such as American Express and Thomas Cook. Note the rates and ask about commission fees; it can sometimes pay to shop around and ask the right questions.

Rarely will Italian hotels accept a dollar-denominated check from your hometown bank as a deposit sent in advance; if you find a hotel that does, it'll probably charge dearly for the conversion. Some hotels accept countersigned traveler's checks sent by mail or a credit card (the latter more commonly done in the larger or higher-grade hotels, but more and more by the smaller hotels such as those suggested in this book) given over the phone.

A few of the smaller hotels still demand a check drawn on an Italian bank when reserving a room from overseas. This can be arranged by a large commercial bank or by a currency specialist like **Ruesch International,** 700 11th St. NW, Suite 400, Washington, DC 20001 (☎ **800/424-2923** or 202/408-1200; www.ruesch.com). Ruesch maintains additional offices in New York, Los Angeles, Chicago, Atlanta, and Boston, though the Washington, D.C., office can supply the bank draft through phone orders.

CREDIT CARDS

Never rely entirely on credit cards, although they can be used almost everywhere. Visa and MasterCard are accepted at most hotels, restaurants, and shops, with American Express trailing behind. Diner's Club is also a favorite. Once you leave the larger or less-visited cities or in some of the smaller, family-run hotels and shops and trattorias, a cash/traveler's-checks-only policy still prevails.

A cash advance against your credit cards, whether from a bank or an ATM, is costly, and usually combines three charges—the surcharge above the interbank rate, the transaction fee, and the financing charge on the loan, which is what a cash advance is (see below).

ATM NETWORKS

The ATM revolution is being felt throughout Italy, rapidly taking hold in both smaller towns as well as larger cities. Although **Bancomat** is the name of a privately owned Italian company, its name has become the generic word for ATMs in Italy where you can withdraw money from your account at home or, more expensively, against your credit card as a cash advance. American Express cardholders can use the ATMs of **Banco Popolare di Milano** throughout Italy or at any American Express office in Italy.

Old worries about PIN numbers not working abroad rarely hold any more, but double-check before leaving home to be sure. On the Internet, check **www.mastercard.com/atm** or **www.visa.com/pd/atm/main.html** to find ATMs where you'll be visiting.

TRAVELER'S CHECKS

Although going the way of the dinosaur, traveler's checks remain the safest method of carrying money because in the event of theft, the value of your checks will be refunded (if you've kept track of each check's number and of those that have already been cashed). Most large banks sell traveler's checks, charging fees averaging 1% to 2% of the value of the checks you buy. If your bank wants more than a 2% commission, it sometimes pays to call the traveler's check issuers directly for the address of outlets where the commission will cost less.

The Italian Lira, the U.S. Dollar & the British Pound

At this writing, US$1 = approximately 2,000L, and this was the rate of exchange used to calculate the dollar values throughout this book. The rate fluctuates from day to day, depending on a complicated series of economic and political factors, and might not be the same when you travel to Italy.

Likewise, the ratio of the British pound to the lira fluctuates constantly. At press time, £1 = approximately 3,230L, an exchange rate reflected in the table below.

Lire	US$	UK£	Lire	US$	UK£
1,000	0.50	0.31	35,000	17.50	10.84
1,500	0.75	0.46	40,000	20.00	12.38
2,000	1.00	0.62	45,000	22.50	13.93
3,000	1.50	0.93	50,000	25.00	15.48
4,000	2.00	1.24	100,000	50.00	30.96
5,000	2.50	1.55	125,000	62.50	38.70
7,500	3.75	2.32	10,000	5.00	3.10
15,000	7.50	4.64	20,000	10.00	6.20
25,000	12.50	7.74	30,000	15.00	9.29

Issuers sometimes have agreements with groups to sell checks commission-free. For example **AAA** clubs sell American Express checks in several currencies without commission.

American Express (☎ **800/221-7282** in the U.S. and Canada; www.americanexpress.com) is one of the largest and most immediately recognized issuers of traveler's checks. The commission is waived for holders of certain types of American Express credit cards.

Citicorp (☎ **800/645-6556** in the U.S. and Canada, or 813/623-1709, collect, from anywhere else in the world; www.citicorp.com) issues its own checks. **Thomas Cook** (☎ **800/223-7373** in the U.S. and Canada; otherwise call 609/987-7300 collect from other parts of the world; www.thomascook.com), issues MasterCard traveler's checks. And **Interpayment Services** (☎ **800/732-1322** in the U.S. and Canada; call 44-17-33-31-89-49 collect from other parts of the world) sells Visa checks, which are issued by a consortium of member banks and the Thomas Cook organization.

5 When to Go

May to **June** and **September** and **October** are the most pleasant months for touring Italy—temperatures are usually mild and the hordes not so intense. But starting in mid-June, the summer rush really picks up, and from July to mid-September, the country teems with visitors.

August (with July a close runner up) is the worst month—not only does it get uncomfortably hot, muggy, and crowded, but the entire country goes on vacation at least from August 15 to the end of the month, and a good percentage of Italians take off the entire month, leaving the cities to the tourists. Many hotels, restaurants, and shops are closed—except along the coast and on the islands, which is where most Italians head.

From **late October to Easter,** most sights go on shorter winter hours or close for renovation periods, many hotels and restaurants take a month or two off between November and February, beach destinations become padlocked ghost towns, and it can get much colder than you'd expect (it may even snow). The crowds thin remarkably, especially outside the Big Three cities (Rome, Florence, and Venice).

High season on most airlines' routes to Rome usually stretches from June to the end of September plus Christmas/New Year's week. This is the most expensive and most crowded time to travel. **Shoulder season** is from Easter time (usually late March or April) to May, late September to October, and December 15 to 24. **Low season** is generally January 6 to mid-March, November 1 to December 14, and December 25 to March 31.

WEATHER

It's warm all over Italy in **summer,** especially inland. The high temperatures (measured in Italy in degrees Celsius) begin in Rome in May, often lasting until some time in late September. July and August can be impossible and explain why life in the cities slows down considerably (and life in the coastline resorts comes alive), and few budget hotels have A/C (and just a handful of hotels in all of Italy have discovered mosquito screens, so when you open the windows for some respite from the heat, you tend to invite dozens of tiny bloodsuckers in as well).

Winters in the north of Italy are cold with rain and snow, and December and January are generally unpleasant unless you're skiing in Cortina. In the south, the weather is mild in the winter months, averaging in the 40s. Sicily's citrus and almond trees are already in bloom in February—but nights can be cold, and Italian hotel's heating systems can be . . . frustrating. Purpose-built, modernized hotels in their own buildings often have independent heating/cooling systems you (or they) can control, but in older hotels and in small ones that take up only part of a building, the heat can often only be turned on for the winter on a pre-established date dictated by the local government, and only left on during certain hours of the day (just one of the many lovely laws still hanging on from the Fascist era). Some of the cheapest hotels in Southern Italy and Sicily don't even have heating systems, so the rare cold snap can leave you shivering.

For the most part, it's drier in Italy than in North America. Since the humidity is lower, high temperatures don't seem as bad; exceptions are cities known for their

Italy's Average Daily Temperature & Monthly Rainfall

Florence

	Jan	Feb	Mar	Apr	May	June	July	Aug	Sept	Oct	Nov	Dec
Temp. (°F)	45	47	50	60	67	76	77	70	64	63	55	46
Rainfall (in.)	3	3.3	3.7	2.7	2.2	1.4	1.4	2.7	3.2	4.9	3.8	2.9

Naples

	Jan	Feb	Mar	Apr	May	June	July	Aug	Sept	Oct	Nov	Dec
Temp. (°F)	50	54	58	63	70	78	83	85	75	66	60	52
Rainfall (in.)	4.7	4	3	3.8	2.4	.8	.8	2.6	3.5	5.8	5.1	3.7

Rome

	Jan	Feb	Mar	Apr	May	June	July	Aug	Sept	Oct	Nov	Dec
Temp. (°F)	49	52	57	62	72	82	87	86	73	65	56	47
Rainfall (in.)	2.3	1.5	2.9	3.0	2.8	2.9	1.5	1.9	2.8	2.6	3.0	2.1

humidity factor, such as Florence and Venice. In Rome, Naples, and the south, temperatures can stay in the 90s for days, but nights are most often comfortably cooler. It's important to remember that this is not a country as smitten by the notion of air-conditioning and central heating as, say, the United States. And remember that the inexpensive hotels we list in this book are often the very places that will remind you of the pros and cons of ancient stone palazzi built with 3-foot-thick walls. Don't expect the comfort of the Ritz.

HOLIDAYS

Offices and shops in Italy are closed on the following dates: **January 1** (New Year's Day), **January 6** (Epiphany, usually called *La Befana* after Italy's Christmas Witch), **Easter Sunday, Easter Monday, April 25** (Liberation Day), **May 1** (Labor Day), **August 15** (Assumption of the Virgin—much of Italy takes its summer vacation from **August 15 to 30**), **November 1** (All Saints' Day), **December 8** (Feast of the Immaculate Conception), **December 25** (Christmas Day), and **December 26** (Santo Stefano); most Italians' **Christmas** holidays last from December 24 though January 6.

Closings are also observed in the following cities on feast days honoring their patron saints: Venice, **April 25** (St. Mark); Florence, Genoa, and Turin, **June 24** (St. John the Baptist); Rome, **June 29** (Sts. Peter and Paul); Palermo, **July 15** (Santa Rosalia); Naples, **September 19** (St. Gennaro); Bologna, **October 4** (St. Petronio); Cagliari, **October 30** (St. Saturnino); Trieste, **November 3** (San Giusto); Bari, **December 6** (St. Nicola); and Milan, **December 7** (St. Ambrose).

Italy Calendar of Events

For more details on each event below, contact the **tourist office** of the city or town where the festival is held (see the individual chapters).

January

- **Epiphany celebrations, nationwide.** All cities, towns, and villages in Italy stage Roman Catholic Epiphany observances. One of the most festive celebrations is the Christmas/Epiphany Fair at Rome's Piazza Navona. From Christmas to January 6.
- **Festival of Italian Popular Song, San Remo (Italian Riviera).** A 3-day festival when major artists and up-and-comers perform the latest Italian pop songs and launch the newest hits. Late January.
- **Foire de Saint Ours, Aosta, Valle d'Aosta.** Observing a tradition that's existed for 10 centuries, artisans from the mountain valleys come together to display their wares—often made of wood, lace, wool, or wrought iron—created during the long winter months. Late January.

February

- ✪ **Carnevale (Carnival), Venice.** Venice's Carnival evokes the final theatrical 18th-century days of the Venetian Republic. Historical presentations, elaborate costumes, and music of all types in every piazza cap the festivities. The balls are by invitation, but the cultural events, piazza performances, and fireworks (Shrove Tuesday) are open to everyone. See the box in chapter 7 for more information. Usually two Fridays before Shrove Tuesday through Shrove Tuesday.
- **Carnevale (Carnival), Rome.** Everyone eats *frappe* (pastry leaves coated with powered sugar) and the kiddies go around dressed in costume for their own version of Halloween (without the candy). The final night, Martedi Grasso (Fat

Tuesday), is the time for big private parties, but little goes on out in the streets. Usually two Fridays before Shrove Tuesday through Shrove Tuesday.

- **Carnevale (Carnival), Viareggio, on the Tuscan coast.** Fireworks, pageants, parades of papier-mâché floats, and a flower show gild this Carnival, which is popular with kids, but not as theatrical and culturally inclined as Venice's rendition. Dates vary; parades take place three consecutive weekends, culminating on Martedì Grasso (Fat Tuesday). Usually two Fridays before Shrove Tuesday through Shrove Tuesday.
- **Almond Blossom Festival, Agrigento (Sicily).** This folk festival includes song, dance, costumes, and fireworks. First half of February.

April

- **Holy Week (Settimana Santa), Rome.** The most notable procession is led by the Pope, passing the Colosseum and Roman Forum up to Palatine Hill. A torch-lit parade caps the observance. Week between Palm Sunday and Easter Sunday; sometimes at the end of March, but often in April.
- **Good Friday and Easter Week observances, nationwide.** Processions and age-old ceremonies—some from pagan days, some from the Middle Ages—are staged. The most colorful and evocative are in **Trapani** and other towns throughout **Sicily.** Beginning on the Thursday or Friday before Easter Sunday, usually in April.
- **Pasqua (Easter Sunday), Piazza di San Pietro, Rome.** In an event broadcast around the world, the Pope gives his blessing from a balcony overlooking a packed St. Peter's Square.
- **Scoppio del Carro (Explosion of the Cart), Florence.** An ancient observance: A cart laden with flowers and fireworks is drawn by three white oxen to the Duomo, where at noon mass a mechanical dove detonates it from the altar by means of a wire that passes through the Duomo's open doors. Easter Sunday.
- **Festa della Primavera (Feast of Spring), Rome.** The Spanish Steps are decked out with banks of azaleas and other flowers, and later orchestral and choral concerts are presented in Trinità dei Monti. Late April or early May.
- ✪ **Maggio Musicale Fiorentino (Musical May Florentine), Florence.** Italy's oldest and most prestigious festival presents opera, ballet, and concerts. It takes place at the Teatro Comunale, the Teatro della Pergola, and various other venues, including Piazza della Signoria and the Pitti Palace courtyard. Maestro Zubin Mehta is the honorary director, often conducting Florence's Maggio Musicale Orchestra, and guest conductors and orchestras appear throughout the festival. Schedule and ticket information is available from Maggio Musicale Fiorentino/Teatro Comunale, Via Solferino 16, 50123 Firenze (☎ **055-211-158;** www.maggiofiorentino.com). Late April to June or July.

May

- **Calendimaggio (Celebration of Holy Week), Assisi.** This pagan celebration of spring is held according to rites dating back to medieval times. First weekend after May 1.
- **International Horse Show, Rome.** This show is held on the Villa Borghese's Piazza di Siena. Usually May 1 to 10, but dates can vary.

Hot Tickets

For major events where tickets should be procured well before arriving on the spot, check with **Edwards & Edwards** (☎ **800/223-6108** in the U.S.).

- **Sagra di Sant'Efisio (Festival of St. Efisio), Cagliari (Sardinia).** At one of the biggest and most colorful processions in Italy, several thousand pilgrims (wearing costumes dating from 1657) accompany the statue of the saint on foot, on horseback, or in a cart. May 1 to 4.

❂ **Corso dei Ceri, Gubbio.** In this centuries-old ceremony, 1,000-pound 30-foot wooden "candles" (*ceri*) are raced through the streets of this perfectly preserved medieval hill town in Umbria. Celebrating the feast day of St. Ubaldo, the town's patron saint, the candles are mounted by statues of the patron saints of the town's medieval guilds and are raced through the narrow streets and up a steep hill to the monastery—where Ubaldo always wins the race. May 15.

- **Voga Longa, Venice.** This 30km (18-mi.) rowing "race" from San Marco to Burano and back again has been enthusiastically embraced since its inception in 1975, following the city's effort to keep alive the centuries-old heritage of the regatta). The event itself is colorful, and every local seems to have a relative or next-door neighbor competing. For details, call ☎ **041-521-0544.** A Sunday in mid-May.

- **Cavalcata Sarda (Sardinian Cavalcade), Sassari.** Traditional procession with over 3,000 people in Sardinian costume, some on horseback. Next to last Sunday in May.

June

- **Estate Fiesolana (Summer in Fiesole), Fiesole.** For this festival, the Roman theater in Fiesole (north of Florence) comes alive with dance, music, and theater. Most of the performances take place in the remains of the A.D. 1st-century Roman theater. You can get information and tickets through **Agenzia Box Office,** Via Alamanni 39, Firenze (☎ **055-210-0804** or 055-261-6049), or at the Roman theater itself on the day of the performance after 4:30pm. A.T.A.F. bus no. 7 travels to Fiesole from Florence's train station and Piazza del Duomo. Late June to August.

- **Calcio Storico (Ancient Football Match), Florence.** For this revival of a raucous 16th-century football match, teams representing Florence's four original parishes, identified by their colors and clad in 16th-century costume, square off against one another in consecutive playoffs on dirt-covered Piazza Santa Croce. It's preceded by an elaborate procession. Afterward, fireworks light up the night sky. See the tourist office for ticket information about numbered seats in the bleachers lining the piazza. There are four matches, usually culminating on June 24, feast day of San Giovanni (St. John), beloved patron saint of Florence.

- **San Ranieri and the Gioco del Ponte (Bridge Game), Pisa.** Two Pisa traditions: First, Pisa honors its own St. Ranieri with candlelit parades followed the next day by eight-rower teams competing in 16th-century costumes. June 16 and 17. The Gioco del Ponte takes place with teams in Renaissance garb taking part in a hotly contested tug-of-war on the Ponte di Mezzo spanning the Arno River. First Sunday of June.

❂ **Spoleto Festival, Spoleto.** Dating from 1958, this festival, until recently known as the Festival dei Due Mondi (Festival of Two Worlds), was the creation of American-born Maestro Gian Carlo Menotti. It's now the country's biggest and most prestigious arts festival. International performers convene in this lovely Umbrian hill town for 3 weeks of dance, drama, opera, concerts, and art exhibits. For more information, contact **Associazione Spoleto Festival,** Piazza del Duomo 8, 06049 Spoleto (PG) (☎ **800-565-600** toll free in Italy, or 0743-220-032; fax 0743-220-321; **0743-44-700** from outside Italy; www. spoletofestival.net; e-mail tickets@spoletofestival.net). Also try the **Teatro Nuovo** (☎ **0743-40-265**). Mid-June to mid-July.

Molto Italiano

Language courses are available at several centers around the Italian peninsula, with the most varied and best recommended usually headquartered in what most Italians refer to as their nation's intellectual and cultural capital, Florence. You can contact any of the following for information about programs across Italy, varying in length, location (city versus rural), short- or long-term, and price: **Italian Cultural Institute** in New York (☎ 212/879-4242), **American Institute for Foreign Study** (☎ 800/727-AIFS;** www.aifs.org), and **Institute of International Education** (☎ 800/445-0443 or 212/984-5413; www.iie.org).

- **Festa di San Giovanni (Feast of St. John), Rome.** This festival is still celebrated with throngs of people singing and dancing and consuming large amounts of stewed snails and artery-clogging *porchetta* (pork) on Piazza San Giovanni in Laterano. June 23.
- **Festa di San Pietro e Paulo (Feast of Sts. Peter and Paul), Rome.** The most significant Roman religious festival is observed with a street fair on Via Ostiense and masses at St. Peter's and St. Paul Outside the Walls. Usually June 29.

Events That Last Throughout the Summer
- **Biennale d'Arte, Venice.** This is Europe's most prestigious—and controversial—International Exposition of Modern Art, taking place in odd-numbered years only. More than 50 nations take part, with art displayed in permanent pavilions in the Public Gardens and elsewhere about town. Many great modern artists have been discovered at this world-famous show. Contact the board at ☎ 041-521-8711 (www.labiennale.org) for more information. June to October.
- **Son et Lumière, the Roman Forum and Tivoli, Rome.** These areas are dramatically lit at night. Early June to the end of September.
- **Shakespearean Festival, Verona.** Ballet, drama, and jazz performances are included in this festival of the Bard with a few performances in English. June to September.
- ✪ **Il Palio, Piazza del Campo, Siena.** Palio fever grips this Tuscan hill town for a wild and exciting horse race from the Middle Ages. Pageantry, costumes, and the celebrations of the victorious contrada mark the well-attended spectacle. It's a no-rules event: Even a horse without a rider can win the race. Tickets (impossible to come by for non-Sienese) usually sell out by January, but consider joining the nonticket-holding crowd that stands in the middle of the square. See the box in chapter 5 for more information. July 2 and August 16.
- **Arena di Verona (Outdoor Opera Season in Verona), Verona.** Culture buffs flock to the open-air, 20,000-seat Roman amphitheater, one of the world's best preserved. The season lasts from early July to August for awesome productions of *Aïda* and others.
- **Music and Drama Festival, Taormina, Sicily.** July and August are the most important months for performances held in the resort town's gorgeously sited ancient Greek amphitheater, with Mt. Etna looming in the distance. The local tourism board distributes tickets.

July
- **Festa de' Noiantri (Festival of We Others), Rome.** Trastevere, the most colorful quarter of Old Rome becomes a gigantic outdoor restaurant, as tons of food and drink are consumed at tables lining the streets. A street fair is held on Viale Trastevere and concerts and plays are performed on Piazza Santa Maria in

Trastevere. This feast was immortalized near the end of Fellini's film *Roma* (the scene in which he interviews Gore Vidal). Mid-July.

- **Umbria Jazz, Perugia.** The Umbrian region hosts the country's (and one of Europe's) top jazz festival featuring world-class artists. Mid- to late July.
- **Festa del Redentore (Feast of the Redeemer), Venice.** This celebration marking the July 1576 lifting of a plague that had gripped the city is centered around the Palladio-designed Chiesa del Redentore on the island of Giudecca. A bridge of boats across the Giudecca Canal links the church with the banks of Le Zattere in Dorsoduro and hundreds of boats of all shapes and sizes fill the Giudecca. It's one big floating festa until night descends and an awesome half-hour *spettacolo* of fireworks fills the sky. Third Saturday and Sunday in July.

August

- **Festa della Madonna della Neve (Festival of the Madonna of the Snows), Rome.** The legendary founding of the Basilica di Santa Maria Maggiore is reenacted with a pretty "snowfall" of rose petals over the congregation during mass. August 5.
- **Torre del Lago Puccini, near Lucca.** Puccini operas are performed in this Tuscan lakeside town's open-air theater, near the celebrated composer's former summertime villa. Contact tourist office in Lucca. Throughout August.
- **Rossini Opera Festival, Pesaro.** The world's top bel canto specialists perform Rossini's operas and choral works at this popular festival on the Italian Adriatic Riviera. Mid-August to late September.
- ✪ **Venice International Film Festival.** Ranking after Cannes, this film festival brings together stars, directors, producers, and filmmakers from all over the world. Films are shown day and night to an international jury and to the public, at the Palazzo del Cinema, on the Lido, and other venues. Contact the tourist office or the Venice Film Festival at ☎ **041-272-6501** or 041-524-1320 (www.labiennale.org). Two weeks in late August to early September.

September

- **Sagra dell'Uva (Festival of the Grape), Rome.** For this festival, grape growers from the region come to the Basilica of Maxentius in the Roman Forum and party in the shade of its half-ruined vaults. This harvest festival of half-price grapes is accompanied by costumed musicians and other market stalls. First week in September.
- **Regata Storica, Grand Canal, Venice.** Just about every seaworthy gondola, richly decorated for the occasion and piloted by *gondolieri* in colorful livery, participates in the opening cavalcade. The aquatic parade is followed by three regattas that proceed along the Grand Canal. You can buy grandstand tickets through the tourist office or arrive early and pull up a piece of embankment near the Rialto Bridge for the best seats in town. First Sunday in September.
- **Giostra del Saracino (Joust of the Saracen), Arezzo.** A colorful procession in full historical regalia precedes the tilting contest of the 13th century with knights in armor in the town's main piazza. First Sunday in September.

Travel Tip

Try to avoid traveling to Italy in August, as this is when most Italians take their vacations (*ferie*) and many shops and restaurants in the cities will be closed. Keep in mind that many of the less-expensive hotels we list don't have air-conditioning, and nights can be intolerable.

Cycling in Italy

Cycling tours are a good way to see Italy at your own pace. Some of the best are featured by the **Cyclists' Touring Club,** 69 Meadrow, Godalming, Surrey GU7 3HS (☎ **01483/417-217** in the U.K.; www.ctc.org.uk). It charges £25 ($45) a year for adults and £12.50 ($23) for those 17 and under for membership, part of which includes information and suggested cycling routes through most European countries. One of the oldest in the United States specializes in walking as well as cycling tours: **Ciclismo Classico** (☎ **800/866-7314** in the U.S.; www. ciclismoclassico.com).

If you want to cycle on your own, head to the Web site of Florence Bike Pages (**www.abeline.it/fbp.htm**). You'll find bike maps of Florence and Tuscany, instructions on how to bike solo, and information on bike supplements for the trains (many trains have a cargo car for bikes; look for a bike icon on train schedules that designates these trains).

For a guided 1-day bike trip, **I Bike Italy** (in Florence ☎ **055-234-2371;** www.ibikeitaly.com; e-mail ibi_tkt_info@ibikeitaly.com) explores the idyllic Tuscan countryside surrounding Florence (walking tours are also arranged). Bikes, a guide, a picnic lunch, and car transfer in and out of the city center are provided.

- **Partita a Scacchi con Personnagi Viventi (Living Chess Game), Marostica.** This chess game is played in the town square by living pawns in period costume. The second Saturday and Sunday of September during even-numbered years.
- **International Antiques Show, Florence.** More than 100 internationally noted dealers hawk their most exquisite pieces—the crowd is as interesting as the wares. The historically potent setting of the massive Renaissance Palazzo Strozzi couldn't be more appropriate, but check for a possible change of venue. Admission is about 15,000L ($8). For information visit the tourist office. Mid-September in odd-numbered years.

October

- **Sagra del Tartufo, Alba, Piedmont.** Honors the expensive truffle in Alba, the truffle capital of Italy, with contests, truffle-hound competitions, and tastings of this ugly but precious and delectable fungus. Two weeks in mid-October.
- **Maratona (Marathon), Venice.** The marathon starts at Villa Pisani on the mainland, runs aongside the Brenta Canal, and ends along the Zattere for a finish at the Basilica di Santa Maria della Salute on the tip of Dorsoduro. For details, call ☎ **041-950-644.** Usually the last Sunday of October.

November

- **Festa della Salute, Venice.** For this festival, a pontoon bridge is erected across the Grand Canal to connect the churches of La Salute and Santa Maria del Giglio, commemorating another delivery from a plague in 1630 that wiped out a third of the lagoon's population; it's the only day La Salute opens its massive front doors (a secondary entrance is otherwise used). November 21.

December

- ○ **La Scala Opera Season, Teatro alla Scala, Milan.** At the most famous opera house of them all, the season opens on December 7, the feast day of Milan's patron St. Ambrogio, and runs into July. Though it's close to impossible to get opening-night tickets, it's worth a try; call ☎ **02-860-787** or 02-860-775 for the box office, 02-7200-3744 for the information line (www.teatroallascala.org).

- **Christmas Blessing of the Pope, Piazza di San Pietro, Rome.** Delivered at noon from a balcony of St. Peter's Basilica. It's broadcast around the world. December 25.

6 Organized Tours, Package Tours & Tour Operators

Before you start your search for the lowest airfare, you may want to consider booking your flight as part of a travel package such as an escorted tour or a package tour. What you lose in adventure, you might gain in time and money saved when you book accommodations, and maybe even food and entertainment, along with your flight. If you're planning on visiting a lot of different destinations throughout Italy, a good tour operator will make sure that you don't have to worry about the logistics of connections, transportation in places where language might be a problem, looking after your own luggage, coping with reservations and payment at individual hotels, and facing other nuts and bolts of travel in a foreign culture. Some travelers may find the biggest compromise is the hotel factor. Most lodging is found in large modern facilities (sometimes on the outskirts of town), not in the small charming places in the *centro storico*. Although several of the best-rated moderately priced tour companies are described below, check as well with a good travel agent, on the Internet, or in your newspaper for the latest offerings and advice.

One of the more moderately priced package-tour operators for travel in Italy is **Italiatour,** part of the Alitalia Group (☎ **800/845-3365** or 212/765-2183; www.italiatour.com), which offers a wide variety of tours at great savings in the off season. The company appeals to the free-at-heart and specializes in tours for independent travelers who ride from one destination to another by train or rental car. In most cases, the company sells pre-reserved hotel accommodations that are usually less expensive than if you had reserved yourself. The range of accommodations provided begins with three-star hotels that, when booked with their bulk discount, can account for a very attractive bottom line. Because of the company's close link with Alitalia, the prices quoted for air passage are sometimes among the most reasonable on the retail market.

Also working with volume and affiliated with Alitalia—and therefore promising big-volume discounts—is the reputable **Central Holidays Tours (CHT)** (☎ **800/935-5000;** www.centralholidays.com), which offers low- and high-season package tours that are escorted, hosted, or independent. This outfitter is also a good choice if you want to mix and match your own arrangements: They'll help with air, hotel, and car rental according to your needs.

There are smaller, equally established agencies that specialize in Italy and often come up with rates comparable to the big guys. **Pino Travel** (☎ **800/247-6578** or

A Specialty Travel Web Site

At the **InfoHub Specialty Travel Guide** (www.infohub.com) you can find tours in Italy (as well as other countries) centered around just about everything: antiques, archaeology, art history, churches, cooking, gay life, nudism, religion, wineries, and much more. If this sounds expensive to you, don't worry—while searching the site, you can even set your own price limit. Two other good resource sites for specialty tours and travels are the **Specialty Travel Index** (www.specialtytravel.com) and **Shaw Guides** (www.shawguides.com).

212/682-5400; www.pinotravel.com) and **Penem Travel** (☎ **800/628-1345** or 212/730-7675) offer a pick-and-choose menu of car rental, air, and hotel; **Maiellano** (☎ **800/223-1616**) specializes in discount car rental but has successfully expanded into all aspects of travel in Italy.

7 Health & Insurance

STAYING HEALTHY

You'll encounter few health problems traveling in Italy. Aside from the occasional sign *acqua non potabile* (water not drinkable), Italy's tap water is generally safe to drink (though, as it's often unfiltered and not subjected to the chemical "purification" barrage of U.S. tap water, it may taste different or appear milky—that's natural calcium). Italy's milk is pasteurized, and its health services are excellent.

Bring along copies of your prescriptions written in the generic (chemical), not brand-name, form (that way foreign pharmacists can fill them more easily). If you need a doctor, your hotel can recommend one or you can contact your embassy or consulate. You can also obtain a list of English-speaking doctors before you leave from the **International Association for Medical Assistance to Travelers (IAMAT),** in the United States at 417 Center St., Lewiston, NY 14092 (☎ **716/754-4883**), or in Canada at 40 Regal Rd., Guelph, ON N1K 1B5 (☎ **519/836-0102;** www.sentex. net/~iamat).

If you suffer from a chronic illness or special medical condition, consider purchasing a Medic Alert identification bracelet or necklace, which will immediately alert any doctor to your condition and will provide Medic Alert's 24-hour hot line phone number so that foreign doctors can obtain medical information on you. The initial membership is $35, and there's a $15 annual fee. Contact the **Medic Alert Foundation,** 2323 Colorado Ave., Turlock, CA 95381-1009 (☎ **800/432-5378;** www. medicalert.org).

INSURANCE

Before purchasing any additional insurance, check your homeowner's, automobile, and medical insurance policies, as well as the insurance provided by your credit card companies and auto and travel clubs. You may have adequate off-premises theft coverage or your credit card company may even provide cancellation coverage if your airline ticket is paid for with a credit card.

Remember, Medicare covers only U.S. citizens traveling in Mexico and Canada, not in Italy or other European countries. Also note that to submit any insurance claim, you must always have thorough documentation, including all receipts, police reports, and medical records.

Travel Guard International, 1145 Clark St., Stevens Point, WI 54481 (☎ **800/ 826-1300;** www.travelguard.com), features comprehensive insurance programs starting as low as $48. The program covers basically everything: trip cancellation and interruption, lost luggage, medical coverage abroad, emergency assistance, accidental death, and a 24-hour worldwide emergency hot line. A pre-existing medical conditions waiver is included.

With **Travel Insured International,** P.O. Box 280568, East Hartford, CT 06128-0568 (☎ **800/243-3174** in the U.S., or 203/528-7663 outside the U.S. between 7:45am and 7pm EST; www.travelinsured.com), trip cancellation and emergency evacuation costs $5.50 for each $100 of coverage. Travel accident and illness insurance goes for $10 for 6 to 10 days, and $500 of insurance for lost, damage, or delayed luggage is $20 for 10 days. **Travelex Insurance Services** (☎ **800/228-9792;** www. travelex-insurance.com) offers cruise and tour insurance packages that include travel-assistance services and financial protection against trip cancellation, trip interruption, flight and baggage delays, sickness, accident-related medical costs, accidental death and dismemberment, and medical evacuation coverage. Application for insurance packages beginning at $67 per person can be made by phone with a major credit card.

In London, you can call **Columbus Travel Insurance** (☎ **020/7375-0011;** www.columbusdirect.co.uk) or **Endsleigh Insurance** (☎ **020/7436-4451;** www.endsleigh.co.uk). In Sydney, contact the **Australian Federation of Travel Agents** (AFTA; ☎ **02/9264-3299;** www.afta.com.au).

8 Tips for Travelers with Special Needs

FOR TRAVELERS WITH DISABILITIES

If you're flying around Europe, the airlines and ground staff will help you on and off planes and reserve seats for you with sufficient leg room, but it's essential to arrange for this assistance in advance by contacting your airline.

Recent laws in Italy have compelled rail stations, airports, hotels, and most restaurants to follow a stricter set of regulations about **wheelchair** accessibility to rest rooms, ticket counters, and so on. Many museums and other sightseeing attractions have conformed to these regulations. Even Venice has now installed wheelchair elevator platforms on many of the hundreds of bridges over the city's canals, effectively opening up well over half the historic center to mobility-impaired visitors (the tourist office map highlights the zones now accessible). **Alitalia,** as Italy's most visible airline, has made a special effort to make its planes, public areas, rest rooms, and access ramps as wheelchair-friendly as possible.

RESOURCES IN THE UNITED STATES   Several agencies can provide advance-planning information. One is the **Travel Information Service,** MossRehab Hospital, 1200 W. Tabor Rd., Philadelphia, PA 19141, which provides information by phone (☎ **215/456-9600** [voice] or 215/456-9602 [TDD] or at its Web site: www.mossresourcenet.org.

You may also want to consider joining a tour for visitors with disabilities. You can get names and addresses of such tour operators and miscellaneous travel info by contacting the **Society for the Advancement of Travel for the Handicapped,** 347 Fifth Ave., Suite 601, New York, NY 10016 (☎ **212/447-7284;** www.sath.org). Annual membership dues are $45 or $25 for seniors and students. Send a self-addressed stamped envelope.

For blind or visually impaired travelers, the best source is the **American Foundation for the Blind,** 11 Penn Plaza, Suite 300, New York, NY 10001 (☎ **800/ 232-5463,** or 212/502-7600 for ordering information booklets; www.afb.org). It offers information on travel and the various requirements for the transport of and border formalities for Seeing Eye dogs.

Contact **Twin Peaks Press** (☎ **800/637-2256** or 206/694-2462; www. pacifier.com/~twinpeak), publisher of the **Directory of Travel Agents for the Disabled** ($19.95), for a list of more than 370 agencies worldwide. Two of the many U.S. agencies that cater to disabled travelers are **Access First Traveler** (☎ **800/ 557-2047;** e-mail accessfir@aol.com) and **Flying Wheels** (☎ **800/535-6790;** www.flyingwheelstravel.com).

Accessible Italy (www.tour-web.com/accitaly/index.html) concentrates on info pertinent to Rome, Florence, Venice, and Milan for the traveler with reduced mobility. This operator can help plan itineraries to a host of other Italian cities as well.

Yahoo! Travel Agents: Special Needs (www.yahoo.com/business_and_economy/shopping_and_services/travel_and_transportation/disabilities/agents) provides information listing travel agents who specialize in planning trips for travelers with disabilities.

RESOURCES IN THE UNITED KINGDOM RADAR (Royal Association for Disability and Rehabilitation), Unit 12, City Forum, 250 City Rd., London EC1V 8AF (☎ **020/7250-3222;** www.radar.org.uk), publishes three holiday fact packs, which sell for £2 each or £5 for all three. The first one provides general information, including planning and booking a holiday, insurance, and finances. The second outlines transport and equipment, transportation available when going abroad, and equipment for rent. The third deals with specialized accommodations. Another good resource is **Holiday Care Service,** 2nd floor, Imperial Building, Victoria Road, Horley, Surrey RH6 7PZ (☎ **01293/77-45-35;** fax 01293/78-46-47), a national service organization that advises on accessible accommodations. Annual membership costs £25. Once you're a member, you can receive a newsletter including information about hotels throughout Europe.

FOR GAYS & LESBIANS

Since 1861, Italy has had liberal legislation regarding homosexuality, but that doesn't mean it's always looked on favorably in a Catholic country (though Taormina has long been a gay Mecca). Homosexuality is much more accepted in the north and larger cities than in the deep south or in the smaller provincial towns. However, all major towns and cities have an active gay life, especially Florence, Milan, Rome, and Bologna.

Milan considers itself the gay capital of Italy (though **Bologna** is a proud contender) and is the headquarters of **ARCI Gay** (www.gay.it), the country's leading gay organization that has branches throughout Italy. **Capri** is the gay resort of Italy, with a predominant Milanese following, with the Amalfi Coast's resort town of Positano (just across the Bay of Naples) just a boat ride away. A gay-operated, English-speaking travel agency in Rome, **Zipper Travel** (V. Francesco Carletti 8, Rome 00154, ☎ **06/488-2730;** fax 06/488-2729; e-mail tptravel@aconet.it) can help create itineraries in both large and small cities, as well as make reservations for travel and hotel.

To learn more about gay and lesbian travel in Italy, you can secure publications and join data-dispensing organizations before you go. Men can order *Spartacus,* the international gay guide ($32.95), or *Odysseus,* a guide to international gay accommodations ($27). Both lesbians and gays might want to pick up a copy of *Gay Travel A to Z* ($16), which specializes in general information, as well as listings of bars, hotels, restaurants, and places of interest for gay travelers throughout the world.

Hungry Minds, Inc., has published its first guide especially for gays and lesbians, ✪ *Frommer's Gay & Lesbian Europe* ($24.99), which includes Rome, Florence, and Venice among its offerings. These books and others are available from **A Different Light,** 151 W. 19th St., New York, NY 10011 (☎ **800/343-4002** or 212/989-4850; www.adlbooks.com), and **Giovanni's Room,** 1145 Pine St., Philadelphia, PA 19107 (☎ **215/923-2960;** fax 215/923-0813; www.giovannisroom.com).

Our World, 1104 North Nova Rd., Suite 251, Daytona Beach, FL 32117 (☎ **904/441-5367;** www.ourworldmag.com), is a magazine devoted to options and bargains for gay and lesbian travel worldwide. It costs $35 for 10 issues in the States. The upscale, reputable *Out and About,* 8 West 19th St., Suite 401, New York, NY 10011 (☎ **800/929-2268;** www.outandabout.com), profiles the best gay or gay-friendly hotels, gyms, clubs, and other places throughout the world. It costs $49 a year for 10 information-packed issues. Both publications are available at most gay and lesbian bookstores.

The **International Gay & Lesbian Travel Association (IGLTA),** 52 W. Oakland Park Blvd. PMB#237, Wilton Manors, FL 33311 (☎ **800/448-8550;** www.iglta.com), encourages gay and lesbian travel worldwide. With around 1,300 member travel agencies, it specializes in networking travelers with the appropriate gay-friendly service organizations or tour specialists. It offers a quarterly newsletter, marketing mailings, and a membership directory that is updated quarterly.

In the United States, the following travel agencies specialize in gay and lesbian travel and offer frequent though erratically scheduled tours to Italy: **Yellowbrick Road Travel** (☎ **800/642-2488** or 312/561-1800); **Kennedy Travel** (☎ **800/988-1181** or 718/347-1818); and **Advance-Damron Vacations** (www.gayweb.com/408/408home.html).

In London, travel agencies offering similar services include **Alternative Holidays** (☎ **020/7701-7040;** fax 020/7708-5668; e-mail info@alternativeholidays.com); **In Touch Holidays** (☎ **020/8742-7749;** fax 020/8742-7407; www.bogo.co.uk/alternatives); **London Handling Ltd.** (☎ **020/7589-2212;** fax 020/7225-1033); and **Zone One** (☎ **020/7730-2347;** fax 020/7730-9756).

FOR SENIORS

Many senior discounts are available, but note that some may require membership in a particular association.

For information before you go, obtain the free booklet *101 Tips for the Mature Traveler,* from **Grand Circle Travel,** 347 Congress St., Boston, MA 02210 (☎ **800/221-2610** or 617/350-7500; www.gct.com).

SAGA International Holidays, 222 Berkeley St., Boston, MA 02116 (☎ **800/343-0273;** www.sagaholidays.com), runs all-inclusive tours for those 50 years old or older. Insurance is included in the net price of their tours.

AARP (American Association of Retired Persons) is the leading organization in the United States for seniors. It offers discounts on car rentals and hotels. For more information, contact AARP at 601 E St. NW, Washington, DC 20049 (☎ **800/424-3410** or 202/434-AARP; www.aarp.org).

Information is also available from the **National Council of Senior Citizens,** 8403 Colesville Rd., Suite 1200, Silver Spring, MD 20910 (☎ **301/578-8800;** www.ncscinc.org), charging $7 annually per person or per couple. You receive a bimonthly magazine, part of which is devoted to travel tips, as well as discounts on hotel and auto rentals.

FOR STUDENTS

IN THE UNITED STATES   Council Travel Service (CTS), a subsidiary of the Council on International Educational Exchange, is America's largest student, youth, and budget travel group, with more than 60 offices worldwide. The main office is at 205 E. 42nd St., New York, NY 10017 (☎ **800/226-8624** or 212/822-2700; www.counciltravel. com). **International Student Identity Cards (ISIC),** issued to all bona fide students for $19, entitle holders to generous travel and other discounts. Discounted international and domestic air tickets are available (nonstudents under 25 are eligible for similar but limited discounts), as well as Eurail passes, YHA (Youth Hostel Association) passes, weekend packages, and hostel/hotel accommodations are also bookable.

Ultra-budget travelers and those keen to meet other traveling students should consider staying in hostels and joining **Hostelling International/American Youth Hostels (HI-AYH).** For information, contact Hostelling Information/American Youth Hostels, 733 15th St. NW, No. 840, P.O. Box 37613, Washington, DC

20013-7613 (☎ **202/783-6161;** www.hiayh.org). Membership costs $25 annually, $10 for 17 and under, $15 for 55 and older.

IN THE UNITED KINGDOM & ABROAD   CTS's (see above) U.K. office is at 28A Poland St. (Oxford Circus), London WIV 3DB (☎ **020/7437-7767**); the **Italy office** is in Rome, near the train station at V. Genova 16, 00184 Roma (☎ **06/46791**). In Canada, **Travel CUTS,** 187 College St., Toronto, Ont. M5T 1P7 (☎ **416/798-2887**), offers similar services.

The **International Student Identity Card (ISIC),** available at CTS offices with proper identification and a copy of a recent grade report or a letter on school letterhead confirming matriculation, is an internationally recognized proof of student status that entitles you to savings on flights, sightseeing, food, and accommodation. It sells for £5 and is well worth the cost. Always show your ISIC when booking a trip—you may not get a discount without it.

USIT Campus Travel, 52 Grosvenor Gardens, London SW1W OAG (☎ **020/ 7730-3402**), opposite Victoria Station (and with a dozen branches throughout England), is Britain's leading specialist in student and youth travel and is open daily. It provides a comprehensive service specializing in low-cost rail, sea, and airfares, holiday breaks, and travel insurance, plus student discount cards.

9 Getting There Without Going Broke

BY PLANE

The upheavals that shook the airline industry during the early 1990s have subsided a bit, but despite relative calm, the industry may still undergo some changes during the life of this edition. For up-to-date conditions, check with a travel agent, consolidators, the various Web sites we suggest or directly with the individual airlines for promotional discounts.

Flying time to **Rome** from New York and the Northeast is 8 hours, from Chicago 10 hours, and from Los Angeles 12½ hours. Flying time to **Milan** from New York is 8 hours, from Chicago 9¼ hours, and from Los Angeles 11½ hours. Consider flying into Rome and out of Milan (or vice versa) if it facilitates your travel arrangements; there is usually no additional cost.

Fares to Italy are constantly changing, but you can expect to pay as low as $350 during winter months and in the range of $500 to $1,000 for a direct round-trip ticket during peak months from New York to Rome in coach class. Consolidators may undercut these rates.

Those interested in an attractive deal combining a stop of a few hours or a few days (or more) in a major European city en route to Italy should consider one of the European carriers below. In order to encourage the public to choose a non-direct alternative, round-trip rates are often handsomely discounted and direct connections sometimes involve no more than an hour or two (check for details and avoid change of airports in London and Paris where possible). By connecting in major European hubs, you may also be able to avoid Milan and Rome by flying into Italy's secondary international airports, like Venice, Pisa, Florence, Naples, or Palermo. **British Airways** (☎ **800/AIRWAYS;** www.britishairways.com/regional/usa) stops over in London, **Lufthansa** (☎ **800/645-3880;** www.lufthansa-usa.com) in Frankfurt, **Air France** (☎ **800/237-2747;** www.airfrance.com) in Paris, and **KLM** (☎ **800/374-7747;** nederland.klm.com) in Amsterdam.

FROM THE UNITED STATES & CANADA

The major Italian carrier, **Alitalia** (☎ **800/223-5730** in the U.S., or 514/842-8241 in Canada; www.alitaliausa.com), offers the most extensive flight schedule. It flies nonstop to both Rome and Milan from a number of North American cities, including New York (JFK International), Newark, Boston, Chicago, Miami, and Los Angeles. Schedules are designed to facilitate easy transfers to all the major Italian cities. Unlike American carriers, Alitalia may add on a small leg to your flight, if your final destination is a secondary airport, for no extra cost (this doesn't apply to all fares). For example, on direct flights from New York to Milan, you may connect and fly on to Venice for the same rate. Many European airlines, including Alitalia, offer students or anyone 12 to 24 a youth fare, which you can buy only within 72 hours of departure; its primary advantage is that it's good for a return trip up to 12 months. Infants under 2 fly for 10% of an adult fare and children under 12 fly for 75% of an adult fare.

Canada's second largest airline, Calgary-based **Canadian Airlines International** (☎ **800/426-7000;** www.aircanada.ca), flies daily from Toronto to Rome.

FINDING THE BEST FARE

HIGH & LOW SEASON **January** and **February** are low-season months when last-minute rates can be remarkably low. **November** and **preholiday December** have recently become as favorable a period for minimum fares. The beginning and cutoff dates designating high season—usually June 1 through September—may vary a little among some airlines. Shoulder season may be April through May, October, and December 15 to 24. Low season is generally November 1 to December 14 and early January to March 31.

APEX FARES Advance-purchase booking (still referred to as APEX by some lines) is often, but not always, the key to getting the lowest fare. Policies may differ from one airline to the next. You generally must be willing to make your plans and buy your tickets as far ahead as possible: The **21-day APEX** is seconded only by the **14-day APEX,** with a stay in Italy of 7 to 30 days. Moreover, since the number of seats allocated to APEX fares is severely limited (sometimes to less than 25% of the capacity of a particular plane), the early bird gets the low-cost seat.

There's often a surcharge for flying on a weekend in either direction, and be aware that the peak season may have a shoulder season, comprising those weeks before and after the peak season, with only slightly lower rates. Cancellation and refund policies can be strict. Absolute freedom is given to those who buy a regular economy fare that has no restrictions and is naturally the most expensive item on the market. One-way tickets are so extreme, it is almost always worth buying a discounted round-trip ticket, and forfeiting the return half.

CONSOLIDATORS Also called "bucket shops," consolidators act as clearinghouses for blocks of excess-inventory tickets that major international airline carriers discount to a wholesaler or consolidator. These aren't charters, and the service is now available in peak periods (when discounts are moderate) as well as in the slow season (when savings can be major). You might even be able to accrue frequent-flyer miles.

This is the factory-outlet approach to ticket shopping; when using the established and trustworthy agencies, the risk is extremely low. Tickets are sometimes priced at up to 35% (and more) off the full fare. Terms of payment can vary—say, anywhere from 45 days prior to departure to last-minute sales offered in a final attempt by an airline to fill an empty aircraft. Restrictions may apply: Inquire about the conditions involved in cancellations, refunds, and re-endorsing to another airline should your carrier delay or cancel. Ask about those frequent-flyer miles. Paying by credit card should be your preference, if allowed, to guarantee further protection.

Since dealing with unknown bucket shops still carries some risk, it's wise to call the Better Business Bureau in your area to see if complaints have been filed against the company from which you plan to purchase a ticket. After booking with the agency, call the airline the agency has booked you on to see if you appear on their confirmed passenger list.

One of the biggest U.S. consolidators is **Travac,** 989 Sixth Ave., 16th floor, New York, NY 10018 (☎ **800/TRAV-800** or 212/563-3303; www.thetravelsite.com), which offers discounted seats throughout the United States to most cities in Europe on commercial airlines. Another branch office is at 2601 E. Jefferson St., Orlando, FL 32803 (☎ **407/896-0014**).

In New York try **TFI Tours International,** 34 W. 32nd St., 12th floor, New York, NY 10001 (☎ **800/745-8000** or 212/736-1140), which offers services to well over 150 cities worldwide.

We've also had good service and good deals by using **1-800-FLY-4-LESS,** 1-800-FLY-CHEAP or Cheap Tickets at 1-800-377-1000 (www.cheaptickets.com).

From the Midwest, explore the possibilities of **Travel Avenue,** 10 S. Riverside Plaza, Suite 1404, Chicago, IL 60606 (☎ **800/333-3335;** www.travelavenue.com), a national agency with ticket prices that keep up with the best deals.

Another possibility is **UniTravel,** 11737 Administration Dr., Suite 120, St. Louis, MO 63146 (☎ **800/325-2222**). It may be your best choice for last-minute and short-notice flights to Europe.

The ultimate free-spirited traveler should contact **Airhitch,** 2641 Broadway, 3rd floor, New York NY 10025 (☎ **800/326-2009** or 212/864-2000; www.airhitch.org). Just pick a 5-day period during which you can fly to a general area of Europe (northern versus southern); most passengers are booked within their first or second day. Here are typical one-way fares: from the northeast United States to Europe $159, Midwest to Europe $209, southeast to Europe $189, West Coast or Northwest to Europe $239.

Similar rates are available to flexible travelers from **Airtech** (☎ **212/219-7000;** www.airtech.com), which caters to carefree travelers who don't mind landing in Zurich instead of Milan on Monday instead of Wednesday. You can get discounted hotel prices on budget accommodations that are potentially short on atmosphere but big on savings.

A California company has started a EurailPass-like approach to air travel within Europe called **Europe by Air** (☎ **888/387-2479;** www.europebyair.com) for U.S. citizens. More than 60 European cities are linked by 13 participating airlines in 20 countries, including Italy. Coupons represent one flight, each costing $90 and valid for 120 days. A minimum of three segments must be purchased.

CHARTER FLIGHTS   Strictly for reasons of economy (and rarely for convenience), some travelers are willing to accept the possible uncertainties of a charter flight to Italy, a dying breed of travel as the major airlines now match charter prices when booked through consolidators.

In a strict sense, a charter flight occurs on an aircraft reserved months in advance for a one-time-only transit to some predetermined point (and often arrives in a major city's secondary airport, such as Rome's Ciampino Airport). Before paying for a charter, check the restrictions. You can wind up paying a stiff penalty or forfeit the ticket entirely if you cancel or change dates. Charters are occasionally canceled when the plane doesn't fill up (more frequent in low season). In some cases, the charter-ticket seller will offer you an insurance policy in case you must cancel (for hospitalization, death in the family, and so on). Don't even think about frequent-flyer miles.

There's no way to predict whether a proposed flight to Rome (very few charters arrive in Milan) will cost less on a charter or less through a consolidator. You'll have to investigate at the time of your trip.

GOING AS A COURIER   This option isn't for everyone. The free tickets of the past offered by courier services now cost a minimum of $150 round-trip from New York to Italy with little notice (with a yearly membership cost often thrown in). Least expensive rates require that you leave within, let's say, 1 to 2 days' notice; otherwise, during peak season and advance booking, you may be paying rates not much less than some consolidator's rates (courier rates sometimes top $499 from New York to Milan); you may also be locked into dates and restrictions imposed by the courier service as they need to be assured of your services to deliver their goods.

Couriers usually must waive their two-piece check-in luggage allowance, which is used by the courier service to transport goods; you travel alone, so flying with a companion becomes problematic. Sometimes when the courier's representative meets you at the airport things go ultrasmoothly, sometimes they don't, and you may spend unnecessary hours at the airport. Some long-time couriers would fly no other way. Only the patient, flexible, light-packing, and adventurous should contact **Halbart Express** (☎ **718/656-8189** 10am to 3pm) or **Now Voyager,** 74 Varick St., Suite 307, New York NY 10013 (☎ **212/431-1616** 10am to 6pm; at other times you'll get a recorded update of destinations and availabilities). Unless you intend to fly with them regularly, yearly membership costs don't make sense.

CHECKING OUT THE NET   You can find lots of great deals on flights by logging on to the Web. For details, see the sidebar "Cyber Deals for Net Surfers," earlier in this chapter.

FROM THE UNITED KINGDOM

Getting to Italy from the United Kingdom has become less expensive in recent years, but savvy folks usually still rely on travel agents for a deal. Charter flights and special air-travel promotions are still the best alternative.

If a special air-travel promotion isn't available or feasible at the time of your visit, then an **APEX ticket** might be the way to keep costs trimmed. These tickets must be reserved in advance. However, an APEX ticket offers a discount without the usual booking restrictions. You might also ask the airlines about a **Eurobudget ticket,** which imposes restrictions or length-of-stay requirements.

British newspapers are always full of classified ads touting slashed fares to Italy. One good source is the magazine *Time Out,* published in London. London's *Evening Standard* has a daily travel section, and the Sunday editions of almost any newspaper will run many ads. Although competition is fierce, one well-recommended company that consolidates bulk ticket purchases and then passes the savings on to you is **Trail-finders** (☎ **020/7937-5400** in London; fax 020/7937-0555). It offers access to tickets on such carriers as SAS, British Airways, and KLM to Milan and Rome, as well as Pisa, Florence, Venice, and other cities.

In London, there are many consolidators or **bucket shops** around Victoria and Earls Court that offer cheap fares on major lines. Make sure the company you deal with is a member of the IATA, ABTA, or ATOL. These umbrella organizations will help you if anything goes wrong.

CEEFAX, a television information service included on many home and hotel TVs, runs details of package holidays and flights to Italy and beyond. Just switch to your CEEFAX channel and you'll find a menu of listings that includes travel information.

Make sure you understand the bottom line on any special deal you purchase—that is, ask if all surcharges, including airport taxes and other hidden costs are cited before committing yourself to a purchase. Upon investigation, some of these deals are not as attractive as advertised. Also, make sure you understand what the penalties are if you're forced to cancel at the last minute.

Both **British Airways (BA)** (☎ **020/8897-4000**; www.british-airways.com) and **Alitalia** (☎ **020/8745-8200**; www.alitalia.it/english/index.html) have frequent flights from London's Heathrow Airport to Rome, Milan, Venice, Pisa, Florence, and Naples. Flying time from London to these cities is anywhere from 2 to 3 hours. BA also has one direct flight a day from Manchester to Rome. A new subsidiary of British Airways, **Go,** opened in 1998 and services flights from London to Rome and Milan (☎ **08456/054-321**; www.go-fly.com.) Virgin Air has also introduced a subsidiary called **Virgin Express** (☎ **0322/752-0505**; www.virgin-express.com) from London to Rome or Milan.

BY TRAIN

If you plan to travel a lot on the European and/or British railways, you'll do well to secure the latest copy of the definitive ***Thomas Cook European Timetable of Railroads.*** This 500-plus-page timetable documents all of Europe's mainline passenger rail services with detail and accuracy. It's available from **Forsyth Travel Library,** 226 Westchester Ave., White Plains, NY 10604 (☎ **800/FORSYTH;** www.forsyth.com), at a cost of $27.95 (plus $4.95 shipping in the U.S., $6.95 in Canada). The timetable is also available at some travel-specialty bookstores such as **Rand McNally,** 150 E. 52nd St., New York, N.Y. 10022 (☎ **212/758-7488**).

TIPS FOR TRAVELERS FROM THE UNITED STATES

EURAILPASSES   One of Europe's greatest bargains, the **EurailPass** permits unlimited first-class rail travel (second-class travel available to those under 26) in any country in western Europe (except the British Isles). It does *not* include travel on the rail lines of Sardinia, which are organized independently of the lines of the rest of Italy.

Here's how it works: The pass is sold only in North America (or rather, you can buy it in Europe, but it costs about 50% more). It costs $554 for 15 days, $718 for 21 days, $890 for 1 month, $1,260 for 2 months, and $1,658 for 3 months. Children under 4 travel free, providing they don't occupy a seat (then they're charged half-fare); children under 12 pay half-fare.

The advantages are tempting: No tickets; simply show the pass to the ticket collector, then settle back to enjoy the scenery. Seat reservations are required on some trains. Many of the overnight trains have *couchettes* (sleeping berths in cabins for four or six) or *wagons lits* (for two), which you can book only by paying an additional fee at the station ticket window before boarding.

Obviously, the heavily peripatetic 2- or 3-month traveler gets the greatest economic advantage—whereas with a 15-day pass, you'd have to spend a great deal of time on the train to get your money's worth. Know in advance what kind of territory you realistically intend to cover to weigh the savings.

EurailPass holders are entitled to considerable reductions on certain buses and ferries. You'll get a 20% reduction on second-class accommodations from certain companies operating ferries between Naples and Palermo or for crossings to Sardinia and Malta.

Travel agents in all towns and railway agents in such major cities as New York, Montréal, and Los Angeles sell these tickets. A EurailPass is available at the North American offices of CIT Travel Service, the French National Railroads, the German Federal Railroads, and the Swiss Federal Railways.

Train Travel

Are you thinking of buying a EurailPass, but just not sure if it'll make financial sense? Here are some examples of how much you'd have to pay if you opt not to use the pass. **Rome/Paris** (16 hours) first class costs $207; second class is $147. **Rome/Amsterdam** (20 hours) first class is $365; second class costs $236. **Rome/Munich** (13.5 hours) first class is $141; second class costs $90. For Italian and European rail information, visit the Web site of **CIT Travel** (the official representative of Italian State Railways) at www.fs-on-line.com or call ☎ **800/ CIT-RAIL.**

Eurail Saverpass is a money-saving ticket offering discounted 15-day first-class travel for groups of two to five people traveling together between April and September or two people traveling together between October and March. The per-person price of a Saverpass, valid all over Europe, is $470 for 15 days, $610 for 21 days, and $756 for 1 month.

Eurail Flexipass is valid in first class and offers the same privileges as the Eurail-Pass. However, it gives you a number of individual travel days you can use over a much longer period. That makes it possible to stay in one city and yet not lose a single day of travel. There are two passes: 10 days of travel in 2 months for $654 and 15 days of travel in 2 months for $862. There's also a **Eurail Saver Flexipass** for two to six people, costing per person $556 for 10 days of travel in 2 months and $732 for 16 days of travel in 2 months.

If you're under 26, you can purchase a **Eurail Youthpass** entitling you to unlimited second-class travel wherever the EurailPass is honored. The pass costs $388 for 15 consecutive days, $623 for 1 month, or $882 for 2 months. There's also a **Eurail Youth Flexipass** for travelers under 26. Two passes are available: 10 days of travel in 2 months for $458 and 15 days of travel in 2 months for $599.

EUROPASSES   Introduced by the EurailPass folks, the **EuroPass** lets you travel in five EuroPass countries: Italy, France, Germany, Spain, and Switzerland with the purchase of a 5-, 6-, or 8-day pass of unlimited first-class train travel in a 2-month period; discounts available for two adults traveling together. A 5-day pass costs $298 for each of two adults, $348 traveling alone; a 6-day pass $314 for each of two adults, $358 traveling alone; an 8-day pass $382 for each of two adults, $448 traveling alone. You can opt for a 10- or 15-day pass or extend your range of travel by adding a sixth or seventh country.

For travelers under 26, the **Euro Youth Pass** (available in the U.S.) allows unlimited second-class travel (not an option for those over 26) in these same five countries. A 5-day pass in a 2-month period costs $233, a 6-day pass $253, an 8-day pass $313, and so on. Also available are a 10-day ($383) and 15-day ($513) pass in a 2-month period, and the chance to add a sixth or seventh country. All EuroPasses offer the option of purchasing an associated country, such as Austria, Benelux, Greece, or Portugal—each additional country costs $45, two additional countries will run you $78.

TIPS FOR TRAVELERS COMING FROM THE UNITED KINGDOM

Train travel is not the least expensive manner to get to Italy, but it is one of the most leisurely, allowing the opportunity to stop off along the way. It's about a 20-hour rail ride from London to Milan, direct.

Many rail passes are available in the United Kingdom for travel within Europe or direct to Italy; point-to-point tickets are the alternative for those on time-restricted itineraries. **Italian State Railways,** Marco Polo House, 3–5 Landsdowne Rd, Croydon, Surrey (☎ 020/8686-0677; e-mail ciao@citalia.co.uk), books all manner of train travel to and from Italy as well as within Italy. So does **European Rail Ltd.,** phone sales only at ☎ 020/7387-0444. General information can be acquired from **European Rail Inquires** (☎ 020/7803-4800).

The popular **International** has been absorbed by its former competition, **Wasteels,** just next door, adjacent to platform 2, Victoria Station, London SW1V 1JY (☎ 020/7834-7066; fax 020/7630-7628). All of the most popular rail passes are available, including the **EurailPass** and **EuroYouth** (available in Europe) offered only to travelers under 26 (see above), entitling them to unlimited second-class travel in 26 European countries. The unlimited travel 15-day pass for £265 is the least expensive. These passes can be issued only to those who have been in the United Kingdom or Europe for less than 6 months, and so are appropriate for U.S. citizens on their way to Italy.

Citizens of the United Kingdom under 26, or anyone under 26 who can prove they have been in the United Kingdom for more than 6 months, will do as well with the **Inter-Rail Pass** (The Inter-Rail+26, available to those above the magic age, is not valid for travel to or within Italy). It permits unlimited travel to and within Italy for 22 days for £159, or 1 month £209.

Call **Campus Travel** (☎ 020/7730-3402; www.usitcampus.co.uk) or any of its many branches throughout the United Kingdom for direct London to Italy train travel for any age. Through Campus Travel, you can get all the variations of the EurailPass and its cousin passes and the Inter-Rail passes.

Wasteels (see above) will sell a **Rail Europe Senior Pass** to bona fide U.K. residents for £5. With it, a British resident over 60 can buy discounted rail tickets on many of the rail lines of Europe. To qualify, you must present a valid British Senior Citizen rail card, available for £16 at any BritRail office if proof of age and British residency is presented.

BY BUS

Eurolines is the leading operator of scheduled coach services across Europe. Its comprehensive network of services includes regular departures to destinations throughout Italy, including Turin, Milan, Bologna, Florence, and Rome—plus summer services to Verona, Vicenza, Padua, and Venice.

Eurolines' services to Italy depart from London's Victoria Coach Station and are operated by modern coach, with reclining seats and a choice of smoking or non-smoking areas. Departures are 9am Wednesday and Saturday (with extra departures added during summer months), arriving in Rome 6:30pm the next evening, and can be booked up until the day of departure (one week advance purchase is recommended during high season). Return tickets are valid for up to 6 months, and passengers may leave the return date open. For information and reservations by credit card, call ☎ 01582/40-45-11, or book in person at Eurolines, 52 Grosvenor Gardens, Victoria, London SW1 (opposite Victoria Rail Station; an additional Eurolines desk can be found within Victoria Station in The Ticket Hall; no phone). A ticket from London to Rome using as direct a route as possible costs £125 round-trip (£112 under 26), and from £88 (£78 under 26) one-way, depending on the season. Passengers can interrupt their journey, pending available space on subsequent legs of their trip, in Paris or Milan en route.

In the United States, Eurolines is represented by **DER Travel** (☎ 800/782-2424), which offers Eurolines 1-month passes but not point-to-point. Peak-season passes cost $359 for 30 days ($309 for youth and senior passes); 60-day passes $439 ($389 for youth and senior passes). These passes offer unlimited travel to 30 cities within 16 European countries including Italy.

BY CAR

If you're already on the continent or are based in London, you may want to drive to Italy. London to Rome is 1,124 miles via Calais/Bologna/Dunkirk or 1,085 miles via Oostende/Zeebrugge, not counting Channel crossings, by either Hovercraft, ferry, or the Chunnel. Milan is some 400 miles closer to Britain than Rome. Once you've arrived at one of the continental ports, you still face a 24-hour drive. Most drivers play it safe and budget 3 days for the journey, 5 for an only marginally more leisurely tool along some of Europe's most scenic highways.

Most of the roads from western Europe leading into Italy are toll-free, with some notable exceptions. If you use the **Swiss superhighway network,** you'll have to buy a special tax sticker at the border. You'll also pay to go through the **St. Gotthard Tunnel** into Italy. Unfortunately, the **Mont Blanc Tunnel** from France is still closed following the devastating March 1999 fire as this book goes to press. It might reopen by fall 2001 at the earliest. To arrive from France avoiding mountain passes, you must head first to the French Riviera, drive east along the coast though Menton, then head east and south into Italy along the Italian Riviera in the direction of San Remo. The latter is the most popular and least grueling route from London or northern France—who wouldn't welcome a little R&R en route in any of the small towns along the Côte d'Azur?

10 Getting Around Affordably

BY PLANE

Italy's domestic air network on **Alitalia** (see "Getting There Without Going Broke," above) is one of the largest and most complete in Europe. Some 40 airports are serviced regularly from Rome, and most flights take less than an hour. Fares vary, but some discounts are available. Tickets are discounted 50% for children 2 to 12; for passengers 12 to 24, there's a youth fare. Prices are still astronomical for domestic flights and you're almost always better off taking a train, except for long-distance hauls (like Palermo to Venice) where you'd rather spend the money than the time—unless you can stop off along the way: In Italy, there's never a shortage of major sites to see.

BY TRAIN

Trains provide a medium-priced means of transport, even if you don't buy the Eurail-Pass/Europass or one of the special Italian Railway tickets (see below). As a rule of thumb, second-class travel regardless of the destination usually costs about two-thirds the price of an equivalent trip in first class, and the difference in quality is minimal. Save for a handful of privately run local lines scattered about, most Italian trains are run by the national **Ferrovie dello Stato,** or **FS** (☎ **01478-88-088** in Italy only; www.fs-on-line.it).

Most **InterCity trains** (designated **IC** on train schedules) are modern air-conditioned trains that make limited stops; compared to the far slower direct or regional trains, the supplement can be steep, but a second-class IC ticket will provide a first-class experience. **EuroCity (EC)** is just an InterCity train that crosses a national boundary; **EuroNight (EN)** and **InterCity Night (ICN)** trains run past midnight and have couchettes

Fly by Night

When traveling on domestic flights in Italy, you can get a 30% reduction by taking a flight that departs at night.

and/or sleeper cars. There are also brand-new, super fast **Eurostar (ES*) trains** (formerly known as *Pendolino*), the most expensive, which service only the principle cities.

Seat reservations are recommended during peak seasons and on weekends or holidays; they must be booked in advance at the station for a small fee (usually less than $10); on some high-speed trains, seat reservation is already included in the cost of your ticket. Children 4 to 11 receive 50% off the adult fare, and children under 4 travel free with their parents.

Seniors get a break, too. Anyone 60 and over can buy a *Carta d'Argento* by presenting proof of age at any rail station. The card, which can be purchased only in Italy, allows a 20% discount off the price of any second-class ticket (30% off in first class) between points on the Italian rail network. It's good for 1 year and costs about 45,000L ($22.50), as does the *Cartaverde,* which offers the same deal and discounts for anyone under 26.

An **Italy Railcard (IRC)** allows non-Italians to ride as much as they like on the entire rail network of Italy. Buy the pass in the United States, have it validated the first time you use it at any rail station in Italy, and ride as frequently as you like within the time validity. An 8-day pass costs $273 in first class and $182 in second, a 15-day pass $341 in first class and $228 in second, a 21-day pass $396 in first class and $264 in second, and a 30-day pass $478 in first class and $318 in second.

The **Italian Flexirail Card (IFR)** entitles holders to a predetermined number of days of travel on any rail line of Italy within a certain period. It's ideal for passengers who plan in advance to spend several days sightseeing before boarding a train for another city. A pass giving 4 possible travel days out of a block of 1 month costs $216 in first class and $144 in second, a pass for 8 travel days in 1 month costs $302 in first class and $202 in second, and a pass for 12 travel days in 1 month costs $389 in first class and $259 in second.

Another option (good for families or small groups) is the *Biglitto Chilometrico* (Kilometric Pass), a pass that allows you to travel either 3,000km, 20 trips, or 2 months, whichever comes first. Up to five people can be listed on one pass, but each person's kilometers counts—if three of you make a 50km trip together, 150km is subtracted from the total. The benefit is 10% to 30% off regular fares (the longer the haul, the greater the discount), but you still must get in line at the ticket window every time so they can fill out the pass and stamp it. First-class passes are 350,000L ($175), second class 214,000L ($107); kids between ages 4 and 12 on the pass only use up half the actual kilometers ridden (for example, an adult and 10-year-old child taking a 100km journey together will "cost" only 150km).

None of the rail passes covers the **supplement** you must pay to ride on Eurostar (ES*) trains; with the Biglietto Chilometrico, you also need to pay supplements to ride IC, EC, or EN/ICN trains.

You can buy any of these passes in the United States from a travel agent or at **CIT Tours,** the official representative of Italian State Railway, with offices at 15 W. 44th St., 10th floor, New York, NY 10173 (☎ **800/248-8687** or 212/730-2121; fax

Be Rid of Excess Baggage

Left luggage offices in train stations across Italy have been more-or-less standardized. The charge is 5,000L ($2.50) a bag for each 12-hour period. The offices are generally open 6:30am to noon and 2 to 8pm, though in major cities they may not close for *riposo* and may close later or open earlier.

Travel Times Between the Major Cities

Cities	Distance	Air Travel Time	Train Travel Time	Driving Time
Florence to Milan	298km/185 mi	55 min	2 hr, 30 min	3 hr, 30 min
Florence to Venice	281km/174 mi	2 hr, 5 min	4 hr	3 hr, 15 min
Milan to Venice	267km/166 mi	50 min	3 hr, 30 min	3 hr, 10 min
Rome to Florence	277km/172 mi	1 hr, 10 min	2 hr, 30 min	3 hr, 20 min
Rome to Milan	572km/355 mi	1 hr, 5 min	5 hr	6 hr, 30 min
Rome to Naples	219km/136 mi	50 min	2 hr, 30 min	2 hr, 30 min
Rome to Venice	528km/327 mi	1 hr, 5 min	5 hr, 15 min	6 hr
Rome to Genoa	501km/311 mi	1 hr	6 hr	5 hr, 45 min
Rome to Torino	669km/415 mi	1 hr, 5 min	9–11 hr	7 hr, 45 min

212/730-4544), and 6033 West Century Blvd., Suite 980, Los Angeles, CA 90045 (☎ **310/338-8616;** fax 310/670-4269). Its Web address is **www.cittours.com**. In previous years, Italian Railway authorities have required that the IRC and the IFR be bought only outside Europe. These rules have relaxed considerably, and at press time you could buy them in Italy (the Biglittto Chilometrico has always been available there). Check with CIT before your departure, as this might change at any time.

BY BUS

Italy has an extensive and intricate bus network, covering all regions. But because rail travel is inexpensive, the bus isn't the preferred method of travel. You cannot book or pay for bus tickets in advance or over the phone; in fact, you're lucky if anyone answers when you call. If they do, it will be only in Italian.

There are dozens of bus companies throughout Italy. Some of the larger ones, servicing the most touristed areas, include semi-nationwide lines **SITA,** Via Santa Caterina da Siena, in Florence (☎ **055-214-721**), and **ANAC,** Piazza Esquilino 29, in Rome (☎ **06-4482-0531**); **Autostradale,** Piazzale Castello, in Milan (☎ 166-845-010 or **02-801-161**), which serves a large chunk of northern Italy; and **Lazzi,** Piazza della Stazione 4–6, in Florence (☎ **166-856-010**), which goes through Tuscany, including Siena and much of central Italy.

Where these widespread services leave off, local bus companies operate in most regions, particularly in the hill sections and in the alpine regions where travel by rail is not possible. For more information about local services, refer to the "By Bus" sections under "Getting There" in the various destination sections.

BY CAR

Driving can be very expensive in Italy. However, there are several strategies you can pursue to make renting a car more affordable, especially for a group of several people.

RULES & REGULATIONS   Technically, U.S. and Canadian drivers must carry, in addition to your state driver's license, an **International Driver's Permit** (nothing more than a multilingual translation of your license) when touring Italy. You can apply for it at any **AAA** branch. You must be at least 18 and have two 2×2-inch photographs, a $10 fee, and a photocopy of your U.S. driver's license with a AAA application form. To find the AAA office nearest you, check the local phone directory or contact AAA's national headquarters at 1000 AAA Dr., Heathrow, FL 32746-5063

(☎ **407/444-7000**). Remember that an international driver's license is valid only if physically accompanied by your original driver's license. In Canada, you can get the address of the **Canadian Automobile Association** closest to you by calling its national office at ☎ **613/247-0117.**

The **Automobile Club d'Italia (ACI)** is the Italian equivalent of AAA. It has offices throughout Italy, including the head office, V. Marsala 8, 00185 Rome (☎ **06-49-981**), open Monday to Saturday 8am to 2pm. The 24-hour **Information and Assistance Center (CAT)** of the ACI is at V. Magenta 5, 00185 Roma (☎ **06-4477**). Both offices are near the main rail station (Stazione Termini).

RENTALS   Many of Italy's most charming landscapes lie far away from the rail network. For that, and for sheer convenience, renting a car is usually the best way to explore the country. It's also the most expensive (Italy's rates have always been some of the highest in Europe) and is usually a consideration only for the budgeteer traveling with one or more companions to split the cost. Also, note that it's much cheaper to book a rental car in your home country than it is once you get to Italy. If you're already in Italy, and you need a car immediately, have someone back home reserve it for you.

The legalities and contractual obligations of renting a car in Italy (where accident and theft rates are very high) are more complicated than those in almost any other country in Europe. You must have nerves of steel, a sense of humor, a valid driver's license (with photo), a valid passport, and be over 25 (some places accept 21). Payment and paperwork are much easier if you present a valid credit card with your completed rental contract (many companies won't even consider a non–credit card payment). If that isn't possible, you'll likely be required to pay a substantial deposit, sometimes in cash. Insurance on all vehicles is compulsory, though what kind and how much is up to you and your credit card company: Ask the right questions and check with your credit card company before leaving home.

The three major rental companies are **Avis** (☎ **800/331-2112;** www.avis.com), **Budget** (☎ **800/472-3325;** www.budgetrentacar.com), and **Hertz** (☎ **800/ 654-3001;** www.hertz.com). Smaller U.S.-based companies specializing in European car rentals—and often cheaper than the Big Three—are **Auto-Europe** (☎ **800/ 223-5555;** www.autoeurope.com); **Europe by Car** (☎ **800/223-1516,** 800/252-9401 in California, or 212/581-3040 in New York; www.europebycar.com); **Kemwel** (☎ **800/678-0678;** www.kemwel.com) and **Maiellano** (☎ **800/ 223-1616**). In addition, although they're most frequently contacted for package deals and air travel, many of the tour operators listed under "Organized Tours, Package Tours & Tour Operators" (see above) also offer discounted car rentals. No matter who you call (and do call all of them), never settle for the first figures quoted: Prices can vary greatly from agency to agency, and even day to day, depending on special promotions. In some cases, slight discounts may be offered to members of the American Automobile Association (AAA) or the American Association of Retired Persons (AARP).

Each company offers a collision-damage waiver (**CDW**) costing $14 to $21 per day (depending on the value of the car). Some companies include CDWs in the prices they quote; others don't. In addition, because of Italy's rising theft rate, most major U.S.-based companies insist you also carry theft and break-in protection policies. For pickups at most airports in Italy, all three impose a 12% government tax (called an airport tax or surcharge). To avoid that, consider picking up your car at an inner-city location if this is convenient for you. There's also an unavoidable 20% government value-added tax (VAT) (called IVA in Italy); though that is usually already included in the rates they quote, always ask to avoid last-minute surprises. Automatic shift (the vast majority of available cars are standard/stick shift) and air-conditioning will raise your rates, as will the option of picking up your car in one city and dropping it off in another. Principal cities have both airport and downtown locations; picking up your car at one and dropping it off at the other, even though within the same city, will most likely cost you. Dropping off outside Italy is even more expensive: Make sure you ask all the right questions when calling around.

GASOLINE Gasoline (called *benzina*) is expensive in Italy, as are highway tolls. Carry enough cash if you're going to do extensive motoring. Filling the tank (*al pieno*) of a medium-size car will usually cost around 70,000L ($35).

Gas stations (*distributori di benzina*) on autostrade are often open 24 hours, but on regular roads gas stations are rarely open on Sunday, may close between noon and 3pm for lunch, and shut down after 7pm. Others will have self-service machines accepting 10,000L bills. Make sure the pump registers zero before an attendant starts refilling your tank. A popular scam, particularly in the south, is to fill your tank before resetting the meter so you pay not only your bill but also the charges run up by the previous motorist.

ROAD MAPS The best touring maps are published by the **Touring Club Italiano (TCI),** or you can buy the maps of the Carta Automobilistica d'Italia, covering Italy in two maps on the scale of 1:800,000 (1cm = 8km). These two maps should fulfill the needs of most motorists. If you plan to explore one region of Italy in depth, consider one of 15 regional maps (1:200,000; 1cm = 2km), published by Grande Carta Stradale d'Italia.

All maps mentioned above are sold at some autostrada gas stations, certain newsstands, and all major bookstores, especially those with travel departments. Many travel bookstores in the United States also carry them. If U.S. outlets don't have these maps, they often offer Michelin's red map (no. 988) of Italy, which is on a scale of 1:1,000,000 (1cm = 10km). This map covers all of Italy in some detail.

BREAKDOWNS/ASSISTANCE In case of car breakdown or for any tourist information, foreign motorists can call ☎ **116** (nationwide telephone service). For road information, itineraries, and all sorts of travel assistance, call the Rome headquarters ☎ **06-499-8234** of **ACI/Automobile Club d'Italia,** a branch of the Touring Club Italiano.

11 Tips on Accommodations

Italy and its regional boards control the prices of its hotels, designating a minimum and a maximum rate. Many hotels are opting to go with one year-round rate to avoid confusion (discounting it during slow periods and off-season); others maintain two separate high- and low-season tariffs. Prices can also vary due to a room's location, size, decor, and whether it offers a private or shared bathroom; however, if there is a range of rates listed for any hotel in this book that range *always* implies a seasonal variation unless the review specifically says otherwise.

Italian hotels are classified by **stars,** indicating mostly the amenities offered: five stars for deluxe, four for first class, three for second, two for third, and one for fourth. Government ratings don't depend on the decoration, quality of the mattresses, or frescoed ceilings but rather on facilities, such as elevators, the presence of an in-house restaurant, amenities (air-conditioning, TVs, minibars, in-room safes, hairdryers), and the like. Many of the finest hostelries in Italy are rated second class because they serve only breakfast (a blessing for those seeking to escape the board requirements, a dying obligation in European hotels these days). Generally speaking, this guide book concentrates on three- and two-star hotels to keep prices low but standards comfortable, but remember you might pay the same for a two-star hotel in Venice off-season as you will pay for a four-star hotel in Lucca in high season.

Few big city hotels have private **garages,** but most either have an arrangement with a local garage, or will give you a permit to park on the street; some of the cheapest one-star hotels leave you to your own devices for parking, merely pointing out the closest public lot or garage.

Government regulation stipulates that **breakfast** is not mandatory and must be charged separately. Almost all hotel owners, however, include it in the cost of the room. If breakfast is only a "continental" breakfast—rolls and/or *cornetti* (croissants) with cappuccino and maybe juice—it is almost invariably overpriced at anywhere from 5,000L to 15,000L ($2.50 to $7.50); you can get the same thing at the corner bar for around 3,000L ($1.50). It can, however, be a welcomed convenience if it's an all-you-can-eat buffet from which you can filch a few pastries and some fruit to snack on later. Check it out before you insist on having breakfast elsewhere.

The Italian term *albergo* is more and more commonly being replaced by the international word *hotel. Locanda* once meant a rustic inn or carriage stop, though it's now used to sometimes refer to a place quite charming or fancy. The **pensione** system of yesteryear has pretty much disappeared, and with it the obligation to share bathrooms and eat three meals a day prepared by the families that once owned them. They are now one- and two-star hotels, with many of them retaining the word *pensione* in their names to connote a small, often family-run hotel of character or charm (not always the case!). In 2000, Italy also introduced *"il Bed and Breakfast"* classification to encourage more of the smaller pensioni or larger rental-room operations to stop hiding from the tax collector and officially incorporate as a business.

Reservations are always advised, even in the so-called slow months of November to March when you might find towns such as Verona and Bologna (not to mention the large cities) booked solid with conventions and trade fairs. Travel to Italy peaks from May through October, when many of the best (or at least best-known) moderate and budget hotels are often filled up a few days to a few weeks in advance.

APARTMENTS, VILLAS & PALAZZI

Millions of properties are put up for rent by their Italian owners—you'll have to do your homework and legwork. Groups or families of four to six people may find villa or apartment rental an enjoyable savings.

These organizations rent villas or apartments, generally on the pricey side, but stipulate your price range when inquiring. Least expensive will be an Italian B&B organization that offers more than 60 historic palazzos and villas in 10 regions where rooms range from $30 to $95 per person: Order their guidebook from **Caffeletto,** 23 Marciola, 50020 San Vicenzo a Torri, Florence (☎ **055-730-9145;** fax 055/768-121). Pricier possibilities include some lower-end choices through **Hideaways International,** 767 Islington St., Portsmouth, NH 03801 (☎ **800/843-4433** or 603/430-4433), and **At Home Abroad,** 405 E. 56th St., Suite 6H, New York, NY 10022-2466 (☎ **212/421-9165;** fax 212/752-1591). One of the most reasonably priced agencies is **Villas and Apartment Abroad, Ltd.,** 420 Madison Ave., New York, NY 10017 (☎ **800/433-3020** or 212/759-1025; fax 212/755-8316). **Vacanze in Italia,** 22 Railroad St., Great Barrington, MA 01230 (☎ **800/533-5405** or 413/528-6610; www.homeabroad.com), handles hundreds of rather upscale properties.

FARMHOUSES

Another option is to stay in a farmhouse, an apartment, or a bedroom on a working Italian farm (wine-producing estates make up a large part of these) as part of a nationwide program known as *agriturismo*. Most of the farms lie in rural areas within easy reach of town centers or principal cities, such as those in Umbria, Tuscany, and Lazio. You can share the setup with the owners (staying in a guest bedroom in the main house) or have the place to yourself (free-standing converted stalls, mills, worker's quarters on the grounds offering more privacy), the former being the less expensive of course. Contact boards of tourism for listings of *agriturism* situations for a do-it-yourself reservation and daily double rates that usually start at 45,000L ($26.50) with breakfast.

The U.S.-based **Italy Farm Holidays (IFH),** 547 Martling Ave., Tarrytown, NY 10591 (☎ **914/631-7880;** fax 914/631-8831), represents about 50 working farms (a number owned by Americans or foreigners). Most properties require minimum stays of 3 to 7 days and payment in full in advance. Many offer meals (usually breakfast) as part of the arrangement; others provide amenities like free use of bikes or optional horseback riding. Only a few of the places contain more than seven rentable accommodations, most have private bathrooms, and many contain kitchens of their own.

Weekly rates for two begin at around $600 in low season in a modest apartment or B&B, and go way up for high season villas or castles that accommodate up to 10 occupants.

12 Tips on Dining

For a quick bite, go to a *bar*—while it does serve alcohol, it functions mainly as a cafe. Prices here have a split personality: *al banco* is standing at the bar, while *à tavola* means sitting at an indoor or outdoor table where you'll be waited on and charged two to four times as much—but consider it rent, and you won't be rushed even after reading the newspaper and finishing your postcards. In bars, you can find *panini* (**sandwiches**) on various rolls and *tramezzini* (**giant triangles of white-bread sandwiches with the crusts cut off**). These both run 2,000L to 6,000L ($2 to $3). A *toast* is a grilled ham-and-cheese Italian style, stuck in a kind of tiny press to flatten and toast it so the crust is crispy and the filling hot and gooey; microwaves have invaded and are everywhere, and many bars now offer quick one-course hot lunches of a pasta or mixed salads for 5,000L to 8,000L ($2.50 to $4).

Pizza à taglio or *pizza rustica* indicate a place where you can order pizza by the slice—though the quality can vary wildly. You'll fare somewhat better at a *pizzeria,* a casual sit-down restaurant that cooks large, round pizzas with very thin crusts in wood-burning ovens with lots of toppings and varieties to keep you coming back. A *tavola calda* (literally "hot table") serves ready-made hot foods you can either take away for a picnic or eat at one of the few small tables often available. The food is usually very good, and you can get away with a full meal at a *tavola calda* for well under 20,000L ($10). A *rosticceria* is the same type of place with some chickens roasting on a spit in the window and the smell of *arrista* (**roast pork with rosemary**) and roast potatoes luring you in.

Eating lunch (*pranzo*) or dinner (*cena*) in Italy can be a pretty elaborate affair, although the serious three-course lunch—an *antipasto* (**appetizer**), *primo* (**first course**) of pasta, soup, or risotto, *secondo* (**second course**) of meat or fish, possibly accompanied by a *controno* (**side dish**) of veggies, *dolce* (**dessert**), and finished off with a *caffè* (**espresso coffee**)—is fast being reduced to the rushed American standard.

Once upon a time, restaurant terms—*osteria, trattorie,* or *ristorante*—actually meant something. *Osterie* were basic tavernlike inns where you could get a plate of spaghetti and a glass of wine; *trattorie* were casual family-run establishments serving full meals of filling, simple fare; and *ristoranti* were fancier places, with bow-tied waiters, printed menus, linen tablecloths, a serious wine list, and hefty prices. Nowadays, fancy restaurants often go by the name of *trattoria* to cash in on the associated charm factor, trendy spots use *osteria* to show they're of-the-moment hip, and casual inexpensive places sometimes tack on *ristorante* to ennoble themselves.

The more casual the ambience, the less you'll feel inclined to order the full-blown Italian repast. Put your nose to the window and see for yourself: If it's full of locals with low prices, head on in; if it's empty or full only of tourists, steer clear (the locals do, and there must be a good reason). Better yet, follow our suggestions and eliminate the suspense. It's hard not to eat well in the country that gave us pasta and Chianti.

SET-PRICE MENUS

At many restaurants, especially larger ones and in cities, you'll find a *menù turistico* (tourists' menu), costing anywhere from 10,000L to 35,000L ($5 to $18), sometimes called *men del giorno* (menu of the day). This set-price menu usually covers all meal incidentals—including table wine, cover charge, and 15% service charge—along with a primo and secondo, but it almost always offers an abbreviated selection of uninspired dishes (with portions that may be less than the standard): spaghetti in tomato sauce and roast chicken.

Sometimes a *menu à prezzo fisso* (fixed-price menu) is better. It usually doesn't include wine but sometimes covers the *coperto* (bread and cover charge) and often offers a wider selection of better dishes, occasionally house specialties and local foods. A *menu degustazione* is a tasting menu of the chef's best or local specialties, and can run from 35,000L ($18) way up to 80,000L ($40), often including wines. Ordering à la carte, however, offers you the best chance for a memorable meal for a price that needn't be too much more. Regardless of where you eat, check the bill to see if a 15% service charge is included (*servizio incluso*); it is usually added. If not, leave 10% to 15% on the table if service was satisfactory.

FOOD & WINE

The *enoteca* (wine bar) is an increasingly popular marriage of wine bar and *osteria*, where you can sit and order from a host of local and regional wines by the glass (usually 2,000L to 10,000L/$2 to $5) while snacking on finger foods (and usually a number of simple first-course possibilities) that reflect the region's fare. Relaxed, full of ambience and good wine, these are great spots for light and inexpensive lunches, and the perfect venue to educate your palate and recharge your batteries.

FOOD STORES

It's also possible and inexpensive to get meals at the familiar *alimentari* (small general food stores) throughout the country: Have sandwiches prepared on the spot or buy the makings for a picnic lunch to be enjoyed in a park or shady piazza. Supermarkets are everywhere in Italy but (happily) Italian food shopping is still rooted in visiting a string of specialty shops and selecting each purveyor's freshest offerings at the *forno* or *panetteria* (bakery), *fruttivendolo* (fruit and vegetable stand), *latteria* (milk and cheese store), *maccelleria* (butcher), and *pasticceria* (pastry shop).

Bread & Cover

In all Italian restaurants, you must pay a *coperto* (cover charge) of 1,500L to 10,000L (75¢ to $5)—the unavoidable charge merely for the privilege of sitting at the table with a basket of bread.

Getting the VAT (IVA) Back

If you make a purchase in Italy and your bill at any one store totals 300,000L ($150), you're eligible for a value-added tax (called IVA in Italy) rebate up to 19% (the IVA varies according to item and is already included in the price). Ask the store for a formal receipt, and before leaving Italy, bring your receipt and purchase (the item must be available for inspection) to Italian Customs at the airport before check-in. The Customs agent will stamp your receipt and give you further directions. The stamped receipt gets sent back to the store and your reimbursement will be credited against your credit card or sent to you by check; either can take months.

Be sure to allow enough time before you board your flight home, and note that if you're leaving Europe from another EU country (which includes all of Western Europe except Switzerland), you can bring all your receipts for each country to the airport from which you depart; so if you're flying home from Paris, you can take your Italian and French receipts to the customs agent at Charles de Gaulle airport. If you're intending to shop, check with **Global Refund** in the United States (☎ **800/566-9828**; www.taxfree.se) for details.

Fast Facts: Italy

American Express   Each major city chapter in this book has a "Fast Facts" section listing the local AMEX office for changing traveler's checks, receiving mail, and booking travel tickets.

Banks   They're open Monday to Friday 8:30am to 1 or 1:30pm and 2 or 2:30 to 4pm and closed all day Saturday, Sunday, and national holidays. Hours change slightly from city to city.

Business Hours   Local business hours can vary greatly and change seasonally. Regular business hours are usually Monday to Friday 9am (sometimes 9:30am) to 1pm and 3:30 (sometimes 4) to 7 or 7:30pm, with Saturdays being half or full days depending on the season or type of business. In July or August, some offices, stores, and businesses may not open in the afternoon until 4:30 or 5pm. An exaggerated *riposo* (siesta), early afternoon closing is often observed in Rome, Naples, and most cities of southern Italy. However, in the bigger cities (especially northern and central ones) the custom has been cut back considerably, with many shops now posting *orario no-stop* (meaning they stay open through *riposo*). Most shops are closed on Sunday, except for pastry stores/bars and certain barbershops that are open on Sunday morning. Sights and museums tend to close Mondays and Sunday afternoons. By law, most restaurants close one day a week, usually Sunday or Monday.

Drug Laws   Penalties are severe and could lead to imprisonment or deportation. Selling drugs to minors is dealt with particularly harshly.

Drugstores   *Farmacie* take turns staying open at night and on Sunday. At every farmacia, a list is posted of those in town whose turn it is to stay open during these off-hours. In bigger cities, there will be a 24-hour pharmacy or two, often on a major square and/or in the train station.

Electricity   The electricity in Italy varies considerably. It's usually alternating current (AC), varying from 42 to 50 cycles. The voltage can be anywhere from 115 to 220. You need both a transformer (to bring down the volts and up the cycles) and an adapter plug (Italian outlets have two round holes) to use U.S. devices that aren't special dual-voltage travel items (like some hairdryers and shavers). Most modern laptop computers and camcorder battery chargers automatically sense the voltage and adjust themselves accordingly.

Embassies/Consulates   Embassies and their consulates (consulates are for citizens—lost passports and other services; embassies are mostly only for diplomats) are all located in Rome, though such other major cities as Milan and Florence often also have consular offices. Each major city chapter in this book has a Fast Facts section listing local embassies/consulates and their open hours for the U.S., Canada, U.K., Ireland, Australia, and New Zealand.

Emergencies   Dial ☎ **113** for an ambulance, police, or fire. In case of a breakdown on an Italian road, dial ☎ **116** at the nearest telephone box; the Automobile Club of Italy (ACI) will be notified to come to your aid.

Legal Aid   The consulate of your country is the place to turn, though offices can't interfere in the Italian legal process. They can, however, inform you of your rights and provide a list of attorneys. You'll have to pay for the attorney out of your pocket, as there's no free legal assistance. If you're arrested for a drug offense, about all the consulate will do is notify a lawyer about your case and perhaps inform your family.

Liquor Laws   Wine with meals has been considered a normal part of family life for hundreds of years in Italy. Children are exposed to wine at an early age, and alcoholic consumption isn't considered anything out of the ordinary—and, as a result, heavy drinking doesn't become a factor of teenage rebellion. There's no legal drinking age for buying or ordering alcohol. There are no restrictions on the sale of wine or liquor in Italy.

Mail   At post offices, General Delivery service is available in Italy. Correspondence can be addressed c/o the post office by adding *Fermo Posta* to the name of the locality. You can pick up mail at the local central post office by showing your passport and paying a small fee (AMEX cardholders can get the same service for free from local American Express offices, listed in each city). In addition to the post offices, you can buy stamps at little *tabacchi* (tobacco stores) throughout any city.

Mail delivery in Italy is notoriously bad and doesn't seem to be improving. If you're writing for hotel reservations (bad idea), it can cause much confusion—visitors may arrive in Italy long before their hotel deposits do. Fax machines speed up the process tremendously, e-mail better yet. Postcards, aerogrammes, and letters weighing up to 20 grams to the United States, Canada, or Oceania cost 1,400L (70¢), to the United Kingdom and Ireland 800L (40¢).

Newspapers/Magazines   In major cities, it's possible to find the *International Herald Tribune* (published by the *New York Times/Washington Post* group), *USA Today, Time,* and *Newsweek,* as well as other English-language newspapers and magazines at hotels and news kiosks.

Pets   A veterinarian's certificate of good health is required for dogs and cats and should be obtained by owners before entering Italy. Dogs must be on a leash or muzzled at all times. Other animals must undergo examination at the border or port of entry. Certificates for parrots or other birds subject to psittacosis must state that the country of origin is free of disease. All documents must be certified first by a notary public, then by the nearest Italian consulate.

Police   Dial ☎ **113,** the all-purpose number for police emergency assistance in Italy.

Rest Rooms   All airport and rail stations have rest rooms, often with attendants, who expect to be tipped. Bars, nightclubs, restaurants, cafes, and all hotels have facilities; public toilets are found near many of the major sights. Ask *"Dov'è il bagno?"*

Usually rest rooms are designated as *W.C.* (water closet) or *toilette* and marked as *donne* (women) or *uomini* (men). The most confusing designation is *signori* (gentlemen) and *signore* (ladies), so watch those final i's and e's!

Safety   Violent street muggings are uncommon in Italy. The most usual menace, especially in all large cities (particularly Rome) is the plague of **pickpockets** and the roving gangs of gypsy children who surround you, distract you, and in all the confusion, steal your purse or wallet. Never leave valuables in a car (even unseen in a locked trunk), and never leave your car unlocked.

Foil pickpockets by keeping passport, credit cards, plane tickets, traveler's checks, and all other valuables in a **money belt** (a flat pouch worn under the clothes, either around the waist or around the neck), leaving just a day's spending money in your wallet.

Taxes   As a member of the European Union, Italy imposes a tax on most goods and services that's already included in the price. It's a **value-added tax,** called **IVA** in Italy. The tax affecting most visitors is that imposed at hotels, which, at about 9% in first- and second-class hotels, is usually incorporated into the bill.

Telegrams/Telephone/Telex/Fax   A **public telephone** is always near at hand in Italy. Local calls cost 200L/10¢, and you can use 100L, 200L, or 500L coins. Most phones also accept a multiple-use precharged **phone card** called a *scheda telefonica* or *carta telefonica,* which you can buy at all *tabacchi* and newsstands in increments of 5,000L, 10,000L, or 20,000L. To use this card, break off the corner, insert it into the slot in the phone, then dial. A digital display will keep track of how many lire you use up. The card is good until it runs out of lire, so don't forget to take it with you when you hang up.

International calls to the United States and Canada can be dialed directly. Dial **00** (the international code from Italy), then the country code (1 for the United States and Canada), the area code, and the number you're calling. Calls dialed directly are billed on the basis of the call's duration only. A reduced rate is applied 11pm to 8am Monday to Saturday and all day Sunday. Other country codes are as follows: the United Kingdom 44, Ireland 353, Australia 61, New Zealand 64.

Calling Italy

To call Italy from the United States, dial the **international prefix, 011;** then Italy's **country code, 39;** then the **number.** Old Italy hands will recall the old city codes— for example, 06 for Rome—but those have now been incorporated into the numbers themselves and you must now dial them (including the initial zero, which you used to drop) at all times, whether you're outside Italy, within Italy, or even in the city itself. Note that **numbers in Italy** do indeed range from six to twelve digits in length.

If you wish to make a **collect call** from a pay phone, simply deposit 200L/10¢ (you get it back when you're done), dial **170,** and an international (and usually English-speaking) operator will come on the line. For **calling-card calls,** drop in the refundable 200L, then dial the appropriate number for your card's company to be connected with an operator in the United States: for AT&T, **172-1011;** for MCI, **172-1022;** and for Sprint, **172-1877.**

Don't count on all Italian phones having **Touch-Tone** service! Even in some of the larger and more expensive hotels you'll find rotary dials, and most push-button phones use the pulses as well. You may not be able to access your voice mail or answering machine if you call home from Italy.

If you make a **long-distance call** from a public phone, there's no surcharge. However, hotels (especially the more expensive ones) have been known to double or quadruple the cost of the call with taxes and surcharges, so be duly warned. It's one of travel's biggest (legal) scams; they'll often even charge you for what should be a toll-free call to AT&T or MCI! Direct-dial calls from the United States to Italy are much cheaper, so arrange for whomever to call you at your hotel at a prearranged hour if possible.

Chances are your hotel will send or receive a **fax** for you, sometimes at inflated prices per page or minute. You can send a fax from the post office to any country in the world, with the exception of the United States. Otherwise, most *cartolerie* (stationery stores), *copisti* or *fotocopie* (photocopy shops), and some *tabacchi* (tobacconists) offer fax services: Look for SERVIZIO FAX signs in their windows. For **telegrams,** ITALCABLE operates services abroad, transmitting messages by cable or satellite. Both internal and foreign telegrams may be dictated over the phone (dial ☎ **186**).

Time   In terms of standard time zones, Italy is 6 hours ahead of Eastern Standard Time in the United States (when it's noon in NYC, it's 6pm in Rome). Daylight savings time goes into effect in Italy each year from the last Sunday in March through the last Sunday in October. Italy uses the 24 hour clock (a.k.a. military time), so 6pm is written 18:00. Also know that in Italy, dates are abbreviated numerically day/month/year, rather than month/day/year as in the U.S., so you could be trying to book a hotel for November 6 by writing 11/6/2001, but they'll mark you down for June 11! I avoid confusion by writing out the month name longhand.

Tipping   This custom isn't practiced with the same flair in Italy as in the United States, even though many people depend on tips to supplement their livelihoods. In hotels, the service charge is already added to a bill. In addition, it's customary to tip the chambermaid a minimum of 1,000L (50¢) per day and the bellhop or porter 2,000L ($1) per bag. If your concierge has helped to resolve a problem or procure a ticket to a sold-out concert, acknowledge this effort with 5,000L ($2.50) or more.

In **restaurants,** 15% to 20% is almost always added to your bill (*servizio incluso*). An additional tip (1,000L/50¢ for each diner) for particularly good service is expected in upscale eateries. If service isn't included, leave about 15% (only if warranted). Washroom attendants expect at least 300L to 500L (15¢ to 25¢), more in nicer restaurants and hotels. Taxi drivers expect at least 10% to 15% of the fare from foreign customers, though Italians tip infrequently.

Water   It's generally safe to drink the water, though the taste may be different from what you're accustomed to.

Rome: The Eternal City

3

by Lynn A. Levine

An antique Gotham that's laid the groundwork for history, **Rome (Roma)** continues to exert an enormous influence on civilizations all over the world, be it for religion, architecture, art, anthropology, or a hearty red sauce of pancetta and onions. Rome is so thoroughly monumental that no matter how deep you dig beneath its surface, you'll come up with something to add to the annals of history—another ancient temple or emperor's palace that underscores how limited the city's Metropolitana (subway) system will always be.

In anticipation of my first trip to Rome, I read not one guidebook, leaving the details up to my love interest at the time, who was Italian. On New Year's Eve, we were picked up in town by friends for a drive out to the host's candlelit home—a 14th-century monastery built of man-sized stones and wood beams. I was ignorant and inexperienced enough to think of the city in vague yet momentous historic terms, completely oblivious to the remnants of the floodlit arena suddenly looming outside the car's window. I was looking at the *Colosseum*—whose name alone suggested the enormity of the icon—and my escort, long desensitized to the city's wonders, hadn't thought to prep me.

That evening was my first experience with the word *fresco*, as well as with the paper-thin slices of a salty delicacy called prosciutto and the woodsy wine that wouldn't leave me with a headache the next day. Still slightly plump from my college cafeteria days, I was tickled when our host insisted I put on some weight. This is the true Rome: a melding of old and new, a taking for granted of an ancient peristyle several meters beneath the pavement combined with a profound reverence for the treasures of the kitchen. For days, we strolled through ochre-colored alleys, passed thoughtlessly by ancient basilicas, and blew off the Sistine Chapel because it would be too inconvenient to visit. Instead, we spent our time making countless stops for caffè,conversing around friends' kitchen tables, and walking hand-in-hand over the Tiber. I had been to the City of Light, but *this* was the Eternal City.

I'm still enchanted by this magical and often maniacal city built over layer upon layer of history. But despite the proliferation of Internet cafes, the whirring of Alfa Romeos around Piazza Venezia, and the fresh coats of paint camouflaging centuries of decay, Rome's magnetism for the first-time visitor inevitably turns to the distant past, to the celebrity lineup of rulers considered sanctified (Augustus, Claudius, Octavian, Vespasian, Trajan, Hadrian) and schizophrenic (Tiberius, Caligula, Nero, Domitian). Challenging this order was the church, from its earliest stages as a rebellious pagan movement rejecting the emperor as the embodiment of religious power to the potent empire that would direct the progression of religious, cultural, artistic, and political thought for centuries to come.

Exploring Rome is like walking through the pages of a life-size pop-up book—over there is the baroque beauty of Piazza Navona, over there the papal fortifications of Castel Sant'Angelo, over there the evocative ruins of the Roman Forum and Imperial Forums, and over there the monumental perfection of the Pantheon. The artistic legacy can become overwhelming in a city wrapped in medieval, Renaissance, and baroque churches designed by the likes of Bramante, Bernini, and Borromini and enriched by Byzantine-era mosaics or frescoes, sculptures, and paintings by the likes of Giotto, Michelangelo, Raphael, Leonardo, and Caravaggio.

Obviously, if you're planning to "do" Rome in a week, you're going to be grievously disappointed, especially if you focus only on the city's top draws. Just as important as those 3 hours spent trudging through the Vatican Museums is the 3 hours spent dining and sipping local wine on the cobblestones of Campo de' Fiori or picnicking among the joggers and Frisbee-catching dogs on the Circus Maximus. And don't be discouraged by the often last-minute variations in hours and schedules—this is all part of the Roman experience of constant surrender to the unpredictable; to an ordered chaos even locals can't comprehend. Roll with it and remember that you're in Rome, so it's time to do as the Romans do.

1 Arriving

BY PLANE

Most international flights land at **Leonardo da Vinci International Airport,** also called **Fiumicino** (☎ **06-65-951;** www.adt.it), 30km (18 mi.) west of the city. Beyond customs is a **visitors' info booth** with good free maps and brochures, open daily 8:15am to 7:15pm. If you've booked a charter flight or are flying in on a budget airline, chances are you'll be landing at the smaller **Ciampino Airport** (☎ **06-7934-0297**), 15km (9 mi.) south of the city.

GETTING FROM THE AIRPORTS TO ROME   To get downtown from **Fiumi-cino,** follow the signs marked TRENI for one of the hourly **nonstop trains** (30 min.; 16,000L/$8) to Stazione Termini, Rome's main rail station. If the temperamental ticket machines are on the fritz, head to the train ticket office in the tiny airport station. If you're really pinching lire, take one of the **local trains** marked "Orte" or "Fara Sabina" (45 min.; 8,000L/$4) leaving from the same track and get off at Rome's Stazione Tiburtina, the secondary train station, where you can catch the Metropolitana (subway) line B to Termini station. You can also catch line B by getting off at the train at the Ostiense stop and walking to the Piramide Metro stop or you can hop on bus 175 to Termini. The amount you save by taking the local isn't worth the inconvenience unless your hotel is in Trastevere (get off at the Trastevere stop) or the Aventine (get off at Ostiense). For arrivals between 11:30pm and 5am, a **night bus** leaves Fiumicino for Tiburtina at 1:15, 2:15, 3:30, and 5am. If you're headed to Termini, the 40N bus connects Tiburtina and Termini at night.

To get downtown from **Ciampino,** catch one of the **COTRAL buses** (2,000L/$1) leaving from outside the terminal every half an hour for the 20-minute trip to Anagnina, the terminus of Metro line A, where you can grab a subway to Stazione Termini (1,500L/75¢).

Taxis to/from either airport cost about 80,000L ($35), plus around 5,000L ($2.50) for bags during the daytime (more at night and on Sunday). Taxis also charge an "airport" supplement of 11,500L ($6) from Fiumicino into town, 14,000L ($7) from town to Fiumicino, and 10,000L ($5) to or from Ciampino.

A Train Ticket Tip

If you're landing at Rome's Fiumicino Airport but plan to head straight to, say, Florence the instant you get to Stazione Termini (Rome's main train station), you can save loads of time by using the **airport train terminal's ticket desk** to buy your Rome-to-Florence rail ticket rather than braving the ludicrously long lines at Termini. And at the **Alitalia office** inside Termini at track no. 22 you can buy tickets for the direct train to Fiumicino airport (*don't waste time waiting in the regular ticket lines*). See "By Plane," above for details on how to get to the airport.

GETTING TO FIUMICINO FROM ROME   At track no. 22 in **Stazione Termini** is an **Alitalia/Fiumicino desk,** open daily 6:30am to 9pm. The first airport train (30 min.; 16,000L/$8) leaves Termini at 6:50am (arriving 7:23am), while the rest run hourly on the 20-minute mark. If you have no luggage to check, you can check in for most Alitalia flights here as well (*except* flights AZ640/AZ642 to Newark or AZ650 to Toronto).

If you have an **early flight,** the first local train out of Rome's **Stazione Tiburtina** leaves at 5:04am (48 min.; 8,000L/$4), then continuously every 20 minutes. To get to the airport **late at night,** you'll have to take a taxi or catch the night bus 40N (every 20 to 30 min.) from Termini to Tiburtina, then catch the COTRAL bus to the airport (30 min.; 7,000L/$3.50) at 12:30, 1:15, or 2:30pm and 3:45am.

BY TRAIN

There are at least three trains an hour from **Florence** running anywhere from 1½ to 3½ hours, depending on whether you ride one of the state-run (**FS**) trains (some depart from Stazione Campo di Marte) or opt for one of the high-speed trains (**Eurostar** or **Intercity**). The fare is either 26,300L ($13) or 51,500L ($26). There are 10 direct and 2 night trains daily from **Venice** (4.5 to 7 hrs.; 46,900L/$23 or 66,000L/$33) and hourly departures from **Milan** (4.5 to 9 hrs.; 50,500L/$25 or 70,100L/$36). From **Naples** (2 to 2.5 hr.; 18,600L/$9 or 30,000L/$15), there are two to three runs hourly and limited service on Sunday.

Rome's main train station is **Stazione Termini** (☎ **1478/88-088** toll free, or 06-4730-6599), at the northeast corner of the *centro storico* (historic center). A few long-haul trains stop only at Rome's secondary **Stazione Tiburtina,** in the southern part of the city (see "By Plane," above). Termini is divided into three sections: You'll be exiting the train in the area of the **tracks** or platforms, where on Track 4, you'll find a small **tourist office,** open daily 8am to 9pm; the **main hall,** filled with shops and services like newsstands, eateries, banks, the **Metro** entrance, and a 24-hour pharmacy; and then the **ticketing hall.** Outside the ticketing hall is Piazza del Cinquecento, a huge square containing **taxi stands** and Rome's major **bus terminus,** where some two dozen routes converge. (During the Jubilee year, the depots of a number of buses were diverted down the road to Piazza della Repubblica to take some of the load off of Termini; if you have questions, check with the tourist information kiosk just beyond the taxi rank to the right.)

A Train Station Tip

When arriving in Rome by train, stock up on bus and Metro tickets at the *tabbacchaio* (tobacconist) located inside the platform area just before passing into the main hall. There's no point in heading straight to the bus terminus empty-handed.

BY BUS

Rome has coach connections with every major city in Italy, but train travel is invariably the more comfortable choice, as buses take longer, are less comfortable, and cost about the same. They can, however, be handy (but crowded) when the rail system goes on strike (a frequent occurrence). For 24-hour info on all bus lines into and out of Rome, call ☎ **0166/845-010.** Most intercity buses arrive either near Stazione Termini (the main train station) or at one of several suburban bus stations (each near a Metro stop).

BY CAR

The saying "all roads lead to Rome" still rings true in Italy, even if none of them leads you directly (or logically) into the center of town. The capital is at the convergence of a dozen highways, including the **A1 autostrada,** which connects Rome with Florence, Milan, and Naples. The **Grande Raccordo Annulare,** called the **"GRA,"** is a highway ring around the greater Roman urban area into which all incoming roads feed. As Rome is such a headache to drive in, it's best to use the GRA to circle around to the side of the city closest to your final destination rather than trying to cut across downtown. For **parking,** see "Getting Around," below.

2 Essentials

VISITOR INFORMATION

TOURIST OFFICES The **main tourist office** (☎ 06-4889-9253; fax 06-4889-9228; www.informaroma.it; Metro: Repubblica) is off of Piazza della Repubblica at Via Parigi 5, behind the Baths of Diocletian; it's open Monday to Friday 8:15am to 7:15pm (Saturday to 1:45pm). There's an **information booth** in the International Arrivals terminal at Fiumicino Airport, open daily 8:15am to 7:15pm, as well as a **small office** on Track 4 at Stazione Termini (☎ 06-4890-6300), open daily 8am to 9pm (it's often difficult to find behind the mass of people).

For the lowdown on **events,** see "Newspapers & Magazines," under "Fast Facts," below.

INFORMATION KIOSKS The Comune di Roma prepared for Papal Jubilee by setting up a number of **information kiosks,** open daily 9am to 7pm. Look for them on Piazza dei Cinquecento, outside Stazione Termini's main entrance, past the taxi stand and to the right (☎ 06-4782-5194); on Piazza di Spagna/Largo Goldoni (☎ 06-6813-6061); on Via Nazionale in front of the Palazzo delle Esposizioni (☎ 06-4782-4525); on Piazza Tempio della Pace, near the Fori Imperiali (☎ 06-6992-4307); on Piazza Navona/Piazza Cinque Lune (☎ 06-6880-9240); at Castel Sant'Angelo/Piazza Pia (☎ 06-6880-9707); on Piazza San Giovanni in Laterano (☎ 06-7720-3535); in Trastevere on Piazza Sonnino (☎ 06-5833-3457); and outside Santa Maria Maggiore (☎ 06-4788-0294).

ENJOY ROME The private firm of **Enjoy Rome,** Via Marghera 8/a, near Stazione Termini (☎ 06-445-1843 or 06-445-6890; fax 06-445-0734; www.enjoyrome.com; e-mail: info@enjoyrome.com; Metro: Termini), has expanded into a full-service travel

Calling for Tips

Suggestions on restaurants and shopping tips are but a phone call away. Useful travel tips and general information on arts, culture, and entertainment are now available in five languages from **Call Center Rome** at ☎ 06-3600-4399 (daily 9am to 7pm).

agency. It began as a walking tour outfit in the early 1990s but soon became the first stop in Rome for budget travelers, students, and backpackers. In addition to offering walking and bike tours of the city, the Enjoy Rome people dabble in the hotel business with the youth hostel Fawlty Towers (see below) and run a convenient bus trip to Pompeii. The young staff, from English-speaking countries, provides lots of info on the city and a free room-finding service (see "Affordable Places to Stay," below). It's open Monday to Friday 8:30am to 2pm and 3:30 to 6pm and Saturday 8:30am to 2pm.

WEB SITES   Though Rome's official sites are **www.romapreview.com** (in English) and **www.comune.roma.it** and **www.informaroma.it** (both in Italian), there are several good privately maintained sites. Try **Dolce Vita** (www.dolcevita.com), **Enjoy Rome** (www.enjoyrome.com), **Virtual Rome** (www.virtualrome.com/english/index. html), **Ancient Sites** (www.ancientsites.com/users/COCCIEIUSCAESAR), **Christus Rex** (www.christusrex.org), the **Vatican** (www.vatican.va), **Time Out** (www.timeout. com/rome), and **Traveling with Ed and Julie** (www.twenj.com/romevisit.htm).

FESTIVALS & EVENTS   Not to be missed are **Carnevale (Carnival),** ending on Martedi Grasso (Fat Tuesday); the **Festa di Primvera (Feast of Spring),** when the Spanish Steps are covered with azaleas; **Holy Week,** when pilgrims flood the city to attend church, see the pope say mass at the Colosseum on Good Friday, and hear him speak a blessing from his balcony in the Vatican overlooking St. Peter's Square on Easter Sunday; **Rome's Birthday** on April 21, celebrated with ceremonies on the Campidoglio and candles set to flicker along the city's stairways and palazzo rooftops; the **International Horse Show;** the **May Day (May 1)** free rock concert on the piazza in front of San Giovanni in Laterano; the **Estate Romana's** summertime lineup of outdoor concerts, exhibits, movies, and performances; the outdoor performances of the **Rome Opera;** the **Festa di San Giovanni (Feast of St. John)** and **Festa di San Pietro e Paolo (Feast of Sts. Peter and Paul);** the **Festa dei Noiantri (Festival of We Others),** immortalized near the end of Fellini's film *Roma* (the scene in which he interviews Gore Vidal); and the pope's **December 25 Urbi et Orbi** blessing from his Vatican window overlooking St. Peter's. See the "Italy Calendar of Events," in chapter 2 for more details.

CITY LAYOUT

Rome is strung along an S-shaped bend of the **Tevere (Tiber River),** with the bulk of the *centro storico* (historic center) lying east of the Tevere. While there are official administrative districts, the Romans themselves think in terms of an address being near this *piazza* (square) or that major monument, so I'll do the same.

The north end of the *centro storico* is the oval **Piazza del Popolo.** From this grand obelisk-sporting square, three major roads radiate south: **Via del Babuino, Via del Corso,** and **Via di Ripetta.** The middle one, Via del Corso (usually just called the Corso), divides the heart of the city in half.

To the east of the Corso lie the **Spanish Steps** (where Via del Babuino ends) and **Trevi Fountain.** Surrounding these monuments are Rome's most stylish shopping streets—including the boutique-lined **Via dei Condotti,** running straight from the Spanish Steps to the Corso. To the west of the Corso spreads the medieval Tiber Bend area, home to landmarks like the long, bustling **Piazza Navona,** the ancient **Pantheon,** the market square of **Campo de' Fiori,** countless churches, a few small museums, and the medieval **Jewish Ghetto.**

The Corso ends at about Rome's center in **Piazza Venezia.** This major traffic circle and bus juncture is marked by the overbearing garish white (locals call it the "wedding cake") **Vittorio Emanuele Monument.** Leading west from Piazza Venezia is **Via Plebescito,** which, after passing through the archaeological site and major bus stop

Mapping It Out

The maps in this chapter will help you orient yourself and find sights, hotels, and restaurants. For a more detailed map, take along the pocket-sized laminated **Streetwise Rome,** which covers central Rome very well and includes a street index; it's available at your local bookstore or travel shop for $5.95. For wider coverage and even more detail, get **Michelin map no. 38,** a large sheet map of Rome with a street finder ($12.95). Available in Rome at newsstands and bookstores, the **De Agostini map** (1:12,000 scale) is complete and comes with a street index (9,000L/$4.50). If you're searching for an address, stop into any bar or ask your hotel if you can look at their *Tuttocittà,* a magazine mapping every little alley (only Rome residents can obtain it).The bookstore chain Feltrinelli carries a commerical equivelent of a *Rome A to Z;* look in the Rome or Italy travel section, usually a prominent display near the registers.

Largo di Torre Argentina, becomes **Corso Vittorio Emanuele II.** Corso Vittorio Emanuele is a wide street that effectively bisects the Tiber Bend as it heads toward the river and the Vatican. (Piazza Navona and the Pantheon lie to the north, Campo de' Fiori and the Jewish Ghetto to the south.)

If you're at Piazza Venezia and facing south, go to the right around the Vittorio Emanuele Monument—behind which stretches the archaeological zone of the **Roman Forum**—to see the stairs leading up to **Capitoline Hill,** ancient Rome's seat of government. Around the left side of the monument is **Via dei Fori Imperiali,** a wide boulevard that makes a beeline from Piazza Venezia to the **Colosseum,** passing the Roman Forum on the right (slung into the low land between the **Capitoline** and **Palatine Hills**) and the **Imperial Forums** on the left. South of the Forum and Colosseum rises the shady residential **Aventine Hill,** beyond which is another hill, the old working-class quarter **Testaccio,** which has recently become a trendy restaurant and nightclub district.

Those are the areas of Rome where you'll spend most of your time. But the grid of 19th-century streets surrounding the main train station, **Stazione Termini,** defines the eastern edge of the *centro storico.* You may also want to venture out at mealtimes to the area east of Termini to the University and intellectuals' district of **San Lorenzo,** home to some fantastic restaurants.

To the northwest of Termini (east of the Spanish Steps area) is a boulevard zone where many foreign embassies lie, the highlight being the cafe-lined **Via Veneto,** of the fashionable 1950s *La Dolce Vita* fame. Via Veneto ends at the southern flank of the giant **Villa Borghese** park, studded with museums and expanding northeast of the *centro storico* (it's also accessible from Piazza del Popolo).

Across the Tiber are two major neighborhoods you may be interested in. Mussolini razed a medieval district to lay down the wide **Via della Conciliazione** linking the Ponte Vittorio Emanuele Bridge with **Vatican City** and **St. Peter's Basilica.** South of there, past the long, parklike **Janiculum Hill,** lies the once medieval working-class, then trendy, and now touristy district of **Trastevere,** with lots of bars, restaurants, and movie theaters.

Neighborhoods in Brief

Around Ancient Rome   This catchall category covers the heart of the ancient city, from the **Colosseum** through the **Roman Forum** and **Imperial Forums** to the **Capitoline** and **Esquiline Hills, Piazza Venezia,** and the streets surrounding them to the river. Antiquity buffs will want to spend a lot of their visit in this vast archaeological zone, but it offers few good hotels and even fewer decent restaurants (most cater to entire tour buses with bad food at high prices).

Around Campo de' Fiori & the Jewish Ghetto   This working-class neighborhood of the Tiber Bend, strung between the river and Corso Vittorio Emanuele II, has lots of good restaurants, a daily market on **Campo de' Fiori,** Renaissance palaces lining Via Giulia, and a burgeoning nightlife scene. More impressive is that many of the area boutiques are bucking the trend to close at lunchtime. The eastern half of the area—between Via Arenula and Via di Teatro Marcello and below Largo di Torre Argentina—has been home to Europe's oldest Jewish population ever since it was a walled **ghetto** in the 16th century. Roman Jewish cooking is some of the city's best, and you'll find delicious and relatively inexpensive examples in trattorie scattered throughout this zone.

Around Piazza Navona & the Pantheon   This is the true heart of medieval Rome, with a host of sights and monuments like the lively **Piazza Navona,** the ancient and beautiful **Pantheon,** churches hiding Caravaggio paintings or Michelangelo sculptures, and plenty of pedestrian-only elbow room. It has a host of excellent restaurants, lots of nightlife possibilities, and a few choice hotels that won't break the bank. You're also within easy walking distance of both the Vatican and the ruins of ancient Rome. It's a toss-up between this and the Spanish Steps area when it comes to choosing the absolute best place to base yourself in Rome (sightseeing fanatics will want to book here and shoppers nearer the Spanish Steps, hardcore budget-seekers may have to look elsewhere).

Around the Spanish Steps & Piazza del Popolo   Since the 18th century, this has been one of the most popular expatriate areas, full of Brits and Germans and lots of *passeggiata* (evening stroll) action. Today, the streets around **Piazza di Spagna** comprise the heart of Rome's shopping scene, with boutique-lined streets like Via de' Condotti sporting the biggest names in Italian and international fashion. It's also one of the most touristy areas of the center, with "public living rooms" and universal tourist magnets like the baroque off-center sweep of the **Spanish Steps** and the gushing mountain of white marble called the **Trevi Fountain.** It's no coincidence that Rome's top hotels cluster at the Spanish Steps' summit or that the American Express is on Piazza di Spagna itself (and that Italy's first McDonald's opened a few doors down in 1986). Moving about this neighborhood is often an exercise in weaving among large clots of camera-clicking tour groups, but the area certainly stays animated and most roads are blessedly closed to cars.

Around Via Veneto & Piazza Barberini   In the 1950s, this was the heartbeat of *La Dolce Vita* ("the sweet life") made famous by Fellini films. **Via Veneto** still has the cafes of its heyday, but today they're overpriced and patronized mainly by tourists, and its grand old hotels are similarly expensive and booked mostly by guided and packaged tours. The area around Via Veneto and **Piazza Barberini** is also full of baroque and 19th-century palazzi, today home to everything from embassies to one of Rome's best painting galleries (in Palazzo Barberini) to newspaper headquarters.

Termini   Aside from some churches and a great museum, the 19th-century neighborhood around the main train station is a pretty boring part of town and too far from the bulk of Rome's sights for even a comfortably long walk. However, it's hard to discount the abundance of cheap hotels in this area, which has actually improved dramatically in recent years. The streets just to the **north of Termini** have undergone the most noticeable improvements, but the immediate Termini area in general still has a ways to go.

The Aventine & Testaccio   The **Aventine Hill** south of the Palatine and next to the river is one of central Rome's quietest, leafiest, and most posh residential sections, with a couple of ancient churches set on curving roads. Few tourists venture here, where Rome's urban sprawl becomes a distant memory. It's a good place to stay if you want a vacation from the urban chaos but still want the convenience of proximity to a nearby bus or Metro stop.

South of the Aventine and up against the river where it turns south again is one of Rome's greatest working-class neighborhoods, **Testaccio,** home of the old slaughterhouse and once Rome's port on the Tiber. Its name means "ugly head" and refers to the small man-made hillock that hems in the neighborhood on the east. Just as the Tiber docklands in ancient times, Testaccio received countless barges carrying amphorae full of wine and olive oil. These ceramic vases were off-loaded and their merchandise measured into smaller, more salable containers; then the amphorae were discarded onto a pile that eventually grew into the 165-foot hill of Testaccio, now covered with grass. Since all that ceramic keeps constant temperature and moisture levels, grottoes were dug into the mound for storing wine and food, and many of Rome's most authentic restaurants still line Testaccio, their dining rooms and cellars burrowed back into the artificial hill of pot shards and their kitchens turning out ultra-traditional cuisine. The area's also become rather fashionable, and most of Rome's hottest nightclubs appear in old warehouses (and often disappear after a few months).

Trastevere   Trastevere (across the Tiber) was another of Rome's great medieval working-class neighborhoods, one that spoke its own dialect and had a tradition of street fairs and poetry—still echoed in the July **Festa de' Noiantri (Feast of We Others).** But after Trastevere became trendy in the 1970s and 1980s, popular with both the Roman upper middle class and lots of expat Americans, it sold out to tourism in the 1990s. It always had lots of restaurants and excellent tiny trattorie, but this boom in popularity has filled it beyond bursting with eateries, pubs, dance halls, funky boutiques, sidewalk vendors and fortune tellers, and a stifling crush of "trendoids" and tourists. Trastevere has become a requisite stop for coach tours and a guided walk in travel books. It's still one of Rome's most colorful quarters, much like Paris's Latin Quarter and New York's SoHo, and the best place to come if you just want to wander into a good restaurant at random.

Around the Vatican   Called the **Borgo,** the area surrounding the **Vatican** and **St. Peter's Basilica** is full of overpriced restaurants and businesses that cater to the tour bus crowds, but you'll also find many modestly priced (if mostly boringly modern) hotels. Expanding north and northeast of the Borgo is the residential and shopping zone of **Prati**—no sightseeing, just a good glimpse into the daily life of middle-class Romans.

GETTING AROUND

Rome is a town to explore on foot. From little baroque churches with ancient columns to a roving knife sharpener working the pedal of his portable grindstone, you never know what you may come across while walking down a Roman street. Rome, however, isn't quite a walker's paradise—the sidewalks are too narrow (or often nonexistent) and the traffic far too heavy. Fortunately, much of the historic center has now been pedestrianized save for a few main thoroughfares.

Beware: Rome's hard, uneven cobblestones are rough on your feet, your shoe soles, and your ankles.

All city transport uses the same 1,500L (75¢) *biglietto* (ticket). This simple one-way ticket gives you unlimited transfers for a maximum of 75 minutes within the city of Rome, including Ostia Antica but not the airport or Tivoli (you can enter the

Metro system only once). There's also a **daily pass** (6,000L/$3) and **weekly pass** (24,000L/$12). Tickets and passes for buses, trams, and the Metro are available from *tabacchi* (tobacconists), most newsstands, Metro stations, or machines at major bus stops (the machines accept only coins and 1,000L or 10,000L notes, not 5,000L bills). Children 10 and under ride free on all public transportation.

BY METRO (SUBWAY)   Rome's **Metropolitana** (Metro for short) isn't very extensive, with only two lines etching a rough "X," with Termini at the intersection. **Line A** runs from Ottaviano (a dozen blocks from the Vatican), through such stops as Flaminio (near Piazza del Popolo), Spagna (Spanish Steps), Termini, and San Giovanni (Rome's cathedral). **Line B** is most useful to shuttle you quickly from Termini to stops for the Colosseo (Colosseum), Circo Massimo (Circus Maximus), and Piramide (at Rome's Tiburtina train station and near Testaccio). The Metro runs daily 5:30am to 11:30pm.

BY BUS & TRAM   At press time, the tourist offices were distributing three contradictory "updated" maps of Rome's extensive bus system. The bus map is available free at these offices, but I've never found it useful; though it's color-coded, you're never really sure what route a particular bus takes or where to pick it up. Notwithstanding the confusion, Rome's bus and tram system is much more extensive than the Metro, and you usually don't have to walk far for a connection.

To handle the massive overflow of visitors for the Jubilee, many bus lines were diverted or even created with alarming frequency, so don't get too frustrated (and don't blame me) if the buses aren't where they're supposed to be (keep an eye on the **23,** listed frequently below, which was recently deviated; confirm its usefulness before getting on).

One of the most useful lines is the **64,** making a beeline from Stazione Termini to the Vatican (heavily used by tourists and thus thieves and known as the Pickpocket Express). Until a recent temporary deviation, the 64 stopped at Piazza Venezia (with the Vittorio Emanuele Monument), near to the "back door" entrance to the Roman Forum and within walking distance of the Colosseum along Via dei Fori Imperiali. Check with the tourist office to find out if they've set it back on its regular course. Set into motion for the Jubilee is the **J** bus, connecting a system of parking lots and checkpoints (for incoming tour buses, no longer permitted in the center) and highly useful for making the rounds of major sights.

The **492** and **175** from Stazione Termini will run you over to Via del Tritone near the Trevi Fountain and the Spanish Steps; if you're coming from the Vatican, hop on the **62.** Buses **116, 117,** and **119** are electric minibuses designed to navigate the narrow cobbled pedestrian streets of the *centro storico,* but not on Sunday. The **116T** line runs evenings and follows, to some extent, the 116 route, diverging on occasion to pass by Rome's various performing arts theaters. The city has instituted a new "ecologically correct" (exhaust-free) **231** bus to run Saturday and Sunday 9 to 7pm, transporting people through the parks of Villa Gloria, Villa Ada, and Villa Borghese. And on Sunday, the special **204** (listed here as 204F for *festivi*) hits much of the historic center.

Validate That Ticket

Always remember to validate your ticket *before* you enter the Metro or board a bus or tram (on buses, stamp your ticket in the orange box) and hold on to it until you're off the bus or out of the Metro station. While the ticket only costs 75¢, the fine will set you back $50!

Most buses run daily 5:30am to midnight, with a separate series of night buses whose route numbers are prefaced by an "N" (or look for the cute little owl over the phrase *bus notturno*). For **bus information**, call ☎ **800/431-784** Monday to Friday 8am to 6pm or 06-4695-4444. Many buses start their routes at the large **Piazza dei Cinquecento** in front of Stazione Termini (for the Jubilee, many of these were rerouted through Piazza della Repubblica). There are also four major spots in the *centro storico* where multiple bus lines converge for easy transfers: **Largo di Tritone/Piazza Barberini, Piazza Venezia/Via Plebescito, Via Plebescito/Largo di Torre Argentina,** and **Piazza San Silvestro** (just off the Corso, between the Spanish Steps and Trevi Fountain). For all of these squares, some buses pause at one of several stops arranged around the piazza itself, many others at a series of stops near the outlets of tributary streets feeding into the square.

BY TAXI   Despite the outrageous fares that appear on the meters, at one time or another you're likely to find yourself worn out and in need of a taxi. Generally you don't hail a cab in the street but summon one by calling a licensed taxi company and providing your location (call ☎ **06-4994**, 06-3570, 06-6645, 06-5551, or 06-4157). You'll be given the ID name and number of the taxi to pick you up (like Bologna/177), but since the dispatch systems are often voice recordings in Italian, you may want to have a local make the call for you (ask your concierge or even the barman). Sticker shock is augmented by the fact that the meter begins running as soon as you make the call, so that if the dispatcher tells you to expect the taxi to arrive in 8 rather than in 2 minutes, you may want to cancel the order. It's also possible to find a taxi at one of the **designated stands** at major piazze, including Piazza Venezia and Largo Argentina; at the Pantheon; and in front of Stazione Termini.

No matter what the meter says at the end of the ride, you'll likely wind up paying more. The initial charge is 4,500L ($2.25), plus 200L (20¢) per kilometer. There are also additional charges for luggage (2,000L/$1 per bag), travel at night (5,000L/$2.50), and travel on Sundays and holidays (2,000L/$1.20). There's even a supplement for bringing your dog along.

BY CAR   Having a car in Rome is a pain, so if you have a choice, don't drive here. Not only are Italian drivers even more manic in the city, but the system of one-way roads seems specially designed to keep you from driving anywhere near your destination. Much of the historic center is pedestrian-only anyway, but you are allowed to drive in to your hotel to drop off luggage. Meanwhile, finding a parking spot is almost impossible, unless you don't mind dropping 30,000L/$15 to 40,000L/$20 per day on a garage. If you plan to rent a car in Rome to tool about the countryside, wait to pick it up until the day you set out and make your first stop back into town the rental agency lot.

Your hotel may have its own garage or an arrangement with one nearby, or you may be lucky enough to be staying in one of the few parts of the historic center that haven't yet been designated a *zona blu*. Most parking spaces have been painted with blue stripes, meaning you must pay a parking meter (usually a box at the end of the block that issues a time slip) or buy a parking "ticket" (2,000L/$1) at the nearest *tabacchi* (tobacconist) or newsstand and place it on the dashboard—note that the meter maids are out in numbers, checking that you're back before your time runs out. **Public garages** are generally cheaper, the biggest being **Parcheggio Borghese** (1,800L/90¢ for the first 3 hours; 23,000/$13 maximum per day) under the Villa Borghese park. The entrance is on Viale del Muro Torto, which leads off into the park from the traffic circle at Porta Pinciana, where Via Veneto, Corso d'Italia, and Via Pinciana converge.

Two- and Four-Wheel Deals

If you arrive in Rome by train and bring your canceled train ticket to **Treno e Scooter** (below), you get a 30% (bicycle) or 10% (scooter) discount on your first day of rental (valid only on the day you arrive in town). **Bici & Baci** has an arrangement with local businesses, including an Internet cafe and various pubs and restaurants, to get clients discounts of up to 50%.

If you don't mind driving around in a used car, Baccina Travel, Via Collina 50, north of Stazione Termini (% 06-482-6915; e-mail: baccina@pronet.it), can get you an economy-sized car for the pleasingly rock-bottom rate of 60,000L ($30) per day. Another factor in your favor is that they have agencies abroad, allowing them to rely on a completely legal billing system, where you save the 20% IVA tax.

BY BICYCLE OR SCOOTER   The best prices on rental bikes or scooters are offered at **Treno e Scooter,** at Track 1 inside Stazione Termini (☎ **06-4890-5823;** Metro: Termini), but you pick up the bikes outside the station on the right; **Bici & Baci,** Via del Viminale 5, near Stazione Termini (☎ **06-482-8443;** Metro: Termini); and **I Bike Rome,** Via Veneto 156, in section 3 of the underground parking lot near Villa Borghese (☎ **06-322-5230**). The rates at all are about 10,000L to 35,000L ($5 to $18) per hour and up; the best deal is 15,000L ($7.50) per day for a regular bicycle (10 speeds and mountain bikes are available but more expensive). Scooters come with a helmet (required by law) and lock.

Warning: Rome's chaotic traffic, widespread pedestrian zones, and one-way streets make trying to get around challenging, if not downright dangerous, so even with a helmet, this should definitely not be your first time on a scooter.

Fast Facts: Rome

American Express   The office is just to the right of the Spanish Steps at Piazza di Spagna 38 (☎ **06-67-641;** Metro: Spagna), open Monday to Friday 9am to 6:30pm and Saturday 9am to 2:30pm; it closes an hour earlier during the 2 weeks of Ferragosto (August 15 to September 1). To report lost or stolen traveler's checks, call ☎ **1678-72-000;** for lost or stolen AMEX cards, call ☎ **722-80-371.**

Business Hours   As in most of Italy, almost all shops and offices, most churches, and many museums observe a siesta-like midafternoon shutdown called *riposo,* about 12:30 or 1 to 3 or 4pm (or as late as 5pm in summer). Capitalism (or demand) has recently begun to show its ugly but irresistible head, as more and more stores in the center have adjusted to *orario continuato* (non-stop open hours). Nevertheless, it's a good idea to figure out the few sights in town that remain open during *riposo* to maximize your sightseeing—or you can just give in to the rhythm and enjoy a leisurely lunch to fill this time. Shop-keepers ease into the week by opening on Monday from about 3 or 4 to 8pm. "Normal" hours are Tuesday to Saturday 9am to 1pm and 3 or 4 to 8pm. Not so for food or gastronomy stores, which open on Monday mornings but close Thursday afternoons.

Doctors & Dentists   The **U.S. Embassy** (☎ **06-46-741**) keeps an updated list of English-speaking doctors and dentists, though you'll find that most doctors have some proficiency in English. First aid is available 24 hours in the emergency room *(pronto soccorso)* of major hospitals (see "Hospitals," below) or by calling the **24-Hour Medical Service** hotline at ☎ **06-482-6741.** You can also try the **International Medical Center,** Via Giovanni Amendola 7 (☎ **06-488-2371;** Metro: Termini).

Embassies & Consulates   The **U.S. Embassy** is at Via Vittorio Veneto 121 (☎ **06-46-741;** Metro: Barberini; Bus: 52, 53, 61, 62, 63, 80, 95, 116, 116T, 204F). For passport and consular services, head to the consulate, to the left of the embassy's main gate at no. 119, open Monday to Friday 8:30am to 1pm and 2 to 5:30pm. The **Canadian Consulate** is at Via Zara 30, fifth floor (☎ **06-445-981;** Bus: 36, 60), open Monday to Friday 8:30am to noon and 1:30 to 4pm. The **U.K. Consulate** is at Via XX Settembre 80/A (☎ **06-852-721** or 06-482-5441; Metro: Repubblica; Bus: 910), open Monday to Friday 8am to 1pm. The **Australian Consulate** is at Via Alessandria 215 (☎ **06-852-721;** Tram 3, Bus: 19, 38, 80, 88, 313), open Monday to Thursday 9am to noon and 1:30 to 5pm and Friday 9am to noon. The **New Zealand Consulate** is at Via Zara 28 (☎ **06-440-2928;** Bus: 36, 60), open Monday to Friday 8:30am to 12:45pm and 1:45 to 5pm.

Emergencies   Dial ☎ **113** in any emergency for the police. You can also call ☎ **112** for the *carabinieri* (the military-trained and more useful of the two police forces), ☎ **118** or 5100 to summon an ambulance, or ☎ **115** for the fire department. *Pronto Soccorso* means first aid and is also the word used for emergency rooms. Call ☎ **116** for roadside assistance (not free).

Hospitals   In an emergency, go to the nearest emergency room (*pronto soccorso*) of any hospital (*ospedale*). Convenient ones in the historic center include **San Giacomo,** Via Canova 29, off Via del Corso, two blocks from Piazza del Popolo (☎ **06-36-261**); **Fatebenefratelli,** on Tiber Island (☎ **06-683-7299**); and **Ospedale Santo Spirito in Sassia,** Lungotevere in Sassia 1 on the river just south of Castel Sant'Angelo (☎ **06-68-351**). The new "H" bus line makes a circular route of all the major hospitals.

English-speaking doctors are always on duty at the **Rome American Hospital,** Via Emilio Longoni 69 (☎ **06-22-551**), and at the privately run **Salvator Mundi International Hospital,** Viale della Mura Gianicolensi 67 (☎ **06-586-041**). Most hospitals will be able to find someone to help you in English, and with Italy's partially socialized medical system, you can usually pop into an emergency room, get taken care of speedily without dealing with insurance forms, and be sent on your way with a prescription and a smile. Just for the record: European Union citizens in possession of their E111 form are entitled to free health care; Australians must present a valid Medicare Card.

Laundry   Self-service *lavanderie* (Laundromats) are all over town. Try the **Bolle Blu,** Via Milazzo 20, where they do the wash for you in an hour for 14,000L ($7), soap included. For coin-operated Laundromats, hit the **Ondablu chain,** with central locations at Via Principe Amadeo 70b (south of Termini) and Via Vespasiano 50 (near the Vatican). The cost is 13,500L ($7), soap included.

The bulk of *lavanderie,* though, are full-service, charging ridiculous by-the-piece rates (4,000L/$2 for a pair of pants, 2,000L/$1 for socks) to wash, dry, press, and wrap up your T-shirts and undies like a Christmas present. Always ask first if service is *a peso* (by weight, the cheap way) or *al pezzo* (by the piece). However, these full-service joints also usually provide *lavasecco* (dry-cleaning) service at prices comparable to those in the States. Your hotel (which will invariably have their own service at equally extortionistic prices) will be able to point out the nearest one.

Mail & E-mail   The Italian mail system is notoriously slow, and friends back home may not receive your postcards for anywhere from 1 to 8 weeks (if ever). Postage for international postcards and letters costs 800L to 1,500L (40¢ to 75¢), depending on the destination. Stamps are available at the numerous post offices around town as well as any *tabacchi* (tobacconists; signs have a white "T" on a brown or black background), which have longer hours than the post offices. The **main post office** is at Piazza San Silvestro 19, 00187 Roma, Italia (off Via del Corso, south of the Spanish Steps); it's open Monday to Friday 9am to 6pm, Saturday 9am to 2pm, and Sunday 9am to 6pm. Enter and head around to the right to buy *francobolli* (**stamps**) at windows 22 and 23. If you want your letters to get home before you do, use the **Vatican post office** instead. It costs the same—but you must use Vatican stamps, available only at their post offices. There are three offices: to the left of the basilica steps, just past the information office; a less crowded branch behind the right-hand colonnade of Piazza San Pietro (where the alley dead-ends beyond the souvenir stands); and upstairs in the Vatican Museums entrance, near the gift shop.

To **receive mail** while in Rome (for a modest pick-up fee), have it sent to the main post office above, addressed to Your Name, FERMO POSTA, Roma, Italia. Holders of AMEX cards can get the same service for free by having their mail sent in care of American Express, Piazza di Spagna 38, Roma, Italia. Have the sender specify on the envelope that it's "Client Mail."

You can log onto the **Internet** in central Rome at **Thenetgate,** Piazza Firenze 25 (☎ **06-689-3445**), open in summer Monday to Saturday 10:30am to 12:30pm and 3:30 to 10:30pm and in winter daily 10:40am to 8:30pm. On Saturday there are happy half-hours 10:30 to 11am and 2 to 2:30pm when Internet access is free, but you must already have an account there (sign-up is free). Thenetgate also has branches at Borgo Santo Spirito 17r (☎ 06-6813-4082), at Via in Arcione 103 (☎ **06-6992-2320**), and in Stazione Termini near Via Marsala (☎ **06-8740-6008**). **Internet Point,** Via Gaeta 25 (exit Termini to the right onto Via Marsala, turn left onto Via Marsala, and follow to Via Gaeta; ☎ **06-4782-3862**) is heavily frequented by students and backpackers and open daily 9am to midnight. North of Castel Sant'Angelo is **Xplore,** Via dei Gracchi 85 (☎ **06-320-2072**), stocked with 20 computer stations. You can order off a typical pub menu (which in Italy includes stuffed *foccaccie*, thank heavens), plus beer, wine, and cocktails. It's open Monday to Saturday 3pm to 1am.

If you're bringing your own access, don't rely on updated phone jacks at your hotel room's bedside that slide effortlessly into your modem port. Most hotels have modernized their phone systems, but those older incompatible phone connections are just as prevalent in smaller hotels. If you can't live even a week without your laptop, you may want to cover your bases and pick up an Italian three-pronged wall jack and phone wire (for sale among the travel paraphernalia at JFK airport, among others, or at a hardware store in Rome; though, if you wait to pick it up in Italy, you may have to buy the handset as well).

Newspapers & Magazines   Expatriate magazines *Wanted in Rome* (1,500L/75¢; www.wantedinrome.com) and the more British *Metropolitan* (1,500L/75¢; www.nettuno.it/electric-italy/metropolitan.html) have calendar-of-events sections along with classified ads and articles on Rome and Italy from the foreigner's point of view. You'll find them at most newsstands, especially around tourist areas like the Vatican. Free at tourist offices and kiosks is *L'Evento,* a bimonthly published by the city of Rome with information on exhibits, concerts, theater, and other special events. *Un Ospite a Roma* is free at the finer hotel desks around town (they won't throw you out if you act like you belong) and has details on what's going on around town. If you want to try your hand at Italian, the Thursday edition of the newspaper **La Repubblica** contains the indispensable magazine insert **TrovaRoma** (www.repubblica.it), a complete guide to entertainment, events, galleries, and show listings for the coming week. Two other prime resources are the excellent weekly magazine **Roma C'è** (2,000L/$1), which has a "This Week in Rome" section at the end in English, and the Rome edition of **Time Out** (4,500L/$2.25), which comes out every 2 months; both are available at newsstands. **Aut,** published monthly and available free at bars, is the gay/lesbian magazine of Rome, good for listings, new venues, and news.

Pharmacies   *Farmacie,* recognizable by the green semi-neon cross, follow a rotation schedule for night, Sunday, and holiday hours, so there's always a pharmacy open in every neighborhood. The rotation schedule is posted in the window of every pharmacy, or you can head to a 24-hour pharmacy. **Farmacia della Stazione** is on Piazza dei Cinquecento, in front of Stazione Termini at the corner of Via Cavour (☎ **06-488-0019;** Metro: Termini); **Piram** at Via Nazionale 228 (☎ **06-488-0754**); and **Internazionale** at Piazza Barberini 49 (☎ **06-487-1195;** Metro: Barberini), which returns to a rotation schedule on weekends.

Police   Dial ☎ **113** in emergencies (see also "Emergencies," above).

Safety   Random violent crime is extremely rare in Rome, but pickpocketing runs rampant in tourist areas, where a desperate thief may go as far as slitting open purses or backpacks with knives. Thieves favor buses that run between Stazione Termini and the major sites (particularly bus 64 to the Vatican), so try to maintain a healthy distance between you and your traveling companions. Other pickpocketing areas are near the Forums and Colosseum, in Piazza del Popolo, around the Vatican, and around Termini, though the station is now staffed with private security officials. The Porta Portese flea market in Trastevere is another prime target. Men should keep their wallets in their front pockets and their hands on it while riding buses; women should wear their purses diagonally across their chests with the flaps facing in. It's all too common for young thieves on Vespas to effectively pull off a drive-by purse snatching. Keep your purse on the wall side of the sidewalk and try not to walk too close to the sidewalk's edge.

Gypsy children present an unexpected face of crime, working in packs around tourist areas. These kids aren't physically dangerous, but whenever they're around, a tourist and his money will soon be parted. They approach looking pitiful, begging and occasionally waving scraps of cardboard scrawled with a few words in English. If you see a group of dirty kids headed your way, yell *Va via!* (scram!) or loudly invoke the *polizia.* If they get too close, shove them away violently—don't hold back just because they're kids. They congregate outside Stazione Termini by the bus depots, at the Colosseum, at the Forum entrances, and in subway tunnels. Gypsy mothers usually stick to panhandling, but I've heard of Oliver Twist–type tales of scams involving swaddled babies flying through the air. The mother tosses what appears to be her baby, usually a doll in blankets (but sometimes the real thing!) at you. When in your surprise you rush to catch it, they or their accomplices are poised to empty your pockets.

Country & City Codes

The **country code** for Italy is **39.** The **city code** for Rome is **06;** use this code when you're calling from outside Italy, within Rome, and within Italy.

Telephone   Local calls in Italy cost 200L (10¢). There are two types of public pay phones, those that take both coins and phone cards and those that only take **phone cards** (*carta telefonica* or *scheda telefonica*). You can buy these prepaid phone cards at any *tabacchi* (tobacconist), most newsstands, and some bars in denominations of 5,000L ($2.70), 10,000L ($5), and 15,000L ($8). Break off the corner before inserting it and don't forget to take the card with you when you leave the phone!

To make calling card calls, insert a phone card or 200L—which will be refunded at the end of your call—and dial the local number for your service: **AT&T** at ☎ **172-1011, MCI** at ☎ **172-1022,** or **Sprint** at ☎ **172-1877.** These numbers will raise an American operator, and you can also use any one of them to place a collect call even if you don't carry that particular phone company's card.

Italy has recently introduced a series of **international phone cards** (*scheda telefonica internazionale*) for calling overseas, sold at the same outlets as regular phone cards. They come in increments of 50 (12,500L/$7), 100 (25,000L/$14), 200 (50,000L/$27), and 400 (100,000L/$54) *unita* (units). Each *unita* is worth 250L (15¢) of phone time; it costs 5 *unita* (1,250L/70¢) per minute to call within Europe or to the United States or Canada and 12 *unita* (3,000L/AUS$2.95) per minute to call Australia or New Zealand. You don't insert this card into the phone; merely dial ☎ **1740,** then push "*2" for instructions in English when prompted.

Tipping   Increasingly in restaurants, a *servizio* (service charge) of 15% is automatically added to your bill, so always ask *"È incluso il servizio?"* ("Is service included?") when you get the check. If not, leave 15%; if yes, it's still customary to leave an extra 1,000L (55¢) per person at the table. At a bar, put a 100L or 200L piece on the counter with your receipt when you order your espresso or cappuccino; if you're ordering at a table, leave about 500L per person. Tip taxi drivers about 10%.

Travel Agencies   In Stazione Termini, you'll find desks for **CTS** (☎ **06-467-9254**) and **Wasteels** (☎ **06-482-5537**), offering discounts (under 26) and assistance (all ages), but only for *international* train travel; both are open daily 8:30am to 8:30pm. If you need full-service attention, head over to their respective main offices: **Wasteels,** Via Milazzo 8c (☎ **06-445-6679**), and **CTS,** Corso Vittorio Emanuele II 297 (☎ **06-687-2672**).

3 Affordable Places to Stay

Cost-conscious travelers to Italy are in luck: Because of requirements imposed by European Union membership, even the most unsightly of one-star pensions have already completed or are in the process of completing cosmetic overhauls, giving you access to small but comfortable rooms overlooking the Pantheon, near the Spanish Steps, or hidden in Trastevere. Just because you're frugal doesn't mean you have to settle for cheap, often squalid rooms around the train station; I've picked out the good ones—just be careful walking these streets at night.

The most visible improvement has been in the methods of fireproofing, which have resulted in new bedspreads and window treatments, as well as top-to-bottom cover-ups of pockmarked and scuffed walls with fire-retardant wallpaper. Enjoy the newness of it all, because it won't take long for the paper to peel and careless smokers to burn holes in the upholstery.

Hotels claim to have high and low seasons, with prices quoted accordingly, but it doesn't take long to find out that low season arbitrarily falls when there aren't any people (usually in winter). With tourism raging in Italy, "low season" has withered to a few weeks during January and February.

Note: Unless otherwise specified, all units come with private bathrooms. And parking rates usually apply for small to midsize cars; you may have to pay more for larger models.

ROOM-FINDING SERVICES   The **tourist offices** (see "Visitor Information," earlier in this chapter) will help you track down a room but are often loathe to do so when there's a long line behind you. Tourist offices aren't allowed to play favorites regarding specific hotels, so the employees will arbitrarily look for any available room in your price range. (Some people are kind enough to try and stick you close to the center.)

You may have more luck and certainly better service at **Enjoy Rome** (see "Visitor Information," earlier in this chapter), which specializes in finding budget accommodations, even at the last minute. The English-speaking staff will help you for free via phone, in person, or via e-mail. The clerks often try to convince you to stay in hostels or other dormlike rooms (often in their own hostel), especially if you're under 30—just remind them you're willing to pay a bit more for a private room.

AROUND ANCIENT ROME

Casa Kolbe. Via San Teodoro 44 (bordering the west side of the Palatine archaeological zone), 00186 Roma. ☎ **06-679-4974.** Fax 06-6994-1550. 63 units. TEL. 112,000L ($56) single; 144,000L ($72) double. Breakfast 8,000L ($4). AE, MC, V. Street parking only. Bus: H, 44, 81, 95, 160, 170, 628, 715, 716, 780.

For those who love archaeology but don't need much in the way of amenities, this huge converted convent may be perfect. It's as hidden as you can get in the heart of Rome, around the corner from the Forum's "back door" on a little-traveled side street hugging the west flank of the Palatine Hill. Most rooms overlook the palm-filled gardens in back, resulting in a monastic silence. Second-floor street-side rooms enjoy a low panorama of the Palatine's ruins and a few Forum columns. The units are large and fairly basic, with an institutional feel reminiscent of the convent that still occupies the top floor. Another bonus: The big names like Piazza Navona and the Pantheon are just a short walk away.

Perugia. Via del Colosseo 7 (near the corner of Via Tempio della Pace), 00184 Roma. ☎ **06-679-7200.** Fax 06-678-4635. 13 units, 7 with bathroom. TV TEL. 105,000L ($53) single without bathroom, 135,000L ($68) single with bathroom; 135,000L ($68) double without bathroom, 175,000L ($88) double with bathroom. Rates include breakfast. AE, DC, MC, V. Parking 30,000L–40,000L ($15–$20) or free on street. Bus: **75**, 85, 87, **115**, 117, **175**, 186, 810, 850. Metro: Colosseo.

A well-run but rundown inn a block behind the Forum entrance, the side-street Perugia is a study in trade-offs. The funky 1970s-reject furnishings are on their last disco legs and that single 40-watt bulb doesn't quite illuminate your room, but the street's fairly quiet so you can open the windows for light, and everything's kept tolerably clean. Bounce on a few beds before choosing, as some will be kinder to your spine. You won't

A Note on Buses & Trams

In each listing's list of buses and trams that pass near the hotel, **boldface** indicates lines you can take directly from the main train station, Stazione Termini (either from the bus terminus on Piazza del Cinquecento out front or from a stop on the streets ringing the piazza).

Getting the Best Deal on Accommodations

- Reserve well in advance to get the best budget room. Rome is predictably popular, and none of the centrally located bargains is a secret; they all fill up quickly, especially in summer.

- Always ask for off-season rates October to Easter or for other special rates for students, seniors, teachers, or professionals—you never know what might work.

- Ask for the cheapest room, as prices often vary according to size, view, amenities, and so on.

- Settle for a room without a private bath—it'll invariably be cheaper.

- Be aware that a double bed (*letto matrimoniale*) is still sometimes cheaper than two twin beds (*due letti*) in a double room.

- If possible, opt out of the hotel breakfast; you can get the same *cornetto* (croissant) and cappuccino at the corner bar for a third of the price.

find the best mattress in room 26, but the room overlooks a minuscule courtyard full of hanging ivy. If you've set your sights on basing yourself in this area, try the Casa Kolbe first.

AROUND CAMPO DE' FIORI & THE JEWISH GHETTO

Campo de' Fiori. Via del Biscione 6 (off the northeast corner of Campo de' Fiori), 00186 Roma. ☎ **06-687-4886** or 06-6880-6865. Fax 06-687-6003. 27 units, 9 with bathroom. TEL. 160,000L ($80) double without bathroom, 250,000L ($125) double with bathroom; 250,000L ($125) double apt. Extra person 50,000L ($25) each (up to five). Rates include breakfast. MC, V. Parking 30,000L ($15). Bus: 46, 62, **64**, 116, 116T.

The units vary greatly at this central inn, from rustic ones with brick arches and wood-beamed ceilings to those in a more romantic (read: floral) decor. Although only 9 rooms come with private baths, it's also possible to book a room with a shower so that only the toilet in the hall is shared (190,000L/$95 double). Some rooms are just big enough to fit a double bed, but most are sizable, and all the shared facilities are clean. The main downside is the lack of an elevator, and the appearance of wear on the carpet increases the farther up you go. The reward for making it up to the top is that the duplex roof terrace affords a 360° vista of the city's rooftops and domes (room 602 enjoys a private view). The nightly party noise wafting up from the piazza can be annoying, so request a room off the front if you want to sleep more soundly.

Della Lunetta. Piazza del Paradiso 68 (off Via del Paradiso, a block from Corso Vittorio Emanuele II), 00186 Roma. ☎ **06-686-1080.** Fax 06-689-2028. 35 units, 15 with bathroom. TEL. 90,000L ($45) single without bathroom; 140,000L ($75) double without bathroom, 190,000L ($95) double with bathroom. Rates include breakfast. MC, V. Free parking on piazza (if you can find a spot). Bus: 46, 62, **64**, 116, 116T.

The Della Lunetta's accommodations may feel a bit institutional, with ranks of two to three cots and modular furnishings, but this hotel has the best prices in the neighborhood. Most baths are new, with enclosed shower stalls, but a few suffer from the curtainless spigot in the wall and drain in the floor arrangement. In all, this is a last-choice option in this cluster of hotels above Campo de' Fiori, though it's quieter than those closer to the campo itself.

Rome Accommodations

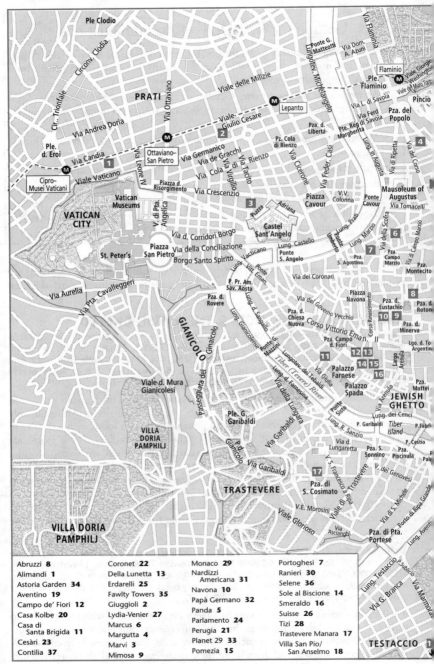

Pomezia. Via dei Chiavari 12 (between Largo Pollaro and Via Giubbonari), 00186 Roma. ☎ and fax **06-686-1371.** 25 units, 12 with bathroom. TEL. 100,000L ($50) single without bathroom, 150,000L ($75) single with bathroom; 150,000L ($75) double without bathroom, 200,000L ($100) double with bathroom. Rates 10% lower in winter. Rates include breakfast. AE, DC, MC, V. Bus: 46, 62, **64,** 116, 116T.

This spare but comfortably furnished inn has been in the same family since 1932, and the current generation of three brothers keeps it in pretty good shape. The most recent update shows in the new reception and breakfast room, though the labor would've been put to better use in the dismal (but clean) shared baths. The rooms with private baths were renovated in the mid-1990s, and it's worth springing for them. You may not have an elevator to help you reach the top-floor rooms, but they do catch some rooftop views and a little less street noise. In fact, the double-paned windows don't do much good, and the walls are thin, so a room on the *cortile* air shaft is best for light sleepers.

Smeraldo. Vicola dei Chiodaroli (between Via Chiavari and Via Monte della Farina), 00186 Roma. ☎ **06-687-5929.** Fax 06-6880-5495. 50 units, 42 with bathroom. A/C TV TEL. 80,000L ($40) single without bathroom, 130,000L ($65) single with bathroom; 130,000L ($65) double without bathroom, 180,000L ($90) double with bathroom. Breakfast 9,000L ($4.50). AE, MC, V. Parking 30,000–40,000L ($15–$20). Bus: **H,** tram 8, 46, 56, 60, 62, **64, 70,** 81, 87, **115,** 116, 186, **492,** 628, **640**.

The Smeraldo offers the utmost comfort and lots of amenities at reasonable prices. Most rooms have fresh and comfortable mattresses, spanking new baths, and functional but pleasant built-in furnishings, though the pebbly stone tile floors should probably be replaced. The rooms are extremely quiet, except for some distant traffic rumble on the Via Monte della Farina side. There's a sunny rooftop offering a panorama of Rome and a shady fourth-floor terrace.

Sole al Biscione. Via del Biscione 76 (½ block north of Campo de' Fiori), 00186 Roma. ☎ **06-6880-6873.** Fax 06-689-3787. 62 units, 40 with bathroom. TV TEL. 115,000L ($58) single without bathroom, 140,000–150,000L ($70–$75) single with bathroom; 170,000L ($85) double without bathroom, 210,000–220,000L ($105–$110) double with bathroom. Rates include breakfast. No credit cards. Parking 30,000–40,000L ($15–$20). Bus: 46, 62, **64,** 116.

Founded in 1462, Rome's oldest hotel has always worked toward self-improvement, and all rooms with baths were renovated for the Jubilee. Those not redone in this round are still in pretty good shape, and the big old-fashioned wood furnishings are nicely tooled or inlaid. However, even the double-glazed windows on the streetside rooms can't block out the late-night revelers, so request one overlooking the garden courtyard. Fourth-floor rooms boast a rooftop view encompassing a few domes and hundreds of TV aerials. Check out the basement garage, where bits of Pompey's Theater (55 B.C.) remain. This inn is popular, so book ahead.

WORTH A SPLURGE

✪ **Casa di Santa Brigida.** Via Monserato 54 (just off Piazza Farnese). Postal address: Piazza Farnese 96, 00186 Roma. ☎ **06-6889-2596.** Fax 06-6889-1573. E-mail: brigida@mclink.it. 20 units. A/C TEL. 145,000L ($85) single; 250,000L ($148) double. Rates include breakfast. V. Bus: 46, 62, **64,** 116.

Rome's best (and poshest) convent hotel is run by the curt sisters of St. Bridget in the house where the Swedish saint died in 1373. The location is optimal, across from the Michelangelo-designed Palazzo Farnese and a block from the daily market and nightlife of Campo de' Fiori. The splurge prices are a bit high but justified by the comfy and rather roomy old-world rooms with antiques or reproductions on parquet (lower level) or carpeted (upstairs) floors. The baths are a little old but at least have shower curtains, and the beds are firm. There's a roof terrace, library, and church. This retreat is highly requested, so reserve as far in advance as possible.

AROUND PIAZZA NAVONA & THE PANTHEON

✪ **Abruzzi.** Piazza della Rotonda 69, 00186 Roma. ☎ **06-679-2021.** 26 units, none with bathroom. 75,000–105,000L ($38–$53) single; 150,000L ($75) double. No credit cards. Bus: 46, 56, 60, 62, **64**, **70**, 81, 87, **115**, 116, 186, **492**, 628, **640**.

When for well under $100 you can look out your window and see the Pantheon less than 100 feet away, you've found something special. Of course, a cheap hotel this perfectly placed is no secret, and you need reserve and send an international money order with a night's deposit *way* in advance. Though not all rooms are blessed with the view (the three singles are on the back courtyard), most are large and clean yet utterly basic. The shared baths are a bit rundown, but the beds are brand new and firm. Since the piazza is a popular hangout until late, the noise can get annoying, but with this location and that view, who cares?

✪ **Coronet.** Piazza Grazioli 5, 00186 Roma. ☎ **06-679-0653.** Fax 06-6992-2705. E-mail: hotelcoronet@tiscalinet.it. 13 units, 10 with bathroom. TEL. 140,000–180,000L ($70–$90) single in double with bathroom; 160,000–200,000L ($80–$100) double without bathroom; 180,000–250,000L ($90–$125) double with bathroom. Rates include breakfast. AE, MC, V. Free parking on piazza (ask hotel for permit). Bus: 46, 56, 60, 62, **64**, **70**, 81, 87, **115**, 186, **492**, 628, **640**.

Here's your chance to live like an aristocrat in a high-ceilinged room in the 15th-century Palazzo Doria-Pamphilj. Simona Teresi and her son preside over baronially sized rooms with modest but comfortably mismatched tasteful furnishings—some functional, others antique style. Most rooms have orthopedic mattresses, and there are three hall bathrooms for the three rooms without private facilities. Rooms 34, 35, and 45 have wood ceilings and sitting corners with sofas. The piazza isn't very noisy, but use whatever excuse you need to request a room overlooking the private gardens.

✪ **Marcus.** Via del Clementino 94 (in the renamed final block of Via Fontanella Borghese before Piazza Nicosia, south of Augustus's Mausoleum), 00186 Roma. ☎ **06-6830-0320.** Fax 06-6830-0312. 20 units. A/C MINIBAR TV TEL. 100,000–150,000L ($50–$85) single; 200,000–250,000L ($100–$125) double. Rates include breakfast. AE, MC, V. Bus: **70**, 81, 87, **115**, 116, 186, 116T, 186, 628.

This updated pensione in a central 18th-century palazzo is easily one of Rome's best two-star hotels. The Marcus is managed by Frommer's-loving Salvatore and his wife, who keep a pot of brewed coffee going all day. Care for visitors shows up as well in the occasional classy antique furnishing, the firm beds, the decent baths, the Persian rugs on the patterned tile floors, and the walls hung with Roman prints and art deco lights. Salvatore believes in running a hotel he'd want to stay in, so the windows have formidable double-glazing. The highest rate includes use of the air-conditioning, and the larger rooms have futon chairs that can sleep an extra person.

Mimosa. Via Santa Chiara 61, 00186 Roma. ☎ **06-6880-1753.** Fax 06-683-3557. E-mail: hotelmimosa@tin.it. 12 units, 5 with bathroom. 90,000L ($45) single without bathroom; 140,000L ($70) double without bathroom, 170,000L ($85) double with bathroom. 10% discount in slow periods of winter. Breakfast 7,000–10,000L ($3.50–$5). No credit cards. Parking 30,000L ($15). Bus: **H**, tram 8, 46, 56, 60, 62, **64**, **70**, 81, 87, **115**, 186, **492**, 628, **640**.

This friendly little pensione offers a fantastic price for such a central location, but prepare for a trip back to the trappings of the local frat house. Things are a bit threadbare but well cared for, and the Cappelletto family has promised to redo some of the rooms very soon. The room furnishings are built-in or modular, with multiple beds (springy yet firm) for families on a budget. The welcoming atmosphere and homey touches separate this modest inn from the real student dives.

✪ **Navona.** Via dei Sediari 8 (off Corso del Rinascimento, between Piazza Navona and the Pantheon), 00186 Roma. ☎ **06-6821-1391.** Fax 06-6880-3802. 30 units, 28 with bathroom/shower. 140,000L ($70) single with bathroom; 190,000L ($95) double with bathroom. Rates include breakfast. No credit cards. Free parking on street (ask hotel for permit). Bus: **70,** 81, 87, **115,** 116, 186, **492,** 628.

Boasting Valentino bath tiles, new made-to-order furnishings, and smart curtains and bedspreads you might easily choose for your own home, the four-star-worthy Navona is the product of the discerning in-house architect/owner. It also wins points for retaining its one-star designation, a clever tactic that keeps the prices down. The hotel is located up two easy flights in an antique building, and air conditioning is available in about half of the rooms (doubles with bath only; add 35,000L/$18). A top-floor suite with a kitchenette is available on a weekly basis. The hotel accepts credit cards only to hold reservations.

If the Navona is full, the Natales may accompany you up to the equally nice **Residence Zanardelli,** which they recently finished renovating in a building off the north end of Piazza Navona. The rooms there come with phones and air-conditioning, and doubles run around 250,000L ($125).

WORTH A SPLURGE

Cesàri. Via di Pietra 89A (just off the Corso, a block south of Piazza Colonna). ☎ **06-679-2386.** Fax 06-679-0882. E-mail: www.venere.it/roma/cesari. 47 units. A/C TV TEL. 215,000–290,000L ($108–$145) single; 300,000–340,000L ($150–$170) double. Rates include breakfast. DC, MC, V. Parking 50,000–60,000L ($25–$30). Bus: 56, 60, 62, 81, 85, 95, 116, 117, 160, **175, 492,** 628, 850.

You couldn't ask for a location more central than halfway between the Pantheon and the Trevi Fountain, the Spanish Steps, and the Forum. In the Cesàri's 200-plus years, it has hosted the likes of Stendhal and Garibaldi, but a 1990s remodeling has left it with a modern style that hums with standardized comforts. The furnishings are built-in, the double-glazed windows particularly effective in blocking street sounds, the baths *modernissimo* (heated towel racks, hair dryers), and the waxed hardwood floors scattered with Persian rugs. Most rooms are modestly sized, but a few are big enough for families.

Portoghesi. Via di Portoghesi 1 (a block west of Via della Scrofa), 00186 Roma. ☎ **06-686-4231.** Fax 06-687-6976. 28 units. 230,000L ($115) single; 310,000–340,000L ($155–$170) double; 340,000–380,000L ($170–$190) suite. Rates include breakfast. MC, V. Parking 40,000L ($24). Bus: **70,** 87, 116, 116T, 186.

On a little-trafficked fork in Rome's medieval streets, the Portoghesi is only a few minutes' walk from Piazza Navona. The neighbors aren't too shabby either: a baroque church next door and a medieval tower across the street. In return for your splurge, you can expect antiques in the halls, comfortably carpeted rooms with built-in wood or lacquered units, and modern baths. Except for the larger antique-accented suites, the units are of average size without being too cramped, and there are even some with

---

A Breakfast Tip

Roman hotels, pensions, and *alberghi* have become so accommodating to foreign travelers that breakfast includes an abundant serving of weak American coffee (along with hot milk, if you've asked for a *caffè latte*). If you've grown accustomed to a more potent awakening, you'll have to specify by asking for a *caffè latte con caffè italiano* (hot milk with espresso) or a cappuccino.

views of the neighborhood (the best views are from rooms 4, 20, 22, 24, 38, 40, and 42). The inn is small and has a roster of devoted regulars, so reserve well in advance.

AROUND THE SPANISH STEPS & PIAZZA DEL POPOLO

Erdarelli. Via due Macelli 28, 00187 Rome. ☎ **06-679-1265.** Fax 06-679-0705. 48 units, 42 with bathroom. TEL. 105,000L ($52.50) single without bathroom, 128,000L ($64) single with bathroom; 140,000L ($70) double without bathroom, 168,000L ($84) double with bathroom. A/C 20,000L ($10) per day. Rates include breakfast.AE, DC, MC, V. Bus: 116, 116T, 117, 119, 590. Metro: Spagna.

The authentic image of a family-style pensione is alive and well at the Erdarelli, welcoming guests since 1935 only yards to the Spanish Steps. One of the Erdarellis will greet you with a warm welcome before shooing you down the narrow lobby corridor for access to the elevator. The pensione is characterized by mismatched wooden furniture and old garret-style showers or baths in the rooms, but most important, everything is painstakingly clean. The dorm-style TV room is dressed in red vinyl. Book at least a month in advance and considerably more for one of the four rooms with private terraces.

Lydia-Venier. Via Sistina 42 (almost a block from Piazza Trinità dei Monti), 00187 Roma. ☎ **06-679-1744.** Fax 06-679-7263. 28 units, 14 with bathroom. TV TEL. 90,000–120,000L ($45–$60) single without bathroom, 120,000–170,000L ($60–$85) single with bathroom; 130,000–200,000L ($65–$100) double without bathroom, 180,000–220,000L ($90–$120) double with bathroom. Rates include breakfast. AE, DC, MC, V. Parking 25,000L ($14). Bus: 52, 53, 56, 58, 58/ 60, 61, 62, 95, 116, 117, **175, 492**. Metro: Spagna or Barberini.

A block from the top of the Spanish Steps, the Lydia-Venier is one of a handful of hotels that continues to provide basic units at rock-bottom prices. The building's sweeping marble staircase leads up the one flight to the hotel, where you'll first encounter the friendly house matron, who'll show you to one of her spick-and-span rooms. The built-in furnishings are new, the mattresses are some of the firmest in town, and the abundant continental breakfast is worth a mention. Rooms 208 and 209 share a ceiling of gilded stuccoes, and room 105 has a frescoed ceiling; the wall-to-wall carpeting helps dampen noise, but the rooms on the back are quietest. If the place isn't booked solid (unlikely), you may want to look at a few of the rooms before choosing—most are huge, but a few are a bit cramped.

Margutta. Via Laurina 34 (2 blocks from Piazza del Popolo between Via Babuino and Via del Corso), 00187 Roma. ☎ **06-322-3674.** Fax 06-320-0395. 24 units. TEL. 170,000L ($85) single; 190,000 ($95) double; 250,000 ($125) triple. Rates include breakfast. AE, DC, MC, V. Bus: 117, 628, 926. Metro: Flaminio.

The Margutta isn't for those who need a lot of elbow room, but it offers reliability and a touch of style for an inexpensive central choice. The hardworking management likes to joke around, providing efficient service with a smile in rapid-fire English. Curly wrought-iron bed frames give the rooms a classy feel, but the lumpy beds barely pass muster for firmness. Most rooms are immaculate but on the small side of cozy, and some baths are positively minuscule. The double-glazed windows keep the street noise down, but since you're already on a side street, things are pretty tranquil.

Panda. Via della Croce 35, 00187 Rome. ☎ **06-678-0179.** Fax 06-6994-2151. 20 units, 4 with bathroom. 80,000L ($40) single without bathroom, 120,000L ($60) single with bathroom; 140,000L ($70) double without bathroom; 180,000L ($90) double with bathroom. 10,000L ($5) per person discount in low season. Rates include breakfast. AE, MC, V. Bus: 116, 116T, 117. Metro: Spagna.

This hotel is just two blocks from the Spanish Steps, but you'll have to trade comfort for location—there are no amenities like phones and an elevator, and few private baths. The linoleum-floored second-floor rooms are decidedly inferior and no-frills, so request a first-floor room (with touches like frescoed ceilings, wrought-iron fixtures, and firm beds set on terra-cotta floors). All rooms are clean, but none is very large. The rooms facing the (mostly pedestrian) street have double-glazed windows, so at least you won't be counting cherubs in those lower front rooms.

● **Parlamento.** Via delle Convertite 5 (at intersection with Via del Corso, near Piazza San Silvestro), 00187 Roma. ☎ **06-679-2082.** Fax 06-6992-1000. 23 units. TV TEL. 170,000–180,000L ($85–$90) single; 190,000–200,000L ($95–$100) double. Rates include breakfast. AE, DC, MC, V. Parking 40,000L ($20). Bus: 52, 53, 58, 58/, 61, 71, 85, 116, 116T, 160, 850 (to Piazza San Silvestro); 56, 60, 62, 95, **115, 175,** 492 (to Largo Chigi/Via Tritone).

The Parlamento has four-star class at two-star prices. After a few stairs, there's an elevator to the third floor and a friendly reception area. The room furnishings are antique or good reproductions and the firm beds backed by carved wood or wrought-iron headboards. A *double set* of double-glazed windows blocks out the street traffic. Fifteen rooms have air-conditioning (installation is tentatively planned for additional rooms; try to negotiate out of the charge), and the baths were recently redone with hair dryers, heated towel racks, phones, and (in a few) marble sinks. You can enjoy the trompe-l'oeil breakfast room or carry your cappuccino to the small roof terrace with its view of San Silvestro's bell tower (several upper-floor rooms share this vista). Some larger units are great for families, including the triple no. 82 with big old antiques and no. 108 with two bedrooms and a small terrace.

Suisse. Via Gregoriana 54 (near the intersection with Via Capo le Case), 00187 Roma. ☎ **06-678-3649.** Fax 06-678-1258. 13 units. TEL. 155,000L ($78) single; 230,000L ($115) double; 310,000L ($155) triple. Rates include breakfast. MC, V. Bus: 52, 53, 56, 58, 58/, 60, 61, 62, 95, 116, 117, **175, 492.** Metro: Barberini.

A long block down a quiet street from the astronomically priced hotels atop the Spanish Steps, the sterile Suisse is run like a tight ship—probably in no small part due to the frau at the head of this small third-floor hotel. The furnishings are old but tasteful, with stiff mattresses on wooden boards. All the baths are new, and a few of the roomy units retain old ceiling stuccoes. The open spaces are scattered with antiques, but the TV/sitting room you share with the family is more like a comfortable old salon. They'll sell you cheap sodas and water from a little fridge. The Suisse is popular, so book ahead. You can pay only half your bill with a credit card, and there's no one at the desk to buzz you in from 2 to 6am.

AROUND VIA VENETO & PIAZZA BARBERINI

Monaco. Via Flavia 84 (parallel to Via XX Settembre, near Via San Tullio.), 00187 Roma. ☎ **06-4201-4180.** Fax 06-474-4335. 12 units, 5 with bathroom. 55,000L ($28) single without bathroom, 70,000L ($35) single with bathroom; 80,000L ($40) double without bathroom, 100,000L ($50) double with bathroom. Rates include breakfast.No credit cards. Parking 30,000–40,000L ($18–$20); free on street. Bus: **16,** 37, **38, 38/,** 60, 61, 62, 136, 137, **319, 360,** 910.

Maria Tomassi, her sister Elena, and her grown children run this bare-bones hotel at the edge of an upscale neighborhood. Most rooms are quite sizable, with just a few pieces of mismatched functional furniture and tiny baths (no shower curtains). The mattresses range from thin and stiff to soft and springy, so you may want to test a few before choosing your room. It's all a bit institutional, with shared baths straight out of a college dorm, but the friendly Tomassis keep it clean and the prices are fantastic. The streets can be noisy by day, but quiet down at night. There's sometimes a midnight curfew, so ask before heading out.

Tizi. Via Collina 48 (east of Piazza Sallustio and west of Via Piave), 00187 Roma. ☎ **06-482-0128.** Fax 06-474-3266. 20 units, 10 with bathroom. 70,000L ($35) single without bathroom; 90,000L ($45) double without bathroom, 110,000L ($55) double with bathroom. Rates include breakfast.No credit cards. Parking 25,000–30,000L ($13–$15). Bus: **38**, **38**/, 56, 58, 58/. **319**, 490, 495.

The family-run Tizi is in a posh neighborhood just south of Villa Borghese park. A few antique-style pieces in the reception hall give way to mostly new modular furnishings in the rooms, but the orthopedic mattresses rest on old-fashioned metal bed frames. The ceilings are high and airy, some with stuccowork, and the private baths are in good working order, with box showers. There's one shared bath for every two rooms. This inn is a favorite with young travelers in search of peace and a friendly atmosphere rather than beer and parties.

WORTH A SPLURGE

Ranieri. Via XX Settembre 43 (near Via San Tullio), 00187 Roma. ☎ **06-481-4467.** Fax 06-481-8834. www.venere.it/roma/ranieri. E-mail: hotel.ranieri@italyhotel.com. 47 units. A/C MINI-BAR TV TEL. Weekdays 195,000–210,000L ($98–$105) single; 255,000–285,000L ($128–$143) double. Weekends 155,000L ($78) single; 210,000L ($105) double. Rates include breakfast. AE, DC, MC, V. Valet parking 30,000–40,000L ($15–$20). Bus: **16**, 37, **38**, **38**/, 60, 61, 62, 136, 137, **319**, 910.

The staff at this large modern hotel love Frommer's readers and obviously love being in the hospitality business. In the refurbished rooms, the carpets, double-paned windows, and fabric wall padding combine to create a dead silence. The built-in wood-and-marble units and armoires are of bland earth tones, but extra amenities abound, such as trouser presses, international outlets you can plug anything into, and phone jacks for computer hookups.

NORTH OF STAZIONE TERMINI

Bus information is included for the hotels below, but you'll notice none is boldface. Each hotel is within a few blocks of Termini train station.

Astoria Garden. Via V. Bachelet 8 (3½ blocks north of Termini), 00185 Roma. ☎ **06-446-9908.** Fax 06-445-3329. www.hotelastoriagarden.it. E-mail: astoria.garden@flashnet.it. 33 units, 32 with bathroom. A/C TV TEL. 140,000L ($70) single; 200,000L ($100) double. AE, DC, MC, V. Rates include breakfast. Parking 30,000L ($15). Bus: H, 9, tram 14, 16, 36, 36/, 38, 38/, 64, 70, 75, 105, 115, 157, 170, 175, 310, 317, 319, 492, tram 516, 640, 714, 910. Metro: Termini or Castro Pretorio.

The prices are fantastic considering what you get at this hotel in a late-19th-century palazzo with stucco ceilings and an old-world atmosphere. However, until the renovations are complete, the units will vary greatly. The old rooms have squishy beds and modular furnishings with chipped lacquer and can't compare to the reproduction furnishings and soft carpets in the High Turin–style quarters of one wing. There's a garden shaded by palm, banana, and orange trees with a glassed-in veranda, and rooms on this side enjoy the best views. For optimal tranquility, opt for one of the several bungalow-like units across the garden. If you'll be staying several days, tell manager Francesco Cusato you're traveling with Frommer's and you may get a discount. They'll pick you up at the airport for 100,000L ($50) for two.

Fawlty Towers. Via Magenta 39 (a block north of Termini, between Via Milazzo and Via Marghera), 00185 Roma. ☎ and fax **06-445-0374.** www.enjoyrome.it. 12 units, 3 with bathroom; 2 shared units, neither with bathroom. 70,000L ($35) single without bathroom, 85,000L ($43) single with bathroom; 100,000L ($50) double without bathroom, 110,000–130,000L ($55–$65) double with bathroom; 35,000L ($18) bed in shared unit. Rates include breakfast. No credit cards. Bus: H, 9, 16, 36, 36/, 38, 38/, 64, 70, 75, 105, 115, 157, 170, 175, 310, 317, 319, 492, 640, 714, 910. Tram: 14, 516. Metro: Termini.

This hotel/hostel is a fave of students and the younger international set who are primarily of the clean-scrubbed variety. It's owned by Enjoy Rome, staffed by a crew of friendly English-speakers, and has the cleanest and most comfy hostel-style accommodations in town. The shared dorms are on the fifth floor (there's an elevator) and private rooms on the sixth. The hostel rooms sleeping three or four are as bare as you'd expect but not squalid (no bunk beds, just soft cots). The simple singles and doubles have firm mattresses and functional furnishings. Four bathless rooms have at least a sink and a shower, and there's a solarium with a TV, fridge, and microwave as well as a small terrace. No curfew.

Papà Germano. Via Calatafimi 14a (4 blocks west of Termini), 00185 Roma. ☎ **06-486-919.** Fax 06-4782-5202. www.hotelpapagermano.it. E-mail: info@hotelpapagermano.it. 17 units, 7 with bathroom. TV TEL. 55,000L ($22.50) single without bathroom; 90,000L ($45) double without bathroom, 100,000L ($50) double with bathroom; 130,000L ($65) triple with bathroom; 30,000L ($15) bed in shared unit without bathroom. Rates include breakfast. AE, DC, MC, V. Parking 25,000L ($13). Bus: 16, 36, 36/, 37, 38, 38/, 60, 61, 62, 136, 137, 317, 319. Metro: Repubblica.

Gino is a terrifically friendly guy who loves to help visitors settle into Rome. As the owner, he holds cleanliness in the highest regard and repaints or repapers every year or two. The mattresses are firm to the point of being hard, but just about everything—from the built-in units and box showers to the double-glazed windows and hair dryers in every room—is spotless and either new or kept looking that way. The shared baths are great, but units with private baths also have satellite TVs. Six bathless rooms can become dorms (you can save by bunking with two or three strangers). All the guidebooks list this inn, so call ahead.

Planet 29. Via Gaeta 29 (near Piazza Indipendenza), 00185 Roma. ☎ **06-486-520.** Fax 06-484-141. E-mail: cristina@mclink.it. 10 units. 90,000–100,000L ($45–$50) single; 110,000–120,000L ($55–$60) double. Rates include breakfast. AE, DC, MC, V. Bus: H, 9, tram 14, 16, 36, 36/, 38, 38/, 64, 70, 75, 105, 115, 157, 170, 175, 204F, 310, 310, 317, 319, 492, tram 516, 640, 714, 910. Metro: Castro Pretorio.

At these prices, few would expect orthopedic beds. But you get these and more, including a quiet night's sleep in a clean comfortable environment in a central location. Most rooms come with a fully operable kitchen area (10,000L/$5 more), complete with necessities like plates, cutlery, and pans, further enabling you watch your budget by not blowing it all on meals; the management provides minibars on request. There's an (unrelated) Internet cafe at street level. Alas, these types of bargains are no longer a secret, so book *very* early.

SOUTH OF STAZIONE TERMINI

✪ **Nardizzi Americana.** Via Firenze 38 (just off Via XX Settembre), 00184 Roma. ☎ **06-488-0368.** Fax 06-488-0035. 22 units. A/C TV TEL. 90,000–130,000L ($45–$65) single; 140,000–200,000L ($70–$100) double. Rates include breakfast. AE, DC, MC, V. Parking 25,000L ($13). Bus: 37, 60, 61, 62, **64, 70, 115,** 116T, 136, 137, 170, **175, 492, 640, 910** (to Largo Santa Susanna/Via V.E. Orlando); . Metro: Repubblica.

The Nardizzi has always been a steal, and even with everything recently renovated, Nik and Fabrizio have managed to keep the rates reasonably low (quote this guide for the best prices). The new style is inspired by ancient Rome, with street lamps on the narrow terrace and a patterned tile decor giving an inlaid stone look to the walls and floors of the public areas. The rooms have tiled floors and new baths, and a few have wood-beam ceilings; the smaller ones contain built-in dressers and the larger ones walk-in closets. Nik and Fabrizio will even come to the airport to get you and one of your closest friends for an astonishingly low 70,000L ($35).

Selene. Via dei Viminale 8, 00184 Roma. ☎ **06-482-4460.** Fax 06-4782-1977. www. hotel-selene-roma.com. E-mail: . 27 units. TV, TEL. 100,000L ($50) single; 150,000L ($75) double. Rates include breakfast. AE, DC, MC, V. Bus: 16, 75, 84, 105, 110, 157, 204F, 360, 590, 649, 714. Metro: Termini.

To bring this former *pensione* up to speed, the earnest new owner, Luigi, has undertaken major renovations. Don't be put off by the squalid exterior and neglected sign: The Selene is a work in progress but already boasting mattresses and pillows your chiropractor would approve of and freshly tiled baths. The units are generally spacious (the baths aren't) and outfitted in streamlined IKEA furniture (antiques line the halls). The neighborhood may not be the greatest, but the Teatro dell'Opera is across the street and Santa Maria Maggiore three blocks away.

WORTH A SPLURGE

Contilia. Via P. Amadeo 81 (near Via Gioberti, 2 blocks from Termini), 00185 Roma. ☎ **06-446-6942.** Fax 06-446-6904. www.hotelcontilia.com. E-mail: contilia@tin.it. 41 units. A/C TV TEL. 110,000–180,000L ($55–$90) single; 110,000–220,000L ($55–$110) double; 150,000-300,000L ($75–$150) triple. Rates include breakfast. AE, DC, MC, V. Parking 30,000L ($17.65); free on street. Bus: 9, tram 14, 16, 70, 71, 75, 105, tram 516, 714. Metro: Termini.

As the automatic doors part to reveal a stylish marble lobby of Persian rugs and antiques, you may double-check the address. The old-fashioned pensione Tony-Contilia has taken over this building's other small hotels and gentrified itself into one of the best choices in this dicey neighborhood. The rooms have been redone in modern comfort with satellite TVs and safes. The double-glazed windows keep out traffic noise, and the rooms overlooking the cobblestone courtyard are even more quiet. The unrenovated baths are a bit small and lack shower curtains; those with new Jacuzzis cost 25,000L ($13) extra.

ON THE AVENTINE

To get to these hotels from the airport, take the *local* train into Rome (not the express to Stazione Termini) and get off at the Ostiense station, just several trafficky blocks from the Aventine. For the trio of San Anselmo/Aventino hotels, no bus saves you from a long walk uphill, so it may be worth it to take a taxi from Ostiense.

WORTH A SPLURGE

Aventino. Via San Domenico 10 (address correspondence to, and check in at, the nearby San Anselmo hotel; see below). ☎ **06-574-3547.** Fax 06-578-3604. 23 units. TV TEL. 170,000L ($85) single; 250,000L ($125) double. Rates include breakfast. AE, DC, MC, V. Free parking at hotel (first-come, first-served) or on street. Bus: 23 , 715, 716, 719. Metro: Piramide.

The Aventino is more downscale than its sibling hotels on this hill (where you'll have to check in and check out; see below), and its exterior is a bit more decrepit—the shutters and walls could use a good scraping and paint job—but the interior is tidier, and it's still got that Aventine villa style and at much lower rates. It's set in some gardens, and the rooms have parquet or tile floors, eclectic furnishings and soft beds. No. 346 has a long columned balcony overlooking the road and surrounding mansions.

Villa San Pio / San Anselmo. Via Santa Melania 19 (where Via San Domenico and Via San Anselmo end at Via Porta Lavernale), 00153 Roma. ☎ **06-574-3547.** Fax 06-578-3604. 110 units. TV TEL. 210,000L ($105) single; 320,000L ($160) double. Rates include breakfast. AE, DC, MC, V. Free parking at hotel (first-come, first-served) or on street. Bus: 23 (watch for deviations), 715, 716, 719. Metro: Piramide.

These inns retain their distinct flavors even though both (and the Aventino, above) share a single management—they won't let you book into one specifically, but you can always ask when you check in. The San Anselmo is the posh centerpiece; the Villa San Pio the stylish hideaway; and the Aventino the budget gem. Of these two pricier inns, the Villa San Pio is the best buy; the San Anselmo has more consistently classy units, but the best rooms at the friendlier San Pio definitely outshine.

The public salons and halls of the **San Anselmo** (Via San Anselmo 2) are fitted with oriental rugs, chandeliers, and other accouterments of the 18th and 19th centuries. The rooms feature antiques or reproductions, rich wall fabrics, firm beds, and modern baths; third-floor units also have air-conditioning. The **Villa San Pio** consists of two buildings bridged by a magnolia-shaded garden and solarium. The decor varies widely (some rooms with modular furnishings, others in grand 19th-century style), but all contain firm beds. The choice rooms are in the structure beyond the gardens, where on the first floor you're most likely to find the best reproduction furnishings, Persian rugs, painted ceilings, and ultramod baths with Jacuzzis. The roof terrace has splendid tranquil views.

IN TRASTEVERE

To get to your Trastevere hotel from the airport, hop on the local train toward Tiburtina (instead of the express into Stazione Termini), which will stop at Trastevere's train station, where you can catch tram 8 up Viale Trastevere.

✪ **Trastevere Manara.** Via L. Manara 24a–25, 00153 Roma. ☎ **06-581-4713.** Fax 06-588-1016. 9 units. TV TEL. 130,000L ($65) single; 170,000L ($85) double; 200,000L ($100) apt for 4, 250,000 ($125) apt for 5. Rates include breakfast. AE, DC, MC, V. Free parking on street. Bus: **H**, tram 8.

In 1998, what was Trastevere's dingiest hotel renovated itself into the classiest and is now one of Rome's best bargains. It offers cushy amenities at fantastic prices, a location at the heart of Trastevere's restaurants and nightlife, and a nearby daily market for fresh picnic pickings. The gentrified rooms are still pensione cavernous, but with fresh tiles and painted stucco, massive modular wood furnishings, and new baths. All except smaller (and dreary) nos. 1 and 2 overlook the market square of San Cosimato—be prepared for a dawn wake-up. The hotel offers an airport transfer at 100,000L ($50) for two.

AROUND THE VATICAN

Take special care in confirming the bus listings in the neighborhoods around the Vatican. The Jubilee Year upsets and bus reroutings were no more pronounced around the city than here.

Alimandi. Via Tunisi 8 (at Via Veniero and the base of the steps up to Viale Vaticano), 00192 Roma. ☎ **06-3972-3941.** Fax 06-3972-3943. www.alimandi.org. E-mail: alimandi@tin.it. 35 units. A/C TV TEL. 160,000L ($80) single; 230,000L ($115) double 260,000L ($130) triple. Breakfast 15,000L ($8). AE, DC, MC, V. Parking 30,000L ($15). Bus: 49 (take bus 492 from Termini to any stop on Via Crescenzio, after Piazza Cavour, to transfer to the 49). Metro: Ottaviano–San Pietro.

This is a tour group–style hotel, but one of the better ones, and that probably explains the *free airport transfer* (pickups according to a specific timetable). The location is great for the district, three blocks from Rome's best daily food market (on Via Andrea Doria) and a short staircase down from the Vatican Museums entrance. The rooms are modern and comfortable, holding few surprises in the built-in wood units and newish baths. The firm beds sport fresh foam mattresses. There's a faux medieval bar, a billiards room, and a roof terrace with no particular view but good sun and caged exotic birds.

Giuggioli. Via Germanico 198 (between Via Principe Emilio and Via F. Massimo), 00192 Roma. ☎ **06-324-2113.** 5 units, 1 with bathroom. Single on request; 150,000L ($75) double without bathroom, 180,000L ($90) double with bathroom. Rates include breakfast. No credit cards. Bus: 32, **70**, 81, 186, 280, 913, 994, 999. Metro: Lepanto.

Signora Gasparina Giuggioli has been running her little pensione for more than 50 years, and though she talks of retiring, she loves the job too much to quit. To go with the high ceilings, patterned rugs on tile floors, and firm mattresses, most units have sturdy old functional furnishings; enormous no. 6 (the one with a bath) enjoys classier antique pieces. No. 4 features a balcony jutting into the profusion of leafy branches that block the boring street from view (it's a bit trafficky, but the double-glazed windows help cut the noise). Signora Giuggioli smiles as she pours you a cup of stovetop espresso or a *digestivo* (digestive liqueur) when you return home from dinner.

Marvi. Via Pietro delle Valle 13 (off Via Crescenzio a block west of Piazza Adriana, the north arm of Castel Sant'Angelo's star-shaped park), 00193 Roma. ☎ and fax **06-6880-2621** or 06-686-5652. 8 units. TEL. 100,000L ($50) single; 150,000L ($77) double. Rates include breakfast. No credit cards. Parking 25,000–30,000L ($13–$15). Bus: 34, 40, 49, **70**, 87, 186, 280, **492**, 913, 926, 990. Metro: Ottaviano–San Pietro.

Since 1969, a friendly guy from Orvieto has run this clean little hotel on a side street of the Borgo (the zone between the Vatican and the river). His rooms are simple, and some of the hodgepodge furnishings are actually quite nice; the baths, though, are tiny. Brand-new cot springs support stiff foam mattresses covered by fashionable bed-spreads. Nos. 10 and 14 have stucco ceiling decorations, and no. 11 gets lots of light from windows on two sides. The third-floor rooms tend to be pretty quiet.

4 Great Deals on Dining

Ever notice that food tastes best when you're starving, diminishing in fabulousness the fuller you get? Well, don't be bullied into eating more than you can realistically hold and don't be intimidated by that incredulous "*E dopo?*" or "*Basta così?*" (meaning "Then what would you like?" or "That's all you're having?").

Dining out is an event for Italians, and it's unheard of not to have at least two plates, generally a *primo* (first course) and a *secondo* (second or main course). Sometimes you can slide by with an antipasto and *primo,* but in Rome, even these tend to be of exaggerated portions. With so many courses expected of you, it's easy to drop 50,000L ($25) and upwards of 70,000L ($40) in overpriced tourist trattorie in the center. Stick to your guns and order only what you want, except in finer restaurants, when ordering only one plate is bad form. It's always a good idea to prepare your waiter for a lack of appetite; I haven't been turned away from an Italian table yet.

At *osterie* (cheap eateries frequented by locals) and *fiaschetterie* (old-fashioned wine bars serving a few inexpensive dishes) you can get basic, filling Roman meals for under 35,000L ($21). Many are just steps from the most touristy sights of the *centro storico,* so if you can resist the temptation to live *la dolce vita* along Via Veneto, you'll have no problem on a budget. If you want to wander and find a restaurant on your own, be aware that the strongest concentration of eateries is in Trastevere. In addition, all around town you'll find trendy **"wine bars"** (called that even in Italian) where you can drink remarkable wines by the glass and nibble on cheese platters, salamis, and often inventive small dishes all pretty cheaply. And if you're looking for a simple but meal-sized salad, try one of **Insalata Ricca's** outlets (see below).

A typical Roman meal begins with an *antipasto* (appetizer or "before the pasta"), which most often means a simple *bruschetta* (a slab of peasant bread grilled, rubbed with garlic, drizzled with olive oil, and sprinkled with salt; *al pomodoro* adds a pile of cubed tomatoes on top). If you see *carciofi* (artichokes), *alla giudea* or otherwise (especially if you're in the Jewish Ghetto), snap up one of Rome's greatest specialties—

tender and lightly fried in olive oil. A favorite that found it's way across the Atlantic some time ago is ***prosciutto e melone***, a surprisingly good combination of salt-cured ham draped over a slice of sweet cantaloupe (in summer, it may be figs instead of melon).

Your ***primo*** (first course) could be a soup—try ***stracciatella*** (egg and parmesan in broth)—or a pasta. Available on just about every Roman menu are traditional favorites like ***bucatini all'Amatriciana*** (in a spicy tomato sauce studded with pancetta and dense with onions), ***spaghetti alla carbonara*** (spaghetti mixed with eggs, bacon, and loads of black pepper—the heat of the pasta cooks the eggs), and ***pasta al pomodoro*** (in a plain tomato sauce). Also try ***penne all'arrabbiata*** ("hopping mad" pasta quills in a spicy tomato sauce), ***tagliolini alla gricia*** (thin egg noodles with parmesan and pig's jowl, which is sort of like bacon), ***tagliolini*** or ***spaghetti cacio e pepe*** (with black pepper and grated pecorino cheese), ***pasta e fagioli*** (pasta with beans), ***pasta e ceci*** (pasta with chickpeas), or ***gnocchi*** (potato-based pasta dumplings).

Secondi (second courses) include traditional local dishes like the eyebrow-raising but delicious ***coda alla vaccinara*** (braised oxtail with tomatoes), ***pajata*** (calves' intestines still clotted with mother's milk and often put in tomato sauce on rigatoni pasta), and ***trippa*** (good old-fashioned tripe). Less adventurous main courses include ***involtini*** (veal layered with prosciutto, cheese, and celery and then rolled and cooked with tomatoes), ***polpette*** (meatballs), ***bocconcini di vitello*** (veal nuggets, usually stewed with potatoes and sage), ***pollo arrosto*** (roast chicken, often excellently sided *con patate,* with roast potatoes), ***pollo e peperoni*** (chicken smothered in roast red and yellow peppers), ***straccetti con rughetta*** (strips of beef tossed with torn rughetta lettuce), ***arrosto di vitello*** (simple roast veal steak), or ***abbacchio a scottaditto*** (grilled tender Roman spring lamb chops; so good the name declares you'll "burn your fingers" in your haste to eat them). One of the best Roman secondi is ***saltimbocca*** ("jumps-in-the-mouth"), a tender veal cutlet cooked in white wine with sage leaves and a slice of prosciutto draped over it.

Roman **pizza**—the kind from a cheap sit-down pizzeria or *pizza al forno*—is large, round, flat, and crispy (unlike its breadier Neapolitan cousin). A "plain" tomato sauce, mozzarella, and basil pie is called ***pizza margherita***. The adventurous may want to try a ***cappriciosa***, a selection of toppings that often includes anchovies, prosciutto, olives, and an egg cracked onto the hot pizza, where it fries in place. You can also get the Roman version of pizza by the slice, ***pizza rustica*** (a.k.a. ***pizza à taglio***) from hole-in-the-wall joints (see "Quick Bites," later in this section).

The ***contorni*** (sides) on the menu are vegetables dishes (*melanzana* is eggplant, *fagioli* are beans, *patate* are potatoes, and *zucchini* are obvious). End your meal with ***tiramisù*** (a layer cake of espresso-soaked lady fingers and sweetened, creamy mascarpone cheese dusted with cocoa), a ***tartufo*** (the mother of ice-cream balls—a fudge center, then vanilla, then chocolate, dusted with cocoa or bittersweet chocolate chunks), or simple ***biscotti*** (twice-baked hard almond cookies).

Although the capital's restaurants are usually blessed with wine cellars that draw on the best vineyards throughout Italy, table wine in Rome is usually a light, fruity white from the hills south of the city, either a **Frascati** or the slightly inferior **Castelli Romane.**

AROUND ANCIENT ROME

Birreria Peroni. Via San Marcello 10 (north of Piazza Santissimi Apostoli). ☎ **06-679-5310.** Reservations not accepted. Dishes 7,500–20,00L ($3.75–$10); buffet items 5,000–11,500L ($2.50–$6). MC, V. Mon–Fri 12:30–11:30pm, Sat 8pm–midnight. Closed up to 4 wks. in Aug. Bus: H, 56, 60, 62, 64, 70, 81, 85, 95, 117, 160, 170, 640, 175, 492, 628, 850. ROMAN/GERMAN/BUFFET.

Getting the Best Deal on Dining

- Take lunch in a less-expensive *tavola calda* (like a tiny cafeteria or hot foods deli) or pizzeria instead of a restaurant.
- Note that some expensive restaurants have cheaper lunch menus, which offer you a chance to sample their fine cuisine at two-thirds the cost.
- Don't just go for any *menu turistico*. Look for good-value menus that offer choices within each course and include wine and cover charge.
- Eat anywhere that's full of locals. Empty restaurants and ones crowded with tourists are places locals steer clear of—you'd be wise to follow their example.
- Order the *vino della casa* (house wine); it'll usually be excellent and always cheaper than any bottle on the wine list.
- Stand at bars and cafes rather than taking a table, where the same food costs twice as much.
- Check your bill to see if service is included in the total (*servizio incluso*). You wouldn't want to tip twice.

At few places in the historic center can you get good food so cheap, fast, and filling. This Italian beer hall has been in this vaulted space since 1906, and the edges of the room were frescoed in the 1940s with art nouveau sportsman drinking beer and espousing homilies like "Beer makes you strong and healthy." The buffet includes prosciutto, goose salami, stuffed or piccante olives, beans with tuna, and marinated artichokes, while plates cover the requisite *bucatini all'amatriciana, trippa,* and *pollo arrosto con patate.* The indecisive should try the *arrosto misto alla Peroni* (a huge mix of lots of German beer hall–style eats, like sausage with sauerkraut and goulash with potatoes). To wash it all down order a Peroni beer or the "blue ribbon" Nastro Azzurro label.

✪ **La Piazzetta.** Vicolo del Buon Consiglio 23/A (near Via del Colosseo). ☎ **06-699-1640.** Primi 10,000–12,000L ($5–$7); secondi 12,000–25,000L ($7–$13). AE, DC, MC, V. Mon–Sat noon–3pm and 7–11pm. Bus: 75, 84 , 85, 87, 117, 175, 186, 810, 850. Metro: Colosseo. ROMAN.

Barely on its third-month anniversary the day I arrived, La Piazzetta is a breath of fresh air for anyone looking for a serene setting and optimum fare. The management accommodates just about any request, including those that extend their lunchtime hours (within reason), assuming you won't mind feasting on what's left of their savory *antipasti* or the day's special *paste.* Try the chef's *mezze maniche alla vegitariana* ("short sleeve" pasta with tomatoes and goat cheese) or, my favorite, the *raviolone* with sage, butter, and saffron. For heartier fare, you can dine without overdoing it on *polpette di carne* (not just your average meatball) or succulent *tagliata di manzo* (rare beef topped with parmesan and arugula). The chef outdoes himself in the dessert area, crafting delicacies like *millefeuilles, sfogliato* (with custard and pignoli nuts), and *baba* dripping in limoncello.

AROUND CAMPO DE' FIORI & THE JEWISH GHETTO

Vegetarians looking for monstrous salads—or if you just want to lay off the heavy Italian for a meal—can find great food at **Insalata Ricca,** Largo dei Chiavari 85 (☎ **06-6880-3656**; Bus: 46, 62, 64, 80, 116). It's open daily 12:30 to 5pm and 6:30pm to 12:30am.

Rome Dining

☉ Da Giggetto. Via Portico d'Ottavia 21–22. ☎ **06-686-1105.** Reservations recommended. Primi 12,000–18,000L ($7–$9); secondi 18,000–27,000L ($9–$14). AE, MC, V. Tues–Sun 12:30–3pm and 7–11pm. Closed Aug. Bus: H, 23, 44, 81, 95, 160, 170, 280, 628, 715, 716, 780. ROMAN JEWISH.

This third-generation eatery in the ghetto is one of the classics of Rome dining. In room after room, drying herbs and spices hang from the wood beams until the time comes to drop a sprig into one of the traditional recipes. The starters rely on fried dishes like *carciofi alla giudia* (flattened fried artichokes) and *fiori di zuccine ripieni* (fried zucchini flowers stuffed with mozzarella and anchovies). Expect well-prepared Roman dishes as well, like *bucatini all'amatriciana, penne all'arrabbiata, saltimbocca,* and *costolette di abbacchio a scottaditto.* With so much excellent food, it's easy to go overboard, so keep an eye on that mounting bill. Call ahead if you want one of the coveted tables wedged between the ancient Roman temple columns sprouting out of the sidewalk.

Da Benito. Via dei Falegnami 14 (near Via Arenula). ☎ **06-686-1508.** Primi 7,000–8,000L ($3.50–$4); secondi 10,000L ($5). No credit cards. Mon–Sat 6am–10pm. Bus: H, Tram 8, 23, 40, 46, 62, 63, 64, 70, 87, 186, 204F, 280, 630, 780, 810. ROMAN/ITALIAN.

Da Benito, a humble working person's trattoria, offers no-frills tables that fill with regulars looking for good food at great prices. Near the door hangs a handwritten menu to use as a guideline for when you step up to the food case, since they'll make whatever you want (within reason). You may want to stick with a salad, like the plate of smoked salmon and mini mozzarella balls on a bed of potatoes and arugula, or combine it with a *tramezzino* (sandwich sliced in a triangle) or a simple primo of *penne al ragù.* Heartier fare leans toward *saltimbocca all romana* (veal cutlet with prosciutto, sage, and marsala wine) or *salsiccia con contorno* (sausage with a side dish, generally potatoes). The friendly staff will help if you don't know how to order or pay (at the cashier on your way out).

Da Pancrazio. Piazza del Biscione 92 (off northeast corner of Campo de' Fiori). ☎ **06-686-1246.** Reservations highly recommended. Primi 15,000–22,000L ($8–$11); secondi 16,000–36,000L ($8–$18); *menu tipico* with wine 48,000L ($24). AE, DC, MC, V. Thurs–Tues 12:30–2:30pm and 7:30–11pm. Closed 25 days in Aug. Bus: 46, 62, 64, 116. ROMAN/ITALIAN.

It doesn't get more atmospheric than a restaurant with basement rooms set into the restored arcades of Pompey's 55 B.C. theater. Though these historic downstairs rooms are often booked by tour groups, try your darndest to get a seat there—though there's nothing wrong with the coffered wood ceiling and brick arches upstairs (in warm weather, everybody sits out on the piazza). For a touristy restaurant, the cooking is surprisingly excellent. Among the top dishes are *spaghetti alla carbonara,* delicious *cannelloni alla Pancrazio* (pasta tubes stuffed with spinach and meat), and *spaghetti con la bottarga* (with gray mullet eggs). Follow up with *involtini, abbacchio al forno con patate, tournedos di filetto alla Rossini* (beef tournedos in Madeira sauce with liver pâté), or fresh fish.

☉ Hosteria Romanesca. Campo de' Fiori 40. ☎ **06-686-4024.** Reservations recommended. Primi 12,000–14,000L ($6–$7); secondi 14,000–21,000L ($7–$11). No credit cards. Tues–Sun noon–4pm and 7pm–midnight. Closed 20 days in Aug. Bus: 46, 62, 64, 116. ROMAN CASARECCIA (HOMESTYLE).

If you're looking to buck the tourists packing the famous but much-declined La Carbonara but still want a seat on the cobbles of lively Campo de' Fiori, head to Armando and Enzo's little 110-year-old osteria to line up for a table. It's the piazza atmosphere and well-tuned traditional dishes you come for, not the service, which some evenings seems nonexistent (there are just too many diners for two waiters and two cooks). Dishes include tried-and-true Roman faves like excellent *pasta all'amatriciana, saltimbocca alla*

If It's Tuesday, It Must Be. . . .

In addition to their regular offerings, the menus of many smaller Roman eateries still follow the traditional weekly rotation of dishes: Tuesday *zuppa di farro* (barleylike emmer soup), Wednesday *trippa*, Thursday *gnocchi*, and Friday *baccalà* and/or *pasta e ceci*.

romana, and *cervello d'abbacchio* (fried lamb's brains; much better than boiled). In colder weather, the streetside tables disappear, and diners retreat under the wood beams of the tiny interior.

L'Angolo Divino. Via dei Balestrari 12 (a block southeast of Campo de' Fiori). ☎ **06-686-4413.** Reservations not accepted. Dishes 6,000–16,000L ($3–$8). MC, V. Daily 10am–2:30pm and 5:30pm–1am. Closed Sun lunch (all day in July) and Mon dinner. Bus: 11. WINE BAR/LIGHT MEALS.

Massimo Crippa and his brothers successfully transformed their grandmother's wine shop into a fashionable wine bar just off Campo de' Fiori. Though old-fashioned in style, with wood ceilings and shelves of vino, the place is trendy in concept. That the menu is translated into English may be due to its location, for the crowd remains overwhelmingly Roman. Like most wine bars, it offers mixed platters of cheeses, salamis, smoked fish, and bruschetta, plus daily dishes like lasagna, *rustica ripiena* (a cousin to quiche), salads, and delectable vegetable terrines. There's a vast selection of wines by the glass, particularly strong in Italian vintages but with a good number of foreign labels as well.

✪ **Sora Margherita.** Piazza Cinque Scole 30 (east of Via Arenula). ☎ **06-686-4002.** Reservations not accepted. Primi 12,000L ($7); secondi 15,000L ($8). No credit cards. Mon–Fri noon–3pm. Closed Aug. Bus: H, 280, tram 8. ROMAN JEWISH.

With nothing but a piece of paper bearing the restaurant name written in felt-tipped pen taped to the door to indicate her presence, Margherita Tomassini opened this nine-table osteria 40 years ago as an outlet for her uncle's Velletri wine. The vino still comes from the family farm (as does the olive oil), and it keeps getting better and better. Margherita keeps busy in the kitchen making the *agnolotti* (meat-stuffed ravioli in ragout), *fettuccine cacio e pepe* (with pecorino and pepper), and *gnocchi* (on Thursday). She began serving her legendary *polpette* (meatballs) almost 20 years ago so her infant son would have something soft to eat—patrons were soon clamoring for them to be added to the menu. Try the heavenly *parmigiana di melanzane*—she doesn't fry the eggplant slices but loads them down with mozzarella and bakes them long and slow in tomato sauce.

WORTH A SPLURGE

✪ **Ditirambo.** Piazza della Cancelleria 74–75 (at northern corner of Campo de' Fiori). ☎ **06-687-1626.** Reservations required. Primi 12,000–15,000L ($6–$8); secondi 18,000–22,000L ($9–$11). MC, V. Daily 8–11:30pm; Tues–Sun 1–3pm. Bus: 46, 62, 64, 116. REGIONAL ITALIAN.

In their spare time, a group of artists, actors, writers, and musicians planned this restaurant, and the results are outstanding. After only 4 years, it has established a coveted spot in the series of highly revered Italian and now American guidebooks. My best advice on ordering is to trust your waiter, as the menu changes daily. You can always count on the freshest pastas, bread, and desserts (made by a Calabrian mother-daughter team) and on a wide variety of vegetable-based dishes like velvety zucchini mousse and savory endive strudel. I opted out of an entirely non-meat meal by ordering the beef carpaccio, perfectly accompanied by fresh pea pods drizzled with balsamic vinegar. If you pop in without a reservation, your selection will be limited—to ensure the high quality of the ingredients, the management orders only what they plan on clearing out that day. If they're all sold out, cross the street for a more traditional Roman meal at its brand-new sibling Hosteria.

AROUND PIAZZA NAVONA & THE PANTHEON

This neighborhood is typical for one whose livelihood comes from tourism. If you're looking for a meal-size salad, try **Insalata Ricca 2,** Piazza Pasquino 72, southwest of Piazza Navona (☎ **06-6830-7881;** Bus: 46, 62, 64, 70, 80, 81, 87, 116, 186, 492, 628). It's open daily noon to 5pm and 6:30pm to 12:30am. A perfectly placed and reliable spot is **Il Delfino,** Corso Vittorio Emanuele II 67, at the corner of Largo Argentina (☎ **06-686-1208;** Tram: 8), an unremarkable *tavola calda* where you'll rub elbows with lunchtime professionals looking for a fast meal. It's open Tuesday to Sunday 7am to 9pm. Otherwise, relax along with the rest of them at one of the places below.

Al Piedone. Via Piè di Marmo 28 (southeast of the Pantheon). ☎ **06-679-8628.** Reservations recommended. Primi 7,000–9,000L ($4.10–$5); secondi 10,000–19,000L ($6–$11). No credit cards. Mon–Sat noon–3pm and 7–11pm. Closed 2 wks in Aug. Bus: 46, 56, 60, 62, 64, 70, 81, 85, 87, 95, 115, 117, 160, 175, 186, 492, 628, 640, 850. ROMAN.

My co-author tracked down this true Roman-style eatery based on a cookbook recipe that came from its kitchens, an *amatriciana bianca* sauce that predates the 16th-century advent of tomatoes from the New World. In wood-paneled rooms filled with businesspeople and a few British expatriates you can discover the joy of this powerful sauce made from pancetta fried with garlic in pepperoncino-spiked olive oil, tossed with fresh ribbons of pasta, and dusted with parmesan. Other worthy dishes are *tortelloni ricotta e spinaci* (leaves of white and green pasta wrapped around ricotta and spinach in a light tomato sauce), *fettuccine al porcino* (noodles with porcini mushrooms), and *involtini alla romana*.

✪ **Antica Taverna.** Via Monte Giordano 12 (near Palazzo del Governo Vecchio). ☎ **06-880-1053.** Reservations suggested. Primi 8,000–14,000L ($4–$7); secondi 12,000–22,000L ($7–$11). AE, DC, MC, V. Daily noon–11pm. Bus: 40, 46, 62, 64, 70, 81, 87, 98, 116, 116T, 186, 204F, 280, 492, 870, 881. ROMAN.

At this taverna on a picturesque back street you'll find a warm family welcome, intimate surroundings, and great food. My taste buds were stimulated by the marinated antipasti and blown away by the *mozzarella di bufala* (ultrafresh buffalo-milk cheese). By the arrival of the *rigatoni melanzane e zucchini* (with eggplant and zucchini), my dining companions and I were nearing capacity, but I had quite a time keeping their forks out of my *spaghetti alla carbonara*. Less impressive were the secondi; specifically the *trippa* (tripe, boiled) and the *osso bucco alla romana*, but I'll attribute this to personal taste and not to the execution of the dishes. The contorni are worth a mention: I don't generally like potatoes but scarfed up a plate of the *patate al forno* (thinly sliced and roasted).

Corallo. Via del Corallo 10–11 (near Chiesa Nuova). ☎ **06-830-7703.** Primi 10,000–14,000L ($5–$7); secondi 15,000–24,000L ($8–$12). AE, DC, MC, V. Daily 7pm–1am. Bus: 40, 46, 62, 64, 70, 81, 87, 116, 116T, 186, 204F, 492. ROMAN.

Though not mentioned in any guidebook (until now), Corallo is that unpretentious yet welcoming trattoria you've been looking for. The golden glow of the interior draws you into a dining room under a large arch, where antipasti are displayed and the sound of satisfied chatter is at its height. The roasted meats are especially good, or if you hit it on Wednesday or Friday, you're in time for heaps of fresh fish. The pizzas are made as crispy as you like (or not) in the wood oven, and if you show the management this book, you'll get a complimentary kir or prosecco with your meal.

Da Gino. Vicola Rosini 4 (an alley off Piazza del Parlamento). ☎ **06-687-3434.** Reservations not accepted. Primi 7,500–12,000L ($3.75–$7); secondi 15,000–22,000L ($8–$11). No credit cards. Mon–Sat 1–3pm and 8–10:30pm. Closed Aug. Bus: 81, 116, 117, 492, 628. ROMAN.

Relying on the menu that has brought it success for years, Da Gino remains a pure local trattoria to which few tourists venture. The lunch hour is hurried, attracting mostly politicos and journalists from Parliament across the street. Crowded under the trompe-l'oeil frescoed vaults, the zealous sink their forks into primi such as *ravioli burro e salvia* (cheese-stuffed pasta with butter and sage), *spaghetti all'amatriciana,* or Gino's specialty *tonnarelli alla ciociara* (pasta with peas and pancetta). Two secondi not to miss: *coniglio al vino* (rabbit cooked in white wine) and *agnello alla cacciatora.* Be sure to leave space for the best tiramisù you'll eat on your trip. Arrive before 1:15pm or forget about eating lunch here.

✪ **Enoteca Corsi.** Via del Gesù 88 (off Via del Plebescito). ☎ **06-679-0821.** Reservations not accepted. Primi 8,000L ($4.70); secondi 12,000L ($7). AE, DC, MC, V. Mon–Sat noon–3:30pm. Closed Aug. Bus: 46, 56, 60, 62, 64, 70, 81, 87, 115, 186, 492, 628, 640. ROMAN.

Corsi has kept up with the times, but luckily not the prices, so while the *enoteca* inside the main entrance is every inch the *vini olii* shop of yesteryear (1937, to be specific), behind it and next door are large fan-cooled rooms to hold the lunchtime crowds at long tables. Your choices are limited to three primi and half a dozen secondi, so though the dishes are excellent in their simplicity, you may want a selection of "tapas" or a drink rather than a full meal. The chalkboard menu changes daily but may run from *penne all'arrabbiata, saltimbocca, trippa,* and *arrosto di vitello* to delectable dishes like tepid *pasta e patate* soup and *zucchine ripiene* (zucchini flowers stuffed with minced meats, then baked).

La Danesina. Via del Governo Vecchio 125. ☎ **06-686-8693.** Reservations suggested. Primi 8,000–14,000L ($4–$7); secondi 14,000–29,000L ($7–15); *menù turistico* without wine 20,000L ($10). AE, DC, MC, V. Tues–Sun noon–3:30pm and 7:30–11:30pm. Bus: 40, 46, 62, 64, 70, 81, 87, 116, 116T, 186, 204F, 492. ROMAN.

Specializing in the highest-quality beef imported from Denmark, this restaurant, opened by two determined young women, sits on the corner of a characteristic Roman piazza. La Danesina cooks its succulent slabs of meat over not charcoal but lava stones. The *tagliata* and *bistecca con porcini* ooze as rare as you like them; for the slightly less carnivorous, the *tagliata* is cut thin enough to ensure some level of thorough-cooking. The chef exercises a bit more control in the primi, with Neapolitan dishes like *spaghetti alla carbonara* and *mezza maniche* with tomatoes, peas, pancetta, and sausage. Baskets of homemade foccaccia may stuff you even before you've begun, but be sure to leave room for the *crostata* or *pasta frolla con marmellata* (marmalade-filled cookies), served free at the end of your meal.

Lilli. Via Tor di Nonna 26 (at the base of steps down from Lungotevere Tor di Nonna). ☎ **06-686-1916.** Reservations required. Primi 13,000–14,000L ($6–$7); secondi 14,000–18,000L ($7–$9). AE, MC, V. Mon–Sat 1–3pm and 8–11pm. Closed 15 days in Aug. Bus: 280. ROMAN.

It's hard to go wrong at this family-owned trattoria, and if you stick to the cheaper dishes you can make this an affordable authentic meal. The crowd is mainly locals who don't mind the long waits between courses while the staff huddles around the kitchen TV to catch a soccer match. When it's warm, the crowds abandon the tiny room filled with mementos of owner Silvio Ceramicola's sporting past to sit out on the cobblestones of this dead-end alley. The time-tested primi include *tagliolini cacio e pepe, penne all'arrabbiata,* and *bucatini all'amatriciana* and the secondi include *trippa alla romana, pollo con peperoni,* and *polpettine in umida con fagioli* (tiny meatballs stewed with beans). However, the true specialty is delicious *fornata con patate al forno* (oven-roasted veal breast with potatoes).

Pizzaria Baffetto. Via del Governo Vecchio 114 (at corner of Via Sora). ☎ **06-686-1617.** Reservations not accepted. Pizza 6,000–11,000L ($3.55–$6). No credit cards. Mon–Sat 6:30pm–1am (Mar–Oct daily). Closed Aug 10–30. Bus: 46, 62, 64. PIZZA.

Reviews of Baffetto are mixed: Do people line up simply because it's Rome's most famous pizzeria or because the food is truly good? Whatever the answer, there's always a wait for a table at this institution, where the service is fast and furious. The pizzas are the thin-crust wood-oven variety with tables surrounded by photos of the directors, artists, and other international types who've shown up over the past 40 years. The night's pizzas are chalked on a board, so when the waiter whisks past be ready to order a *piccolo* (small), *media* (medium), or *grande* with the toppings of your choice; "plain" margherita is the most popular. Get here early to avoid the adolescent crush.

WORTH A SPLURGE

Terra di Siena. Piazza Pasquino 77–78 (southwest of Piazza Navona). ☎ **06-6830-7704.** Reservations highly recommended. Primi 15,000–18,000L ($8–$9); secondi 20,000–50,000L ($10–$25). AE, MC, V. Tues–Sun 1–3pm and 7:30–11pm. Closed 3 wks. in Aug. Bus: 46, 62, 64, 70, 81, 87, 115, 116, 116T, 186, 492, 628. TUSCAN.

The family that runs the capital's best Tuscan restaurant celebrates the cooking from their homeland south of Siena. You can dine amid rustic wood beams and softly lit goldenrod walls or, in nice weather, at a communal table on the lively piazza. The menu changes seasonally, but you can always start with *crostini misti* (toast rounds spread with liver pâté, spicy tomato sauce, or mushrooms), followed by *pici all'aglione* (hand-rolled fat spaghetti in garlicky tomato sauce) or *pappardelle al sugo di cinghiale* (wide noodles in wild boar sauce). In winter, dig into a hearty *ribollita* (stewlike vegetable-and-bread soup). Your secondo could be the pungent *cinghiale alla maremmana* (wild boar stewed with tomatoes) or the lighter *cacio toscano con le pere* (pears with ewe's-milk cheese). Stick with the good house wines—the bottled vintages are overpriced.

AROUND THE SPANISH STEPS & PIAZZA DEL POPOLO

For a super-cheap eat, head to **Il Brillo Parlante,** Via della Fontanella 12, a block south of Piazza del Popolo (☎ **06-324-3334;** Metro: Flaminio or Spagna; Bus 117, 119), where you can choose from over 1,000 bottles of wine and a menu of creative Italian cuisine, till 1am on weekends. It's open Monday to Saturday noon to 2am.

Edy. Vicola del Babuino 4 (off Via del Babuino, 3 blocks from Piazza del Popolo). ☎ **06-3600-1738.** Reservations highly recommended. Primi 11,000–18,000L ($5–$9); secondi 11,000–25,000L ($6–$13). AE, DC, MC, V. Mon–Sat noon–3:30pm and 7pm–midnight. Closed 1 wk in Aug. Bus: 117. ROMAN/SEAFOOD.

In an otherwise upscale area, Edmondo and Luciana offer genuine Roman cooking at downscale prices. You can sit under an old coffered and painted ceiling or at candlelit tables on the cobblestones to sample recipes that change seasonally. *Cartoccio con frutti di mare,* a spaghetti-and-seafood extravaganza baked and served in foil, is always on the menu; with any luck you can try the *ravioli agli asparagi* (ravioli with asparagus) or the excellent *tagliatelle con ricotta e carciofi* (in ricotta-and-artichoke sauce), For a secondo, try the *abbacchio Romanesco con patate* (spring lamb with potatoes), *bocconcini di vitello* (veal nuggets stewed with tomatoes, peas, and couscous), or *rombo alla griglia con patate* (grilled turbot with potatoes). Don't leave without ordering one of the homemade desserts.

✪ **Fiaschetteria Beltramme (da Cesaretto).** Via della Croce 39 (4 blocks from Spanish Steps). No phone. Reservations not accepted. Primi 16,000L ($8); secondi 20,000L ($10). No credit cards. Mon–Sat noon–2:30pm and 8–11pm. Closed 2 wks in Aug. Bus: 117. Metro: Spagna. ROMAN.

At this hole-in the wall, little has changed since 1886, except the menu's a bit longer and the place has been declared a national monument. At lunch, businesspeople and local workers line up to cram into communal tables under whirling fans and framed whatnots on the walls. Dinner is just as crowded, but there are more families and visitors. Good primi choices are *antipasto misto, rigatoni al cesareto* (pasta with arugula, cherry tomatoes, mozzarella, olive oil, and herbs), and *tagliatelle ai funghi* (noodles with mushrooms). The secondi are traditional, like *bollito misto* (mix of boiled meats) and *abbacchio scottaditto*.

✪ **PizzaRé.** Via di Ripetta 14. ☎ **06-321-1468.** Reservations recommended. Pizza 9,000–18,000L ($4.50–$9). AE, DC, MC, V. Daily 12:45–3:30pm and 7:30pm–12:30am. Closed 1 wk in Aug. Metro: Flaminio. Bus: 95, 117, tram 225, 490, 495, 628, 926.

Another contender in the pizza wars, PizzaRé is the preeminent outpost for the increasingly popular *pizza alta,* the thick and chewy crust imported from Naples. Many die-hard purists order the margherita, but exceptional as it is, you may want to try one of the 40 varieties or the traditional calzone, oozing with tomatoes, mozzarella, and ham. Despite the inevitable backup at the door (unless you arrive when it opens), the service is cheerful and crisp, but with such competition for the ovens, you may want to split an appetizer of the *frittura mista* (fried starters) or one of the many abundant salads while you wait.

WORTH A SPLURGE

Al 34. Via Mario de' Fiori 34 (a block from Spanish Steps). ☎ **06-679-5091.** Reservations highly recommended. Primi 10,000–32,000L ($5–$16); secondi 15,000–32,000L and up for specials ($8–$16); set menus 58,000–69,000L ($29–$35). AE, DC, MC, V. Tues–Sun 12:30–3pm and 7–11:30pm. Closed Aug 10–31. Bus: 116, 117. Metro: Spagna. ROMAN/INNOVATIVE ITALIAN.

This is a fashionable post-shopping restaurant, serving such flavorful food I can forgive the prices. The most coveted tables are out on the cobblestones, but the interior is a pleasant mix of rustic wood beams, brick arches, and Liberty-style mirrors and prints. Three set menus offer choices based on traditional local fare, "surf" ("Sireneuse"), or "turf." The Sicilian-inspired "Oscar" menu gets you *spaghette al pesto di Trapani* (short pasta in a pesto of basil and almonds), *maccheroni alla Positano* (with eggplant and provolone), and steak or Messina-style *involtini di pesce spada* (swordfish rolls), along with specialties from regional kitchens. The "Roma" menu offers *bombolotti* (thin pasta tubes) *all'amatriciana* and *rigatoni con pagliata,* followed by *trippa alla romana* and *coda alla vaccinaara* or a less adventurous but enormous serving of *abbachio al forno.*

NORTH OF STAZIONE TERMINI

Cantina Cantarini. Piazza Sallustio 12 (east of Via Veneto; turn up Via San Tullio from Via XX Settembre and bear left). ☎ **06-485-528.** Reservations recommended. Primi 8,000–17,000L ($4–$9); secondi 14,000–22,000L ($7–$11). AE, DC, MC, V. Mon–Sat 12:30–3:30pm and 7:30–10:30pm. Closed 3 wks in Aug, last wk Dec/1st wk Jan. Bus: 16, 37, 60, 61, 62, 136, 137, 910. MARCHIGIANA/ROMANA.

In an upscale neighborhood, this 100-year-old trattoria mixes Roman faves with specialties from the Marches region. Courteous, fast service and a reasonable prices ensure the arrival of a throng of locals accustomed to dining elbow to elbow at simple wooden tables or one of the sidewalk tables. *Spaghetti alla carbonara* and *alla matriciana* (very good) make their appearance alongside *fettuccine al salmone* or, in season, *ai funghi porcini*. The archetypal secondo is *fegato marchigiana* (breaded veal liver sautéed with sage), but you can also order *bollito misto* (mix of boiled meats) or *coniglio alla cacciatore* (hunter's style rabbit). For variety, stop by on Thursday evening through Saturday, when fresh fish selections like *spaghetti al nero di seppia* (squid ink) are added to the menu.

Il Restorantino. Via Servio Tullio 8–10 (near Via XX Settembre). ☎ **06-487-2027.** Primi 8,000–12,000L ($4–$7); secondi 10,000–16,000L ($5–$8). AE, DC, MC, V. Daily noon–3pm and 7:30pm–midnight. Closed Sat lunch and Sun dinner. Bus: 16, 36, 60, 61, 62, 84, 90.

On a back street above the imposing Palazzo delle Finanze, this spot would look less out of place in beachside Wilmington, North Carolina. The decor is peachy and modern, but the recipes are the greats of the Italian kitchen, taking traditional Roman fare to new levels. Unable to decide between two mouthwatering primi, I convinced the waiter to give me a half portion of both: a huge plate of dreamy *risotto ai carciofi* (risotto in artichoke sauce) and a huge and even tastier plate of *risotto al radicchio e gamberi* (with radicchio and prawns). Il Restorantino has a huge selection of fish, but then you'd have to pass up a tasty *vitella tonata* (veal in a sauce with tuna). The chef tips his hat to non-meat eaters with *involtini vegetariani*. Note that the *panna cotta* (cream custard) tasted like it came from a box.

✪ Trimani Il Wine Bar. Via Cernaia 37b (at Via Goito). ☎ **06-446-9630.** Primi 9,000–16,000L ($4–$8); secondi 12,000–40,000L ($7–$20); salads and cheeses 14,000–20,000L ($7–$10). AE, DC, MC, V. Mon–Sat 11:30am–3pm and 5:30pm–12:30am. Closed Aug. Bus: 60, 61, 62, 136, 137 (to Via Cernaia); 37, 116T, 175, 492, 910. Metro: Repubblica. ITALIAN/WINE BAR/LIGHT MEALS.

For a gourmet experience that won't break the bank, head to this postmodern wine bar, attached to the historic wine cellar of the same name. For Marco and Carla Trimani, serving fine foods to accompany wine chosen from their thousands of labels is merely an extension of the family's 170-plus years in the vino trade. The tiny rooms, long stylish bar, and outdoor gazebo are tinged with elegance. The daily changing menu may include Andalusian gazpacho or strongly flavored *trittico di crostini*, a trio of bread slices generously topped with gorgonzola, stilton, and Roquefort, then baked and drizzled with chestnut honey. In addition to wine accompaniments like cheeses and salamis, there are main dishes like *polenta con involtini di vitello alle erbe aromatiche e pancetta* (polenta with veal roll-ups flavored with herbs and pancetta) and aromatic rice pilaf *sformato alle verdure* (baked with vegetables).

IN SAN LORENZO

✪ Arancia Blu. Via dei Latini 65 (at Via Arunci). ☎ **06-445-4105.** Reservations highly recommended. Primi 16,000L ($8); secondi 14,000–15,000L ($7–$8). V. Daily 8pm–midnight. Closed 2 wks in Aug. Bus: 71. INVENTIVE VEGETARIAN ITALIAN.

This trendy spot serves Rome's best vegetarian cuisine, superior food even for the unconvinced. In the glow of soft lighting and wood ceilings, surrounded by wine racks and university intellectuals, the friendly waiters will help you compile a menu to fit any need, such as allergies or weight restrictions. The dishes are inspired by peasant cuisines from across Italy and beyond, and everything's made with organic and natural ingredients. Appetizers range from hummus and tabbouleh to zucchini-and-saffron quiche and *insalata verde con mele, gorgonzola naturale e aceto balsamico* (salad with apples, gorgonzola, and balsamic vinegar). The main courses change seasonally and may include couscous *con verdure* (vegetable couscous) or *ravioli ripieni di patate e menta* (ravioli stuffed with potatoes and mint, served under fresh tomatoes and

Sardinian sheep's cheese). They offer almost 100 wines, cheese platters, and inventive desserts like *pere al vino* (pears cooked in wine, scented with juniper, and served with a semifreddo of orange honey).

Tram Tram. Via dei Reti 44–46 (at the corner of Via dei Piceni). ☎ **06-490-416.** Reservations highly recommended. Primi 11,000–18,000L ($6–$9); secondi 16,000–24,000L ($8–$12). DC, MC, V. Tues–Sun 12:30–3pm and 7:30pm–12:30am. Closed 2–3 wks in Aug. Bus: Tram 19, tram 30/, 71, 492. SOUTHERN ITALIAN/ROMAN.

This crowded trattoria is run by the di Vittorio sisters, under the invaluable tutelage of their mother, Rosanna, who has infused some of her native Apulia into the menu. The dishes are well balanced between meat and fish, with a *lasagna vegetale* halfway between. Primi include *cavatelli alla siciliana* (short pasta with swordfish and eggplant), handmade *orecchiette broccoli e vongole* (ear-shaped pasta with broccoli and clams) or *alla norma* (with tomato, eggplant, and hard ricotta), and *rigatoni alla paiata.* The decibel levels are pretty high, in part due to the nearby tram rumbling by, causing the silverware and glasses to tinkle every few minutes and voices to rise to steady levels. The trams have inspired not only the steady chatter but also the decor: old trolley signs and photos, even tram benches as seats.

WORTH A SPLURGE

Pommidoro. Piazza Sanniti 44 (turn off Via Tiburtina onto Via degli Ansoni). ☎ **06-445-2692.** Reservations highly recommended. Primi 12,000–15,000L ($7–$8); secondi 16,000–18,000L ($8–$9). AE, DC, MC, V. Mon–Sat noon–3pm and 7:30pm–midnight. Closed Aug. Bus: 71, 492. ROMAN.

The Bravi family—these days Anna (cook), Aldo (hunter), and their brood—have for four generations been satisfying everyone from downtown cognoscenti and neighborhood cronies to intellectuals and celebrities like Pier Pasolini and Maria Callas. There's a glassed-in deck on the piazza, but the inside's more atmospheric, with a huge old fireplace grill. Or you can head downstairs to dine under low arches of hand-cast brick. Roman specialties reign supreme, from *amatriciana* and excellent *carbonara* to peppery *spaghetti cacio e pepe* and *rigatoni con pajata.* Wintery fare leans toward porcini mushrooms tossed with fettuccine, *pappardelle al sugo cinghiale* (wide noodles in boar sauce), and gamey dishes made with quail, woodcock, and duck. For those whose palate extends beyond the norm, there's *animelle alla cacciatore* (sweetbread stew) and chicken livers.

IN TESTACCIO

Da Felice. Via Maestro Giorgio 29 (at the corner of Via A. Volta). ☎ **06-574-6800.** Reservations highly recommended. Primi 7,500–8,500L ($3.75–$4.25); secondi 13,000–20,000L ($7–$10). No credit cards. Mon–Sat 12:30–2:30pm and 8–10:30pm. Closed Aug. Bus: 13, 23, 27, 75, 673, 715, 716, 719. Metro: Piramide. ROMAN.

The food is good traditional fare, but that's not the draw of this neighborhood trattoria. It's the thrill of victory when grouchy old Felice gives you the once-over, accepts you, and then leads you inside. "*Riservato*" signs occupy every empty table, even on traditionally slow Monday nights, so Felice can say "*siamo completo*" (no vacancy) to anyone who rubs him the wrong way. There's no sign or menu, but every seat fills up for the plentiful cheap food. Felice ambles around the high-ceilinged room in his waiter's jacket (which is why the service is so slow), his son mans the kitchen, and his grandson helps serve. The dishes change with the days of the week and are made from the freshest market ingredients. My primo choice is usually the minestrone or the remarkable *tonarelli cacio e pepe* or *al sugo.* The most popular secondi—*involtino al sugo* and *spezzatino di vitello con peperoni* (veal smothered with bell peppers)—are equally good.

✪ **Il Torricella.** Via E. Torricelli 2–12 (at Via G. B. Bodoni, just off the Lungotevere a few blocks up from Ponte Testaccio). ☎ **06-574-6311.** Primi 10,000–19,000L ($5–$9); secondi 10,000–23,000L ($5–$12). AE, MC, V. Tues–Sun 12:30–3:30pm and 7:30–11:30pm. Closed a few days in Aug. Bus: 27,95, 673, 719. Metro: Piramide. ROMAN.

This ultratraditional *osteria* is set in the echoey tiled rooms of what appears to be an old dock warehouse, with tall arches, soccer team photos on the walls, and a die-hard crowd of neighborhood families. It's anything but fancy and they could polish up that old welcome wagon, but Il Torricella gets a star for its genuineness and huge portions. The menu lists basic favorites like *spaghetti ai frutti di mare* (spaghetti with seafood), homemade *gnocchi* (on Thursdays), *rigatoni con pagliata*, tasty *bucatini all'amatriciana*, *saltimbocca alla romana*, *abbacchio à scottaditto*, *bistecca di manzo ai pepi verdi* (steak in cream sauce with green peppercorns), and fresh *sogliole* (sole), *spigola* (sea bass), *rombo* (turbot), and other fish.

WORTH A SPLURGE

✪ **Checchino dal 1887.** Via di Monte Testaccio 30 (at the south end of Testaccio). ☎ **06-574-6318.** www.checchino-dal-1887.com. Reservations required for dinner. Primi 19,000–21,000L ($10–$11); secondi 20,000–35,000L ($10–$18). AE, JCB, DC, MC, V. Tues–Sat 12:30–3pm and 8pm–midnight. Closed Aug and 1 wk at Christmas. Bus: 27, 719. Metro: Piramide. ULTRAROMAN.

Rome's greatest splurge is the Mecca for people who classify eating as an art. The Mariani family started this temple of traditional cuisine six generations ago as a blue-collar wine shop patronized by workers from the slaughterhouse across the street. These men received the undesirable refuse of the day's butchering (offal, tails, feet, and so on), and Checchino turned these into culinary masterpieces—it even made oxtail a staple by inventing and perfecting *coda alla vaccinara* (stewed with tomatoes, celery, white wine, bittersweet chocolate, pine nuts, and raisins). Only for the adventurous is the *insalata di zampe* (salad with jellied trotters); otherwise, stick with the house specialty *abbacchio alla cacciatore* (spring lamb browned in olive oil and flavored with anchovies, vinegar, and pepperoncini). Be sure to try some of the two dozen cheeses or a homemade dessert, each accompanied by the perfect glass of wine from among the 500 labels in the extensive wine cellar.

IN TRASTEVERE

Da Augusto. Piazza de' Renzi 15 (between Vicola del Cinque and Via del Moro). ☎ **06-580-3798.** Reservations not accepted. Primi 5,000–10,000L ($2.50–$5); secondi 8,000–14,000L ($4–$7). No credit cards. Mon–Fri noon–3pm and 8pm–midnight; Sat noon–3pm. Closed mid-Aug to mid-Sept. Bus: 280. ROMAN.

This modest place has found its way into virtually every guidebook as a poster child for the Trastevere *osteria*. But even with all the press, the bulk of patronage remains neighborhood cronies. Maybe visitors just can't find the place, tucked into a forgotten corner of the area on a tiny square used as a parking lot. The lucky few, sitting elbow-to-elbow in the pair of rooms or at a handful of tables squeezed into the triangular piazza, get to dig into standbys like *rigatoni all'amatriciana, fettuccine cacio e pepe, trippa alla romana, involtini,* and succulent *abbacchio*. It gets rather busy, so don't expect solicitous service; just excellent home cooking.

Dar Poeta. Vicola del Bologna 45 (off Piazza Santa Maria della Scala, not to be confused with Via del Bologna, off which it branches) ☎ **06-588-0516.** Reservations recommended. Pizza 7,000–16,000L ($3.50–$8). AE, DC, MC, V. Tues–Sun 8pm–midnight. Bus: 280. PIZZA.

The pizza wars have called a truce here, where uncompromising thin-crust eaters sit side by side with those who prefer their pizza "high." Using the slow-rise method introduced in recent years by nouvelle pizza guru Angelo Iezzi, Dar Poeta's offerings have crispy or fluffy bases and creative toppings, including *taglialegna* (mixed vegetables, mushrooms, sausage, and mozzarella) and *bodrilla* (apples and Grand Marnier). The varied bruschette are first-rate, and you can eat till late.

❂ Il Duca. Vicola del Cinque 52–56 (around the corner from Piazza Sant'Egidio, behind Piazza Santa Maria in Trastevere). ☎ **06-581-7706.** Reservations recommended. Primi 11,000–16,000L ($6–$8); secondi 13,000–26,000L ($7–$13); pizza 10,000–12,000L ($5–$7). AE, DC, MC, V. Tues–Sat 7pm–midnight; Sun noon–3pm and 7pm–midnight. Bus: 23, 280. ROMAN/PIZZA.

The noisy banter of Trasteverino and Roman dialects echo through the brick arches and wood-ceilinged interior of this institution—always a good sign. The walls, fantastically muraled with scenes of Rome, are as much of an attraction as the excellent cooking. But no matter how good the quality of the food or how extensive the choice, everyone comes for the lasagna, so wonderful it has made it off the occasional daily special menu and into the permanent annals of Il Duca. If you're unlucky enough to arrive after the last serving is gone, try the *spaghetti alla carbonara, spaghetti alla gricia,* or *gnocchi alla gorgonzola.* For a secondo, the *saltimbocca alla romana, pollo arrosto con patate,* and *abbacchio à scottaditto* are divine.

Ivo a Trastevere. Via San Francesco a Ripa 158 (from Viale di Trastevere, take a right onto Via Fratte di Trastevere, then left on Via San Francesco a Ripa). ☎ **06-581-7082.** Reservations not usually necessary. Primi 15,000L ($8); secondi 16,000–20,000L ($8–$10) and up to 30,000L ($15) for fish; pizza 12,000–16,000L ($7–$8). AE, DC, MC, V. Wed–Mon 12:30–3pm and 7:30–11:30pm. Bus: H, tram 8, 44, 75. PIZZA/ROMAN.

Trastevere's huge, bustling pizza parlor is always thronged with locals and foreigners (is there any guidebook that doesn't list it?), but the hordes haven't led it to compromise taste or prices. The tables outside are hard to come by, but the street's fairly trafficked, so I always choose the crowded, closely spaced tables inside. The service is swift and brusque, but Ivo is an excellent place to introduce yourself to Roman-style wood-oven pizza. The "plain" margherita is the favorite, but also good are *al prosciutto* and *capricciosa* (likely to include anchovies, prosciutto, olives, and a fried egg). There are plenty of pastas to choose from as well.

La Tana dei Noiantri. Via della Paglia 1–3 (the street leading west out of Piazza Santa Maria in Trastevere). ☎ **06-580-6404.** Reservations highly recommended. Primi 7,000–14,000L ($4.10–$8); secondi 15,000–25,000L ($9–$15); pizza 11,000–15,000L ($7–$9). AE, MC, V. Wed–Mon noon–3pm and 7:30–11:30pm. Bus: H, tram 8, 23, 280. ROMAN/ITALIAN/PIZZA.

La Tana dei Noiantri has a vast menu of quite good food, but everybody really comes for the romance of dining out on the cobblestone piazza, under the illuminated eye of Santa Maria in Trastevere. The interior is a bit more formal, with wood ceilings and painted coats of arms above baronial fireplaces, staffed by waiters who've been around forever. There are no surprises among the primi, while the best secondi are the *abacchio arrosto con patate* and the *fritto cervello di abbacchio* (fried lambs brains and zucchini). The sizable selection of fresh fish and seafood includes *cozze alla marinara* (mussels in tomato sauce).

Taverna della Scala. Piazza della Scala 19. ☎ **06-581-4100.** Reservations recommended. Primi 9,000–20,000L ($4.50–$10); secondi 12,000–24,000L ($7–$12); pizza 9,000–12,000L ($4.50–$7). AE, MC, V. Wed–Sun 12:30–3pm and 7pm–midnight. Bus: 23, 280. ROMAN/PIZZA.

This ever-popular basic trattoria offers a few tables set on the out-of-the-way piazza, but most diners end up in the small ground-floor dining room or in the stuccoed basement room surrounded by odd modern art. All the Roman staples are here: *bucatini all'amatriciana, penne all'arrabbiata, spaghetti alla puttanesca* (spicy "whore's pasta," with black olives, capers, garlic, and anchovies), and *farfalle alle mutandine rose* (bow-tie pasta "pink panties," in a rosé tomato-and-cream sauce). For a secondo, try the *ossobuco romano* (veal shank cooked with tomatoes; the marrow is considered a delicacy), *scaloppina al vino* (veal scallop in wine), or fresh fish like *spigola* (sea bass) or *orata* (sea bream) grilled.

WORTH A SPLURGE

Il Ciak. Vicola del Cinque 21 (just south of Piazza Trilussa, north of Piazza Santa Maria in Trastevere). ☎ **06-589-4774.** Reservations highly recommended. Primi 12,000–17,000L ($7–$9); secondi 18,000–26,000L ($9–$13). AE, DC, MC, V. Tues–Sun 8–11:30pm. Closed end July–beginning Aug. Bus: 23, 280. TUSCAN/GAME.

When locals occasionally tire of Roman food, they head out for a variation on a theme. Il Ciak offers hearty Tuscan fare in a cozy rustic space, featuring wooden benches and a big bottle of pay-what-you-drink Chianti on each table. Movie stills from owner Paolo Celli's former life as an actor cover the walls, but proof is in the pudding that no true Tuscan ever leaves his culinary roots. Celli hails from Lucca, a Tuscan city (see chapter 5) renowned for its olive oil, wines, and hearty barley soup. Typical primi are *papardelle al sugo di cinghiale* (wide noodles in wild boar sauce), *minestra di farro con fagioli* (barley soup with beans), and *ribollita* (vegetable soup made thick with bread). For a secondo, try the mighty *Fiorentina originale* (a steak barely grilled rare; if you can't handle this 800-gram/28-ounce slab, you can order the 400-gram *mezza*), *braciole di maiale* (pork chop), *cinghiale alla boscaiola* (woodsman's-style wild boar), or *starna al crostone* (partridge on toasted bread).

✪ **Sora Lella.** Via Ponte Quattro Capi 16 (on Tiber Island, at the foot of Ponte Fabricio). ☎ **06-686-1601.** Reservations highly recommended. Primi 18,000–24,000L ($9–$12); secondi 22,000–34,000L ($11–$17). AE, DC, MC, V. Mon–Sat 12:50–2:40pm and 7:50–10:40pm. ROMAN/INVENTIVE ITALIAN.

This classic is refined rustic, with rough-hewn beams, elegant place settings, good service, and a great wine list. Aldo Trabalza and his sons honor the memory of his mother, Sora Lella Fabbrizi—cook, unlikely star of Italian TV, and Roman character—by serving traditional essentials alongside innovative lighter fare and half-forgotten Roman dishes with centuries of pedigree. The specialty primo is *tonnarelli alla cuccagna* (pasta with sausage, eggs, walnuts, cream, and a dozen other ingredients), but also good are *bombolotti alla ciafruiona* (pasta with tomatoes, artichokes, peas, and tuna) and *rigatoni con pagliata*. For a secondo, try the *abbacchio brodettato* (lamb in a sauté of eggs, lemon, parmesan, and parsley) or *maialino al forno "antica romana"* (sweet-and-sour suckling pig with prunes, raisins, pine nuts, almonds, and baby onions).

AROUND THE VATICAN

The no. 6 branch of the wildly popular Roman chain of salad-and-light-meals restaurants, **Inslata Ricca,** is across from the Vatican walls at Piazza del Risorgimento 5–6 (☎ **06-3973-0387;** Bus: 23, 32, 49, 51, 81, 492, 982, 990, 991). It's open daily

The Best Gelaterie & Cafes

Though Rome boasts no true gelato tradition of its own, Romans are demanding and remain loyal to only the cream-of-the-crop purveyors, so to speak. **Giolitti**, Via Uffici del Vicario 40, a few long blocks north of the Pantheon (☎ **06-699-1243**; www.giolitti.it), was the unchallenged leader in the *centro storico*, until **San Crispino** opened a branch at Via Panetteria 32 near the Trevi Fountain (☎ **06-679-3924**). Using the "northern" recipe (made from a cream-based custard; Tuscan gelato uses a milk-based custard, and the Sicilian recipe uses the milk but ditches the egg yolks), San Crispino, with its pioneer location at Via Acaia, 56/56A, near the Baths of Caracalla (☎ **06-7045-0412**), is the winner. Its signature flavor is a subtle pistachio—get it in a cup, as cones are verboten here—expanding on the preservative- and additive-free principle of using only the finest ingredients (like honey from its own apiary or 20-year-old reserve Marsala wine).

Known for its yummy tartufo (see the beginning of this section for a description), **Tre Scalini**, Piazza Navona 28–32 (☎ **06-6880-1996**), is a popular but unsightly bar that continues to draw crowds. Here are some other historic cafes you may want to pop into: Near the "tempietto" (small temple) of Santa Maria della Pace is the **Antico Caffè della Pace**, Via della Pace 4–7 (☎ **06-686-1216**), an early-1900s cafe abuzz with Romans drinking outrageously priced coffee until 3am. The **Antico Caffè del Greco**, Via Condotti 96 (☎ **06-679-1700**), opened in 1760, just in time for Casanova to wile away the hours waiting to meet in secret with his lovers and for German author Goethe to become a regular during his prolonged stay in Rome. Nearby, just to the left of the Spanish Steps, is one of Rome's bastions of the Anglo-American expat scene, **Babington's Tea Rooms**, Piazza di Spagna 23 (☎ **06-678-6027**), started by two little old ladies in 1893 and little changed since. Stop in to raise your pinkies to a very proper afternoon tea in this staunchly (and slightly uncomfortable, with hard wooden chairs) British reminder of the genteel 19th century. A pot of tea runs 12,000L ($7) on up, but excellent British cakes, sandwiches, and dishes are also available.

Near the Pantheon lies the cafe of **Sant'Eustachio**, Piazza Sant'Eustachio 82 (☎ **06-686-1309**), a traditional Italian stand-up bar serving since 1938 what's widely held to be Rome's best caffè, made with water carried into the city on an ancient aqueduct and with enough froth to disguise the miniscule amount of liquid at the bottom of the cup. The **Pasticceria Strabbioni**, Via Servio Tullio 2 (☎ **06-487-3965**), is a cafe/pastry shop with fancifully decorated vaults, a courteous staff, and excellent pastries.

Piazza del Popolo is *the* place to see and be seen, drawing a nightly parade of Ferrari- and Maserati-driving couples to pose in the **Cafe Rosati**, Piazza del Popolo 4–5 (☎ **06-322-5859**). The cafe still retains its 1922 art nouveau decor, but the Rosati's real draw is the nostalgia for the directors and producers of yesteryear that prompted countless budding *artistes* to stake out a table in wait for their big break. The cafe rests on its laurels, though its outdoor tables are preferable to those of its rival **Canova** across the square. If you want to capture some of that lingering *Dolce Vita* spirit on Via Veneto, head to its old queen of Roman bars, the **Cafe Doney**, Via Veneto 145 (☎ **06-482-1788**), which in its heyday was the epicenter of the glamour crowd (Marcello Mastroianni, Ava Gardner, Anita Ekberg).

noon to 3:30pm and 7 to 11:30pm. If you're looking for an Italian pub with food, head to **Armando's Cafe,** Via Paolo Emilio 17, at Via Cola di Rienzo (☎ **06-324-3111;** Bus: 81), open Thursday to Tuesday noon to 3pm and 7 to 11pm.

Il Matriciano. Via dei Gracchi 55 (at corner of Via Silla). ☎ **06-321-3040** or 06-321-2327. Reservations highly recommended. Primi 18,000L ($9); secondi 22,000–30,000L ($11–$15). AE, DC, MC, V. May–Oct Sun–Fri 12:30–3pm and 8–11:30pm; Nov–Apr Thurs–Tues 12:30–3pm and 8–11:30pm. Closed Aug 6–21 and New Year's. Bus: tram 19, 32, 51, 81, 492, 907, 990, 991, 982. Metro: Ottaviano–San Pietro. ROMAN.

For more than 80 years, this classy classic *ristorante* has been beloved by Rome cognoscenti, Prati residents, and film directors for business lunches. Obviously *they* know what they want, because you may have to ask a few times to see a menu or wine list. At these prices, the portions could be larger and sauces more ample, but better quality than quantity, no? Antipasti include *mozzarella di bufala* (made from buffalo milk) and a *fritto misto* of zucchini flowers and broccoli. For a primo, try the superb namesake *bucatini alla matriciana, fettuccine casarecce* (with tomatoes and basil), or *tagliolini alla gricia.* The pride of the secondi are the *abbacchio al forno con patate* (lamb with tasty oven-roasted potatoes), *ossobuco cremoso con funghi* (ossobuco with mushroom-cream sauce), and *filetto di bue* (ox steak).

ON VIA APPIA ANTICA

Hosteria l'Archeologica. Via Appia Antica 139 (across from San Sebastiano catacombs, at the corner of Vicola della Basilica). ☎ **06-788-0494.** Reservations recommended. Primi 15,000–20,000L ($8–$10); secondi 15,000–35,000L ($8–$18). AE, DC, MC, V. Fri–Wed 12:15–3pm and 8–11pm. Bus: 218, 660 (Sun: 760F to end, then continue on foot about ½ mile toward San Sebastiano catacombs). ROMAN/ITALIAN.

Perfect for a post-catacombs lunch, this is one of Rome's few remaining countryside trattorie, where extended families gather for Sunday lunch under masses of wisteria (the road is closed to traffic on Sunday). The garden seating extends back from the original roadside inn, with its tightly spaced tables under cozy wood-beam ceilings and painting-covered walls. Kick off with the *bucatini all'amatriciana, gnocchi al cinghiale* (homemade gnocchi in a hearty tomato sauce enriched with chunks of wild boar), or *rigatoni al cuore di carciofo* (pasta with artichoke hearts). The secondi are simple, often grilled meats, like *bistecca di manzo all griglia* (grilled steak) and a good *abbacchio alla scotta ditto.*

5 Seeing the Sights

A note on hours: Though many museums, monuments, and archaeological sites expanded their hours for the Papal Jubilee, they may or may not continue to do so into 2001 and beyond. The opening times given in the entries below will most certainly be outdated by the time you get to Rome. In general, hours are shorter in winter and prolonged on weekend evenings in summer. Also, keep in mind that ticket offices close between a half hour to an hour before final closing. To circumvent most of the idiosyncrasies of Italian planning, call ☎ **800/991-199** (in Rome toll free) or pick up a free **Official City Map** at the tourist office or nearest kiosk (the back has the most up-to-date hours for all the sites around town). To be absolutely safe, check directly with the museum ahead of time.

ST. PETER'S & THE VATICAN

Did you know that Rome's greatest church and greatest museum are technically not even in Italy? The **Vatican** is the world's second-smallest sovereign state, a theocracy ruled by the pope with about 1,000 residents (some 550 of whom are Vatican citizens)

Bronze Door (Portone di Bronzo) **7**
Excavations Office (Ufficio Scavi) **11**
Grottoes Entrance **10**
Hall of Audiences **14**
House of Pius IV **5**
Michelangelo's *Pietà* **9**
Palace of the Governorship **4**
Sacristy & Treasury **12**

St. Peter's Basilica **10**
Sistine Chapel **6**
Statue of St. Peter **10**
Vatican Gardens **2**
Vatican Museum Entrance **1**
Vatican Post Office **8** & **13**
Vatican Radio **3**

living on 44 hectares of land. the Vatican is protected (theoretically) by its own militia, the curiously uniformed (some say by Michelangelo) Swiss Guards. It's been that way ever since the 1929 Lateran Pact with Italy's government. But don't worry, your lire (and soon your euros) are still good here, though the efficient Vatican post office does use different stamps.

✪ **Basilica di San Pietro (St. Peter's Basilica).** Piazza San Pietro (there's an info office/bookshop on the left side of the basilica steps). ☎ **06-6988-4466.** Admission free to church, sacristy, and crypt; dome 7,000L ($3) for foot access or 8,000L ($4) for elevator most of the way up; treasury 8,000L ($4). Church Apr–Aug daily 7am–7pm (Sept–Mar to 6pm); dome Mar–Sept daily 8am–6pm (Oct–Feb to 4:45pm); crypt Apr–Sept daily 8am–6pm (Oct–Mar to 5pm); treasury Apr–Sept daily 9am–6:15pm (Oct–Mar to 5:15pm). Free guided tours in English leave from the information office Mon–Sat at 2:15pm, Mon and Wed–Fri at 3pm, and Sun at 2:30pm. Bus: 23, 32, 34, 46, 46/, 51, 62, 64, 81, 98, 492, 881, 982, 990. Metro: Ottaviano–San Pietro.

St. Peter's is one of the holiest basilicas in the Catholic faith, the pulpit for a parish priest we call the pope, one of the grandest creations of Rome's Renaissance and baroque eras, and the largest church in Europe. It was the biggest in the world but the basilica has since been surpassed in size several times over. St. John the Divine in New York City will hold the title for largest church—if they ever finish it.

St. Peter's is unimaginably huge, longer than two football fields and 145 feet high inside, but since every part of it is oversized (even the cherubs would dwarf a 6-foot man), it doesn't appear nearly that large—until you look 614 feet down to the

A St. Peter's Tip

St. Peter's (and all churches, for that matter) has a strict dress code: no shorts, no skirts above the knee, and no bare shoulders. *You will not be allowed in if you don't come dressed appropriately.* In a pinch, both men and women can buy a big cheap scarf from a nearby souvenir stand and wrap it around their legs as a long skirt or throw over their shoulders as a shawl.

opposite end and see the specks of people in the distance. Mocking bronze plaques set in the floor of the central nave mark just how short the world's other great cathedrals come up. The basilica itself takes at least an hour to see—not because there are many specific sights; it just takes that long to walk down to one end of it and back. A more complete visit will take 2 to 3 hours, including climbing Michelangelo's dome and descending to the papal crypt.

THE PIAZZA   You approach the church through the embracing arms of Bernini's oval colonnade, which encompasses **Piazza San Pietro (St. Peter's Square).** Actually, this "oval" is a perfect ellipse described by the twin arms of 284 Doric columns, arranged in four rows and topped by 96 statues of saints. Straight ahead is the facade of the basilica (Sts. Peter and Paul are represented by statues in front, Peter carrying the keys to the kingdom), and to the right, above the colonnade, are the dark brown buildings of the **papal apartments** and the **Vatican Museums.** In the center of the piazza is an **Egyptian obelisk,** brought from the ancient city of Heliopolis on the Nile delta. Flanking the obelisks are two 17th-century **fountains:** the one on the right (as you face the basilica) by Carlo Maderno, who designed the facade of St. Peter's, and the other by Carlo Fontana. Note that the ellipse creates a neat special effect: Between either of the fountains and the obelisk is a marble disk in the ground. Stand here to see the rows of the colonnade closest to you line up, appearing to be only one column deep.

THE BASILICA   The **Basilica di San Pietro,** which replaced a crumbling 4th-century version, has gone through many architects, each attempting to realize his own personal vision. It was started by Bramante in 1506 (on a Greek cross floor plan), continued by Raphael (who adapted it to a Latin cross plan), then by Peruzzi (back to Greek cross), Antonio Sangallo the Younger (Latin cross again), Michelangelo (Greek cross again, though his major contribution was raising the dome), and Giacomo della Porta and Carlo Fontana (who completed it in 1590 more or less in line with Michelangelo's designs). Then in 1605, they tore down the facade and brought in Carlo Maderno, who—tell me you didn't see this coming—lengthened the nave so as to finish it off in a Latin cross plan by 1626. For a baroque flourish, Bernini, in addition to creating the piazza out front, took care of much of the interior decor from 1629 through the 1650s.

To the right as you enter the basilica is the greatest single sight, Michelangelo's *Pietà* (1500). The beauty and unearthly grace of sweet-faced Mary and her dead son, Jesus, with details that seem exactly perfect and yet are exaggerated for effect—the Virgin's lap is mountainously large in order to support the body of a full-grown man without seeming unbelievable—led some critics of the day to circulate a rumor that the 25-year-old Florentine sculptor could never have carved such a work. An indignant Michelangelo returned to the statue and did something he never did before or after: He signed it, chiseling his name right across the Virgin's sash. The *Pietà* has been behind protective glass since the 1970s, when a hammer-wielding lunatic attacked it.

Attending a Papal Audience

If the pope is at home (and has time), he holds a public audience every Wednesday at 10am (sometimes as early as 9am in summer). This basically means you get to attend a short service performed by the pope, either in the Vatican's large Paolo IV Hall or, when it's really crowded, out on the piazza. You need a ticket for this (see below), but not for the brief Sunday noon blessing the pope tosses out his office window to the people thronging Piazza San Pietro below.

Audience tickets are free, but you must get them ahead of time (available Monday or Tuesday 9am to 1pm). Apply in person at the **Prefecture of the Papal Household** (☎ **06-6988-3273**), located through the bronze door where the curving colonnade to the right of the church begins on Piazza San Pietro. You can also obtain tickets by writing at least 2 weeks beforehand to **Prefettura della Casa Pontifica,** Città del Vaticano, 00120 ITALIA. Specify your nationality, the number of tickets you need, and date you'd like (Wednesday only). Mid-July to mid-September, His Holiness often cools his heels at his estate in nearby Castel Gandolfo, so there are few audiences then.

Under the fabulous dome is Bernini's twisty-columned **baldacchino** (1524), a 96-foot-high ridiculously fancy canopy for the papal altar constructed with bronze purloined from the Pantheon (this altar is placed over St. Peter's tomb). Of the four great piers supporting the dome, the first on your right is a backdrop for Arnolfo di Cambio's late-13th-century bronze of *St. Peter.* Cambio, architect of Florence's Gothic palazzi, was also an underrated sculptor, and his greatest work in Rome does double duty as a piece of art and a holy good-luck talisman for the faithful—you'll often see a line of people sidling up to touch or kiss his outstretched foot, by now worn to a shiny nub.

Alongside the usual collection of embroidered vestments, gilded chalices, and other bejeweled accouterments of the faith in the **treasury** (entrance just before the left transept) is the enormous bronze slab tomb of Pope Sixtus IV, cast by early Renaissance master Antonio del Pollaiuolo in 1493 and edged with bas-relief panels personifying the scholarly disciplines.

THE CRYPT   Recessed into that pier with the statue of St. Peter are the steps down to the **papal crypt** (a.k.a. **Vatican grottoes**); sometimes the entry is moved to another of the central piers. Along with the **tomb chapels** of lots of dead popes (plus Queen Christina of Sweden), you get to see 15th-century **bronze plaques** on the lives of Sts. Peter and Paul by Antonio del Pollaiuolo and remaining bits of Constantine's original basilica. See the crypt last, as they usually route you right from this up to the dome, then out onto the piazza, ending your visit.

THE SUBCRYPT   If the papal crypt isn't enough, you can also tour the **subcrypt around St. Peter's tomb,** with tombs and a necropolis dating all the way back to the origins of Christianity. St. Peter was probably martyred in the Circus of Nero, which lies under part of the current basilica, but the actual site of his grave was argued over for centuries. Then excavations in the 1940s uncovered here what many thought was merely a medieval myth: the Red Wall, behind which St. Peter was known to be buried and on which early Christian pilgrims scratched prayers, invocations, thanks, and many a "Killroyus was here" in Latin. Sure enough, behind this wall was found a small pocket of a tomb in which doctrine now holds the first pope was buried (however, there's no evidence other than circumstantial that the set of human bones found here actually belonged to Heaven's Gatekeeper). The only way to visit the subcrypt and necropolis is by reservation. You must apply at least 20 days in advance at the **Ufficio Scavi** (☎/fax **06-6988-5518**), through the arch to the left of the stairs up the basilica. You specify your name, the number in your party, your language, and the date you'd like to visit; they'll notify you by phone of your admission date and time. Guided tours are 15,000L ($8) and audio tours 6,000L ($3).

THE DOME   The last great thing to do at the Vatican is climb **Michelangelo's dome,** 450 feet from the ground at its top and 138.6 feet in diameter (Michelangelo made his dome 5 feet shorter across than the Pantheon's, which he studied before beginning this one). If you don't want to climb all the way (once you start you can't turn back), you can ride an elevator for parts of the ascent (you'll still have 320 steps to go), but you'll likely have to wait in a long line—buy your elevator ticket when you pay admission. Once at the dome base, you wander through a little village of souvenir shops to the backside of the facade for a view over Piazza San Pietro. More stairs lead up to Carlo Maderno's lantern for a fantastic and dizzying **panorama of Rome** laid out at your feet. On a clear day, from this perch you can see far beyond the city to the low mountains and countryside beyond.

Note: Professors and scholars from Rome's North American College offer free tours of the basilica Monday to Friday at 2:15 and 3pm, Saturday at 10:15 and 2:15pm, and Sunday at 2:30pm. Meet in front of the Vatican info office to the left of St. Peter's main steps.

۞ Musei Vaticani (Vatican Museums) & Cappella Sistina (Sistine Chapel). Viale Vaticano (on the north side of the Vatican City walls, between where Via Santamaura and the Via Tunisi staircase hit Viale Vaticano; about a 5- to 10-min. walk around the walls from St. Peter's). ☎ **06-6988-3333.** www.vatican.va or www.christusrex.org/www1/vaticano/ 0-Musei.html. Admission 18,000L ($9) adults, 12,000L ($7) students under 26 and kids under 14. Free (but crowded!) last Sun of each month. Mar–Oct and Dec 20–30 Mon–Fri 8:45am–3:30pm (to 12:30pm Sat, last Sun of month, and all other days). Last admission 30 min. before closing. Closed Jan 1 and 6, Feb 11, Easter Mon, May 1, June 29, Aug 15 and 16, Nov 1, Dec 8 and 25, and many other religious holidays. Bus: 49 (or tram 19, 23, 32, 49, 51, 64, 81, 492, 907, 982, 990, 991). Metro: Ottaviano–San Pietro.

The Vatican harbors one of the world's greatest museum complexes, a series of some 12 collections and apartments whose highlights include Michelangelo's incomparable Sistine Chapel and the Raphael Rooms. It would be impossible to try to see it all in one day—a complete tour, including every nook and cranny in the collection, would cover a whopping 14km (8.7 mi.)! It's a good idea to get up extra early and be at the grand new monumental museum entrance (next door to the old one and under scaffolding as of this writing) before it opens—30 minutes before in summer—or be prepared to wait behind a dozen busloads of tourists.

There are **four color-coded itineraries** you can follow, depending on your interests and time constraints. Plan A takes about 90 minutes—it shuttles you through the Raphael Rooms to the Sistine—and plan D takes upward of 5 hours and hits most of the highlights. To any tour add 30 to 45 minutes for waiting in lines.

Note: My suggestion for the best *short* visit (2½ hours total) is that before you hop on the plan A route, head to the right when you get to the end of the awning-covered corridor to run quickly (20 to 30 minutes) through the *pinacoteca* (picture gallery), which isn't included on the short itinerary but really should be.

۞ PINACOTECA (PICTURE GALLERY)   One of the top painting galleries in Rome shelters Giotto's *Stefaneschi Triptych* (1320), Perugino's ***Madonna and Child with Saints*** (1496), Leonardo da Vinci's unfinished ***St. Jerome*** (1482), Guido Reni's ***Crucifixion of St. Peter*** (1605), and Caravaggio's ***Deposition from the Cross*** (1604), alongside works from Simone Martini, Pietro Lorenzetti, Fra' Angelico, Filippo Lippi, Melozzo da Forlì, Pinturicchio, Bellini, Titian, Veronese, and Il Guercino.

But the most famous name here is Raphael, the subject of room VIII, where you'll find his *Coronation of the Virgin* (1503) and *Madonna of Foligno* (1511) surrounded by the Flemish-woven tapestries executed to the master's designs. In the center of the room hangs Raphael's last and greatest masterpiece, ✪ *Transfiguration* (1520). This 13½-foot-high study in color and light was discovered almost finished in the artist's studio when he died suddenly at age 37, and mourners carried it through the streets of Rome during his funeral procession.

✪ STANZE DI RAFFAELLO (RAPHAEL ROOMS)   Pope Julius II didn't like his predecessor's digs (the Borgia Apartments, see below), so in 1508—a few months after commissioning Michelangelo to paint the ceiling of the Sistine Chapel—Julius hired Raphael to decorate these new chambers. As Raphael's fame and commissions grew, he turned more of his attention away from this job and let his assistants handle much of the painting in the first and last rooms you visit. But in the restored Stanza della Segnatura and Stanza di Eliodoro (the first two actually painted), the master's brush was busy. Note that the order in which you visit the rooms is also occasionally rearranged.

The first room, the **Stanza dell'Incendio,** was actually the third one painted (1514 to 1517); it was done during the reign of Pope Leo X (also a Raphael fan), which explains why the frescoes detail exploits of previous popes named Leo. The best is the *Borgo Fire,* which swept the Vatican neighborhood in A.D. 847 and was extinguished only when Pope Leo IV hurled a blessing at it from his window in the background. The setting, though, is classical, showing Aeneas carrying his jaundiced father, Anchises, and leading his son, Ascanius, as they escape the fall of Troy (eventually, according to Virgil in *The Aeneid,* Aeneas will make it to the village started by Romulus and found the city of Rome). Though pupils like Giulio Romano painted most of the fresco, some experts see the master's hand at work in the surprised woman carrying a jug on her head and possibly in the Aeneas group.

The second room is perhaps the highlight, the **Stanza della Segnatura** (1508 to 1511), containing Raphael's famous *School of Athens.* This mythical gathering of the philosophers from across the ages is also a catalog of the Renaissance, with many philosophers actually bearing portraits of Raphael's greatest fellow artists, including his mentor, the architect Bramante (on the right as balding Euclid, bent over while drawing on a chalkboard), Leonardo da Vinci (as Plato, the bearded patriarch in the center pointing heavenward), and Raphael himself (looking out from the lower-right corner next to his white-robed buddy Il Sodoma). In the midst of painting this masterpiece, Raphael took a sneak peek at what his rival Michelangelo was painting on the ceiling down the hall and was so impressed he returned to the *School of Athens* and added a sulking portrait of Michelangelo (as Heraclitus) sitting on the steps in his stonecutter's boots. It was a true moment of growth for the cocky young master, who realized even he could learn from the genius of another (in fact, he soon adapted his style and color palate, reflecting Michelangelo's influence).

Another important fresco here is the *Disputation of the Sacrament,* with three more portraits. Toward the middle of the right side, half hidden behind a golden-robed church dignitary, stands a dour man in red with a laurel-leaf crown—the poet Dante, whose *Inferno* revolutionized Italian literature by using the Tuscan vernacular rather than Latin (though Sicilians dispute this point). Look also on the far left for a pious man in black with just a wisp of white hair remaining—it's a portrait of the monastic painter Fra' Angelico, whose great work in Rome lies just after these rooms. Bramante (again) bends over the railing in front and thumps a book (probably arguing some finer point of architecture).

The third room is the **Stanza di Eliodoro** (1510 to 1514). The title fresco, *Heliodorous Expelled from the Temple,* shows the king's lackey trying to carry out orders to steal a Hebrew temple's sacred objects; a heavenly knight appears to help the faithful chase him off while a time-traveling Pope Julius II—a warrior pope whose battle against church enemies this fresco is metaphorically celebrating—looks on from his litter to the left. There's also the darkly dramatic *Freeing of St. Peter from Prison,* a Renaissance example of using "special effects" (the angel's brilliant glow would be enhanced by the natural light streaming through the window below). Another scene shows Pope Leo I (bearing Julius II's face) calling forth the armed and floating Sts. Peter and Paul in A.D. 452 to scare off a marauding Attila the Hun—the miracle actually happened at Mantua, but Raphael painted a Roman aqueduct and the Colosseum into the background! Pudgy-faced Cardinal Giovanni de' Medici, a Raphael patron and soon-to-be successor to Julius as Pope Leo X, looks on from his horse at the far left.

The Miracle of Bolsena depicts the origin (1264) of the feast of Corpus Christi, when a Bohemian priest who doubted transubstantiation (the miraculous transformation of the wafer and wine into the body and blood of Christ) was saying mass in the town of Bolsena and the Eucharist wafer suddenly began to drip blood onto the altar cloth. Attending the scene at the lower right are members of the papal Swiss Guards; this detail provided some of the historic evidence on which the guards' current retro-Renaissance outfits are based.

The fourth room, the **Sala di Constantino** (1517 to 1524), is the least satisfying, having largely been painted after Raphael's death, according to his hastily sketched designs. Giulio Romano and Rafaellino del Colle adapted some of their master's cartoons into the newly fashionable Mannerist style of painting. They probably did most of the *Battle at the Milvian Bridge* (Emperor Constantine the Great fights his would-be deposer, Maxentius), the *Vision of the Cross* (under whose miraculous sign the emperor wins), and the *Donation of Rome* (the now-converted Emperor Constantine gives princely power over Rome to Pope Silvester I), while a less apt pupil of Raphael's finished off the cycle with a weak *Baptism of Constantine.*

APPARTAMENTO BORGIA (BORGIA APARTMENTS) & CAPPELLA DI NICHOLAS V (CHAPEL OF NICHOLAS V) After visiting the Raphael Rooms' Sala di Constantino, you pop out into the **Sala dei Chiaroscuro,** with a 16th-century wooden ceiling bearing the Medici arms and in the corner, a little doorway many people miss and most tour groups skip. Their loss. Through this doorway is the Vatican's most gorgeous hidden corner, the closet-size ✪ **Chapel of Nicholas V** (1447 to 1449), colorfully frescoed floor-to-ceiling with early Renaissance Tuscan genius by that devout little monk of a painter, Fra' Angelico.

The **Borgia Apartments** downstairs from the Raphael Rooms were occupied by the infamous Spanish Borgia pope Alexander VI and are now hung with bland pieces of modern art. But the walls and ceilings retain their rich frescoes, painted by Pinturicchio with early Renaissance Umbrian fantasy. A co-pupil of Raphael's under master Perugino, Pinturicchio had a penchant for embedding fake jewels and things like metal saddle studs in his frescoes rather than painting these details in. And while his art is not necessarily at its top form in these rooms, it's worth a look. From here you can climb back up and head straight to the Sistine Chapel or continue downstairs to visit the Modern Art Museum first.

MUSEO PIO-CLEMENTINO (PIO-CLEMENTINO MUSEUM) This is the best of the Vatican's ancient Greek and Roman sculpture collections. In the octagonal Belvedere Courtyard (Cortile del Belvedere)—the original core of the Vatican museums—you'll find the famed *Laocoön* group, a 1st-century B.C. tangle of a man

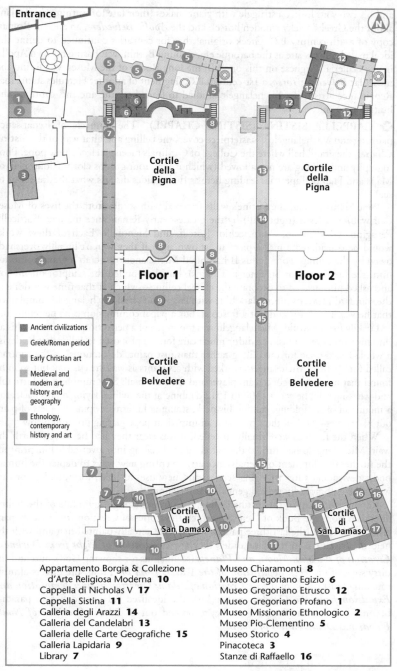

The Vatican Museums

Entrance

Cortile della Pigna

Floor 1

Cortile della Pigna

Floor 2

Cortile del Belvedere

Cortile del Belvedere

- Ancient civilizations
- Greek/Roman period
- Early Christian art
- Medieval and modern art, history and geography
- Ethnology, contemporary history and art

Cortile di San Damaso

Cortile di San Damaso

Appartamento Borgia & Collezione
d'Arte Religiosa Moderna **10**
Cappella di Nicholas V **17**
Cappella Sistina **11**
Galleria degli Arazzi **14**
Galleria del Candelabri **13**
Galleria delle Carte Geografiche **15**
Galleria Lapidaria **9**
Library **7**

Museo Chiaramonti **8**
Museo Gregoriano Egizio **6**
Museo Gregoriano Etrusco **12**
Museo Gregoriano Profano **1**
Museo Missionario Ethnologico **2**
Museo Pio-Clementino **5**
Museo Storico **4**
Pinacoteca **3**
Stanze di Raffaello **16**

and his two sons losing a struggle with giant snakes (their fate for warning the Trojans about the Greeks' tricky wooden horse); and the *Apollo Belvedere,* an ancient Roman copy of a 4th-century B.C. Greek original that for centuries continued to define the ideal male body (as late as the baroque era, a young Bernini was basing his own Apollo in the Galleria Borghese on this one). In the long Room of the Muses, you'll find the muscular *Belvedere Torso,* a 1st-century B.C. fragment of another Hercules statue that Renaissance artists like Michelangelo studied to learn how the ancients captured the human physique.

✪ **CAPPELLA SISTINA (SISTINE CHAPEL)**   The pinnacle of Renaissance painting and Michelangelo's masterpiece covers the ceiling and altar wall of the **Sistine Chapel,** the grand hall where the College of Cardinals meets to elect a new pope. Photography and talking are not allowed (which is why tour groups clot the long Hall of Maps and Hall of Tapestries leading here as their guides discuss what they're about to see).

Pope Sixtus IV had the Sistine's walls frescoed with scenes from the lives of Moses (left wall) and Jesus (right wall) by the greatest early Renaissance masters: Botticelli, Perugino, Ghirlandaio, Pinturicchio, Roselli, and Signorelli. Each of these works would be considered a masterpiece in its own right if they weren't literally overshadowed by the ceiling. Pope Julius II had hired Michelangelo to craft a grand tomb for him (see the listing for St. Peter in Chains), but then pulled the sculptor off the job and asked him instead to decorate the chapel ceiling—which at that time was done in the standard Heavens motif, dark blue with large gold stars. Michelangelo complained that he was a sculptor and not a frescoist, but a papal commission can't be rebuffed.

Luckily for the world, Michelangelo was too much of a perfectionist not to put his all into his work, even at tasks he didn't much care for. He proposed to Julius that he devise a whole fresco cycle for the ceiling rather than just paint "decorations" as the contract called for. At first, Michelangelo worked with assistants as was the custom, but soon he found that he wasn't a good team player and fired them all. So, grumbling and irritable and working solo, he spent 1508 to 1512 daubing at the ceiling, laying on his back atop a mountain of scaffolding, craning his neck, straining his arms, wiping droplets of paint out of his eyes—and all the while with an impatient pope glaring up from below.

When the frescoes were finally unveiled, it was clear they had been worth the wait. Michelangelo had turned the barrel-vaulted ceiling into a veritable blueprint for the further development of Renaissance art, inventing new ways to depict the human body, new designs for arranging scenes, and new uses of light, form, and color that would be embraced by several generations of painters.

Refer to the map of the Sistine ceiling. The scenes along the middle of the ceiling are taken from the Book of Genesis and tell the stories of Creation (the first six panels) and of Noah (the last three panels, which were actually painted first and with the help of assistants). In thematic order, they are: *Separation of Light from Darkness; Creation of the Sun, Moon, and Planets* (scandalous for showing God's butt and the dirty soles of his feet); *Separation of the Waters from the Land;* the fingers-almost-touching artistic icon of the ✪ *Creation of Adam; Creation of Eve; Temptation and Expulsion from the Garden* (notice how the idealized Adam and Eve in paradise become hideous and haggard as they're booted out of Eden); *Sacrifice of Noah; Flood;* and *Drunkenness of Noah.*

A Sistine Chapel Tip

To get the best view of the Sistine Chapel's ceiling, bring along binoculars.

The Sistine Chapel's Ceiling Frescoes

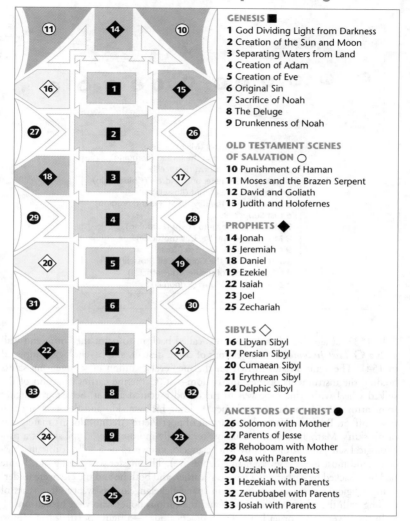

GENESIS ■
1 God Dividing Light from Darkness
2 Creation of the Sun and Moon
3 Separating Waters from Land
4 Creation of Adam
5 Creation of Eve
6 Original Sin
7 Sacrifice of Noah
8 The Deluge
9 Drunkenness of Noah

OLD TESTAMENT SCENES OF SALVATION ○
10 Punishment of Haman
11 Moses and the Brazen Serpent
12 David and Goliath
13 Judith and Holofernes

PROPHETS ◆
14 Jonah
15 Jeremiah
18 Daniel
19 Ezekiel
22 Isaiah
23 Joel
25 Zechariah

SIBYLS ◇
16 Libyan Sibyl
17 Persian Sibyl
20 Cumaean Sibyl
21 Erythrean Sibyl
24 Delphic Sibyl

ANCESTORS OF CHRIST ●
26 Solomon with Mother
27 Parents of Jesse
28 Rehoboam with Mother
29 Asa with Parents
30 Uzziah with Parents
31 Hezekiah with Parents
32 Zerubbabel with Parents
33 Josiah with Parents

These scenes are bracketed by a painted false architecture to create a sense of deep space (the ceiling is actually nearly flat), festooned with chubby cherubs and 20 *ignudi,* nude male figures reaching and stretching, twisting and turning their bodies to show off their straining muscles and male physiques—Michelangelo's favorite theme. Where the slight curve of the ceiling meets the walls, interrupted by pointed lunettes, Michelangelo ringed the ceiling with Old Testament prophets and ancient Sibyls (sacred fortune-tellers of the classical age in whose cryptic prophecies medieval and Renaissance theologians liked to believe they found foretellings of the coming of Christ). The triangular lunettes contain less impressive frescoes of the Ancestors of Christ, and the wider spandrels in each corner depict Old Testament scenes of salvation.

The Sistine Chapel's Wall Frescoes

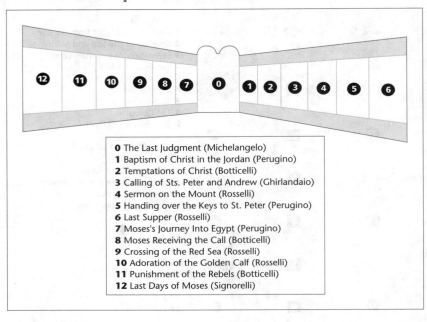

0 The Last Judgment (Michelangelo)
1 Baptism of Christ in the Jordan (Perugino)
2 Temptations of Christ (Botticelli)
3 Calling of Sts. Peter and Andrew (Ghirlandaio)
4 Sermon on the Mount (Rosselli)
5 Handing over the Keys to St. Peter (Perugino)
6 Last Supper (Rosselli)
7 Moses's Journey Into Egypt (Perugino)
8 Moses Receiving the Call (Botticelli)
9 Crossing of the Red Sea (Rosselli)
10 Adoration of the Golden Calf (Rosselli)
11 Punishment of the Rebels (Botticelli)
12 Last Days of Moses (Signorelli)

In 1535, at age 60, Michelangelo was called back in to paint the entire end wall with a ✪ *Last Judgment,* a masterwork of color, despair, and psychology completed in 1541. The aging master carried on the medieval tradition of representing saints holding the instruments of their martyrdom—St. Catherine carries a section of the spiked wheel with which she was tortured and executed and St. Sebastian clutches some arrows. Look for St. Bartholomew holding his own skin and the knife used to flay it off. St. Bart's face (actually a portrait of poet Pietro Aretino) doesn't match that of his skin's. Many hold that the almost terminally morose face on the skin is a psychological self-portrait of sorts by Michelangelo, known to be a sulky, difficult character (and most likely a severe manic-depressive). The master was getting old, Rome had been sacked by barbarians a few years earlier, and both he and the city were undergoing religious crises—not to mention that Michelangelo was weary after years of dealing with the whims of the church and the various popes who were his patrons.

In the lower-right corner is a political practical joke—a figure portrayed as Minos, Master of Hell, but in reality a portrait of Biagio di Cesena, Master of Ceremonies to the pope and a Vatican bigwig who protested violently against Michelangelo's painting all the shameless nudes here (though some of the figures were partially clothed, the majority of the masses were originally naked). As the earlier Tuscan genius Dante had done to his political enemies in his poetic masterpiece *Inferno,* Michelangelo put Cesena into his own vision of Hell, giving him jackass ears and painting in a serpent eternally biting off his testicles. Furious, Cesena demanded that the pope order the artist to paint his face out, to which Pope Paul III reportedly said, "I might have released you from Purgatory, but over Hell I have no power."

Twenty-three years and several popes later, the voices of prudence (in the form of Pope Pius IV) got their way and one of Michelangelo's protégés, Daniele da Volterra, was brought in—under protest—to paint bits of cloth draped over the objectionable bits of the nude figures. These loincloths stayed modestly in place until many were

The Ruins Before & After

To appreciate the Roman Forum, Colosseum, and other ruins more fully, buy a copy of the small red book called ***Rome Past and Present*** (Vision Publications), sold in bookstores or on stands near the Forum. Its plastic overleafs show you how things looked 2,000 years ago.

---

removed during the politically charged cleaning from 1980 to 1994, which also removed centuries of dirt and smoke stains from the frescoes. Some critics claim that Michelangelo himself painted some of the cloths on after he was done and that too many were removed; others wanted all the added draperies stripped from the work. It seems that the compromise, with the majority of figures staying clothed but a few bare bottoms uncovered, pleased nobody. In addition, the techniques used and the amount of grime—and possibly paint—taken off are bones of contention among art historians.

One thing is for certain. Since the restorations of both the ceiling and the *Last Judgment,* Michelangelo's colors just pop off the wall in warm yellows, bright oranges, soft flesh tones, and rich greens set against stark white or brilliant azure backgrounds. Many still prefer the dramatic, broodingly somber and muddled tones of the pre-cleaning period. For all the controversy, the revelations provided by the cleanings have forced artists and art historians to reevaluate everything they thought they knew about Michelangelo's palette, his technique, his painterly skills, and his art.

OTHER VATICAN COLLECTIONS   The Vatican has many more museums; it would take months to go through them all. Among them are good collections of **Egyptian, Etruscan, paleo-Christian,** and **ancient Roman artifacts,** including the **Museo Gregoriano Profano (Gregorian Musuem of Pagan Antiquities),** with a fantastic floor mosaic from an ancient Roman dining room "littered" with banquet leftovers.

The **Collezione d'Arte Religiosa Moderna (Collection of Modern Religious Art)** features papal robes designed by Matisse, while the **Pontificio Museo Missionario-Etnologico (Ethnological Museum)** covers 3,000 years of history across all continents (the Chinese section is particularly good). There's also a 2-hour foot-and-bus tour of the 16th-century **Giardini Vaticani (Vatican Gardens).** Book this a day or two in advance at the Vatican Information Office to the left of St. Peter's entrance (☎ **06-6988-4466** or 06-6988-4866). Visits generally run Monday, Tuesday, and Thursday to Saturday at 10am; tickets are 20,000L ($10).

Castel Sant'Angelo. Lungotevere Castello. ☎ **06-681-9111.** Admission 10,000L ($5) adults; free under 18 and over 60. Tues–Fri and Sun 9am–7pm, Sat to 8pm (check for extended hours). Closed 2nd and 4th Tues of each month. Bus: 34, 49, 80, 87, 280, 492, 990. Metro: Lepanto.

Hadrian's massive brick cylindrical tomb was transformed in the Middle Ages into Rome's greatest castle, serving triple duty as a papal military stronghold, a prison, and a place of torture (it's still connected to the Vatican by a raised brick viaduct that allowed the pope movement between the two). The castle takes its name from a miracle that occurred during the plague of 590: According to legend, the apparition of an angel in a symbolic stance of grace atop the mausoleum resulted in the end of the pestilence. In honor of the angel, the name of the castle was changed and the crowning statue was placed atop the structure.

Today, beyond Hadrian's burial chamber and the original 2nd-century brick-walled spiraling ramp, the castle is a museum with a hodgepodge of exhibits. The collections range from 16th-century ceiling frescoes to a small arms and armor museum covering everything from a 6th-century B.C. Etruscan gladiator's helmets to an officer's uniform from 1900, with some deadly swords, daggers, spears, guns, pikes, halberds, and the likes in between. The castle is slowly being transformed into a space for temporary exhibits, but it's worth a peek for the wonderful views of the Tiber and the statue-lined Ponte Sant'Angelo from the ramparts.

THE FORUM, COLOSSEUM & BEST OF ANCIENT ROME

✪ Foro Romano (Roman Forum). Entrances currently at Piazza del Colosseo (near the Arch of Constantine) and at the back of Campidoglio. ☎ **06-699-0110.** Free admission (to Forum area only; see Palatine listing, below); audio guide in English 7,000L ($3.50); archaeologist-accompanied visits in English (daily at 10:30am; call to confirm) 6,000L ($3). Apr–Sept Mon–Sat 9am–6pm, Sun to 1pm; Oct–Mar Mon–Sat 9am–3pm, Sun to 1pm. Closed Christmas and New Year's. Bus: 60, 63, 75, 81, 84, 85, 87, 115, 117, 160, 175, 186, 204F, 628, 673, 810, 850. Metro: Colosseo.

Slung between the Palatine and Capitoline Hills, the Forum was the cradle of the Roman Republic, a low spot whose buildings and streets became the epicenter of the ancient world. It takes a healthy imagination to turn what are now dusty chunks of architrave jumbled on the ground, crumbling arches, and a few shakily re-erected columns into the glory of ancient Rome, but this archaeological zone is amazing nonetheless. You could wander through in an hour or two, but many people spend 4 or 5 hours and pack a picnic lunch to eat on the Palatine. It gets hot and dusty in August, so visit in the cool morning, wear a brimmed hat and sunscreen, and bring bottled water.

The early Etruscan kings drained this swampy lowland, and under Republican rule it became the heart of the city, a public "forum" of temples, administrative halls, orators' podiums, markets, and law courts. Standing ranks of columns here and there mark the sites of once-important temples and buildings. Much of it means little to those of us who aren't fresh from a class in ancient history, so I'll highlight a few of the more visually spectacular sights.

At the entrance to Via Sacra ("Holy Way," down which triumphal military parades and imperial processions marched) at Piazza del Colosseo is the **Arco di Costantino (Arch of Constantine),** one of the largest of Rome's ancient triumphal arches, celebrating Emperor Constantine the Great's A.D. 312 victory over Maxentius at the Milvian Bridge. Though the arch's reliefs were primarily pirated from earlier sites and make no mention of the battle itself, it was perhaps one of the most significant of all ancient Rome's wars. It was during this battle that the emperor asked for a sign from the gods and in reply had a vision of a Cross. After winning, Constantine dutifully converted himself—and then the entire Roman Empire—to Christianity.

At the top of Via Sacra is the second great surviving triumphal arch, the A.D. 81 **Arco di Tito (Arch of Titus),** on which one relief depicts the carrying off of treasures from Jerusalem's temple—look close to see a menorah among the booty. This arch glorifies the war that ended with the expulsion of Jews from the colonized Judea, signaling the beginning of the Jewish Diaspora throughout Europe. From here, you can enter and climb the only part of the Forum archaeological zone that still charges admission, the **Palatine Hill** (see below). To continue in the free area, turn right at the arch, climbing between some overgrown ruins and medieval additions under the shade trees, then head left to enter the massive brick remains and coffered ceilings of the. 4th-century **Basilica di Costantino e di Massenzio (Basilica of Constantine and Maxentius).** These were Rome's public law courts, and their architectural style was adopted by early Christians for their houses of worship (the reason so many ancient churches are called basilicas).

At the time of this writing, the area of the basilica was fenced in, so you may have to backtrack a bit, heading down the dirt ramp straight into the main artery of the Forum. Just beyond on your left is the partially reconstructed 3rd- to 4th-century **Casa delle Vestali (House of the Vestals)** against the south side of the grounds. This was home to

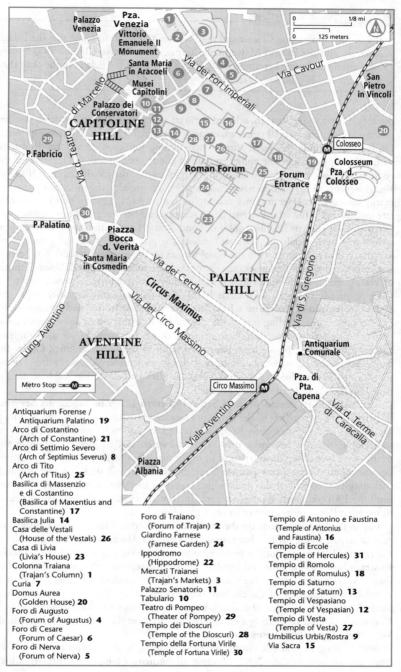

Palazzo Venezia
Pza. Venezia
Vittorio Emanuele II Monument
Santa Maria in Aracoeli
Musei Capitolini
Palazzo dei Conservatori
CAPITOLINE HILL
P.Fabricio
P.Palatino
Piazza Bocca d. Verità
Santa Maria in Cosmedin
AVENTINE HILL
Metro Stop
Via dei Fori Imperiali
Via Cavour
San Pietro in Vincoli
Roman Forum
Colosseo
Colosseum Pza. d. Colosseo
Forum Entrance
Via dei Cerchi
PALATINE HILL
Circus Maximus
Via dei Circo Massimo
Via di S. Gregorio
Antiquarium Comunale
Circo Massimo
Pza. di Pta. Capena
Via d. Terme di Caracalla
Lung. Aventino
Viale Aventino
Piazza Albania
Via di Marcello
Via d. Teatro
0 1/8 mi
0 125 meters

Antiquarium Forense / Antiquarium Palatino **19**
Arco di Costantino (Arch of Constantine) **21**
Arco di Settimio Severo (Arch of Septimius Severus) **8**
Arco di Tito (Arch of Titus) **25**
Basilica di Massenzio e di Costantino (Basilica of Maxentius and Constantine) **17**
Basilica Julia **14**
Casa delle Vestali (House of the Vestals) **26**
Casa di Livia (Livia's House) **23**
Colonna Traiana (Trajan's Column) **1**
Curia **7**
Domus Aurea (Golden House) **20**
Foro di Augusto (Forum of Augustus) **4**
Foro di Cesare (Forum of Caesar) **6**
Foro di Nerva (Forum of Nerva) **5**

Foro di Traiano (Forum of Trajan) **2**
Giardino Farnese (Farnese Garden) **24**
Ippodromo (Hippodrome) **22**
Mercati Traianei (Trajan's Markets) **3**
Palazzo Senatorio **11**
Tabulario **10**
Teatro di Pompeo (Theater of Pompey) **29**
Tempio dei Dioscuri (Temple of the Dioscuri) **28**
Tempio della Fortuna Virile (Temple of Fortuna Virile) **30**

Tempio di Antonino e Faustina (Temple of Antonius and Faustina) **16**
Tempio di Ercole (Temple of Hercules) **31**
Tempio di Romolo (Temple of Romulus) **18**
Tempio di Saturno (Temple of Saturn) **13**
Tempio di Vespasiano (Temple of Vespasian) **12**
Tempio di Vesta (Temple of Vesta) **27**
Umbilicus Urbis/Rostra **9**
Via Sacra **15**

A Money-Saving Tip

If you plan to visit the Colosseum, the Palatine, the Baths of Caracalla, the Palazzo Altemps, and the Palazzo Massimo alle Terme, you can save 10,000L ($5) by buying a **combination ticket** for 30,000L ($15). It's sold at the ticket booths of all these museums and is valid for up to 5 days.

the consecrated young women, selected between ages 6 and 10 from patrician families to serve as priestesses for 30 years, who tended the sacred flame in the Temple of Vesta. During their tenure, the Vestal Virgins were among Rome's most venerated citizens, with unique powers like the ability to pardon condemned criminals. The cult of the goddess Vesta was quite serious about the "virgin" part of the job description: If any of Vesta's servants were found to have "misplaced" their virginity, the miscreant was summarily buried alive. (Her amorous accomplice was merely flogged to death.) A similar fate awaited her if the sacred eternal flame went out on her watch. The overgrown rectangle of their gardens has lilied goldfish ponds and is lined with heavily worn broken statues of senior Vestals on pedestals (and, at any given time when the guards aren't looking, two to six visitors posing as Vestal Virgins on the empty pedestals). Just beyond is a bit of curving wall that marks the site of the little round **Tempio di Vesta (Temple of Vesta),** rebuilt several times after fires started by the sacred flame housed within.

Opposite (don't worry, we'll circle back) is a medieval church grafted onto and above the **Tempio di Antonino e Faustina (Temple of Antonius and Faustina),** the eight columns still standing free of the church fabric at the top of some steps (it was built in A.D. 141 by Antonius Pius in honor of his late wife, Faustina). Continue toward the arch. Just before it on your right is Julius Caesar's large brick **Curia,** the main seat of the Roman Senate and remarkably well preserved (partly from being transformed in the Middle Ages into a church; if it's unlocked, pop inside to see the marble-inlaid floor, a 3rd-century original).

The A.D. 203 triumphal **Arco di Settimio Severo (Arch of Septimius Severus)** displays time-bitten reliefs of the emperor's victories in what are today Iran and Iraq. During the Middle Ages when Rome was forced to cede to its wealthier rival, Constantinople, the city became a provincial backwater, and frequent flooding of the nearby river helped rapidly bury most of the Forum. This former center of the empire became, of all things, a cow pasture. Some bits of it did still stick out aboveground, including the top half of this arch, which was used to shelter a barbershop! It wasn't until the 19th century that people became interested in excavating these ancient ruins to see what Rome in its glory must once have been like.

Just to the left of the arch are the remains of a cylindrical lump of rock with some marble steps curving off it. That round stone was the **Umbilicus Urbus,** considered the center of Rome and of the entire empire, and the curving steps of the **Imperial Rostra,** where great orators and legislators stood to speak and the people gathered to listen. Against the back of the Capitoline Hill—the modern building of which is raised on a foundation of the ancient **Tabularium,** where the ancients stored their State Archives—you'll see the much-photographed trio of fluted columns with Corinthian capitals supporting a bit of architrave to form the corner of the **Tempio di Vespasiano (Temple of Vespasian).**

Start heading to your left toward the eight standing Ionic columns comprising the front and corners to the 42 B.C. **Tempio di Saturno (Temple of Saturn),** which housed the first treasury of Republican Rome. It was also where one of the city's biggest annual blowout festivals took place—the December 17 feast of Saturnalia. After a bit of tweaking, we now celebrate this as Christmas. Here you turn left to start heading back east, walking along the Forum's southern side past the worn steps and stumps of brick pillars (19th-century reconstructions) that outline the enormous **Basilica Julia**, built by Julius Caesar. Past it are three standing Corinthian columns of the **Tempio dei Dioscuri (Temple of the Dioscuri)**, dedicated to the original Gemini twins, Castor and Pollux. Actually, these identical twin gods were part of a fraternal triplet, all born out of the divine egg laid by Leda, whose transformation into a swan didn't do much to dampen Zeus' amorous advances. Who was the other triplet? Helen of Troy, a woman so beautiful the ancient Greeks went to war with the Trojans over her.

Palatino (Palatine Hill) & Museo Palatino (Palatine Museum). Main entrance inside the Roman Forum (see above). ☎ **06-699-0110.** Admission 12,000L ($7); archaeologist-accompanied visits (daily at 10:30am) 6,000L ($3). Museum Apr–Sept Mon–Sat 9am–5pm, Sun to noon; Oct–Mar Mon–Sat 9am–2pm, Sun to noon. Palatine Gardens Apr–Sept Mon–Sat 9am–6pm, Sun to 1pm; Oct–Mar Mon–Sat 9am–3pm, Sun to 1pm. Bus: 75, 85, 87, 115, 117, 175, 186, 810, 850. Metro: Colosseo.

The Palatine Hill was where Rome began as a tiny Latin village (supposedly founded by Romulus) in the 8th century B.C. Later it was covered with the palaces of patrician families and early emperors. Today it's a tree-shaded hilltop of gardens and fragments of ancient villas that few visitors bothered to climb even before there was an admission charge. So it can make for a romantic, scenic escape from the crowds, a place where you can wander across the grassy floors of ancient palaces and peer down the gated passageways that were once the homes of Rome's rich and famous.

In 1998, the **Museo Palatino** (at the back of the gardens; follow the main cobbled ramp straight up the hill) finally reopened after 13 years, displaying an excellent collection of Roman sculpture and finds from the ongoing digs in the Palatine villas. In summer, there are daily guided tours in English (see above); call in winter to see if they're still running. If you ask the museum's custodian, he may take you to one of the nearby locked villas and let you in for a peek at surviving frescoes and stuccoes.

From the Palatine's southern flank, you can look out over the long grassy oval that was the **Circo Massimo (Circus Maximus)**, where Ben-Hur types used to race chariots (now mainly used by joggers and dog walkers).

✪ **Colosseo (Colosseum).** Piazza del Colosseo. ☎ **06-700-4261.** Admission 10,000L ($5); audio guide 7,000L ($3.50); guided tour in English (six times daily) 6,000L ($3). Mon–Sat 9am–7pm, Sun to 8pm. Bus: Tram 30/, 75, 81, 85, 87, 117, 175, 186, 204F, 673, 810, 850. Metro: Colosseo.

This wide, majestic oval is the world's most famous sports arena, even though it's been well over 1,500 years since gladiators fought each other to the death and condemned prisoners were thrown to the lions. Since then, the most impressive aspect of the Colosseum has been viewing it from afar, admiring that unmistakable silhouette, symbol of

Seeing the Sights at Night

In recent years, some of Rome's most popular (and newly renovated) monuments, archaeological sites, and museums have begun not only staying open until 8 or 10pm during summer but also engaging in "**Art and Monuments Under the Stars,**" special summer schedules wherein they re-open one or more nights a week from around 8:30 to 11:30pm. The offering includes guided tours (often in English), concerts, or simply general admission to sights for night owls, including tours of some ancient sites usually closed to the public, like the Tomb of Augustus and the Stadium of Domitian (under Piazza Navona). This is a developing phenomenon, so I can't give many specifics, but keep your eyes peeled in the events guides and in tourist brochures.

Rome Attractions

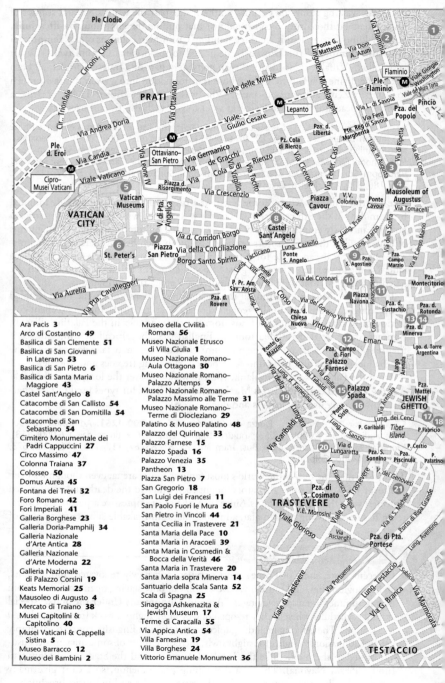

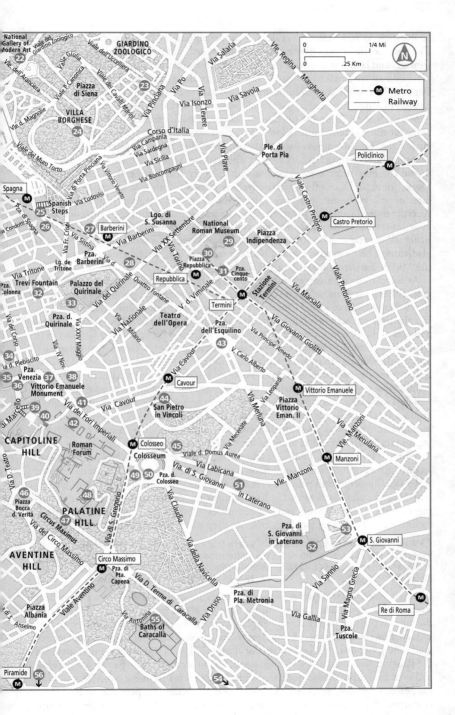

Rome itself, as you walk up Via dei Fori Imperiali (see the front cover of this guide). The Colosseum fell into disuse as the empire waned, earthquakes caused considerable damage, and later generations used its stones and marble as a stone quarry rich in pre-cut building materials. The scavenging came to an end during the tenure of Pope Benedict XIV, who's conservationist streak led him to consecrate the Colosseum to the passion of Jesus, honoring it as a site of Christian martyrdom.

Started in A.D. 70 on the filled-in site of one of Nero's artificial fish ponds (see the entry for the Golden House below), this grand amphitheater was the "bread and cir-cus" of the Roman Empire. Architecturally, the Colosseum is a poster child for classi-cal order, built of three levels of arcades whose niches were once filled with statues and whose columns became more ornate with each level, following the Greek order of Doric, Ionic, and Corinthian, respectively. A plainer fourth level supported an appa-ratus of pulleys, beams, and canvas that created a retractable roof, winched out by a specially trained troupe of sailors to shade the seats from sun and rain (Astrodome, eat your heart out). This arena of blood and gore could amuse 50,000 at a time—the inaugural contest in A.D. 80 lasted 100 days and killed off 5,000 beasts and countless gladiators. These contests eventually drove to extinction several creatures, including the Middle Eastern lion and North African elephant.

As for man-to-man (or woman) combat, professional gladiators were young men who, either poor or ruined, slaves or criminals, were lured by the promise of prize riches to sell themselves into a kind of slavery to the trainers and lead brutish, dangerous lives. If a gladiator was seriously but not mortally wounded, he stretched out on the ground and raised his left arm for mercy. The victor then decided his opponent's fate; however, whenever the emperor was around, he made the call, giving us gestures that we still use today—the thumbs-up (spare the man) and thumbs-down (finish him off). The only release from gladiatorial life was death in the ring or the granting by the emperor of the *rudis,* a wooden sword that signaled a dignified, well-earned retirement from the games.

The Colosseum has now become the turnstile for Rome's largest traffic circle, around which thousands of cars whip daily, spewing exhaust all over this venerable monument. Ambitious plans are underway to rebuild 500 square meters of the floor-ing and install an elevator to allow visitors to explore the interior more fully by 2002. Preparation for the Papal Jubilee set an international team of archaeologists to work to reconstruct a portion of the wood floor, a section that once covered the long-exposed skeleton of underground passages that served as the green room for a cast of charac-ters. Now classical Greek tragedies have brought the drama back to the arena, debut-ing with the suitably ghastly story of Sophocles' *Oedipus Rex.* The stage will remain, so future events, barring rock concerts, can keep the aged monument alive.

✪ **Domus Aurea (Golden House).** Via della Domus Aurea. ☎ **06-3974-9907** for reser-vations (2,000L/$1 fee) or 06-481-5576 (information and sales). Admission 10,000L ($5). Audiocassette guide 3,000L ($1.50). Wed–Sun 9am–7:45pm, Sat to 11pm. Ticket window closes 7pm sharp. Bus: 30/, 85, 87, 117, 186, 204F, 810, 850. Metro: Colosseo.

After 20 years of excavations, one of the most monumental discoveries of ancient Rome is now open. The Domus Aurea, built on Nero's orders in A.D. 64, following the famous fire that leveled Rome, displayed a megalomania and an excessiveness that bordered on the grotesque. The opulent palace (most notable for its preponderance of gold) and grounds comprised an area of almost 200 acres (80 hectares) that included the Palatine, Celio, Oppio, and Esquiline Hills, an area of woods, pastures, vineyards, and even a lake. But Nero's clock was ticking and so was that of the palace: A year after his death, Vespasian, to reverse the injustices done during the previous "year of three emperors," began to restore the grounds to the people. The lake was drained to sup-port the foundations of the Flavian Amphitheater, known today as the Colosseum.

The palace survived only until A.D. 104, when its rooms were stripped of all their ornamentation and filled in with tons of dirt, providing a solid foundation for the Baths of Trajan. It was probably this act that permitted the palace to survive somewhat intact. The site was rediscovered in the 15th century, when passersby fell through the ceiling of the pavilion (this opening is seen on the tour). The discovery of such a wealth of frescoes resulted in the diffusion of the style called "the art of the grotesque," and 200 years later, the most famous names in Renaissance art (Pinturicchio, Raphael, Ghirlandaio, and so on) found their way here to check out the works.

The 45-minute tours depart every 15 minutes (it's best to reserve at the number above). Bring a sweater, as the site, now submerged and more like a cave, maintains a constantly chilly temperature (12°C/53°F in summer; 4°C/39°F in winter). The tour includes only 32 chambers, with most of the 150 identified rooms still buried, unreachable, or being restored. Lacking the gold, ivory, marble, and jewels that once adorned it, the structure is a shadow of what it once was, with bare arches, fragments of mosaics, and faded frescoes, but the visit nevertheless is an eye-opener. Highlights include the **Case Repubblicane (Republican House Rooms),** with its tract of mosaic flooring in an unusual but regular rhomboidal design; the **Ninfeo di Ulisse e Polifemo (Nimphaeum of Ulysses and Polyphemus),** named for the partially damaged mosaic on the ceiling; and the **Sala di Achille a Skyros (Hall of Achilles and Skyros),** one of two symmetrical rooms flanking the Sala Ottagona (below) and containing the only completely conserved painting in the pavilion. The tour ends at the **Sala Ottagona (Octagonal Hall),** remarkable not only for its architectural uniqueness (in those days rooms were generally rectangular) but also for its dome, which becomes hemispheric near to the oculus in deference to the room's measurements.

Fori Imperiali (Imperial Forums). Via dei Fori Imperiali, near Via Cavour. ☎ **06-3751-1250** or 06-3974-6221 (reservations by computer). Admission with mandatory guide: 10,000L ($5). Tours with audioguide daily at 1 and 4:30pm; archaeologist-led tours in English daily at 10, 11:40am, and 3pm. Tours free with admission. (Other language tours also available; check with site for departure times.) Mon–Fri 9am–6pm, Sat to 1pm. Bus: 60, 63, 64, 70, 75, 84, 85, 87, 117, 170, 175, 186, 640, 810, 850. Metro: Colosseo.

With the growth of late Republican Rome into the great metropolis of the Empire, the burgeoning population began to crowd the Roman Forum's public buildings and temples. A succession of leaders and emperors, starting with Julius Caesar, began building new forums and markets east of the original Forum in ambitious bouts of urban expansion that provided for the populace, curried favor with the elite, and improved the city infrastructure all at the same time. Demolitions and concrete reconstructions of these Imperial Forums began in full force during the reign of the House of Savoie, but the Fascists had other ideas, bulldozing Via dei Fori Imperiali right down the center of the most significant, if not the largest, open-air museum in the world. Today, visitors, accompanied by guides (who do little more than operate the sound system), make their way through the labyrinth of excavations, past archaeologists who'll be kept busy for years to come. The tour lasts about an hour.

The **Foro di Cesare (Forum of Caesar)** is the only one on the west side of Via dei Fori Imperiali, tucked between the huge Vittorio Emanuele Monument, the Capitoline, and the Roman Forum. It was the first of these new *fori,* begun by Julius Caesar in 54 B.C. and completed by Augustus after Julius's death. The popular general (with his eye on the dictatorship) used the money he'd made during his successful Gaulish wars to buy up all the private property flanking the Roman Forum, tear down the houses, and build public temples and markets in their stead. The three standing Corinthian columns were part of his Temple to Venus Genetrix, a goddess from whom Caesar claimed direct descent through Rome's legendary founder, Aeneas.

The first major forum on your right is the **Foro di Augusto (Forum of Augustus).** The stairs and column stumps in the center once belonged to the 2nd-century B.C. Temple of Mars Ultor. Richly decorated, this square temple was lined with statues of *summi veri,* the imperial figures of Roman history, and ongoing excavations have uncovered depictions of the families of Caesar and Augustus. The only thing left of the public square and formal gardens of the **Foro di Vespasiano (Forum of Vespasian),** begun by the emperor after the capture of Jerusalem in A.D. 71 and dedicated 4 years later after the fall of Masada, are the remains of the **Tempio della Pace (Temple of Peace).** Pliny considered this temple, built by Vespasian to inaugurate an era of protracted peace, one of Rome's three most beautiful buildings. It contained treasures stripped from the Temple of Jerusalem and art from the Domus Aurea (see above), gathered by Nero from all over the empire.

Not much more than the ancient two-story houses are left of the **Foro di Nerva (Forum of Nerva),** begun by Domitian and inaugurated by Nerva in A.D. 97. The **Tempio di Minerva (Temple of Minerva)** was demolished in the 16th century (some decorative items survived) under the orders of Pope Paul V, who used the stones to build the Acqua Paola fountain on the Janiculum and the Borghese Chapel in Santa Maria Maggiore.

More dramatic are the last set of ruins, **Mercato di Traiano (Trajan's Market)** and **Foro di Traiano (Trajan's Forum);** admission to Trajan's Market is 3,750L ($1.90), and it's open Tuesday to Sunday 9am to 7pm (free the last Sunday of the month). Of the five imperial *fori* unearthed here, Trajan's is the grandest and most remarkable because of the massive covered market he had built at its flank in the 2nd century. It consisted of over 100 shops built on three levels, a grand bazaar lined with stalls boasting marble porticos and barrel-vaulted ceilings. What's left are some fragments and sculptural bits, but a few have remarkably sharp and well-preserved detailing. Climb up to the top terrace for a bird's-eye panorama and explore the four stories of 150 empty *tabernae* (shops) that made up the world's first multilevel shopping mall. This site is also marked by several rows of re-erected columns that comprised the central part of the huge Basilica Ulpia, Rome's largest basilican law courts.

Behind them rises the area's most stunning sight, the 98-foot ✪ **Colonna Traiana (Trajan's Column),** topped by a 16th-century statue of St. Peter. Around the column wraps a cartoon strip of deep bas-relief carvings that would measure 660 feet if stretched out; it uses a cast of 2,500 to tell the story of Trajan's victorious A.D. 101 to 106 campaigns to subdue the Dacians. A spiral staircase inside leads to the top (closed), and the emperor's ashes were kept in a golden urn entombed at the base. Recent excavations have uncovered countless pieces of ornamented porticos and two colossal white marble **statues of Dacian prisoners** in a good state of preservation (casts of the carvings are kept at the Museo della Civiltà Romana, below).

✪ **Pantheon.** Piazza della Rotonda. ☎ **06-6830-0230.** Admission free. Mon–Sat 9am–6:30pm, Sun to 1pm. Bus: 116; H, tram 8, 46, 62, 63, 64, 70, 81, 87, 116, 116T, 186, 204F, 492, 628, 640, 810.

"Simple, erect, severe, austere, sublime." That's the poet Lord Byron groping for words to capture the magic of Rome's best-preserved ancient building, a "pantheon," or temple to all the gods. An architectural achievement like no other, the temple was built by Emperor Hadrian (an accomplished architect) in the early 2nd century, drawing on his advanced engineering skills to create a mathematically exacting and gravity-defying space inside. (Hadrian constructed the Pantheon over a temple erected by Marcus Agrippa but modestly kept the dedicatory inscription from Agrippa on the architrave of the porch's pediment.)

The **bronze entrance doors**—1,800-year-old originals—weigh 20 tons each. The rotunda is circular and the **coffered ceiling** a perfect half-sphere of a dome, with an 18-foot **oculus** (eye) in the center (this is the only source of light and it lets in rain in inclement weather). The dome is 143 feet across and the building 143 feet high—if you could find a soccer ball big enough, it would fit perfectly in this space. An engineering marvel such as this remained unduplicated until the Renaissance, and it was only relatively recently that Hadrian's secret was revealed. The roof is made of poured concrete (a Roman invention) composed of light pumice stone, and the weight of it doesn't bear down but is distributed by brick arches embedded sideways into the walls and channeled into a ring of tension around the lip of the oculus. It also helps that the walls are 25 feet thick. The decoration is spare (its niches once contained white marble statues of Roman gods) but includes the **tombs** of Italy's short-lived 19th-century monarchical dynasty (three kings total yet only two are here, Vittorio Emanuele II and Umberto I) and that of the great painter Raphael.

The Pantheon has survived the ages because it was left alone by the barbarians, who recognized its beauty, and by overzealous temple-destroying Christians, who reconsecrated it as a church in 609. Later Christians weren't as charitable. When Pope Urban VIII, a prince of the Barberini family, removed the bronze tiles from the portico and melted them down to make 80 cannons and St. Peter's baldacchino, it prompted one wit to quip, "What even the barbarians wouldn't do, Barberini did." The Pantheon is now a church dedicated to Santa Maria ad Martyres (St. Mary of the Martyrs)—every year on Pentecost, the 50th day after Easter, hundreds of thousands of red rose petals are dropped through the oculus, commemorating the descent of the Holy Spirit in the form of tongues of fire.

ATTRACTIONS NEAR ANCIENT ROME

Musei Capitolini (Capitoline Museums) & Capitolino (Capitoline Hill). Piazza del Campidoglio 1. ☎ **06-6710-2071.** Admission (covers both museums) 10,000L ($5) adults, 5,000L ($2.50) students. Admission free (and crowded) the last Sun of the month. Tues–Sun 9am–7pm. Bus: 44, 46, 60, 62, 63, 64, 70, 81, 84, 87, 95, 160, 170, 186, 204F, 628, 640, 716, 780, 781, 810.

The **Capitoline Hill,** behind Piazza Venezia's Vittorio Emanuele Monument, has been the administrative seat of Rome's civic government since the 11th century and was a venerated spot used for the highest state occasions in Republican Rome. The trapezoidal **Piazza del Campidoglio** at its top, reached by a long set of low sloping steps meant to accommodate carriages, was laid out by an elderly Michelangelo, who also designed the palace facades on its three sides. It's one of Rome's most unified open spaces and a prime example of High Renaissance ideals in aesthetics, architecture, and spatial geometry. At the square's center is a 2nd-century bronze equestrian statue of Marcus Aurelius, his outstretched hand seeming to bless the city (this is a copy; the original is in the Palazzo Nuovo). During restoration of a 1920 addition built by Mussolini, excavators uncovered the most famous temple of ancient Rome, the **Tempio di Giove (Temple of Jupiter).**

A Tip to a View

Standing on Piazza del Campidoglio, walk around the right side of the Palazzo Senatorio to a terrace overlooking the city's best panorama of the Roman Forum, with the Palatine Hill and the Colosseum as a backdrop. Return to the square and walk around the left side of the Palazzo Senatorio to you'll find a stair winding down past the Forum wall, passing close by the upper half of the Arch of Septimius Severus—a nifty little back door.

Cheap Thrills: Exploring Rome for Free (or Almost)

- **Wandering the medieval streets.** Note that the best value in Rome is undoubtedly simply wandering the streets of the center, past ancient ruins, Renaissance churches, and baroque palaces. Grab a bus map from the ticket booths outside the train station so you can learn the main routes and use public transport wisely and sparingly.

- **Checking out the churches.** You can get in free to all the city's 900-odd **churches,** many of which seem to be nothing more than consecrated walls serving as backdrops for Renaissance and baroque masterpieces by Caravaggio, Pinturrichio, Michelangelo, Leonardo, Giotto, Lippi, and Bernini. If that's not enough to draw a crowd, many offer outstanding **classical and liturgical concerts** on Sundays. **Sant'Ignazio di Loyola,** Piazza Sant'Ignazio, has mass at 10am, 11:30am, and 6pm; **Gesú e Maria,** Via del Corso 45, has a 10am and 6pm mass in Latin; **Santa Maria del Popolo,** Piazza del Popolo, chimes its bells at midnight, 8am, 9am, 10am, 11am, and noon; and **San Paolo Entro le Mura,** Via Nazionale, performs mass in Italian at 8:30 and 10:30am and in Spanish at 1pm. The mass at the **Basilica di Sant'Eustachio,** Piazza Sant'Eustachio, is accompanied by organ music on Thursday and Saturday at noon and 7pm, adding guitar-toting nuns at services Monday to Friday. During the Jubilee, the Benedictine monks offered free classical concerts before Latin vespers on the first and third Sunday of each month (excluding August) at the **Abbey of the Aventine,** Piazza Cavalieri di Malta 5. Call ☎ **06-579-1319** to confirm that this is ongoing.

- **Taking advantage of free admission days.** On the last Sunday of the month, several of the big names in culture suspend their entrance fees and open their doors free to the public. The **Vatican Museum** opens 8:45am to 12:45pm, packing 'em in (unless a public holiday falls on that day, overriding any freebees) to the point that the crush propels you forward regardless of your own intentions to stop and admire a work of art. You'll find no such indignity at **Trajan's Markets,** where between 9am and 1pm you can wander the open spaces to your heart's desire. The **Capitoline Museums** address the crowding issue by opening its doors 9am to 7pm, and the **Palazzo del Quirinale** (President's Palace) on Via XX Settembre opens to an unsuspecting public every second and fourth Sunday of the month 8:30am to 12:30pm.

The discovery of this 6th-century B.C. temple opened up a can of worms, exposing artifacts (like tombs of children) dating from the 16th century B.C. and shedding light on the origins of the Capitoline Hill.

The central **Palazzo Senatorio** houses the mayor's office and the side palaces house the **Capitoline Museums,** the world's oldest collection of public art, occupying two buildings. On the left is the **Palazzo Nuovo,** filled with ancient sculpture like the *Dying Gaul,* busts of ancient philosophers, the *Mosaic of the Doves,* and the original statue of Marcus Aurelius (the regilded bronze had been tossed into the Tiber, and when Christians later fished it out, they thought it was Constantine the Great, the first Christian emperor, a misinterpretation that saved it from being hacked to pieces). On the right is the **Palazzo dei Conservatori,** whose entrance is to the left of a courtyard filled with the oversized marble head, hands, foot, arm, and kneecap of what was once a 40-foot statue of Constantine II. The collections have their share of antique statuary, including the

- **Seeing the free sights.** Don't forget that the **Pantheon,** one of the most perfectly preserved ancient temples in the world and a masterpiece of architecture and aesthetic beauty, won't cost you a lira. Ditto for the **Roman Forum,** the heartbeat of the ancient city that controlled Europe, North Africa, the Near East, and parts of Asia 2,000 years ago. And note that the newly restored **Vittoriano (Vittorio Emanuele Monument),** Piazza Venezia's unmistakable monument (better know as the "Wedding Cake"), has been opened to the public. Access is permitted Tuesday to Sunday 10:30am to 4:30pm, with guided tours (in Italian), leaving from Piazza Aracoele at 10:30am, noon, and 3pm. You'll mostly get to climb around the enormous staircase, terraces, and portico, each vantage point enjoying its own superb view of the city

- **People-watching on a piazza.** When in Rome, do as the Romans do and set up camp in one of the cafe tables on Piazza Navona or Piazza della Rotonda (Pantheon) for some priceless people-watching, all for the price of a cappuccino or an afternoon Campari.

- **Indulge in some Roman lore.** Local mythology has it that one coin tossed over you shoulder into the Trevi Fountain ensures a return to the Eternal City. But few are onto the bonus: two coins will get you a fling with an Italian, and three coins buys you the wedding ring. Confirm your partner's sincerity over at the Mouth of Truth , where questions answered falsely are said to cause the stoney teeth to clamp down.

- **Enjoy nighttime panormas.** Wander around the backside of the mayor's palace on Piazza del Campidoglio to see the Rome of the Caesars floodlit in a solemn and shadowy light. Or end your evening (after a hearty Trastevere dinner) with a walk along the walls of the Gianicolo hill stretching north toward the Vatican with a sweeping vista of the city.

- **Seek out Rome's exceptional views**. The sprawl of Rome twinkles below the Gianicolo, the hill above Trastevere reachable by hiking up Via Garibaldi, (or take bus 870). By night, couples congregate in the moonlight high above the city. The Aventine boasts one of Rome's most picturesque gardens in the Giardino degli Aranci, where peeping through the keyhole of the Priorato di Malta, you'll get a memorable view of the dome of the Vatican.

Resting Faun, a Roman sculpture that inspired Nathaniel Hawthorne's 19th-century novel *The Marble Faun;* in the gallery for temporary exhibits is the celebrated 6th-century B.C. Etruscan bronze *She-Wolf,* whose suckling **Romulus and Remus** (see "The Founders of Rome," below), added in the 16th century and temporarily weaned after 500 years, are displayed in the adjoining room. The picture gallery is impressive, with works by Guercino, Veronese, Titian, Rubens, Cortona, and Caravaggio—standouts are the *Gypsy Fortune Teller* and the scandalously erotic *St. John the Baptist,* where the nubile young saint twists to embrace a ram and looks out at us coquettishly.

Note: The museum is undergoing a $20-million restoration that will more than double the total exhibition area by the end of 2001. The mostly cosmetic improvements of Phase I, completed in April 2000, include the opening of the **Tabularium.** This subterranean gallery, connecting the two palaces, was once a warehouse used for the archiving of hundreds of thousands of public records (tablets).

Santa Maria in Aracoeli. Via Teatro di Marcello (up many steps, between Piazza Venezia's Vittorio Emanuele Monument and Piazza dei Campidoglio). ☎ **06-679-8155.** Admission free. Daily 7am–noon and 3:30–5:30pm. Bus: 44, 46, 60, 62, 63, 64, 70, 81, 84, 87, 95, 160, 170, 186, 204F, 628, 640, 716, 780, 781, 810.

Santa Maria in Aracoeli was old when it was first mentioned in the 7th century, but its current incarnation dates from the Franciscans in A.D. 1250. Legend holds that the Tiburtine Sibyl told Emperor Augustus that on this lofty spot would be an "altar to the first among gods," whereupon he had a vision of the heavens opening up and a woman bearing a child in her arms on the hilltop. Augustus dutifully built an *aracoeli* (Altar in the Sky) up here, but Christians later interpreted the prophecy as a reference to their God and replaced it with a church.

Past the unfinished brick facade is a slightly baroqued Romanesque interior hung with chandeliers but retaining a Cosmatesque pavement and 22 mismatched columns recycled from pagan buildings. The elegant wood ceiling is carved with naval emblems and motifs to commemorate the great victory at Lepanto (1571). The worn **tomb of Giovanni Crivelli** to the right of the door was cast by Donatello, and the **first chapel** on the right was frescoed by Umbrian Renaissance master Pinturicchio, one of his greatest masterpieces.

To the left of the altar, with a 10th-century *Madonna d'Aracoeli* painting, is the chapel that once housed a highly venerated statue of the baby Jesus called the *Santo Bambino,* supposedly carved from an olive tree in the Garden of Gethsemane and imbued with miraculous powers to heal the sick and answer the prayers of children (he spent half his time making the rounds of Rome's hospitals to visit the sickbeds of the terminally ill). The bambino received thousands of letters from around the world every year (most addressed simply "Santo Bambino, Roma"); they were left in his chapel, unopened, until they were burned so the prayers in them could waft heavenward. Roman children came to recite little speeches or sing poetry in front of the little holy statue, especially at Christmastime. Alas, the *Santo Bambino* was stolen in 1994.

Santa Maria in Cosmedin & Bocca della Verità (Mouth of Truth). Piazza Bocca della Verità 18. ☎ **06-678-1419.** Admission free. Church daily 10am–1pm and 3–5pm; portico (containing Mouth of Truth) daily 10am–5pm (in summer sometimes to 8pm). Bus: H, 23, 44, 63, 81, 95, 160, 170, 204F, 628, 630, 716, 780, 781, 810.

At the Palatine Hill's western foot sit two small 2nd-century B.C. temples—the square **Tempio di Portunus (Temple of Portunus)** and the round **Tempio di Ercole Vincitore (Temple of Hercules Victor),** Rome's oldest marble structure—as well as **Santa Maria in Cosmedin,** with its early-12th-century bell tower and Cosmatesque floors. The church's front porch draws crowds who want to stick their hands inside the **Mouth of Truth,** a 4th-century B.C. sewer cover carved as a bearded face with a dark slot for a mouth (remember the scene with Gregory Peck and Audrey Hepburn in *Roman Holiday?*). Medieval legend holds that if you stick your hand in its mouth and tell a lie, it will clamp down on your fingers and bite them off (apparently, a priest once added some sting to this belief by hiding behind the mouth with a scorpion, dispensing justice as he saw fit).

Up Via di Teatro Marcello from the piazza out front, you can see the outer wall of what looks like a midget Colosseum with a 16th-century palace grafted atop its curve. This was actually the model for the Colosseum, the **Teatro di Marcello,** built by Augustus in 11 B.C. and dedicated to his nephew Marcellus.

San Pietro in Vincoli (St. Peter in Chains). Piazza San Pietro in Vincoli 4 (just south of Piazza Cavour). ☎ **06-488-2865.** Admission free. Daily 9am–noon and 3–6pm. Metro: Cavour. Bus: 75, 84, 117.

Besides the **chains** that supposedly once bound St. Peter in prison (now on display under the altar), this 5th-century church with the Renaissance portico facade is famous for containing one of Michelangelo's greatest masterpieces—and one of his most bitter failures. In 1505, Pope Julius II commissioned Michelangelo to create for him a tomb, and the master came up with a grandiose mausoleum to be festooned with 40 statues. The pope sent the sculptor off to the mountains of Carrara to search for marble, but when Michelangelo returned Julius set him to work painting the Sistine Chapel ceiling instead. Julius died in 1512, a few months after Michelangelo completed the ceiling.

As he doggedly tried to continue work on the tomb over the next several decades, Michelangelo kept reducing his plans as other projects took up his time and Julius's descendants squabbled over how much they'd invest in the project. The master managed to finish two *Slaves,* which now reside in the Louvre in Paris, and roughed out five more, now in Florence's Accademia alongside his *David* (see chapter 4). He also crafted one of the figures destined for the upper corners of the tomb, a muscle-bound ✪ *Moses* with satyrs horns on his head (symbolizing the holy rays of light from medieval iconography), the Commandments tablets clutched in a hand and a portrait of Michelangelo hiding in his flowing beard.

And that's pretty much all poor old Pope Julius got in the end. This (relatively) modest wall monument, with a few other niched statues, was mostly executed by Michelangelo's assistants (though the master probably had a hand in the more delicate Rachel and Leah figures flanking Moses). In a final twist of fate, this is a monument only, not a tomb. Julius himself lies buried and forgotten in an unassuming grave in a corner of the Vatican.

Basilica di San Clemente. Via San Giovanni in Laterano/Via Labicana 95. ☎ **06-7045-1018.** Admission to church free; excavations 4,000L ($2). Mon–Sat 9am–12:30pm and 3:30–6pm, Sun 10am–noon and 3:30–6pm. Bus: 85, 87, 117, 186, 204F, 810, 850. Metro: Colosseo.

Nowhere else in this city is the layering effect of Rome's history more evident than in this 12th-century church built atop a 4th-century church built atop a late-2nd-century pagan temple. This situation is far from unique in Rome—almost the entire city is built directly on top of the ancient one—but what's special about San Clemente is that you can actually climb down into those lower levels to explore Rome's sandwich of history.

The **upper church**—built in 1108 and run by the convent of Irish Dominican monks who rediscovered the lower levels in the 19th century—is beautiful enough to stand out on its own. It features a **pre-Cosmatesque pavement,** an ornate **marble choir** (a 6th- to 9th-century piece from the lower church), recently restored frescoes of the *Life of St. Catherine* (1228) by Masolino and his young disciple Masaccio in the first chapel on your right, and a 12th-century *Triumph of the Cross* mosaic in the apse. This last work shows a crucified Christ in the center, with the Tree of Life growing in twisting vine tendrils all around, loaded with medieval symbolism (Christ and the Apostles pose as sheep along the bottom; the Rivers of Paradise flow from the base of the cross from which the faithful, represented by stags, drink; doves flutter about; and the Hand of God reaches down from the canopy of the Heavens).

Off the right aisle is a postcard-lined passage and the entrance to the **lower church,** built in the 4th century and largely demolished by barbarian sackings in 1084. It preserves a few crude frescoes, including the *Life of St. Clement* on the wall before you enter the nave and the *Story of St. Alexis* on the left wall of the nave. After you've had your fill of this Dark Ages church, descend another flight of stairs to the ancient pagan **Mithraic temple** and the adjacent 1st-century **Roman palazzo.** Both later church's altars are placed directly above this pagan one to Mithras, which depicts the god sacrificing a bull. As you wander in and out of the brick vaulted rooms of the grand palazzo, you'll hear the sound of rushing water, and in one room you can even take a drink from the sweet spring water gushing out of an ancient pipeline to be routed along a small aqueduct set into the wall.

Basilica di San Giovanni in Laterano (St. John Lateran). Piazza San Giovanni in Laterano 4. ☎ **06-6988-6433.** Admission to church and baptistry free; cloisters and museum 4,000L ($2). Church daily 7am–7:30pm; baptistery daily 9am–1pm; cloisters and museum daily 9am–6pm. Bus: 16, tram 30/, 81, 85, 87, 117, 186, 218, 590, 650, 714, 810, 850. Metro: San Giovanni.

The cathedral of Rome (St. Peter's is merely a holy basilica on Vatican property) is oddly one of the least interesting of the city's grand churches. San Giovanni in Laterano has an illustrious history, however—founded by Constantine as Rome's first Christian basilica in A.D. 314 and the model for all Christian basilicas—but after going through seven cycles of destruction and rebuilding (due to fires, earthquakes, barbarian invasions, or wholesale remodeling), today's basilica is primarily a Borromini construction from the 1640s (and even parts of that were destroyed and are being restored after a 1993 bombing).

The massive Alessandro Galilei facade boasts stacked porticoes with a line of colossal saints, apostles, and Christ standing along the top. The gargantuan interior (230 feet long) has a unified decorative scheme designed by Borromini and a fine medieval Cosmatesque floor. On the aisle side of the first pillar on the right is a fresco by the proto-Renaissance genius Giotto (all that survives of a series of frescoes the master painted here in the early 14th century). The scene shows Boniface VIII proclaiming the first Jubilee Holy Year on this spot in 1300. The cloisters off the left transept are a peaceful oasis amid the bustle of Rome, a quadrangle of twisty columns inlaid with Cosmati stoneworks and the walls lined with fragments from earlier incarnations of this cathedral.

ATTRACTIONS NEAR PIAZZA NAVONA & THE PANTHEON

Note that this neighborhood's greatest sight, the **Pantheon,** is covered under "The Forum, Colosseum & Best of Ancient Rome," above.

✪ **Piazza Navona.** North of Corso Vittorio Emanuele II. Bus: 46, 62, 64, 70, 81, 87, 116, 116T, 186, 204F, 492, 628.

Closed to traffic, studded with fountains, lined with cafes, and filled with tourists, street performers, artists, kids playing soccer, and couples cuddling on benches, Piazza Navona is one of Rome's archetypal open spaces. It's also one of the best places to kick back and relax in the heart of the city. The piazza owes its long, skinny, round-ended shape to the **Stadium of Domitian,** which lies mostly unexcavated underneath (buried under a bank on Piazza di Tor Sanguigna, just outside the piazza, is one travertine entrance arch from the north curve of the stadium).

The **Fontana del Moro (Fountain of the Moor)** on the piazza's south end was designed by Giacomo della Porta (1576), the **Fontana di Nettuno (Fountain of Neptune)** at the north end by Antonio della Bitta and Gregorio Zappalà (1878), and the

---

The Founding of Rome

Rome was legendarily founded by twin brothers, **Romulus** and **Remus,** who had been abandoned in the woods and raised by a she-wolf. Romulus later quarreled with and killed Remus à la Cain and Abel—which is why you're visiting Rome and not Reme—but that heroic she-wolf with the overactive motherly instincts became the most famous of the trio and since ancient times has been the symbol of Rome and all it stands for.

soaring ✪ **Fontana dei Quattro Fiumi (Fountain of Four Rivers)** in the center by Gianlorenzo Bernini (1651). This last is a roiling masterpiece of rearing mer-horses, sea serpents, and muscle-bound figures topped by an obelisk; the giant figures at the corners represent the world's four great rivers (or at least those known in the 1650s): the Danube (Europe), the bearded Ganges (Asia), the bald Plate (Americas), and the Nile (Africa, with his head shrouded since the source of the Nile was unknown at the time). Borromini's curvaceous facade of **Sant'Agnese in Agone** rises next to the fountain, and tour guides love to tell the legend that Bernini designed a slight to Borromini in the figure of Plate, rearing back and throwing his arm up in a gesture of protection against the church facade falling on him. It's true that the two architects were archrivals, but the facade was started in 1653—2 years after Bernini finished the fountain.

The stadium's tradition as a place for chariot races and games was kept alive throughout the ages with medieval jousts, Renaissance festivals, and the 17th- to 19th-century practice of flooding it on August weekends for the populace to wade in and the nobles to parade around in the shallow pools in their carriages. It was a market from 1477 to 1869, and for quite some time has hosted a Christmastime fair selling traditional crèche figurines and statues along with toys and dolls of the Christmas Witch La Befana, who traditionally brings Italian children presents on January 6.

✪ **Santa Maria sopra Minerva.** Piazza della Minerva 42 (southeast of the Pantheon). ☎ **06-679-3926.** Admission free. Daily 7am–noon and 4–7pm. Bus: 116; H, tram 8, 46, 60, 62, 64, 70, 81, 87, 186, 492, 628, 640.

Rome's only Gothic church was built in 1280 over the site of a Temple to Minerva (hence the name "St. Mary over Minerva"). The piazza out front sports a **whimsical statue** by Bernini of a baby elephant carrying a miniature Egyptian obelisk on its back (1667). The interior was heavily restored in the 19th century and contains some masterpieces by Tuscan Renaissance artists and the bodies of important Tuscan Renaissance personalities.

The last chapel on the right retains a sumptuous cycle of ✪ **frescoes** by Filippino Lippi (you insert coins in a light box and the works are briefly illuminated). In the scene of **St. Thomas Condemning the Heretics** on the lower half of the right wall, the two boys in the group on the right are Giovanni and Giulio de' Medici. These two grew up to become Pope Leo X and Pope Clement VII, respectively, and are buried in the apse in tombs by Antonio Sangallo the Younger. St. Catherine of Siena (1347 to 1380), a skilled theologian and diplomat whose letters and visits were instrumental in returning the papacy from Avignon to Rome, is allegedly buried under the altar (a claim also made by the monks of St. Catherine's monastery at Mt. Sinai), but since the saint's martyrdom resulted in a gruesome decapitation, I can say with certainty that her head is enshrined at her home in Siena.

To the left of the altar steps is Michelangelo's ✪ **Risen Christ** (1514 to 1521), leaning nonchalantly on a diminutive Cross (such a strong, virile, and quite naked Christ wasn't to everyone's taste, and the church later added bronze drapery to cover the Lord's loins). In a corridor to the left of the choir, behind a small fence, is the **tomb slab of Fra' Angelico,** the early Renaissance master and devout monk who died in the attached convent in 1455. Pope Nicholas V, who had commissioned a Vatican chapel from the painter 10 years earlier and was touched by the little monk's piety, modesty, and skill, wrote the epitaph.

Galleria Doria-Pamphilj. Piazza del Collegio Romano 1A (off Via del Corso near Piazza Venezia). ☎ **06-679-7323.** Admission 14,000L ($7) adults; tour of apts. 6,000L ($3); ticket includes use of audioguide. Gallery Fri–Wed 10am–5pm; apts. Fri–Wed 10:30am–noon. Closed Aug 15–31. Bus: 56, 60, 62, 81, 85, 95, 117, 160, 175, 492, 628, 850.

This formerly private art collection is now open to the public, with the layout preserved and paintings displayed more or less as they were in the 19th century. Since the works are jumbled like a giant jigsaw puzzle on the dimly lit walls, you need to use the list of artists and titles handed out at the entrance to match to the numbers on the works themselves. Among masterworks by Tintoretto, Correggio, Annibale and Lodovico Carracci, Bellini, Parmigianino, Jan and Pieter Brueghel the elders, and Rubens, you'll find two stellar paintings by Caravaggio, *Mary Magdalen* and the *Rest on the Flight into Egypt,* as well as a copy he made of his *Young St. John the Baptist,* now in the Capitoline Museums. Also here are Titian's *Salome with the Head of St. John the Baptist* and Bernini's *Bust of Innocent X,* whose sister-in-law started this collection.

۞ Museo Nazionale Romano (National Roman Museum)—Palazzo Altemps. Piazza di Sant'Apollinare 44 (2 blocks north of Piazza Navona). ☎ **06-683-3566.** Admission 10,000L ($5) adults; audio guide 7,000L ($3.50); guided tours on summer evenings 6,000L ($3). Tues–Sat 9am–6pm, Sun to 8pm. Bus: 70, 81, 87, 116, 116T, 186, 204F, 492, 628.

The new home to the famed Ludovisi ancient sculpture collection is an example of Italy's ability to craft a 21st-century museum respecting the gorgeous architecture and frescoes of the Renaissance space in which it's installed and the aesthetic and historic value of the classical collection it contains. What was once a single National Roman Museum—which languished for decades inside the Baths of Diocletian—has split up across the city in four collections: the Ludovisi, Mattei, and Altemps collections of classical statuary here; more statuary and exquisite ancient Roman mosaics, bronzes, frescoes, coins, and jewelry at the Palazzo Massimo alle Terme (below); bathhouse art and colossal statuary in the Aula Ottagona (below); and artifacts relating to the foundation of Rome at the recently restored Baths of Diocletian (below).

The 16th- to 18th-century Palazzo Altemps is gorgeous, with a grand central court-yard and many surviving frescoes and original painted wood ceilings, especially upstairs, where you can wander onto a bust-lined loggia frescoed as a "Garden of Delights" in the 1590s. Statues aren't crammed into every nook and cranny—a few choice pieces have been set in each room, encouraging you to examine each statue carefully, walk around it, and read the placard (in English and Italian) explaining its significance and showing which bits are original and which were restored in the 17th century. Seek out the 2nd-century giant *Dionysus with Satyr;* a 1st-century B.C. copy of master Greek sculptor Phidias's most famous statue (now lost), the 5th-cenutry B.C. *Athena* that once held the place of honor in Athens's Parthenon; 2nd-century B.C. Ptolemaic **Egyptian statuary;** a pair of lute-playing *Apollos;* plenty of **imperial busts;** and an 3rd-century **sarcophagus** carved from a single block of marble and depicting in incredible detail the Roman legions fighting off invading Ostrogoth Barbarians.

San Luigi dei Francesi. Piazza San Luigi dei Francesi 5 (just east of Piazza Navona). ☎ **06-688-271.** Admission free. Fri–Wed 8:30am–12:30pm and 3:30–7pm, Thurs 3:30–7:30pm. Bus: 70, 81, 87, 116, 116T, 186, 204F, 492, 628.

France's national church in Rome is a must-see for Caravaggio fans: In the last chapel on the left (insert coins to operate the lights for a short time) is his famous St. Matthew cycle of paintings. These huge canvases depict ۞ *The Calling of St. Matthew* on the left, the best of the three and amply illustrating Caravaggio's mastery of light and shadow to create mood and drama; *The Martyrdom of St. Matthew* is on the right; and *St. Matthew and the Angel* is over the altar. Interestingly, that scene with the angel inspiring St. Matthew to write his Gospel is not the one Caravaggio originally painted for the chapel. The church objected to that version, which showed the saint as a rough, illiterate peasant, the angel directly guiding his hand as he wrote. A wise collector not affiliated with the church bought that version (now destroyed), but its legacy appears here—Matthew's stool tips over the edge of the painting, as though about to tumble onto the altar. Before you leave, check out the **Domenichino frescoes** in the second chapel on the right aisle.

San Agostino. Piazza San Agostino (northeast of Piazza Navona). ☎ **06-6880-1962.** Admission free. Mon–Sat 8am–noon and 4:30–7:30pm. Bus: 70, 81, 87, 116, 116T, 186, 204F, 492, 628.

Around the corner from San Luigi dei Francesi is another stop on the Caravaggio tour, the early Renaissance San Agostino. The first altar on the left contains Caravaggio's almost Mannerist ✪ *Madonna del Loreto,* with pair of dirty-footed pilgrims kneeling before the velvet-robed Virgin, who's carrying a ridiculously oversized (if marvelously lifelike) Christ child. The picture's beautiful but a bit weird. Against the entrance wall is a shrine to the *Madonna del Parto,* a pregnant Virgin Mary (carved by Jacopo Sansovino in 1521) surrounded by thousands of votive offerings sent in supplication, especially by women who want to ensure a safe childbirth. The third pillar on the right side has a fresco by Raphael of *Isaiah* showing the influence of Michelangelo on the young painter.

THE SPANISH STEPS, PIAZZA DEL POPOLO & NEARBY ATTRACTIONS

Fontana dei Trevi (Trevi Fountain). Piazza di Trevi, a block south of Via Tritone. Bus: 52, 53, 60, 61, 62, 71, 95, 116, 116T, 175, 492.

This huge baroque confection of thrashing mer-horses, splashing water, and striding Tritons all presided over by a muscular Neptune is one of Rome's most famous sights. It was sculpted in 1762 by Nicolà Salvi to serve as an outlet for the waters carried into Rome by the 13-mile Acqua Vergine aqueduct, built in 19 B.C. and still running (it also supplies the fountains in Piazza Navona and Piazza di Spagna). Tourists and young folk just hanging out on the curving steps throng the cramped little piazza from early morning till after midnight, making it one of the most densely crowded but scenic spots to squeeze into a marble seat and people-watch.

Legend and movies like *Three Coins in the Fountain* hold that if you toss a coin into this fountain, you're guaranteed to return to the Eternal City. General weathering and the chemical damage from all those rusting coins forced the fountain's restoration in 1990, and now the monies are collected regularly and donated to the Red Cross. Some say you must lob the coin with your right hand backward over your left shoulder. Others insist you must use three coins. Historians point out the original tradition was to drink the fountain's water, but unless you like chlorine, I'd stick to tossing lire.

Scala di Spagna (Spanish Steps). From Piazza di Spagna to Piazza Trintà dei Monti. Metro: Spagna. Bus: 116, 116T, 117.

The off-center yet graceful curves of the **Spanish Steps** rising from the hourglass-shaped Piazza di Spagna are decorated with bright azaleas in spring and teeming with visitors, Roman teens, and poseurs year-round. This monumental baroque staircase was built by Francesco de Sanctis in the 18th century and funded almost entirely by the French to lead up to their twin-towered **Trinità dei Monti** church—with paintings by Michelangelo protégé Daniele da Volterra and frescoes by Raphael's pupil Giulio Romano inside. (The steps are officially called the Scalinata di Trinità dei Monti, and the piazza at the bottom is called the Spanish Square after the Spanish Embassy, which once was located nearby.) At the bottom is the beloved **Barcaccia** ("Ugly Boat") fountain, sculpted by a teenage Bernini and his father, Pietro, who together managed to solve the dilemma of low water pressure at this point in the Acqua Vergine aqueduct system by forgoing the usual dramatic sprays and jets and instead crafting a sinking boat overflowing with water.

Historically, Piazza di Spagna has been Rome's Anglo-American center. British and American artists lived or had studios (many still do) on Via Margutta (parallel to Via del Babuino); the Anglican church is just down the road; the Grand Tour's poshest hotels still huddle at the top of the steps; Italy's first McDonald's and the American Express office are just a few yards up the piazza; and flanking the steps are the British 19th-century bastions of Babington's Tea Rooms and the house where John Keats spent his final months with Joseph Severn by his side. Inside the young Romantic poet's apartment at Piazza di Spagna 26 is the **Keats Memorial** (☎ **06-678-4235**). It was here in 1821, with a view over the steps, that Keats died of consumption (tuberculosis) at age 25. The rooms are stuffed with mementos, letters, Keats's death mask, portraits, and around 10,000 books by Shelley, Byron, Leight Hunt, and of course Keats. It's open Monday to Friday 9am to 1pm and 3 to 6pm and Saturday 11am to 2pm. Admission is 5,000L ($2.50).

Ara Pacis (Altar of Peace). Via di Ripetta at Lungotevere in Augusta/Piazza Augusto Imperatore. ☎ **06-6880-6848** or 06-6710-3819 for guided tours. Visits by appointment. *Note:* Closed for restoration at press time. Admission 4,000L ($2) adults. Bus: 13, 81, 204F, 590, 628, 913, 926.

Augustus had this "altar" built from 13 to 9 B.C. to celebrate the peace his campaigns to unify the new Empire had brought to Europe, northern Africa, and the Near East. It has been reconstructed in a huge aquarium along the Lungotevere, and though you can admire it through the glass walls, I suggest you pay the low admission to examine up close the decorative bas-relief panels depicting mythological figures and processions of prominent Roman citizens above a Greek key band and lower frieze of acanthus leaves and swans. These carvings are not only beautiful but also represent the point at which Roman art finally significantly broke from Greek models to make a strong classical statement all its own.

Since the 16th century, bits of decorative frieze have been recovered from beneath buildings lining the Corso, most making their way to collections in the Louvre, the Vatican, and the Uffizi. The bulk of the altar, however, lay under the water table serving as the foundation for several palazzi. Mussolini, always looking for ways to link the concept of his new Fascist empire with that of ancient Rome, ordered the rest excavated in 1937. His archaeologists came up with the brilliant plan of freezing the water in the soil, building new supports for the palaces above, and extracting the chunks of marble altar before the ground thawed again. The reconstructed Ara Pacis is close to complete, with casts replacing the bits Rome hasn't been able to repatriate from museums. Nearby is Augustus's Mausoleum (below).

Mausoleo di Augusto (Augustus's Mausoleum). Piazza Augusto Imperatore. ☎ **06-6710-3819.** Admission by appointment 4,000L ($2). Appointments Wed–Fri 9am–1pm only for visits Sat–Sun 10am–1pm. Bus: 32, 81, 628, 913, 926.

Completing the Ara Pacis "complex" and filling up one of Rome's most hideous Fascist-designed piazze lies Augustus's Mausoleum, a neglected brick rotunda that once housed the remains of Rome's first emperor; his family; his general, Agrippa; and every Roman emperor up to Nerva (died A.D. 98). This awesome ring of brick 287 feet in diameter was once crowned with a dirt mound and cypress trees but has been so abused throughout the centuries—it was a fortress in the Middle Ages, then an amphitheater in the baroque era (used for cockfights and bear baiting), and finally a concert hall until 1936—we're lucky the body survives with a few plaques of the old marble still in place.

Santa Maria del Popolo. Piazza del Popolo 12 (at the Porta del Popolo). ☎ **06-361-0836.** Admission free. Mon–Sat 7am–noon and 4–7pm, Sun 8am–noon and 4:30–7:30pm. Bus: 95, 117, tram 225, 490, 495, 628, 926. Metro: Flaminio.

Although the first church on this site was built in 1099 to exorcise Nero's ghost from local walnut trees, the current Renaissance/baroque structure dates from the 1470s. You'll have to search out the light switches and light boxes (bring lots of coins) in the shadowy Santa Maria del Popolo, but it's worth the trouble. Many of Rome's architectural celebrities had a hand in the church's reconstruction, namely Bregno, Pinturicchio, and Pontelli, with later additions by Bramante and Bernini.

The much-restored **frescoes** in the first chapel on the right are by the Umbrian early Renaissance master Pinturicchio (who also did the vault frescos in the apse). Duck behind the altar to see the coffered shell-motif **apse**—one of Bramante's earliest works in Rome (flip on the lights at the box to your left). Sansovino carved the **Tomb of Sforza** and **Tomb of Girolamo Basso** (1505 to 1507) here, combining classical triumphal arches with surprising sarcophagal depictions of the deceased; these Renaissance cardinals recline comfortably on cushions, only half asleep, without the lying-in-state look of medieval tombs. Set higher in the walls are Rome's first **stained-glass windows,** commissioned in 1509 from the supreme French master Guillaume de Marcillat.

In the first transept chapel to the left of the altar is a juxtaposition of rival baroque masters Annibale Carracci and Caravaggio. Crowd-pleasing Annibale was more popular in his day, as the highly modeled colorful ballet of his *Assumption of the Virgin* in the center suggests, but posterity has paid more attention to the moody chiaroscuro of Caravaggio's tensely dramatic original style. He used overly strong and patently artificial light sources to enhance the psychological drama of *The Conversion of St. Paul* and *The Crucifixion of St. Peter* and to draw you right into the straining muscles, wrinkled foreheads, dirty feet, and intense emotions of his figures.

When banking mogul Agostino Chigi commissioned his favorite artist, Raphael, to design a memorial chapel tomb for him, he had no idea he'd need it so soon. Both patron and artist died in 1520, by which time Raphael had barely begun construction on the pyramid-shaped tombs of Agostino and his brother for the second-on-the-left **Cappella Chigi (Chigi Chapel).** Chigi Pope Alexander VII later hired others to complete the ceiling mosaics to Raphael's designs, with God in the center of the dome seeming to bless Agostino's personal horoscope symbols, surrounding him. Lorenzetto carved the smoother-bodied statues of Jonah and Elijah to match Raphael's sketches, but Bernini stuck to his own detailed style to depict Habakkuk with the angel and Daniel getting his foot licked by a bemused-looking lion. (Actually, Bernini is telling a Bible story; the angel is about to carry Habakkuk and his picnic basket across the chapel to feed Daniel, starving in the lion's den). The altarpiece is by Sebastiano del Piombo and the macabre flying skeleton in the floor by Bernini.

✪ **Galleria Borghese.** Piazzale Scipione Borghese 5 (in the northeast corner of Villa Borghese park, off Via Pinciana). ☎ **06-328-101** for reservations (Mon–Fri 9:30am–6pm; 2,000L/$1 surcharge) or 06-841-7645 for main desk. Admission 12,000L ($7) plus 2,000L ($1) obligatory reservation fee. Audioguide 7,000 ($3.50). Summer Tues–Sat 9am–10pm, Sun to 8pm; winter Tues–Sat 9am–5pm, Sun to 1pm. Bus: 95, 490, 495 (to middle of park); 52, 53, 910 (to Via di Porta Pinciana).

Reopened in 1997 after a 14-year restoration, this small museum packs a punch and is an absolute must-see. The new ticket reservation policy is annoying, but in summer

Making Reservations

Note that you need to make reservations to enter these three sights: the **Domus Aurea,** the **Fori Imperiali,** and the **Galleria Borghese.**

the museum can be sold out for days, so try to book at least a day before (earlier if possible). You'll spend 45 to 90 minutes wandering around this frescoed 1613 villa admiring the classical statues and mosaics, Renaissance paintings, and fabulous marble sculptures of the baroque, with frequent stops to return your lower jaw to its rightful position. Most of these compelling pieces were acquired by the villa's original owner, Cardinal Scipione Borghese (who bought Caravaggio's works when no one else wanted them).

The entrance to the **Pinacoteca (Picture Gallery)** is inside the villa (to the left of the exterior grand staircase) on an upper floor, accessible via two flights of a circular stairs. The 30-minute limit puts the pressure on, but if you rent the audiocassette guide, you'll breeze through with no trouble. Here you'll find most of the painting collection, featuring a humbling lineup of Italian Renaissance masters like Andrea del Sarto, Perugino, Girlandaio, Fra' Bartolomeo, Lorenzo di Credi, Antonella Messina, Pinturicchio, and Corregio. Just when you think the lineup will end, a masterful 1507 *Deposition* by the young Raphael or a *Madonna col Bambino e San Giovannino* by Botticelli appears. The foreign schools have their representation as well, and it's not difficult to spot a Titian, Dürer, or Rubens.

Exit the gallery and villa, circle the building (you may want to stop in the new cafe near the baggage check) and head up the grand staircase to gain access to the ✪ **sculpture gallery.** The main room is a temple to ancient Rome—indeed, looking around, you'll understand why all the great archaeological sites are empty. The best stuff is here. Roman mosaics cover the floor, with depictions of gladiators and scenes of the hunt, while several alarmingly large busts stand watch. Beginning counterclockwise, enter the room to the left, where you'll find five Caravaggios, including the powerful *Madonna of the Serpent,* a.k.a. *Madonna dei Palafrenieri* (1605); the *Young Bacchus, Ill* (1653), the earliest surviving Caravaggio, said to be a self-portrait from when the painter had malaria; and *David with the Head of Goliath* (1610), in which Goliath may be another self-portrait. The Egyptian room contains objects brought back by Napoléon; notice the pyramids in the ceiling fresco and the woman figure—representative of the gift of life and of the Nile, whose water sustains all life in Egypt.

Four rooms are each devoted to an early masterpiece by the baroque's greatest genius, Gianlorenzo Bernini. His *Aeneas and Anchises* (1613) was done at age 15 with the help of his father, Pietro, and the *Rape of Persephone* (1621) is a powerful narration in marble. Also here is ✪ *Apollo and Daphne* (1624), in which the 26-year-old sculptor captures the moment the nymph's toes take root and her fingers and hair sprout leaves as her river god father transforms her into a laurel tree to help her escape from a Cupid-struck Apollo. Bernini's vibrant ✪ *David* (1623 to 1624) is a baroque answer to Michelangelo's Renaissance take on the subject in Florence's Accademia. Michelangelo's *David* is pensive, all about proportion and philosophy. Bernini's *David* is a man of action, his body twisted as he's about to let fly the stone from his sling. Bernini modeled the furrowed brow and bitten lip of *David*'s face on his own.

The grand finale is in the last room: a deceptive masterpiece in gleaming white marble. Neoclassical master Canova's sculpted portrait of Napoléon's notorious sister ✪ *Pauline Bonaparte as Venus* (1805) reclining on a couch was quite the scandal in its time. When asked whether she wasn't uncomfortable posing half-naked like that, Pauline reportedly responded, "Oh, no—the studio was quite warm." (It's ironic that this sculpture is one of the gallery's stars—Pauline Bonaparte married Prince Camillo Borghese in 1807 and sold many of the pieces of the original collection.)

✪ **Museo Nazionale Etrusco di Villa Giulia (Etruscan Museum).** Piazzale di Villa Giulia 9 (on Viale delle Belle Arti, in the northern reaches of Villa Borghese park).

☎ **06-320-6571.** Admission 8,000L ($4) adults. Tues–Sat 9am–7pm, Sun and holidays to 8pm. Bus: Tram 19, tram 30/, 95, tram 225, 628, 926. Metro: Flaminio.

Housed in a 16th-century Mannerist villa built for Pope Julius III by Ammanati, Vasari, and Vignola, this museum is dedicated to the Etruscans, who may have immigrated to Italy from Turkey in the 9th century B.C. They were the peninsula's first great culture, concentrated in what are today the provinces of Tuscany, Umbria, and the north half of Lazio (Rome's province). The height of their power as an association of loosely organized city-states was from the 7th to 5th centuries B.C., when their Tarquin dynasty even ruled Rome as its first kings. Etruscan society is a mystery to us since what little we know of it comes down mainly through vases and funerary art (it's hard to reconstruct an entire culture based solely on its cemeteries). But from what we can gather, they enjoyed a highly developed society, had a great deal of equality between the sexes, and appreciated the finer things in life like banqueting, theater, and art.

This museum houses the most important Etruscan collection in Italy, unrivaled by anything even in Tuscany. The greatest piece is the touching and remarkably skilled 6th-century B.C. terra-cotta ✪ **Sarcophagus of Newlyweds** from nearby Cerveteri, whose lid carries full-size likenesses of a husband and wife sitting down to their eternal banquet. Also look for the 4th-century B.C. **Ficoroni Cist,** a bronze marriage coffer richly engraved with tales of the Argonauts, and a large painted terra-cotta statue of ✪ **Apollo** (ca. 500 B.C.), which once topped a temple to Minerva at Veio. The Castellani collection of ancient jewelry spans Minoan civilization through the Hellenistic and Roman eras as well as some Asian pieces. But what strikes most visitors about the Villa Giulia are the miles upon miles of **pots,** from native pre-Etruscan styles through the Etruscan and Greek eras to the Roman one, many beautifully painted. Be sure to seek out the **Faliscan Krater,** with a scene of Dawn riding her chariot across the sky, and the early 7th-century B.C. **Chigi Vase,** showing hunting scenes and the Judgment of Paris.

Galleria Nazionale d'Arte Moderna (National Gallery of Modern Art). Viale delle Belle Arti 131 (in the Villa Borghese park). ☎ **06-322-981.** Admission 12,000L ($7) adults. Tues–Sat 9am–7pm, Sun and holidays to 8pm (sometimes closes 2pm in winter). Bus: Tram 19, 52, 95, tram 225, 495, 628, 926. Metro: Flaminio.

In the heart of Villa Borghese, Rome's main modern art gallery concentrates on late-19th- and early-20th-century European and Italian art. There's art nouveau by Galileo Chini, futurism by Gino Severini, and *macchaioli* (a Tuscan variant on impressionism) by Giovanni Fattori and Silvestro Lega. Assorted foreign schools are represented by Klimt, Duchamp, Mondrian, Cézanne, Degas, Van Gogh, Modigliani, Goya, Ingres, Gauguin, Whistler, and Münch.

THE CATACOMBS OF THE APPIAN WAY

The arrow-straight **Via Appia Antica** was the first of Rome's great consular roads, completed as far as Capua by 312 B.C. and soon after extended the full 370km (222 mi.) all the way to Brindisi in Apulia, the heel of Italy's boot. Its initial stretch in Rome is lined with ancient tombs of Roman families—burials were forbidden within the city walls as early as the 5th century B.C.—and, beneath the surface, miles of tunnels hewn out of the soft tufa stone.

These tunnels, or **catacombs,** were where early Christians buried their dead and, during the worst times of persecution, held church services discreetly out of the public eye. A few are open to the public, so you can wander through mile after mile of musty-smelling tunnels whose soft walls are gouged out with tens of thousands of burial niches—long shelves made for two to three bodies each. The requisite guided tours, hosted by priests and monks, feature a smidgen of extremely biased history and a large helping of sermonizing.

Via Appia Antica has been a popular **Sunday picnic site** for Roman families following the half-forgotten pagan tradition of dining in the presence of one's ancestors on holy days. This practice was rapidly dying out in the face of the traffic fumes that were choking the venerable road, but a 1990s initiative closed Via Appia Antica to cars on Sundays, bringing back the picnickers and bicyclists—along with in-line skaters and a new Sunday-only bus route to get out there.

You can take bus 218 from the San Giovanni Metro stop, which follows Via Appia Antica for a bit, then veers right onto Via Ardeatina at the Domine Quo Vadis church. After another long block, the 218 stops at Largo M. F. Ardeatine, near the gate to San Callisto catacombs. From there, you can walk right on Via delle Sette Chiese to the San Domitilla catacombs or left down Via delle Sette Chiese to the San Sebastiano catacombs. Alternately, you can ride the Metro to the Colli Albani stop and catch bus 660, which wraps up Via Appia Antica from the south, veering off at the San Sebastiano catacombs (if you're visiting all three, you can take the 218 to the first two, walk to the San Sebastiano, and then catch the 660 back to the Metro stop at Colli Albani). On Sundays, bus 760F works its way from the Circo Massimo Metro stop down Via Appia Antica, turning around after it passes the Tomb of Cecilia Metella.

Catacombe di San Sebastiano (Catacombs of St. Sebastian). Via Appia Antica 136. ☎ **06-785-0350** or 06-788-7035. Admission 8,000L ($4) adults, 4,000L ($2) ages 6–14. Mon–Sat 8:30am–noon and 2:30–5pm. Closed Nov. Bus: See above.

Though the tunnels run for 10km (7 miles) and the venerable bones of Sts. Peter and Paul were once hidden here for safekeeping, the St. Sebastian tour is one of shortest and least satisfying of all the catacombs visits. The highlight is a chance to see a few well-preserved Roman (not Christian) tombs from what used to be an aboveground necropolis adjacent to the catacombs. Since this pagan graveyard was buried for centuries, the stucco decorations on the ceilings and frescoes inside were almost perfectly preserved.

Catacombe di San Callisto (Catacombs of St. Callixtus). Via Appia Antica 110. ☎ **06-5130-1580** or 06-513-6725. Admission 8,000L ($4) adults, 4,000L ($2) ages 6–14. Thurs–Tues 8:30am–noon and 2–5pm. Closed Feb. Bus: See above.

These catacombs have the biggest parking lot and thus the largest crowds of tour bus groups—as well as the cheesiest, most Disneyesque tour, full of canned commentary and stilted jokes. Some of the tunnels, however, are phenomenal, 70 feet high and less than 6 feet wide, with elongated tomb niches pigeonholed all the way up to the top. Of all the catacombs, these are among the oldest and certainly the largest (19km/ 12 miles of tunnels more than 33 acres and five levels housing the remains of half a million Christians) and were the final resting place of 16 early popes. You also get to ogle some of the earliest Christian art—frescoes, carvings, and drawings scratched into the rock depicting ancient Christian symbols like the fish, anchor, and dove and images telling some of the earliest popular Bible stories.

✪ Catacombe di San Domitilla (Catacombs of St. Domitilla). Via delle Sette Chiese 283. ☎ **06-511-0342.** Admission 8,000L ($4) adults, 4,000L ($2) ages 6–14. Wed–Mon 8:30am–noon and 2:30–5pm. Closed Jan. Bus: See above.

This oldest of the catacombs is the winner for the most enjoyable experience. The groups are small, most guides are entertaining and personable, and (depending on your group and guide) the visit may last 20 minutes or over an hour. You enter through a sunken 4th-century church. There are fewer "sights" here than in the other catacombs—though the 2nd-century fresco of the *Last Supper* is impressive—but some guides actually hand you bones out of a tomb niche so you can rearticulate an ancient Christian hip. (Incidentally, this is the only catacomb where you'll get to see bones; the rest have emptied their tombs to rebury the remains on the inaccessible lower levels.)

MORE ATTRACTIONS
AROUND VIA VENETO & PIAZZA BARBERINI

Cimitero Monumentale dei Padri Cappuccini (Capuchin Crypt). In Santa Maria Immacolata Concezione, Via Veneto 27. ☎ **06-487-1185.** Donation of 2,000L ($1) expected. Fri–Wed 9am–noon and 3–6pm. Metro: Barberini. Bus: 52, 53, 60, 61, 62, 95, 116, 116T.

The Capuchins are monks with a death wish—or, depending on how you look at it, with a healthy attitude toward their own mortality. They're a weird lot, very polite but with a penchant for making mosaics out of the bones of their brethren. That's what happened in the crypt of this church, where five chambers were filled between 1528 and 1870 with mosaics made from over 4,000 dearly departed Cappuccini (first dried out by temporary burial in the floors filled with dirt from Jerusalem). These fantastic displays form morbid patterns and baroque decorative details, from rings of knuckle-bones and garlands of pelvises to walls made from stacked skulls and scapulae used to create butterflies or hourglasses in an all-too-fitting *memento mori* motif. A few bodies lean against the walls in varying states of desiccated decay, and the full skeletons of two Barberini princelings adorn the last chamber, near a placard that drives home the ashes-to-ashes point in several languages, "What you are, we used to be. What we are, you will become."

⊘ **Galleria Nazionale d'Arte Antica (National Gallery of Ancient Art).** Via Quattro Fontane 13 (just up from Piazza Barberini). ☎ **06-481-4591.** Admission 8,000L ($4) adults. Tues–Sat 9am–7pm, Sun to 1pm. Metro: Barberini. Bus: 52, 53, 60, 61, 62, 95, 116, 116T, 175, 492.

When a Barberini was finally made pope (Urban VIII) in 1624, the fabulously wealthy family celebrated by hiring Carlo Maderno to build them a huge palace, which Borromini and Bernini later embellished with window frames and doorways. Since 1949, it has housed half of Rome's National Gallery of paintings, works that span the 13th to the 17th century (the other half is in Trastevere's Palazzo Corsini, below).

The masterpieces are numerous, but while you're admiring the paintings hung on the walls, don't fail to look up at the ceilings, many of which were decorated by one of the masters of Roman baroque frescoes, Pietro da Cortona. Keep an eye out especially for the Great Hall, where Pietro frescoed his masterpiece, the allegorical ⊘ *Triumph of Divine Providence* (1633 to 1639). It celebrates the Barberini dynasty in a sumptuously busy but masterful trompe-l'oeil space open to the heavens, with the Barberini bees swarming up to greet Divine Providence herself, who's being crowned by Immortality (most baroque pontiffs weren't known for their modesty).

As for the works on the walls, you'll pass icons of art like Filippo Lippi's *Annunciation* and *Madonna and Child;* Andrea del Sarto's *Holy Family;* Peruzzi's *Ceres;* Bronzino's *Portrait of Stefano Colonna;* Guido Reni's *Portrait of a Lady* believed to be Beatrice Cenci (condemned for murdering her father); and three Caravaggios, *Narcissus,* an action-packed gory *Judith Beheading Holofernes,* and an attributed *St. Francis in Meditation.* But the star painting has to be Raphael's bare-breasted ⊘ *Fornarina,* a racy portrait of the artist's girlfriend, a baker's daughter named Margherita. Some critics claim it's actually a painting of a courtesan by Raphael's pupil

Giulio Romano, but this wouldn't explain why the lass wears an armband bearing Raphael's name. Other great artists here are Filippino Lippi, Sodoma, Beccafumi, El Greco, Tintoretto, Titian, Paul Brill, and Luca Giordano.

NEAR STAZIONE TERMINI

Basilica di Santa Maria Maggiore. Piazza Santa Maria Maggiore. ☎ **06-483-195.** Admission to church free; loggia 5,000L ($2.50). Church daily 7am–7pm; loggia daily 9:30am–5pm. Metro: Termini or Cavour. Bus: 16, 70, 71, 75, 204F, 360, 590, 649, 714.

This is the greatest and by far the best preserved of Rome's four basilicas, marking the city skyline with Rome's tallest bell tower, a graceful 14th-century addition. The main facade is a baroque mask that uses arcades and loggias to partially hide the fantastically mosaicked earlier facade (1294 to 1308). Often you can climb stairs to view these mosaics up close, like scenes recounting the legend that this basilica was founded in the 350s by Pope Liberius, who, one night in August, had a vision of the Madonna telling him to raise the church on the spot and rebuild along an outline that would be demarcated by a miraculous snowfall the next morning. Every August 5, a special Mass takes place with the snowfall beautifully reenacted using pale flower petals.

The basilica's basic design and decor have been preserved from the 6th century. The gargantuan space is some 284 feet long, a dark echoey environment suited to religious pilgrimages. The glowing coffered ceiling was the work of Giuliano da Sangallo, said to be gold leafed using the very first gold brought back from the Americas by Columbus (a gift from Ferdinand and Isabella to the pope). The floor was inlaid with marble chips in geometric patterns by the Cosmati around 1150, while the mosaics lining the nave and covering the triumphal arch before the altar are glittering testaments to the skill of 5th-century craftsmen (the apse's *Coronation of the Virgin* mosaics were designed by Iacopo Torriti in the 1290s). The most striking later additions are the two magnificent and enormous late Renaissance and baroque chapels flanking the altar to form a transept (the Cappella Sistina on the left is particularly sumptuous).

✪ **Museo Nazionale Romano (National Roman Museum)—Palazzo Massimo alle Terme.** Largo di Villa Peretti (where Piazza dei Cinquecento meets Via Viminale). ☎ **06-4890-3500** or 06-520-726. Admission 12,000L ($7) adults. Tues–Sat 9am–7pm, Sun to 2pm (extended hours in summer). Bus: H, 64, 70, 116T, 170, 175, 492, 640, 910. Metro: Termini or Repubblica.

Opened in 1998, this museum (paired with its sibling collection in the Palazzo Altemps, above) blows away anything else you'll find in Rome when it comes to classical statues, frescoes, and mosaics. The 19th-century Palazzo Massimo alle Terme boasts a modernized museum of advanced lighting systems, explanatory placards in English, and a curatorial attention to detail heretofore unseen on the dusty old Roman museum scene.

There are no boring ranks of broken marble busts here—portrait busts are aplenty, but most are masterworks of expression and character, giving you an opportunity to put marble faces to the names of all those emperors and other ancient bigwigs. Among them is a **statue of Caesar Augustus** wearing his toga pulled over his head like a shawl, a sign he'd assumed the role of a priest (actually, of the head priest, which in Latin is Pontifex Maximus, a title that the Christian popes later adopted). Also on the ground floor are an **altar** from Ostia Antica whose reliefs bear a striking resemblance to 15th-century frescoes of the Nativity and a hauntingly beautiful 440 B.C. **statue of a wounded Niobid,** collapsing as she reaches for her back, where one of Apollo and Artemis's arrows struck. Among the masterpieces on the first floor are a **discus thrower,** a bronze **Dionysus** fished out of the Tiber, bronze bits from **ancient**

shipwrecks on Lake Nemi, and an incredibly well-preserved **sarcophagus** featuring a tumultuous battle scene between Romans and Germanic barbarians (all from the 2nd century).

On the second floor are **Roman frescoes, stuccoes,** and **mosaics** spanning the 1st century B.C. to the A.D. 5th century, most never seen by the public since they were discovered in the 19th century. You can visit only on a 45-minute guided tour, which is included in the price of your admission (your museum ticket will have a time printed on it; be on the second floor at that time for the tour; you can visit the rest of the museum afterward). The frescoes and stuccoes are mainly countryside scenes, decorative strips, and a few naval battles, all carefully restored and reattached into spaces that are faithful to the original dimensions of the rooms from which they came. Also up here are halls and rooms lined with incredible mosaic scenes, among them the famous ✪ *Four Charioteers* standing with their horses in the four traditional team colors (red, blue, green, and white) that ran the races around the Circus Maximus. There are also several rare 4th-century *opus sectile* (marble inlay) scenes from the Basilica di Giunio Bassa.

The basement has two sections. The first contains **ancient jewelry, gold hair nets, ivory dolls,** and the **mummy of an 8-year-old girl.** The second is an oversized vault containing Rome's greatest **numismatic collection.** It traces Italian coinage from ancient Roman Republic monies through the pocket change of Imperial Rome, medieval Italian empires, and Renaissance principalities to the Italian lira, the euro, and a computer live feed of the Italian stock exchange.

Museo Nazionale Romano (National Roman Museum)—Terme di Diocleziano (Baths of Diocletian). Viale Enrico E. Nicola 78. ☎ **06-3996-7700.** Admission 8,000L ($4) adults, 4,000L ($2) students. Tues–Sun 9am–7:45pm. Last ticket sold an hour before closing. Bus: 60, 61, 62, 136, 137. Metro: Repubblica.

In mid-2000, the Baths of Diocletian finally opened. This massive complex was the largest of all the bath complexes in Rome—twice the size of the Baths of Caracalla and capable of accommodating 3,000 people at any given time. A rectangular area of 376m by 361m (1,234 by 1,184 feet, an entire residential block) was razed for its construction, taking advantage of the abundance of water converging here from three of the city's aqueducts. After over a year of sporadic and interminable closings, the Baths of Diocletian inaugurate the National Antiquities arm of the National Museum, a coherent exhibit on the foundations of Rome. Many new rooms have been unveiled, including those displaying artifacts never before seen by the public, with medals, funerary items, mosaics, and paintings.

Museo Nazionale Romano (National Roman Museum)—Aula Ottagona. Via G. Romita 3 (entrance between Piazza della Repubblica and the tourist office on Via Parigi). ☎ **06-488-0530.** Admission free. Tues–Sun 9am–7:45pm. Bus: 60, 61, 62, 136, 137. Metro: Repubblica.

Flanking the Baths of Diocletian is the Octagonal Hall, whose rectangular exterior camouflages the domed geometric interior—perfect for the planetarium installed here in the 1920s. The hall probably connected the complex's gardens and open-air gymnasium with the caldarium and is now ringed with statues that came from various bath complexes around the empire. Look for the 2nd-century *Lyceum Apollo* found near the Baths of Trajan here in Rome; the 1st-century *Aphrodite of Cyrene,* a Hellenistic work from Libya; and two magnificent bronze figures, *The Boxer,* signed by Appollonius from Athens, and *The Prince,* whose pose is identical to Lysippos's *Alexander the Great.*

THE AVENTINE & SOUTH

Terme di Caracalla (Baths of Caracalla). Via delle Terme di Caracalla 52.
☎ **06-575-8626.** Admission 8,000L ($4); guided visit in Italian 2,000L ($1). May 2–Oct
Tues–Sun 9am–7:30pm; Nov–Jan 15 Tues–Sun to 4:30pm; Jan 16–Feb 15 Tues–Sun to 5pm;
Feb 16–Mar 15 to 5:30pm. Year-round Mon 9am–2pm. Bus: 628, 760. Metro: Circo Massimo.

Public baths complexes were meant to exercise the minds and the bodies of ancient
Roman citizens. These built by Emperor Caracalla in A.D. 212 could hold up to 1,600
bathers at a time and are among the largest to survive from the Imperial age. The plan
of the visit changes regularly as sections close for restoration, but you usually start
where the ancient bathers did, in the *palestra* (gym). After your exercises, you pro-
ceeded to the *laconicum* (Turkish bath) to scrape your sweaty body clean, then move
on to the boiling hot *caldarium,* followed by a spell soaking in the lukewarm *tepidar-
ium,* and finally a pore-closing dip in the cold waters of the *frigidarium.* After this you
could get a rub down, continue to the open-air *natatio* (swimming pool), or visit the
onsite library or art gallery.

San Paolo Fuori le Mura (St. Paul Outside the Walls). Viale di San Paolo/Via Ostiense.
☎ **06-541-0341.** Admission free. Daily 7:30am–6pm (cloisters close 1–3pm). Metro: San
Paolo.

Another of Rome's four grand pilgrimage basilicas, St. Paul Outside the Walls burned
down in 1873, but it has been faithfully reconstructed using as many elements as possible from the original. The **Byzantine doors,** with 11th-century incised bronze panels, were badly damaged in the fire but survived to be preserved on the inside of the
west wall, between the central and south portals. The altar is said to mark the spot of
St. Paul's burial (a 1st-century tomb discovered beneath seems to support this tradition), and sheltering the altar is a late-13th-century *ciborium* by Arnolfo di Cambio.
Nearby is a weird, giant **marble candlestick** carved in the 12th century with a whirl
of medieval scenes. The restored **apse mosaics** were executed by Venetian craftsmen
in the 1220s. The one part of the church to survive the fire almost intact is still its
greatest draw, the lovely early-13th-century ✪ **cloisters,** whose columns are a cornucopia of variety, many twisted or paired and inlaid with gems, mosaics, or colored
marble chips in glittering patterns.

TRASTEVERE

Santa Maria in Trastevere. Piazza Santa Maria in Trastevere. ☎ **06-581-9443.** Admission
free. Daily 8am–12:30pm and 4–7pm. Bus: H, tram 8, 280.

Rome's oldest church dedicated to the Virgin was established before A.D. 337 on the
site of an inn where a well of olive oil sprang from the floor at the precise moment
Christ was born (look for this detail in the mosaics of the apse inside). The current
structure was raised in 1140, with a Romanesque bell tower and a 12th- to 13th-
century facade mosaic (lit at night) of the Madonna and 10 women. The interior preserves a gorgeous Cosmatesque-like *opus sectile* floor, 21 columns pilfered from nearby
ancient buildings, and a 1617 wood ceiling by Domenichino.

   Filling the apse are some of Rome's most beautiful mosaics, the half dome pictur-
ing *Christ and the Madonna* (1140) and, below that, six scenes from the *Life of the
Virgin* by Pietro Cavallini (1291). These show the artist's remarkable use of color
tones and foreshortening to create depth and facility with expressing character psychology and story line. (Cavallini was really the only artist in Rome who, as a slightly
earlier contemporary of Florence's Giotto, was helping break art from its static Byzantine traditions to plunge it into a vibrant proto-Renaissance mode.)

Santa Cecilia in Trastevere. Piazza di Santa Cecilia 22. ☎ **06-589-9289.** Admission to church free; excavations and crypt 4,000L ($2); donation expected for Cavallini fresco. Sun–Tues and Thurs–Fri 8am–6pm, Wed and Sat 4–6pm; Cavallini fresco Sun 10am–noon, Tues and Thurs 10–11:30am. Bus: H, tram 8, 44, 280.

The bland 18th-century interior of this convent church hides the fact that it dates from 824 and contains not only one of the greatest frescoes from late medieval Rome but also the ruins of a Roman patrician house beneath. It was ostensibly the home of St. Cecilia, killed in A.D. 230 for political reasons and—since the Roman prosecutors used her practice of the illegal cult of Christianity as the chief accusation against her—an early martyr.

The mosaic **apse** dates from the 9th century, when Pope Paschal I rebuilt the church and brought Cecilia's body from the catacombs to rebury her beneath the altar. Under the present **altar,** with its Guido Reni painting and beautiful Arnolfo di Cambio *baldacchino* (1283), lies Stefano Maderno's touching 17th-century statue of *St. Cecilia.* Maderno was on hand to make sketches when Cardinal Sfondrati opened the saint's tomb in 1599, and they found Cecilia perfectly preserved under a gold funeral shroud. The cut across her neck tells of her famous martyrdom: After locking her in her own steam room for 3 days failed to do her in—indeed, Cecilia came out singing, for which she later was declared the patron saint of music—the executioners tried decapitating her. The three allowed strokes of the axe failed to finish the job, however, and Cecilia held on for another 3 days, slowly bleeding to death and converting hundreds with her show of piety (and this obvious evidence of the power of the God protecting her).

You can descend to those **Roman ruins** beneath the church, but be sure afterward to ask the nun on duty if you can please see the *affreschi di Cavallini* (if no one is on duty, ring the bell at the door on the left aisle; you'll have to bribe the nun a few thousand lire to walk you up to the frescoes). The 18th-century interior redecorators slapped plaster over most of the bottom half of Cavallini's masterful ✪ *Last Judgment* on the entrance wall but had to leave room for a large built-in balcony so the cloistered nuns could attend mass unseen. In doing so, they unintentionally preserved the fresco's top half, and what remains here of Christ, the angels, and apostles is stunning. Cavallini painted this in 1293 in a magnificent break from formulaic Byzantine painting. For the first time, each character has a unique face and personality, and all are highly modeled with careful shading and color gradients.

Villa Farnesina. Via della Lungara 230. ☎ **06-6880-1767** or 06-683-8831. Admission 6,000L ($3) adults, 4,000L ($2) ages 14–18. Mon–Sat 9am–1pm. Bus: 280.

Baldassare Peruzzi built this modestly sized but sumptuously decorated villa for banking mogul Agostino Chigi from 1508 to 1511. Chigi loved to show off his vast wealth and had good taste in artists, so he hired Raphael, Sodoma, and Peruzzi to decorate the interior of his new villa. The room off the ground-floor loggia has a ceiling painted by Peruzzi with Chigi's horoscope symbols, lunettes by Sebastiano del Piombo with scenes from Ovid's *Metamorphosis,* and the ✪ *Trionfo di Galatea (Triumph of Galatea)* by Raphael (a perfectly composed Renaissance fresco depicting the nymph and her friends attempting to flee on the backs of pug-nosed dolphins from their mermen admirers). The ceiling in the **Loggia di Psiche (Loggia of Psyche)** is frescoed as an open pergola of flowers and fruit framing scenes from the myth of Psyche, a woman so beautiful Cupid himself fell in love with her. The fresco cycle was executed between 1510 and 1517 (restored in the 1990s) by Raphael's students Giulio Romano, Raffaellino del Colle, and Francesco Penni.

In the grand **Sala delle Prospettive (Hall of Perspectives)** upstairs, Peruzzi frescoed every inch of the walls to masterfully carry trompe l'oeil to its extremes and allow Chigi to glimpse an imagined world of Roman countryside and cityscapes between the painted marble columns of a (fake) open loggia. Even with the frescoes faded by time, Peruzzi's painterly and architectural tricks create a pretty convincing optical illusion. Notice how, from the correct angles, the room's real flooring and coffered ceiling are continued into the painted space with perfect perspective. The imperial army of Charles V, sacking the city in 1527, didn't seem to have much respect for this talent, scratching into the frescoes' plaster antipapal epithets in Gothic German script and signing their names and in one place the date (at the time, it was vandalous graffiti; time has turned it into a precious historic record to be preserved behind Plexiglas shields). The small **bedchamber** off this room was frescoed with a delightful scene of the *Wedding Night of Alexander the Great* by Sodoma.

Galleria Nazionale di Palazzo Corsini (National Gallery of Palazzo Corsini). Via della Lungara 10. ☎ **06-6880-2323.** Admission 8,000L ($4) adults. Tues–Thurs and Sat 9am–7pm, Fri to 2pm, Sun to 1pm. Bus: 280.

This 15th-century palace houses the original half of Rome's National Gallery of paintings (the other half is in the Palazzo Barberini, above). The paintings are hung for space rather than composition, but search out especially Murillo's *Madonna and Child,* Caravaggio's *St. John the Baptist,* a **triptych** by Fra' Angelico, and Guido Reni's *Salome with the Head of St. John the Baptist.* Also be on the lookout for fine works by Andrea del Sarto, Rubens, Van Dyck, Joos van Cleve, Guercino, and Luca Giordano.

ROME'S PARKS & GARDENS

Rome's greatest central slice of nature is the **Villa Borghese** park, 226 acres of gardens, statue- and bust-lined paths, fountains, and artificial lakes containing a biopark zoo, three top museums (reviewed above), and the 19th-century Pincio Gardens rising above Piazza del Popolo. The grand park is truly a breath of fresh air in an otherwise polluted city, especially now that the transverse roads have been closed to motor traffic. You can rent bikes, paddleboat on the small lake (there's a tiny 19th-century Greek-style temple on a mini-island), and take the kids to the newly revamped zoological biopark (see "Especially for Kids," below).

Rising above Trastevere, south of the Vatican, is a long ridge paralleling the Tiber called the **Gianicolo (Janiculum),** famously *not* one of the Seven Hills of Rome. There are a few sights up here, but the most attractive feature is simply the sweeping ✪ **view of Rome across the river,** taking in everything from the Pincio Gardens on the left past the domes of the city center beyond the curve of the Colosseum on the right. This panorama is thrilling by day and beautiful by night, when the Gianicolo doubles as Rome's Lover's Lane (lots of steamy Fiat windows and lip-locked lovers stationed every 10 feet along the walls).

Toward the Gianicolo's southerly end is the **Acqua Paolo fountain,** a gargantuan 17th-century basin and fountain made from marble taken from the Forum that serves as both the outlet for Trajan's aqueduct and the requisite backdrop for all Roman newlyweds' wedding photos.

ESPECIALLY FOR KIDS

Kids are bound to tire out well before you, becoming ornery and just plain bored. Pace yourselves and keep up the kids' interest with breaks, picnics, a few sights just for them (more on that in a minute), and generous amounts of yummy gelato.

There are several sights that seem to fire children's enthusiasm and imagination more than others. Some favorites (see above for details) are the arms and armor collection in **Castel Sant'Angelo** (okay, it's a boy thing), the gruesome bone montages of the **Capuchin Crypt,** the miles of subterranean passages of the **catacombs,** the **Mouth of Truth,** the **mummies** in the Egyptian wing of the Vatican, some of the **fountains** and **statues** like Bernini's baby elephant obelisk, and the exploreable ruins of the **Roman Forum** and **Trajan's Markets.** And few people, regardless of age, aren't seriously impressed by the **Colosseum** and the **Sistine Chapel.**

Part of an international initiative that began with the 1899 foundation of the Children's Museum of Brooklyn is the at-press-time opening of the **Museo dei Bambini (Children's Museum),** Via Flaminio 80, a stimulating interactive learning environment geared to kids 3 to 12. The complex is even constructed of recycled and recyclable materials. For further information, contact the Associazione Museo dei Bambini at ☎ **06/361-3741** or log onto the Web at www.mdbr.it. Several museums have separate spaces or programs for kids, with audiocassette guides recorded for them and pamphlets so they can follow along. The **Museo Barracco,** Corso Vittorio Emanuele II 158, highlights the sculpture collection in the Egyptian, Mesopotamian, and Greek rooms for 6- and 7-year-old historians; the **Museo della Civiltà Romana** (above) prepares tours for 8- and 9-year-olds; and the **Pinacoteca Capitoline** (above) gears its tours to kids 10 to 12. For information, contact the **Colleo del Museo** at ☎ **06-3908-0730.** For a more hands-on experience, the **Villa Giulia** runs a didactic kids' program that includes a simulation of an archaeological dig and a ceramic laboratory. Visits are by reservation, so contact the **Organizzazione Cooperativo Arte in Gioco** at ☎ **06-4423-9949.** Other kid-oriented events are run independently or in conjunction with one of the organizations above (sometimes at the **Galleria Borghese** or the **Museii Capitolini**); the **Comune di Roma** puts out a periodic brochure with a calendar of events, available at any tourist information kiosk.

The **Villa Borghese** park is good for kids of all ages. There are facilities for renting bikes, a merry-go-round on the Pincio, and paddleboats on the Giardino del Lago: Also here is the renovated **Bioparco,** Piazzale del Giardino Zoologico 1 (☎ **06-360-8211**), which has been retooled from a zoo of cages to a biological garden of natural habitat enclosures that primarily house endangered species and injured animals that are being rehabilitated to return to the wild. It has become a teaching zoo, with placards at each enclosure that show via pictograms what threats the animal faces in the wild (climate changes, pollution, habitat destruction, hunting); the bears, wolves, lions, and apes are especially popular. Admission is 10,000L ($5) adults or 7,000L ($3.50) ages 6 to 12. It's open daily 9:30am to 7pm (to 5pm November to February).

The **Gianicolo (Janiculum Hill)** offers great city panoramas, a merry-go-round, and on Piazzale del Gianicolo the ✪ **Teatrino di Pulcinella al Gianicolo** (☎ **06-582-7767** or 0349-170-6874), an open-air puppet theater showing the Neapolitan hand-puppet Pulcinella (Punch, of Punch and Judy fame). Shows of this traditional Italian entertainment currently run daily between 3 and 8pm (whenever enough kids show up; *always* call ahead for times) and Sundays at 3:30 and 6:30pm. It's free, but you're welcome to leave a donation. Get there any day at noon for the sounding of the Janiculum cannon.

ORGANIZED TOURS

Enjoy Rome, Via Marghera 8/a (☎ **06-445-1843** or 06-445-6890; fax 06-445-0734; www.enjoyrome.com; e-mail: info@enjoyrome.com; Metro: Termini), has a young staff from various English-speaking countries who run both 3-hour **walking tours** (maximum 15 to 20 people; those of Ancient Rome and Rome at Night run daily, those of the Vatican about three times weekly) and daily 4-hour **bike tours** (bike and helmet included; maximum 10 people). Walking tours cost 30,000L ($15) adults or 25,000L ($13) if you're under 26; bike tours (including the bike) cost 35,000L ($18).

For 15,000L ($8), city-run **ATAC bus 110** (☎ **06-4695-2252**) offers a 2½-hour circuit of the major sights whose primary down side is that you get only 15 minutes to explore the Colosseum and the Vatican. The hostesses provide you with an explanatory leaflet. The Jubilee Year schedule of half-hourly departures from outside Stazione Termini may be scaled back in 2001 and beyond to the former schedule of 10:30am and 2, 3, 5, and 6pm; check with the tourist office or anywhere tickets are sold. ATAC also offers a 3-hour tour of **Rome's major basilicas** (Linea delle Basiliche), also at 15,000L. Tours leave from Stazione Termini at 10am and 2.30pm, with stops at St. Peter's (20 min), San Paolo fuori le Mura (15 min.), and San Giovanni in Laterano (15 min.). Tickets are sold daily 9am to 7pm at the ATAC kiosk on Piazza dei Cinquecento in front of Termini, at the ATAC kiosk near Platform C (cash or credit), or on the bus (cash only; surcharge applies).

A number of other organizations offer hop on/hop off tours, the most economical being **Stop 'n' go City Tours** (☎ **06-321-7054**), with 9 departures daily and 14 selected stops. The hostesses are multilingual, and the cost for a day is 20,000L ($10; discounts available for multiple days). Buses leave from Stazione Termini. The **Ciao Roma Trolley Tour** (☎ **06-474-3795**); charges 30,000L ($15), with a 5,000L ($2.50) discount per person if you begin your tour after 1:30pm. There are five departures daily to 11 points of interest around the city, including the Galleria Borghese, and you get a headset with recorded explanations of the sites.

If you want live commentary, you'll have to pony up at least 60,000L ($30) to **American Express,** Piazza di Spagna 38 (☎ **06-6764-2413**), for its 4-hour introductory tours, which depart at 9:30am and/or 2:30pm daily, depending on the season. One tour gives a general overview of all Rome and the Vatican and the other focuses mainly on ancient Rome.

6 Shopping

THE SHOPPING SCENE

Rome's **best buys** are in antiquities, high fashion, wine, ecclesiastical knickknacks, designer housewares, and flea-market bargains.

The capital's toniest boutique zone radiates out from the **Spanish Steps,** centered on the matriarch of high-fashion streets, **Via dei Condotti.** Condotti runs arrow-straight from the base of the steps and has become rather too famous for its own good, sprouting such downscale abominations as a Footlocker and other international chain outlets. This zone is bounded by **Via del Corso,** ground zero for Rome's most fashionable see-and-be-seen *passeggiata* evening stroll. It too is lined with generally expensive bigger stores—great for window shopping, but if you're looking for bargain prices, head to **Via Nazionale** and **Via del Tritone.**

Via dei Coronari, running west off the north end of Piazza Navona, has always been the heart of Rome's antiques district. Almost every address here is a dealer or restorer, and many of their wares or works-in-progress spill out onto the narrow cobbled street. For art, the highest concentration of dealers and studios lies along **Via Margutta,** a side street parallel to Via del Babuino.

But while the locals do turn out to *passeggiata* on the Corso and window shop on Via dei Condotti, the actual shopping in these parts is pretty touristy. To Romans, the true shopping nexus of the city is the upper-middle-class residential zone of **Prati,** just northeast of Vatican, with the economic activity centered on wide **Via Cola di Rienzo.** Here you'll find generally lower prices, more down-to-earth stores, and a much better opportunity to see how the citizens of Rome really live and shop.

SHOPPING A TO Z

ANTIQUITIES   How much is a Grecian urn? Well, if you have to ask, you can't afford it. Pieces cost anywhere from 200,000L to 9,500,000L ($100 to $4,750) at **M. Simotti Rocchi,** Largo Fontanella Borghese 76 (☎ 06-687-6656), a dealer in Etruscan, Greek, and Roman antiquities. That cheapest painted vase would be a 4-inch piece from the ancient equivalent of a child's tea set. Here you can pick up Roman coins, tiny terra-cotta ex-voto heads, or oil lamps starting at 150,000L ($75). Marble statues can cost up to 150,000,000L ($7,500)—still, it's about one-third the price you'd find at Sotheby's in New York or London.

For lower prices, visit **Gea Arte Antica,** Via dei Coronari 233A (☎ 06-6880-1369), where small oil lamps go for as little as 120,000L to 200,000L ($60 to $100)—though the more nicely decorated ones, not to mention larger vases, start around 900,000L ($450). If you'd prefer to wear your classical acquisitions, check out **Massimo Maria Melis,** under "Jewelry," below.

BOOKS   Among the better English-language bookstores are the venerable **Lion Bookshop and Cafe,** Via dei Greci 33–36 (☎ 06-3265-4007); the large **Anglo-American,** beyond the Spanish Steps at Via della Vite 102 (☎ 06-679-5222); and the even larger **Economy Bookshop,** Via Torino 136 (☎ 06-474-6877), which also offers a wide selection of cheap, used paperbacks and a free "Rome Travel Pack" with map and guides to the city's services.

Italy's version of Barnes & Noble is the Feltrinelli chain, and you'll find a wide selection of books in English at the huge **Feltrinelli International,** Via V. E. Orlando 84–86, off Piazza della Repubblica (☎ 06-487-0999; www.feltrinelli.it). Other branches are at Largo di Torre Argentina 5A (☎ 06-6880-3248), Via del Babuino 49–40 (☎ 06-3600-1873), and next door to the "International" one at Via V. E. Orlando 78–81 (☎ 06-487-0171).

Remainders, Piazza San Silvestro 27–28 (☎ 06-679-2824), is what the name says—a shop selling overstock books up to 50% off, including lots of glossy art and coffee-table books. **La Grotta del Libro,** Via del Pellegrino 172 (☎ 06-687-7567), and **Libreria Vecchia Roma,** Via del Pellegrino 94, both look like garages piled to the ceiling with books, advertising even cheaper coffee-table books at 50% to 80% off, but not as consistent a selection. **Le Pleiadi Librerie,** Via del Giubbaonari 76–77 (☎ 06-6880-7981), is classier, with a wider selection of recently printed books on art and the city of Rome up to 50% off. Also don't miss the **antiquarian book and print market** on Piazza Borghese, with good deals on dated art books as well as spiffy Roman prints. And the **Libreria Babele,** Via dei Bianchi Vecchi 116 (☎ 06-687-6628; Bus: 46, 62, 64, 80, 116, 116T), is Rome's most central all-gay/lesbian bookstore.

DEPARTMENT STORES   Italy's top two chains are a bit pricey. In Rome, the designer label–driven **La Rinascente,** Via del Corso/Piazza San Silvestro (☎ 06-679-7691), is set apart by its cover-all-bases selection, English-language information and tax-free shopping desk, and central location in its own 19th-century high rise. **Coin,** Piazzale Appio 7 (☎ 06-708-0020; Metro: San Giovanni), has recently been muscling in on La Rinascente territory by going more upscale in look and attitude, with stylish displays of upper-middle-class fashions—a chic Macy's.

For more everyday shopping, head to **Standa,** at Viale Trastevere 62–64 (☎ **06-589-5342**) and Via Cola di Rienzo 173 (☎ **06-324-3319**), where Italians buy their socks and underwear. It runs back-to-school specials and carries bulk dish detergent, frying pans, lamps, cake mix, and other everyday items and clothes—an upscale Kmart with a supermarket in the basement. **Upim,** Piazza di Santa Maria Maggiore (☎ **06-446-5579**), is another national chain that's just slightly above Standa.

DESIGN & HOUSEWARES Italians are masters of industrial design, making the most utilitarian items into memorable art pieces. Rather than a percolator, they create the Pavoni espresso machine, and a lowly teapot becomes a whimsical Alessi master-piece the MoMA is proud to display.

In a teeny storefront in Trastevere is **Azi,** Via San Francesco a Ripa 170 (☎ **06-588-3303**), selling household items with more emphasis on form than function. If you're willing to fork over lots of lire or just want to browse among the bounty, check out **Spazio Sette,** Via dei Barbieri 7 off Largo di Torre Argentina (☎ **06-686-9747**), Rome's slickest housewares emporium. It goes way beyond the requisite Alessi tea kettles to fill three huge stories with the greatest names and latest word in Italian and international design. Even if you aren't in the market for the living-room furnishings on the top floor, climb up anyway to gawk at the frescoed ceilings. Another good bet is **Bagagli,** Via Cam. Marzio 42 (☎ **06-687-1406**), with a dis-count section in back. You'll find a good selection of Alessi, Rose and Tulipani, and Villeroy & Boch china in a pleasantly kitschy old Rome setting (cobblestone floors and so on).

Bargain hunters should head to one of **Stock Market's** two branches: Via dei Banchi Vecchi 51–52 (☎ **06-686-4238**) and Via Tacito 60 near the Vatican (☎ **06-3600-2343**). You'll find mouthwatering prices on last year's models, over-stock, slight irregulars, and artistic misadventures that the pricier boutiques haven't been able to move. Most is moderately funky household stuff, but you never know when you'll find a gem of design hidden on the shelves. If the big names don't do it for you, you may prefer **c.u.c.i.n.a.,** Via dei Babuino 118A (no phone), a stainless-steel shrine to everything you need for a proper Italian kitchen, sporting designs that are as beautiful in their simplicity as they are utilitarian.

DISCOUNT FASHION Rome has several stock houses selling last year's fashions, irregulars, and overstock at cut-rate prices. One of the best is **Il Discount dell'Alta Moda,** with branches at Via di Gesù e Maria 16A near the Spanish Steps (☎ **06-361-3796**) and Via Viminale 35 near Stazione Termini (☎ **06-482-3917**). The selection of such labels as Versace, Donna Karan, Armani, Dolce & Gabbana, Venturi, Krizia, and Ferré shifts constantly, with prices that are still inflated at up to 50% off. Both men's and women's clothing are sold, plus accessories and outerwear.

Firmastock, Via delle Carrozze 18 (☎ **06-6920-0371**), carries everything from Levi's and Hugo Boss to Valentino, Armani, and Max Mara at 50% to 70% off already outrageous prices. The small, eclectic, and ever-changing inventory includes men's and women's suits, dresses, overcoats, and shoes. **New Fashion,** Via Simone de Saint Bon 85–87 in Prati (☎ **06-3751-3947**), carries women's suits and skirts from top design-ers like Moschino, Valentino, Max Mara, and Dolce & Gabbana as well as lesser-known "Made in Italy" labels. The prices are higher than at the other stock houses listed here, but the discounts are honest and the outfits tend to be more consistently fashionable.

FOOD Rome's top food emporium—after the fresh **food markets** around town—is undoubtedly **Castroni,** a legend since 1932 with the main shop at Via Cola di

Rienzo 196 in Prati (☎ **06-687-4383**) and an offspring store at Via Flaminio 28–32 just north of Piazza del Popolo (☎ **06-361-1029**). Castroni carries a stupefying collection of the best foods, both fine and common, from around the world, including such exotic concoctions as peanut butter and Vegemite. Next door to the main Castroni is **Franchi,** Via Cola di Rienzo 204 (☎ **06-687-4651;** www.franchi.it), a more traditional Italian-style *alimentari.* The excellent prepared foods include *calzoni fritti* and *calzoni al forno* (fried and baked versions of pizza pockets wrapped around cheese and ham)—the best in town by a long shot, with the daily long lines awaiting their appearance at 5pm to prove it.

Romans come from all over town and the 'burbs to buy their cheeses and milk products from among the fantastic selection at **Latteria Micocci,** Via Collina 16 (☎ **06-474-1784**). For some offbeat food shopping in Trastevere, hit **Drogheria Innocenzi,** Piazza San Cosimato 66 (☎ **06-581-2725**), an old-fashioned bit-of-everything grocery store with a newfangled eclectic stock. Part natural health food emporium, part gourmet international foods store, and part medieval spice shop, it's the only place I've ever been able to find all the odd ingredients called for by the recipes in Apicius's ancient Roman cookbook.

GIFTS   I've always thought that the greatest Roman gifts come from the combination of kitschy and holier-than-thou **Vatican gift shops** and souvenir stands encircling St. Peter's and the Vatican. You'll find everything from a light-up plastic Michelangelo's *Pietà,* pictures showing a smiling Christ from one angle and a crucified one from another, and models of the Virgin Mary that weep on command to your-name-here papal indulgences and even a "pope-ener" (an anthropomorphic corkscrew—by twisting the medallion printed with the pope's head, you cause his "arms" to raise slowly in benediction).

For singular timepieces, visit **Guaytamelli,** Via del Moro 59 in Trastevere (☎ **06-588-0704**), where Argentinean Adrian Rodriguez crafts beautiful hour candles, hourglasses, and sundials in the form of rings, sticks, pendants, and flip-top boxes—all of quality workmanship at rather low prices (from 15,000L/$8 for a sundial ring). There's even a tiny flat pendant sextant; turn the sandwich of engraved disks until they align with the stars and it'll tell you the time at night. A bit more discreet are the delectable coffee accessories at **Caffé Sant'Eustachio,** Piazza Sant'Eustachio 82 (☎ **06-686-1309**), at prices so surprisingly low you'll have to ask twice (an elegant espresso set for six only 35,000L/$18).

JEWELRY   For traditional pieces, **Tresor,** Via della Croce 71B–72 (☎ **06-687-7753**), crafts classically worked 18-karat gold jewelry at prices not much higher than the market value of the raw material. At **Massimo Maria Melis,** Via dell'Orso 57 (☎ **06-686-9188**), 21-karat gold is hand-worked to encase genuine coins and pieces of glass or carved stone from the Etruscan, Roman, and medieval eras. A pair of earrings set with Imperial Roman coins will set you back about 500,000L ($250).

MARKETS   The mother lode of Roman bazaars is **Porta Portese,** a flea market off Piazza Ippolito Nievo that began at the close of World War II as a black and gray market but has grown to be one of Europe's premier garage sales. You'll find everything from antique credenzas to used carburetors, bootleg CDs to birds that squawk "Ciao," previously owned clothes to Italian comic books to used Leicas, all in a carnival atmosphere of haggling and hollering, jostling and junk jockeying, beggars, pickpockets, and shrewd stall owners, swirling around auditory pockets of badly dubbed dance music and the scents of sweet roasting corn. It runs every Sunday dawn to lunchtime. Hang on to your wallet.

Snuggled up along a stretch of the Aurelian Wall off Via Sannio are the half-covered stalls of the **San Giovanni clothing market,** the best place to pick up inexpensive new and cut-rate used clothing (or cheap army surplus in case you need an extra pack, sleeping bag, or tent) and outfit yourself like a true Roman. It runs Monday to Friday 10am to 1pm and Saturday 10am to 5pm.

Campo de' Fiori, once the site of medieval executions, is today one of Rome's most lively squares. This cobblestone expanse starts bustling in the pre-dawn hours as the florists arrange bouquets of flowers and fruit and vegetable vendors set up their stalls, imbuing the piazza with a burst and swirl of color and scents. The lively workaday life winds down after lunch, but the piazza reanimates later in the evening with adolescent Romans and tourists in a carnival of dining and nightlifing.

MUSIC   Italy's biggest chain of record stores is **Ricordi,** with major branches in Rome at Via del Corso 506 (☎ **06-361-2370**), Via C. Battisti 120D (☎ **06-679-8022**), and on Piazza Indipendenza (☎ **06-444-0706**). All have a wide selection of Italian and international music and listening stations, as well as the definitive collection of books and classical scores. For a good selection of used and new CDs, tapes, and vinyl, visit **Millerecords** (☎ **06-495-8242**), with two shops on Via dei Mille at no. 29 (jazz, rock, and pop) and no. 41 (classical). For underground selections, all the Italian DJ's head to **Goody Music,** Via Cesare Beccaria 2 (☎ **06-361-0959**). The latest British and American independent releases are at **Disfunzioni Musicali,** Via degli Etruschi 4–14 (☎ **06-446-1984**), just a few steps from the university.

SHOES & ACCESSORIES   Unless you're shopping for plastic shoes, much of the good stuff gets exported or sold here at prices weighted down by more zeros than you'd care to write a check out for. For middle of the range footwear, the **Bati** chain keeps up with the trends but not inflation. Two of the more centrally located stores are at Via Nazionale 88A and at Via due Macelli 45.

For classically inspired and beautifully crafted shoes, sandals, and half-boots starting around 300,000L ($150), check out the boutique of **Fausto Santini,** Via Frattina 120 (☎ **06-678-4114**). It also does purses and bags along clean modernist lines. If you like Santini's style but not the prices, head to Via Cavour 106 (☎ **06-488-0934**), the designer's discount outlet for last year's models at 100,000L to 200,000L ($50 to $100) and remainders at 20,000L to 70,000L ($10 to $35).

Want a wider range of accessories at stock shop prices? **Il Discount delle Firme,** on the tiny road off Largo del Tritone called Via dei Serviti 27 (☎ **06-482-7790**), carries perfumes, purses, ties, scarves, shoes, wallets, and belts from all the top names (and a few lesser-known Italian designers) at 50% off. Near the Vatican, your best bet is **Grandi Firme,** Via Germanico 8 (☎ **06-3972-3169**), with a rotating accessory stock of purses, ties, belts, scarves, and shoes also up to 50% off from names like Fendi, Dior, Missoni, and Ferré.

If you want to hook yourself up with one of those colorful **Invicta** backpacks that seem a required part of every school uniform for Italian students from kindergarten through grad school, visit their showroom at Via del Babuino 27–28 (☎ **06-3600-1737**).The **Standa** and **Upim** chains also carry these knapsacks, generally in the kid's section.

TOYS   Rome's best toy store is **La Città del Sole,** Via della Scrofa 65 (☎ **06-6880-3805**). Since 1977, this owner-operated branch of the national chain has sold old-fashioned wooden brainteasers, construction kits, hand puppets, 3-D puzzles, and science kits. There's even a tot's book section in case you want to start junior on his Italian early. These are the sorts of toys that, while being gobs of fun, also help youngsters (and some adults) push and stretch their minds, encouraging creativity and imagination.

For slightly more mass-market toys—but still fantastic and largely European-made—visit one of the **Giorni** branches in Prati. At Via dei Gracchi 31–33 (☎ **06-321-7145**), you'll find only models, from build-it-yourself to ready out of the box, including the Bburago series of cast-metal cars. The softer side is at Via M. Colonna 26 (☎ **06-321-6929**), where you'll find dolls, stuffed animals, and music boxes. For a more general selection, visit the Via Pompeo Magno 86 shop (☎ **06-321-3540**), where the playthings are appropriate for ages up to 10, or head next door to Via Pompeo Magno 84 (☎ **06-321-4736**), the toy outlet "for ages 8 to 99."

WINE & LIQUOR   Rome's most peculiar inebriatory experience has to be **Ai Monasteri,** off the north corner of Piazza Navona at Piazza   Cinque Lune 76 (☎ **06-6880-2783**). Here are gathered the liqueurs, elixirs, *digestivi,* extracts, apéritifs, and other alcoholic ingestibles that are concocted by industrious monks at various monasteries, abbeys, and convents across Italy. Sort of a central outlet shop for the country's collective monastic liquor cabinet/organic shop (it deals in soaps and oils too).

The granddaddy of Rome's wine stores is **Trimani,** Via Goito 20 (☎ **167-014-625** toll free or 06-446-8351), a family business since 1821 with literally thousands of bottles in a huge shop and even more in the cellars. This place ain't cheap, but it isn't unreasonable either. You'll find plenty of quaffable stuff for under 10,000L ($5)—you just have to search it out between lots of classy, aged, high-profile bottles that can easily run upwards of 200,000L ($100).

La Vecchia Cantina, Via Viminale 7B (☎ **06-460-737**), is a good spot to pick up a cheap but decent bottle of *vino* for that picnic. For more atmosphere and selection, try the **Enoteca al Parlamento,** Via Prefetti 15 (☎ **06-687-3446**), a stylish and old-fashioned wood-lined wine emporium where you rub shoulders with politicians and other business suits as you sample wine by the glass at the counter and choose from the select stock, which also includes liqueurs, champagnes, honeys, and marmalades. Another historic wine shop is **Buccone,** Via di Ripetta 19–20 (☎ **06-361-2154**), with a selection so enormous it covers selections of cheap Valpolicella as well as the wines costing upwards to 1,000,000L ($500).

7 Rome After Dark

True Roman nightlife consists of lingering over a full restaurant meal until after midnight, with lots of good wine and good conversation among friends. For a more culturally related evening or a late night of bar hopping, check out the listings below and the events guides described under "Newspapers & Magazines" in "Fast Facts," earlier in this chapter.

THE PERFORMING ARTS

CLASSICAL MUSIC   Always check the events listings for information about concerts being held in Rome's medieval and baroque churches and, in summer especially, outdoor evening performances in evocative, archaeological settings surrounded by ancient columns and ruins.

One of Italy's premier musical associations, the **Accademia Nazionale di Santa Cecilia,** finally has a permanent seat at the **Auditorio,** Via della Concilliazione 4 (☎ **06-6880-1044,** 06-361-1064 for the Via Vittoria 6 office; or 06-3938-7297 for tickets). The season runs October to May, with symphonic concerts Saturdays to Tuesdays and soloist and ensemble chamber music Fridays. In summer, there are outdoor concerts in the Villa Giulia's theatrical *nymphaeum.*

The **Accademia Filarmonica Romana,** which performs in the **Teatro Olimpico** north of the center at Piazza Gentile da Fabriano 17 (☎ **06-323-4890** or 06-3938-7297 for tickets), was founded in 1821 and puts on Thursday concerts October to June that range from chamber music and classical hits to folk and ethnic music. The Accademia also hosts international ballet and dance companies. The **Orchestra Regionale del Lazio** performs at the **Teatro Nazionale,** Via Viminale 51 (☎ **06-485-494** or 06-487-0614) January to June, with a program from baroque classics to contemporary composers directed by mainly up-and-coming young Italian and international conductors and musicians.

OPERA & BALLET   After years of languishing without funding or respect, Rome's newly restored late-19th-century **Teatro dell'Opera,** Piazza Beniamino Gigli 1, at the intersection of Via Torino and Via Viminale (☎ **167-016-665** toll free, 06-481-601 office, or 06-4816-0255 box office; www.themix.it), has a new superintendent and musical director who've are attracting fine musicians, conductors, and performers for their opera and ballet seasons. The preseason runs October to December and the official season January to June. The July and August season changes venue every year, and though those high notes were causing irreparable damage to the Baths of Caracalla, resulting in a total ban from the ruins, operas are frequently held outdoors (in the Stadio Olimpico; Bus: 32 from Via Ottaviano). Tickets can go as low 25,000L ($13) or 15,000L ($8) for an outdoor event; check with the box office (closed Monday) or any Banca di Roma location (getting tickets by phone ☎ **147/882-211** is frustrating and futile).

DISCOS & NIGHTCLUBS

Romans don't necessarily like their own discos, preferring instead to pile into cars for a midnight drive to the club-king towns of **Rimini** and **Riccione** (along the Adriatic coast). Those left behind (or uninterested in the groggy wee-morning drive home) congregate in local bars, creating their own bar/discos by commandeering the floor, rather than dropping up to $20 on a night out in a club geared to hip-hop gangs with bad taste in music. **Via della Pace** near Piazza Navona is a popular nighttime strip, attracting a healthy mix of trendoids from the neighborhood as well as tourists. Bar hoppers will find plenty of hunting grounds in the neighborhoods of **Trastevere** and **San Lorenzo,** and the **Testaccio** quarter gets pretty lively after dark, with everyone's first stop at the increasingly Latin **Four XXXX Pub,** Via Galvani 29/29a (☎ **06-575-7296**), closed in August.

If you put all of Rome's nightclubs back to back, you could easily fill several football fields and definitely blow out an eardrum. Many have followed the dangerous road into hardcore techno music, so I've decided to cover only those slightly more mainstream.

Rome's attempt at a major Manhattan- or London-style disco is **Alien,** Via Velletri 13–19 (☎ **06-841-2212**), with a funky sci-fi decor in an underground garage setting, with (mainly 20-something) dancing bodies. The music is cutting edge, and on Tuesdays, it about-faces to become a New Age club. September to May, it's open Tuesday to Sunday 11pm to 4am (June and July, Friday and Saturday only). Admission is 20,000L to 30,000L ($10 to $15).

Clochard, Via del Teatro Pace 29–30 (☎ **06-6880-2029**), is a restaurant/nightclub in a 15th-century palazzo. The disco spins funk and 1970s flashback tunes and features a live band most evenings. It's open Wednesday to Saturday 8:30pm to 3:30am; the atmosphere is pretty laid back, and you have to pay only 15,000L ($8) to get in Fridays and Saturdays for that obligatory drink.

In the heart of the center is the slightly creepy **Gilda,** Via Mario de' Fiori 97 (☎ **06-678-4838**), a famous disco/nightclub patronized by a fair lot of politicians (hence the creepiness factor) but also plenty of Romans of all ages and lots of visitors, who arrive in droves to this club to act excruciatingly trendy but seemingly with no clear idea why. The admission is a scandalous 40,000L ($20) and includes a drink; September to June, it's open Tuesday to Sunday 10:30pm to 4am.

LATIN MUSIC CLUBS

Romans go crazy for Latin music, and two of the best clubs where you can enjoy it are in Trastevere. **Berimbau,** Via dei Fienaroli 30B (☎ **06-581-3249**), is a flashy and colorful South American club with a strict menu of samba and South American rhythms. There are free Latin dance lessons so you don't embarrass yourself and a DJ for dancing after the live concert. September to June, it's open 10:30pm to 3am. Including a drink, admission is 10,000L ($5) on Wednesday, Thursday, and Sunday; 15,000L ($8) on Friday; and 20,000L ($10) on Saturday. You can also get free dance lessons Tuesdays at **Bossa Nova,** Via Orti di Trastevere 23 (☎ **06-581-6121**), a Brazilian joint with live music nightly. Admission is 12,000L ($7), including a drink; September to July, it's open Tuesday to Sunday 10:30pm to 3am.

JAZZ & BLUES CLUBS

If you make time for only one jazz club, make it **Alexanderplatz,** Via Ostia 9 in Prati (☎ **06-3974-2171**), open nightly 9:30pm to 1:30am). It's Rome's only club with a heavy dose of respect on the international jazz circuit, drawing names like Winton Marsalis, Lionel Hampton, and George Coleman along with top Italian players. Meals are served starting at 9pm (not included in membership pass but reasonable), with concerts beginning at 10:30pm and lasting to 1:30am or later. In summer, it moves outside to the gardens of Villa Celimontana. It's closed Sundays, and a pass good for 2 months is 12,000L ($7).

Another solid choice for live jazz performances is the **New Mississippi Jazz Club,** Via B. Angelico 18a (☎ **06-6880-6348**), where you can hear some of Italy's top artists and the occasional American artist passing through town. It's open Thursday to Saturday 9:30pm to 2am, and the one-time admission pass is 12,000L ($7).

The Roman home of the blues is in Trastevere at **Big Mama,** Vicola San Francesco a Ripa 18 (☎ **06-581-2551**), which since 1984, has been hosting some of the world's top blues musicians when they come to Rome, sprinkling the offerings with funk and jazz as well. A monthly pass is 10,000L ($5), but the prices sometimes go up for particular shows. The music is strictly live, so it's open only when there's someone on the ticket (closed July and August; call ahead).

BARS, PUBS & *ENOTECHE*

AROUND CAMPO DE' FIORI   You'll find a full gamut of nightspots in this corner of town. The exceedingly popular but old-fashioned wine bar called **Vineria Reggio,** no. 15 (☎ **06-6880-3268**), is still holding its own amid the nightly crowds on this piazza. This spot is also known affectionately as Da Giorgio, and everyone calls in here sooner or later for decent wine by the glass from 2,000L ($1), though you can also avail yourself of the beers on tap. During the day and the early evening, it throngs with locals and historic expatriates; at night, it's a seriously hip hangout for bright young things. It's also a good place to pick up a bottle after hours.

Next door is the "casual but chic" **Taverna del Campo,** no. 16 (☎ **06-687-4402**), a crowded stop for a quick bite where it's easy to fill up unexpectedly on *crostini, panini,* or even oysters and champagne. A few more doors down, you can cool your heels to the live-DJ music (and air-conditioning) of the American-style **The Drunken Ship,** nos. 20–21 (☎ **06-6830-0535**). Off the campo itself, things chill out quickly, though if you want some understated modernist digs with cocktails, pop two blocks over to trendy **Chiavari,** Via dei Chiavari 4–5 (☎ **06-683-2378**).

NEAR PIZZA NAVONA & THE PANTHEON   Steer your beer cravings toward the basement rooms of the **Black Duke,** Via della Maddalena 29B (☎ **06-6830-0381**), an Irish pub serving pub grub just north of the Pantheon. Another lively Irish pub is the **Abbey Theatre,** Via del Governo Vecchio 51–53 (☎ **06-686-1341**), a "Guinness bar"—the Irish beer company sells prefab rustic-style pubs, complete from the woodsy decor down to the kitschy Brit paraphernalia and dart board. Even more genuine is the **St. Andrew's Pub,** Vicola della Cancelleria 36 (☎ **06-683-2638**), so Scottish it's got tartan on the walls. There's Tennent's on tap along with that excellent Edinburgh double-malt red ale Devil's Kiss and Caffrey's stout (that one's Irish, but it's still good).

The most bizarre nightspot in the area is without doubt ✪ **Jonathan's Angels,** Via della Fossa 16 (☎ **06-689-3426**), a temple to weirdo kitsch down a side street strung with Christmas lights. The owner was a circus acrobat and restaurateur before opening this funky, dark, casual bar and turning his energies to painting and sculpting. The walls are completely covered with representations of his artistic vision; note that the faces on all the portraits (even the nun) are his. If nothing else, come to use the over-the-top bathroom (where there'll inevitably be a line), complete with its own full-sized cherub fountain.

Henry's Pub, Via Tor Millinia 34a (☎ **06-686-9904**), is a pretty gross joint with outdoor seating on the heart of the action off Piazza Navona's northwest end. Beware of what you drink—there's a sangria punch bowl into which the barman dumps the leftovers from mixed drinks. Next door at no. 32 is the **Vineria La Botticella** (☎ **06-686-1107**), a little vineria cum American-style bar with Devil's Kiss on tap. Down on Piazza Sant'Andrea della Valle is the ever-popular **John Bull Pub,** Corso Vittorio Emanuele II 107 (☎ **06-687-1537**), serving John Bull ale and Strongbow cider to a mainly young crowd (lots of American students); a barroom brawl isn't an uncommon form of entertainment.

The pièce de résistance of all meat-market spots is **Trinity College,** Via del Collegio Romano, off Via del Corso near Piazza Venezia (☎ **06-678-6472**). At the very least, go here to watch stereotypically dressed American exchange students in ponytails congregating under the watchful gaze of the Mediterranean Male, while the more sexually liberated Italian girls try to intercept. They say nobody leaves here alone.

NEAR THE SPANISH STEPS & PIAZZA DEL POPOLO   Every Italian town has one bar that serves as the area's living room, and in Rome that place is the dubiously named (there's an unmentionable four-letter-word translation in there) **Bar del Fico,** Piazza del Fico 27–28 (☎ **06-686-5205**). As sure as night becomes day, by 11pm this hangout is bursting at the seams, as large groups converge, drinks in hand, to decide where that evening will take them. By day, this bar/cafeteria is a bit more mellow, serving lunch around regulars glued to a game of checkers or chess. The bar is open 8am to 3am.

The **Birreria Viennese,** Via della Croce 21 (☎ **06-679-5569**), is a Bavarian-tinged *bierhaus* with a woodsy dark interior and pretzels hanging at each table; you can order Austrian grub and beer by the liter mug. Down the block, the **Enoteca Antica di Via**

della Croce, Via della Croce 76b (☎ **06-679-0896**), is a friendly and relaxed spot; a perfect place to rest your weary shopping feet. Sort of a traditional *enoteca* gone trendy, it offers wine bar fare like salads and sampler platters of cheese and salamis along with wine by the glass, beer, and harder drinks.

A Brit expat landmark for years, the **Victoria House Pub,** Via Gesù e Maria 18 (☎ **06-320-1698**), is a genuine English pub—though most of the ale on tap is Scottish (Tennent's) or Irish (Cafferey's). Italians flock to this little corner of England, going so far as to tolerate pub grub like shepherd's pie and the no-smoking bar/sitting room at the back. If you fancy a spot of pool in a contemporary pub on a busy road near the Trevi Fountain (just before the tunnel off Piazza Trionfale), head to **The Albert,** Via del Traforo 132 (☎ **06-481-8795**).

IN TRASTEVERE   New bars and clubs open in Trastevere every month—and about half are closed by the next one. Fortunately, Trastevere seems to know no limit of critical mass when it comes to nightlife, so even the remaining half is still enough to keep you busy after hours. The following places seem here to stay. **Birreria La Scala,** Piazza della Scala 60 (☎ **06-580-3763**), is a raucous Italian-style beer hall and disco/pub. It's open to 1am and has lots of good food, snacks, and desserts, plus a decent selection of beers and wines. There's live music Tuesday, Thursday, and Sunday (preceded on Thursday and Sunday by a magic show). **Molly Malone Pub,** Via dell'Arco di San Calisto 17, near Piazza Santa Maria in Trastevere (☎ **06-5833-0904**), is more of an American bar. The ever-popular **Artú,** Largo Fumasoni Biondi 5 (no phone), is part pub, part wine bar, and part cafeteria/tea salon serving decadent homemade desserts; there's also an ample menu for heartier appetites (closed Monday).

One of Trastevere's greatest stops for traditionalists doesn't even have a name or a sign. Out front of Via della Scala 64 is the moniker **Vini Olii** (Wines and Oils), harkening to a simpler era with its "name" spray-painted on the concrete door lintel. Come for cheap glasses of vino while you stand at the minuscule counter with the neighborhood's old men. The **Bar San Callisto,** Piazza San Callisto 3–4 (no phone), is just a run-of-the-mill *bar* (in the Italian sense of the word), a bit dingier than most, that somehow has become a requisite stop for everyone from trendoids to tourists to Trasteverini. But it's just a first stop since it closes at 10pm.

GAY & LESBIAN CLUBS

Many gay clubs in Italy have subscribed to the use of an **Arci-Gay card,** an annual membership card costing 20,000L ($10). You can buy the card at any of these clubs, but some bars have their own membership cards as well, usually around 3,000L ($1.50).

The hottest gay event in Rome these days is La Mucca Assassina party on Fridays at **Alpheus,** Via del Commercio 36 (☎ **06-574-7826**; Metro: Piramide), where even Rome's heterosexual club-kids go to see and be seen. The kitchy fountain and sculpture along with the pink bar make it all a bit cheesy and "rave" at the same time. Admission on Fridays with your first drink is 20,000L ($10). The rest of the week (September to June, Tuesday to Sunday; July and August, Friday and Saturday only), the club goes straight.

Gay Rome created such a winner in **Alibi,** Via Monte Testaccio 40–44 (☎ **06-574-3448**), that the club's appeal has crossed over into mainstream nightlife. It has a rotating schedule of DJs and three rooms, with blaring disco, garage music, underground tunes, a mix of pop and dance hits, or house music. The energy and surprise theme parties as well as the extraordinary terrace ensure big crowds. Admission is 20,000L ($10) on Thursday to Saturday and 15,000L ($7.50) on Sunday (free on Wednesday); it's open to 4am.

Rome's oldest gay club is **The Hanger,** Via in Selci 69 (☎ **06-488-1397**), run by an American/Italian gay couple and these days frequented mainly by the under-30 crowd and Anglo-American visitors. Mondays draw the biggest crowds with high-quality skin flicks; this is the only night women aren't allowed. Admission is free with an Arci-Gay card, and it's open Wednesday to Monday 10:30pm to 2am.

The **New Joli Coeur,** Via Sirte 5 (☎ **06-8621-5827**), is a women-only disco open Saturdays 11pm to 5am. It's divided into three sections: a games room, a cabaret or floor show with the occasional karaoke event, and a dance hall. Admission is 12,000L ($7). While there are plenty of squalid S&M clubs, not all homosexuals are on the prowl. At **Shelter,** Via dei Vascellari 35 (no phone), both gays and lesbians congregate and chat over coffee, cocktails, or dessert. Admission is free with a membership card, and it's open daily 9pm to 3am.

8 Side Trips: Ostia Antica & Tivoli

OSTIA ANTICA: ROME'S ANCIENT SEAPORT

The ruins of Rome's ancient seaport, 23km (14 mi.) west of the city, are just as impor-tant and almost as fascinating as those of Pompeii, with the smell of saltwater in the air but without the crowds. Just a Metro ride from Rome's center, **Ostia Antica** (☎ **06-5635-8099**) is only partly excavated, much of it overgrown with tall grasses and umbrella pines that give the place a romantic touch missing from so many tourist-ridden archaeological sites these days. Bring a picnic and make a day of it.

Most of the buildings date from between the 1st and the 4th century A.D., though the city was founded in the 4th century B.C. The site plan handed out at the gate is very good, and most of the structures inside the park are now placarded in English. Most visitors follow the **Decumanus Maximus** (Latin for Main Street) from begin-ning to end, but take the time to explore the side streets where you'll find intact shops, black-and-white floor mosaics, a few frescoes clinging to walls, and millstones hiding in the weeds behind baker's shops.

Make sure to stop at the well-preserved 1st- and 2nd-century **Theater,** which could seat 2,700 people. Several giant marble theater masks still survive on tufa columns at the stage. The **Casa di Diana (House of Diana)** is a typical three-story house with shops on the ground floor, some frescoes on the walls inside, and a courtyard fountain of the huntress goddess that gave the house its name. Don't miss Ostia's on-site **museum** (☎ **06-563-5801**), which houses all the bits that unscrupulous types might try to carry off (as the Dark Ages barbarians and early baroque-era excavators did with wild abandon).

On the town's Forum you'll find the **Capitolum,** an important temple with an imposing flight of steps and most of the brick cella still standing. Finally, search out the **Terme dei Sette Sapienti,** a well-preserved baths complex named for the seven "sages" painted on the wall and spouting bathhouse homilies. The central hall retains its magnificent floor mosaic of hunting scenes.

Admission to the site is 8,000L ($4), and it's open Tuesday to Sunday 9am to an hour before sunset (the museum is open 9am to 1:30pm). Take Rome's Metro line B to the San Paolo stop, where you can catch a twice-hourly local train to the Ostia-Scavi stop (1,500L/75¢). If you fancy a day at Rome's very crowded **beach,** you can also ride this Metro line to Ostia-Lido or continue to it's the last stop, Cristoforo Colombo, then it's another 8km (5 miles) to the area's nude/gay (but innocuous) beach.

TIVOLI & ITS VILLAS

The little city of **Tivoli,** 32km (19 mi.) from Rome, was already 4 centuries old when the Eternal City itself was founded, and it became a popular spot for countryside villas during both the Imperial period and the Renaissance. To get there, take Rome's Metro line B to the Ponte Mammolo stop, where you catch the COTRAL bus (3,000L/$1.50) to Tivoli–Villa d'Este (every 30 min.) or Tivoli–Villa Adriana (every hour).

In the center of town is the **Villa d'Este** (☎ **0774-312-070**), started by Piero Ligorio for the fabulously wealthy Cardinal Ippolito II d'Este in 1550 (the construction outlived both of them and the gardens were added to up until 1927). This site is renowned less for the (relatively) modest villa itself than for the spectacular ✪ **gardens,** a baroque fantasy of some 500 fountains terraced down a hillside and surrounded by artificial grottoes and scads of umbrella pines, cypresses, ilexes, elms, and cedars. Call before making the trip out here to be sure the fountains will be going at full blast that day, for the play of water against the sunlight is what the Villa d'Este is all about (the best time is sunny weekends). Though what's here is spectacular (including the high jets of the Neptune Fountain and the long wall of One Hundred Fountains whose decorative frieze is overgrown with moss) imagine what it must've been like when the famous Water Organ fountain was still working and playing its songs and the Fontana della Civitta was creating birdsong and the screeching of an owl. The villa is open Tuesday to Sunday 9am to an hour before sunset, and admission is 8,000L ($4).

Five kilometers (3 mi.) before the town on the road to Rome lie the ruins of the most fabulous palace built during the Empire, the ✪ **Villa Adriana** (☎ **0774-530-203**). The Emperor Hadrian was quite an accomplished architect, designing not only Rome's Pantheon but also his own lavish palace in A.D. 118, a countryside retreat within easy reach of the capital and so architecturally advanced it even included central heating. The well-traveled Hadrian picked up so many architectural ideas from his voyages that he decided to re-create his own versions of famous buildings here. That's why today you can wander the long pool inspired by the Egyptian city of **Canopus,** a statue-lined canal with a beautiful curved colonnade at one end and a Temple of Serapis at the other. Recent reinterpretation of the statues suggest that the whole ensemble may be meant to represent the Mediterranean world, with the temple at the end portraying Egypt, the statues that imitate the caryatids from Athens's Acropolis in the middle symbolizing Greece, and the statues of Amazons at the other end standing for Asia Minor.

To honor the genius of the ancient Greeks, Hadrian built himself a peristyle—a giant cloister measuring 766 by 320 feet—called the **Pecile,** loosely modeled after Athens's Stoa Poikile (Painted Porch), under which the great philosophical school of Stoicism was founded. The **Teatro Marittimo** was a retreat for the emperor, who could escape with his thoughts to this circular structure in the middle of a pond and pull the wooden bridges after him for seclusion. The **Imperial Palace** is grouped around four courtyards; in the staff wing are preserved some fine mosaics, and you can see some good portions of both the **Small Baths** and the **Large Baths** still standing at the compound's west end. The grounds of this archaeological park are vast, and parts are still being excavated. Wander for as long as you can, looking for the **Greek Theater** and the ruins of the **Accademia** and pausing in the two **small museums** to get a better grip on the original layout. Bring a picnic lunch and stay the whole day. The villa is open Tuesday to Sunday 9am to an hour before sunset, and admission is 8,000L ($4).

4 Florence: Birthplace of the Renaissance

by Reid Bramblett

Five hundred years ago, the rich and beautiful city of **Florence (Firenze)** was the heart of European life. The Renaissance was born and developed here in the 15th century, giving rise to many of the most important developments in art, science, literature, and architecture through luminaries like Giotto, Donatello, Brunelleschi, Leonardo da Vinci, Michelangelo, and Pisa-born Galileo. Florence may no longer be the axis around which the cultural world revolves, but the Renaissance's elegance and aesthetic sensibility are still alive and well. The city boasts Europe's greatest concentration of artistic wealth, some of which you can see or sense without even entering any of its world-class museums.

Europe's cultural revolution was financed in large part by the Medicis (and those who flourished under their commercial success), Florence's unrivaled ruling family throughout much of the Renaissance. They came to power as bankers and used their unprecedented acumen and wealth to foster artistic and intellectual genius. The city is filled with this heritage: Fully half a dozen of Italy's principal museums, as well as myriad churches and palazzi, house major paintings and sculpture of that golden period when Florence was, as D. H. Lawrence described it, "Man's perfect center of the Universe."

However, it's not only the sights and history that make Florence a special place. The nuts and bolts of where you stay and what you eat will make this city special in- and off-season. Many of the affordable hotels I've listed are housed in imposing palazzi from the time of the Medicis and Michelangelo. You may find yourself sleeping beneath a ceiling decorated with colorful old frescoes or sampling a glass of Chianti in the cantina of a palazzo built before the locally born Giovanni da Verrazzano set eyes on New York Harbor. The rustic though delicious cuisine of this region, *cucina toscana,* from the heart of the nation's wine- and olive-producing farmland, is one of the finest in Italy—certainly one of the most sought after in the world. But don't worry, it's possible to get a dinner fit for a Florentine duke for merely a song.

1 Arriving

BY PLANE

Several European airlines are now servicing Florence's expanded **Amerigo Vespucci Airport** (☎ **055-373-498** or 055-306-1700 for national flight info; 055-306-1702 for international flight info;

www.safnet.it), also called **Peretola,** just 5km (3.1 mi.) northwest of town. There are no direct flights to/from the United States, but you can make easy connections through London, Paris, Amsterdam, Frankfurt, and so on. The regularly scheduled **city bus no. 62** connects the airport with Piazza della Stazione downtown, taking about 30 minutes and costing 1,500L (75¢). Slightly more expensive (6,000L/$3) but without the local stops is the hourly **SITA bus** to/from downtown's bus station at Via Santa Caterina 15r (☎ **055-214-721**), behind the train station. Metered **taxis** line up outside the airport's arrival terminal and charge about 25,000L ($13) to most hotels in the city center.

The closest major international airport is **Pisa's Galileo Galilei Airport** (☎ **050-500-707;** www.pisa-airport.com), 97km (60 mi.) west of Florence. Two to three **trains** per hour leave the airport for Florence (70–100 min.; 10,500L/$5). If your flight leaves from this airport and you'll be going there by train from Florence, you can check in your baggage and receive your boarding pass at the Air Terminal on Track 5 in Florence's Stazione Santa Maria Novella; show up 30 minutes before your train departure. Early-morning flights may make train connections from Florence to the airport difficult: The solution is the regular train from Florence into downtown Pisa, with a 10-minute 5,000L ($2.50) taxi from the Pisa train station to the nearby Pisa airport; the no. 7 bus makes the same hop in twice the time for 1,500L (75¢).

BY TRAIN

Most Florence-bound trains roll into the **Stazione Santa Maria Novella,** Piazza della Stazione (☎ **055-288-765** or toll free in Italy 800-888-088), which you'll often see abbreviated as **S.M.N.** The station is on the northwestern edge of the city's compact historic center, a 10-minute walk from the Duomo and a 15-minute walk from Piazza della Signoria and the Uffizi. The best budget hotels are immediately east of there around Via Faenza and Via Fiume.

With your back to the tracks, you'll find a tiny **info office** with a hotel-booking service office (charging 4,500L to 15,000L/$2.25 to $8) toward the station's left exit next to a 24-hour pharmacy. The **train information office** is near the opposite exit to your right. Walk straight through the central glass doors into the outer hall for tickets at the *biglietteria.* At the head of Track 16 is a 24-hour luggage depot where you can drop your bags (5,000L/$2.50 per piece for 12 hours) while you search for a hotel. You'll find a rank of taxis outside the station.

Some trains stop at the outlying **Stazione Campo di Marte** or **Stazione Rifredi,** which are worth avoiding. Though there's 24-hour bus service between these satellite stations and S.M.N., departures aren't always frequent and taxi service is erratic and expensive.

BY BUS

Dozens of companies run frequent service to Florence from cities within Tuscany and Umbria to two bus hubs, one on each side of the Stazione Santa Maria Novella: **SITA,** Via Santa Caterina da Siena 17r (☎ 055-214721), is important for those busing to San Gimignano or Siena; **Lazzi,** Piazza della Stazione 4–6 (☎ **166-856-010** toll free within Italy), specializes in service to Lucca, Pisa, and the coast (Viareggio, Forte dei Marmi).

BY CAR

Driving to Florence is easy; the problems begin once you arrive. Almost all cars are banned from the historic center—only residents or merchants with special permits are allowed in. You'll likely be stopped at some point by the traffic police, who'll assume from your rental plates that you're a visitor heading to your hotel. Have the name and address of the hotel ready and they'll wave you through. You can drop off baggage there (the hotel will give you a sign for your car advising traffic police you're unloading), then you must relocate to a parking lot. Ask your hotel which is most convenient: Special rates are available through most of the hotels and their nearest lot.

Standard rates for parking near the center are 2,000L to 5,000L ($1 to $2.50) per hour; many lots offer a daily rate of 25,000L to 50,000L ($13 to $25). Least expensive at 15,000L ($8) is the vast underground **Parterre lot** at Piazza della Libertà; you must show a hotel receipt to get that tourist rate when you pay upon retrieving your car. Don't park your car overnight on the street; towing and ticketing are the likely result, and they'll set you back substantially—the headaches to retrieve your car are beyond description.

2 Essentials

VISITOR INFORMATION

TOURIST OFFICES The city's **largest tourist office** is at Via Cavour 1r (☎ **055-290-832;** fax 055-276-0383), about three blocks north of the Duomo. This office offers lots of literature, including details on current (sometimes extended) museum hours and concert schedules. March to October, it's open Monday to Saturday 8:15am to 7:15pm and Sunday 8:30am to 6:30pm; November to February, hours are Monday to Saturday 8:15am to 1:45pm (though lately they've been experimenting with keeping it open to 7:15pm in winter).

At the head of the tracks in Stazione Santa Maria Novella is a **tiny info office** with some maps and a hotel-booking service (see "Getting the Best Deal on Accommodations," below) open Monday to Saturday 9am to 9pm (to 8pm November to March). But the station's **main tourist office** (☎ **055-212-245;** www.firenze.turismo. toscana.it) is outside at Piazza della Stazione 4. With your back to the tracks, take the left exit, cross onto the concrete median, and turn right; it's about 100 feet ahead. The office is usually open Monday to Saturday 8:30am to 7pm (often to 1:30pm in winter) and Sunday 8:30am to 1:30pm.

Ignore publications carrying the address of the **information office** just off Piazza della Signoria at Chiasso Baroncelli 17r; it relocated in 1998 to an obscure side street south of Piazza Santa Croce, Borgo Santa Croce 29r (☎ **055-234-0444**), open Monday to Saturday 9am to 7pm and Sunday 9am to 2pm.

PUBLICATIONS At the tourist offices, pick up the free monthly *Avvenimentia* or the bimonthly *Firenze Oggi* (2,000L/$1). The bilingual *Concierge Information* magazine, free from the front desks of top hotels, contains a monthly calendar of events and details on attractions. *Firenze Spettacolo,* a 3,000L ($1.50) Italian-language monthly sold at most newsstands, is the most detailed and up-to-date listing of nightlife, arts, and entertainment. Arci-Gay/Arci-Lesbica publishes a free gay guide (in Italian and English) to Florence and Tuscany called *Il Giglio Fuscia,* listing gay bars, beaches, useful addresses, and resources. It's available at the Arci-Gay offices (see "Florence After Dark," later in this chapter), gay nightspots, and some bookstores.

WEB SITES The official Florence information, **www.firenze.turismo.toscana.it,** is as yet only in Italian (English is coming) but contains a wealth of up-to-date information on Florence and its province, including a searchable hotels form allowing you to specify amenities, categories, and the like, and it spits out a list where you can get contact info and see current room rates.

Firenze By Net (www.mega.it/florence), **Firenze.Net** (http://english.firenze.net), and **FlorenceOnLine** (www.fol.it) are all Italy-based Web sites with English translations and good, general information on Florence. **Informacittà** (www.informacitta.net) is an excellent little guide to this month's events, exhibits, concerts, and theater; the English version is still pending, however. Other sites worth checking out are **Your Way to Florence** (www.arca.net/florence.htm), **Time Out** (www.timeout. com/florence), **Know It All: Know Tuscany** (www.knowital.com), **The Heart of Tuscany** (www.nautilus-mp.com/tuscany/index.html), and **Chianti Doc Market-place** (www.chianti-doc.com).

FESTIVALS & EVENTS   Not to be missed are the **Maggio Musicale (Musical May)**, Italy's oldest music festival and one of Europe's most prestigious; the **Estate Fiesolana (Summer in Fiesole)**, when the Roman theater in nearby Fiesole comes alive with dance, music, and theater; the **Calcio Storico**, a no-holds-barred combination of rugby, soccer, and wrestling that crowns the feast day for San Giovanni; the **Florence Dance Festival**, held in Cascine Park's beautiful amphitheater; and the **International Antiques Show**, held in mid-September in uneven years. See the "Calendar of Events," in chapter 2, for more details.

CITY LAYOUT

Florence is a compact city best negotiated on foot. No two sights are more than a 20- or 25-minute walk apart, and all the hotels and restaurants in this chapter are in the relatively small *centro storico* **(historic center).** The center is loosely bounded by the Stazione Santa Maria Novella (S.M.N.) to the northwest, Piazza della SS. Annunziata to the northeast, Piazza Santa Croce to the east, and the Arno River to the south. South of the river is the **Oltrarno** (on the other side of the Arno), a "Left Bank" adjunct to the *centro storico* and home to the Pitti Palace, the Boboli Gardens, and the lookout-point Piazzale Michelangiolo.

In the *centro storico*, **Piazza del Duomo** is dominated by Florence's magnificent tri-color-marble **cathedral,** freestanding bell tower, and baptistry. You'll inevitably walk along many of the streets radiating from this imposing square. **Borgo San Lorenzo,** a narrow street running north from the baptistry, is best known for the excellent outdoor market at its far end, the **Mercato San Lorenzo,** selling everything from mar-bleized paper-wrapped boxes and frames to leather bags and jackets. It borders the train station neighborhood, where you'll find a cluster of the city's cheapest hotels.

Via dei Calzaiuoli, Florence's most popular pedestrian thoroughfare and shopping street, runs south from the Duomo, connecting the church with the statue-filled **Piazza della Signoria,** off of which opens the Uffizi Gallery. West of and parallel to this is **Via Roma,** which becomes **Via Por Santa Maria** on its way to the famed **Ponte Vecchio,** a bridge over the Arno lined with tiny goldmith's shops. Midway between the two is **Piazza della Repubblica,** a busy cafe-ringed square surrounded by expensive-to-moderate shopping streets. Farther west is **Via dei Tornabuoni,** Florence's boutique-lined shopping drag, and its elegant offshoot, **Via della Vigna Nuova.**

From Piazza della Signoria, **Via D. Gondi** leads east, becoming **Borgo dei Greci** on its way to **Piazza Santa Croce** at the center's eastern edge.

The Red & the Black

Unlike in other Italian cities, there are two systems of street numbering in Florence: **black (*nero*)** and **red (*rosso*).** Black numbers are for residential and office buildings and hotels, while red numbers (indicated by an "r" following the number) are for commercial enterprises like restaurants and stores. The numbering systems operate independently of each other—so the doorways on a given street may run 1r, 2r, 3r, 1 (black), 4r, 2 (black). Florence plans to eventually eliminate this system and renumber everything, creating the major confusion they've resisted for centuries, but it'll be years before this is put into effect.

Neighborhoods in Brief

Florentines generally divide their city into the two banks of the Arno River—the northern bank around the Duomo and Piazza della Signoria and the Oltrarno southern bank around the Palazzo Pitti. I've broken it down further, mostly into the visitor-oriented neighborhoods surrounding particular sites or churches, to facilitate the location of hotels, restaurants, and so on. It's an arbitrary designation to help you understand the flavor of each, decide where you want to stay, and plan your days.

AROUND THE DUOMO & PIAZZA DELLA SIGNORIA   This is as central as you can get and offers the greatest concentration of attractions (the Duomo, Uffizi, Bargello, Palazzo Vecchio), restaurants, hotels, and so on. Real estate is understandably the most expensive, and visitors help pay for this. For centuries, the **Duomo** has been Florence's religious hub and **Piazza della Signoria** its civic hub. Many streets still follow the ancient grid pattern laid down by the Romans, and the narrow back streets of truncated medieval towers and stalwart palazzi are some of the most picturesque and evocative. While shops along the neighborhood's western boundary of the boutique-lined **Via dei Tornabuoni** belong to the high priests of made-in-Italy glamour, the area generally offers something for everyone: The same is true of hotels and restaurants that can range from the refreshingly unpretentious to the over-the-top-priced tourist traps.

NEAR THE TRAIN STATION, THE MERCATO SAN LORENZO & SANTA MARIA NOVELLA   North and northwest of the Duomo area, but still easily accessible by foot, this neighborhood is one of the busiest due to train-station traffic and marketplace shoppers. Colorful, yes; peaceful, hardly. However, it doesn't carry the stigma of Rome's train station area (often seedy) or Venice's (inconvenient to most sites). The budget-hotel strips of Via Faenza and Via Fiume are nondescript but passable for those looking to cut costs; there's no danger to speak of. The blocks surrounding the **Medici Chapels, Basilica di San Lorenzo,** and vast **Mercato San Lorenzo** are overwhelmed by hundreds of pushcart stalls, a potential plus for the shopping fiend; this is also where restaurant chefs and Florentines do their daily shopping. The 13th-century **Santa Maria Novella** church lends a note of quiet grace to the otherwise commercial and bustling area.

NEAR SAN MARCO & SANTISSIMA ANNUNZIATA   Defining the northern limits of the *centro storico,* Piazza San Marco is light-years away from the square by the same name in Venice. Traffic has taken over this square, and nearby high schools and university buildings keep it packed, too. It's home to the important **Museo San Marco,** dedicated to the work of Fra' Angelico, and the expansive **Piazza SS. Annunziata,** said to be one of the Renaissance's most beautiful. However, make no mistake that the area's greatest magnet is Michelangelo's *David* in the **Accademia.** The relatively quiet side streets are removed enough from the Duomo crush to make this a preferred area for alternative hotel choices, though the walk to and from Duomo-area sites can be tiresome.

NEAR SANTA CROCE   This large neighborhood-like area east of the busy Via Proconsolo (and east of the Bargello and Uffizi in the Duomo area) is dominated by the Gothic **Santa Croce** church—by far the most visited of this area's sites. Nonetheless, it's an area that offers its fair share of genuine residential character in a city fast succumbing to fast-food bars and tourist shops. An alluring choice of restaurants and quiet side streets and a must-do visit to the Pantheon-like burials and frescoes for which Santa Croce is famous means you'll probably visit this eastern end of the *centro storico* at least once.

THE OLTRARNO   The "Other Side of the Arno" is often referred to as the city's Left Bank. Escaping the prohibitive costs of the Duomo-dominated scenario north of here, it has been the alternative location for artists and artisans for centuries, but escalating costs today are slowly changing the neighborhood's dynamics—something not immediately obvious to visitors. The nightlife that revolves around the outdoor bars and restaurants of the tree-shaded **Piazza Santa Spirito** are still redolent of those bohemian days. Its historic sites are limited though important: The picture gallery at the **Palazzo Pitti** is second only to the Uffizi, and the frescoes of the Brancacci Chapel at **Santa Maria del Carmine** were some of the most seminal in the early years of the Renaissance. The Oltrarno was once the edge of the countryside, and it retains a sense of separateness and removal from the northern bank of the Arno, a 5-minute walk away. The side streets still accommodate the centuries-old workshops of wood carvers, furniture restorers, leather workers, and jewelry makers. Together with Santa Croce, this is one of the more residential neighborhoods, but with a spirited mix of restaurants, small shops, and wine bars.

IN THE HILLS   The oppressive weather of valley-trapped Florence has residents and visitors alike taking to the hills for a moment's respite from both the heat and the crowds. Although **Fiesole** (to the north) is considered a city in its own right, it's often seen as a suburb of Florence, and its views and restaurants make it a favorite escape (see "A Day Trip to Fiesole," later in this chapter). On the southern Oltrarno bank of the Arno and across from the area of Santa Croce is the lofty perch of **Piazzale Michelangiolo** and its postcard-perfect view of Florence and the Duomo (and Fiesole beyond). A visit to the lovely Romanesque **San Miniato** church, an easy stroll south of the piazzale, is recommended for a late-afternoon gelato break when Gregorian vespers are sung at the church and the sun sets on Florence's terra-cotta rooftops. Those in shape can walk here from the Ponte Vecchio by taking **Via San Nicolo,** which initially runs parallel to the river and then turns south and passes through the ancient gate of the city, Porta San Nicolo, and heads up toward the piazzale, becoming a stepped pathway called the **Via del Monte alle Croci.** Alternatively, from the Ponte alle Grazie, east of the Ponte Vecchio on the Oltrarno side of the river, take the **bus no. 13** for the 10-minute trip. A taxi from the center of town will probably cost around 15,000L ($8), but you may risk being stuck without return transportation—they usually won't wait unless paid (but you can always take a bus or walk back).

GETTING AROUND

Florence—with almost all of its relatively small *centro storico* closed to commercial traffic—is one of the most delightful cities in Europe to explore on foot. The best city map is the pocket-sized **LAC Firenze** with the yellow-and-blue jacket, available at most newsstands for 5,000L ($2.50).

BY BUS   You'll rarely need to use Florence's efficient **ATAF bus system** (☎ **055-565-0222;** www.ataf.net) since the city is so wonderfully compact. Many visitors accustomed to big cities like Rome step off their arriving train and onto a city bus out of habit, thinking to reach the center; within 5 minutes, they find themselves in the suburbs. The cathedral is a mere 5- to 7-minute walk from the train station.

     Bus **tickets** cost 1,500L (75¢), and you must buy them before boarding. A **four-pack** (*biglietto multiplo*) is 5,800L ($2.90) and a **24-hour pass** 6,000L ($3). Tickets are sold at *tabacchi* (tobacconists), bars, and most newsstands. Once on board, validate your ticket in the box near the rear door to avoid a steep fine. If you intend to use the bus system, you should pick up a **bus map** at a tourist office. Since most of the historic center is limited as to traffic, buses make runs on principal streets only.

BY TAXI   You can't hail a cab, but you can find one at **taxi ranks** in or near major piazze, or call one to your restaurant or hotel by dialing ☎ **4242,** 4798, or 4390. Taxis charge 1,500L (75¢) per kilometer, but there's a whopping minimum fare of 6,500L ($3.25), and most hops average about 10,000L to 15,000L ($5 to $8); don't forget to include a 10% tip. Taxis are really worth considering only for getting to/from the train station with luggage.

BY BICYCLE   Despite the relatively traffic-free historic center, biking has never caught on here, though local authorities are trying to change that. **Firenze Parcheggi,** the public garage authority (☎ **055-500-0453**), has set up temporary sites about town (look for stands at the train station, Piazza Strozzi, Via della Nina along the south side of Palazzo Vecchio, and large public parking lots) where bikes are furnished free 8am to 8pm; you must return the bike to any of the other sites. For now, the program is summer only, though it may go year-round soon (and may charge a nominal 1,000L/50¢).

If no bikes are left, you'll have to pay for them at a shop like **Alinari,** Via Guelfa 85r (☎ **055-280-500**), renting bikes by the hour (4,000L to 5,000L/$2 to $2.50) and day (20,000L to 30,000L/$10 to $15). It also rents scooters and mopeds by the hour (respectively 9,000L to 60,000L/$4.50 to $30) or the day (35,000L to 180,000L/$18 to $90).

BY RENTAL CAR   Don't rent a car for exploring pedestrianized Florence itself; but for day-tripping in the Chianti or exploring Tuscan hill towns, a car is vital. Arrange your rental from home for the best rates. But, if you need to do it on the spot, auto-rental agencies in Florence are centered around the Europa Garage on Borgo Ognissanti. **Avis** is at no. 128r (☎ **055-239-8826**) and **Europcar** nearby at no. 53r (☎ **055-290-438**); **Hertz** is at Via Fininguerra 33r (☎ **055-282-260**). Most rental services have representatives at the Florence and Pisa airports, though you'll probably pay more to pick up a car there and drop it off in town.

Fast Facts: Florence

American Express   AMEX (☎ **055-50-981**) is on Piazza Cimatori/Via Dante Alghieri 22r. It will act as a travel agent (for a commission), accept mail on your behalf (see "Mail & E-mail," below), and, of course, cash traveler's checks at no commission (they don't have to be AMEX checks). It's open Monday to Friday 9am to 5:30pm and Saturday 9am to 12:30pm.

Consulates   The consulate of the **United States** is at Lungarno Amerigo Vespucci 38, near the intersection with Via Palestro (☎ **055-239-8276**); it's open Monday to Friday 8:30am to 1pm and 2 to 5:30pm. The consulate of the **United Kingdom** is at Lungarno Corsini 2, near Via dei Tornabuoni (☎ **055-284-133**); it's open Monday to Friday 9:30am to 12:30pm and 2:30 to 4:30pm. Citizens of **Australia, New Zealand,** and **Canada** should consult their embassies in Rome (see "Fast Facts: Rome," in chapter 3).

Doctors/Dentists   A **Walk-in Clinic** (☎ **055-483-363** or 0330-774-731) is run by Dott. Giorgio Scappini. Tuesday and Thursday office hours are 5:30pm to 6:30pm or by appointment at Via Bonifacio Lupi 32 (just south of the Tourist Medical Service; see "Hospitals," below); Monday, Wednesday, and Friday go to Via Guasti 2 from 3 to 4pm (north of the Fortezza del Basso). **Dr. Stephen Kerr** keeps an office at Piazza dei Giuochi 5–6r, near American Express (☎ **0335-836-1682** or 055-436-8775 at home), with home visits or clinic appointments 24 hours.

For general dentistry, try **Dr. Camis de Fonseca,** Via Nino Bixio 9, northeast of the city center off Viale dei Mille (☎ **055-587-632**), open Monday to Friday 3 to 7pm; he's also available for emergency weekend calls. The U.S. consulate can provide a list of other English-speaking doctors, dentists, and specialists. See also "Hospitals," below, for medical translator service.

Emergencies   Dial ☎ **113** for an **emergency** of any kind. You can also call the **Carabinieri** (the national police force, more useful than local branches) at ☎ **112,** dial an **ambulance** at ☎ **118,** and **report a fire** at ☎ **115.** All these calls are free from any phone. For **car breakdowns,** call ☎ **116.**

Hospitals   The **ambulance number** is ☎ **118.** There's a special **Tourist Medical Service,** Via Lorenzo il Magnifico 59, north of the city center between the Fortezza del Basso and Piazza della Libertà (☎ **055-475-411**), open 24 hours; take bus 8 or 80 to Viale Lavagnini or bus 12 or night bus 91 to Via Poliziano.

Thanks to socialized medicine, you can walk into most any Italian hospital when ill but not an emergency and get taken care of speedily with no insurance questions asked, no forms to fill out, and no fee charged. They'll just give you a prescription and send you on your way. The most central are the **Arcispedale di Santa Maria Nuova,** a block northeast of the Duomo on Piazza Santa Maria Nuova (☎ **055-27-581**), and the **Misericordia Ambulance Service,** on Piazza del Duomo across from Giotto's bell tower (☎ **055-212-222** for ambulance).

For a **free translator** to help you describe your symptoms, explain the doctor's instructions, and aid in medical issues in general, call the volunteers at the **Associazione Volontari Ospedalieri (AVO)** (☎ **055-425-0126** or 055-234-4567) Monday, Wednesday, and Friday 4 to 6pm and Tuesday and Thursday 10am to noon.

Laundry/Dry Cleaning   Though there are several coin-op shops (mostly of the OndaBlu chain), you can get your wash done for you even more cheaply at a pay-by-weight *lavanderia*—and you don't have to waste a morning sitting there watching it go in circles. The cheapest are around the university (east of San Marco), and one of the best is a nameless joint at **Via Alfani 44r** (☎ **055-247-9313**), where they'll do an entire load for 11,000L ($6), have it ready by afternoon, and even deliver it free to your hotel. It's closed Saturday afternoon and Sunday. At other, non-self-service shops, check the price *before* leaving your clothes—some places charge by the item. Dry cleaning (*lavasecco*) is much more costly and available at *lavanderie* throughout the city (ask your hotel for the closest).

Mail & E-mail   You can buy *francobolli* (**stamps**) from any *tabacchi* (tobacconists) or from the central post office. The most **central post office** is at Via Pellicceria 3, under the arcade at Piazza della Repubblica, to the left of the Banco Nazionale del Lavoro (☎ **160** for general info or 055-211-147). September to July, it's open Monday to Saturday 8:15am to 7pm and Sunday 8:30am to 7pm (on Sundays and holidays, you can enter only from Piazza Davazanti 4, around the back of the building). In August, it's open daily 8:30am to 1:30pm. It's closed January 1, May 1, Easter, August 15, and December 25.

Drop **postcards and letters** into the boxes outside. To mail larger **packages,** drop them at *sportello* (window) 9/10, but first head across the room to window 21/22 for stamps. If that window is closed, as it often is, you buy your stamps at the next window, 23/24, which is also the pickup for *Fermo Posta* (***poste restante,*** or held-mail; see below).

You can also send packages via **DHL,** Via della Cupola 243 (☎ **055-308-877** or 800-345-345 for free pick-up) or **UPS,** Via Pratignone 56a in Calenzano (☎ **055/882-5501**).

To **receive mail** at the central post office, have it sent to (your name)/Fermo Posta Centrale/50103 Firenze, Italia/ITALY. They'll charge you 300L (15¢) per letter when you come to pick it up at window 23/24; bring your passport for ID. For people without an AMEX card, this is a much better deal than American Express's similar service, which charges 3,000L ($1.50) to receive and hold non-cardholder's mail. For AMEX members, however, this service is free, so you can have your mail sent to (your name)/Client Mail/American Express/Via Dante Alghieri, 22r/50123 Firenze, Italia/ITALY.

To check or send e-mail, head to the **Internet Train** (www.fionline.it), with locations at Via dell'Oriuolo 25r, three blocks from the Duomo (☎ **055-263-8968**); Via Guelfa 24a near the train station (☎ **055-214-794**); and Borgo San Jacopo 30r in the Oltrarno (☎ **055-265-7935**). Access is 10,000L ($5) per hour or 8,000L ($4) for students. You get a free membership and e-mail address with your first hour, and they also provide printing, scanning, Webcam, and fax services. So does **www village,** Via Alfani 11–13r (☎ **055-247-9398**), where on-line charges are 3,000L ($1.50) for 15 minutes, 10,000L ($5) per hour (9,000L/$4.50 for students), or 8 hours for 60,000L ($30). **Netgate,** Via Sant'Egidio 10–20r (☎ **055-234-7967**), has similar rates, but also offers a Saturday "happy hour" of free access 10:30 to 11am and 2 to 2:30pm. All are open daily from around 10am to midnight or later (Sundays, www village opens 2 to 8pm; Netgate closes at 10:30pm, 8:30pm in winter).

Newspapers & Magazines   You can pick up the *International Herald Tribune* and *USA Today* from almost any newsstand and will find the *Wall Street Journal Europe* and the *London Times,* along with *Time* and *Newsweek,* at most larger kiosks. There's a 24-hour newsstand in the train station. For upcoming events, theater, and shows, see "Visitor Information," earlier in this chapter.

Pharmacies   For pharmacy information, dial ☎ **110.** There are **24-hour pharmacies** (also open Sundays and state holidays) in **Stazione Santa Maria Novella** (☎ **055-216-761;** ring the bell between 1 and 4am); at **Piazza San Giovanni 20r,** just behind the baptistry at the corner of Borgo San Lorenzo (☎ **055-211-343**); and at **Via Cazzaiuoli 7r,** just off Piazza della Signoria (☎ **055-289-490**).

Police   For **emergencies,** dial ☎ **112** for the **Carabinieri** police. To report **lost property** or passport problems, call the *questura* (urban police headquarters) at ☎ **055-49-771.** Also see "Emergencies," above.

Safety   Central Italy is an exceedingly safe area with practically no random violent crime. There are, as in any city, plenty of **pickpockets** out to ruin your vacation, and Florence has the added joy of light-fingered Gypsy children (especially around the train station), but otherwise you're safe. Do steer clear of the Cascine Park after dark, when it becomes somewhat seedy and you may run the risk of

Country & City Codes

The **country code** for Italy is **39.** The **city code** for Florence is **055;** use this code when you're calling from outside Italy, within Florence, and within Italy.

being mugged. And you probably won't want to hang out with the late-night heroin addicts shooting up on the Arno mudflats below the Lungarno embankments on the edges of town.

Telephone   See "Fast Facts: Rome," in chapter 3.

Tipping   See "Fast Facts: Rome," in chapter 3.

3 Affordable Places to Stay

Many budget hotels are concentrated in the area around the Stazione Santa Maria Novella. You'll find most of the hotels in this convenient and relatively safe, if charmless, area on noisy Via Nazionale and its first two side streets, Via Fiume and Via Faenza; an adjunct is the area surrounding the Mercato San Lorenzo. The area between the Duomo and Piazza della Signoria, particularly along and near Via dei Calzaiuoli, is a good though invariably more expensive place to look.

Peak season is mid-March to mid-July, September to early November, and December 23 to January 6. May and September are particularly popular whether in the city or in the outlying Tuscan hills.

NEAR THE DUOMO & PIAZZA DELLA SIGNORIA

Aldini. Via dei Calzaiuoli 13 (3rd floor; south of Piazza del Duomo), 50122 Firenze. ☎ **055-214-752.** Fax 055-291-621. www.pronet.it/hotelaldini. E-mail: hotelaldini@ pronet.it. A/C MINIBAR TV TEL. 14 units. 150,000L ($75) single; 240,000L ($120) double; 300,000L ($150) triple; 360,000L ($180) quad. Rates include continental breakfast. Rates discounted 20% low season. AE, DC, MC, V. Nearby garage parking 50,000L ($25). Bus: A, 1, 6, 11, 14, 17, 22, 23, 36, 37.

There's little hyperbole in the Aldini's claim to being near the Duomo (it'll sound as if the bells are under your pillow). Within centimeters of the magnificent tricolored marble Duomo and its 14th-century campanile, the Aldini is in a 13th-century palazzo above the marginally less expensive Costantini (see below). But the Aldini is more distinguished—a handsome, comfortable place with terra-cotta floors covered by Persian runners and large rooms whose floral bedspreads, matching drapes, and spacious baths reflect a recent renovation. The front rooms have windows with partial views of the Duomo, though the clip-clop of horse-drawn carriages and the chatter of late-night strollers may disturb you.

Alessandra. Borgo SS. Apostoli 17 (between Via dei Tornabuoni and Via Por Santa Maria), 50123 Firenze. ☎ **055-283-438.** Fax 055-210-619. www.hotelalessandra.com. 25 units, 17 with bath. TV TEL. 120,000L ($60) single without bath, 190,000L ($95) single with bath; 190,000L ($95) double without bath, 250,000L ($125) double with bath; 250,000L ($125) triple without bath, 320,000L ($160) triple with bath. Rates include breakfast. Ask about low-season rates. AE, MC, V. Parking in nearby garage 30,000L ($15). Bus: B, 6, 11, 36, 37.

The etched-glass street doors hint of the architectural significance of the Alessandra's palazzo nobile, designed in 1507 by Baccio d'Angnolo, a pupil of Michelangelo. This is a good spot to opt for a room without a private bathroom, since only seven rooms share four nearby communal bathrooms, all large and newly redone. The attentive housekeeping and spacious high-ceilinged rooms are most welcome, as is the free air-conditioning (request it on reserving, as only 23 rooms have it). There's a 12:30am curfew, though an all-night concierge can buzz you in after that.

Casci. Via Cavour 13 (between Via dei Ginori and Via Guelfa), 50129 Firenze. ☎ **055-211-686.** Fax 055-239-6461. www.hotelcasci.com. 25 units. A/C TV TEL. 170,000L ($85) single; 220,000L ($110) double; 300,000L ($150) triple; 380,000L ($190) quad. Rates

> # Getting the Best Deal on Accommodations
>
> • Book early to secure the hotel and price category you want.
> • Remember that the information office inside the train station provides a hotel-booking service (see "Arriving," earlier in this chapter).
> • Get out of paying for breakfast at your hotel and enjoy an inexpensive stand-up breakfast at one of Florence's cafes. Hoteliers are more likely to bend on this rule in off-season. Clarify the breakfast situation when checking in.
> • Ask how many rooms share each hall bathroom: One or two is minimum traffic, but three or four may mean problems with housekeeping and availability. With a good ratio, the option of a room without a private bathroom should become a real consideration.

include buffet breakfast. Off-season rates 20%–30% less; check Web site for special offers, especially Nov–Feb. AE, DC, MC, V. Valet parking 40,000L ($22). Bus: 1, 6, 11, 17.

The friendly Lombardi family transformed this student pensione into an attractive hotel for an older, more discerning guest several years ago. Signora Lombardi is a stickler for cleanliness (most bathrooms literally gleam), and she and her son offer amenities like hair dryers, laundry service, and tour-booking services. The central location means some rooms (with double-paned windows) overlook busy Via Cavour, so for more quiet, ask for a room facing the inner courtyard's magnolia tree. They serve an ample breakfast buffet in a frescoed room, offer free Internet access in the little bar off the reception area, and plan soon to add minibars to the rooms. Rossini, legendary composer of *The Barber of Seville* and *The William Tell Overture*, lived in this palazzo from 1851 to 1855.

Costantini. Via dei Calzaiuoli 13 (2nd floor; south of Piazza del Duomo), 50122 Firenze. ☎ **055-213-995.** tel./fax 055-215-128. 15 units. A/C TEL TV. 140,000L ($70) single; 240,000L ($120) double; 360,000L ($180) triple; 480,000L ($240) quad. Rates include breakfast. AE, DC, MC, V (can use credit card to pay for only half the bill). Bus: A, 1, 6, 11, 14, 17, 22, 23, 36, 37.

This formerly nondescript two-star hotel remains a favorite for its great location, relatively low prices, and recently refurbished rooms. The Costantini is housed in what's left of the two 13th-century towers long ago joined to create a palazzo, and its biggest draw are the rooms with an askance view of Giotto's bell tower (from 101, 102, and 106; just a bit from 110 and 111, but they're over a courtyard and much quieter) and the tricolored Duomo. For those who find the proximity of the frequent church bells glorious and not annoying and for whom cleanliness is paramount, this is an excellent choice. The rooms feature dark wood furnishings, orthopedic beds, and new bathrooms with box showers. Breakfast tastes especially wonderful beneath modern frescoes (the owner didn't like the old ones, so he painted over them), which also grace two of the guest rooms (these are period, though).

Firenze. Piazza Donati 4 (on Via del Corso, off Via dei Calzaiuoli), 50122 Firenze. ☎ **055-268-301** or 055-214-203. Fax 055-212-370. 60 units. TV TEL. 110,000L ($55) single; 150,000L ($75) double; 215,000L ($107.50) triple; 260,000L ($130) quad. Rates include continental breakfast. No credit cards. Bus: A, 14, 23.

A recent renovation has transformed this former student hangout (still partly used as a study-abroad dorm) into a two-star hotel on its own little piazza at the heart the

Florence Accommodations & Dining

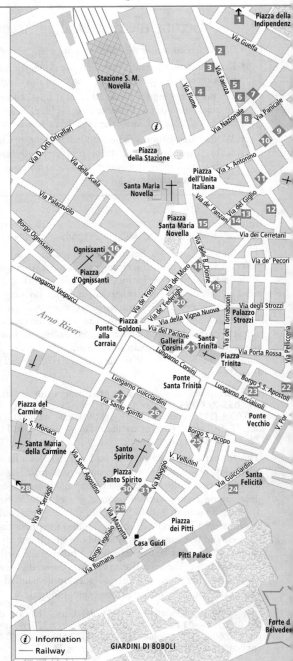

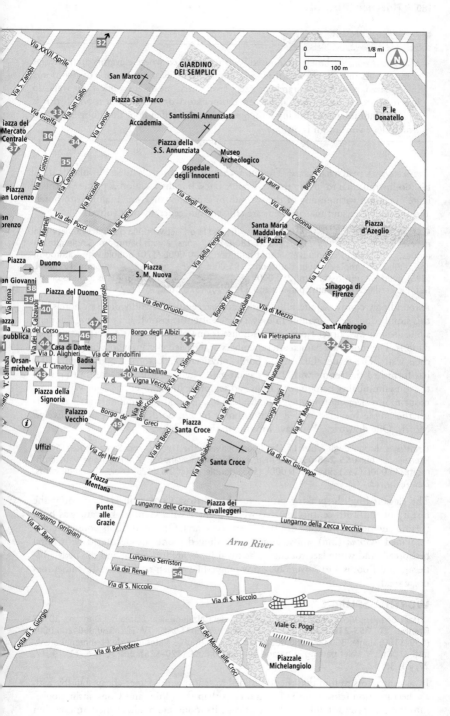

Via XXVII Aprile

Via S. Zanobi

32

GIARDINO
DEI SEMPLICI

0   1/8 mi
0   100 m

San Marco

Via Guelfa

33

Via San Gallo

Piazza San Marco

Via Cavour

Accademia

Santissimi Annunziata

P. le
Donatello

iazza del
Mercato
Centrale

36

34

Piazza della
S.S. Annunziata

Museo
Archeologico

37

Via de' Ginori

35

Via Cavour

i

Piazza
an Lorenzo

Ospedale
degli Innocenti

Borgo Pinti

Via Laura

Via della Colonna

an
orenzo

V. de' Martelli

Via dei Pucci

Via Ricasoli

Via de' Servi

Via degli Alfani

Santa Maria
Maddalena
dei Pazzi

Piazza
d'Azeglio

Via della Pergola

Via L. C. Farini

Piazza
an Giovanni

Duomo

Piazza
S. M. Nuova

Via Roma

38

Piazza del Duomo

39

Via dell'Oriuolo

Borgo Pinti

Via Fiesolana

Via di Mezzo

Sinagoga di
Firenze

Via del Proconsolo

40

Via del Corso

47

Via del Calzaiuoli

Borgo degli Albizi

51

Sant'Ambrogio

azza
lla
pubblica

44

45

46

48

Via Pietrapiana

52 53

1

Casa di Dante

Via D. Alighieri

Via de' Pandolfini

V. d. Cimatori

Badia

V. d.

50

Via Ghibellina

Orsan-
michele

V. Calimala

43

Vigna Vecchia

Via d. Stinche

V.M. Buonarroti

Piazza della
Signoria

V. de' Benci

Borgo de'

Via de' Bentaccordi

Via G. Verdi

Via de' Pepi

Borgo Allegri

Via de' Macci

i

Palazzo
Vecchio

49

Greci

Piazza
Santa Croce

Uffizi

Via del Neri

Via Magliabechi

Santa Croce

Via di San Giuseppe

Piazza
Mentana

Piazza dei
Cavalleggeri

Lungarno Torrigiani

Via de' Bardi

Ponte
alle
Grazie

Lungarno delle Grazie

Lungarno della Zecca Vecchia

Arno River

Lungarno Serristori

Via dei Renai

54

Costa di S. Giorgio

Via di S. Niccolo

Via di S. Niccolo

Via del Monte alle Croci

Viale G. Poggi

Via di Belvedere

Piazzale
Michelangiolo

An Elevator Warning

Many *centro storico* hotels are housed in historic palazzi where elevators aren't always common. As one-, two-, and three-star hotels, many exist on just one or two floors in a palazzo, with a lobby rarely at street level—that means it's a one-floor walk-up just to get to the front desk and often another story or two to your room. If this is an issue, inquire when booking if there's an elevator, which floor the lobby is on, and which floor your room is on.

centro storico's pedestrian zone. The rooms are simple, brightly tiled but bland. It's a bit too institutional to justify the mid-range rates, but the location *is* prime. This is a large operation without any of the warmth or ambiance of a small family-run hotel, and the concierge and management are efficient but generally uninvolved.

☮ **Maria Luisa de' Medici.** Via del Corso 1 (2nd floor; between Via dei Calzaiuoli and Via del Proconsolo), 50122 Firenze. ☎ **055-280-048.** 9 units, 2 with bathroom. Single rate on request; 110,000L ($55) double without bathroom, 140,000L ($70) double with bathroom; 150,000L ($75) triple without bathroom, 195,000L ($98) triple with bathroom; 192,000L ($96) quad without bathroom, 250,000L ($125) quad with bathroom. Rates include breakfast. No credit cards. Nearby parking about 40,000L ($20). Bus: A, 14, 23.

Astoundingly comfy, wonderfully quirky, and exceedingly friendly one-star hotels like this simply don't exist anymore in Italy. Named after the last Medici princess, this pensione around the corner from Dante's house is one of Italy's most eclectic accommodations. The rooms are named after members of the Medici clan, whose portraits grace their walls. The owner, Dr. Angelo Sordi (physician, collector, art and design buff), has furnished the rooms with 1960s avant-garde Italian furniture—contrasting with the museum-quality baroque paintings and sculpture in the foyer and hall. With enormous rooms sleeping up to five, the Maria Luisa is good for families, who'll also relish the ample breakfast served in the rooms by Dr. Sordi's Welsh partner, Evelyn Morris. One drawback: You have to walk up three flights.

Orchidea. Borgo degli Albizi 11 (1st floor; between the Duomo and Santa Croce), 50122 Firenze. ☎/fax **055-248-0346.** E-mail: hotelorchidea@yahoo.it. 7 units, none with bathroom. 75,000L ($38) single; 110,000L ($55) double; 150,000L ($75) triple. No credit cards. Bus: A, 14, 23.

The elegant English-speaking proprietor, Maria Rosa Cook, will gladly recount the history of this 13th-century palazzo where Dante's wife, Gemma Donati, was born (Dante's home and the Casa di Dante aren't far away). One of its floors houses an old-fashioned *locanda* (inn) whose large high-ceilinged rooms are decorated with floral bedspreads and white lace touches. The furnishings are functional and the beds a little squishy. Rooms 4 to 7 overlook a tiny jungle-like garden rather than the sometimes noisy road.

WORTH A SPLURGE

Chiari Bigallo. Vicolo degli Adimari 2 (off Via dei Calzaiuoli near Piazza del Duomo), 50122 Firenze. ☎ **055-216-086.** Fax 055-214-496. 27 units. A/C TV TEL. 180,000–200,000L ($90–$100) single; 300,000–350,000L ($150–$175) double. Rates include continental breakfast. AE, MC, V. Valet parking in garage 40,000–50,000L ($20–$25). Bus: A, 1, 6, 11, 14, 17, 22, 23, 36, 37.

I was quite cross to find that they'd decided to renovate this super-cheap standby with *the* best location (closer to the Duomo even than the Aldini and Constantini above) into three-star status (and double the prices). Its rooms are modular modern now, but in the location competition, it still wins for being above the Loggia del Bigallo on the corner of Piazza del Duomo. If you get one of the few rooms facing the Duomo, you'll have a view like no other, within poking distance of Giotto's bell tower. The traffic-free zone doesn't mean you won't have significant pedestrian noise that drifts up from the cobbled street below, as this is the city's most tourist-trammeled intersection.

They renovated this place to bring it in line with their other three hotels, including, a few blocks away on Via delle Oche and with side views of this living postcard, the quieter **Lanzi** (☎/fax **055-288-043**), with doubles at 330,000L ($165).

Pendini. Via Strozzi 1 (at Piazza della Repubblica), 50123 Firenze. ☎ **055-211-170.** Fax 055-281-807. www.florenceitaly.net. E-mail: pendini@dada.it. 42 units. A/C TV TEL. 150,000–200,000L ($75–$100) single; 200,000–280,000L ($100–$140) double; 280,000–380,000L ($140–$190) triple; 320,000–450,000L ($160–$225) quad; 320,000–590,000L ($160–$190) family suite. Rates include continental breakfast. AE, DC, MC, V. Valet garage parking 40,000–60,000L ($20–$30). Bus: A, 6, 11, 22, 36, 37.

The concept of the classic family-run pensione, quickly disappearing in Italy, is alive and well here: David and Emmanuele Abolaffio have kept intact the old-fashioned hominess of this century-old pensione. The nine spacious rooms overlooking Piazza della Repubblica are the most popular (guests don't seem to mind the late-night live music that comes from the square's cafes in summer); the rooms overlooking the inner courtyard are quieter. The family suites have two small bedrooms with a bathroom in common. The Pendini has been renovated but still exudes 19th-century elegance, for the owners rescued deserving original period pieces and supplemented them with convincing reproductions. A long corridor of parquet flooring covered with Persian runners leads to the inviting sitting room and the sunny breakfast room.

✪ **Torre Guelfa.** Borgo SS. Apostoli 8 (between Via dei Tornabuoni and Via Por Santa Maria), 50123 Firenze. ☎ **055-239-6338.** Fax 055-239-8577. www.italyhotel.com. E-mail: torre.guelfa@flashnet.it. 16 units. A/C MINIBAR TV TEL. 200,000L ($100) single; 300,000L ($150) double; 390,000L ($195) triple; 420,000L ($210) quad. Rates include continental breakfast. Ask about off-season discounts. AE, MC, V. Bus: B, 6, 11, 36, 37.

The first of many reasons to stay here is to drink in the breathtaking 360° view from the 13th-century tower, Florence's tallest privately owned tower. Though you're just steps from the Ponte Vecchio, you'll want to put sightseeing on hold and linger in your canopied iron bed. So many people request room no. 15, with a huge private terrace and a view similar to the tower's, they've had to tack 20,000L ($11) onto the price. Follow the strains of classical music to the salon, whose vaulted ceilings and lofty proportions hark back to the palazzo's 14th-century origins.

The owners' newest hotel endeavor is the 18th-century **Palazzo Castiglione,** Via del Giglio 8 (☎ **055-214-886;** fax 055-274-0521), with four doubles (300,000L/$150) and two suites (380,000L/$190); breakfast is served in your room. Also ask them about their new Tuscan hideaway, the **Villa Rosa** in Panzano (☎ **055-852-577;** fax 055-856-0835), a 35km (22-mi.) drive from Florence in the heart of the Chianti, where the 15 doubles are 200,000L to 240,000L ($100 to $120).

NEAR THE TRAIN STATION, MERCATO SAN LORENZO & SANTA MARIA NOVELLA

Inexpensive hotels proliferate in this area (generally safe but short on picturesque charm), particularly on **Via Faenza** and **Via Fiume,** where some buildings house as many as six pensioni. It makes most sense to walk to these hotels—all these are within a few blocks of the train station (which would be the bus stop anyway).

Armonia. Via Faenza 56 (1st floor), 50123 Firenze. ☎ **055-211-146.** 7 units, none with bathroom. 50,000–70,000L ($25–$35) single; 90,000–110,000L ($45–$55) double; 135,000L ($68) triple; 160,000L ($80) quad. No credit cards. Bus: 7, 10, 11, 12, 25, 31, 32, 33.

Owned by Mario and Marzia, a young English-speaking brother and sister, this pensione is a reliable no-frills choice when your budget keeps you near the train station. An occasional touch sets it apart: Some whitewashed rooms have nice bedspreads, and breakfast is served in your room at no extra charge. The three rooms in the back are the quietest. You'll have the key to the front door, so you won't need to wake the night porter after hours. In a quirky promotion, throughout 2001 they'll give you a 5% discount if you have the same last name as a famous actor (Mario's quite the film buff, as the photo gallery plastered around the reception desk attests).

Azzi. Via Faenza 56 (1st floor), 50123 Firenze. ☎/fax **055-213-806** (fax in 2001 may be 055-264-8613). E-mail: hotelazzi@hotmail.com. 12 units, 8 with shower and sink, 3 with bathroom. 70,000L ($35) single without bathroom; 100,000L ($50) double with shower, 130,000L ($65) double with bathroom; 120,000L ($60) triple without bathroom, 150,000L ($75) triple with bathroom; 160,000L ($80) quad with or without bathroom. 40,000L ($20) bed in shared room. Rates include breakfast. Off-season rates about 20% less. AE, DC, MC, V. Parking in nearby private garage 30,000L ($15). Bus: 7, 10, 11, 12, 25, 31, 32, 33.

Musicians Sandro and Valentino, the new young owners of this ex-pensione (a.k.a. the Locanda degli Artisti/Artists' Inn), are creating here a haven for artists, artist manqués, and students. It exudes a relaxed bohemian feel—not all the doors hang straight and not all the bedspreads match, though strides are being made (and they've even recently discovered some old frescoes in room 3 and 4). You'll love the open terrace with a view where breakfast is served in warm weather, as well as the small library of art books and guidebooks so you can enjoy a deeper understanding of Florence's treasures.

In the same building, under the same management and with similar rates, are the **Anna** (8 units, 4 with bathroom; ☎ **055-239-8322**) and the **Paola** (7 units, 4 with bathrooms and some with frescoes; ☎ **055-213-682**).

✪ **Bellettini.** Via dei Conti 7 (off Via dei Cerretani), 50123 Firenze. ☎ **055-213-561.** Fax 055-283-551. www.firenze.net/hotelbellettini. E-mail: hotel.bellettini@dada.it. A/C TV TEL. 28 units. 150,000L ($75) single; 230,000L ($115) double; 275,000L ($138) triple; 345,000L ($173) quad. Rates include buffet breakfast. AE, DC, MC, V. Nearby parking 35,000L ($18). Bus: A, 1, 6, 14, 17, 22, 23, 36, 37.

A hotel has existed in this Renaissance palazzo since the 1600s. Gina and Marzia, sisters who are third-generation hoteliers, run this gem of terra-cotta tiles, wrought-iron or carved wood beds, antiques, stained-glass windows, and hand-painted coffered ceilings. Room 44 offers a tiny balcony that, blooming with jasmine and geraniums by late spring, makes it second best only to room 45 with its view of the Medici Chapels and the Duomo's dome. The two bedrooms of no. 20 make it perfect for families. Breakfast is an impressive spread. In 2000, they added a lovely six-room annex with frescoes, marble baths, minibars, and coffeemakers; rooms are about 20,000L ($10) more than at the main hotel.

The hotel shares management with the 26-room **Le Vigne,** Piazza Santa Maria Novella 24 (☎ **055-294-449;** fax 055-230-2263), which absorbs some of the overflow into large but simple renovated rooms. The rates are slightly lower than at the Bellettini, and duplex 119 is great for families.

Boston. Via Guelfa 68 (west of Via Nazionale), 50129 Firenze. ☎ **055-496-747.** Fax 055-470-934. 18 units, 14 with bathroom. A/C TV TEL. *For Frommer's readers:* 100,000L ($50) single without bathroom, 140,000L ($70) single with bathroom; 195,000L ($98) double with bathroom; 240,000L ($120) triple with bathroom; 280,000L ($140) quad with bathroom.

Rates include continental breakfast. Ask about 15% low-season discounts. No credit cards. Valet parking 30,000L ($15). Bus: 7, 10, 11, 12, 25, 31, 32, 33.

The Boston is a dignified place filled with original art and blessed with a shaded patio where breakfast becomes an idyllic way to start your day. The first two floors were built in the 17th century and have exposed wooden beams and plenty of charm (rooms on the newer third floor, equally recommended, are accessible by elevator). Via Guelfa gets some traffic, so ask for a quiet room overlooking the patio, whose only noise is the clink of china at breakfast. When booking with the amenable Viti family, be sure to mention you're a Frommer's reader to be eligible for the discounted rates above.

✪ Burchianti. Via del Giglio 6 (off Via de Panzani), 50123 Firenze. ☎/fax **055-212-796.** 11 units, 5 with shower only, 6 with bathroom. 65,000L ($33) single without bathroom, 75,000L ($38) single with bathroom; 120,000L ($60) double with shower, 150,000L ($75) double with bathroom; 150,000L ($75) triple with shower, 190,000L ($95) triple with bathroom. Continental breakfast 8,000L ($4). Ask about off-season discounts. No credit cards. Nearby parking 50,000L ($25). Bus: A, 1, 6, 14, 17, 22, 23, 36, 37.

Opened in the late 19th century by the Burchianti sisters (the last of whom died in 1973) in a 17th-century palazzo, this pensione gets a star for sheer theatricality. It has hosted royals and VIPs (you may get Benito Mussolini's room), and much of that grandeur is intact though now faded a bit. Leaded and stained-glass windows and doors, frescoed walls and ceilings (in some, best in room 6), hand-painted coffered ceilings (in some), and antique furniture fill the high-ceilinged public areas and rooms (steer clear of the two ultra-plain rooms). Prefabricated shower stalls stuck in corners and sinks bolted onto 19th-century frescoed walls with the toilet down the hall are some eyesore additions. Yet the sunny salon and handsome breakfast room seem right out of a Merchant Ivory film.

✪ Centrale. Via dei Conti 3 (2nd floor; off Via Cerretani), 50123 Firenze. ☎ **055-215-761.** Fax 055-215-216. 18 units, 15 with bathroom. TV TEL. 168,000L ($84) single with bathroom; 168,000L ($84) double without bathroom, 198,000L ($99) double with bathroom; 215,000L ($108) triple without bathroom, 250,000L ($125) triple with bathroom. Rates include buffet breakfast. Rates discounted in Aug. AE, DC, MC, V. Bus: A, 1, 6, 14, 17, 22, 23, 36, 37.

The presence of Normandy-born manager Mariethérése Blot is everywhere in this pensione converted from a 14th-century palazzo. Most of the large bright rooms contain matching antique armoires and headboards, and many rooms overlook the Medici Chapels. Throughout you'll note the careful housekeeping and touches like dried flower bouquets under the occasional stuccoed ceiling. This is a perfect place for families, and off-season guests who stay for four nights minimum but pay for only three. Plus you get the most ample buffet breakfast in town at this price.

Centro. Via Ginori 17 (north of Piazza San Lorenzo), 50123 Firenze. ☎ **055-230-2901.** Fax 055-212-706. www.hotelcentro.net. E-mail: centro@pronet.it. 16 units, 14 with bathroom. TV TEL. 110,000L ($55) single without bathroom, 150,000L ($75) single with bathroom; 190,000L ($95) double with bathroom; 300,000L ($150) triple with bathroom. Rates include buffet breakfast. AE, DC, MC, V. Nearby garage 35,000L ($18). Bus: 1, 6, 11, 17.

A block north of the Mercato San Lorenzo, this refurbished hotel occupies a palazzo that was home to Renaissance master painter Raphael in 1505 and 1506. There's precious little he'd recognize in its contemporary reincarnation, with ample-sized rooms outfitted in pastel bedspreads and blond-wood furnishings; the bathrooms are tiled in white and brightly lit. New owners Andrea and Sandra Vendali continue to upgrade with amenities like hair dryers and safes. Second-floor rooms have air-conditioning (most of the rest get ceiling fans).

Fiorita. Via Fiume 20 (3rd floor), 50123 Firenze. ☎ **055-283-189.** Fax 055-272-8153. www.hotelfiorita.com. 13 units, 10 with bathroom. A/C MINIBAR TV TEL. 120,000L ($60) single without bathroom, 140,000L ($70) single with bathroom; 210,000L ($105) double with bathroom; 290,000L ($145) triple with bathroom. Rates include buffet breakfast. Low-season discount 25%. AE, DC, MC, V. Valet parking 35,000L ($18). Bus: A, 4, 7, 10, 11, 12, 13, 14, 25, 28, 31, 32, 33, 36, 37, 62.

In 1999, the friendly Maselli family gussied up its old one-star to meet two-star standards, but the addition of welcomed amenities like TVs and air conditioning hasn't encroached on the venerable charm inherent in the original stained-glass doors and windows that hint of the palazzo's late 19th-century origins. Approximately half the rooms and bathrooms have been fully refurbished and, at no extra cost, are the ones to ask for.

Merlini. Via Faenza 56 (3rd floor), 50123 Firenze. ☎ **055-212-848.** Fax 055-283-939. 10 units, 2 with bathroom. 65,000–75,000L ($33–$38) single without bathroom; 95,000–105,000L ($48–$53) double without bathroom, 125,000L ($63) double with bathroom; 135,000–140,000L ($68–$70) triple without bathroom. Breakfast 9,000L ($4.50). Off-season rates about 15% less. MC, V. Bus: 7, 10, 11, 12, 25, 31, 32, 33.

Family-run by a Sicilian, this cozy walk-up boasts rooms appointed with wooden-carved antique headboards and furnishings (and a few modular pieces to fill in the gaps). It's one of only two hotels in all Florence with mosquito screens. The optional breakfast is served on a sunny glassed-in terrace decorated in the 1950s with frescoes by talented American art students. Enjoy your cappuccino with a view of the Medici Chapel's cupola, Florence's bell towers, and the city's terra-cotta roofscape. This is a notch above your average one-star place, the best in a building full of tiny pensioni. There's a 1am curfew.

Mia Cara. Via Faenza 58 (2nd floor), 50123 Firenze. ☎ **055-216-053.** Fax 055-230-2601. 22 units, 9 with bathroom. *For Frommer's readers:* Single with/without bathroom (call for rates); 90,000L ($45) double without bathroom, 105,000L ($53) double with bathroom. Extra bed 35% more. Ask about off-season discounts. No credit cards. Four parking spots 10,000–15,000L ($5–$8). Bus: 7, 10, 11, 12, 25, 31, 32, 33.

The only way you'll pay less than at this one-star hotel is at the Noto family's hostel on the ground floor. At the hotel, you'll find double-paned windows, spacious no-frills rooms, renovated plumbing (no shower curtains), and attractive iron headboards. Now if they'd only up the wattage of the light fixtures. The rooms overlooking the small garden out back are more tranquil than those on the street side. Angela, the English-speaking daughter, can be reached at the above numbers or ☎ **055-290-804** for info on the downstairs **Archi Rossi Hostel,** where units sleep four to six, without bathroom for 30,000L ($15) per person and with bathroom for 35,000L ($18)—lower rates in low season. Both the hotel and the hostel have their own TV room and public phone.

Monica. Via Faenza 66 (1st floor; at Via Cennini), 50123 Firenze. ☎ **055-283-804.** Fax 055-281-706. 15 units, 2 with shower only, 10 with bathroom. A/C TV TEL. 140,000L ($70) single without bathroom, 160,000L ($80) single with bathroom; 190,000L ($95) double without bathroom, 220,000L ($110) double with bathroom; 280,000L ($140) triple without bathroom, 320,000L ($160) triple with bathroom. Rates include buffet breakfast. Ask for discounts in low season. AE, DC, MC, V. Bus: 7, 10, 11, 12, 25, 31, 32, 33.

Gracious polyglot Rhuna Cecchini has supervised the facelift of this hotel, resulting in a bright airy ambiance and refinished baths. The prices have increased but so have the amenities. Highlights are the terrazzo floors, wrought-iron bedsteads, exposed-brick archways, and wonderful terrace, which begins hosting breakfast the minute the weather turns warm. Most rooms are in the back of the building over the terrace, ensuring a quiet stay and pleasant rooftop views.

✪ **Nuova Italia.** Via Faenza 26 (off Via Nazionale), 50123 Firenze. ☎ **055-268-430** or 055-287 508. Fax 055-210-941. E-mail: hotel.nuova.italia@dada.it. 20 units. A/C TV TEL. *For Frommer's readers:* 155,000L ($78) single; 205,000L ($103) double; 255,000L ($128) triple; 305,000L ($153) quad. Rates include continental breakfast. AE, DC, MC, V (but 8% discount if you pay in cash or traveler's checks). Valet garage parking 35,000L ($18). Bus: 7, 10, 11, 12, 25, 31, 32, 33.

This top-notch hotel is watched over by affable English-speaking Luciano and Canadian-born Eileen Viti and their daughter, Daniela. Eileen met Luciano more than 30 years ago, when she stayed at his family's hotel on the recommendation of an old *Frommer's Europe on $5 a Day.* Their hotel is a work in progress: One season, triple-paned windows and rare mosquito screens were installed; the next, bathrooms were retiled and air-conditioning and new carpeting appeared. Expected by the time you get there is new furniture custom-designed by Eileen. Dry cleaning and laundry services are available. The family's love of art is manifested in all the framed posters and paintings, and Eileen is a great source about local exhibits.

Serena. Via Fiume 20 (2nd floor), 50123 Firenze. ☎ **055-213-643.** Fax 055-280-447. 8 units, 2 with shower only, 3 with bathroom. TEL TV. Single rate on request; 130,000L ($65) double without bathroom, 150,000L ($75) double with bathroom. Extra person 50,000L ($25). Ask about off-season discounts. AE, DC, MC, V. Bus: A, 4, 7, 10, 11, 12, 13, 14, 25, 28, 31, 32, 33, 36, 37, 62.

Run with pride by the Bigazzi family, this unpretentious but dignified one-star place offers pleasant surprises: some brand-new nicely tiled baths, molded ceilings, and early 1900s stained-glass French doors. The rooms are airy and bright and kept clean as a whistle by the owner's wife. If this place is full, try the smaller and less expensive **Otello Tourist House** upstairs (☎/fax **055-239-6159**); it has just four simple but lovely units, two with bathroom, and is run by English-speaking Anna and her husband, Otello.

WORTH A SPLURGE

Mario's. Via Faenza 89 (1st floor; near Via Cennini), 50123 Firenze. ☎ **055-216-801.** Fax 055-212-039. www.webitaly.com/hotel.marios. E-mail: hotelmarios@hotelmarios.com. 16 units. A/C TV TEL. 110,000–230,000L ($55–$115) single; 160,000–310,000L ($80–$155) double; 210,000–380,000L ($105–$190) triple. Rates include continental breakfast. AE, DC, MC, V. Valet parking 35,000–45,000L ($18–$23). Bus: 7, 10, 11, 12, 25, 31, 32, 33.

In a traditional Old Florence atmosphere, Mario Noce and his enthusiastic staff run a first-rate ship. Your room may have a wrought-iron headboard and massive reproduction antique armoire and look out onto a peaceful garden; the amenities include hair dryers and fresh flowers and fruit. The beamed ceilings in the common areas date from the 17th century, though the building became a hotel only in 1872. I'd award Mario's a star if not for its location—it's a bit far from the Duomo nerve center. Hefty discounts during off-season months (as low as the lowest rates listed above) de-splurge this lovely choice.

NEAR PIAZZA SAN MARCO

Cimabue. Via Benifacio Lupi 7 (west of Via San Gallo), 50129 Firenze. ☎ **055-471-989.** Fax 055-463-0906. www.venere.it/firenze/cimabue. E-mail: hotelcimabue@tin.it. 16 units. TV TEL. 150,000–170,000L ($75–$65) single; 200,000–240,000L ($100–$120) double; 260,000–300,000L ($130–$150) triple; 300,000–350,000L ($150–$175) quad. Rates include buffet breakfast. AE, DC, MC, V. Nearby garage 30,000L ($15). Bus: 1, 7, 8, 12, 25, 33, 80.

Looking for a hotel with lots of charm and character and a spirited multilingual couple that runs it all with pride? The small Cimabue may have only two stars, but they're two shining stars, from the firm orthopedic mattresses to the best freshly ground breakfast cappuccino. When Igino Possi and his Belgian wife, Daniele Dinau, renovated their acquisition in 1993, they saved what they loved best in this 1904 palazzo and renovated around it: the original terra-cotta pavement, ceiling frescoes in six rooms, suites of art-nouveau headboards, and mirrored armoires. During a recent visit, the guests were an interesting mix of two retired British professors, an American priest, a young Canadian couple on their honeymoon, and a stylish German art historian.

IN THE OLTRARNO

Much more convenient than the remote though beautiful IYHF youth hostel in the hills of Fiesole (Ostello Villa Canerata, Viale Augusto Righi 2/4, 50137 Firenze; ☎ **055/60-14-51;** fax 055/61-03-00), the privately run **Ostello Santa Monaca,** Via Santa Monaca 6, 50124 Firenze (☎ **055-268-338;** fax 055-280-185; www.ostello.it), is a lively gathering spot for the collegiate and newly graduated crowd, as well as a great place to trade budget tips and meet travel companions; beds cost 25,000L ($13) each.

✪ **La Scaletta.** Via Guicciardini 13 (2nd floor; near Piazza de Pitti), 50125 Firenze. ☎ **055-283-028** or 055-214-255. Fax 055-289-562. www.lascaletta.com. 12 units, 11 with bathroom. TEL. 100,000L ($50) single without bathroom, 180,000L ($90) single with bathroom; 190,000L ($95) double without bathroom, 210,000–240,000L ($105–$120) double with bathroom; 200,000L ($100) triple without bathroom, 250,000–270,000L ($125–$135) triple with bathroom; 280,000–300,000L ($140–$150) quad with bathroom. Rates include continental breakfast. Ask about off-season discounts. MC, V. Nearby parking 20,000–40,000L ($10–$20). Bus: D, 11, 36, 37.

Order an iced tea and head for the umbrella-shaded roof terrace at sunset, then marvel at the stunning 360° panorama overlooking the Pitti Palace. In one of only two historic palazzi on the street to survive World War II, this top-floor pensione is run by Barbara Barbieri and her son, Manfredo. The spacious rooms boast terra-cotta floors, whitewashed walls, sturdy furnishings, and waffle towels in the modest bathrooms. Four have air-conditioning, including one without bathroom, and you may have a TV on request. Those downstairs are more old-fashioned, with *pietra serena* door jambs, and there's even a huge family-style room with a fireplace. The rooms fronting Via Giucciardini have double-paned windows, while the quieter ones in back overlook the Boboli Gardens. On request, Manfredo whips up a fixed-price dinner for 20,000L ($11).

Sorelle Bandini. Piazza Santo Spirito 9, 50125 Firenze. ☎ **055-215-308.** Fax 055-282-761. 13 units, 5 with bathroom. Single rate on request; 184,000L ($92) double without bathroom, 224,000L ($112) double with bathroom; 254,000L ($127) triple without bathroom, 308,000L ($154) triple with bathroom. Extra person 35% more. Rates include continental breakfast. No credit cards (for now). Bus: D, 11, 36, 37.

This pensione occupies a landmark Renaissance palazzo on one of the city's great squares. You can live like the nobles of yore in rooms with 15-foot ceilings whose 10-foot windows and oversize antique furniture are proportionately appropriate. Room 9 sleeps five and offers a Duomo view from its bathroom window; room B is a double with a fantastic cityscape out the window. On closer inspection, you'll see the resident cats have left their mark on common-area sofas, and everything seems a bit ramshackle and musty. But that seems to be the point. The highlight is the monumental roofed veranda where Mimmo, the English-speaking manager, oversees breakfast and encourages brown-bag lunches and the chance to relax and drink in the views. Zeffirelli used the pensione for some scenes in *Tea With Mussolini.*

Worth a Splurge

✪ **Silla.** Via dei Renai 5 (on Piazza Demidoff, east of Ponte delle Grazie), 50125 Firenze. ☎ **055-234-2888.** Fax 055-234-1437. www.hotelsilla.it. 35 units. A/C MINIBAR TV TEL. 210,000L ($105) single; 290,000L ($145) double; 350,000L ($175) triple. Rates include buffet breakfast. Ask about off-season discounts. AE, DC, MC, V. Parking in hotel garage 25,000L ($12.50). Often closes late Nov to late Dec. Bus: C, D, 12, 13, 23.

On a shaded riverside piazza, this 15th-century palazzo's second-floor patio terrace is one of the city's nicest breakfast settings (in winter, there's a breakfast salon with chandeliers and oil paintings). The Silla's most recent renovation was in 1997, with a few rooms redone in 1994. Many overlook the Arno and, when winter strips the leaves off the front trees, the spire of Santa Croce on the opposite bank. Every room is unique— some with beamed ceilings and parquet floors, others with floral wallpaper and stylish furnishings. The attention to detail and friendly skilled staff should make this hotel better known; word-of-mouth keeps it regularly full in pricey Florence despite its refreshing low profile.

4 Great Deals on Dining

Italian **meals** consist of three primary courses: the *antipasto* **(appetizer),** the *primo* **(first course, usually a pasta or soup),** and the *secondo* **(the main course of meat or fish)**—to which you must add a separate *contorno* if you want a side of veggies. You're expected to order at least two courses, if not all three.

Almost all the places below specialize in *cucina povera* or *cucina rustica,* based on the region's rustic and hearty cuisine. Despite its simplicity, Flortentine cooking remains one of the most renowned in Italy for its well-balanced flavors and high-caliber ingredients.

Slabs of crusty bread are used for *crostini,* spread with chicken-liver pâté as the favorite Florentine antipasto. Hearty Tuscan peasant soups often take the place of pasta, especially *ribollita* **(a stew-like minestra of twice-boiled cabbage, beans, and bread)** or *pappa al pomodoro* **(a similarly thick bread soup made from tomatoes and drizzled with olive oil).** Look for *pasta fatta in casa* **(the homemade pasta of the day),** such as Tuscan pappardelle, thick flat noodles, often served *al cinghiale* **(with a wild boar sauce)** or with a simple tomato sauce. Your *contorno* will likely be the classic *fagioli all'uccelletto* **(cannellini beans smothered in a sauce of tomatoes and rosemary or sage),** sometimes *fagioli* are served plain, dressed only with extra-virgin olive oil.

Grilled meats are a specialty, the jewel being ✪ *bistecca alla fiorentina,* an inch-thick charcoal-broiled steak on the bone: It's usually the most expensive item on the menu but is often meant to be shared by two (if you're not a sharer, tell the waiter it's *per una persona sola*). A wonderful splurge! Florentines also sing the praises of *trippa alla fiorentina,* but cow's stomach cut into strips and served with onions and tomatoes isn't for everyone.

Though you won't swoon over the unfussy and limited desserts, the pudding-like *tiramisù* made with whipped mascarpone cheese is almost always great, if not typically Florentine. Some travelers could care less about the art, culture, or shopping in Florence; they come just for the *gelato,* a denser, richer, and more heavenly cousin to ice cream (see "Taking a Gelato Break," later in this section).

Tuscany's most famous red **wines** are from the designated area known as **Chianti** between Florence and Siena. You may be pleasantly surprised with the far less expensive *vino della casa* (house wine). Either a full bottle is brought to the table—you'll be charged *al consumo,* according to the amount you consume—or you'll be served by the quarter or half carafe as you request.

Note: You can locate the restaurants below on the "Florence Accommodations & Dining" map on p. 178.

NEAR THE DUOMO & PIAZZA DELLA SIGNORIA

Alimentari Orizi. Via Parione 19r (off Via dei Tornabuoni). ☎ **055-214-067.** Sandwiches 4,000–6,000L ($2–$3). AE, MC, V. Mon–Fri 8am–3pm and 5–8pm, Sat 8am–8pm. Closed Aug 1–15. SANDWICH BAR.

Surprisingly few spots will make sandwiches to your specifications, and even fewer will give you the chance to pull up a seat and enjoy your food with a glass of wine at no extra cost. At this small *alimentari* (grocery store), Signor Orizi offers a choice of crusty rolls and breads and quality meats and cheeses to be sliced and arranged as you like (now with ketchup, mayonnaise, and mustard, too). There's a bar and half a dozen stools, but if the sun is shining you can ask for your creation *da portare via* (to take away) and find a piazza bench with a view (Piazza della Repubblica to the east or Piazza Santa Maria Novella to the west). The new coffee machine and fresh pastries make this a good breakfast option.

Caffè Caruso. Via Lambertesca 16r (off Via Por Santa Maria). ☎ **055-281-940.** Primi 8,000–9,000L ($4–$4.50); secondi 10,000–12,000L ($5–$6); pizza and soda 15,000L ($8). AE, MC, V. Mon–Sat 8am–6pm. ITALIAN.

On a quiet side street between Via Por Santa Maria and the Uffizi, a block from the Ponte Vecchio, this family-run caffè serves a variety of inexpensive hot dishes in what amounts to an expanded bar/*tavola calda* (small cafeteria). It's busy with locals at lunch, but the continuous hours promise less commotion if your appetite is flexible (however, the variety diminishes after the lunch crush). Choose from the display of four or five pastas, a few roast meats (chicken, pork, roast beef), a dozen pizzas, or lots of vegetable side dishes (making this place great for light eaters and vegetarians). It isn't fancy, but the prices are rock bottom for this area.

Caffè Italiano. Via Condotta 56r (off Via dei Calzaiuoli). ☎ **055-291-082.** Primi 8,000L ($4); secondi 12,000L ($6); salads 13,000L ($7). No credit cards. Daily 12:30–3pm and 8–10pm. Bar daily: winter 7:30am–1am, summer to 8pm. ITALIAN.

Umberto Montano, the young owner of this handsome caffè, has created an early 1900s ambiance in the second-floor dining room and offers a delicious lunch to standing-room-only crowds (come early). The delicate but full-flavored soups, mixed platter of salamis and cheeses, and unusual variety of vegetable *sformati* (terrines) top the list of choices, or you can order one of a dozen oversized salads. Stop by in the afternoon for dessert: Made on the premises by a talented pastry chef, they go perfectly with the exclusive blend of African coffees. You may hear that Montano owns two other restaurants, the **Osteria del Caffè Italiano** and **Alle Murate,** but I don't recommend them. Stick with Caffè Italiano.

Closed for Vacation

Despite Florence's importance as a modern-day Grand Tour destination, almost all restaurants (and stores and offices) close *per ferie* (for vacation) at some point in July or August from 2 to 6 weeks. The date may vary from year to year, so call any of the following establishments during this period before showing up: Your hotel will always know of a reliable choice in the neighborhood. In August, no one ever goes hungry, but your choices are considerably diminished.

Getting the Best Deal on Dining

- Choose a casual eatery where you'll feel comfortable ordering just one course (easier done at lunch)—though whether a modest pasta dish will satisfy your appetite may be another matter. You won't get the heaping portions common-place in many American restaurants serving Italian food.
- If the weather is nice, grab a *panino* (sandwich) to go, choose a different piazza every day for lunch and a lesson on neighborhood life, and leave more lire for an evening's trattoria experience.
- Consider the *menù turistico,* a potential bargain, but first ask about what's included—the selection is often limited and one of the courses is probably a vegetable side dish.
- Try the local *vino della casa* (table wine) instead of a finer bottled wine.
- Round off your dinner with dessert elsewhere: Order an ice cream to go at a neighborhood gelateria and stroll the city's deserted side streets.
- For a splurge evening, you needn't go to Florence's white-glove restaurants and Michelin-starred choices. The more modestly priced trattorie in this chapter can bring you up to another level of spending—and enjoyment—when you leave restraint at the door and go for the sampling of antipasti to start, a choice of the more expensive grilled meats (and that fabled bistecca alla fiorentina) and an extra fine bottle of Chianti Classico. Il Latini, Trattoria Antellesi, and Trattoria Sostanza can guarantee you that special evening for a few thousand lire more (usually just beyond 50,000L/$25). If you're a wine rookie, ask your waiter to help you choose from the best of the regional wines: Remember that the premier wines of the designated Chianti area are grown in Florence's backyard.

✪ **Cantinetta del Verrazzano.** Via dei Tavolini 18–20r (off Via dei Calzaiuoli). ☎ **055-268-590.** Focaccia sandwiches 1,500–6,000L (75¢–$3); glass of wine 2,500–10,000L ($1.25–$5). AE, DC, MC, V. Mon–Sat 8am–9pm. WINE BAR.

Owned by the Castello di Verrazzano, one of Chianti's best-known wine-producing estates (see chapter 5), this wood-paneled *cantinetta* with a full-service bar/*pasticceria* and seating area helped spawn a revival of stylish wine bars as convenient spots for fast-food breaks. It promises a delicious self-service lunch or snack of focaccia, plain or studded with peas, rosemary, onions, or olives; buy it hot by the slice or as *farcite* (sandwiches filled with prosciutto, arugula, cheese, or tuna). Try a glass of their full-bodied chianti to make this the perfect respite. Platters of Tuscan cold cuts and aged cheeses are also available.

Trattoria Belle Donne. Via delle Belle Donne 16r (north off Via della Vigna Nuova). ☎ **055/238-2609.** Reservations not accepted. Primi 10,000L ($5); secondi 10,000–15,000L ($5–$8). MC, V. Mon–Fri 12:30–2:30pm and 7:15–10:30pm. Closed most of Aug. TUSCAN.

Tucked away on a narrow street (whose name refers to the women of the night who once worked this then-shady neighborhood) parallel to exclusive Via dei Tornabuoni, this packed-to-the-gills lunch spot (with no identifying sign) immediately drew the area's chic boutique owners and sales staff. It now tries to accommodate them and countless others (no lingering over lunch; dinner isn't as rushed). Tuscan cuisine gets reinterpreted and updated by the talented young chef, who placates the local palate without alienating it: Traditional dishes appear in the company of innovative alternatives like cream of zucchini and chestnut soup or lemon-flavored chicken. The regulars seem inured to the occasional rush job, so don't take it personally.

Trattoria Croce al Trebbio. Via delle Belle Donne 49r (west of Via dei Tornabuoni). ☎ **055/287-089.** Reservations recommended only for groups over 4. Primi 7,500–13,000L ($3.75–$7); secondi 14,000–20,000L ($7–$10). AE, DC, MC, V. Tues–Sun noon–2:30pm and 7–10:30pm (daily Mar–Oct). Closed Aug. TUSCAN.

Locals head for their regular tables near the kitchen, where spirited conversation turns to politics, soccer, and how last year's wine was better (they say that every year). Overseeing everything is the affable Signor Riccardo, who has run this trattoria for over 20 years. The menu is straightforward and delicious, and the well-priced *menu Toscano* (23,000L/$12) provides a choice of six primi and seven secondi plus a side dish and dessert. Simplicity is paramount in dishes like *pollo arrosto con potate* (tender free-range chicken, roasted with baby potatoes and spiced with rosemary and sage). It tastes better if you're seated at one of the few tables in the 15th-century terra-cotta wine cellar.

Ristorante Casa di Dante (da Pennello). Via Dante Alighieri 4r (between Via dei Calzaiuoli and Via del Proconsolo). ☎ **055-294-848.** Reservations suggested. Primi 10,000–14,000L ($5–$7); secondi 12,000–22,000L ($6–$11); *menù turistico* 30,000L ($15) without wine. AE, DC, V. Tues–Sat noon–3pm and 7–10:30pm, Sun noon–3pm. Closed Aug. ITALIAN.

This is one of Florence's oldest restaurants, housed since the 1500s in a palazzo that once belonged to a Renaissance artist (Cellini, Pontormo, and Andrea del Sarto used to dine here). Its claim to fame is the antipasto table, groaning under the day's changing array of two dozen appetizers. Prices vary, but expect to spend 10,000L to 15,000L ($5 to $8) for a good sampling. Continue by ordering the *tris di primi a piacere,* your choice of any three pastas for a minimum of two (20,000L/$10 per person). Lesser appetites may be as happy with a simple pasta and perfectly grilled chop for about the same cost.

Trattoria le Mossacce. Via del Proconsolo 55r (a block south of the Duomo). ☎ **055-294-361.** Reservations suggested for dinner. Primi 7,500–8,500L ($3.75–$4.25); secondi 9,000L–22,000L ($4.50–$11). AE, MC, V. Mon–Fri noon–2:30pm and 7–9:30pm. ITALIAN.

This is a straightforward place for *cucina toscana,* deftly prepared and served in a lively and pleasant atmosphere. Favorites on the menu are the thick *ribollita* or any of the daily changing pastas. If the thought of a thick slab of steak is your idea of heaven, indulge in the regional specialty, the *bistecca alla fiorentina,* a splurge worth 22,000L ($11).

NEAR THE TRAIN STATION, THE MERCATO SAN LORENZO & SANTA MARIA NOVELLA

✪ **Il Latini.** Via Palchetti 6r (off Via della Vigna Nuova). ☎ **055-210-916.** Reservations required. Primi 10,000–12,000L ($5–$6); secondi 15,000–20,000L ($8–$10); fixed-price meal 55,000L ($28). AE, MC, V. Tues–Sun 12:30–2:30pm and 7:30–10:30pm. ITALIAN.

Octogenarian Narcisio Latini and his sons, Giovanni and Torello, operate one of the busiest tavernlike trattorias in town. There's always a line waiting for a cramped seat at one of the long wooden tables. But the delicious adventure is worth the wait, with most of the wines and many of the menu choices coming from the Latini's estate in Chianti. There's a written menu, but you probably won't see it, for one of the brothers will explain the selection in a working version of English. Gargantuan eaters can indulge in the *menu completo*—a meaty fixed-price feast for 55,000L ($28), plus all the wine and mineral water you can drink. More restrained appetites and wallets should just order à la carte.

Taking a Gelato Break

Florence is a good spot for **gelato** (ice cream), with a number of great sources around town. The following are not only the best but also have the largest selections and are the most central. Ask for a *cono* (cone) or *coppa* (cup) from 2,000L to 10,000L ($1 to $5)—point and ask for as many flavors as can be squeezed in (you can have a field day with the 10,000L size).

Of all the centrally located gelaterie, **Festival del Gelato,** Via del Corso 75r, just off Via dei Calzaiuoli (☎ **055-239-4386**), has been the only serious contender to the premier Vivoli (below), offering about 50 flavors along with pounding pop music and colorful neon. It's open Tuesday to Sunday: summer 8am to 1am and winter 11am to 1am.

Vivoli, Via Isole delle Stinche 7r, a block west of Piazza Santa Croce (☎ **055-239-2334**), is still the city's institution. Exactly how renowned is this bright gelateria? Taped to the wall is a postcard bearing only "Vivoli, Europa" for the address, yet it was successfully delivered to this world capital of ice cream. It's open Tuesday to Sunday 9am to 1am (closed August and January to early February).

One of the major advantages of the always crowded **Gelateria delle Carrozze,** Piazza del Pesce 3–5r (☎ **055-23-96-810**), is its location at the foot of the Ponte Vecchio—if you're coming off the bridge and about to head on to the Duomo, this gelateria is immediately off to your right on a small alley that forks off the main street. In summer, it's open daily 11am to 1am; in winter, hours are Thursday to Tuesday 11am to 8pm.

A block south of the Accademia (pick up a cone after you've gazed upon *David*'s glory) is what local purists insist is Vivoli's only deserving contender to the throne as gelato king: **Carabé,** Via Ricasoli 60r (☎ **055-289-476**). It offers genuine homemade Sicilian gelato in the heart of Florence, with ingredients shipped in from Sicily by the hard-working Sicilian owners. Taste for yourself and see if Florentines can hope to ever surpass such scrumptiousness direct from the island that first brought the concept of ice cream to Europe. May 16 to September, it's open daily 10am to midnight; February 15 to May 15 and October to November 15, hours are Tuesday to Sunday 10am to 8pm.

Nerbone. In the Mercato Centrale, entrance on Via dell'Ariento, stand no. 292 (ground floor). ☎ **055-219-949.** Primi 4,000–6,000L ($2–$3); secondi 7,000L ($3.50). No credit cards. Mon–Sat 7am–3pm. ITALIAN.

One of the city's best basic eateries, this red-and-green food stand is inside the covered meat-and-produce marketplace. Packed with marketgoers, vendors, and working-class types, it offers four small tables next to a meat counter. Daily specials include a limited choice of pastas, soups, huge plates of cooked vegetables, sausages, and fresh sandwiches. The service is swift, and wine and beer are sold by the glass. If at first you can't find Nerbone, just ask. It's worth the hunt and promises lots of local color and good eats.

✪ **Trattoria Antellesi.** Via Faenza 9r (near the Medici Chapels). ☎ **055-216-990.** Reservations required. Primi 10,000L–14,000L ($5–$7); secondi 16,000L–28,000L ($8–$14). AE, DC, MC, V. Mon–Sat noon–2:30pm and 7–10:30pm. ITALIAN.

This is an attractive spot in a converted Renaissance palazzo. As their restaurant empire expands, the young Florence/Arizona combination of chef Enrico and manager/sommelier Janice Verrecchia are around less these days, but their skilled staff guarantees a lovely Tuscan dining experience. Never without a smile, they'll talk you through a memorable dinner that should start with their signature antipasto of pecorino cheese and pears. Follow with *crespelle alla fiorentina* (crêpes stuffed with ricotta and spinach and baked) or *spaghetti alla chiantigiana* (pasta with chianti-marinated beef cooked in tomato sauce). This is the spot to try *bistecca alla fiorentina*— and one of the excellent moderately priced red wines.

Trattoria I Cafaggi. Via Guelfa 35r (west of Via dei Ginori). ☎ **055-294-989.** Reservations suggested for dinner. Primi 12,000–13,000L ($6–$7); secondi 16,000–25,000L ($8–$13). AE, DC, MC, V. Wed–Mon noon–2:30pm and 7:30–10:30pm. Closed 2 weeks in late July or Aug. TUSCAN.

This roomy plain-Jane trattoria looks like it has always been here. The simple old-fashioned decor isn't worth describing, but the cooking is. Maybe not as good as mamma's, but this is a satisfying second choice. In the same family for generations, it was long ago discovered by the tourist trade, but the mix of diners still leans toward Florentine fans, who come for moderately priced meals and quality fish in a carnivorous town. Budget watchers should take a look at the fixed-price menus available at lunch and dinner; don't overlook the napoleon-like *millefoglie* or any of the homemade desserts.

Trattoria I' Toscano. Via Guelfa 70r (west of Via dei Ginori). ☎ **055-215-475.** Reservations suggested for dinner. Primi 10,000–14,000L ($5–$7); secondi 14,000–22,000L ($7–$11); fixed-price lunch 27,000L ($14). AE, DC, MC, V. Wed–Mon noon–2:30pm and 7:30–10:30pm. Closed Aug 1–15. TUSCAN.

This flower-filled somewhat formal space showcases enduring old-time Florentine recipes made to seem new again. For a delicious crash course on *cucina fiorentina*, start with the delicious homemade ravioli, outshone only by the truffle-sauced gnocchi. Typical of Tuscany's meat-heavy specialties and dictated by the season, game (*cacciagione*) plays an important role; those so inclined should sample wild boar, venison, rabbit, and pheasant. More predictable and my own favorite is the *arista di maiale con patate arroste* (rosemary-flavored roast pork loin with potatoes). Fresh fish, so very un-Florentine despite Tuscany's strip of nearby coastline, is especially prominent on Friday.

Trattoria Le Fonticine. Via Nazionale 79r (at Via dell'Ariento, north end of the Mercato Centrale). ☎ **055-282-106.** Reservations recommended. Primi 7,000–20,000L ($3.50–$10); secondi 14,000–25,000L ($7–$13). AE, DC, MC, V. Tues–Sat noon–3pm and 7–10pm. Closed Aug. TUSCAN/BOLOGNESE.

Bruna Grazia, the talented Bologna-born chef and co-owner of this art-filled restaurant on the edge of the Mercato Centrale (look next door for the 16th-century Luca della Robbia wall fountain from which the restaurant takes its name), serves as an unofficial guarantee that you'll leave with a smile. Silvano Bruci, Bruna's Florentine-born husband (and the collector of the modern art) sees that his hometown's cuisine doesn't get short shrift. Tortellini are the traditional pasta of Bologna and are hand-made and hand-stuffed here daily, with a hearty *alla bolognese* sauce that overshadows the menu's admirable roster of competing primi (ask about the pasta sampler). If you're seated in the back room, you'll pass the open kitchen and be rewarded a glimpse of the action.

Palle d'Oro. Via Sant'Antonio 43–45r (near the Mercato Centrale). ☎ **055-288-383.** Reservations suggested for dinner. Primi 5,000–8,000L ($2.50–$4); secondi 8,000–15,000L ($4–$8). AE, DC, MC, V. Mon–Sat noon–2:30pm and 6:30–9:45pm. Closed Aug. ITALIAN.

Everyone seems to prefer this trattoria's front bar area, usually packed with the market's vendors and shoppers enjoying a quick lunch of pasta, soup, and vegetable side dishes. The prices aren't much higher for table service in the less-crowded back room, but the front area's advantage is you don't have to order a full meal and can eat and run. Look for the house specialty pasta, *penne della casa* (with porcini mushrooms, prosciutto, and veal). For a cholesterol boost with a kick, try the homemade *gnocchi alla gorgonzola.*

✪ **Trattoria Sostanza (aka Il Troia).** Via Porcellana 25r (near Borgo Ognissanti). ☎ **055-212-691.** Reservations strongly suggested. Primi 6,000–12,000L ($3–$6); secondi 12,000–28,000L ($6–$14). No credit cards. Mon–Fri noon–2:30pm and 7:30–9:30pm. Closed Aug. FLORENTINE

The insider's choice for the best *bistecca alla fiorentina* has long been Sostanza. Nowadays there are a few more contenders worth considering, but Sostanza continues to guarantee a blue-ribbon beefsteak experience. Popularly called Il Troia (The Feeding Trough), this white-tiled former butcher shop puts hoi polloi and wide-eyed visitors elbow to elbow at rough-finished tables for a thoroughly enjoyable Tuscan evening. The *petti di pollo al burro* (plump chicken breasts lightly fried in butter) gives the bistecca a run for its money. The house's third specialty, tripe, understandably finds favor mostly with the regular Florentine customers. The degree of conviviality always runs high.

Trattoria 13 Gobbi (Tredici Gobbi). Via Porcellana 9r (north of Borgo Ognissanti). ☎ **055-284-015.** Reservations recommended for dinner. Primi 9,000–19,000L ($4.50–$10); secondi 16,000–35,000L ($8–$18). AE, DC, MC, V. Tues–Sun noon–2:30pm and 7–10:45pm, Mon 7–10:45pm. TUSCAN.

La Fiorentina refers to both the Florentine beefsteak and the local soccer team—both available at the newly recharged and reopened "13 Hunchbacks." It offers soccer habitués a relaxed atmosphere with exposed 15th-century beams and terra-cotta floors. Those who choose to dine alfresco can watch the neighbors' laundry billow overhead and catch a glimpse of the campanile of the Ognissanti church. Introduce yourself to the delicious Tuscan *pici,* a homemade spaghetti-like pasta rarely found outside country kitchens. Meat-lovers can go straight for the *tagliata di bistecca all'acetto balsamico,* tender steak grilled, sliced, sautéed with balsamic vinegar, and presented on a bed of arugula. The choice of wines is a winning one, with some of the best not appearing on the menu.

Trattoria Zà-Zà. Piazza Mercato Centrale 26r. ☎ **055-215-411.** Reservations recommended. Primi 8,000–13,000L ($4–$7); secondi 12,000–25,000L ($6–$13); *menù turistico* 20,000L ($10). AE, DC, MC, V. Mon–Sat noon–3pm and 7–11pm. Closed Aug. ITALIAN.

The walls are lined with chianti bottles and photos of old movie stars and not-so-famous patrons, the long wooden tables crowded with visitors and locals. Serving Tuscan favorites at reasonable prices amid a cheerful clatter, this trattoria is a good spot to try the fabled *bistecca fiorentina* without losing your shirt. Things don't change much here, except for the tables that've been set up on an unremarkable piazza and a new wine bar under the same management next door at no. 27r. Daily 7pm to 2am, **John Torta** (☎ 055-214-655) offers a wide range of Tuscan wines by the glass for 4,000L to 18,000L ($2 to $9).

Zà-Zà has a serious competitor in the bare-bones **Da Mario,** around the corner at Via Rosina 2; it's open for lunch only (closed Sunday) and absorbs the overflow.

NEAR SANTA CROCE

Il Che C'è, C'è. Via Magalotti 11r (off Via Proconsolo and Borgo dei Greci). ☎ **055-216-589.** Reservations recommended. Primi 7,000–14,000L ($3.50–$7); secondi 14,000–30,000L ($8–$18). AE, MC, V. Tues–Sun noon–3pm and 7–11:30pm. Closed 3 wks late Aug and early Sept. TUSCAN.

First of all, the name: It's a local expression that approximately translates to "What you see is what you get." You won't have to hope for more and certainly won't be settling

A Moveable Feast

In Florence, there are few supermarkets. Cold cuts are sold at a *salumeria,* which also sells cheese, though for a wide selection or for yogurt you'll have to find a *latteria.* Vegetables and fruit can be found at a produce stand and store called a *fruttivendolo* or *orto e verdura* and often at a small *alimentari,* the closest thing to a neighborhood grocery store. For bread to put all that between, visit a *forno,* which, along with a *pasticceria,* can supply you with dessert. And for a bottle of wine, search out a shop selling *vino e olio.* **Via dei Neri,** beginning at Via de' Benci near Piazza Santa Croce and stretching over toward Piazza della Signoria, has a handful of small specialty food shops and is a good area for picnic pickings.

If you prefer to find all you need under one roof, visit the colorful late 19th-century **Mercato Centrale,** a block-long two-story marketplace that's a must-see and not just for food shoppers. Open Monday to Friday 7am to 2pm and Saturday 7am to 2pm and 4 to 8pm, it's at Via dell'Ariento 12, looming in the midst of the open-air Mercato San Lorenzo, on the block between Via San Antonino and Via Panicale.

If you're just as happy to have someone else make up your sandwiches, seek out **Forno Sartoni,** Via dei Cerchi 34r, with fresh rolls and breads in front; the crowd in back waits for pizza bubbling from the oven, sold by the slice and weighed by the ounce—the average slice is 2,500L ($1.50). It also makes up a limited but delicious selection of fresh sandwiches (with prosciutto, mozzarella, and arugula, for example, at about 4,000L/$2) on freshly baked focaccia. Sartoni is predominantly a baker, so for a greater variety of quality cold cuts stop by **Alimentari Orizi** (above) and have the combination panino of your choice made up as you wait.

The **Boboli Gardens,** on the opposite side of the Arno behind the Palazzo Pitti (see "Seeing the Sights," below), is without a doubt the best green picnic spot in town. A grand amphitheater behind the palazzo provides historic seating, but it's worth the hike to the top, where the grounds join with those of the Fortezza Belvedere for the breathtaking view and green grass. If you'd just as soon pull up a park bench in the *centro storico,* a number of the city's most beautiful piazzas have stone benches and open spaces: **Piazza Santa Croce** comes to mind as much for its church's three-toned marble facade as for its proximity to Vivoli's for a post-lunch gelato. **Piazza Santa Maria Novella** offers stone benches and the only plots of grass in any of the city's squares. And if summer has set in, there are just two shady piazzas with benches: **Piazza Massimo d'Azeglio** east of the Accademia and lovely **Piazza Santo Spirito** in the Oltrarno near the Palazzo Pitti.

for less, for everything is excellently prepared. The irreverent name is compatible with the casual, family-run atmosphere, but the quality of the menu that's Tuscan in spirit hints of the chef/owner's formal training in the kitchens of London. Everything is kept simple, but the ingredients are obviously the best and the results full flavored. Unlike on many full-throttle Tuscan menus, fish is given its share of the limelight here. There are set-price menus for the economically minded (20,000L/$10) and those curious to expand their culinary horizons without breaking the bank (50,000L/$25).

Il Pizzaiolo. Via de' Macci 113r (at the corner of Via Pietrapiana). ☎ **055-241-171.** Reservations required for dinner. Pizza 9,000–16,000L ($4.50–$8); primi 12,000–20,000L ($6–$10); secondi 12,000–18,000L ($6–$9). No credit cards. Mon–Sat 12:30–3pm and 7:30pm–midnight. PIZZERIA/TRATTORIA.

The crowd milling about on the sidewalk (and they have reservations!) is confirmation this place serves the best pizza in town. Italy remains proudly regionalistic about its food: Southerners contend they're the best pizzamakers on the peninsula. And so Florence was elated to welcome Carmine, who headed north after 30 years in Naples, bringing along his family, his expertise, and integral ingredients like garlic and oregano. The simple *pizza margherita* (fresh tomatoes, mozzarella, and basil) is perfection, as is the more endowed *pizza pazza* (fresh tomatoes, artichokes, olives, mushrooms, and oregano).

Pizzeria I Ghibellini. Piazza San Pier Maggiore 8–10r (at the end of Borgo degli Albizi east from Via del Proconsolo). ☎ **055-214-424.** Reservations suggested for dinner. Pizza 6,000–12,000L ($3–$6); primi 6,000–8,000L ($3–$4); secondi 8,000–20,000L ($4–$10). AE, DC, MC, V. Thurs–Tues noon–4pm and 7pm–12:30am. ITALIAN/PIZZERIA.

With exposed brick walls and ceilings and curved archways inside and umbrella-shaded tables on the picturesque piazzetta, I Ghibellini is a good bet year-round. Pizza is the draw, and there's a long list to make your choice difficult: Try the house specialty, *pizza alla Ghibellini* (prosciutto, mascarpone, and pork sausage). The many pastas include *penne alla boccalona,* whose tomato sauce with garlic and a pinch of hot pepper is just spicy enough.

✪ **Ristorante Acqua al Due.** Via della Vigna Vecchia 40r (at Via dell'Acqua). ☎ **055-284-170.** Reservations required. Primi 10,000–11,000L ($5–$6); secondi 10,000–25,000L ($5–$13); *assaggio* 13,000L ($7) for pasta, 7,000L ($3.50) for dessert. AE, MC, V. Daily 7:30pm–1am. ITALIAN.

This is the perfect place to sample as much as you can at one sitting without breaking the bank or bursting your seams. The specialty is the *assaggio di primi,* a sampling of five types of pasta (with the occasional risotto thrown in) in various shapes and sauces. These aren't five full-size portions, but don't expect to have room for an entree after. There are also *assaggi* of *insalate* (salads) and *dolci* (sweets). Low prices and late hours make this comfortable place popular with a young international crowd.

Trattoria Cibreo. Via de' Macci 122r. ☎ **055-234-1100.** Primi 10,000L ($5); secondi 18,000L ($9). AE, DC, MC, V. Tues–Sat 1–2:30pm and 7:30–11pm. TUSCAN.

This is the casual trattoria of celebrated chef/owner Fabio Picchi; its limited menu comes from the same creative kitchen that put on the map his premier and more than twice as expensive *ristorante* next door. The trattoria moved from its back alley location to the main street in 1999, and this higher visibility has only made the lines to get in even longer. Picchi takes his inspiration from traditional Tuscan recipes, and the first thing you'll note is the absence of pasta. After you taste the velvety *passata di peperoni gialli* (yellow bell-pepper soup), you won't care much. The stuffed roast rabbit demands the same admiration. My only complaint: They rush you through your meal in an un-Italian fashion in order to free up tables. Enjoy your after-dinner espresso at the Caffè Cibreo across the way.

IN THE OLTRARNO

Bar Ricchi. Piazza Santo Spirito 9r. ☎ **055-215-864.** Primi 7,000L ($3.50); secondi 10,000L ($5). AE, V. Mon–Sat noon–2:30pm. (Bar winter Mon–Sat 7am–8:30pm; summer Mon–Sat 7am–1am.) ITALIAN.

Don't miss this bar when spring arrives and tables appear on one of Florence's best piazzas; its great inexpensive lunch menu is available year-round—if only they'd repeat the performance at dinner. Four or five pastas are made up on order and, as an alternative to the usual entrees, try one of the super salads (8,000L/$4). A shady piazza table is ringside, but take a look inside at the 350 framed designs from a 1980 contest to complete the unfinished facade of Brunelleschi's Santo Spirito church.

Borgo Antico. Piazza Santo Spirito 6r. ☎ **055-210-437.** Reservations suggested for dinner. Pizza 10,000L ($5); primi 10,000L or 25,000L ($5 or $13); secondi 18,000–25,000L ($9–$13). AE, MC, V. Daily 12:45–2:30pm and 7:45pm–midnight. ITALIAN/PIZZERIA.

In the spirit of the Oltrarno's Left Bank atmosphere, the Borgo Antico is a relaxed spot where you can order as little or as much as you want and enjoy it among a mix of visitors and Florentines. The scene inside is always buzzing, but from April to September, tables are set out where the million-dollar view of Brunelleschi's church is free. There are a dozen great pizzas and a number of combination super salads. Specialties of the day get equally creative (and expensive!). It's almost always hectic—if you get the hint they'd like your table, you'd do well not to linger.

Il Cantinone. Via Santo Spirito 6r (off Piazza Santa Trinita). ☎ **055-218-898.** Crostoni 8,000–10,000L ($4–$5); primi 9,000–25,000L ($4.50–$13); secondi 14,000–40,000L ($7–$20). AE, MC, V. Tues–Sun 12:30–2:30pm and 7:30–10:30pm. TUSCAN/ENOTECA.

In the brick-vaulted wine cellar of a 16th-century palazzo, this candlelit wine bar can seem more jovial than romantic on nights when the wine gets flowing—and you'll find a fine selection of Chianti's best. Five or six reds are available by the glass, but don't overlook a liter of the good house wine. Order a number of appetizers and first courses and you'll understand why they call Tuscany's peasant fare the food of kings. Crostoni are large slabs of home-baked bread slathered with prosciutto, *funghi* (mushrooms), tomatoes, mozzarella, or *salsiccia* (sausage). Primi choices may be a hearty *pappa al pomodoro* or *ribollita* soup or pasta of the day.

Osteria del Cinghiale Bianco. Borgo San Jacopo 43r (off Piazza Santa Trinita). ☎ **055-215-706.** Reservations suggested for dinner. Primi 7,000–12,000L ($3.50–$6); secondi 13,000–22,000L ($7–$11). No credit cards. Thurs–Mon noon–2:30pm and 7–10:30pm. TUSCAN.

In a medieval tower, with exposed stone walls setting the ambience, this friendly trattoria is dedicated to the *cinghiale,* the wild boar so ubiquitous in the Tuscan hills and traditional cuisine. Its presence is felt strongly during the fall game season, but you'll usually see year-round dishes like pappardelle pasta with cinghiale sauce and wild boar sausage (*salsiccia*) antipasto. But most of the menu is cinghiale-free, such as the delicious *strozzapreti* (literally "priest stranglers"—don't ask), baked pasta with a ricotta-and-spinach mix, served with melted butter. Things are relaxed here during lunch, where the owners have added an *insalata dello chef* (chef's salad). A few niches have been created for the romantically inclined, and it's a comfortable place to linger over dinner.

✪ **Trattoria Angiolino.** Via Santo Spirito 35r (west of Piazza Santa Trinita). ☎ **055-239-8976.** Reservations recommended. Primi 9,000–10,000L ($4.50–$5); secondi 15,000–20,000L ($8–$10). AE, DC, MC, V. Tues–Sun noon–2:30pm and 7:15–10:30pm. Closed Aug. FLORENTINE.

Local noble families fill this Florentine classic on Sundays, while artisans and antiques store owners file in the rest of the week. I hope there'll be room for you to experience a perfect Florentine meal in this traditional rustic trattoria. From the first hint of the extra-virgin olive oil used in the house specialty of marinated fresh vegetables (eggplant, bell peppers, zucchini—whatever's in season) to the *penne all'Angiolino* (with a chianti-flavored tomato-and-meat sauce), you'll appreciate the recent restoration that brightened the place but left the great food and atmosphere intact. The open kitchen provides between-the-bites entertainment.

Trattoria Casalinga. Via Michelozzi 9r (between Via Maggio and Piazza Santo Spirito). ☎ **055-267-9243.** Primi 5,500–7,000L ($2.75–$3.50); secondi 8,500–16,000L ($4.25–$8). Mon–Sat noon–2:30pm and 7–10pm. AE, DC, MC, V. ITALIAN.

Casalinga refers to the home cooking that keeps this recently expanded unpretentious place always full. Along with the expansion came the frayed nerves of the help and a sometimes erratic performance from the kitchen. So maybe they won't win any culinary awards, but the menu is straightforward Tuscan: Try the hearty *ribollita* or the *ravioli al sugo di coniglio* in rabbit-flavored sauce. Save dessert or an after-dinner caffè for one of the cafes on nearby Piazza Santo Spirito.

5 Seeing the Sights

Seeing all of Florence in a short time requires organization. It's not just that there's so much to see in this great city; it's also that establishments (stores, churches, and so on) close for long lunch breaks, and some museums close for the day at 2pm or sooner (remember that the last entrance is at least 30 minutes, sometimes 45 to 60 minutes, before closing). Many museums are closed on Monday. The first thing you should do: Stop by a tourist office (see "Essentials," above) for an up-to-the-minute listing of museum hours or ask at your hotel.

Over the past few years, summer hours have been extended more and more, and recently this phenomenon has been spreading into the off-season as well, so it's a good idea to get the most up-to-date hours from the tourist office. Churches and the markets are good alternatives for afternoon touring time, since they usually remain open to 7pm. You won't waste precious hours if you plan in advance and purchase tickets to the top museums ahead of time (see below).

ON & AROUND PIAZZA DEL DUOMO

✪ **Duomo (Cathedral of Santa Maria del Fiore).** Piazza del Duomo. ☎ **055-230-2885.** Cathedral, free; cupola, 10,000L ($5); excavations, 4,000L ($2). Cathedral, Mon–Sat 10am–5pm, Sun 1:30–5pm (open Sun morning for services only); cupola, Mon–Fri 8:30am–7pm, Sat 8:30am–5pm. Closes 3:30pm on the first Sat of every month; cathedral may stay open to 7pm in winter. Last entrance to ascend cupola 40 min. before closing.

The red-tiled **dome** of Florence's magnificent Duomo dominates the skyline in the early 21st century just as it did when it was built more than 5 centuries ago. At the time it was completed in 1434, it was the world's largest unsupported dome, meant to dwarf the structures of ancient Greece and Rome. In Renaissance style, it's a major architectural feat and was the high point of architect Filippo Brunelleschi's illustrious career. Brunelleschi had to invent many new winch-and-pulley systems to raise his dome, an ingenious piece of engineering constructed of two shells, both of which thin as they approach each other and the top. You can climb 463 spiraling steps (no elevator) and clamber up between these two layers to the lantern at the summit for a spectacular panorama (you can enjoy a similar view, with fewer steps to climb, from the campanile, below); entrance to the stairs is from outside the church, on the south (bell tower) side, through the door marked "Cupola di Brunelleschi."

The bands of marble (white, red, and green—the colors of the Italian flag) on the cathedral's **exterior** were taken from Tuscan quarries and added in the late 19th century, when Florence briefly became the capital of a united Italy. This tricolored-marble mosaic, repeated on the baptistry and campanile, is an interesting contrast to the sienna-colored medieval fortress-like palazzi throughout the city. Though much of the

Florence Attractions

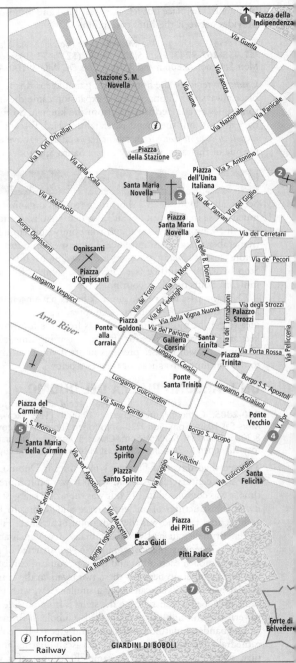

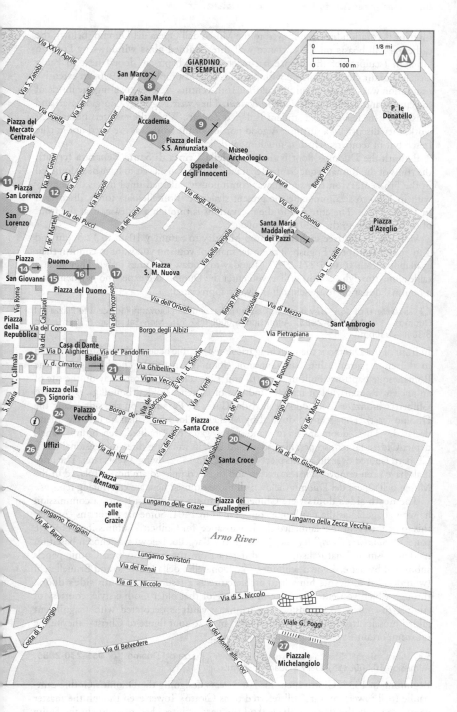

Via XXVII Aprile

Via S. Zanobi

Via Guelfa

Via San Gallo

GIARDINO
DEI SEMPLICI

San Marco ✕
8

Piazza San Marco

P. le
Donatello

Piazza del
Mercato
Centrale

Via Cavour

Accademia
10

9 ✝

Piazza della
S.S. Annunziata

Museo
Archeologico

Via de' Ginori

ⓘ

Via Cavour

Via Laura

Borgo Pinti

11
Piazza
San Lorenzo

12

Via Ricasoli

Ospedale
degli Innocenti

Via della Colonna

13

Via dei Pucci

Via dei Servi

Via degli Alfani

San
Lorenzo

V. de' Martelli

Via della Pergola

Santa Maria
Maddalena
dei Pazzi

Piazza
d'Azeglio

Piazza
14 ✝

Duomo

Piazza
S. M. Nuova

San Giovanni

15 **16** ✝

17

Via L. C. Farini

Piazza del Duomo

Via dell'Oriuolo

Borgo Pinti

Via di Mezzo

18

Via Roma

Via dei Calzaiuoli

Via Fiesolana

Piazza
della
Repubblica

Via del Corso

Borgo degli Albizi

Via Pietrapiana

Sant'Ambrogio

Casa di Dante

Via D. Alighieri

Via de' Pandolfini

22

V. d. Cimatori

Badia ✝

21

Via Ghibellina

Via d. Stinche

V. d.

Vigna Vecchia

Via G. Verdi

19

V. M. Buonarroti

S. Maria

V. Calimala

Piazza della
Signoria

23

24

Palazzo
Vecchio

Borgo de'

Via de'
Bentaccordi

Greci

Piazza
Santa Croce

Via de' Pepi

Borgo Allegri

Via de' Macci

ⓘ

25

Via de' Benci

20 ✝

Via di San Giuseppe

26

Uffizi

Via del Neri

Via Magliabechi

Santa Croce

Piazza
Mentana

Via dei Renai

Lungarno delle Grazie

Piazza dei
Cavalleggeri

Ponte
alle
Grazie

Lungarno Torrigiani

Via de' Bardi

Lungarno della Zecca Vecchia

Arno River

Lungarno Serristori

Via dei Renai

Via di S. Niccolo

Via di S. Niccolo

Viale G. Poggi

Costa di S. Giorgio

Via di Belvedere

Via del Monte alle Croci

27
Piazzale
Michelangiolo

interior decoration has been moved to the Museo dell'Opera del Duomo (below), the cathedral still boasts on the entrance wall three **stained-glass windows** by Lorenzo Ghiberti (sculptor of the bronze bas-reliefs on the baptistry doors) next to Paolo Uccello's **giant clock** decorated with portraits of four prophets. In 1996, an extensive restoration was completed on the colorful 16th-century frescoes covering the inside of the cupola and depicting the *Last Judgment.* They were begun by Giorgio Vasari and finished by his less talented student Federico Zuccari. When the restorers began their work, they discovered a surprise: A good portion of the work was executed not in true fresco but in tempera, which is much more delicate.

Beneath the Duomo's floor is the **Scavi della Cripta di Santa Reparata (crypt),** the ruins of the Romanesque Santa Reparata Cathedral, believed to have been founded in the 5th century on this site. It was continuously enlarged until it was done away with in 1296 to accommodate the present structure. Brunelleschi's tomb, discovered in 1972, is here. The entrance to the excavations is through a stairway near the front of the cathedral, to the right as you enter.

Volunteers offer **free cathedral tours** Monday to Saturday 10am to 12:30pm and 3 to 5pm. Most speak English; if there are many of you and you want to confirm their availability, call ☎ **055-271-0757** (Tuesday to Friday, mornings only). They sit at a table along the right (south) wall as you enter the Duomo and expect no payment, but a nominal donation to the church is always appreciated.

✪ **Battistero di San Giovanni (Baptistry).** Piazza di San Giovanni (adjacent to Piazza del Duomo). ☎ **055-230-2885.** Admission 5,000L ($2.50). Mon–Sat noon–6:30pm, Sun 8:30am–1:30pm.

In front of the Duomo is the matching tricolored-marble octagonal baptistry, dedicated to the city's patron saint, San Giovanni (John the Baptist). The highlight of the Romanesque baptistry, built in the 11th and 12th centuries (most likely on the site of an ancient Roman villa or temple) and one of Florence's oldest buildings, is Lorenzo Ghiberti's bronze exterior doors called the **Gates of Paradise,** on the side facing the Duomo (east). They were so dubbed by Michelangelo, who, when he first saw them, declared, "These doors are fit to stand at the gates of Paradise." Ten bronze panels depict Old Testament scenes, like Adam and Eve, in stunning three-dimensional relief. Ghiberti labored over his masterpiece from 1425 to 1452, dying 3 years later. The originals have been removed for restoration and those completed are now displayed in the Museo dell'Opera del Duomo (below); all those exposed here are convincing replicas.

The **north side's doors** were Ghiberti's warm-up to the east doors, a commission he won at age 23 as the result of a contest held in 1401. Some art historians consider this to be the event that launched the Renaissance, for Ghiberti's submission (a bronze panel of *Abraham Sacrificing Isaac,* now in the Bargello, below) was chosen based on its dynamism and naturalism—very different from the static, stylized Gothic panels submitted by better-known sculptors, like Donatello, della Quercia, and Brunelleschi (who decided to devote himself to architecture as a result). The **south side's doors,** through which you enter, are a good example of that older Gothic style, courtesy of Andrea Pisano in 1336. Inside, the baptistry **vault** is decorated with magnificent gilded mosaics from the 1200s, dominated by a 26-foot figure of Christ—they're the most important Byzantine mosaics in Florence.

✪ **Campanile di Giotto (Giotto's Bell Tower).** Piazza del Duomo. ☎ **055-230-2885.** Admission 10,000L ($5). Daily 8:30am–7:30pm.

Beginning in 1334, Giotto spent his last 3 years designing the Duomo's Gothic campanile (bell tower), and it's still referred to as Giotto's Tower even though the master completed only the first two levels (and the next architect had to overhaul the faulty design—Giotto was an astoundingly great painter but a lousy engineer). Banded in the same three colors of marble as the cathedral and the baptistry, it's 20 feet shorter than the dome.

The **bas-reliefs** on its slender exterior are copies of works by Andrea Pisano, Francesco Talenti, Luca della Robbia, and Arnoldi (the originals are in the Museo dell'Opera del Duomo). The view from the top is about equal to that from the Duomo; there are, however, a mere 414 steps here and fewer crowds, but you won't get the chance to get up-close with Brunelleschi's masterpiece. Both offer remarkable cityscapes over a preserved historic center that was never permitted to build higher than the cathedral's dome.

Museo dell'Opera del Duomo (Museum of the Duomo). Piazza del Duomo 9. ☎ **055-230-2885.** Admission 10,000L ($5). Mon–Sat 9:30am–6:30pm, Sun 8am–2pm.

Opened in 1891, this museum behind the cathedral contains much of the art and furnishings that once embellished the Duomo and reopened in 2000 after a 2-year renovation. A **bust of Brunelleschi** at the entrance is a nod to the architect of the magnificent cupola (some of his original equipment and a death mask are housed in the first small room), and over the door hang two glazed **della Robbia terra-cottas.** In the second inner room to your left are **sculptures** from the old Gothic facade (destroyed in 1587 to make way for today's neo-Gothic facade, which wasn't completed until the late 1800s), including work by the original architect, Arnolfo di Cambio, who was also responsible for the Palazzo Vecchio. Of the various statues, the most noteworthy are Donatello's weather-worn but noble *St. John* and Nanni di Banco's intriguing *San Luca.*

The highlights of the center room upstairs are the enchanting twin white marble *cantorie* (**choirs**) from the 1430s by Donatello and Luca della Robbia. But don't miss the two Donatello statues: his haggard figure of *Mary Magdalene* (a late work in polychrome wood originally in the baptistry) and *Lo Zuccone* (*Pumpkin Head*) from Giotto's bell tower. In the next room are the original **bas-reliefs** that decorated the first two stories of the exterior of Giotto's campanile.

One of the museum's most important displays is ✪ four of the original bronze panels from Ghiberti's **Gates of Paradise** door for the baptistry (the other six will appear after restoration). There's also a priceless 14th- to 15th-century silver-gilt **altarpiece** with scenes from the life of St. John, as well as one of Michelangelo's last *Pietà* sculptures, carved when the master was in his 80s and originally intended for his own tomb until he became so unsatisfied with it he attacked it with a hammer. He later let his students carry it away and finish off a few of the characters—they left the figure of Nicodemus untouched, it's said, because it was a self-portrait of Michelangelo.

A Note About Museum & Church Hours

Remember that most stores close for long lunch break, many of the museums close for the day at 2pm or earlier (the last entrance is at least 30 minutes before closing), and many are closed Monday. First thing, stop by the tourist office for an up-to-date listing of museum hours and possible extended hours (in 2000, some museums stayed open—and empty—to 11:30pm). Also note that museum bookshops often close 15 to 30 minutes before the collections, an annoying practice that has cheated many tourists of their postcards or museum books if they wait until the guards are shooing them out of the Uffizi to leave. Some churches stay open through *riposo,* so save them for after lunch. And there's always the stalls of the open-air San Lorenzo market Monday to Saturday 9am to 7pm.

ON & AROUND PIAZZA DELLA SIGNORIA

In Florence all roads lead to elegant **Piazza della Signoria**—the cultural, political, and social heart of the city since the 14th century. Named after the *signoria,* the oligarchy that ruled medieval Florence, it serves as a picture-perfect outdoor sculpture gallery replete with pigeons, horse-and-buggies, tons of tourists, and outdoor cafes. It's one of Italy's most beautiful public squares.

The enormous **Fontana di Nettuno (Neptune Fountain;** Ammanati, 1576) was purportedly derided by Michelangelo as a waste of good marble. A small disk in the ground in front of it marks the spot where religious fundamentalist **Savonarola** was burned at the stake for heresy in 1498—a few years after inciting the original "bonfires of the vanities" while ruling the city during the Medici's temporary exile from Florence (even Botticelli got caught up in the fervor and is said to have tossed in a painting to fuel the flames). Flanking the life-size copy of Michelangelo's *David* (the original is in the Accademia) are copies of Donatello's *Judith and Holofernes* (original in the museum inside) and the *Marzocco* (original in the Bargello), the heraldic lion of Florence. Unfortunately placed next to David's anatomical perfection (across the stone steps) is Baccio Bandelli's *Heracles* (1534), which comes across looking like the "sack of melons" Cellini described it to be.

On the south side of Piazza della Signoria is the 14th-century **Loggia dei Lanzi** (also called Loggia della Signoria, or, after its designer, Loggia di Orcagna), Florence's captivating outdoor sculpture gallery. It has finally been freed of its scaffolding, and the loggia is open for the first time in decades. Benvenuto Cellini's bronze ✪ *Perseus* (1545) was cleaned and restored in the 1990s and replaced in the prime corner spot in 2000. Giambologna's important *Rape of the Sabine* is also an original, a three-dimensional study in Mannerism, alongside his *Hercules Slaying the Centaur* and *Duke Cosimo de' Medici.* The wallflower statues standing against the back are ancient Roman originals.

✪ **Galleria degli Uffizi (Uffizi Gallery).** Piazzale degli Uffizi 6 (south of Palazzo Vecchio and Piazza della Signoria). ☎ **055-238-8651.** Admission 12,000L ($6). Summer Tues–Fri 8:30am–6:50pm, Sat 8:30am–10pm, Sun 8:30am–7pm; winter Tues–Sat 8:30am–6:50pm, Sun 8:30am–8pm.

The Uffizi is one of the world's most important art museums and should be the first stop in Florence for anyone interested in the rich heritage of the Renaissance (be sure to make a reservation—see details in the box). Six centuries of artistic development are housed in this impressive Renaissance palazzo, built by Giorgio Vasari (also a painter and Europe's first art historian) for Grand Duke Cosimo I de' Medici in 1560 to house the Tuscan Duchy's administrative offices (*uffizi* means "offices" in local dialect). The collection, whose strong point is Florentine Renaissance art but includes major works by Flemish and Venetian masters, was amassed by the Medicis and bequeathed to the city in 1737 in perpetuity by Anna Maria Ludovica, the last of the Medici line, who stipulated the unmatched collection of masterworks could never leave Florence.

The gallery consists of 45 rooms where paintings are grouped into schools in chronological order, from the 13th to the 18th century—but as you wander, don't overlook the rich details of the building itself, including frescoed ceilings, inlaid marble floors, and tapestried corridors. The superb collection begins in room 2 with Giotto's *Maestà* (1310), one of the first paintings to make the transition from the Byzantine to the Renaissance style. Look for the differences between Giotto's work and his teacher Cimabue's *Maestà* (1280) nearby. Some of the best-known rooms are dedicated to 15th-century Florentine painting, the eve of the Renaissance. In room 7 are major works by Paolo Uccello, Masaccio, and Fra' Angelico, as well as the only works by Piero della Francesca in Florence. As you proceed, look for the elegant *Madonnas*

Reserving Tickets for the Uffizi & Other Museums

As tourism to Italy increases, so do the lines at major museums. Much of the problem behind the often alarming wait at the Uffizi is the security policy regulating the number of visitors inside at any one time. Now you can buy tickets in advance for a designated time and day, eliminating an often 3-hour wait. Call **Firenze Musei** at ☎ **055-294-883** (www.firenzemusei.it) a minimum of 24 hours in advance (or weeks, if possible). Each reservation request adds 2,000L ($1) to the museum admission—but this is more than worth it to save the wait. Advance tickets are possible for the Uffizi, Accademia, Palazzo Pitti, Cappelle Medicee, Museo di San Marco, Museo Nazionale del Bargello, and a handful of lesser museums, but I find it usually necessary (and highly recommended) only for the Uffizi and Accademia.

of Filippo Lippi and Pollaiolo's delightful little panels that influenced Botticelli, whose masterworks are next.

For many, the Botticelli rooms (10 to 14) are the undisputed highlight. Arguably the most stunning are the recently restored **Primavera (*The Allegory of Spring*)**, whose three graces form the principal focus, and **The Birth of Venus** (commonly referred to as "Venus on the Half-Shell"). Botticelli's **Adoration of the Magi** is interesting for the portraits of his Medici sponsors incorporated into the scene, as well as a self-portrait of the artist on the far right in yellow.

Other notable works are Leonardo da Vinci's unfinished **Adoration of the Magi** and his famous **Annunciation** in room 15, Lukas Cranach's **Adam and Eve** in room 20, Michelangelo's circular **Doni Tondo** or **Sacra Famiglia (*Holy Family*)** in room 25, Raphael's **Madonna with the Goldfinch** in room 26, Titian's **Flora** and **Venere di Urbino (*Venus of Urbino*)** in room 28, Tintoretto's **Leda** in room 35, Caravaggio's **Medusa and Bacchus** in room 43, two **Rembrandt self-portraits** in room 44, and Canaletto's **Veduta del Palazzo Ducale di Venezia (*View of the Doge's Palace in Venice*)** in room 45.

Since the May 1993 bombing that damaged 200 works (37 seriously) and killed five (including the museum's director), the Uffizi has staged an amazing recovery. Only four of those works damaged were superior examples from the Italian Renaissance; two were destroyed beyond repair. Restorators have been working around the clock to repair the substantial damage to the fabric of the building itself. In December 1998, Italy unveiled the "New Uffizi," a $15-million renovation that repaired all damaged rooms, added more than 20,000 square feet of museum space, and displayed more than 100 works that had never been seen before. It's part of a larger project to triple exhibit space by the beginning of 2001. A handsome ground-floor book/gift store and the reopening of the elegant terrace cafe (at the end of the west wing) were part of the welcomed renovation.

The **Corridoio Vasariano (Vasari Corridor)** is an aboveground "tunnel" running along the rooftops of the Ponte Vecchio buildings and connecting the Uffizi with Duke Cosimo I's residence in the Pitti Palace on the other side of the Arno. The corridor is lined with portraits and self-portraits by a stellar list of international masters, such as Bronzino, Reubens, Rembrandt, and Ingres. The damage incurred from the 1993 bombing has been repaired and the corridor officially reopened at press time, but it still requires special admission and an accompanying guide; inquire at the ticket window.

The Uffizi

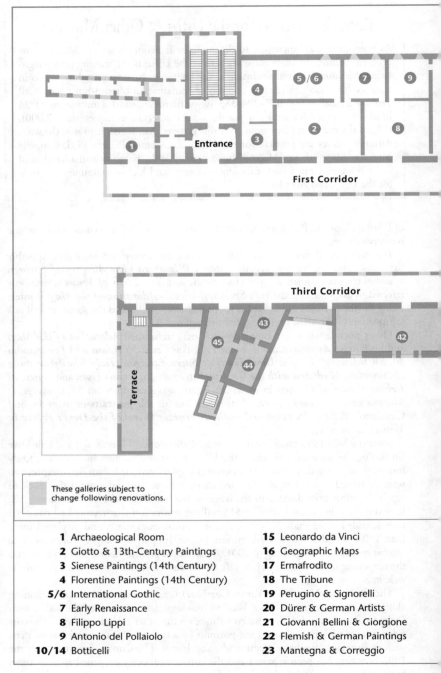

These galleries subject to change following renovations.

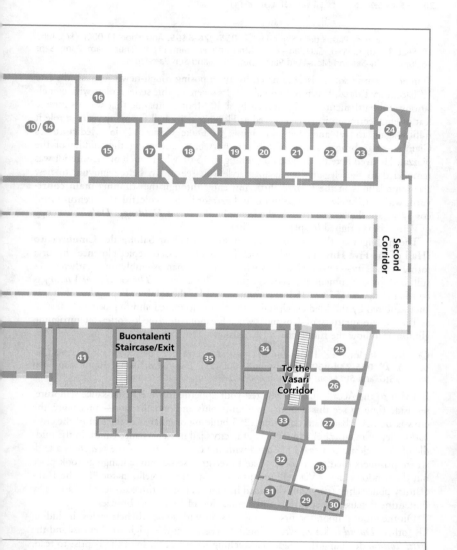

24 Miniatures

25 Michelangelo & Florentine Artists

26 Raphael & Andrea del Sarto

27 Pontormo & Rosso Fiorentino

28 Tiziano

29 Parmigianino

30 Emilian Paintings

31 Dosso Dossi

32 Sebastiano del Piombo & Lorenzo Lotto

33 16th-Century Paintings

34 Veronese

35 Tintoretto & Barocci

41 Rubens

42 Niobe

43 Caravaggio

44 Rembrandt

45 18th-Century Paintings

Palazzo Vecchio. Piazza della Signoria. ☎ **055-276-8465.** Admission 11,000L ($6). June 15–Sept 15 Tues, Wed, Sat 9am–7pm, Mon and Fri 9am–11pm, Thurs 9am–2pm; Sept 16–June 14 Fri–Sat and Mon–Wed 9am–7pm, Thurs and Sun 9am–2pm.

Florence's central square is dominated by an imposing rough-hewn fortress, the late 13th-century Palazzo Vecchio (Old Palace). Its severe Gothic style, replete with crenellations and battlements, is highlighted by a 308-foot campanile that was a supreme feat of engineering in its day. It served as Florence's city hall for many years (a role it fulfills again today) and then was home to Duke Cosimo I de' Medici (that's Giambologna's bronze statue of him on horseback anchoring the middle of the piazza). He lived here for 10 years beginning in 1540, when much of the interior was remodeled to the elegant Renaissance style you see today, before moving to new accommodations in the Palazzo Pitti. You enter through the stunning **main courtyard,** with intricately carved columns and extraordinarily colorful 16th-century frescos by Vasari; the central focus is the fountain of a *Putto Holding a Dolphin,* a copy of Verrocchio's original (displayed upstairs).

The highlight of the interior is the massive first-floor **Salone dei Cinquecento (Hall of the Five Hundred),** whose rich frescoes by Vassari depict Florence's history; formerly the city's council chambers where the 500-man assembly once gathered, it's still used for government and civic functions. The statue of *The Genius of Victory* is by Michelangelo (1533 to 1534); commissioned for the tomb of Pope Julius II, it was later acquired by the Medici. Upstairs, the richly decorated and frescoed salons, such as the private quarters of Cosimo's wife, Eleanora de Toledo, offer an intriguing glimpse into how the ruling class of Renaissance Florence lived.

✪ **Museo Nazionale del Bargello (Bargello Museum).** Via del Proconsolo 4 (at Via Ghibellina). ☎ **055-238-8606.** Admission 8,000L ($4). Tues–Sat 8:30am–1:50pm. Also open the 1st, 3rd, and 5th Mon; closed the 2nd and 4th Sun of each month.

If a visit to the Accademia has whetted your appetite for fine Renaissance sculpture, set aside time to see this national museum's outstanding collection—amazingly, the crowds are never bad. This daunting 1255 building originated as the seat of the city's *podestà* (chief magistrate) and served as the city's jail in Renaissance times. In the middle of the majestic courtyard plastered with the coats of arms of the *podestà* is a tank where prisoners used to be tortured and executed; some public hangings took place out the windows facing Via del Proconsolo. Today, the Bargello, named for the 16th-century police chief (*bargello*) who ruled from here, houses three stories of treasures by Florentine Renaissance sculptors and a collection of Mannerist bronzes.

On the ground floor, the first room kicks off with some Michelangelos, including his "other" *David* (a.k.a *Apollo,* sculpted 30 years after the original), *Brutus,* and the *Pitti Tondo,* depicting the Madonna teaching Jesus and St. John the Baptist to read. Take a look at his *Bacchus* (1497): It was done at age 22 and was the artist's first major work, effortlessly capturing the Roman god's drunken posture. Among the other important sculptures are Ammanati's *Leda and the Swan,* his student Giambologna's significant *Winged Mercury,* and several Donatellos, including his *St. George, St. John the Baptist,* and sexually ambiguous *David,* the first nude statue to be done by an Italian artist since classical times. In another room are the two **bronze plaques** by Brunelleschi and Donatello's master, Ghiberti, made for the competition in 1401 to decide who'd sculpt the baptistry's second set of doors—Ghiberti's won.

✪ **Ponte Vecchio.** At Via Por Santa Maria, north bank, and Via Guicciardini, south bank.

Linking the north and south banks of the Arno River at its narrowest point, the Ponte Vecchio (Old Bridge) has long been a landmark symbol of the city. It was destroyed and rebuilt many times before the construction of the 1345 bridge you see today, designed by Taddeo Gaddi, and has stood lined with these same goldsmith's shops for centuries. Many of the exclusive gold and jewelry stores are owned by descendents of the 41 artisans set up on the bridge in the 16th century by Cosimo I de' Medici. No longer able to tolerate the smell from the bridge's old butchers and skin tanners on his trips to and from the new Medici residence in the Palazzo Pitti on the other side of the river, Cosimo booted them out and moved in the classier goldsmiths (and upped the rent).

Florentines tirelessly recount the story of how in 1944, Hitler's retreating troops destroyed all the bridges crossing the Arno (all since reconstructed, often with the original material or at least according to archival designs) with the exception of the Ponte Vecchio. To compensate, the Germans bombed both bridgeheads to block Allied access to it, resulting in the 1950s look of those buildings in the otherwise medieval areas of Via Por Santa Maria and Via Guicciardini.

Orsanmichele. Via Arte della Lana 1/Via dei Calzaiuoli. ☎ **055-284-944.** Admission free. Church, daily 9am–noon and 4–6pm; museum, daily 9–9:45am, 10–10:45am, 11–11:45am. Both closed the 1st and last Mon of month. Bus: A.

This 14th-century boxlike church is Florence's last remnant of ornate Gothic architecture and was originally built as a covered market with an upstairs granary. The downstairs was eventually converted into an oratory—the open archways were bricked up and the outside's **tabernacles** decorated with donations from the city's powerful *arti* (guilds), such as the tanners, silk weavers, bankers, furriers, and goldsmiths; their patron saints fill the 14 niches surrounding the exterior. Masters like Ghiberti, Donatello, and Giambologna were commissioned to cast the saints' images. They virtually comprise a history of Florentine sculpture from the 14th to the 16th century, though almost all have been relocated to the second-floor museum (below) and replaced by copies. In the candle-lit interior—among the vaulted arches, stained-glass windows, and 500-year-old frescoes—is the colorful encrusted 14th-century **Gothic tabernacle** by Andrea Orcagna. It supports and protects the 1348 *Madonna and Child* painted by Giotto's student Bernardo Daddi.

Across Via dell'Arte della Lana from the Orsanmichele's main entrance is the 1308 **Palazzo dell'Arte della Lana.** Up the stairs inside, you can cross over the hanging walkway to the first floor of the Orsanmichele. These are the old granary rooms, now housing a **museum** containing statues that once surrounded the exterior. A few are still undergoing restoration, but eight of the original sculptures are here, well labeled, including Donatello's marble *St. Mark* (1411 to 1413); Ghiberti's bronze *St. John the Baptist* (1413 to 1416), the first life-sized bronze of the Renaissance; and Verrocchio's *Incredulity of St. Thomas* (1473 to 1483).

NEAR PIAZZA SAN MARCO & PIAZZA SANTISSIMA ANNUNZIATA

✪ **Galleria dell'Accademia (Accademia Gallery).** Via Ricasoli 60 (between Piazza del Duomo and Piazza San Marco). ☎ **055-238-8609.** Admission 15,000L ($7.50). Tues–Sun 8:30am–7pm (to 10pm Sat).

The Accademia is home to Michelangelo's ✪ *David* (1501 to 1504), his (and perhaps the world's) greatest sculpture. Michelangelo was just 29 and only recently recognized for his promising talents following the creation of the *Pietà* in Rome's St. Peter's Basilica. Sculpted from a 17-foot column of white Carrara marble that had been quarried for another sculptor's commission, worked on, then deemed unworkable and left abandoned, *David* looms in stark masculine perfection atop a 6-foot marble stand beneath the rotunda of the main room built exclusively for its display in 1873, when it was moved here from Piazza della Signoria (a life-size copy stands in its place; a second copy lords over Piazzale Michelangiolo).

Cheap Thrills: What to See & Do in Florence for Free (or Almost)

- **Window shopping.** In what was traditionally one of Europe's great reasonably priced shopping Meccas, prices aren't what they used to be, but the window shopping still is. Every display is an homage to the timeless made-in-Italy phenomenon that still flourishes, centuries after the Medicis gave free reign to their artisans to create, embellish, and raise their crafts to an unprecedented level of artistry. Gold, leather goods, embroidery, fashion—maybe you can talk yourself into at least one instant heirloom. You can salivate your way along the temples of the high priests of fashion: Global names like Versace, Gucci, and Armani are concentrated along **Via dei Tornabuoni** and **Via della Vigna Nuova.** You can seek other pipe-dreams along the gold-laden **Ponte Vecchio** and its dozens of jewelry stores. Less extremely priced retail stores line **Via Por Santa Maria, Via Roma** and, connecting Piazza della Signoria with Piazza del Duomo, **Via dei Calzaiuoli** (to name just a few).

- **Wandering the Florentine markets.** Little in Italy compares to the sprawling outdoor **Mercato San Lorenzo** surrounding the San Lorenzo church and the covered early 1900s **Mercato Centrale.** The latter is a vast marketplace whose street-level stalls are occupied by butchers, fish vendors, and cheesemongers and saturated with local color galore; the upstairs is mostly given over to the fertile region's heady bounty of produce, fruit, and flowers—you'll never again see so many varieties of salad greens, pyramids of artichokes and plump tomatoes, porcini mushrooms as wide as Frisbees, and pearl-sized wild strawberries. The outdoor market is comprised of hundreds of canvas-awninged stalls hawking tourist stuff, a lot of which is worth a walk-through for the guaranteed (and not infrequent) finds. Shop here for souvenirs first before hitting the city's countless tourist retail stores whose overhead hikes their prices.

- **Biking the streets.** Florence isn't yet Amsterdam, but local authorities are encouraging the two-wheeler as transportation within the *centro storico* as traffic is clearly but slowly being forbidden within the *zona blu.* Florence is generally flat, so track down the half dozen stands around town that offer free bikes for the day (see "Getting Around," near the beginning of this chapter).

- **Taking free tours.** Church volunteers await you in the **Duomo** for free English-language guided tours of this early Renaissance wonder (see "On & Around Piazza del Duomo," earlier in this chapter). Free guided tours are also being offered in some of the museums and churches, such as the **Palazzo**

The museum houses several other Michelangelos, including four never-finished ✪ *Prisoners* or *Slaves* struggling to free themselves, commissioned for the tomb of Julius II; Michelangelo believed he could sense their very presence captured within the stone and worked to release their forms. They offer a fascinating insight of how he approached each block of marble that would yield his many masterpieces. The *Palestrina Pietà* here was long attributed to Michelangelo but most scholars now believe it's the work of his students. The statue of *St. Matthew* (begun in 1504) is by the master. A number of 15th- and 16th-century Florentine painters are also represented here; search out the *Madonna del Mare (Madonna of the Sea),* attributed to Botticelli or his student Filippino Lippi.

Vecchio, Santa Maria Novella, and the **Brancacci Chapel** in Santa Maria del Carmine, during specially extended evening hours. Check with the tourist office to see if these tours are continuing.

- **Enjoying free museums and extended hours.** Not many museums in town offer free admission, except for the **Museo Stibbert,** which opens on Sundays free of charge. But check with the tourist office for other museums that may follow suit, and don't forget to request a listing of extended hours. **Church visits,** for the moment, remain free, except for special admission fees to fresco-rich chapels like the Brancacci (Santa Maria del Carmine) and the Chiostro Verde (Santa Maria Novella).

- **Catching the daily vespers.** Florence's most beautiful Romanesque church (and one of its oldest), **San Miniato,** is the only venue for late-afternoon vespers. A handful of monks sing their timeless Gregorian chant, transporting you back to the nascent days of the hilltop church's 11th-century origin.

- **Watching a postcard-perfect sunset.** To see the Technicolor sunset over the Duomo amid the *centro storico*'s terra-cotta rooftops plastered on a million postcards, hike on up to the Oltrarno's **Piazzale Michelangiolo.** Here you'll find Michelangelo's second larger-than-life copy of the fabled *David* (the other is in Piazza della Signoria), standing vigil over Florence. Daytime sees the piazza transformed into a parking lot for tour-group buses; nighttime feels like a locals' lovers-lane-meets-the-looking-for-excitement-after-hours crowd. Dusk is no less popular, with a truly magnificent *spettacolo* over the Arno trellised by its many bridges and offset by the hills of Fiesole rising up behind.

- **Listening to Music in Piazza della Repubblica.** The historic **Café Paszkowski** has been the site of alfresco evening music in this central square for generations. The recent transformation of parking lot to dignified piazza of old was a welcomed return to the way things were, including the addition of the occasional planters-cum-seats from which to enjoy the crowd-gathering live music until the wee hours without having to pay the steep cover charges imposed by the cafes. Paszkowski's elegant next-door neighbor, **Gilli's,** is the traditional favorite cafe of choice, where you can nurse a Campari for hours for less than 12,000L ($6) while eavesdropping on the classic, pop, and light jazz tunes that fill the piazza.

✪ **Museo di San Marco.** Piazza San Marco 3 (north of the Duomo on Via Cavour). ☎ **055-238-8608.** Admission 8,000L ($4). Tues–Fri 8:30am–1:50pm, Sat to 7pm; 2nd and 4th Sun of each month 8:30am–8pm; 1st, 3rd, and 5th Mon of each month 8:30am–1:50pm.

Built in the 13th century and enlarged and rebuilt by Michelozzo as a Dominican monastery in 1437, this small museum is a monument to the devotional work of friar/painter Fra' Angelico, an early master of the 15th-century Renaissance. To your right upon entering is a room containing Florence's largest collection of his **painted panels** and **altarpieces.** The Chapter House nearby is home to Fra' Angelico's powerful large *Crucifixion* fresco. The ground-floor Refectory was decorated by Domenico Ghirlandaio (under whom a young Michelangelo apprenticed) with a realistic

Cenacolo (*Last Supper*), one of the most important of Florence's nine such *Last Suppers* found in ancient refectories (the tourist office has a list of the others).

At the top of the stairs to the second-floor monks' cells is Fra' Angelico's masterpiece, the *Annunciation*. Each of the 44 small dorm cells is decorated with frescoes from the life of Christ painted by Fra' Angelico or one of his assistants under the master's direction from 1439 to 1445 and intended to aid in contemplation and prayer. The frescoes in cells 1, 3, 6, and 9 are the most beautiful. Larger and more luxurious, cells 38 and 39 were designated for the occasional use of Cosimo il Vecchio, originator of the Medici dynasty who financed the enlargement of the monastery, and were frescoed with the aid of Angelico's student Benozzo Gozzoli.

At the end of the corridor is the **cell of Girolamo Savonarola,** which includes a stark portrait of the monastery's former prior by his convert and student, Fra' Bartolomeo, as well as his sleeping chamber, his notebook, his rosary, and remnants of the clothes worn at his execution. Savonarola was a religious fundamentalist who ruled Florence briefly at the head of a mob-rule theocracy, inspiring the people to burn priceless artwork and precious hand-illuminated books. After the pope threatened to excommunicate the entire city for following the mad preacher, Savonarola was found guilty of heresy, hanged, and burned at the stake on Piazza della Signoria in 1498, as depicted here in an anonymous 16th-century painting.

Santissima Annunziata. Piazza SS. Annunziata. ☎ **055-239-8034.** Admission free. Daily 7:30am–12:30pm and 4–6:30pm.

On your way to or from your visit to Michelangelo's *David* at the Accademia, stop by **Piazza SS. Annunziata** for a moment's respite in what has been called the most perfectly proportioned Renaissance square. It's surrounded on three sides by loggias, but at its center stands the **equestrian statue** of Grand Duke Ferdinando I de' Medici, the last work of Giambologna, cast after his death by Tacca (who's also responsible for the fountains on either side). Facing south is the 13th-century **Santissima Annunziata** church (reconstructed during the Renaissance by Michelozzo) with a number of major works by Andrea del Sarto (who's also buried here, along with Cellini and Il Pontormo). In Florence, brides don't toss their bouquets: For good luck, they bring them here and place them in front of a **tabernacle** designed by Michelozzo (to the left as you enter). It houses an allegedly miraculous portrait of the *Annunciation* (after whom the church was named), whose Madonna's face was said to have been painted by an angel. On the right as you enter the church is del Sarto's important *Birth of the Virgin* (1513); his *Madonna del Sacco* in an area off the cloisters is not always available for viewing.

As you exit the church, you'll see on your left the **Ospedale degli Innocenti (Hospital of the Innocents),** Europe's oldest foundling hospital. Its portico was designed by Brunelleschi and the area between its arches adorned with glazed terra-cotta reliefs of swaddled babies by Andrea della Robbia. It still functions as an orphanage in a limited capacity, but the small opening where Florentines could leave their unwanted infants in the dark of night, ring the bell, and run, is no longer in use. The **museum** (☎ **055-249-1708**) upstairs houses some fine Renaissance paintings by the likes of

The Master's Famous Scribbles

A large number of charcoal sketches, confirmed to be by Michelangelo himself, were discovered by sheer chance in the 1980s in a room beneath the sacristy at the Medici Chapels. They're now available to the public for viewing for no additional admission but only on special request: Ask at the ticket booth on your arrival.

Ghirlandaio, Pontormo, and a young Botticelli. Admission is 5,000L ($2.50), and it's open Thursday to Tuesday 8:30am to 2pm.

NEAR THE TRAIN STATION, THE MERCATO SAN LORENZO & SANTA MARIA NOVELLA

Basilica di San Lorenzo & Biblioteca Medicea-Laurenziana. Piazza San Lorenzo. ☎ **055-216-634.** Admission free. Basilica daily 7am–noon and 3:30–6:30pm; Biblioteca Medicea-Laurenziana, Mon–Sat 9am–1pm.

San Lorenzo, whose barren unfinished facade looms semi-hidden behind market stalls hawking soccer banners and synthetic-silk scarves, was the Medicis's parish church, as well as the resting place for most of the clan's early bigwigs, including Cosimo il Vecchio, founder of the family fortune and patron to Donatello (memorialized in front of the high altar with a plaque proclaiming him *pater patriae,* "father of his country"). Donatello's two **pulpits,** his final works, are worth a look, as is the second chapel on the right, with Rosso Fiorentino's *Marriage of the Virgin.* Designed by Brunelleschi and decorated by Donatello, the **Old Sacristy,** off the left transept, contains several important works.

The key feature of the main part of the church is the **Biblioteca Medicea-Laurenziana** (1524), a stunning bit of architecture by Michelangelo housing one of the world's largest and most valuable collections of manuscripts and codices, a few of which are on display. An elaborate Michelangelo **stone staircase** leads to it from the quiet cloister (off the left aisle), the one real reason to peak in here after a visit to the church next door. Though the Laurentian Library is closed at press time, it's scheduled to reopen by the time you get here, possibly with new hours. San Lorenzo is best known, however, for the **Cappelle Medicee (Medici Chapels),** but you can't reach them from the church: You enter by going around through the Mercato San Lorenzo to the back of the church (see below).

Cappelle Medicee (Medici Chapels). Piazza Madonna (at the end of Borgo San Lorenzo, around the back side of San Lorenzo). ☎ **055-238-8602.** Admission 11,000L ($6). Tues–Sat 8:30am–5pm; also 1st, 3rd, and 5th Sun each month and 2nd and 4th Mon each month (same hours).

On entering, you first pass through the massively overwrought marble wonderland of the **Cappella dei Principi (Chapel of the Princes),** added in 1604 but not finished until 1962. Your goal is the far more serene ✪ **Nuova Sacrestia (New Sacristy),** containing the Michelangelo-designed tombs for Lorenzo II de' Medici, Duke of Urbino and grandson of Lorenzo il Magnifico (with the sculptor's famous statues of female *Dawn* and male *Dusk*) on the left as you enter. On the opposite wall is the tomb of Giuliano de' Medici, Duke of Nemours (with the more famous female *Night* and male *Day*). These two pairs are some of Michelangelo's greatest works (1521 to 1534). Never overlooked by guides is that *Dawn* and *Night* make obvious the virility with which Michelangelo sculpted females—only marginally less masculine and muscular than males, with breasts tacked on almost as an afterthought.

✪ **Palazzo Medici-Riccardi & Cappella dei Magi (Chapel of the Magi).** Via Cavour 3 (north of Piazza del Duomo). ☎ **055-276-0340.** Palazzo free; Cappella dei Magi 8,000L ($4). Mon–Tues and Thurs–Sun 9am–7pm.

Built by Brunelleschi's student Michelozzo for Cosimo il Vecchio (the Elder), founder of the Medici dynasty and grandfather of Lorenzo il Magnifico, this austere palazzo was the private home of the Medici clan from 1460 to 1540 (before Cosimo I moved with his new Spanish wife, Eleanora de Toledo, to the Palazzo Vecchio and eventually the Palazzo Pitti on the other side of the Arno) and was held as the prototype for subsequent residences of the nobility. Only two rooms are open to the public, but they make your trip worthwhile.

A staircase to the right off the entrance courtyard leads to the ✪ **Cappella dei Magi (Chapel of the Magi).** The jewel-box chapel takes its name from the gorgeously dense frescoes by Benozzo Gozzoli (completed in 1463), who worked into his depictions of the Wise Men's journey through the Tuscan countryside several members of the Medici family (the last Magi with the golden locks is a highly idealized version of a young Lorenzo il Magnifico) as well as his master, Fra' Angelico. He even added himself on the right wall as you enter (look on the far left for a young man wearing a red hat inscribed "Opus Benotii," beneath the man wearing a light-blue hat). Upstairs is an elaborate 17th-century **baroque gallery** commissioned by the subsequent owners, the Riccardi; amid the gilt and stucco are masterful Luca Giordano frescoes, illustrating the Apotheosis of the Medicis. The palazzo now houses government offices, though parts of it are frequently used for temporary and traveling exhibits.

✪ **Basilica di Santa Maria Novella.** Piazza Santa Maria Novella (just south of train station). ☎ **055-210-113** or 055-282-187 for museum. Basilica free; Museo 5,000L ($2.50). Basilica Mon–Fri 7am–noon and 3:30–6pm, Sat 7am–noon and 3:30–5pm, Sun 3:30–5pm; Museo Sat–Thurs 9am–2pm.

Begun in 1246 and completed in 1360 (with a green-and-white marble facade, the top portion of which wasn't added until the 15th century), this cavernous Gothic church was built to accommodate the masses who'd come to hear the Word of God as delivered by the Dominicans. To educate the illiterate, they filled it with cycles of frescoes that are some of the most important in Florence—a claim not to be taken lightly.

In the **Cappella Maggiore (Main Chapel)** behind the main altar, with a bronze crucifix by Giambologna, Domenico Ghirlandaio created a fresco cycle supposedly depicting the *Lives of the Virgin and St. John the Baptist,* when in fact what we see is a dazzling illustration of daily life in the golden days of Renaissance Florence. It's sprinkled with local personalities and snapshot vignettes, and a number of the faces belong to the Tornabuoni family, who commissioned the work. In the **Cappella Filippo Strozzi,** to the right of this, are frescoes by Filippino Lippi (son of Filippo Lippi). To the extreme right is the **Cappella dei Bardi,** covered with 14th-century frescoes; its lunette frescoes of the *Madonna* are believed to be by Cimabue (ca. 1285). To the left of the Cappella Maggiore is the **Cappella Gondi** and a 15th-century crucifix by Brunelleschi, his only work in wood. And to the extreme left is the **Cappella Gaddi,** with frescoes by Nardo di Cione (1357); the altarpiece is by Nardo's brother, Orcagna. The chapel awaits the return of Giotto's 13th-century crucifix, now at the restorer. Adjacent is the **sacristy,** worth a peek for the delicate glazed terra-cotta *lavabo* (sink where priests would wash their hands) by Giovanni della Robbia.

In the left aisle near the main entrance is Masaccio's 1428 ✪ *Trinità* fresco, the first painting in history to use perfect linear mathematical perspective. Nearby is Brunelleschi's 15th-century **pulpit** from which Galileo was denounced for his heretical theory that Earth revolved around the Sun.

If you're not yet frescoed out, exit the church and turn right to visit the museum, comprised of the **Chiostro Verde (Green Cloister),** sporting Paolo Uccello's 15th-century fresco cycle of *Noah and the Flood* (ironically, it was heavily damaged in the 1966 Arno flood), and the **Cappellone degli Spagnoli (Spanish Chapel),** whose captivating series of Andrea de Bonaiuto early Renaissance frescoes (recently restored) glorify the history of the Dominican church. The chapel got its name from the nostalgic Eleanora de Toledo, wife of Cosimo de' Medici, who permitted her fellow Spaniards to be buried here.

Museo Stibbert. Via Stibbert 26. ☎ **055-475-520.** Admission 8,000L ($4). Easter to early Oct Mon–Wed 10am–1pm, Fri–Sun to 6pm; winter Mon–Wed 10am–2pm, Fri–Sun to 6pm. Bus: 4.

Anyone even remotely interested in armor and the historic days of chivalry should spend some time in the musty formerly private home of wealthy Scotch-Italian collector Frederick Stibbert. Opened to the public since shortly after his death in 1906 and considered one of the most important private collections in the world, Stibbert's house/museum is filled to the brim with—among countless other objects and antiques from the 16th to the 19th century—thousands of pieces of armor from East and West (with Europe's largest collection of Japanese armor) and all the bellicose trappings: maces, pole-axes, crossbows, blunderbusses, and the like.

The **Sala della Cavalcata (Hall of the Cavalcade)** is the high point of the house, with a dozen life-size models of knights on war horses dressed in full-body battle armor. In the **Salone della Cupola,** 50 men-at-arms wearing glistening suits of plate armor represent all parts of the world. Some of the historic armor is as striking as body sculptor, as decorative as body jewelry. The last few years (and the arrival of a new female European curator) have seen radical improvements in the museum's evolution, garnering the more appropriate attention it has long deserved.

NEAR SANTA CROCE

✪ **Basilica di Santa Croce & Cappella Pazzi (Pazzi Chapel).** Piazza Santa Croce. ☎ **055-244-619.** Basilica free; Pazzi Chapel 8,000L ($4). Basilica, summer Mon–Sat 9:30am–5:30pm, Sun 3–5:30pm; winter Mon–Sat 8am–12:30pm and 3–5:30pm, Sun 3–5:30pm. Pazzi Chapel, Mar–Oct Thurs–Tues 10am–7pm; Nov–Feb Thurs–Tues 10am–6pm.

Begun in 1294 by Arnolfo di Cambio, the original architect of the Duomo, the cavernous Santa Croce is the world's largest Franciscan church. The humble presence of St. Francis is best felt in the **two chapels** to the right of the main altar: Entirely covered with faded but important early 14th-century frescoes by Giotto, they depict the life of the Assisi-born saint and scenes from the Bible. The Bardi is the more famous of the two, if only as a setting for a scene in Merchant Ivory's film *A Room with a View;* its deathbed scene of St. Francis is one of the church's most important frescoes. To the left of the main altar is a wooden **crucifix** by Donatello, whose portrayal of Christ was thought too provincial by early 15th-century standards (his buddy Brunelleschi once commented "Why Donatello, you've put a peasant on the Cross!").

Santa Croce is the final resting place for many of the Renaissance's most renowned figures. Over 270 **tombstones** pave the floor of the church, but attention deservedly goes to **monumental tombs** like that of Michelangelo, designed by Vasari, the first on the right as you enter; the three allegorical figures represent Painting, Architecture, and Sculpture. Dante's empty tomb is right next to him (he was exiled from Florence in 1302 for political reasons and was buried in Ravenna in 1321; there's also a statue dedicated to him on the left side of the steps leading into the church), while Machiavelli rests in the fourth. Galileo and Rossini, among others, were also laid to rest here. Off the right transept and through the sacristy and gift shop is one of Florence's most renowned **leather shops,** where you can watch the artisans at work (great quality; not cheap).

The entrance to the tranquil **Cappella Pazzi (Museo dell'Opera di Santa Croce)** is outside the church, to the right of the main doors. Commissioned in 1443 by Andrea de' Pazzi, a key rival of the Medici family, and designed by Filippo Brunelleschi, the chapel is a masterful example of early Renaissance architecture. The 12 glazed-terra-cotta roundels of the *Apostles* are by Luca della Robbia, finished in 1452. Next door, the 13th-century **refectory** serves as the church's museum, housing many works from the 13th to the 17th century, highlighted by one of Cimabue's finest works, the *Crucifixion,* which suffered serious damage in the 1966 flood of the Arno. Completely submerged when floodwaters rose to 3 feet in the church and 5 feet in the museum, it has now been restored and is displayed on an electric cable that'll lift it out of reach of future harm.

Casa Buonarroti (Buonarroti's House). Via Ghibellina 70 (5 blocks east of the Bargello). ☎ **055-241-752.** Admission 12,000L ($6). Wed–Mon 9:30am–2pm.

This graceful and modest house, which Michelangelo bought late in life for his nephew, was turned into a museum by his heirs. Today, it houses two of the master's most important early works: *Madonna alla Scala* (*Madonna on the Stairs*) and *Battaglia dei Centauri* (*Battle of the Centaurs*), both sculpted in his teenage years, when he was still working in bas-relief and before he created the Rome *Pietà*. The museum also houses a sizable collection of his drawings and scale models, particularly the one for the facade of San Lorenzo that was never realized.

Tempio Isrelitico & Jewish Museum. Via Farina 4. ☎ **055-234-6654.** Admission 6,000L ($3) adults, 4,000L ($2) students. Sun–Thurs 10am–1pm and 2–4pm (to 5pm in summer), Fri 10am–1pm; obligatory 45-min. guided tours every 25 min. Bus: 6, 31, 32.

The 19th-century green copper–domed Tempio Isrealitico warrants a visit by those interested in architecture or the heritage of Florence's Jewish community. It's a 15-minute walk east of the Duomo (but closer to Santa Croce) in an area of Florence that sees little tourism (unless you're lucky enough to be staying at Florence's only Relais & Châteaux hotel, the Regency). The neo-Moorish temple dates from the 1860s, when the Mercato Vecchio (Old Market) and its bordering Jewish Ghetto were cleared away to make way for Piazza della Repubblica. This oriental-inspired synagogue was begun in 1874, when its first stone arrived from Jerusalem, and heavily damaged by the Nazis in 1944 (it was completely restored soon after). A small museum houses a selection of Judaica dating back to the 17th century and includes a number of photos of the ghetto before it was razed.

IN THE OLTRARNO & BEYOND

✪ **Palazzo Pitti (Pitti Palace).** Piazza Pitti. **Galleria Palatina:** ☎ **055-238-8614;** admission 14,000L ($7); Tues–Fri 8:30am–6:50pm, Sat to 10pm, Sun to 7pm (may stay open later daily in summer). **Galleria d'Arte Moderna:** ☎ **055-238-8616;** admission 8,000L ($4). **Galleria del Costume:** ☎ **055-238-8713;** admission 8,000L ($4). **Museo degli Argenti:** ☎ **055-238-8709;** admission 4,000L ($2). All three daily 8:30am–1:50pm. **Museo della Porcellana:** ☎ **055-238-8709;** admission 4,000L ($2); daily 9am–1:30pm. All closed 1st, 3rd, and 5th Mon and 2nd and 4th Sun of each month.

It's ironic that this rugged golden palazzo, begun in 1458 (presumably by Brunelleschi) for wealthy textile merchant/banker Luca Pitti, in an attempt to keep up with the Medicis, was bought by Medici descendants in 1549 when Pitti's heirs spiraled into bankruptcy. They used it as their official residence as rulers of Florence. The Medicis, beginning with Cosimo I and his wife, Eleanora di Toledo, who moved here from the Palazzo Vecchio, tripled its size, elaborately embellished it, and graced it with the Boboli Gardens (see below) that still fan up the hill behind it, once the quarry from which the palazzo's *pietra dura* was taken. Today, it's home to seven museums, the largest collection of galleries in Florence under one roof.

✪ **GALLERIA PALATINA (PALATINE GALLERY)**　These 26 art-filled rooms on the first floor are the stars of the palazzo. Home to one of the finest collections of Italian Renaissance and baroque masters in Europe, this gallery is the most important collection in Florence after the Uffizi's. The art of the 16th century is the forte of the Palatina, in particular that of Raphael and Titian. Of the outstanding Raphaels

Pitti Cumulative Ticket

In 2000, you could buy a 20,000L ($10) **cumulative ticket** (15,000L/$8 after 4pm) that gets you into the Galleria Palatina, Boboli Gardens, Galleria d'Arte Moderna, and Museo degli Argenti.

displayed here, look for the prized *Madonna of the Chair* (the best known of his many interpretations of the Madonna) and his second most famous, *La Fornarina* also known as *La Velata (The Veiled Woman)*, a portrait of his baker's daughter and young mistress; if she looks particularly Madonna-like, it's because she most likely posed for most of his Madonna commissions.

The gallery's treasures include a large collection of works by Andrea del Sarto; Fra' Bartolomeo's *San Marco* and his beautiful last work, *Descent from the Cross;* some superb works by Rubens, including *The Four Philosophers;* and canvases by Tintoretto and Veronese. There are stunning portraits by Titian, including *Pope Julius II, The Man with the Gray Eyes,* and *The Music Concert*—his collection is regarded as some of the museum's most important, a hard call to make from such a cavalcade of superstars. Also represented are Caravaggio (namely, his *The Sleeping Cupid,* 1608), Pontormo, Van Dyck, and Botticelli.

After wandering past the jigsaw-puzzle walls of the painting-lined Galleria Palatina, you may want to rest your eyes with a stroll through the green Boboli Gardens (see below) or allow for a brief visit in the second-most-visited museum in the palazzo, the Appartamenti Monumentali, no less extravagant than what you've just seen but with a far less attention-riveting art collection.

APPARTAMENTI MONUMENTALI (MONUMENTAL APPARTMENTS)
These restored apartments, gilded and chandeliered, contain some paintings (look for Caravaggio's *Portrait of a Knight of Malta*), tapestries, and over-the-top furnishings from the resplendent days of the Medici and later the dukes of Lorraine.

GALLERIA D'ARTE MODERNA (MODERN ART GALLERY) You may not have come to Florence to view modern art, but those with any concentration left should head upstairs to this gallery. It houses an interesting array of 19th-century Italian impressionists (known as the *Macchiaioli* school after the *macchie* or "spots" used in their Impressionist style); the leader of the movement, Giovanni Fattori, is well represented here, as are Lega, Signorini, and early 20th-century predecessors.

OTHER MUSEUMS OF INTEREST Among the least visited of the Pitti's panoply of small museums is the **Museo degli Argenti (Silver Museum),** on the ground floor, 16 rooms filled with the priceless, private treasure of the Medici family. Other small museums that follow their own drum when it comes to hours and closures include the **Museo della Porcellana (Porcelain Museum),** currently open; the **Museo delle Carozze (Coach Museum),** closed indefinitely; and the **Galleria del Costume (Costume Gallery).** The latter concentrates on costumes from the 18th to the 20th century, with some earlier exceptions.

Giardini di Boboli (Boboli Gardens). Directly behind the Pitti Palace. ☎ **055-265-1816.** Nov–Feb daily 9am–4:30pm, Mar and Oct daily to 5:30pm, Apr–May and Sept daily to 6:30pm, June–Aug 8:15am–8pm. Closed the first and last Mon of every month; fortress hours vary with exhibits. Admission to gardens 4,000L ($2); to fortress grounds free, but exhibit admission varies.

The expansive Giardini Boboli begin behind the Pitti Palace and fan up to the star-shaped Fortezza Belvedere crowning the hill. Enter the gardens via the rear exit of the

Pitti Palace if you're visiting the museum or the entrance to the left facing the palace if you're bypassing the museum. The green gardens, particularly beautiful in spring, were laid out in the 16th century by the great landscape artist Tribolo. They're filled with an amphitheater, graveled walks, grottoes, and antique and Renaissance statuary and are the best spot in Florence for a picnic lunch. The view from the fortress (1590 to 1595) is stunning, but there's not much to see inside unless there's a special exhibit; ask at the tourist office or look for posters around town.

✪ **Santa Maria del Carmine & Cappella Brancacci.** Piazza Santa Maria del Carmine (west of Piazza Santo Spirito in the Oltrarno). ☎ **055-238-2195.** Church free; Cappella Brancacci 6,000L ($3). Mon and Wed–Sat 10am–5pm, Sun 1–5pm.

This baroque church dates from the 18th century, when a fire ravaged the 13th-century structure built for the Carmelite nuns; the smoke damage was major, but the fire left the Brancacci Chapel miraculously intact. This was a miracle indeed, as the frescoes begun in 1425 by Masolino and continued by his brilliant student Masaccio were a watershed in art history, crucial to the development of the Renaissance. They were painstakingly restored in the 1980s, removing not only the dirt and grime but also the prudish fig leaves trailing across Adam's and Eve's privates. Now more clearly evident is the painters' unprecedented expression of emotion as well as their pioneering use of perspective and chiaroscuro.

Masaccio's *Expulsion of Adam and Eve* (extreme upper-left corner) best illustrates anguish and shame hitherto unknown in painting, while *The Tribute Money* (just to its right) is a study in unprecedented perspective. The bulk of the frescoes depict the *Life of St. Peter* (who appears in a golden orange mantel). The lower panels were finished by Filippino Lippi (son of the great Filippo Lippi) in 1480, 50 years after the premature death of Masaccio at 27; he faithfully imitated the young master's style and technique. Even later masters like Leonardo da Vinci and Michelangelo came to see what they could learn from this mastery of perspective, light, colors, and realism.

✪ **San Miniato al Monte & Piazzale Michelangiolo.** Via del Monte alle Croci/Viale Galileo Galilei (behind Piazzale Michelangiolo). San Miniato: ☎ **055-234-2731.** Admission free. Easter to early Oct daily 8am–noon and 2–7pm, winter daily 8am–noon and 2:30–6pm. Bus: 12, 13.

No trip up to the green lofty heights of Piazzale Michelangiolo for sunset is complete without a visit first to **San Miniato,** an outstanding example of Florentine Romanesque architecture and the oldest religious building in Florence after the baptistry. From the Ponte Vecchio and points below, you can marvel at its multicolored facade and glimmering 13th-century fresco, but it's worth the trip up if only for the breathtaking view of the city from the church steps. Construction of the present building began in 1013 (with the geometrical-design marble facade added later that century) on the site where St. Minias, a 3rd-century martyr, was said to have carried his severed head from the city below before collapsing dead at this precise spot.

The dark interior appears more mystical because of its undulating 13th-century oriental-carpetlike **pavement mosaic** with signs of the zodiac. In the center of the nave is a **chapel** by Michelozzo (1447) whose glazed terra-cotta ceiling is by Luca della Robbia. A visit to the 11th-century **crypt** with frescoes by Taddeo Gaddi (architect of the Ponte Vecchio) and with fine columns and original capitals is evocative of the church's early days. Stay for the daily vespers sung in Gregorian chant at 4:30pm (followed by mass) by the handful of monks who live here. You can imagine why Florentine nobility prefers to attend Christmas mass and brides dream of being married here. The adjacent **cemetery** is worth a stroll in search of the gravestone of Tuscan-born Carlo Lorenzini, also known as Carlo Colladi, author of *Pinocchio*.

Now stroll on over to the **Piazzale Michelangiolo** to catch sunset over Florence, take a photo of the second copy of Michelangelo's *David,* and enjoy the view you've seen on 1,000 postcards.

ESPECIALLY FOR KIDS

While children may feel like this museum-rich city is filled with stuff way too old for them to relate to, Florence's biggest plus for parents is the city's accessibility and compact layout in relatively traffic-free streets. Much of your visit will be spent strolling the ancient streets of a city that's one big open-air museum. Young legs that can sustain a 400-plus step workout should head up to **Brunelleschi's cupola** (see the Duomo) and/or the top of **Giotto's campanile** for an awesome view of the city and swarms of ant-sized tourists. Your kids (and you) can recharge their batteries during **picnic lunches** in the green Boboli Gardens or, higher yet, on the grounds of the Forte Belvedere above.

If you're visiting in June, try to catch one of the four processions and games of the **Calcio Storico** (see the "Calendar of Events," in chapter 2) with their historic costumes and armored knights on steeds. And your kids won't let you miss tasting your way through the many excellent **gelaterie,** whose variety (they can squeeze four or five flavors into some of those cups) and quality makes Baskin Robbins look ho-hum.

As Florentine authorities encourage residents to take up bike riding as the historic center's pedestrian zone grows, **bicycle stands** become more predominant. If your child can handle a two-wheeler well, you have the blessing of tooling around a flat city (Florence is no hill town) in a generally traffic-free zone (but the cobblestones can do you in).

The **Stibbert Museum's** unusually extensive collection of armor (see above) is also a guaranteed pleaser. And don't even think about leaving town without rubbing the nose of the famous bronze statue of the *porcellino* **(wild boar)** on the south side of the Straw Market (a.k.a. the Mercato Nuovo or New Market), ensuring good luck and a return to Florence.

ORGANIZED TOURS

American Express (see "Fast Facts," above) teams with **CAF Tours,** Via Roma 4 (☎ **055-283-200**), to offer two half-day bus tours (57,000L/$29), including visits to the Uffizi, the Medici Chapels, and Piazzale Michelangiolo. They also offer several walking tours for 35,000L to 45,000L ($18 to $25); day trips to Pisa, Siena/San Gimignano, and the Chianti region for 57,000L to 83,000L ($29 to $42); and farther afield to Venice and Perugia/Assisi for 140,000L to 180,000L ($70 to $90). You can book the same tours through most other travel agencies around town.

Recently introduced is a daily walking tour called **Enjoy Florence** (☎ **800-274-819** toll-free from anywhere in Italy; www.florencewalkingtours.com). It departs Monday to Saturday at 10am (sometimes with a second tour on Monday, Wednesday, and Friday at 5pm) from the Thomas Cook exchange office just off the Ponte Vecchio on the Duomo side of the river; it lasts 3 hours and costs 30,000L ($15) for those over 26 and 25,000L ($13) for those under 26. **Walking Tours of Florence** (☎ **055-234-6225;** www.artviva.com) offers 3-hour tours Monday to Saturday at 10am for 35,000L ($18) adults or 10,000L ($5) children. Meet at the doors of Caffè Giubbe Rosse on Piazza della Repubblica. They also provide private guides and custom requests.

Call **I Bike Italy** (☎ **055-234-2371;** www.ibikeitaly.com) to sign up for 1-day rides in the surrounding countryside (Fiesole, Chianti, or a 2-day trip to Siena) March to November, or you can book **Country Walks in Tuscany** year-round at the same number. Guided walks are 75,000L ($38) and guided bike rides (21-speed bikes supplied) 95,000L ($48). A shuttle bus picks you up at 9am at the Ponte delle Grazie and drives you to the outskirts of town, and an enjoyable lunch in a local trattoria is included. You're back in town by 5pm. It may stretch your budget, but you should get out of this tourist-trodden stone city for a glimpse of the incomparable Tuscan countryside. To see some of Tuscany on your own, see chapter 5.

6 Shopping

In terms of good-value shopping, Florence is easy to categorize: It's paradise. This one-time capitalist capital, where modern banking and commerce first flourished, has something for every taste and price range. Whether you can afford little more than a bargain-priced wool sweater in the open-air market or are interested in investing in a butter-soft leather jacket that'll burst your budget, Florence is for you. Florentine merchants are not the born histrionic negotiators of the south or yesteryear, and few will encourage bargaining. Only if you're buying with traveler's checks and buying a number of items should you even broach the subject, and only in the most civilized manner. Good luck.

THE SHOPPING SCENE

BEST BUYS   "Alta moda" fashion is alive and well and living on **Via dei Tornabuoni** and its elegant offshoot, **Via della Vigna Nuova,** where some of the high priests of Italian and international design and fashion share space with the occasional bank (which you may have to rob in order to afford any of their goods). But it makes for great window-shopping.

Between the Duomo and the river are the pedestrian-only **Via Roma** (which becomes **Via Por Santa Maria** before reaching the Ponte Vecchio) and the parallel **Via dei Calzaiuoli;** lined with fashionable jewelry and clothing stores (and the city's two largest department stores, **La Rinascente** and **Coin**), they're the city's main shopping streets. Stores here were traditionally only slightly less high fashion and less high priced than those on the gilded Via dei Tornabuoni—but there has been a recent trend to head down market. A stop at any of the area's **gelaterie** is a guaranteed spirit-lifter for the nonshoppers among you. **Via del Corso** and its extension east of Via del Proconsolo, **Borgo degli Albizi,** is another recommended shopping street, boasting historic palazzi as well as less pretentious and more approachable boutiques though fewer in number.

Unless you have a Medici-size fortune and hope to leave with a Renaissance trinket, window-shop (only) the stores with museum-quality antiques on **Borgo Ognissanti** near the Arno and the perpendicular **Via dei Fossi. Lungarno Corsini** and **Lungarno Acciaiuoli** run along the river, where you'll find merchants offering fine paintings and sculpture, objets d'art, and antiques and miscellany. But perhaps the most impressive antiques row is **Via Maggio** in the Oltrarno and, to a far lesser degree, its perpendicular offshoot, **Via Santo Spirito.**

Florence is probably most famous for its ✪ **leather.** Many travelers are happily, albeit mistakenly, convinced they can buy a leather coat for a song. No European city can hold a candle to Florentine quality and selection, but prices are higher than those rumors you may have heard. Expect to spend $150 to $300 for a leather jacket with moderate workmanship, detail, and quality. The shops around **Piazza Santa Croce** are the best places for leather and aren't much more expensive than the pushcarts at the San Lorenzo Market. Leather apparel may be beyond your budget, but consider the possibilities of small leather goods, from wallets and eyeglass cases to fashion accessories like shoes, belts, and bags.

Florence has been known for its gold for centuries, and jewelry shops of all price levels still abound. Dozens of exclusive gold stores line both sides of the pedestrian **Ponte Vecchio.** Gold is almost always 18 karat (ask them to point out the teensy stamp), beautifully crafted and, though not a bargain, reasonably priced—think instant heirlooms.

MARKETS   There's nothing in Italy, and indeed perhaps nothing in Europe, to compare with Florence's bustling, sprawling, open-air ✪ **Mercato San Lorenzo.** Hundreds of awninged pushcarts crowd along the streets around the Basilica di San Lorenzo and the Mercato Centrale, offering countless varieties of hand-knit wool and mohair sweaters, leather jackets, handbags, wallets, and gloves—not to mention the standard array of souvenir T-shirts and sweatshirts, wool and silk scarves, and other souvenirs. (If you remember the place being filled with Gucci and Fendi knock-offs, you'll be disappointed that the police have done away with them almost entirely. The follow-up act is the easy availability of Prada and Moschino bags sold by Senagalese sidewalk vendors around town and on the Ponte Vecchio after store hours).

The market stretches for blocks between Piazza San Lorenzo behind the Medici Chapels to Via Nazionale, along Via Canto de' Nelli and Via dell' Ariento, with stalls also along various side streets in between. Mid-March to October, the market operates daily 9am to 7pm (closed Sunday and Monday the rest of the year), though extremely slow periods (or during heat waves and inclement weather) may result in many or all of the vendors staying home. Many vendors accept credit cards. These hundreds of tchotchke vendors buzz around the early 1900s **Mercato Centrale** food market (entrance on Via dell'Ariento), a riotous two-floor feast for all senses; whether you breeze through looking for picnic goodies or photo-ops, it'll leave you breathless and hungry.

Much smaller, but still worth a look, is the outdoor **Mercato del Porcellino,** once known as the Straw Market and today commonly known as the **Mercato Nuovo (New Market),** where a couple of dozen stalls crowd beneath an open-sided arcade two blocks south of Piazza della Repubblica. Vendors offer mostly handbags, scarves, embroidered tablecloths, and miscellaneous souvenirs. The market is named for the bronze boar (*porcellino*) on the river side of the arcade, whose snout has been worn smooth by the countless Florentines who've touched it for good luck. Hours are generally 9am to 6pm: daily mid-March to November 3 and Tuesday to Saturday the rest of the year.

The **Mercato delle Pulci** on small Piazza Ciompi (follow Via Oriuolo east out of Piazza del Duomo) is a rather unimpressive flea market open Tuesday to Saturday 8:30am to 7pm; it doubles in size the last Sunday of every month. The **Mercato delle Cascine** takes place every Tuesday 8am to 2pm in the grassy riverside park west of the Teatro Comunale. This is where the locals shop, so don't expect tourist merchandise; do expect more contained prices on household goods and everyday clothes. You may also want to check out Tuscany's major flea market in **Arezzo** (accessible by bus or direct train in an hour) the first weekend of every month.

SHOPPING A TO Z

ACCESSORIES   Silk and pseudosilk scarves and 100% wool mufflers and shawls are some of the best buys at the **Mercato San Lorenzo** (see above). Those wanting to graduate to the label-conscious level and price point of designer ties and labeled scarves of world-known designers will thrill at the selection in the small **Mr. Aramis,** Via Condotta 4r (☎ **055-282-881**). It's one-stop shopping for men and women, conservative to fashion forward. If you don't see what you want, ask about their second, nearby location.

BOOKSTORES   Even the smaller book shops in Florence these days have at least a few shelves devoted to English-language books. **Feltrinelli International,** Via Cavour 12 (☎ 055-292-196) is one of the few of any size. For English-only shops, hit **Paperback Exchange,** Via Fiesolana 31r (☎ 055-247-8154)—not the most central, but the best for books in English, specializing in titles relating in some way to Florence and Italy. Much of their stock is used, and you can't beat the prices—dog-eared volumes and all Penguin books go for only 4,000L to 6,000L ($2 to $3). You can also trade in that novel you've finished for another. **BM Bookshop,** Borgo Ognissanti 4r (☎ 055-294-575), is a bit smaller but more central and with only new volumes. They also have a more well-rounded selection—from novels and art books to cookbooks and travel guides.

G. **Vitello,** Via dei Servi 94–96r (☎ 055-292-445) sells coffee-table books on art and all things Italian at up to half off the price you'd pay in a regular bookstore. There are other branches at Via Verdi 40r (☎ 055-234-6894) and Via Pietrapiana 1r (☎ 055-241-063). The **Libreria Il Viaggio,** Borgo degli Albizi 41r (☎ 055-240-489), is a cozy niche specializing in travel guides, related literature, and maps, with a sizable selection in English. It's a good place to find specialty guides—hiking in the Chianti, touring Elba, wine estates that offer *agriturismo,* and the like.

CERAMICS   **Sbigoli,** Via Sant'Egidio 4r, east of the Duomo (☎ 055-247-9713), has a large selection of hand-painted Tuscan ceramics, particularly 16th- and 17th-century reproductions. Products of skilled craftsmanship are never cheap (and shipping, which this store offers, is bound to double your expense), but here, you'll find colorful terra-cotta mugs, ashtrays, and other small items that are reasonable. Short-term classes are available in the store's studio. **La Botteghina,** Via Guelfa 5r, north of the Mercato San Lorenzo (☎ 055-287-367) specializes in a more discerning selection from the ceramics capitals of Deruta and Montelupo. This is better quality, but you'll find small items for 25,000L to 50,000L ($13 to $25). Around the corner from the Medici Chapels is another favorite, **Ceramiche Ricceri,** Via dei Conti 14r (☎ 055-291-296), with typically Tuscan platters and dishes but occasionally small items that are less intimidating in price.

DEPARTMENT STORES   **Standa,** Via dei Panzani 31r (☎ 055-239-8963), is the last of the mid- to low-end department stores where you can come up with the occasional find in accessories, household goods, and miscellaneous items. The clothes are classic and poor or nice quality, but expensive. It's also a good spot to pick up needed toiletries. **Coin,** Via dei Calzaiuoli 56r (☎ 055-280-531), is as close to Macy's as you'll get in Florence: four floors of made-in-Italy apparel and accessories for men, women, and children. Moderately priced items are mixed in with the high-end merchandise, and it all makes for enjoyable browsing even for those not buying. Check out the sales amid the January and July crowds. The newest arrival is the six-story branch of the national chain **La Rinascente,** Piazza della Repubblica 1 (☎ 055-219-113). Often compared to Bloomingdale's, it's the nicest (and largest) to represent the best of made-in-Italy merchandising.

DESIGN & HOUSEHOLD ITEMS   On your way to or from a visit to the Accademia to see *David,* check out the collection at **Viceversa,** Via Ricasoli 53r (☎ 055-239-8281), showcasing the most interesting items from the creative studios of Milan. Much of this looks like it belongs in the Museum of Modern Art, with a number of small items that embody the latest in Italian design and make great souvenirs. You can spend a fortune or concentrate on bottle openers, key rings, ashtrays, pens, and hot plates all for under 25,000L ($13). For a balanced mix of the cutting edge and traditional, time-tested kitchenware and household goods Italian style, head to **La Menagere,** Via dei Ginori 8r, near the Mercato San Lorenzo (☎ **055-213-875**).

DISCOUNT FASHION   To get your high fashion at bargain-basement prices, head to one of the branches of **Stock House Grandi Firme.** The Borgo degli Albizi 87r store (☎ **055-234-0271**) carries mainly the past season's models, the Via dei Castellani 26r branch (☎ **055-294-853**) carries spring/summer remaindered collections, and the Via Verdi 28r (☎ **055-247-8250**) and Via Nazionale 38r (☎ **055-215-482**) stores sell outfits from the past winter. **Stock House Il Giglio,** Via Borgo Ognissanti 86 (no phone), and **Stock House Pattaya 2,** Via Cavour 51r (☎ **055-210-151**), also carry big name labels at 50% to 60% off.

HERBS & SPICES   Just a palazzo or two removed from Piazza della Signoria is the **Erboristeria Palazzo Vecchio,** Via Vacchereccia 9r (☎ **055-239-6055**), an old-world herbal store whose traditions and origins (and some of its recipes and formulas) go back centuries. There are natural pomades and elixirs for everything from dandruff to the blues, but you'll be most interested in the nicely packaged scented soaps, room scents, essences, candles, and sachets. Packaged seasonings and spices used in the *cucina italiana* make nice gifts for Italophile friends. While this Erboristeria is affordable, the theatrical landmark **Farmacia Santa Maria Novella,** Via della Scala 16r (☎ **055-216-276**), is not. But this is some place to see, though browsing is limited and the help notoriously unhelpful. The 16th-century setting alone is worth the trip, and you may be able to scrape up enough lire for some of their famous potpourri or beautifully packaged soaps and room scents.

JEWELRY   If you have the financial solvency of a small country, the place to buy your baubles is the **Ponte Vecchio,** famous for its goldsmiths and silversmiths since the 16th century. The craftsmanship at all the stalls is usually of a very high quality, and so they seem to compete instead over who can charge the highest prices. A more moderately priced boutique is Milan-based **Mario Buccellati,** Via dei Tornabuoni 71r (☎ **055-239-6579**), which since 1919 has been making thick, heavy jewelry of high quality. In the back room is the silver.

Florence is also a good place to root around for classy bijoux. **Bijoux Cascio,** Via Por Santa Maria 1r (☎ **055-238-2851**), is a good place to go if you don't want your faux jewels to look fake. The shop faithfully apes the popular top patterns and produces some tasteful pieces of its own design. The audacious bijoux at **Angela Caputi,** Borgo San Jacopo 82r (☎ **055-212-972**), aren't for the timid. Much of Angela's costume jewelry—from earrings and necklaces to brooches and even a small clothing line—is oversize and bold and often ultraflamboyant . . . and low priced.

LEATHER   The city is awash in leather stores of all quality ranges. The low end of the gamut is a departure point worth considering: the **Mercato San Lorenzo** (see above). A good 80% of the leather jackets are too cheaply made, but a fair number are passable to decent and sometimes even very good. The problem is in finding them—you'll have to wade through a ton of mediocre stuff. Check seams and lining and suppleness of leather. Don't bank on alterations once you get home: Few tailors do leather, and those that do will charge dearly.

If you're not of the market mentality, try the respectable **Leather School** in the Basilica di Santa Croce, Piazza Santa Croce (☎ **055-244-533;** www.leatherschool.it). The fine quality of the varied selection of leather goods from wallets and key chains to bags and attaché cases isn't cheap, but it's not overpriced either. The same goes for the selection at **Madova Gloves,** Via Guicciardini 1r, on the south side of the Ponte Vecchio (☎ **055-239-6526;** www.madova.com). A reasonable alternative to the pricey designer labels of Via dei Tornabuoni is **Anna,** Piazza Pitti 38–41r (☎ **055-283-787**), which provides fine quality and a professional staff who know their stuff. The apparel is classic to fashionable, and the price point is high but reasonable considering the goods. Alterations can be done by seasoned tailors in 24 hours.

PAPER GOODS Marbleized paper and the myriad items it covers (agendas, albums, boxes, diaries, pencils, and pencil holders) is a centuries-old craft that has experienced a resurgence. For the unknowing, little-deserving, or innocent child awaiting their souvenirs back home, the low-quality photocopy quality of what is sold at the **Mercato San Lorenzo** will suffice. But for all else, the best value is at **Il Torchio,** Via de' Bardi 17 (☎ **055-234-2862**), whose artisans take great pride in the quality of their hand-printed papers and the carefully crafted items they cover (they'll also consider custom work). Its easy-to-reach Oltrarno location east of the Ponte Vecchio keeps prices lower than those in the high-rent Duomo neighborhood. More central, with five locations in Florence, is **Il Papiro,** whose largest branch is at Via Tavolini 13r (☎ **055-213-823**).

SHOES Quality shoe stores abound, from the exquisite Florentine institutions of Via dei Tornabuoni to the fun and ultracheap. For the latter, try **Peppe Peluso,** Via del Corso 1, at Via Proconsolo (☎ **055-268-283**), the cheapest shoe store in town, its large rooms chockablock with medium-quality knock-offs of yesterday's and some of tomorrow's runway fashions. Men's and women's shoes are arranged according to size, with styles from out-of-date to the up-to-date, priced as low as 59,000L ($30).

7 Florence After Dark

Florence doesn't have the musical cachet or grand opera houses of Milan, Venice, or Rome, but there are two symphony orchestras and a fine music school in Fiesole. The city's public theaters are certainly respectable, and most major touring companies stop in town on their way through Italy. Get tickets to all cultural and musical events at the city's main clearinghouse, **Box Office,** Via Alamanni 39 (☎ **055-210-0804** or 055-261-6049).

Many concerts and recitals staged in major halls and private spaces are sponsored by the **Amici della Musica** (☎ **055-609-012** or 055-608-420; www.mega.it/amici.musica), so contact them to see what concerts may be on while you're in town. When Florentines really want a fine night out at the theater, they skip town and head to nearby Prato for the **Teatro Metastasio,** one of Italy's finest (see chapter 4).

THE PERFORMING ARTS

CONCERT HALLS & OPERA The **Teatro Comunale,** Corso Italia 16 (☎ **055-211-158**), is the city's main music hall. It opens its season in September with concertos and recitals. Opera season runs December to mid-January, following which are symphonies and orchestral concerts through April. Mediocre plays are staged throughout the year.

The **Teatro Verdi,** Via Ghibellina 99–101 (☎ **055-212-320** or 055-281-792), is Florence's opera and ballet house, with the nice habit of staging Sunday-afternoon shows during the January-to-April season. The **Orchestra della Toscana** (☎ **055-281-993;** www.dada.it/ort) plays classical concerts here December to May. The theater also offers a bit of theater, but not of the caliber of La Pergola (below).

THEATER The biggest national and international touring companies stop in Florence's major playhouse, the **Teatro della Pergola,** Via della Pergola 12 (☎ **055-247-9651;** www.pergola.firenze.it). La Pergola is the chief purveyor of classical and classic plays from the Greeks and Shakespeare through Pirandello, Samuel Beckett, and Italian modern playwrights. Performances are professional and of high quality, if not always terribly innovative (and, of course, all in Italian).

CHURCH CONCERTS   Many Florentine churches fill the autumn with organ, choir, and chamber orchestra concerts, mainly of classical music. The tiny **Santa Maria de' Ricci** on Via del Corso seems always to have music wafting out of it; slipping inside to occupy a pew is occasionally free and sometimes a modest 5,000L to 20,000L ($2.50 to $10). Around the corner at Santa Margherita 7, the **Chiesa di Dante** (☎ **055-289-367**) puts on quality concerts of music for, and often played by, youths and children (tickets required). The **Florentine Chamber Orchestra,** Via E. Poggi 6 (☎ **055-783-374;** www.ats.it/orchest), also runs an autumn season in the **Orsanmichele;** tickets are available at Box Office (see above) or at the door an hour before the 9pm shows.

LIVE-MUSIC CLUBS

In 1979, Andrea Ardia opened his laid-back tavern **Chiodo Fisso,** Via Dante Alighieri 16r (☎ **055-238-1290**), to give his fellow singer/songwriters a place to play. It opens at 8 or 9pm with light meals; the performer takes the tiny stage around 10:30 or 11pm; the cover is 5,000L ($2.50) upon your first visit for an annual pass. For more action, head to **Dolce Zucchero,** Via dei Pandolfini 38r (☎ **055-247-7894**). "Sweet Sugar" is one of the better recent efforts to spice up Florence's nightlife and is popular with all ages. Under high ceilings are a long bar and a small dance floor with a stage for the nightly live musicians, usually a fairly talented cover act cranking out American and Italian dance songs for the packed crowd. The 10,000L ($5) cover includes one drink.

DISCOS & NIGHTCLUBS

Full Up, Via della Vigna Vecchia 23–25r (☎ **055-293-006**), remains year after year one of the trendiest clubs in town and also one of the more elegant. People dress up to come here, whether they plan to sip drinks on the velvet sofas around the piano bar or hit the smallish disco floor to groove to pop, dance, and hip-hop. It's open September to June only, Monday to Saturday 11pm to 4am. The 10,000L ($5) cover— 25,000L ($13) on weekends—includes one drink. Forever known as Yab Yum and recently reincarnated with a new attitude is **Yab,** Via Sassetti 5r (☎ **055-215-160**), just behind the main post office on Piazza della Repubblica. This dance club for 20-somethings is a perennial favorite, a relic of a 1980s disco that's open Monday and Wednesday to Saturday 9pm to 3am.

You'll have to wait a long time in line and fork over upwards of 20,000L to 30,000L ($10 to $15) to get into **Meccanò,** Viale degli Olmi 1, at the entrance to the Cascine Park, Piazza Vittorio Veneto ☎ **055-331-371**), Florence's biggest, baddest disco, open 11pm to 4am daily except Monday and Wednesday. The Cascine is pretty seedy after dark, so be careful as you leave and head straight for the Viale. Right in the *centro storico,* **Space Electronic,** Via Palazzuolo 37 (☎ **055-293-082** or 055-680-089), is a middlin' big-city dance club in a small-city setting. It's open Tuesday to Sunday 10pm to 2am or so, and cover begins at 15,000L ($8).

PUBS & BARS

There's an unsurprising degree of similarity among Florence's half dozen **Irish-style pubs** (7,000L to 8,000L/$3.50 to $4 for a pint of Guinness or cider) dark, woody interiors usually with several back rooms and plenty of smoke; and a crowd (stuffed to the gills on weekends) of students and 20- and 30-something Americans and Brits along with their Italian counterparts. The better ones are the Florence branch of the successful Italian chain **Fiddler's Elbow,** Piazza Santa Maria Novella 7r (☎ **055-215-056**); **The Old Stove,** Via Pellicceria 4r (☎ **055-284-640**), just down from Piazza della Repubblica; and, under the same management, **The Lion's Fountain,** Borgo Albizi 34r (☎ **055-234-4412**), on the tiny but lively Piazza San Pier Maggiore near Santa Croce. You'll find plenty of others around town—they pop up like mushrooms these days, but often disappear just as quickly.

Red Garter, Via de' Benci 33r (☎ **055-234-4904**), is a speakeasy attracting a 20s-to-30s crowd of Italians and some Americans, Australians, and English. The hooch will run you 8,000L ($4) and up. There's a small bilevel theater room in the back with live music some nights—the last time I was here, it was a one-man band playing American and Italian rock hits with some blues mixed in.

GAY & LESBIAN BARS

Florence has one of Italy's largest gay communities, with a tradition of gay tolerance that goes back to the early days of the Renaissance and some of the Medicis' homosexual proclivities (and Michelangelo didn't specialize in male nudes for nothing). The Florentine fondness for *buon gusto* and inherent discretion remain all-important, however—except for the remarkable transvestites who populate the somewhat seedy Cascine Park after dark.

The **Arci-Gay/Arci-Lesbica** office is at Via San Zanobi 54r (☎/fax **055-476-557** or 055-488-288; www.agora.stm.it/gaylesbica.fi), offering advice, psychological counseling, HIV testing, and information on the gay community and sponsoring gay-related events. It's open Monday to Saturday 4pm to 8pm, with Monday theme nights and Wednesday evenings devoted to lesbians and Saturday afternoons to the younger set. It also publishes the free gay guide *Il Giglio Fuscia.*

Tabasco, Piazza Santa Cecilia 3, near Piazza della Signoria (☎ **055-213-000**), is Florence's (and Italy's) oldest gay dance club. The crowd is mostly men in their 20s and 30s. The dance floor is downstairs, while a small video room and piano bar are up top. There are occasional cabaret shows and karaoke. The club is open Thursday to Tuesday 10pm to 3am, with a 15,000L to 30,000L ($8 to $16) cover.

Florence's leading gay bar, **Crisco,** Via San Egidio 43r, east of the Duomo (☎ **055-248-0580**), is for men only. Its 18th-century building contains a bar and a dance floor open Sunday, Monday, Wednesday, and Thursday 10:30pm to 3:30am and Friday and Saturday 10:30pm to 5 or 6am. The cover is 12,000L to 16,000L ($6 to $9). In summer at the **Flamingo Bar** (formerly Santanassa), Via del Pandolfini 26, near Piazza Santa Croce (☎ **055-243-356**), the crowd is international. Thursday to Saturday, it's a mixed gay/lesbian party; the rest of the week, it's men only. On the street level is a crowded bar, sometimes with a live piano player; on Friday and Saturday, the cellar becomes a disco. It's open Sunday to Thursday 10pm to 4am and Friday and Saturday 10pm to 6am. The bar is open year-round; the disco, only September to June. Cover, including the first drink, is 12,000L ($6) Sunday to Thursday and 15,000L to 20,000L ($8 to $11) Friday and Saturday.

CAFFÈS

Florence no longer has a glitterati or intellectuals' cafe scene, and when it did—from the late 19th-century Italian *Risorgimento* era through the *dolce vita* of the 1950s—it was basically copying the idea from Paris. Although they're often overpriced tourist spots today, Florence's high-toned caffès are fine if you want designer pastries and hot cappuccinos served to you while you sit on a piazza and people-watch.

At the refined, wood-paneled, stucco-ceilinged, and very expensive **Gilli,** Piazza della Repubblica 39r/Via Roma 1r (☎ **055-213-896**), tourists gather to sit with the ghosts of Italy's *Risorgimento,* when the cafe became an important meeting place of the heroes and thinkers of the unification movement from the 1850s to the 1870s.

The red-jacketed waiters at **Giubbe Rosse,** Piazza della Repubblica 13–14r (☎ **055-212-280**), must've been popular during the 19th-century glory days of Garibaldi's red shirt soldiers. This was once a meeting place of the Florentine futurists, but aside from organized literary encounters on Wednesdays, it, too, is mainly a tourists' cafe with ridiculous prices. Once full of history, now mainly full of tourists, **Rivoire,** Piazza della Signoria/Via Vacchereccia 4r (☎ **055-214-412**), has a chunk of prime real estate on the Piazza della Signoria. Smartly dressed waiters serve smartly priced sandwiches to cappuccino-sipping patrons.

WINE BARS

The most traditional wine bars are called *fiaschetterie,* after the word for a flask of Chianti. They tend to be hole-in-the-wall joints serving sandwiches or simple food along with glasses filled to the brim—usually with a house wine, though finer vintages are often available. The best are **I Fratellini,** Via dei Cimatori 38r (☎ **055-239-6096**); **Antico Noé,** off Piazza San Pier Maggiore (☎ **055-234-0838**); and **La Mescita,** Via degli Alfani 70r (☎ **055-239-6400**). There's also a traditional wine shop in the Oltrarno called simply **La Fiaschetteria,** Via de' Serragli 47r (☎ **055-287-420**), that, like many, doubles as a small locals' wine bar with 1,000L (50¢) glasses.

A more high-toned spot is the **Cantinetta Antinori,** Piazza Antinori 3 (☎ **055-292-234**). It's housed in the palace headquarters of the Antinori wine empire at the top of Florence's main fashion drag, Via dei Tornabuoni. For a trendier wine bar focusing on hand-picked labels offered with plates of cheese and other snacks, head to the Oltrarno and a real oenophile's hangout, **Il Volpe e L'Uva,** Piazza de' Rossi, behind Piazza Santa Felicita off Via Guicciardini (☎ **055-239-8132**).

8 A Day Trip to Fiesole

For a more extensive choice of full day trips from Florence, take a look at the next chapter and the nearby towns of Lucca, San Gimignano, and Siena. For a quickie, consider Fiesole, an independent *comune* easily accessible by public bus, where Florentines take to the hills to escape the crowds and heat of the valley-locked city below.

Situated 8km (5 mi.) north of town on a green hill rising above Florence, **Fiesole** is an important archaeological site, once a pre-Roman Etruscan settlement, and later a prominent Roman town. In more recent centuries, families of means have fled the city's summer heat, history's rash of plagues, family feuds, and urban ennui by taking to the cool cypress-studded environs above. It has long been known for its magnificent ancestral villas and million-dollar views. Many of the historic villas are now associated with the dozens of American university programs, such as that of the famous art historian/critic Bernard Berenson, who left his Villa I Tatti to his alma mater Harvard University (today, it's a postdoctorate center for studies of Renaissance topics), and the Rockefellers' Villa Le Balze, bequeathed to Georgetown University.

GETTING THERE

Fiesole is an easy half-day excursion, accessible by public bus, so you may find yourself surrounded by fellow tourists. It can be reached in 30 minutes with bus no. 7 (costing the standard 1,500L/75¢) from Piazza della Stazione or Piazza San Marco to the end of the line.

A Money-Saving Tip

Most sites in Fiesole are open in winter Wednesday to Monday 9:30am to 5pm and in summer daily 9:30am to 5pm. A **single admission ticket** of 10,000L ($5) gets you into all the major sights and museums. Fiesole's private villas aren't on view to the public, though other historic sites are, and most visitors come for the change of air, gorgeous views looking south over Florence, and a piazza-side aperitif, light meal, or evening performance at the amphitheater.

EXPLORING THE TOWN

The Etruscans founded ancient Faesulae centuries before the Romans established the riverside trading colony and army retirement camp of Fiornetina down below. You can still feel the presence of these cultures at the important archaeological site called the **Teatro Romano,** a vast area of 2,000-year-old Etruscan and Roman ruins (☎ **055-59-477**). Its highlight is the 3,000-seat 1st century B.C. Roman theater used for the Estate Fiesolana music, dance, and theater festival (see the "Calendar of Events," in chapter 2). The admission includes the **Museo Civico (Museo Faesulanum),** whose finds prove the importance of Fiesole over Florence in their nascent days, and the little **Museo Bardini** to the left of the archaeological site entrance, housing 13th- to 15th-century Florentine paintings.

The town center surrounds a large square dedicated to sculptor Mino da Fiesole (ca. 1430 to 1484). Fronting the square is the Romanesque **Cattedrale di San Romolo,** from 1000 (though the columns inside are even older, pilfered from neighboring Roman structures) and much altered during the Renaissance. On the right side of the raised presbytery are several important sculptures and tombs carved in the 15th century by Mino da Fiesole. Also on the piazza is the 17th-century **Palazzo Arciverscovado (Bishop's Palace)** and **Santa Maria Primerana** church.

But Fiesole is all about its lofty **views** over the Arno Valley, and no one leaves without a look at the splendid panorama of Florence and the countryside. For a heart-stopping view (in every sense of the word), you'll have to hike up the very steep pedestrian-only Via di San Francesco west (left) out of the main square—not for the weak of heart. At the top are a church and museum that follow temperamental hours, but halfway up lies a ✪ **terrace belvedere** and a view that never ends.

You'll have worked up an appetite by now, but Fiesole's abundant restaurants, bars, and cafes principally work as tourist traps. Sip a Campari or order a gelato while waiting for the bus back to reality, but don't plan on eating here.

Tuscany & Umbria 5

by Reid Bramblett

Tuscany (**Toscana**) and **Umbria** share much of the same cultural and artistic heritage, a history dating from the pre-Roman Etruscans, a cuisine, and to some degree, a similarity in landscape. However, it'll behoove you never to mention these two regions in the same breath to a Tuscan or an Umbrian. Like two first cousins, Tuscany and Umbria are just as often fiercely individualistic in the characteristics and traditions they've preserved and nurtured over the centuries.

Italians are rarely modest about their unabashed love for the region they call home. But nowhere is this emotion-packed loyalty of provincia so deservedly heartfelt as in Tuscany, one of the country's most visited rural destinations. Richly endowed with a wide variety of topography, from the Apennine Mountains in the northwestern corner to the open rolling plains of the Maremma area in the south, Tuscany is also endowed with a coastal riviera (admittedly less alluring than Liguria's, but with the benefit of wide sandy beaches) and a number of idyllic islands in the Ligurian Sea of which Elba, Napoléon's exile retreat, is the largest and most renowned.

Almost three-quarters of Tuscany are comprised of gentle hills, terraced by farmers over time to prevent erosion while providing more room for crops. It's not hard for visitors to recapture the magical beauty of a Merchant Ivory movie: Hollywood would never think of filming on location elsewhere. Tuscans are only half-joking when they tell you that God may be responsible for the beauty that is Tuscany's, but the local genius Michelangelo drew up the plans.

The Umbrian cities featured in this chapter haven't changed much since the Middle Ages, but you'll never mistake them for museum cities: They're very much alive, fueled by their cultural interests and thriving economies only partially sustained by tourism. Two of Italy's most important summer festivals take place here, the Umbrian Jazz Festival in Perugia and the Spoleto Festival in Spoleto.

Most of the tourist offices in the towns and cities can supply you with lists of *affittacamere,* bed-and-breakfast accommodations that often offer the best deal in town. In many places, there's also the possibility of *agriturismo* accommodations in the countryside, ranging from the very basic to working farms with swimming and horseback riding. Lists are available, though they do little to describe or recommend one over the next.

A Taste of Tuscany & Umbria

The Tuscan and Umbrian *cucina* draws heavily from the grains, beans, and ingredients of the farmer's simple pantry and the woods and forests covering its hills. Nouvelle cuisine it's not. Rustic *salsicce* (sausage) antipasti, *cacciagione* (game), and tender quality meats roasted or *alla griglia* are the highlight of every meal—the mighty *bistecca alla fiorentina* being the fabled (and bill boosting) entree you'll want to try at least once. The unquestioned prominence of **olive oil** makes an appearance from the acclaimed groves of Lucca and Spoleto, the Tuscan and Umbrian suppliers of Europe's best *olio di oliva*. Renowned **Chianti wines** from the scenic pocket between Florence and Siena and distinctive **Orvieto whites** make this area an oenophile's dream—and you most likely won't be disappointed with the humble *vino della casa* **(house wine).** Umbria's touted claim to gastronomic fame is the underground *tartufo* **(truffle)** from Norcia, Spoleto, or San Miniato. Preciously grated over pastas and pizzas, it's expensive but its acquired taste is considered sublime by gourmand palates. This is the place to try it: not only for the local expertise and abundance, but for the moderate prices (moderate when compared to over-the-top American ones).

1 Pisa & Its Tipping Tower

77km (48.5 mi.) W of Florence, 21km (13 mi.) W of Lucca, 335km (211 mi.) N of Rome, 98km (62 mi.) NW of San Gimignano

Legions descend on **Pisa** just to see the famous tower that just won't stand up straight. Few other buildings have captured the world's imagination. Most surprising is the realization that the Leaning Tower—which may reopen to visitors in 2001 (see below)—is but one of three principle structures occupying the vividly green piazza called Campo dei Miracoli and is the Duomo's free-standing (well, barely) campanile (bell tower). Also surprising may be the fact that Pisa is a large riverside city with a population of 100,000—vibrant, contemporary, bustling, and relatively indifferent to its icon—something that may or may not appeal to those who expect a quaint Tuscan town.

Pisa is one of Italy's great ancient cities, its Roman roots going back more than 1,000 years before the building of the campanile. The mouth of the Arno River has long since silted up, placing Pisa inland 8km (5 mi.) from the coast, but it was once a vital port and naval base for imperial Rome and for centuries fought to keep the Tyrrhenian coast free of invading Saracens. From the 11th to the 13th century, it grew to rival the three other maritime powers—Genoa, Amalfi, and Venice—and gloried in its military supremacy in the western Mediterranean. This was the city's Golden Age, when its artistic splendor flourished.

But internal rivalries and external strife from nearby Lucca and Florence chipped away at its political stability, and in 1406, it was defeated by the Florentines. There was a brief period of well-being under the Medicis and the flourishing of its prestigious university (established in 1343) and an even briefer period of independence from 1494 to 1509. But for the most part, Pisa's history melded with that of Florence's from the early 1500s until Italian unification in the 1860s.

ESSENTIALS

GETTING THERE **By Train** There are more than 20 trains daily from **Rome** (regional: 4 hr., 28,400L/$14; high speed: 3 hr., 42,300L/$21). From **Florence,** 35 daily trains make the trip (80–90 min.; 7,700L/$3.85). There are trains about hourly from **Siena** (100–110 min.; 10,500L/$5). And **Lucca** zips 24 runs here every day (20–30 min.; 3,200L/1.60). On the Lucca line, get off at the **Stazione San Rossore,** just a few blocks west of Piazza del Duomo and its campanile. All other trains, and the Lucca one eventually, pull into **Stazione Pisa Centrale.** From here, bus 1, 3, or 11 will take you to Piazza del Duomo.

By Bus   Lazzi (☎ **0583-584-876**) runs hourly buses from **Lucca** (20–30 min.; 3,700L/$1.85), where you can connect for hourly runs from **Florence** (2–2½ hr. total from Pisa; 12,300L/$6). Pisa's bus station is at Piazza Vittorio Emanuele II, just north of the main train station.

By Car   There's a Florence-Pisa autostrada along the Arno valley. Take the SS12 or S12r from Lucca; the A12 comes down the coast from the north, and the SS1 runs north and south along the coast.

By Plane   Tuscany's main international airport, **Galileo Galilei** (☎ **050-500-707**), is 3km (2 mi.) south of Pisa. Trains zip you downtown to the train station in 5 minutes (1,700L/85¢). A taxi to town takes only about 5 minutes (about 15,000L/$8)— some people even walk from town in about 20 minutes.

VISITOR INFORMATION   The **main tourist office** is just outside the Porta Santa Maria on the west end of the Campo dei Miracoli at Via C. Cammeo 2 (☎ **050-560-464;** www.pisa.turismo.toscana.it). May to October, it's open daily 8am to 8pm; November to April, hours are Monday to Saturday 9am to 5pm, and Sunday 10:30am to 3:30pm. A helpful **private tourism consortium** (supported by the state) shares office space there (☎ **050-830-253;** fax 050-830-243; www.traveleurope.it/pisa.htm); among other services, it'll book hotel rooms for free. There's a **small tourist office** to the left as you exit the train station (☎ **050-42-291**). These tourist offices can hand out maps and pamphlets, but they're oddly uninformed on the city of Pisa.

Usually, considerably more knowledgeable "Custodians of the Duomo" hang around the Museo dell'Opera del Duomo desk. The administrative **APT tourist office** is at Via Benedetto Croce 26 (☎ **050-40-096** or 050-40-202; fax 050-40-903). To find out what's going on in town, pick up a copy of the free weekly *Indizi e Servizi* at some newsstands and hotels.

FESTIVALS & MARKETS   The most important holiday is the that of the local patron, **San Ranieri,** on June 16 and 17, when the banks of the Arno are illuminated with torches (the Luminaria), followed by a regatta the following day. It also means the arrival of the **Gioco del Ponte (Bridge Game),** celebrated on the last Sunday of June. On the Ponte di Mezzo, teams from the north and south banks of the Arno dress in Renaissance costume and reenact a reverse tug-of-war, trying to run each other over with a 7-ton decorated cart. An extravagant procession of 600 people in historic costume precedes the "battle."

Pisa's old-fashioned **food market** (Monday to Saturday 8am to 1:30pm) is centered on the picturesque 16th-century Piazza delle Vettovaglie, west off the arcaded shopping street of Borgo Stretto on the north side of the Arno. On the second weekend of every month (except in July and August), an **antiques fair** fills the side streets on both sides of the Ponte di Mezzo, with many stores in the area staying open on Sunday as well.

SEEING THE LEANING TOWER & MORE

The **Campo dei Miracoli (Field of Dreams),** aptly named by Italian poet Gabriel D'Annunzio but more parochially known as **Piazza del Duomo,** sits within the northwestern stretch of the ancient city walls. The trio of elegant buildings on the piazza bear testimony to the importance of the Pisan Republic during the first 2

Tuscany & Umbria

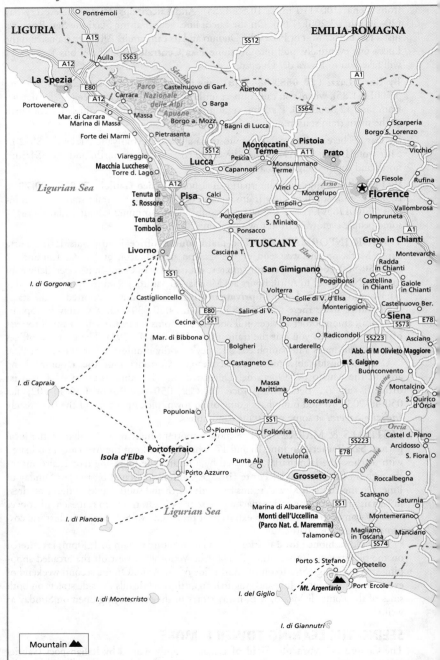

LIGURIA

EMILIA-ROMAGNA

Pontrémoli

A15

SS12

Aulla

SS63

A12

A1

La Spezia

E80

Parco
Nazionale
delle Alpi
Apuane

Castelnuovo di Garf.

Abetone

Portovenere

A12

Carrara

SS64

Mar. di Carrara
Marina di Massa

Massa

Barga

Scarperia

Borgo S. Lorenzo

Forte dei Marmi

Borgo a. Mozz.

Bagni di Lucca

Vicchio

Pietrasanta

Montecatini
Terme

Pistoia

Viareggio

SS12

Pescia

A11

Prato

Macchia Lucchese

Lucca

Monsummano
Terme

Fiesole

Rufina

Torre d. Lago

Capannori

Arno

A12

Vinci

Montelupo

Florence

Ligurian Sea

Tenuta di
S. Rossore

Pisa

Calci

Empoli

Vallombrosa

Impruneta

Tenuta di
Tombolo

Pontedera

S. Miniato

A1

Ponsacco

TUSCANY

Greve in Chianti

Livorno

Casciana T.

Montevarchi

SS1

San Gimignano

Radda
in Chianti

I. di Gorgona

Poggibonsi

Castellina
in Chianti

Gaiole
in Chianti

Volterra

Castiglioncello

Colle di V. d'Elsa

Castelnuovo Ber.

E80

SS1

Saline di V.

Monteriggioni

Siena

Cecina

Pornaranze

SS73

E78

Mar. di Bibbona

Radicondoli

SS223

Asciano

Bolgheri

Larderello

Abb. di M Oliveto Maggiore

Castagneto C.

S. Galgano

Buonconvento

Massa
Marittima

Montalcino

Roccastrada

S. Quirico
d'Orcia

Populonia

Orcia

Piombino

SS1

Follonica

Castel d. Piano

Portoferraio

SS223

Arcidosso

Isola d'Elba

E78

S. Fiora

Punta Ala

Vetulonia

Porto Azzurro

Roccalbegna

Grosseto

I. di Capraia

Scansano

Saturnia

SS1

I. di Pianosa

Ligurian Sea

Marina di Albarese

Montemerano

Monti dell'Uccellina
(Parco Nat. d. Maremma)

Magliano
in Toscana

Manciano

Talamone

SS74

I. di Montecristo

Porto S. Stefano

Orbetello

Mt. Argentario

Port' Ercole

I. del Giglio

I. di Giannutri

Mountain ▲▲

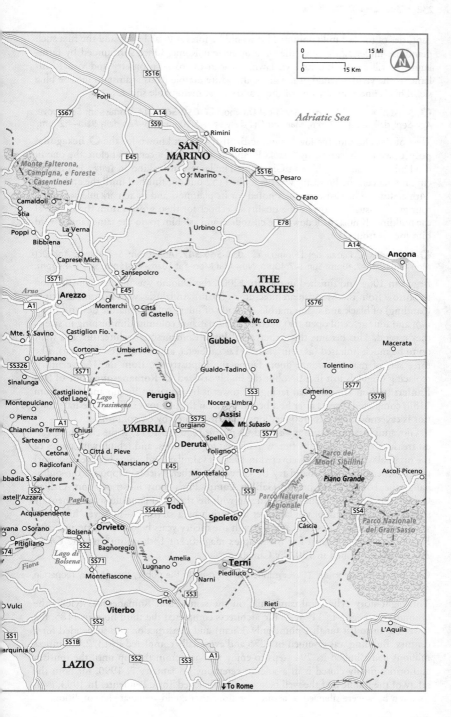

centuries of the last millennium: This would be forever Pisa's legacy and the first such grandiose undertaking since the time of ancient Rome. Once surrounded by farm-lands, it still sits within its own lawn, a paean to spatial geometry and visual bril-liance—the vivid emerald of the grass, the white marble icons against an intense blue sky. This is undoubtedly one of the world's most memorable squares.

✪ **Battistero (Baptistry).** Piazza del Duomo. ☎ **050-560-547.** Admission: See above. Apr–Sept daily 8am–7:20pm; Mar and Oct daily 9am–5:20pm; Nov–Feb daily 9am–4:20pm.

West of the Duomo, the lovely Gothic Baptistry is best known for the ✪ **hexagonal pulpit** beautifully carved by Nicola Pisano in 1260, half a century before the one in the Duomo created by his son Giovanni. The largest of its kind in Italy (348 feet in circumference), the Baptistry was begun in 1152 but not finished until the end of the 14th century. The vast interior is noted for its plainness and its remarkable acoustics; tour guides usually illustrate the quality of echoes for their groups from the center of the building. If not, track down the custodian and ask him to do the same (and reward him for his trouble).

✪ **Cattedrale.** Piazza del Duomo. ☎ **050-560-547.** Admission: See above. Apr–Oct Mon–Sat 10am–7:40pm, Sun 1–7:40pm; Nov–Mar Mon–Sat 10am–12:45pm, Sun 3–4:45pm.

Begun in 1064 and finished in the late 1200s, the Duomo was the first construction to borrow from the Moorish architecture of Spain's Andalusia, with horizontal stripes (banding) of black and white marble, a facade of inlaid colored-marble design (*intarsia*), and four graceful open-air galleries of mismatched columns diminishing in size as they ascend. This became the archetype of Pisan Romanesque architecture and went on to be much imitated (as your visits to Lucca, Siena, and elsewhere will attest). The three sets of massive bronze doors facing the Baptistry are from the 16th century, replacing originals lost in a fire, but the highly stylized ✪ **Romanesque door of San Ranieri** (patron saint of Pisa) facing the tower is by Bonanno Pisano and dates from 1180, completed 7 years after he'd begun work on the bell tower. The cathedral's inte-rior is cavernous, close to 400 feet long and interrupted by 68 columns.

Giovanni Pisano's intricately carved ✪ **pulpit** (1301 to 1311) is the church's great-est treasure, destroyed in the fire, warehoused for centuries, and rebuilt with pieces of the original when it was rediscovered in 1926. It's similar (and, some believe, superior) to an earlier one in the Baptistry by Giovanni's father, Nicola. Opposite the pulpit hangs the 16th-century bronze **Galileo Lamp.** Pisa's most illustrious son, Galileo Galilei (1564 to 1642), allegedly came up with his theory of pendulum movement by studying the swinging of the lamp set in motion by a sacristan—however, historians say the astronomer/physicist came up with the theory years before the lamp was cast. Having survived the great fire is the apse's magnificent 13th-century mosaic *Christ Pantocrator,* finished in 1302 by Cimabue.

✪ **Campanile (Leaning Tower).** Indefinitely closed to the public, though may reopen in 2001 (see below).

This eight-story cylindrical campanile, in the same Pisan Romanesque style as the Duomo, was begun in 1174. As the architects completed the third floor in 1185, the tower began to list (at that point only 3.8cm) and construction was suspended for a century. Building was resumed in 1275 and eventually completed in 1372. Countless millions had climbed its 294 steps to enjoy the view from the top until the tourism authorities finally closed it in a solemn ceremony on January 7, 1990, for both the safety of the public and the well being of their beloved Torre Pendente. In 1993, even its seven bells were silenced to avoid vibrations that could aggravate its condition.

Pisa

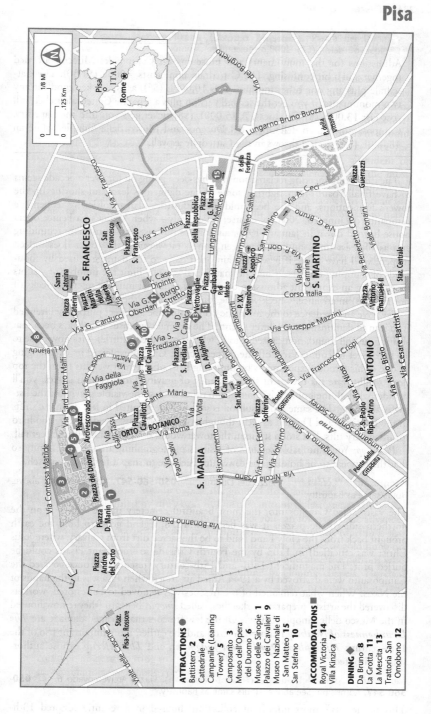

ATTRACTIONS ●
Battistero 2
Cattedrale 4
Campanile (Leaning Tower) 5
Camposanto 3
Museo dell'Opera del Duomo 6
Museo delle Sinopie 1
Palazzo dei Cavalieri 9
Museo Nazionale di San Matteo 15
San Stefano 10

ACCOMMODATIONS ■
Royal Victoria 14
Villa Kinzica 7

DINING ◆
Da Bruno 8
La Grotta 11
La Mescita 13
Trattoria San Omobono 12

Campo dei Miracoli Admissions

Admissions for the monuments and museums on Campo dei Miracoli are tied together and a bit confusing. The Cattedrale alone costs 3,000L ($1.50). The Cattedrale plus any one other monument is 10,000L ($5), as is a ticket good for any two monuments (if you get the second version plus a separate Cattedrale ticket, it'll cost just 13,000L/$7 for three). A 15,000L ($8) ticket gets you into the Baptistry, Camposanto, Museo dell'Opera del Duomo, and Museo delle Sinopie, while an 18,000L ($9) version throws in the Cattedrale as well.

The drastic engineering reclamation that has been going on for over a decade seems to have finally paid off in righting some of the dangerous lean and shoring up the tower's foundations, and I've been told the authorities plan to officially reopen the campanile on June 16, 2001 (of course, this is Italy—when Venice's La Fenice opera house burned down in January 1996, authorities promised an immediate rebuilding and as of press time, nothing has been done). However, if the tower does indeed reopen, we'll have to see if it will remain open daily to the damage caused by thousands of tramping tourists. It may be that they'll severely limit the number of visitors by charging an exorbitant admission on very few slots that must be reserved weeks (if not months) in advance. Check with the tourist office for the latest news.

Few give any credence to the romantic notion that the architect purposely intended it to lean to demonstrate his clever talents: The general consensus has always been that shifting subsoil foundation caused it to slowly list over the centuries—it's now close to 14 to 17 feet (accounts vary) off the perpendicular. Galileo exploited its overhanging in one of his famous experiments by dropping balls of different weights from the top floor to illustrate his theory of the constancy of gravity. From certain angles, you'll wonder what all the hubbub is about; from other angles, the visible gravity of the listing is alarming. The same sandy subsoil is said to have resulted in less dramatic shifts in the Baptistry and Duomo as well, though you may go cross-eyed looking too hard for imaginary tilts. If it stood straight, the tower would be approximately 185 feet tall.

Photo op: You'll probably see lots of visitors photographing friends and family so that they appear to be holding the tower up. Feel free to snap a few shots yourself.

Camposanto (Cemetery). Piazza del Duomo. ☎ **050-560-547.** Admission: See above. Hours same as Baptistry.

The vast walled Camposanto, the most beautiful cemetery in the world, is on the northern side of the piazza. It was begun in 1278, legend goes, to hold the earth brought back from the Holy Land (said to be the sacred dirt from Calvary, where Jesus Christ was crucified) in 1203 by the Fourth Crusade so important Pisans could be buried in it. The magnificent 14th- and 15th-century frescoes that once covered the Camposanto were destroyed by a 1944 Allied air attack when Pisa was in the hands of the Nazis. When what remained of the frescoes was removed to be restored, workers discovered the artists' preparatory sketches, called *sinopie*, beneath (they're now housed in the Museo delle Sinopie, below). Of the few frescoes that escaped damage are *The Drunkenness of Noah* by Benozzo Gozzoli and the earlier, more important trio of the 14th-century *Triumph of Death, Last Judgment,* and *The Inferno,* whose authorship is disputed.

Museo dell'Opera del Duomo (Duomo Museum). Piazza Arcivescovado 6. ☎ **050-560-547.** Admission: See above. Hours same as Baptistry.

This is the city's most important collection, housed in a recently restored 13th-century palazzo. Used as the Duomo's Chapter House and later as a Capuchin monastery, it's now divided into 19 rooms that are home to a wealth of artworks from the campo's buildings. Sculptures by the various members of the Pisano family and their students are the highpoints of the museum. From Giovanni Pisano, whose pulpit is the focal point of the Duomo, is his important statuette of *Madonna and Child* (1300), whose figures lean in to the natural curve of the ivory tusk from which the work is carved; it was found on the Duomo's main altar.

Another highpoint is the precious **Pisan cross** that led the local contingent off to the First Crusade in 1099. A 12th-century **bronze griffin,** a masterpiece of Islamic art, was picked up as war booty from the Saracens and placed in the Duomo before being relocated here. The Islamic influence felt in many of the pieces is testimony to Pisa's history as a powerful maritime republic in the Mediterranean; see the examples of the **inlaid marble intarsia** of Moorish-influenced designs that once decorated the Duomo's facade. The last few rooms house a small Roman and Etruscan **archaeological collection** from the Camposanto. Most important are the 19th-century **etchings** of its Renaissance frescoes (being restored at that time) that are the only record of the artwork that was destroyed when the cemetery was bombed in 1944.

Museo delle Sinopie. Piazza del Duomo. ☎ **050-560-547.** Admission: See above. Hours same as Baptistry.

Of limited interest except to those particularly intrigued by the story of the Camposanto and its frescoes, this well-arranged museum is the newest of the Campo dei Miracoli's additions. Created exclusively in a 13th-century hospice to display the preliminary fresco sketches found beneath those destroyed in 1944 by a bomb attack (see the Camposanto entry, above), the museum is dedicated to the *sinopie* or reddish-brown sketches made from Sinope clay. They're all that remain of the majority of the Camposanto's frescoes by leading early Renaissance masters. There's also an explanation of how frescoes were created in those days.

MORE PISAN SIGHTS

Take an easy 10-minute stroll down Via Santa Maria from Piazza del Duomo and make a left onto Via dei Mille, and you'll find yourself in **Piazza dei Cavalieri (Square of the Knights).** There would be a lot more hype about its architectural attributes if it didn't have the Campo dei Miracoli to vie with. The square was built on the site of the old Roman Forum and takes its name from the Order of St. Stephen, a military/religious order founded in 1561 by the Medicis to protect the Mediterranean from the Turkish infidels. Next to the 16th-century **San Stefano,** designed by Vasari, is the fabulously (and recently restored) graffiti-covered **Palazzo dei Cavalieri,** once used to train the knights until Napoléon took over and founded the Scuola Normale Superiore in 1810. The Medicis (and not Napoléon) are represented by the **statue of Grand Duke Cosimo I** (1519 to 1574) standing outside. The third most important building on the square is the **Palazzo dell'Orologio (Clock Tower),** two medieval towers joined by Vasari and today, housing the library for the Scuola Normale Superiore.

Museo Nazionale di San Matteo (National Museum). Lungarno Mediceo (near Ponte Fortezza). ☎ **050-541-865.** Admission 8,000L ($4). Tues–Sat 9am–7pm, Sun 9am–2pm. Bus: 5, 7, 13.

Most of the major paintings from Pisa's churches are now displayed here around the 15th-century cloister of the convent of San Matteo. Fourteenth-century religious works, from Pisa's final period of prosperity, make up the bulk of the collection that spans the 12th to the 17th century and includes mostly minor works by Simone Martini, Masaccio, Gentile da Fabriano, Donatello, Fra' Angelico, Gozzoli, and Ghirlandaio, plus Nino Pisano' beautifully sculpted *Madonna del Latte.*

Davidus Jones's Locker

In 1998, workers expanding the San Rossore train station stumbled across what Italy's culture minister dubbed a "marine Pompeii": 10 remarkable **ancient Roman wooden ships**—riverboats to seafaring vessels and what may be the only Roman warship ever recovered intact, spanning the 1st century B.C. through the Imperial Age. Pisa's forgotten ancient port was buried by silt in the 12th century (which has since moved the shoreline 8km/5 mi. west), and these docks where the Arno once met the sea were probably half marshy flatlands, half lagoon—much like modern-day Venice. Alas, this sort of harbor is prone to flash flooding during storms, which is probably what sank these ships.

Fortunately, the sudden demise of these ships meant that much of their contents has survived, from holds filled with clay amphorae (whose seals have preserved shipments of olives, cherries, walnuts, and wine for 2,000 years) to sailors' quarters still kitted out with their belongings (leather sandals, sewing kits, clothing, and even a wax writing board). Once archaeologists get the ships excavated, the city plans to open a maritime archaeology museum in the old Medici Arsenale; besides seeing the displayed ships' contents, you'll be able to watch the arduous restoration work on the vessels. Check with the tourist office for the projected opening date.

AFFORDABLE PLACES TO STAY

Pisa is the quintessential day trip from Florence, and the selection of hotels is limited, with very reasonable prices. All the buses disgorging their passengers at the Leaning Tower will return them to their hotels in Florence at the end of the day. Should you have a problem with availability, call the **Consorzio Turistico** (it shares space with the tourist office at Via C. Cammeo—see above) and ask them to reserve a hotel for you at no cost.

If the Royal Victoria (below) is full, try the family-run **Villa Kinzica** just off Piazza del Duomo at Piazza Arcivescovado 2 (☎ **050-560-419;** fax 050-551-204; www.pisaonline.it/hotelvillakinzica), where doubles with a view of the tower cost 180,000L ($90), breakfast included.

✪ **Royal Victoria.** Lungarno Pacinotti 12, 56126 Pisa (near Ponte di Mezzo). ☎ **050-940-111.** Fax 050-940-180. www.royalvictoria.it. E-mail: mail@royalvictoria.it. 48 units, 40 with bathroom. TV TEL. 100,000–105,000L ($50–$53) single without bathroom, 155,000L ($78) single with bathroom; 115,000L–120,000L ($58–$60) double without bathroom, 185,000L ($93) double with bathroom. Rates include buffet breakfast. AE, DC, MC, V. Parking 30,000L ($15) in garage. Bus: 1 or 7 (toward Pratalle), 4 (toward I Passi), or 3 (from airport).

"I fully endorse the above," wrote Teddy Roosevelt in one of the yellowed guest books, and what was good for him will be good for you. Built in 1839 by the great-grandfather of the two current owners, this is Pisa's oldest and only hotel full of character, charm, and (during Sunday and Thursday lessons) tango music. It links several medieval structures (rooms. 101, 201, 301, and 401 are in a 10th-century tower) facing the Arno and has done much to keep its old-world atmosphere, with original pavements, etched-glass doors, antique furniture, and frescoed ceilings and walls in many rooms. The rooftop terrace offers river views and bar service. The Piegaja brothers undertake regular renovations—new firm mattresses one year, tastefully arranged silk-flowers another—and rent bikes for 5,000L ($2.50) per hour or 30,000L ($15) per day (10,000L/$5 per day if you're using the garage). To get a better picture of this hotel, flip to the back cover of this book.

GREAT DEALS ON DINING

Even if you're one of Pisa's countless day-trippers, try to arrange your day around a nice lunch at any of the following. Pisa has become a city for food lovers, and the new wave of young restaurateurs has brought it up a gastronomic notch in the last few years. Sharing the spotlight with La Grotta (below) is Pisa's other favorite trattoria, **Da Bruno,** Via Luigi Bianchi 12, north of the Campo dei Miracoli outside the Porta Lucca (☎ **050-560-818**), a bastion of tried-and-true Pisan specialties and one of the few restaurants open on Sunday; its prices are marginally higher. Du Bruno is open Monday noon to 3pm and Wednesday to Sunday noon to 3pm and 7 to 10:30pm; reservations are recommended.

La Mescita. Via D. Cavalca 2 (just off Piazza Vettovaglie). ☎ **050-544-294.** Reservations recommended. Primi 13,000–15,000L ($7–$8); secondi 15,000L–24,000L ($8–$12). No credit cards. Apr–Sept Tues–Sun 1–2pm and 8–11pm; Oct–Mar Tues–Thurs 8–11pm, Fri–Sun 1–2pm and 8–11pm. Closed 20 days in Aug. PISAN/ENOTECA.

This small trattoria's marketplace location means its crowd is colorful and its ingredients are the best and freshest; it becomes an enoteca (wine bar) in its late hours. The *cucina* is both local *pisana* and nontraditional but always interesting and delicious and served in a fun atmosphere. Often on the menu are soufflélike *sformati* based on fresh seasonal vegetables like *melanzane* (eggplant) and *zucca* (pumpkin or squash). A more regional standby is the excellent *baccalà* (salt codfish) made with chickpeas and potatoes.

A block away in the marketplace neighborhood is an equally favorite spot, the family-owned ✪ **Trattoria San Omobono,** Piazza San Omobono 6 (☎ **050-540-847**). The prices and menu choices are similar for a delicious casual meal in the company of locals, university professors, and market shoppers. It's open Monday to Saturday 12:30 to 2:30pm and 7:30 to 10pm.

La Grotta. Via San Francesco 103 (at the corner of Via Case Dipinte). ☎ **050-578-105.** Reservations strongly recommended. Primi 9,000L–15,000L ($4.50–$8); secondi 13,000L–25,000L ($7–$13). No credit cards. Mon–Sat 7:30–11:30pm. Closed Aug and Dec 24–Jan 7. Bus: 2, 3, 7. TUSCAN/ITALIAN.

Just east of the store-lined Borgo Stretto running from the river to the Campo dei Miracoli, this charming trattoria is always full and always serving great regional specialties to happy-looking Pisans. There's an old-fashioned warmth between the staff and the locals who've frequented this faux-grotto for generations, as much for the traditional Tuscan specialties as for the unpretentious service. You can't go wrong with any of the roasted and grilled meats with herb-crusted potatoes or the *coniglio ripieno alle castagne* (rabbit stuffed and roasted with chestnuts). The dining room is small, so be ready to reserve in advance or arrive early—or join those who patiently wait, knowing it's worth the effort.

2 Lucca & Its Renaissance Walls

72km (45 mi.) W of Florence, 21km (13 mi.) E of Pisa, 336km (209 mi.) N of Rome, 96km (60 mi.) NW of San Gimignano

You'll always remember the great walls of this unspoiled (albeit no longer undiscovered) Tuscan town: Brick ramparts rebuilt most recently in the 16th and 17th centuries encircle this graceful city in their Renaissance swath. Although **Lucca** boasts a population of 90,000, only a marginal percentage lives within the ancient walls, where a thriving small-town atmosphere prevails. The city preserves much of its tangible past: A flourishing colony of Rome in 180 B.C., its ancient legacy is still evident in the grid pattern of its streets.

A sophisticated silk and textile trade reinterpreting the luxurious silks from the Orient made this small town famous around Europe in the Middle Ages and early Renaissance, and the streets are still lined with handsomely preserved medieval towered palazzi reflecting Lucca's heyday. However, the town's power slowly dissipated—it tenaciously kept its independence from neighboring Pisa and Florence for many centuries but finally fell to Napoléon, who in 1805, handed it over to his sister Elisa Baciocchi as a principality; in 1815, it was absorbed into the Tuscan Grand Duchy. The quiet streets—where 25,000 workers once kept 3,000 hand looms operating—open onto small picturesque squares, each anchored by a marble-faced church. Lucca's medieval highlights are the Duomo and the elaborate San Michele, both exquisite examples of Pisan-Lucchese architecture.

Proximity to Pisa's Galileo Galilei Airport makes this an excellent first or last stop in Tuscany, recommended above the larger city of Pisa despite its legendary Leaning Tower (stay in Lucca and make a day trip to Pisa). The lack of traffic enhances Lucca's unhurried air, where moneyed matriarchs, whose noble family histories have survived the centuries, do their daily shopping around town on battered bicycles. The hotel situation doesn't bode well for budget travelers, but once you find a place to settle down, you'll discover the general lack of mass tourism is the city's, and your, greatest blessing.

ESSENTIALS

GETTING THERE   By Train   Lucca is on the Florence-Viareggio train line, with 21 trains daily from **Florence** (70–90 min.; 7,000L/$3.50). **Pisa** zips 24 runs here every day (20–30 min.; 3,200L/1.60). Lucca's **train station** is a short walk south of the Porta San Pietro, or you can take *navetta* minibus no. 16 into town.

By Car   The A11 runs from Florence through Prato, Pistoia, and Montecatini before hitting Lucca. The SS12 runs straight up here from Pisa.

By Bus   Lazzi buses (☎ **0583-584-876**) run hourly from both **Florence** (70 min.; 8,600L/$4.30) and **Pisa** (20–30 min.; 3,700L/$1.85) to Lucca's Piazzale Verdi.

VISITOR INFORMATION   The main **tourist office** is just inside the city walls at Piazza Santa Maria 35 (☎ **0583-91-991;** fax 0583-469-964; www.lucca.turismo. toscana.it). April to October, it's open daily 9am to 7pm (November to March to 2pm). It provides an excellent free pocket map and good pamphlets on Lucca and the Garfagnana. For events and theater, pick up the English-language monthly *GrapevinE* for 3,000L ($1.50) at most newsstands.

FESTIVALS & MARKETS   Musical festivals celebrate the town's melodious history. April to June, the churches take part in a **Festa della Musica Sacra (Festival of Sacred Music).** All September long, the **Settembre Lucchese** brings concerts and Puccini operas performed in the theater where many premiered, the Teatro Comunale on Piazza del Giglio. On September 13, an 8pm candlelit procession from San Frediano to the Duomo honors Lucca's most prized holy relic, the **Volto Santo** statue of Christ that tradition holds was carved by Nicodemus himself.

A huge **antiques market,** one of Italy's most important, is held the third Sunday (and preceding Saturday) of every month on Piazza Antelminelli and the streets around the Duomo. It's great fun but also leaves rooms hard to find and restaurants booked, especially at lunch (even those normally closed Sunday reopen for this one). It's spawned a local **art market** on Piazza del Arancio on the same dates, and the final Sunday of the month sees an **artisans' market** on Piazza San Giusto. There's a cute little **Christmas market** on Piazza dell'Anfiteatro from December 8 to 26, and September 13 to 29 brings an **agricultural market** to Piazza San Michele, featuring Lucca's wines, honeys, and D.O.C. olive oils.

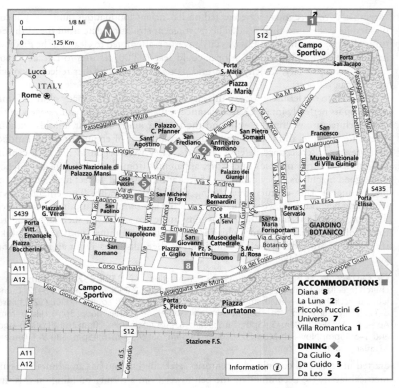

GETTING AROUND   A set of *navette* (**electric minibuses**) whiz dangerously down the city's peripheral streets, but the flat town is easily traversable on foot.

To really get around like a Lucchese, though, you need to **rent a bike.** There are four main rental outfits. There's the **city-sponsored stand** on Piazzale Verdi (☎ **0583-442-937;** closed November to mid-March), and **Cicli Barbetti,** Via Anfiteatro 23, near the Roman amphitheater (☎ **0583-954-444**), open Monday to Friday 9am to 12:30pm and 2:30 to 6pm, and Saturday 2:30 to 6pm (also Saturday morning and Sunday if the weather is nice). **Antonio Poli,** Piazza Santa Maria 42 (☎ **0583-493-787**), is open daily 8:30am to 7:30pm (closed Sundays mid-November to February and Monday mornings year-round). You can also try **Cicli Bizzarri** next door (☎ **0583-496-031**), open Monday to Saturday 8:30am to 1pm and 2:30 to 7:30pm, and Sundays March to mid-September. Rates are the same at all: 4,000L ($2) per hour or 20,000L ($10) per day (6,000L/$3 or 30,000L/$15, respectively, for a mountain bike).

Taxis rank at the train station (☎ **0583-494-989**), Piazza Napoleone (☎ **0583-492-691**), Piazzale Verdi (☎ **0583-581-305**), and Piazza Santa Maria (☎ **0583-494-190**).

SEEING THE SIGHTS

The aerial photograph of Lucca's **Anfiteatro Romano (Roman Amphitheater),** between Via Fillungo and Via Mordini, on local postcards is remarkable, showing the perfect elliptical shape of the theater built here in the 2nd century; the buildings from varying eras you see today were erected on its ancient foundations, and many incorporated its arches into their walls. The most recent structures date from the 19th century, when Napoléon's sister Elisa, as city governor, attempted to clean up the medieval jumble. The amphitheater, which once could seat 10,000, testifies to Lucca's importance as a Roman city; the city's neat grid pattern of streets further reflects its origin as a Roman outpost.

Succumb to the leisurely pace of this city and stroll or bike the shady 4km (2.5-mi.) path atop its perfectly intact ✪ **Renaissance walls.** Here, you can enjoy a view of the city's architecture within the walls and the lovely countryside that unfolds without. These are the city's third set of walls, an enormous feat of engineering and Europe's best-preserved Renaissance defense ramparts. They were begun in the 16th century long after centuries of feuds and strife, apparently from the belief that good fences make good neighbors. They measure 115 feet at the base and 40 feet high, with a double avenue of 19th-century trees lining their 60-foot width. The emerald lawns stretching beyond them weren't planted until the last century. You can access the tree-lined promenade at any of the 11 bastions (there are six gates), such as behind the tourist office on Piazzale Verdi (which is where, during summer, you can rent a bike; see "Getting Around," above). A full circuit of the walls takes about an hour by foot and 20 minutes by bike.

✪ **Cattedrale di San Martino.** Piazza San Martino. ☎ **0583-957-068.** Admission to church free. Ilaria tomb (in sacristy) 3,000L ($1.50) adults, 2,000L ($1) children 6–12. Cumulative ticket for tomb, Museo, and San Giovanni 7,000L ($3.50) adults, 4,000L ($2) children 6–12. Daily 7am–5pm (to 7pm in summer; sometimes closes noon–3pm). Illaria tomb Apr–Oct Mon–Fri 9:30am–5:45pm, Sat 9:30am–6:45pm, Sun 9am–10pm and 11:30am–noon and 1–5:45pm; Nov–Feb Mon–Fri 9:30am–4:45pm, Sat 9:30am–6:45pm, Sun 9–10am and 11:30am–noon and 1–5pm.

Started in 1060 and completed 2 centuries later, the Duomo has an admirable asymmetrical facade (to accommodate the bell tower from a former building on this site) with three galleries of slender mismatched twisting columns and early 13th-century bas-reliefs. It's one of the finest examples of the exuberant Pisan-Romanesque architecture for which this area of Tuscany is known (Pisa's Duomo is usually held as the supreme archetype). The star of the church's interior and Lucca's most precious relic is the robed figure of Jesus on the cross: The hauntingly beautiful wooden *Volto Santo* **(Holy Face)** is enshrined in its own elaborate 15th-century Tempietto (marble chapel) by Lucchese sculptor Matteo Civitali. The darkened crucifix is said to have been carved by Nicodemus, a fervent follower of Christ who helped lower him from the cross, and is believed to be a true image of Jesus (art historians attribute the work to 12th-century Eastern origin). Set adrift at sea, it was miraculously transported from the Holy Land across the Mediterranean and washed up on Tuscany's shores near La Spezia; the bishop of Lucca transported it here in 782. Local merchants spread the word throughout Europe, and Lucca gained fame for its portrait of Christ throughout the Middle Ages and became a point of pilgrimage for those on their way to Rome. Each September 13 and 14, the town turns out in a special evocative procession to carry the venerated statue dressed up in kingly jewel-encrusted robes through the streets illuminated by candlelight.

Competing for historic importance is the recently restored ✪ **Tomb of Ilaria del Carretto Guinigi,** now in the former sacristy along with the superb **Madonna and Saints altarpiece** by Domenico Ghirlandaio (1494), the young Michelangelo's fresco master. Sculpted with her beloved dog at her feet (representing fidelity) by Sienese master Jacopo della Quercia (1408), who breathed softness into the silklike folds of her dress, Ilaria was the young wife of a prominent lord of Lucca, in a politically arranged marriage that became a true union of love. She died at 26 after giving birth to their daughter, and is a much beloved figure in local history—the marble tomb is the Duomo's masterpiece. Look into the second chapel on the left for a 1598 painting by Bronzino, the *Presentation of Mary at the Temple,* and the third chapel on the right for the *Last Supper* (1590 to 1591) by Tintoretto and his students.

On the joint ticket described above, you can visit the **Museo della Cattedrale (Cathedral Museum)** across the street (☎ **0583-490-530**); April to October, hours are daily 10am to 6pm, and November to March, hours are Monday to Friday 10am to 3pm (Saturday and Sunday to 6pm). Opened in 1992, this small museum displays choice pieces of art such as paintings, silver chalices and reliquaries, and wooden and marble statuary from the Duomo's original collection. The restoration was severe, but there's still much left to admire in the space created by joining a 13th-century tower, a 14th-century palazzo, and an adjacent 16th-century church. Future plans are to relocate the Tomb of Ilaria to the museum, though there's no projected date. In the meantime, don't miss the early 15th-century statue of *St. John the Baptist* (once gracing the Duomo's facade) by the tomb's sculptor, Jacopo della Quercia, and the bejeweled regalia the *Volto Santo* wears on the days it's carried through town.

Nearby **San Giovanni** and its baptistry (open the same hours as the museum), recently reopened after years of work where stratum on stratum of archaeological foundations was unearthed, provides a one-stop look into the cathedral's and city's distant past. The deepest and lowest level you can visit is the original Roman foundation from the 1st century B.C., the latest is the foundation of the church's most recent reincarnation from the late Middle Ages.

✪ **San Michele in Foro.** Piazza San Michele. ☎ **0583-48-459.** Admission free. Daily 7:40am–noon and 3–6pm.

San Michele is the social and geographic, if not the religious, center of town, built on the original site of the Roman Forum (hence its name). Understandably mistaken as the Duomo by visitors, San Michele, begun in 1143, is second in importance only to the Duomo and dedicated to the winged archangel Michael, who crowns its facade. It's a wonderful example of the Pisan-Lucchese architecture influenced by Pisa's Duomo. The **remarkable facade** begins with ground-level arches, above which four tiers of twisted, patterned columns of every variety, size, and thickness are displayed; the facade soars considerably higher than the church itself. A number of national patriots, such as Cavour and Garibaldi, were added during a heavy 19th-century restoration. The impressive campanile is the city's highest.

Things are decidedly less exuberant inside since money ran out after completion of the facade, but there's a beautifully framed **painting of several saints** by Filippino Lippi, student of Botticelli; among the most important of his works, it's on the far wall in the right transept. A glazed **terra-cotta bas-relief** by Andrea della Robbia (some say it was by his uncle Luca) is inset on the first altar on the right.

Take a minute to stroll past the buildings lining the piazza; some dating back to the 13th century, while others are as recent as the 15th and 16th centuries. **Giacomo Puccini** was born in 1858 just a block from here on Via di Poggio 30. Both his father and his grandfather were organists here, and young Giacomo sang in the choir.

San Frediano. Piazza San Frediano. ☎ **0583-493-627.** Admission free. Mon–Sat 8:30am–noon and 3–5pm, Sun 10:30am–5pm.

A colorful 13th-century *Christ in Majesty* mosaic on the stark-white facade of San Frediano sets it apart from the city's countless other churches, one reason it figures on the short list (with the Duomo and San Michele) of Lucca's most visited. Also typical of the local Pisan-Lucchese style, but minus the open loggias full of ornate columns, it's dedicated to the 6th-century Irish Bishop St. Frigidian, who is said to have brought Christianity to Lucca (the first town in Tuscany to embrace it) and buried under its high altar. Upon entering, you'll see one of the church's highlights, an elaborately carved huge 13th-century **baptismal font.** Beyond the font and high on the wall is the glazed terra-cotta *Annunciation* by Andrea della Robbia. Behind the font is the chapel of St. Zita, the patron saint of domestics and ladies-in-waiting. Her feast day is April 26, when the Piazza San Frediano is carpeted with flowers and her lace-enwrapped body is carried out to be glorified by the locals.

If you've already visited the Duomo (above), you'll have seen the Tomb of Ilaria Caretto by master Sienese sculptor Jacopo della Quercia, whose marble reliefs on an altar and a pair of tombstones (1422) are here in the **Capella Trenta,** the fourth chapel on the left. Nearby, in the second chapel you can find the 16th-century frescoes of *The Life of San Frediano* and *Arrival of the Volto Santo* by Amico Aspertini (the yearly procession of the holy relic begins at the Duomo and ends here).

As you leave the church, head around the left side to Via Battisti to the 17th-century **Palazzo Pfanner** (☎ **0583-491-243**), whose sumptuous walled gardens were used as location shots for the 1996 film *The Portrait of a Lady.* March to November 15, it's open daily 10am to 6pm; admission is 3,000L ($1.50) each to the gardens or the palazzo or 5,000L ($2.50) for both. (If you tool around the city's ramparts you can look down into the gardens for free.)

Museo Nazionale di Palazzo Mansi (National Museum). Via Galli Tassi 43. ☎ **0583-55-570.** Admission 8,000L ($4). Tues–Sat 9am–7pm, Sun to 2pm.

This small-scale museum is both impressive and appropriate for a city of this size and historic background. This was the town dwelling of the Mansi, a wealthy local family that still lives in the family country villa outside town. The 16th- to 19th-century palazzo is now used as a picture gallery for works by Guido Reni, Bronzino, Pontormo, and others, though not their most important pieces. Don't leave without seeing the **Camera degli Sposi (Bridal Chamber),** an elaborate 17th-century Versailles-like alcove of decorative gold leaf, putti, and columns, where trembling Mansi brides awaited their conjugal duties amidst the sumptuous Luccan silks and heavy brocades.

AFFORDABLE PLACES TO STAY

The hotel situation in Lucca continues to be disheartening. Most of the one- and two-star hotels are in the newer, less interesting section of town outside the walls. In high season, be sure to make a hotel reservation in advance, or you may have to stay in Florence, nearby Pisa, or (if you have a car) one of the seaside resorts.

If there's no vacancy within the walls, don't think twice about staying in the charming B&B operated by the Favilla family at their **Villa Romantica,** Via N. Barbantini 246 (☎ **0583-496-872;** fax 0583-957-600; www.villaromantica.it), a tree-shaded Liberty villa with six comfortable doubles; it's a 5-minute walk to the walls and 10 minutes into the center of town. Rates are 120,000L to 135,000L ($60 to $68) for the single use of a double, 150,000L to 170,000L ($75 to $85) for a double, and 180,000L to 200,000L ($90 to $100) for a four-poster suite. Continental breakfast is 15,000L ($8) and buffet breakfast 20,000L ($10). I hesitate to recommend the cheapest thing going within the walls: the **Diana,** Via Molinetto 11 (☎ **0583-492-202;** fax 0583-47-795), which has passable-enough plain doubles with phones and TVs for around 115,000L ($58) and is just half a block from the Duomo. But the staff can turn from seemingly friendly to downright nasty at the drop of a hat.

La Luna. Corte Compagni 12, 55100 Lucca (off Via Fillungo near Amphitheater). ☎ **0583-493-634.** Fax 0583-490-021. E-mail: laluna@onenet.it. 30 units. A/C MINIBAR TV TEL. 120,000L ($60) single; 180,000L ($90) double; 280,000L ($140) suite. Buffet breakfast 15,000L ($8). AE, DC, MC, V. Parking 20,000L ($10) in garage. Closed Jan 6–Feb 7.

Located in a small courtyard a block from the amphitheater and near San Frediano for more than 2 centuries, this choice may have a little less charm than the Piccolo Puccini but offers better availability in high season. The rooms are well thought out and decorated in a fresh contemporary vein—though those who splurge on the suites (sleeping two to four) will find more space, with early 1900s ceiling frescoes, original fireplaces, and large sitting areas. Late risers with big appetites can tuck into the ample breakfast buffet and later skip lunch—though that would be a shame given Lucca's choice of eateries. An alternative to the pricey breakfast is the lobby bar, where coffee and a croissant will keep costs down.

✪ **Piccolo Puccini.** Via di Poggio 9, 55100 Lucca (just off Piazza San Michele). ☎ **0583-55-421.** Fax 0583-53-487. www.hotelpuccini.it. 14 units. TV TEL. 100,000L ($50) single; 145,000L ($73) double. Continental breakfast 5,000L ($2.50). AE, DC, MC, V. Free parking nearby.

This charming three-star hotel occupies a 15th-century palazzo in front of the building where Puccini was born, and some of the rooms overlook the small piazza and its bronze statue of Puccini. Paolo and Raffaella, the enthusiastic young couple that has recently taken over, have brightened up the place with a marble-tiled lobby, flower arrangements in the public areas, and an extremely friendly attitude. A perfect choice for those who appreciate tasteful attention and discreet professionalism. Breakfast is optional, so head for any of the cafes on Piazza San Michele, one of Lucca's loveliest squares. Book early to make sure you find room at this inn: Word is out.

Universo. Piazza del Giglio 1, 55100 Lucca (off Piazza Napoleone). ☎ **0583-493-678.** Fax 0583-954-854. www.lunet.it/aziende/hoteluniverso. 58 units. TV TEL. 160,000L ($80) single; 260,000L ($130) double. Rates include buffet breakfast. MC, V. Ten free parking spaces (ask for permit) or lot 500m away for 2,000L ($1).

This hotel-with-an-attitude aspires to be the grandest of Lucca's limited roster, and an ongoing renovation is resuscitating the rooms to their former 19th-century charm. Ask for one of the refurbished rooms overlooking small Piazza del Giglio and its Teatro Comunale (others overlook expansive Piazza Napoleone, recently pedestrianized). They vary greatly in decor from contemporary to period, with the occasional added treats of molded ceilings, antiques, and hand-painted tiles in the baths. Only a few rooms also have air-conditioning and minibars (specify when booking).

GREAT DEALS ON DINING

✪ **Da Giulio.** Via Conce 45, Piazza San Donato (nestled in the northwest corner of the walls). ☎ **0583-55-948.** Reservations recommended. Primi 8,000–10,000L ($4–$5); secondi 8,000–14,000L ($4–$7). AE, DC, MC, V. Tues–Sat and third Sun of month noon–2:30pm and 7:30–10:15pm. Closed 10 days in Aug and 10 days around Christmas. LUCCHESE/TUSCAN HOME COOKING.

Delighted foreigners and locals agree that this big, airy, and forever busy trattoria is one of Tuscany's undisputed stars. Though casual, Da Giulio isn't the place to occupy a much-coveted table for just pasta and a salad. Save up your appetite and come for a full-blown Tuscan feast, trying all the rustic specialties. Begin with the thick *farro* soup made with a local barleylike grain or the fresh *maccheroni tortellati* pasta stuffed with fresh ricotta and spinach, both perfection. Perfect also are the grilled and roasted meats, like the *arrosti misti* of beef and turkey and the *pollo al mattone,* chicken breast flattened and roasted under the weight of heated bricks. The waiters know not to recommend certain local favorites to non-Italians, unless you look like the tripe, *tartara di cavallo* (horsemeat tartare), or veal snout type. Fixed-price menus come and go at about 30,000L ($15).

Da Guido. Via Cesare Battisti 28 (near Piazza Sant'Agostino and San Frediano, west of Roman Amphitheater). ☎ **0583-476-219.** Primi 4,000–6,000L ($2–$3); secondi 7,000–10,000L ($3.50–$5); *menu turistico* 17,000L ($9) with wine. AE, MC, V. Mon–Sat noon–2:30pm and 7:30–10pm. Closed 3–4 weeks in Aug. LUCCHESE/TUSCAN.

The amiable proprietor, Guido, welcomes local cronies and hungry out-of-towners with the same warm smile and filling meals that keep 'em all happy. The bar in the front and the TV locked into a sports channel create a laid-back atmosphere that'll make you want to linger; the fresh tortellini made on the premises and the simplicity of the roast *coniglio* (rabbit) or *vitello* (veal) will wipe out any conflicting inclinations to do otherwise. This is a cut below the price and quality level of Giulio's (above), but you're guaranteed a good home-cooked meal in a no-frills, family-run trattoria.

Da Leo. Via Tegrimi 1 (just north of Piazza San Michele). ☎ **0583-492-236.** Reservations recommended. Primi 6,000–8,000L ($3–$4); secondi 10,000–15,000L ($5–$8). No credit cards. Mon–Sat noon–2:30pm and 7:30–10:30pm. TUSCAN/LUCCHESE.

There's usually an English menu floating around somewhere—the good-natured waiters are used to dealing with foreigners who've discovered one of the most authentic lucchese dining spots in town, run by the amiable Buralli family. This isn't as much a bare-bones tavern as Guido's, not quite as polished an operation as the well-regarded Giulio's, but still as beloved by a devoted local following nonetheless. Its location, two steps from the central Piazza San Michele, draws tourists who happen by, lured into the peach-colored rooms by the aroma of roasting meats and the scent of rosemary. The ubiquitous *farro* soup made from emmer (a kind of barley) followed by the simple but delicious *pollo fritto con patate arroste* (fried chicken with roast potatoes) with the good house wine is my stock order.

SIDE TRIPS FROM LUCCA

A number of villas of historic importance are within biking distance of Lucca's center. The **Villa Reale** in Marlia (☎ **0583-30-108**) was once home to Napoléon's sister Elisa Baciocchi; March to November, you can take a 10,000L ($5) guided tour of its grounds daily on the hour 10am to noon and 3 to 6pm. March to November 12, the **Villa Torrigiani** in Camigliano (☎ **0583-928-008** or 0368-320-9614) is open Wednesday to Monday 10am to 12:30pm and 3 to 6:30pm, admission is 15,000L ($8) to the villa and grounds or 10,000L ($5) for just the park. Visit Lucca's tourist board for a map and a listing of occasional summer concerts that take place in their gardens.

Lucca is also convenient to **Pisa,** where you can spend half a day seeing the Leaning Tower and its Duomo and Baptistry (see the Pisa section for details). On the Tuscan coast to the northwest in the direction of the Italian Riviera (follow the green autostrada signs saying DIREZIONE MARE on A11/12 northwest) lie the seaside resorts of **Viareggio** (25km/15.8 mi.) and the tonier and more picturesque **Forte dei Marmi** (34km/21.4 mi.). In summer, CLAP and LAZZI buses leave frequently from Lucca's Piazzale Verdi bus station. Avoid these towns in the dismal winter, when little remains open except, to some degree, on weekends.

3 San Gimignano & Its Medieval Towers

57km (35 mi.) SW of Florence, 65km (40 mi.) SE of Lucca, 90km (56.7 mi.) SE of Pisa, 42km (26 mi.) NW of Siena, 100km (62 mi.) SE of Lucca

For centuries, **San Gimignano** has arrested the traveler's imagination as the quintessential Tuscan hill town. Its stunning skyline bristles with medieval towers (there remain 14 of an estimated 70) whose construction dates from the 12th and 13th centuries, when they were built as much for defensive purposes as for the prestige of outdoing the neighbors. San Gimignano is on the ancient Francigena road that transported medieval trade and pilgrims from northern Europe to Rome (imagine the impressive sight it was to those approaching from afar, with its 70-odd towers heralding the town's prominence)—it was quite the wealthy agricultural town in its 14th-century heyday and could afford to build handsome palazzi and impressively frescoed churches. It has held on to its rugged good looks and gained the sobriquet of the "Medieval Manhattan," and much is written about its distinctive profile and its towers being the archetypes for today's skyscrapers (some of the remaining towers are over 150 feet high). San Gimignano boasts the perfect combination of a rural small-town atmosphere, stunning views, a crop of great restaurants, and enough history and museums to occupy the curious and impress the discerning.

ESSENTIALS

GETTING THERE   By Train   The 20 or so daily trains on the line between **Siena** (20–45 min.; 3,200L/$1.60) and Empoli, where you can connect from **Florence** (60–75 min.; 7,000L/$3.50), stop at Poggibonsi (☎ **0577-933-646** or 0577-936-462). From **Poggibonsi,** 19 buses make the 20-minute run to San Gimignano Monday to Saturday, but only two run on Sunday (7:20am and 12:55pm).

By Car   Take the Poggibonsi exit off the **Florence-Siena** autostrada or the SS2. San Gimignano is 12km (7.5 mi.) from Poggibonsi.

By Bus   You almost always have to **transfer buses at Poggibonsi** (see "By Train"). SITA runs 26 buses daily from **Florence** to Poggibonsi (50–90 min.; 10,000L/$5), 13 of which meet right up with the connection to San Gimignano. There's also a **Sunday direct bus from Florence** (1 hr., 20 min.) at 8:30am. **Tra-in** (☎ **0577-204-111** or 0577-937-207) runs about 33 daily buses from **Siena** to Poggibonsi (35–45 min.; 8,600L/$4.30). In San Gimignano, buy bus tickets at the tourist office.

VISITOR INFORMATION   The **tourist office** is at Piazza del Duomo 1 (☎ **0577-940-008;** fax 0577-940-903; www.sangimignano.com). It's open daily March to October 9am to 1pm and 3 to 7pm, and November to February 9am to 1pm and 2 to 6pm.

SPECIAL EVENTS & MARKETS   San Gimignano has two patron saints, **San Gimignano** himself (a 4th-century bishop from Modena), whose feast day is celebrated January 31, and **Santa Fina** (who died in 1253, at age 15), whose feast day is on March 12. Both are celebrated with a High Mass in the Duomo and an all-day outdoor fair in the main square.

San Gimignano also boasts one of Tuscany's more animated **Carnevale,** held each of the four Sundays before Ash Wednesday. The third weekend of June is the **Fiera delle Messi,** when the town effortlessly resuscitates its medieval character during a weekend of outdoor markets, musical and theatrical events, and a jousting tournament of knights on horseback, all in medieval costume. Since 1924, mid-June to August has been dedicated to dance and music performances for the **Estate Sangimignese** festival, when you can look for art exhibits, outdoor classical concerts, alfresco opera, or ballet in Piazza della Cisterna. See the tourist office for a schedule. Santa Fina shows up again for the first Sunday of August's **Festa di Ringraziamento;** the next day, a small fair takes place in the main square. The only market in town worth a look is the bustling **biweekly produce market** on Piazza del Duomo Thursday and Saturday mornings.

SEEING THE SIGHTS

If it has reopened in 2001 as expected, spend a few minutes in the **Museo d'Arte Sacra** (Museum of Sacred Art) to see its medieval tombstones and wooden sculptures—enter from Piazza Pecori, under the arch to the left of the Duomo's facade. It's expected to keep the same hours as the Museo Civico (below), with a 5,000L ($2.50) admission.

✪ **Collegiata.** Piazza del Duomo. ☎ **0577-940-316.** Admission on cumulative ticket (above) or 6,000L ($3) adults, 3,000L ($1.50) ages 6–18. Apr–Oct Mon–Fri 9:30am–7:30pm, Sat to 5pm, Sun 1–5pm; Nov–Mar Mon–Sat 9:30am–5pm, Sun 1–5pm. Closed Jan 27–Feb 28.

Because there's no longer a bishop of San Gimignano, the Duomo (cathedral) has been demoted to a Collegiata (though it'll forever be a Duomo in the locals' eyes) and is a prime example of not judging a 12th-century church by its facade. It was never finished outside, but its interior is heavily frescoed with Bible scenes, testimony to the city's past prosperity and one of Tuscany's, perhaps Italy's, most lavishly decorated churches. On the north wall are three levels with 26 scenes from the Old Testament by Bartolo dei Fredi (1367); on the south wall are 22 scenes from the life of Christ by Lippo Memmi (1333 to 1341); the entrance end of the interior nave wall is decorated with scenes from the *Last Judgment,* attributed to Taddeo di Bartolo (1410); and against the west wall Benozzo Gozzoli painted a *Martyrdom of St. Sebastian* (1464)— brilliant colors set off by the black-and-white-striped marble arches of Pisan-Romanesque architecture. Don't miss the tiny ✪ **Cappella di Santa Fina** in the southwest corner for the frescoes by Florentine Renaissance master Domenico Ghirlandaio (1475) recounting the life of a young girl named Fina born in San Gimignano in 1238. The town's towers appear in the background of the scene depicting her funeral. Fina spent most of her 15 years in prayer and is the patron saint (though never officially canonized, but don't bring this up with the locals), together with St. Gimignano, of the town. Be sure to find another of Ghirlandaio's superb works, ✪ *The Annunciation* (1482), gracing a loggiaed courtyard adjacent to the Baptistry.

Museo Civico (Civic Museum) & Torre Grossa (Big Tower). In the Palazzo del Popolo, Piazza del Duomo. ☎ **0577-940-340** (ask for *museo*). Admission on cumulative ticket (above) or Museum 7,000L ($3.50) adults, 5,000L ($2.50) ages 6–18; Tower 8,000L ($4) adults, 6,000L ($3) 6–18; combined ticket 12,000L ($6) adults, 9,000L ($4.50) ages 6–18. Mar–Oct daily 9:30am–7:20pm; Nov–Feb Tues–Sun 9:30am–12:50pm and 2:30–4:50pm.

Labor to the top of the 14th-century Palazzo del Popolo's 117-foot **Torre Grossa** (1311), the highest of San Gimignano's towers and the only one in town you can climb. You'll feel as if you're on top of a flagpole with heart-stopping views of the town, its towers, and the bucolic sweep of country beyond. It may just be the best

---

A Money-Saving Tip

The **cumulative ticket** covers the Torre Grossa, the Collegiata, and all the museums in town *except* the privately run Torture Museum. It costs 18,000L ($9) adults and 14,000L ($7) ages 6 to 18. The prices below are for individual entries to each sight.

San Gimignano

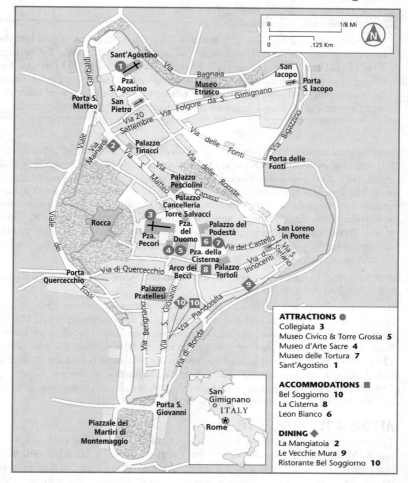

ATTRACTIONS ●
Collegiata **3**
Museo Civico & Torre Grossa **5**
Museo d'Arte Sacre **4**
Museo delle Tortura **7**
Sant'Agostino **1**

ACCOMMODATIONS ■
Bel Soggiorno **10**
La Cisterna **8**
Leon Bianco **6**

DINING ◆
La Mangiatoia **2**
Le Vecchie Mura **9**
Ristorante Bel Soggiorno **10**

tower-top view of its kind in Tuscany—and that's saying something. Once you've gotten that out of your system, backtrack to see some of the **Civic Museum**'s collection. The first public room, the **Sala di Dante,** is frescoed with hunting scenes and is the spot where the poet Dante, as ambassador from pro-pope (Guelph) Florence, came to pro-emperor (Ghibelline) San Gimignano in 1300 to plead for unity. Here you'll find the museum's—and the town's—masterpiece, a *Maestà* by Sienese Lippo Mimmi (1317). The second-floor *pinacoteca* **(picture gallery)** is composed mostly of 12th- to 15th-century paintings from the Sienese school, with highlights by Bennozzo Gozzoli, Pinturicchio, Filippino Lippi, and a late 14th-century Taddeo di Bartolo painting of San Gimignano himself holding the town in his lap.

Museo della Tortura (Torture Museum). Via del Castello 1 (just off Piazza della Cisterna). ☎ **0577-942-243.** Admission 15,000L ($8) adults, 10,000L ($5) students. Mar–Nov 3 daily 10am–8pm, Nov 4–Feb Mon–Sat 10am–5:30pm, Sun 10am–7pm.

Is it karmic happenstance or a quirk of history that this museum of medieval torture is housed in the 13th-century Palazzo del Diavolo (Devil's Palace)? One of Tuscany's

Guided Countryside Walks

April to October, the San Gimignano tourist office offers guided excursions into the countryside two to three days a week (usually weekends), costing 20,000L to 30,000L ($10 to $15) per person. Since the country edges right up to San Gimignano's walls, you can easily set out on your own to wander with a good map—the tourist office will soon sell a map and catalog marked with suggested hikes and walks, or you can pick up a regional map from any of the local souvenir stands.

more unusual attractions, this surprisingly expansive chamber of horrors contains over 100 instruments of torture. Most are original pieces, and all are thoughtfully and impressively displayed and explained in Italian and English. This is good, because items like knuckle- and skull-crushers and iron gags to stifle screams aren't always immediately recognizable to the innocent. It's worth the admission just to see the cast-iron chastity belts. As unsettling as some of the original prints depicting the atrocities of the 15th-century Inquisition are, many of the item descriptions, such as that accompanying the garrote—a punishment used in Spain until 1975—are still used in South America today.

Sant'Agostino. Piazza Sant'Agostino. ☎ **0577-940-008.** Admission free. Daily 7am–noon and 3–7pm (Oct–Apr to 6:30pm).

If you're not all frescoed out after a visit to the Collegiata, visit the large 13th-century Sant'Agostino in the north end of town by following the flagstone Via San Matteo through one of San Gimignano's less commercial corners. The church's simple Romanesque exterior contrasts with its rococo interior completed in the mid-1700s. The interior's highlight is the cycle of frescoes covering the choir behind the main altar and showing 17 scenes from ✪ *The Life of St. Augustine* by Benozzo Gozzoli, a 15th-century Florentine painter. Hired after yet another plague passed through town in 1464, Gozzoli was commissioned to cover the walls floor to ceiling.

AFFORDABLE PLACES TO STAY

The hotels in this most popular hill town aren't cheap. If you arrive without a reservation, **Siena Hotels Promotion,** Via San Giovanni 125 (☎/fax **0577-940-809;** hotsangi@tin.it), will help you find a room. Those watching their lire may want to stay in the more modern satellite community of Santa Chiara, a few minutes' walk from the Porta San Giovanni. You can check out pictures of all the hotels below (and others) at **www.sangimignano.com.** Ask the tourist office for a list of B&B or farm accommodations in the countryside.

The **Ostello della Gioventù (Youth Hostel),** Via dei Fonti 1, 53037 San Gimignano (☎ **0577-941-991** or 055-807-7009; fax 055-805-0104; www.alfaweb.it/franchostel), has 75 beds in 9 rooms costing per person 23,000L ($12) in a larger dorm or 35,000L ($18) in a shared double or quad. Breakfast is 7,000L ($3.50).

Bel Soggiorno. Via San Giovanni 91, 53037 San Gimignano (near the Porta San Giovanni). ☎ **0577-940-375.** Fax 0577-907-521. www.hotelbelsoggiorno.it. 22 units. A/C TV TEL. 180,000–310,000L ($90–$155) double; 250,000–290,000L ($125–$145) suite. Buffet breakfast 15,000L ($8). AE, DC, MC, V. Parking 20,000L ($10) in garage outside walls. Closed Jan–Feb.

Close to the San Giovanni city gate and a 5-minute walk uphill toward the main square, this well-known hostelry of simply decorated rooms gets two thumbs up. One is for the dozen or so rooms (three of which share a large patio) commanding awesome views of the hills of Tuscany's Val d'Elsa (add 15,000L/$8 to a double rate for the view. The second is for the acclaimed restaurant Bel Soggiorno (see "Great Deals on Dining," below) where guests are encouraged though not obliged to have their meals (no great hardship).

If you have access to wheels and long for a more rural environment, ask at the desk about their country property, the 50-room **Le Pescille** (☎ **0577-943-165;** fax 0577-940-186), a converted farmhouse/hotel boasting a lovely setting 4km (2.5 mi.) out of town, with a pool, tennis court, and reasonable rates comparable to those above; it's open mid-March to October.

La Cisterna. Piazza della Cisterna 23–24, 53037 San Gimignano. ☎ **0577-940-328.** Fax 0577-942-080. E-mail: lacisterna@iol.it. 49 units. TV TEL. 125,000L ($63) single; 165,000L–205,000L ($83–$103) double; 235,000L ($118) suite. Half and full pensione available. Rates include buffet breakfast. AE, DC, MC, V. Closed Jan 7–Mar 3.

This is the town's nicest hotel in this price category, housed in a series of truncated towers flanking central Piazza della Cisterna and run by the Salvestrini family since 1919. Like the Bel Soggiorno, it includes one of the town's better restaurants, Le Terrazze (open Friday to Tuesday for lunch and dinner, Wednesday for dinner only). Upstairs you'll find some large rooms, many of which have balconies offering spellbinding panoramas. However, the rest are small and have no view, making them seem even smaller. The hotel has been used as the setting for films, from *Where Angels Fear to Tread* to *Tea with Mussolini*.

Leon Bianco. Piazza della Cisterna 8, 53037 San Gimignano. ☎ **0577-941-294.** Fax 0577-942-123. E-mail: leonbianco@www.see.it. 25 units. A/C TV TEL. 160,000L ($80) single use of double; 190,000L ($95) double standard; 215,000L ($108) superior double; 250,000L ($125) triple. Rates include buffet breakfast. AE, DC, MC, V. Parking in public lots. Closed mid-Nov to Christmas and Jan 15–early Feb.

Across from La Cisterna, this smaller hotel occupies a beautifully restored palazzo. The central part is in a 12th-century patrician home that was expanded in the next century with a medieval tower on either side, parts of which are incorporated into the hotel. The modernized rooms are historically offset with exposed brick walls, vaulted ceilings, archways, and terra-cotta floors and priced according to size and view: Five overlook the piazza, nine have countryside views, and all others overlook an enclosed courtyard. The superior rooms are, for the most part, merely larger and have minibars. May to September, the brick courtyard is the lovely setting for breakfast, and the sunny roof terrace is perfect for postcard writing. There's no restaurant, but try La Cisterna's or the Bel Soggiorno's down the street.

GREAT DEALS ON DINING

✪ **La Mangiatoia.** Via Mainardi 5 (near the Porta San Matteo). ☎ **0577-941-528.** Reservations recommended. Primi 13,000L–20,000L ($7–$10); secondi 18,500L–23,000L ($9–$12). MC, V. Wed–Mon 12:30–2:30pm and 7:30–10pm. Closed Nov 4–Dec 7. TUSCAN.

"The Eatin' Trough" is a quirky mix of largish but still cozy rooms boasting heavily stuccoed stone walls inset with back-lit stained-glass cabinet doors. This place is fond of Latin quips and dramatic classical music, and the staff is friendly. Alas, the food's a mix, too—stick to the more unusual dishes, intriguing and excellently prepared choices where the cooks seems to try harder. The *gnocchi deliziose* (spinach gnocchi in Gorgonzola sauce) is great, as is the *tagliatelle dell'amore* (with prosciutto, cream, tomatoes, and a little hot spice). After, you can try the *coniglio in salsa di carciofi* (rabbit with artichokes), but I'd choose the more adventurous *cervo in dolce et forte* (an old

Wining & Dining in Chianti's Backyard

A stroll up **Via San Giovanni** will impress you with the number of wine shops whose windows are stocked floor-to-ceiling with the fruits of the surrounding Chianti vineyards. The gently rolling hills of Tuscany supply Italy's finest red wines, while San Gimignano itself is well known for its celebrated **Vernaccia,** a distinctive white wine unique to this corner of Italy and old enough to have been mentioned in Dante's *Divine Comedy.* The curious and the *appassionati* should make a beeline for **Da Gustavo,** Via San Matteo 29 (☎ **0577-940-057**), an old-time wine bar run by the Becucci family since 1946; summer hours are daily 8am to midnight and winter hours Saturday to Thursday 8am to 8pm. You can orchestrate an informal wine tasting from over 20 types of Tuscan and Italian whites and reds by the glass (generally 3,000L to 5,000L/$1.50 to $2.50 per glass). There's no place to sit, but fresh panini are made to order, and you can choose from a delicious selection of the region's top-quality cheeses and salamis. Take your picnic and head west of here (behind the Duomo) to the Rocca, the remains of the 14th-century fortress atop the ramparts, now a public park with wonderful views.

recipe of venison cooked with pine nuts and a strong sauce of pinoli, raisins, vinegar, and chocolate—traditionally used to cut the gaminess of several-day-old venison). The desserts are excellent.

Le Vecchie Mura. Via Piandornella 15 (a twisty walk down the first right off Via San Giovanni as you walk up from the Porta San Giovanni). ☎ **0577-940-270.** E-mail: vecchiemura@iol.it. Reservations recommended. Primi 11,000L ($6); secondi 15,000L–23,000L ($8–$12). AE, DC, MC, V. Wed–Mon 5–10pm. Closed Dec–Feb. TUSCAN/ITALIAN.

The first thing you must do is see if either of the two comfortable bedrooms with baths is available (70,000L/$35 double). If not, console yourself with a marvelous meal downstairs in the cool brick-vaulted trattoria in what served as a patrician family's stables in the 1700s. The thick *ribollita* (cabbage-based bread soup) and home-made *tagliatelle al cinghiale* (pasta with wild-boar sauce) are deservedly the house specialties. The regional specialty of wild boar shows up as a favorite entree, marinated in the local Vernaccia white wine and then grilled. Across the narrow graveled road is a small alfresco terrace whose gorgeous views out over the ancient city walls and valley beyond may make concentrating on your meal difficult.

Ristorante Bel Soggiorno. Via San Giovanni 41 (near the Porta San Giovanni). ☎ **0577/94-31-49.** Reservations recommended. Primi 10,000–15,000L ($5–$8); secondi 18,000–25,000L ($9–$13); *menù turistico* from 40,000L ($20). AE, DC, MC, V. Thurs–Tues 12:30–2:30pm and 7:30–10pm. TUSCAN.

This spacious rustic restaurant boasts a menu that shares the spotlight with the glorious countryside framed by the oversize windows. Tuscan bigwigs who work in the area's wine industry entertain their important buyers here, assured of the *bella figura* they'll make with a meal that's casual but of top Tuscan quality. Many of the kitchen's limited-production ingredients are from the owners' private estate: olive oil, honey, grappa, and wines labeled AZIENDA AGRICOLA PESCILLE. Thick-crusted bread and wide pappardelle noodles are made fresh daily—if it's autumn, look for the latter traditionally prepared with a tomato sauce flavored with *alla lepre* (hare) or *al cinghiale* (wild boar). The specialty of meats simply prepared on the grill is ultra-Tuscan; ultra-delicious is the homemade *crostata di ficchi* dessert, a delicate fig tart that proves you can measure happiness by the slice. You can stay at the family's country inn or in their guest rooms just upstairs (see "Affordable Places to Stay," above).

4 The Chianti Road

The fabled ✪ **Chianti** stretches between Florence and Siena along **La Chiantigiana (the Chianti Road),** known as the **SS222.** This 104.5-square-kilometer (65-square-mile) stretch of land is many people's idea of Paradise on Earth—tall hills topped by medieval castles and valleys dotted with small market towns. Ten thousand acres of these rolling hills are blanketed with grapevines producing the Chianti wines that have long made this region famous.

The name *Chianti,* probably derived from the name of a local noble Etruscan family Clantes, has been used to describe the hills between Florence and Siena for centuries, but it wasn't until the mid–13th century that Florence created the *Lega del Chianti* to unite the region's three most important centers—Castellina, Radda, and Gaiole—who chose the black rooster as their symbol. In 1716, the boundaries of the Chianti were officially established, making it the world's first officially designated wine-producing area.

Along the way, look for the sign DEGUSTAZIONE or VENDITÀ DIRETTA, advising wine operations that offer tastings and sales direct to the public. The sign AZIENDA AGRICOLA, TENUTA, or FATTORIA indicates the wine-producing operations—some multimillion-dollar affairs, others unsung and family run. Each will offer its own unique experience.

ESSENTIALS

GETTING AROUND   The only way to explore the Chianti effectively is to **drive.** But know that many of the roads off the major SS222 (La Chiantigiana) are unpaved and sometimes heavily potholed. **Biking** through the Chianti can be one of Tuscany's most rewarding and scenic strenuous workouts. See chapter 2 for tour companies, or go on your own by renting a bike in Greve at **Marco Ramuzzi,** Viale Falsettacci 6 (☎ **055-853-037**). The region's low mountains and stands of ancient forest are also excellent for **hiking.** For exploring by any means, you'll need a good map; both the huge Edizione Multigrafic (EMG) 1:50,000 map and the smaller free 1:70,000 sheet called "Il Chianti" put out by the Florentine tourist board are excellent for backroads exploring. (*Drivers be warned:* These maps do, on occasion, mark dry streambeds as "unpaved roads.")

You can visit the major towns by **bus,** but be prepared to stay a while until the next ride comes along. **SITA** (☎ **055-483-2651**) from Florence services Strada (40 min. from Florence), Greve (65 min.), Panzano (75 min.), Radda or Castellina (95 min.), and Gaiole (2 hrs.); it leaves at least hourly for stops up through Greve and Panzano, and at least 1 to 3 times a day all the way through to Gaiole. About eight (Monday to Saturday) **Tra-in** buses (☎ **0577-204-245**) from Siena hit Radda, Gaiole, and Castellina; and you can get to Impruneta with a **CAP** bus (☎ **055-214-637**) from Florence.

VISITOR INFORMATION   You can pick up some info at the **Florence** or **Siena** **tourist office.** The unofficial capital of the area is Greve in Chianti, and its tiny **tourist office,** Via Luca Cini (☎ **055-854-5243**) makes an effort to provide some Chianti-wide info. Easter to October, it's open Monday 9:30am to 1pm and 2:30 to

7pm, Tuesday 9:30am to 1pm and 2:30 to 5pm, Wednesday 9:30am to 3:30pm, Friday 9:30am to noon and 2 to 6pm, Saturday 9:30am to 1pm and 2:30 to 5pm, and Sunday 9:30am to 1pm. In winter, the official hours are "frequently closed" (from experience, I'd say try weekday mornings).

WINE FESTIVALS   The second weekend in September, Greve hosts the main annual **Rassegna del Chianti Classico** (☎ **055-854-243**), a bacchanalian festival of food and dancing that showcases wine from all the region's producers. Radda sponsors its own **wine festival** on the last weekend in May, where buying the 10,000L ($5) commemorative glass lets you sample 50 to 60 wines for free. There's also a free concert, evening snacks, and a communal grappa tasting at 10pm.

THE FLORENTINE CHIANTI

EN ROUTE TO GREVE   Cross Florence's eastern Ponte San Niccolò and follow the signs from Piazza Ferrucci on the other side toward Grassina and the SS222. The SS222 takes you through **Strada in Chianti,** where a Donatello-school crucifix rests in the church of San Cristofano.

At the bend in the road called Le Bolle is a right turnoff for **Vicchiomaggio** (☎ **055-854-079;** fax 055-853-911; www.vicchiomaggio.it), a Lombard fortress modified in the 15th century and today one of the best preserved of the Chianti castles. Its estate, under British ownership, produces well-regarded wines, which you can taste Monday to Friday 9am to 12:30 and 3 to 5pm. You can visit the cellars with one day's notice. They also offer cooking courses (anywhere from an hour or two to several days) and rent rooms.

A bit farther along on the right is the turnoff for the **Castello di Verrazzano** (☎ **055-854-243;** fax 055-854-241), the 12th-century seat of the Verrazzano family (Giovanni Verrazzano, born here in 1485, discovered New York City). The estate has been making wine at least since 1170, and you can sample it Monday to Friday 8am to 6pm. (On weekends, you can buy the wine at the small stand on SS222; ☎ **055-853-211.**)

Just before you get to Greve, a left turn signposts the ✪ **Castello di Uzzano** (☎ **055-854-032;** fax 055-854-375) built around A.D. 1100 but transformed into a sumptuous villa in the 16th and 17th centuries. From Easter to October, 8:30am to 6pm, you can tour its formal Italianate gardens and sample the wine once preferred by Francesco Datini, the famed 14th century "Merchant of Prato." In winter, call at least a day ahead to set up a tasting.

GREVE IN CHIANTI   Greve (*Grey*-vey) is the Chianti's main market town, dating back to the 13th century and today serving as the region's center of the wine trade and unofficial capital. The central **Piazza Matteotti** is a rough triangle of mismatched arcades centered on a statue of **Giovanni Verrazzano,** and at the narrow end of the piazza sits the pretty little church of **Santa Croce** with an *Annunciation* by Bicci di Lorenzo and a 13th-century triptych.

Greve is the host of the Chianti's annual September wine fair, and there are, naturally, dozens of wine shops in town. The better ones are the **Bottega del Chianti Classico,** Via Cesare Battisti 4 (☎ **055-853-631**), and the **Enoteca del Chianti Classico,** Piazzetta Santa Croce 8 (☎ **055-853-297**). At Piazza Matteotti 69–71 is one of Italy's most famous butchers, **Macelleria Falorni** (☎ **055-852-029**), a wonderland of prosciutto and salami established in 1700. **Tourist information** (☎/fax **055-854-5243**) is available in the dollhouse 1960s "castle" on Via Luca Cini at the corner of a large car park.

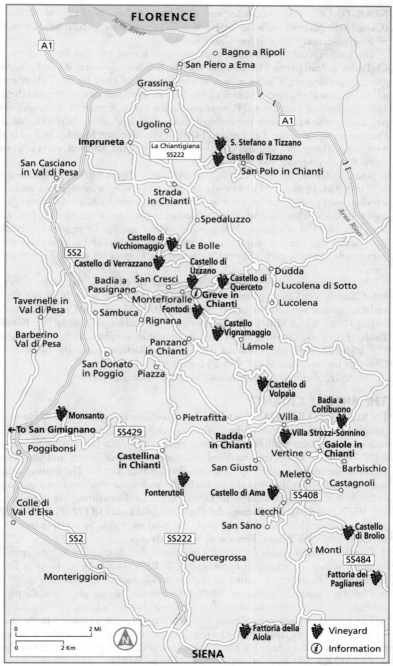

FLORENCE

Arno River

A1

Bagno a Ripoli

San Piero a Ema

Grassina

A1

Ugolino

Impruneta

La Chiantigiana SS222

S. Stefano a Tizzano

Castello di Tizzano

San Polo in Chianti

San Casciano
in Val di Pesa

Arno River

Strada
in Chianti

Spedaluzzo

Castello di
Vicchiomaggio

Le Bolle

Castello di
Uzzano

Dudda

Castello di Verrazzano

San Cresci

Castello di
Querceto

Lucolena di Sotto

SS2

Badia a
Passignano

Montefioralle

i Greve in
Chianti

Lucolena

Tavernelle in
Val di Pesa

Sambuca

Fontodi

Rignana

Castello
Vignamaggio

Barberino
Val di Pesa

Panzano
in Chianti

Lámole

San Donato
in Poggio

Piazza

Castello di
Volpaia

Monsanto

Badia a
Coltibuono

←To San Gimignano

SS429

Pietrafitta

Villa

**Radda
in Chianti**

Villa Strozzi-Sonnino

Poggibosi

**Gaiole in
Chianti**

Vertine

**Castellina
in Chianti**

San Giusto

Barbischio

Meleto

Castagnoli

Colle di
Val d'Elsa

Fonterutoli

Castello di Ama

SS408

Lecchi

Castello
di Brolio

San Sano

SS2

SS222

Monti

Quercegrossa

SS484

Monteriggioni

Fattoria dei
Pagliaresi

0   2 Mi
0   2 Km

N

Fattoria della
Aiola

🍇 Vineyard

i Information

SIENA

NEAR GREVE   One kilometer east of Greve perches the medieval hamlet of **(Castello di) Montefioralle,** an evocative stone village of one circular street, with the pretty 10th-century Pieve di San Cresci just outside the walls.

The road beyond Montefioralle continues over several miles of dirt roads to the ✪ **Badia a Passignano** (☎ **055-807-1278**), dramatically situated amid a cypress grove atop vineyards. The monastery was established in 1049 by the Vallombrosan order. Its small Romanesque church of San Michele got a baroque overhaul in the late 1500s courtesy of local artist Il Passignano. Sundays at 3pm, meet at the church for a free tour of the monastery; the highlight is the Ghirlandaio brothers' (Davide and Domenico) fresco of the *Last Supper* (1476) in the refectory. Monday to Friday the monastery's closed, but you can visit the *bottega* to buy the Antinori wines produced in the Badia's vineyards and tour the cellars.

South of Greve, the SS222 takes you past the left turn for **Villa Vignamaggio** (☎ **055-854-4840** or 055-854-661; fax 055-854-4468; www.vignamaggio.com), whose elegant gardens served as the set for Kenneth Branagh's *Much Ado About Nothing* (1993). The 14th- or 15th-century villa itself was once home to the *Mona Lisa,* born here in 1479. Vignamaggio wines are counted among the region's top bottles. Book ahead and you can tour the cellar and ornate gardens and sample three wines with simple snacks or more elaborate wines and snacks (plus vin santo). They also rent rooms.

The Chiantigiana next cuts through **Panzano in Chianti;** the tourist office is **InfoChaniti,** Via Chiantigiana 6 (☎ **055-852-933**). The town is known for its embroidery and for another famed butcher, **Antica Macelleria Cecchini,** Via XX Luglio 11 (☎ **055-852-020**). Panzano sports two excellent wine shops: The **Enoteca Baldi,** Piazza Bucciarelli 25, on the main traffic triangle at the Chiantigiana (☎ **055-852-843**); and. **Enoteca del Chianti Classico,** down the block at Via Giovanni da Verrazzano 8 (☎ **055-852-495**).

The SS222 continues south toward Castellina in Chianti (below).

THE SIENESE CHIANTI

EN ROUTE TO RADDA   **Castellina in Chianti,** an Etruscan town and Florentine bastion against Siena, is one of the more medieval-feeling hill towns of the region. The tourist office is the **Colline Verdi** travel agency, Via della Rocca 12 (☎ and fax **0577-740-620**). Castellina's medieval walls survive almost intact, and the central piazza is dominated by the imposing crenellated **Rocca** fortress. The nearby soldier's walk **Via delle Volte** is an evocative tunnel street with open windows facing out to the valley below. The best local wine-tasting is at **La Castellina,** Via Ferrucio 26 (☎ **0577-740-454**). The **Bottega del Vino,** Via della Rocca 13 (☎ **0577-741-297**), is a good wine shop. Outside town on the road to Radda is a 6th-century B.C. Etruscan tomb, the **Ipogeo Etrusco di Montecalvario.**

From here you can shoot 18km (11.2 mi.) down the Chiantigiana to Siena, past the medieval village and winery of **Fonterutoli** (☎ **0577-740-212**), in the same family since 1435. The direct sales office in town is usually locked; the *ristorante* across the way has a bar (open daily 10am to 10:30pm) where you can sample wines (the person behind the bar will open the sales office if you want to buy a case).

The road continues on to Siena, passing through **Quercegrossa,** the birthplace of Siena's great sculptor Jacopo della Quercia. But if you want to explore what many consider the best of the Chianti, it's time to cut east into the rugged mountainous heart of the old Lega del Chianti along the SS429 toward Radda.

Just before you hit Radda, a signposted right turn will take you a winding 7km (4.3 mi.) past the **Castello di Ama,** a top-rated vineyard whose Frenchified wine-making methods you can experience at the **Rinaldi Palmira** direct sales office (☎ 0577-746-021; open year-round, though tastings available only Easter to September) down the road in the hamlet of **Lecchi.** From here, the road continues to **San Sano** (see "Affordable Places to Stay," below)

RADDA IN CHIANTI & ENVIRONS   **Radda in Chianti** has retained its importance as a wine center along with its medieval street plan and a bit of the walls. The center of town is the 15th-century **Palazzo del Podestà,** studded with the mayoral coats of arms of past mayors; it contains the tourist office (☎/fax **0577-738-494;** e-mail: proradda@chiantinet.it), open Monday to Saturday 10am to 1pm and 3:30 to 7:30pm. Again, we have a local butcher, in Radda's case **Luciano Prociatti,** who runs an alimentari on Piazza IV Novembre 1 at the gate into town (☎ **0577-738-055**).

Seven kilometers north of Radda on a secondary road is the perfectly stony-medieval **Castello di Volpaia** (☎ **0577-738-066;** fax 0577-738-619), a first-rank wine estate. The central tower has an enoteca for drop-in tastings of one of the wines that helped found the Chianti Consorzio in 1924, with direct sales 10am to 6pm (closed February and Tuesdays November to March) of their wines, award-winning olive oils, and vinegars. You can also tour the winery, installed in a series of buildings throughout the little village, by calling ahead, preferably a week in advance. They also rent apartments and two small villas and lease out a small hotel on a neighboring hill.

Three kilometers (2 mi.) east of Radda, get on the left byroad for a 19km (11.8 mi.) trip to the beautifully isolated **Badia a Coltibuono** (☎ **0577-749-498;** fax 0577-749-235). The abbey was expanded by the Vallombrosan monks from 770 through the early 1800s, when it became an agricultural estate. Today, the estate is owned by the Stucci-Prinetti family, whose current matriarch—married into the Medici line—is the internationally renowned cookbook author Lorenza de' Medici. She hosts her famed culinary school here in summer, and her son Paolo runs the fine restaurant (☎ **0577-749-424**), closed Mondays and November to February. There's a direct sales office for their products at the "osteria" (☎ **0577-749-479**) down at the main road.

EN ROUTE TO SIENA   Follow the scenic road leading south out of Radda toward Siena and you'll see, on the left side, the ✪ **ceramic workshop** and showroom of master **Giuseppe Rampini** (☎ **577-738-043**).

Heading south directly from Badia a Coltibuono on the SS408 will take you through **Gaiole in Chianti,** the third member of the Lega del Chianti. The tourist office is at Via Ricasoli 50 (☎ **0577-749-411;** e-mail: gaiole@chiantinet.it), open Monday, Wednesday, and Friday 4 to 7pm. This is an ancient market town like Greve but is basically modernized without much to see, aside from the wine shops the **Cantina Enoteca Montagnani,** Via B. Bandinelli 13–17 (☎ **0577-749-517**), and the **Cantinetta del Chianti,** Via F. Ferruci 20 (☎ **0577-749-125**).

Farther south of Gaiole, the SS484 branches east toward Castelnuovo Berardenga and the famous 15th century ✪ **Castello di Brolio** (☎ **0577-749-066**), in the Ricasoli family since 1141 (save for a brief—near disastrous—1980s interlude as part of the Seagram's empire). The first official formula for Chianti Classico wine was concocted here in the mid–19th century by "Iron Baron" Bettino Ricasoli—nobleman, experimental agriculturalist, and the second Prime Minister of Italy. The Iron Baron's Chianti recipe balanced Sangiovese, Canaiolo, Trebbiano, and Malvasia grapes, and was used when Italy's wine-governing DOC and DOCG laws were written up in the 1960s. Today, Chianti laws have been much relaxed and many estates (including Brolio) are making Chianti out of pure Sangiovese grapes, but this vineyard remains at the forefront of Tuscan viticulture. Monday to Saturday 9am to noon and 3 to 7pm (to 6pm Sunday) you can pull the bell at the main door to visit some of the castle grounds, including the small chapel where Bettino is buried and the gardens and walk along the wall for nice Chianti views.

To buy their award-winning wines, visit the modern bottling rooms/cantina, the **Barone Ricasoli Cantina di Brolio** (☎ **0577-7301;** turn-off a few hundred feet from the long driveway to the castle). They offer cantina tours, with free tastings at the end, Monday to Friday at 10 to 11am or 2 to 3:30pm; call at least a few days in advance. The store itself is open year-round Monday to Friday 8am to 7pm (to 6pm in winter). By early 2001, they'll move this wine shop, tasting room, and cantina tour away from the modern bottling center and up to a building at the foot of the road to the *castello*, near the quite good **Osteria del Castello** restaurant (☎ **0577-747-277**).

The westerly byroad out of here leads most quickly to join the SS408 as it heads south, out of the land of the black rooster and into Siena (see the next section).

AFFORDABLE PLACES TO STAY

✪ **Borgo Argenina.** Località Argenina (near San Marcellino Monti), 53013 Gaiole in Chianti. ☎/fax **0577-747-117.** 5 units, 2 apts. MINIBAR TEL. Ask about single and triple rates; 220,000L ($110) double; 280,000L ($140) apt. Off-season discounts. Rates include country breakfast. No credit cards.

You'll need your own transportation to get to this little slice of the Tuscan dream 15km (9.5 mi.) north of Siena. From the flagstoned terrace of Elena Nappa's newly opened hilltop B&B (she bought the whole medieval hamlet), you can see the farmhouse where in 1996 Bertolucci filmed his cinematographically gorgeous *Stealing Beauty* (required viewing for those planning a visit to Tuscany). Against remarkable odds (she'll regale you with the anecdotes), doting hostess Elena has created the rural retreat of her dreams. It doesn't get any better than this. Her innate design talents and keen attention to charm and detail is the stuff of country design magazines. This is the untrammeled corner of vine-covered Chianti you've been looking for, but it's not easy to find. English-speaking Elena will fax you directions when you reserve.

San Sano. Località San Sano, 53010 Lecchi in Chianti. ☎ **0577-746-130.** Fax 0577-746-156. www.chiantinet.it. 14 units. A/C TEL. 180,000–230,000L ($90–$115) single; 200,000–250,000L ($100–$125) double; 320,000L ($160) triple. Rates include buffet breakfast. AE, DC, MC, V. Closed mid-Nov to mid-Mar.

Giancarlo Matarazzo and his German wife, Heidi, traded in their jobs as schoolteachers in Germany for this idyllic niche of Chianti and opened a special rural hideaway. The lack of TVs in the rooms is meant to enhance the tranquillity, and the medieval jumble of 13th-century stone buildings boasts a beautifully sited pool nestled amid the vineyards. The decor is rustic, simple, and perfect—and so are the views. The Matarazzos will help map out a day trips over scenic back roads to wine estates and hill towns (Radda and Gaiole are both about 10km/6.3 mi. away) and the chance to sample local trattorie—but most guests wind up gravitating back here to the cozy country kitchen for optional dinners of *cucina toscana* and animated dinner talk. And Siena is a lovely 20km (12.6-mi.) drive away.

5 Siena & the Palio delle Contrade

34km (21 mi.) S of Florence, 100km (63 mi.) SE of Pisa, 42km (26 mi.) SE of San Gimignano, 230km (143 mi.) NE of Rome, 107km (66 mi.) NW of Perugia

✪ **Siena** is often bypassed by the mad rush of visitors traveling the Rome-Florence autostrada. Others allot it minimum time to revel in its perfectly preserved medieval charm. You'll see almost nothing of the baroque so prevalent in Rome or the

Renaissance character of nearby Florence. Founded as Sena by the Etruscans and colonized by ancient Rome as Saena Julia, Siena flourished as a republic in the Middle Ages from the wool and textile trade and pre-Medici banking. It was one of the major cities of Europe in its day and became a principal center of art and culture as well. Piazza del Campo, the imposing palazzi, the Duomo, and the churches you see today were the result of a building boom that flourished during those years. Its noted university dates from that period, founded in 1240. But beginning in 1348, prosperity was aborted after devastating and recurring bouts with the bubonic plague that diminished the city's population from 100,000 to 30,000. Today's population is over 60,000, one still proud of its rich medieval heritage.

Locking horns over the centuries with its powerful neighbor Florence and never having fully stabilized after its brush with the Black Death, it finally succumbed to Florence after an 18-month siege in 1554 to 1555, became part of the Grand Duchy of Tuscany under Medici rule, and was reduced to a small provincial town. Florence's disinterest in Siena during the golden years of the Renaissance is your great fortune: Seemingly frozen in time, it's one of the country's best-preserved medieval cities. Because of the days when coffers overflowed, it boasts some of the most beautiful Gothic cathedrals, town halls, and main squares (Piazza del Campo) in all of Italy.

The Monte dei Paschi Bank in the postcard-perfect Piazza Salimbeni was founded in 1472; it's Europe's (many say the world's) oldest bank and still one of Italy's most solvent. It has long played a large role in sponsoring much of the city's cultural life. But while Siena's architectural expansion may have never progressed beyond the early Renaissance, Siena is still a very vital city, as you can witness during the early-evening *passeggiata* hour when the city's folk take to strolling Via di Città and Via Banchi di Sotto and Via Banchi di Sopra. Proud, handsome, fashionably turned out, and more welcoming than the ultrareserved Florentines, the Sienese still stand by the famous inscription at the ancient Porta Camolia: "Siena opens up its heart to you more than any other."

Siena is an ideal gateway for central and southern Tuscany for those with and without cars. From here, you can meander off to experience the various hill towns and hamlets in the Siena orbit of patchwork farmland and vine-draped estates. While the rest of Tuscany sleeps, return here for its artistic riches and marginal dash of cosmopolitan cultural life and a number of dining choices. Best of all, finish your day with that after-dinner gelato in any of the cafes ringing beautiful Piazza del Campo, the best place around to sit and take in your extreme good luck.

ESSENTIALS

GETTING THERE   By Train   The bus is often more convenient, since Siena's train station is outside town. Some 19 trains daily connect Siena with **Florence** (1½ to 2¼ hrs.; 8,500L/$4.25). Siena's **train station** (☎ 0577-280-115) is at Piazza Fratelli Roselli, about 3km (2 mi.) north of town. Take the C minibus to Piazza Gramsci in Terza di Camollia or a taxi (☎ 0577-49-222).

By Car   There's an autostrada highway direct from **Florence** (it has no route number; follow the green autostrada signs toward Siena), or you can take the more scenic routes: down old Via Cassia SS2 or the Chiantigiana SS222 through the Chianti (see above). From **Rome,** get off the A1 north at the Val di Chiana exit and follow the SS326 west for 50km (31 mi.). The SS223 runs 70km (43 mi.) here from **Grosseto** in the Maremma. From **Pisa,** take the highway toward Florence and exit onto the SS429 south at Empoli (100km/62 mi. total).

Trying to drive into the one-way pedestrian-zoned center isn't worth the headache. Siena **parking** (☎ 0577-22-871) is now coordinated, and all the lots charge 2,500L

Siena

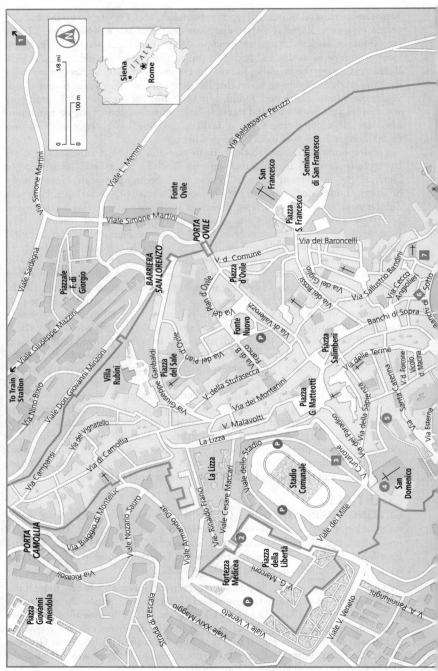

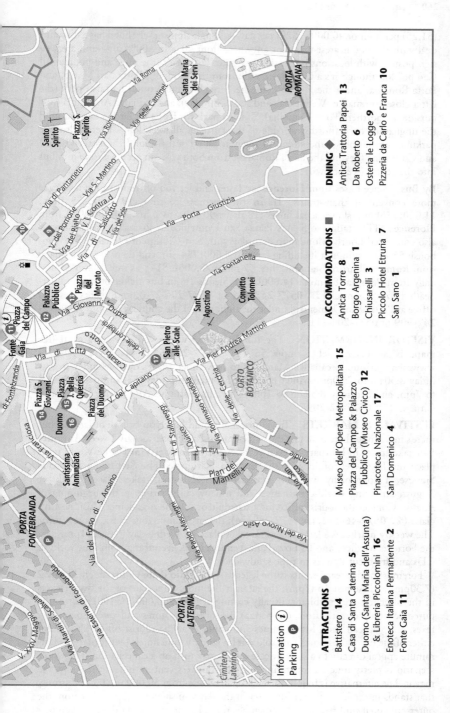

ATTRACTIONS ●

Battistero **14**
Casa di Santa Caterina **5**
Duomo (Santa Maria dell'Assunta)
& Libreria Piccolomini **16**
Enoteca Italiana Permanente **2**
Fonte Gaia **11**

Museo dell'Opera Metropolitana **15**
Piazza del Campo & Palazzo
Pubblico (Museo Civico) **12**
Pinacoteca Nazionale **17**
San Domenico **4**

ACCOMMODATIONS ■

Antica Torre **8**
Borgo Argenina **1**
Chiusarelli **3**
Piccolo Hotel Etruria **7**
San Sano **1**

DINING ◆

Antica Trattoria Papei **13**
Da Roberto **6**
Osteria le Logge **9**
Pizzeria da Carlo e Franca **10**

Information (*i*)
Parking (P)

259

($1.25) per hour or 40,000L ($20) per day—though almost every hotel has a discount deal with the one nearest them for anywhere from 40% to 100% off—and are well sign-posted, with locations just inside city gates Porta Tufi (the huge and popular "Il Campo" lot, though it's a 20-minute walk from the Campo!), Porta San Marco, and Porta Romana; under the Fortezza (another large lot) and around La Lizza park (the latter closed on market Wednesday and soccer Sunday); and at Piazza Amendola (just outside the northern Porta Camollia). You can **park for free** a bit farther away around the unguarded back (northwest) side of the Fortezza all week long. There's also free parking outside the southeast end of town at Due Ponti (beyond the Porta Pispini) and Coroncina (beyond the Porta Romana); from both you can get a *pollicino* minibus into the center (see below).

By Bus   Since buses from **Florence** are faster and let you off right in town, they're more convenient than trains. **Tra-in** runs express coaches (19 daily; 75 min.; 11,000L/$6) and slower local buses (18 daily, 90 min. to 2 hrs.; 11,000L/$6) from **Florence**'s SITA station to Siena's Piazza San Domenico or Piazza Gramsci. Siena is also connected hourly Monday to Saturday with **San Gimignano** (change in Poggibonsi; 55 to 65 min. not including layover; 8,600L/$4.30), and there are 5 to 7 daily from **Rome**'s Tiburtina Station (2 hrs. 47 min.; 27,000L/$14), as well as 2 to 4 buses daily from **Perugia** (85 min.; 14,000L/$7). Siena's Tra-in **bus ticket office** is underneath Piazza Gramsci (☎ **0577-247-934** or 0577-204-270), and there's a **small office** at Piazza San Domenico, under the right side of the church exterior (☎ **0577-247-909** or 0577-204-111).

VISITOR INFORMATION   The **tourist office,** where you can get a great free map, is at Piazza del Campo 56 (☎ **0577-280-551;** fax 0577-270-676; www.siena.turismo.toscana.it). March 22 to November 10, it's open Monday to Saturday 8:30am to 7:30pm; winter hours are Monday to Friday 8:30am to 1pm and 3 to 7pm, and Saturday 8:30am to 1pm. The administrative **APT office** is at Via di Città 43 (☎ **0577-42-209**).

FESTIVALS & MARKETS   Travel material would have you believe otherwise, but there's more to see here than just the twice-annual Palio horse race. A 2-week **Antiques Fair** takes place in February of even years. A **Settimana dei Vini** (Wine Week) takes place the first week of June at the Enoteca Nazionale. The **Settimana Musicale Sienese,** a noteworthy weeklong classical musical festival, takes place in July or August, attracting world-class names and usually culminating in the beginning of August. Contact the tourist office for a schedule or call the Accademia Musicale Chigiana (☎ **0577-46-152;** fax 0577-288124), the city's prestigious music conservatory. The **weekly market** is a large affair and takes place on Wednesday (8am to 1pm) near the Fortezza Medicea and La Lizza Park. Vendors hawk everything from tube socks to CDs and fresh-cut flowers to tripe sandwiches.

Foremost of the year's events is the legendary ✪ **Palio delle Contrade,** held July 2 (7:30pm) and August 16 (7pm); the latter is the more important of the two. Tickets in the bleachers are exorbitant, usually costing at least 200,000L ($100) and can be purchased only directly from the piazza's 30-some-odd stores and cafes; some have faxes, and you can get a list of names and contacts at the tourist office. Tickets for either of the two Palios usually are sold out by January (and hotels by February); a last-minute appeal directly to a store or cafe owner may turn up a cancellation. The whole scenario is pretty much a frustrating and often useless venture unless you know the mayor. The alternative is to join the crowd, anywhere from 50,000 to 100,000 strong, that stands in the inner piazza (the later in the day you show up, the farther from the outer rail you'll find free space); remember this all happens during the peak summer

A Money-Saving Tip

Siena offers several **cumulative tickets** you can pick up at any of the participating museums or sights. These are ostensibly seasonally based (you can buy some only in summer, others only in winter), but they don't seem to enforce this rule. Note that this initiative mutates every year, so be ready for the specifics to change.

November to March 15, you can get a 3-day 8,500L ($4.25) ticket that includes the **Libreria Piccolomini** (inside the Duomo), **Museo dell'Opera Metropolitana,** and **Baptistry.** Or you can buy the more complete 7-day 25,000L ($13) version covering the above sights also granting admission to the **Museo Civico, Santa Maria della Scala,** and the new contemporary art gallery in the **Palazzo delle Papesse** on Via di Città (where admission is normally 7,000L/$3.50).

March 16 to October, the more restricted 3-day 9,500L ($4.75) ticket includes the **Libreria Piccolomini, Museo dell'Opera Metropolitana, Baptistry,** and **Oratorio di San Bernardino** (for 13,000L/$7, you can also visit **Sant'Agostino**). The more complete 7-day 32,000L ($16) summer combo includes all those sights (including Sant'Agostino), plus the **Museo Civico, Santa Maria della Scala,** and **Palazzo delle Papesse.**

You can now **book tickets and entry times** to most of Siena's museums via e-mail (moira@comune.siena.it), the Web (www.comune.siena.it/cultura/prenot-bigl.htm; it's in Italian, just click on FORM), or fax (☎ 0577-226-265 or 0577-46-829) at least a week in advance. Siena tends not to be overly crowded, so this isn't strictly necessary, but there's the curious added benefit that it **saves you 1,000L (50¢)** on each admission to any of the civic museums—though for all other city museums and sights, the usual rule applies and you're *charged* an extra 1,000L (50¢) fee per ticket for this reservation service. So perhaps just reserve the Palazzo Pubblico and pay for the others as you go.

heat, vision is limited, and emotions run high. But hey, it's free. For more on the Palio, see the box.

CITY LAYOUT   Siena is splayed out like a Y along three ridges with deep valleys in between, effectively dividing the city into thirds, called *terze.* The *terze* are each drawn out along three main streets following the spines of those ridges. The southern arm, the **Terza di San Martino,** slopes gently down around **Via Banchi di Sotto** (and the various other names it picks up along the way). To the west lies the **Terza di Città** (home to the Duomo and Pinacoteca), centered on **Via di Città.** The **Terza di Camollia** runs north around **Via Banchi di Sopra.** These three main streets meet at the north edge of **Piazza del Campo (Il Campo),** Siena's gorgeous scallop-shaped central square.

Tip: Each *terza*'s main ridge-topped street is relatively flat—for Siena—while off either side medieval alleys drop precipitously. If you hate climbing hills, the shortest (or at least less strenuous) distance between two points in Siena isn't a straight line but a curve that follows the three main drags as much as possible.

GETTING AROUND   Although it looks and feels like a small Tuscan hill town, Siena truly is a city (albeit a small one), and its sights are widely spread. There's no efficient public transport system in the center, so it's up to your feet to cover the territory. There are plenty of steep ups and downs, and no shortcuts from one *terza* to another without a serious workout.

The city does run **minibuses** called Pollicini (☎ **0577-204-246** or 0577-204-111), which dip into the city center 6am to 9pm. The B services the Terza di San Martino and out the Porta Pispini gate, as do buses 22, 23, 25, and 27 (there's also an "N" night bus on this route 9pm to 1am). The C runs from the train station down into the northern bit of the Terza di Camollia. Confusingly, there are four "A" buses, differentiated by color. "A pink" goes around the Terza di San Martino (and out the Porta Romana), as does bus 26; "A green" and "A yellow" cover the Terza di Città (green from the Porta Tufi to the Duomo and yellow from the Porta San Marco to the Duomo); and "A red" takes care of the southerly part of the Terza di Camollia (from Piazza della Indipendenza out the Porta Fontebranda), a route also followed by buses 20 and 21.

You can call for a radio **taxi** at ☎ **0577-49-222** (7am to 9pm only); they also queue at the train station and in town at Piazza Matteotti.

EXPLORING SIENA

✪ **Piazza del Campo & Palazzo Pubblico aka Palazzo Comunale (Museo Civico).** Piazza d. Campo. ☎ **0577/29-22-63.** Admission to Museo Civico 12,000L ($6) adults, 7,000L ($3.50) students and over 60; Torre del Mangia 10,000L ($5); combined admission 18,000L ($9). Mar 16–Oct daily 10am–7pm; Nov–Mar 15 daily 10am–6:30pm (Torre del Mangia to 4pm).

PIAZZA DEL CAMPO (Il CAMPO)   You'll see posters and postcards with aerial shots of the unusual fan-shaped piazza, though they don't prepare you for its sheer breadth or monumental beauty. All roads and events, all visitors and residents gravitate toward it; you can catch a glimpse of its sunlit expanse from a dozen narrow alleys that lead down and empty into it. Built at the point where the city's three hills converge and the Roman forum once rose, Il Campo is divided into nine marble-trimmed strips representing the city's Government of Nine, established in 1290, but is also said to imitate the folds in the cloak of the Virgin Mary, protector of the city since time immemorial. The piazza has always been center stage—the one-time place of executions, bullfights, and demonstrations—and is today lined with handsomely restored 13th- and 14th-century palazzi and their ground-floor cafes and stores.

The piazza is still a great place to hang out, like the Ramblas in Barcelona and the Spanish Steps in Rome. Locals meet, gossip, shop, and cross it at every angle; university-goers loiter about; and seniors congregate against this backdrop of matchless harmony. At its highest point is the piazza's famous **Fonte Gaia,** dedicated to the ancient mythological goddess of the seas (though many sources say its name translates as gay and carefree). It's a poor 19th-century copy of the early 15th-century fountain by local master Jacopo della Quercia (you can find some of the much-decayed original marble reliefs in the Palazzo Pubblico's Museo Civico) and is fed by a 15-mile aqueduct that has supplied the city with fresh water since the 14th century.

PALAZZO PUBBLICO & TORRE DEL MANGIA   Also known at the **Palazzo Comunale,** this palace is a stunning symbol of civic pride and still the site of the Town Hall and takes up nearly all Piazza del Campo's south side. Its elegant Gothic facade, completed in 1310 and expanded in the 17th century, is slightly curved in keeping with the piazza's unusual parameter. The adjacent 320-foot brick bell tower, the marble-crowned **Torre del Mangia,** is the highest medieval tower in Italy after Cremona's and was named after its first bell ringer, nicknamed *mangiagaudagni* (literally profit-eater) because of his notorious idleness. Its bells were used to announce the opening and closing of the city gates, threat of attack, and special events like the arrival of a pope. Its 505 steps will provide you with vertigo-inducing views over Il Campo,

Siena's *centro storico,* and the Tuscan countryside that picks up where the modern city sprawl beyond the city walls diminishes (the other heart-stopping view in town is from atop the Facciatione, adjacent to the Duomo; see below). At the base of the tower is the **Cappella di Piazza** (1352 to 1376), erected by the grateful Sienese people in thanksgiving for the passing of the Black Death in 1348. It's not open to the public.

MUSEO CIVICO Within the Palazzo Pubblico, this museum houses some of the Sienese school of art's most significant works. One of the two important rooms is the **Sala del Mappamondo (Globe Room),** named after a long-lost map of the world and frescoed in 1315 with two important works by the prominent local artist Simone Martini, a student of Duccio. On the left is his splendidly restored ✪ *Maestà* (1315) and on the opposite wall ✪ *Guidoriccio da Folignano* (1328), a captain of the Sienese army in full battle regalia; both were meant to protect the city from harm and pestilence (the latter fresco had always been attributed to Martini until recent controversy that keeps historians divided).

The next room, the **Sala di Pace (Hall of Peace),** was the meeting place for the medieval Government of Nine and today contains the two famous allegorical frescoes by local master Ambrogio Lorenzetti: ✪ *Allegory of Good and Bad Government and Their Effects on Town and Countryside* (1337 to 1339). You won't have a hard time determining which is which. They're some of the earliest and most important secular artworks to survive from medieval Europe. Lorenzetti is believed to have died from the plague not long after completing the fresco cycle.

✪ **Duomo (Santa Maria dell'Assunta).** Piazza del Duomo. ☎ **0577-283-048.** www.operaduomo.it. Admission to Duomo free; Libreria Piccolomini 2,000L ($1). Mar 15–Oct daily 9am–7:30pm; Nov–Mar 14 daily 10am–1pm and 2:30–5pm.

Begun in 1196, this black-and-white-marble-striped Duomo dedicated to Our Lady of the Assumption tops Siena's highest hill and is one of Italy's most beautiful Gothic churches. If you arrive by bus in Piazza San Domenico, look for its perfect view from afar. Much of what you see was completed in the 13th century. The unfinished free-standing construction to the right of the cathedral is what the Sienese call the **Facciatone (Big Facade).** In 1339 (when Siena was reaching its medieval zenith and felt the need to keep up with its old-time rival Florence, which had just built an enormous Duomo), plans were launched to build an even greater Duomo that would incorporate the extant structure as the transept and become Christendom's largest church outside Rome. Work was abandoned forever when money ran short, the bubonic plague of 1348 altered local history, and the economy fell apart.

The exterior's extravagant marble bands (borrowed from Pisan-Lucchese architecture) are reflected in the interior. Your entry can be visually startling, with your focus soon being drawn to the priceless ✪ **pavement of masterful mosaics,** 56 etched and inlaid marble panels created by more than 40 artisans between the mid–14th and 16th centuries, with some finished in the 19th century. They're partially roped off and many are covered by protective cardboard, but all are uncovered for a few weeks before and after the August 15 feast day of the Assumption (and sometimes into September).

Beneath the central vault is the octagonal **pulpit,** whose famous upper panels depicting the life of Christ were carved by master Tuscan sculptor Nicola Pisano in 1265, assisted by his son Giovanni (who designed the Duomo's lower facade in 1284) and Arnolfo di Cambio. It's his masterpiece, even greater and more elaborate than his then-recent work in Pisa's baptistry, and is one of the Duomo's (and the city's) most important artistic treasures. Within the Duomo at an entrance in the north (left) aisle is the lavish ✪ **Libreria Piccolomini,** built in the late 15th century by Cardinal

The Palio delle Contrade

Twice a year, Siena packs Piazza del Campo with dirt, and the city's traditional *contrade*—the neighborhood wards that still govern many aspects of Sienese life—hold a fast-paced, bareback horse race called the Palio. It is the highlight of a week of trial runs, feasts, parades, spectacles of skill, and solemn ceremonies, a tradition that goes back, in one form or another, to at least 1310.

Ten *contrade* are chosen by lot each year to ride in the **July 2** Palio. The other seven, plus three from the July race, run the even bigger Palio on **August 16.** Lest you think the Palio is a race of skill: Your chance to ride, your horse, and the order you're lined up are each chosen by separate lots—even your jockey (always a hired outsider) is a wild card, since you may not pay him more than a rival is bribing him to throw the race. The jockey exists mainly to lash at other riders with his short whip; in the end, it's the horse that wins (if no rivals have drugged it), whether there's a rider still on it or not. The prize for all this mayhem? The *palio* is merely a banner painted with the image of the Virgin Mary. Well, you also win the honor of your *contrada* for the coming year. The Palios really start on June 29/August 13, when the lots are drawn to select the racers and the trial runs begin for the next two days. Each Palio holds *contrade* a pre-Palio feast that lasts until the Palio day's 7:45am Jockey's Mass in the Campo's Cappella della Piazza. There's a final heat at 9am, but the highlight is the 3pm (3:30pm in July) Blessing of the Horse in each *contrada*'s church. Unless invited by a *contrada*, you're not going to get into any of the packed churches for this, so your best strategy is to stick around the Campo all day. Standing in the piazza's center is free; the grandstands require tickets. Stake out a piazza spot close to the start/finish line before 2pm. Just before 5pm, the pageantry begins, with processions including the *palio* banner carried in a War Chariot drawn by two white oxen. *Contrada* youths in Renaissance costume juggle huge colorful banners in a *sbandierata* flag-throwing display.

At 7:30pm (7pm in July) nine of the horses start lining up between two ropes, waiting for the tenth horse to come galloping up from behind and start the race—three laps; a minute and a half. Then it's time for the winning *contrada* to burst into song, the losers to cry, and those suspecting their jockeys of taking bribes to chase the riders through the streets. Save for the winners, the banquets that night, at long tables laid out on the streets of each *contrada*, are more solemn than the feasts of the night before.

Francesco Piccolomini (the future Pius III—for all of 18 days in office before he died) to house the important illuminated book collection of his uncle, Pope Pius II, the quintessential Renaissance man/humanist. The elder pontiff's life is the subject of 10 brilliantly colored giant frescoes, the masterpiece of Umbrian artist Pinturicchio (1509); he was assisted by his students, including a young Raphael. One of the most famous frescoes depicts the canonization of Siena-born St. Catherine, the third fresco on the left as you enter. An ancient Roman copy of a Greek-inspired statue of the **Three Graces** stands in the center. As you leave the library, on your right you'll see the late 15th-century **Piccolomini altar** adorned with four statues attributed to a young Michelangelo; though commissioned to do 15, he left early for Florence to create his *David*.

○ **Museo dell'Opera Metropolitana (Duomo Museum).** Piazza del Duomo 8.
☎ **0577-283-048.** www.operaduomo.it. Admission 6,000L ($3). Mar 15–Sept daily
9am–7:30pm; Oct daily 9am–6pm; Nov–Mar 14 daily 9am–1:30pm.

Located in the "new" part of the Duomo that was never finished, with the adjoining
Facciatone, this museum houses much of the sculpture and artwork that formerly
graced the cathedral inside and out. Most interesting is the first-floor's collection of
weather-worn Gothic facade statuary by Giovanni Pisano with an important contribution by Donatello, a marble tondo of the *Madonna and Child.* Upstairs in a room
by itself is the ○ *Maestà* (1311), the museum's most celebrated work, once the
Duomo's altarpiece. It's a complex work by Duccio di Buoninsegna, a student of
Cimabue and a native son of Siena, and has long been considered one of the most
important late medieval paintings in Europe. Follow signs for access to the top of the
Facciatone (no elevator) for an ○ **inspiring view** over Siena, arguably better than the
view from the Torre del Mangia. During peak months when hours allow, try to make
it for sunset.

Battistero (Baptistry). Piazza San Giovanni (down the stairs around the back-right flank of
the Duomo). ☎ **0577-283-048.** www.operaduomo.it. Admission 3,000L ($1.50). Mar
15–Sept daily 9am–7:30pm; Oct daily 9am–6pm; Nov–Mar 14 daily 10am–1pm and
2:30–5pm.

Due to its separate entrance and obscure placement down the stairs and around the
back-right flank of the Duomo, few people visit this baptistry. Look for the 15th-
century hexagonal ○ **baptismal font** by local son Jacopo della Quercia, adorned with
gilded bronze bas-reliefs panels by Donatello and Ghiberti. If you've already visited
Lucca, you'll have seen his important Tomb of Ilaria in the sacristy of the local
Duomo.

○ **Pinacoteca Nazionale (National Picture Gallery).** Via San Pietro 29.
☎ **0577-281-161.** Admission 8,000L ($4). Summer Mon 8:30am–1:30pm, Tues–Sat
9am–7pm, Sun 8am–1pm; winter daily 8:30am–1:30pm (to 1pm Sun), plus Tues–Sat afternoon visits at 2:30, 4, and 5:30pm.

If you've already visited the Duomo Museum or the Museo Civico, you'll recognize
some of the names and styles of the Sienese school of painters, whose works are displayed here in the 14th-century Gothic Palazzo Buonsignori. Though it can't hold a
candle to what was transpiring simultaneously in Florence, this sliver of local art history is fascinating. Visitors usually bypass the ground floor and head to the second
floor's treasures, highlighted by the works of Duccio, antiquity's last great painter and
the most acclaimed of Siena's movement; in his works you can follow artistic advance-
ments in composition, perspective, and expression. His student Simone Martini is also
represented, as are brothers Pietro and Ambrogio Lorenzetti. The use of gold hung on
longer in the Sienese school than in the Florentine, perhaps because the patrons who
commissioned the works wanted to have them shine in gloomy chapels. Florence
moved onto more advanced developments, while Siena was slow to break with its religious compositions.

Enoteca Italiana Permanente (Permanent Italian Wine Cellar). Fortezza Medicea
(beyond the Stadium, at the northwest corner of town). ☎ **0577-288-497.** Free admission;
glass of wine 2,500–6,000L ($1.75–$3). Mon noon–8pm, Tues–Sat to 1am.

There could be no better setting to showcase Italy's timeless wine culture, making this
a unique destination for serious connoisseurs and casual oenophiles. Set within the
massive military fortress built by Cosimo de' Medici in 1560 after Siena had fallen to
Florence, this wine-tasting bar provides a wide selection of vintages to be enjoyed

inside and out, where tables are set on a terrace. It's most popular in the late afternoon or early evening, when local wine devotees and a young crowd drop in for an *aperitivo,* choosing from dozens of wines sold by the glass (or by the bottle). The emphasis is on Tuscan wines—many made around Siena—but this enoteca is a national concern owned/operated by the government to support the Italian wine tradition. Its 750-label collection is representative of the various regions and one of the most prodigious selections of its kind in Italy.

Casa di Santa Caterina. Costa di Sant'Antonio (between Via della Sapienza and Via Santa Caterina). No phone. Free admission. Easter–Oct daily 9am–12:30pm and 2:30–6pm; daily winter 9am–12:30pm and 3:30–6pm.

This is the 14th-century birthplace and home of St. Catherine of Siena, patron saint of Italy (together with St. Francis of Assisi) and one of the first women ever elevated to Doctor of the Church. If you've arrived at a time when a tour group or other crowd is present, wait until they leave so you can fully absorb the serenity of this simple and reflective place. After you cross through a brick-lined courtyard, the points of interest are the **small chapel** on your right where a painted 13th-century **crucifix** is said to be the one in front of which she received the stigmata in 1375, and an **oratory** to the left built on the spot of the family home, with wide steps leading down to her cell. St. Catherine died at 33 in 1380, the year that St. Bernard of Siena was born (d. 1444). Their mysticism exerted a deeply felt grip on the age, a time of heightened spirituality during an onslaught of droughts, bubonic plagues, and declining economies. The eloquent St. Catherine is perhaps most remembered for her instrumental involvement in persuading Pope Gregory XI to return the seat of the papacy to Rome from Avignon in France after a 67-year exile. She was canonized in 1464, and her home transformed into this pilgrimage site not long thereafter.

San Domenico. Piazza San Domenico. No phone. Free admission. Apr–Oct daily 7am–12:55pm and 3–6:30pm; Nov–Mar daily 9am–12:55pm and 3–6pm.

This monastic church has always been closely linked with St. Catherine, who had taken the Dominican veil in 1355 after her first vision of Christ. This barnlike 13th-century church juts above a high position affording beautiful views of the Duomo and the rooftops. But it's most visited for the ✪ **Cappella di Santa Caterina (Chapel of St. Catherine)** halfway along the nave on the right wall, added in 1460 to house the saint's severed head in a gilded tabernacle. In 1526, Il Sodoma frescoed all but the right wall with scenes from the saint's life. Catherine experienced most of her trances and visions of Christ in this church and received her stigmata in the raised **Cappella delle Volte (Chapel of the Vaults)** in the west end of the church (on your right as you enter). Over the chapel's altar, a contemporary portrait of her by one of her friends, Andrea Vanni (ca. 1380), is said to be the only authentic depiction of her.

SHOPPING

Siena puts up a noble effort to keep up with its centuries-old rival Florence as a shopping destination but pales in comparison. It is, however, far better in variety and quantity than any of the other cities in this chapter, with the only close contenders being Perugia and Deruta (a side trip from Perugia for those interested in ceramics alone).

The elegance of the Sienese is obvious in the cluster of stores along the principle streets covered in "City Layout" earlier in this section. There are the predictable designer and accessories boutiques of top names, but you may be more interested in its ceramics stores and shops selling artisanal crafts (*prodotti toscani*). The ceramics store **Zina Provvedi,** Via di Città 96 (☎ **0577-286-068**), has one of the best selections with the nicest of quality and will even ship. On this same block are at least five other ceramics shops selling everything from spoon rests to turkey-sized platters, simply decorated (less expensive) or elaborately covered (very expensive). Also nearby is **Il Papiro,** Via di Città 37 (☎ **0577-284-241**), whose attractive paper goods you may have seen in its hometown of Florence, but in this retail outpost you'll also find a handsome series of postcards and note cards of watercolor vignettes depicting Siena's loveliest medieval palazzi.

If you've meandered about, you may have happened on any of the five **Nannini** bars or pasticcerie, sacred local institutions. The Nannini name is known beyond the confines of Siena, if not for its famous packaged sweets than for the pop singer Gianna Nannini (a cross between Madonna and a Streisand wannabe). Their largest and oldest bar/cafe is on Via Banchi di Sopra near Piazza del Campo (☎ **0577-41-591**). Although the fruit-and-nut cake *panforte* and the cookie-like *ricciarelli* sweets made of almond paste are associated with Siena and Nannini's, food connoisseurs will guide you to the city's best one-stop-shop for gourmet products, the **Enoteca San Domenico,** Via del Paradiso 56, just off Piazza San Domenico (☎ **0577-271-181**). Here the just-sweet-enough *ricciarelli* are marvelous, and the selection of regional wines, oils, dried herbs, and other handsomely packaged gourmet goods will cover every hard-to-shop-for person on your list, yourself included.

AFFORDABLE PLACES TO STAY

There are no youth hostels in town; ask at the tourist office about the two a few miles outside town (one in a lovely corner of Chianti). Both are under the same management as the hostel in San Gimignano (see earlier in this chapter). If all the hotels below are full, try the English-speaking **Prenotazioni Alberghiere (hotel reservations) stand** on Piazza San Domenico (☎ **0577-288-084;** fax 0577-280-290; e-mail: info@hotelsiena.com), where you'll pay 3,000L to 8,000L ($1.50 to $4) per reservation according to the category of hotel. In summer, the office is open Monday to Saturday 9am to 8pm (to 7pm in winter).

For **long stays,** Siena's fabled Piccolomini family has opened one of its Renaissance palazzi as furnished rentals by the week or month. Close to Piazza del Campo, top-floor apartments with a view sleeping two or three rent for $1,015 per week in low season or $1,450 in high season; the one sleeping four or five runs $1,500 in low season or $2,150 in high season. To all rates you must add utilities; prices get progressively less for longer stays. In New York, contact Manfredi Piccolomini at ☎ **212/932-3480** (fax 212/932-9039; www.palazzoantellesi.com). In Italy, call his mother's Florence number at ☎ **055-244-456** (fax 055-234-5552).

✪ **Antica Torre.** Via di Fieravecchia 7, 53100 Siena. ☎/fax **0577-222-255.** 8 units. TV TEL. 170,000L ($85) single; 205,000L ($103) double. Prices lower in slow periods. Continental breakfast 13,000L ($7). AE, DC, MC, V. Parking in streets around hotel or public lot nearby.

Installed in a 16th-century tower (one of Siena's more recent constructions) with a time-worn travertine stairwell, this unusual and charming hotel offers cozy—some might call them small—rooms. The higher-floors rooms are slightly larger and feature lovely views over the rooftops and green hills. Most rooms have cool terra-cotta pavements, exposed-beamed ceilings, white-lace curtains, and beds with wrought-iron headboards; the baths are compact and new. TVs are available on request. Though the hotel is on a quiet side street in a relatively residential niche of town, it's only a 10-minute walk to Piazza del Campo. You can even breakfast there in one of the expensive outdoor cafes for less than what you'd pay at the hotel. The breakfast room, a 14th-century potter's *bottega* on top of which the tower was built, is charming but not for claustrophobics—especially before morning coffee.

Chiusarelli. Viale Curtatone 15 (near San Domenico), 53100 Siena. ☎ **0577-280-562.** Fax 0577-271-177. 49 units, 48 with bathroom. A/C TV TEL. 102,000L ($51) single without bathroom, 130,000L ($65) single with bathroom; 190,000L ($95) double with bathroom; 255,000L ($128) triple with bathroom; 330,000L ($165) quad with bathroom; suites up to 280,000L ($140). Buffet breakfast included. AE, MC, V. Free parking (7 spaces, first come, first served) or around 35,000L ($18) in garage.

Two regal palms stand guard before the columned facade of this neoclassical 19th-century villa turned hotel. It's an easy block walk from the bus station for those with light luggage and also an easy walk uphill to the central piazza once you're ready to sightsee. Availability is slightly better in prime months if you book in advance. The plain modernized rooms are prettied up with rose chenille or flowered bedspreads—light sleepers should request a room overlooking the green stadium behind, not terribly picturesque but quieter (except during Sunday matches) than those on Via Curatone. This is a "proper" hotel with a bar, a breakfast terrace, a restaurant (avoid it and go to one of my suggestions below), and tour groups.

✪ **Piccolo Hotel Etruria.** Via Donzelle 3, 53100 Siena (off Via Banchi di Sotto). ☎ **0577-288-088.** Fax 0577-288-461. E-mail: hetruria@tin.it. 13 units, 12 with bathroom. TV TEL. 70,000L ($35) single without bathroom, 80,000L ($40) single with bathroom; 130,000L ($65) double with bathroom. Extra bed 38,000L ($19). Continental breakfast 8,000L ($4). AE, DC, MC, V. Parking in public facilities. Closed around Dec 10–27.

This hotel is lovely enough to be your base in Tuscany—it's too great a find to be used as a one-night stop. The proud Fattorini family oversaw every painstaking detail in its recent renovation, and the taste and quality level are something you usually find in hotels at thrice the cost. The rooms are simple but thoughtfully decorated and charming; the use of terra-cotta pavements and blond wood is ubiquitous. They're divided between the main building and a *dipendenza* across the street; some guests prefer the privacy of the latter and others the friendly presence of the Fattorinis in the former. The many appreciated touches include floral bedspreads, sheer white curtains, and hair dryers in the new baths. The Fattorinis' new in-house restaurant specializes in home-style cuisine. In high season, book well in advance—this secret is out.

GREAT DEALS ON DINING

Antica Trattoria Papei. Piazza del Mercato 6 (behind Palazzo Pubblico). ☎ **0577-280-894.** Reservations suggested. Primi 10,000L ($5); secondi 8,000L–15,000L ($4–$8). AE, MC, V. Tues–Sun noon–3pm and 7–10:30pm. SIENESE.

It's rather ambitious, in a city whose origins date from the Roman Empire, for a restaurant to call itself the "Ancient Trattoria" when it's been around for a mere 50 years. But three generations of the proud Papei family have put this wonderful restaurant on the map from day one. You'll understand why its future is secure when the homemade *pappardelle alla cinghiale* (flat noodles in a wild-boar tomato sauce) arrive at your outdoor table on one of the city's oldest piazze. The theme continues with *coniglio all'arrabiata* (rabbit marinated in white wine and simmered with sage and a pinch of hot pepperoncino). One of the myriad possibilities for non-hunters is the homemade *pici*, a hand-rolled egg pasta that looks like fat spaghetti and is served with a full-flavored fresh tomato sauce. Though the place has been discovered by foreigners, locals rigorously hang on (they avoid the modern room to the right as you enter, and so should you).

Da Roberto. Via di Calzoliera (between Banchi di Sopra and Banchi di Sotto, off Piazza Tolomei). ☎ **0577-285-080.** Reservations recommended. Primi 7,000L–10,000L ($3.50–$5); secondi 8,000L–14,000L ($4–$7); pizza 5,000L–10,000L ($2.50–$5); fixed-price menu 24,000L ($12) without wine. No credit cards. Wed–Mon 12:30–2:30pm and 7:30–11:30pm. SIENESE/PIZZA.

The delicious wood-oven pizzas indubitably overshadow the restaurant menu, but you're welcome to opt out of Roberto's special *pizza alla fattoressa* (smothered with tomato, mozzarella, and thinly-sliced potatoes sprinkled with fresh rosemary) and order from the full menu. Homemade *pici alla pettitosa* are a hard-to-find spaghetti-like pasta with a faintly spicy tomato sauce; follow them with *cosce di maiale* (roasted leg of pork fragrant with rosemary). This is *cucina toscana* as you can only hope to find at these prices.

Pizzeria da Carlo e Franca. Via di Pantaneto 138 (near Via di Pispini). ☎ **0577-220-485.** Pizza 5,500–8,000L ($2.75–$4). Thurs–Tues noon–3pm and 5pm–midnight. No credit cards. PIZZERIA.

This unpretentious pizzeria is always crowded—the pizza is too good and the prices are too moderate to expect otherwise. The plain wooden tables with paper placemats can't accommodate the lines, so the more impatient patrons know to grab a *pizza al taglio* (by the slice) and eat it on the run. But if you come a little early you can sit, order an appetizer of *bruschetta* (small slabs of toasted bread brushed with garlic and drizzled with olive oil) and peruse at leisure the 30 types of pizza and calzone. Most opt for the house specialty: *pizza alla boscaiola,* with tomatoes, sausage, mushrooms, mozzarella, and garlic.

WORTH A SPLURGE

✪ **Osteria le Logge.** Via del Porrione 33 (just off the Campo). ☎ **0577-48-013.** Reservations required. Primi 10,000L–20,000L ($5–$10); secondi 25,000L–30,000L ($13–$15). AE, DC, MC, V. Mon–Sat noon–3pm and 7–10:30pm. Closed Nov 15–Dec 6. SIENESE/TUSCAN.

Owner Gianni Brunelli is passionate about what he does, and so is his legion of devotees. This is one of those rare Sienese eateries for which you should reserve before arriving in town rather than risk settling for one of Gianni's cookbooks when the standing-room-only scenario turns you away. There's always a fresh homemade pasta to launch a memorable meal, followed by entrees that are all about the simple perfection of grilled meats, though I've seen vegetarians looking mighty content, too. The excellent choice of extra-virgin olive oil is enough to confirm the owner's seriousness, seconded by a small but discerning wine list that's topped by his own limited production of Rosso and Brunello di Montepulciano. You won't understand how exceptional this atmospheric locale is (a cabinet-lined former pharmacy) until you've eaten elsewhere in Siena.

SIDE TRIPS FROM SIENA

The wine-producing towns of southern Tuscany are still relatively unknown compared to those found along the Chianti Road (see earlier in this chapter), being just a mile too many away for Florence-based day trippers. They're more easily accessible from Siena and can generally be reached by public transportation, though a rental car will facilitate enormously the logistics and flexibility of a day trip.

MONTALCINO   Located 43km (27 mi.) south of Siena, sleepy and small but well-to-do Montalcino is the home of the powerhouse DOCG ✪ **Brunello di Montalcino wine** and its lighter-weight cousin Rosso di Montalcino. The town has remained unchanged since the 16th century, and you'll find an especially lovely vista from the 14th-century **Fortezza** (☎ **0577-849-211**), which moonlights as its enoteca. April to October, it's open daily 9am to 8pm; November to March, hours are Tuesday to Sunday 9am to 1pm and 2 to 6pm. By-the-glass wines begin at 3,000L ($1.50), but head right for the Brunello at 7,000L ($3.50) and a savory plate of the local cheeses or salami for Montalcino's perfect meal. Admission to the fortress's ramparts is 3,500L ($2) adults and 2,000L ($1.15) students, or you can buy a 10,000L ($6) cumulative ticket that also gets you into the Museo Civico. Another wonderful place for wine tasting is the **Caffè/Fiaschetteria Italiana,** Piazza del Popolo 6 (☎ **0577-849-043**), open Friday to Wednesday 7:30am to midnight. In a 19th-century ambience or at a few choice tables outside, you can revel in a self-styled Brunello tasting, with three or four varieties by the glass for 8,000L to 20,000L ($4 to $10). You can buy a bottle to bring home with you, if you want to part with 100,000L ($50).

In the handsomely restored former St. Augustine monastery, Montalcino's small **Museo Civico (Civic Museum),** Via Ricasoli 31 (☎ **0577-846-014**), is a collection of Sienese paintings dating from the 1400s to the Renaissance. It's open Tuesday to Sunday: January to March 10am to 1pm and 2 to 5pm, and April to December to 6pm. Admission is 8,000L ($4). Two of the area's most alluring experiences are outside the town walls, however.

The 12th-century Cistercian abbey of ✪ **Sant'Antimo** (☎ **0577-835-659**) rests in its own pocket-sized vale amid olive trees and cypresses 10km (6.3 mi.) south of Montalcino. One of Tuscany's most perfectly intact Romanesque churches, it's especially worth visiting during the Gregorian chants performed daily by a handful of monks who still live there. It's open daily 10:30am to 12:30 and 3 to 6:30pm. While at Sant'Antimo, follow the signs for the nearby ✪ **Fattoria Barbi** (☎ **0577-848-277**), one of the most respected producers of Brunello, in the same family since the 16th century. Wine tastings are available Monday to Saturday plus Sunday afternoon, but so are excellent country meals, with most products direct from the estate's farm. Rustic accommodations at the inn will tempt you to stay on indefinitely. Barbi is open Monday to Saturday 9:30am to noon and 2 to 5:30pm.

From Siena, there are a dozen or so Tra-in **buses** to Montalcino (60–90 min., 6,000L/$3). Montalcino's **tourist office** is at Via Costa dei Municipio 8 (☎/fax **0577-849-331**), open Tuesday to Sunday 10am to 1pm and 2 to 6pm.

PIENZA This Renaissance jewel (24km/15 mi. from Montalcino and 52km/33 mi. from Siena) is easy to reach from Montalcino by public bus. But with just two or three bus departures from Siena and no trains, a rental car will make your life easier. Film director Franco Zeffirelli found the perfect backdrop awaiting him here to film *Romeo and Juliet* in 1968, bypassing "fair Verona" as the obvious choice. Pienza was also used in the Oscar-winning epic *The English Patient.*

Pienza is most noteworthy as testament to the ego of a quintessential Renaissance man. Pope Pius II (of Siena's illustrious Piccolomini family) was born here in 1405 when it was called Corsignano and in 1459 (a year after becoming pope) commissioned Florentine architect Bernardo Rossellino to level the medieval core of town and create the first stage of what would become the model High Renaissance city (and renamed it Pienza, in his own honor). The grand scheme didn't get very far (the pope died in 1464), but what was done remains now perfectly preserved (and protected by UNESCO)—just look at the graceful ✪ **Piazza Pio II.** Visit the piazza's **Palazzo Piccolomini** (the pope's private residence, lived in by descendents of the Piccolominis until 1968) and the **Duomo;** walk behind the Duomo for sweeping **views** of the dormant Mt. Amiata and the wide Val d'Orcia. The piazza is also the location for the **tourist office** (☎/fax **0578-749-071**). Ask about free guided tours of the town during summer.

You can see most of the town, with a population of 2,500, in just half a day. It'll take only 5 minutes to cover Pienza's main drag, **Corso Rossellino,** whose food stores specialize in the gourmet products from this bountiful corner of Tuscany, namely wines, honey, and its famous ✪ **pecorino cheese** (also known as *cacio*). Cheese tasting is more popular than wine tasting here, and stores offer their varieties of *fresco* (fresh), *semistagionato* (partially aged), *pepperocinato* (dusted with hot peppers), or *tartufato* (embedded with truffles). Taste as much cheese as you will, but by all means save room for lunch at the town's well-known and reasonably priced **Dal Falco,** Piazza Dante Alighieri 7 (☎ **0578-749-856**), open Saturday to Thursday noon to 2:45pm and 7 to 10pm (closed 10 days each February, July, and November). A meal of homemade pici pasta and a delicious grilled meat will cost around 32,000L ($17). There are six simple doubles upstairs for 100,000L ($50).

AREZZO   Only 74km (47 mi.) east of Siena and an easy hour train trip from Florence (81km/51 mi.), Arezzo boasts a lovely medieval demeanor that was introduced to the world as the backdrop for the first part of Tuscan native Roberto Benigni's Oscar-winning film *La Vita è Bella* (*Life Is Beautiful*). It's worth a day's stay for a meander through its medieval *centro storico* and a visit to Piero della Francesca's stunning fresco cycle, the ✪ *Legend of the True Cross* (1452 to 1466), in the 14th-century **San Francesco** church on Piazza San Francesco. In 2000, a hugely successful 15-year restoration to bring the frescoes back to colorful glory was completed. Nearby is the wonderfully charming lopsided ✪ **Piazza Grande,** lined on one side by a loggia designed by local boy Giorgio Vasari, though all you get of the 12th-century **Santa Maria della Pieve** church is the apse end; for the stacked Lombard-Romanesque facade, you'll have to walk around to the Corso Italia side.

Arezzo is transported back to the Dark Ages with its much-felt historic ✪ **Giostra del Saracino (Saracen Joust)** held in the off-kilter main piazza the last Sunday in August and the first Sunday in September; for tickets contact the tourist office (below). If you can't get tickets for the joust itself, go for the elaborate *corteo* (procession) wending through the narrow cobblestone streets beforehand—the rich costumes and authentic armor (on knights and horses alike) are the result of meticulous archival research and the theatrical know-how of Tuscan-born Franco Zeffirelli. If you can time it right, Italy's best and largest **antiques fair** the first weekend of every month fills the main piazza.

Should you arrive in town and nothing much is happening, go for lunch or dinner at everyone's favorite trattoria in town, the **Osteria L'Agania,** Via Mazzini 10, two blocks from San Francesco church (☎ **0575-295-381**). It's open Tuesday to Sunday noon to 3pm and 7 to 10:30pm. If it's full, you'll be happy next door at the **Trattoria del Saraceno,** no. 6 (☎ **0575-27-644**), for a similarly casual ambience. It's open Thursday to Tuesday noon to 4pm and 7 to 10pm. Arezzo's finest restaurant, the **Buca di San Francesco,** Via San Francesco 1 (☎ **0575-23-271**), is housed in the frescoed cellar of a 14th-century palazzo next door to the San Francesco church. It's a bit more expensive (average dinner is 40,000L to 50,000L/$20 to $25 without wine) and a lot more dramatic, and the traditional Tuscan menu is delicious. It's open Wednesday to Monday noon to 2:30pm and Wednesday to Sunday 7 to 10pm. The **tourist office** is at Piazza della Repubblica 22, just outside the train station (☎ **575-377-678;** fax 575-20-839). You can get to Arezzo **from Florence by train,** dozens daily, in 60 to 90 minutes; **from Florence by bus** isn't as convenient: CAT buses take 80 minutes to 2 hours. A few LFI **buses leave Siena** daily (trip time: 1 hr. 30 min.—because it makes local stops).

6   Perugia: Capital of Umbria

80km (50 mi.) SE of Arezzo, 188km (117 mi.) NE of Rome, 154km (96 mi.) SE of Florence, 26km (16 mi.) NW of Assisi, 75km (47.3 mi.) NE of Orvieto, 110km (69 mi.) SE of Siena

Umbria is the "green heart of Italy" and **Perugia** its commercial and economic capital. Close your eyes to the charmless modern-day sprawl you pass through on your way into the elegant heart of the ancient city. Principally known today for its celebrated university and as home to Biuttoni and Perugina chocolate (now part of Nestlés), Perugia is a prosperous city dressed in medieval hill town clothing. It's a good base for travelers with and without cars who'd like to visit Umbria's many characteristic hill towns, like Assisi, Gubbio, and Spoleto and the ceramics town Deruta. Even Orvieto is a feasible day trip (about 50 mi.) for those with wheels. Perugia's historic center's cosmopolitan and urban bustle is a vibrant contrast to the rustic sleepiness of Umbria's hinterland for those inclined to venture afield.

As the easternmost satellite of the 12 Etruscan League cities, Perugia boasts a strategic position that made it a Roman stronghold in the 3rd century B.C. Perugia asserted itself through the Dark and Middle Ages as a strong progressive city, an independent commune with the griffin as its emblem; trade and the arts flourished, and its still prominent university was founded in 1270. This was Perugia's heyday, and much civic architecture was constructed on the Roman foundations, which had been built on the Etruscan foundations. The **Arco Etrusco (Etruscan Arch)** is the city's oldest testimony. It later was topped by a Renaissance fortification when the pope subdued the city in the 1500s and left behind the Rocca Paolina fortress to remind the Perugini who was now in charge (with Italian Unification in the 19th century, the castle was torn down, but its massive brick foundations remain, still incorporating that Etruscan arch). You can peel away the epochs and follow the story of Perugia's legendary past, counting the appearances of the griffin around town.

If everyone you see seems to be 21 (and playing hooky), it's because, in addition to the ancient state university, one of Italy's largest, there's also a Università per Stranieri, the country's most prestigious school teaching the Italian language and culture to foreigners. Set up by Mussolini to improve the image of Italy abroad, it now enrolls more than 5,000 students representing more than 110 countries. This explains the proliferation of concerts, pizzerie, and music stores as well as the air of energy and vitality that crescendos during the annual Umbria Jazz Festival, since 1973 one of Europe's foremost music events.

ESSENTIALS

GETTING THERE   By Train   Coming from **Rome,** there are five direct trains (2¼ hr.; 10,500L/$5) and about eight more requiring a transfer at Foligno. From **Florence,** take one of the dozen daily trains to Terontola/Cortona that meet up with a connecting train to Perugia (2–2½ hr. total; 14,500L/$7). From **Assisi,** there are some 24 trains daily direct (20 min.; 3,200L/$1.60). These lines are part of the FS state-run rail system and stop at the **Fontiveggie Station** on Piazza Vittorio Veneto, a 15-minute ride on bus 26, 27, 29, or 32 to 36 from Piazza Italia in the center of Perugia.

Perugia also sits on the privately run FCU train line serving Umbria. Fourteen daily trains run north from Terni through **Todi** (35–45 min.; 4,900L/$2.45), pulling into the outlying Ponte San Giovanni Station (☎ **075-393-615**), then chugging 8 minutes up a capillary line to the Santa Anna Station in town (☎ **075-572-3947**), under the curve of Viale Roma under the Piazza Italia end of town. All outgoing trains depart first from the Santa Anna Station.

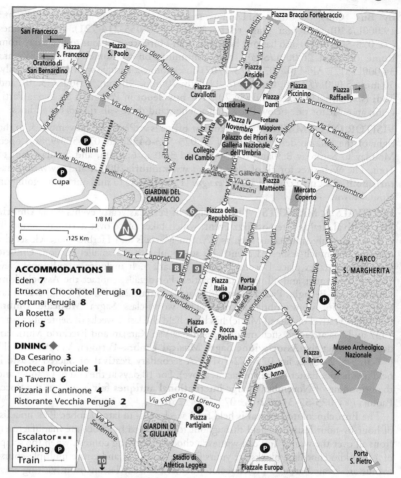

San Francesco

Piazza S. Francesco

Oratorio di San Bernardino

Via della Sposa

Via S. Francesco

Via Francolina

Via dei Priori

Piazza S. Paolo

Via dell'Aquilone

Piazza Cavallotti

Acquedotto

Via Cesare Batisti

Via U. Rocchi

Piazza Ansidei

Cattedrale

Via Bartolo

Piazza Danti

Piazza Piccinino

Via Bontempi

Piazza Raffaello

Via Cartolari

Via G. Alessi

Piazza Braccio Fortebraccio

Via Pinturicchio

P Pellini

Viale Pompeo Pellini

P Cupa

Via della Cupa

5

Via Ritorta

4 **3**

Piazza IV Novembre

Fontana Maggiore

Palazzo dei Priori & Galleria Nazionale dell'Umbria

Collegio del Cambio

Via Boncambi

Corso Vannucci

Galleria Kennedy

Via G. Mazzini

Piazza Matteotti

Via XIV Settembre

Mercato Coperto

GIARDINI DEL CAMPACCIO

6 Piazza della Repubblica

0   1/8 Mi

0   .125 Km

N

Via C. Caporali

Corso Vannucci

7

8 **9**

Via Bonazzi

Piazza Italia

P

Porta Marzia

Viale Indipendenza

Via Oberdan

Via Baglioni

PARCO S. MARGHERITA

Via Tancredi Ripa di Meana

Via XIV Settembre

P

ACCOMMODATIONS ■
Eden **7**
Etruscan Chocohotel Perugia **10**
Fortuna Perugia **8**
La Rosetta **9**
Priori **5**

DINING ◆
Da Cesarino **3**
Enoteca Provinciale **1**
La Taverna **6**
Pizzaria il Cantinone **4**
Ristorante Vecchia Perugia **2**

Viale Indipendenza

Piazza del Corso

Rocca Paolina

Via Masi

Corso Cavour

Piazza G. Bruno

Museo Archeologico Nazionale

Via Marconi

Stazione S. Anna

Via Fiume

Piazza G. Bruno

Via Fiorenzo di Lorenzo

Via XX Settembre

P Piazza Partigiani

GIARDINI DI S. GIULIANA

Stadio di Atletica Leggera

Piazzale Europa

P

Porta S. Pietro

Escalator ▪▪▪
Parking **P**
Train ┅┅┅

10

By Car   From Florence, take the A1 south to the Valdichiana exit and the SS75bis to Perugia. The SS326 also leads to this interchange from Siena. From Rome, exit the A1 north at Orte to take the SS204 to the SS3bis north. The SS3 and SS3bis cross at Perugia to connect with northern and southern Umbria. The center is closed to traffic, though you may drop off your baggage at your hotel.

Parking is fairly abundant, with the most convenient being the underground pay lot at Piazza Partigiani, at 1,500L (75¢) for the first hour and 2,000L ($1) each subsequent hour; or you can pay when you first arrive at the special tourist rate of 16,000L ($8) per day for the first 2 days, then 10,500L ($5) per each additional day (you get a temporary parking pass ticket that lets you come and go as you please). The lot is south of the city, but there's an underground escalator through the buried medieval city up to Piazza Italia. Two other pay lots are under the Mercato Coperto (elevator up to Piazza Matteotti) and at Pellini (escalator up to Via dei Priori). Below the latter is free parking on Piazza della Cupa, with an escalator up to Pellini.

By Bus   Only one daily SITA bus makes the trip from Florence (1¾ hr.; 19,000L/$10), and you must reserve a seat (☎ **055-214-721**). SULGA lines (☎ **075-500-9641**) also has one bus daily from **Florence,** and four to five a day from **Rome** (2½ hr.; 26,000L/$13), some continuing on to Rome's airport (3¼ hr.; 34,000L/$17). APM (☎ **075-573-1707**) buses connect Perugia with **Assisi** (six daily, 50 min.; 5,000L/$2.50), **Gubbio** (8–11 daily, 70 min., 10 min.; 7,400L/$3.70), and **Todi** (six daily, 1¼ hr.; 9,400L/$4.70). The **bus depot** in Perugia is on Piazza Partigiani, an escalator ride below Piazza Italia. The stand there sells tickets for all lines.

VISITOR INFORMATION   The **tourist office** is at Piazza IV Novembre 3, to the right of the Palazzo dei Priori steps (☎ **075-573-6458;** fax 075-573-9386), open Monday to Saturday 8:30am to 1:30pm and 3:30 to 6:30pm, and Sunday 9am to 1pm. The Web sites for all of Umbria are **www.umbria2000.it** and **www.umbria-turismo.it**. Pick up a copy of *Viva Perugia* (1,000L/50¢) to find out what's going on around town.

FESTIVALS & MARKETS   The highlight of Perugia's yearly events is the **Umbria Jazz Festival,** Italy's foremost jazz event, which takes place over a 10-day period in early or mid-July (musicians such as Wynton Marsalis and Herbie Hancock set the tone for this much-respected event). It's so popular that a smaller version, **Umbria Jazz Winter,** takes place December 29 to January 5. It includes a traditional New Year's Eve banquet and all-night jazz parties. For details, contact the **Associazione Umbria Jazz–Perugia,** Piazza Danti 28, Casella Postale 228 (☎ **075-573-2432;** fax 075-572-2656; www.umbriajazz.com). The world-class **Sagra Musicale Umbra** (Umbrian Festival of Sacred Music) has been held the last 2 weeks of September since 1937 and has attracted such major maestros as Van Karajan and Riccardo Muti. For details, contact the **Associazione Sagra Musical Umbra–Perugia,** Via Podianai 11 (☎ **075-572-1374;** fax 075-572-7614). A secondary **Festival of Sacred Music** is held just before Easter (same contact as above). For 10 days at the end of October and the beginning of November, a large **international antiques fair** is held in the Rocca Paolina (☎ **075-57-31-322;** fax 075-5724725).

The **Eurochocolate Festival** is held for 1 week mid- to late October. Pick up a list of hour-by-hour festivities held throughout town, staged by chocolate manufacturers from all over the world. You can witness a chocolate-carving contest, when the scraps of 1,000-kilo chocolate blocks are yours for the sampling, and entire multiple-course menus are created around the chocolate theme. Half-day lessons from visiting chefs are also available. Contact the **Eurochocolate Organization,** Via d'Andreotto 19, 06124 Perugia (☎ **075-573-2670;** fax 075-573-1100; www.chocolate.perugia.it).

For picnic provisions, the **daily market** (Monday to Saturday mornings only) takes place in the Mercato Coperto (Covered Market) east of the Palazzo dei Prior; entrance is from Piazza Matteotti. The much larger **weekly market** takes place every Saturday morning near the Stadium (behind the train station) on Piazza Umbria Jazz. An unusual **organic food market,** Umbria Terraviva, takes place the first Sunday of every month; check with the tourist office for its new location.

CITY LAYOUT   The main pedestrian thoroughfare is **Corso Vannucci,** lined with historic cafes, bars, the city's best stores, and palazzi, with narrow vaulted streets branching off west and east and invariably lead down, often with steps built into them. The Corso is anchored on the north end by **Piazza IV Novembre** and its the Fontana Maggiore, the city's social hub, with the Duomo just beyond it; and on the south end (after widening briefly into **Piazza della Repubblica**) by **Piazza Italia,** home to the shaded Giardini Carducci, with benches and a super view over the Tiber Valley. Beneath the gardens are the foundations of the 16th-century Rocca Paolina and the *scala mobile* network of escalators that bring you down through the ruins of the fortress to the town's lower level, main public parking lot, and long-distance bus station at Piazza Partigiani.

SEEING THE SIGHTS

If ever there was a venue on which to see and be seen, it's Perugia's **Corso Vannucci,** the city's north-south pedestrian nerve center. Small clumps of the young and beautiful; people at tables collecting signatures supporting human rights, local politicians, or the cause of the moment; matrons with their dogs; pensioners with their cronies discussing soccer and union dues increases; cafe tables capturing the sun (or shade)— you'll find that and much more. Siena's major strip was named after Pietro Vannucci, better known as Perugino (1445–1523), Perugia's most celebrated local painter, whose works you can see in the National Gallery.

The ✪ **Fontana Maggiore (Great Fountain)** is the elaborately decorated two-tiered centerpiece of picturesque **Piazza IV Novembre.** The fountain resurfaced in 1999 from the glass-domed bubble that protected it during a 5-year renovation and once again gleams as the city's greatest artistic treasure. Designed in 1278 by a local monk/architect, Fra' Bevignate (known in his time for his involvement in the construction of Orvieto's Duomo), to commemorate the completion of the town's aqueduct, it was decorated with a lower tier of 50 bas-relief panels by Gothic master sculptor Nicolò Pisano, already known for the pulpits commissioned for Siena's Duomo and his hometown of Pisa's baptistry; this was his last major work. The panels of the Fontana Maggiore depict everything from Aesop's fables and signs of the zodiac to episodes from Genesis and the origin of ancient Rome. The upper tier of 24 statuettes and panels is attributed to Nicolò's son, Giovanni.

The plain-faced **Cattedrale (Cathedral)** to the north of the fountain was built after the fountain's completion. It was begun in 1347, and its external walls have been left in their uncompleted state. A number of 15th- and 16th-century paintings decorate the baroque interior, but the most curious item is the alleged wedding band of the Virgin Mary, displayed (though hidden within 15 boxes that graduate in size, each locked by a key kept under safekeeping with a different church official) in the **Cappella del Sant'Anello (Chapel of the Holy Ring),** the first chapel on the left.

✪ **Palazzo dei Priori & Galleria Nazionale dell'Umbria (National Gallery).** Corso Vannucci 19 (at Piazza IV Novembre), Perugia. ☎ **075-574-1247.** Admission 8,000L ($4). Daily 9am–8pm (often Sat to 11pm in summer).

The bulk of the impressive **Palazzo dei Priori (Priors' Palace)** lines the west side of Corso Vannucci, but its oldest facade presides over Piazza IV Novembre. From the 13th century, the pink-tinged facade is distinguished by a grand staircase (used by tired visitors and by students enjoying a social moment between classes) and bronze copies of the 13th-century griffin (the city symbol) and the Guelph (papal) lion holding the massive chains that were once used to close the city gates of Siena, taken from the town after a Perugian victory in 1358. It's crowned by a row of bristling crenellations above rows of Gothic windows. Used as the town hall for hundreds of years, the Palazzo dei Priori is one of the greatest extant examples of secular architecture from its period.

On the Corso Vanucci side is an entrance to the **Collegio del Cambio** (below) and an entrance for the stairs to the fourth-floor **Galleria Nazionale,** which has just undergone an extensive renovation and reorganization. This showcase of Umbrian art traces the school's chronology from the 13th to the 18th century as well as the schools that influenced it. The rooms dedicated to Tuscan masters like Duccio, Fra' Angelico, and Piero della Francesca just about steal the show. But a dozen or so paintings by local celebrity Pietro Vannucci, alias Perugino, are the treasure, particularly his *Pietà* and late 15th-century *Adoration of the Magi.* Known for his gentle landscapes and as being the teacher of both Pinturicchio and Raphael, Perugino is one of the principal figures of the Italian Renaissance, certainly the most illustrious of the Umbrian school of painting. Others may contend that the deep colors of Pinturicchio—the one responsible for the Piccolomini Library in Siena's Duomo—demand their fair share of attention.

Other than very minor damage done to the Duomo, the Palazzo dei Priori absorbed the brunt of the 1997 serial earthquakes that shook Umbria and were felt marginally in Perugia (see the Assisi section following). The scaffolding is down, but the fissures in the palazzo's ancient facade remain, with massive steel bolts securely holding things together, visible from both the outside and the inside.

✪ **Collegio del Cambio (Exchange Guild) & Collegio della Mercanzia (Merchants' Guild).** Corso Vannucci 25 and 15 (both part of the Palazzo dei Priori). ☎ **075-572-8599.** Admission to Collegio del Cambio 5,000L ($2.50); admission to Collegio della Mercanzia 2,000L ($1); joint admission 6,000L ($3). Mar–Oct and Dec 20–Jan 6 Mon–Sat 9am–12:30pm and 2:30–5:30pm, Sun 9am–12:30pm. Nov 1–Dec 19 and Jan 7–Feb 28 Tues–Sat 8am–2pm (Collegio della Mercanzia to 4:30pm Wed and Sat), Sun 9am–12:30pm.

The work of Perugino is the highlight of the small 15th-century **Collegio del Cambio,** the precursor of Perugia's commodities exchange. This was the seat of the Exchange Guild, whose affluent members chose Perugino, the finest artist of the time, to fresco their offices (1496 to 1500). These vibrant frescoes are his masterpieces—including scenes from the bible, the prophets, and female figures representing the virtues—and a vivid depiction of late 15th-century fashion. Perugino didn't overlook including his own self-portrait on a trompe-l'oeil column on the left wall as you enter. Pinturicchio and 17-year-old apprentice Raphael were said to have collaborated with him. The Exchange Guild's neighbors in the Merchant's Guild had their headquarters, the **Collegio della Mercanzia** (☎ **075-573-0366**), decorated in the 15th century with carved woodwork on the walls and ceiling.

Museo Storico di Perugina (Perugina Museum). Località San Sisto, Nestlé Italiana. ☎ **075-527-6796.** Admission free. Mon–Fri 9am–12:30pm and 2:30–5pm; Sat by appointment.

The Perugina chocolate industry is a Perugia success story. Founded in 1907 by two local families, it grew from strength to strength, heightened by the creation of the *bacio* (kiss) candy in 1922. It currently produces 200 million *baci* per year, to be found in stores worldwide (though the exported ones often lack the fortune cookies–style love-oriented quotes inside the wrapper). A popular runner-up in popularity is the gaily wrapped Easter eggs that are as much a tradition as the holiday itself. Opened in 1997 for the 90th anniversary of the manufacturer, the Perugina Museum explores the long history of the trademark. You can also visit the factory floor itself but you must book ahead for that. The rest of the year, you can buy Perugina goodies in just about any bar/cafe, though there's no Perugina outlet per se. A well-stocked choice is always the Caffè del Cambio (see "Great Deals on Dining," below), any of the other bar/cafes on Corso Vanucci, or the Perugina store on the east side of Piazza Italia.

AFFORDABLE PLACES TO STAY

Promhotel Umbria is a local travel agency that can book you into one of more than 80 hotels in Perugia and throughout Umbria (☎ **0678-62-033** toll free in Italy, or 075-500-2788; fax 075-500-2789; e-mail: promhotelumbia@krenet.it). For info about the city's **youth hostel,** call ☎ **075-572-2880.**

Also note that the **Hotel Eden,** Via Cesare Caporali 9, west off Piazza Italia, 06123 Perugia (☎ **075-572-8102;** fax 075-572-0342), offers 20 contemporary rooms with

TVs and phones for 60,000L ($30) single, 100,000L ($50) double, 135,000L ($68) triple, and 170,000L ($85) quad. And at the **Etruscan Chocohotel Perugia,** Via Campo di Marte 134, 06123 Perugia (☎ **075-583-7314;** fax 075-583-7314; e-mail: etruscan@chocohotel.it; www.chocohotel.it), all the 94 air-conditioned rooms have modern Italian-style furniture and large baths. The real draw, though, is staying in a "chocohotel": Each floor is dedicated to a type of chocolate (milk, dark, gianduia) and each room has a "chocodesk." The restaurant features a cocoa-based menu, and in the chocostore you can sample many concoctions. Nonchocolate amenities include a large roof deck with a panoramic view and a good-sized pool. Rates are 90,000L to 150,000L ($45 to $75) single and 140,000L to 200,000L ($70 to $100) double, and there's free parking.

✪ **Fortuna Perugia**. Via Bonazzi 19 (west of Piazza Italia), 06123 Perugia. ☎ **075-572-2845**. Fax 075-573-5040. www.umbriahotels.com. 34 units. A/C MINIBAR TV TEL. 120,000–140,000L ($60–$70) single; 180,000–200,000L ($90–$100) double. Rates include buffet breakfast. AE, DC, MC, V.

The charming Fortuna offers four-star accommodations at three-star rates. Beveled- and leaded-glass doors welcome you to this hotel where thoughtful service and details like silk- and dried-flower arrangements and white-lace doilies hint of a provincial inn. The coziness continues in most of the rooms, where a contemporary character prevails despite the floral bedspreads and upholstery and blond-wood headboards and tables. New management took over in 1998, and work is being done here and there—during which they discovered 18th-century frescoes on the third floor, making room 309 highly requested. For the guests who don't snag it, there's always the frescoed salon with a Murano chandelier—or rooms 408, 501, and 502, which require climbing a short flight of stairs but reward you with great countryside panoramas. Other rooms have views over the rooftops or the Umbrian valley. In warm weather, breakfast is served on the roof garden/terrace with stunning vistas; your cappuccino will never taste this good again.

La Rosetta. Piazza Italia 19 (at southern end of Corso Vanucci), 06121 Perugia. ☎/fax **075-572-0841**. www.perugiaonline.com/larosetta. 90 units. MINIBAR TV TEL. 145,000L ($73) single; 220,000L ($110) regular double, 278,000L ($139) superior double. Extra person 72,000L ($36). Rates include breakfast. AE, DC, MC, V. Parking 30,000L ($15) in garage with valet.

This favorite of the international music crowd that descends for the Umbria Jazz Festival began as a small inn in 1927 and has gradually expanded, explaining its almost labyrinthine layout and the variety in the quality and decor of the rooms. Some are quite grand with parquet floors and frescoed ceilings and others more modest with carpeting and more contemporary furnishings. But they're all peaceful and well maintained—this is a four-star hotel with rates that are comfortably low. An accommodating staff and perfect location augment its appeal, with an excellent (though slightly expensive) restaurant (open daily for lunch and dinner). Huge room 55, with a spectacular trompe-l'oeil frescoed ceiling vault and view into the medieval courtyard (beware noisy guests returning late), carries a special splurge price tag of 303,000L ($152).

Priori. Via dei Priori (west off Corso Vannucci), 06123 Perugia. ☎ **075-572-3378**. Fax 075-572-3213. www.perugia.com/hotelpriori. E-mail: hotelpriori@perugia.com. 56 units. TEL. 100,000L ($50) single; 140,000L ($70) double; 190,000L ($95) triple; 230,000L ($115) quad. Rates include buffet breakfast. Ask about discounts for stays of 2 nights and longer (not available during holidays or Jazz Festival). MC, V. Parking 20,000–30,000L ($10–$15). Closed Dec 22–30.

Three short blocks down Via dei Priori and behind the Palazzo dei Priori, this modernized hotel still enjoys the fruits of a 1995 renovation. Half the spacious rooms with terra-cotta floors overlook San Filippo Neri, the lucky ones overlook the hotel terrace and the valley beyond. The terrace is surprisingly spacious, given the typical hill-town problems of limited space. When weather permits, breakfast here beneath the white canvas umbrellas. TVs are available on request for 10,000L ($5) per day, and a new annex in an adjoining historic palazzo means five new rooms with air-conditioning at 30,000L ($15) extra per day (request on booking).

GREAT DEALS ON DINING

In addition to the restaurants below, stop by some of the lovely local cafes, such as the **Caffè Sandri,** Corso Vanucci 32; **Caffè Ferrari,** Corso Vanucci 43; and **Caffè del Cambio,** Corso Vanucci 29. They're all reasonably priced central spots for a light lunch, offering sandwiches and even primi for 5,000L to 11,000L ($2.50 to $6) at the bar or at tables indoors and out. Caffè Sandri is the local favorite, small but rich with atmosphere, its wood-paneled 19th-century interior cramped but cozy. It quadruples in seating capacity when warm weather permits it to set up outdoor tables in the middle of the corso's pedestrian catwalk. The new meeting spot in town, the **Caffè di Perugia,** Via Mazzini 10–14, off the Corso Vanucci, is elegantly housed in a medieval palazzo, comfortably looking like it has always been there. Fixed-price lunches include a primi plus vegetable side dish (16,000L/$8), or you can spend half that at the busy bar for a sandwich and drink.

Food fans should make sure to have at least one casual meal at the **Enoteca Provinciale,** Via Ulisse Rocchi 18 (☎ **075-572-4824**), where substantial bruschette and platters of salads or regional cheeses and salami are just a savory side; the draw here is the 5 to 10 red and white regional wines available by the glass in a beautifully restored 13th-century palazzo. It's open Monday to Saturday 10am to 9:30pm, and Sunday 10am to 3pm.

✪ **Da Cesarino.** Piazza IV Novembre 4–5 (west of the Fontana Maggiore). ☎ **075-572-8974.** Reservations recommended. Primi 13,000L ($7); secondi 13,000–20,000L ($7–$10). AE, DC, MC, V. Thurs–Tues 12:30–3pm and 7:30–11pm. UMBRIAN.

Cesarino's new location is easy to find on the piazza anchored by the Fontana Maggiore, with preferred outdoor tables offering a view of this most characteristic corner of time-locked Perugia. The cooking is a hats-off salute to the bounty and wonder of simple home-style cooking—traditional *cucina umbra* at its best. Whatever today's special pasta is, order it. If you eat indoors, you'll be privy to free cooking lessons if seated near the open kitchen where white-capped signoras roll out fresh pasta while a white-aproned man tends to the open hearth and its crackling and sizzling meats on a spit.

✪ **La Taverna.** Via delle Streghe 8 (off Corso Vanucci). ☎ **075-572-4128.** Reservations recommended. Primi 10,000–20,000L ($5–$10); secondi 18,000–28,000L ($9–$14). AE, DC, MC, V. Tues–Sun 12:30–3:30pm and 7:30–9pm. UMBRIAN.

The location of this eatery in the cantina of a 14th-century palazzo reached via a dark stepped alley curiously called the Street of the Witches is too much to resist. Surprisingly, the space is bright and welcoming, even elegant with waiters in jackets and white ankle-length aprons hovering over candlelit tables beneath high barrel-vaulted brick ceilings. The menu is as traditional as it is innovative, the latter half hinting of the Umbrian chef's experience abroad—in Florida, no less. The trappings of La Taverna may strike you as a splurge choice, but unless you let loose with any of the discerning wine list's better options and overindulge in the justifiably well-known dessert cart, the cost of a lovely and romantic dinner here needn't set you back.

Pizzeria il Cantinone. Via Ritorta 6 (west of the Fontana Maggiore). ☎ **075-573-4430.** Reservations suggested. Primi 10,000–14,000L ($5–$7); secondi 18,000–25,000L ($9–$13); pizze 6,000–12,000L ($3–$6). AE, MC, V. Wed–Mon noon–3pm and 7:30pm–midnight. PIZZERIA/UMBRIAN.

If you're in search of something casual and inexpensive in the area of Corso Vannucci or Piazza IV Novembre, wander down the narrow street west of the Fontana Maggiore and, where the pedestrian traffic flows right, look to the left, where you'll find this popular pizzeria in a cool brick-vaulted medieval setting. Despite its central location, the prices are kept moderate while the lure of their pizzas (evenings only) keeps the place full. There's a full menu of local specialties as well, though the steady patrons are pizza devotees who return for the *pizza alla gorgonzola e porcini* (made with Gorgonzola and mushrooms) or any one of the dozens of others. There's even a no-smoking room.

Ristorante Vecchia Perusia. Via Ulisse Rocchi 9 (north of Piazza IV Novembre), Perugia. ☎ **075-572-5900.** Reservations suggested. Primi 9,000–16,000L ($4.50–$8); secondi 13,000–18,000L ($7–$9). No credit cards. Mon–Sat 12:30–2:30 and 7–11pm. UMBRIAN.

There are just 10 tables in this homey trattoria where the aroma from the open kitchen is enough to make you order one of everything. If you don't have an Umbrian grandmother, come here for the genuine *cucina umbra* you've been missing (though not Grandma's smile; the service leaves *much* to be desired). Every day a new *pasta fresca* appears (look for the *tagliatelle con porcini freschi,* made with fresh mushrooms), but happy habitués seem to go with the *crepe alla perusia* (crêpes spread with four cheeses and ham, rolled, smothered with mushroom-cream sauce, and baked). The menu also offers traditional Umbrian game (*faraona*/pheasant, *coniglio*/rabbit) and the simplicity of a grilled pork or veal chop.

A SIDE TRIP FOR CERAMICS

Known since the Middle Ages as a ceramic center, the tiny town of **Deruta** lies 20km (12.6 mi.) south of Perugia by car (or take the S3 bus; there are a few daily 30-minute buses but no train service—check the tourist office for the schedule and make sure not to miss the last bus back). Deruta's embarrassment of choices can be mind boggling, for you'll find store after store, particularly along Via Tiberina. Making ceramics since the 15th century (the city's history of ceramic production is recorded as far back as the 12th century), the family of Ubaldo Grazia guarantees one of the best selections of original Deruta patterns, some from the 16th century and some refreshingly modern and unusual. And yes, you probably did see his wares in Saks or Neiman Marcus. Credit cards aren't accepted, but personal checks and traveler's checks are. The store is at Via Tiberina 16 (☎ **075-971-0201;** fax 075-972-018). The **Museo Regionale della Ceramica (Regional Museum of Ceramics),** Largo San Francesco (☎ **075-971-1000**), houses a precious collection of Deruta ceramics of various periods from the Middle Ages to the 1930s. April to September, it's open daily 10am to 1pm and 3:30 to 7pm; October to March, hours are Wednesday to Monday 10am to 1pm and 3:30 to 7pm (check for shorter hours off-season). Admission is 5,000L ($2.50).

7 Assisi & the Basilica di San Francesco

190km (120 mi.) SE of Florence, 26km (16 mi.) SE of Perugia, 177km (111.5 mi.) NE of Rome, 48km (30 mi.) N of Spoleto

More than 700 years—and countless billions of pilgrims and tourists—have passed since St. Francis lived and died in the small hill town of **Assisi,** with its muted pink-and-white stone, sitting on the wooded slopes of Mt. Subasio. It's Umbria's most visited city and yet, despite the mania of shops selling St. Francis everything—from ashtrays and pot holders to embroidered tea towels and glow-in-the-dark rosary beads—the spirit of the young barefoot monk who forsook these very material goods to preach poverty, chastity, and obedience lives on. His spirit may seem diminished at times when unparalleled crowds and heat reach their peak, but it's easy to find it again, in a quiet moment at the saint's crypt below the Lower Basilica or during a delightful walk to the shaded serenity of the unspoiled hermitage outside the city's medieval walls. The universality of his humanity and love for nature and the animal kingdom transcend all nationalities and religions, and Francis is often held as a medieval flower child, an environmentalist of the Middle Ages who wrote the first poems in the Italian language. If the church had to create a figure that would endure the last millennium and go forward bravely into the next and be embraced by so many, it couldn't have outdone this disarmingly simple character who lived to love God and all those who inhabited this planet—a welcomed departure from the doom-and-gloom strictures of the Dark Ages.

Born in 1182 to a local well-to-do family of textile merchants, Francis renounced his social status and youthful carousing only after a number of apparitions and visions. He traveled on foot through Italy, Spain, and Egypt, a revolutionary spirit who took the Roman Catholic church back to the basics when the papacy was rotten with corruption. Dante compared him to John the Baptist; his fame grew quickly beyond the confines of Umbria and even Italy. In 1210, he founded an order of mendicant monks that became known thereafter as the Franciscans. Within 15 years, there was a growing community of 5,000 who followed the barefoot asceticism of *Il Poverello* (the Poor One), and he enjoyed great veneration and acceptance in his lifetime. In 1224, he was the first ever to receive the "stigmata" wounds in his hands, feet, and side at a hilltop retreat in Tuscany called La Verna—mirroring the same wounds inflicted on Jesus Christ during his Crucifixion. His friendship with the lovely Chiara (Clare), a local girl of a minor noble family who followed him, would soon follow by her founding the Second Order of St. Francis, the nuns known as the Sorelle Clarisse, the Poor Sisters of St. Clare (more simply known as the Poor Clares), in 1212 when she was just 17; together they pushed this sleepy Umbrian town unto the church's center stage, where it has remained ever since. Today it's the largest of all Catholic orders and St. Francis, made patron saint of all Italy in 1939, is the most beloved of Christendom's galaxy of saints.

St. Francis's spirit somehow survives the unashamed commercialization of the town. Young groups of Italian and European students who come for seminars; art lovers who descend on the Basilica of St. Francis for its glorious frescoes by Giotto, Cimabue, Simone Martini, and the Lorenzetti; and pilgrims from the earth's four corners who come to pay homage to one of the holiest men to have walked this planet find in these narrow back streets something of the town as it was in the saint's own time. As a former Roman stronghold, Assisi reached its medieval zenith in the years surrounding the lives of Francis and Clare. Much of what you see today is true to its 13th-century origins, and the city, with its patrician palazzi made of a local pink-tinged stone, is handsomely preserved.

Atheists, agnostics, and devotees alike continue to visit Assisi as a site of pilgrimage, artistic appreciation, and cultural curiosity; during peak months, numbers are legion. Moderate-priced accommodations are very good (and the restaurants serving Umbrian specialties even better) and numerous, but booking ahead during busy months is almost obligatory. Things quiet down in the evening—the majority of pilgrims and religious groups usually lodge outside town in the larger roadside hotels—but you may want to move on after the day or two spent seeing the sites.

Umbria Shook, Rattled & Rolled

On September 26, 1997, serial earthquakes (5.7 and 5.6 on the Richter scale) with the epicenter just outside Assisi violently shook this otherwise serene corner of Umbria. More than 13,000 Umbrians were left homeless, and the structure that sustained the most damage was Assisi's crown jewel, the Basilica di San Francesco. During an a second quake, two monks and two inspectors were killed by the 2 tons of debris that crashed from the basilica's vaulted ceiling, and entire sections of priceless frescoes—some of the world's most important—were destroyed. Pope John Paul visited in January 1998, encouraging the area's residents to bear up "in a Franciscan spirit" and heal the wounds of their hearts and of their homeland. Work began immediately, and much of the scaffolding is already down from repair work that has been completed on all but the most damaged sites (you'll continue to see scaffolded buildings throughout Umbria in the years to come). The Basilica di San Francesco actually managed to reopen for the Jubilee Year 2000 (a minor miracle in itself), with the only major "victims" some of the lesser ceiling frescoes by Cimabue—almost all of Giotto's fabulous work was saved.

ESSENTIALS

GETTING THERE   By Train   From **Perugia** there are about 20 trains daily (25–30 min.; 3,200L/$1.60). From **Florence** there are 11 daily Rome-bound trains, from which you transfer at Terontola/Cortona for Assisi (2–3 hr. traveling time, often with long layovers; 16,500L/$8). Coming from **Rome,** nine daily trains make the connection through Foligno (2–3 hr. total; 16,500L/$8).

The **station** (☎ 075-804-0272) is in the modern valley town of Santa Maria degli Angeli, about 5km (3 mi.) from Assisi, with bus connections to Assisi every 20 minutes (1,200L/60¢); or you can take a **taxi** for 18,000L to 20,000L ($9 to $10), plus 1,000L (50¢) per bag.

By Bus   Eight **APM/Sit** buses (☎ 075-573-1707 or 0743-212-211) run daily from **Perugia** (1 hr.; 5,000L/$2.50). They also run about five buses from **Gubbio. Sulga** (☎ 075-500-9641) runs two buses daily from **Rome**'s Tiburtina Station (3 hr.; 30,000L/$15), and one daily from Piazza Adua in **Florence** (2½ hr.; 25,000L/$13). In Assisi, you can get tickets in any *tabacchi* or at the tourist office. Most buses leave Assisi from Piazza Matteotti, northeast of Piazza del Comune, though most also pass by the lower half of Piazza San Pietro (at the bottom of the big traffic curve) at the other end of town.

By Car   From Perugia, head southeast on SS3; at the junction of Route 147 follow signs east for Assisi. It's a half-hour drive. The entire historic center is closed to traffic, but traffic police will let you drop off your bags at a hotel; check with hotel for special agreements they may have with nearest municipal parking lot.

VISITOR INFORMATION   The **tourist office** (☎ 075-812-534; fax 075-813-727) has been hop-scotched around to different offices on Piazza del Comune ever since the quake, though it hopes by 2001 to take up residence in its new permanent seat at nos. 22–23. Ask about its list of Case Religiose di Ospitalità, 17 local religious convents, monasteries, and religious-run hostelries that offer doubles for 50,000L to 100,000L ($25 to $50). The office is open Monday to Friday 8am to 2pm and 3:30 to 6:30pm, Saturday 9am to 1pm and 3:30 to 6:30pm, and Sunday 9am to 1pm.

FESTIVALS & MARKETS   The **Settimana Santa (Holy Week)** that precedes Easter is understandably commemorated with numerous processions between churches, including evocative night processions by torchlight. The feast day of the ✪ **Calendimaggio** is the year's largest event and is celebrated during a 3-day period the first week of May (starting the first Thursday after May 1). The entire town turns out in elaborate medieval costume to reenact the rivalry between two upper and lower factions of town that can be traced back to the 1300s; there are competitions of concerts, crossbows, and flag-throwing, to name a few.

Oddly, **San Rufino** (after whom the Duomo is named) and not St. Francis is the patron saint of Assisi, and his feast day is celebrated on August 11 with a procession and crossbow contest in medieval costume. It's followed by the feast day of **Santa Chiara (St. Clare)** on August 12. On October 3 and 4, the **Festa di San Francesco** commemorates the saint's death; as patron saint of Italy, he's duly honored with great pageantry.

The yearly **Assisi Antiquariato antiques fair** is held for 2 weeks in the end of April and the beginning of May in the suburb of Bastia. And a **weekly market** fills Piazza Matteotti every Saturday morning.

EXPLORING ASSISI

Mt. Subasio is a protected regional park and offers an extensive network of footpaths that attracts do-it-yourself trekkers and mountain bikers. A map called **Sentieri di Mt. Subasio (Footpaths of Mt. Subasio)** is sometimes available at the tourist office. If it's out of stock, look for two alternatives maps that are usually on sale in local shops: the map put out by **C.A.I. (Club Alpino Italiano)** for 9,000L ($4.50) or **Kompass** 10,000L ($5). Half-hearted walkers who are happy with a brisk amble but nothing more taxing should consider the Eremo delle Carceri (see below).

Piazza del Comune is the heart of Assisi, and much of what you see dates from the 12th to the 14th century and the very days of economic prosperity that Francis and Clare eschewed. Its most ancient component is the white ✪ **Tempio della Minerva (Temple of Minerva),** the majestic Corinthian-columned temple on its north side that dates as far back as the 1st century B.C.; so perfect in classical design and proportion, "one could never stop looking at its facade," wrote an enthralled Goethe during his 18th-century Italian journey. Its most recent reincarnation is that of a baroque church that provides, at most, a pew and a cool moment for reflection. Facing the temple and dominating the south side of the piazza is the **Pinacoteca** (closed due to heavy earthquake damage, though admission used to be 6,000L/$3, with it closed Mondays), the town's unremarkable picture gallery, housed in the 14th-century Palazzo dei Priori. Check the tourist office for its new hours when it reopens.

Beneath the flagstoned piazza, and unbeknownst to the flocks of tourists that fill it, sit the remains of the ancient Roman Forum. Glimpses of its ongoing renovation are part of the draw of the generally overlooked **Museo Civico e Foro Romano (Civic Museum and Roman Forum),** entrance on Via Portica off the western edge of Piazza del Comune (☎ **075-813-053**), and its collection of Etruscan and Roman artifacts;

A Church Warning

With the exception of the Basilica di San Francesco, all **churches** in Assisi are open 7am to noon and 2pm to sunset. There's a strict **dress code** for the Basilicas of San. Francesco and Santa Chiara; entrance is forbidden to those showing bare knees, shoulders, or midriffs (so no shorts, miniskirts, or tank tops).

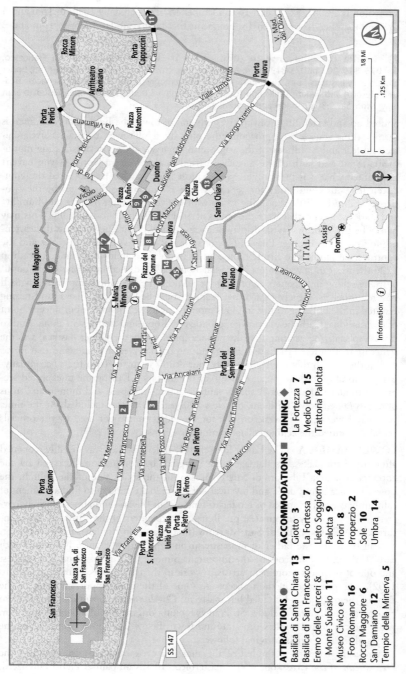

Assisi

ATTRACTIONS ●
Basilica di Santa Chiara **13**
Basilica di San Francesco **1**
Eremo delle Carceri &
  Monte Subasio **11**
Museo Civico e
  Foro Romano **16**
Rocca Maggiore **6**
San Damiano **12**
Tempio della Minerva **5**

ACCOMMODATIONS ■
Giotto **3**
La Fortessa **7**
Lieto Soggiorno **4**
Palotta **9**
Priori **8**
Properzio **2**
Sole **10**
Umbra **14**

DINING ◆
La Fortezza **7**
Medio Evo **15**
Trattoria Pallotta **9**

ITALY
Rome
Assisi

Information ⓘ

1/8 Mi
.125 Km

San Francesco

Rocca Minore
Porta Cappuccini
Via Carceri
Porta Nuova
V. Mad. del Olivo

Rocca Maggiore
Porta Perlici
Anfiteatro Romano
Piazza Matteotti
Via Villamena
Viale Umberto
Porta di
Via Perlici

Porta S. Giacomo
Via Metastasio
Via San Francesco
Via Fontebella
Via Frate Elia
Piazza Unità d'Italia
Porta S. Francesco
Piazza S. Pietro
Porta S. Pietro
San Pietro
Via del Fosso Cupo
Via Borgo San Pietro
Viale Marconi

Via S. Paolo
V. Seminario
Via Fortini
V. Brizi
Via Ancaiani
Via A. Cristofani
Via Apollinare
Via Vittorio Emanuele II

S. Maria Minerva
Piazza del Comune
Vicolo D. Castello
Piazza S. Rufino
Duomo
Via S. Gabriele dell'Addolorata
Via S. Rufino
Corso Mazzini
Piazza S. Chiara
Santa Chiara
Via Sant'Agnese
T. Ch. Nuova
Porta Moiano
Porta del Sementone
Via Vittorio Emanuele II
Via Borgo Aretino

SS 147

Piazza Sup. di San Francesco
Piazza Inf. di San Francesco

283

admission is 4,000L/$2. March 16 to October 15, it's open daily 10am to 1pm and 3 to 7pm; October 16 to March 15, hours are Tuesday to Sunday 10am to 1pm and 2 to 5pm.

✪ **Basilica di San Francesco (Basilica of St. Francis).** Piazza di San Francesco. ☎ **075-819-001** or 075-819-0084. Admission free. Lower church daily 6:15am–6pm; upper church daily 8:30am–6pm. Sun morning visits allowed only for those attending services. Treasury (Tesoro) and Perkins Collection (Collezione Perkins) 3,000L ($1.50); open Easter to Sept only, Mon–Sat 9:30am–noon and 2–6pm.

Shored up and extending from the western end of town, the Basilica of St. Francis is the first thing you see on approaching this pink-hued hill town. It was a massive architectural feat and is still one of the engineering marvels and most outstanding monuments to art and faith of the medieval period in the Western world. If you haven't pinpointed what it is that bothers you, it most likely is what has bothered the Franciscan religious community for centuries: The commanding figure cut by the two-tiered basilica has little if nothing to do with the vows of utter poverty and humility and stark asceticism that were the tenets of St. Francis's back-to-basics life. This may hardly be the Vatican's lavish display of extravagance, but it's nevertheless disheartening to know that Brother Elias of Cortona, one of Francis's earliest disciples and the controversial monk who firmly took control in the years following Francis's death in 1226 (he was canonized almost immediately in 1228), cashed in on the saint's popularity by selling indulgences across Europe (Brother Leone, who sympathized with Il Poverello's beliefs, futilely argued that Francis would be horrified). Elias's fund-raising resulted in the building of this impious monument to wealth and importance, a point of international Catholic pilgrimage seconded by Rome and Bethlehem alone. And so it was especially devastating that the basilica (particularly the Upper Basilica) was the structure that suffered the most damage during the 1997 earthquakes and that it was within the church that the region's only four deaths occurred (two friars accompanying two local officials who came to survey the damage). During the unexpected second earthquake, the Upper Basilica's vaulted ceilings collapsed and more than 2 tons of debris rained down on them, priceless 700-year-old frescos included. At the time, you may have seen this scene on TV, for the video equipment used by the officials actually captured the ceiling collapse and their deaths.

LOWER BASILICA   The Lower (and slightly older) Basilica was speedily reopened after the earthquakes, its damage only marginal by comparison. Reached by the entrance in Piazza Inferiore di San Francesco on the south side of the church, the Lower Basilica is low, dark, and mystical—if you're lucky enough to find a moment of calm in between the arrival of fender-to-fender tour buses—and almost entirely covered with frescoes by the greatest pre-Renaissance painters of the 13th and 14th centuries. The ✪ **Cappella di San Martino** (first chapel on the left), dedicated to St. Martin of Tours, the father of monasticism in 4th-century France, is covered with early 14th-century frescoes by the important Simone Martini of Siena. The earliest and one of the most prominent artists to work in the church was Cimabue (1240 to 1302), whose frescoes in the transept are some of the most important here. To the right of the main altar, his faded but masterful ✪ *Madonna, Child and Angels* (also known as the *Maestà*) includes St. Francis looking on, the popular depiction of him you'll see duplicated endless times around town. Below Cimabue's paintings are the tombs of five of Francis's original followers.

Across the transept to the left of the altar is a cycle of frescoes surrounding the *Deposition of the Cross,* one of the masterpieces of Tuscan painter Pietro Lorenzetti, a contemporary of Simone Martini from Siena. But the frescoes creating one of art history's greatest controversies are those attributed to Cimabue's most famous student,

Giotto (1226 to 1337)—both Cimabue and Giotto worked extensively in the Upper Basilica as well. In the early 1900s, most art historians had decided it was nameless followers or fellow apprentices of Giotto, and not the master himself, who had covered much of both basilicas with cycles of frescoes. His work, they believed, was far too mature for the 20-something student who hadn't yet proven himself in his epochal work covering Perugia's Arena Chapel; these frescoes depicted an expression and emotion that broke with the static icons of the rigid Byzantine school and heralded the onset of the Renaissance. The 1995 completion of the restoration of the **Cappella della Maddalena (Chapel of St. Mary Magdalen),** the third and final one to the right of the nave close to the altar, provided the confirmation of Giotto's authorship (1307) in the eyes of many Italian scholars. To keep everyone happy, authorship is still attributed to "Giotto and workshop." Vespers are sung by the friars in the Lower Basilica Monday to Saturday, at 5pm in summer and 6pm in winter.

CRYPT   From the Lower Basilica halfway up the nave you can reach the Crypt (free admission) where the saint's body wasn't discovered until 1818; a new and typically simple stone tomb was built in the early 1900s. Four of his closest followers are buried together with St. Francis.

TESORO (TREASURY) & COLLEZIONE PERKINS (PERKINS COLLECTION)   From another entrance in the Lower Basilica (behind the main altar to the right) you can reach this collection, where glass cases display the likes of chalices and silver objects, but of most note are the saint's original gray patchwork sackcloth (the brown tunic was adopted by the order much later), the white tunic worn during the last year of his life, a knotted rope belt, and worn slippers. On a more somber note is the stone upon which he rested his head in his coffin and the suede cloth used to cover his stigmata. The Perkins Collection is a small but rich collection bequeathed by an American philanthropist with some surprisingly important Tuscan Renaissance artworks.

UPPER BASILICA   From the south transept of the Lower Basilica, stairs lead to the Upper Basilica (1230 to 1253), built on the Romanesque framework of the lower church. Where the lower spaces encouraged awe, contemplation, and meditation, the upper reaches of the airy Gothic basilica are another experience entirely. Tall, bathed in light, it was created, it would seem, as the blank canvas on which Giotto was to create the masterpiece frescoes depicting the ✪ *The Life of St. Francis* (1296 to 1304). These are the highlights of the basilica and generally escaped the earthquakes' wrath intact. Twenty-eight scenes (the last four not attributed to Giotto) unfold left to right beginning in the transept. One of the most famous and charming of panels is the *Sermon to the Birds* found on the entrance wall, underlining the saint's tenet that all nature is the reflection of God. In many of the narrations, you'll see medieval Assisi illustrated much as you see it now, starting with the first panel's *Homage in Piazza del Comune.*

Giotto was believed to be just 29 when he began this cycle of frescoes, already a longtime lay follower of St. Francis. He seemed to particularly embrace the message of St. Francis, whose love of man and warmth of expression is reflected in Giotto's radical break from the lifeless images of the Byzantines' icons. The single undivided nave was meant to accommodate the masses, and Giotto's extensive pictorial narrations were meant to educate them about Assisi's native son while attempting to express his love for nature and humanity. Francis broke with the traditional excesses of the medieval papacy as Giotto revolutionized the art world with his break from the lifeless Byzantine order. Other highlights are the 15th-century **choir,** made of 105 inlaid stalls. The choir's central "throne" was reserved for the pope, the only papal throne outside St. Peter's Located behind and above in the left transept is a cycle of time- (and not earthquake-) damaged cycles by Cimabue dominated by his dramatic ✪ *Crucifixion,* the pigments oxidized by time into a sort of photo negative fresco.

Ermeo delle Carceri & Monte Subasio. Via Ermeo delle Carceri (4km/2.5 mi. east of the Porta Cappuccini). ☎ **075-812-301.** Admission free. Ermeo delle Carceri daily 6:30am–7pm. Walk or take a taxi from Piazza Santa Chiara for about 17,000-20,000L ($9-$10).

St. Francis and his followers spiritually "imprisoned" themselves in prayer at this isolated retreat on the ilex- and oak-wooded slope of Monte Subasio. They lived in tiny *carceri* (cells) naturally carved out of the stone centuries before the extant friary was built. A timeworn holm oak, thought to be at least 1,000 years old, still stands supported by metal crutches near the saint's cave where he meditated and prayed. The gnarled tree is said to have shaded Francis and the birds that gathered to listen to his sermons; they once flew off in the four cardinal directions, symbolizing how the Franciscans would one day leave Assisi to bring the word of Francis to all corners of the world.

Leave behind the crowds in the basilica and the town's tourist shops; it's an easy 1-hour walk from the town's eastern gate, the Porta Cappuccini (leaving from the Rocca Minore north of the Porta isn't recommended as the pathway isn't as clearly marked) on a signposted paved road past cypresses and with wide-open views used by pedestrians and cars. A handful of friars still live at the retreat established by St. Bernard of Siena (who lived here after Francis from 1438 to 1440) and act as guides; a donation is appreciated as the friars live by alms alone. A visit here better conveys the spirit and serenity of St. Francis than the cavernous basilica built by his followers.

Basilica di Santa Chiara. Piazza Santa Chiara. ☎ **075-812-282.** Admission free. Daily 7am–noon and 2pm–dusk.

St. Clare died surrounded by her nascent following of nuns in the Convent of San Damiano down below on August 12, 1253; just 12 years later this pink-and-white basilica made from local marble was dedicated to her and became the home of the Poor Clares (the small community is currently living in Perugia until earthquake repairs are finished). The interior is Spartan, due to the 17th-century whitewashing of elaborate frescoes by orders of a German bishop who attempted to discourage tourism and the temptations it would supply the nuns. The **Oratorio del Crocifisso (Oratory of the Crucifix)** houses a few relics of the saint and the 12th-century **Crucifix of San Damiano** that spoke to a young St. Francis in 1209, informing him of his calling. It's indefinitely closed to the public while earthquake repairs continue. The crypt containing the remains of St. Clare is open. An anonymous crucifix older than the church itself hangs over the main altar. The adjacent small **San Giorgio** church predates the basilica; it was the site of Francis's early schooling and where his remains awaited the completion of the basilica upon his death. On the basilica's terracelike piazza, lovely views of the surrounding countryside and Umbrian plains draw locals and visitors at any hour of the day, particularly during sunset hours.

San Damiano. Via San Damiano (1.5km/1 mi. from the Porta Nuova). ☎ **075-812-273.** Admission free. Daily 10am–12:30pm and 2–6pm.

If you stand alone amid the olive groves and wildflowers, in the serenity of the Spoleto Valley, this quiet spot will easily evoke the time and atmosphere of a young Francis who came here (the church dates from the 11th century) to escape the wrath of his father. It was in this church in 1209 that a wooden crucifix told a restless world-weary 27-year-old Francis to "Go and repair the Church," referring to the decadent papacy and corrupt monastic orders (the crucifix is now housed in Santa Chiara, above). Francis took the orders literally, however, and sold his father's textile stock and offered the money to St. Damian's priest, who threw the money pouch back at him. In 1210, he found the approval of Pope Innocent III to create his own order of mendicant monks and, in 1212, a second order for women. St. Clare later lived here at San Damiano as abbess, her Order of Poor Clares moving up to the newly constructed Basilica di Santa Chiara after her death; you can visit the simple 13th-century convent's dormitory where a cross marks the spot of the saint's death in 1226.

The cloisters and refectory still have the original tables and benches where the nuns shared their meager meals. St. Francis visited just once during Clare's stay here and is said to have composed his famous *Canticle of the Creatures* here. To get here: From Piazza Santa Chiara or the Basilica di Santa Chiara, take Via Borgo Aretino and at the Porta Nuova (the eastern gate to the city) take a right and head south down a steep road to San Damiano following the signs. It's 20 to 30 minutes downhill; a road for vehicle traffic runs parallel to a pedestrian road. Taxis that have dropped passengers off are usually lingering about to take you back uphill for 20,000L to 30,000L ($10 to $15) one way.

AFFORDABLE PLACES TO STAY

Advance hotel reservations are a must. If the following places are full and you need help finding a room, contact the **Consorzio Alberghi ed Operatori Turistiche,** Via A. Cristofani 22a (☎ **075-816-566;** fax 075-812-315; www.krenet.it/assisihotels) or Viale Marconi (☎ **075-813-599**), a kind of clearinghouse for local hotels that'll help you stick to your budget by booking a hotel category you request with no fee involved.

Unless you have no choice or it's all the same to you, make sure you insist on being in the historic center of town and not the satellite town of Santa Maria degli Angeli (which always tries to pass itself off as *Assisi centro* to unwitting tourists) down near the train station or, worse yet, the town of Bastia, where tour buses usually put up their groups 4km (2.5 mi.) outside town. If the town is full (or closed—a number of hotels and restaurants close up in January and February), don't overlook using Perugia as your base.

With an average of seven rooms at about 85,000L to 110,000L ($43 to $55), a number of small hotels in the center fill up fast and are often closed in winter. Try **La Fortezza,** Vicolo dei Fortezza 19b (☎ **075-812-418;** www.assind.perugia.it/hotel/fortezza); **Lieto Soggiorno,** Via A. Fortini (☎ **075-816-191**); **Palotta,** Via San Rufino 6 (☎/fax **075-812-649**); and **Properzio,** Via San Francesco 38 (☎ **075-813-188;** fax 075-815-201).

Giotto. Via Fontebella 41 (just east of Piazza San Francesco), 06082 Assisi. ☎ **075-812-209.** Fax 075-816-479. E-mail: htlgiotto@tin.it. 85 units. A/C MINIBAR TV TEL. 165,000L ($83) single; 252,000L ($126) double. Up to 30% discount Jan 7–Mar 31 and Nov 15–Dec 20. Rates include breakfast. AE, DC, MC, V. Free garage parking.

This stately hotel, Assisi's largest, is in the western part of town not far from the Basilica of St. Francis. It has five floors built into the side of the hill with wonderful views from almost all its rooms. If you ask when booking, the staff will do its best to hold one of the five rooms sharing a large terra-cotta terrace. A wonderful outdoor breakfast terrace comes with the same expansive view that includes the Romanesque San Pietro below. The rooms are nice in an old-fashioned way, with brass headboards and baths that'll soon need a facelift but are fine for the moment. Gracious aspects of its public areas—open landings of patterned gray-and-white marble tiles, wrought-iron handrails, and Persian runners on the wide marble steps—are reminiscent of better days.

Priori. Corso Mazzini 15 (1 block east of the Piazza del Comune), 06081 Assisi. ☎ **075-812-237.** Fax 075-816-804. www.assisihotel.net. E-mail: hpriori@edisons.it. 34 units. A/C TV TEL. 132,000–148,000L ($66–$74) single; 190,000–210,000L ($95–$105) standard double, 250,000–270,000L ($125–$135) superior double; triple and quad rates on request. Rates include buffet breakfast. Ask about off-season discounts. AE, DC, MC, V. Parking nearby 14,000–21,000L ($7–$11). May close Jan–Feb.

A stay in this 16th-century palazzo with stained-glass windows will take you back in time when local families made their fortunes in trade and textiles and lived like royalty. Royal rates are something this book avoids, but I find the lovely rooms in this hotel housed in a landmark building to be more than reasonable; spend the extra lire and book one of the 10 superior *camere dei Priori*, replete with 19th-century frescoed ceilings. Persian runners and valuable antiques and handsome prints decorate the public rooms and guest rooms, all of which have been refreshed by a 1998 renovation. This is the type of character and history you'd never be able to afford in a similar hotel in Rome or Florence.

Sole. Corso Mazzini 35 (between Piazza del Comune and Santa Chiara), 06081 Assisi (PG). ☎ **075-812-373.** Fax 075-813-706. www.umbria.org/hotel/sole. 37 units, 35 with bathroom. TEL. 75,000L ($38) single; 120,000L ($69) double; 140,000L ($80) triple. Pensione plan available. Breakfast 12,000L ($7). AE, DC, MC. V. Open year-round (restaurant closed in winter).

This is one of the loveliest family-run hotels for these prices I've seen in Umbria. Its excellent location is enhanced by the charm of the freshly redone rooms on the top two floors and those across the street in the annex (even those not yet refurbished are nice enough). There's an elevator in the annex, though not in the principal building, yet I prefer the latter, whose spacious rooms have generally been done with more charm. Furnishings range from contemporary to antique (and antique-inspired) wrought-iron painted beds and thoughtfully chosen framed prints. The family's restaurant, the Hostaria Ceppo della Catena, is set in theatrically stone-vaulted rooms in a 15th-century palazzo above the restaurant, where half board can be arranged (85,000L/$50 per person, double occupancy); open March to October.

✪ **Umbra.** Via dei Archi 6 (15 paces off the west end of Piazza del Comune), 06081 Assisi (PG). ☎ **075-812-240.** Fax 075-813-653. www.caribusiness.it/carifo/az/hotelumbra. 25 units. A/C MINIBAR TV TEL. 125,000L ($63) single; 160,000L–215,000L ($91–$123) double. Rates include breakfast. AE, DC, MC, V. Parking 18,000L ($11) in garage. Closed Jan–Easter; restaurant closed Sun.

The majority of this three-star hotel dates from the 15th century, but the basement's laundry and kitchen area boast ancient Roman foundations. Three generations of a local family have proudly run this hotel, known for its well-respected alfresco restaurant (fixed-price 35,000L/$23; closed all day Sunday and Wednesday at lunch). Patrons dine in a shaded garden patio where birdsong easily reminds you that St. Francis was born just blocks away and lamp-lit dinners are no less romantic. Most rooms are highlighted with well-worn 18th- and 19th-century antiques. When booking, ask for one of the rooms overlooking the Umbrian Valley; a few are double blessed with balconies. The main square is just paces away, but it's easy to feel removed from the pilgrimage jostle.

GREAT DEALS ON DINING

✪ **La Fortezza.** Vicolo della Fortezza/Piazza del Comune (up the stairs near the Via San Rufino end). ☎ **075-812-418.** www.assind.perugia.it/hotel/fortezza. Reservations recommended. Primi 9,000L–15,000L ($4.50–$8); secondi 11,000L–20,000L ($6–$10); fixed-price menu 25,000–38,000L ($13–$19) without wine. MC, V. Fri–Wed 12:30–2:30pm and 7:30–9:30pm. UMBRIAN/CREATIVE.

Up a stepped alley from Piazza del Comune, this lovely restaurant has been family run for over 40 years and is prized for its high quality and reasonable prices. An exposed ancient Roman wall to the right of the entrance establishes the antiquity of this hand-somely refurbished palazzo with brick-vaulted ceilings (the rest dates from the 13th century). The delicious homemade pastas are prepared with sauces that follow the sea-son's fresh offerings, while the roster of meats skewered or roasted on the grill (*alla brace*) range from veal and lamb to duck. The ubiquitous *tartufo nero* (black truffle) is available here). La Fortezza also rents seven rooms upstairs (see "Affordable Places to Stay," above).

Medio Evo. Via dell'Arco dei Priori 4B (a dogleg down from Piazza del Comune). ☎ **075-813-068.** Reservations strongly recommended. Primi 8,000L–35,000L ($4–$18); secondi 20,000L–30,000L ($10–$15). AE, DC, MC, V. Thurs–Tues noon–2:30pm and 7:30–10pm. Closed Jan 7–Feb 8. UMBRIAN/ITALIAN.

Down a steep S-curve from the center of town, Medio Evo offers well-spaced tables under magnificent stone-vaulted medieval ceilings. For antipasto, treat yourself to simple but exquisite aged *prosciutto di Parma*. There are concessions to local ingredi-ents in dishes like *conchiglie alla Norcina* (shell pasta with black truffles and sausage) but also creations that smack of northern Europe, like *pennette alla moscavita* (with salmon, vodka, and tomatoes). For your second course, the Valdichiana beefsteak reigns supreme, and you can order it *alla Fiorentina* (grilled with a bit of olive oil and pepper), as an *entrecôte "Madagascar"* with green peppers, or as a flambéed fillet *alla moda dello chef.* Pork, mutton, and veal are available for lighter appetites, or try the superb *fritto misto* with fried meats and vegetables, cheese, olives, and salami.

Trattoria Pallotta. Via San Rufino 4 (just up from Piazza del Comune on the way to the Duomo). ☎ **075-812-649.** Reservations recommended. Primi 7,000L–11,000L ($3.50–$6); secondi 8,000L–18,000L ($4–$9); *menù turistico* 26,000L ($13) with wine; tasting menu 40,000L ($20) without wine. AE, MC, V. Wed–Mon noon–2:30pm and 7:15–9:30pm. Closed a week in late Feb. UMBRIAN.

Pallotta's pair of brightly lit stone-and-plaster rooms sees its share of tourists siphoned off from nearby Piazza del Comune, but it hasn't wavered from serving good Umbrian food at fair prices. The *antipasto misto* is a meal in itself, with Assisi's *torta al testa*, cros-tini, sliced meats, and more. The *strangozzi alla Pallotta* are served with a pesto of olives, mushrooms, and some pepperoncino for kick, and the *ravioloni al burro e salvia* come in a butter-and-sage sauce. Move on to *coniglio alla cacciatore* (rabbit in tomato sauce with a side of plain *torta al testo*) or a *pollo arrosto* (roast chicken). Although the *menù turistico* includes wine, the tasting menu offers better food choices. Ask about the comfortable rooms for rent upstairs (see "Affordable Places to Stay," above).

8 Gubbio

39km (24.5 mi.) NE of Perugia, 170km (107 mi.) SE of Florence, 200km (126 mi.) N of Rome; 90km (57 mi.) SE of Arezzo, 54km (34 mi.) N of Assisi

An austere, proud mountain outpost, the tiny no-nonsense stone town of ✪ **Gubbio** hangs on to its medieval charm and wonderful flavor of authenticity despite its grow-ing popularity with off-the-beaten-trackers looking for a picturesque hill town minus the tourists. Untrammeled it is not, but compared to, say, San Gimignano, you can consider Gubbio downright quiet, undiscovered, and cocooned in the middle of nowhere. The last few years have shown a commendable growth in the accommoda-tions scene, with renovations and a handsome new hotel in an enviably located his-toric palazzo.

Set into the rugged steep slope of forest-clad Mt. Ingino, Gubbio was a modestly prosperous Roman settlement, Iguvium, whose Roman amphitheater from the time of Augustus still sits at the foot of today's town. Like its Umbrian neighbor Spoleto, south of here, it flourished from its strategic location on the heavily trafficked Via Flaminia, linking ancient Rome and the imperial capital of Ravenna on the Adriatic. Today's visitor can easily evoke the Eugubium of the Dark Ages, a busy little market center, when its most important local personality, the sage Bishop Ubaldo Baldassini (now Gubbio's beloved patron saint) sidestepped destruction by the fierce hand of Barbarossa (Red Beard) in 1155. Its second-most celebrated resident was the ferocious Wolf of St. Francis fame. The 13th-century saint, from the nearby town of Assisi, strove to save the life of the hungry animal, which had been attacking flocks and terrorizing residents. After an alleged heart-to-heart, the saint convinced the wolf to change its ways and accepted its paw in peace. The townsfolk agreed to feed it regularly and a pact was sealed. This simple tale of *The Taming of the Wolf of Gubbio* has survived more than 7 centuries though the part about the repenting wolf bursting into tears after striking the deal with St. Francis may be discounted as historic embellishment.

Much of the Gubbio that welcomes visitors today was built in the early 14th century, when local master architect Matteo Gattapone, responsible for the famous arched bridge of Spoleto, constructed the Palazzo dei Consoli on the much-photographed central Piazza Grande. From 1387 to 1508, the Montefeltro counts of Urbino oversaw a long, if not brilliant, period of rule. It was during this time, as happened with its Umbrian neighbor Deruta, that Gubbio became widely known as a center for the high-quality glazed ceramics and majolica that came from its workshops; many are still operating, but don't expect the quantity of choice you'll find in Deruta. Maestro Giorgio Andreoli (1465 to 1552), one of the world's greatest masters of the craft, developed a particularly intense ruby-red glaze that was never discovered by neighboring towns. He is the city's most famous resident after St. Ubaldo and that pesky wolf.

ESSENTIALS

GETTING THERE   By Train   The closest **station** is at Fossato di Vico (☎ **075-919-230**), 19km (12 mi.) away on the Rome-Anacona line. Ten trains run daily from **Rome** (2¼ hr.; 18,600L/$9) and nine daily from **Spoleto** (40–60 min.; 6,100L/$3.05). Nine daily buses (six on Sunday) connect the train station with Gubbio (30 min.).

By Car   The SS298 leads north from Perugia through rugged scenery. The most convenient **parking** lot is off Piazza 40 Martiri (1,000L/$ per hour; pay at the Easy Gubbio office). There's also free parking off Via del Teatro Romano on the south edge of town and at the base station for the *funivia,* outside the east walls.

By Bus   ASP (☎ **075-922-0918**) has 11 buses Monday to Saturday (four on Sunday) from **Perugia**'s Piazza Partigiani (70 min.; 7,400L/$3.70). If you're coming from the north, you'll probably have to change in **Umbertide,** from which there are three daily ASP runs to Gubbio (45 min.). From **Florence,** take the daily 5pm **SULGA** bus (☎ **075-500-9641**) to Perugia, where within 40 to 70 minutes (no connection on Sunday) there's the ASP connection to Gubbio described above. The total traveling time is about 3 hours. Monday to Saturday, there's a 4pm SULGA bus from **Rome**'s Tiburtina Station (3½ hr.; 25,000L/$13). Buses to Gubbio arrive at/leave from Piazza 40 Martiri. Tickets are available at the newsstand on the piazza or at Easy Gubbio.

VISITOR INFORMATION   A private company, **Easy Gubbio,** just up from the bus stop at Via Repubblica 11 (☎ **075-922-0066**), is open daily in summer 8am to midnight (winter to 10pm), but closed Tuesday mornings year-round. It has some sightseeing material and rather long hours, but not as much information as the **official tourist office** at Piazza Oderisi 6, a wide spot on Corso Garibaldi (☎ **075-922-0693** or 075-922-0790; fax 075-927-3409). It's open Monday to Friday 8:15am to 1:45pm and 3:30 to 6:30pm, Saturday 9am to 1pm and 3:30 to 6:30pm, and Sunday 9:30am to 12:30pm. (November to March, afternoon hours are 3 to 6pm.)

FESTIVALS & MARKETS   The end-all festival in town is the ✪ **Corso dei Ceri** on May 15, the eve of the Festa di Sant'Ubaldo, Gubbio's patron saint. Three 16-foot-high wooden "candles" (*ceri*) weighing 400 kilos each (880 lbs.) crowned with small statues of Sts. Ubaldo, George, and Anthony are vertically raced through town to the hilltop Basilica di San Ubaldo. Oddly, St. Ubaldo always wins, but that doesn't diminish the excitement level—or the number of folks who show up to follow all the events that take place before, during, and after the race. To keep May a merry month, the last Sunday is dedicated to the **Palio della Balestra,** a crossbow competition against its ancient rival Sansepolcro in medieval costume (the rematch in Sansepolcro takes place in mid-September). An internal competition among four local teams is held on August 14.

Two weeks of **classical music concerts** take place in the end of July to the beginning of August, with performances held in the evocative venue of the ancient Roman Amphitheater and an illuminated Gubbio as dramatic backdrop. *Spettacoli Classici* (Classical Plays) in Italian take place in the Roman Amphitheater mid-July to mid-August. Umbria's town of Nocera may be famous for its black truffle, but Gubbio's rare albino rendition is the reason for the annual **Mercato del Tartufo Bianco** during the last weekend of October: Expect to pay at least 300,000L ($150) per 100 grams.

SEEING GUBBIO

The wide open expanse of the brick-paved ✪ **Piazza Grande** is the center stage of the **Città Alta (High City).** A good chunk of the old medieval town was razed and leveled to make way for this square and the crenellated **Palazzo dei Consoli** (☎ **075-927-4298**) and its slender campanile that dominates it. Meant to represent the power and pride of a small medieval commune in the golden age of its 14th-century political and economic might, it does just that. Behind the nondescript facade is the palazzo's cavernous municipal council chamber, the **Salone dell'Arengo;** the **Pinocoteca** (Picture Gallery); and the **Museo Civico,** whose **Tavole Eugubine (Eugubine Tablets)** are by far the museum's highlight. The seven bronze tablets discovered by a shepherd in 1444 are held to be Umbria's most important archaeological find, the oldest known documents detailing religious practices in Europe (best the scholars can figure, these tablets instruct priests how to interpret omens). The only extant example of the ancient written Umbrian language, they may date back as far as the 3rd to 1st centuries B.C. The museum also houses the city's only work of ceramics (1527) by Gubbio's master artisan Mastro Giorgio (d. 1552); with none to their name, the city bought it at Sotheby's for an undisclosed sum in 1992. Admission to the Palazzo dei Consoli, Pinacoteca, and Museo is 7,000L/$3.50; it's open daily 10am (10:30am April to September) to 1pm and 3 to 6pm.

From here, head up Via Ducale following signs for the Palazzo Ducale and the Duomo. The **Palazzo Ducale,** Via Federico da Montefeltro, at Via Ducale and Via della Cattedrale (☎ **075-927-5872**), was built in the 1470s as a scaled-down version of the ruling Duke Federico di Montefeltro's more lavish palace in Urbino. Most of the lordly trappings and furnishings are gone, but its worth a visit for some of the original frescoes, a smattering of baroque paintings, and the hanging gardens with a view that are open in summer. Admission is 6,000L/$3; it's open Monday to Saturday 9am to 1:30pm and 2:30 to 7pm, and Sunday 9am to 1:30pm.

If you weren't blown away by the Palazzo Ducale, you may want to save yourself a visit to the 12th-century **Duomo** across the way, a Gothic pile that pales when compared to some of those in the region you've likely seen in Spoleto, Orvieto, or Assisi (no phone; free admission; open daily 9am to noon and 3 to 5pm).

From behind the Duomo, follow the signs for one of Gubbio's two popular treks for the sturdy of knee. The least taxing is the paved road to the **Basilica di Sant Ubaldo,** on the hillside above town at 2,690 feet. The walk up steep Via Sant Ubaldo is 2km (1.3 mi.) along a consistent incline—most Eugubians drive it, reaching the basilica for their Sunday-afternoon stroll. There's also an open *funivia* (cable car) departing from the Porta Romana (a remaining 13th-century tower that permitted access to town), east of Piazza Grande (open daily 9am to sunset, with a 1:15 to 2:30pm break October to June; tickets are 5,000L/$2.50 one-way or 6,500L/$3.25 round-trip). The quiet 16th-century basilica holds the remains of the city's 12th-century patron saint in a glass casket and the three massive wooden *ceri* that turn the town upside down every May 15 when they're raced in a folkloric feast second only to Siena's Palio in terms of local hysteria (see "Festivals & Markets," above).

Got your second breath? You can continue by foot (the way is signposted) from the Basilica another 15 minutes or so to the remains of the 12th-century military fortress **La Rocca,** on the 3,000-foot pinnacle of Monte Igino, for one-of-a-kind views of the wild Appenine Mountains and the Umbrian plains.

SHOPPING

You can't miss the fact that Gubbio is still famous for **ceramics** after all these years. The two main shopping strips are **Via dei Consoli,** heading west out of Piazza Grande, and **Via XX Settembre,** heading east from the piazza, though you can find small shops selling the town's artisanal crafts along its secondary streets too. You'll find everything from items of amateur quality to those appropriate for serious collectors, the latter represented by the well-situated **La Mastro Giorgio di Valentino Biagioli,** Piazza Grande 3 (☎ **075-927-1574**). Another excellent retail outlet/workshop is **Rampini Ceramiche d'Arte,** Via Leonardo da Vinci 94 (☎ **075-927-2963**), where traditional patterns influence contemporary and modern designs.

Copies of medieval *balestre* (crossbows) are but a sampling of the exquisite *ferro battuto* (wrought-iron) craftsmanship handed down over the centuries. The best store/laboratory in town is **Artigianato Ferro Artistico,** Via Baldassini 22 (☎ **075-927-3079**). Handsomely crafted leather goods are the reason to search out the stores/workshops of **Maistri Librai,** Via dei Consoli 48 (☎ **075-927-7425**), and **Officina Libris,** Via Baldassini 16 (☎ **075-927-6650**).

AFFORDABLE PLACES TO STAY

Off-season rates are also offered by some hotels in winter, as well as the slow months of June and July (considered high season in other towns).

Bosone Palace. Via XX Settembre 22 (near Piazza Grande), 06024 Gubbio (PG). ☎ **075-922-0688.** Fax 075-922-0552. www.mencarelligroup.com. E-mail: hotel.bosone@libero.it. 30 units. MINIBAR TV TEL. 120,000–140,000L ($60–$70) single use of double; 170,000–190,000L ($65–$95) double; 280,000L ($140) 4-person junior suite; 350,000L ($175) 4-person Renaissance suite. Rates include expanded continental breakfast. AE, DC, MC, V. Free parking nearby. Often closed Jan–Feb.

Until the Relais Ducale opened, the Bosone was the city's most atmospheric hotel. Built in the 1300s and enlarged during the Renaissance, it's steps from Piazza Grande and allows you to enjoy a return to lifestyles of the rich and famous of other centuries. Owned by the local patrician Raffaelli clan, this formerly private residence once hosted an exiled Dante Alighieri (persona non grata in his hometown of Florence for trumped-up political charges). Its lobby's monumental marble staircase leads to standard rooms that are comfortable, simple, and spacious, and whose baths are mostly new (so much for time travel). Ask for one of the three with small terraces and big views. For the remarkable, book one of the two dramatic Renaissance suites with stuccoed ceilings elaborately frescoed in the 17th century and reproduction period furnishings.

Gattapone. Via Beni 6. ☎ **075-927-2489.** Fax 075-927-2417. www.mencarelligroup.com. 18 units. MINIBAR TV TEL. 120,000–140,000L ($60–$70) single; 160,000–180,000L ($80–$90) double; 210,000–250,000L ($105–$125) triple. AE, MC, V. Parking 5,000L ($2.50) in Piazza 40 Martiri nearby. Closed Jan 8–Feb 1.

After reopening in 1999 following a complete refurbishment, the long-loved Gattapone deservedly graduated to three-star status, but with prices that are more than reasonable given the quality and style. It's housed in a medieval building on a stepped alley down from Piazza Grande; many rooms overlook the Romanesque church and bell tower of San Giovanni. The redesigned rooms, however, reflect little of the hotel's ancient roots, with the exception of an occasional wood-beamed ceiling left intact. The tiles in the brand-new baths pick up the color scheme of each room. If you call on arrival, the hotel will send its van to collect you and your luggage. This is a sibling hotel of the Bosone, a more imposing palazzo but not yet slated for a facelift.

WORTH A SPLURGE

✪ **Relais Ducale.** Via Galeotti 19/Viale Ducale 2 (can also enter from the cafe in the center of Piazza Grande). ☎ **075-922-0157.** Fax 075-922-0159. www.mencarelligroup.com. 32 units. A/C MINIBAR TV TEL. 190,000L ($95) standard single, 220,000L ($110) superior single; 290,000L ($145) standard double, 340,000L ($170) superior double; 400,000L ($200) junior suite. Rates include breakfast. AE, DC, MC, V.

Housed in the aristocratic guest quarters of the ruling Dukes of Urbino, nestled between their Palazzo Ducale (above) and Piazza Grande (below), this new hotel offers a combination of historic importance and unrivaled panoramic location, with hanging gardens shaded by regal palms and scented by jasmine. The timeless view that must have bedazzled the guests of the ruling Montefeltro Dukes is the same one enjoyed by today's guests lingering over breakfast in the gardens or gazing out from many of the elegantly appointed rooms. Parquet floors, damask bedspreads and matching curtains, and the occasional historic touch (stone vaulted ceilings) or modern luxury (Jacuzzi baths) make this Gubbio's unrivaled premier hotel. If you're not staying here, stop by the Caffè Ducale at Piazza Grande 5 (the hotel rises above the cafe, carved into many levels and medieval structures), the most refined of the city's watering holes.

GREAT DEALS ON DINING

Taverna del Buchetto. Via Dante 30 (at the Porta Romana). ☎ **075-927-7034.** Reservations recommended. Primi 6,000L–15,000L ($3–$8); secondi 12,000L–22,000L ($6–$11); pizze 6,000L–15,000L ($3–$8); set-price menus 23,000L–30,000L ($13–$15) without wine. AE, DC, MC, V. Tues–Sun noon–3pm and 7–11pm. Closed 2 weeks in Feb. UMBRIAN/ITALIAN.

Simple, straightforward, and a real pleasure describes the menu and the ambience of this neighborhood trattoria/tavern. Since it's in an atmospheric 13th-century warehouse near the funicular that heads up to the basilica, this is a great place to come for lunch before heading up for a late afternoon or sunset moment at the basilica. The menu is testimony to the pleasures of Umbria's peasant fare: Delicious homemade pappardelle noodles are a quasi-constant (I hope you'll find them prepared with wild hare/tomato sauce). The homemade gnocchi are the best regardless of their changing sauce. Things are kept simple and delicious with a number of meats (or, when in season, plate-sized porcini mushrooms) sizzled *alla griglia.*

○ **Taverna del Lupo.** Via Ansidei 21 (on the corner of Via Repubblica, a few blocks uphill from Piazza 40 Martiri). ☎ **075-927-4368.** Reservations strongly recommended. Primi and secondi 16,000L–35,000L ($8–$18); tasting menu 80,000L ($40) without wine. AE, DC, MC, V. Tues–Sun 12:15–3pm and 7pm–midnight. UMBRIAN/EUGUBINA.

The Mencarelli empire that today includes the hotels above started here over 30 years ago in what continues to be Gubbio's culinary landmark. The family-run restaurant is large but divided into vaulted and brick-walled rooms that are handsomely appointed with Umbrian ceramics and prints. The atmosphere is one of elegant coziness, with a professional kitchen that rarely goes wrong with the regional specialties and well-chosen wine list. Flexible hours accommodate those trying to see the sites and sample local gastronomy on a limited day trip. The fixed-price menu is an interesting splurge, but I opt for anything *tartufo* (truffle) enhanced (beginning with the full-flavored sauce used for their special homemade tagliatelle). It's worth the extra lire.

9 Spoleto & the Spoleto Festival

129km (80 mi.) N of Rome, 209km (130 mi.) S of Florence, 48km (30 mi.) SE of Assisi, 64km (40 mi.) SE of Perugia

The world-famous ○ **Spoleto Festival** (until recently known as the Festival dei Due Mundi/Festival of Two Worlds) put Spoleto back on the map after centuries of historical obscurity. However, it was that obscurity that was responsible for the town's untouched medieval preservation, which still makes it worth visiting, even when the world-class arts festival isn't turning it on its ear. Established by Italian-American composer/maestro Gian Carlo Menotti in 1957, the celebrated arts festival brings together performers from all over the world for 3 weeks of dance, concerts, art, and drama known for their diversity and quality.

Much is made of the city's Roman past. As Spoletium, it was one of the empire's most important outposts. Strategically situated on the well-trafficked Via Flaminia linking Rome and the late imperial capital of Ravenna, it flourished for centuries and proudly held out when fiercely attacked by Hannibal in the 3rd century. It became the capital of the important Lombard Duchy of Spoleto from the 6th to the 8th century. The arrival of the emperor Barbarossa in 1155 saw widespread destruction of the region, after which the city only partially recovered before falling into the hands of the church and the stifling Papal States. The 15th-century Pope Alexander VI presented the town to his teenage daughter, Lucrezia Borgia, and appointed her governor. And that was pretty much the cap on excitement until Maestro Menotti arrived in 1957. Spoleto was far enough away from the epicenter of Umbria's 1997 earthquakes to have escaped with little to no damage.

There's no traipsing through countless museums and dimly lit churches in Spoleto. The much-used adjectives *quaint* and *charming* are put to excellent use here. After a visit to the Duomo—whose lovely, sloping piazza passes for one of the country's most evocative outdoor venues during the festival's closing-night concert—your time will be spent wandering the vaulted back streets and poking around small antiques shops and gourmet-stocked stores, always winding up in ancient Piazza del Mercato, a perfect reminder of the city's ancient roots as a market town during its day in the Dark Ages.

ESSENTIALS

GETTING THERE   By Train   Spoleto is a main station on the Rome-Ancona line, and all 16 daily trains from **Rome** stop here (about 1½ hr.; 12,500L/$6). From **Perugia,** take one of the 20 daily trains to Foligno (25 min.) to transfer to this line for the final 20-minute leg (6,100L/$3.05 total). The C bus heads from the **station**

(☎ 0743-48-516) up to Piazza Libertà in the upper town (bus D stops at Piazza Garibaldi in the lower town). Make sure you ask the driver if the bus is going toward the *centro storico.*

By Bus   Spoleto's bus company, **SIT** (☎ 0743-212-211), runs buses into Piazza della Vittoria (connected to Piazza Garibaldi) from **Perugia** (two afternoon runs, weekdays only, 1 hr.; 10,000L/$5) and **Rome** (an early morning and midafternoon run to Terni, where you can switch to many Spoleto-bound coaches, 2½ hr. total; 10,000L/$5). If you can reach Foligno by other means, there are lots of buses from there.

By Car   Spoleto is literally on the SS3 (the road tunnels under the city), the old Roman Via Flaminia running north from Rome and connecting in Foligno with the SS75 from Perugia. Parking in the old town is free only along Via Don Bonilli next to the soccer stadium and off Viale dei Cappuccini (turn left off the SS3 onto Viale G. Matteotti, then left again). There's also a parking lot off Piazza della Vittoria on the north end of lower Spoleto. Parking in the metered "zona blu" spaces in the center generally costs 1,000L (55¢) per hour.

VISITOR INFORMATION   The large **tourist office,** Piazza della Libertà 7 (☎ 0743-220-311; fax 0743-46-241; www.umbria2000.it), hands out scads of info and an excellent, if oversize, map. It's open Monday to Friday 9am to 1pm and 4 to 7pm, and Saturday and Sunday 10am to 1pm and 4 to 7pm.

FESTIVALS & MARKETS   For 3 weeks beginning in the last week of June, Spoleto turns its attention to the ✪ **Festival di Spoleto (Spoleto Festival),** the American-Italian arts-and-music festival. World-class symphonies and music ensembles as well as dance and drama troupes come from all over the world, culminating in the final evening's standing-room-only symphonic performance on Piazza del Duomo. There are often 5 to 10 events happening daily at different indoor/outdoor venues. Tickets usually go on sale mid-April. Edinburgh-type fringe and alternative performances are finding their way into the program to resuscitate some of the cutting-edge energy of the festival's early years, and tickets can often be found at the last moment. For general program information and instructions for ticket purchase after mid-April, contact the **Associazione Spoleto Festival** (☎ 800-565-600 toll free in Italy, or 0743-220-032; fax 0743-220-321; 0743-44-700 from outside Italy; www.spoletofestival. net). Also try the **Teatro Nuovo** at ☎ 0743-40-265.

To keep the cultural activity level at a consistent high, the relatively new **Spoleto-estate (Spoleto Summer)** arts festival picks up where its big-sister festival leaves off, organizing performances around town from July to September. See the tourist office for listings.

A daily morning **produce-and-flower market** (except Sunday) takes over ancient Piazza del Mercato, originally the site of the Roman Forum, in fragrant and organized chaos. The second Sunday of every month, a **Mercato delle Briciole** takes place here and in neighboring piazzas (pick up information at the tourist office), where merchants hawk collectibles and choice antiques together with junky stuff.

SEEING THE SIGHTS

With the exception of the Duomo, there isn't much to see here. But a walk through town will illustrate the antiquity of a city that's still very much alive and doesn't live for tourism's sake alone. Just west of the main Piazza della Libertà is the **Teatro Romano (Roman Theater)** from the 1st century, when Spoleto was a thriving Roman city. It has recently been restored and is a popular venue for festival performances (admission 4,000L/$2; Monday to Saturday 9am to 7pm, and Sunday 9am to 1pm).

From Piazza della Libertà, take a right on Via Brignone and a left on Via Arco di Druso, which leads into **Piazza del Mercato,** a window to centuries past. Stores around its periphery sell the gourmet products of Umbria, including the prized black truffles from nearby Norcia. Outdoor cafes like the **Bar Primavera** (no. 8; excellent gelato) set up tables outside as alfresco command posts for taking in the piazza life. Explore the vaulted alleys and hidden corners just off the piazza or follow the characteristic **Via dei Duchi** north out of Piazza del Mercato to window-shop on one of the city's most pleasant streets. At its end, turn left onto Via del Mercato or right onto Via Fontesecca for more streets evocative of the city's medieval past, now inhabited by tasteful shops, antiques stores, and boutiques.

It's a short walk east to Piazza del Duomo and the ✪ **Duomo,** a 12th-century building (on the site of a 7th-century church) whose simple but elegant facade is graced by five rose windows and crowned with a mosaic by Solsterno (1207). The most illustrious (recently restored and mercifully untouched by the 1997 earthquakes) pictorial masterpiece of the city is found in the domed apse—the last works done by Florentine painter Filippo Lippo (1467 to 1469). From left to right they're the *Annunciation,* the *Passage of the Virgin Mary,* and the *Nativity;* the *Coronation* fills the space above. In the scene of the Virgin's death, you'll find self-portraits of the painter and his son Filippino to the right. His premature death, rumor goes, came from poisoning when he was found to have seduced the nubile daughter of a noble family. It was bad enough that, as a monk, he'd taken up with Lucrezia Buti, a nun who posed as the Madonna in many of his works. Filippino, the son of Filippo and Lucrezia (and student of his father's old protégé Botticelli), designed his father's tomb found in a chapel in the right transept, funded by Florence's Lorenzo de' Medici, the master's patron; the body mysteriously disappeared for a brief period 2 centuries later, stolen, they say, by descendants of the compromised girl.

The other work of note is the fresco cycle in the **Cappella di Erioli,** at the beginning of the right nave. The author was a 17-year-old Pinturicchio, not yet famous for his future work in the Piccolomini Library in Siena's Duomo. The Duomo is open 8am to 1pm and 3 to 5:30pm (March to October to 6:30pm). Down the steps on the west side of Piazza del Duomo are the shaded hanging gardens of **Piazza della Signoria,** whose benches and postcard views of the valley make this the city's most idyllic picnic spot (buy your provisions at the open-air market before vendors pack up at 1pm).

The decade-long renovation of the towered and crenellated papal **Rocca fortress** (☎ **0348-700-4829**) was completed in 2000, and you can now tour some of its frescoed halls and peer into the archaeological excavation pits. Built by the Gubbio-born architect Gattapone from 1359 to 1363 for the tireless papal envoy Cardinal Albornoz (also responsible for the Rocca above Assisi), it was temporary home to the Lucrezia Borgia, teenage daughter of 15th-century Pope Alexander VI. It was also used as a prison, most recently having housed Pope John Paul II's would-be assassin Ali Agha for a brief period. It's currently open Monday to Friday 3 to 6pm, and Saturday and Sunday 4 to 10pm, but those hours will probably change, so call ahead to be sure. Take a walk, if only for the town's best picture-perfect views, around the right side of the Rocca to the 14th-century ✪ **Ponte delle Torri (Bridge of the Towers).** Gattapone built it on the foundation of an ancient Roman aqueduct. Its 10 Gothic arches span a 760-foot-wide chasm 240 feet above a torrent and to this day, it's held as an awe-inspiring engineering endeavor for that period. A favorite summertime hike is to the rural **monastery of Monteluco,** once favored by St. Francis and St. Bernardino of Siena, who came to live here after him (open daily 9am to noon and 3 to 6pm). If the

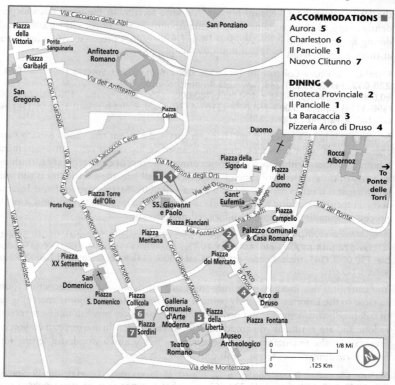

ACCOMMODATIONS ■
Aurora **5**
Charleston **6**
Il Panciolle **1**
Nuovo Clitunno **7**

DINING ◆
Enoteca Provinciale **2**
Il Panciolle **1**
La Baracaccia **3**
Pizzeria Arco di Druso **4**

footbridge is closed, as it often is, you can catch a bus from Piazza della Libertà (2,600L/$1.30) for the 8km (5-mi.) ride. The tourist office can supply you with maps of walking paths to Monteluco and other sites of interest in the immediate country-side.

AFFORDABLE PLACES TO STAY

Rates are usually discounted November to March (low season). If you plan to visit during the festival, book 2 to 3 months in advance (last-minute cancellations are rare); you may also consider commuting by car or bus from Perugia or the neighboring towns during the festival when the town is at zero vacancy. Note that prices during the 3-week festival may be higher than those quoted below: Hoteliers charge whatever they believe the demand will support.

✪ **Aurora.** Via Apollinare 3 (near Piazza della Libertà), 06049 Spoleto (PG). ☎ **0743-220-315.** Fax 0743-221-885. www.umbria.org/hotel/aurora. E-mail: hotelaurora@virgilio.it. 23 units. MINIBAR TV TEL. 70,000–90,000L ($35–$45) single; 90,000L–146,000L ($45–$73) double. Rates include breakfast. AE, DC, MC, V. Free parking.

Off Piazza della Libertà in a small courtyard that ensures a central location but quiet nights, this popular hotel is especially recommended if you can procure any of the renovated rooms (*camere nuove*)—ask when booking. Rather stylish for these rates, the new rooms boast a coordinated decor of wall-to-wall carpeting, discreetly patterned wallpaper, and deep-mauve curtains. The other rooms—with baths harking back to the 1970s—have been kept up but are due for a facelift. In the hotel but independently managed is the acclaimed Ristorante Apollinare, one of the city's more upscale dining spots; its menu offers regional Umbrian specialties prepared with a light, and at times creative, hand (half and full pensione plans are available).

Charleston. Piazza Collicola 10 (near San Domenico), 06049 Spoleto (PG). ☎ **0743-220-052.** Fax 0743-221-244. www.qsa.it/hotelcharleston. 18 units. A/C MINIBAR TV TEL. 60,000–115,000L ($30–$58); 100,000L–180,000L ($50–$90) double; 180,000–230,000L ($90–$115) triple; 210,000–260,000L ($105–$130) quad. Buffet breakfast 15,000L ($8). AE, DC, MC, V. Parking 15,000L ($8).

Much of this hotel's centuries-old character survived a recent renovation by new management, with open fireplaces, chestnut-beamed ceilings, and terra-cotta pavements admirably intact. Within such a historic context, the mix of contemporary furnishings and artwork is seamless and tasteful. Despite its small size, the Charleston is run with an efficient air, offers amenities like a sauna (20,000L/$10 per person) and Internet access, organizes walking tours and bike outings in the immediate area, and is in the process of installing an enoteca and several more rooms.

Il Panciolle. Via del Duomo 3–5 (2 blocks west of Piazza della Signoria), 06049 Spoleto. ☎/fax **0743-45-677.** 7 units. MINIBAR TV TEL. 70,000L ($35) single; 100,000L ($50) double; 130,000L ($65) triple. Continental breakfast 8,000L ($4). Rates discounted 20%–25% low season. No credit cards.

You can't beat this inexpensive family-run place for new and nicely decorated rooms so close to the Duomo. The newly painted white walls offset the rooms' matching sets of oak headboard, armoire, and bedside table; the baths are smallish but were recently redone and are as nice as you could hope for at these rates. In warm weather, you can breakfast on the restaurant's flagstone terrace, which is also a wonderful setting for a home-style dinner (see "Great Deals on Dining," below).

Nuovo Clitunno. Piazza Sordini 6 (just west of Piazza della Libertà), 06049 Spoleto. ☎ **0743-223-340.** Fax 0743-222-663. www.hotelclitunno.com or www.spoleto1.com/ hotelclitunno.html. 45 units. TV TEL. 85,000–110,000L ($43–$55) single; 125,000–135,000L ($63–$68) standard double, 140,000–150,000L ($70–$75) "Old Style" double; triple rates on request. Rates include buffet breakfast. AE, DC, MC, V. Free parking available. Closed Feb (but not in 2001).

Little is left from the time when this 19th-century palazzo was a firehouse. But the Tomassoni family's welcome augments the comfort and warmth of the public area's fireplace, beamed ceilings, and gold-plastered walls. To accommodate disparate tastes, the rooms have recently been refitted in two styles. Request "old style" and you'll have reserved one of 18 lovely rooms with terra-cotta floors, antique iron beds, armoires, and rough-hewn ceiling beams. The majority of rooms are decorated in "standard" style (less expensive than the old-style rooms), with stylish contemporary furnishings in warm pastel colors. All have new baths but only 15 of the standard rooms offer a handsome view over the Vale Spoletino. Not all rooms have air-conditioning; it is available at no extra cost but should be requested when booking.

GREAT DEALS ON DINING

Enoteca Provinciale. Via Aurelio Saffi 7. ☎ **0743-220-484.** Primi 7,000L–15,000L ($3.50–$8); secondi 6,000L–20,000L ($3–$10); wine from 2,500L ($1.25) per glass; menù turistico 20,000L ($10) with wine. AE, DC, MC, V. Wed–Mon 10am–4pm and 6–10:30pm (summer to midnight). UMBRIAN/SPOLETINA.

Make at least one of your lunches, light dinners, or snacks in the converted livestock stalls of this medieval tower, where casual meals are accompanied by wine tastings.

Meals consist of the region's simplest, and in this case the most delicious, offerings. The toasted *bruschetta all'olio di Spoleto* showcases the local olive oil; homemade *strangozzi al tartufo* pasta is just an excuse to revel in its unrivaled truffle sauce; *polenta alla spoletina* is made with a barleylike flour (not the usual cornmeal) and heaped with sausage and lentils. You can a sample a cross section of more than 30 red and white Umbrian wines by the glass, but toast the night with the very unusual *amaro di tartufo*, a bitter liqueur made from the ubiquitous truffle. Eat and drink as little or as much as you want; the atmosphere is relaxed and jovial and you'll be welcomed into the fold the longer you stay and the more you imbibe.

Il Panciolle. Via del Duomo 3–5. ☎ **0743-45-598.** Reservations recommended. Primi 12,000L–25,000L ($6–$13); secondi 13,000L–25,000L ($7–$13). AE, MC, V. Thurs–Tues 12:30–2:30pm and 7:45pm–10:45. Closed Aug 1–12. SPOLETINA.

This family-run restaurant, popular with performers during the festival, offers two wonderfully distinctive eating experiences: a wintertime evening in the cantina's stone-walled room with beamed ceilings and an open fireplace, where the aroma of roasting meat teases your appetite before you're even seated; and in warm weather a dinner on the open flagstoned terrace, shaded by a huge pine and presented with an open view of the Spoleto Valley. What remains invariable is the *cucina umbra casalinga*, the home cooking that's the kitchen's specialty. Homemade *strangozzi* pasta can be enjoyed simply prepared with *aglio e olio* (garlic and olive oil) or dressed up royally with *funghi e tartufi* (truffles and mushrooms). The meats *alla brace* (grilled over an open fire) are delicious, but also sample the grilled mozzarella or the smoke-cured cheese *scamorza alla brace*, a peasant's dish you could serve to a king. For the restaurant's charming rooms, see "Affordable Places to Stay," above.

۞ La Barcaccia. Piazza Fratelli Bandiera (north of Piazza del Mercato), Spoleto. ☎ **0743/22-11-71.** Reservations suggested. Primi 8,000–18,000L ($4–$9); secondi 16,000–25,000L ($8–$13); *menù turistico* 28,000L ($17). AE, DC, MC, V. Wed–Mon 12:30–2:30pm and 7:30–11pm. UMBRIAN.

This is one of Spoleto's finer restaurants, where you can have a modestly priced dinner if you resist, alas, the allure of its otherwise highly recommended truffle dishes. A safe way to dine is with the well-priced *menù turistico*, which includes a choice of truffle-free pasta, a meat entree, a fresh vegetable, fruit, and service—everything except a glass of the local Umbrian wine. A covered terrace extends the length of the restaurant in front, though the small piazza's use as a parking lot does little to romanticize the view. Truffle-deprived and -innocent diners should employ the carpe diem approach to dining in Umbria and try any of the truffle-sprinkled first courses. An entree of mixed roast meats (*grigliata alla brace*) is the house's deservedly promoted specialty.

Pizzeria Arco di Druso. Via Arco di Druso 25 (off Piazza del Mercato), Spoleto. ☎ **0743/22-16-95.** Reservations suggested. Primi and pizzas 7,000–13,000L ($3.50–$7); secondi 10,000–22,000L ($5–$11); *menù turistico* 25,000L ($13). MC, V. Tues–Sun 12:30–2:30pm and 7–11pm. PIZZERIA/UMBRIAN.

Since this place is practically in the lively daily market, there's little doubt that what winds up on your plate was a farmer's freshly picked special this morning. The wood-burning stove turns out a stellar *pizza al tartufo* and *pizza con funghi porcini* with mushrooms. Ceilings alternate between vaulted brick and exposed wooden beams, redolent of the palazzo's origins in the 1400s as horse stables. Humans now chow down in two busy rooms with murals and pink linen tablecloths, a fancy setting for such simple offerings as the delicious *polenta con funghi porcini*. Any of the season's changing pastas are good; ask which is the day's *pasta fatta a casa* (homemade specialty).

10 Orvieto

45km (28.3 mi.) W of Todi, 87km (55 mi.) W of Spoleto, 86km (54 mi.) SW of Perugia; 152km (95.8 mi.) S of Florence, 121km (75.6 mi.) N of Rome

One of the most dramatically sited hill towns in Italy, **Orvieto** is perfectly situated between Florence and Rome, atop a volcanic plateau over 1,000 feet above a wide valley. It's an amazing sight, one visible from miles away, when the setting sun is reflected off the glittering mosaic facade of the Duomo—which, by the way, is one of Italy's most outstanding cathedrals.

Orvieto was of Etruscan origin—one of the original league of 12 important satellite cities and possibly its religious center—and later destroyed in 264 B.C. by the Romans, who transformed it into their own stronghold. As the Etruscans before them, they sculpted the porous tufa butte into a labyrinth of tunnels, storage caves, cisterns, wells, and living spaces (you can visit parts of the **"Orvieto Underground"** daily with an English-speaking guide for 10,000L/$5, usually at 11am and 4pm; contact the tourist office or call ☎ **0763-375-084**). The Middle Ages saw a thriving period as an influential *commune*, enjoying its golden days in the 13th and 14th centuries, when many palazzi and churches were built. Orvieto was also a prominent papal seat: As many as 33 pontiffs had their summer residence here. The proximity to the Vatican was a plus, as was the high-altitude tabletop setting that made it a natural fortress while guaranteeing cool weather during Rome's infernal summers.

Those intending to stay overnight and longer may have to fend off not the day-trippers, but the possible disappointment of its limited sites. Those with cars, however, will enjoy using Orvieto as a base for visiting the area's prominent vineyards and other charming hill towns, such as Todi and Spoleto.

ESSENTIALS

GETTING THERE   By Train   Fourteen trains on the main **Rome-Florence** line stop at Orvieto daily (1¾ hr. from Florence, 16,500L/$8; 1½ hr. from Rome, 12,500L/$6). From **Perugia**, take the train to Terontola (16 daily) for this line heading south toward Rome (1¼ hr. total; 10,500L/$5).

Orvieto's station is in the boring new town of Orvieto Scalo in the valley. To reach the city, cross the street and take the **funicular,** a modern version of the steep cog railway that ran on hydraulic power in the 19th century. You can buy a funicular-only ticket for 1,200L (60¢) or a combined funicular-and-bus ticket for 1,500L (75¢) that lets you hop on a minibus at the top of the funicular run (Piazza Cahen) and ride into the center of town: The "A" bus heads to Piazza del Duomo and the "B" bus to central Piazza della Repubblica via Piazza XXIX Marzo (it then doubles back to the Duomo). Or you may wish to get the "Carta Unica" combination ticket that covers the funicular, bus, and museums (see below). From in front of the train station, you could also grab bus 1 that runs to Piazza XXIX Marzo in the city (get two tickets—one for the return trip—at the bar inside the station, as they're hard to come by in town).

By Bus   Train transportation to any of the above destinations is generally preferred to the extremely limited bus service to and from Orvieto. For bus information, call ☎ **0763-301-234** or visit the tourist office.

By Car   If you're coming from **Todi,** the SS448 is the fastest route, but the twisty SS79bis is more scenic; from **Perugia,** shoot down the SS3bis through Deruta to Todi and branch off from there. The SS71 runs here from just east of **Chiusi** in southern Tuscany, and the A1 autostrada between **Florence** and **Rome** has an exit at the valley town Orvieto Scalo.

The most convenient **free parking** is in Orvieto Scalo outside the train station (take the funicular to town; see "By Train," above); at the top of the funicular run on Piazza Cahen (with both free and pay spaces); and, if you can find room, the free lot off Via Roma. There's a new large pay lot (500L/30¢ per hour; 10,000L/$6 for 24 hours) at the ex Campo della Fiera in the valley below the south end of town with elevators to take you up to Orvieto level.

VISITOR INFORMATION The **tourist office** is opposite the Duomo at Piazza del Duomo 24 (☎ 0763-341-772; fax 0763-344-433), open Monday to Friday 8am to 2pm and 4 to 7pm, and Saturday and Sunday 10am to 1pm and 3:30 to 7pm.

FESTIVALS & MARKETS Seven weeks after Easter, **Pentecost Sunday** (usually falling in June) is festively celebrated in Orvieto. On this day, **La Palombella** commemorates the descent of the Holy Spirit on the Apostles amid much fanfare. Nine weeks after Easter, **Corpus Christi** (usually the first half of June) reenacts an event in 1264 in the time of Pope Urban IV (see the Duomo listing, below). Since 1950, the precious, ancient relic (the Holy Corporal) kept in the Duomo is carried through the streets, accompanied by a *corteo* of 400 people in costume, evoking the period when Orvieto was a prominent papal seat. For 5 days surrounding New Year's Eve (and ending January 3rd), **Umbria Jazz Winter,** the relatively new mini jazz festival has been catching on.

Every Thursday and Saturday, a morning market fills **Piazza del Popolo** with fresh produce and fruits, as well as an interesting smattering of stalls hawking clothing, ceramics, and miscellaneous items.

SEEING THE SIGHTS

✪ **Duomo.** Piazza del Duomo. ☎ **0763-341-167.** Admission to Cappella di San Brizio (☎ **0763-342-477**) 3,000L ($1.50), under 10 free (or cumulative ticket). Tickets available at tourist office across piazza. Daily 7:30am–12:45pm and 2:30pm–sunset (San Brizio Chapel opens 10am but is closed Sun morning).

This city's singular draw is its spacious Piazza del Duomo and 13th-century **Duomo,** one of Italy's treasures. It's noted for its breathtaking facade influenced by dozens of architects and artists; inside, the Duomo contains one of the greatest fresco cycles of the Renaissance in the ✪ **Cappella di San Brizio (Chapel of San Brizio),** recently reopened after a lengthy period of restoration. The cycle, begun by Fra' Angelico and completed by Luca Signorelli, depicts in vivid detail the Last Judgment, one that was said to have influenced Michelangelo and his own interpretation in the Sistine Chapel. Leonardo da Vinci wouldn't give it the time of day.

The Duomo was built to shelter the relic of the Miracle of Bolsena, an incident that happened in 1263 just a few miles south of Orvieto and has since been celebrated by the Catholic church as the feast of the Corpus Christi. A doubting priest who questioned the sacrament of the Transfiguration (one of the church's most sacred mysteries: that the consecrated communion Host contains the incarnation—the actual body and blood—of Christ), witnessed that the bleeding host had stained the linen altar

---

A Money-Saving Tip

The useful "Carta Unica" **cumulative ticket** (20,000L/$10) adults and 17,000L/$9 students and over 60) gets you into the Duomo's Cappella di San Brizio, the Museo Claudio Faina, the Torre del Moro, and the Orvieto Underground tour—plus either one funicular-plus-one-bus ride *or* five hours in the Campo della Fiera parking lot. It's available at the tourist office, all those sights, and the funicular depots.

cloth. This precious relic is now protected in a gold-and-enamel reliquary (1339) that mimics the facade of the cathedral in the **Cappella del Corporale,** a chapel to the left of the main altar, and it's paraded through town once a year to major fanfare (see "Festivals & Markets," above). It spawned what would become the construction of Orvieto's cathedral, one of the most important in Italy (and that's saying something).

Much attention is given to the glittering **mosaics** of the elaborate facade, but in fact they weren't added until the 17th and 18th centuries and aren't major works. Work continued as recently as this century: The Duomo's controversial (mainly because they're contemporary) central **bronze doors** were made in 1964 by Sicilian sculptor Emilio Greco. Some of the earliest work are the **bas-reliefs** on the lower parts of the pillars (protected by Plexiglas due to threats of vandalism in the 1960s)—the work of Sienese master Lorenzo Maittani, one of the original architects involved in the cathedral's early years until his death in 1330. The facade's delicate **rose window** was the work of Florentine Andrea Orcagna from the mid–14th century. If you're still in town at sunset, join the small knot of savvy visitors who know to be nowhere else when the moment occurs; the lighting of the window is something unforgettable.

CRAFTS & WINE

The shopping scene is limited but varied, representing Orvieto's tradition of centuries-old crafts: lace and embroidery work, woodwork (carved objects, inlays, and veneers), ceramics, and wine (with the local DOC white wine Orvieto Classico holding out as everyone's favorite purchase). Shops are concentrated around the area of the Duomo and along the pedestrian shopping strips west of the Duomo, namely **Via del Duomo** and **Via Cavour.**

Visit **Michelangeli,** Via Gualtiero Michelangeli 3 (☎ **0763-342-660**), for the most creative woodwork and inlays in town. One of the very few lace workers left in town is the gracious **Maria Moretti,** Via Maurizio 1 (☎ **0763-341-714**). Ceramics are the easiest to come by, with a number of artisan shops along the pedestrian strips mentioned above. Wine lovers should give some time and attention to the city's many *cantine* and *enoteche* open to the public: The **Enoteca Barberani,** Via Michelangeli 14 (☎ **0763-341-532**), sells excellent wines and oils from its own estate, as well as a sampling of other food products like truffles, preserves, and liqueurs (they can arrange to have you visit their wine-growing estate about 16km/10 mi. outside town); **Cantina Foresi,** Piazza del Duomo 2 (☎ **0763-341-611**), represents a number of local wine producers, as does **La Bottega del Buon Vino,** Via del. Cava 26, which sits above ancient Etruscan excavations (ask the friendly shopkeeper if you can take a peek; consider hanging around for lunch as well, at the enoteca's popular trattoria). The tourist office has a brochure and map called *Andar per Vigne* (*Visiting the Vineyards*), with information about a dozen major producers in the region within a 5- to 20km (3- to 13-mi.) radius of Orvieto and their visiting hours. The **Castello di Sala** of the storied Antinori family probably wins out as the most picturesque, replete with a medieval castle, an ideal setting, and important vintages.

AFFORDABLE PLACES TO STAY

Orvieto Promotion, associated with the local travel agency Effe & G Viaggi, Piazza Fracassini 4 (☎ **0763-344-666;** fax 0763-343-943; e-mail: effegiviaggi@effegiviaggi. it), will help with hotel reservations free of charge if the following hotels are full. Specify the category or price range you're interested in.

Strict budgeteers may want to contact the **Hotel Virgilio,** Piazza del Duomo 5–6 (☎ **0763-341-882;** fax 0763-343-797), which has 13 very basic modern rooms with some of the ugliest lamps I've ever seen, but it's smack on Piazza del Duomo. Doubles run 100,000L to 165,000L ($50 to $83), and the hotel is closed mid-January to mid-February.

⊙ **Palazzo Piccolomini.** Piazza Ranieri 36 (2 blocks down from Piazza della Repubblica), 05018 Orvieto (TR). ☎ **0763-341-743.** Fax 0763-391-046. E-mail: piccolomini.hotel@ orvienet.it. 32 units. A/C MINIBAR TV TEL. 163,000L ($82) single; 236,000L ($118) double; 386,000L ($183) suite. Rates include buffet breakfast. AE, DC, MC, V. Parking 20,000L ($10) in garage.

The 1998 opening of this converted Renaissance palazzo is the sole reason behind the suspiciously low prices. Pray they stay this low through 2001, but know that their days are numbered and act now. Looking very pretty in pink, this 16th-century palazzo was the Orvieto home of the illustrious Tuscan family that gave us two popes. It's back in operation following a complete refurbishment that has kept the historic shell and its grand dimensions, plus vaulted ceilings and wide halls, while creating an uncluttered ambience that's quasi-minimalist with terra-cotta floors and white slipcovered furniture.

WORTH A SPLURGE

⊙ **La Badia.** Loc. La Badia 8 (about 3km south of town off the road to Bagnoreggio), 05019 Orvieto (TR). ☎ **0763-301-959.** Fax 0763-305-396. E-mail: labadia.hotel@tiscalinet.it. 26 units. A/C MINIBAR TV TEL. 235,000–255,000L ($118–$128) single; 325,000–365,000L ($163–$183) standard double, 340,000–380,000L ($170–$190) deluxe double; 480,000–590,000L ($240–$295) suite. Rates include continental breakfast. AE, MC, V. Free parking. Closed Jan–Feb.

La Badia (the Abbey) is an ecclesiastical enclave of golden-stone buildings dating as far back as the 8th century (and then enlarged as a Benedictine monastery in the 12th). Outside of Orvieto proper, it's gorgeously sited amid the quiet and birdsong in the countryside. The rural hotel lends itself to seminars, wedding receptions, and group tours, and the remote other-worldliness the monks once knew can get lost amid the one-night traffic. But it remains a highly unique h hotel made more attractive during the low season rates above (March to May and October 15 to December). The hotel likes to encourage half board (the stone-vaulted dining hall and open hearth is high on drama), though it's not mandatory. Country club amenities like tennis courts and a pool make this a good spot to settle in for a few days R&R. The size of the rooms varies greatly, and the whole place is aging, but it carries its age well. Ten rooms have views of Orvieto, some overlook the abbey's 12th-century, 12-sided bell tower, said to be the only one of its kind in the world. If you don't have car, you can take a taxi here from the train station for about 20,000L ($10).

GREAT DEALS ON DINING

If you're in between meals or just looking for a nibble, consider the **Enoteca Barberani** (see "Crafts & Wine," above) or the **Bar/Caffe Montanucci,** Via Cavour 21, for the best coffee in town. You can shop for delicious picnic ingredients at either of the two best delicatessens: **Dai Fratelli,** Via del Duomo 10, or **Antonia Carraro,** Via Cavour 101. Piazza del Duomo is ground zero for tourist spots but also the location for the **Cantina Foresi,** no. 2, perfect for a tasty sandwich and a glass of local wine, and the **Gelateria del Duomo,** no. 14, for the best ice cream in town.

⊙ **Osteria dell'Orso.** Via della Misericordia 18–20. ☎ **0763-341-642.** Reservations recommended. Primi 6,000L–14,000L ($3–$7); secondi 12,000L–22,000L ($6–$11). AE, DC, MC. Wed–Sun 12:30–2:30pm and 7:30–10pm, Mon 12:30–2:30pm. Closed Feb, July, and Nov. UMBRIAN/ABRUZZESE.

The ubiquitous *umbrichelli* (Umbria's homemade spaghetti-like specialty) is best here *alla campagnola* ("country style" with zucchini, eggplant, and onions). Any of the fresh pastas, in fact, is a must-try at this unprepossessing trattoria full of locals, somewhat free of tourists because of its location one step too far off the beaten path (it's a 10-min. stroll from the Duomo). The ingredients of fresh market offerings and home-grown herbs help confirm the impression of a day in the country. The simplest of dishes—an omeletlike frittata of asparagus or potatoes—is a wonderful surprise, full of the season's flavor and the masterful touch of chef Gabriele di Giandomenico.

✪ **Tipica Trattoria Etrusca.** Via Lorenzo Maitani 10 (1 block from the Duomo). ☎ **0763-344-016.** Reservations recommended. Primi 9,500L–23,000L ($4.75–$12); secondi 7,000L–26,000L ($3.50–$13); fixed-price menu 35,000L ($18) without wine. AE, DC, MC, V. Tues–Sun noon–2:45pm and 7:30–10pm. Closed Jan 7–Feb 5. ORVIETANA.

Precede or cap off a visit to Orvieto's Duomo with a meal here and you'll have orchestrated the perfect day at moderate cost and immense personal pleasure. The Etrusca offers a cool respite during a hot Umbrian afternoon, on the ground level of a 15th-century palazzo whose roots (like much of Orvieto) are lost in Etruscan times. A much requested primo is the regional homemade pasta *umbrichelli,* an almost chewy flour-and-water spaghetti served here *alla orvietana* (a slightly spicy tomato sauce with bacon). To complete a meal typical of this game-rich region, try the tried-and-true Umbrian specialty of rabbit, *coniglio all'Etrusca* in a savory sauce of herbs and spices. Stay close to home with fresh ricotta cheese from a local supplier, dusted with sugar and covered with fresh berries for a light dessert. A thoughtful selection of Umbrian and Tuscan wines fills the restaurant's wine cellars, carved into the ancient Etruscan foundations below.

TODI: A SIDE TRIP FROM ORVIETO

With so little to see or do in **Todi,** it's always surprising that this medieval hill town is on everyone's itineraries these days. Smack-dab between Orvieto to the west and Spoleto to the east (each about 45km/28 mi.), Todi also makes the perfect day's jaunt from those setting up base in Perugia, equidistant to the north (unless you're based in Perugia, bus service isn't good; you'll need your own wheels). The twisting, winding back roads that lead you there are some of the loveliest through southern Umbria's less trammeled corners.

What you do once you arrive is up to you. For 10 days at the end of August and the beginning of September, the classy **Festival di Todi** aspires to be a small version of the world-famous festival in Spoleto. Todi's growing popularity with Rome's arts and media set and as the preferred summer retreat of choice of an Anglo-American artist community (as an alternative destination to the always more "crowded" Tuscany) is the result of the camera crews and on-location film crews that have "discovered" the fairy-tale medievalism of this town and spread the word. There's no discounting its small-town charm, just don't expect your days to be filled with sightseeing—strolling and snacking, yes.

✪ **Piazza del Popolo** has long been described as one of medieval Italy's loveliest compendium of secular and religious palazzi, generally from the 13th-century period when Todi was a thriving commercial *commune.* Here also is **Umbria,** Via San Bonaventura 13, just off Piazza del Popolo though the archway (☎ **075-894-2390**), Todi's finest restaurant, with special views from its terrace tables as well as regional cuisine with a nod to Roman specialties. An average meal for one without wine is 40,000L ($20). It's open Wednesday to Monday 12:30 to 2:30pm and 7:30 to 10:30pm. The **Enoteca dell'Academia dei Convivianti,** Todi's best enoteca wine store, is next door.

The second most important site in town is **San Fortunato** on Piazza della Repubblica; its size alone is testimony to Todi's medieval might. The church was begun in 1291 but not finished until 1459, so the initial Gothic style is mingled with that of the Renaissance. Finishing off the triumvirate of sites is **Santa Maria della Consolazione,** a late Renaissance church 99 years in the making. Inspired by plans by Bramante, architect of Rome's St. Peters, it is often written about as a Renaissance masterwork and, by the time it was finished in 1607, had been collaborated on by a series of architects, including Sangallo the Younger and Vignola.

Todi's **tourist office** is under the arches on Piazza del Popolo (☎ **075-894-3456** or 075-984-3395). It's open Monday to Saturday 9am to 1pm and 3:30 to 6:30pm, and Sunday 9:30am to 12:30pm.

6

Bologna & Emilia-Romagna

by Reid Bramblett

Emilia-Romagna comprises two ancient lands: Emilia, named for the Roman road that bisects its plains and art cities, and Romagna, named for its prominence in the Roman Empire. History has left its mark here on some of Italy's most beautiful cities—**Ravenna,** last capital of the empire and later the stronghold of the Byzantines and the Visigoths; **Ferrara,** center of art and culture for much of the Renaissance; **Parma,** one of the most powerful duchies in Europe under the Farnese family; **Modena,** famous for vinegar and opera stars; and **Bologna,** a university center since the Middle Ages and Italy's most youthful and exuberant city.

Many travelers whiz through Emilia-Romagna on high-speed trains and autostrade en route to and from Florence, Milan, Venice, or Rome. They're not only bypassing some of Italy's finest art and architecture but also are missing the opportunity to experience a way of life that has been largely unaffected by those two great demons of the 20th century: mass tourism and massive industrialization.

1 Bologna: Home of Europe's Oldest University

105km (63 mi.) N of Florence, 210km (126 mi.) SE of Milan, 210km (126 mi.) S of Venice, 380km (220 mi.) N of Rome

Bologna is known the world over as the home of the oldest university in Europe, and this venerable institution accounts for much of what you'll see of the city's past and present. By the 13th century, scholars had begun descending upon the city in droves, and the city took shape to accommodate them. Bologna's famous loggias, 40km (21 mi.) of them total, are covered sidewalks that have given students and locals the opportunity to stroll and discourse in any kind of weather. Palazzi and churches were built by the burgeoning community, and artists came from throughout Italy to decorate them. These treasures remain amid a handsome cityscape of ocher-colored buildings, red-tile rooftops, and the occasional tower constructed by powerful medieval families to display their wealth and power. The students remain a vibrant presence in Bologna, giving the city a youthful exuberance.

ESSENTIALS

GETTING THERE   By Plane   European flights land at **Aeroporto G. Marconi** (☎ 051-647-9615), 8km (4 mi.) north of the city and connected to the train station by Aerobus, which runs every 15 minutes; the trip takes 15 minutes and service runs from 6am to 11:35pm and costs 8,000L ($4).

By Train Trains arrive from and depart for the following major Italian cities almost hourly: **Florence** (1 hr.; 14,400L/$7), **Rome** (2¾–3½ hr.; 51,500–65,000L/ $26–$33), **Milan** (regional: 2½ hr., 18,600L/$9; Intercity: 1¾ hr., 29,400L/$15), and **Venice** (2 hr.; 14,500–33,000L/$7–$17). Buses 25 and 30 make the run from the station to Piazza Maggiore in the center of the city, which is within a comfortable walking distance of about 15 minutes down Via Indipendenza, Bologna's major avenue.

By Bus Bologna relies more on trains than it does on buses for service to other cities. But **ATC buses** serve suburban towns from a terminal just outside the train station (☎ **051-290-290**). One bus that may be of interest to travelers is the hourly one to **Ferrara** (65 min.; 9,800L/$4.90).

By Car Bologna lies directly on the A1 autostrada, which runs up the center of the peninsula and connects Rome and Milan. Using this high-speed corridor, Bologna is only an hour from Florence and 2 hours from Milan. Bologna is also linked by the A13 autostrada to Venice (about 2 hr.) and by the A14 to Rimini (a little over an hour) and the other Adriatic cities.

VISITOR INFORMATION The **main tourist office** is in the Palazzo Comunale on Piazza Maggiore (☎ **051-239-660;** fax 051-231-454; www.comune.bologna.it), open Monday to Saturday 9am to 7pm and Sunday 9am to 2pm (July and August, Saturday 8:30am to 2pm, Sunday closed). The **branch office** in the train station (☎ **051-246-541**) will book rooms Monday to Saturday 9am to 7pm. The **airport office** (☎ **051-647-2036**) is open Monday to Saturday 9am to 1pm and 2 to 4pm (during trade fairs, daily 9am to 7pm).

FESTIVALS & MARKETS If you're in Bologna April to October, you can spend your evenings at the classical and jazz concerts and other events that are part of the **Bologna Festival** and held in church cloisters and other scenic settings throughout the city center. The most recent season included a range from Mozart (*The Magic Flute*) to Leonard Bernstein (*West Side Story*), the St. Petersburg, Russia, Philharmonic, and Chick Corea. Tickets start from 10,000L to 20,000L ($5 to $10); for details, call ☎ **051-649-3397,** or check out **www.bolognafestival.it**.

A Taste of Emilia-Romagna

With such a collection of exquisite cities at hand, the pleasures of the region are primarily urban. No small part of the delight of visiting these cities is to partake of the bounty of the rich farmland that lies around them and comes to the tables of the region's simple but excellent restaurants—prosciutto, parmigiano reggiano cheese, fruits and vegetables, salamis, the cream and butter used in the rich sauces that top tortellini and other pastas, and, from the nearby Adriatic, a wealth of seafood. This is a moneyed province, and the food tends to be rich: *Alla Bolognese* means served with a thick meat sauce; *lasagna verde,* made with spinach noodles, contains layer upon layer of meat, béchamel sauce, and parmigiano. Meat dishes are plentiful, and it's indicative of the culinary preferences here that most restaurants serve a good *bollito misto,* a selection of boiled beef, tongue, pig's foot, capon, pork sausages, and maybe oxtail (the choices vary) that's rolled to the table on a cart and topped with a *salsa verde* (herbs and capers).

Emilia-Romagna

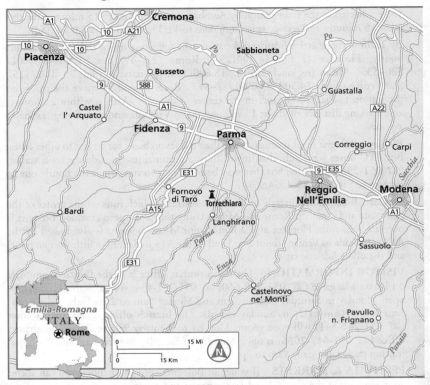

A much less tame event is the **Made in Bo** festival (☎ **051-533-880**), a series of late-night outdoor disco events held in July and August in Parco Nord (bus no. 25 or 91a serves the area from the train station; free buses from Piazza Maggiore are provided for some events). Ask the tourist office for details on both these festivals, as well as the many other concerts, dance and theater performances, and other events the city stages throughout the year.

CITY LAYOUT   The center of Bologna is **Piazza Maggiore,** about a 10-minute walk down **Via dell'Indipendenza** from the train station. All sights are more or less on a short radius from this central square, where the Neptune Fountain, the Basilica di San Petronio, the Palazzo Comunale, and other sights of monumental Bologna are located.

Since old Bologna is densely concentrated within the ring roads that follow the lines of its old walls, anything of interest is only a 10- to 15-minute walk from the Piazza Maggiore. For instance: Following **Via Rizzoli,** which skirts the north end of the piazza, you come to Bologna's famous leaning towers, and from there **Via Zamboni** leads northeast toward the university and the Pinacoteca Nazionale; **Via Ugo Bassi** runs west from the piazza to **Via del Pratello** and the surrounding area, with its antique shops and osterie; and **Via degli Orefici** takes you southeast into the midst of Bologna's colorful food markets and toward the San Stefano church complex.

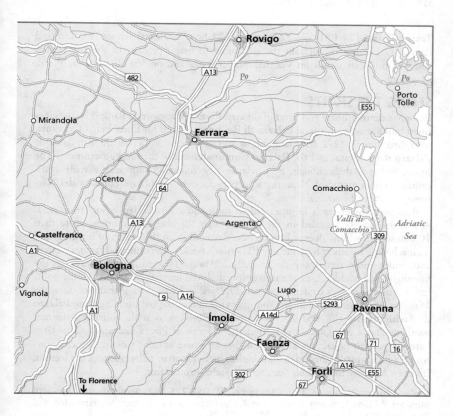

FAST FACTS **Bookstore** National chain **Feltrinelli International,** Via Zamboni 7b (☎ **051-268-070;** www.feltrinelli.it), sells a large selection of English-language titles. **Libreria Il Portico,** Via Rizzoli 9 (☎ **051-231-074**), is a discount bookstore with a couple of bookcases of English-language books (maybe two-thirds classics and literature) at the same cut rates as the rest of their merchandise.

Crime Bologna reportedly has a low incidence of purse snatching and other crimes against tourists; however, beware of pickpockets in and around the train station. In recent years, there has been an alarming and highly visible increase in the number of heroin addicts, especially in the streets off Via dell'Indipendenza.

Drugstores The pharmacy at Piazza Maggiore 6 (☎ **051-239-690**) is open 24 hours.

Emergencies As in all of Italy, the general emergency number is ☎ **113.** The military Carabinieri at ☎ **112** are the most useful police force. To report a fire, call ☎ **115;** for medical emergencies, call ☎ **333-333.**

Hospitals Hospitals in and near the city center are **Ospedale Santa Orsola,** Via Massarenti 9 (☎ **051-636-3111**), and **Ospedale Maggiore,** Via 1 Nigrisoli 2 (☎ **051-647-8111**).

Mail The **main post office** is on Piazza Minghetti, a few blocks southeast of Piazza Maggiore, off Via Farini (☎ **051-223-598**). It's open Monday to Friday 8:15am to 6:30pm and Saturday 8:15am to 12:20pm. All other offices are open Monday to Saturday 8:30am to 1:30pm. The postal code for central Bologna is 40100.

Taxis **Il Taxi** (☎ 051-372-727) provides 24-hour radio taxi service. You can find taxis at taxi stands throughout the city, often in major piazzas. In the city center, you will find taxi stands on Via dell'Indipendenza and on Via Rizzoli near Piazza Maggiore.

SEEING THE SIGHTS

Bologna's central square and heart of the city, **Piazza Maggiore,** is flanked by the city's finest buildings: the medieval **Palazzo di Rei Enzo,** named for Enzo, king of Sardinia, who died here in 1272 after languishing in captivity for 23 years; the Romanesque **Palazzo del Podesta;** and the **Palazzo Comunale,** seat of the local government. The square is dominated, though, by a relative newcomer: an immodestly virile 16th-century bronze statue of Neptune, who presides over the ornate **Fontana del Nettuno,** inhabited by sensual sirens.

Bologna's **university** is Europe's oldest, rooted in a Roman law school from A.D. 425 and officially founded in the 10th century. By the 13th century, more than 10,000 students from all over Europe were descending on this center of learning, and their scholarly numbers have included Thomas à Becket, Copernicus, Dante, Petrarch, and, much more recently, Federico Fellini. Always forward-thinking, even in the unenlightened Middle Ages, the university employed female professors, and the political leanings of today's student body are displayed in leftist slogans that emblazon the 15th- to 19th-century buildings. You may visit one of the old buildings, the **Palazzo di Archiginnasio** (☎ 051-236-488 or 051-276-811), near the university district, south of Piazza Maggiore, just behind the Duomo at Piazza Galvani 1. This large baroque palazzo houses an anatomical theater where ancient wooden benches surround a much-used marble slab and skinless carved human pillars support the lectern. It's open Monday to Saturday 9am to 1pm; admission is free.

Basilica di San Petronio. Piazza Maggiore. ☎ **051-225-442.** Admission free. Apr–Sept Mon–Sat 7:15am–1pm and 2–6pm, Sun 7:30am–1pm and 2–6:30pm. Museum Mon and Wed–Sat 9:30am–12:30pm. Bus: 10, 11, 17, 20, 25, 27, 30, 37.

Massive as this church is, it's not nearly as big as its 14th-century architects intended it to be. Rome got wind of the Bolognese scheme to build a church bigger than St. Peter's and cut off the funds. Even so, the structure that was erected over the next 3 centuries is impressively grand, fronted by a facade partially striped in white and red, the city's heraldic colors, and punctuated by one of the great works of the Italian Renaissance: a **marble doorway** surrounded by bas-reliefs depicting the Madonna and Child and scenes from the Bible, carved by Jacopo della Quercia and now sadly weather-worn.

The cavernous interior beyond (where Charles V was crowned Holy Roman Emperor in 1530) is richly decorated with frescoes, the best of which are in the chapels to the left as you enter. One contains Lorenzo Costa's *Madonna and Child,* and the other (fourth on the left) is enlivened with colorful depictions of *Heaven and Hell,* the *Life of St. Petronius,* and *Stories of the Magi* by Giovanni da Modena (who also

Driving in Bologna

Much of central Bologna is closed to cars without special permits daily 7am to 8pm (including Sundays and holidays). A permit is required to park in the center; hotel guests can obtain one through their hotel for 8,000l ($4) a day, which included a 6,000L ($3) all-day bus pass!

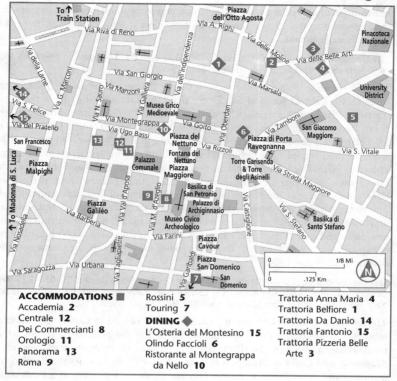

did the frescoes in and around the left aisle's first chapel). All chapels are equipped with 200L (10¢) light boxes.

Embedded in the floor of the left aisle is an enchanting curiosity—Italy's largest **sundial,** a 221-foot astronomical clock that the astronomer Cassini installed in 1655. The two-room "museum" at the end of the left aisle contains drawings and wooden models of the church and various plans for its facade, some fine illuminated choir books, and the usual gilt and silver reliquaries, robes, and chalices.

Basilica di Santo Stefano. Via Santo Stefano 24. ☎ **051-223-256.** Admission free. Daily 9am–noon and 3:30–6pm. Bus: 11, 18, 25, 27.

This remarkable assemblage of hallowed buildings incorporates four churches from the 4th to the 13th century. A walk through the complex provides a remarkable overview of the history of Bologna. The first church you enter is the **Crocifisso,** begun in the 11th century (as you enter, notice the pulpit built into the facade). San Petronio, Bologna's patron saint, lies in the church to the left, the most charming in the group, the 12th-century **San Sepolcro,** a polygon modeled after the church of the Holy Sepulchre in Jerusalem. According to legend, the basin in the courtyard is the one in which Pontius Pilate absolved himself after condemning Christ to death (in truth, it's an 8th-century Lombard piece). The oldest church is the 5th-century **Santi Vitale e Agricola,** incorporating fragments of a Roman temple to Isis; Charlemagne allegedly worshiped here in the 8th century. Just beyond is the 13th-century **Trìnita** and the complex's 11th-century **cloisters,** where plaques honor Bologna's war dead. A small museum/gift shop opens off the back, containing some unmemorable paintings and frescoes spanning the 13th to the 18th century. Here is yet another church: the tiny **Cappella della Benda.**

San Domenico. Piazza San Domenico 13. ☎ **051-640-0411.** Admission free. Tues–Mon 7am–1pm and 2:30–7pm, Sun 2:30–7pm. Bus: 17, 30.

Here, in the sixth chapel on the right, is one of the great treasures of Bologna, the beautifully crafted ○ **tomb of San Domenico (St. Dominic),** founder of the teaching order that bears his name, who died in Bologna in 1221 (and whose venerated X-ray decorates the chapel wall). These saints and angels are a joint effort of Michelangelo, Pisano, and, most notably, Nicolo di Bari, who was so proud of his work on the cover of the tomb (*arca*) that he dropped his last name and is better known as Nicolo dell'Arca. Postcards near the entrance to the chapel show you who carved what; a 20-year-old Michelangelo did the candle-bearing angel at the lower right and the statue of San Petronius bearing a tiny model of Bologna up on the tomb toward the left. He also carved San Proculus, with his cloak slung over one shoulder, on the tomb's backside, but you can no longer walk around back to see it thanks to a new fence and gate. The chapel's apse fresco is by Guido Reni, who's buried in the baroque chapel across the nave. The two striking stilt-tombs on the piazza out front date from 1298 and 1300.

San Giacomo Maggiore & Oratorio di Santa Cecilia. Piazza Rossini. ☎ **051-225-970;** Oratorio 051-648-7580. Admission free. Church daily 7am–noon and 3:30–6pm; Oratorio daily 10am–1pm and 3–7pm (2–6pm in winter). Bus: 25, 27, 30, 37, 50.

The masterpiece in this 13th-century church, which took on its Gothic appearance in subsequent centuries, is the chapel/burial chamber of the Bentivoglio family, which ruled Bologna through the 15th century. Among the masterpieces here are a *Madonna and Child* by Francesco Francia, along with the **frescoes** the Bentivoglios commissioned from Ferrarese master Lorenzo Costa to depict life in a Renaissance court, an apt decoration for Bologna's most influential (and tyrannical) clan. An underground passage connects the chapel to the spot, now occupied by the Teatro Comunale, where the family's palazzo stood until it was razed by an angry mob in the 16th century.

Entered from Via Zanobi 15 (toward the back of the left flank of the church), the **Oratorio di Santa Cecilia** was frescoed with scenes from the lives of St. Catharine and her husband, St. Valerian, by the best artists working in Bologna in the 16th century. These included Il Francia (the two scenes closest to the altar on either side), Lorenzo Costa (the two panels abutting Il Francia's), and Amico Aspertini (the two scenes closest to the entry door on either side; he may have had a hand in the four middle panels as well).

○ **Torre Garisenda & Torre degli Asinelli.** Piazza Porte Ravegna. Torre degli Asinelli, admission 5,000L ($2.50). May–Sept daily 9am–6pm, Oct–Apr daily 9am–5pm. Bus: 11, 13, 17, 18, 25, 27, 30, 37.

Of the more than 200 towers that once rose above Bologna—built by noble families as symbols of their wealth and prestige—only these and a scattering of others still stand, but barely—the 165-feet-tall **Torre Garisenda** tilts a precarious 10 feet off the perpendicular, and the 320-feet-tall **Torre degli Asinelli** leans 7½ feet. A climb up the 500 steps of the Torre degli Asinelli rewards you with a stunning view of Bologna's red-tile rooftops and the surrounding hills. At the base of the towers, the seven main streets of medieval Bologna spread out from Piazza Porta Ravegna.

A Money-Saving Tip

A cumulative ticket for all the city's civic museums (including the archaeology and medieval ones reviewed here) is available for 12,000L ($6) for 1 day or 16,000L ($8) for 3 days.

Museo Civico Archeologico (Archaeological Museum). Via dell'Archiginnasio, 2. ☎ **051-233-849.** Admission 8,000L ($4), 4,000L ($2) ages 15–18, students, and over 60. Free under 15. Tues–Fri 9am–2pm, Sat–Sun 9am–1pm and 3:30–7pm. Bus: 11, 17, 25, 30, 37.

The Etruscan and Roman finds from the surrounding region and many fine Egyptian antiquities make this museum one of Italy's best collections of antiquities. The Egyptian holdings have been reorganized and are now housed in well-lit quarters on the lower level; they include a portion of the ***Book of the Dead*** and **bas-reliefs** from the tomb of Horemheb. As you move up through the building, you walk through another relatively new ground-floor exhibit, a wing housing replicas of well-known Greek and Roman statues, to the peaceful central courtyard, which is littered with ancient milestones from Via Emilia. The next floor is filled with the museum's impressive Etruscan collection (crowded into glass cases à la the 19th century), which includes many remnants from Bologna's own beginnings as the Etruscan outpost Felsina. Among the burial items and other artifacts is a bronze urn from the 5th century B.C., the **Situla di Certosa,** decorated with a depiction of a ceremonial procession.

Museo Civico Medioevale (Medieval Museum). Via Manzoni 4. ☎ **051-203-930.** Admission 8,000L ($4), 4,000L ($2) ages 15–18, students, and over 60. Free under 15. Mon–Fri 9am–2pm, Sat–Sun 9am–1pm and 3:30–7pm. (Note: Word on the street is the hours will change to Tues–Sun 9am–6:30pm, but it's not yet official.) Bus: 10, 11, 17, 20, 25, 27, 30, 37.

Though a Roman wall runs through the courtyard, the collection here is determinedly devoted to depicting life in medieval Bologna. It also has a healthy handful of medieval objects from cultures around the world (collections left over from previous incarnations of the museum). During the Middle Ages, the city revolved around its university, and the most enchanting treasures are the sepulchers of professors, surrounded for eternity by carvings of dozing and mocking students. Also on view are some fascinating cooking utensils from daily life in medieval Bologna, some illuminated manuscripts, and a sizeable collection of arms and armor. The museum's name hasn't kept it from squirreling away a few small Renaissance and baroque bronzes by the likes of Giambologna, Bernini, and Algardi.

Pinacoteca Nazionale (National Picture Gallery). Via delle Belle Arti 56. ☎ **051-243-222.** Admission 8,000L ($4) adults, free under 18 and over 65. Tues–Sat 9am–2pm (to 7pm Thurs), Sun 9am–1pm. Bus: 18, 20, 32, 33, 37.

Many of these second-floor galleries, which are badly in need of better lighting and signage, are devoted to Bolognese painters or painters from elsewhere who worked in Bologna. The galleries house, for instance, Italy's largest repository of paintings by Bologna's most illustrious artist, Guido Reni (1575 to 1642). Perhaps his best-known work, ***Ritratto della Madre,*** a portrait of his mother, is here, and in the same room hang many of his other works, including ***Samson the Victorious.*** More striking, however, is a work by an earlier Bolognese artist, Vitale da Bologna: the 14th-century ***St. George and the Dragon.*** The museum's most sought-out work is not by a native son but by Raphael, whose ***Ecstasy of St. Cecilia*** is one of the great achievements of Renaissance painting.

AFFORDABLE PLACES TO STAY

High season in Bologna is any time the city is hosting one of its trade fairs; low season is during much of the summer—especially in August, when the Bolognese tend to flee the city for cooler realms. Don't be shy about bargaining for a better rate during slow periods; hotelkeepers eager to fill empty rooms will often offer them at rates that are substantially lower than the ones they publish.

Accademia. Via delle Belle Arti 6, 40124 Bologna. ☎ **051-232-318.** Fax 051-263-590. www.hotelaccademia.it. 28 units, 24 with bathroom. TV TEL. 90,000–95,000L ($45–$48) single without bathroom, 130,000L ($65) single with bathroom; 150,000L ($75) double without bathroom,190,000L ($95) double with bathroom. Rates include breakfast (but you may be able to talk them out of it and save 15,000L/$8 a head). No credit cards. Parking 10,000L ($5). Bus: 50.

If you're looking for a high level of comfort and service, don't even consider staying here. On the other hand, the location, on a lively street near the university, is superb, and the surroundings are full of character. The rooms are spread across several floors of a centuries-old palazzo, and the lobby and entrance, with well-worn stone flooring and vaulted ceilings, are deceivingly grand, as is the staircase (no elevator). Several years ago, at least, the bright, no-frills, comfortable rooms were refurbished with bland contemporary armoires, desks, and headboards. Alas, I can't say more than that, as the generally disagreeable management refused to let me see any of the rooms. Last I saw, the baths didn't seem to have been updated for a couple of decades, so the fixtures and tiles were worn and the half-size bathtubs can pose a bit of a challenge.

Centrale. Via delle Zecca 2 (off Via Ugo Bassi, 2 blocks west of Piazza Maggiore), 40121 Bologna. ☎ **05l-225-114.** Fax 051-235-162. E-mail: werterg@tin.it. 25 units, 20 with bathroom. TV TEL. 80,000L ($40) single without bathroom, 120,000L ($60) single with bathroom; 130,000L ($65) double without bathroom, 160,000L ($80) double with bathroom; 210,000L ($105) triple with bathroom; 250,000L ($125) quad with bathroom. No breakfast. AE, DC, MC, V. Closed Christmas week and 1 week in mid-Aug. Bus: 25.

This attractive pensione offers one of Bologna's best values: It's cheap, central, and clean and has all the amenities you need. An ancient cage elevator deposits you at the door on the third floor of an old apartment house a few blocks off Piazza Maggiore. Once inside you'll find yourself in the amiable company of the English-speaking owner and an interesting mix of travelers from all over the world. A nicely appointed bar, breakfast room, sitting room, and several of the guest rooms are on this floor, while others are reached via an internal staircase to the floor above. Oriental runners and crystal chandeliers lend an air of elegance to the halls, and the charm extends to the white-tile-floored rooms. All have been redone with crisp modern furnishings and pleasant pastel fabrics. The baths can be small but are newly tiled and nicely fitted out with large sinks and commodious stall showers. Most rooms are unusually spacious for Italy, and several have three and four beds, making this an especially affordable stopover for families (I like no. 18, with a big window overlooking a brick tower and church dome). All the rooms have air conditioning, save the three bathless singles (even the doubles without bath have it).

Panorama. Via Livraghi 1 (off Via Ugo Bassi, 3 blocks west of Piazza Maggiore), 40121 Bologna. ☎ **051-221-802.** Fax 051-266-360. 13 units, 1 with bathroom. TV. 75,000L ($38) single; 100,000L ($50) double without bathroom, 140,000L ($70) double with bathroom; 140,000L ($70) triple without bathroom, 170,000L ($85) triple with bathroom; 160,000L ($80) quad; 180,000L ($90) quint. No credit cards. Bus: 10, 25.

I'm delighted whenever I discover another charming old-fashioned pensione like this still in business. In fact, if you don't mind rooms without baths or air-conditioning (but with fans), you may want to consider staying here even if your budget allows for more luxurious accommodation. The location near Piazza Maggiore is excellent, and the women who own/manage the hotel, which occupies the top floor of an old apartment house, make guests feel like family. The rooms are very large and high ceilinged, and most look through large windows over a pleasant courtyard to the hills above the city (avoid nos. 6 to 10, whose double-paned windows can't keep out the traffic noise). The furnishings are functional but modern and include enough wooden armoires and other homey touches to render them cozy; some rooms sleep four and five.

✪ **Roma.** Via d'Azeglio 9, 40123 Bologna. ☎ **051-226-322.** Fax 051-239-909. E-mail: hotelroma@mailbox.dsnet.it. 85 units. A/C MINIBAR TV TEL. 208,000L ($104) single; 266,000L ($133) double. Rates include buffet breakfast. AE, DC, MC, V. Parking 25,000L ($13).

This gracious hotel enjoys a marvelous location only steps away from Piazza Maggiore and offers many of the amenities you'd expect in larger hotels—including a cozy bar off the lobby, an adequate though not outstanding in-house restaurant, an efficient English-speaking staff at the front desk, porters to carry your bags, and a garage. What really makes this hotel worth seeking out, though, are its unusually comfortable rooms. Most have foyers between the baths and bedrooms that have closets at one end, so they double as dressing rooms. The rooms are large and bright, with brass beds that are often king size, roomy armchairs, and long tables where you can spread out belongings without being messy. (For those who prefer neutral decor, one drawback may be the profusion of tastefully matching floral patterns that dominates the wallpaper, draperies, and comforters.) The green-tiled baths were redone several years ago and tend to be huge, with bidets and luxuriously deep tubs (though you'll have to hold the shower nozzle yourself, and there's rarely a curtain). Ask for one of the rooms on the top floor with a terrace (nos. 301 to 303 and 306 to 309).

Rossini. Via Bibiena 11, 40126 Bologna. ☎ **051-237-716.** Fax 051-268-035. 30 units, 25 with bathroom. TEL. 70,000L ($35) single without bathroom, 110,000L ($55) single with bathroom; 110,000L ($55) double without bathroom, 170,000L ($85) double with bathroom. AE, DC, MC, V. Bus: 50.

Its location in the heart of the university district is what draws many guests to this plain but comfortable hotel, often filled with visiting academics. If you prefer basic comfort at a good price to luxury and fancy amenities, the Rossini will fill the bill, if not thrill. The rooms aren't much more than functional, right down to the no-nonsense small baths. The rooms tend to be large, however, with very firm beds, and the bland modern furnishings include well-lit desks and even reading lights over the beds. A 2000 renovation almost doubled the hotel's size, installed an elevator, granted TVs to the rooms with bath, and added air-conditioning to the eight top-floor rooms. The lobby bar is a fun place to sit around sipping wine and listening to some intellectual chatter.

Touring. Via de' Mattuiani 1–2 (off Via Garibaldi), 40124 Bologna. ☎ **051-584-305.** Fax 051-334-763. www.hoteltouring.it. 36 units. TV TEL. 110,000–200,000L ($55–$100) single; 180,000–350,000L ($90–$175) double; 280,000–450,000L ($140–$225) jr. suite for 2–5. Rates include breakfast. AE, DC, MC, V. Parking 30,000–40,000L ($15–$20) in garage. Bus: 30 to Piazza Tribunale.

This quiet hotel on the edge of the *centro storico* near San Domenico is just finishing up 3 years of renovations (in spring 2001). The stylish rooms are nicely fitted out with shiny hardwood or faux-marble ceramic floors, sleek contemporary furnishings, and (in almost all) air-conditioning (a few just have ceiling fans). The baths are striking, many with gilt-framed mirrors on the white tile walls, deep sinks (there are double sinks in a few), roomy stall showers, and hair dryers and scales. Some rooms are quite large indeed, and many on the third and fourth floors have large balconies. The eight no-smoking rooms also come with minibars. The roof terrace affords wonderful views.

WORTH A SPLURGE

✪ **Dei Commercianti.** Via Pignattari 11, 40123 Bologna. ☎ **051-233-052.** Fax 051-224-733. www.cnc.it/bologna. 34 units. A/C MINIBAR TV TEL. 205,000–370,000L ($103–$185) single; 305,000–525,000L ($153–$263) double. Rates include buffet breakfast. AE, DC, MC, V. Parking 40,000L ($20).

This lovely building faces the flanks of San Petronius, and was built in the 12th century as the city's first seat of government. A recent renovation took full advantage of this provenance, even to the point of showing off some of the original beams and flooring in cutaway views through protective glass, and occasionally even a bit of fresco. There are lovely antique pieces and Oriental carpets in the lobby and vaulting and columns in the breakfast room. The polished woodwork and rustic touches extend down the twisting halls into the stunning rooms, which have been carved out of the centuries-old structure and vary widely in size and shape. Even the smallest, though, are welcoming. Most of the beds are canopied or have iron frames; the fabrics are in rich red, gold, and blue; many of the ceilings are beamed; and lots of rooms have inlaid marble tables. The baths are modern and come with hair dryers and glass-enclosed showers. Some rooms have nicely planted small terraces (a few overlooking San Petronius). Internet access is offered for no more than the cost of the local phone call to connect.

Orologio. Via IV Novembre 10, 40123 Bologna. ☎ **051-231-253.** Fax 051-260-552. www.cnc.it/bologna. 34 units. A/C MINIBAR TV TEL. 205,000–370,000L ($103–$185) single; 305,000–525,000L ($153–$273) double without view, 335,000–580,000L ($168–$290) double with view (a sliver of Piazza Maggiore or of hills); 480,000–770,000L ($240–$385) suite. Rates include buffet breakfast. AE, MC, V. Parking 40,000L ($20).

A loyal cadre of travelers have come to love this recently renovated small hotel, which looks across a small pedestrian street adjacent to Piazza Maggiore, on the clock tower side of the town hall (hence the name). Aside from this wonderful location, two of the attractions are the lounge, with its comfy couches and Internet terminal (you pay for the local phone call), and the adjacent breakfast room, where a generous buffet is served. Another plus is the welcome afforded by the English-speaking staff and members of the Orsi family, who own this and other hotels in central Bologna and whose welcome extends to the loan of a bike for a spin around town. The rooms are small but nicely done with sponge-washed wall coverings and old photos of Bologna, wrought-iron bed frames and handsome contemporary furnishings, and well-equipped modern baths with hair dryers. The suites, while not very large, have two rooms with extra touches like ceiling stuccoes in the baths or marble column capitals serving as end tables. All told, the recent price hike wasn't justified, but the location can't be beat.

GREAT DEALS ON DINING

There's good reason it's called "Bologna the Fat." Chubby tortellini are filled with cheese and meat and topped with cream sauces. Heaping platters of grilled meats are served without a care for cholesterol. Not surprisingly, you can eat very well in Bologna—what is surprising is that you need not spend a fortune doing so.

L'Osteria del Montesino. Via del Pratello 74b. ☎ **051-523-426.** Primi and crostini 5,000–12,000L ($2.50–$6); salads 13,000–18,000L ($7–$9). MC, V. Tues–Sun 8am–1am. SARDEGNAN/WINE BAR.

Of the many osterias lining Via del Pratello, this would be my choice for a light meal. It has a huge selection of crostini, and you can taste all of them when you order a heaping platter of *crostini misti* (12,000L/$6). A daily trio of pastas costs 10,000L ($5) for one, 11,000L ($6) to sample two, or 12,000L ($6) for all three or for the ricotta-

Snacks & Gelato

Many Bolognese claim that the **Gelateria Creperia Gianna** (no phone), Via Montegrappa 11, a short walk from Piazza Maggiore, serves the city's best gelato. ✪ **Bar Giuseppe,** Piazza Maggiore 1 (no phone), is a popular watering hole that stretches for at least a block beneath arcades facing Piazza Maggiore. It's the perfect spot to linger over a glass of wine or one of the many cocktails on the bar menu and watch the human comedy that transpires endlessly in this grand space. Giuseppe is also known for its homemade gelato, which comes in at least 40 flavors and can be enjoyed in a cone (from 3,000L/$1.50) or in elaborate concoctions with fruit, chocolate, whipped cream, and other toppings.

The dark-paneled **Bar Roberto,** Via Orefici 9a (☎ **051-232-256**), is near Bologna's central market. It's probably the only smoke-free place you'll find in Italy. The ban on smoking, according to Roberto, is to ensure the purity of the delicious homemade pastries that attract a loyal breakfast clientele who can be seen waiting at the door when the bar opens at 8am. There's something refreshingly staid about the **Gran Bar,** Via M. d'Azeglio 8 (☎ **051-227-522**); maybe it's the long mahogany bar beneath a ceiling of stained glass. Because it's just a few steps off Piazza Maggiore, this is a handy spot to enjoy a glass of wine or a light snack. You'll find the attractive **Il Caffè della Corte,** Corte Isolani 5b (☎ **051-261-555**), hidden in the newly renovated shopping arcade connecting Strada Maggiore with one of Bologna's favorite landmarks, San Stefano; in fact, this is a good place to relax after touring that lovely church complex. The pastries are excellent.

and-spinach *tortellacci* (weekends only). These *primi*—along with most wines and the various mixed meat and cheese platters—ignore the famed local cuisine and are proudly Sardegnan. The salads are excellent, and many are heaped high with such substantial ingredients as roast chicken and shrimp. The interior rooms are typical Italian tavern, but most regulars queue up for a table on the covered front terrace, usually open except in the chilliest midwinter months.

✪ **Olindo Faccioli.** Via Altabella 15/B. ☎ **051-223-171.** Primi 8,000L ($4); secondi 9,000–15,000L ($4.50–$8). AE, DC, MC, V. Mon–Sat 6pm–2am. Closed Aug. BOLOGNESE.

Wander into this inconspicuous little place for a glass of wine and you may end up spending the entire evening. Nine tables are wedged into two tiny handsome rooms lined high with the more than 400 vintages the proprietor serves. While this selection and the ambience are reason enough to linger, you'll probably want to stay to sample the limited but delicious offerings from the kitchen. There's no menu, but the daily fare is posted on a chalkboard—or, when they forget to do that, recited orally. If you want to eat, try to arrive before nine to ensure that you'll get a table before the rooms fill with patrons who linger over wine into the late evening. A carpaccio of tuna or a selection of bruschetti or *crostini misti* (toasted breads with various toppings) are perfect openers, followed by one of the few specials that change each evening but lean toward lighter vegetarian fare—zucchini flowers stuffed with mozzarella, *crespellini* (cheese-filled little crepes), and *tagliatelle con pesto* (flat noodles topped with homemade pesto). While 2am is the official closing, Carlo, the owner, often chooses to stay open later, and he keeps the restaurant open in August if he doesn't want to take a vacation.

Trattoria Anna Maria. Via Belle Arti 17a. ☎ **051-266-894.** Reservations recommended. Primi 12,000–15,000L ($6–$8); secondi 15,000–22,000L ($8–$11). AE, MC, V. Tues 7:30pm–midnight, Wed–Sun noon–3pm and 7:30pm–midnight. Closed July 27–Aug 27. EMILIA-ROMAGNOLA.

Anna Maria, the friendly proprietor, always seems to be on hand at this animated spot, and she and her staff serve some of the finest trattoria food in Bologna in a big room adorned with old photos of opera stars who've performed at the Teatro Comunale. All the pasta is freshly made and appears in some unusual variations, such as *quadrettini*, four shapes of ricotta-stuffed pasta floating in chicken broth, and a wonderful *tortellini al gorgonzola.* While any of these pasta dishes constitutes a meal in itself, you may be tempted to try one of the substantial second courses, most of which are simple, deliciously prepared dishes from the region and include the likes of *trippa con fagioli* (tripe and beans) and *fegato con cipolli* (liver and onions).

Trattoria Belfiore. Via Marsala 11a. ☎ **051-226-641.** Primi 8,500–11,000L ($4.25–$6); secondi 9,000–23,000L ($4.50–$12); pizze 5,000–10,000L ($2.50–$5). AE, DC, MC, V. Sun–Mon noon–3pm and 7:30pm–midnight. BOLOGNESE.

This series of narrow high-ceilinged rooms is on one of the old streets that run between Via dell'Indipendenza and the university area, and as a result it attracts an incongruous group of students and businesspeople who chatter noisily as friendly waiters run back and forth from the kitchen. This is not the place for a romantic conversation or a foray into haute cuisine—simple is the rule. Dishes don't get much more elaborate than tortellini, risotti, or a platter of *salsiccia al ferri* (grilled sausages) or *pollo arrosto* (roast chicken), but like much of the fare, including the pizzas, they're prepared over an open fire and are delicious and very fairly priced.

Trattoria Da Danio. Via San Felice 50. ☎ **051-555-202.** Primi 7,000–10,000L ($3.50–$5); secondi 8,000–15,000L ($4–$8); menù turistico 13,500L ($7) for one course with wine, 20,000L ($10) for full meal with wine. MC, V. Tues–Sun noon–2:30pm and 7:30pm–10pm. BOLOGNESE.

This simple restaurant, which consists of one brightly lit tiled room, is family run and usually filled with the clamor of families who live in this old neighborhood just east of Piazza Maggiore (follow Via Ugo Bassi its length to Via San Felice). The kitchen sends out good, substantial servings of traditional Bolognese fare: heaping bowls of tortellini topped with Bolognese sauce, delicious gnocchi stuffed with spinach and ricotta, homey chicken and pork dishes, and the like. The 20,000L *menù turistico* (pasta, main course, side dish, wine, water, and cover) is a great deal.

Trattoria Fantoni. Via del Pratello 11/A. ☎ **051-236-358.** Reservations recommended. Primi 8,500–9,500L ($4.25–$4.75); secondi 11,000–16,000L ($6–$8). No credit cards. Tues–Sat noon–4pm and 7pm–midnight, Mon noon–4pm. BOLOGNESE.

Of all the casual eateries along Via del Pratello, this down-to-earth restaurant is probably my favorite. The two simple dining rooms are almost always jammed with people who work in the neighborhood (which is why the management closes on weekends), and the menu reflects their culinary tastes. You can sample horsemeat, which appears on many traditional Bolognese menus, prepared here several ways, including *bistecca cavallo* and *cavallo alla tartara* (horse steak and horsemeat tartare). Or you can opt for nicely prepared versions of more familiar fare, such as *salsiccia* (grilled sausage) or *tacchino alla griglia* (turkey breast). The vegetable dishes are also especially good—the *melanzane al forno* (baked eggplant) and *finocchi lessi* (boiled fennel) constitute meals in themselves. The food is so good and the prices so low that you can expect to wait for a table just about any evening.

Trattoria-Pizzeria Belle Arte. Via Belle Arti 14. ☎ **051-225-581.** Primi 12,000–22,000L ($6–$11); secondi 14,000–30,000L ($7–$15); pizze 6,500–16,000L ($3.25–$8). AE, MC, V. Thurs–Tues noon–2:30pm and 7pm–midnight. Closed part of Jan and Aug. PIZZERIA/ITALIAN/SEAFOOD.

Why do theatergoers flock here after performances at the nearby Teatro Comunale? Because the food is excellent and the kitchen keeps later hours than most Bologna restaurants. Even on weeknights you may have to wait to get a table in the handsome brick- and panel-walled dining room, but once the *tortellini alla panna* (homemade tortellini in cream sauce) or *tagliatelli con funghi porcini* (flat noodles with porcini mushrooms) starts arriving at the table, you'll be glad you waited. Lately, they've been making a go of a fish-and-paella–oriented half of the menu (seafood *paella alla Valenciana* for two 44,000L/$22). Or choose from a stupendous selection of pizzas that emerge from a wood-burning oven. There's also a nice selection of oversize salads.

WORTH A SPLURGE

Ristorante al Montegrappa da Nello. Via Montegrappa 2. ☎ **051-236-331.** Reservations recommended for dinner. Primi 10,000–13,000L ($5–$7); secondi 16,000–30,000L ($8–$15). AE, DC, MC, V. Tues–Sun noon–3pm and 7–11:30pm. Closed Aug. BOLOGNESE.

Just watching the whirl in the clamorous, cavernous dining rooms is part of the experience at this venerable Bologna institution. You can get by with a simple and relatively inexpensive meal here, but you'll probably want to spend the extra lire and sample the excellently prepared fare, which relies on the fresh ingredients of the season, without fiscal constraint. Truffles (which can tack 15,000L/$8 onto the price of a dish) and porcini are hallmarks of the house, and they appear in salads, atop rich pastas, and accompanying grilled meats, which range into wild boar and venison in season. There's a menu, but because the chef only prepares what's fresh at the market that day, it's best just to let the waiters tell you what they're serving; in fact, you can get a preview of the daily offerings in appetizing displays near the entrance.

BOLOGNA AFTER DARK

A good way to keep up with performances in Bologna—whether a poetry reading in the back of a bar or a pop concert at the Stadio Comunale—is to scan the posters that are plastered on walls around the university. The tourist office also distributes updates on cultural events. *Il Bo,* a weekly that covers local events, has many listings; it's in Italian but is sprinkled liberally with English and distributed for free around the city.

THE PERFORMING ARTS The **Teatro Comunale,** Via Largo Respighi 1 (☎ **051-529-011**), hosts Bologna's lively opera, orchestra, and ballet seasons, as well as intriguing shows, such as homages to Frank Zappa or Charlie Chaplin. The box office is open Monday to Friday 3:30pm to 7pm and Saturday 9:30am to 12:30pm and 3:30 to 7pm.

BARS Given its young and restless student population, Bologna stays up later than most Italian cities. The main night-owl haunts are **Via del Pratello** and, near the university, **Via Zamboni** and **Via delle Belle Arte.** You can usually find a place for a drink, a shot of espresso, or a light meal as late as 2am.

Head to the **Cabala American Bar,** Strada Maggiore 10 (☎ **051-265-445**), to hear a pianist who plays nightly and favors American classics and show tunes (open at 7:30pm; music 10pm to 4am). You'll want to retire at 10:30pm to the cellars of a 16th-century palazzo near the university at **Cantina Bentivoglio,** Via Mascarella 4b (☎ **051-265-416;** www.affari.com/bentivoglio). That's when you'll hear some of the best jazz in Bologna. It's also a popular spot for filmgoers, who stop in for some food

---

A Moveable Feast

At the **Enoteca Italiana,** Via Marsala 2b (☎ **051-235-989**), an inviting and aromatic shop-cum-wine bar on a side street just north of Piazza Maggiore, you can stand at the bar and sip on a local wine while enjoying a sandwich. For a moveable feast, you can also stock up on a wide selection of ham, salamis, and cheese at the deli counter, and enjoy a picnic near the gurgles of the Neptune Fountain. It's open daily 10:30am to 3pm and 6 to 9:30pm.

On a stroll through the **Pescherie Vecchie,** the city's market area, you can also assemble a meal. Along the Via Drapperie and adjoining streets, salumerie, cheese shops, bakeries, and vegetable markets are heaped high with attractive displays. The stalls of Bologna's other food market, the **Mercato Clavature,** Via Clavature 12, is open Monday to Wednesday and Friday and Saturday 7am to 1pm (plus 4 to 6pm in summer) and Thursday and Saturday 7am to 1pm.

(most dishes 10,000L to 20,000L/$5 to $10) and tunes after catching one of the first-run movies at the Odeon 2 across the street. It's open Tuesday to Sunday 8pm to 2am.

There's Guinness and Harp on tap and an attendant Anglophone following at the **Irish Times Pub,** Via Paradiso 1 (☎ **051-261-648**), though a well-dressed but not always so well-behaved young Italian crowd predominates in the noisy, smoky, pub-like rooms; open daily 7:30pm to 2am (2:30am Friday and Saturday), with 6,000L ($3) pints during happy hour until 9pm (10:30pm Tuesday). More popular these days is the **Cluricaune Irish Pub,** Via Zamboni 18b (☎ **051-263-419**), a raucous joint near the university with quite good live music some nights (no cover) and seating out under the street's arcade. Happy hour lasts until 8:30pm (10:30pm on Wednesdays) and knocks 2,000L ($1) off most drinks.

The **Birreria del Pratello,** Via del Pratello 24a (☎ **051-238-249**), does a passable Italian imitation of a Munich *bierhalle,* though it lacks that Teutonic coziness. Still, locals flock here for the outdoor seating and the genuine Bavarian brew served in liter-sized mugs for 10,000L ($5). They also do sandwiches, slices of pizza, and pasta dishes for 7,000L to 10,000L ($3.50 to $5); closed Sunday. The **Osteria de Poeti,** Via Poeti 1 (☎ **051-236-166**), is Bologna's oldest osteria and has been in operation since the 16th century—the brick-vaulted ceilings, stone walls, and ancient wine barrels provide just the sort of ambience you would expect to find in such a historic establishment. Stop in to enjoy the live jazz and folk music on tap Tuesday to Sunday 7:30pm to 2:30am (also open for lunch Tuesday to Friday 12:30 to 2:30pm).

GAY BARS Bologna is the seat of Italy's Arci-Gay movement, and that plus the large student population make it rather more open to same-sex couples. **Cassero,** Piazza Porta Saragozza 2 (☎ **051-644-6902;** www.gay.it/cassero), is Bologna's most popular gay bar, with a noisy discolike atmosphere and floor shows daily 9pm to 2am (later Friday and Saturday). Monday to Thursday, they host shows, cabaret, and concerts; Thursday is women's night; Friday to Sunday, it's a full-fledged disco. The biggest attraction here, though, is the setting—the club actually occupies one of Bologna's 13th-century gates, the top of which serves as a roof garden and open-air dance floor in good weather. During the day (weekdays 10am to 1pm and 3 to 9pm), they offer gay-friendly services, including a library and a help line. You need a 20,000L ($10) annual Arci-Gay card to get in (available here); some live acts tack on 5,000L ($2.50) or so.

2 Ferrara: Where the Estes Ruled

45km (27 mi.) N of Bologna, 110km (66 mi.) S of Venice, 250km (150 mi.) SE of Milan, 425km (250 mi.) N of Rome

One family, the Estes, accounts for much of what you'll find in this enchanting city on the plains of Romagna. From 1200 to 1600, the Estes ruled and ranted from their imposing palazzo/fortress that's still the centerpiece of **Ferrara.** They endowed the city with palaces, gardens, and avenues, as well as intrigues, including those of their most famous duchess, Lucrezia Borgia. After the Estes left (when Rome refused to recognize the last heir of the clan as duke), Ferrara fell victim to neglect and finally, during World War II, to bombs. Despite the bombing, much of the Renaissance town remains and has been restored. In fact, this city of rose-colored brick is one of the most beautiful in Italy and, shrouded in a gentle mist from the surrounding plains as it often is, one of the most romantic.

ESSENTIALS

GETTING THERE   By Train   Half-hourly trains arrive from and depart for **Bologna** (35–60 min.; 4,900L/$2.45), and **Venice** (80 min, 10,800–26,500L/$5–$13). There are 1 to 2 trains per hour to **Ravenna** (60–70 min.; 7,000–12,500L/$3.50–$6). One to three trains hourly connect with **Padua** (regional: 80–100 min, 7,600L/$3.80; High speed: 45 min., 20,200L/$10).

The **train station** is a 15-minute walk from the center; just follow Viale Costituzione through the small park in front of the station to Viale Cavour, which leads directly into the center of town. City buses 1, 2, and 9 stop in front of the station and go to the center; buy your ticket (1,400L/70¢) at the newsstand and validate it when you board the bus.

By Bus   Ferrara's **main bus terminal** (☎ 0523-599-492) is south of the center near the city walls on Rampari San Paolo; however, most buses also stop in front of the more conveniently located train station (☎ 0532-599-490). Buses link Ferrara hourly with both **Bologna** (65 min.; 9,800L/$4.90), and **Modena** (1 hr. 50 min.; 9,000L/$4.50).

By Car   Ferrara is about half an hour north of Bologna on A13 and about a little more than an hour south of Venice, which is reached via A13 to Padua and from there A4.

VISITOR INFORMATION   The extremely helpful **tourist office** is in the Castello Estense (☎ **0532-209-370;** fax 0532-212-266; www.comune.fe.it). It's open daily 9am to 1pm and 2 to 6pm.

FESTIVALS & MARKETS   Though not quite as dramatic as its counterpart in Siena, Ferrara's **Palio di San Giorgio** is a much-attended event held in the Piazza Ariostea the last Sunday of May. Two-legged creatures run first, in separate races for

A Money-Saving Tip

A cost-efficient way to tour Ferrara's many museums is to purchase one of the two *biglietto cumulativo.* The 10,000L ($5) adults, 5,000L ($2.50) students and over 60, version covers the Palazzo Schifanoia, Palazzina di Marfisa d'Este, and Museo Civico Lapadario. For 20,000L ($10) adults, 12,000L ($6) students and over 65, you can add to that list the Palazzo Massari museums and six other minor museums. You can purchase it at the ticket offices of any of the participating museums.

young men and young women. They're followed by donkeys and, in the main event, barebacked horses mounted by jockeys representing Ferrara's eight traditional districts.

During summer, the streets of Ferrara seem like one great theater. Excellent jazz and classical concerts are the main events of **Estate à Ferrara,** an outdoor festival that begins in early July (including 9:30pm outdoor concerts on Piazza Municipale) and runs until late August (most official concerts indoors), when the festivities are augmented by street musicians, mimes, and orators who partake in the **Busker's Festival** (☎ **0532-249-337**).

EXPLORING FERRARA

Casa Romei. Via Praisolo and Via Savonarola. ☎ **0532-240-341.** Admission 4,000L ($2), 2,000L ($1) ages 18–25, free under 18 and over 65. Tues–Sat 8:30am–7:30pm, Sun to 2pm.

The most famous visitor to this airy villa, built from 1440 to 1450 by local merchant Giovanni Romei, was Lucrezia Borgia, who retreated here from the rigors and intrigues of court life at the *castello*. (She was the wife of Duke Alfonso I d'Este, and her reputation for murders, poisonings, and other intrigues has been shown by history to be largely unwarranted.) The lovely rooms, connected by loggias that wrap around two peaceful courtyards, are partially filled with frescoes and statues rescued from Ferrara's deconsecrated churches and convents, but it's the elegant architecture of the house that will win you over.

Castello Estense (Este Castle). Via Cavour and Corso Ercole I d'Este. ☎ **0532-299-233.** Admission 8,000L ($4) adults, 6,000L ($3) students, free under 10. Tues–Sun 9:30am–5:30pm.

This imposing moat-encircled castle dominates the city center and much of Ferrara's Renaissance history. It was built in 1385, and it was here in 1435 that Nicolo III d'Este, with a contrivance of window mirrors, caught his young wife Parisina Maletesta *in flagrante delicto* with his son Ugo and had them beheaded in the dank dungeons below. Robert Browning recounted the deed in his poem "My Last Duchess," and today's visitors clamber down a dark staircase to visit the damp cells where the lovers and others who fell out of favor with the Este clan once languished. Not to be overlooked is the fact that the Estes also made Ferrara a center of art and learning, and the infamous (and unjustly maligned) Lucrezia Borgia entertained poets and artists beneath the fragrant bowers of the orangerie.

Most of the palace is now used as offices for the province, but you can still catch a glimpse of the Estes' enlightenment in what remains of their grand salons—the **Sala dell'Aurora** and **Sala dei Giochi (Game Room),** both ornately festooned with frescoes. Another remnant of court life is the marble chapel built for Renta di Francia, the daughter of Louis XII. Those fond of views and stout of heart can climb the 122 steps

---

Pedaling Around

To get around like a true Ferrarese, you can **rent a bike** from the lot just to the left of the train station as you leave the main entrance (☎ **0532-772-190**); it's open 5am to 8pm and rentals are 4,000L ($2) an hour, 12,000L ($6) per day. A few blocks east of the bus station along the city wall is another rental outfit at Viale Kennedy 4 (☎ **0532-202-003**), open daily 9:30am to 1pm and 3 to 7pm; bikes are 4,000L ($2) per hour, 10,000L ($5) per half day, or 20,000L ($10) for a full day. In the center, there's a rental shop at Via della Luna 10 (☎ **0532-206-017**), open daily 9am to 12:30pm and 3:30 to 7:30pm; rates are 3,000L ($1.50) per hour, 10,000L ($5) for a half day, or 15,000L ($8) for a full day.

to the top of the **Torre dei Leoni** (which predates the castle) Tuesday to Sunday 10am to 4:30pm; admission is an extra 2,000L ($1).

Cimitero di Certosa & Cimitero Erbacio (Jewish Cemetery). Both near the walls off Corso Porta Mare. Admission free. Certosa: daily 8am–7:30pm (to 6pm in winter); Cimitero Erbacio: Sun–Fri 9am–6pm (to 4:30pm Oct–Mar).

The centerpiece of the Certosa is **San Cristoforo,** a long graceful sweep of a church by architect Biagio Rossetti. The **Jewish Cemetery,** with its ancient tumble of overgrown tombstones, is the most haunting place in Ferrara. A monument to the Ferrarese murdered at Auschwitz is a reminder of the fate of the city's once sizable Jewish community, whose last days are recounted in the book and film *The Garden of the Finzi-Continis,* evocatively set in the gardens and palaces of Ferrara and required viewing for anyone planning to visit the city. To learn more about Jewish Ferrara, take a guided tour (in Italian, at 10am, 11am, or noon) at the **Museo Ebraico di Ferrara,** Via Mazzini 95 (☎ **0532-210-228**), open Sunday to Thursday; admission is 7,000L ($3.50) adults, 5,000L ($2.50) students.

Duomo. Corso Liberta and Piazza Cattedrale. ☎ **0532-207-449.** Church Mon–Sat 7:30am–noon and 3–6:30pm, Sun 7:30am–1pm and 3:30–7:30pm. Museum (donation requested) Tues–Sat 10am–noon and 3–5pm, Sun 10am–noon and 4–6pm.

With its pink-marble facade highlighted by layers of arches, this handsome 12th-century cathedral reflects a heady mix of the Gothic and the Romanesque. The glory of the otherwise austere structure is its marble porch, where carvings by an unknown artist depict a fearsome *Last Judgment.* An 18th-century renovation relegated many of the paintings, sculptures, and other works that noble families commissioned for the cathedral over the centuries to the **Museo della Cattedrale,** reached by the stairs on the left as you enter.

The pride of the collection is a painting depicting **St. George slaying the dragon** by Cosmè Tura, Ferrara's 15th-century master. Another masterpiece here is Jacopo della Quercia's *Madonna of the Pomegranate,* in which Mary seems to balance the fruit in one hand and the Christ Child in the other. A nearby relief showing the 12 months of the year once graced the exterior of the cathedral, where it served prosaically as a calendar for the largely illiterate citizenry.

The **Loggia dei Mercanti (Loggia of the Merchants),** flanking one side of the church, is still the scene of active secular trade, as it has been since the 18th century, and the surrounding streets and piazzas are filled with lively cafes.

Palazzo dei Diamanti (Palace of Diamonds) & Pinacoteca Nazionale (National Picture Gallery). Corso Ercole I d'Este 21. ☎ **0532-205-844.** Admission 8,000L ($4) adults, 4,000L ($2) ages 10–25, free under 18 and over 65. Tues–Wed and Fri–Sat 9am–2pm, Thurs 9am–7pm, Sun 9am–1pm.

You'll have no problem figuring out where this palazzo gets its name: 9,000 pointed marble blocks cover the facade. Less interesting are the collections in the cluster of museums housed within. The most deserving of a visit is the Pinacoteca Nazionale, containing some notable works by Cosmè Tura, Il Garofalo, and other painters of the Ferrara school, as well as Carpaccio's *Death of the Virgin.* By and large, though, the holdings aren't spectacular. The ground-floor galleries often house temporary exhibits and charge separate admission; check with the ticket office here or the tourist office to see what's on view.

Palazzo Ludovico il Moro. Via XX Settembre. ☎ **0532-66-299.** Admission 8,000L ($4) adults, 4,000L ($2) ages 18–25, free under 18 and over 65. Tues–Sun 9am–8pm.

Ludovico il Moro, famed duke of Milan who married Beatrice d'Este, commissioned this lovely little palazzo as a place to retire from his courtly duties. Unfortunately,

Beatrice died young, and the duke spent his last years as a prisoner of the French. The couple's 15th-century palace, built around a lovely rose garden, contains their furniture and paintings and provides a lovely view of life in Ferrara during its Renaissance heyday. Part of the palazzo houses the small but fascinating collections of the **Museo Archeologico.** The bulk of the treasures are Etruscan and Greek finds unearthed near Ferrara at Spina.

Palazzina Marfisa d'Este. Corso Giovecca 170. ☎ **0532-207-450.** Admission 4,000L ($2), 3,000L ($1.50) students and over 65, free under 18. Tues–Sun 9:30am–1:30pm (to 1pm Oct–Feb) and 3–6pm.

A recent restoration has returned the 16th-century home of this ardent patron of the arts to its former splendor. Period furniture and ceiling frescoes (most retouched in the early 1900s) bespeak the heyday of the Este dynasty, and the little theater in the garden is a reminder that drama, on stage as well as off, was one of the family's great passions.

Palazzo Massari. Corso Porto Mare 9. ☎ **0532-206-914.** Admission: Museo Giovanni Boldoni 8,000L ($4) adults, 4,000L ($2) over 65; Museo Civico d'Arte Moderna 4,000L ($2) adults, 3,000L ($1.50) over 65; cumulative ticket for both 10,000L ($5) adults, 5,000L ($2.50) over 65. Both free under 18, and free for everyone 1st Mon of month. Both daily 9am–1pm and 3–6pm.

The museums housed in this exquisite palace contain Ferrara's modern art holdings, including the **Museo Giovanni Boldini,** with works by the 19th-century Italian painter, and the **Museo Civico d'Arte Moderna (Civic Museum of Modern Art),** largely devoted to the output of Filippo De Pisis—who studied the *metafisica* school of Giorgio de Chirico—plus works by contemporary regional artists.

Palazzo Schifanoia & Museo Civico d'Arte Antica (Civic Museum of Ancient Art). Via Scandiana 23. ☎ **0532-64-178.** Admission 8,000L ($4) adults, 4,000L ($2) students and over 65, free under 18. Tues–Sun 9:30am–7pm.

Borso d'Este, who made Ferrara one of the Renaissance's leading centers of art, commissioned the frescoes you'll find here in the **Salone dei Mesi (Salon of the Months).** It's a fascinating cycle of the months that's both a Renaissance wall calendar and a rich portrayal of life and leisure in the 15th-century Este court. Each of the 12 sections shows Ferrara's aristocrats going about their daily business; looming above them in each, though, is a different god from classical mythology. The work is a composite of the genius of Ferarra's heyday—Francesco del Cossa painted the *March, April,* and *May* scenes, Ercole de'Roberti and other court painters executed the rest, and Cosmè Tura, the official painter of the Este court, oversaw the project. Also here is small collection of coins, bronzes, and other artifacts unearthed from the plains around Ferrara, 14th- and 15th-century ivories, and some medieval and Renaissance ceramics (including a pair of Andrea della Robbia saints).

AFFORDABLE PLACES TO STAY
Rates at the high end of the ranges below apply in summer.

✪ **Borgonuovo Bed & Breakfast.** Via Cairoli 29, 44100 Ferrara. ☎ **0532-211-100.** Fax 0532-248-000. 4 units. A/C MINIBAR TV TEL. 100,000L ($50) single; 160,000L ($80) double; 180,000L ($90) double with kitchenette. Rates include breakfast. AE, DC, MC, V.

This elegant B&B is the most charming hostelry in Ferrara. The gracious owner, Signora Adele Orlandini, has spruced up an apartment that once housed her father's law offices and is in a medieval palazzo on a pedestrian street around the corner from the

Castello Estense. She accommodates her guests in stylish large rooms with a tasteful mix of country-style and art deco antiques and posh new baths (one large double also has a kitchenette). She also provides a hearty breakfast (served in the lovely garden, weather permitting), bicycles, discount coupons for museums and nearby shops, and plenty of advice on how to enjoy her native Ferrara. Book well in advance, since Signora's rooms and hospitality are much in demand; fortunately, she's planning to expand her domain to three or four more rooms in a church complex down the street.

Casa degli Artisti. Via Vittoria 66, 44100 Ferrara. ☎ **0532-761-038.** 21 units, 2 with bathroom. 38,000L ($19) single without bathroom; 60,000L ($30) double without bathroom, 90,000L ($45) double with bathroom. No credit cards.

Though the surroundings are utilitarian, this basic old budget hotel is very reasonably priced, excellently located in the atmospheric medieval Jewish quarter mere blocks from the Duomo, and not without charm. The simple rooms are big, bright, and clean; the heavy 1950s-era pieces are a nice change from the banal furnishings you find in most hotels in this price range; and the shared bath facilities are plentiful and clean. Rooms have orthopedic mattresses, sinks, and bidets. Plus, there are some pleasant and unusual amenities here—guests have use of kitchen facilities at the end of the hall on each floor, and there's a nice terrace on the roof.

Europa. Corso Giovecca 49 (between Via Palestro and Via Teatini), 44100 Ferrara. ☎ **0532-205-456.** Fax 0532-212-120. www.hoteleuropaferrara.com. 39 units. A/C MINIBAR TV TEL. 125,000L ($65) single; 195,000L ($98) double; 240,000L ($120) triple; 250,000L ($125) suite. Rates include breakfast. AE, DC, MC, V. Parking 14,000L ($7).

Built in 1700, this elegant palazzo a block from the Castello Estense has served as a hotel since 1880. Many subsequent renovations have left it with a somewhat contemporary look, though enough of the original architecture remains to render the premises atmospheric. The ground-floor sitting rooms and bar area are furnished in 19th-century antiques, as are several enormous guest rooms on the floor above that have been converted from grand salons and have frescoed ceilings, the original checkerboard terra-cotta tile floors, art nouveau furnishings, and Murano chandeliers (including most along the main street). While the other rooms (same price) are less grand, they are gracious and large, with a nice mix of contemporary furnishings and reproduction Venetian antiques, and you can at least enjoy the modest ceiling frescoes of the breakfast room. All units have gleaming new baths.

San Paolo. Via Baluardi 9, 44100 Ferrara. ☎ **0532-762-040.** Fax 0532-768-333. www.hotelsanpaolo.it. 31 units. TEL TV. 100,000L ($50) single; 140,000L ($70) double; 170,000L ($85) triple; 190,000L ($95) quad. AE, DC, MC, V. Parking free on street or in nearby lot. Bus: 2 from train station.

My favorite budget choice in Ferrara is on the edge of the old Jewish ghetto, with its warren of lanes and small shops, and faces the old city walls. Add to this atmospheric location the attentive service of the proprietors, who rent bikes (10,000L/$5 per day), dispense advice on sightseeing and restaurants, and serve coffee from the little lobby bar. The rooms, on the other hand, are a little bland but comfortable and decorated in inoffensive contemporary blond furnishings, and all but a few have small but functional baths. The hotel expanded in 2000 with some dozen new rooms (orthopedic beds, heated towel racks—but waffle towels—and box showers), and the rest of the premises should be renovated by the time this book hits the shelves. The only thing lacking in the redone rooms will be air-conditioning (about half the rooms already have it; the balance will by late 2001).

Worth a Splurge

✪ Ripagrande. Via Ripagrande 21, 44100 Ferrara. ☎ **0532-765-250.** Fax 0532-764-377. www.4net.com/business/ripa. 40 units. A/C MINIBAR TV TEL. 240,000–270,000L ($120–$135) single; 300,000–340,000L ($150–$170) double; 320,000–400,000L ($160–$200) junior suite. Rates include breakfast. AE, DC, MC, V. Parking free on street or 20,000L ($10) in garage.

Occupying a converted Renaissance palazzo near the center of town, this enchanting hotel provides the perfect atmosphere. The cavernous entrance foyer and public rooms are walled in rose-colored brick, have tall vaulted ceilings, and are built around two cloister-like courtyards and a garden. Upstairs, the rooms are large and distinctive, furnished in a carefully chosen mix of reproductions and contemporary furnishings. About half the rooms are junior suites, most long and narrow but with very high ceilings, and are split into three levels: a bath and dressing room connected by a short staircase to a sitting room, with a loftlike bedroom above. Several top-floor rooms (some of which were being fitted with Jacuzzi tubs when I last visited) open onto large terraces overlooking red-tile rooftops. The price of a room includes the use of bicycles.

GREAT DEALS ON DINING

The walls and Ferrara's other green spaces are ideal for a **picnic.** Buy what you need on narrow brick Via Cortevecchia, near the cathedral. It's lined with salumerie, cheese shops, and bakeries. The nearby **Mercato Comunale,** at the corner of Via Santo Stefano and Via del Mercato, is crowded with food stalls and open Monday to Saturday to 1pm and Friday 3:30 to 7:30pm. At **Negozio Moccia,** Via degli Spadari 9, you can indulge in a chunk of *panpeteto,* Ferrara's hallmark chocolate-covered fruitcake.

✪ Al Brindisi. Via Adelardi 11. ☎ **0532-209-142.** Dishes 6,000–15,000L ($3–$8); tasting menus 18,000–80,000L ($9–$40). DC, MC, V. Tues–Sun 9am–1am. Closed July 10–Aug 20. WINE BAR/OSTERIA.

What claims to be the oldest wine bar in the world (since 1435) serves a staggering selection of wines by the glass (from 3,000L/$1.50) and a wonderful selection of panini and other light fare. In fact, you may want to come here to sample the offerings of the kitchen as well as those of the cellar. The *torta rustica,* a selection of little pies filled with an assortment of vegetables, is perfect as a starter or a light meal; the *tortelli di zucca* (pumpkin ravioli) is sublime here, as is a substantial combination of sausage and potatoes. This excellent food and drink is served in the convivial confines of two timbered rooms stacked to the ceiling with wine bottles. When the weather is nice, you can sit at booth-like tables on a little lane facing a flank of the Duomo. The tourist menu is quite a bargain and includes a feast of appetizers, a special main course of the day, dessert, and a carafe of wine.

Antica Osteria Al Postiglione. Via dei Teatro 4. ☎ **0532-204-937** or 0532-241-509. Sandwiches, pastas, and other dishes 7,000–16,000L ($3.50–$8). AE, MC, V. Mon–Sat 9:30am–3:30pm and 5pm–1am. Closed Sun. WINE BAR.

Dozens of beers and an extensive selection of local wines are available at this cozy wine bar/osteria on a narrow lane near the Teatro Comunale and Piazza Castello. You can also eat very well, and the family members who cook and wait tables pride themselves on such simple home-cooked dishes as grilled *salsiccia* (sweet sausages), *mozzarella al forno* (baked mozzarella), and *pasta e fagioli* (a substantial soup of beans and pasta). The desserts, including a delicious *zuppa inglese* (the Italian version of the English trifle, a decadent concoction of pound cake soaked in rum and smothered in sweet custard cream), are made fresh daily.

Snacks & Gelato

The outdoor terrace and large interior room of the **Duca d'Este,** Piazza Castello 22 (☎ **0532-207-688**), one of several cafes surrounding the Castello, are almost always full of locals who stop by at all times of day and evening for coffee or stronger libations and snacks. A nice selection of sandwiches and salads is served, as is a daily selection of pasta dishes. The main draws here, though, seem to be the gelato, available in 40 flavors, and fresh pastries that can be accompanied by excellent coffee, making this a mandatory stop in the morning.

✪ **Antica Trattoria Volano.** Viale Volano 20. ☎ **0532-761-421.** Primi 13,000–15,000L ($7–$8); secondi 12,000–20,000L ($6–$10). AE, DC, MC, V. Sat–Thurs noon–5pm and 7pm–midnight. Closed 15 days in Aug. FERRARESE.

Just south of the city walls, a block from the traditional market square, this roadside trattoria has been satisfying hungry travelers since the 1700s. The decor is unassuming (and a tad staid), and the traffic noise detracts, but the cooking is superb. The menu is a veritable study in traditional Ferrara specialties. To sample the best of them all, order a *tris di primi,* a trio of *cappellaci di zucca* (squash-stuffed ravioli), *tagliatelle al prosciutto,* and *tortelloni di ricotta;* or warm yourself up with their delicious *cappelletti in brodo* (pasta soup). Stay in the sampler category with the *misto bolliti* (a selection of boiled meats), or try the ultra-traditional *salama di sugo* (local salami diced, cooked in red wine and cognac, and dolloped over mashed potatoes), *trippa alla parmigiana,* or *quaglia alla boscaiola* (roast quail). For dessert, try the excellent *zuppa inglese* (trifle) or the *Mandulin dal Pont* (dry cookies served with sweet Moscato wine).

Buca San Domenico. Piazza Sacrati 22b. ☎ **0532-200-018.** Primi 8,000–11,000 ($4–$6); secondi 10,000–16,000L ($5–$8); pizzas 8,000–11,000 ($4–$6). MC, V. Sat–Thurs noon–2:30pm and 7:30–11:00pm. Closed Aug. PIZZA/PASTA.

This local institution, on a charming square just a couple of blocks from the *castello,* reopened under new ownership mere days before I stopped in for a pizza. But the new management doesn't plan to change much of what kept this informal spot almost always booked solid on Saturday and Sunday evenings. The main dining room is cozy and rustic, with wooden booths and the fragrant odor of baking pizzas and wood smoke wafting from the large rear ovens. (Alas, the adjoining room is modern and garishly lit.) You can dine very well and inexpensively on what many locals consider to be the best pizza in town or venture into the simple menu. The best choices are the homemade soups, including a delicious *tortellini in brodo,* and pastas—I hope the excellent *tortelli di zucca* (pumpkin ravioli) of old makes a comeback.

✪ **La Provvidenza.** Corso Ercole I d'Este 92 (at Vc. Parchetto). ☎ **0532-205-187.** Reservations required. Primi 12,000–18,000L ($6–$9); secondi 18,000–30,000L ($9–$15). AE, DC, MC, V. Tues–Sun noon–3pm and 8–10:30pm. Closed part of Aug. FERRARESE/SEAFOOD.

One of the pleasures of dining at this charming restaurant a few steps from the town walls is to walk here along a stone-paved road leading past the Palazzo dei Diamanti and many of the city's most lovely old mansions and brick-walled gardens. Once inside the dining room, with its cream-colored walls and attractively rustic furnishings, you'll feel you're in the country; there's even an arbor-shaded, partially enclosed garden for outdoor dining in good weather. If you want to eat a full meal, begin with grilled vegetables, salamis, and other selections from the irresistible antipasto buffet. The pastas are excellent and include *cappellaci* (pasta pillows stuffed with squash), *straccetti al granchio* (pasta with crab), *bavette con bottarga* (pasta with dried roe) and tortellini stuffed with Gorgonzola and walnuts. The *salama da sugo* (giant sausage stewed in tomato sauce) comes with mashed potatoes, or order a grilled fish like *rombo* (turbot) or *tonno* (tuna), *anguilla* (eel), or a *misto pesce brace* (mixed seafood grill). The dessert of choice (all pastries are made in house) is a Ferrarese specialty, *torta di tagliatelle.*

3 Ravenna & Its Amazing Mosaics

75km (45 mi.) SE of Bologna, 75km (45 mi.) SE of Ferrara, 135km (81 mi.) NE of Florence

Few cities in Europe are so firmly entrenched in so distant a past. The last days of ancient Western Civilization waned in this flat little city on the edge of the marshes that creep inland from the Adriatic. Though **Ravenna** has been an off-the-beaten-track backwater since the 6th century, it continues to dazzle visitors with its mosaics and other artistic vestiges of the Romans, the Byzantines, and the Visigoths. Aside from its horde of treasures, Ravenna is also a fine place to pass the time in sun-drenched piazzas and pleasant cafes.

ESSENTIALS
GETTING THERE   By Train   Twelve trains travel daily from **Ferrara** to Ravenna (70 min.; 7,000L/$3.50). Ferrara is the connection point for trains to **Venice,** another 2 hours. There are at least hourly direct runs from **Bologna** (60–75 min.; 7,700L/$3.85), and from the Adriatic coastal resort **Rimini** (1 hr.; 4,900L/$2.45). The **train station** is only about a 10-minute-walk down Viale Farini (which becomes Via Diaz) from Piazza del Popolo.

By Bus   While trains link Ravenna with many other cities in Emilia-Romagna, local ATM buses (☎ **0544-35-288;** www.racine.ra.it/atm) connect Ravenna with a number of nearby towns, including some nearby beach resorts. Buses leave from the front of the train station, where you'll also find a ticket office that's open Monday to Saturday 6:30am to 8:30pm (7:30pm in winter) and Sunday 7am to 8pm (7:30am to 7:30pm in winter). At other times, you can buy tickets from a newsstand inside the station.

By Car   Ravenna is about an hour southeast of Bologna on A14 and A13 and a little more than an hour southeast of Ferarra on the slower S309.

VISITOR INFORMATION   The **tourist office** is just off Piazza del Popolo at Via Salara 8 (☎ **0544-35-404;** fax 0544-35-094; www.racine.ra.it/ravennaintorno). It's open Monday to Saturday 8:30am to 7pm (to 6pm October to April) and Sunday 10am to 4pm. The office now gives visitors free bikes to use for the day.

FESTIVALS & MARKETS   Ravenna takes advantage of its lovely piazzas to stage concerts and other performances throughout the summer. The **Ravenna Festival International** in July and August has become world renowned, drawing a top list of classical musicians and stars of the opera. The tourist office provides information, or call ☎ **0544-32-577;** tickets begin at 25,000L ($13). **Ravenna Teatro** is a less glitzy but more accessible affair, offering free concerts (most of them outdoor) throughout the summer. The **Dante Festival,** sponsored by the church of San Francesco the second week of September, honors Ravenna's adopted son with readings and exhibits; check with the tourist office or call ☎ **0544-39-972** or 0544-482-150.

A walk through Ravenna's lively food market, the **Mercato Coperto,** will introduce you to the bounty of the land; it's near the center on Piazza Andrea Costa and is open Monday to Saturday 7am to 2pm and Friday 4:30 to 7:30pm.

Ravenna's Cumulative Ticket & Open Hours

They keep changing the way this works, but currently the **cumulative ticket** covers the Basilica di San Vitale, Basilica di Sant'Apollinare Nuovo, the Mausoleum of Galla Placidia, the Battistero Neoniano, the Museo Arcivescovile/Capella di Sant' Andrea, and the Basilica dello Spirito Santo. It costs 8,000L ($4) November to February, 9,000L ($4.50) June to October, and 10,000L ($5) March to May (though for some reason these months don't include Galla Placidia, which costs another 4,000L/$2). There's a 2,000L ($1) discount on all those rates for students.

The open hours (all daily) for all are as follows: November to February 9:30am to 4:30pm, March and October 9:30am to 5:30pm, April to September 9am to 7pm.

EXPLORING RAVENNA

Most of Ravenna's stunning mosaics adorn buildings that are in and near the city center, most within a 5-minute walk of Piazza del Popolo. The exception is Sant'Apollinare in Classe, 10 minutes away by bus 4 or 44 from the train station or, closer to the center, Piazza Caduti.

Basilica di Sant'Apollinare Nuovo. Via di Roma. ☎ **0544-219-938.** Admission and hours: See "Ravenna's Cumulative Ticket & Open Hours," above.

The famous mosaics in this 6th-century church, punctuated by Greek columns taken from a temple, are clearly delineated by gender. On one side of the church, the side traditionally reserved for women, a procession of 22 crown-carrying virgins makes its way toward the Madonna; on the other side, the men's side, 26 male martyrs march toward Christ. The mosaics near the door provide a fascinating look at the 6th-century city and its environs—one on the right shows the monuments of the city, including Emperor Theodoric's royal palace, and one on the left shows the port city of Classe.

○ **Basilica di San Vitale.** Via San Vitale 17. ☎ **0544-219-938.** Admission and hours: See "Ravenna's Cumulative Ticket & Open Hours," above.

Ravenna's most dazzling display of mosaics adorns the dome of this 6th-century octagonal basilica that's not by accident exotically Byzantine in its design—Emperor Justinian commissioned the church to impose the power of Byzantine Christianity over Ravenna. The emperor and his court appear in splendidly detailed mosaics of deep greens and golds on one side of the church; Theodora, his empress (a courtesan born into the circus whose ambition, intelligence, and beauty brought her to these lofty heights), and her ladies-in-waiting appear on the other; and above and between them looms Christ, clean-shaven in this early representation.

Battistero Neoniano (Baptistry). Via Battistero. ☎ **0544-219-938.** Admission and hours: See "Ravenna's Cumulative Ticket & Open Hours," above.

This enchanting 4th-century octagon was built as the baptistry of a cathedral that no longer stands; it's now behind Ravenna's banal present-day Duomo, built in the 19th century. Fittingly for the structure's purpose, the blue and gold mosaics on the dome depict the baptism of Christ by St. John the Baptist, surrounded by the Twelve Apostles. Entrance to the baptistery includes, and is included in, admission to the nearby Museo Arcivescovile.

Museo Arcivescovile (Archbishop's Museum) & Capella di San Andrea. Piazza Arcivescovado. ☎ **0544-219-938.** Admission and hours: See "Ravenna's Cumulative Ticket & Open Hours," above.

The highlight of this small museum, housed in the 6th-century Archbishop's Palace and in itself a remarkable monument, is another 6th-century treasure—the ivory throne of Emperor Maximilian. Adjoining the museum is a small chapel built in the shape of a cross and dedicated to St. Andrea, every inch of which is emblazoned with dazzling mosaics. Of the early Christian imagery that confronts you here, the most remarkable scene is of a warlike Christ, wearing armor and stepping on a serpent.

Mausoleum of Gallo Placidia. Via San Vitale, behind the Basilica di San Vitale. ☎ **0544-219-938.** Admission and hours: See "Ravenna's Cumulative Ticket & Open Hours," above.

Perhaps the most striking of all Ravenna's monuments is this small and simple tomb of Galla Placidia, lit only by small alabaster windows. The life of this early Christian was not without drama. She was the sister of Honorius, last emperor of Rome and wife of Ataulf, king of the Visigoths. Upon his death, she became regent to her 6-year-old son, Valentinian III, and, in effect, ruler of the Western world. The three sarcophagi beneath a canopy of blue and gold mosaics—a firmament of deep blue lit by hundreds of bright gold stars—are meant to contain Galla Placidia's remains and those of her son and husband, but it is more likely that she lies unadorned in Rome, where she died in A.D. 450.

Sant'Apollinare in Classe. Via Romeo Sud 224, Classe. ☎ **0544-473-643.** Admission 4,000L ($2). Mon–Sat 8:30am–7:30pm, Sun 1–7pm. Bus: 4 or 44 from Piazza Farini in front of the train station (every 20 min.).

This long and high early Christian basilica and its campanile have loomed amid the pine woods near the old Roman port, long ago silted up, since the 6th century. The plain exterior belies the splendor that lies within. At the end of the long, sparse nave, punctuated by Greek columns, you come to the apse, the dome of which is covered with lustrous gold mosaics—made so by the application of gold leaf that suggests a heavenly light; imagine how transporting the effect was when the floor, too, was tiled in gold mosaic. The dominating figure depicted here, flanked by 12 lambs representing the apostles, is St. Apollinare, the bishop of Ravenna to whom the basilica is dedicated.

Tomba di Dante (Dante's Tomb). Via Dante Alighieri. ☎ **0544-30-252.** Admission free. Daily 9am–7pm.

In exile from Florence, the poet Dante Alighieri made Ravenna his home, and it was here that he finished his *Divine Comedy*, of which the *Inferno* is but the first third, and where he died in 1321. Despite efforts by the Florentines to reclaim their famous son's remains, he resides here for eternity, next to the Basilica di San Franceso, beneath an inscription, "Here in this corner lies Dante, exiled from his native land, born to Florence, an unloving mother." The adjoining Museo Dantesco, a small collection of Dante memorabilia, has been closed for years.

AFFORDABLE PLACES TO STAY

Al Giaciglio. Via R Brancaleone 42, 48100 Ravenna. ☎ and fax **0544-39-403.** E-mail: mmambo@racine.ra.it. 19 units, 9 with bathroom. TV. 45,000L ($23) single without bathroom, 55,000L ($28) single with bathroom; 65,000L ($33) double without bathroom, 80,000L ($40) double with bathroom. MC, V.

If your needs don't extend beyond having the basic comforts, look no further than this family-run hotel/restaurant—you're not going to find better lodgings for the price in Ravenna. The rooms are no-frills but bright, clean, and quite comfortable, with a

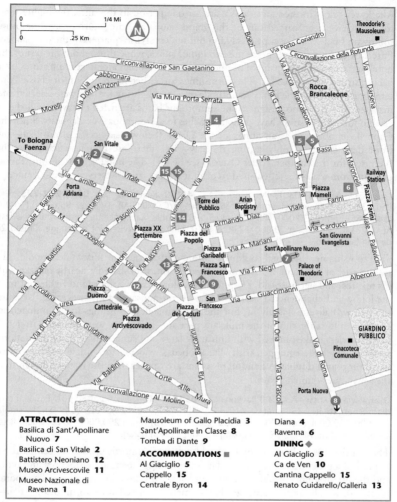

ATTRACTIONS ●
Basilica di Sant'Apollinare Nuovo **7**
Basilica di San Vitale **2**
Battistero Neoniano **12**
Museo Arcivescovile **11**
Museo Nazionale di Ravenna **1**

Mausoleum of Gallo Placidia **3**
Sant'Apollinare in Classe **8**
Tomba di Dante **9**

ACCOMMODATIONS ■
Al Giaciglio **5**
Cappello **15**
Centrale Byron **14**

Diana **4**
Ravenna **6**

DINING ◆
Al Giaciglio **5**
Ca de Ven **10**
Cantina Cappello **15**
Renato Guidarello/Galleria **13**

homey array of mismatched furniture, and almost half have functional baths; shared facilities are plentiful and spotless. The cot springs sag a bit, but not direly. There's a good restaurant downstairs (Al Giaciglio; see below), and the location, 5 minutes from the center and near the train station and Ravenna's medieval castle and its surrounding park, is excellent. Given the prices and these appealing features, you'd be wise to reserve.

✪ **Cappello.** Via IV Novembre 41, 48100 Ravenna. ☎ **0544-219-813.** Fax 0544-219-814. www.ravennabedandbreakfast.it. 7 units. A/C MINIBAR TV TEL. 145,000 ($73) single; 200,000 ($100) double; 160,000–220,000L ($80–$110) jr. suite; 180,000–240,000L ($90–$120) suite. Rates include breakfast. AE, DC, MC, V.

Ravenna now has a hotel that's truly exciting—and remarkably affordable given the luxuries and amenities it provides. Opened in 1998, the Cappello occupies a beautifully restored 14th-century palazzo in the city center. The four suite-category rooms (the lower prices in the ranges above are for one person in the suite, the higher rates for two) have been carved out of the grand salons and are enormous, while other rooms are smaller and occupy less grand but no less stylish quarters of the old palazzo. Fifteenth-century frescoes grace the two junior suites, while throughout the rest of the hotel, terra-cotta floors, painted beamed ceilings, and other architectural features have been restored when possible. The furnishings are either reproduction or classic contemporary designs—the funky sculptural lamps and lighting fixtures were selected and installed by a Bergamo designer. The sumptuous baths are fitted out with stall showers and tubs. Some suites have pullout couches to accommodate extra guests. Since the Cappello is operated as an annex of the Diana (below), services are minimal—the front desk is staffed only during the day—but there are two restaurants on the premises (for the cheaper, cozier Osteria, see below). The hotel is up two short flights of stairs from a hallway often used to exhibit a local artist. Reserve well in advance.

Centrale Byron. Via IV Novembre 14, 48100 Ravenna. ☎ **0544-212-225.** Fax 0544-34-114. www.hotelbyron.com. 53 units. A/C MINIBAR TV TEL. 95,000–110,000L ($48–$55) single; 150,000–180,000L ($75–$90) double. Rates include continental breakfast. AE, DC, MC, V. Parking 20,000–22,000L ($10–$11) in supervised lot or garage. Closed 20 days in Jan or Feb.

True to its name, this hotel couldn't be more central, right off Piazza del Popolo. The second part of the name is a tribute to Lord Byron, who shared a nearby palazzo with his mistress and her husband. Despite these colorful associations (and an elegant marble lobby and chandeliered bar), this hotel is no-nonsense and serviceable. Upstairs, the narrow halls are harshly lit, but the modern-style furnishings in the immaculate rooms, while fairly run-of-the-mill, are pleasant, and most were replaced in 1999. Lone travelers make out well with unusually large and sunny single accommodations, many of which are equipped with "French beds," wider than a single bed but a little narrower than a double. A handful of rooms are smaller than the rest and weigh in at the lower rates quoted above.

Diana. Via G. Rossi 47, 48100 Ravenna. ☎ **0544-39-164.** Fax 0544-30-001. E-mail: hotel-diana@netgate.it. 33 units. A/C TV TEL. 97,000–125,000L ($49–$63) single; 134,000–180,000L ($67–$90) double; 230,000L ($115) triple; 250,000L ($125) quad. Rates include breakfast. AE, D, MC, V. Parking 15,000L ($8) in garage.

Though this stylish hotel occupies an old palazzo just north of the city center, it has the feel of a pleasant country hotel. The surrounding streets are residential and quiet, and the bright lobby, breakfast room, and bar open onto a lovely garden. The rooms, no two of which are the same, are handsomely decorated with an innovative flair— with pretty striped wallpapers and mahogany headboards and armories. Those on the top floor are the most charming, with sloping ceilings and large skylights. All the baths have recently been redone with care and have glass-enclosed tub/shower arrangements, heated towel racks, and hair dryers. The range in rates above applies to three categories of rooms: Standard (slightly smaller with blander, but new, furnishings), Superior (larger with nicer stuff), and De Luxe (main defining factor: minibar).

Ravenna. Via Maroncelli 12, 48100 Ravenna. ☎ **0544-212-204.** Fax 0544-212-077. 26 units, 22 with bathroom. TEL. 60,000–70,000L ($30–$35) single without bathroom, 70,000–80,000L ($35–$40) single with bathroom; 70,000–90,000L ($35–$45) double without bathroom, 80,000–110,000L ($40–$55) double with bathroom; 130,000–145,000L ($65–$73) triple with bathroom. 20,000L ($10) to add another bed. MC, V. Free parking.

Across from the train station, this pleasant hotel is handy for late arrivals and early departures but is also only a 10-minute walk to the sights in the town center. You'll find many more amenities than you'd expect from a hotel in this price range. An elevator has recently been installed, and, for a welcoming touch, the halls and public spaces are attractively enlivened with paintings and prints. The tile-floored rooms, fitted out with standard hotel-issue modern furnishings, feature orthopedic mattresses and are large and immaculately kept (some very large rooms have been equipped with extra beds for families). Most are far enough from the street to be extremely quiet, and all but the few bathless ones have TVs. The baths are up-to-date but tiny, and since many of the showers aren't enclosed (a nozzle, a drain, and no curtain), you'll have to keep your wits about you if you want to keep towels and toiletries dry during your ablutions.

GREAT DEALS ON DINING

The slick-looking **Sorbetteria degli Esarchi,** Via IV Novembre 11, off Piazza del Popolo (☎ **0544-36-315**), seems to supply its offerings to every visitor who sets foot in Ravenna. Esarchi is popular with locals, too, because it uses only the freshest ingredients and follows secret recipes that unfailingly deliver delicious results. The eponymous sorbets are especially notable and come in a dozen or so flavors, depending on what fresh fruit is available. Creamier gelati are also available and, like the sorbets, made on the premises several times a day. It's open daily 11am to 10 or 11pm (closed Mondays in winter).

Al Giaciglio. Via Rocca Brancaleone 42. ☎ **0544-39-403.** Primi 6,000L–9,000L ($3–$4.50); secondi 9,000–18,000L ($4.50–$9); menù turistico 23,000L ($12). AE, DC, MC, V. Tues–Sun 12:20–2:30pm and 7–9:30pm. RAVENNESE.

This comfortable, friendly restaurant comprises a few large paneled rooms on the ground floor of the pensione of the same name (see above). The no-nonsense food is delicious, with a nice selection of basics such as tortellini, spaghetti Bolognese, and *scaloppini alla gorgonzola.* On Friday and Saturday, fish is added to the menu, but without raising prices, as is often the case.

Ca de Ven. Via C. Ricci 24. ☎ **0544-30-163.** Sandwiches and light dishes 1,300–14,000L (65¢–$7); primi 11,000–13,000L ($6–$7); secondi 14,000–25,000L ($7–$13). AE, DC, MC, V. Tues–Sun 11am–2pm and 5:30–10:15pm. Closed Mon. RAVENNESE.

The most atmospheric osteria in Ravenna is tucked away under massive brick vaults on the ground floor of a 16th-century building next to Dante's tomb. In fact, Dante is said to have lived here when the premises served as a lodging house. The ornate shelves that line most of the walls come from a later reincarnation and were installed to outfit a 19th-century spice shop; they now display hundreds of varieties of Emilia-Romagna wines, many of which are available by the glass to accompany a light meal (from 2,700L/$1.35 a glass). *Piadine,* the delicious local flat bread, is a specialty here, topped with cheeses, meat, or vegetables—or served plain as a perfect accompaniment to cheese and assorted salamis. They offer three to four pasta and meat courses daily, and if there are two of you, you can share a *bis di primi* (pick two) for 14,000L ($7) each, or a *tris di primi* (sample three) for 16,000L ($8).

Cantina Cappello. Via IV Novembre 41. ☎ **0544-219-876.** Primi 10,000–15,000L ($5–$8); secondi 12,000–25,000L ($6–$13). AE, MC, V. Mon 7:30–10:30pm, Tues–Sat 12:30–2:30pm and 7:30–10:30pm. WINE BAR.

The high-shuttered windows, timbered ceiling, and ocher-colored walls render this room on the ground floor of the stylish *albergo* of the same name (see above) both chic and inviting. In fact, with the attractive surroundings, friendly service, excellent choices of drink and food, and handy location just off Piazza del Popolo, this is my first choice for a light meal in Ravenna. You can order just about any wine from Emilia-Romagna, and the house choices are available by the glass (from

3,000L/$1.50) or carafe (from 10,000L/$5). The food, however, isn't to be over-looked. You can order a *tavolozza* (a mixed platter of cheeses, crostini, salami, and salad) or choose from the daily pasta and meat specials. From 6 to 8:30pm is *aperitivo* hour, with loads of tiny snacks and tea sandwiches free for anyone who bellies up to the bar for a glass of wine. Don't leave without ordering one of the delicious coffees.

Renato Guidarello/Galleria. Via Mentana 33/Via R. Gessi 9. ☎ **0544-213-684.** Primi 9,000–12,000L ($4.50–$6); secondi 10,000–20,000L ($5–$10); pizze 6,500–14,000L ($3.25–$7); menù turistico 26,500L ($13) without wine. DC MC, V. Daily 12:15–2:30pm and 7:30–9:30pm. ITALIAN/PIZZA.

The cavernous rooms seem to extend forever—or at least to a second entrance around the corner. And even at that, on some nights there never seem to be enough tables to accommodate locals and tourists alike who come here to enjoy pizzas (not the greatest, but okay) and hearty trattoria fare. Roast meats dominate the menu and include several turkey preparations, including a simply prepared *paillard di tacchino* (grilled turkey breast). In deference to tradition and the proximity of the Adriatic, a handful of fresh fish dishes are added to the menu on Friday.

FAENZA: A DAY TRIP FROM RAVENNA

In the 16th century, the local artisans brought fame to this little city by applying new firing techniques to the production of majolica-style pottery and creating faience ware that became the international rage. The tradition, which involves giving a ceramic piece a white glaze, then applying designs in yellow and blue tones, lives on.

GETTING THERE Faenza is only half an hour from Ravenna by train (4,100L/$2.05), but you will have to time your trip carefully. The seven daily trains from Ravenna to Faenza leave very early in the morning (at 6:30 and 7:35am and not again until 11:34am), and from then roughly every 2 hours. Likewise, the return trains leave mainly in the afternoon, though the last train is not until 7:50pm, allowing plenty of time to linger in the museum. From Bologna, 15 trains a day run almost hourly and make the trip in 1 hour and 20 minutes; the one-way fare is 6,200L ($3.10). By car, it is a quick trip of less than half an hour via S253 from Ravenna to Faenza and from Bologna the trip down A14 takes about 45 minutes.

VISITOR INFORMATION Faenza's **tourist office** is in the heart of town at Piazza del Popolo 1 (☎ **0546-25-231**). November to May, it's open Tuesday to Saturday 9:30am to 12:30pm and 4 to 6pm; June to October, hours are daily 9:30am to 12:30pm and 3:30 to 6:30pm (closed Sunday afternoons).

SEEKING OUT CERAMICS Almost as soon as you set foot in town you should visit the **Museo Internazionale delle Ceramiche,** Viale Baccarini 19 (☎ **0546-21-240;** www.micfaenza.org). You'll get an overview of the town's famous craft, a taste of styles from all of Italy's other traditional ceramics centers, as well as a firm grounding in ceramics from the Etruscans and pre-Columbian Peruvians to Chinese masters and contemporary artists, artisans, and designers. The most popular works are those by modern masters not usually associated with ceramics—a platter by Picasso incorporates his famous dove of peace design, and there are works by Matisse, Chagall, and Léger as well. April to October, the museum is open Tuesday to Saturday 9am to 7pm and Sunday 9am to 1pm and 3 to 7pm; November to March, hours are Tuesday to Friday 9am to 1:30pm, Saturday 9am to 1:30pm and 3 to 6pm, and Sunday 9:30am to 1pm and 3 to 6pm. May to September, admission is 15,000L ($8) adults and 7,500L ($3.75) students and over 65; October to April, it's 10,000L ($5) adults and 5,000L ($2.50) students and seniors.

Faenza is still very much an artisan's center, with a major institute for ceramics study, **Instituto d'Arte per la Ceramica,** and many workshops where you can buy the wares of artisans. To save some hoofing from shop to shop, from late June through late October you can get a good overview of the best several dozen artisans and workshops in town by visiting the **Summer Ceramics Show** in the Palazzo delle Esposizioni, Corso Mazzini 92 (☎ **0546-211-145;** www.estateceramica.com). Each workshop has a selection of pieces on display, so you can take notes on the ones you like and, using the handy map keyed to a number system, then go visit the producers that most catch your fancy. (You can buy the display pieces at the show, too, but with a 10% mark-up.) In even-numbered years, this regular exhibit is joined by a fair of antique ceramics on the third week of September. The tourist office can also provide you with that list and map of workshops, or just look for any *bottega* displaying the official oval sign of a handshake.

4 Modena

40km (25 mi.) NW of Bologna, 56km (34 mi.) SE of Parma, 400km (250 mi.) N of Rome

Via Emilia has run through the center of **Modena** since the city was founded as a Roman colony in 183 B.C., and this prominent location seems to have brought nothing but prosperity. Modena is, after all, known the world over for producing the finest balsamic vinegar, Ferrari and Maserati automobiles, prosciutto, and Lambrusco wine (a thick, fizzy red), as well as for the culinary achievements of its chefs and the operatic voices of citizens Luciano Pavarotti and Mirella Freni.

Modena is a treat for the eye too. Visitors will be delighted to find an elegant city of palaces, churches, piazze, and artworks, most of which can be attributed to the Este family. Forced to leave Ferrara at the end of the 16th century, the Estes came to Modena and soon began building suitable quarters—the Palazzo Ducale, which now houses the military academy—and clearing away cramped medieval lanes to create elegant avenues and piazze. You can easily visit Modena on a day trip from Bologna or Parma, but there is enough to see and do to warrant a stopover of at least a night; in fact, given Bologna's proximity and tendency to fill up during its trade fairs, Modena makes a pleasant alternative.

ESSENTIALS

GETTING THERE **By Train** Trains arrive from and leave for **Bologna** 2 to 3 times an hour (25–35 min.; regional: 4,100L/$2.05, High speed: 8,200L/$4.10), and **Parma** (30 min.; regional: 5,300L/$2.65, High speed: 9,400L/$4.70).

The **train station** is a 10-minute walk from the center; follow Corso Vittorio Emanuele and Via Farini to Piazza Grande. Bus no. 7 also runs from the station to the piazza (1,400L/70¢). You can rent a bike from the lot in front of the main entrance to the station for 2,000L ($1) for 2 hours, 500L (25¢) per hour after that, or 4,000L ($2) a day; the lot is open from 6:30am to 8pm.

By Bus Buses, leaving from the station just to the right of the train station off Viale Monte Kosica, serve the surrounding region. Hourly buses also link Modena with **Ferrara** (1 hr. 50 min.; 9,000L/$4.50).

By Car Modena is conveniently located on A1, halfway between Bologna to the south and Parma to the north and only about half an hour from either.

VISITOR INFORMATION The **tourist office** is in the historic center at Piazza Grande 17 (☎ **059-206-660;** fax 059-206-659; www.provincia.modena.it and www.comune.modena.it). It's open Monday to Saturday 9am to 1pm and 3pm to 7pm (closed Wednesday afternoon) and Sunday 9:30am to 12:30pm.

FESTIVALS & MARKETS   In July and August, Modena stages **Sipario in Piazza,** a program of opera and other musical performances; many events are held next to the duomo in the Piazza Grande, and the great Pavarotti himself has been known to grace the stage. The Tourist Office provides schedules, but for tickets (from 15,000 to 50,000L/$8 to $25) go to the Sipario office in the Palazzo Communale in Piazza Grande (☎ **059-206-460;** Monday to Saturday 10am to 12:30pm and 4 to 7pm). All of Modena seems to be a stage during one week each year at the end of June or beginning of July, when vendors, artists, mimes, and other performers take to the streets for the **Settimana Estense;** festivities culminate in a parade in which the town turns out in Renaissance attire.

Fiera d'Antiquariato, the fourth weekend of every month, invites vendors selling antiques, junk, crafts, and ordinary household supplies; there are musical performances and food stalls as well. The fair is held just outside the city center at Ex Ippodromo exhibition park (take bus no. 7); the tourist office can provide further details.

SEEING THE SIGHTS

Duomo. Piazza Grande. ☎ **059-216-078.** Daily 6:30am–12:30pm (to noon July–Aug) and 3:30–7pm.

Built in the 12th century, this cathedral, with its arched and carved facade, is one of the glories of the European Romanesque. Many of these intricate reliefs are the work of the sculptor Wiligemus and depict scenes from the Old Testament; others—including the lions surrounding the main portal and the scenes from the life of Modena's patron saint, late 4th-century Bishop Geminiano, decorating the south entrance—are by Viligelmo. Rising from the rear of the edifice is the **Ghirlandina,** a 12th- to 14th-century bell tower. You may want to retire to one of the cafes facing Piazza Grande to admire this remarkable assemblage before venturing inside, where **polychrome reliefs** depicting the New Testament on the rood screen, a huge painted **Crucifix,** and more **sculpted lions** lend a Byzantine air to the vast space. St. Geminiano's stone coffin lies in the crypt under the choir (which has nice inlaid stalls)—though his arm is encased in silver on the altar—and the coffin is carried through the streets on his feast day, January 31.

Biblioteca Estense (Estense Library). Palazzo dei Musei, Largo Sant'Agostino 337 (at the northwestern end of Via Emilia). ☎ **059-222-248.** 5,000L ($2.50). Mon–Sat 9am–1pm.

One of Europe's most extensive historic libraries contains more than half a million books and some 15,000 incunabula, codices, and other rare manuscripts. While most of the collection is open only to scholars, the gems are displayed in one large room, the Sala Mostra. Among the medieval maps and letters is the most treasured illustrated manuscript of Renaissance Italy: the *Bibbia di Borso d'Este,* a magnificently illustrated 1,200-page Bible.

Galleria Estense. Palazzo dei Musei, Largo. Sant'Agostino 337 (at the northwestern end of Via Emilia). ☎ **059-222-145.** Admission 8,000L ($4). Tues–Sun 8:30am–7:30pm.

A 5-minute walk up Via Emilia from Piazza Grande brings you to another treasure of Modena, the sizeable art collection that the Este family brought with it from Ferrara and continued to gather during its tenure here. Shown off to their best advantage in newly renovated galleries, the works are staggering in their magnitude and array—a *Portrait of Duke Franceso I* by Velazquez next to a bust of him by Bernini, along with canvases by Tintoretto, Correggio, Andrea del Sarto, Guido Reni, Cima da Conegliano, Il Guercino, Ludovico Carracci, and Emilian artist Cosimo Tura. It's a sign of the Estes' wide-ranging tastes that the collection also includes an El Greco and canvases by Flemish masters such as Joos van Cleve, Jan Gossaert, and Pieter Brueghel the Younger.

Galleria Ferrari (Car Museum). Via Dino Ferrari 43, in the town of Maranello (about 10 min. south of the center via no. 2 bus from the bus station, near the train station off Viale Monte Kosica). ☎ **0536-943-204.** www.ferrari.it. Admission 15,000L ($8) adults, 10,000L ($5) under 10. Tues–Sun 9:30am–12:30pm and 3–6pm.

For those whose taste extends beyond vinegar to Modena's other famous product, a visit to the Ferrari showroom and museum, part of the famed automaker's factory, is a must. Racing enthusiasts will find the many trophies that the Ferrari team has won in international competitions over the years—including, after a long dry spell, a major victory in 2000—but pride of place belongs to the gorgeous automobiles the company has produced over the years.

AFFORDABLE PLACES TO STAY

Centrale. Via Rismondo 55, 41100 Modena. ☎ **059-218-808.** Fax 059-238-201. www.hotelcentrale.com. E-mail: info@hotelcentrale.com. 40 units, 38 with bathroom. A/C TV TEL. 80,000L ($40) single without bathroom, 140,000L ($70) single with bathroom; 210,000L ($105) double with bathroom. Buffet breakfast 15,000L ($8). AE, DC, MC, V. Parking 15,000L ($8) in garage or free on street (ask for permit).

The Centrale is indeed in the center of things, wonderfully situated on a charming old street a block from the Duomo. Besides the great location, there's an inviting breakfast room and bar area downstairs and unusually large rooms upstairs. The furnishings are contemporary and bland but spanking new, and the baths are tiny and come with stall showers. Most rooms have nice views over the surrounding palazzi of old Modena, and three of the accommodations include a short corridor leading to a small extra room with a single bed, making them ideal for families.

WORTH A SPLURGE

✪ **Canalgrande.** Corso Canalgrande 6, 41100 Modena. ☎ **059-217-160.** Fax 059-221-674. www.canalgrandehotel.it. 70 units. A/C MINIBAR TV TEL. 210,000L ($105) single; 305,000L ($153) double; 360,000L ($180) triple or jr. suite; 465,000L ($233) suite. Rates include buffet breakfast. AE, DC, MC, V. Parking 15,000L ($8) in garage or free on street (ask for permit).

Chances are you won't regret exceeding your budget on this exquisite hotel, which provides just the sort of ambience you'd expect in a city as atmospheric and elegant as Modena. The ground-floor public areas and breakfast rooms of this 17th-century villa retain splendid terra-cotta floors and elaborate plasterwork and frescoes and are decorated in a pleasing blend of Victorian and traditional furnishings. French doors open to a beautifully planted garden (ask for a room facing this side of the building). Upstairs, ongoing renovations are bringing the guest rooms up-to-date in perfect style—the silk pastel-colored draperies and bed coverings, linen sheets, and Venetian-style or 19th-century reproductions provide handsome surroundings. The new baths are sumptuous and come with amenities like massaging shower heads, hair dryers, and heated towel racks. Service is both efficient and friendly, and there's an osteria-style restaurant in the cellars, La Secchia Rapita.

GREAT DEALS ON DINING

Giusti. Vc. Squallore 46. ☎ **059-222-533.** Reservations required. Primi 20,000–25,000L ($10–$13); secondi 28,000–45,000L ($14–$23). AE, MC, V. Tues–Sat 1–3pm. Closed July 20–Aug 31 and Dec. MODENESE.

I hesitate to mention this five-table eatery only because it can be so hard to procure a table—often, you must reserve at least a month before you plan to be in Modena—but the experience of lunching here is well worth the effort. You enter through a shop fragrant with balsamic vinegars and parmigiano and put yourself in the hands of Nano

---

Living Off the Fat of the Land

Modena's well-deserved reputation for culinary excellence is not confined to the city's elegant restaurants. To equip yourself for a picnic, pick your way through the food stalls of the 1931 **covered market** on Via Albinelli, open weekdays 6:30am to 2pm and Saturday 5 to 7:30pm in summer. Purists may want to procure local hams during tastings at the **Consorzio del Prosciutto di Modena,** Viale Corassori 72 (☎ **059-343-464**), and accompany them with wines from the **Consorzio Tutela del Lambrusco di Modena,** Via Schedoni 41 (☎ **059-235-005**).

More readily available are the balsamic vinegars, prosciutto, and other foodstuffs sold at several gourmet shops throughout the city. Two of these emporia are connected with well-known restaurants (see "Great Deals on Dining," above): **Salumeria Giuseppe Giusti,** Via Farini 75 (☎ **059-441-203**), and **Fini,** Piazza San Francesco (☎ **059-223-314**).

Morandi and Laura Galli, the husband-and-wife proprietors. You'll want to try the capon in two forms—a capon broth with tortellini (which, like all the pastas, is made on the premises) and a crunchy capon salad dribbled with aged balsamic vinegar. A *stinco* (roast joint) of veal or pork is the perfect dish with which to proceed, and even if you feel you can't, do indulge in one of the delicious homemade cakes.

Ristorante Oreste. Piazza Roma 31a. ☎ **059/24-33-24.** Reservations recommended. Primi 8,000–22,000L ($4–$11); secondi 20,000–28,000L ($10–$14). AE, DC, MC, V. Thurs–Tues noon–3pm and 7:30–10:30pm. Closed Sun evening and July 10–31. MODENESE.

Oreste was last redecorated in 1959, and the glass globe lamps, blonde paneling, and Danish-modern furnishings suggest a timelessness that is reflected in the flawless service and an excellent menu of traditional Modenese favorites. You can sample a wonderful assortment of antipasti (including prosciutto supplied directly from a nearby producer and vegetables delivered fresh daily to the kitchen door) at the self-service buffet (8,000L/$4 for a half portion, 16,000/$8 for a full portion). Many vegetarian pastas are available (including a risotto with wild mushrooms and tortellini stuffed with ricotta and spinach), but Oreste is justifiably well known for its flawlessly prepared meat dishes. You would be hard pressed to find a richer *osso buco* or more succulent roast of veal or pork (served with heavenly rosemary-infused potatoes). The attentive staff is happy to help you with the extensive wine list, which includes many local vintages.

WORTH A SPLURGE

Fini. Rua Frati Minori 54. ☎ **059-223-314.** Reservations required. Primi 18,000–35,000L ($9–$18); secondi 18,000–55,000L ($9–$28). AE, DC, MC, V. Wed–Sun 12:30–3pm and 8–11pm. Closed July 23–Aug 26 and Dec 24–Jan 3. MODENESE.

Fini was founded as an annex to a salumeria in 1912 and since then has become one of Italy's most noted restaurants—and it lives up to its far-flung reputation without fail. The surroundings are vaguely art deco and surprisingly relaxed, service is impeccable without being stuffy, and the kitchen sends out meals that are sure to be memorable. An unusual and delectable starter is the pâté of chicken and prosciutto, and carnivores should move on to the house's famous *carrello dei setti tagli di bollito* (a cart with seven kinds of boiled meats to carve, served with an accompaniment of sauces including *mostarda de Cremona*—fruits preserved in mustard sauce). The fare doesn't get too much lighter than fried sweetbreads or kidneys topped with truffle shavings; however, vegetarians will be satisfied with many of the pasta dishes, which change daily and are nicely infused with *funghi porcini* and other fresh ingredients in season. The wine list includes many Lambruscos from Fini's own vineyards.

5 Parma

95km (57 mi.) NW of Bologna, 122km (75 mi.) SE of Milan

Its prosciutto di Parma hams and parmigiano reggiano cheeses are justly famous, as they have been since Roman times, but the pleasures of this exquisite little city extend far beyond the gastronomic. The Farneses, who made their duchy one of the art centers of the Renaissance, were succeeded by Marie-Louise, a Hapsburg and wife of Emperor Napoléon. Her interest in everything cultural ensured that **Parma** never languished as a once-glorious backwater, as was the case with nearby Ferrara and Ravenna. As a result, today's residents of Parma live in one of Italy's most prosperous cities and are surrounded by palaces, churches, and artwork—all of which can also be enjoyed by travelers who choose to spend some time here.

ESSENTIALS
GETTING THERE   By Train   Since Parma is on the busy north-south rail lines, connections are excellent. There are 2 to 4 trains per hour to and from **Bologna** (regional: 65–75 min., 7,700L/$3.85, High speed: 50–55 min., 12,800L/$6); most also stop in **Modena** (30 min.; regional: 5,300L/$2.65, High speed: 9,400L/$4.70), and many continue all the way to **Milan** (regional: 90 min., 12,500L/$6; High speed: 70–85 min., 20,200L/$10).

About four high-speed trains a day connect with **Florence** (2 hr.; 26,300L/$13). The **Parma–La Spezia** line (2½ hr.; 10,500L/$5) runs 9 trains daily and is handy for travelers coming from Liguria (the region's southern tip) or the Tuscan coast (La Spezia lies just north of Pisa and Lucca). The train station is about a 20-minute walk from the center; from the front of the station follow Viale Bottego east for one block to Via Garibaldi, which leads to Piazza Duomo.

By Bus   The bus station, next to the train station on Piazzale Carlo Alberto della Chiesa, serves surrounding towns.

By Car   The A1 autostrada connects Parma with Bologna in less than an hour and with Milan in a little over an hour. Modena, also on the A1, is about halfway between Parma and Bologna.

VISITOR INFORMATION   The **tourist office,** Via Melloni 1B (☎ **0521-218-889;** fax 0521-234-735; http://turismo.comune.parma.it/turismo), is open Monday to Saturday from 9am to 7pm and Sunday 9am to 1pm.

FESTIVALS & MARKETS   Parma celebrates its musical traditions in July and August with **Concerti Nei Chiostri,** when classical concerts are performed in churches, cloisters, and piazzas around the city. The tourist office provides a list of times and locations. To partake of Parma's preoccupation with food, take a walk through the **food market** on Piazza Ghiaia, near the Palazzo della Pilotta. It's open Monday to Saturday 8am to 1pm and 3 to 7pm. There's an **antiques market** every Thursday on Via d'Azelgio and a general **weekly market** Fridays on Piazza Lubiana and Wednesdays and Saturdays on Piazza Ghaia.

SEEING PARMA

✪ Battistero (Baptistry). Piazza del Duomo. ☎ **0521-235-886.** Admission 5,000L ($2.50) adults, 3,000L ($1.50) students and seniors over 65. Daily 9am–12:30pm and 3–6:45pm.

This stunning octagon, begun in 1196 and clad in pink and white marble, is a tribute to the work of Benedetto Antelami, one of the most important sculptors of the Italian Romanesque. His friezes of allegorical animals encircle the base of the structure, which rises in five graceful tiers. Inside is his famous 14-statue cycle depicting the 12 months and winter and spring, now stuck way up in the lower colonnade above the tall niches that once held them. Those niches and the ceiling are covered in 13th-century frescoes by an unknown artist that portray the lives of the apostles, Jesus, and other biblical figures in a stunning display of visual storytelling and color.

Camera di San Paolo. Via Melloni 3 (just off Piazza Pilotta, down a little gated, shade-lined street). ☎ **0521-233-309** or 0521-233-718. Admission 4,000L ($2). Tues–Sun 9am–7:30pm, Mon 9am–2pm. (These extended hours are an experiment, so call to be sure they aren't back to closing at 2pm daily.)

When the abbess of this convent sought to commission an artist to fresco her dining room, she went to Correggio, one of masters of the Italian High Renaissance, who lived and worked in Parma in the early 16th century. He rose to the occasion by turning the room's late Gothic umbrella vaulting into a magnificent deep green pergola framing colorful putti. His portrait of the abbess as Diana, goddess of the hunt (and, more to the point in a convent, of chastity), hangs over the fireplace. These intimate rooms are an excellent place to begin a tour of Parma—you'll encounter Correggio again in the city's churches and its museum, but nowhere else are you able to observe his work so closely. Ask the ticket takers to accompany you to the back of the gardens and unlock the Cella di Santa Caterina, so called after Alessandro Araldi's fresco *The Mystical Marriage of St. Catharine.*

Casa Natale & Museo di Arturo Toscanini (Arthur Toscanini Birthplace). Via R. Tanzi 13. ☎ **0521-285-499.** Admission 3,000L ($1.50) adults, 1,000L (50¢) under 14. Tues–Sat 10am–1pm and 3–6pm, Sun 10am–1pm.

Arturo Toscanini, one of the greatest conductors of the early 20th century, was born in Parma in 1867, and though he traveled the world, he often returned to Parma to conduct at the Teatro Regio. Among the memorabilia exhibited in the house of his birth includes original furnishings, programs, photos, and a copy of every recording he ever made.

San Giovanni Evangelista. Piazzale San Giovanni (just behind the Duomo). ☎ **0521-235-592.** Admission to church and cloisters free, pharmacy 4,000L ($2). Daily 6:30am–noon and 3–6pm; pharmacy daily 9am–1:45pm.

Behind the baroque facade of this church just to the east of the Duomo are works by the two masters of Parma, Correggio and Il Parmigianino. Correggio's dome painting here (placing 500L/25¢ in the box in the left transept lights it up), the *Vision of San Giovanni,* is considered to be one of the great achievements of the High Renaissance; his fresco of the saint writing down his vision is in the left transept, and he also did the narrow frieze around the nave of prophets, sybils, putti, and pagan altars. Il Parmagianino frescoed the first two chapels on the left aisle. Off the cloisters in the adjoining monastery (entrance just left of the church doors) is a *biblioteca* (library) frescoed with grotesques, maps, and battle scenes.

Around the corner is the entrance to the **Spezeria (Pharmacy),** Borgo Pipa 1 (☎ **0521-233-309**), from which the good monks have supplied Parma with potions and poultices (today, honeys, tisanas, and beauty products at the cloister entrance) for nearly 700 years. An array of medieval-looking mortars and jars continues to line the shelves.

✪ **Duomo.** Piazza del Duomo. ☎ **0521-235-886.** Admission free. Daily 9am–12:30pm and 3–7pm.

Parma's Duomo, made of (very dirty) soft pink marble and embellished with three rows of loggias and flanked by a graceful campanile, was built in the 12th century and is one of the great achievements of Italian Romanesque architecture. Once inside, all eyes are lifted to celestial realms: Correggio's great masterpiece, his dramatic *Assumption of the Virgin,* adorns the octagonal cupola. The Virgin and her entourage of putti seem to be floating right through the roof into an Easter egg–blue heaven, and Correggio captured them in what seems to be three-dimensional depth—long before this technique became prominent during the baroque period. Even before Correggio added his crowning embellishment, between 1522 and 1534, the Duomo shone with another masterpiece—a bas-relief of *The Deposition* by the 12th-century sculptor Antelami. Look for it in the right transept.

Galleria Nazionale (National Gallery). Palazzo della Pilotta, Piazzale Marconi. ☎ **0521-233-309.** Admission 12,000L ($6); 4,000L ($2) for just the theater. National Gallery daily 9am–2pm; theater daily 9am–7pm.

This grim-looking massive complex, which the Farnese put up near the banks of the river Parma in 1603, would be an empty shell if it weren't for Marie-Louise, the Hapsburg wife of Emperor Napoléon and niece of Marie Antoinette, who ruled the duchy in the early 19th century. Marie-Louise shared her aunt's passion for art, and under her guidance, paintings from throughout her domain were brought here to fill the rooms the Farnese had left empty when Isabella Farnese assumed the throne of Spain in the 18th century and the clan left Parma for good. Though Allied bombings came close to flattening the palace in May 1944, much of it has been rebuilt. Visitors enter the museum via the **Teatro Farnese,** a wooden jewel box of a theater that Giambattista Aleotti, a student of Palladio, built for the Farnese in 1618, modeling it after the master's Palladian theater in Vicenza (see chapter 8); this was the first theater in Europe to accommodate moving scenery, and its elegant proportions provide a warm, intimate atmosphere.

A tour of the museum's outstanding collections continues up onto the stage and behind it along a series of raised metal walkways through otherwise bare salons. The works of Parma's great masters are here, including Correggio's *Madonna of St. Jerome* and Il Parmigianino's *Schiava Turca,* and good stuff from lesser-known local talents Il Temperelli, Filippo Mazzola, Josaphat and Alessandro Araldi, Del Grano, and Michelangelo Anselmi, who moved to Parma from Siena and worked alongside Correggio and fellow Mannerist Parmigianino. There are also many fine works by other maestros such as Fra' Angelico, Spinello Aretino, Il Francia, Cima da Conegliano, Tintoretto, Il Guercino, El Greco, Tiepolo, Canaletto, Bernini, and several members of the Carracci clan (Agostino even contrived to die here in Parma). Another prize of the

Parks in Parma

The gravel paths, wide lawns, and splashing fountains of the **Parco Ducale,** another Farnese creation across the river from the Palazzo Pilotta, provide a nice retreat from Parma's busier quarters. It's open daily, May to September 6am to midnight; October, March, and April 6:30am to 7pm; November and February 7am to 6pm; and December to January 7am to 5:30pm.

collection is a sketch by Leonardo da Vinci, *La Scapigliata.* Don't miss the racks of 15th-century Faenza majolica floor tiles from the monastery of S. Paolo. Some of the most striking treasures are by non-Italians, reflecting Maria Louisa's worldly tastes— one of Hans Holbein the Younger's most famous portraits, *Erasmus,* is here, and there is a small collection of other works by northern Europeans as well, including canvases by Jan aud Pieter Brueghel the Younger, Paul Brill, and Van Dyck.

Museo Archeologico Nazionale (National Archaeological Museum). Palazzo della Pilotta, Piazzale Marconi. ☎ **0521-233-718.** Admission 4,000L ($2). Tues–Sun 8:30am–7:30pm.

This small collection spans antiquity, with a nicely displayed collection of Egyptian sarcophagi, Etruscan vases, and Greek statues. Pride of place, though, belongs to a local treasure, an engraved Roman tablet excavated near Piacenza at Velleia.

AFFORDABLE PLACES TO STAY

Astoria Executive. Via Trento 9, 43100 Parma. ☎ **0521-272-717.** Fax 0521-272-724. www.piuhotels.com. 80 units. A/C MINIBAR TV TEL. 160,000L ($80) single; 220,000L ($110) double. In *dipendence* (annex), 60,000L ($30) single; 86,000L ($43) double. Buffet breakfast included in main hotel; 10,000L ($5) in dipendence. 32,000L ($16) for a meal in restaurant. AE, DC, MC, V. Parking in garage 15,000L ($7.50).

No-nonsense and businesslike are the terms that come to mind at this modern hotel just steps from the train station. The facade is sheeted in blue-tinted glass, and the lobby, breakfast, and bar area and guest rooms sport a contemporary decor. This doesn't mean the Astoria isn't welcoming—if you don't mind the complete absence of old-world charm, it's an excellent choice. Guest rooms are compact but tidily furnished with wood-veneer cabinetry and firm, low-slung beds and efficient baths. Double sets of double-glazed windows ensure a good night's sleep, even on the side facing the railroad tracks (honest: There's barely a whisper when a train passes). Several Spartan, tile-floored rooms with very basic furnishings (right down to cotlike beds) are located in the one-star *dipendence,* an old building around the corner. These rooms have none of the amenities of the rooms in the main building (including air-conditioning) and are a bit grim, but they're priced accordingly.

Brenta. Via G. B. Borghesi 12, 43100 Parma. ☎ **0521-208-093.** Fax 0521-208-094. www.hotelbrenta.it. 15 units. TEL. 98,000L ($49) single; 155,000L ($78) double. Continental breakfast 8,000L ($4). AE, DC, MC, V. Parking free on street (ask for permit).

One of the nicer hotels near the train station, this is a perfectly decent fallback if the more atmospheric places in town are full. The dark-paneled lobby is a little drab, but don't let that put you off. The English-speaking management is very helpful and eager to point visitors to sights and nearby restaurants, and surroundings brighten considerably as you go upstairs. Guest rooms are large and quite up to date, with functional modern furniture and new baths with stall showers. Most face side streets and are extremely quiet. One convenience the hotel doesn't have is an elevator.

Button. Borgo Salina 7, 43100 Parma. ☎ **0521-208-039.** Fax 0521-238-783. www.italy-hotels.it. 40 units. TV TEL. 120,000L ($60) single; 165,000L ($83) double. Buffet breakfast 15,000L ($8). AE, MC, V. Parking free on street (ask for permit). Closed July 5–31 and 10 days around Christmas.

Just off Piazza Garibaldi, this pleasant hotel, which is usually filled with European tourists, enjoys a central location, but since the surrounding warren of little streets and squares doesn't see much traffic, it's also surprisingly serene. The rooms are large and serviceable though a little somber, with dark floral wallpaper and Spartan modern furnishings. The baths are nicely tiled and have stall showers. Single travelers enjoy quarters that are much larger than the ones to which they are usually relegated, with

"French beds" that are quite a bit wider than standard single beds, and a few of the doubles have small balconies overlooking a piazzetta behind the hotel. The Cortesi, who run the place, are most accommodating, and you're always welcome to join them in the lobby lounge to watch a soccer match.

Park Hotel Toscanini. Viale Toscanini 4, 43100 Parma. ☎ **0521-289-141.** Fax 0521-283-143. www.hoteltoscanini.com. 48 units. A/C MINIBAR TV TEL. 230,000L ($115) single; 330,000L ($165) double. Buffet breakfast included. AE, DC, MC, V. Parking free in spaces in front of hotel, or 30,000L ($15) in garage.

A hotel named after Parma's famous native composer would have to meet high standards, and the thoroughly modern Toscanini, near the center along Parma's lovely riverfront, does so admirably. Service is notably gracious, and the English-speaking staff at the reception desk is more than happy to make restaurant reservations and lend bicycles. The rooms are large (even singles, which enjoy those extra-wide "French" beds) and soothingly contemporary, with pastel-shaded carpeting and draperies; this somewhat nondescript decor is enlivened with reproductions of works by Renaissance and modern masters. Ask for a room in front to enjoy the river views (double-glazed windows keep noise from the busy riverfront avenue to a minimum). Since the hotel caters mostly to businesspeople, the management is usually willing to lower rates considerably during August and other slow periods.

Torino. Via A. Mazza 7, 43100 Parma. ☎ **0521-281-046.** Fax 0521-230-725. 33 units. A/C TV TEL. 115,000L ($58) single; 165,000L ($83) double. Buffet breakfast 15,000L ($8). AE, DC, MC, V. Parking 18,000L ($9) in garage. Closed Aug 1–24.

At my top choice for moderately priced accommodations in Parma, the location in the pedestrian zone near the Duomo is only half the allure; it's also wonderful because the elegant proprietor has fitted out her modern hotel with a careful eye to style and comfort. There are fresh-cut flowers and a collection of antique porcelains in the pretty lobby, with Liberty-style accents like a chandelier and lots of curves. The charming breakfast room and bar area are graced with antiques. Breakfast is something of an occasion, served on china and including fresh pastries, excellent coffee, and a selection of teas and juices, and in summer, you can take it in the pretty little terra-cotta courtyard. The tile-floored rooms are comfortably modern with modular furnishings but natty grace notes, including dramatic headboards emblazoned with reproductions of Correggio frescoes. The baths are clean, if cramped, and fitted with box showers.

GREAT DEALS ON DINING

One of the great pleasures of being in Parma is dipping into the wonderful local bounty, most notably ham (**prosciutto di Parma**) and cheese (**parmigiano**). The favored pastas on Parma tables are tagliatelli and tortellini, often stuffed with pumpkin or squash, and they come to the table with some wonderfully creative sauces. Main courses lean heavily toward meat, including the *filletto di cavallo* (fillet of horsemeat) that is a staple on most menus. Parma's hallmark wine is Lambrusco, a sparking red that may not be to everyone's taste (but it tastes great with pizza).

Enoteca Fontana. Via Farina 24/a. ☎ **0521-286-037.** Panini 3,800–7,500L ($1.90–$3.75). No credit cards. Tues–Sat 9am–3pm and 4:30–9pm. WINE BAR.

In this atmospheric wine bar/shop, you can stand at the ancient old bar or take a seat at one of the long communal tables and sample your choice of hundreds of wines from Emilia-Romgana, many of them from the immediate region (from 2,000L/$1 per glass); all but a few of the cask wines are available by the bottle. You may decide to dine here as well and accompany your tasting with a light meal from the short menu of panini, platters of ham, salami, and cheese, and a few pasta dishes.

Snacks & Gelato

The lively **Gran Caffè Orientale,** Piazza Garibaldi 19, has a prime location on the city's main square, which can be nicely enjoyed from one of the outdoor tables. In warm weather, it's the house gelato that draws the crowds. The **Miss Pym Sala de Te,** Borgo Parmiginao 5 (☎ **0521-206-006**), is a Ye Olde English refuge for footsore shoppers laden with bags from the chic shops between Piazza Garibaldi and the Duomo; they offer dishes (9,000L to 15,000L/$4.50 to $8 for pasta, crepes, and quiches) Tuesday to Saturday noon to 12:30am, Sunday 3:30 to 7:30pm, plus two special meals: an afternoon tea at 4pm, and a light supper at 8pm.

   Pasticerria Torino, with branches at Via Garibaldi 61 (☎ **0521-235-689**) and Via Farini 60 (☎ 0521-282-796), is an elegant, century-old shop-cum-coffeehouse, where you can enjoy Parma violets—a prissy delicacy of violets coated in sugar that you've probably encountered affixed to wedding cakes. Here, they come plain or topping an assortment of cakes and tarts (and they make a great gift for pastry-chef friends back home).

Gallo d'Oro. Borgo Salina 3A. ☎ **0521-208-846.** Primi 10,000–12,000L ($5–$6); secondi 12,000–24,000L ($6–$12). AE, DC, MC, V. Mon–Sat noon–2:30pm and 7:30–11pm. PARMIGIANA.

Diners are wedged in among an odd assortment of antique toys, movie posters, and casks of the wonderful house Lambrusco in this lively, yellow-walled trattoria near Piazza Garibaldi. The kitchen keeps longer hours than most places in town, and the huge platters of prosciutto di Parma and assorted salamis make a satisfying late-night supper. The homemade *tortellini di zucca* (stuffed with pumpkin) is sublime, and the innovative main courses include a thick chicken breast rolled with prosciutto and parmigiano and served in white wine sauce.

Pizzeria La Duchessa. Piazza Garibaldi 1b. ☎ **0521-235-962.** Primi 9,500–12,000L ($4.75–$6); secondi 10,000–30,000L ($5–$15); pizza 8,000–18,000L ($4–$9). DC, MC, V. Tues–Sun noon–2:45pm and 7:30pm–midnight. PIZZA/PASTA.

The most popular pizzeria in Parma is open late and almost always crowded. You'll probably have to wait for a table, especially if you want one outdoors, but there's a lot of activity to watch in the piazza while you're waiting. Although you can eat a full meal here, you're best off with the exquisite pizzas and meal-in-themselves plates of pasta, washed down with a carafe of the house Sangiovese or a bottle of Lambrusco, Italy's best pizza wine.

Ristorante Lazzaro. Via XX Marzo 14. ☎ **0521-208-944.** Primi 12,000–14,000 ($6–$7); secondi 12,000–20,000L ($6–$10). AE, MC, V. Wed–Sun noon–2:15pm and 7:30–10:30pm, Mon–Tues 11:30am–3:30pm. Closed Sun July–Aug. PARMIGIANA.

This white-walled, boisterous trattoria caters to mostly business clientele at lunchtime, and it opens evenings to serve families for whom a meal here is a favorite outing. The menu focuses on meat dishes, beginning with a tray of prosciutto, and the best main courses are the grilled veal and lamb chops; horsemeat is presented in many different variations as well. The homemade pastas are wonderful and served in copious portions; in fact, even herbivores can dine very well here on one of the vegetarian dishes, such as tagliatelle topped with wild mushrooms (the vegetarian menu includes any number of pasta dishes, as well as salads and grilled vegetables).

Hamming It Up in Parma

For a true taste of Parma, in addition to visiting the outdoor food market at **Piazza Ghiaia** (see "Festivals & Markets," above), you should also sniff out **Salumeria Specialita di Parma,** Via Farini 9C (☎ **0521-233-591;** www.specialitadiparma.com), for a huge selection of prosciutto and other meats. Aficionados can tour the factories of the **Consorzio del Parmigiano Reggiano,** Via Gramsci 26c (☎ **0521-292-700**), with two-hour visits Monday to Friday at 8:30am; and **Consorzio del Prosciutto di Parma,** Via M. dell'Arpa 8b (☎ **0521-243-987**), with visits arranged when you call ahead.

WORTH A SPLURGE

○ **La Greppia.** Strada Garibaldi 39A. ☎ **0521-233-686.** Reservations required. Primi 18,000–25,000L ($9–$13); secondi 28,000–45,000L ($14–$23). AE, DC, MC, V. Wed–Sun 1–3pm and 8–10:30pm. Closed July. PARMIGIANA.

My choice for a memorable meal in one of Parma's serious temples of gastronomy manages to be unpretentious while at the same time making you feel you're experiencing a meal of a lifetime. This is due to the presence of wife-and-husband owners Paola Cavassini and Maurizio Rossi, who preside over the plain dining room with grace and ease. While you can enjoy many traditional Parmigiana favorites (their *stracotto,* braised beef, is the city's best), the menu ventures into dozens of exciting dishes that rely on not only Parma's famous hams and cheeses but also its vegetables. Fresh asparagus lightly topped with prosciutto and tortelli stuffed with fresh herbs are a perfect pair of starters. My favorite main course is veal kidneys with truffle shavings, though a very close second is the veal scaloppini with lemon and a light sauce of white wine and herbs. The dessert chef prepares many kinds of fruit tarts, including one made with green tomatoes, and the chocolate cake will convince you that you have indeed enjoyed the meal of a lifetime.

PARMA AFTER DARK

THE PERFORMING ARTS   Parma's opera house, the **Teatro di Regio,** is not too far down the scale of high regard from Milan's La Scala. After all, Verdi was born nearby (see below) and Arturo Toscanini, who often conducted at the theater, is a native son. Tickets can be hard to come by, since they're swallowed up for the entire October-though-March season well in advance by opera buffs from all over Emilia-Romagna. However, the tourist office sometimes sells standing-room tickets, and you should also check the box office (☎ **0521-218-678** or 0521-218-910; www.teatroregioparma.org) on Via Garibaldi near Piazza della Pace, for last-minute cancellations.

The nearby **Teatro Due** is home to the Colletivo di Parma, a world-renowned theater troop. Their performances, as well as other theatrical events, are staged from October to June; inquire at the tourist office or box office (☎ **0521-230-242;** www.teatrostabileparma.com) for details.

BARS & CLUBS   Parma does not have a lively nightlife. The prime night spots are the cafes and bars in and around Piazza Garibaldi; see some of my choices above. Parma's top dance clubs tend to line Via Emilio Lepido: **Dadaumpa** at no. 48 (☎ **0521-483-802**), **Escalier** at no. 47 (☎ **0521-487-453**), and **Ippopatamus** at no. 28 (☎ **0521-487-535**); there's also **Astrolabio** at Via Zarotta 86A (☎ **0521-460-538**).

7

Venice: La Serenissima

by Reid Bramblett

Yes, the tourist hordes have become so relentless there doesn't seem to be a low season anymore. And, yes, the prices here can be double what they are elsewhere in Italy. But, after all, this is the fabled city of canals: This is Venice, *La Serenissima* (the Serene Republic), what Lord Byron described as "a fairy city of the heart." People flock here for a very good reason: Venice is extraordinary, magical, and worth every lira. It shouldn't exist and yet it does, and it's a living, breathing, singular city that seems almost too exquisite to be genuine.

Venice was at the crossroads of the Byzantine and Roman worlds for centuries, a fact that lends to its unique heritage of art, architecture, and culture. And although traders and merchants no longer pass through "La Repubblica Serena" as they once did, it nonetheless continues to find itself at a crossroads: an intersection in time between the uncontested period of maritime power that built it and the modern world that keeps it ever-so-gingerly afloat.

Allot Venice at least a stay of 2 to 3 days (heck, it'll take you half a day just to find your hotel). But if you can, stay longer—it'll most likely be the highlight of your time in Italy. Venice is too special to be rushed—and sometimes difficult to appreciate unless you stick around long enough to see its less-touristy corners and seek out its secrets.

1 Arriving

BY PLANE

You can fly into Venice from North America via Rome or Milan with Alitalia or a number of other lines or by connecting through a major European city with European carriers like KLM, Luftansa, British Airways, Air France, and so on.

Flights land at the **Aeroporto Marco Polo,** 7km (4½ mi.) north of the city on the mainland (☎ **041-260-9260** for flight info or 041-260-6111; www.veniceairport.it). There are two bus alternatives: The **ATVO airport shuttle bus** (☎ **041-520-5530**) connects with Piazzale Roma not far from the Santa Lucia train station, the closest point to Venice's attractions accessible by land. Buses leave for/from the airport about every hour, cost 5,000L ($2.50), and make the trip in 20 minutes. The twice-hourly local **public ACTV bus 5** (☎ **041-528-7886**) costs 1,500L (75¢) and takes 30 to 45 minutes. Buy tickets for either at the newsstand just inside the terminal from the signposted bus stop. With either bus, you'll have to walk to/from the final stop at Piazzale Roma to the nearby *vaporetto* stop for the final connection to your hotel. It's rare to see porters around who'll help with luggage, so remember to pack light.

A **land taxi** from the airport to Piazzale Roma to pick up your *vaporetto* will run about 50,000L ($25).

The most fashionable and traditional way to arrive in Piazza San Marco is by sea. For 17,000L ($9), the **Cooperative San Marco/Alilaguna** (☎ **041-522-2303**) operates a large *motoscafo* (shuttle boat) service from the airport with two stops at Murano and the Lido before arriving after about an hour in Piazza San Marco. Call for the daily schedule of a dozen or so trips (about 6am to midnight), which changes seasonally and is coordinated with the principal arrival/departure of the major airlines (most hotels have the schedule). If your hotel isn't in the Piazza San Marco area, you'll have to make a connection at the *vaporetto* launches (your hotel can help with the specifics if you've booked before leaving home).

A private *taxi acquei* (water taxi), taking 20 to 30 minutes to/from the airport, is convenient but costly—a legal minimum of 87,000L ($44) but usually more around 140,000L ($70) for two passengers with bags. However, it's worth considering if you're pressed for time, have an early flight, have a lot of luggage (a Venice no-no), or can split the cost with a friend or two. It may be able to drop you off at the front (or side) door of your hotel or as close as it can maneuver given your hotel's location (check with the hotel before arriving). Your taxi captain should be able to tell you before boarding just how close he can get you.

BY TRAIN

Trains from **Rome** (Intercity only: 4½ hr., 79,000L/$40), **Milan** (Intercity: 3 hr., 35,700L/$18; regional: 3½ hr., 22,700L/$11), Florence (Intercity: about 3 hr., 46,700L/$23; regional to Mestre, then Intercity: 3¾ hr., 34,600L/$17), and all over Europe arrive at the **Stazione Santa Lucia.** To get there, all must pass through (though not necessarily stop at) a station marked Venezia–Mestre. Don't be confused: Mestre is a charmless industrial city that's the last stop on the mainland. Occasionally trains end in Mestre, in which case you have to catch one of the frequent 10-minute shuttles connecting with Venice; if so, take a moment to look around, as the Mestre station was designed by famed architect Rienzo Piano, who did Paris's Pompidou Center and the New York Times building currently going up in Manhattan. Still, it's inconvenient, so when booking your ticket confirm that the final destination is Venezia–Stazione Santa Lucia.

Between the station's large front doors is a small, understaffed **tourist office** (☎ **041-529-8727**), with lines that can be discouraging and a strict "one person allowed in at a time" policy. It's open daily 8am to 7pm (closed Sunday in winter). The **train info office,** marked with a lowercase "i," is also in the station's main hall and staffed daily 8am to 8pm.

On exiting, you'll find the Canal Grande (Grand Canal) in front of you, making a heart-stopping first impression. You'll find the docks for a number of *vaporetto* lines (the city's public ferries or "water buses") to your left and right. Head to the booths to your left, near the bridge, to catch either of the two lines plying the Canal Grande: the **no. 82 express,** which stops only at the station, San Marcula, Rialto Bridge, San Tomà, San Samuele, and Accademia before hitting San Marco (26 min. total); and the misnamed **no. 1 *accellerato,*** which is actually the local, making 14 stops between the station and San Marco (a 31-min. trip). Both leave every 10 minutes or so, but every other no. 82 stops short at Rialto, meaning you'll have to disembark and hop on the next no. 1 or 82 that comes along to continue to San Marco.

Note: The no. 82 goes in two directions from the train station: left down the Canal Grande toward San Marco—which is the (relatively) fast and scenic way—and right, which also gets you to San Marco (at the San Zaccaria stop) but takes twice as long because it goes the relatively boring way around Dordosuro. Make sure the no. 82 you get on is headed to San Marco.

BY BUS Though rail travel is more convenient and commonplace, Venice is serviced by long-distance buses from all over mainland Italy and some foreign cities. The final destination is Piazzale Roma, where you'll need to pick up vaporetto no. 82 or 1 (see "By Train," above) to connect you with stops in the heart of Venice and along the Grand Canal.

BY CAR The only wheels you'll see in Venice are those attached to luggage. Venice is a city of canals and narrow alleys. No cars allowed—even the police and ambulance services use boats. Arriving in Venice by car is problematic and expensive—and downright exasperating if it's high season and the parking facilities are full (they often are). You can drive across the Ponte della Libertà from Mestre to Venice itself but can go no farther than Piazzale Roma at the Venice end, where many garages eagerly await your lire. Do some research before choosing a garage—the rates vary widely, from 30,000L ($15) per day for an average-size car at the **ASM garage** (☎ **041-272-7301**) to 48,000L ($24) per day at private outfits like **Garage San Marco** (☎ **041-523-2213**) and others. If you have reservations at a hotel, check before arriving: Most offer discount coupons for some of the parking facilities with a special daily rate of 20,000L ($11) to submit on departure when payment is due (ask the hotel at which garage you need to park).

Vaporetto lines nos. 1 and 82 (see "By Train," above) both stop at Piazzale Roma before continuing down the Canal Grande to the train station and, eventually, Piazza San Marco.

2 Essentials

VISITOR INFORMATION

TOURIST OFFICES There's a **small office** in the train station (above), but you'll find a slightly less crowded **larger office** under the arcade at the west end of Piazza San Marco at no. 71, on the left of the tunnel-like street leading to Calle dell'Ascensione (☎ **041-529-8711;** fax 041-523-0399; Vaporetto: San Marco). May to mid-September, it's open daily 9:30am to 6:30pm; winter hours are Monday to Saturday 9:45am to 3:15pm. There's also a **small office/gift shop** at Palazzina del Santi, also called Palazzetto Selva (☎ **041-522-6356** or 041-522-5150; Vaporetto: San Marco), between the small green park on the Grand Canal called the Giardinetti Reali and the famous Harry's Bar. It's open daily 10am to 6pm.

Look for the ubiquitous posters around town with exhibit and concert schedules that are far more helpful, or hope your hotel staff can help, and pick up a copy of the info-packed *Un Ospite di Venezia* (lying around hotel lobbies everywhere). Ask the tourist offices for a schedule of the month's special events and an updated listing of museum and church hours, as these can change erratically (watch for extended nighttime hours in summer). During peak season, a small info booth with erratic hours operates in the Arrivals Hall at the airport.

WEB SITES The city's official tourist board sites is **www.turismovenezia.it**. Several good privately maintained sites are Meeting Venice (**www.meetingvenice.it**), Carnival of Venice (**www.carnivalofvenice.com/uk**), the Venice Italy Index (**www. iuav.unive.it/~juli/venindx.html**), and Doge of Venice (**www.doge.it**).

A Money-Saving Tip

Anyone between 16 and 29 is eligible for the terrific **Rolling Venice pass,** giving discounts in museums, restaurants, stores, language courses, hotels, and bars across the city. It's valid for a year and costs 5,000L ($2.50). Year-round, you can pick one up at the **Informagiovani Assessorato alla Gioventù,** San Marco 1529, on Corte Contarina off the Frezzeria (☎ **041-274-7651;** Vaporetto: San Marco), open Monday to Friday 9:30am to 1pm, plus Tuesday and Thursday 3 to 5pm. July to September, you can stop by the Rolling Venice office set up in the Santa Lucia train station daily 8am to 8pm; in winter, you can get the pass at the Transalpino travel agency (☎ **041-524-1334**) just outside the station's front doors and to the right, at the top of the steps, open Monday to Friday 8:30am to 12:30pm and 3 to 7pm and Saturday 8:30am to 12:30pm.

FESTIVALS & EVENTS   Not to be missed are pre-Lenten **Carnevale,** Venice's most special event, a theatrical resuscitation of the 18th-century bacchanalia that drew tourists during the final heyday of the Serene Republic; the **Voga Longa,** a 30km (18-mi.) rowing "race"; the **Festa del Redentore,** one big floating festa until night descends and an awesome half-hour *spettacolo* of fireworks fills the sky; the **Venice International Film Festival,** the most respected celebration of celluloid in Europe after Cannes; the prestigious **Biennale d'Arte,** one of the world's top international modern-art shows;.the **Regata Storica,** an extravagant seagoing parade in historic costume as well as a genuine regatta; the **Festa della Salute,** when a pontoon bridge is erected across the Grand Canal to connect La Salute and Santa Maria del Giglio, commemorating another delivery from a plague in 1630 that wiped out a third of the lagoon's population; the **Festa della Sensa,** reenacting the ancient ceremony when the doge wed Venice to the sea; the April 25 **feast day of Saint Mark,** beloved patron saint of Venice and of the ancient Republic; and the **Maratona (Marathon).** See the "Calendar of Events," in chapter 2 for more details.

CITY LAYOUT

Keep in mind as you wander seemingly hopelessly among the *calli* (streets) and *campi* (squares) that the city wasn't built to make sense to those on foot but rather to those plying its canals. No matter how good your map and sense of direction, time after time you'll get lost. Just view it as an opportunity to stumble across Venice's most intriguing corners and vignettes.

Venice lies 2½ miles from terra firma, connected to the mainland burg of **Mestre** by the **Ponte della Libertà,** which leads to **Piazzale Roma.** Snaking through the city like an inverted S is the **Canal Grande (Grand Canal),** the wide main artery of aquatic Venice. The "streets filled with water" are 177 narrow *rio* (canals) cutting through the interior of the two halves of the city, flowing gently by the doorsteps of centuries-old palazzi. They'd be endlessly frustrating to the landlubbing visitors trying to navigate the city on foot if not for the 400 footbridges crossing them, connecting Venice's 118 islands.

Only three bridges cross the Grand Canal: the **Ponte degli Scalzi,** just outside the train station; the elegant white marble **Ponte Rialto,** connecting the districts of San Marco and San Polo and by far the most recognizable; and the wooden **Ponte Accademia,** connecting the Campo Santo Stefano area of the San Marco neighborhood with the Accademia museum across the way in Dorsoduro.

A Note on Addresses

Within each *sestiere* (district) is a most original system of numbering the palazzi, using one continuous string of 6,000 or so numbers. The format I've used for addresses in this chapter is the official mailing address: the *sestiere* name followed by the building number in that district, followed by the name of the street or campo on which you'll find that address—for example, San Marco 1471 (on Salizzada San Moisè) means the mailing address is San Marco 1471, and you'll find it in the San Marco district on Salizzada San Moisè. Be aware that San Marco 1471 may not necessarily be found close to San Marco 1475 and that many buildings aren't numbered at all.

The **free street map** offered by the tourist office and most hotels has good intentions, but it doesn't even show, much less name or index, all the *calli* and pathways of Venice. For that, pick up a more detailed map (ask for a *pianta della città*) for sale in any of a number of bookstores or newsstands. The best (and most expensive) available is the easy-to-read, spiral-bound, highly detailed **Touring Club edition** (16,000L/$8). The recognizable red, white, and black map put out by **Nicola Vincitorio Pub.** (6,000L/$3) is just as handy. The newspaper and magazine stand at the train station carries a number of alternatives to the poorly detailed tourist-office freebie. Apparently word got out centuries ago that maps in Venice are a useless thing. If you're lost, you're better off just asking a local Venetian to point you in the right direction.

Neighborhoods in Brief

Beginning in the 12th century and made official in 1711, the city has been divided, for tax-related purposes, into six **sestieri** ("sixths" or districts). The "Canalazzo" or Grand Canal neatly divides them into three on each bank.

San Marco   The most visited (and thus most expensive) of the *sestieri,* this central district is anchored by the magnificent **Piazza San Marco** and the **Basilica di San Marco** to the south and the **Ponte Rialto** (bridge) to the north. It's the city's commercial, religious, and political heart and has been for more than a millennium (it was also its musical heart until a fire destroyed **La Fenice** opera house in 1996; La Fenice now stands a hollow shell, waiting to be rebuilt). Though you'll find glimpses of the real Venice here, ever-rising rents have nudged resident Venetians to look for housing in the outer neighborhoods: You'll be hard-pressed to find a grocery store or dry cleaners in San Marco. But if you're looking for Murano glass trinkets and mediocre restaurants, you'll find an embarrassment of choices. This area is a Mecca for first-class hotels—with direction from Frommer's, however, you can stay here in the heart of Venice without going broke.

Cannaregio   Sharing the same side of the Grand Canal with the San Marco district, Cannaregio stretches north and east from the **Santa Lucia train station** to include the **Jewish Ghetto** and into the canal-hugging vicinity of the **Ca' d'Oro** and the **Ponte Rialto.** Its outer reaches are unspoiled and residential (what tourist crowds? you'll wonder); one-third of Venice's ever-shrinking population of 20,000 is said to live here. Venice's majority of one-star hotels are clustered about the train station—not a dangerous neighborhood, but not one known for its charm either. The gloss and dross of the tourist-shop-lined **Lista di Spagna** strip continues as it morphs into the **Strada Nuova** in the direction of the Rialto Bridge.

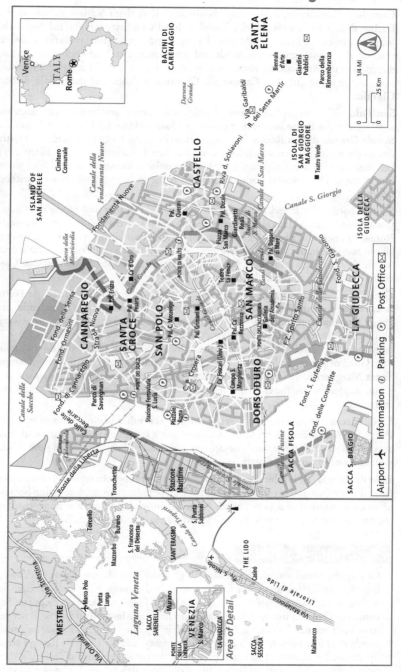

Airport ✈ Information ⓘ Parking ⓟ Post Office ⊠

ITALY
Venice
Rome ★

ISLAND OF
SAN MICHELE

Cimitero
Comunale

Canale della
Fondamenta Nuove

Sacca della
Misericordia

BACINI DI
CARENAGGIO

Darsena
Grande

SANTA
ELENA

Via Garibaldi
R. dei Sette Martir

Biennale
d'Arte
Giardini
Pubblici
Parco della
Rimembranza

CASTELLO

Riva d. Schiavoni

ISOLA DI
SAN GIORGIO
MAGGIORE
■ Teatro Verde

Canale S. Giorgio

Pal.
Querini

Pal. Ducale
Piazza
San Marco
Giardinetti
Reali
Pal. Dogana
di Mare

ISOLA DELLA
GIUDECCA

Fondamenta Nuove

CANNAREGIO

Pal. Erizzo
Ca' d'Oro

PONTE DI RIALTO

Teatro
La Fenice

SAN MARCO

Canale di San Marco

Fond. S. Giacomo

Fond. della Sensa

Fond. Ormesini

Strada Nuova

SANTA
CROCE

Pal.
Pesaro

Pal. C. Morosini

SAN POLO

Pal. Grimani

Pal. Ca'
Rezzonico

Galleria
dell'Accademia

PONTE DELL'ACCADEMIA

F. Z. Spirito Santo

DORSODURO

Fond. delle Convertite

LA GIUDECCA

Canale della Giudecca

Fond. S. Eufemia

Canale delle
Sacche

Parco di
Savorgnan

PONTE DEI SCALZI

Stazione Ferroviaria
S. Lucia

Piazzale
Roma

Calle delle
Beccarie

Ca' Foscari (Univ.)

C. p. Crosera

Campo S.
Margherita

SACCA FISOLA

SACCA S. BIAGIO

Fond. delle Convertite

Tronchetto

Stazione
Marittime

Canal Scomenzera

Canale della Libertà

Ponte della Libertà

MESTRE

Via Orlanda

Via Triestina

Marco Polo
Punta
Lunga

Laguna Veneta

SACCA
SARENELLA

Murano

SACCA
SESSOLA

Torcello

Burano

Mazzorbo

S. Francesco
del Deserto

SANT'ERASMO

Canale di Treporti

S. Punta
Sabbioni

THE LIDO

Casinó

Riv. S. Nicoló

Litorale di Lido

Via Malamocco

Malamocco

VENEZIA
S. Marco
LA GIUDECCA

PONTE
DELLA
LIBERTÀ

Area of Detail

1/4 Mi
.25 Km

351

...o This district, whose tony "boulevard," **Riva degli Schiavoni,** follows the **Bacino di San Marco (St. Mark's Basin),** is lined with first-class and deluxe hotels. It begins just east of Piazza San Marco, skirting Venice's most congested area to absorb some of the crowds and better hotels and restaurants. But head farther east in the direction of the **Arsenale** or inland away from the Bacino and the people traffic thins out, despite major sites like **Campo SS. Giovanni e Paolo** and the **Scuola di San Giorgio.**

San Polo This mixed-bag *sestiere* of residential corners and tourist sites stretches northwest of the **Ponte Rialto** to the principal **Santa Maria dei Frari** church and the **Scuola Grande di San Rocco.** The hub of activity at the foot of the bridge is greatly due to the Rialto market, which has taken place here for centuries—some of the city's best restaurants have flourished here for generations, alongside some of its worst tourist traps. The spacious **Campo San Polo** is the main piazza of Venice's smallest *sestiere.*

Santa Croce North and northwest of the San Polo district and across the Grand Canal from the Santa Lucia train station, Santa Croce stretches all the way to **Piazzale Roma.** Its eastern section is generally one of Venice's least visited sections—making it all the more desirable for curious visitors. Less lively than San Polo, it's as authentic, seemingly light-years away from San Marco. The quiet and lovely **Campo San Giacomo dell'Orio** is considered its heart.

Dorsoduro The residential area of Dorsoduro is on the opposite side of the **Ponte Accademia** from the San Marco district. Known for containing the **Accademia** and **Peggy Guggenheim** museums, it's the largest of the *sestieri* and has been something of an artists' haven (hence the tireless comparison with New York's Greenwich Village—a far cry) until recent rent escalations forced much of the community to relocate. Good neighborhood restaurants, a charming gondola boatyard, the lively **Campo Santa Margherita,** and the sunny quay called **Le Zattere** (a favorite promenade and gelato stop) all add to the character and color that make this one of the city's most visited areas.

La Giudecca Venice shares its lagoon with several other islands. Located opposite Piazza San Marco and Dorsoduro, La Giudecca is a tranquil working-class residential area where you'll find the youth hostel and a handful of hotels (including the deluxe Cipriani, one of Europe's finest).

Lido di Venezia This slim 7-mile-long area is the city's **beach;** separating the lagoon from the open sea and permitting car traffic, it's a popular summer destination because of its concentration of seasonal hotels (these landmark hotels serve as home base for the annual Venice Film Festival), but the Lido is also quite residential.

Beware the *Acqua Alta*

During the notorious tidal *acqua alta* ("high water") floods, the lagoon backwashes into the city, leaving up to 5 or 6 feet of water in the lowest-lying streets (Piazza San Marco, as the lowest point in the city, goes first). They can start as early as late September or October, usually taking place November to March. As many as 50 per year have been recorded since they first started in the late 1700s. The waters usually recede after just a few hours and are often virtually gone by noon. Walkways are set up around town, but wet feet are a given, and the complex system of hydraulic dams being constructed out in the lagoon to cut off these high tides won't be operation for a few years yet.

Mestre   This dreary gateway to Venice is located on the mainland and has nothing to explore. In a pinch, its host of inexpensive hotels are worth consideration when Venice's hotels are full, but that's about it.

Murano, Burano & Torcello   These three islands, northeast of the city and easily accessible by public transportation, are popular tourist destinations. Since the 13th-century **Murano** has exported its glass products worldwide; it's an interesting day trip if you have the time (or the desire to visit a furnace or glass-blowing factory or the noteworthy glass museum), but shoppers can do just as well in Venice's myriad glass stores. The intensely colorful (and I mean that quite literally) fishing village of **Burano** was and still is famous for its lace, an art now practiced by so few that prices are generally unaffordable. **Torcello** is the most remote and least populated, and the 40-minute boat ride is worthwhile for history and art buffs, who'll be awestruck by the cathedral's incredible Byzantine mosaics, some of the finest outside Ravenna.

San Michelle   This cemetery island is the final resting place of celebrities such as Igor Stravinsky and Sergei Diaghilev.

GETTING AROUND

Aside from boats, the only way to explore Venice is by **walking**—and getting lost repeatedly. You'll navigate many twisting streets whose names change constantly and don't appear on any map, streets that may very well simply end in a blind alley or spill abruptly into a canal. And you'll cross dozens of footbridges. Treat getting bewilderingly lost in Venice as part of the fun, and budget more time than you'd ever think necessary to get wherever you're going.

As you wander, look for the ubiquitous **yellow signs** whose destinations and arrows direct you toward five major landmarks: **Ferrovia** (the train station), **Piazzale Roma,** the **Rialto** (Bridge), **Piazza San Marco,** and the **Accademia** (Bridge). If you're in a hurry, follow them. If you're not, turn left when they indicate right to quickly leave the tourist hordes behind and enjoy Venice's local flavor.

BY BOAT   The various *sestieri* are linked by a comprehensive *vaporetto* (water bus/ferry) system of about a dozen lines operated by the Azienda del Consorzio Trasporti Veneziano (ACTV), San Marco 1810, on Calle Fuseri, off the Frezzeria (☎ **041-528-7886** or 041-272-2111; www.actv.it; Vaporetto: San Marco). The *vaporetti* principally serve the Grand Canal (and can be crowded in summer), the outskirts, and the outer islands. The crisscross network of small canals is the province of delivery vessels, gondolas, and private boats. Transit maps are available at the tourist office and most ACTV stations.

The **one-way ticket** is a steep 6,000L ($3), or 5,000L ($2.50) per person for groups of three or more. A **round-trip ticket** is 10,000L ($5), while the **24-hour ticket** at 18,000L ($9) is a good buy if you'll be making more than three trips in a day. Most lines run every 10 to 15 minutes 7am to midnight, then hourly until morning; most *vaporetto* docks (the only place you can buy tickets) have timetables posted. Note that not all stations sell tickets after dark; if you haven't bought a pass or extra tickets beforehand, you'll have to settle up with the conductor on board (you'll have to find him—he won't come looking for you) for an extra 1,000L (50¢) per ticket or gamble on a 40,000L ($20) fine, no excuses accepted.

Also available are **3-day tickets** (35,000L/$18) and **7-day tickets** (60,000L/$30). And there are two **special passes** at 15,000L ($8): One allows you unlimited travel on the Canal Grande for 12 hours, and the Laguna Nord lets you explore the outlying islands (see "Exploring Venice's Islands") for 12 hours.

Cruising the Canals

A leisurely cruise along the ✪ **Canal Grande (Grand Canal)** from Piazza San Marco to the Santa Lucia train station—or the reverse—is one of Venice's must-dos. Hop on *vaporetto* 1 in the late afternoon (grab one of the outdoor seats), when the weather-worn colors of the buildings are warmed by the soft light and when the traffic has eased a bit. Some 200 palazzi, churches, and imposing Republican buildings from the 14th to the 18th century line this 2-mile ribbon of water looping through the city like an inverted S, crossed by only three bridges (the Rialto spans it at midpoint).

Some of the palazzi stand deserted, though many (particularly the larger ones) have been converted into banks, museums, galleries, or even condos. Lower water-lapped floors may now be empty, but the higher floors are coveted by the city's titled families, who've inhabited these glorious places for centuries; others have become the summer dream homes-with-a-view of privileged expats, drawn here as irresistibly as the romantic Venetians-by-adoption who preceded them—Richard Wagner, Robert Browning, Lord Byron, and (more recently) Woody Allen.

As much a symbol of Venice as the winged lion, the **gondola** is one of Europe's great traditions, truly as romantic as it looks (yeah, it's touristy, but who can resist?). Though it's often quoted in print at differing official rates, expect to pay 120,000L ($60) for up to 50 minutes, with up to six passengers, and 60,000L ($30) for an extra 25 minutes. There's a 30,000L ($15) surcharge after 8pm (with 75,000L/$38 for each 25 minutes beyond the first 50), but aim for late afternoon before sundown when the light does its magic on the canal reflections (and bring a bottle of *prosecco*). If the price is too high, ask visitors at your hotel or others lingering about at the gondola stations if they'd like to share it. Establish the cost, time, and route explanation (any of the back canals are preferable to the trafficked and often choppy Grand Canal) with the gondolier before setting off. They're regulated by the **Ente Gondola** (☎ **041-528-5075;** www.gondola-venezia.it), so call if you have any questions or complaints.

And what of the serenading gondolier immortalized in film? A duo of an accordion player and tenor is so expensive it's shared among several gondolas traveling together. A number of travel agents around town book evening sere-nades for 50,000L ($25) per person. The number of *gondolieri* willing to brave the winter cold and rain are minimal, though some come out of their winter hibernation for the Carnevale period.

There are 12 **gondola stations** around Venice, including Piazzale Roma, the Santa Lucia train station, the Ponte Rialto, and Piazza San Marco. There's also a number of smaller stations, with gondoliers standing alongside their sleek 36-ft black wonders looking for passengers. They all speak enough English to com-municate the necessary details.

Just three bridges span the Grand Canal. To fill in the gaps, *traghetti* **skiffs** (over-size gondolas rowed by two standing gondolieri) cross the Grand Canal at eight inter-mediate points 7:30am to 8:30pm (8am to 6:55pm Sunday). You'll find a station at the end of any street named Calle del Traghetto on your map and indicated by a yellow sign with the black gondola symbol. The fare is 1,000L (50¢), which you hand to the gondolier when boarding. Most Venetians cross standing up. For the expe-rience, try the "Santa Sofia" crossing connecting the Ca' d'Oro and the Pescheria fish market, opposite each other on the Grand Canal just north of the Rialto Bridge—

the gondoliers expertly dodge water traffic at this point of the canal where it's the busiest and most heart-stopping.

BY WATER TAXI *Taxi acquei* (water taxis) charge high prices and aren't for visitors watching their lire. For (unlikely) journeys up to 7 minutes, the rate is 27,000L ($14); 500L (25¢) click off for each 15 seconds thereafter. Each bag over 50cm long costs 2,200L ($1.10), plus there's an 8,500L ($4.25) supplement for service 10pm to 7am and a 9,000L ($4.50) surcharge on Sunday and holidays (these last two can't be applied simultaneously). If they have to come get you, tack on another 8,000L ($4). Those rates cover up to four people; if any more squeeze in, it's another 3,100L ($1.55) per extra passenger.

Six **water-taxi stations** serve key points in the city: the Santa Lucia train station (☎ **041-716-286**), Piazzale Roma (☎ **041-716-922**), the Ponte Rialto (☎ **041-523-0575**), Piazza San Marco (☎ **041-522-9750**), the Lido (☎ **041-526-0059**), and Marco Polo Airport (☎ **041-541-5084**). **Radio Taxi** at ☎ **041-522-2303** or 041-723-112 will come pick you up any place in the city.

BY GONDOLA To come all the way to Venice and not indulge in a gondola ride could be one of your biggest regrets. Yes, it's touristy and yes, it's expensive (see "Cruising the Canals," above), but only those with a heart of stone will be unmoved by this quintessential Venetian experience. Don't initiate your trip, however, until you've agreed on a price and synchronized watches. Oh, and don't ask them to sing—if only for your own sake.

Fast Facts: Venice

American Express American Express is at San Marco 1471, on Salizzada San Moisè, 30124 Venezia (☎ **041-520-0844;** Vaporetto: San Marco). In summer, the office is open for banking Monday to Saturday 8am to 8pm (for all other services, 9am to 5:30pm); in winter, hours are Monday to Friday 9am to 5:30pm and Saturday 9am to 12:30pm (for banking and other services).

Bookstores Two centrally located bookstores that carry a line of softcover and hardcover books in English are the **Libreria Sansovino,** San Marco 84, on the Bacino Orseolo, north of Piazza San Marco (☎ **041-522-2623;** Vaporetto: San Marco), and the **Libreria San Giorgio,** San Marco 2087, on Calle Larga XXII Marzo (☎ **041-523-8451;** Vaporetto: San Marco), toward Campo San Stefano. Both carry a selection of books about Venetian art, history, and literature.

Business Hours Standard hours for **shops** are Monday to Saturday 9am to 12:30pm and 3 to 7:30pm. In winter, shops are closed on Monday morning, while in summer it's usually Saturday afternoon. Most **grocers** are closed on Wednesday afternoon throughout the year. In Venice just about everything is closed on Sunday, though **tourist shops** in the tourist areas like San Marco are permitted to stay open during high season. **Restaurants** are required to close at least 1 day per week (*il giorno di riposo*), though the particular day varies from one trattoria to another. Many are open for Sunday lunch but close for Sunday dinner. Many restaurants specializing in fish and seafood also close Monday when the fish market is closed. Restaurants will close for holidays (*chiuso per ferie*), often sometime in July or August, frequently over Christmas, and sometimes in January before the Carnevale rush.

Consulates The nearest **U.S. Consulate** is in Milan, at Largo Donegani 1 (☎ **02-290-351**), open Monday to Friday 9am to 11am for visas only; Monday also open for telephone service info 2 to 4pm. The **U.K. Consulate** at Dorsoduro 1051 (☎ **041-522-7207**), at the foot of the Accademia Bridge just west of the museum in the Palazzo Querini; it's open Monday to Friday 9am to noon and 2 to 4pm. **Canada and Australia** also have consulates in Milan, about 3 hours away by train. Along with **New Zealand,** they all maintain embassies in Rome (see "Fast Facts: Rome," in chapter 3).

Crime Be aware of petty crime like pickpocketing on the crowded *vaporetti,* particularly the tourist routes where passengers are more intent on the passing scenery than watching their bags. Venice's deserted back streets were once virtually crimeproof; occasional tales of theft are circulating only recently. Generally speaking, it's one of Italy's safest cities.

Dentists/Doctors For a shortlist, check with the consulate of the United Kingdom, the American Express office, or your hotel.

Drugstores Venice's pharmacies take turns staying open all night. To find out which one is on call in your area, ask at your hotel, check the rotational duty signs posted outside all drugstores, or dial ☎ **041-523-0573.**

Emergencies In Venice and throughout Italy, dial ☎ **113** to reach the **police.** Most Italians will recommend that you forgo the police and try the military-trained Carabinieri at ☎ **112.** For an ambulance, phone ☎ **523-0000.** To report a fire, dial ☎ **115.** For any **tourism-related complaint** (rip-offs, exceedingly shoddy service, etc.) dial the special agency **Venezia No Problem** toll free at ☎ **800-355-920.**

Holidays Venice's patron saint, San Marco or St. Mark, is honored on April 25.

Laundry The self-service laundry most convenient to the train station is the **Lavaget,** Cannaregio 1269, to the left as you cross Ponte alle Guglie from Lista di Spagna; the rate is about 16,000L ($8) for up to 4.5 kilos (10 lb.). The most convenient to San Marco is **Gabriella,** San Marco 985, on Rio Terrà Colonne (off Calle dei Fabbri), where they wash and dry it for you within an hour or two for 20,000L ($10).

Mail & E-Mail Venice's Posta Centrale is at San Marco 5554, 30124 Venezia, on the San Marco side of the Rialto Bridge at Rialto Fontego dei Tedeschi (☎ **041-271-7111;** Vaporetto: Rialto). This office sells stamps at Window 12 Monday to Saturday 8:10am to 7pm (for parcels, 8:10am to 1:30pm). If you're at Piazza San Marco and need postal services, walk through Sottoportego San Geminian, the center portal at the opposite end of the piazza from the basilica on Calle Larga dell'Ascensione. Its usual hours are Monday to Friday 8:15am to 1:30pm and Saturday 8:15am to 12:10pm. You can buy *francobolli* (stamps) at any *tabacchi* (tobacconists). The limited mailboxes seen around town are red.

For checking or sending e-mail, you can log on 24 hours at **Internet Cafe,** San Marco 2967, on Campo Santo Stefano (☎ **041-277-1190;** Vaporetto: S. Samuele or Giglio). Or try **Venetian Navigator,** Castello 5269, on Calle delle Bande between San Marco and Campo Santa Maria Formosa (☎ **041-522-6084;** www.venetiannavigator.com; Vaporetto: San Marco, Zaccaria, Rialto), open daily 10am to 10pm (to 7:30pm in winter).

Country & City Codes

The **country code** for Italy is **39.** The **city code** for Venice is **041;** use this code when you're calling from outside Italy, within Venice, or from within Italy.

Venetian Dialect: What Would Dante Say?

Even non-Venetian Italians look befuddled when trying to decipher this city's street names and signs (if you can ever find any). Venice's colorful thousand-year history as a once-powerful maritime republic has everything to do with its local dialect, which absorbed nuances and vocabulary from far-flung outposts in the East and from the flourishing communities of foreign merchants who lived and traded in Venice. A linguist could gleefully spend a lifetime trying to make some sense of it all. But for the Venice-bound traveler just trying to make sense of Venetian addresses, the following should give you the basics. (And don't even try to follow a conversation between two gondolieri!)

ca': The abbreviation of the word *casa* is used for the noble palazzi, once private residences and now museums, lining the Grand Canal: Ca' d'Oro, Ca' Pesaro, and Ca' Rezzonico. There's only one palazzo in Venice—the Palazzo Ducale, the former doge's residence. However, as time went on some great houses gradually began to be called palazzi, so today you'll encounter the Palazzo Grassi or the Palazzo Labia.

calle: Taken from the Spanish (though pronounced as if Italian: *cal*-lay), this is the most commonplace word for street, known as *via* or *strada* elsewhere in Italy. There are numerous variations. *Ruga* from the French word *rue* once meant a calle flanked with stores, a designation no longer valid. A *ramo* (literally "branch") is the offshoot of a street and is often used interchangeably with *calle*. *Salizzada* once meant a paved street, implying that all other less important calles were once just dirt-packed alleys. A *stretto* is a narrow passageway.

campo: Elsewhere in Italy, a square is a *piazza*. In Venice the only piazza is the Piazza San Marco (and its two bordering *piazzette*), plus Piazzale Roma. All other squares are *campi* or the diminutive, *campielli*. Translated as "field" or "meadow," these were once small unpaved grazing spots for chickens or cows. Almost every one of Venice's campi carries the name of the church that dominates it (or once did) and most have wells, no longer used, in the center.

canale: There are three principal wide canals: the Canal Grande (affectionately called Il Canalazzo, the Canal), the Canale della Giudecca, and the Canale di Cannaregio. Each of the other 160-odd smaller canals is called a *rio*.

fondamenta: Referring to the foundations of the houses lining a canal, this is a walkway along the side of a rio. Promenades along the Grand Canal near Piazza San Marco and the Rialto are called *riva* as in Riva del Vin or Riva del Carbon, where cargo such as wine and coal were once unloaded.

rio: Any canal other than one of the biggies.

rio terra: This was once a canal; now it's a *calle*. A *piscina* is a filled-in basin, now acting as a campo or piazza.

Porters   When you can find them at the principal *vaporetto* stops (San Marco, Piazzale Roma, and so on), they'll charge 20,000L ($12) for your first piece of luggage and 10,000L ($6) for each additional piece. Leaving from your hotel to the *vaporetto* stop is less problematic, as the hotel will call and have a porter come to pick you up.

Police   In an emergency, dial ☎ **112** or 113.

Tax & Tipping   See "Fast Facts: Rome," in chapter 3.

Telephone   See Fast "Facts: Rome," in chapter 3.

3 Affordable Places to Stay

Few cities boast as long a high season as Venice, beginning with the Easter period. May, June, and September are the best weather-wise and so the most crowded. July and August are hot—at times unbearably so (few one- and two-star hotels offer air-conditioning; when they do it usually costs extra). Like everything else, hotels are more expensive here than in any other Italian city and with no apparent upgrade in amenities. The least special of those below are clean and functional; at best they're charming and thoroughly enjoyable. Some may even provide you with your best stay in Europe.

Most hotels usually observe high- and low-season rates, though they're slowly adopting a single year-round rate. Even where it's not indicated in the listings, be sure to ask when you book or arrive at a hotel whether off-season rates are in effect. High season here is about March 15 to November 5, with a lull in July and August (when discounts are often offered). Some small hotels close (sometimes without notice or to renovate) November or December until Carnevale, opening about 2 weeks around Christmas and New Year's at high-season rates. November to Carnival (save Christmas Eve to January 6) also constitutes low season in the hotels that stay open.

I strongly suggest you reserve in advance, even in the low season. If you don't, arrive as early as you can, definitely before noon. The **Hotel Reservations booth** in the Santa Lucia train station will book rooms for you, but the lines are long and (understandably) the staff's patience is often thin. For 1,000L (50¢) they'll try to find you a hotel of the price range of your choice; on confirmation from the hotel, they'll accept the deposit by credit card and issue you a voucher, and you pay the balance on your arrival at the hotel.

Another alternative for reserving the same day as your arrival is through the **A.V.A. (Venetian Hoteliers Association),** toll free by phone in Italy at ☎ **800-843-006** (041-522-2264 from abroad or 041-522-8004; www.veniceinfo.it). Simply state the price range you want to book and they'll confirm a hotel while you wait. There's no fee for the service, and there are offices at the train station, in Piazzale Roma garages, and at the airport.

State-imposed ordinances have issued deadlines for the updating of antiquated electrical, plumbing, and sewage systems—all costly endeavors. To make up for this, one- and two-star hotels have raised their rates and often applied for category upgrades for which they're now eligible. Even more have stuck TVs on the desks and hairdryers in the baths to garner that extra star so they could inflate their rates for the Jubilee Year 2000. The good news is that now you'll have accommodations of a better quality (or at least with more amenities of questionable necessity), but the bad news is that yesteryear's finds are disappearing. The rates below were compiled in late 2000, with the hoteliers estimating what they'll charge in 2001. You can expect the usual increase of 4% to 8%, but you may be hit with an increase of as much as 20% if the hotel you pick is one that has been redone recently.

A few peculiarities about Venice hotels have everything to do with the fact that this city built on water doesn't consistently offer what you may take for granted: elevators, light, and spaciousness. Hotels here often have tiny baths. The rooms are generally smaller than those elsewhere and can be dark, and canal views aren't half as frequent as we'd like them to be. This doesn't mean a welcoming family-run hotel in an atmospheric neighborhood can't offer a memorable stay. Just don't expect the amenities of the Danieli or Grand Canal vistas.

Note: Unless otherwise specified, all units come with private baths.

IN SAN MARCO

✪ **Ai do Mori.** San Marco 658 (on Calle larga San Marco), 30124 Venezia. ☎ **041-520-4817** or 041-528-9293. Fax 041-520-5328. www.hotelaidomori.com. 11 units, 7 with bathroom. A/C TV TEL. 100,000L ($50) single without bathroom; 160,000L ($80) double without bathroom, 230,000L ($115) double with bathroom; 215,000L ($108) triple without bathroom, 280,000L ($140) triple with bathroom; 260,000L ($130) quad without bathroom, 290,000L ($145) quad with bathroom; 400,000L ($200) 5-person family suite. Ask about lower off-season rates. MC, V. Vaporetto: San Marco (exit Piazza San Marco beneath the Torre dell'Orologio; turn right at the Max Mara store and the hotel is on the left, just before McDonald's).

Antonella, the young owner/manager, creates an efficient yet comfortable ambiance, with special care given to Frommer's readers. The lower-floor rooms (there's no elevator and the hotel begins on the second floor) are slightly larger and offer rooftop views. But, the top-floor rooms boast views of San Marco's cupolas and the Torre dell'Orologio, whose two bronze Moors ring the bells every hour (the large double-paned windows help ensure quiet). A 1998 facelift brought new tiled baths (with hairdryers and heated towel racks), TVs, firm mattresses, and air-conditioning. All but one of the rooms without baths should receive them in 2001. Rooms 4 (a small double) and 5 (a triple) share a bath and a small hallway and can be turned into a family suite.

✪ **Al Gambero.** San Marco 4687 (on Calle dei Fabbri), 30124 Venezia. ☎ **041-522-4384** or 041-520-1420. Fax 041-520-0431. E-mail hotelgambero@tin.it. TEL. 27 units, 15 with bathroom. 95,000L ($48) single without bathroom, 180,000L ($90) single with bathroom; 160,000L ($80) double without bathroom, 245,000L ($123) double with bathroom; 210,000L ($105) triple without bathroom, 320,000L ($160) triple with bathroom; 260,000L ($130) quad without bathroom, 390,000L ($195) quad with bathroom. Rates include continental breakfast. MC, V. Vaporetto: Rialto (turn right along the canal, cross the small footbridge over Rio San Salvador, and turn left onto Calle Bembo, which becomes Calle dei Fabbri; the hotel is about 5 blocks ahead on the left).

Midway on a main strip connecting Piazza San Marco and the Ponte Rialto, one of Venice's former budget hotels underwent a full makeover in 1998 and has another in the works for late 2000 that'll give all the rooms private baths (they were still waiting for permissions at press time). Surrounded by striped damask-like bedspreads and curtains, you can slumber in one of the 14 canal-side rooms (5 with baths, including no. 203 with a small balcony). Only rooms on the first two floors (with bath) now have air-conditioning, TVs, minibars, and high ceilings. Currently the upstairs rooms are without bath and still one-star bland, but most enjoy a piece or two of antique styling. By Venice standards, the one-star Gambero has all the trappings of a three-star hotel at two-star prices. Guests receive a 10% discount in the lively ground-floor Bistrot de Venise (see "Great Deals on Dining," below).

Gallini. San Marco 3673 (on Calle della Verona), 30124 Venezia. ☎ **041-520-4515.** Fax 041-520-9103. TEL. 50 units, 40 with bathroom. 138,000L ($69) single without bathroom, 200,000L ($100) single with bathroom; 200,000L ($100) double without bathroom, 276,000L ($138) double with bathroom; 350,000L ($175) triple with bathroom. Off-season rates about 15% lower. *For Frommer's readers:* Ask for a discount of about 10%. Rates include continental breakfast. AE, MC, V. Closed Nov 15–Carnevale. Vaporetto: Sant'Angelo (follow the zigzagging road south toward Campo Sant'Angelo; exit the campo at the northeast end by taking Calle della Mandola; turn right at the Ottica [optometrist] onto Calle dei Assasini, which becomes Calle della Verona).

Though the 1997 fire at La Fenice opera house doused this neighborhood's spark, it's now business as usual at the Gallini. The amiable Ceciliati brothers, Adriano and Gabriele, have been at the helm since 1952 and offer four floors (no elevator) of bright spacious rooms and big modern baths (all rooms should have baths by the time you

Getting the Best Deal on Accommodations

- Be aware that some hotels offer as much as 30% to 50% discounts in winter (many just shut down entirely).
- Remember that July and August, considered peak season elsewhere in Italy, is low season here.
- When arranging for a room in person, always ask if the price quoted is the best available; in slow periods even during high season, hotels will often entice you with discounted rates rather than have empty rooms, especially if you're standing in front of them, looking to stay for more than 1 night.
- When booking your hotel, confirm whether breakfast is obligatory and, if not, what it costs; you may spend half as much at the neighborhood bar or merely enjoy it more in a cafe setting.
- If you're eligible, get a Rolling Venice pass for discounted rates (see "A Money-Saving Tip," earlier in this chapter); in summer, the Rolling Venice booth at the train station will also help you with reservations for free.
- If Venice's cheap rooms have been snatched up, think about spending the night in Padua (see chapter 8) if you're on a really tight budget, but incorporate the cost of a round-trip train ticket into your projected savings if you don't have a pass for unlimited train travel. Travel between the cities is about 20 to 40 minutes, and trains run early morning to late at night.

get here). Ten rooms overlook narrow Rio della Verona, and a few have air-conditioning (15,000L/$8 daily). This is the largest place I suggest in this area, so look here when the smaller options are full. The housekeeping staff seems to be forever cleaning, and marble floors in green, red, or speckled black alternate with intricate parquet to lend an old-world air.

Fiorita. San Marco 3457 (on Campiello Novo), 30124 Venezia. ☎ **041-523-4754.** Fax 041-522-8043. www.locandafiorita.com. 10 units, 8 with bathroom, in main house; 8 units in annex. A/C TV TEL. Main house: 120,000–140,000L ($60–$70) single without bathroom; 160,000–190,000L ($80–$95) double without bathroom, 180,000–210,000L ($90–$105) double with bathroom. Annex: 220,000–240,000L ($110–$120) double, 230,000–250,000L ($115–$125) family suite. Extra person 30% more at either. Rates include continental breakfast. AE, DC, MC, V. Vaporetto: Sant'Angelo (walk to the tall brick building, then turn right around its side; cross a small bridge and turn left down Calle del Pestrin; a bit farther down on your left is a small square 3 stairs above street level; the hotel is against the back of it).

New owners have created a pretty little hotel in this Venetian red palazzo, parts of which date from the 1400s. In 1999 to 2000, they renovated everything in 18th-century Venetian style. The wisteria vine partially covering its facade is at its glorious best in May or June, but the Fiorita is excellent year-round, for its simply furnished rooms boasting new baths (with hairdryers) and its location on a campiello off the Campo Santo Stefano. Rooms 1 and 10 have little terraces beneath the wisteria pergola and overlook the campiello: They can't be guaranteed on reserving, so ask when you get there. Each of the two bathless rooms has its own private facilities down the hall. A block away is a small *dipendenza* (annex) in a less interesting palazzo, but some of its slightly more elegant rooms overlook a tiny canal, and there's a family suite. A second annex should open by the time you get there.

Remedio. San Marco 4412 (on Calle del Remedio), 30122 Venezia. ☎ **041-520-6232.** Fax 041-521-0485. 12 units. A/C MINIBAR TV TEL. *For Frommer's readers:* 180,000L ($90) single;

300,000L ($150) double; 390,000L ($195) triple; 480,000L ($240) quad. Rates include breakfast. AE, MC, V. Vaporetto: San Marco (exit Piazza San Marco under the Torre dell'Orologio and turn right at the Max Mara store onto Calle Larga San Marco; at the Ristorante All'Angelo, turn left onto Calle va al Ponte dell'Angelo and take the first right onto Ramo del Anzolo; cross the small footbridge onto Calle del Remedio).

Renato is of the new breed of Venice's young hotel owners/managers striving to create charming lodgings at moderate rates. By Venetian standards, the hotel offers unusually large and quiet rooms with fine antiques (and good repros) in an ancient palazzo around the corner from one of St. Mark's busiest streets. Most rooms are on the second floor (no. 27 has lovely ceiling frescoes) off a ballroom-size hall. Renato has just modernized most of the small baths, put new carpeting in the rooms, and attached VCRs to the TVs (movies in English are at the desk). He has also recently renovated, in 18th-century Venetian style, the six-room Querini a few blocks away on tranquil Campo San Giovanni Novo; the rates are slightly lower there.

WORTH A SPLURGE

✪ **Flora.** San Marco 2283 (Calle del Bergamaschi, off Calle Larga XXII Marzo, near Campo San Moisè). ☎ **041-520-5844.** Fax 041-522-8217. www.hotelflora.it. 44 units. A/C TV TEL. 300,000L ($150) single; 400,000L ($200) double. Extra person 100,000L ($50). Rates include continental breakfast. AE, DC, MC, V. Vaporetto: San Marco. (Walk down Calle Valleresso and turn left on to the Via XXII Marzo. After crossing the San Moisè Bridge and passing the Deutsche Bank, you'll see a sign on the left side of the street for the hotel, located down a narrow passage off the Via XXII Marzo.)

The Flora's simple name refers to its greatest attribute, a jewel-like patio garden visible beyond the lobby. A delightful place to have breakfast, afternoon tea, or an aperitif, it's enclosed by climbing vines and ivy-covered walls, with an antique well, potted flowers, and blooming plants. Seamlessly run by two generations of the highly professional Romanelli family and their friendly staff, the Flora has long been one of Venice's favorite spots. The rooms, small to standard in size, vary greatly in decor. Several are rather plain; some done in 18th-century Venetian style; and others graced with stucco decorations and Liberty-style furnishings. However, the small baths could do with a facelift. On the top-floor, room 47 looks onto the alleged Desdemona's palazzo (of Shakespeare's tragedy *Othello*), with the dome of La Salute beyond. The hotel's popularity and perfect location mean you should book ahead—but note that renovations will keep it closed until mid-February 2001.

IN CANNAREGIO

Expect most (but not all) of these suggestions to be in or near the Santa Lucia train station neighborhood, one full of trinket shops and budget hotels. This area is comparatively charmless (though safe), and in the high season is wall-to-wall with tourists who window-shop their way to Piazza San Marco, an easy half-hour to 45-minute stroll away. Vaporetto connections from the train station are convenient.

Adua. Cannaregio 233A (on Lista di Spagna), 30121 Venezia. ☎ **041-716-184.** Fax 041-244-0162. 13 units, 9 with bathroom. A/C TV TEL. 90,000–130,000L ($45–$65) single without bathroom, 150,000–160,000L ($75–$80) single with bathroom; 110,000–140,000L ($55–70) double without bathroom, 180,000–220,000L ($90–$110) double with bathroom. Extra bed about 50% more. Breakfast 10,000L ($5). AE, DC, MC, V (but you must tell them you'll be using a credit card when you arrive). Vaporetto: Ferrovia (exit the train station and turn left onto Lista di Spagna).

The Adua family, in the low-end hotel business more than 30 years, completed a welcome renovation in 1999, giving the largish rooms a unified summery look with contemporary wood furnishings painted pale green. An independent palazzo across the street with six refurbished rooms (without baths, TVs, or air conditioning, but

Venice Accommodations & Dining

Near the Stazione FS. S. Lucia

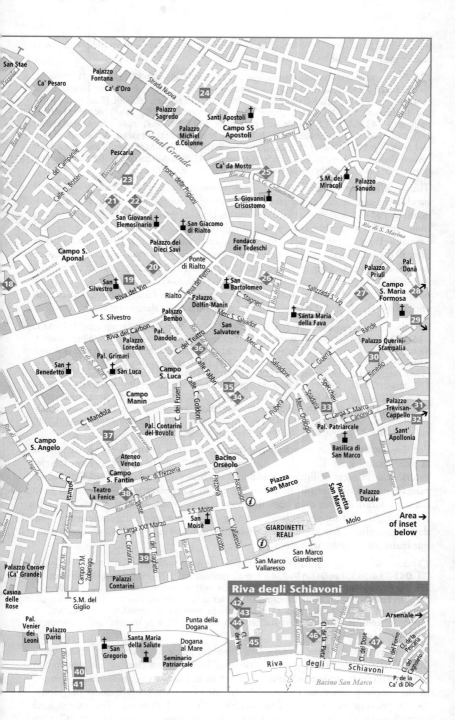

San Stae
Ca' Pesaro
Palazzo Fontana
Ca' d'Oro
Strada Nuova
24
Palazzo Sagredo
Santi Apostoli
Palazzo Michiel d.Colonne
Campo SS Apostoli
Canal Grande
Pescaria
Fond. delle Prigioni
Ca' da Mosto
Rio di S.G. Crisostomo
25
S.M. dei Miracoli
Palazzo Sanudo
23
S. Giovanni Crisostomo
Pal. Donà
Calle D. Botteri
21 **22**
San Giovanni Elemosinario
San Giacomo di Rialto
Rio di S. Marina
Palazzo Priuli
Campo S. Aponal
Palazzo dei Dieci Savi
Fondaco die Tedeschi
Palazzo Sanudo
27
Campo S. Maria Formosa
28
18
20
San Silvestro **19**
Ponte di Rialto
San Bartolomeo
26
Salizzada S. Lio
29
Riva del Vin
Rialto
Palazzo Dolfin-Manin
C. Stagneri
Santa Maria della Fava
C. Bande
Palazzo Querini-Stampalia
S. Silvestro
Palazzo Bembo
Merc S. Salvador
San Salvatore
C. Guerra
30
Riva del Carbon
Pal. Dandolo
C. del Teatro
Merc S.
Salvadore
Rimedio
Pal. Grimani
Palazzo Loredan
36
Calle Fabbri
Salizzada
C. Spechieri
Palazzo Trevisan-Cappello
31
San Benedetto
San Luca
Campo S. Luca
35
34
C. Fiubera
Merc Orlogio
Larga S. Marco
C. Canonica
32
Campo Manin
Calle C. Goldoni
Sant' Apollonia
C. Mandola
Pal. Contarini del Bovolo
33
Pal. Patriarcale
37
Campo S. Angelo
Ateneo Veneto
Basilica di San Marco
Campo S. Fantin
Pisc. di Frezzeria
Bacino Orseolo
Teatro La Fenice **38**
Rio delle Veste
Frezzeria
Piazza San Marco
Piazzetta San Marco
Palazzo Ducale
C. Ascension
(i)
Palazzo Corner (Ca' Grande)
C. Larga XXII Marzo
S.S. Moise
San Moise
C. Vallaresso
C. Ricotto
GIARDINETTI REALI
(i)
Molo
Area → of inset below
39
Campo S.M. Zobenigo
Palazzi Contarini
San Marco Vallaresso
San Marco Giardinetti
Casina delle Rose
S.M. del Giglio

Riva degli Schiavoni

Pal. Venier dei Leoni
Palazzo Dario
Punta della Dogana
42
43
Arsenale →
44
San Gregorio
Santa Maria della Salute
Dogana al Mare
C. del Vin
45
46
47
40
Seminario Patriarcale
Riva   degli   Schiavoni
41
Bacino San Marco
P. de la Ca' di Dio

363

with ceiling fans) costs 20% less. The street's noisy but convenient to the station, and there's really little else to be said for this place.

☉ Bernardi-Semenzato. Cannaregio 4366 (on Calle de l'Oca), 30121 Venezia. **☎ 041-522-7257.** Fax 041-522-2424. E-mail mtpepoli@tin.it. Hotel: 18 units, 10 with bathroom; annex: 7 units. A/C MINIBAR TV TEL. *For Frommer's readers:* 69,000L ($35) single without bathroom, 92,000L ($46) single with bathroom, 93,000L ($47) double without bathroom, 143,000L ($72) double with bathroom; 133,000L ($67) triple without bathroom, 160,000L ($80) triple with bathroom. Rates include continental breakfast. Ask about off-season rates. AE, MC, V. Vaporetto: Ca' d'Oro (walk straight ahead to Strada Nova, turn right toward Campo SS. Apostoli, and look for Cannaregio 4309, a stationery/toy store on your left; turn left on Calle Duca, then take the first right onto Calle de l'Oca).

This weather-worn palazzo's exterior doesn't hint at its 1995 renovation, which left hand-hewn ceiling beams exposed, air-conditioned rooms with antique-style headboard/spread sets, and modernized tiled baths. Upstairs rooms enjoy higher ceilings and more light. The enthusiastic young English-speaking owners, Maria Teresa and Leonardo Pepoli, aspire to three-star style and received two stars at press time, but they offer all the amenities at one-star rates (prices get even better off-season). The *dipendenza* (annex) three blocks away gives you the chance to feel as if you've rented an aristocratic apartment, with parquet floors and Murano chandeliers—room 5 is on a corner with a beamed ceiling and fireplace, 6 (a family-perfect two-room suite) overlooks the confluence of two canals, and 2 overlooks the lovely garden of a palazzo next door.

Dolomiti. Cannaregio 72–74 (on Calle Priuli ai Cavalletti), 30121 Venezia. **☎ 041-715-113.** Fax 041-716-635. www.ciaovenezia.com/dolomiti. E-mail hoteldolomiti@ntt.it. 49 units, 20 with bathroom. TEL. *For Frommer's readers* (except during festivals and holidays, when slightly higher official rates apply): 100,000L ($50) single without bathroom, 150,000L ($75) single with bathroom; 120,000–140,000L ($60–$70) double without bathroom, 190,000–220,000L ($95–$110) double with bathroom; 180,000L ($90) triple without bathroom, 250,000L ($125) triple with bathroom; 210,000L ($105) quad without bathroom, 280,000L ($140) quad with bathroom. Inquire about low-season discounts. Rates include breakfast. DC, MC, V. Closed Nov 15–Jan 31. Vaporetto: Ferrovia (exit the train station, turn left onto Lista di Spagna, and take the first left onto Calle Priuli).

For those who prefer to stay near the train station, this is an old-fashioned reliable choice. Because it has large, clean, but ordinary rooms spread over four floors (no elevator), your chances of finding availability are better at this hotel, one of the larger places I suggest. It's been in the Basardelli family for generations—the current head manager, Graziella, was even born in a second-floor room—and they and their efficient polyglot staff supply umbrellas, dining suggestions, and a big smile after a long day's sightseeing. They hope to add air-conditioning by early 2001, and rooms without baths always come with sinks.

☉ San Geremia. Cannaregio 290A (on Campo San Geremia), 30121 Venezia. **☎ 041-716-245.** Fax 041-524-2342. E-mail: mkoca@tin.it. 20 units, 14 with bathroom. TV TEL. *For Frommer's readers:* 150,000L ($75) double without bathroom, 220,000L ($110) double with bathroom. Ask about rates/availability for singles, triples, and quads and about off-season rates (about 20% cheaper). Rates include continental breakfast. AE, DC, MC, V. Vaporetto: Ferrovia (exit the train station, turn left onto Lista di Spagna, and continue to Campo San Geremia).

Mention Frommer's when booking and show this guide when checking in and you'll get the rates above. If this gem of a two-star hotel had an elevator and was in San Marco, it'd cost twice as much and still be worth it. Consider yourself lucky to get one of the tastefully renovated rooms—ideally, one of the seven overlooking the campo (better yet, one of three top-floor rooms with small terraces). The rooms have blond-wood paneling with built-in headboards and closets or whitewashed walls with deep-green or burnished rattan headboards and matching chairs. The small baths offer hairdryers and heated towel racks. Everything is overseen by an English-speaking staff and owner/manager Claudio, who'll give you helpful tips and free passes to the winter Casino.

Santa Lucia. Cannaregio 358 (on Calle della Misericordia), 30121 Venezia. ☎ **041-710-610.** Fax 041-715-180. 18 units, 12 with bathroom. TEL. 95,000L ($48) single without bathroom; 150,000L ($75) double without bathroom, 180,000L ($90) double with bathroom. Extra person 30,000L ($15) without bathroom, 40,000L ($20) with bathroom. Rates include continental breakfast. AE, DC, MC, V. Generally closed Dec 20–Feb 10. Vaporetto: Ferrovia (exit the train station, turn left onto Lista di Spagna, and take the second left onto Calle della Misericordia).

This contemporary building with a garden-enclosed flagstone patio/terrace is one of the nicer choices in this area. Bordered by roses, oleander, and ivy, the patio is a lovely place to enjoy breakfast, with coffee and tea brought in sterling silver pots. The kindly owner, Emilia Gonzato; her son, Gianangelo; and his wife, Alessandra, oversee everything with pride and it shows: The large rooms are simple but bright and clean, with modular furnishings and a print or pastel to brighten things up.

IN CASTELLO

✪ Al Piave. Castello 4838–40 (on Ruga Giuffa), 30122 Venezia. ☎ **041-528-5174.** Fax 041-523-8512. www.elmoro.com/alpiave. E-mail hotel.alpiave@iol.it. 11 units; 3 apts. A/C TV TEL. *For Frommer's readers:* 220,000–260,000L ($110–$130) double; 320,000–360,000L ($160–$180) triple; 320,000–380,000L ($160–$190) quad; 360,000–450,000L ($180–$225) family suite for 3–5 or apt for 2–5. Discounts if you pay cash and in late July–Aug. Rates include continental breakfast. Closed Jan 7–Carnevale. AE, DC, MC, V. Vaporetto: San Zaccaria (walk straight ahead on Calle delle Rasse to small Campo SS. Filippo e Giacomo, take a right on Calle San Provolo, and cross over the canal to Campo San Provolo; take a left, cross the first small footbridge, and follow the zigzagging calle that becomes Ruga Giuffa).

The Puppin family's tasteful hotel is a steal: This level of attention coupled with the sophisticated *buon gusto* in decor and spirit is rare in a two-star. You'll find orthopedic mattresses under ribbon-candy-print or floral spreads, immaculate white lace curtains, stained-glass windows, new baths, and even (in a few rooms) tiny terraces. The family suites—with two bedrooms, minibars, and shared baths—are particularly good deals, as are the small but stylishly rustic apartments with kitchenettes, minibars, and washing machines (in the two smaller ones). A savvy international crowd has discovered this classy spot, so you'll need to reserve far in advance.

Casa Verardo. Castello 4765 (at the foot of the Ponte Storto), 30122 Venezia. ☎ **041-528-6127.** Fax 041-523-2765. www.chipsandcolors.com/casaverardo. 26 units. A/C TEL TV. 150,000–180,000L ($75–$90) single; 250,000–320,000L ($125–$160) double; 340,000–470,000L ($170–$235) suite for 3–4. Rates include breakfast. Prices much lower in off-season; ask when you book. AE, MC, V. Vaporetto: San Zaccaria (walk straight ahead on Calle delle Rasse to Campo SS. Filippo e Giacomo; continue straight through the small campo to take Calle Chiesa to cross the first small bridge, Ponte Storto, to find the hotel on the left).

In 2000, Daniela and Francesco took over this one-star pensione and transformed it into a fine three-star hotel (and more than doubled its size), while still maintaining the feel of a Venetian palazzo romantically faded by time. The wood-paneled lobby is anchored by an ancient stone well. The rooms are done in chipped-stone floors, Murano chandeliers, and eclectic furnishings from imposing armoires and repro 17th century to pseudo deco and modern functional; three have small terraces. The best accommodations come with stucco wall decorations and scraps of old ceiling frescoes—and tops are the six overlooking a little canal. The airy main hall doubles as a breakfast room. Renovation work that will close the hotel from January to mid-February 2001 should be finished by summer.

Fontana. Castello 4701 (on Campo San Provolo), 30122. ☎ **041-522-0579.** Fax 041-523-1040. www.hotelfontana.it. 14 units. TV TEL. 100,000–170,000L ($50–$85) single; 150,000–280,000L ($75–$140) double; 230,000–360,000L ($115–$180) triple; 280,000–410,000L ($140–$205) quad. Rates include buffet breakfast. AE, DC, MC, V. Vaporetto: San Zaccaria (from Riva Schiavoni, take any narrow street north to Campiello SS. Filippo e Giacomo; exit this small campo from east side, in direction of Campo San Zaccaria, until reaching Campo San Provolo).

Three generations of Stainers have been behind the front desk since 1967 (for centuries prior to that the Fontana was a convent for Austrian nuns), and their warmth seems to pour out the lobby's leaded-glass windows. The four-story hotel offers a pensionelike family atmosphere coupled with a professional operation and comfortable rooms containing lovely antique furnishings but a decided lack of wattage in the overhead lights. The choice two on the upper floor have private terraces. There's no elevator, but those who brave the climb to the top floors are compensated by views of San Zaccaria's 15th-century facade.

Foresteria Valdese (Palazzo Cavagnis). Castello 5170 (at the end of Calle Lunga Santa Maria Formosa), 30122 Venezia. ☎ **041-528-6797.** Fax 041-241-6238. www. doge.it/valdesi. 6 units, 2 with bathroom, 4 without bathroom, 3 dorms (8, 12, and 16 beds), none with bathroom. 2 mini-apts. (sleeping 4 and 5, minimum stay often required) with kitchen and bathroom. 32,000–33,000L ($16–$17) dorm bed; 90,000–95,000L ($45–$48) double without bathroom; 120,000L ($60) double with bathroom; 180,000–190,000L ($90–$95) apt. Rates include breakfast except in apts. Closed 3 weeks in Nov. MC, V, but with a 35% charge. Vaporetto: Rialto. (Head southeast to Campo Santa Maria Formosa; look for the Bar all'Orologio and turn right on Calle Lunga Santa Maria Formosa begins; follow it to the end and over the bridge. The campo is just about equidistant from Piazza San Marco and the Rialto Bridge.)

Those lucky enough to get a place at this weathered 16th-century palazzo will find simple accommodations in a charming *foresteria*, a religious institution that traditionally provided lodging for pilgrims and guests. Affiliated with Italy's Waldesian and Methodist churches, the large dorm-style rooms are often booked by church groups, though everyone is warmly welcomed. Each plainly furnished room in this once-noble residence opens onto a balcony overlooking a quiet canal, and the frescoes gracing the high ceilings in two of the doubles and two of the dorms are by the same artist who decorated the Museo Correr. The two apartments with kitchens are the best budget choice for families of four or five. A complete renovation is nearing its completion (by mid-2001, the dorms may shrink but get more baths in exchange). The reception is open daily 9am to 1pm and 6 to 8pm and Sunday 9am to 1pm. *Note:* You can't book for the dorms.

WORTH A SPLURGE

✪ **Campiello.** Castello 4647 (on Campiello del Vin), 30122 Venezia. ☎ **041-520-5764.** Fax 041-520-5798. www.hcampiello.it. 16 units. A/C TV TEL. 200,000L ($100) single; 300,000L ($150) double. Extra person 25% more. Ask about discounts in low season. Rates include buffet continental breakfast. AE, DC, MC, V. Vaporetto: San Zaccaria (Calle del Vin is the alley left of the Savoia e Jolanda).

This gem is on a tiny campiello just off prestigious Riva degli Schiavoni. The atmosphere is airy and bright, its relaxed hospitality and quality service due to the Bianchini sisters, Monica and Nicoletta. A 1998 renovation transformed much of the rooms' contemporary style into a more traditional decor; most are now done in 18th-century and art nouveau antiques—inlaid dressers and bas-reliefs on the headboards. The building's 15th-century marble-mosaic pavement is still evident, a vestige of the days when it was a convent under the patronage of the nearby San Zaccaria—you'll catch a glimpse of it in the lounge area opening onto the pleasant breakfast room.

Frommer's Discounts

Reading Frommer's has its privileges. Many hotels recognize the name, appreciate the business we bring them, and want to give readers a Frommer's discount, which I'm only too happy to pass along to you. Just show the book when you check in. A lot of the prices listed in the book apply only to the likes of you and me—people who use this book.

IN DORSODURO

Alla Salute (Da Cici). Dorsoduro 222 (on Fondamenta Ca' Balà), 30123 Venezia. ☎ **041-523-5404.** Fax 041-522-2271. E-mail hotel.salute.dacici@iol.it. 58 units, 12 with shower only, 30 with bathroom. TEL. 140,000L ($70) single without bathroom, 190,000L ($95) single with shower; 180,000L ($90) double without bathroom, 250,000L ($125) double with bathroom; 260,000L ($130) triple without bathroom, 330,000L ($165) triple with bathroom. Ask about units sleeping 4–5. Discounts given Mar, July, and Aug. Rates include continental breakfast. MC, V (by 2001). Often closes in Jan or Feb for upkeep. Vaporetto: Salute (facing La Salute, turn right and head to the first small bridge; cross it and walk as straight ahead as possible to the next narrow canal, then turn left, before crossing the bridge, onto Fondamenta Ca' Balà).

An airy lobby with beamed ceilings and cool marble floors, a small but lovely terrace garden, and a cozy cocktail bar occupy the ground level of this converted 17th-century palazzo on Rio della Fornace. Upstairs, the comfortable rooms have high ceilings and huge windows (10 with canal views and 4 facing the garden), many of them large enough to accommodate families of four or even five at 60,000L ($30) per person extra. Breakfast is served in the garden in warm weather.

Galleria. Dorsoduro 878A (at the foot of the Ponte Accademia), 30123 Venezia. ☎ **041-523-2489.** Fax 041-520-4172. www.hotelgalleria.it. 10 units, 6 with bathroom. 110,000L ($55) single without bathroom; 160,000L ($80) double without bathroom, 190,000–230,000L ($95–$115) double with bathroom. Extra bed 30% more. Rates include continental breakfast. AE, DC, MC, V. Vaporetto: Accademia (with the Ponte Accademia behind you, the hotel is just to your left, next to the Totem Il Canale gallery).

If you've always dreamed of flinging open your hotel window to find the Grand Canal in front of you, choose this 17th-century palazzo. But reserve way in advance—these are the cheapest rooms on the canal and the most charming at these rates, thanks to new owners Luciano Benedetti and Stefano Franceschini. All are done in a modestly sumptuous 17th- and 18th-century style. Six overlook the canal; others have partial views that include the Ponte Accademia over an open-air bar/cafe (which can be annoying to anyone hoping to sleep before the bar closes). The baths are small but were renovated between 1998 and 2000. Breakfast, with oven-fresh bread, is served in your room.

Messner. Dorsoduro 216–217 (on Fondamenta Ca' Balà), 30123 Venezia. ☎ **041-522-7443.** Fax 041-522-7266. E-mail messner@doge.it. Main house, 11 units; annex, 20 units. Main house, A/C TV TEL; annex TEL. *For Frommer's readers* (main house only): 180,000L ($90) single; 250,000L ($125) double; 300,000L ($150) triple; 340,000L ($170) quad. Annex (no discounts): 160,000L ($80) single; 200,000L ($100) double; 260,000L ($130) triple; 290,000L ($145) quad. Rates include continental breakfast. AE, DC, MC, V. Closed Dec 1–27. Vaporetto: Salute (follow the small canal immediately to the right of La Salute; turn right onto the third bridge and walk straight until seeing a white awning just before reaching Rio della Fornace).

The Messner and Alla Salute (above) are the best bets in the Guggenheim area (the choice of those looking for a quiet alternative to San Marco), at budget-embracing rates. The Messner is a two-part hotel: In the *casa principale* (main house) are the handsome beamed-ceiling lobby and public rooms of a 14th-century palazzo and modernized guest rooms with comfortable modular furnishings and Murano chandeliers (three overlook picturesque Rio della Fornace). The 15th-century *dipendenza* (annex) 20 yards away doesn't show quite as close an attention to detail in the decor but is perfectly nice. In summer, you get to take breakfast in a small garden.

✪ La Calcina. Dorsoduro 780 (on Zattere al Gesuati), 30123 Venezia. ☎ **041-520-6466.** Fax 041-522-7045. www.italyhotel.com/venezia/calcina. E-mail la.calcina@libero.it. 29 units, 26 with bathroom. A/C TEL. 110,000L–130,000L ($55–$65) single without bathroom, 150,000L ($75) single with bathroom, 170,000L ($85) single with bathroom and canal view; 200,000–230,000L ($100–$115) double with bathroom, 260,000L–300,000L ($130–$150) double with bathroom and canal view. Rates include continental breakfast. AE, DC, MC, V. Vaporetto: Zattere (follow the Zattere east; the hotel is on the water before the first bridge).

British author John Ruskin holed up here in 1876 when penning *The Stones of Venice* (you can request his room, no. 2, but good luck), and this hotel has remained a quasi-sacred preference of writers, artists, and assorted Bohemians. You can imagine their horror when a recent overhaul of the place was announced—but it was done so sensitively that the third-generation owners refused to add TVs. However, the rates have begun creeping up. Half the unfussy but luminous rooms overlook the Giudecca Canal in the direction of Palladio's 16th-century Redentore. The outdoor floating terrace and the rooftop terrace are glorious places to begin or end any day.

WORTH A SPLURGE

American. Dorsoduro 628 (on Fondamenta Bragadin), 30123 Venezia. ☎ **041-520-4733.** Fax 041-520-4048. www.hotelamerican.com. 27 units. A/C MINIBAR TV TEL. 230,000L ($115) single; 400,000L ($200) double; 370,000L ($185) double with canal view. Rates include buffet breakfast. Extra person 85,000L ($43). AE, MC, V. Vaporetto: Accademia (veer left around the Galleria dell'Accademia, taking the first left turn, and walk until you cross the first small footbridge; turn right to follow the Fondamenta Bragadin running alongside the Rio di San Vio canal; the hotel is on your left).

Despite its potentially unromantic name, this is a splurge recommendation for its style and substance, one of the nicest of Venice's three-star hotels. The perfect combination of old-fashioned charm and utility, the American offers a dignified lobby and breakfast room with oriental carpets and marble flooring, polished woods, and leaded-glass windows and French doors. The best choices are the nine rooms overlooking a quiet canal, especially the large corner ones; some have small canal-side terraces. All rooms contain traditional Venetian-style furnishings that usually include hand-painted furniture, beveled mirrors, and even Murano chandeliers. The baths feature nice touches like sink counters (rarely a given in Italy) and heated towel racks.

✪ Accademia. Dorsoduro 1058 (Fondamenta Bollani, west of the Ponte Accademia), 30123. ☎ **041-521-0188.** Fax 041-523-9152. www.pensioneaccademia.it. 27 units. A/C MINIBAR TV TEL. 140,000–220,000L ($70–$110) single; 240,000–420,000L ($120–$220) double; 400,000–480,000L ($200–$240) triple. AE, DC, MC, V. Vaporetto: Accademia (step off the vaporetto and turn right down Calle Gambara, which doglegs first left and then right; it becomes Calle Corfu, which ends at a side canal; walk left for a few feet to cross over the bridge, then head to the right back up toward the Grand Canal and the hotel).

You'll have to reserve far in advance to get any room here, let alone one overlooking the breakfast garden, which is snuggled into the confluence of two canals. Formally called the Villa Maravege (Villa of Wonders), the 17th-century building is fitted with period antiques in its first-floor "superior" rooms, and the atmosphere is old-fashioned and elegant (the Pensione Fiorini, where Katharine Hepburn's character lived in the 1955 film *Summertime*, was modeled on this pensione). Its outdoor landscaping (a flowering patio on the small Rio San Trovaso that spills into the Grand Canal and the grassy formal rose garden behind) and interior details (original pavement, wood-beamed and decoratively painted ceilings) still create the impression of being a privileged guest in an aristocratic Venetian home from another era. I do wish they'd stop jacking up the prices, though.

IN SAN POLO

✪ **Guerrato.** San Polo 240A (on Calle Drio or Dietro la Scimia, near the Rialto Market), 30125 Venezia. ☎ **041-522-7131.** Fax 041-528-5927. web.tiscalinet.it/pensioneguerrato. E-mail hguerrat@tin.it. 14 units, 9 with bathroom. TEL. Ask about single rates. 140,000–160,000L ($70–$80) double without bathroom, 180,000–210,000L ($90–$105) double with bathroom; 190,000–200,000L ($95–$100) triple without bathroom, 250,000L ($125) triple with bathroom; 300,000L ($150) quad with bathroom. Pay in cash, get 10% off. Rates include buffet breakfast. MC, V. Closed Dec 22–26 and Jan 10–31. Vaporetto: Rialto (from the north side of the Ponte Rialto, walk straight ahead through the stalls and market vendors; at the corner of Banca di Roma, go 1 more short block and turn right; the hotel is halfway down the narrow street).

The Guerrato is as reliable and clean a one-star hotel as you're likely to find at these rates. Brothers-in-law Piero and Roberto own this former pensione in a 13th-century convent and manage to keep it full (mostly with Americans). The firm mattresses, good modernish baths, and flea-market finds (hand-carved antique or deco headboards and armoires) show their determination to run a budget hotel in pricey Venice. They don't exaggerate when calling their breakfast, accompanied by classical music, *buonissimo.* The Guerrato is in the Rialto's heart, so think of 7am noise before requesting a room overlooking the marketplace (with a peek down the block to the Grand Canal and Ca d'Oro). Piero and Roberto have recently acquired the building's top floor (great views; no elevator, 70 steps) and will install five new rooms sometime in 2001 or 2002 (Venice's historical status makes getting renovation permits hard).

Roberto also rents (2-night minimum) two fully equipped lovely **apartments** between San Marco and the Rialto. The one-bedroom is 220,000L to 240,000L ($110 to $130) for two or 300,000L to 350,000L ($150 to $175) for four (though it would be cramped), while the much larger two-bedroom (on three levels) goes for 300,000L to 400,000L ($150 to $200) for four.

WORTH A SPLURGE

Sturion. San Polo 679 (on Calle dello Sturion), 30125 Venezia. ☎ **041-523-6243.** Fax 041-522-8378. www.locandasturion.com. 11 units. A/C MINIBAR TV TEL. 220,000L ($110) single; 340,000L ($170) double without Grand Canal view, 390,000L ($195) double with Grand Canal view; 440,000L ($220) without Grand Canal view, 490,000L ($245) triples with Grand Canal view. Quads available. Ask for discounts Jan–Mar 1 and July–Aug. Rates include buffet breakfast. AE, MC, V. Vaporetto: Rialto (cross the bridge, turn left at the other side, and walk along the Grand Canal; Calle dello Sturion will be the 4th narrow alley on the right, just before San Polo 740.

There has been a pensione on this site since 1290—paintings in the Accademia prove it—and a recent gutting and rebuilding have made the Sturion into a tasteful three-star hotel decorated with 18th-century Venetian-style furniture, stone-chip floors, and Murano chandeliers. It's managed by the charming Scottish-born Helen and co-owners Sergio and Flavia, who also run Le Bistrot de Venise (see "Great Deals on Dining," below), where guests get a 10% discount. The reception is perched four flights (and 69 challenging steps) above the Grand Canal (and, depending on your room's location, there could be even more stairs involved). Alas, only two rooms offer views of the Ponte Rialto (no. 1 larger than no. 2), as does the delightful breakfast room. Most rooms are big enough for families or groups of three or four; the others have views over the Rialto rooftops. Considerate extras include in-room coffeemakers, an Internet terminal, and some books on Venice.

IN SANTA CROCE

✪ **Ai Due Fanali.** Santa Croce 946 (on Campo San Simeone Profeta), 30125. ☎ **041-718-490.** Fax 041-718-344. www.aiduefanali.com. 16 units. A/C MINIBAR TV TEL. 170,000–280,000L ($85–$140) single; 200,000–360,000L ($100–$180) double. Extra bed 25% more. Rates include continental breakfast. AE, DC, MC, V. Vaporetto: Ferrovia (from the train station, cross the Grand Canal on the Ponte degli Scalzi, then turn left just before the street dead-ends, across a small canal, and make your first left into the campo).

Checking in at the 16th-century altar-turned-reception-desk is your first clue that this is the hotel of choice for lovers of aesthetics and impeccable taste. The hotel is on a quiet square in Santa Croce, a 5-minute walk across the Grand Canal from the Santa Lucia train station but a 20-minute stroll from the Ponte Rialto. Signora Marina Stea and her daughter Stefania have beautifully restored part of the 14th-century Scuola of San Simeon Grando with their innate *buon gusto*. It's evident all the way from the lobby with its period pieces to the third-floor breakfast terrace with a glimpse of the Grand Canal. The rooms boast headboards painted by local artisans, high-quality bed linens, chrome and gold bath fixtures, and fluffy towels. Prices drop considerably November 8 to March 30, with exception of Christmas week and Carnavale.

Ask about the four equally classy lagoon-front **apartments** with a view and kitchenette on Riva degli Schiavoni, near Vivaldi's La Pietà east of Piazza San Marco, sleeping four to five people for 280,000L to 700,000L ($140 to $350), depending on the size and season.

Falier. Santa Croce 130 (on Salizzada San Pantalon) 30135 Venezia. ☎ **041-710-882.** Fax 041-520-6554. www.hotelfalier.com. 19 units. A/C TV TEL. 260,000L ($130) single; 310,000L ($155) double. Rates discounted in low season. Rates include continental breakfast. AE, MC, V. Vaporetto: Ferrovia (from the train station, cross the Ponte degli Scalzi, turn right along the Grand Canal for 150 feet, then turn left toward the Tolentini Church; continue along the Salizzada San Pantalon in the general direction of Campo Santa Margherita).

Owned by the fellow who put the American (above) on Venice's three-star map, the Falier is his savvy interpretation of less expensive lodging, particularly worthy when low season rates apply. Renovated in the early 1990s, its standard-size rooms (and modern baths) are attractively decorated with white lace curtains, flowered bedspreads, and functional furniture, and some have wood-beamed ceilings. The old-world lobby sets your first impression with potted ferns and Doric columns and marble floors, and there's a small vine-shaded summer terrace. The neighborhood needs mentioning, as detractors may feel the need to be closer to Piazza San Marco, when the truth is the Falier is much closer to the real Venice, in a lively area lined with stores and bars. It's between the large Campo Santa Margherita, one of the city's piazzas with the most character, and the Frari Church.

4 Great Deals on Dining

Eating cheaply in Venice isn't easy, though by no means impossible. So plan well and don't rely on the serendipity that may serve you in other cities. If you've qualified for a Rolling Venice card, ask for the guide listing dozens of restaurants offering discounts. Bear in mind that Venice is a city of early meals compared to Rome and other points south: You should be seated by 7:30 to 8:30pm. Most kitchens close at 10 or 10:30pm, even though the restaurant may stay open to 11:30pm or midnight.

Italian **meals** consist of three primary courses: the *antipasto* (appetizer), the *primo* (first course, usually a pasta or soup), and the *secondo* (the main course of meat or fish)—to which you must add a separate *contorno* if you want a side of veggies. You're expected to order at least two courses, if not all three.

Fishy Business

If you order fresh fish or seafood, know it'll hike the price of an average meal. And don't forget that the menu price commonly refers to *l'etto* (100 grams), a fraction of the full cost (have the waiter estimate the full cost before ordering); larger fish are intended to feed two. Eating a meal based on the day's catch (restaurants are legally bound to print on the menu when the fish is frozen) will be enjoyable but never inexpensive, so avoid splurging on fish or seafood on Mondays, when the Fish Market (and most self-respecting fish-serving restaurants) is closed.

Venetian *cicchetti* are tapas-like finger foods such as calamari rings, speared fried olives, potato croquettes, and grilled polenta squares, traditionally washed down with an *ombra* (shadow), a small glass of wine. Venice has countless cafes and neighborhood bars called *bacari* where you can order a selection of *cicchetti,* a *panino* (sandwich on a roll), or a *toast* (grilled ham-and-cheese sandwich). All of the above will cost about 1,500L to 2,500L (75¢ to $1.25) if you stand at the bar or as much as double if you sit at a table. Bar food is displayed on countertops or in glass counters and usually sells out by late afternoon, so don't rely on it for a light dinner, though light lunches are a delight. You'll find a concentration of well-stocked bars along the Mercerie shopping strip connecting Piazza San Marco with the Ponte Rialto, the always lively Campo San Luca (look for Bar Torino, Bar Black Jack, or Leon Bianco), and Campo Santa Margherita. Avoid the tired-looking pizza (reheated by microwave) sold in most bars—informal sit-down neighborhood pizzerias offer savory and far fresher renditions for a minimum of 6,000L ($3), plus your drink and cover charge.

On Venetian menus you'll see things you won't see elsewhere, plus local versions of time-tested Italian favorites. For primi, both pasta and risotto (more liquidy in the Veneto than usual) are commonly prepared with fish or seafood: *risotto alla sepie* or *alla seppioline* (tinted black by cuttlefish ink and also called *risotto nero,* or black risotto) or *spaghetti alle vongole* or *alle vorace* (with clams; clams without their shells aren't a good sign!) are two common specialties. Both also appear with *frutti di mare* ("fruits of the sea"), which can be a little bit of whatever looked good at that morning's fish market. *Bigoli,* homemade whole-wheat pasta, isn't commonly found elsewhere, while creamy *polenta,* often served with *gamberetti* (small shrimp) or *schie* (tiny shrimp) or as an accompaniment to *fegato alla veneziana* (calf's liver with onions Venetian style), is a staple of the Veneto and perhaps Venice's only non-fish specialty. Fish and seafood to look out for are *branzino* (sea bass), *rombo* (turbot or brill), *moeche* (small soft-shelled crab), *granseola* (crab), and *sarde in saor* (sardines in a sauce of onion, vinegar, pine nuts, and raisins).

From a host of good local **wines,** try the dry white tocai and pinot from the Friuli region and the light, champagne-like *prosecco* Venetians consume almost like a soft drink (it's the base of Venice's famous Bellini drink made with white peach purée). Popular reds include merlot, cabernet, raboso, and refosco. The quintessentially Italian bardolino, valpolicella, and soave are from the nearby Veneto area. **Grappa,** the local firewater, is an acquired taste and often offered in a dozen variations. Neighborhood *bacari* (wine bars) provide the chance to taste the fruits of leading wine producers in the grape-rich regions of the Veneto and neighboring Friuli.

Note: You can locate the restaurants below on the "Venice Accommodations & Dining" map on p. 362.

Getting the Best Deal on Dining

- If you qualify for a Rolling Venice pass (see "A Money-Saving Tip," near the beginning of this chapter), ask for the guide listing dozens of restaurants offering 10% to 30% discounts.

- Remember that standing up at a bar, cafe, or *rosticceria* is uniformly less expensive than sitting down—but once you sit down, you're rarely rushed.

- Pizza may not be a local specialty, but it's certainly a delicious way to save money (or consider a picnic lunch in one of the piazzas), leaving more lire for dinner.

- Save your wine consumption for before or after dinner at a characteristic old *bacaro* (wine bar), not at the restaurant.

- Look for the words *servizio incluso* on your menu or at the bottom of your bill—you won't need to leave a 10% to 15% tip if service is already included.

- Check out the breakdown of a *menù turistico* and determine just how hungry you are—you may spend less and be more satisfied with just pasta and a salad à la carte.

- Avoid surprises: Fish is the basis of Venice's traditional cuisine but will hike up your bill substantially. Have the waiter approximate the cost of the entree before you order, as the price typically appears per 100 grams (by the *etto*) on the menu.

IN SAN MARCO

✪ **Bistrot de Venise.** San Marco 4687 (on Calle dei Fabbri), below the Albergo al Gambero. ☎ **041-523-6651.** www.bistrotdevenise.com. Primi 14,000–22,000L ($7–$11); secondi 26,000–38,000L ($13–$19); classic French tasting menu 60,000L ($30). MC, V. Daily 9am–1am. Vaporetto: Rialto (turn right along the canal, cross the small footbridge over Rio San Salvador, turn left onto Calle Bembo, which becomes Calle dei Fabbri; the Bistrot is about 5 blocks ahead in the direction of Piazza San Marco). VENETIAN/FRENCH.

This relaxed spot offers outdoor and indoor seating (even a no-smoking section), young English-speaking waiters, and an eclectic menu. It's a popular meeting spot for Venetians and young artists, and you're made to feel welcome to write postcards over a cappuccino, enjoy a simple lunch like risotto and salad, or dine when most of Venice is shutting down. Linger over an elaborate meal that may include local favorites like *figa' de vedelo a la venexiana* (Venetian calf's liver) and the odd *morete a la caorlotta* (tagliolini made with cocoa, topped by a festival of crustaceans) or dishes from 15th-century Venetian recipes or a classic French cookbook. Peek in the back room (or check the Web site) to see what's going on in the evening—art exhibits, cabarets, live music, or poetry readings.

Osteria alle Botteghe. San Marco 3454 (on Calle delle Botteghe, off Campo Santo Stefano). ☎ **041-522-8181.** Primi 8,000L ($4); secondi 14,000L ($7); *menù turistico* 17,000L ($9). DC, MC, V. Mon–Sat 11am–4pm and 7–10pm. Vaporetto: Accademia or Sant'Angelo (find your way to Campo Santo Stefano by following the stream of people or asking; take narrow Calle delle Botteghe at the Gelateria Paolin across from Santo Stefano). PIZZERIA/ITALIAN.

Easy on the palate, easy on the wallet, and even easy to find (if you've made it to Campo Santo Stefano), this is a great casual choice for pizza, a light snack, or a full meal. You can have stand-up *cichetti* and fresh sandwiches at the bar or windowside counter, while more serious diners can head to the tables in back to enjoy the dozen pizzas, the pastas, or the *tavola calda,* a glass counter filled with prepared dishes like eggplant parmigiana, lasagna, and fresh-cooked vegetables in season, reheated when you order.

Rosticceria San Bartolomeo. San Marco 5424 (on Calle della Bissa). ☎ **041-522-3569.** Pizza and primi 6,500L–15,000L ($3.25–$8); secondi 13,000L–24,000L ($7–$12); *menù turistico* 16,000L–45,000L ($8–$23). Prices about 20%–30% higher upstairs. AE, MC, V. Summer daily 9am–9:30pm; winter Tues–Sun 9am–2:30pm and 4:30–8:40pm. Vaporetto: Rialto (with the bridge at your back on the San Marco side of the canal, walk straight ahead to Campo San Bartolomeo; take the underpass slightly to your left marked Sottoportego della Bissa; you'll come across the rosticceria at the first corner on your right; look for "Gislon" [its old name] above entrance). ITALIAN/TAVOLA CALDA.

With long hours and a central location, this refurbished old-timer is Venice's most popular *rosticceria* (and for good reason), so the continuous turnover guarantees fresh food. With a dozen pasta dishes and as many fish, seafood, or meat entrees, San Bartolomeo can satisfy any combination of culinary desires. Since the ready-made food is displayed under a glass counter, you don't have to worry about mistranslating—you'll know exactly what you're ordering. There's no cover charge if you take your meal standing up or seated at the stools in the aroma-filled ground-floor area. For those who prefer to linger, head to the dining hall upstairs—though it costs more and you could do much better than this institutional setting.

Rosticceria Teatro Goldoni. San Marco 4747 (at the corner of Calle dei Fabbri). ☎ **041-522-2446.** Pizza and primi 10,000L–15,000L ($5–$8); combination salads 15,000L–19,000L ($8–$10); secondi 8,000L–28,000L ($4–$14); *menù turistico* 23,000L ($12). AE, DC, V. Daily 8am–10pm. Vaporetto: Rialto (walk from the San Marco side of the bridge to Campo San Bartolomeo and exit it to your right in the direction of Campo San Luca). ITALIAN/INTERNATIONAL/FAST FOOD.

Bright and modern (though it has been here for over 50 years), this showcase of Venetian-style fast food tries to be a bar, cafe, *rosticceria,* and *tavola calda* on the ground floor and a pizzeria upstairs. A variety of sandwiches and pastries beckons from a downstairs display counter, and another offers prepared foods (eggplant parmigiana, roast chicken, *pasta e fagioli,* lasagna) that'll be reheated when ordered; there are also a dozen pasta choices. The combination salads are freshest and most varied for lunch and a welcome concession to Americans. This won't be your most memorable meal in Venice, but you won't walk away hungry or broke.

✪ Trattoria da Fiore. San Marco 3561 (on Calle delle Botteghe). ☎ **041-523-5310.** Reservations suggested. Primi 10,000–24,000L ($5–$12); secondi 20,000–35,000L ($10–$18). AE, MC, V. Wed–Mon noon–3pm and 7–10pm. Vaporetto: Accademia (cross the bridge to the San Marco side and walk straight ahead to Campo Santo Stefano; exit the campo at the northern end, take a left at the Bar/Gelateria Paolin onto Calle delle Botteghe). VENETIAN.

Don't confuse this laid-back trattoria with the expensive Osteria da Fiore. You may not eat better here, but it'll seem that way when your relatively modest bill arrives. Start with the house specialty, the *pennette alla Fiore* for two (with olive oil, garlic, and seven in-season vegetables) and you may be happy to call it a night. Or try the *frittura mista* (over a dozen varieties of fresh fish and seafood). The bouillabaisse-like *zuppa di pesce alla chef* is stocked with mussels, crab, clams, shrimp, and tuna—at only 25,000L ($13), it doesn't get any better and is a meal in itself. This is a great place to snack or make a light lunch out of *cichetti* at the Bar Fiore next door (10:30am to 10:30pm).

✪ **Vino Vino.** San Marco 2007 (on the Ponte delle Veste near La Fenice). ☎ **041-523-7027.** www.anticomartini.com/vinovino.htm. Primi 8,000L ($4); secondi 10,000–16,000L ($5–$8). AE, DC, MC, V. Wed–Mon 10am–midnight, Sat 10am–1am. Vaporetto: San Marco (with your back to the basilica, exit Piazza San Marco through the arcade on the far left side; keep walking straight, pass American Express, cross over the canal, and, before the street jags left, turn right onto Calle delle Veste). WINE BAR/ITALIAN.

Vino Vino is an informal wine bar serving well-prepared simple food, but its biggest pull is the impressive selection of local and European wines sold by the bottle or glass (check out the Web site), with great *cichetti* to accompany them. The Venetian specialties are written on a chalkboard but also usually displayed at the glass counter. After placing your order, settle into one of about a dozen wooden tables squeezed into the two storefront-style rooms. The high quality is attributable to the owner—the eminent (and expensive) Antico Martini, a few doors down, with whom it shares a kitchen. At dinner, the food often runs out around 10:30pm, so don't come too late.

IN CASTELLO

Da Aciugheta. Castello 4357 (in Campo SS. Filippo e Giacomo, east of Piazza San Marco) ☎ **041-522-4292.** Pizzas and primi 8,000–18,000L ($4–$9); secondi 18,000–28,000L ($9–$14); *menù turistico* 25,000–30,000L ($13–$15). AE, MC, V. Daily 8am–midnight (closed Wed Nov–Mar). Vaporetto: San Zaccaria (walk north on Calle delle Rasse to Campo SS. Filippo e Giacomo). VENETIAN/WINE BAR/PIZZERIA.

A long block north of the chic Riva degli Schiavoni hotels lies one of Venice's best wine bars, expanded to include an elbow-to-elbow trattoria/pizzeria in back. Its name refers to the toothpick-speared marinated anchovies that join other *cichetti* lining the popular front bar, where you can enjoy an excellent wine selection of Veneto and Italian wines by the glass. The staff is relaxed about those not ordering full multiple-course meals—a pasta and glass of wine or pizza and beer will keep anyone happy. There's an unusually long list of half bottles of wine, and an even more unusual no-smoking room. Tables move out onto the small piazza when the warm weather moves in.

Pizzeria/Trattoria al Vecio Canton. Castello 4738a (at the corner of Ruga Giuffa). ☎ **041-528-5176.** Reservations not accepted. Primi 12,000–17,000L ($6–$9); secondi 15,000–30,000L ($8–$15); pizze 9,000–17,000L ($4.50–$9); *menù turistico* 20,000L ($10) without wine. AE, DC, MC. Wed 7–10:30pm, Thurs–Mon noon–2:30pm and 7–10:30pm. Vaporetto: San Zaccaria (from the Riva degli Schiavoni waterfront, walk straight ahead to Campo SS. Filippo e Giacomo, then turn right and continue east to the small Campo San Provolo; take a left heading north on the Salizzada San Provolo, cross the first footbridge and you'll find the pizzeria on the first corner on the left). ITALIAN/PIZZA.

Good pizza is hard to find in Venice—literally. Tucked in a northeast corner behind Piazza San Marco on a well-trafficked route connecting it with Campo Santa Maria Formosa, the Canton boasts a taverna-like atmosphere and great pizzas that are worth the time you'll spend looking for the place. There's a full trattoria menu as well, with a number of pasta and side dishes (*contorni*) of vegetables providing a palatable alternative. The new ownership in 1998 didn't sit well with locals who don't relish change: The jury is still out, divided between those who pine for the old days and those who feel the change (including live music Wednesdays at 9pm) has been positive.

Trattoria alla Rivetta. Castello 4625 (on Salizzada San Provolo). ☎ **041-528-7302.** Primi 9,000–12,000L ($4.50–$6); secondi 11,000–24,000L ($6–$12). AE, MC, V. Tues–Sun noon–2:30pm and 7–10pm. Vaporetto: San Zaccaria (with your back to the water and facing the Hotel Savoia e Jolanda, walk straight ahead to Campo SS. Filippo e Giacomo; the trattoria is tucked away next to a bridge off the right side of the campo). SEAFOOD/VENETIAN.

Lively and frequented by gondoliers (always a clue of quality dining for the right price), merchants, and visitors drawn to its bonhomie and bustling popularity, this is one of the safer bets for genuine Venetian cuisine and company in the touristy San Marco area, a 10-minute walk east of the piazza. All sorts of fish—the specialty—decorate the window of this brightly lit place. Another good indicator: There's usually a bit of a wait, even off-season.

○ **Trattoria da Remigio.** Castello 3416 (on Calle Bosello near the Scuola San Giorgio dei Greci). ☎ **041-523-0089.** Reservations required. Primi 6,000–10,000L ($3–$5); secondi 10,000–25,000L ($5–$13). AE, DC, MC, V. Mon 1–3pm, Wed–Sun 1–3pm and 7–11pm. Vaporetto: San Zaccaria (follow Riva degli Schiavoni east until you come to the white Chiesa della Pietà; turn left onto Calle della Pietà, which jags left into Calle Bosello). ITALIAN/VENETIAN.

Famous for its straightforward renditions of classics, Remigio (well known though not easy to find—just ask any local) is the kind of place where you can order simple *gnocchi alla pescatora* (homemade gnocchi in tomato-seafood sauce) and *frittura mista* (a cornucopia of fried seafood that makes a flavorful but light secondo) and know it'll be memorable. It bucks the current Venetian trend by offering excellent food and service at reasonable prices. The English-speaking head waiter, Pino, will talk you through the day's perfectly prepared fish dishes (John Dory, sole, monkfish, cuttlefish) or the dozen meat choices. There are two pleasant but smallish dining rooms.

WORTH A SPLURGE

○ **Al Covo.** Castello 3968 (on Campiello del Pescheria, east of Chiesa della Pietà in the Arsenale neighborhood). ☎ **041-522-3812.** Reservations suggested. Primi 16,000–27,000L ($8–14); secondi 40,000L ($20); 3-course fixed-price lunch 57,000L ($29). No credit cards. Fri–Tues 12:45–2pm and 7:30–10pm (kitchen hours). Closed Dec 15–Jan 15 and 2 weeks in Aug. Vaporetto: Arsenale (walk a short way back in the direction of Piazza San Marco, turn right at the Bar/cafe il Gabbiano, and the restaurant is on your left; otherwise, take an enjoyable 20-minute stroll along the waterfront Riva degli Schiavoni from Piazza San Marco, past the Chiesa della Pietà and the Metropole Hotel. VENETIAN/SEAFOOD.

For years, this restaurant has been popular with American food writers, but this has never compromised the incredible dining at this welcoming spot, where you'll find an excellent selection of moderately priced wines. Much of its friendly atmosphere is due to co-owner Texan Diane Rankin, a dessert whiz. She'll eagerly talk you through a fish-studded menu that can seem like Greek to non-Venetians. Her husband, Cesare Benelli, is known for his infallible talent in the kitchen. There's always one non-seafood selection at each course for landlubbers. If you want one of the tables set on the flagstones of the little campo out front, make sure you request it upon booking.

Osteria Alle Testiere. Castello 5801 (on Calle. del Mondo Novo off Salizzada San Lio). ☎ **041-522-7220.** Reservations required. Primi 22,000L ($11); secondi 30,000–33,000L ($15–$17). MC, V. Mon–Sat noon–2pm and two dinner seatings (7 and 9pm). Vaporetto: Rialto or San Marco (find the store-lined Salizzada San Lio, west of Campo Santa Maria Formosa, and from there ask where to turn off on Calle del Mondo Novo). VENETIAN/SEAFOOD.

The seating for just 24 lucky patrons at butcher-paper-covered tables, relaxed young staff, and upbeat tavernlike (no-smoking!) atmosphere belie the seriousness of this newcomer. This is your guaranteed choice if you're a foodie, curious to experience the increasingly interesting Venetian culinary scene without going broke. Start with the carefully chosen wine list, most of whose 90 labels (average 30,000L/$15) you can order by the half bottle. The delicious homemade *gnocchetti ai calamaretti* (with baby squid) makes a frequent appearance, as does the secondo specialty *scampi alla busara*, a secret shrimp recipe, some of whose ingredients are tomato, cinnamon, and a dash of hot pepper. Cheese is a rarity in these parts, except for Alle Testiere's exceptional choice of a half dozen winners.

IN DORSODURO

Brasserie ai Pugni. Dorsoduro 2839 (at the foot of the Ponte dei Pugni). ☎ **041-523-9831.** Dishes, sandwiches, salads, and pizze 5,500–11,500L ($2.75–$6); *menù turistico* 20,000L ($10). AE, DC, MC, V. Tues–Sun noon–3pm and 7–11:30pm. Vaporetto: Ca' Rezzonico (walk due west toward Campo San Barnaba; the restaurant is in front of the floating produce boat). ITALIAN/INTERNATIONAL.

Visitors seek out this no-frills canal-side pub/bistro for the relaxed setting and young locals for the unusual value for their money. With service included and no cover, there are no hidden fees for the simple but welcome meals even when you order à la carte or linger over a beer. Over 50 interesting sandwiches and some 60 pizza combinations are on offer. The *menù turistico* includes daily pasta or soup specials, *cotoletta alla milanese* (a northern Italian version of breaded Wiener schnitzel), and a house salad. You can't leave Venice without experiencing this residential corner nestled between two lovely piazze: Campo San Barnaba and Campo Santa Margherita. The area's pièce de résistance is the produce barge moored outside the pub—the last such floating market still used in Venice.

Taverna San Trovaso. Dorsoduro 1016 (on Fondamenta Priuli). ☎ **041-520-3703.** Pizze and primi 8,000–14,000L ($4–$7); secondi 13,000–27,000L ($7–$14); *menù turistico* 30,000L ($15); fixed-price 4-course menu 65,000L ($33). AE, MC, V. Tues–Sun noon–2:50pm and 7–9:50pm. Vaporetto: Rialto (walk to the right around the Accademia and take a right onto Calle Gambara; when this street ends at the small Rio di San Trovaso, turn left onto Fondamenta Priuli). VENETIAN.

Wine bottles line the wood-paneled walls and low vaulted brick ceilings augment the sense of character in this canal-side tavern. The *menù turistico* includes wine, an ample *frittura mista* (assortment of fried seafood), and a dessert. The gnocchi is homemade; the local specialty of calf's liver and onions is great, and the simply grilled fish is the taverna's claim to fame. There's also a variety of pizzas. For a special occasion that'll test your budget but not bankrupt you, consider the four-course menu: It starts with a fresh antipasto of seafood followed by pasta and a fish entree (changing with the day's catch) and includes side dishes, a dessert, and wine. While in the neighborhood, stroll along Rio San Trovaso toward the Giudecca Canal: On your right will be the Squero di San Trovaso, one of the few boatyards that still makes and repairs gondolas.

Trattoria Ai Cugnai. Dorsoduro 857 (on Calle Nuova Sant'Agnese). ☎ **041-528-9238.** Primi 9,500–15,000L ($4.75–$8); secondi 10,000–29,000L ($5–$15). AE, MC, V. Tues–Sun 12:30–3pm and 7–10:30pm. Vaporetto: Accademia (head east of the bridge and the Accademia in the direction of the Guggenheim Collection; on the straight street connecting the two museums; the restaurant is on your right). VENETIAN.

The storefront of this long-time favorite does little to announce that herein lies some of the neighborhood's best dining. The name refers to the brothers-in-law of the three women chefs, all sisters, who serve classic *cucina venexiana*, like the reliably good *spaghetti alle vongole verace* (with clams) or *fegato alla veneziana*. The homemade gnocchi and lasagna would meet any Italian grandmother's approval (you won't go wrong with any of the menu's *fatta in casa* choices of daily homemade specialties). Equidistant from the Accademia and the Guggenheim, Ai Cugnai is the perfect place to recharge after an art overload.

IN SAN POLO

✪ **A Le Do Spade.** San Polo 860 (on Sottoportego do Spade). ☎ **041-521-0574.** Primi 10,000–16,000L ($5–$8); secondi 14,000–18,000L ($7–$9); *menu fisso* 28,000L ($14). AE, MC, V. Mon–Wed and Fri–Sat 9am–3pm and 5–11pm, Thurs 9am–3pm. Vaporetto: Rialto or San Silvestro (at the San Polo side of the Ponte Rialto, walk away from the bridge and through the open-air market until you see the covered fish market on your right; take a left and then take the second right onto Sottoportego do Spade). WINE BAR/VENETIAN.

Since 1415, workers, fishmongers, and shoppers from the nearby Mercato della Pescheria have flocked to this wine bar. There's bonhomie galore amid the locals here for their daily *ombra*—a large number of excellent Veneto and Friuli wines are available by the glass. A counter is filled with various *cichetti* (potato croquettes, fried calamari, polenta squares, cheeses) and a special *picante panino* whose secret mix of super-hot spices will sear your tastebuds. Unlike at most *bacari*, this quintessentially Venetian cantina has added a number of tables and introduced a sit-down menu, accounting for my star here over its competitor, Cantina do Mori (below), which is a better choice for stand-up bar food.

○ **Alla Madonna.** San Polo 594 (on Calle della Madonna). ☎ **041-522-3824.** Reservations not accepted. Primi 15,000–18,000L ($8–$9); secondi 15,000–20,000L ($8–$10). AE, MC, V. Thurs–Tues noon–3pm and 7–10:30pm. Closed 2 weeks in Aug and most of Jan. Vaporetto: Rialto (from the foot of the Ponte Rialto on the San Polo side of the Grand Canal, turn left and follow Riva del Vin along the Grand Canal; Calle della Madonna [also called Sottoportego della Madonna] will be the second calle on your right [look for the big yellow sign]; the restaurant is on your left). ITALIAN/VENETIAN.

Packing them in for more than 50 years, this Venetian institution has it all: a convenient location, five large dining rooms, a mix of locals and foreigners, a decor of high-beamed ceilings and walls frame-to-frame with local artists' work, and a professional kitchen that prepares a menu of fresh fish and seafood to perfection. With all of this and (by Venetian standards) moderate prices, it's no surprise this place is always jumping (too bad you can't reserve). So don't expect the waiter to smile if you linger over dessert. Most of the first courses are served with seafood, like the spaghetti or risotto with *frutti di mare* or the pasta with *sepie* (cuttlefish), blackened from its own natural ink. Most of the day's special fish selections are best simply and deliciously prepared *alla griglia* (grilled).

Cantina do Mori. San Polo 429 (entrances on Calle Galiazza and Calle Do Mori). ☎ **041-522-5401.** Sandwiches and *cichetti* bar food 1,500–3,000L (75¢–$1.50). No credit cards. Mon–Sat 8:30am–9:30pm. Vaporetto: Rialto (cross the Ponte Rialto to the San Polo side, walk to the end of the market stalls, turn left, then immediately right, and look for the small wooden cantina sign on the left). WINE BAR/SANDWICHES.

Since 1462, this has been the watering hole of choice in the market area; legend even pegs Casanova as a habitué. Here's the best place to try *tramezzini*—you're guaranteed fresh combinations of thinly sliced meats, tuna, cheeses, and vegetables, along with tapas-like *cichetti*. They're traditionally washed down with an *ombra*. Venetians stop to snack and socialize before and after meals; if you don't mind standing (there are no tables), do as they do. And now with a limited number of primi like *melanzane alla parmigiana* (eggplant parmigiana) and *fondi di carciofi saltati* (lightly fried artichoke hearts), my obligatory stop here is more fulfilling than ever.

Da Sandro. San Polo 1473 (on Campiello dei Meloni). ☎ **041-523-4894.** Primi 7,500–14,000L ($3.75–$7); secondi 8,000–25,000L ($4–$13); pizze 7,500–16,000L ($3.75–$8); fixed-price menus 22,000–28,000L ($11–$14). AE, MC, V. Sat–Thurs 11:30am–11:30pm. Vaporetto: San Silvestro (with your back to the Grand Canal, walk straight to store-lined Ruga Vecchia San Giovanni and take a left; head toward Campo San Polo until you come on Campiello dei Meloni). ITALIAN/PIZZERIA.

Like most pizzerie/trattorie, Sandro offers a dozen varieties of pizza (his specialty) as well as a full trattoria menu of pastas and entrees. But if you're looking for a 12,000L ($6) pizza-and-beer meal, this is a reliably good spot on the main drag linking the Rialto to Campo San Polo. You won't raise any eyebrows if you order just a pasta or a pizza and pass on the meat or fish. There's communal seating at a few wooden picnic tables placed outdoors, with eight small tables stuffed inside.

IN SANTA CROCE

Pizzeria alle Oche. Santa Croce 1552 (on Calle del Tintor south of Campo San Giacomo dell'Orio). ☎ **041-524-1161.** Reservations recommended for weekends. Primi 8,000–14,000L ($4–$7), secondi 10,000–20,000L ($5–$10), pizze 6,000–14,000L ($3–$7). MC, V. Tues–Sun noon–3pm and 7pm–midnight (in summer open daily). Vaporetto: Rio San Biasio, San Stae (you can walk here in 10 min. from the nearby train station; from the vaporetto station, find your way to the Campo San Giacomo dell'Orio and exit the campo south onto Campo del Tintor). PIZZERIA.

When I' m looking for a carbo overload (and what better country to be in?), I head for the Baskin-Robbins of Venice's pizzerie. Italians are zealously unapologetic about tucking into a good-size pizza and a pint of beer (with more than 20 here from which to choose); the walk to and from this slightly peripherally located hangout (with outside eating during warm weather) allays thoughts of calorie counts. A whopping 85 varieties of imaginative pizza fill the menu, a dozen of the tomato sauce–free *pizza bianca* ("white") variety. The crowd is a mixed bag of young and old, students and not, Venetian and visitors—most happily putting away the classically wonderful Margherita version.

IN CANNAREGIO

Brek, Lista di Spagna 124 (☎ **041-244-0158;** Vaporetto: Ferrovia), that Northern Italian chain of upscale cafeterias, has just opened up a popular Venice branch near the train station; it's open daily 11:30am to 10:30pm.

✪ **Ai Tre Spiedi.** Cannaregio 5906 (on Salizzada San Cazian). ☎ **041-520-8035.** Primi 6,000L–12,000L ($3–$6); secondi 16,000L–30,000L ($8–$15); *menù turistico* 26,000–35,000L (13–$18) without wine. AE, MC, V. Tues–Sun noon–3pm and 7–10pm, Mon noon–3pm. Vaporetto: Rialto (on the San Marco side of bridge, walk straight ahead to Campo San Bartolomeo and take a left, passing the post office, Coin department store, and San Crisostomo; cross the first bridge after the church and turn right at the toy store onto Salizzada San Cazian). VENETIAN.

Venetians bring their visiting friends here to make a *bella figura* (good impression) without breaking the bank, then swear them to secrecy. Rarely will you find as pleasant a setting and appetizing a meal as in this casually elegant small trattoria with some of the most reasonably priced fresh fish dining that'll keep meat-eaters happy as well. Their *spaghetti O.P.A.* (with parsley, pepperoncino, garlic, and olive oil) is excellent and their *spaghetti al pesto* the best this side of Liguria.

PICNICKING

You don't have to eat in a fancy restaurant to have a good time in Venice. Prepare a picnic, and while you eat alfresco, observe the life of the city's few open piazzas or the aquatic parade on its main thoroughfare, the Grand Canal. And you can still indulge in a late dinner *alla veneziana.* Plus, doing your own shopping for food can be an interesting experience because there are very few supermarkets as we know them and small *alimentari* (food shops) in the highly visited neighborhoods (where few Venetians live) are scarce.

MERCATO RIALTO   Venice's principal open-air market is a sight to see, even for non-shoppers. It has two parts, beginning with the **produce section,** whose many stalls, alternating with souvenir vendors, unfold north on the San Polo side of the

Ponte Rialto (behind these stalls are a few permanent food stores whose delicious cheese, cold cuts, and bread selections make the perfect lunch). The vendors are here Monday to Saturday 7am to 1pm, with a number who stay on in the afternoon.

At the market's farthest point, you'll find the covered **fresh-fish market,** with its carnival atmosphere, on the Grand Canal opposite the magnificent Ca' d'Oro. The area is filled with a number of small *bacari* frequented by market vendors and shoppers where you can join in and ask for your morning's first glass of *prosecco* with a *cichetto* pick-me-up. The fish merchants take Monday off and work mornings only.

CAMPO SANTA MARGHERITA   Tuesday to Saturday 8:30am to 1 or 2pm, open-air stalls selling fresh fruit and vegetables set up shop here. You should have no trouble filling out your picnic spread with the fixings available at the various shops around the campo, including an exceptional *panetteria* (bakery), Rizzo Pane, at no. 2772; a fine *salumeria* (deli) at no. 2844; and a good shop for wine, sweets, and other picnic accessories next door. There's even a conventional supermarket, **Merlini,** just off the campo in the direction of the quasi-adjacent Campo San Barnabà at no. 3019. This is also the area where you'll find Venice's heavily photographed **floating market** operating from a boat moored just off Campo San Barnabà at the Ponte dei Pugni. This market is open daily 8am to 1pm and 3:30 to 7:30pm, except Wednesday afternoon and Sunday. You're almost better off just buying a few freshly prepared sandwiches (*panini* when made with rolls, *tramezzini* when made with white bread).

THE BEST PICNIC SPOTS   Alas, picnicking in Venice means you won't have much in the way of green space (it's not worth the boat ride to the Giardini Publici past the Arsenale, Venice's only green park). An enjoyable alternative is to find some of the larger piazze or campi that have park benches, and in some cases even a tree or two to shade them, such as **Campo San Giacomo dell'Orio** (in Santa Croce). The two most central are **Campo Santa Margherita** (in Dorsoduro) and **Campo San Polo** (in San Polo). Personally, I like staking out a sliver of canal-front *fondamenta* and picnicking simply, dangling my feet off the marble embankment over the water.

For a picnic with a view, scout out the **Punta della Dogana (Customs House)** area near La Salute for a prime viewing site at the mouth of the Grand Canal. It's directly across from Piazza San Marco and the Palazzo Ducale—pull up a piece of the embankment here and watch the water activity against a canvaslike backdrop deserving of the Accademia. In this same area, the small **Campo San Vio** near the Guggenheim is on the Grand Canal and even boasts a bench or two. If you want to create a real Venice picnic, you'll have to take the no. 12 boat out to the near-deserted island of **Torcello,** with a hamper full of bread, cheese, and wine, and reenact the romantic scene of Katharine Hepburn and Rossano Brazzi from *Summertime.*

5 Seeing the Sights

Venice is notorious for changing and extending the opening hours of its museums and, to a lesser degree, its churches. Before you begin your sightseeing, ask at the tourist office for the season's list of museum and church hours. During the peak months, you can enjoy extended museum hours—some places stay open to 7 or even 10pm. Alas, these hours aren't released until about Easter of every year. Even then, little is done to publicize the information, so you'll have to do your own research.

Check with a tourist office for **free tours** being offered (erratically and usually during high season) in some of the churches, particularly the Basilica di San Marco and occasionally the Frari.

IN SAN MARCO

Basilica di San Marco (St. Mark's Basilica). San Marco, Piazza San Marco. ☎ **041-522-5205** or 041-522-5697. Basilica, free; Museo Marciano (also called La Galleria, includes Loggia dei Cavalli), 3,000L ($1.50) adults, 1,500L (75¢) students; Tesoro (Treasury), 4,000L ($2) adults, 2,000L ($1) students; Pala d'Oro (altar screen), 3,000L ($) adults, 1,500L (75¢) students. Basilica, Tesoro, and Pala d'Oro: summer Mon–Sat 9:45am–5pm, Sun 2–4:30pm; winter Mon–Sat 9:45am–4pm, Sun 2–4pm. Museo Marciano: summer daily 9:45am–5pm; winter daily 9:45am–4pm. Vaporetto: San Marco.

For centuries, Venice was Europe's principal gateway between the Orient and the West, so it shouldn't be surprising that the architectural style for this sumptuously Byzantine basilica, with five mosquelike bulbed domes, was borrowed from Constantinople. Legend has it that in 828, two enterprising Venetian merchants smuggled St. Mark the Evangelist's remains from Alexandria in Egypt by packing them in pickled pork to bypass the scrutiny of Muslim guards. And so St. Mark replaced the Greek St. Theodore as Venice's patron saint, and a small chapel was built on this spot in his honor. Through the subsequent centuries (much of what you see was built in the 11th century), wealthy Venetians vied with one another in donating gifts to expand and embellish this church, the saint's final resting place and, with the Palazzo Ducale, a symbol of Venetian wealth and power. Exotic and mysterious, it's unlike any other Roman Catholic church you'll visit.

And so it is that the Basilica di San Marco earned its name as the **Chiesa d'Oro** (Golden Church), every inch of its cavernous interior exquisitely gilded with Byzantine mosaics added over some 7 centuries (the earliest from the 11th century). For a close look at many of the most remarkable ceiling mosaics and for a better view of the oriental carpet–like patterns of the intricate undulating pavement mosaics below, pay the museum admission to go upstairs to the **Galleria and Museo Marciano** (the entrance to these is in the atrium at the principal entrance). This was originally the *matroneum* (women's gallery), and one room showcases the restored *Triumphal Quadriga* of four gilded-bronze horses (2nd or 3rd century) brought in 1204 to Venice from Constantinople (though probably cast in Imperial Rome) together with the Lion of St. Mark (the patron saint's icon and Venice's mascot) and other booty from the Crusades. The statue group was a symbol of the unrivaled Serene Republic and is the only *quadriga* (four horses tethered together) to have survived from the classical era.

From the Galleria you can also climb out onto the outdoor **Loggia dei Cavalli,** an unexpected highlight providing an excellent view of the piazza and what Napoléon called "the most beautiful salon in the world" upon his arrival in Venice in 1797. The emperor later carted the *quadriga* (a replica of which now stands on the loggia) off to Paris, but it was returned after the fall of the French Empire. The 500-year-old Torre dell'Orologio (Clock Tower) stands to your right; to your left is the Campanile (Bell Tower) and beyond, the glistening waters of the open lagoon and Palladio's San Giorgio on its own island.

The church's greatest treasure is behind the main altar, whose green marble canopy on alabaster columns covers the tomb of St. Mark: the magnificent Gothic altarpiece known as the **Pala d'Oro (Golden Alterpiece),** encrusted with close to 2,000 precious

A St. Mark's Warning

The basilica is open Sunday morning for those wishing to attend mass; all others are strongly discouraged from entering (see hours above). At all times, guards stand at the entrance and are serious about forbidding entry to anyone in inappropriate attire, including shorts, short skirts, and anything baring the shoulders.

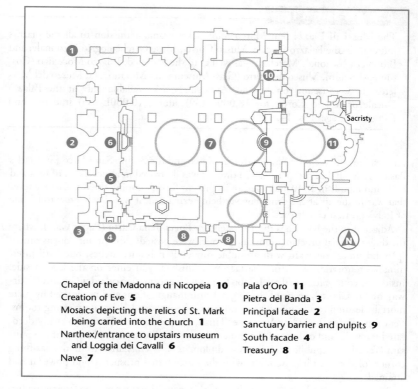

Chapel of the Madonna di Nicopeia **10**
Creation of Eve **5**
Mosaics depicting the relics of St. Mark being carried into the church **1**
Narthex/entrance to upstairs museum and Loggia dei Cavalli **6**
Nave **7**

Pala d'Oro **11**
Pietra del Banda **3**
Principal facade **2**
Sanctuary barrier and pulpits **9**
South facade **4**
Treasury **8**

gems and 255 enameled panels. It was created as early as the 10th century and embellished by master Venetian and Byzantine artisans between the 12th and the 14th century. Also worth a visit is the **Tesoro (Treasury),** to the far right of the main altar, housing a collection of the Crusaders' plunder from Constantinople and other icons and relics amassed by the church over the years. Much of the Venetian booty has been incorporated into the interior and exterior of the basilica in the form of marble, columns, capitals, and statuary. Second to the Pala d'Oro in importance is the 10th-century *Madonna di Nicopeia,* a bejeweled icon absconded from Constantinople and exhibited in its own chapel to the left of the main altar. She's held as one of present-day Venice's most protective patrons.

In July and August (with much less certainty the rest of the year), church-affiliated volunteers give **free tours** Monday to Saturday, leaving four or five times daily (not all are in English), beginning at 10:30am; groups gather in the atrium, where you'll find posters with schedules.

✪ **Palazzo Ducale (Doge's Palace) & Ponte dei Sospiri (Bridge of Sighs).** San Marco, Piazza San Marco. ☎ **041-522-4951.** Admission only with cumulative ticket (see above). Excellent "Itinerari Segreti" guided tour in English 10:30am Thurs–Tues (by reservation only) 24,000L ($12) adults, 14,000L ($7) students, 8,000L ($4) ages 6–14 (includes cumulative ticket). Apr–Oct daily 9am–7pm; Nov–Mar daily 9am–5pm. (*Note:* Ticket office closes 90 min. earlier). Vaporetto: San Marco.

The pink-and-white marble Gothic **Palazzo Ducale,** residence/government center of the officials and doges ("dukes," elected for life) who ruled Venice for more than 1,000

A Money-Saving Tip

The **Musei di Piazza San Marco** joint ticket grants admission to all the piazza's museums—the Palazzo Ducale, Museo Correr, Museo Archeologico Nazionale, and Biblioteca Nazionale Marciana—as well as to the Museo di Palazzo Mocenigo (Costume Museum), Museo del Vetro (Glass Museum) on Murano, and Museo del Merletto (Lace Museum) on Burano. Annoyingly, it's available only at the Palazzo Ducale or Museo Correr for 18,000L ($9) adults, 10,000L ($5) students, and 6,000L ($3) ages 6 to 14.

---

years, stands between the Basilica di San Marco and the Bacino San Marco (St. Mark's Basin). A symbol of prosperity and power, it was destroyed in a succession of fires and built and rebuilt in 1340 and 1424 in its present form, escaping the Renaissance fever that was in the air at the time. Forever being expanded, it was slowly grew to be one of Italy's greatest civic structures.

Adjacent to the basilica is the 15th-century **Porta della Carta (Paper Gate),** where the doges' official proclamations and decrees were posted; this entrance opens onto a splendid inner courtyard with a double row of Renaissance arches, but until interminable restoration work on the facade is finished, you enter on the lagoon side. Inside the courtyard, you'll see Jacopo Sansovino's enormous **Scala dei Giganti (Stairway of the Giants),** scene of the doges' lavish inaugurations and never used by mere mortals, leading to the interior's wood-paneled courts and elaborate meeting rooms. Venetian masters including Veronese, Titian, Carpaccio, and Tintoretto richly decorated the walls and ceilings of the principal rooms to illustrate the history of the puissant Venetian Republic and impress diplomats and emissaries from the far-flung corners of the Maritime Republic with the uncontested prosperity and power it had attained.

If you want to understand something of this magnificent palace, the fascinating history of the 1,000-year-old Maritime Republic, and the intrigue of the government that ruled it, rent an **audio guide** at the entrance (7,000L/$3.50) or, even better, sign up for the fantastic "Secret Itineraries" tour (see below).

The first room you'll come to is the **Sala delle Quattro Porte (Hall of the Four Doors),** whose ceiling is by Tintoretto. The next main room, the **Sala del Anti-Collegio** (adjacent to the **Sala del Collegio,** whose ceiling is by Tintoretto), is where foreign ambassadors waited to be received (and thus the embellishment of its canvases, serving as self-aggrandizement) by the Collegio committee's 25 members: It's decorated with Tintorettos and Veronese's *Rape of Europe,* one of the palazzo's finest. It steals some of the thunder from Tintoretto's *Three Graces* and *Bacchus and Ariadne*—the latter considered one of his best by some critics. A right turn from this room leads into one of the most impressive of the spectacular interior rooms, the richly adorned **Sala del Senato (Senate Chamber),** with Tintoretto's ceiling painting, *The Triumph of Venice.* Here laws were passed by the Senate, a select group of 200 chosen from the Great Council. The latter was originally an elected body but from the 13th century and onward, it was an aristocratic stronghold that could number as many as 1,700.

After passing again through the Sala delle Quattro Porte, you'll come to the Veronese-decorated **Stanza del Consiglio dei Dieci (Room of the Council of Ten),** of particular historic interest as it's where justice was dispensed and decapitations ordered. Formed in the 14th century to deal with emergencies, the Council of Ten was considered more powerful than the Senate and feared by all. Just outside the adjacent

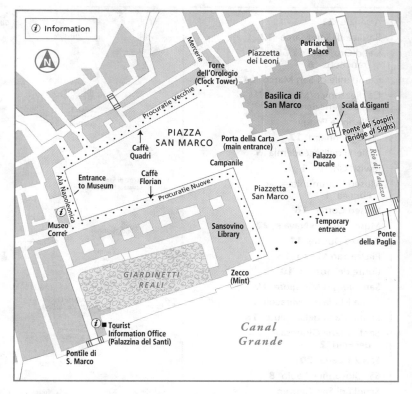

chamber, the **Sala della Bussola (Compass Chamber),** notice the **Bocca dei Leoni (Lion's Mouth),** a slit in the wall into which anyone could slip a signed and witnessed denunciation or accusation of alleged enemies of the state for quick action by the much feared Ten (signed and witnessed to avoid back-stabbing; if the accused was found innocent, the accuser himself would have to face the Ten!).

The main sight on the next level down—indeed of the entire palace—is the **Sala del Maggior Consiglio (Great Council Hall).** This enormous space is made special by Tintoretto's huge *Paradiso* at the far end of the hall above the doge's seat (he was in his 70s when he undertook the project with the help of his son and died 6 years later). Measuring 23 by 75 feet, it is the world's largest oil painting; together with Veronese's gorgeous *Il Trionfo di Venezia (The Triumph of Venice)* in the oval panel on the ceiling, it affirms the power emanating from the Council sessions held here. Tintoretto also did the **portraits of the 76 doges** encircling the top of this chamber; note that the picture of the Doge Marin Falier, the only doge to be convicted of treason (beheaded in 1355), has been blacked out. Venice has never forgiven him. Although elected for life since sometime in the 7th century, over time *il doge (doe*-jay*)* became nothing but a figurehead (they were never allowed to meet with foreign ambassadors alone); the power rested in the Great Council.

Exit the Great Council Hall via the tiny doorway on the opposite side of Tintoretto's *Paradiso* to find the enclosed **Ponte dei Sospiri (Bridge of Sighs),** which connects the Doge's Palace with the grim **Palazzo delle Prigioni (Prisons).** The bridge took its current name only in the 19th century, when visiting northern

Venice Attractions

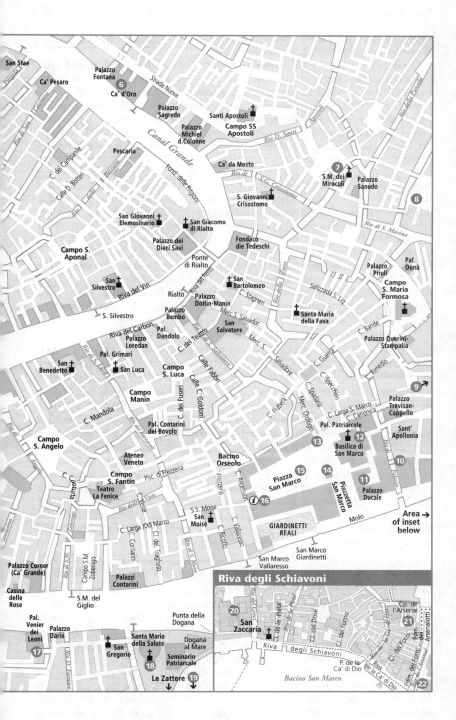

San Stae

Ca' Pesaro

Palazzo Fontana
6
Ca' d'Oro

Strada Nuova

Palazzo Sagredo

Santi Apostoli

Campo SS
Apostoli

Palazzo Michiel d.Colonne

Canal Grande

Rio D. Santi

Pescaria

Ca' da Mosto

Rio di S.G. Crisostomo

7
S.M. dei Miracoli

Palazzo Sanudo

8

C. del Campanile

Calle D. Botteri

Fond. delle Prigioni

S. Giovanni Crisostomo

Rio di S. Marina

San Giovanni Elemosinario

San Giacomo di Rialto

Palazzo dei Dieci Savi

Fondaco die Tedeschi

Campo S. Aponal

Ponte di Rialto

Palazzo Priuli

Pal. Donà

Campo S. Maria Formosa

San Silvestro

Riva del Vin

Rialto

San Bartolomeo

Salizzada S. Liq

C. Stagneri

S. Silvestro

Palazzo Dolfin-Manin

Merc S. Salvador

Santa Maria della Fava

C. Bande

Palazzo Bembo

San Salvatore

Merc. S.

Palazzo Querini-Stampalia

Riva del Carbon

Pal. Dandolo

C. del Teatro

C. Guerra

C. Rimedio

Palazzo Loredan

Riva di S. Luca

Salvadore

Pal. Grimari

Campo S. Luca

C. Specchieri

9

San Benedetto

San Luca

Calle Fabbri

C. Frubera

Merc Orologio

C. Spadaria

Palazzo Trevisan-Cappello

Campo Manin

C. dei Fuseri

C. C. Goldoni

C. Larga S. Marco

Canonica

Sant' Apollonia

C. Mandola

Pal. Contarini del Bovolo

Pal. Patriarcale

Campo S. Angelo

13

Basilica di San Marco

12

10

Ateneo Veneto

Bacino Orseolo

14

11

Campo S. Fantin

15

Piazza San Marco

Piazzetta San Marco

Palazzo Ducale

Teatro La Fenice

Pisc. di Frezzeria

i 16

S.S. Moisè
San Moisè

Area →
of inset
below

C. Larga XXII Marzo

GIARDINETTI REALI

San Marco Giardinetti

Molo

Palazzo Corner
(Ca' Grande)

Palazzi Contarini

San Marco Vallaresso

Casina delle Rose

S.M. del Giglio

Pal. Venier dei Leoni

Palazzo Dario

Punta della Dogana

20

San Zaccaria

Cp. de l'Arsenal

21

17

San Gregorio

Santa Maria della Salute

Dogana al Mare

Riva degli Schiavoni

18

Seminario Patriarcale

Le Zattere 19

P. de la Ca' di Dio

22

Bacino San Marco

The Secrets of the Palazzo Ducale

I can't recommend the new **Itinerari Segreti (Secret Itineraries) guided tours** highly enough. They offer an unparalleled look into the world of Venetian politics over the centuries and are the only way to access the otherwise restricted quarters and hidden passages of this enormous palace, such as the doge's private chambers and the torture chambers where prisoners were interrogated. The story of Casanova's imprisonment and escape is the tour highlight. Reserve in advance by phone (tours are often sold out a day or two in advance at least) or in person at the ticket desk.

European poets romantically envisioned the prisoners' final breath of resignation upon viewing the outside world one last time from its little window before being locked in their fetid cells awaiting the justice of the Terrible Ten. Some of the stone cells still have the original graffiti of past prisoners, many of them locked up interminably for petty crimes. But Venice's most famous prisoner had to have been 18th-century lothario Giacomo Casanova who, following his arrest in 1755 (he was accused of being a Freemason and spreading anti-religious propaganda), was locked away in "The Leads," low cells tucked into the attic of the Doge's Palace itself. He was one of the rare few to escape 15 months after his imprisonment, alive, returning to Venice 20 years later. ("Secret Itineraries" tours—especially those in English—play this story up for dramatic effect and give you all the harrowing details, should you not have time to read the man's memoirs.)

Campanile di San Marco (Bell Tower). San Marco, Piazza San Marco. ☎ **041-522-4064.** Admission 10,000L ($5) adults, 5,000L ($2.50) students. Apr–Oct daily 9am–9pm; Nov–Mar daily 9am–7:30pm (may shorten hours in deepest winter). Vaporetto: San Marco.

It's an easy elevator ride up to the top of this 324-foot bell tower for a breathtaking view of the cupolas of St. Mark's. It's the highest structure in the city, offering a pigeon's-eye view that includes the lagoon, its neighboring islands, and the red rooftops and church domes and bell towers of Venice—and, oddly, not a single canal. On a clear day you may even see the outline of the distant snow-capped Dolomite Mountains. It was built in the 9th century and then rebuilt in the 12th, 14th, and 16th centuries, when the marble loggia at its base was added by Jacopo Sansovino. It collapsed unexpectedly in 1902, miraculously hurting no one except a cat. It was rebuilt exactly as before, using most of the same materials, only shorter (solving the structural problem). They even rescued one of the five historic bells still used today (each bell was rung for a different purpose, such as war, the death of a doge, religious holidays, and so on).

Torre dell'Orologio (Clock Tower). San Marco, Piazza San Marco. No phone. Scheduled to reopen in 2001. Admission and hours weren't set at press time. Vaporetto: San Marco.

As you enter the magnificent Piazza San Marco, the Clock Tower is one of the first things you see, standing on the north side, next to and towering above the Procuratie Vecchie (the ancient administration buildings for the Republic). The Renaissance tower was built in 1496 and the clock mechanism of that same period still keeps perfect time but has gotten a cleaning up by Piaget, the sponsor of a renovation that has kept it closed for years now. The two bronze figures up top, known as Moors because of the dark color of the bronze, pivot to strike the hour. The base of the tower has always been a favorite *punto di incontro* for Venetians ("meet me at the tower") and is the entrance to the ancient Mercerie (from the word for merchandise), the principal souklike retail street of both high-end boutiques and trinket shops that zigzags its way to the Ponte Rialto. Visits to the top will resume on the tower's reopening.

Museo Correr. San Marco, under the arcade at the west end of Piazza San Marco. ☎ **041-522-5625** or 041-522-4951. Admission and hours same as Palazzo Ducale (above). Vaporetto: San Marco.

This museum is no match for the Accademia but does include some interesting paintings of Venetian life, plus a fine collection of artifacts (like coins, costumes, the doges' ceremonial robes and hats, and an incredible pair of 15-inch platform shoes) that gives an interesting feel for aspects of daily life in the city's heyday. Bequeathed to Venice by the aristocratic Correr family in 1830, the museum is divided into three sections: the **Painting Section,** the **History Section,** and the **Museum of the Risorgimento** (Italy's 1797 to 1866 unification movement). The latter two aren't worth much mention. Of the painting collection from the 13th to the 18th century, Vittorio Carpaccio's *Le Cortigiane (The Courtesans),* in room 15 on the upper floor, is one of the museum's most famous works (though there's a question as to whether the subjects are actually courtesans or respectable noble ladies), as are the star-attraction paintings by the Bellini family, father Jacopo and sons Gentile and Giovanni. For a lesson in just how little this city has changed in the last several hundred years, head to room 22 and its anonymous 17th-century **bird's-eye view of Venice.** Most of the rooms have a sign with a few paragraphs in English explaining the significance of the contents.

IN DORSODURO

✪ **Galleria dell'Accademia (Accademia Gallery).** Dorsoduro, at the foot of the Ponte Accademia. ☎ **041-522-2247.** Admission 12,000L ($6); under 12 free. Tues–Sat 8:30am–7:30pm, Sun 9am–7pm, Mon 9am–2pm. Vaporetto: Accademia.

The glory that was La Serenissima lives on at the Accademia, the definitive treasure house of Venetian painting and one of Europe's great museums, contained in a deconsecrated church and its adjoining scuola (confraternity hall). The collection is exhibited chronologically from the 13th to the 18th century, and there's no one hallmark masterpiece; rather, this is an outstanding and comprehensive showcase of works by all the great masters of Venice. It includes Paolo and Lorenzo Veneziano from the 14th century; Gentile and Giovanni Bellini (and Giovanni's brother-in-law Andrea Mantegna from Padua) and Vittore Carpaccio from the 15th century; Giorgione (whose *Tempest* is one the gallery's top highlights), Tintoretto, Veronese, and Titian from the 16th century (works by Tintoretto and Veronese are found frequently in Venice's churches and scuolas but the bulk of Titian's work is here; exceptions are those found in La Salute and the Frari); and from the 17th and 18th centuries, Canaletto, Piazzetta, Longhi, and Tiepolo, among others.

Most of all, the works open a window onto the Venice of 500 years ago—you'll see in the canvases how little Venice has changed over the centuries. Admission is limited, due to fire regulations, and lines can be daunting (check for extended evening hours in the peak months), but put up with the wait and don't miss it. **Guided tours** in English (10,000L/$5) are given at 10am, 11am, and noon (book at ☎ **041-520-0345** or 199-199-100 in Italy); **audio tours** cost 7,000L ($3.50) for one person and 10,000L ($5) for two people.

Collezione Peggy Guggenheim. Dorsoduro 701 (on Calle San Cristoforo). ☎ **041-240-5411.** Admission 12,000L ($6) adults, 8,000L ($4) students. Wed–Mon 10am–6pm (Apr–Oct Sat to 10pm). Vaporetto: Accademia (walk around the left side of the Accademia, take the first left, and walk straight ahead following the signs—you'll cross a canal, then walk alongside another, until turning left when necessary).

One of the most comprehensive and important collections of modern art in the world and one of the most visited attractions in Venice, this collection of painting and sculpture was assembled by eccentric and eclectic American expatriate Peggy Guggenheim.

A Dorsoduro Photo-Op

Just north of the Zattere (the wide walkway running along the Giudecca Canal), the **Squero San Trovaso** is next to the church of San Trovaso on the narrow Rio San Trovaso (near the Ponte Accademia). One of Venice's most photographed sights, this small boatyard from the 17th century is surrounded by Tyrolian-looking wooden structures (a rarity in this stone city built on water) home to the multigenerational owners and original workshops for the traditional Venetian boat, the sleek black gondola. The workers don't mind if you watch them at work from across the narrow Rio di San Trovaso, but don't try to invite yourself in. It's the perfect midway photo-op after a visit to the Accademia and a trip to the gelateria Da Nico, Zattere 922, whose chocolate gianduiotto is not to be missed.

She did an excellent job of it, with particular strengths in cubism, European abstraction, surrealism, and abstract expressionism since about 1910. Max Ernst was one of her early favorites (she even married him), as was Jackson Pollock. Among the major works are Magritte's *Empire of Light,* Picasso's *La Baignade,* Kandinsky's *Landscape with Church (with Red Spot),* Metzinger's *The Racing Cyclist,* and Pollock's *Alchemy.* The museum is also home to several haunting canvases by Ernst, Giacometti's unique figures, Brancusi's fluid sculptures, and numerous works by Braque, Dalí, Léger, Mondrian, Chagall, and Miró.

On the Grand Canal, the elegant 18th-century Palazzo Venier dei Leoni, never finished and thus its unusual one-story structure, was purchased by Peggy Guggenheim in 1949 and became her home in Venice until her death in 1979. The graves of her canine companions share the lovely interior garden with several works of the **Nasher Sculpture Garden,** while the canal-side patio watched over by Marino Marini's *Angel of the Citadel* is one of the best spots to linger and watch the canal life. A new book/gift shop and cafe/bistro (expensive) has opened in a separate wing across the inside courtyard where temporary exhibits are often housed.

Check the tourist office for an update on hours; it's often open when many others are closed and sometimes offers a few hours a week of free admission. Don't be shy about speaking English with the young staff working on internship; most are American, and they run **free educational talks** on specific works daily at 11am, noon, and 3, 4, and 5pm, plus a **free guided tour** of the collections Saturdays at 7pm.

Ca' Rezzonico (Museo del '700 Veneziano; Museum of 18th-Century Venice). Dorsoduro (on the Grand Canal on Fondamenta Rezzonico). ☎ **041-520-4036.** Admission 12,000L ($6) adults, 8,000L ($4) students. Summer Sat–Thurs 10am–5pm; winter Sat–Thurs 10am–4pm (these hours are predicted for the opening at press time; call to check when you arrive) Vaporetto: Ca' Rezzonico (walk straight ahead to Campo San Barnabà, turn right at the piazza, and go over one bridge, then take an immediate right for the museum entrance).

This museum was expected to reopen at press time—but it's been "expected to reopen" for several years. This home on the Grand Canal offers an intriguing look into what living in a grand Venetian palazzo was like in the final years of the Venetian Republic. Begun by Baldassare Longhena, 18th-century architect of La Salute, the palazzo is a sumptuous backdrop for a collection of period paintings (most important, works by Venetian artists Tiepolo and Guardi and a room dedicated to the dozens of works by Longhi), furniture, tapestries, and artifacts. Through it you can see the tastes and fashions of the Rezzonico merchant family—the lavishly frescoed ballroom alone will evoke the lifestyle of the idle Venetian rich. English poet Robert Browning, after

Cheap Thrills: What to See &
Do in Venice for Free (or Almost)

- **Touring the Basilica di San Marco.** Straddling East and West, the ancient basilica is unlike any other Roman Catholic church in the Western world. Try for one of the free guided tours given by church-affiliated volunteers; check with the tourist office for days and times.

- **Lingering in Piazza San Marco.** The small three- and four-piece orchestras playing at the historic cafes lining the magnificent Piazza San Marco will make your cappuccino a worthwhile one. Take in the scenario for free by sitting on the steps on the south and west side of the piazza with a friend or your thoughts. The moon-illuminated mosaic-covered facade of the basilica is magic.

- **Drinking in the scene.** For a dollar or two, hang out at the bar of one of Venice's countless neighborhood *bacari* (wine bars). Regional wines by the glass and the tasty finger foods that accompany them are a draw, but not half as interesting as the experience itself. What language barrier?

- **Eating gelato.** Gelato is commonplace the farther south you venture, but Venice has two wonderful gelaterias, Paolin and Nico (see "Venice After Dark," later in this chapter), that would pass muster with any Roman or Neapolitan. To go or to stay, it'll only augment the day's enjoyment.

- **Cruising the Grand Canal.** It may be easier and faster to get there by foot, but if you board the *vaporetto* 1 (ticket 6,000L/$3) and ply the full length of the 2-mile Grand Canal (the world's most celebrated boulevard), you'll get a front-row look at the palazzo-lined aquatic thoroughfare whose buildings never moved beyond the 18th century.

- **Taking advantage of two-for-one admission.** Be aware that the admission to the Palazzo Ducale includes admission to the Museo Correr and vice versa. Don't miss out by setting aside time to see only one.

- **Enjoying the views.** Buy a crusty *panino* or just some fresh fruit and cheese and pull up a piece of the embankment at La Dogana (Customs House) at the mouth of the Grand Canal (and east of La Salute), across from the Palazzo Ducale and Piazza San Marco. This is the same heart-stopping first glimpse of the Serene Republic as seen by visiting diplomats and foreign merchants who arrived during the glorious 1,000 years when Venice held sway.

the death of his wife, Elizabeth Barrett Browning, made this his last home and died here in 1889.

Santa Maria della Salute (La Salute). Dorsoduro (on Campo della Salute). ☎ **041-522-5558.** Church, free; sacristy, 2,000L ($1). Daily 9am–noon and 3–5:30pm. Vaporetto: Salute.

This crown jewel of 17th-century baroque architecture proudly reigns at a commercially and aesthetically important point, almost directly across from Piazza San Marco, where the Grand Canal empties into the lagoon. The first stone was laid in 1631 after the Senate decided to honor the Virgin Mary of Good Health for delivering Venice from a plague (and after the completion of the neighboring San Giorgio). They accepted the revolutionary plans of a relatively unknown young architect, Baldassare Longhena (who went on to design, among other projects, the Ca' Rezzonico). He dedicated the next 50 years of his life to overseeing its progress (he died a year after its inauguration but 5 years before its completion). The octagonal Salute is recognized for its exuberant exterior of volutes, scrolls, and more than 125 statues and rather sober interior, though one highlighted by a small gallery of important works in the **Sacristy** (you have to pay to enter and the entrance is through a small door to the left of the main altar). A number of ceiling paintings and portraits of the Evangelists and church doctors are all by Titian (few paintings of his can be found in Venice outside the Accademia and the Frari). On the right wall is Tintoretto's *Marriage at Cana,* one of his best.

IN SAN POLO

✪ **Scuola Grande di San Rocco (Confraternity of St. Roch).** San Polo 3058 (on Campo San Rocco adjacent to Campo dei Frari). ☎ **041-523-4864.** Admission 9,000L ($4.50) adults, 6,000L ($3) students. Apr–Oct daily 9am–5:30pm; Nov–Mar daily 10am–4pm. Vaporetto: San Tomà (walk straight ahead on Calle del Traghetto and turn right and immediately left across Campo San Tomà; walk as straight ahead as you can, on Ramo Mandoler, Calle larga Prima, and Salizzada San Rocco, which leads into the campo of the same name—look for the crimson sign behind the Frari).

This Renaissance men's clubhouse is a dazzling monument to the work of Tintoretto—the largest collection of his work anywhere. The series of the more than 50 dark and dramatic works took him more than 20 years to complete, making this the richest of the many confraternity guilds (*scuole*) that once flourished in Venice. Jacopo Robusti (1518 to 94), called Tintoretto because his father was a dyer, was a devout, unworldly man who traveled beyond Venice only once. His epic canvases are filled with phantasmagoric light and intense, mystical spirituality.

Begin upstairs just off the Great Hall in the **Sala dell'Albergo,** where the most notable of the enormous, powerful canvases is *La Crocifissione (The Crucifixion).* In the center of the gilt ceiling of the **Great Hall** itself is *Il Serpente di Bronzo (The Brazen Serpent).* Among the eight huge, sweeping paintings downstairs, each depicting a scene from the New Testament, *La Strage degli Innocenti (The Slaughter of the Innocents)* is the most noteworthy, so full of dramatic urgency and energy that the figures seem almost to tumble out of the frame. As you enter the room, it's on the opposite wall and at the far end. A useful guide to the paintings inside is posted on the wall just before the entrance to the museum. There are a few Tiepolos among the paintings, as well as a solitary work by Titian. Note that the works on or near the staircase are not by Tintoretto.

Venice's second most important and richly decorated scuola is that of San Giorgio degli Schiavoni (see below).

For Church Fans

The **Associazione Chiesa di Venezia** (☎ **041-275-0462;** www.chorus-ve.org) now curates most of Venice's top churches. Each of the association's churches charges 3,000L ($1.50) admission and (with a few exceptions) is open Monday to Saturday 10am to 5pm and Sunday 1 to 5pm. If you're a real church afficionado, the 15,000L ($8) 3-day cumulative ticket allows you to visit six of your choice: Santa Maria Gloriosa dei Frari, Il Rendatore, Santa Maria del Giglio, Santo Stefano, Santa Maria Formosa, Santa Maria dei Miracoli, San Polo, San Giacomo dell'Orio, San Stae, Alvise, Madonna dell'Orto, San Pietro di Castello, San Sebastiano, and San Marco cathedral's treasury.

Santa Maria Gloriosa dei Frari (Church of the Frari). San Polo 3072 (on Campo dei Frari). ☎ **041-522-2637** or 041-275-0462. Admission 3,000L ($1.50). Mon–Sat 9am–6pm, Sun 1–6pm. Vaporetto: San Tomà (walk straight ahead on Calle del Traghetto, then turn right and left across Campo San Tomà; walk as straight ahead as you can on Ramo Mandoler, then Calle larga Prima, and turn right when you reach the beginning of Salizzada San Rocco).

Known simply as I Frari, this immense 13th- to 14th-century Gothic church is around the corner from the Scuola Grande di San Rocco (above). Built by the Franciscans (*frari* is dialect for *frati* or "brothers"), it's one of Venice's largest churches after San Marco. The Frari has long been considered something of a memorial to the ancient glories of Venice. Since St. Francis and the order he founded emphasized prayer and poverty, it's not surprising that the church is austere both inside and out. Yet it houses a number of important works, including two of Titian's masterpieces, the more striking being the ***Assumption of the Virgin,*** over the main altar, painted when the artist was only in his late 20s. His ***Virgin of the Pesaro Family*** is in the left nave; Titian's wife posed for the figure of Mary (then died soon after in childbirth) for this work commissioned by one of Venice's most powerful families. The church's other masterwork is in the Sacristy (take the door on the right as you face the altar): Giovanni Bellini's ***Madonna and Child*** triptych, one of his finest portraits of the Madonna. There's also an almost primitive-looking wood carving by Donatello of ***St. John the Baptist.*** The grandiose **tombs** of two famous Venetians are also here: Canova (d. 1822), the Italian sculptor who led the revival of classicism, and Titian, who died in 1576 during a deadly plague. **Free tours** in English are sometimes offered by church volunteers during high season; check at the church.

IN CASTELLO

SS. Giovanni e Paolo (Sts. John and Paul). Castello 6363 (on Campo SS. Giovanni e Paolo). ☎ **041-523-5913.** Free admission. Mon–Sat 8am–12:30pm and 3–6pm, Sun 3–5:30pm. Vaporetto: Rialto.

This massive Gothic church, built by the Dominican order from the 13th to the 15th century, is tied with I Frari as second in size only to St. Mark's. An unofficial Pantheon where 25 doges are buried (a number of tombs are part of the unfinished facade), the church, commonly known as Zanipolo in Venetian dialect, is also home to a number of artistic treasures. Visit the **Cappella del Rosario** through a glass door off the left transept to see the three recently restored ceiling canvases by Paolo Veronese, particularly ***The Assumption of the Madonna.*** Also recently restored is the brilliantly colored ***Polyptych of St. Vincent Ferrer*** (ca. 1465), attributed to a young Giovanni Bellini, in the right aisle. You'll also see the **foot of St. Catherine of Siena** encased in glass.

Adjacent to the church is the **Scuola di San Marco,** an old confraternity-like association now run as a civic hospital, most noteworthy for its beautiful 15th-century Renaissance facade. Anchoring the large campo, a popular crossroads for this area, is the ✪ **statue of Bartolomeo Colleoni,** the Renaissance *condottiere* (mercenary captain) who defended Venice's interests at the height of its power and until his death in 1475. This 15th-century work by Florentine Andrea Verrocchio is his best and one of the world's great equestrian monuments.

San Zaccaria (St. Zacchary). Castello, Campo San Zaccaria. ☎ **041-522-1257.** Free admission. Daily 10am–noon and 4–6pm. Vaporetto: San Zaccaria.

Behind (east of) the Basilica di San Marco is this 9th-century Gothic church with its original 13th-century campanile (bell tower) and splendid late-15th-century Renaissance facade by Venetian Mario Codussi. Of the interior's many artworks is the recently restored ***Madonna Enthroned with Four Saints*** by Giovanni Bellini (1505), above the second altar in the left aisle. In the fan vaults of the **Cappella di San Tarasio**

Carnevale a Venezia

Venice's top event is ✪ **Carnevale** (☎ 041-241-0570; www.venicecarnival.
iti.it), a theatrical resuscitation of the bacchanalia Napoléon outlawed upon his
arrival. The festival marks the unbridled celebration preceding Lent, the period
of penitence and abstinence prior to Easter, and its name is derived from the
Latin *carnem levare* ("to take meat away"), since many people gave up meat for
the duration of Lent. Today's Carnevale events, masked balls, and costumes usually evoke that 18th-century swan song. Many of the concerts around town are
free, when baroque to samba to gospel to Dixieland jazz fill the piazze and
byways; check with the tourist office for a list of events.

The masked balls are often private; those where (exorbitantly priced) tickets
are sold are sumptuous, with candlelit banquets calling for extravagant period
costumes you rent by the day from special shops. If you'll be in town for
Carnevale and want a splurge you'll never forget, try to get tickets to the **Ballo
del Doge (Doge's Ball)** (www.ballodeldoge.com), a jet-set party held in the
16th-century Palazzo Pisani-Moretta on the Grand Canal (between the Rialto
and the Foscari), boasting Tiepolo frescoes and all the other accoutrements of
18th-century Venice. Those not invited to any ball will be just as happy having
their faces painted and watching the ongoing street theater from a ringside cafe.
There's a daily market of Carnavale masks and costumes on Campo Santo Stefano (10am to 10pm).

Although Carnevale lasts no more than 5 to 10 days today (culminating in the
Friday to Tuesday before Ash Wednesday), 18th-century revelers came from all
over Europe to take part in festivities that began months ahead, gaining
crescendo until their raucous culmination at midnight on Shrove Tuesday. As the
Venetian economy declined and its colonies and trading posts fell to other powers, the Republic in its swan song turned to fantasy and escapism. The faster its

---

are the faded ceiling frescoes of the Florentine-born artist Andrea del Castagno, the
first to bring the spirit of the Renaissance to Venice. Apply to the sacristan to see the
Coro delle Suore (Sisters' Choir), with works by Tintoretto, Titian, Il Vecchio, Van
Dyck, and Bassano. The paintings aren't labeled, but the sacristan will point out the
names of the artists.

Museo Storico Navale (Naval History Museum) & Arsenale (Arsenal). Castello 2148
(on Campo San Biasio). ☎ **041-520-0276.** Admission 3,000L ($1.50). Mon–Fri 8:45am–
1:30pm, Sat 8:45am–1pm. Vaporetto: Arsenale.

The **Naval History Museum's** most fascinating exhibit is its collection of model ships.
It was once common practice for vessels to be built not from blueprints but from precise scale models like you see here. The prize of the collection is a model of the legendary *Bucintoro,* the lavish ceremonial barge of the doges. Another section of the
museum contains an array of historic vessels. Walk along the canal as it branches off
from the museum to the Padiglione delle Navi (Ships' Pavilion), where the historic
vessels are displayed.

To reach the **Arsenal** shipyards from here, walk up the Arsenale Canal and cross the
wooden bridge to Campo del'Arsenale and you'll soon reach the land gate of the Arsenale, not open to the public. The marble-columned Renaissance gate with the republic's winged lion above is flanked by four ancient lions, booty brought at various times
from Greece and points farther east. It was founded in 1104 and at the height of

decline was, the longer and more unlicensed became its anything-goes merry-making. Masks became ubiquitous, affording anonymity and pardoning 1,000 sins. They permitted the fishmonger to attend the ball and dance with the baroness, the properly married to carry on as if they were not. The doges condemned it and the popes denounced it, but nothing could dampen Carnevale spirit until Napoléon arrived in 1797.

Resuscitated in 1980 by local powers to fill the empty winter months, Carnevale is calmer nowadays, though just barely. The born-again festival got off to a shaky start, met at first with indifference and skepticism, but in the years since, it has grown from strength to strength. The new Carnevale is at its dazzling best now with 2 decades under its belt, a harlequin patchwork of musical and cultural events, many of them free. At any given moment, musical events are staged in any of the city's dozens of piazze—from reggae and zydeco to jazz to baroque and chamber music—and special art exhibits are mounted at museums and galleries. The recent involvement of international corporate commercial sponsors has met with a mixed reception, though it seems to be the direction of the future.

Carnevale isn't for those who dislike crowds—the crowds are what it's all about. Truly enjoying Carnevale means giving in to the spontaneity of magic and surprise around every corner, the mystery behind every mask. Period masks and costumes are everywhere. Groups travel in coordinated getups ranging from a contemporary passel of Felliniesque clowns to the court of the Sun King in all its wigged-out drag-queen best. The places to be seen in costume (only appropriate costumes need apply) are the historic cafes lining Piazza San Marco, the Florian being the unquestioned Command Post. Don't expect to be seated in full view at a window seat unless your costume is straight off the stage of the local opera house.

Venice's power employed 16,000 workers who turned out merchant and wartime galleys on an early version of the assembly line at speeds and in volumes unknown until modern times. Occupying one-fifth of the city's total acreage, the Arsenal was once the very source of the republic's maritime power. It's now used as a military zone, as closed as Fort Knox to the curious.

Scuola di San Giorgio degli Schiavoni. Castello 3259 (on Calle Furlani). ☎ **041-522-8828.** Admission 5,000L ($2.50). Tues–Sat 9:30am–12:30pm and 3:30–6:30pm, Sun 9:30am–12:30pm. Often closed afternoons in Aug. Vaporetto: San Zaccaria.

At the St. Antonino Bridge (Fondamenta dei Furlani) is Venice's second most important guild house. The Schiavoni were a wealthy trading colony of Dalmatian merchants who built their own *scuola* (the coast of Dalmatia, today in Croatia, was once ruled by the Greeks and thus the scuola's alternative name of San Giorgio dei Greci). Between 1502 and 1509, Vittore Carpaccio (himself of Dalmatian descent) painted a **pictorial cycle** of nine masterpieces illustrating episodes from the lives of St. George and St. Jerome, Dalmatia's patron saints. These appealing pictures freeze in time moments in the lives of the saints: St. George charges his ferocious dragon on a field littered with half-eaten bodies and skulls (a horror story with a happy ending); St. Jerome leads his lion into a monastery, frightening the friars; St. Augustine has just taken up his pen to reply to a letter from St. Jerome when he and his little dog are transfixed by a miraculous light, and a voice telling them of St. Jerome's death.

IN GUIDECCA & SAN GIORGIO

San Giorgio Maggiore. On the island of San Giorgio Maggiore, across St. Mark's Basin from Piazzetta San Marco. ☎ **041-522-7827.** Free admission. Apr–Oct Mon–Sat 9:30am–12:30pm and 2:30–6:30pm, Sun 2:30–6:30pm; Nov–Mar Mon–Sat 10am–12:30pm and 2:30–4:40pm, Sun 2:30–4:40pm. Vaporetto: Take the Giudecca-bound no. 82 from Riva degli Schiavoni and get off at the first stop, the island of San Giorgio Maggiore.

This church, on the island of San Giorgio Maggiore, is one of the masterpieces of Andrea Palladio, the great Renaissance architect from nearby Vicenza (see chapter 8). Best known for his country villas for Venice's wealthy merchants, Palladio was commissioned to build two churches (the other is the Redentore on neighboring Giudecca), beginning with San Giorgio, designed in 1565 and completed in 1610. To impose a classical facade on the traditional church structure, he designed two interlocking facades, with repeating triangles, rectangles, and columns that are harmoniously proportioned. Palladio reinterpreted the church's interior, begun as early as the 10th century, with whitewashed surfaces, stark but majestic. The main altar is flanked by two epic paintings by an elderly Tintoretto, *The Fall of Manna* to the left and the more noteworthy *Last Supper* to the right, famous for its chiaroscuro. Through the doorway to the right of the choir leading to the **Cappella dei Morti (Chapel of the Dead)** you'll find Tintoretto's *Deposition.* To the left of the choir is an elevator you can take to the top of the **campanile** (3,000L/$1.50) to experience an unforgettable view of the island itself, the lagoon, and the Palazzo Ducale and Piazza San Marco across the way. A handful of remaining Benedictine monks gather for Sunday mass at 11am, sung in Gregorian chant (you can hear it only if you arrive on time and stay for the whole mass).

IN CANNAREGGIO

Ca' d'Oro (Galleria Giorgio Franchetti). Cannaregio between 3931 and 3932 (on Calle Ca' d'Oro north of the Ponte Rialto). ☎ **041-523-8790.** Admission 6,000L ($3) adults, 3,000L ($1.50) students 18 to 25, free under 12. Daily 8:15am–2pm (sometimes to 7pm in summer). Vaporetto: Ca' d'Oro.

The 15th-century Ca' d'Oro is one of the best preserved and most impressive of the hundreds of patrician palazzi lining the Grand Canal. After the Palazzo Ducale, it's the city's finest example of Venetian Gothic architecture. A restoration of its delicate pink-and-white facade (its name, the "Golden Palace," refers to the gilt-covered facade that faded long ago) was completed in 1995. Inside, the ornate beamed ceilings and palatial trappings provide an attention-grabbing backdrop for the private collection of former owner Baron Franchetti, who bequeathed his palazzo and artwork to the city during World War I.

The core collection, expanded over the years, now includes sculptures, furniture, 16th-century Flemish tapestries, an impressive collection of bronzes (12th to 16th century), and a gallery whose most important canvases are Andrea Mantegna's *San Sebastiano* and Titian's *Venus at the Mirror,* as well as lesser paintings by Tintoretto, Carpaccio, Van Dyck, Giorgione, and Jan Steen. For a delightful break, step out onto the palazzo's **loggia,** overlooking the Grand Canal, for a view up and down the aquatic waterway and across to the Pescheria, a timeless vignette of an unchanged city. Off the loggia is a small but worthy ceramics collection open 10am to noon.

Santa Maria dei Miracoli. Cannareggio, Rio dei Miracoli. ☎ **041-275-0462.** Admission 3,000 ($1.50). Mon–Sat 10am–5pm, Sun 1–5pm. Vaporetto: Rialto (midway between the Ponte Rialto and Campo SS. Giovanni e Paolo).

At a charming canal-crossing hidden in a corner of the residential section of Canareggio, the small 15th-century Miracoli is once again open after a laborious 10-year renovation. It's one of the most attractive religious buildings in Europe, with one side of the precious polychrome-marbled facade running alongside a canal, creating shimmering reflections. The architect, Pietro Lombardo (a local artisan whose background in monuments and tombs is obvious) went on to become one of the founding fathers of the Venetian Renaissance. The less romantic are inclined to compare it to a large tomb with a dome, but the untold couples who've made this perfectly proportioned gem their choice for weddings will dispel such insensitivity.

The small square in front is the perfect place for gondolas to drop off and pick up the newlyweds. The inside is intricately decorated with early Renaissance marble reliefs, its pastel palette of pink, gray, and white marbles making an appropriately elegant venue for all those weddings. In the 1470s, an image of the Virgin Mary was responsible for a series of miracles (including bringing back to life someone who'd spent half an hour at the bottom of Giudecca Canal) that led pilgrims to leave gifts and, eventually, enough donations to have this church built. Look for the icon now displayed over the main altar.

Il Ghetto (Jewish Ghetto). Cannaregio, Campo dei Ghetto Nuovo. Vaporetto: Guglie or San Marcuola (from either stop or if walking from the train station area, locate the Ponte delle Guglie; walking away from the Grand Canal along the Fondamenta di Cannaregio, look for a doorway on your right with Hebrew etched across the threshold; this is the entrance to Calle del Ghetto Vecchio that leads to Campo del Ghetto Nuovo.)

Venice's relationship with her longtime Jewish community has fluctuated over time from acceptance to borderline tolerance, attitudes often influenced by the fear that Jewish moneylenders and merchants would infiltrate other sectors of the Republic's commerce under a government that thrived on secrecy and control. In 1516, 700 Jews were forced to move to this then-remote northwestern corner of Venice, to an abandoned site of a 14th-century foundry (*ghetto,* old Venetian dialect for "foundry," soon was used throughout Europe and the world to depict isolated minority groups).

As was commonplace with most of Venice's hundreds of islands, this too was totally surrounded by water. Its two access points were controlled at night and early morning by heavy gates manned by Christian guards (paid for by the Jews), protecting and segregating its inhabitants. Within one century, the community grew to more than 5,000, representing many languages and cultures. Though the original **Ghetto Vecchio (Old Ghetto)** was expanded to include the **Ghetto Nuovo (New Ghetto)** and later the **Ghetto Nuovissimo (Newest Ghetto),** land was limited and quarters were always cramped. A small, ever-diminishing community of Jewish families continues to live here today: Some 2,000 are said to live in all of Venice and Mestre together.

Museo Communità Ebraica. Cannaregio 2902 (on Campo del Ghetto Nuovo). ☎ **041-715-359.** Museum admission 5,000L ($2.50) adults, 3,000L ($1.50) students; museum and synagogue tour 12,000L ($6) adults, 9,000L ($4.50) students. Museum Apr–Sept Sun–Fri 10am–7pm; Oct–Mar Sun–Fri daily 10am–5:30pm. Synagogue tours hourly 10:30am–4:30pm. Vaporetto: Guglie.

The only way to visit any of the area's **five 16th-century synagogues** is through one of the Museo Communità Ebraica's frequent organized tours conducted in English. Your guide will elaborate on the commercial and political climate of the times, the unique "skyscraper" architecture (overcrowding resulted in many buildings having as many as seven low-ceilinged stories with no elevators), and the daily lifestyle of the Jewish community until the 1797 arrival of Napoléon, who declared the Jews free citizens. Venice's first kosher restaurant, **Gam Gam,** recently opened on Fondamenta di Cannaregio 1122 (☎ **041-715-284**), near the entrance to the Ghetto and nearby the Guglie vaporetto stop. Owned/run by Orthodox Jews from New York, it serves lunch and dinner every day except Saturday, with an early Friday closing after lunch.

ESPECIALLY FOR KIDS

It goes without saying that a **gondola ride** will be a thrill for any child or adult. If that's too expensive, consider the convenient and far less expensive alternative: ✪ **vaporetto 1.** They offer two entirely different experiences, that of seeing Venice through the back door (and a ride past Marco Polo's house), and a tool down its aquatic Main Street, the Grand Canal, respectively. Look for the ambulance boat, the garbage boat, the firefighters boat, the funeral boat, even the Coca-Cola and McDonald's delivery boats. Best sightings are the special gondolas filled with flowers and rowed by gondolieri in livery taking the happy bride and groom to the church.

Judging from the squeals of delight, **feeding the pigeons in Piazza San Marco** (purchase a bag of corn and you'll be draped in pigeons in a nanosecond; these birds have radar) could be the epitome of your child's visit to Venice, and it's the optimal photo op. Be sure your child won't be startled by the all the fluttering and flapping (or the scrabbling feet; that's what I remember from age 11 when my parents did this to me). A jaunt to the neighboring island of **Murano** can be as educational as recreational—follow the signs to any *fornace* where a glass-blowing performance of the island's 1,000-year-old art is free entertainment. But be ready for the almost guaranteed sales pitch that follows.

Before you leave town, take the elevator to the top of the **Campanile di San Marco** (the city's highest structure) for a pigeon's-eye view of Venice's rooftops and church cupolas, or get up close and personal to the *Triumphal Quadriga* on the facade of the Basilica San Marco. Its outdoor loggia with a view holds the copies of the famous *quadriga* (you can see the real ones in the Basilica's Museo Marciano), but the view from here is something hard for you or your children to forget.

Many children enjoy the **Museo Navale** and the **Arsenale** with its ship models and old vessels, and the many historic artifacts in the **Museo Correr** that are a vestige of when Venice was a world unto itself.

ORGANIZED TOURS

Most of the central travel agencies will have posters in their windows advertising half- and full-day walking tours of the city's sights. Most of these tours are piggy-backed onto those organized by **American Express** (see "Fast Facts: Venice," above) and should cost the same: about 40,000L ($22) for a 2-hour tour and 65,000L ($35) for a full day, per person.

A welcome newcomer is the **Enjoy Venice** (www.enjoyvenice.com) walking tour: 30,000L ($16) or 25,000L ($14) for those under 26. Just show up Monday to Saturday for the 10am departure at the Thomas Cook office off the Rialto (Castello 5144) or call ☎ **800-274-819** toll free from anywhere in Italy. Free organized tours of the Basilica di San Marco and some of the other churches can be erratic, as they're given by volunteers.

Organized 3- to 4-hour visits to "**The Islands of the Venetian Lagoon**" include brief stops on Murano, Burano, and Torcello (see "Exploring Venice's Islands," at the end of this chapter).

6 Shopping

THE SHOPPING SCENE

A mix of low-end trinket stores and middle-market to upscale boutiques lines the narrow zigzagging **Mercerie** running north between Piazza San Marco and the Ponte Rialto. More expensive clothing and gift boutiques make for great window-shopping on **Calle Larga XXII Marzo,** beginning west of Piazza San Marco and wending its way to the expansive Campo Santo Stefano near the Accademia. The narrow **Frezzeria,** also west of the piazza and not far from Piazza San Marco, offers a grab bag of bars, souvenir shops, and tony clothing stores.

In a city that for centuries has thrived almost exclusively on tourism, remember this: Where you buy cheap, you get cheap. You'll find few bargains, and there's nothing to compare with Florence's San Lorenzo Market; the nonproduce part of the Rialto Market is as good as it gets, where you'll find cheap T-shirts, glow-in-the-dark plastic gondolas, and tawdry glass trinkets. Venetians aren't known for bargaining. You'll stand a better chance when paying in cash or buying more than one of some item.

Venice is uniquely famous for several local crafts that have been produced here for centuries and are hard to get elsewhere: the **glassware** from the island of Murano, the delicate **lace** from Burano, and the *cartapesta* (papier-mâché) **Carnevale** masks you'll find in endless *botteghe,* where you can watch artisans paint amid their wares.

Now here's the bad news: There's such an overwhelming sea of cheap glass gew-gaws it becomes something of a turn-off (shipping and insurance make most things unaffordable; the alternative is to hand-carry something so fragile). There are so few women left on Burano willing to spend countless hours keeping alive the art of lace-making that the few pieces you'll see not produced by machine in Hong Kong are sold at stratospheric prices; ditto on the truly high-quality glass (though trinkets can be cheap and fun). Still, you can find exceptions in all of the above, and when you find them you'll know.

SHOPPING A TO Z

ANTIQUES   The interesting **Mercatino dell'Antiquariato (Antiques Fair)** takes place three times yearly in the charming Campo San Maurizio between Piazza San Marco and Campo Santo Stefano. Dates change yearly for the 3-day weekend market but generally are the first weekend of April, mid-September, and the weekend before Christmas. More than 100 vendors sell everything from sublime Murano glass to quirky dust collectors. Early birds may find reasonably priced finds like Murano candy dishes from the 1950s, Venetian-pearl glass beads older still, old Italian posters advertising Campari-sponsored regattas, or postcards of Venice that could be from the 1930s or the 1830s—things change so little. Those for whom price is less an issue might pick up antique lace by the yard or a singular museum-quality piece of hand-blown glass from a local master.

CRAFTS   The small **Murano Art Shop,** San Marco 1232, on the store-lined Frezzeria, parallel to the western border of, and close to, Piazza San Marco (☎ **041-523-3851;** Vaporetto: San Marco), is a cultural experience. At this precious shop, every inch of wall space is draped with the whimsical crafts of the city's most creative artisans. Fusing the timeless with the contemporary and whimsical—with a nod to the magic and romance of Venice past—the results are a dramatic and ever-evolving collection of masks, puppets, music boxes, marionettes, costume jewelry, and the like. It's all expensive, but this rivals a visit to the Doge's Palace.

When it seems as if every gift-store window is awash with collectible bisque-faced dolls in elaborate pinafores and headdresses, go to **Bambole di Trilly,** Castello 4974, on Fondamenta dell'Osmarin, off Campo San Provolo on your way east out of Piazza San Marco toward San Zaccaria (☎ **041-521-2579;** Vaporetto: San Marco), where the hand-sewn wardrobes of rich Venetian fabrics and painstakingly painted faces are particularly exquisite; the perfect souvenir starts at 35,000L ($21) in this well-stocked work space.

EMBROIDERED LINENS   A doge's ransom will buy you an elaborately worked tablecloth at **Jesurum,** San Marco 4856, on the busy Mercerie shopping strip

Two Venice Shopping Strategies

There are two rules of thumb for shopping in Venice: If you have the good fortune of continuing on to Florence or Rome, save shopping for clothing, leather goods, and accessories for there, as most things are more expensive here. However, if you happen on something that strikes you, consider it twice on the spot (not back at your hotel), then buy it. Don't plan on returning: In this web of alleys you may never find that shop again.

zigzagging from Piazza San Marco to the Ponte Rialto (☎ **041-520-6085;** Vaporetto: San Marco), but some of the small items make gorgeous affordable gifts for discerning friends for under 20,000L ($12): drawstring pouches for your baubles, hand-embroidered linen cocktail napkins in different colors, or hand-finished doilies and linen coasters.

FOOD   Food lovers will find charmingly packaged food products for themselves or friends at **Giacamo Rizzo,** Cannaregio 5778, on Calle San Giovanni Grisostomo, northeast of the Ponte Rialto (☎ **041-522-2824;** Vaporetto: Rialto). Pasta made in the shape of gondolas, colorful Carnavale hats, and dozens of other imaginatively shaped possibilities (colored and flavored with squash, beet, spinach) cost 7,000L to 13,000L ($3.50 to $7) per package. Those with a sweet tooth should head in the opposite direction, to **Pasticceria Marchini,** San Marco 2769, at the Ponte San Maurizio, just before Campo Santo Stefano (☎ **041-522-9109;** Vaporetto: S. Samuele or Giglio). A selection of traditional cookies is beautifully prepackaged for traveling—the delicate *baicoli,* cornmeal raisin *zaleti,* and S-shaped *buranelli.*

GLASS   Cut to the chase and visit the spacious emporium of quality glass items at **Marco Polo,** San Marco 1644, on on the Frezzerie, just west of Piazza San Marco (☎ **041-522-9295;** Vaporetto: San Marco). The front half of the first floor offers a variety of small gifts (candy dishes, glass-topped medicine boxes, paperweights). Cheap they are not, but no one else has such a lovely representation of handblown Murano glassware. Consider a pair of lovely Murano drinking glasses or champagne flutes. Glass beads are called "Venetian Pearls," and an abundance of exquisite antique and reproduced baubles are the draw at **Anticlea,** Castello 4719, on Campo San Provolo, in the direction of San Zaccaria (☎ **041-528-6946;** Vaporetto: S. Zaccaria). Once used for trading in Venice's far-flung colonies, they now fill the coffers of this small shop east of Piazza San Marco, sold singly or already strung. The open-air stall of **Susie and Andrea,** Riva degli Schiavoni, near the Pensione Wildner (just ask), has handcrafted beads that are new, well made and strung, and moderately priced. The stall operates from February to November.

LEATHER   You usually think of Florence when thinking of Italian leather goods. But the plethora of mediocre-to-refined shoe stores in Venice is testimony to the tradition of small shoe factories along the nearby Brenta Canal that supplies most of Italy and much of the world with its made-in-Italy footwear. If you're not going on to Florence and are in the market for a handbag or small leather goods, the two-storied **Marforio,** on the Merceria Due Aprile, San Marco 5033, near the Ponte Rialto (☎ **041-25-734;** Vaporetto: Rialto), stocks small leather goods and accessories as well as bags according to color and style (evening, casual, shoulder-strapped, back-pack style). Not a good place just to browse, but a great place if you know what you're looking for. There are some designer labels, but less expensive lines are abundant and the selection is probably the largest in Venice.

MASKS   A shortage of mask *bottegas* in Venice isn't your problem; the challenge is ferreting out the few exceptionally talented artists producing one-of-a-kind theatrical pieces. Only the quality-conscious should shop at **La Bottega dei Mascareri,** San Polo 80, at northern end of the Ponte Rialto (☎ **041-522-3857;** Vaporetto: Rialto), where the charming Boldrin brothers' least elaborate masks begin under 25,000L ($13). Anyone who thinks a mask is a mask is a mask should come here first for a look-see.

MUSIC   If you attended any of the many marvelous concerts in Venice's churches and scuole, you'll want to bring some of the musical magic home with you. **Nalesso,** San Marco 2765, on your left just before Campo Santo Stefano if you're arriving from Piazza San Marco (☎ **041-520-3329;** Vaporetto: S. Samuele or Giglio), specializes in classical musical recording, particularly the entire works of Vivaldi and 18th-century Venetian music. You can also pick up tickets here to most of the concerts around town.

7 Venice After Dark

Visit one of the tourist offices for current English-language schedules of the month's special events. The monthly *Ospite di Venezia* is distributed free and extremely helpful but usually available only in the more expensive hotels. If you're looking for nocturnal action, you're in the wrong town. Your best bet is to sit in the moonlit Piazza San Marco and listen to the caffès' outdoor orchestras, with the illuminated basilica before you—the perfect opera set.

THE PERFORMING ARTS

Venice has a long and rich tradition of classical music, and there's always a concert going on somewhere. Several churches regularly host classical music concerts (with an emphasis on the baroque) by local and international artists. This was, after all, the home of Vivaldi, and the ✪ **Chiesa di Vivaldi** (officially the Chiesa Santa Maria della Pietà), Riva degli Schiavoni (between Rio dei Greci and Rio della Pietà), is the most popular venue for the music of Vivaldi and his contemporaries. A number of other churches and confraternities (like San Stefano, San Stae, the Scuola di San Giovanni Evangelista, and the Scuola di San Rocco) also host concerts, but the Vivaldi Church, where the red priest was the choral director, offers perhaps the highest-quality ensembles (with tickets slightly more expensive). If you're lucky, they'll be performing *Le Quattro Staggioni (The Four Seasons)*. Tickets are sold at the church's box office (☎ **041-523-1096** or 041-917-257; www.vivaldi.it) on Riva degli Schiavoni, at the front desk of the Metropole Hotel next door, or at many of the hotels around town; they're usually 40,000L ($20) adults or 20,000L ($10) students. Information and schedules are available from the tourist office; tickets for most concerts should be bought in advance, though the frequency of concerts mean they rarely sell out.

The city stood still in shock as the famous ✪ **Teatro La Fenice,** San Marco 1965, on Campo San Fantin (☎ **041-521-0161** or 041-3265-8010; www.teatrolafenice.it), went up in flames in January 1996. For centuries it was the city's principal stage for world-class opera, music, theater, and ballet. Carpenters and artisans were on standby to begin working around the clock to re-create the *teatro* (built in 1836) according to archival designs; however, little progress has been made in all this time because political factions have been bickering. The Orchestra and Coro della Fenice now perform in a substitute venue, a year-round tent-like structure called the **PalaFenice** (☎ **041-520-4010**), in the unlikely area of the Tronchetto parking facilities near Piazzale Roma, convenient to many vaporetto lines. To say it ain't the same is something of an understatement. Tickets for the PalaFenice start at about 30,000L ($15), and the box office is open Monday to Friday 9am to 6pm.

CAFFÈS

Venice is a quiet town in the evening and offers very little in the way of nightlife. For tourists and locals alike, Venetian nightlife mainly centers around the many caffè/bars in one of the world's most remarkable piazzas: Piazza San Marco (Napoléon called it the "most beautiful drawing room of the world"). It's also the most expensive and touristed place to linger over a Campari or cappuccino but a splurge that should not be dismissed too readily.

The nostalgic 18th-century **Caffè Florian,** San Marco 56A–59A, on the south side of the piazza, is the most famous (closed Wednesday in winter) and most theatrical inside; have a Bellini (*prosecco* and fresh peach nectar) at the back bar and spend half what you'd pay at an indoor table; alfresco seating is even more expensive when the band plays but worth every lira for the million-dollar scenario. It's said that when Casanova escaped from the prisons in the Doge's Palace, he stopped here for a coffee before fleeing Venice. On the opposite side of the square at San Marco 133–134 is the old-world **Caffè Lavena** (closed Tuesday in winter) and at no. 120 is **Caffè Quadri** (closed Monday in winter). At all these spots, a cappuccino, tea, or Coca-Cola at a table will set you back about 10,000L ($5). But no one will rush you, and if the sun is warm or the moon is bright and the orchestras are playing, I can think of no more beautiful public open-air salon in the world.

Around the corner (no. 11) and in front of the pink-and-white Palazzo Ducale with the lagoon on your right is the best deal, ✪ **Caffè Chioggia** (closed Sunday). Come here at midnight and watch the Moors strike the hour atop the Clock Tower from your outside table, while the quartet or pianist plays everything from quality jazz to pop until the wee hours (and without taking a break every 6 minutes; they also take requests). If the weather is chilly or inclement, or for no reason other than to revel in the history and drama of Venice's grand dame hotel, dress up, look confident, and stroll into the Danieli's landmark lobby's **Bar Dandolo,** Castello 4196, on Riva degli Schiavoni east of Piazza San Marco. Tea or coffee will set you back only 8,000L ($4) and you can sit forever, taking in what once was the former residential palazzo of a 15th-century doge. A pianist plays 7 to 9pm and 10pm to 12:30am. Drinks are far more expensive; ask to see the price list before ordering.

CLUBS, BARS & GELATERIE

Although Venice boasts an old and prominent university, clubs and discos barely enjoy their 15 minutes of popularity before changing hands or closing down (some are open only in summer). Young Venetians tend to go to the Lido or mainland Mestre.

For just plain hanging out in the late afternoon and early evening, popular squares that serve as meeting points are **Campo San Bartolomeo,** at the foot of the Ponte Rialto, and nearby **Campo San Luca;** you'll see Venetians of all ages milling about engaged in animated conversation, particularly 5pm to dinnertime. In late-night hours, for low prices and a low level of pretension, there's huge open **Campo Santa Margherita,** about halfway between the train station and Ca' Rezzonico. Look for the popular **Green Pub** (no. 3053), **Bareto Rosso** (no. 2963), and **Bar Salus** (no. 3112). **Campo Santo Stefano** is also worth a visit, namely to sit and sample the goods at the **Bar/Gelateria Paolin** (no. 2962), one of the city's best ice-cream sources. Its runner-up, **Gelateria Nico,** is at Dorsoduro 922, on the Zattere, south of the Accademia. For occasional evenings of live music, cabaret, or just a relaxed late-night hangout for a drink and a bite, consider the ever-popular **Le Bistrot de Venise** (see "Great Deals on Dining," above).

Note: Most bars are open Monday to Saturday 8pm to midnight.

The **Devil's Forest Pub,** San Marco 5185, on Calle Stagneri (☎ **041-520-0623;** www.devilsforest.com; Vaporetto: San Marco), offers the outsider an authentic chance to take in the convivial atmosphere and find out where Venetians do hang out. It's popular for lunch with the neighborhood merchants and shop owners and ideal for relaxed socializing over a beer and a host of games like backgammon, chess, and Trivial Pursuit. A variety of fresh sandwiches runs 6,000L to 8,000L ($3 to $4). It's open daily 10am to 1am. **Bácaro Jazz,** San Marco 5546, just north of Campo San Bartolomeo (☎ **041-285-249;** Vaporetto: Rialto), is a happening tapas bar with restaurant seating in the back (tasty Venetian cuisine from 6,000L/$3). It's open Thursday to Tuesday 11am to 2am (happy hour 3 to 8pm).

Good food at reasonable prices would be enough to regularly pack **Paradiso Perduto,** Cannaregio 2540, on Fondamenta della Misericordia (☎ **041-720-581;** Vaporetto: Ferrovie), but its biggest draw is the live jazz performed on a small stage several nights a week. Popular with Americans and other foreigners living in Venice, this bar was once largely devoid of tourists, primarily because of its hard-to-find location, but lately it looks as if the word is out. The good selection of well-prepared pizzas and pastas is under 10,000L ($5); arrive early for a table. It's open Thursday to Tuesday 7pm to 1 and sometimes 2am.

DANCE CLUBS

Venice is a quiet town at night and offers little in the line of dance clubs. Evenings are best spent lingering over a late dinner, having a pint in a *birreria,* or nursing a glass of *prosecco* in one of Piazza San Marco's tony outdoor cafes. Dance clubs barely enjoy their 15 minutes of popularity before changing hands or closing; some of those that have survived are open only in summer.

University-age Venetians tend to frequent the Lido or mainland Mestre, but if you really need that disco fix, you're best off at **Piccolo Mondo,** Dorsoduro 1056, near the Accademia (☎ **041-520-0371;** Vaporetto: Accademia). Billed as a disco/pub, it serves sandwiches during lunch to the tune of America's latest dance music and offers a happy hour in the late afternoon in winter. But the only reason you'd want to come is if you want a disco night (summer only); the club is frequented mostly by curious foreigners and the young to not-so-young Venetians who seek them out. It's open daily: 10pm to 4am in summer and 10am to 4pm and 5 to 8pm in winter. There's live music and a 20,000L ($10) cover.

Another that seems to be surviving is **Casanova,** Cannaregio 158a, on Lista di Spagna near the train station (☎ **041-275-0199** or 041-534-7479; www.casanova.it). The bar and restaurant open at 6pm, but at 10pm the bar becomes a disco open to 4am (the restaurant stays open to around midnight). Admission is often free (if you arrive before midnight), though sometimes there's a 10,000L ($5) or more cover that includes a drink. Wednesday is Salsa night; Thursday is rock, pop, alternative, and indie; Friday is dance music; and Saturday brings the house and progressive DJ.

GAY & LESBIAN BARS

There are no gay bars in Venice, but you'll find some in nearby Padua, a lovely old city about 35 minutes from Venice by train (see chapter 8 and see *Frommer's Gay & Lesbian Europe*). However, Venice does have a local division of a government-affiliated agency, **Arci-Gay Arci-Lesbica,** Santa Croce 1507, on Campo San Giacomo dell'Orio (☎ **041-721-842** or 041-721-197). It serves as a home base for the gay community, with info on AIDS services, gay-friendly accommodations, and such. The best hours to call (it's hard to find) are Wednesday, Thursday, and Saturday 6 to 10pm.

THE CASINO

May to October, the **Casino Municipale di Venezia,** in the Palazzo Vendramin Calergi, Cannaregio 2400, on Fondamenta Vendramin (☎ **041/529-7111;** Vaporetto:

Marcuola), moves to its nondescript summer location on the Lido, where a visit isn't as strongly recommended as during winter, when it's housed in this handsome 15th-century palazzo on the Grand Canal. Venice's tradition of gambling goes back to its glory days, and they live on here in this august Renaissance palace built by Mauro Codussi. Though not of the caliber of Monte Carlo, and occasionally slow on a midweek winter's night, this is one of only four casinos on Italian territory—and what a remarkable stage setting it is! Richard Wagner lived and died in a wing of this palazzo in 1883. Check with your hotel before setting forth; some offer free passes for guests. Otherwise, if you're not a gambler or curiosity seeker, it may not be worth the 18,000L ($9) admission. A passport is required and the casino is open daily 4pm to 2:30am.

8 Exploring Venice's Islands

Venice shares its lagoon with three other principal islands: **Murano, Burano,** and **Torcello.** Guided tours of the three are operated by a dozen agencies with docks on Riva degli Schiavoni/Piazzetta San Marco (all interchangeable), but I'd recommend a do-it-yourself visit (easy and cheaper). The 3- and 4-hour tours run 25,000L to 40,000L ($13 to $20), usually include a visit to a Murano glass factory (you can easily do that on your own, with less of a hard-sell), and leave daily around 9:30am and 2:30pm (times change; check in advance).

You can also visit the islands on your own conveniently and easily using the *vaporetti.* Lines 12, 13, 41, 42, and the *navetta* make the journey to Murano from Fondamente Nove (on the north side of Castello), and line 12 continues on to Burano and Torcello. You can get a special 15,000L ($8) **Laguna Nord day ticket** to cover the entire journey. The islands are small and easy to navigate, but check the schedule for the next island-to-island departure (usually hourly) and eventually your return so you don't spend most of your day waiting for connections.

MURANO & ITS GLASS

The island of **Murano** has long been famous throughout the world for the products of its glass factories, but there's little to find in variety or prices you won't find in Venice. A visit to the **Museo Vetrario (Museum of Glass Art),** Fondamenta Giustinian 8 (☎ **041-739-586**), will put the island's centuries-old legacy into perspective and is recommended for those considering major buys. Hours are Thursday to Tuesday 10am to 5pm (to 4pm November to March), and admission is 8,000L ($4) adults and 5,000L ($2.50) students and over 65 or free with the cumulative San Marco ticket (see earlier in this chapter). Dozens of *fornaci* (furnaces) offer free shows of mouth-blown glassmaking almost invariably hitched to a hard-sell ("No obligation! Really!") tour of the factory outlet. These retail showrooms of delicate glassware can be enlightening or boring, depending on your frame of mind. Almost all the places ship, often doubling the price. On the other hand, these pieces are instant heirlooms.

Murano also has two worthy churches: **San Pietro Martire,** with its altarpieces by Tintoretto, Veronese, and Giovanni Bellini, and the ancient **Santa Maria e Donato,** with an intricate Byzantine exterior apse and a 6th-century pulpit and columns inside resting on a fantastic 12th-century inlaid floor.

BURANO & ITS LACE

Lace is the claim to fame of tiny, colorful **Burano,** a craft kept alive for centuries by the wives of fishermen waiting for their husbands to return from sea. It's still worth a trip if you have time to stroll in the island's opera-set of back streets, whose canals are lined with the remarkably brightly colored simple homes of *buranesi* fisherman. The local government continues its attempt to keep its centuries-old lace legacy alive with subsidized classes. Visit the **Scuola di Merletti (School of Lace Making),** Piazza Galuppi (☎ **041-730-034**), to understand why anything so exquisite shouldn't be left to fade into extinction. It's open Wednesday to Monday 10am to 5pm (to 4pm November to March), and admission is 8,000L ($4) adults and 5,000L ($2.50) children or free with the cumulative San Marco ticket (see "A Money-Saving Tip" near the beginning of the "Seeing the Sights," section earlier in this chapter).

TORCELLO & ITS MOSAICS

Nearby **Torcello** is perhaps the most charming of the islands. It was the first of the lagoon islands to be called home by the mainland population fleeing persecution (from here they moved to the area around the Ponte Rialto), but today it consists of little more than one long canal leading from the *vaporetto* landing past sad-sack vineyards to a clump of buildings at its center.

Torcello boasts the oldest Venetian monument, the **Cattedrale di Torcello (Santa Maria Assunta),** whose foundation dates from the 7th century (☎ **041-270-2464**). It's famous for its outstanding 11th- to 12-century Byzantine mosaics—a *Madonna and Child* in the apse and a *Last Judgment* on the west wall—rivaling those of Ravenna and St. Mark's Basilica. The cathedral is open daily 10:30am to 5:30pm (shorter hours in winter), and admission is 5,000L ($2.50). Also of interest is the adjacent 11th-century church dedicated to **St. Fosca** and a small **archaeological museum** (☎ **041-730-761**); both hours are the same as the cathedral's, but the museum is closed Monday. Museum admission is 3,000L ($1.50).

Peaceful Torcello is uninhabited except for a handful of land-working families and is a favorite **picnic spot** (you'll have to bring the food from Venice, since on the island there are no stores, and only one bar/trattoria and one rather expensive restaurant—the **Cipriani,** of Hemingway fame). Once the tour groups have left, it offers a very special moment of solitude and escape when St. Mark's bottleneck becomes oppressive.

THE LIDO & ITS BEACHES

Though a convenient 15-minute *vaporetto* ride from San Marco, Venice's **Lido beaches** aren't much to write home about. The Adriatic has had pollution problems in recent years, and for bathing and sun-worshiping there are much nicer beaches in Italy. But the parade of wealthy Italian and foreign tourists (plus a good number of Venetian families with children) who frequent this *litorale* throughout summer is an interesting sight indeed, though you'll find many of them at the elitist beaches affiliated with such deluxe hotels as the legendary Excelsior and the Hotel des Bains.

There are two beach areas at the Lido. **Bucintoro** is at the opposite end of Gran Viale Santa Maria Elisabetta (referred to as the Gran Viale) from the *vaporetto* station Santa Elisabetta. It's a 10-minute walk; walk straight ahead along Gran Viale to reach the beach. **San Nicolò,** a mile away, can be reached by bus B. You'll have to pay 20,000L ($10) per person (standard procedure at Italy's beaches) for use of the cabins (you can't change on the beach) and umbrella rental. Alternatively, you can patronize the more crowded and noisier public beach, Zona A at the end of Gran Viale. If you stay at any of the hotels on the Lido, most of them have some kind of agreement with the *bagni* (beach establishments).

The Lido's limited sports amenities, such as golf and tennis, are affiliated with its deluxe hotels. Although there's car traffic, the Lido's wide, shaded boulevards are your best bet for jogging while you're visiting Venice. A number of bike-rental places along Gran Viale rent bicycles for 5,000L to 6,000L ($2.50 to $3) per hour. *Vaporetto* lines 1, 6, 14, 52, 82, and N cross the lagoon to the Lido from the San Zaccaria–Danieli stop near San Marco.

8

The Veneto & South Tyrol

by Reid Bramblett

For centuries, the Venetian Republic ruled most of the northeastern region called the **Veneto,** turning its attentions inland once its maritime power was well established throughout the Mediterranean and eastward. Many of the inland cities of the Veneto, though, had been around for centuries when the city of Venice was officially founded with the election of its first doge in A.D. 726. As ancient Roman strongholds, these cities had already lived through their own period of glory. This rich heritage makes a tour through the Veneto a rewarding and often fascinating trip. Verona's wealth of Roman sites and magnificent ancient amphitheater have garnered it the nickname "Little Rome." Still standing in the main squares of Padua, Vicenza, and Verona are columns topped by the winged-lion mascot of St. Mark— a symbol of the distant and often glorious days of the Most Serene Republic of Venice. Venetian Renaissance palazzi, frescoed churches, and basilicas proudly line the cities' main drags. Shakespeare may have never stepped foot in these parts, but he was sufficiently fascinated that he chose to place many of his best works in "fair Verona" and the surrounding area.

Until the arrival of Napoléon in 1797, the Veneto, sharing the bounty of the Serene Republic, was built up and embellished. Many of the Palladian villas dotting the hills were the extravagant summer legacy of wealthy Venetian merchants whose urban palazzi lined Venice's Grand Canal. The Byzantine-Oriental influence so prominent in Venice's Gothic architecture can be seen in the region's churches and municipal buildings—the earlier structures adorned by the frescoes of Giotto and his ilk; the later ones decorated by the Venetian masters Veronese, Titian, Tintoretto, and Tiepolo.

The Veneto is a region of great physical diversity. The northeastern boundaries of the region reach up to the pink-tinged mountain range of the regal Dolomites, which separate Italy from the Tyrol. Farther south, the alluvial plains surrounding the mighty Po River are relentlessly flat, though punctuated by the Berici Mountains south of Vicenza and the Euganean Hills near Padua. The region's rivers—the Po, Adige, Brenta, Piave, and others—provide a fertile breeding ground for the surrounding hills, where vineyards, fruit orchards, and lucrative small-scale farms thrive.

A very different landscape dominates the **Dolomites.** Two mountain ranges, the Alps and the Dolomites, cut into this region, which stretches north from Lombardy and the Veneto. Here you'll discover

A Taste of the Veneto

The foods of the Veneto are as diverse as its geography. From the mountains and the foothills comes a proliferation of mushrooms and game. Much of the cuisine is based on the rice and corn grown here; **polenta** makes frequent appearances on most menus, served with a hearty game stew with hints of Austrian influences. Rice is commonly prepared as **risotto,** a first course served along with the season's vegetables or, more characteristically, offerings from the Adriatic on the east. The olive oil of Tuscan cuisine is used here only minimally—it's not unusual to sense the use of butter, more commonly associated with Emilian food. But above all it's the Adriatic that dictates the regional cuisine, even here in the landlocked environs of the Veneto, where fish and shellfish feature heavily in the local diet. Outside influences are also behind the proliferation of desserts, a throwback to the two times in history when the Veneto was ceded to Austria—sweet remnants of the occupation are still evident in many pastry shops. The now universal favorite **tiramisù** is said to have originated in the Veneto.

Wine is an integral element in any meal; it's no compromise to limit yourself to the local wines, which are some of Europe's finest. The Veneto—and in particular Verona—plays an all-important role in the production and exportation of such world-renowned wines as **Soave, Bordolino,** and **Valpolicello.** No other region in Italy produces as many DOC (Denominazione di Origine Controllata, zones of controlled name and origin) red wines as the Veneto. The rich volcanic earth of the Colli Euganei yields a good number of these reds, while a light and *frizzante* **Prosecco** hails from the hills around Asolo.

an Italy that often doesn't seem very Italian at all. Most of the Dolomites and **South Tyrol**—which encompasses the Trentino and Alto Adige regions—belonged to Austria until it was handed over to Italy at the end of World War I, and many residents (especially in and around Bolzano, Merano, and Bressanone) still prefer the ways of the north to those of the south. They speak German (to them, these towns are Bozen, Meran, and Brixen), eat Austrian food, and go about life with Teutonic crispness. And they live amid mountain landscapes that are more suggestive of Austria than of Italy.

The region's two mountain ranges are physical opposites: The eastern Alps are gentle and beautiful; the dramatically craggy peaks of the Dolomites, a little farther to the east, are actually coral formations that only relatively recently reared up from ancient seabeds. Throughout Trentino-Alto Adige, soaring peaks, highland meadows, and lush valleys provide a paradise for hikers, skiers, and rock climbers; set amid these natural spectacles are pretty and interesting towns to explore.

1 Padua & Giotto's Fabulous Frescoes

42km (26 mi.) W of Venice, 81km (50 mi.) E of Verona, 32km (20 mi.) E of Vicenza, 234km (147 mi.) E of Milan.

The University of Bologna had already grown to 10,000 students by the time **Padua** (Padova) founded its university in 1222. Padua was an ancient Roman stronghold that became the academic heartbeat of the powerful Venetian Republic. For this reason, it is one of the most important medieval and Renaissance cities in Italy. Dante and Copernicus studied here; Petrarch and Galileo taught here. When you wander the narrow, cobbled, arcaded side streets in the timeless neighborhoods surrounding the "Bo" (named after a 15th-century inn that once stood on the present-day site of the university), you will be transported back to those earlier times.

The Veneto & South Tyrol

A Taste of South Tyrol

The cuisine of the Alto Adige is more or less Austrian, with a few Italian touches. *Canederli* (dumplings) often replace pasta or polenta and are found floating in rich broths infused with liver; *speck* (smoked ham) replaces prosciutto; and *Wiener schnitzel grostl* (a combination of potatoes, onions, and veal—the local version of corned beef hash) and pork roasts are among preferred *secondi*. As you move east into Friuli–Venezia Giulia, the cuisine remains firmly of the mountain variety, with some exotic and hard-to-pronounce variations reflecting the region's mixed cultural heritage. Among these are *cvapcici*, Trieste's signature meatball dish, and *brovada*, a *secondo* that combines turnips, grape skins, and pork sausage—a farmer's supper if ever there was one. San Daniele, probably the best **prosciutto** in all Italy (no small claim), comes from this region. The preferred spirit is heady *grappa*, made from grape skins and sure to take the chill out of the night air.

Padua is a vital city, with a young university population that gets about on bicycles and keeps the city's piazzas and cafes humming. The historic hub of town is still evocative of the days when the city and its university flourished in the late Middle Ages and Renaissance as a center of learning and art.

Pilgrims have also secured Padua's place on the map: For more than 700 years, the enormous Basilica di Sant'Antonio has drawn millions from around the world. A mendicant Franciscan monk born in Lisbon, Antonio spent his last years in Padova. He died here in 1231, was canonized almost immediately, and the basilica—a fantastic mingling of Romanesque, Byzantine, and Gothic architecture—was begun within a year. St. Anthony is one of the Roman Catholic Church's most beloved saints, known best, perhaps, for his powers to locate the lost. Countless handwritten messages left on his tomb inside the great domed church call upon this power to help find everything from lost love to lost limbs. Both the church and the miracle worker are simply referred to as "il Santo." The church warrants a visit as much for its artistic treasures and architectural importance as for its religious significance; it remains one of Europe's principal destinations of pilgrimage.

Pilgrims of another ilk have long made the journey here to admire Giotto's magnificent frescoes in the Scrovegni Chapel—to some, even more brilliant than his more famous cycle in Assisi. Alas, the chapel will be closed for renovation for most of 2001.

ESSENTIALS

GETTING THERE   By Train   The main train station is at Piazza delle Stazione (☎ **049-875-1800**), in the northern part of town, just outside the 16th-century walls. Padova is well connected by frequent train service to points directly west and east: Verona (regional: 70 min., 8,300L/$4.15; High speed: 50 min., 12,800L/$6.40), Venice (regional: 30–40 min., 4,400L/$2.20, High speed: 20–30 min., 8,200L/$4.10), Vicenza (regional: 20–30 min., 4,400L/$2.20, High speed: 15–20 min., 8,200L/$4.10), and Milano (regional: 3 hr., 20,600L/$11; High speed: 2½ hr., 33,100L/$17). From the train station, take bus 3, 8, or 14 downtown.

By Bus   The main SITA bus station is located behind (east of) the Scrovegni Chapel and Arena Gardens area on Via Trieste 40/Piazzale Boschetti (☎ **049-820-6844**). Frequent bus service to Venice and Verona costs approximately the same as train tickets, though tourists and locals alike seem to use this station principally for the smaller outlying cities, such as the two to three per hour for Bassano del Grappa (75 min., 6,100L/$3.50).

By Car   Padua is on the A4 autostrade that links Venice with Milan. All the points of interest listed below are located within the city's historical center, which is closed to traffic.

VISITOR INFORMATION   The **tourist office** is in the train station (☎ **049-875-2077;** fax 049-650-794; www.padovanet.it/apt). April to October, it's open Monday to Saturday 9:15am to 7pm and Sunday 9am to noon; November to March, hours are Monday to Saturday 9:20am to 5:45pm and Sunday 9am to noon. From the train station, bus 8 heads downtown (as do nos. 12 and 18 Monday to Saturday and no. 32 Sunday).

There are two **offices downtown:** one at the cathedral on Piazza del Santo (☎ **049-875-3087**), open Monday to Saturday 9am to 6pm (may close for *riposo* in winter), Sunday 9am to 12:30pm.; the other in Galleria Pedrocchi (☎ **049-876-7927**), open Monday to Saturday 9:30am to 12:30pm and 3:30 to 7pm.

Southwest of Padua is a small but renowned wine area, and at the tourist office you can get a **"Strada dei Vini"** wine route map (when in stock!). It also leads you to the small city of Terme di Abano, famous as a center for radioactive springs and mud treatments unique to this volcanic range.

FESTIVALS & MARKETS   The beloved **Sant'Antonio** celebrates his feast day June 13, when his relics are carried about town in an elaborate procession joined by the thousands of pilgrims who come from all over the world.

The **outdoor markets** (Monday to Saturday) in the twin Piazza delle Erbe (**fresh produce**) and Piazza della Frutta (**clothing and dry goods**) flanking the enormous Palazzo della Ragione are some of Italy's best. The third Sunday of every month sees the area of the Prato delle Valle inundated by more than 220 **antiques and collectibles dealers,** one of the largest antiques fairs in the region (☎ **049-820-5856**). Only early birds will beat the large number of local dealers to the good stuff. Antiques lovers with a car might want to visit Italy's second-largest **Mercato dell'Antiquariato** the last Sunday of every month at the 18th-century Villa Contarini, in Piazzola sul Brenta (☎ **0329-237-2475**), a lovely 30-minute drive that can be combined with a visit to some of the other Palladian and Palladian-inspired country villas along the Brenta Canal (see "Day Trips from Padua," below). An estimated 320 vendors hawk their wares; the villa is open for visits during those hours.

Less important, but far more frequent, is the weekly **Saturday outdoor flea market** of non-antique goods (clothes, pet food, household goods—nothing fascinating, but an interesting peek into local life and a good place to pick up kitchen items to recreate the *cucina Italiana* back home), also held in the Prato della Valle. The market's large number of inexpensive shoe stands is testament to the many shoe factories for which the nearby Brenta Canal area is famous. Even if you don't buy anything, visiting either market will give you a chance to see the 18th-century Prato delle Valle, one of the largest piazzas in Europe. Just southwest of the Basilica di Sant'Antonio, it's ringed by a canal and populated by more than 80 statues.

WHAT TO SEE & DO

✪ **Cappella degli Scrovegni (Scrovegni Chapel or Arena Chapel).** Piazza Ermitani 8 (off Corso Garibaldi). ☎ **049-820-4550** for entry reservation. www.padovanet.it/turismo. E-mail (for reservations): musei.comune@padovanet.it. *Note:* The chapel will be closed during most of 2001 for restoration work. Admission (joint ticket with the Museo Eremitani) 10,000L ($5) adults, 7,000L ($3.50) kids. Feb–Oct, Tues–Sun 9am–7pm; Nov–Jan, Tues–Sun 9am–6pm. Entrance through the Museo Eremitani. Bus: 3, 8, 10, 12, 32, 42.

This is the one uncontested must-see during your stay in Padua, so be prepared for lines in high season, a wait made even longer by the small numbers of controlled groups allowed to enter the chapel at any one time (limits of 20-minute visits are often imposed during peak periods; check when buying your ticket so you can plan your visit accordingly). Once inside, art lovers armed with binoculars behold the scene in awe—the recently renovated cycle of **vibrant frescoes** by Giotto that revolutionized 14th-century painting is still considered among the most important early Renaissance art. A brilliant cobalt blue is the dominant color of the illustrations, which are easy to understand and painted in typical medieval comic-strip format; here they take on an unprecedented degree of realism and emotion.

This cycle is even larger, more complete, and better preserved than the famed St. Francis frescoes Giotto later painted in Assisi. Giotto worked from 1303 to 1306 to completely cover the ceiling and walls with 38 scenes illustrating the lives of Mary and Christ from floor to ceiling. With your back to the front door, the three bands that cover the walls are: top right, Life of Joachim; top left, Life of the Virgin; right center, The Childhood of Christ; left center, Christ's Public Life; right bottom, The Passion of Christ (the third panel of Judas kissing Christ is perhaps the best known of the entire cycle); left bottom, Christ's Death and Resurrection. Above the entrance is the fresco of the Last Judgment: Christ, as judge, sits in the center, surrounded by the angels and apostles. Below him, to the right, are the blessed; while to the left, Giotto created a terrible hell in which devils and humans are condemned to eternal punishment.

The area around the ancient Roman Arena where the chapel now stands (and hence the chapel's alternative name) was purchased in 1300 by a wealthy Paduan, Enrico Scrovegni. He built an extravagant palazzo (destroyed in 1820) and a family chapel, which stands next to it, whose exterior remains simple and unadorned. Dedicated to his father, an unethical usurer so notorious in his time that he was refused a Christian burial, the son hoped to atone for his father's ways and commissioned Tuscan-born Giotto, whose work he had seen in the Basilica di Sant'Antonio. Giotto felt obligated to include the father in the portrait of the Last Judgment's blessed souls. Dante felt otherwise, immortalizing him by placing him amid the usurers condemned to hell in his epic *Inferno*.

Musei Civici Eremitani (Civic Museum of the Hermits). Piazza Eremitani 8 (off Corso Garibaldi and adjacent to the Cappella Scrovegni). ☎ **049-820-4550.** For admission and hours, see Cappella Scrovegni, above.

The centuries-old cloisters that were once home to the monks (*eremitani* means hermits) who officiated in the adjacent Scrovegni Chapel (officially part of the museum complex) have been handsomely renovated to provide an airy display space as the city's new civic museum. Its prodigious collection begins on the ground floor with the Archeological Museum's division of Egyptian, Roman, and Etruscan artifacts and antiquities. The upstairs collection represents an impressive panorama of minor Venetian works from major Venetian artists from the early 15th century to the 19th century. You'll find works by Titian, Tiepolo, and Tintoretto, whose *Crucifixion* is the museum's finest work. Special mention is given to Giotto's unusual wooden *Crucifix* and Bellini's *Portrait of a Young Senator.*

Chiesa degli Eremitani (Church of the Hermits). Piazza Eremitani (off Corso Garibaldi). ☎ **049-875-6410.** Free admission. Mon–Sat 8:15am–12:15pm and 4–6pm, Sun 9:30am–12:15pm and 4 to 6pm. Bus: 3, 8, 10, 12, 32, 42.

Padua's worst tragedy was the complete destruction of this church by Nazi bombings in 1944; some art historians consider it the country's greatest artistic wartime loss. It has been remarkably restored to its original early 13th-century Romanesque style, but the magnificent cycle of frescoes painted from 1454 to 1457 by the 23-year-old

Padua

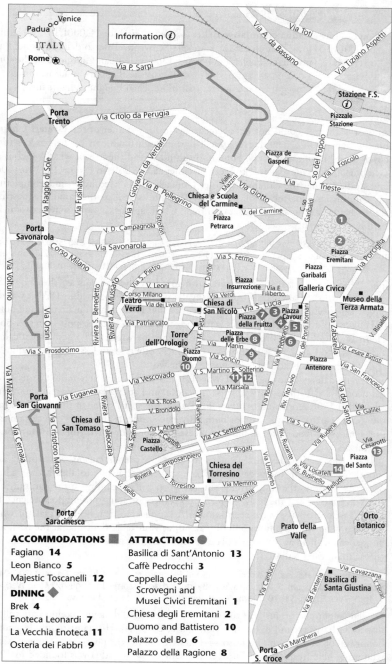

Information ⓘ

Stazione F.S. ⓘ
Piazzale Stazione

Porta Trento

Via Citolo da Perugia

Piazza de Gasperi

Chiesa e Scuola del Carmine

Piazza Petrarca

V. del Carmine

Porta Savonarola

Via Savonarola

Piazza Eremitani

Piazza Garibaldi

Galleria Civica

Museo della Terza Armata

Piazza Insurrezione

Via E. Filiberto.

Chiesa di San Nicolò

Via Verdi

Via S. Lucia

Piazza Cavour

Teatro Verdi

Corso Milano

V. Leoni

Via del Livello

Piazza della Fruitta

Torre dell'Orologio

Via Patriarcato

Piazza delle Erbe

Via Manin

Piazza Duomo

Via Soncin

Piazza Antenore

Via Vescovado

V. S. Martino E. Solferino

Via Marsala

Porta San Giovanni

Chiesa di San Tomaso

Via S. Rosa
V. Brondolo

Via I. Andreini

Piazza Castello

Via XX Settembre

Chiesa del Torresino

V. Rogati

Piazza del Santo

Basilica di Sant'Antonio

Porta Saracinesca

Prato della Valle

Orto Botanico

Porta S. Croce

Basilica di Santa Giustina

ACCOMMODATIONS ■
Fagiano **14**
Leon Bianco **5**
Majestic Toscanelli **12**

DINING ◆
Brek **4**
Enoteca Leonardi **7**
La Vecchia Enoteca **11**
Osteria dei Fabbri **9**

ATTRACTIONS ●
Basilica di Sant'Antonio **13**
Caffè Pedrocchi **3**
Cappella degli Scrovegni and Musei Civici Eremitani **1**
Chiesa degli Eremitani **2**
Duomo and Battistero **10**
Palazzo del Bo **6**
Palazzo della Ragione **8**

411

A Money-Saving Tip

You can buy a **Padua cumulative ticket** (*biglietto unico*) for 15,000L ($7.50) adults, 10,000L ($5) kids, that covers the Cappella Scrovegni, Palazzo della Ragione, Baptistry, Musei Antoniani, Scoletta del Santo, Oratorio di San Giorgio, and the Orto Botanico. It's a decent savings if you plan to visit the Ragione, as admission just to that and the Scrovegni Chapel would cost more when bought individually.

Andrea Mantegna could not be salvaged, except for a corner of the **Ovetari Chapel** on the right of the chancel. Here you'll find enough fragments of the frescoes (discovered in the rubble after the bombing) to understand the loss of what was considered one of Italy's great artistic treasures. Mantegna was born in Padua (1431 to 1506) and studied under the Florentine master Donatello, who lived here while completing his commissions for the Basilica di Sant'Antonio as well as the famous equestrian statue that now stands in the piazza before it. Classical music concerts are occasionally held in the church.

✪ **Caffè Pedrocchi.** Via VIII Febbraio 15 (at Piazza Cavour). ☎ **049-820-5007.** Admission to historical salons upstairs 5,000L ($2.50), open Tues–Sun 9:30am–12:30pm and 3:30–6:30pm. Bar: admission free (but drinks expensive!), open daily 7am–midnight.

The Pedrocchi is a historic landmark, as beloved by the Paduans as "their" own St. Anthony (who actually hailed from Portugal). When it first opened in 1831 it was the largest cafe in Europe—whom were they expecting? Famous are the literary and political characters and local luminaries who made this their command post—French-born Henri Beyle, a.k.a. Stendhal, had it in mind when he wrote: "The best Italian cafe is almost as good as the Parisian ones." Countless others were less reserved, calling it arguably the most beautiful coffeehouse in the world.

Heavily damaged during World War II, it has been completely rebuilt in its original neoclassical 19th-century stage-set splendor, and after a laborious renovation and a heralded 1998 reopening that was, for Padua, the social event of the year, it's again the social heartbeat of the city for both university students and ladies of a certain age. On a more prosaic note: It has the nicest restrooms in town, for the use of cafe patrons.

In warm weather, Pedrocchi opens its doors (hence its curious description as a "doorless cafe") onto the pedestrian piazza; sit here for awhile to absorb the Paduan spirit. As is always the case, drinks cost less when you're standing at the bar, but then you will have missed the *dolce far niente* (sweetness of doing nothing) experience for which Pedrocchi has always been known. A cappuccino, tea, beer, or glass of white Prosecco wine will cost from 5,000L ($2.50) at your table (half that at the bar), and hunger can be held at bay with a plate of dainty teatime pastries or a grilled ham-and-cheese toast, each 5,000L ($2.50).

Bo (Università Palazzo Centrale). Via VIII Febbraio (south of Piazza Cavour). ☎ **049-820-9773.** Admission 7,000L ($3.50). By guided tour, some in English, Mon, Wed, Fri 3–4pm, Tues, Thurs, Sat 10–11am. Ask at tourist office for status of renovation.

Galileo taught here from 1592 to 1610, and his battered desk and podium are still on display in Italy's second-oldest university (after Bologna). His name joins a legendary honor roll of students and professors—Petrarch, Dante, the poet Tasso, Copernicus—who came here from all over Europe. The University of Padua was founded in 1222 and grew to become one of the most famous and ambitious learning centers in Europe reaching its zenith in the 16th and 17th centuries.

Today, a number of buildings are spread about town, but the **Palazzo del Bo** (named after the long-gone "Bo," or Ox Inn, a favorite student hangout in the 15th century) is the university's main seat. Ongoing restoration keeps most of it off-limits, but the perfectly preserved **Teatro Anatomico (Anatomical Theater)** is one of the few sites open for a visit. Built in 1594, it was here that William Harvey most probably developed his theory of the circulation of blood when getting his degree in 1602.

Palazzo della Ragione (Law Courts), Piazza delle Erbe & Piazza della Frutta. ☎ **049-820-5006.** Admission to palazzo 7,000L ($3.50), more during frequent exhibits. Tues–Sun 9am–7pm. Bus: 8.

Just south of Caffè Perocchi and an inevitable destination for those meandering about the historic center of town, the picturesque open-air markets of **Piazza delle Erbe (Square of the Herbs)** and **Piazza della Frutta (Square of Fruit)** frame the massive 13th-century palazzo at their center; together they have stood as the town's political and commercial nucleus for centuries. Before being distracted by the color, smells, and cacophony of the sprawling outdoor fruit and vegetable market stalls, turn your attention to the magnificent **Palazzo della Ragione,** whose interior is as impressive as its exterior.

Food shops by the dozen fill its ground floor, and stand-up bars and outdoor cafes make this lunch central. The two-story loggia-lined "Palace of Reason" is topped with a distinctive sloped roof that resembles the inverted hull of a ship, the largest of its kind in the world. It was built in 1219 as the seat of Padua's parliament and was used as an assembly hall, courthouse, and administrative center to celebrate Padua's newly won independence as a republican city. Considered a masterpiece of civil medieval architecture, it was heavily damaged by a fire in 1420 that destroyed, among other things, an elaborate cycle of frescoes by Giotto and his students that adorned **il Salone (the Great Hall).** The Hall, 270 feet long, was almost immediately rebuilt and is today the prime draw, both for its floor-to-ceiling 15th-century frescoes immediately commissioned after the fire—similar in style and astrological theme to those that had been painted by Giotto (and one of the very few complete zodiac cycles to survive into modern times)—and a large wooden sculpture of a horse that some art historians have attributed to Donatello. Museum-quality exhibits are often held at this impressive venue, giving you twice the reason to visit.

On the far (west) side of the adjoining piazzas' canvas-topped stalls, flanking the Palazzo della Ragione, is the **Piazza dei Signori,** most noteworthy for the 15th-century clock tower that dominates it, the first of its kind in Italy.

✪ **Basilica di Sant'Antonio.** Piazza del Santo (east of Prato delle Valle). ☎ **049-824-2811.** Free admission. Summer daily 6:30am–7:45pm; winter daily 7am–7pm. Bus: 8, 12, or 18.

This enormous basilica's imposing interior is richly frescoed and decorated, filled with a number of tombs, works of art, and inlaid checkerboard marble flooring. It's all there to honor one man, Padua's patron St. Anthony (Sant'Antonio). Simply and commonly referred to as "il Santo," Anthony was born in Lisbon in 1195 and died just outside

When Venice Overflows

Padua is convenient to both Venice and Verona. It doesn't offer a wide choice of desirable hotels in the *centro storico,* but you'll pay close to half the rates of comparable accommodations in Venice. Plus, you'll find the commute, just 19 miles, an easy and inexpensive one (and often a necessary one when Venice is booked full).

of Padua in 1231. Work began on the church almost immediately but was not completed until 1307. Its eight domes bring to mind the Byzantine influence also found in Venice's St. Mark's Basilica, which predates Padua's Romanesque-Gothic construction by more than two centuries. A pair of octagonal, minaret-like bell towers enhances its Eastern appearance.

The faithful could care less about the architecture; they flock here year-round to caress the **tomb** holding the saint's body (off the left aisle) and pray for his help in finding what they've lost. The tomb is always covered with flowers, photographs, and handwritten personal petitions left by devout pilgrims from every corner of the globe whose numbers have remained constant over the centuries. The saint is the patron of lost or mislaid objects, and the faithful who flock here come to find everything from lost love to lost health. The series of nine bronze bas-reliefs of scenes from the saint's life are some of the finest works by 16th-century Northern Italian sculptors. The seven bronze statues and towering central *Crucifixion* that adorn the main altar are by Donatello (1444 to 1448) and are the basilica's artistic highlight.

In his lifetime, St. Anthony was known for his eloquent preaching, so interpret as you will the saint's perfectly (some say miraculously) preserved tongue, vocal chords, and jawbone on display in the **Cappella del Tesoro** in the back of the church directly behind the main altar. These treasured relics are carried through town in a traditional procession every June 13 to celebrate the feast day of *il Santo.* You'll also see one of the original tattered tunics belonging to *il Santo* dating from 1231.

Standing out amid the smattering of stalls across the large piazza in front of the basilica selling St. Anthony–emblazoned everything, is Donatello's famous *Gattamelata* equestrian statue. The first of its size to be cast in Italy since Roman antiquity, it is important for its detail, proportion, and powerful contrast between rider (the inconsequential Venetian condottiere Erasmo da Narni, nicknamed the "Spotted Cat") and horse. It would have a seminal effect on Renaissance sculpture and casting and restore the lost art of the equestrian statue.

AFFORDABLE PLACES TO STAY

When making reservations, note that low season is usually considered December and January, and July and August. Inquire about discounts if you'll be in Padua at this time of year.

Fagiano. Via Locatelli 45 (west of Piazza del Santo), 35122 Padova. ☎ **049-875-0073.** Fax 049-875-3396. E-mail: alfagiano@libero.it. 30 units, 27 with bathroom. A/C TV TEL. 50,000L ($25) single without bathroom; 95,000L ($47.50) single with bathroom; 70,000L ($35) double without bathroom, 130,000L ($65) double with bathtoom; 150,000L ($75) triple with bathroom. Breakfast 6,000–12,000L ($3–$6). AE, DC, MC, V. From train station: bus no. 8, 12, 18, or 32.

Although small, this newly renovated hotel is a great value-for-your-money deal. It doesn't exactly ooze coziness and charm, but given the less-than-encouraging hotel situation in town, the Fagiano's bright, modern, and clean rooms are still a standout. The baths have also been redone and include niceties like hair dryers. And you rarely find air-conditioning and TVs at these rates. Just a few steps off the expansive Piazza del Santo (its most appealing asset), the family-run Fagiano shouldn't be confused with the recently renamed Hotel Buenos Aires, formerly known as the Fagiano and just a block away.

Leon Bianco. Piazzetta Pedrocchi 12 (at Via Cavour), 35122 Padova. ☎ **049-657-225.** Fax 049-875-0814. www.toscanelli.com. 22 units. A/C MINIBAR TV TEL. 145,000L ($73) single; 177,000–184,000L ($88–$92) double. Buffet breakfast 16,000L ($8). AE, DC, MC, V. Parking in garage 27,000L ($14). Bus: 3 or 8.

This is the three-star sibling of the four-star Majestic Toscanelli below, and the most centrally located of its competitors. In fact, it's the best in terms of location regardless of category: The heartbeat of town—the landmark Caffè Pedrocchi and the open-air marketplace—is just outside your front door. The 100-year-old palazzo is done up in an uninspired once-contemporary theme that's in need of a facelift (though I hope they never lose the funky 1970s-designer lamps), with an art collection hung in the public areas. A top-floor alfresco terrace redeems things considerably: Brown-bag a drink or snack (unless you're willing to spring for the overpriced breakfast) under white canvas umbrellas with views over Palazzo della Ragione and the center's medieval rooftops. Some of the simply furnished rooms are noteworthy for their parquet floors strewn with Persian rugs; others offer more than ample space, a good choice for families of three or four. Though the decor hasn't aged well, the housekeeping is attentive, the service very good, and the place well maintained.

WORTH A SPLURGE

✪ **Majestic Toscanelli.** Via dell'Arco 2 (2 blocks west of Via Roma and south of Piazza delle Erbe), 35122 Padova. ☎ **049-663-244.** Fax 049-876-0025. www.toscanelli.com. 34 units. A/C MINIBAR TV TEL. 175,000L ($88) single; 267,000L ($134) double. Rates include buffet breakfast. Rates discounted July 14–Aug 31. AE, DC, MC, V. Parking in garage 27,000L ($14).

A four-star hotel this nice would cost a great deal more in nearby Venice, which is why the Toscanelli often finds itself with guests who make this their home base while visiting neighboring cities and the surrounding area. A 1992 redo has kept the hotel's old-world charm fresh and handsome, with rooms tastefully done in classic decor with coordinated pastel themes, burnished cherry-wood furniture, and large bathrooms bright with white ceramic and marble tiles. Work in 2000 freshened up the lobby with highlights of gold leaf that hint of the Venetian rococo era. Off the lobby is an American bar, while a good buffet breakfast is available on an indoor balcony that overlooks the lobby on one side and is lit by picture windows on the other. This quiet, historic neighborhood is entirely closed to traffic, with porticoed alleyways lined with antiques shops and wine bars. From here it's an easy walk to Via Roma and Piazza delle Erbe.

GREAT DEALS ON DINING

Brek. Piazza Cavour 20. ☎ **049-875-3788.** Reservations not accepted. Primi and pizza 6,000–10,000L ($3–$5); secondi 7,000–13,000L ($3.50–$7). Daily 11:30am–3pm and 6:30–10:30pm. DC, MC, V. ITALIAN CAFETERIA.

Brek is self-service *all'italiana,* a homegrown Northern Italian chain of upscale cafeterias that make concessions to the time-pressed modern world without sacrificing old-world quality. Put your language problems and calorie counting aside as you help yourself to pastas made up fresh while you wait, along with the sauce of your choice. There's a counter just for omelets made express, another for entrees and pizza. The dessert cart groans under a copious array of cheeses, fresh fruits, fruit salads, and fruit-topped tarts and cobblers. Join the thoroughly local eat-on-the-run lunch crowd from the university and surrounding shops, and save your day's budget for dinner.

✪ **Enoteca Leonardi/La Corte dei Leoni.** Via Pietro d'Abano 1 (on a side street leading north of Piazza della Frutta). ☎ **049-875-0083.** Reservations suggested. Primi 16,000–18,000L ($8–$9); secondi 25,000–28,000L ($13–$14). Tues–Sat 12:30–2:30pm and 6:30pm–12:30am, Sun 12:30–2:30pm. Closed 1 week in Aug. AE, CB, DC, V. WINE BAR/ PADUAN.

After a heady wander amid the sights, sounds, and smells of Padua's open-air market-place, head for this new enoteca. Your head need spin no longer, despite the 700 labels in its well-stocked wine cellar (at least 30 are available to sample by the glass at 3,500L to 8,500L/$1.50 to $4). The stylishly minimal white-and-moss-green interior is attractive, but the outdoor courtyard where centuries-old horse stables have been converted for human grazers is the warm-weather draw. The interesting antipasti are as sophisticated as the setting: Look for the *mousse di fegato grasso d'oca tartufato,* a lighter-than-air foie gras heightened by a hint of truffles; or a platter of various Italian cheeses or salumi, each a perfect complement to Leonardi's very impressive selection of wines. Only a handful of dishes is offered, but each is excellently prepared, such as *mezzelune* (a kind of ravioli) stuffed with ricotta and eggplant in a sauce of fresh mushrooms and mountain cheese, or a *petto d'anatra in salsa d'uva* (duck breast cooked with grapes that somehow escaped their fate as wine).

✪ **Osteria dei Fabbri.** Via dei Fabbri 13 (on a side street south of Piazza delle Erbe), ☎ **049-650-336.** Reservations suggested. Primi 12,500–14,500L ($6–$7); secondi 22,000–30,000L ($11–$15). Mon–Sat 12:30–3pm and 7:30pm–1am. DC, MC, V. PADUAN.

This rustic old-fashioned tavern (osteria) is a lively spot where intellectual types share tables with Zegna-suited bankers, and students stop by for a tipple or to find a quiet corner in which to pore over the newspaper (a pastime not encouraged during hours when meals are served). Some of the day's specials are displayed on the heavy oak bar—antipasti of grilled vegetables, rosemary potatoes, seafood salads—while hot dishes pour out of the kitchen. There's always at least one homemade pasta choice to start with, and osso buco, the specialty of the house, is especially memorable when accompanied by any of the local (and excellent) Venetian wines available by the bottle or glass. Stop by at least for a *dopo cena* (after-dinner drink) to top off your day in Padua. If this restaurant is full, head two blocks over to the reliable **Osteria L'Anfora** at Via del Soncin 13, east of Piazza del Duomo (☎ **049-65-66-29**), for inexpensive wine and good food.

WORTH A SPLURGE

✪ **La Vecchia Enoteca.** Via San Martino e Solferino 32 (just south of Piazza delle Erbe). ☎ **049-875-2856.** Reservations recommended. Primi 10,000–14,000L ($5–$7); secondi 22,000–30,000L ($11–$15). Mon 7:45–10pm, Tues–Sat 12:45–2pm and 7:45–10pm. Closed 2 weeks mid-Aug. MC, V. PADUAN.

The sophistication of the Veneto's prodigious viticulture is shown off here in an appropriately refined venue. Cozy, in a elegantly rustic kind of way, La Vecchia Enoteca is for that special evening of white linen and smooth service when you'd like the full-blown experience of Paduan cuisine and top-notch wines (hence its placement in our splurge department). Prices are contained enough to encourage diners to indulge in both a delicious menu and a commendable selection of regional and Italian wines. The menu showcases the bounty-rich Veneto: The traditional polenta and risotto change with the season, as does the homemade gnocchi. Meat possibilities are numerous and tempting, while the influence of the Adriatic appears in entrees like the *branzino in crosta di patate,* sea bass roasted in a light crust of potatoes.

PADUA AFTER DARK

The classical-music season usually runs October to April at different venues around town. Among them, the historic **Teatro Verdi** at Via dei Livello 32 (☎ **049-876-0339**) is the most impressive. Programs are available at the tourist office. Look for posters advertising performances by the world-class Solisti Veneti, who are Paduans but spend most of the year, alas, traveling abroad.

As a university city, Padua's student population makes its presence known at all times—everyone looks 22 and in search of themselves. You can network with the student crowd at any of the popular **cafes along Via Cavour,** or the **osterie,** wine bars, and beer dives in the porticoed medieval side streets encircling the Palazzo della

Ragione (the area around the Bo) and its bookends Piazza delle Erbe and Piazza della Frutta.

A DAY TRIP FROM PADUA: THE FORGOTTEN RIVIERA

The navigable **Brenta Canal** links Padua with Venice in the east and gave its name to the **Riviera del Brenta.** This area is ambitiously called the "Forgotten Riviera" because of the dozens of historic summer villas built here by Venice's aristocracy and wealthy merchants; you visit by car or boat. Some of the villas are far more outstanding than others. Only one was designed by the 16th-century master architect Palladio (Villa Foscari), but many are Palladian-inspired (see "Vicenza: City of Palladio," below, for background on Palladio and how to visit his villas). The best way to see them all is on a cruise down the Brenta (see below).

You can view more than 30 villas from the boats (some only partially or at a great distance) but visit only 3. The important 18th-century **Villa Pisani** in Stra was commissioned by the family of a Venetian doge and is famous for its ballroom frescos by Tiepolo and the hedge maze in its gardens. Easter to October, it's open Monday and Tuesday 9am to 6pm and Wednesday to Sunday 9am to 7pm (winter daily 9am to 5pm). Admission is 10,000L ($5) for the villa or 5,000L ($2.50) for just the park and gardens.

The other two biggies are in Mira. The 18th-century **Villa Valmarana** (☎ 041-560-9350) is dramatically set amid weeping willows, open Sunday only April to June, September, and October by 10,000L ($5; free under 14), on tours that leave every half hour 10am to 11:30am and 2:30 to 5:30pm (in July and August, you can only visit as part of a large group, such as with the cruises detailed below). The **Villa Foscari** (a.k.a. **Villa Malcontenta,** "The Unhappy Woman"; ☎ 041-424-156), is one of Palladio's finest examples. It's open May to September Tuesday to Friday 10am to 6pm, Saturday and Sunday 10am to 7pm; March, April, October, and November Tuesday to Friday 10am to 5pm, Saturday and Sunday 10am to 6pm; requisite 8,000L ($4) guided tours (3,000L/$1.50 under 10 and over 60) leave every hour from 10:15 on.

The most popular **Brenta cruise** is **Il Burchiello,** run by Siamic Express, Via Trieste 42 (☎ **049-660-944;** fax 049-662-830; . It can be disorganized, however (they lose reservations, change hours without advising those who have booked, and sometimes forget passengers at stops along the way). A similar outfit, with which I have no experience, is **I Batelli del Brenta,** Via Porciglia 34 (☎ **049-876-0233,** fax 049-876-3410; antoniana.it/batellidelbrenta).

Il Burchiello leaves Padua at 8am Wednesday, Friday, and Sunday and takes you by bus from their office in Padua (on public bus terminus Piazzale Boschetti just northeast of the Ermetani) to the first stop, Stra and its Villa Pisani. After a tour of the villa, you board the boat, stop at the other two big villas and once for lunch, and arrive in Venice at 6:20pm. If you're doing the Brenta in the other direction, they leave from Venice's Pietà dock on Riva degli Schiavoni at 9am Tuesday, Thursday, and Saturday, arriving in Padova at 6:40pm. I Batelli del Brenta embarks in Padova from the Scalinata del Portello at 8:30am Saturday and Sunday, arriving in Venice at 7:30pm; from Venice's Riva degli Schiavoni dock in front of Caserma Cornolid, they leave Saturdays at 8:50am, finishing in Padova at 7:30pm.

Both charge 110,000L ($55) adults or 65,000L ($33) for ages 6 to 17 for the trip, which includes admission to the Villa Malcontenta/Foscari and the Villa Widmann, but not the Villa Pisani (an additional 10,000L/$5). The optional seafood lunch is another 43,000L ($21.50). The return trip is not included, so either catch one of the cheap, frequent trains back, or ask about taking your luggage on board so that you can simply continue your trip from the end point.

If you want to **do the tour yourself,** the largest concentration of country villas can be found between Stra and Mira. The secondary road S11 runs alongside some of the canal; at certain points it departs from the canal but remains the best of any extant roadways for viewing the villas. Don't try this without wheels: Erratic public bus connections make this tour close to impossible if you don't have a car. Still, a car tour requires some planning, as visiting hours and days differ from villa to villa and season to season. See the tourist office about a map.

2 Vicenza: City of Palladio

32km (20 mi.) W of Padua, 74km (46 mi.) W of Venice, 51km (32 mi.) E of Verona, 204km (128.5 mi.) E of Milan.

Vicenza pays heartfelt homage to Andrea di Pietro della Gondola (born in Padua in 1508, died in Maser in 1580). He came to Vicenza at age 16 and lived out his life and dreams here under the name Palladio at a time when Vicenza was under the sway of Venice's still-powerful Republic. Although not highly innovative, he was the most important architect of the High Renaissance, one whose living monuments inspired and influenced architecture in the Western world over the centuries to this very day. Vicenza and its surroundings are a Mecca for the architecture lover, a living museum of Palladian and Palladian-inspired architectural monuments and consequently one designated a protected UNESCO World Heritage Site in 1994. Even if you've never heard of Palladio, you'll appreciate an evening stroll through the town's illuminated piazzas and along boutique-lined streets—and you may just leave a rookie architecture buff: A day in Vicenza is worth a semester back in school.

Vicenza today is one of the wealthiest cities in Italy, thanks in part to the burgeoning local computer-component industry (Federico Faggin, inventor of the silicon chip, was born here). It is also the traditional center of the country's gold manufacturing industry (one-third of Italy's gold is made here, and each year three prestigious international gold fairs make finding a hotel in these parts impossible) and one of Europe's largest producers of textiles. The average Vicentino is well off and it shows; join the entire town for the daily *passeggiata* and pick up on the palpable attitude.

ESSENTIALS

GETTING THERE   By Train   The train station is in Piazza Stazione, also called Campo Marzio (☎ **0444-325-046**), at the southern end of Viale Roma. Frequent service (2 to 3 per hour) connects Vicenza with Venice (regional: 67 min., 6,800L/$3.40; High speed: 52 min., 10,400L/$5); Padua (20 min., 4,400–8,200L/$2.20–$4.10); and Verona (30 min., 5,500–9,700L/$2.75–$4.85).

By Bus   The FTV bus station (☎ **0444-223-115,** or 0444-223-127) is on Viale Milano, just to the west (left) of the train station. Buses leave frequently for all the major cities in the Veneto and to Milano; prices are comparable to train travel.

By Car   Vicenza is on the A4 autostrada that links Venice to the east with Milano to the west. Coming from Venice (about 1 hr.), you'll bypass Padua before arriving in Vicenza.

VISITOR INFORMATION   The **tourist office** is at Piazza Matteotti 12 (☎ **0444-320-854;** fax 0444-327-072; www.ascom.vi.it/aptvicenza or www.comune. vicenza.it), next to the Teatro Olimpico. The office is open Monday to Saturday 9am to 1pm and 2:30 to 6pm and Sunday 9am to 1pm. Mid-October to mid-March, closing time is 5:30pm. During summer, an office at the train station is open Monday to Saturday 9am to 2pm and Sunday 1 to 6pm. April to October, the tourist office offers 2-hour walking tours of the city every Saturday at 3pm. Technically, they're free, but only if you buy the 20,000L ($10) Vicenza Card (see below), which gets you admission to all the sights you visit.

FESTIVALS   The well-established summertime series of **Concerti in Villa** (☎ **0444-399-104**) takes place in June and July; a few concerts are held outdoors at Vicenza's famed Villa la Rotonda, for others, you will need a car. The tourist office will have the schedule and availability of seats; tickets usually cost around 30,000L ($15). The stage of the delightful **Teatro Olimpico** (☎ **0444-540-072** or 044-222-101) hosts shows from September to October, mainly classical plays (this year was *The Oedipus Cycle*) or Shakespeare (*Henry V* and *Hamlet* are sort of strange in Italian). Tickets are 20,000L to 35,000L ($10 to $17.50).

EXPLORING THE PALLADIAN HERITAGE

Vicenza's primary sights are now all grouped onto one of several **cumulative admission tickets;** which one you buy depends on how much you want to see. The basic ticket costs 12,000L ($6), 6,000L ($3) students, and covers the Teatro Olimpico, Pinacoteca di Palazzo Chiericati, and Museo Naturalistico Archeologico di San Corona. Add the Museo del Risorgimento e della Resistenza a Villa Guiccioli for 14,000L ($7) adults, 7,000L ($3.50) students. You can no longer get individual tickets for any of those.

Vicenza Cards cover all the above, plus several sights for which you can buy separate admissions. Upgrade to the 20,000L ($10) adults or 15,00L ($8) students Vicenza Card to add the Basilica Palladiana, Palazzo Barbaran da Porto, and Gallerie di Palazzo Leoni Montanari. If you're planning to visit the outlying villas, you can spring for the 40,000L ($20) adults or 33,000L ($17) students card that adds in La Rotonda and the Villa Valmarana "ai Nani."

Which offers the best deal? Quite frankly, some of the above sights aren't terribly engaging. You can visit all the sights recommended below, including the villas, for a total of 32,000L ($16) by just buying the basic 12,000L cumulative ticket and then paying for the villa admissions separately.

PIAZZA DEI SIGNORI

South of Corso Palladio on the site of the ancient Roman Forum and still the town hub, this central square should be your first introduction to the city and Palladio, the local boy wonder.

The magnificent bigger-than-life ✪ **Basilica Palladiana** is not a church at all and was only partially designed by Palladio. Beneath it stood a Gothic-style Palazzo della Ragione (Law Courts and Assembly Hall) that Palladio was commissioned to convert to a High Renaissance style befitting a flourishing late 16th-century city under Venice's benevolent patronage. It was his first public work and as such secured his favor and reputation with the local authorities. He created two superimposed galleries, the lower with Doric pillars, the upper with Ionic. The roof was destroyed by World War II bombing, but has since been rebuilt in its original style. It's open April to September Tuesday to Sunday 10am to 7pm, October to March Tuesday to Sunday 9am to 5pm. Admission is currently free, but a small fee may be in place by the time you visit.

The towering 12th-century **Torre Bissara** (or Torre di Piazza) bell tower belonged to the original church and stands near two columns in the piazza's east end (the Piazza Blade), one topped by the winged lion of Venice's Serene Republic, the other by the *Redentore* (Redeemer). Of note elsewhere in the piazza are the **Loggia del Capitaniato** (1570), begun but never finished according to plans by Palladio except for the four massive red-brick columns (on the north side of piazza alongside the well-known Gran Caffè Garibaldi). Behind the Basilica (to the south) is the **Piazza delle Erbe,** site of the daily produce market.

CORSO ANDREA PALLADIO

This is Vicenza's main street, and a grand one it is, lined with the magnificent palazzi of Palladio and his students (and *their* students, who centuries later were still influenced by the mastery of Palladio's work), today converted into cafes, swank shops, and imposing banks. To reach the first one of note, starting from its southwest cap near the Piazza Castello, you'll have to detour a few steps left up Corso A. Fogazzaro to no. 16, the **Palazzo Valamarana**, begun by Palladio in 1566 and perhaps his most eccentric work. Back on the main Corso, on the right you'll see the **Palazzo del Comunale**, the town hall built in 1592 by Scamozzi (1552 to 1616), a Vicenza native and Palladio's protégé and star pupil. This is said to be Scamozzi's greatest work.

From Corso Palladio heading northeast, take a left onto the town's second most important street, the Contrà Porti, with its wealth of Palladian and Gothic palazzi. The two designed by Palladio are the **Palazzo Barbarano Porto** at no. 11, and (opposite) **Palazzo Thiene** at no. 12 (now the headquarters of a bank); Gothic palazzi of particular note can be found at nos. 6 to 10, 14, 16, 17, and 19.

Returning to Corso Palladio, look for no. 145/147, the pre-Palladian **Ca d'Oro (Golden Palace),** named for the gold leaf used in the frescoes that once covered its facade. It was bombed in 1944 and rebuilt in 1950. The simple 16th-century palazzo at no. 163 was **Palladio's home.**

Before reaching Piazza Matteotti and the end of Corso Palladio you'll see signs for **Santa Corona,** set back on the left on Contrà Santa Corona 2 (☎ **0444-323-644**); it's open daily 8:30am to noon and 2:30 to 6pm. An unremarkable 13th-century Gothic church, it shelters two masterpieces (and Vicenza's most important church paintings) that make this worth a visit: Giovanni Bellini's *Baptism of Christ* (fifth altar on left) and Veronese's *Adoration of the Magi* (third chapel on right). This is Vicenza's most interesting church, far more so than the cavernous Duomo southwest of Piazza dei Signori, but worth seeking out only if you've got the extra time. At the northeastern end of Corso Palladio is Palladio's world-renowned Teatro Olimpico and, across the street, the Museo Civico in the Palazzo Chiericati.

✪ **Teatro Olimpico (Olympic Theater) & Museo Civico (Civic Museum).** Piazza Matteotti (at Corso Palladio). ☎ **0444-222-800** or 0444-321-348. Admission, see above. June 19–Aug daily 9am–7pm (Teatro opens 10am); Sept–June 18 daily 9am–5pm.

The splendid **Teatro Olimpico** was Palladio's greatest urban work, and one of his last. He began the project in 1580, the year of his death at age 72; it was completed 5 years later by his student Vicenzo Scamozzi. It was the first covered theater in Europe, inspired by the theaters of antiquity. The seating area, shaped in a half-moon like the old arenas, seats 1,000. The stage seems profoundly deeper than its actual 14 feet, thanks to the permanent stage "curtain" and Scamozzi's clever use of trompe l'oeil added after Palladio's death. The stage scene represents the ancient streets of Thebes, while the faux clouds and sky covering the dome further the impression of being in an outdoor Roman amphitheater. Drama, music, and dance performances are still held here year-round; check with the tourist office.

Across the Piazza Matteotti is another Palladian opus, the **Palazzo Chiericati,** which houses the **Museo Civico (Civic Museum).** Looking more like one of the country villas for which Palladio was equally famous, this major work is considered one of his finest and is visited as much for its two-tiered, statue-topped facade as for the collection of Venetian paintings it houses on the first floor. Here are paintings by Venetian masters such as Tiepolo, Tintoretto, and Veronese, as well as lesser-known works from the Vicenzan (founded by Bartolomeo Montagna) and Bassano schools of painting.

VILLAS & A BASILICA NEARBY

To reach the two important villas in the immediate environs of Vicenza, southeast of the train station, you can walk, bike, or take the no. 8 bus. First stop by the tourist office for a map, and check on visiting hours, which tend to change from year to year.

The ✪ **Villa Rotonda** (☎ **0444-321-793**), also referred to as the Villa Capra Valmarana after its owners, is considered one of the most perfect buildings ever constructed and has been added to the World Heritage List by UNESCO; it is a particularly important must-do excursion for students and lovers of architecture. Most authorities refer to it as Palladio's finest work. Obviously inspired by ancient Greek and Roman designs, Palladio began this perfectly proportioned square building topped by a dome in 1567; Scamozzi completed it after Palladio's death, between 1580 and 1592. You will perhaps recognize it, for it is the model that inspired Thomas Jefferson's Monticello, the Chiswick House near London, myriad plantation homes in America's Deep South, and countless other noble homes and government buildings in the United States and Europe. It is worth a visit if only to view it from the outside (you can see much of it from the gate). Admission for outside viewing is 5,000L ($2.50), 10,000L ($5) if you want to see the lavishly decorated interior as well. March 15 to November 4, the grounds are open Tuesday to Sunday 10am to noon and 3 to 6pm; the interior is open only Wednesday and Saturday during the same hours.

From here, it's only a 5-minute walk along a path to the **Villa Valmarana,** also called "ai Nani" ("dwarfs") after the statues that line the garden wall (☎ **0444-543-976**). Built in the 17th century by Mattoni, an admirer and follower of Palladio, it is an almost commonplace villa that is worth a visit for an interior covered with remarkable 18th-century frescoes by Giambattista Tiepolo and his son Giandomenico. Admission is 10,000L ($5); 14,000L ($7) if you want to visit outside regular hours, which are complicated. It's open mornings as follows: March 15 to November 5, Wednesday, Thursday, Saturday, and Sunday 10am to noon. It's open afternoons Tuesday to Sunday, as follows: March 15 to April, 2:30 to 5:30pm; May to September, 3 to 6pm; and October to November 5, 2 to 5pm.

Also in this area is the **Basilica or Santuario di Monte Berico** (☎ **0444-320-998**), built in 1668 by a Bolognese architect—and, if you've already visited the Villa Rotonda, you will understand where he got his inspiration. The interior's most important work is in a chapel to the right of the main altar, a *Lamentation* by Bortolomeo Montagna (1500), founder of the local school of painting and one of the Veneto's most famous. The terrace in front of the church affords beautiful views of Vicenza, the Monti Berici, and the nearby Alps. The basilica is open Monday to Saturday 6:15am to 12:30pm and 2:30 to 7:30pm, Sunday 6:15am to 8pm (earlier closing in winter months); admission is free.

AFFORDABLE PLACES TO STAY

Unlike Padua, which gets the overflow when Venice is full, or the tourism-magnet Verona, Vicenza can be very quiet in high season, August, or winter months when trade fairs are not in town; some hotels close without notice for a few weeks if the demand is low. Make sure you call in advance; the city's number of hotels is limited.

Cristina. Corso San Felice 32 (west of Salvi Gardens), 36100 Vicenza. ☎ **0444-323-751.** Fax 0444-543-656. E-mail: hotel.cristina@keycomm.it. 33 units. A/C MINIBAR TV TEL. 180,000L ($90) single; 230,000L ($115) double; triples and quads available. Rates include buffet breakfast. Discounts possible in low season. AE, DC, MC, V. Parking 12,000L ($6).

Located west of the Piazza Castello and the green Giardino Salvi, this recently refurbished hotel is still within easy walking distance of the historic center's principal sites.

It's a perfect choice for those with wheels and a few extra dollars. A contemporary approach, with occasional exposed beams and marble and parquet flooring, results in a handsome, well-maintained lodging that is one of Vicenza's preferred three-star properties. An internal courtyard provides welcome parking space, and guests have access to bicycles for touring the traffic-free center of town as well as the nearby villas just southeast of the train station. After a day of cycling, you can coast back to the hotel and luxuriate in the recently added Finnish sauna.

Due Mori. Via Do Rode 26 (1 block west of Piazza dei Signori), 36100 Vicenza. ☎ **0444-321-886.** Fax 0444-326-127. 26 units, 23 with bathroom. TEL. 75,000L ($37.50) single with bathroom; 80,000L ($40) double without bathroom, 130,000L ($65) double with bathroom. Add a third bed for 15,000L ($7.50). Breakfast 10,000L ($5). AE, MC, V. Closed last 2 wks July.

A full renovation in 1996 has resulted in this fresh, bright, inexpensive hotel choice. Add to that the family-run hotel's history as the oldest in Vicenza and its convenient location on a quiet side street just west of the sprawling Piazza dei Signori, and you have deservedly the most popular spot in town for the budget sensitive. In other words: Book early. In the modernized shell of a centuries-old palazzo, tasteful and authentic 19th-century pieces distinguish otherwise plain rooms whose amenities are kept at a minimum (though in 1999, they did add hair dryers)—but then, so are the prices. This is as good as it gets in the very center of Palladio's hometown.

Palladio. Via Oratorio dei Servi 25 (east of the Piazza dei Signori), 36100 Vicenza ☎ **0444-321-072.** Fax 0444-547-328. E-mail: hotelpalladio@libero.it. 25 units, 16 with bathroom. TEL TV. 70,000L ($35) single without bathroom, 95,000L ($47.50) single with bathroom; 100,000L ($50) double without bathroom, 120,000L ($60) double with bathroom; 160,000L ($80) triple with bathroom. Buffet breakfast included. AE, DC, MC, V. Parking 3,000L ($1.50) on street (5 spaces). Bus from station: 2, 3, 4, 5.

A popular two-star choice spread over three floors (no elevator), the Palladio is the friendliest of the city's few hotels worth mentioning. Just a two-minute walk from the Piazza dei Signori (and equidistant from the Piazza Matteotti and the Teatro Olimpico), this family-run hotel offers small, no-frills rooms in a quiet neighborhood. The beds may be cots, but boards underneath ensure a good night's sleep. Most rooms on the back along a side courtyard have balconies; top floor no. 32 even has a small terrace.

GREAT DEALS ON DINING

Antica Casa della Malvasia. Contrà delle Morette 5 (between Corso Palladio and Piazza dei Signori). ☎ **0444-543-704.** Reservations suggested during high season. Primi 7,500L ($3.75) at lunch, 8,000–10,000L ($4–$5) at dinner; secondi 9,500–11,500L ($4.75–$6) at lunch, 12,000–18,000L ($6–$9) at dinner. AE, MC, V. Tues–Sun noon–3pm and 7pm–midnight (sometimes later). VICENTINO.

This ever lively, tavernalike osteria sits on a quiet, characteristic side street that links the principal Corso Palladio with Piazza dei Signori. The informal service comes with a smile, and the cooking is homemade and regional (there's usually one waiter or more whose English will help eliminate the guessing game). The food is reliably good, but it's just an excuse to accompany the selection of wines (80), whiskies (100), grappas (150), and teas (over 150). No wonder this place always buzzes. Even if you don't eat here, stop in at least for a late-night toddy, Vicentino-style—it's a favorite spot for locals and visitors alike, and live music is often offered on Tuesday and Thursday evenings.

Gran Caffè Garibaldi. Piazza dei Signori 5. No phone. DC, MC, V. Thurs–Tues 8am–midnight. CAFE.

If it's a lovely day, set up camp here in the shade of an umbrella at a table that overlooks Vicenza's grand piazza. The most historically significant cafe in Palladio's city is as stage-set-impressive inside as you would imagine. The upstairs restaurant is too expensive for what it offers, but the outside terrace gives you the chance to sit and gaze upon the wonders of the whale-sized Basilica, yet another Palladian masterpiece. A 15,000L ($8) chef's salad, like the Insalata Garibaldi, makes a great lunch, as do any of the sandwiches and panini, at 6,000L ($3) or less. Or just nurse a cappuccino or aperitivo for the same lire at your outside table; prices are slightly less at the bar, but go for the front-row seats and the theater-in-the-round that the city's beautiful Piazza dei Signori offers.

Righetti. Piazza del Duomo ¾. ☎ **0444-543-135.** Primi 5,000L ($2.50); secondi 8,000–16,000L ($4–$8). No credit cards. Mon–Fri noon–2:30pm and 7–10pm. VICENTINO/ ITALIAN.

For a self-service operation, this place is a triple surprise: The diners are all local (and loyal); the food is reliably good—of the home-cooked, generous-portions variety; and the interior is rustic, welcoming, and pleasant considering its inexpensive profile. But it's the opportunity to sit outdoors in the quiet, traffic-free Piazza Duomo that's the biggest draw here. First stake out a table by setting it, and then order your food at the counter (prepared fresh on the spot). When you're finished, tell the cashier what you had, and he'll add up the bill. There are three or four first courses to choose from (Tuesday and Friday are risotto days) and as many entrees. Evenings offer the added option of grilled meats (which makes eating indoors in the cold winter months more enjoyable), though this is the perfect relaxed place to revel in a simple lunch of pasta and a side vegetable, while opting for a more special dinner venue.

WORTH A SPLURGE

✪ **Trattoria Tre Visi.** Corso Palladio 25 (near Piazza Castello). ☎ **0444-324-868.** Reservations suggested. Primi 15,000L ($8); secondi 22,000–30,000L ($11–$15). Tues–Sun 12:30–2:30pm; Tues–Sat 7:30–10pm. AE, MC, DC, V. VICENTINO/ITALIAN.

Operating since the early 1600s just around the corner until 1997, this Vicentino institution is now located on an important palazzo-studded street in a setting somewhat less dramatic than the 15th-century palazzo it previously occupied—though the new address offers an alfresco courtyard. The menu has stayed unchanged, however, and that's good. Ignore items that concede to foreign requests and concentrate on the regional dishes it knows best. Almost all the pasta is made fresh daily, including the house specialty, *bigoli con anitra,* a fat spaghetti-like pasta served with duck ragout. The region's signature entree, *baccalà alla vicentina,* a traditional "poor man's" dish, is a tender salt codfish simmered in a stew of onions, herbs, anchovies, garlic, and parmigiano for hours before arriving at your table as a work of perfection. When it's prepared properly, as it is here, it's delicious. Ask your kind waiter for help in selecting from Veneto's wide spectrum of very fine wines: Yes, your bill will be enhanced, but so will the memories you'll bring home with you.

DAY TRIPS FROM VICENZA

In addition to visiting the two villas located in the immediate outskirts of Vicenza, a tour of the dozens of country **ville venete** farther afield is the most compelling outing from Vicenza. Check at the tourist office for availability of organized tours, something that has been on-again and, more frequently, off-again for the last few years. You most probably will have to do it yourself, which means having access to wheels. The tourist office will arm you with reams of information to help you sort out the problem of erratic visiting hours (many of the villas are still privately owned and inhabited, and not all can be toured; others permit visits to the grounds but not the interiors). The tourist office also has maps and a host of varied itineraries outlining the most important villas; many are UNESCO protected sites. Public transportation to these villas is close to nonexistent. If you do have access to a car, ask about the summer concert series in June and July, Concerti in Villa (see "Festivals," above), which has drawn some first-class talent in the classical music world.

Bassano di Grappa, about 37km (22 mi.) north of Vicenza, can be incorporated into a tour of the villas. Renowned for both its centuries-old production of ceramics and grappa, it is a picturesque town located on the Brenta River. A covered wooden bridge built by Palladio in 1568 is a highlight of the small *centro storico.* The facades of the city's arcaded homes are painted in the traditional manner, and small squares make this a lovely break from the art-laden larger towns discussed in this chapter. Bassano's yearly **Opera Estate Festival** takes place from early July through August, with alfresco performances of opera, concerts, and dance. For information, call the **tourist office,** Largo Corona d'Italia 35 (☎ **0424-524-351;** fax 0424-525-301). It's open Monday to Friday 9am to 12:30pm and 2 to 5pm and Saturday 9am to 12:30pm. To get here from Vicenza, you can take one of two dozen daily **FTV** buses (☎ **0424-30-850**) that make the 1-hour trip (frequent buses from Padua to Bassano take half the time, making fewer stops); one-way tickets from both cost 5,600L ($2.80).

The delightful medieval walled village of **Marostica,** about 28km (17 mi.) north of Vicenza (and 7km/4.4 miles west of Bassano), comes alive à la *Brigadoon* every other summer, in even years only, when the entire town dresses up to commemorate a true centuries-old chess game between two enamored knights for the hand of Lionora. (Are you surprised? This is the region that gave us Romeo and Juliet.) The chivalric *Partita a Scacchi* is re-enacted on the main piazza with real people as the pieces, dressed in full elaborate Renaissance costume, preceded by a flag-throwing procession with everyone in town taking part; the evocative torch-lit nighttime setting is gorgeous. The next performance is the second Sunday of September 2002. A few of the worst seats are usually available each day of performance, but it's best to purchase tickets months in advance. Tourist information is at Piazza Castello 1 (☎ **0424-72-127;** fax 0424-72-800; www.telemar.it/marostica.htm; e-mail: promarostica@telemar.it). Marostica's engaging **Sagra del Ciliege (Cherry Festival)** takes place in June. You can get here on one of two dozen daily buses from Vicenza (40 min.; 4,500L/$2.25). Dozens of local buses daily do the short run from Bassano to Marostica (it's only 7km/4.4 mi. away). By car, head west on S248.

3 Verona: Home to Juliet & Her Romeo

114km (71 mi.) W of Venice, 80km (50 mi.) W of Padua, 61km (38 mi.) W of Vicenza, 157km (99 mi.) E of Milan.

Suspend all disbelief regarding the real-life existence of Romeo and Juliet, and your stay in **Verona** will be magical. After Venice, this is the Veneto's most visited city. Verona reached a cultural and artistic peak during the 13th and 14th centuries under the powerful, often cruel, and sometimes quirky Della Scala, or Scaligeri, dynasty that took up rule in the late 1200s. In 1405, it surrendered to Venice, which remained in charge until the invasion of Napoléon in 1797.

During the time of Venetian rule, Verona became a prestigious urban capital and controlled much of the Veneto and as far south as Tuscany. You'll see the emblem of the *scala* (ladder) around town, heraldic symbol of the Scaligeri dynasty. The city retains its locked-in-time character that recalls its medieval and Renaissance heyday, and the magnificent medieval palazzi, towers, churches, and stagelike piazzas you see today are picture-perfect testimony to its centuries-old influence and wealth.

And what about Romeo and Juliet? Did they really exist? Originally a Sienese legend, first put into novella form in 1476, this story was subsequently retold in 1524 by Veneto-born Luigi da Porto. He chose Verona in the years 1302 to 04, during the reign of the Scaglieri, and renamed the young couple Romeo and Giulietta. The popular *storia d'amore* was translated into English and became the source of and inspiration for Shakespeare's tale (no one ever said it was original, though the 1998 film *Shakespeare in Love,* a highly enjoyable fictionalized tale, will have you believing it's the Bard's own). Translated into dozens of languages and performed around the world (just look at the number of Asian and Eastern European tourists who flock to Juliet's House), this is a tale of pure love in the tempestuous times of a medieval city whose streets were stained with the blood of feuding families. It's universal and timeless in its content—and no other city setting is so authentically stagelike (though Zeffirelli chose to film his classic 1968 interpretation in the tiny Tuscan town of Pienza, south of Siena—see chapter 5).

Remarkably, visitors spend precious little time in this beautiful medieval city. Statistics clock most tourists stopping for a mere overnight stay (or less). I recommend a stay of at least 2 nights. While it offers a short list of attractions, Verona is a handsome town to take in and enjoy at a leisurely pace.

ESSENTIALS

GETTING THERE   By Train   Verona is easily accessed on the west-east Milan-Venice line as well as the north-south Brennero-Rome line. At least 30 trains daily run west from **Venice** (regional: 2 hr., 10,800L/$5; High speed: 87 min., 17,400L/$9). Even more arrive from Milan (regional: 2 hr., 12,500L/$6; High speed: 85 min., 20,600L/$10).

Trains also connect Verona with Vicenza (30–50 min., 6,000L/$3; High speed: 30 min., 9,400L/$4.70); Padua (regional: 55 min., 8,700L/$4.35; High speed: 50 min. 12,800L/$6); and Bologna (regional: 90 min.–2 hr. 40 min., 10,500L/$5; High speed: 80 min., 17,100L/$9).

The Stazione Porta Nuova **train station** (☎ **045-590-688**) is located rather far south of the Piazza Brà (and Arena) area and is serviced by at least half a dozen local bus lines. The bus network in the historic center is limited, so if you have luggage you'll most probably want a taxi to get to your hotel. To get downtown from the train station, walk straight out to the bus island marked "marciapiede f" (parallel to the station) to catch minibus no. 72 or 73 (1,600L/80¢ tickets at the newsstand in the station or the AMT booth on "Marciapiede A"). Get off on Via Stella at Via Cappello for the center. Alternatively, over half the buses from the station stop at Piazza Brà, so just peruse the posted route signs.

By Bus   The bus station, **APT** (Azienda Provinciale Trasporti; ☎ **045-800-4129**) is at Piazza XXV Aprile directly across from the train station. Buses leave from here for all regional destinations, including Largo di Garda (see chapter 9). Although there is bus service to Vicenza, Padua, and Venice (only the summertime departures for Venice are direct; in other months there's a change), it is easier and cheaper to travel by train.

By Car   The A4 autostrada links Venice and Milan; the exit for downtown Verona is Verona Sud. Coming from the north or south, use the A22 autostrada, taking exit Verona Nord.

VISITOR INFORMATION   The main **tourist office** is at Via degli Alpini 9, at Piazza Bra adjacent to the Arena (☎ **045-806-8680;** fax 045-800-3638; www.verona-apt.net), open daily 9am to 7pm (may close at 6pm in winter). A **small office** is at the train station (☎ **045-800-0861**), open Monday to Saturday 9am to 7:30pm.

Will the Fat Lady Sing?

The well-known **opera season** that takes place every July (usually beginning the last few days of June) and August in **Verona's Arena,** the ancient amphitheater, began in 1913 with a staging of *Aïda* to commemorate the 100th anniversary of Verdi's birth. *Aïda* in all of its extravagant glory has been performed yearly ever since; when I last attended, in 2000, modern dance and minimalist scenery had been incorporated to great effect. Expect to see other Verdi works such as *Un Ballo in Maschera, Nabucco, La Traviata,* and *Rigoletto.*

Those seated on the least expensive, unreserved stone steps costing 42,000L ($21) Friday and Saturday or 38,000L ($19) otherwise, enjoy fresh air, excellent acoustics, and a view over the Arena's top to the city and surrounding hills beyond. The rub is that Jose Carreras will appear to be only about 1 inch high. Numbered seats below cost from 180,000L ($90) to 290,000L ($145); all tickets are subject to an advance booking fee of 5,000L to 38,000L ($2.50 to $19)—worth it, unless you're willing to tough it out by lining up at 4 or 5pm for the 6pm opening of the gates for unreserved seating (and the show doesn't start until 9pm).

The **box office** is on Via Dietro Anfiteatro 6b; credit card purchase accepted by phone or online (☎ **045-800-5151;** fax 045-801-3287; www.arena.it). You pick up tickets the night of the performance. If you hope to find tickets upon arrival, remember that *Aïda* is everyone's most requested performance; weekend performances are usually sold out. As a last-minute resort, be nice to your hotel manager or concierge—everyone has a connection, or a relative with a connection. And even on the most coveted nights (weekend performances by top names), scalpers abound.

FESTIVALS & MARKETS   The Teatro Romano is known for its **Festival Shakespeariano (Shakespeare Festival)** from June to August, which celebrated its 50th anniversary in 1998 with a week of English-language performances by the Royal Shakespeare Company, repeated in 1999 and 2000. Festival performances begin in late May and June with jazz concerts. In July and August there are a number of ballets (such as Prokofiev's Romeo and Juliet) and modern dance performances. Check for the schedule (☎ **045-807-7500** or 045-806-6485 or with the tourist office). Last-minute tickets go on sale at the Teatro Romano box office at 8:15pm (most performances start at 9pm). Tickets range from 15,000L to 40,000L ($8 to $20) plus booking charges.

During Verona's summer-long **festival of the arts,** frequent free concerts (jazz, tango, classical) in the Piazza dei Signori keep everyone out until the wee hours. And for something truly unique, check out **Sognando Shakespeare (Dreaming Shakespeare):** Follow this *teatro itinerante* (traveling theater) of talented young actors in costume as they wander the medieval corners of Verona from site to site, reciting *Romeo e Guilietta* (in Italian only) *in situ,* as Shakespeare would've loved to see it. For information, contact the tourist office.

Other important events are the famous 4-day **horse fair, Fieracavalli,** in early November and the important 5-day **VinItaly wine fair** (which overlaps with the equally important **Olive Oil Fair**) in mid-April. (Verona's schedule of fairs is long and varied; while not many are of interest to those outside the trades involved, their frequency can create problems for tourists in regard to hotel availability.) The Piazza San Zeno hosts a traveling **antiques market** the third Saturday of every month; come early.

GUIDED TOURS   An air-conditioned **"bus turistico"** departs thrice Tuesday to Sunday (10am, 11:40am, and 3:30pm, plus a 9pm Saturday run) for a 1½-hour Giro Turistico tour of the city's historic center every day except Monday June 30 to September 6. The cost is 20,000L ($10) for a recorded spiel in four languages. It leaves from the Gran Guardia in the Piazza Brà, diagonally across from the tourist office. The Saturday afternoon tour features a real live tour guide, which ups the cost to 35,000L ($18).

SEEING THE CITY

The city lies alongside the banks of the S-shaped Adige River. The impressive ancient Roman amphitheater, the **Arena,** sits at the southern end of the city's hub in cafe-ringed **Piazza Brà.** The piazza is linked by the popular pedestrian **Via Mazzini** to **Piazza delle Erbe** and its adjacent **Piazza dei Signori.** The grid of pedestrian-only streets in between is lined with handsome shops and cafes and makes up the principal strolling and window-shopping destination in town.

If you're in town the first Sunday of any month, check to see if entry is still free for the following sites (projected but not confirmed at time of printing): Castelvecchio Museum, the Roman Theater, and Juliet's Tomb.

THE TOP ATTRACTIONS

✪ **Arena di Verona.** Piazza Brà ☎ **045-800-3204.** Admission 6,000L ($3) adults, 4,000L ($2) students, 2,000L ($1) ages 7–14. Tues–Sun 9am–6:30pm. During the July–Aug summer opera season, daily 9am–3pm.

The best-preserved Roman amphitheater in the world and the best known in Italy after Rome's Colosseum, the elliptical Arena was built out of a slightly pinkish marble around the year A.D. 100 and stands in the very middle of town with the Piazza Brà on its southern flank. Built to accommodate more than 20,000 people (outdone by Rome's contender, which could seat more than twice that), it is in remarkable shape today, despite a 12th-century earthquake that left only four arches of the outer ring standing—beloved testimony to the pride and wealth of Verona and its populace.

Its acoustics, astoundingly good for an open-air venue, have survived the millennia and make it one of the wonders of the ancient world and one of the most fascinating venues for live performances today, conducted without microphones. If you're in town during the summer opera performances in July and August, do everything possible to procure a ticket (see "Will the Fat Lady Sing?," above) for any of the outdoor evening performances. Even opera-challenged audience members will take home the memory of a lifetime.

The cluster of outdoor cafes and trattorias/pizzerias on the western side of the Piazza Brà line a wide marble esplanade called Il Liston; they stay open long after the opera performances end, and some serious after-opera people-watching goes on here.

✪ **Piazza delle Erbe.** Between Via Mazzini and Corso Porta Borsari. Open-air produce and flower market Mon–Sat 8am to 7pm.

This bustling marketplace—the palazzi-flanked Square of the Herbs—sits on the former site of the Roman Forum, where chariot races once took place. The herbs, spices, coffee beans, and bolts of silks and damasks that came through Verona after landing in Venice from faraway Cathay have given way to the fresh and aromatic produce of one of Italy's wealthiest agricultural regions—offset by the inevitable ever-growing presence of T-shirt and French-fry vendors, as the piazza has become something of a tourist trap. But the perfume of fennel and vegetables fresh from the earth still assaults the senses in the early morning, mixing with the cacophony of vendors touting their plump tomatoes, dozens of different variations of salad greens, and picture-perfect fruits that can't possibly taste as good as they look, but do. Add to this the canary lady, the farmer's son who has brought in a half a dozen puppies to unload, and the furtive pickpocket who can spot a tourist at 50 paces—and you have one of Italy's loveliest little outdoor markets. A ground-zero rest stop is one of the steps leading up to the small 14th-century fountain in the piazza's center and a Roman statue dubbed "The Virgin of Verona."

✪ Piazza dei Signori (Piazza Dante).

To reach Piazza dei Signori from Piazza delle Erbe, exit under the Arco della Costa (Arch of the Rib), which you'll be able to spot by the enormous whalebone hanging overhead. It was placed here 1,000 years ago, when it was said to have been unearthed during excavations on this spot, indicating that the area was once underwater. Local legend goes that the rib will fall on the first person to pass beneath it that has never told a lie—thus explaining the nonchalance with which every Veronese passes under it.

The perfect antidote to the color and bustle of Piazza delle Erbe, the serene and elegant Piazza dei Signori is a slightly sober square, one of Verona's innermost chambers of calm. Its center is anchored by a large 19th-century statue of the "divine poet" Dante, who found political exile from Florence in Verona as a guest of Cangrande I and his Scaligeri family (in appreciation, Dante wrote of his patron in his poem "Paradiso"). If entering from the Archway, you'll be facing the Scaligeri's 13th-century crenellated **residence** before it was taken over by the governing Venetians. Left of that, behind Dante's back, is the **Loggia del Consiglio (Portico of the Counsel),** a 15th-century masterpiece of Venetian Renaissance style. Opposite that and facing Dante is the 12th-century Romanesque **Palazzo della Ragione,** whose courtyard and fine Gothic staircase should be visited. This piazza is Verona's finest microcosm, a balanced and refined assemblage of historical architecture. Secure an outdoor table at the square's legendary command post, the **Antico Caffè Dante,** and take it all in over a late-afternoon Campari and soda.

✪ Museo Castelvecchio. Corso Castelvecchio 2 (at Via Roma, on the Adige River). ☎ **045-592-985** or 045-594-734. Admission 6,000L ($3). Free 1st Sun of each month. Tues–Sun 9am–6:30pm.

A 5-minute walk west of the Arena amphitheater on Via Roma and nestled on the banks of the swift-flowing Adige River, the "Old Castle" is a crenellated fairy-tale pile of brick towers and turrets, protecting the bridge behind it. It was commissioned in 1354 by the Scaligeri warlord Cangrande II to serve the dual role of residential palace and military stronghold. It survived centuries of occupation by the Visconti family, the Serene Republic of Venice, and then Napoléon, only to be destroyed by the Germans during World War II bombing. The acclaimed Venetian architect Carlos Scarpa initiated a painstaking restoration in 1958 and the castle reopened in 1964. It's now a fascinating home to some 400 works of art.

The ground-floor rooms, displaying statues and carvings from the Middle Ages, lead to alleys, vaulted halls, multileveled floors, and stairs, all as architecturally arresting as the Venetian masterworks from the 14th to 18th centuries—notably those by Tintoretto, Tiepolo, Veronese, Bellini, and the Verona-born Pisanello—that you'll find throughout. Don't miss the large courtyard with the equestrian statue of the warlord Cangrande I (a copy can be seen at the family cemetery at the Arche Scaligeri) with a peculiar dragon's head affixed to his back (it appears to be his armor's helmet removed from his head and resting behind him). A stroll across the pedestrian bridge behind the castle affords you a fine view of the castle, the **Ponte Scaligeri** (built in 1355 and also destroyed during World War II; it was reconstructed using the original materials), and the river's banks.

Verona

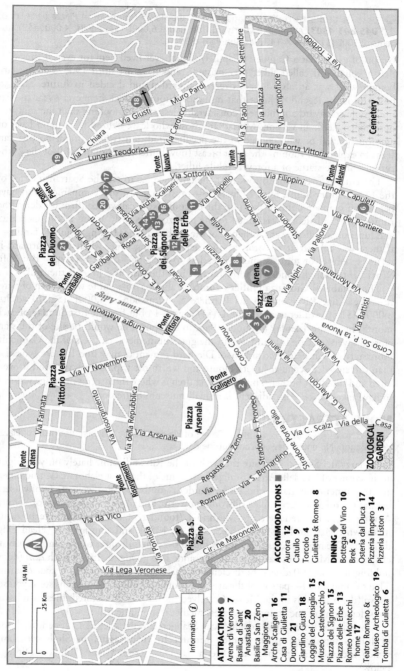

ATTRACTIONS
Arena di Verona **7**
Basilica di Sant' Anastasia **20**
Basilica San Zeno Maggiore **1**
Arche Scaligeri **16**
Casa di Giulietta **11**
Duomo **21**
Giardino Giusti **18**
Loggia del Consiglio **15**
Museo Castelvecchio **2**
Piazza dei Signori **15**
Piazza delle Erbe **13**
Romeo Montecchi home **17**
Teatro Romano & Museo Archeologico **19**
Tomba di Giulietta **6**

ACCOMMODATIONS ■
Aurora **12**
Catullo **9**
Torcolo **4**
Giulietta & Romeo **8**

DINING ◆
Bottega del Vino **10**
Brek **5**
Osteria dal Duca **17**
Pizzeria Impero **14**
Pizzeria Liston **3**

Information ⓘ

0 — 1/4 Mi
0 — .25 Km

✪ **Casa di Giulietta (Juliet's House).** Via Cappello 23 (southeast of Piazza delle Erbe). ☎ **045-803-4303.** Admission: courtyard free; house 6,000L ($3) adults, 4,000L ($2) students, 2,000L ($1) ages 7–14. Tues–Sun 9am–6:30pm.

No proof exists that a Capuleti (Capulet) family ever lived here (or even if they did, that a young girl called Juliet ever existed), and it wasn't until 1905 that the city bought what was an abandoned, overgrown garden and decided its future. Still, so powerful is the legend of Juliet that millions of tourists flock here every year to visit the simple courtyard and home—considerably less affluent-looking than the sumptuous Franco Zeffirelli version. Myriad are those who leave behind layer upon layer of amorous graffiti or who engage in the peculiar tradition (whose origin no one can seem to explain) of rubbing the right breast (now buffed to a bright gold) of the 20th-century bronze statue of a forever-nubile Juliet.

The curious may want to fork over the entrance fee to see the Spartan interior of the 13th-century home, restored in 1996—most do it just so a companion who stays below can snap a picture of them on the balcony. No local will confirm (or deny) the rumor that the balcony was added to the palazzo as recently as the 1920s. Ceramics and furniture on display are authentic of the era but did not belong to Juliet's family—if there was a Juliet at all. Stop by just before closing time, when the courtyard is relatively empty of tourists and it is easiest to imagine Romeo uttering, "But Soft! What light through yonder window breaks? It is the east, and Juliet is the sun!"

The **Tomba di Giulietta (Juliet's Tomb)** is about a 15-minute walk south of here, near the Adige River on Via del Pontiere 5. Admission is 5,000L ($2.50) adults, 3,000L ($1.50) students, and 2,000L ($1) ages 7–14 but free the first Sunday of each month; hours are Tuesday to Sunday 9am to 6:30pm. The would-be site of the star-crossed lovers' suicide is found within the graceful medieval cloisters of the Capuchin monastery of San Francesco al Corso. Die-hard romantics may find it more evocative than the crowded scene at Juliet's House and worth the trip. Others will find it overrated and shouldn't bother. The adjacent church is where their secret marriage was said to have taken place. Also adjacent is a small museum of frescoes.

MORE ATTRACTIONS

Arche Scaligeri (Scaligeri Tombs). Corner of Via degli Arche Scaligeri, northeast of Piazza delle Signori. No entry; viewed from outside only.

Exit Piazza dei Signori opposite the Arch of the Rib and immediately on your right, at the corner of Via delle Arche Scaligeri, are some of the most elaborate Gothic funerary monuments in Italy—the raised outdoor tombs of the Scaligeri family (seen behind the original decorative grillwork), powerful and often ruthless rulers of Verona. Among those interred here are Mastino I (founder of the dynasty, date of death unknown), Mastino II (Mastiff the Second, d. 1351), and Cansignorio (Head Dog, d. 1375). The most interesting tomb is found over the side door of the family's private chapel Santa Maria Antica—that of Cangrande I (Big Dog, d. 1329), with *cani* (dogs) holding up a *scala* (ladder), both elements that figure in the Scaligeri coat of arms. That's Cangrande I—patron of the arts and protector of Dante—and his steed you see above (the original is in the Museo Castelvecchio). Recently restored, these tombs are considered one of the country's greatest medieval monuments.

Around the corner on Via degli Arche Scaligeri 2 is the alleged 13th-century home of Juliet's significant other, **Romeo Montecchi (Montague, in Shakespearian),** which incorporates the popular Osteria dal Duca (See "Great Deals on Dining," below).

Basilica San Zeno Maggiore. Piazza San Zeno. ☎ **045-592-813.** Admission 3,000L ($1.50). Mar–Oct Mon–Sat 9am–6pm, Sun 1–6pm; Nov–Feb Tues–Sat 10am–4pm, Sun 1–6pm.

This is one of the finest examples of Romanesque architecture in northern Italy, built between the 9th and the 12th century. Slightly out of the old city's hub but still easily reached by foot, San Zeno, dedicated to the city's patron saint, is Verona's most visited church. Spend a moment outside to appreciate the fine, sober facade, highlighted by the immense 12th-century rose window, the **Ruota della Fortuna (Wheel of Fortune).**

As lovely as it is, the window pales in importance compared with the ✪ **entrance below**—two pillars supported by marble lions and massive doors whose 48 bronze panels were sculpted from the 9th to the 11th century and are believed to have been some of the first castings in bronze since Roman antiquity. They're among the city's most cherished artistic treasures and worth the trip even if the church is closed. Not as sophisticated as those that would adorn the Baptistry doors of Florence's Duomo in the centuries to come, these panels are more like a naive illustration from a children's book, meant to educate the illiterate masses with scenes from the Old and New Testaments and the life of San Zeno. They're complemented by the stone bas-reliefs found on either side of the doors, the 12th-century work of Niccolo, who was also responsible for the Duomo's portal. The 14th-century tower on the left belonged to the former abbey while the freestanding slender campanile on the right was begun in 1045.

The massive interior is filled with 12th- to 14th-century frescoes and crowned by the nave's ceiling, designed as a wooden ship's keel. But the interior's singular highlight is the famous triptych of the ***Madonna and Child Enthroned with Saints*** by Andrea Mantegna (1459), behind the main altar. Napoléon absconded with the beautiful centerpiece—a showcase for the Padua-born Mantegna's sophisticated sense of perspective and architectural detail—which was eventually returned to Verona, although two side panels stayed behind in the Louvre and in Tours. Look for the colored marble statue of a smiling San Zeno, much loved by the local Veronesi, in an act of blessing; it can be found in a small apse to the left of the altar.

Basilica di Sant'Anastasia. Piazza Anastasia at Corso Anastasia. ☎ **045-592-813.** Admission 3,000L ($1.50). Mar–Oct Mon–Sat 9am–6pm, Sun 1–6pm; Nov–Feb Tues–Sat 10am–4pm, Sun 1–6pm.

Built between 1290 and 1481, Verona's largest church is the city's finest example of Gothic architecture, even though the facade remains unfinished. A lovely 14th-century campanile bell tower is adorned with frescoes and sculptures. The church's interior is typically Gothic in design, highlighted by two famous *gobbi* (hunchbacks) who support the holy-water fonts, an impressive patterned pavement, and 16 side chapels containing a number of noteworthy paintings and frescoes from the 15th to the 16th century. Most important is Verona-born Pisanello's ***St. George Freeing the Princess of Trebisonda*** (1433) which, after several relocations, is now back in its original spot

A Church Tip

Verona's churches have banded together as the **Associazione Chiese Vive** (☎ **045-592-813**). Admission to any one is 3,000L ($1.50), or you can get a cumulative ticket for 8,000L ($4) adults, 7,000L ($3.50) students and over 65, granting admission to Sant'Anastasia, San Zeno, San Lorenzo, San Fermo, and the Duomo complex (the last only between noon and 4pm on this cumulative ticket).

way up above the terra-cotta-filled **Cappella Pellegrini** in the right transept. It's one of his best paintings and is of the armed-knight-and-damsel-in-distress genre—with the large white rump of St. George's steed one of its focal points. Also worth scouting out are the earlier 14th-century frescoes by the Giotto-inspired Altichiero in the **Capella Cavalli** next door.

Teatro Romano (Roman Theater) & Museo Archeologico (Archaeolocical Museum). Via Rigaste Redentore (over the Ponte Pietra bridge behind the Duomo, on the north banks of the Adige). ☎ **045-800-0360** or 045-594-734. Admission 5,000L ($2.50) adults, 3,000L ($1.50) students; free under 14, and for everyone 1st Sun of each month. Tues–Sun 9am–7pm.

The oldest Roman monument in Verona dates from the time of Augustus when the Arena was built and Verona was a strong Roman outpost at the crossroads of the Empire's ancient north/south, east/west highways. There's something almost surreal about attending an open-air performance of Shakespeare's *Two Gentlemen of Verona* or *Romeo and Juliet* here—even if you can't understand a word (see "Festivals & Markets," above). Classical concerts and ballet and jazz performances are also given here, with evocative views of the city beyond. A tour of a small **Archaeological Museum** housed above in a lovely old monastery is included in the admission ticket.

Duomo. Piazza del Duomo (at Via del Duomo). ☎ **045-592-813.** Admission 3,000L ($1.50). Duomo, daily 11am–4:50pm (possibly shorter in winter). Baptistry and Santa Elena. Mar–Oct Mon–Sat 9:30am–6pm, Sun 1:30–6pm; Nov–Feb Tues–Sat 10am–4pm, Sun 1:30–6pm.

Begun in the 12th century and not finished until the 17th, the city's main church still boasts its original main doors and portal, magnificently covered with low reliefs in the Lombard Romanesque style that are attributed to Niccolo, whose work can be seen at the Basilica of San Zeno Maggiore. You enter, however, way around to the right. The church was built upon the ruins of an even more ancient paleochristian church dating to the late Roman Empire. Visit the Cappella Nichesola, the first chapel on the left, where Titian's serene but boldly colorful *Assumption of the Virgin* is the cathedral's principal treasure, with an architectural frame by Sansovino (who also designed the choir). Also of interest is the semicircular screen that separates the altar from the rest of the church, attributed to Sanmicheli. To its right rises the 14th-century tomb of Saint Agatha.

The excavations of **Santa Elena** church, also in the Duomo complex, reveal a bit of 6th-century mosaic floor; the Baptistry contains a Romanesque font carved with scenes from the Nativity cycle.

Don't leave the area without walking behind the Duomo to the river: Here you'll find the 13th-century **Torre di Alberto della Scala** tower and nearby **Ponte della Pietra** bridge, the oldest Roman monument in Verona (1st century B.C.; rebuilt in the 14th century). There has been a crossing at this point of the river since Verona's days as a 1st-century Roman stronghold, when the Teatro Romano was built on the river's northern banks and the Arena at its hub.

VIEWS & GARDENS

The view of Verona from the **Roman Theater** is beautiful any time of day, but particularly during the evening performances—the ancient Romans knew a thing or two about dramatic settings. For other views, you can take a rickety elevator to the 10th-century **Santa Libera** above the theater, or to the former monastery and cloisters of **San Girolamo,** which now houses a small archaeological museum. Above this is the **Castel San Pietro,** whose foundations go back to the times of the Romans and whose terraces offer the best view in town.

Nearby are the well-known, multitiered **Giardino Giusti** (☎ 045-803-4029), gardens whose formal 16th-century layout and geometrical designs of terraces, fountains, statuary, and staircases inspired, among many, Mozart and Goethe. The gardens are open daily 9am to dusk; admission is 8,000L ($4) adults and 3,000L ($1.50) students and under 18.

SHOPPING

Unlike in Venice, all these people walking the boutique-lined pedestrian streets are locals, not tourists. Come to Verona to spend some time doing what the locals do, shopping and stopping in any of the myriad cafes and *pasticcerie*. Unlike Venice, Verona does not live for tourism alone, and it shows: Only the most predictable souvenirs are found in the tourist trinket market. Shopping is mostly for the Veronesi, and upscale clothing and accessories boutiques line the two most fashionable shopping streets, **Via Mazzini** (connecting the Arena and the Piazza delle Erbe) and **Via Cappello,** heading southeast from the piazza and past Juliet's House. Also check out **Corso Borsari** and **Corso Sant'Anastasia** (heading west and east, respectively, out of the Piazza delle Erbe); the latter has a concentration of interesting antiques stores.

AFFORDABLE PLACES TO STAY

Although the following prices reflect peak season rates, expect inflated prices during the July/August opera season (when Venice is offering low season discounts) or when one of the major trade fairs is in town. With these exceptions, low season is November through mid-March. The **C.A.V. (Cooperativa Albergatori Veronesi)** is an organization of dozens of two-to five-star hotels that will help you with bookings for a fee determined by your choice of hotel category (☎ **045-800-9844;** fax 045-800-9372; www.cav.vr.it).

Aurora. Piazza delle Erbe 2 (southwest side of piazza), 37121 Verona. ☎ **045-594-717.** Fax 045-801-0860. 19 units, 17 with bathroom. A/C TV TEL. 90,000–120,000L ($45–$60) single without bathroom; 160,000–210,000L ($80–$105) double with bathroom. Rates include buffet breakfast. AE, DC, MC, V. Parking free on street. Bus: 72 or 73 to Piazza delle Erbe.

Until now, it was location, location, location that had loyal guests returning to the Aurora. After a 1996 refurbishing of all guest rooms and en suite bathrooms, it was the updated decor as well. Six doubles are blessed with views of one of the world's great squares, the Piazza delle Erbe and its white-umbrella stalls that make up the daily marketplace. Consider yourself blessed if you snag the top-floor double (there is an elevator!) with a small balcony. Another terrace for the guests' use overlooks the *mercato* from the second floor, just above the breakfast room where the hotel's daily ample buffet is served.

Catullo. Via Catullo 1 (just north of Via Mazzini), 37121 Verona. ☎ **045-800-2786.** Fax 045-596-987. 21 units, 6 with bathroom; 60,000L ($) single without bathroom; 90,000L ($45) double without bathroom; 110,000L ($55) double with bathroom; 155,000L ($77.50) triple without bathroom; 165,000L ($82.50) triple with bathroom; 210,000L ($105) quad suite with bathroom. No credit cards. Parking free in street. From train station: any bus going to Piazza Brà.

It's a three-floor hike to this homey pensionelike place that has been run by the affable Pollini family for more than 25 years, but it's ultracentral and the rooms are spacious and clean, the baths nice and bright. The prices attract the 20- and 30-something lire-counters who make up the majority of the hotel's clientele. With impressive details such as decorative plaster molding, French doors, and marble or parquet floors, the hanging tapestries and dried flower arrangements become almost superfluous. Single rooms are large and come equipped with a sink; solo travelers feel comfortable in the prevailing family atmosphere. No breakfast service is available, but the bar downstairs couldn't be more convenient.

○ **Torcolo.** Vicolo Lisone 3 (just 1 block off the Piazza Brà), 37121 Verona. ☎ **045-800-7512.** Fax 045-800-4058. 19 units. A/C MINIBAR TV TEL. 90,000–125,000L ($45–$65) single; 120,000–178,000L ($60–$89) double; 150,000–222,000L ($75–$111) triple. Breakfast 13,000–18,000L ($6.50–$9). AE, DC, MC, V. Parking free on street, or 18,000L ($9) in garage. Closed Jan 5–Feb 5. From train station: all buses to Piazza Brà.

Lifelong friends Signoras Silvia and Diana are much of the reason behind the deserving success of this small, comfortable hotel just one peaceful block off the lively Piazza Brà. Bright and homey, it is inviting for its unfussy but tasteful decor throughout. Each guest room is individually done, one lovely for its wrought-iron bed, another for the intricate parquet floor, another still in 19th-century furnishings. No. 31 is a country-style sunny top-floor room (the hotel has an elevator) with exposed ceiling beams, while nos. 16 (a triple), 18, 21, and 34 are done with original Liberty-style furnishings. The recently redone bathrooms have amenities such as hair dryers. They truly care about your comfort here: You'll find orthopedic mattresses on stiff springs, double-paned windows (though it's quiet already), extra air-conditioners on the top floor, and extra-wide single beds. Considerations are even made for different travel tastes: pets are accepted in a nod to Swiss travel habits, a few rooms have tubs for Japanese guests, and softer beds are available for the French. You can take the rather expensive breakfast outdoors on the small patio, in a breakfast nook, or in your room.

WORTH A SPLURGE

○ **Giulietta & Romeo.** Vicolo Tre Marchetti 3 (south of Via Mazzini, 1 block east of the Arena), 37121 Verona ☎ **045-800-3554.** Fax 045-801-0862. www.giuliettaeromeo.com. 30 units. A/C MINIBAR TV TEL. 190,000L ($95) single; 310,000L ($155) double; 350,000L ($175) triple. Rates include buffet breakfast. Mention Frommer's when booking and show book upon arrival for a 10% discount. AE, DC, MC, V. Parking nearby 20,000–30,000L ($10–$15) in garage, or free in open lot. From train station: all buses going to Piazza Brà.

A block from the Arena is this handsomely refurbished palazzo-hotel recommended for its upscale ambience and cordial can-do staff. The brightly lit guest rooms are warmed by burnished cherry-wood furnishings, and the large marble-tiled baths are more like those you'd find in tony first-class hotels at less reasonable rates. The hotel takes its name seriously—there are two small marble balconies à la Juliet on the facade (and some more prosaic ones at the back), but the view from either is unremarkable. The hotel is on a narrow side street that's quiet and convenient to everything.

GREAT DEALS ON DINING

○ **Bottega del Vino.** Via Scudo di Francia 3 (off Via Mazzini), Verona. ☎ **045-800-4535.** www.ifinet.it/bottega. Reservations necessary for dinner. Primi 12,000–20,000L ($6–$10); secondi 15,000–40,000L ($8–$20). Wed–Mon noon–3pm (bar 10:30am–3pm) and 7pm–midight (bar 6pm–midight). AE, DC, MC, V. VERONESE/WINE BAR.

Oenophiles can push an evening's meal here into the stratosphere if they succumb to the wine cellar's 80,000-bottle selection, the largest in Verona. This atmospheric bottega first opened in 1890, and the old-timers who spend hours in animated conversation seem sprung from that era. The atmosphere and conviviality are reason enough to come by for a tipple at the well-known bar, where five dozen good-to-excellent wines are for sale by the glass (1,500L to 20,000L/75¢ to $10). There's no mistaking Verona's prominence in the wine industry here. At mealtimes the regulars head home, and the next shift arrives: Journalists and local merchants fill the few wooden tables, ordering simple but excellent dishes flavored with regional wines, like the *risotto al Amarone*, sauced with Verona's most dignified red.

Brek. Piazza Brà 20. ☎ **045-800-4561.** No reservations accepted. Primi and pizzas 5,100–8,000L ($2.55–$4); secondi 7,500–15,000L ($3.75–$8). AE, MC, V. Daily 11:30am–3pm and 6:30–10pm. CAFETERIA.

The Veronesi (and Italians in general; Brek is part of a Northern Italian restaurant chain) are forever dismissing this place as a mediocre tourist spot, but who are all these Italian-speaking locals with their trays piled high, cutting in front of me in line at the pizza station and clamoring for all the best tables outside with a brilliant view of the sun-kissed Arena? This strip of Piazza Brà is lined with pleasant alfresco alternatives such as the more serious Olivo and Tre Corone, but Brek is an informal, inexpensive preference of mine for a casual lunch where you can splurge (a lot) and walk away satisfied and still solvent. Yes, this is fast food *alla Veronese*—but do the Italians ever really go wrong in the culinary department? Inside it's a food fest, with various pastas and fresh vegetables made up as you wait, and some self-service where fruit salads and mixed green salads are displayed.

✪ **Osteria dal Duca.** Via Arche Scaligeri 2 (east of Piazza dei Signori). ☎ **045-594-474.** Reservations not accepted. Primi 10,000L ($5); secondi 15,000L ($7.50); *menù turistico* 21,000L ($10.50). MC, V. Mon–Fri noon–2:15pm and 6:45–10pm, Sat noon–2:15pm. VERONESE.

There are no written records to confirm that the Montecchi (Montagues) family once owned this 13th-century palazzo, and, thankfully, the discreet management never considered calling this place the "Ristorante Romeo." But here you are, nonetheless, dining in what is believed to be Romeo's house, a characteristic medieval palazzo, and enjoying one of the nicest meals in town in a spirited and friendly neighborhood ambience. You may find *penne con pomodoro e melanzane* (fresh tomato sauce with eggplant) or a perfectly grilled chop with rosemary-roasted potatoes. It'll be simple, it'll be delicious, you'll probably make friends with the people sitting next to you, and you'll always remember your meal at Romeo's Restaurant. Even the most adventurous palates might want to avoid anything on the menu that has *cavallo* or *asino* in it, unless you want to sample horse meat, a local specialty.

Pizzeria Impero. Piazza dei Signori 8. ☎ **045-803-0160.** No reservations accepted. Primi and pizzas 12,000–15,000L ($6–$8); secondi 14,000–30,000L ($7–$15). D, MC, V. Summer daily noon–2am. Winter Thurs–Tues noon–3pm and 6pm–midnight. PIZZERIA/TRATTORIA.

Location is not everything, but sitting with a pleasant lunch or moonlit dinner in this most elegant of piazzas will be one of those Verona memories that stays with you. Impero makes a perfectly respectable pizza (with a full trattoria menu to boot), and any of the two dozen or so varieties will taste pretty heavenly if you're sharing an outdoor table with your Romeo or Juliet.

If Impero is full and the Arena area is more convenient to your day's itinerary, try the well-known and always busy **Pizzeria Liston,** a block off Piazza Brà at Via Dietro Listone 19 (☎ **045-803-4003**). It also serves a full trattoria menu (all credit cards accepted; closed Wednesday), and its pizzas are said to be better, but the side-street setting—even with outdoor tables—doesn't match that of the Impero.

CAFES, PASTRIES & WINE BARS

When all is said and done in Verona, one of the most important things to consider is where you'll stop to sip, recharge, socialize, nibble, and revel in this handsome and affluent town.

CAFES & PASTRIES   Verona's grande dame of the local cafe society is the ✪ **Antico Caffè Dante** in the beautiful Piazza dei Signori (no phone). Verona's oldest cafe, it is rather formal indoors (read: expensive) where meals are served. But it's most recommended for those who want to soak up the million-dollar view of one of Verona's loveliest ancient squares from the outdoor tables smack in the midst of it all. During the Arena summer season, this is the traditional après-opera spot. It's open daily 9am to 4am.

The oldest of the cafe/bars lining Verona's market square is **Caffè Filippini,** Piazza delle Erbe 26 (☎ **045-800-4549**). Repeated renovations have left little of yesteryear's character or charm, but centuries-old habits die hard: It's still the command-post of choice whether indoors or out (preferably out), a lovely spot to take in the cacophony and colorful chaos of the market. It's open 8am to 1am: daily in summer and Thursday to Tuesday in winter.

An old-world temple of caffeine, **Caffè Tubino,** Corso Porta Borsari 15/d, 1 block west of the Piazza delle Erbe (☎ **045-803-2296**), is stocked with packaged blends of Tubino-brand teas and coffees displayed on racks lining parallel walls in a small space made even smaller by the imposing crystal chandelier. The brand is well known, nicely packaged, and makes a great gift. It's open daily from 7am to 11pm. On the same street is **Pasticceria Bar Flego** (Corso Porta Borsari 9; ☎ **045-803-2471**), a beloved institution with eight tiny tables for two. Order a frothy cappuccino along with a sampling of their deservedly famous bite-size pastries, sold by the piece at 1,000 to 2,000L (50¢ to $1) each. Sample the regional specialty, *zaletti,* traditional cookies made with corn flour, raisins, and pine nuts—much better tried than described! It's closed on Monday.

One of Verona's oldest and most patronized pasticcerias is **Cordioli,** a moment's stroll from Juliet's house on Via Cappello 39 (☎ **045-800-3055**). There are no tables and it's often three-deep at the bar, but with coffee this good and pastries this fresh (made on the premises), who cares? Verona's perfect souvenir? Try the homemade *baci di Guilietta* (vanilla meringues called "Juliet's kisses") or *sospiri di Romeo* ("Romeo's sighs," chocolate hazelnut cookies). It's closed Sunday afternoon and Wednesday.

WINE BARS   Verona is the epicenter of the region's important viticulture (Veneto produces more DOC wine than any other region in Italy), but the old-time wine bars are decreasing in number and atmosphere. Recapture the spirit of yesteryear at **Carro Armato,** in a 14th-century palazzo at Vicolo Gatto 2A/Vicolo. San Piero Martire, a block south of Piazza Sant'Anastasia (☎ **045-803-0175**), a great choice for afterhours or any hour when you want to sit and sample some of the 30 or so regional wines by the glass (2,000L to 5,000L/$1 to $2.50) and make an informal meal out of the fresh, inexpensive bar food. Oldsters linger during the day playing cards or reading the paper at long wooden tables, while a younger crowd fills the place in the evening. A small but good selection of cheeses and cold cuts or sausages might be enough to take the edge off, but there is always an entree or two and a side of fresh vegetables on offer. It's open Monday to Friday 10am to 2pm and 5pm to 2am (Saturday and Sunday nonstop).

The wonderfully characteristic old wine bar, **Enoteca dal Zovo,** on Vicolo San Marco in Foro ⅞ (off Corso Porta Borsari near the above-mentioned Caffè Tubino; ☎ **045-803-4369**), is run by Oreste, who knows everyone in town. They all stop by for his excellent selection of Veneto wines averaging 2,000L ($1) a glass, or you can go for broke and start with the very best at 4,000L ($2). Oreste's *simpatica* American-born wife, Beverly, can give you a crash course. Salami, olives, and finger foods will help keep you vertical, since the few stools are always occupied by senior gentlemen who are as much fixtures of the place as the hundreds of dusty bottles of wines and grappa that line the walls. Open Tuesday to Sunday 8am to 1pm and 2 to 8pm.

SIDE TRIPS FROM VERONA

The ancient Greeks called Italy *Enotria*—the land of wines. It produces more wine than any other country in the world, so the annual ✪ **VinItaly** wine fair held every April in Verona is an understandably prestigious event. The Veneto produces more DOC (Denominazione di Origine Controllata, zones of controlled name and origin) than anywhere else in Italy, particularly the Veronese trio of Bardolino and Valpolicella (reds) and Soave (white). The costly, dry Valpolicella wine known as Amarone comes from the vineyards outside of Verona. ✪ **Masi** is among the region's most respected producers, one of many in the Verona hills whose *cantine* are open to the public for wine-tasting stops. Visit Verona's tourist information office for a listing of wine estates open to the public. No organized tours are available, and you'll need your own wheels, but oenologically-minded visitors will want to taste some of Italy's finest wines at the point of their origin.

4 Trent

230km (143 mi.) NW of Milan, 101km (63 mi.) N of Verona, 57km (35 mi.) S of Bolzano.

Surrounded by mountains, this beautiful little city on the banks of the Adige River definitely has an alpine flair. Yet unlike other towns here in the far north, which tend to lean heavily on their Austrian heritage, **Trent (Trento)** is still essentially Italian. The piazzas are broad and sunny, the palaces are ocher-colored and tile-roofed, Italian is the lingua franca, and pasta is still a staple on menus. With its pleasant streets and the remnants of its most famous event, the 16th-century Council of Trent, Trent is a nice place to stay for a night or to visit en route to Bolzano (see section 5 below) and other places in the Trentino-Alto Adige.

ESSENTIALS

GETTING THERE   By Train   Strategically located on a main north-south rail line between Italy and Austria, Trento is served by some 30 trains a day to and from **Verona** (regional: 67 min., 8,500L/$4.25; High speed 58 min., 14,200L/$7), a major transfer point for trains to Milan, Florence, Rome, Venice, Trieste, and all points south. There are about 40 trains a day from **Bolzano** (32 min., 5,700L/$2.85).

By Bus   **Atesina** buses (☎ **0461-821-000**), which leave from a terminal next to the train station, are the major links to outlying mountain towns. There's also hourly service to and from **Riva del Garda** on Lago di Garda (see chapter 9; 1 hr. 40 min., 5,500–6,000L/$2.75–$3).

By Car   The A22 autostrada connects Trento with Verona in about an hour; from Verona you can connect with the A4 for Milan (total trip time between Milan and Trento is about 2½ hr.) and with A22 to Modena and from there A1 for Florence and Rome (Trento is a drive of about 3½ hr. from Florence and about 6½ hr. from Rome). A22 also runs north to Bolzano, a little over half an hour away; the slower S12 also connects Trento and Bolzano, and from it you can get on the scenic Strada di Vino.

VISITOR INFORMATION   The **tourist office,** near the Duomo at Via Manci 2 (☎ **0461-983-880,** fax 0461-984-508, www.trento.it), is open daily 9am to 7pm.

FESTIVALS & MARKETS   In May and June, churches around the city are the evocative settings of performances of the **Festivale di Musica Sacra (Festival of Sacred Music).** Its final performances coincide with **Festive Vigiliane,** a medieval pageant for which townspeople turn up in the Piazza del Duomo appropriately decked out. An ambitious program aptly named **Superfestival** stages musical performances,

Getting a Lift Out of Town

For a breezy view of Trento and a heart-thumping aerial ride as well, take the cable car from Ponte di San Lorenzo near the train station up to **Sardagna,** a village on one of the mountainsides that enclose the city. You may want to provision yourself at the market and enjoy an alpine picnic on one of the grassy meadows nearby. The cable car (☎ **0461-822-075**) runs daily, every 30 minutes 7am to 6:30pm and the fare is 1,500L (75¢) each way.

historic dramas, and reenactments of medieval and Renaissance legends in castles surrounding Trento; it runs from late June through September.

A small **daily food market** covers the paving stones of Piazza Alessandro Vittorio daily 8am to 1pm. A larger **market,** this one with **clothing, crafts,** and **bric-a-brac,** is held Thursday from 8am to 1pm in Piazza Arogno near the Duomo, and this same piazza hosts a **flea market** the third Sunday of every month.

WHAT TO SEE & DO

To reach the center of town from the train station, where you will also find parking, follow the Via Pozzo through several name changes until it reaches the Piazza del Duomo as Via Cavour. As you amble around this lovely town, you'll soon learn that much of what's notable about Trento is in some way connected with the **Council of Trent,** called by the Vatican from 1545 to 1563 to counter the effects of the new wave of Protestantism that was sweeping down from the north.

The outcomes of the many council sessions were announced in the 13th- to 16th-century **Duomo** (☎ **0461-234-419**), which is delightfully situated on the wide expanse of the cafe-filled Piazza del Duomo. This square, with a statue of Neptune at its center, is referred to as the city's *salotto* (sitting room), so popular is it as a place to pass the time. More specifically, the decrees that came out of the Council were read in the Duomo's Chapel of the Crucifix, beneath an enormous 15th-century cross. Under the altar of the main church is the Basilica Paleocristiana, a 6th-century church later used as a crypt for the city's powerful prince-bishops. But a few scraps of mosaic and carvings remain. The Duomo is open Monday to Saturday 9:30am to 12:30pm and 2:30 to 6pm; its crypt is open 10am to noon and 2:30 to 6pm. Admission to the crypt is 2,000L ($1), but admission is free with the Museo Diocesano ticket (see below).

The Duomo's **Museo Diocesano Tridentino** (☎ **0461-234-419**) is housed in the adjoining, heavily fortified palace of these bishops. The museum displays some fascinating paintings of Council sessions that serve almost as news photos of the proceedings (one provides a seating plan for delegates), as well a collection of medieval and Renaissance paintings, 16th-century tapestries and statuary, and other objects from the Duomo's treasury. The Museo is open Monday to Saturday 9:30am to 12:30pm and 2:30 to 6pm; admission is 5,000L ($2.50), which includes the Duomo's crypt (see above).

Many Council sessions were held in the **Castello di Buonconsiglio,** which you can reach by walking north from the Duomo along Via Belenzani, then east on Via Roma—both, especially the former, are lined with palaces, many with faded frescoes on their facades, built to house the church officials who came to Trento to attend the council sessions. The mazelike Castello incorporates the 13th-century Castelvecchio, surrounded by medieval fortifications, and the elegant Magno Palazzo, a palace built for a prince-bishop in the 15th century. Within the vast complex is the Museo Provincale d'Arte, where the pride of the collection is the 15th-century ✪ *Ciclo dei Mesi*

(*Cycle of the Months*) housed in the Torre dell'Aquila, or Eagle's Tower (for admission, ask the guards at the Loggia del Romanino). It's an enchanting fresco cycle that presents a detailed look at life at court and in the countryside, showing amusements among the lords and ladies and much hard work among the peasants.

You can also visit the cell where native son Cesare Battiste was held in 1916 for his part in the Irredentist movement, which sought to return Trento and other parts of the region to Italy. This indeed came to pass with the Treaty of Versailles in 1919, but not before Battiste was hanged in the moat that surrounds the Castelvecchio.

July 15 to October, the complex is open Tuesday to Sunday 10am to 6pm; November to July 14, Tuesday to Sunday 9am to noon and 2 to 5:30pm. Admission is 10,000L ($5).

AFFORDABLE PLACES TO STAY

Al Cavallino Bianco. Via Cavour 29, 38100 Trento. ☎ **0461-231-542.** 24 units, 6 with bathroom. 47,000L ($23.50) single without bathroom, 67,000L ($33.50) single with bathroom; 72,000L ($36) double without bathroom, 95,000L ($47.50) double with bathroom; 130,000L ($65) triple with bathroom. AE, DC, MC, V. Closed June 16–29 and Dec 16–29.

The surrounding neighborhood near the Duomo is charming, but this hostelry is basic—you should come here only if the Venezia is booked. Still, these prices and the privacy that the spacious rooms afford make this a good base from which to explore the expensive region. The lobby is actually quite amusing—with green pressed-felt carpeting, picnic tables, and a cartoonish mural of alpine meadows. The guest rooms don't have much more than a bed and a chair, and most don't have baths—but they do have in-chamber showers, sinks, and bidets.

Aquila d'Oro. Via Belezani 76, 38100 Trento. ☎ **0461-986-822.** 20 units. MINIBAR TV TEL. 100,000L ($50) single; 140,000L ($70) double. Rates include breakfast. AE, DC, MC, V.

A recent renovation of an older hotel that in turn occupied a centuries-old palazzo has created some of the nicest rooms in Trento, with a wonderful location right around the corner from the Piazza del Duomo. Decor throughout is stylishly contemporary, with a nice smattering of Oriental carpets, vaulted ceilings, and other interesting and cozy architectural touches in public rooms. The guest rooms are a little plainer, but have glossy, streamlined new furnishings and gleaming tile bathrooms. All this may change, however, when new management takes over in 2001 (the retiring owners have no idea what the new ones plan). Call ahead.

Venezia. Via Belezani 70 at Piazza Duomo, 38100 Trento. ☎ **0461-234-559.** 40 units, 34 with bathroom. 50,000L ($25) single without bathroom, 65,000L ($33) single with bathroom; 70,000L ($35) double without bathroom, 90,000L ($45) double with bathroom. MC, V.

This old hotel is a sight nicer than the Cavallino Bianco, above, but it's just about as charmless. Marked by 1950s-style furnishings, the simple, high-ceiling rooms are a bit dowdy but offer solid, old-fashioned comfort (unfortunately, some beds still bear the sags left by generations of travelers). Its selling point: The rooms in the front come with stunning views over the Piazza Duomo. Some of the younger members of the family who run the hotel speak English and are more than happy to dispense advice on what to see and do in town and the surrounding area.

GREAT DEALS ON DINING

It's almost a requirement to stroll down Trento's renaissance streets with a gelato from **Torre Verde-Gelateria Zanella** on Via Suffragio 6 (☎ **0461-232-039**). Many of the flavors are made from fresh, local fruits in season, while others make no such attempt at wholesomeness and incorporate the richest chocolate and cream.

Birreria Pedavena. Piazza Fiera 13 at Via Santa Croce. ☎ **0461-986-255.** Wed–Mon noon–2:15pm and 6pm–12:15am (bar and light meals 8:30am–12:15am). Primi 6,500–9,000L ($3.25–$4.50); secondi 8,900–16,900L ($4.45–$8); pizze 6,500–11,000L ($3.25–$6). MC, V. BEER HALL/PIZZERIA.

It seems as if this dark cavernous beer hall–style cafeteria can feed all of Trento, and it just might. It draws a big crowd for coffee and pastries in the morning and keeps serving a huge mix of pastas, *würstel, canederli,* and pizza all day. You will probably be happiest if you order simply, maybe a plate of *würstel* (essentially, hot dogs) or goulash or one of the excellent pizzas. Pedavena keeps some of the latest hours in town, making this something of a late evening spot in a town where the nightlife is scarce.

La Cantinota. Via San Marco 24. ☎ **0461-238-527.** Reservations recommended. Fri–Wed noon–3pm and 7–11pm (piano bar, 10:30pm–2am). Primi 9,000–13,000 ($4.50–$7); secondi 15,000–25,000L ($8–$13). ITALIAN/TYROLEAN.

With its white tablecloths, excellent service, and reasonably priced menu, La Cantinota could be the most popular restaurant in Trento. The color red is used with abandon, and a goose wanders among the tables in the atrium garden. The fare includes Italian and Tyrolean dishes and is truly inspired, making use of fresh local ingredients: wonderful homemade gnocchi, *strangola preti* (spinach dumplings coated in melted butter), rich risottos with porcini mushrooms, grilled sausages with polenta, and *vitello barolo* (veal in a rich red wine sauce). The adjoining piano bar is popular with the local talent who tend to intersperse Frank Sinatra renditions with yodeling.

Pizzeria Duomo. Piazza del Duomo 22. ☎ **0461-984-286.** Sun–Fri, 11:30am–2:30pm and 5–11:30pm. Primi 7,000–11,000L ($3.50–$6); secondi 9,000–16,000L ($4.50–$8); pizze 7,000–11,000L ($3.50–$6). MC, V. PIZZERIA/ITALIAN.

This pleasant eatery facing the Duomo has a no-frills tile-floor-and-white-walled dining room, but offers much more romantic dining on its terrace overlooking the church and its square. While it's possible to eat a full meal of the standard pasta and veal variety here, the pizzas are the big draw—topped with everything from tomatoes to *würstel.* Be prepared to wait in line on Friday and Sunday nights.

EN ROUTE TO BOLZANO: THE STRADA DI VINO

Some of Italy's finest wines are produced on the vines that cloak the hillsides between Trento and Bolzano. (These local wines include many pinot grigios and pinot noirs among whites, and Vernatsch, the most common red of the region.) If you are traveling by car between the two cities you can make the trip on the well-marked Strada di Vino (Weinstrasse). Leave Trento on S12; 15km (9 mi.) north you'll come to the main turn-off for the village of Lavis; follow this turn-off, and from here easy-to-follow yellow signs will lead you along a series of twisting roads through seemingly endless vineyards and around Lago di Caldaro to Bolzano. Many of the vineyards have tasting rooms open to the public and sometimes offer cheese, sandwiches, and other refreshment as well. If you don't have your own wheels, the tourist offices in Trento and Bolzano can provide lists of local tour companies that lead wine tours.

5 Bolzano

154km (92 mi.) N of Verona, 118km (73 mi.) S of Innsbruck, 57km (35 mi.) NE of Trento.

Without even crossing a border, you'll find yourself in a place that doesn't resemble Italy at all. During its long history, this pretty town at the confluence of the Talvera and Isarco rivers has been ruled by the bishops of Trent, the counts of Tirol, and the Hapsburgs, to name but a few of the empires to which it has belonged. **Bolzano** has

---

Free Bikes!

The best way to get about town—certainly out to the castles and to Gries—is on one of the free bikes offered by the commune. There's a stand on the left side of Viale Stazione just before Piazza Walther, and another on Piazza Gries. Just leave a 10,000L ($5) deposit, have a passport or driver's license handy (they write the number down), and bring it back by 7pm.

---

been part of Italy since the end of World War I, but as you explore the narrow streets and broad piazzas and stroll through the parks that line the town's two rivers, you get the sense that the city is more Nordic than Italian—a notion underscored by the city's high-gabled, Tyrolean-style houses and preference for the German tongue.

ESSENTIALS

GETTING THERE   By Train   Bolzano is on the north-south rail line that links Verona with Innsbruck, Austria, via the Brenner Pass. Some 30 trains run daily from **Verona** (regional: 1 hr. 45 min., 12,500L/$6.25; High-speed 90 min., 20,200L/ $10.10); forty trains a day from **Trento** (32 min., 5,700L/$2.85). Hourly train service links Bolzano with **Merano** (38 min., 6,300L/$3.15).

By Bus   Bolzano is the hub of the excellent **SAD bus network,** serving even the most remote mountain villages (☎ **0471-450-111**). Hourly buses run to and from **Merano** (1 hr.; 5,500L/$2.75), and **Bressanone** (1 hr.; 7,200L/$3.60). Two daily morning buses (currently 9:15 and 11:10am) make the trip to **Cortina,** with a change in Dobbiaco (about 4 hr.; 21,100L/$10.55). The extremely helpful staff at the bus station, the round building one block up from the train station and on the left, will help you make sense of the routing.

By Car   The A22 autostrada connects Bolzano with Trento in a little over half an hour and with Verona (where you can connect with the A4 for Milan and Rome) in a little over an hour; and, farther south, Modena (where you can connect with the A1 for Florence and Rome); A22 runs north to Innsbruck.

VISITOR INFORMATION   The city **tourist office,** near the Duomo at Piazza Walther 8 (☎ **0471-307-000;** fax 0471-980-300; www.sudtirol.com/bolzano.it), dispenses a wealth of information on Bolzano and the South Tyrol. It's open Monday to Friday 9am to 6:30pm and Saturday 9am to 12:30pm.

FESTIVALS & MARKETS   Bolzano celebrates spring with weekend **concerts** throughout April and May in Piazza Walther, and adds a **flower show,** with more music, around the first of May. The city's most serious musical event is the **Concorso Internazionale Piantistico F. Busoni,** an international piano competition held the last 2 weeks of August. The **Festival del Teatro di Strada** draws wandering musicians, mimes, puppeteers, and other performers to the streets of the Old City in October. One of the more colorful events in the region is the **Bartolomeo Horse Fair,** which brings together the region's most beautiful equines on the Renon plateau, which can be reached by funicular (see "Funiculars," below).

One of the most enjoyable walks in the Old City takes you through the stalls of the **fruit and vegetable market** in Piazza delle Erbe, which operates Monday through Saturday from 8am to 7pm. From November 28 to December 23 the city hosts a much-attended **Mercatino di Natale** (Christkindlmarkt), in which handmade ornaments, wooden toys, and other seasonal crafts, along with Christmas pastries and mulled wine, are sold from booths in a festively decorated Piazza Walther.

A **flea market** fills the Passegiata del Talvera along the River Talvera (follow Via Museo from the center of town) the first Saturday of every month, opening at 8am and closing at 4pm.

WHAT TO SEE & DO

With its two rivers, surrounding hills, expansive greens, and medieval center, Bolzano is an extremely appealing city that melds urban sophistication with an appreciation for nature. The compact medieval Old City is still the heart of town, and at its center **Piazza Walther** honors a 12th-century wandering minstrel. The piazza seems to capture the mood of its lighthearted historical associations with a fringe of cafe tables to one side and the brightly tiled roof and lacy spire of the **Duomo** on the other. The interior of this 12th- to 14th-century church is far plainer than its exterior, but is enlivened somewhat by much-faded frescoes and an intricately carved pulpit (☎ **0471-978-676;** open Monday to Friday 9:45am to noon and 2 to 5pm and Saturday 9:45 to noon; Sunday for services only).

A far more enticing church is the **Chiesa dei Domenicani** (☎ **0471-973-133**), just a few steps west of the Duomo. Inside this 13th-century structure are two sets of frescoes that comprise the city's greatest artistic treasure. From the 15th century, on the walls of the cloisters, one depicts court life. The other, in the Capella di San Giovanni (under the arch behind the altar and to the right; 500L/25¢ light box), is a 14th-century religious cycle attributed to the school of Giotto, including the **Triumph of Death.** In these rich frescoes, a heady dose of realism comes through, along with the beginnings of the use of such elements as perspective and foreshortening, which suggests the influence of the early Renaissance. It's open Monday to Saturday 9:30am to 6pm; Sunday for services only.

There is one more church to see in Bolzano, but before you reach it, you will be distracted by the considerable worldly pleasures this city has to offer. If you walk north from Piazza Walther you will soon come to the lively clamor of **Piazza dell'Erbe,** actually one long, wide street that winds past a statue of *Neptune* through the old town and is so named because it has hosted Bolzano's fruit and produce market for centuries. The piazza is lined with shops selling bread, cheese, strudel, wine, and other comestibles, which spill into stalls along the pavement to create a cheerful, open-air supermarket. At the north end is Bolzano's atmospheric main shopping street, **Via dei Portici,** also closed to traffic. It's lined with 15th-century houses whose porticoes overhang the sidewalk to create a cozy effect that definitely feels more northern European than Italian.

The aforementioned church, **Chiesa dei Francescani** (☎ **0471-977-293**), is across Via dei Portici on Via Francescani. Inside is a sumptuously carved altar from 1500, one of the Gothic masterpieces of the Trentino-Alto Adige. The 14th-century cloisters are charming—intimate, frescoed on one side, gracefully vaulted and beautifully planted. It's open Monday to Saturday 10am to noon and 2:30 to 6pm; Sunday for services only).

Bolzano's newest and by far most popular sight is the thoroughly modernized ✪ **Museo Archeologico dell'Alto Adige,** Via Museo at Via Cassa di Risparmio (☎ **0471-982-098;** www.iceman.it), better known as "Ötzi's House" since it was remodeled in 1998 to house the famed 5,300-year-old "Iceman." This mummy made headlines in 1991 when a pair of German hikers discovered him sticking out of a melting glacier high in the Tyrol mountains—though whether he was of Alpine origin or was merely trying to cross the Alps is still being debated (his equipment and one of his last meals seem to have come from lower-altitude valleys, nearer Verona). Along with the mummy were preserved remnants of clothing (including shoes and a bear-skin hat), a flint dagger, a copper ax, and a quiver with flint-tipped arrows he was in the process of making. The museum is open May to September Tuesday to Sunday 10am to 6pm (to 8pm Thursday), October to April Tuesday to Sunday 9am to 5pm (to 8pm Thursday). Admission is 13,000L ($7) adults, 7,000L ($3.50) students under 28, 9,000L ($4.50) seniors over 65, or 26,000L ($13) family card (2 adults plus kids under 14). The recommended audioguides are an extra 3,000L ($1.50).

A walk across the River Talvera (follow Via Museo west across the Ponte Tavera) brings you into the newer **"Italian" section** of Bolzano, constructed in the 1920s when the Mussolini government encouraged workers from other parts of Italy to settle here in the newly won territory. Those who answered the call were either inspired or intimidated by the imposing Fascist-era structures put up along Corso Libertá (including the **Monumento della Vittoria,** a triumphal arch that is frequently the target of attacks by German-speaking groups who want the region to revert to Austrian rule).

In a few blocks, though, the Corso brings you into the pleasant confines of **Gries,** once an outlying village and now a quaint, leafy neighborhood built around the **Abbazia dei Benedettini di Gries,** a Benedictine abbey (not usually open to the public) prettily surrounded by vineyards and gardens. Just beyond is the **Vecchia Parrochiale di Gries,** the village's parish church, whose treasures include a 12th-century crucifix and an elaborately carved 15th-century altar (☎ **0471-283-089;** open Monday to Friday 10:30am to noon and 2:30 to 4pm; closed November to March). If you wish to continue walking, Gries is the terminus of the **Passeggiata del Guncina,** a beautiful maintained, 8km (5 mi.) trail that leads through parklike forests planted with many botanical specimens to a belvedere.

CASTLES   Of the many castles that surround Bolzano, the closest to the center is the **Castel Mareccio,** just a short walk along the River Talvera (from the Piazza delle Erbe, follow the Via Museo west to the Ponte Tavera and from there the Lungo Talvera Bolzano north for less than half a kilometer/a quarter of a mile). Though it's now used as a convention center and its five towers rise from a residential neighborhood of recent vintage, this 13th-century fortress is stunning, all the more so since it's surrounded by a generous swath of vineyards that've been saved from urban encroachment, and backed by forested hills. You can step inside for a glimpse at the stone-walled medieval interior and enjoy a beverage at the bar; the castle is open to the public Wednesday to Monday 9am to 6pm (hours vary when conferences are in session; ☎ **0471-976-615**).

A longer walk of about 2km (a little over a mile; or take the free bus from Piazza Walther) leads out of Bolzano north to the 13th-century **Castel Roncolo** (☎ **800-210-003** or 0471-329-808), beautifully ensconced high above the town and beneath a massive, foreboding cliff face; from the Chiesa dei Francescani follow the Via Castel Roncolo north; you will pass one side of the Castel Mareccio, at which point posted signs will lead you along Via Beatro Arrigo and Via San Antonio for a gradual uphill climb to Castel Roncolo. The interior is decorated with faded but fascinating ✪ **frescoes** from the 14th and 15th centuries that depict secular scenes from the story of *Tristram and Isolde* and other tales of romantic love and chivalry. These painted scenes are remarkably moving in their almost primitive craftsmanship that nonetheless reveals a certain worldliness. Admission is 10,000L ($5) adults, 6,000L ($3) students and over 60, 20,000L ($10) family card for 4; hour-long guided tours in English cost an extra 5,000L ($2.50) per person. The castle is open Tuesday to Saturday: September 16 to June 14 10am to 6pm and June 15 September 15 10am to 8pm.

FUNICULARS   Several cable cars will whisk you right from the center of Bolzano into the surrounding mountains. The most dramatic ride takes you from a terminal near the train station 3,000 feet up to the **Altopiano del Renon,** a pasture-covered plateau that provides dizzying views down to Bolzano and up to higher Dolomite peaks. The funicular deposits you in **Soprabolzano (Oberbozen),** where you can sip a beer and enjoy the view, then venture farther by footpath or an electric tram into a bizarre landscape of spindly rock spires—worn needle-thin by erosion and each seeming to balance a boulder on the top—that surrounds the village of **Collabo.** The cable car (☎ **0471-978-479**) makes the ascent in 15 minutes and operates daily from a terminus 500 meters (about 1,500 feet) east of the train station on Via Renon; it operates hourly 7am to 8pm; the round-trip, 15 minutes each way, costs 9,400L ($4.70) and includes tram fare between Soprabolzano and Collabo (7,200L/$3.60 if you skip the tram).

The **Funivia di San Genesio** whisks you up a forested hillside to the pretty village of San Genesio Atesino, surrounded by woods and mountain peaks. Cable cars (☎ **0471-978-436**) leave hourly from 7am to 7pm (from 8am on Sunday) from a terminus on Via Sarentino on the northern outskirts of Bolzano (take bus 12 or 14). The trip takes 15 minutes and the round-trip fare is 6,500L ($3.75). San Genesio's little tourist office (☎ **0471-355-196,** fax 0471-354-085) is open Monday to Friday 9am to 1pm (July to November also 3 to 5pm).

AFFORDABLE PLACES TO STAY

Feichter. Via Grappoli 15, 39100 Bolzano. ☎ **0471-978-768.** Fax 0471-974-803. www.paginegialle.it/feichter. 49 units. TV, TEL. 90,000L ($45) single, 140,000L ($70) double, 170,000L ($85) triple. Rates include breakfast. MC, V. Parking 10,000L ($5) in garage (10 spots). Closed 3 weeks in Feb.

This charming little inn is one of the few hotels in the Old City. For the location and atmosphere it provides, it's one of the city's better lodging values. On the main floor are a Tyrolean-style lobby and a bar and self-service restaurant that resemble a *weinstube* (rustic wine pub). The rooms may not be full of mountain ambience (and the bathrooms are cramped), but they offer serviceable, modern furnishings that are comfortable; the extremely firm beds are equipped with that wonderful local luxury: thick down quilts. A narrow courtyard is set with picnic tables and shaded by a grape arbor.

Regina. A. Via Renon 1, 39100 Bolzano. ☎ **0471-972-195.** Fax 0471-978-944. www.gattei.it/regina. 40 units. TV TEL. 90,000–100,000L ($45–$50) single on front, 100,000–110,000L ($50–$55) single on back; 130,000–140,000L ($65–$70) double on front, 140,000–150,000L ($70–$75) double on back; 195,000–204,000L ($98–$102) triple on front, 204,000–210,000L ($102–$105) triple on back; 220,000L ($110) quad on front, 230,000L ($115) quad on back; 250,000L ($125) mansard quint on back. Rates include breakfast. MC, V. Parking free on street.

For pleasant and affordable lodgings in Bolzano, you need look no further than this modern hotel across the street from the train station—a decent location, as you're still only three blocks from the main square. The rate disparity above, however, reflects the noisiness of the busy main street out front. Families take note: The bright rooms are unusually large, and there are several quads and one mansard quint on hand. While accommodations are quite plain, they're very nicely decorated with streamlined Scandinavian furnishings, and all offer a level of comfort and amenities that you would expect in a much more expensive hotel—including large bathrooms nicely equipped with stall showers. Lower-ceilinged mansard rooms are offered for 10,000L ($5) less than the rates quoted above.

Stadt Hotel Citta. Piazza Walther 21, 39100 Bolzano. ☎ **0471-975-221.** Fax 0471-976-688. 102 units. A/C TEL TV. 150,000–190,000L ($75–$95) single, 200,000–280,000L ($100–$140) double. Rates include breakfast. AE, DC, MC, V. Parking 18,000L ($9).

This modernized old hotel, with an attractive arcaded facade typical of the city's distinctive architecture, commands a sunny corner of Bolzano's main piazza, and was massively overhauled by its new owners, the Hotel Alpi, in 2000/2001. The large and bright guest rooms, many with small terraces, have been done in a contemporary style with echoes of old Bolzano, and the baths are spanking new. The best rooms overlook the square and the Duomo; Mussolini stayed in one of them (no. 303), a suite with a corner balcony. The ground-floor bar and cafe that opens to the square is a popular gathering spot, and the handsome paneled and terra-cotta-tiled lobby is also a much-used meeting place.

GREAT DEALS ON DINING

Some of the least expensive meals in towns are supplied by the **vendors** who dispense a wide assortment of *würstel* from carts in the Kornplatz and Piazza dell'Erbe.

Batzenhasul. Via Andreas Hofer/Andreas Hoferstrasse 30. ☎ **0471-976-183.** Primi 8,000–12,000L ($4–$6); secondi 16,000–35,000L ($8–$18). No credit cards. Wed–Mon 6:30pm–2am (Sun to 1am). TYROLEAN.

The two floors of dining rooms are charming and cozy, with dark carved Tyrolean benches, hardwood floors, and heavily beamed ceilings; the downstairs is primarily a *weinstube*, a tavernlike room where you are welcome to linger over a beer and a plate of cheese. On both floors you can also order from a menu that, like those in many other restaurants in town, is typically Tyrolean, which means mostly Austrian with some Italian touches. While an excellent minestrone is sometimes available, this is also the place to sample *leberknödelsuppe*, a thick broth with a liver dumpling floating in it. Pork loin, roast beef with potatoes, and other heavy Northern fare dominate the entree choices.

Cavallino Bianco. Via Bottai/Bindergasse 6. ☎ **0471-973-267.** Primi 6,500–11,000L ($3.25–$6); secondi 8,000–27,000L ($4–$14). No credit cards. Mon–Fri 8am–1am, Sat 8am–3pm. TYROLEAN.

This atmospheric *stube* (beer hall) is darkly paneled and decorated with carved wooden furniture to create a cozy, typically Tyrolean atmosphere. The restaurant opens early to operate as a cafe, dispensing coffee and pastry for breakfast, and remains opens well into the night, sending out hearty lunches and dinners of local fare with only a slight Italian influence. Fried Camembert, herrings, and assorted salami are among the dozens of appetizers, while a pasta dish (and there are many to choose from) is likely to be followed by a main course of Wiener schnitzel or *würstel*.

Ristorante Hostaria Argentieri. Via Argentieri 14. ☎ **0471-981-718.** Reservations highly recommended. Primi and secondi 25,000–35,000L ($12.50–$37.50). DC, MC, V. Mon–Sat noon–2:30pm and 7 to 10:30pm. SEAFOOD.

You'll feel as if you've come back to Italy when you step into this attractive cream-colored, tile-floored room. The menu offers several risottos and a grilled steak, but most of the offerings are seafood—unusual, and much in demand, up here in the Dolomiti. You can start with tasty *tagliolini al salmone, bigoli alla veneta* (homemade pasta with anchovies and capers), followed by grilled *branzino, rombo*, or *trancio di spada* (swordfish steak). In good weather there is dining on a tiny terrace in front of the restaurant, facing an attractive cobblestone street that is indeed Tyrolean in character.

Vogele. Via Goethe 3. ☎ **0471-973-938.** Primi 6,500–14,000L ($3.25–$7); secondi 17,000–31,000L ($9–$16). V. Mon–Fri 9am–midnight, Sat 9am–3pm. TYROLEAN.

If you ask someone in Bolzano where to eat, there's a very good chance you'll be sent to this attractive *weinstube*/restaurant just off Piazza dell'Erbe. One of the two long cross-vaulted rooms is set up as a cafe and the other as a dining room (or you can eat under the arcade out front). Both have traditional, woody Tyrolean furnishings, and wherever you sit you can order lightly, or relatively so, if you wish, from the long appetizer menu—perhaps a platter of speck or *affumicato della casa* (smoked meats). First and second courses alike include many traditional favorites; start with a wonderful *zuppa di vino* (a soup with a white wine and cream base) or *canederli* (dumplings that here are laced with liver, bacon, or ham), followed by a *stinco di maiale* (roast pork shank) or other roast meat.

BARS & CAFES

Nightlife in Bolzano—and daytime wine tasting—centers around the long curve of **Piazza dell'Erbe,** and you'll find plenty more wine bars, pubs, *stubes,* and tiny live-music venues in addition to the following.

To sample the local wines (from 2,000L/$1 a glass), step into this tiny little stand-up bar at **Etti's Thekki** at Piazza dell'Erbe 11 (☎ **0471-971-705**). The chic **Exil** at Piazza del Grano/Kornplatz 2 (☎ **0471-971-814**) is filled with a young crowd night and day, providing a welcome alternative to the many *weinstubes* around town. Exil has the ambience of a coffeehouse (excellent coffee, pastries, and sandwiches are served) and a bar as well, with many kinds of beers from Italy and north of the Alps on tap. On weekend evenings, the elegant **Park Hotel Lauren** on Via Laurino 4 (☎ **0471-311-000**) turns its Art Nouveau–decorated lobby—a sumptuous room overlooking the hotel's private park—into a jazz club. An enthusiastic crowd turns out, making this one of the most popular places in town to be.

You won't find a more distinctive locale in Bolzano than **Fishbanke** at Via di Streiter 26A (☎ **0471-971-714**) in which to bend your elbow; in fact, a stop at this outdoor wine bar is mandatory if your visit coincides with one of its seasonal openings. Wine, beer, and a few snacks (cheese and bruschetta) are served on the well-worn stone slabs of Bolzano's centuries-old former fish market, an unusual experience that attracts a friendly crowd of regulars who, along with the animated proprietor, are always pleased to welcome strangers into their midst.

6 Merano

86km (53 mi.) N of Trento, 28km (17 mi.) NW of Bolzano.

The well-heeled resort of **Merano,** tucked into a valley half an hour west of Bolzano, sports Europe's northernmost outdoor palm trees—the product of a mild microclimate ensuring that summers are never too hot or humid and winter temperatures remain above freezing, even though the surrounding slopes fill with snow.

Austrian nobility and, in their wake, bourgeois vacationers from all over the continent have been descending on Merano since the 19th century. But the town flourished long before that. In fact, the counts of Venosta were lords of all of what would become Austria from here through much of the 13th and 14th centuries; the name "Tyrol" came from the Castel Tirolo, just above Merano, from which they ruled. The capital of the vast territories that passed from the house of Vernosta to the Hapsburgs wasn't moved from Merano to Innsbruck until 1420.

With its handsome, shop-lined streets, riverside promenades, and easy access to mountainous wilderness, Merano is a nice place to visit for a day or two of relaxation or hiking.

ESSENTIALS

GETTING THERE   By Train   Hourly train service links Merano with **Bolzano** (38 min., 6,300L/$3.15).

Late May through September, a stand outside the station will provide you with a **bike for free!**

By Bus   SAD buses arrive and depart from the train station and stop in the center of town, connecting Merano with **Bolzano** hourly (1 hr.; 5,500L/$2.75) and with villages throughout the region.

By Car   Route S38, a pretty road that cuts through vineyards and mountain meadows, links Merano and Bolzano in less than half an hour.

VISITOR INFORMATION   The **tourist office** on Corso Libertà/Freiheistrasse 35 (☎ **0473-235-223,** fax 0473-235-524, www.meraninfo.it), is open March to September, Monday to Friday 9am to 6:30pm, Saturday 9:30am to 6pm, Sunday 10am to 12:30pm; October to February, Monday to Friday 9am to 12:30pm and 2:30 to 6:30pm, Saturday 9:30am to 12:30pm.

Another good source of information on hiking the region is the local office of the **Club Alpino Italiano** at Via K. Wolf 15 (☎ **0473-448-944**). It's open Monday to Friday 9am to 1pm (plus Thursday 7 to 8:30pm). For events, pick up "MeMo" from the tourist office or log on to **www.memopolis.com**.

FESTIVALS & MARKETS   The Piazza del Duomo is the scene of Merano's civic life. A morning **fruit and produce market** is held here from 8am to 1pm Monday to Saturday, and from late November through Christmas it fills with stalls selling carved ornaments and other seasonal paraphernalia during the town's **Christkindlmarkt.** From late August through September the town hosts **Settimane Musicali Meranesi** in several concert halls and churches around town (☎ **0473-221-447;** www. meranofestival.com). On the second Sunday of October, enthusiasts of the grape take over the square for a festival honoring the **wines and grape juice** produced by local vineyards.

WHAT TO SEE & DO

The charming old town that is a vestige of Merano's noble past clusters around the **Piazza del Duomo,** where the namesake 14th-century **Cathedral** has a crenellated facade and heavy buttresses that make it look almost like a castle. A dollhouse-size castle is nearby, just to the west on Via Galilei. **Castello Principesco,** built by the counts of Tyrol in 1470, is still filled with the austere furnishings they installed, along with a collection of armor and musical instruments; the castle (☎ **0473-250-329**) is open Tuesday to Saturday 10am to 5pm and Sunday 10am to 1pm (July and August, Sunday hours are 4 to 7pm only); admission is 4,000L ($2) adults or 3,000L ($1.50) students and over 60.

Merano's picturesque main shopping street, **Via Portici** (leading west from Piazza del Duomo), is lined with Tyrolean-style houses whose porticoes extend over the sidewalk. The preferred places to stroll in Merano, though, are along any number of scenic promenades. Two follow the banks of the river Passer: the **Passeggiata d'Inverno** (**Winter Walk,** facing south) and the delightful **Passegiata d'Estate** (**Summer Walk,** facing north) which, after 1km (½ mi.), turns into a very well-tended, parklike mountain wilderness.

The top of the Passeggiata is just below **Castel Tirolo** (☎ **0473-220-221**), which you can also reach by car or by walking along Via Monte San Zeno for 5km (3 mi.) from Merano. Here, amid stony splendor, you can see the throne room from which the Counts of Tyrol ruled much of present-day Austria and Northern Italy—and you can also enjoy a magnificent view that hasn't changed much since then—as well as a beautifully frescoed Romanesque chapel with a 1330 carved wood *Crucifix.* Unfortunately, until August 2001 (at the earliest), much of the interior remains closed while a new museum on Tyrolean history and culture is installed; once it's finished, admission rates will definitely go up (probably double), but hours may lengthen, and it will

---

Taking the Cure

With its mild climate and mineral-rich springs bubbling up from beneath the town, Merano has long enjoyed a reputation as a spa town. To this day, one of Merano's most popular pastimes is taking the cure. You can have a complete treatment (mud bath, mineral wrap, hydrotherapy) at the **Terme di Merano** (☎ **0473-237-724**), in the center of town but across the river at Via Piave 9, or just take a dip in the pool of mineral-rich water (12,500L/$6). A poor man's version of an elaborate spa regimen—but one you can follow only when grapes from the vineyards surrounding the town ripen in late September and early October—is Merano's famous *cura delle uva* **(grape cure).** One drastic form of the grape cure, which is allegedly beneficial for digestive disorders, requires eating two pounds of grapes a day. A more palatable approach calls for drinking several glasses a day of the delicious fresh *spermuta di uva fresca/traubensaft* (grape juice) that appears in cafes in the early fall.

---

probably stay open in winter. Currently, the castle is open Easter through November, Tuesday to Sunday 10am to 5pm; admission is 5,000L ($2.50), 4,000L ($2) students, 10,000L ($5) family ticket (two adults with kids under 18). To get here without too much hoofing take the half-hourly bus from Merano's train station or center to village of Tirol, then finish the beautiful 15-minute walk along a trail amid grapevines and apple groves.

THE NATIONAL PARKS

For more strenuous excursions, Merano is the gateway to two national parks. The tourist office in town provides information on them, as does the Club Alpo Italiano (see "Visitor Information" above); both parks also have visitor centers within their boundaries.

PARCO NAZIONALE DELLA STELVIO   In this vast 1.3-million-acre wilderness east of Merano, elk and chamois roam the mountainsides and craggy snowcapped peaks pierce the sky. A network of trails crisscross almost-virgin wilderness, and some of Europe's largest glaciers provide year-round skiing. The official **park office** (☎ **0342-903-030**) is in the center of the park, open March to November daily 9am to 1pm and 4 to 6pm; in winter, call ☎ **0342-903-300.** It dispenses maps, lists of hiking trails and other information, and assigns *rifugi* (huts where hikers can overnight) in the park; several buses a day run from Merano to Silandro, at the park entrance, which is about 30km (18 mi.) east via route S38.

PARCO NAZIONALE DI TESSA   This alpine wonderland surrounds Merano with a pleasant terrain of meadows and gentle, forest-clad slopes. A relatively easy path, the southern route of the Meraner Hohenweg, allows even the most inexperienced hiker to cross the park effortlessly (in two days if you wish to follow the entire route) and is conveniently interspersed with restaurants and farmhouses offering rooms. The northern route is much more isolated, difficult, and scenic, with snack-bar-equipped *rifugi* conveniently placed every few hours or so along the route. The **park office** in Naturno, about 15km (9 mi.) west on Route S44 (Via dei Campi 3 ☎ **0473-668-201**), provides a wealth of information on hiking trails, meals, and accommodations. Hourly buses run between Merano and Naturno; the half-hour trip costs 2,500L ($1.25).

AFFORDABLE PLACES TO STAY

April, August through October, and the Christmas holidays constitute high season in Merano, when rates are highest and rooms are scarce. The two hotels in the center of town are easy enough to find; for the **Hotel Castel Labers** (see below), follow the yellow arrows on *"alberghi"* road signs (Merano has a complicated color-coded, geographical breakdown for all its hotels; just trust me and follow the yellow arrows) until a small brown-on-white hotel sign for the Schloss tells you otherwise.

Europa Splendid. Corso Liberta 178, 39012 Merano. ☎ **0473-232-376.** Fax 0473-230-221. www.europa-splendid.com. 54 units. MINIBAR TV TEL. 94,000–140,000L ($47–$70) single; 150,000–210,000L ($75–$105) double. Rates include breakfast. AE, DC, MC, V. Parking 16,000L ($8).

Conveniently located in the center of town a block off the river Passer, the Europa is an old-fashioned hotel that caters to guests who return year after year. The decor is charmingly faded, with an elegant, Regency-style salon and Tyrolean-style bar downstairs. The large, bright guest rooms upstairs haven't been redecorated since the 1960s, but they're bright and very comfortable, with handsome, sturdy furnishings and old but well-maintained bathrooms. A few accommodations even have Art Deco–style interiors. Many of the rooms have small, flower-filled balconies, and a large, sunny hotel terrace is on the first floor. The rates above reflect both season and room type (cheaper category "B" rooms suffer either from less space, a poorer view, or more noise). Corner rooms (208, 308, 408) are choice, with windows on two sides and small balconies.

WORTH A SPLURGE

● **Hotel Castel Labers.** Via Labers 25, Merano 39012 (in Maia Alta, 3km/2 mi east of town). ☎ **0473-234-484.** Fax 0473-234-146. 30 units. TEL. 217,500–270,000L ($109–$135) single; 290,000–400,000L ($145–$200) double, depending on type of accommodation; 260,000L ($130) per person in suite. Rates include breakfast. For 3 nights or more, includes half-pension (meals available à la carte if stay fewer than 3 nights). AE, MC, V. Parking free outside or 20,000L ($10) in garage. Closed Nov 4–Apr 5.

The Stapf-Neubert family turned its pitch-roofed castle (begun in the 11th century) into a hotel in 1885, and in so doing has provided a remarkable lodging. The library, salons, and billiard and dining rooms of the former residence have been converted seamlessly to guest rooms, many with small terraces. Upper floors house distinctive and gracious accommodations, no two of which are alike—in some, cozy conversation nooks are tucked into towers; others are luxurious garret-like arrangements under the eaves, and some are simply commodious, high-ceilinged, and elegantly appointed. The grounds meander down to surrounding grapevine-covered hillsides, and contain a heated swimming pool, tennis courts, and a pleasant terrace overlooking the valley below and the peaks that hem it in. It's a good 10-minute drive high above downtown, though, so don't even consider it without a car.

GREAT DEALS ON DINING

Yes, this region has crisp, excellent wines, but make sure to set aside time for at least one *Prost!* (German for "cheers!") over a frosty glass of **Forst,** a rich and slightly bitter golden beer brewed here in Merano—and the best beer in Italy, in my opinion.

Café Darling. Passeggiata d'Inverno 5–9. ☎ **0473-237-221.** Pastries from 2,000L ($1), sandwiches from 4,000L ($2). MC, V. Thurs–Tues 7:30am–1am. CAFE.

The so-called Winter Walk (see above) along the banks of the River Passer is lined with cafes, and this one is especially pleasant. There's an awning out front, but the tables stretch much farther along the cobblestones until they're practically hanging over the river. The comfortable interior room has a casual ambience that's not too common in this staid, refined resort. You'll probably feel comfortable passing some time reading a book here while sipping a beer or a glass of the house grape juice. Pastries and light sandwiches are also available.

Kavalier. Via Carducci 29. ☎ **0473-236-561.** Primi 8,000–12,000L ($4–$6); secondi 20,000–31,000L ($10–$16); pizze 9,500–15,000L ($4.75–$8). MC, V. Thurs–Tues 11am–2:30pm and 5:30–9:30pm. ITALIAN/TYROLEAN.

Just a few steps off the river (you can hear it from the terrace) near Piazza Teatro, this informal restaurant, with a pleasant arbor-shaded terrace to one side, is a handy stop and can accommodate any level of hunger. A full menu of mostly Tyrolean fare is served, featuring heaping platters of speck, a hearty beef goulash, the odd *Kavalierplatte* (Wiener schnitzel with pineapple, banana, rice, and mushrooms), and an amazingly filling pasta dish, *gnocchetti alla spinachi con prosciutto e panna* (little spinach gnocchi filled with ham in a cream sauce). You can also dine lightly on salads and omelets, or just stop by for pizza.

Rothaler Weinstube. Via Portici 41. No phone. Cheese and meat plates about 6,000–8,000L ($3–$4). No credit cards. Mon–Fri 8am–midnight, Sat 8am–noon. WEINSTUBE.

If you want a big dose of the Tyrol, you need only step into this cozy tavern on Merano's arcaded main street. Up front is a simple, contemporary bar where many shoppers and workers go for a glass of wine or beer. But to get the full experience, you must step into the back room, which is half-paneled, heavily frescoed with images of grapes and vineyards, and lit by a collection of rustic lanterns that have been electrified. The offerings seem to vary by the hour, but typically include a wheel of Parmesan or other cheese, speck (the region's cured and aged ham), and *carre di miale affumiata* (smoked pork loin).

7 Bressanone

40km (24 mi.) N of Bolzano, 68km (41 mi.) E of Merano.

Tucked neatly in the Val d'Isarco between the Eisack and Rienz rivers and surrounded by orchards and vineyards that climb the lower flanks of the surrounding peaks, **Bressanone (Brixen)** is a gem of a Tyrolean town with a hefty past that today's quaint, small-town atmosphere belies. From 1027 to 1803, Bressanone was the center of a large ecclesiastical principality, and its bishop-princes ruled over much of the South Tyrol. Their impressive monuments arise amid the town's heavily gabled, pastel-colored houses and narrow cobblestone streets.

ESSENTIALS

GETTING THERE **By Train** Bressanone lies on the same north-south rail line as Bolzano and Verona, making connections between those cities extremely easy, with more than 30 trains a day from **Bolzano** (35 min., 6,300–8,200L/$3.25–$4.10), where you can change for **Merano.** From **Trento,** trains run almost hourly (75 min., 8,500L/$4.25; High speed: 60 min., 14,200L/$7).

By Bus SAD buses (☎ 0472-801-075 or 800-846-047) leave from the front of the train station and connect Bressanone and **Bolzano** (1 hr.; 7,200L/$3.60) and outlying villages, including several daily (half-hourly in ski season) to **Sant'Andrea,** a good base for hiking and skiing (see below; 20 min.; 2,200L/$1.10); service is augmented by a ski bus that is free for pass holders. There are also two daily buses to **Cortina,** with a change at Dobbiaco (about 2¾ hr; 15,000L/$8).

By Car   Bressanone is about a half-hour drive north of Bolzano on A22. It's easy to get around Bressanone by foot—it's compact, and many of its streets are closed to cars. If you arrive by car, you will probably use the large parking lot on the south of the city on Via Dante (you'll pass it as you drive into the city from the autostrada); the center is 5 minutes away up the Via Roma. From the train station follow Viale Stazione for about 10 minutes to the center.

VISITOR INFORMATION   The **tourist office,** at the *centro storico* end of Via Stazione leading from the train station at no. 9 (☎ **0472-836-401,** fax 0472-836-067), is open Monday to Friday 8:30am to 12:30pm and 2:30 to 6pm and Saturday 9am to 12:30pm.

FESTIVALS & MARKETS   With its cozy, twisting medieval lanes and snug Tyrolean-style houses, Bressanone is especially well suited to Christmas celebrations. The main holiday event is a **Christkindlmarkt (Christmas market)** from late November to Christmas Eve; stalls on and around Piazza del Duomo sell hand-carved ornaments, crafts, holiday pastries, and other seasonal merchandise. A **fruit-and-vegetable market** enlivens Piazza Parrocchia near the Duomo Monday to Saturday 8am to noon and 3 to about 6pm.

WHAT TO SEE & DO

The center of town is the **Piazza del Duomo,** a rectangular tree-shaded square with cafes on one side and the white facade of the Duomo on the other. A baroque renovation to the tall exterior, flanked by two bell towers, has masked much of the cathedral's original 13th-century architecture, which you'll see more of in the interior and in the crypt. The heavily frescoed cloisters (entered through a door to the right of the main one) are especially charming, even though the view of *Judgement Day* they portray is gloomy. Open daily 6am to noon and 3 to 6pm; there are guided tours (in Italian and German) Monday through Saturday at 10:30am and 3pm.

Just south of Piazza del Duomo, on the adjoining Piazza Vescovile, stands the palace of the prince-bishops, whose power over the region—and the fragility of that power—is made clear by the surrounding moat and fortifying walls. The massive 14th-century palace now houses the **Museo Diocesano,** where more than 70 rooms display wooden statuary, many somewhat unremarkable Renaissance paintings by local artists, and what is considered to be the museum's treasure and the objects most likely to capture your attention—an extensive and enchanting collection of antique Nativity scenes, one of the largest such assemblages anywhere, filling eight rooms. The collections were put in storage in 2000 for a special exhibit, but all should be back in place by May 2001, though the following hours and admission prices may change. The museum (☎ **0472-830-505;** www.dioezesanmuseum.bz.it) is open March 15 to October 31, Tuesday to Sunday 10am to 5pm; the Nativity-scene galleries only open again from December 15 to February 10, Tuesday to Sunday 2 to 5pm (closed December 24 and 25); admission to the complete museum collection is 7,000L ($3.50), to the Nativity-scene exhibit only is 3,000L ($1.50).

AFFORDABLE PLACES TO STAY

Cremona. Via Vittorio Veneto 26, 39042 Bressanone. ☎ **0472-835-602.** Fax 0472-200-794. 12 units, 10 with bathroom. 50,000L ($25) single without bathroom, 100,000L ($50) double with bathroom. No credit cards. Closed Jan 7 to mid-Feb.

Like many of the other well-heeled resorts in this part of the world, Bressanone doesn't offer many inexpensive beds. That's why this small, plain hotel near the train station and about a 10-minute walk to the center of town is a good find. The neighborhood is not as quaint as much of the rest of Bressanone, but it's safe, and the tiny reception area and rooms are more functional than charming. All but the two bathroomless singles are large, and the beds are firm and covered with the feather quilts that are standard issue in this part of the world.

Goldene Krone/Corona d'Oro. Via Fienili 4, 39042 Bressanone. ☎ **0472-835-154.** Fax 0472-835-014. www.hotelkrone.it. 35 units. MINIBAR TV TEL. 120,000–150,000L ($60–$75) single; 160,000–220,000L ($80–$110) double. Rates include breakfast. Half-board 25,000L ($12.50) more per person. MC, V. Parking 10,000L ($5). Closed Jan 6–Feb 6.

Everything about this amiable hotel at the edge of the old city suggests solid comfort, from the homey, wood-paneled lounge to the *weinstube*-style bar to the breakfast room and restaurant, where booth-like tables are lit by pretty shaded lamps. There are two categories of guest rooms, and hence the range of prices. Those in the lower range are pleasant enough, with streamlined modern furnishings, and many have terraces. The more expensive rooms are really quite special, though, and well worth the extra expense. They're actually suites, with separate sitting and sleeping areas, equipped respectively with roomy couches and armchairs and king-size beds. The bathrooms are grand, with double sinks and large tubs equipped with Jacuzzi jets.

WORTH A SPLURGE

Elefante. Via Rio Bianco 4. 39042 Bressanone. ☎ **0472-832-750.** Fax 0472-836-579. www.acs.it/elephant. 44 units. TV TEL. 136,000–150,000L ($68–$75) single; 300,000–330,000L ($150–$165) double. Breakfast 24,000–26,000L ($12–$13). AE, DC, MC, V. Parking 12,000L ($6). Closed Jan 7–Feb 28 and Nov 5–30.

One of Italy's oldest and most famous inns is named for a 16th-century guest—an elephant accompanying Archduke Maximilian of Austria on the long trek from Genoa to Vienna, where the beast was to become part of the royal menagerie. During its two-week stay the pachyderm attracted onlookers from miles around, and the innkeeper renamed his establishment and commissioned a delightful elephant-themed fresco that still graces the front of the building. Today's hotel matches its provenance with excellent service and extraordinary environs that include dark-paneled hallways and grand staircases. The distinctive old rooms are full of nooks and crannies and furnished with heavy Tyrolean antiques and some tasteful modern pieces, include wonderfully solid beds. Many guests choose to take all their meals in the justly famous restaurant (half- and full-board available); the generous buffet breakfast emphasizes delicious Austrian pastries. The hotel also has a large garden and a pleasant swimming pool.

GREAT DEALS ON DINING

Fink. Via Portici Minori 4. ☎ **0472-834-883.** Primi 7,000–16,000L ($3.50–$8) downstairs, 8,000–21,000L ($4–$10.50) upstairs; secondi 13,000–21,000L ($6.50–$10.50) downstairs, 22,000–31,000L ($11–$15.50) upstairs. AE, DC, MC, V. Thurs–Mon noon–2:30pm and 7–10pm, Tues noon–2:30pm. Closed July 1–14. TYROLEAN.

It only seems right that Bressanone's charmingly arcaded main street should have a restaurant like this one, dishing out excellent local cuisine amid paneling hung with antlers and oil paintings. Fink offers many mountain-style dishes you may find only within a close radius of Bressanone, including a *piatto alla Val d'Isarco*, a platter of locally cured hams and salamis, and a *zuppa di vino*, a traditional Tyrolean soup made with white wine that here includes crusty pieces of cinnamon toast. The *miale gratinato*, a pork roast topped with a cheese sauce, is surprisingly light and absolutely delicious, as are the local cheeses served for dessert. If in doubt about what to order, just ask—the English-speaking staff is extremely gracious. An upstairs dining room has a slightly more refined cuisine and atmosphere to go with the higher prices.

Hitting the Slopes

Bressanone's major playground is **Monte Plose,** and the gateway to ski slopes and hiking trails alike is the outlying village of **Sant'Andrea** (see "Getting Here by Bus," above). Skiing here is not as glamorous as it is in better-known resorts like Cortina, but it is excellent and much less expensive. A ski pass is 44,000–50,000L ($22–$25) a day, and can be purchased at one of the outlets near the Sant'Andrea funicular, which costs 16,000L ($8) round-trip and runs July through mid-September weekdays 9am to noon and 1 to 6pm, Saturday and Sunday 9am to 6pm; and from December through May daily 9am to 4:30pm. (Winter schedules vary considerably with snow conditions; a summer ascent will take you to a network of alpine trails near the stop at Valcroce.) The tourist board in Bressanone provides maps, information on skiing, mountain refuges, and other details you need to know to enjoy this mountain wilderness.

Finsterwirt. Vicolo Duomo 3. ☎ **0472-835-343.** Salads and light meals from 13,000L ($6.50). AE, DC, MC, V. Tues–Sat 10am–midnight, Sun 10am–3pm. Closed Jan 10–Feb 2 and June 15–30. WINE BAR.

Occupying the same quarters as Oste Scuro restaurant (see below) and run by the same family, this ground-floor tavern near the cathedral also shares the same dark paneling and leaded-window ambience. The fare and service, however, are much more casual, though excellent, and you are welcome to settle into one of the nooklike tables for as long as you'd like to enjoy a beer or glass of local wine (from 2,000L/$1) and a plate of fresh goat cheese or a platter of speck and salami. A lovely rear garden, candlelit at night, is open throughout the summer and well into the chillier days when people from more southerly climes wouldn't think of sitting outdoors.

Oste Scuro. Vicolo Duomo 3. ☎ **0472-835-343.** Reservations recommended. Primi 8,000–15,000L ($4–$7.50); secondi 23,000–34,000L ($11.50–$17). AE, DC, MC, V. Tues–Sat noon–2pm and 7–9pm, Sun noon–2pm. Closed Jan 10–Feb 2 and June 15–30. TYROLEAN.

What may be Bressanone's temple of gastronomy (Fink, above, is a close contender) occupies a welcoming series of intimate candlelit rooms above the Finsterwirt *weinstube* (see above). The first of these rooms contains a standup bar where patrons stop by just to order one of the excellent wines by the glass. It would be a shame not to dine here, though, because the kitchen excels at simple but innovative preparations of the freshest local ingredients. A *tartina di ricotta* is a concoction of creamy cheese atop a bed of lightly sauteed spinach; even if you have found the region's steady diet of *canederli* (dumplings) heavy, try them here because they are light and infused with fresh wild mushrooms. The kitchen excels at meat dishes, included an herb-infused veal roast. Fresh berries top off a meal in season, and the strudels are perfection.

EN ROUTE TO CORTINA: THE STRADA DI DOLIMITI

The **Great Dolomite Road,** the scenic route between Bolzano (follow signs to Eggental/ Val d'Ega) and Cortina going east, S241 and S48, is 110km (66 mi.) of stunning views. The road curves around some of the highest peaks in the Dolomites, including 10,000-foot-tall Marmolda, and goes through a scattering of mountain villages and ski resorts before dropping out of a high pass into Cortina. Some tour buses follow this route (the tourist offices in Bolzano and Cortina can provide a list of tour operators; check with the bus station in Bolzano), as do two daily buses of the SAD network from July through September (check with the bus station in Bolzano or call ☎ 0471-450-111). However, you may want to rent a car if only for a day to make the spectacular round-trip, one of Europe's most scenic drives (allow at least 2½ hr. each way over the twists and turns of the passes). Keep in mind, though, that the Strada di Dolomiti is often closed to vehicles because of heavy snow in the winter months, and you will often need to put chains on your tires between November and April.

8 Cortina d'Ampezzo

133km (82 mi.) E of Bolzano, 166km (100 mi.) N of Venice.

Italy's best-known mountain resort, put on the international map when it hosted the 1956 Winter Olympics, has a glamorous, moneyed reputation. Long before the Olympics, though, **Cortina** was attracting European alpine enthusiasts, who began coming here for stays in the town's first hotels as early as the 1860s. In 1902, Cortina hosted its first ski competitions, and in 1909, the completion of the first road in and out of the town, the magnificent Strada di Dolomiti (built by the Austro-Hungarian military), opened the slopes to more skiers.

Even without its 90 miles of ski runs and 50 cable cars and chair lifts that make the slopes easily accessible, Cortina would be one of Europe's most appealing alpine towns. The surrounding Dolomite peaks are simply stunning. Eighteen of them rise more than 10,000 feet, ringing Cortina in an amphitheater of craggy stone. In full light the peaks are a soft bluish-gray, and when they catch the rising and setting sun they take on a welcoming rosy glow.

True to its reputation for glamour, Cortina can be expensive (especially in August and the high ski season months of January through March). Many well-to-do Italians have houses here, and a sense of privilege prevails. What's often forgotten, though, is that for all the town's fame, strict zoning has put a damper on development, and, as a result, Cortina is still a mountain town of white timbered houses, built aside a rushing stream and surrounded by forests, meadows, and, of course, the stunning Dolomite peaks.

ESSENTIALS

GETTING THERE   By Bus   Frequent **SAD** bus service provides the only public transportation in and out of Cortina; (☎ **800-846-047**). There are two daily buses each from **Bolzano** (about 4 hr.; 21,100L/$12), stopping in **Bressanone** (about 2¾ hr; 15,000L/$8), that head to Cortina, but with a change in Dobbiaco. There's also one daily bus to and from Venice (☎ **035-237-641;** 4 hr. 20 min.; 18,000L/$9) and a daily bus to and from Milan (☎ **02-801-161;** 6½ hr.; 58,000–67,000L/$29–$36). The bus station in Cortina is located in the former train station on Via Marconi.

By Train   The closest train station to Cortina is the one at Calalzo di Cadore, 30km (19 mi.) south. There are ten trains a day to Calalzo from **Venice,** but only 2 are direct (2 hr. 20 min.); with connections, allow 3 to 4 hours (12,l00L/$6). There are also six daily direct runs from **Padua** (3 hr. 14,000L/$7). From Calalzo, 30 daily buses connect with Cortina (4,500L/$2.25 plus 1,500L/75¢ for each bag).

By Car   The spectacularly scenic Strada di Dolomiti (see above) links Bolzano and Cortina, while S51 heads south toward Venice, connecting south of Belluno to Autostrada A27, for a total trip time of about 3 hours between Cortina and Venice.

VISITOR INFORMATION The **tourist office,** Piazetta San Francesco 8 (☎ **0436-3231,** fax 0436-3235, www.sunrise.it/dolomiti), is open daily 9am to 12:30pm and 4 to 7pm. In addition to a list of accommodations, the English-speaking staff will also provide a wealth of information on ski slopes, hiking trails, and bus schedules.

FESTIVALS & MARKETS The Piazza Italia near the bus station doubles as Cortina's **marketplace.** Stalls sell produce, mountain cheeses, clothing, housewares, and other items on Tuesday and Friday mornings from 8:30am to 1pm. While chic Cortina concerns itself mostly with secular pursuits, the town turns out for a solemn religious procession down the main street, Corso Italia, on **Good Friday.**

WHAT TO SEE & DO

The main in-town activity in Cortina appears to be walking up and down the main street, the pedestrian-only **Corso Italia,** wearing the most fashionable skiwear money can buy. Most of the buildings are new but pleasingly low-scale and alpine in design, and at the town center is the pretty 18th-century church of **Santi Filippo e Giacomo,** with a charming bell tower eclipsed only by the surrounding majestic peaks. It is on the slopes of these peaks that most visitors set their sights, enjoying an amazing array of outdoor activities.

EXPLORING PEAKS Skiers and nonskiers alike will enjoy the eye-popping scenery on a trip up the mountainsides on the funicular systems that leave right from town. The most spectacular trip is the ascent on the **Freccia nel Cielo (Arrow of the Sky),** which departs from a terminus near the Stadio Olimpico del Ghiacchio (Olympic Ice Skating Stadium), about a 10-minute walk north and west of the town center. The top station is at **Tafano di Mezzo,** at 10,543 feet; the round-trip is 45,000L ($23). For nonskiers interested in viewing mountain scenery, it is less expensive (30,000L/$15) and just as satisfying to make the trip only as far as **Ra Valles,** the second stop, at 8,500 feet. The views over glaciers and stony peaks are magnificent, and a bar serves sandwiches and other refreshments on an outdoor terrace. The funicular runs mid-July to late September and mid-December to May 1, with departures every 20 minutes 9am to 4 or 5pm, depending on the time of sunset; ☎ **0436-5052** for information.

The **Funivia Faloria** (☎ **0436-2517**) arrives and departs from a terminus on the other side of town, about a 10-minute walk southeast of the town center. The ride is a little less dramatic than the one on the longer Freccia nel Cielo. Even so, the ascent over forests and meadows, then up a sheer cliff to the 7,000-foot-high ski station at Faloria, is not without thrills, and the view from the terrace bar at Faloria down to Cortina and to the curtain of high peaks to the north is one you won't soon forget. Like the Freccia nel Cielo, the Funivia Faloria runs mid-July to late September and mid-December to May 1, with departures every 20 minutes 9am to 4 or 5pm, depending on time of sunset. The round-trip fare is 24,500L ($22.25). .

Another trip for funivia enthusiasts is the one from the top of **Passo Falzarego,** 25km (15 mi.) west of Cortina, to **Lagazoul,** a little skiing and hiking station at the 8,500-foot level. In summer, you can follow a network of trails at the top and scamper for miles across the dramatic, rocky terrain. The ride is a nearly vertical ascent up the rocky face of the mountain, and as an eerie alternative to the funicular you can make the climb up or down through a series of tunnels dug into the cliff during World War I. Falzarego is the last pass through which you descend if you follow the Strada di Dolimiti into Cortina, so you may want to stop and board the funicular for a scenery-filled introduction to the region. If you are not driving, five buses a day make the 35-minute trip between Cortina and the funicular stop at the top of the Passo Falzarego; the fare is 3,000L ($1.50) each way. The funivia runs mid-July to late September and mid-December to May 1, with departures every 30 minutes; the round-trip fare is 18,000L ($9). For more information, call ☎ **0436-867-301.**

DOWNHILL SKIING Cortina is Italy's leading ski resort, and it lives up to its reputation with eight exceptional ski areas that are easily accessible from town. Two of the best, **Tofana-Promedes** and **Faloria-Tondi,** can be reached by funiculars that lift off from the edges of town (see "Exploring Peaks," above), as can the novice slopes at **Mietres.** You can enjoy these facilities fairly economically with one of the comprehensive **Dolomiti Superski passes** that provide unlimited skiing (including all chairlift and funicular fees, as well as free shuttle bus service to and from Cortina and the ski areas) at all eight of Cortina's ski areas and those at 10 outlying resorts. You can get passes for any number of days up to 21; a few sample prices: during high season, December 24 to January 6 and February 4 to March 10, is 63,000L ($32) for 1 day, 178,000L ($88) for 3 days, and 332,000L ($162) for 7 days. Shave off about 7,000L ($3.50) per day for low season, January 7 to February 3 and March 11 to 24. For more information, contact the tourist office or Dolomiti Superski, Via Castello 33, 32043 Cortina (☎ **0436-862-171** or 0471-795-397; www.DolomitiSuperski.com).

For **lessons,** contact the **Scuola di Sci Cortina,** Corso Italia (☎ **0436-2911,** http://cortina.dolomiti.org/scuolascicortina), which offers 6 consecutive mornings of group lessons for 316,000L ($158) in high season and 260,000L ($130) in low season (add about 120,000L/$60 and they'll throw in ski rentals as well). Private lessons cost 67,000L ($33.50) per hour for one person, plus 20,000L ($10) each additional person.

You can **rent** skis at many outlets throughout town, including stands at the lower and upper stations of the Freccia nel Cielo cable car and other funiculars; rentals average 20,000L to 45,000L ($10 to $22.50) for skis—plus 8,000L to 20,000L ($4 to $10) for boots—or 35,000L to 45,000L ($17.50 to $22.50) for snowboards.

HIKING & ROCK CLIMBING In this mountainous terrain, these two activities are often synonymous. The tourist office can provide maps of hiking trails throughout the surrounding region. For high-altitude hiking, canyoning, and rock climbing, you may want to join one of the excursions led by **Gruppo Guide Alpine Cortina,** Corso Italia 69A (☎ **0463-868-505;** www.mnet-climb.com/GuideCortina), open 8am to noon and 4 to 8pm.

HORSEBACK RIDING **Fattoria Memguto,** in outlying Fraina (☎ **0463-860-441**), offers group and individual riding through the lovely valleys surrounding Cortina; the stables are open from late spring through late fall from 9am to noon and 3 to 7pm and rides cost 16,000L ($8) for 30 minutes and 32,000L ($16) for an hour.

ICE SKATING At the **Stadio Olimpico del Ghiacchio,** just to the northwest of the town center on Via del Stadio (☎ **0436-4380**), you can practice turns on the two recently refurbished rinks where Olympians vied for the gold in the 1956 games. Admission plus skate rental is 13,000L ($6.50).

MOUNTAIN BIKING The roads and tracks leading into the peaks provide arduous biking terrain; many serious cyclists from all over the world come to Cortina to practice for events. If you want to test your mettle, you can rent a bike from the **Mountain Bike Center,** Corso Italia 294 (☎ **0336-494-770**). Rentals are 20,000L ($10) for 2 hours, 40,000L ($20) for 4 hours, and 60,000L ($30) for a day. The English-speaking staff will point you in the direction of routes that match your abilities.

AFFORDABLE PLACES TO STAY

Cortina is booked solid during the high season: August, Christmas, and late January through March. You should reserve well in advance. Rates are lowest in late spring and early fall. Keep in mind that many innkeepers prefer to give rooms to guests who will stay several days or longer and who will take meals at the hotel. Given the scarcity of reasonably priced restaurants in town, you will probably be happy settling for a half- or full-board plan. The tourist board provides a list of private homes that take in guests, a way to keep costs down while enjoying the local hospitality, which is considerable.

Bellaria. Corso Italia 266, 32043 Cortina d'Ampezzo. ☎ **0436-2505.** Fax 0436-5755. http://cortina.dolomiti.org/bellaria. 22 units. TV TEL. 80,000–150,000L ($40–$75) single; 160,000–300,000L ($80–$150) double. Rates include breakfast. Half-pension available. DC, MC, V. Closed 1 month in fall or spring.

The Majoni family, which owns this pleasant hotel a short walk from the center on the northern edge of town, did a complete refurbishing recently, and they chose to keep prices down for the benefit of the patrons who come here season after season. As a result, they still provide some of Cortina's most reasonably priced accommodations, housing their guests in handsome, sunny rooms that overlook the mountains and have fresh alpine-style pine furnishings, firm new beds, and crisp fabrics. All of the bathrooms have been redone and outfitted with heated towel racks. Downstairs is a lovely paneled lounge, a dining room, a pleasant terrace in front of the house, and a lawn out back.

✪ **Montana.** Corso Italia 94, 32043 Cortina d'Ampezzo. ☎ **0436-862-126.** Fax 0436-868-211. www.cortinanet.it/alberghi. 30 units. TV TEL. 82,000–106,000L ($41–$53) single; 148,000–406,000L ($74–$203) double; 188,000–248,000L ($94–$124) suite. Rates include breakfast. AE, DC, MC, V. Closed Nov and June.

Right in the center of town, this hotel occupies a tall, pretty alpine-style house and is run by the amiable Adriano and Roberta Lorenzi, who provide some of the resort's nicest lodgings for the price. Guest rooms are pleasant and cozy, with old-style armoires, hardwood floors, and down quilts on the beds, and many open to balconies overlooking the peaks. Most of the doubles are quite large, and many are beautifully paneled and have separate sitting areas. Half the rooms here are singles, making this an ideal spot for solo travelers or cranky twosomes who need to get away from each other. There is no restaurant, but breakfast is served in a pleasant room where guests tend to linger through much of the morning.

Villa Nevada. Via Ronco 64, 32043 Cortina d'Ampezzo. ☎ **0436-4778.** Fax 0436-4853. 11 units. TV TEL. 80,000–125,000L ($40–$62.50) single; 150,000–220,000L ($75–$110) double. Rates include breakfast. No credit cards. Closed first Sun Oct–Dec 1 and after Easter to mid-June.

On a grassy hillside overlooking the town, valley, and mountains, the Villa Nevada is a low-slung alpine building that has the appearance of a private home. The same ambience prevails inside, where an attractive, paneled lounge is grouped around a hearth and opens to a sunny terrace, inviting guests to linger as they might in a living room. The guest rooms are large and bright and afford wonderful views over the alpine landscape; they are nicely furnished with dark-stained pine pieces and thick rugs or carpeting, and they all have large balconies. Located on the road to the outlying settlement of Ronco, this is probably a better option for those with a car than for those without—the center of Cortina is a pleasant 20-minute walk downhill, but it could be a long uphill trek home in bad weather or late at night.

WORTH A SPLURGE

Hotel Menardi. Via Majon 110, 32043 Cortina d'Ampezzo. ☎ **0436-2400.** Fax 0436-862-183. www.sunrise.it/hmenardi. 49 units. TV TEL. 95,000–150,000 ($47.50–$75) single; 190,000–300,000L ($95–$150) double. Rates include breakfast. Half-pension 135,000–230,000L ($67.50–$115) per person. DC, MC, V. Parking free, or 15,000L ($7.50) in garage. Closed Apr 10–June 15 and Sept 20–Dec 20.

One of the oldest and most charming hostelries in Cortina successfully combines the luxury and service of a fine hotel with the homelike comfort of a mountain inn. The Menardi family, which converted its farmhouse into a guesthouse in the 1920s, has, over the years, beautifully appointed the public rooms with antiques and comfortable furnishings, and done up the high-ceilinged, wood-floored guest rooms simply but tastefully with painted or pine armoires and bedsteads, down quilts, and attractive floral fabrics. Rooms in the rear of the house are especially quiet and pleasant, looking across the hotel's spacious lawns to the forests and peaks; some newer (but still panel-and-pine alpine) rooms are located in an annex next door, many of which have large balconies with picnic tables. Most guests take half-board to avail themselves of the excellent meals in a dining room converted from the former stalls (at the turn of the 20th century they rented extra horses to pull carriages on the mountain roads), but it is also possible to make bed-and-breakfast arrangements when the hotel is not fully booked. A pretty, public foot trail leads from the back lawn into town in 15 minutes.

GREAT DEALS ON DINING

Inexpensive meals are hard to come by in Cortina—even pizzerias are few and far between. For a low-cost meal, you might want to equip yourself for a **picnic** at **La Piazzetta,** Corso Italia 53, with a mouth-watering assortment of salamis, cheeses, breads, and other fare. Another source of supplies is the department store **La Cooperativa,** Corso Italia 40 (☎ **0436-861-245**), the largest, best-stocked supermarket for miles around.

Al Camin. Via Alvera 99. ☎ **0436-862-010.** Reservations recommended. Primi 12,000–15,000L ($6–$7.50); secondi 14,000–30,000L ($7–$15). MC, V. Tues–Sun noon–3pm and 7–11:30pm. ALPINE.

If you follow the Via Alvera along the Ru Bigontina, a rushing mountain stream, about 10 minutes east from the center of town, you'll come to this charming, rustic restaurant. The tables in the wood-paneled dining room are grouped around a large stone fireplace, and the menu offers many local favorites. Your meal may include what is known in this part of the region as *kenederli* (dumplings flavored with liver that are known as *canelderli* outside of the immediate vicinity of Cortina), as well as a few dishes, many of them seasonal, that you may find nowhere else—these include *radicchio di prato*, a mountain green that appears in early spring and is served dressed with hot lard, and, in winter, *formaggio fuso con funghi e polenta*, a lush combination of creamy melted mountain cheese and wild mushrooms served over polenta.

La Tavernetta. Via dello Stadio 27 a/b. ☎ **0436-867-494.** Reservations recommended. Primi 13,000–18,000L ($7–$9); secondi 20,000–35,000L ($10–$18). AE, MC, V. Thurs–Tues noon–2:30pm and 7:30–11pm. ALPINE.

A former barn just steps from the Olympic ice-skating stadium has been delightfully converted to a very stylish yet reasonably priced restaurant, with handsome paneled walls, timbered ceilings, and tile floors. The menu relies on local ingredients and typical dishes of the Alto Adige, and the rustic environs may inspire you to eat heartily. You might want to begin with a dish of polenta delicately infused with *asparagi selvatici* (the tips of fresh wild asparagus) or *gnocchi di spinachi* (gnocchi filled with spinach and topped with a rich wild game sauce), and then move on to a robust *stinco di vitello con patate* (veal shank served with creamy potato) or *cervo in salsa di mirtilli* (venison with a sauce of myrtle berries with polenta).

Ospitale. Locale Ospitale. ☎ **0436-4585.** Primi 10,000–12,000L ($5–$6); secondi 15,000–22,000L ($8–$11). AE, MC. Tues–Sun noon–2:30pm and 7–10pm. ALPINE.

A trip out to this roomy restaurant in a high-gabled house (about 5 miles north of Cortina on the road to the village and lake of Dobbiaco) is a favorite outing for residents of Cortina. Many members of the Alvera family are on hand in the series of comfortable, wood-floored dining rooms and in the kitchen, preparing and serving local specialties as well as traditional Italian dishes. In season, fresh vegetables appear in such pasta dishes as *pappardelle ai porcini* (flat noodles with porcini mushrooms) and *casunziei rossi,* a short, local pasta mixed with beets, or *gnocchi di zucca con ricotta* (gnocchi made from squash and stuffed with ricotta). The *goulash con polenta* is one of any number of substantial main courses. If you don't have a car, you can take one of the hourly buses out here from the bus station in Cortina, but that is only an option at lunch.

Milan, Lombardy & the Lakes

by Reid Bramblett

There's a lot more to Italy's most prosperous province, **Lombardy (Lombardia)**, than the factories that fuel its economy. Many of the attractions here are urban—in addition to Milan, a string of Renaissance cities dots the Lombardian plains, from Pavia to Mantua. To the north, the region bumps up against craggy mountains and romantic lakes and to the south it spreads out in fertile farmlands fed by the Po and other rivers. The Lombardians, who over the centuries have been ruled by feudal dynasties (the Spanish, Austrians, French), are a little more continental than their neighbors to the south, faster talking, and a little faster paced as well. They even dine a little differently, tending to eschew olive oil for butter and often forgoing pasta for polenta and risotto.

Among the region's greatest treasures (aside from some notable works of art and architecture) are the Italian lakes, admired over the centuries from poets and writers from Catullus to Ernest Hemingway. Backed by the Alps and ringed by lush gardens and verdant forests, each has its own charms and, accordingly, its own enthusiasts. Not least among these charms are their easy accessibility to many Italian cities, making them ideal for short retreats: Lago Maggiore (Lake Maggiore) and Lago di Como (Lake Como) are both less than an hour's distance from Milan, and Lago di Garda (Lake Garda) is tantalizingly close to Venice, Verona, and Mantua.

1 Milan: More than *The Last Supper*

552km (343 mi.) NW of Rome, 288km (179 mi.) NW of Florence, 257km (160 mi.) W of Venice, 140km (87 mi.) NE of Turin, 142km (88 mi.) N of Genoa.

Milan (Milano) is Italy's financial center, business hub, and fashion capital, as well as one of its most industrialized major cities. But it's crowded, noisy, hot in summer and damp and foggy in winter, less easygoing, and more expensive than most Italian cities—in short, not as appealing as Venice, Florence, or Rome. Milan, though, reveals its long history in a pride of monuments, museums, and churches—its cathedral is one of Europe's great Gothic monuments, and another church contains Leonardo's *The Last Supper*. It also sets one of Italy's finest tables and supports a cultural scene embracing La Scala (one of the world's top opera houses), high-fashion boutiques and shows, and throbbing nightlife. With its dazzling shop windows and sophisticated

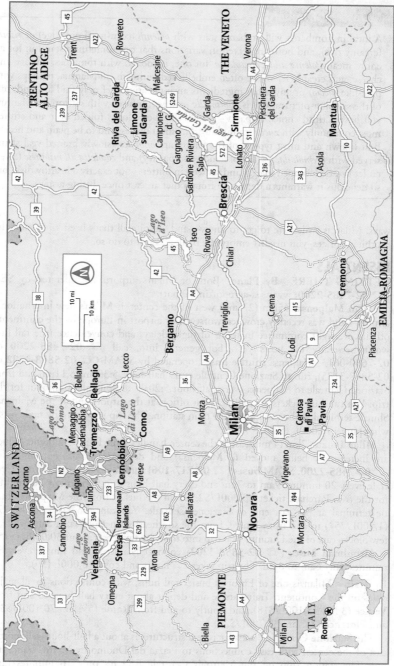

A Taste of Lombardy

A meal in Lombardy will probably start with *polenta* (corn-meal porridge) or *risotto* (creamy rice), and both are served in variations that can sometimes stand in for an entire meal. *Polenta alla Bergamasca,* for one, is cooked with tomatoes, sausage and cheese, and creamy *risotti* are often embellished with fish (in Mantua, perhaps with pike-like *luccio*) or any other ingredients an innovative chef may find at hand; one of the simplest preparations is *risotto alla milanese,* infused with saffron. In Mantua, you have a third choice of pasta—tortelli, little envelopes folded over and stuffed most commonly with *zucca* (pumpkin). The meat dishes tend to be plain and hearty. Best known and most typical of the region are *ossobuco* (slowly braised veal shank served with *gremolada,* a sauce of lemon and parsley) and *cotoletta all milanese* (a veal cutlet breaded, dipped in egg, and sautéed in butter—not exactly a healthy dish, but so delicious it warrants a departure from a diet at least once during a stay).

---

ways, Milan is a pleasure to get to know—and, despite all that's been said about the exorbitant prices, you needn't empty the bank account to do so.

ESSENTIALS

GETTING THERE   By Plane   Both of Milan's airports are operated by **SEA** (☎ **02-7485-2200;** www.sea-aeroportimilano.it).

Milan Malpensa, 45km (27 mi.) west of the center, is Milan's new international airport—and was recently crowned worst major airport in Europe by the continent's official oversight committee in terms of flight delays and convenience (the rail link won't be ready for years yet). For general info, call ☎ **02-7485-2200** or 02-7680-0613. Malpensa **shuttle buses,** operated by STAM (☎ **02-5858-3202** or 02-5858-3185), run to Stazione Centrale every half-hour 5:30am to 11pm and from Stazione Centrale to Malpensa every half-hour 5:20am to 8pm; allow an hour for the trip. You can buy tickets (13,000L/$7) at offices at the airport and at the Malpensa Shuttle terminal at the east end of the train station. The trip into town by **taxi** costs a whopping 140,000L ($70).

Milan Linate, 7km (4 mi.) east of the center, handles some European flights (which are increasingly being moved to Malpensa) and domestic flights. For info, dial ☎ **02-7485-2200.** STAM **buses** (☎ **02-717-106**) run from Linate to Stazione Centrale every 20 minutes 7am to 7pm and every half hour 7 to 9pm; allow 20 minutes for the trip. Purchase tickets (5,000L/$2.50) on the bus or from the Malpensa Shuttle terminal at the east end of Stazione Centrale. You can also take city bus 73 (1,500L/75¢) to and from Linate, from the southeast corner of Piazza San Babila, a few blocks east of the Duomo. The trip into town by **taxi** costs about 30,000L ($15).

Airpulman buses (☎ **02-5858-3202**) connect Malpensa and Linate every 90 minutes daily 6am to 8pm. The trip takes 1¼ hours and costs 18,000L ($9).

By Train   Milan is one of Europe's busier rail hubs, with connections to all major cities on the Continent. Trains arrive and depart about every half hour to and from **Venice** (3 hr., 35,100L/$18), and hourly to and from **Rome** (5½ hr., 70,100L/$35) and **Florence** (3½ hr., 39,700L/$20).

The **Stazione Centrale,** a vast Facist-era structure, is about a half-hour walk northeast of the center, with easy connections to Piazza del Duomo by Metro, tram, and bus. The station stop on the Metro is Centrale F.S.; it's only 10 minutes (and 1,500L/75¢) away from the Duomo stop, in the city's heart. If you want to see something of the city en route, take bus 60 from the station to Piazza del Duomo. If you decide to walk, follow Via Pisani through the district of high-rise office buildings around the station to the equally cheerless Piazza della Repubblica, and from there continue south on Via Turati and Via Manzoni to Piazza del Duomo. Chances are you'll arrive at Stazione Centrale, but some trains serve Milan's other train stations: **Stazione Nord** (with service to/from Como, among other cities), **Porta Genova** (with service to/from Alessandria and Asti), and **Porta Garibaldi** (with service to/from Lecco).

By Bus   Given Milan's excellent rail links with other cities in Lombardy and throughout Italy, it's usually unnecessary to travel by long-distance buses, which tend to take longer and cost more than the trains do. If you choose to travel by intercity bus, expect to arrive at and depart from **Autostradale,** in front of the Castello Sforzesco on Piazza Castello (Metro: Cairoli). The ticket office (☎ **166/845-010,** 500L/25¢ per minute) is open daily 6:30am to 9:30pm. A few common runs are the 12 daily buses to and from **Turin** (2 hr.; 17,200L/$9) and, for Milanese ski and out-door enthusiasts, the two daily buses (more in winter) to and from Aosta (2½-3½ hr.; 21,500L/$11).

By Car   Milan is well served by Italy's superhighway (*autostrada*) system. The A1 links Milan with Florence and Rome (Florence is a little over 3 hours away by car, Rome is a little under 6), and the A4 connects Milan with Verona and Venice to the east and Turin to the west (Venice is about 2½ hours from Milan by car, Turin a little over an hour). Driving and parking in Milan are not experiences to be relished; in fact, much of the central city is closed to traffic. Many hotels make parking arrangements for guests; ask when you reserve a room.

VISITOR INFORMATION   The **main tourist office** is in the Palazzo del Turismo at Via Marconi 1 on Piazza del Duomo (☎ **02-7252-4300;** fax 02-7252-4350; Metro: Duomo); hours are Monday to Friday 8:30am to 8pm, Saturday 9am to 1pm and 2 to 7pm, and Sunday 9am to 1pm and 2 to 5pm. There's also an **office in Stazione Centrale** (☎ **02-669-0532** or 02-7252-4360), open Monday to Saturday 9am to 7pm and Sunday 9am to 12:30pm and 1:30 to 6pm. These offices issue maps, museum guides, hotel and restaurant listings, and a wealth of other information; but they're now privately run, so they charge nominal fees for most of the useful pamphlets, including 2,000L ($1) for *Milano: Where, When, How.* But still free are the monthly events brochures *Milano Mese* and *Hello Milano* (www.hellomilano.it), with extensive listings of museum exhibits, performances, and other events.

Throughout the year, the tourist office leads English-language **sightseeing tours** of the city's monuments and museums, costing 20,000L ($10) for tours within Milan and 40,000L ($20) for tours outside the center. Milan tours include a visit to the Duomo, Galleria Vittorio Emanuele II, La Scala, Museo Poldi-Pezzoli, Pinacoteca Ambrosia, and Pinacoteca di Brera.

FESTIVALS & MARKETS   Though overshadowed by Venice's goings-on, Milan's pre-Lenten **Carnevale** is becoming increasingly popular, with costumed parades and an easygoing good time, much of it focusing around Piazza del Duomo beginning a week or so before Ash Wednesday. Before the city shuts down in mid-August (trust me: stay away!), the city council stages a series of **June and July dance, theater, and music events** in theaters and open-air venues around the city; call ☎ **02-8646-4094** for details.

In a city as well dressed as Milan, it only stands to reason that some great-looking castoffs are bound to turn up at **street markets.** Milan's largest street market is the one held on **Via Papiniano** in the Ticinese/Navigli district (Metro: Sant'Agostino) on Tuesdays 8am to 1pm and Saturdays 9am to 7:30pm; many of the stalls sell designer's seconds as well as barely used high-fashion wear. There's an **antiques market on Via Fiori Chiari** (Metro: Moscova) in the Brera district the third Saturday of each month 9am to about 7:30pm (but not in August) and another last Sunday of each month on the quays along the **Canale Grande** in the Navigli district the last Sunday of each month 9am to about 7:30pm (☎ 02-8940-9971; Metro: Sant'Agostino). Every Sunday morning there's a large **flea market,** with everything from books to clothing to appliances, at the **San Donato Metro stop.** A fascinating array of handicrafts, from different regions of Italy and around the world, is on sale at the market around **Viale Tunisia** (☎ 02/2940-8057; Metro: Porta Venezia), open Tuesday to Sunday 9:30am to 1pm and 3 to 7:30pm. The city's largest **food market** is the one at **Piazza Wagner** (Metro: Piazza Wagner), just outside the city center due west of Santa Maria delle Grazie (follow Corso Magenta and its extension, Corso Vercelli to Piazza Piemonte; the market is a block north). It's held Tuesday to Saturday 8am to 1pm and 4pm to 7:30pm and Monday 8am to 1pm; the displays of mouthwatering foodstuffs fill an indoor market space and stalls that surround it.

CITY LAYOUT   Think of Milan as a series of concentric circles radiating from Piazza del Duomo at the center. Within the inner circle, once enclosed by the city walls, are many of the churches, museums, and shops that'll consume your visiting hours. For a general overview of the lay of the land, obtain one of the serviceable maps, with indices, the tourist offices provide for free.

The city's major neighborhoods encircle the hub, **Piazza del Duomo.** Looking east from the Duomo, you can see the imposing **Castello Sforzesco,** at one end of the well-heeled **Magenta neighborhood.** You can walk to the Castello in about 15 minutes by following **Via Orefici** to **Piazza Cordusio** and from there **Via Dante.** The other major draw in Magenta is **Santa Maria delle Grazie** (*The Last Supper*); to reach it, leave Via Dante at **Via Meravigli,** which becomes **Via Magenta** and leads to the church (total walking time from Piazza del Duomo to the church is about 20 minutes).

Heading north from Piazza del Duomo, walk through the city's glass-enclosed shopping center (the world's first), the **Galleria Vittorio Emanuelle II.** Emerging from the northern end of the Galleria, you'll be steps away from **Piazza della Scala** and Milan's famous opera house, **La Scala.** A walk northeast of about 5 minutes along **Via Manzoni** takes you to **Via Montenapoleone** and the city's high-fashion shopping district, the epicenter of Italian design. A walk of about 10 minutes north of Piazza della Scala along **Via Brera** brings you into the atmospheric **Brera neighborhood,** where cobblestone streets and old palazzos surround the city's major art collection, the **Pinacoteca di Brera.**

Another neighborhood to set your sights on is **Ticinese/Navigli,** usually referred to by the last word in that combination, which translates as "canals." Due south of Piazza del Duomo, the Navigli's old quays follow what remains of an elaborate canal system, designed in part by Leonardo da Vinci, that once laced through the city. The moody charm of this area isn't lost on prosperous young Milanese, who are converting old lofts and moving into former quarters of the working classes. The attendant bars, shops, and restaurants on the ground floors have appeared to serve their needs. You can walk to the Navigli in about 30 minutes from Piazza del Duomo by following **Via Torino** south to **Corso Porta Ticinese,** but a Metro ride to the Porta Genova will get you there more quickly.

GETTING AROUND   An extensive **subway** system (Metropolitana Milanese), trams, and buses make it very easy to move around Milan. The Metro closes at midnight, though buses and trams run all night. **Tickets** good for one Metro ride (or 75 minutes of surface transportation) cost 1,500L (75¢). You can buy them at most news-stands and *tabacchi* (tobacconists) or from machines at Metro stations and major bus terminals (though many still accept only coins). You can also purchase a **block of 10 tickets** for 14,000L ($7) or get a ticket good for unlimited travel for **1 day** (5,000L/$2.50) or **2 days** (9,000L/$4.50). For details about Milan public transportation, visit the **ATM info office** in the Duomo Metro stop (☎ **800-016-857;** www.atm-mi.it), open Monday to Saturday 7:30am to 7:30pm.

FAST FACTS: MILAN

American Express   The office is at Via Brera 3, just north of La Scala and near the Pinocoteca di Brera (☎ **02-7200-3693;** Metro: Cairoli), open Monday to Thursday 9am to 5:30pm and Friday 9am to 5pm. Card members can arrange cash advances, receive mail (the postal code is 20121), and wire money.

Bookstores   Milan has two English-language bookshops. The **American Bookstore,** Via Camperio 16, at the corner of Via Dante, between the Duomo and Castello Sforzesco (☎ **02-878-920;** Metro: Cardusio), is open Monday 1 to 7pm and Tuesday to Saturday 10am to 7pm. The **English Bookshop,** Via Mascheroni 12 at Via Ariosto (☎ **02-469-4468;** Metro: Conciliazione), is open Monday to Saturday 9am to 8pm.

Consulates   The **U.S. Consulate** is at Via Principe Amadeo 2/10 (☎ **02-290-351;** Metro: Turati), open Monday to Friday 8:30am to 5pm. The **Canadian Consulate** is at Via Pisani 19 (☎ **02-67-581;** Metro: F.S. Centrale or Repubblica), open Monday to Thursday 8:45am to 12:30pm and 1:30 to 5:15pm. The **U.K. Consulate** is at Via San Paolo 7 (☎ **02-723-001;** Metro: Duomo), open Monday to Friday 9:15am to 12:15am and 2:30 to 4:30pm. The **Australian Consulate** is at Via Borgogna 2 (☎ **02-7770-4217;** Metro: San Babila), open Monday to Thursday 9am to noon and 2 to 4pm and Friday 9am to noon. The **New Zealand Consulate** is at Via Arezzo 6 (☎ **02-4801-2544;** Metro: Pagano), open Monday to Friday 9am to noon.

Crime   For **police** emergencies dial ☎ **113;** you can reach the English-speaking staff at the **tourist police** at ☎ **02-863-701.** There's a police station in Stazione Centrale and the main station, the Questura, is just west of the Giardini Pubblici at Via Fatebenefratelli 11 (☎ **02-622-61;** Metro: Turati). Milan is generally safe, with some notable exceptions, especially at night, including the public gardens, Parco Sempione, and the area to the west of Stazione Centrale. The train station is notorious for pickpockets, whose favorite victims seems to be distracted passengers lining up for the airport buses at the east side of the building. You should likewise be vigilant for pickpockets on all public transportation and at street markets.

Drugstores   Pharmacies rotate 24-hour shifts; dial toll free ☎ **800-161-070** to find ones open around the clock on a given day or look for signs posted in most pharmacies announcing which shop is on a 24-hour schedule. In the main train station, the **Farmacia Stazione Centrale** (☎ **02-669-0735**) is open 24 hours daily, and some of the staff speak English.

Emergencies   The general number for **emergencies** is ☎ **113.** For the **Carbinieri** (the most effective police force), call ☎ **112;** for **first aid** or an **ambulance,** dial ☎ **118.**

Hospitals   The **Ospedale Maggiore Policlinico,** Via Francesco Sforza 35, a 5-minute walk southeast of the Duomo (☎ **02-55-031,** 02-550-3259, or 02-550-3240; Metro: Duomo or Missori). Some of the medical personnel speaks English.

Laundry   A handy place is **Adriana,** Via Tadino 5. A full load—wash, dry, and soap included—costs 11,000L ($6) for 7 kg. or 16,000L ($8) for 12 kg.; it's open daily 7:30am to 9:30pm.

Mail & E-mail The main post office, **Poste e Telecommunicazioni,** Via Cordusio 4, is just west of Piazza del Duomo (☎ **02-7248-2126** or 02-8669-2136; Metro: Cardusio). It's open Monday to Friday 8am to 7pm and Saturday 8:30am to 1pm. Most branch offices are open Monday to Saturday 8:30am to 1:50pm. There's also a post office in the Stazione Centrale, open Monday to Friday 8am to 7pm and Saturday 9:30am to 1pm.

You can check on and send e-mails at **Internet Point,** Via Manara 1 (☎ **02-5518-2221;** Tram: 4, 9, 29, 30), open Monday to Friday 9am to 1am; **Internet Enjoy,** Via Medici 6 off Via Torino (☎ **02-7209-4544;** Tram: 2, 3, 14, 20), open Monday to Saturday 10am to midnight and Sunday 3pm to midnight; **Nashuatec/Digicopy,** Via Larga 9 (☎ **02-5831-5546;** Metro: Missori), open Monday to Friday 9am to 7pm.

Taxis To find a **taxi** in Milan, walk to the nearest taxi stand, usually near major piazzas and major Metro stops. In the center, there are taxi stands at Piazza del Duomo and Piazza della Scala. Or call a **radio taxi** at ☎ 02-6767, 02-8585, 02-5353, or 02-8383 (the desk staff at many hotels will be happy to do this for you, even if you aren't a guest). Cab meters start at 6,000L ($3) and add a nighttime surcharge of 5,000L ($2.50).

SEEING THE SIGHTS

✪ **Duomo & Museo del Duomo.** Piazza del Duomo. ☎ **02-8646-3456.** www.internet-landia.com/duomo. Duomo free; admission to roof 6,000L ($3) on foot, 9,000L ($4.50) by elevator; treasury and crypt 2,000L ($1); baptistery 3,000L ($1.50), free under 6; Museo del Duomo 10,000L ($5) adults, 5,000L ($2.50) students and over 65. Combo ticket to roof and museum (buy at roof entry) 12,000L ($6). Duomo daily 7:15am–6:45pm. Roof daily 9am–5:30pm (to 4pm Oct–Feb). Treasury and crypt daily 9am–noon and 2:30–6pm. Baptistry daily 9am–5:15pm. Museo del Duomo and Museo Civico d'Arte Contemporanea Tues–Sun 9:30am–12:30pm and 3–6pm. Metro: Duomo.

When Milanese think something is taking too long, they refer to it as *la fabricca del duomo* (the making of the Duomo), recalling the 5 centuries it took to complete this magnificent Gothic cathedral. The last of Italy's great Gothic structures—begun by the ruling Visconti family in 1386—is the world's fourth-largest church (after St. Peter's in Rome, Seville's cathedral, and a new one on the Ivory Coast), with 135 marble spires, a stunning triangular facade, and 3,400-some statues flanking the massive but almost fanciful exterior.

The cavernous **interior,** boasting brilliant stained-glass windows, seats 40,000 but is unusually Spartan and serene, divided into five aisles by a sea of 52 columns. Poet Percy Bysshe Shelley used to sit and read Dante amid monuments like a gruesomely graphic statue of *St. Bartholomew Flayed* and the tombs of Giacomo de' Medici, two Viscontis, and many cardinals and archbishops. Alfred, Lord Tennyson, rhapsodized about the ✪ **view** of the Alps from the roof (elevators on the church's exterior northeast corner; stairs on the exterior north side), and on a clear day you'll do the same. You're joined high above Milan by a gold statue of the *Madonnina* (*Little Madonna*), the city's beloved protectress. The **crypt** contains the remains of San Carlo Borromeo, one of the early cardinals of Milan. A far more interesting descent is the one down the staircase to the right of the main entrance to the **Battistero Paleocristiano,** the ruins of a 4th-century baptistry believed to be where St. Ambrose baptized Saint Augustine. To aid in your explorations of the interior and the crypt, you can rent an **audio guide** wand for 5,000L ($2.50) for one person or 4,000L ($2) per person for two or more.

The Duomo displays many of its treasures across the piazza from the left transept in the Palazzo Reale, where you'll find the **Museo del Duomo** (☎ **02-860-358).**

Milan

Cimitero Monumentale

Porta Garibaldi Station

Stazione Centrale

Via C. Farini

Via Ceresio

Viale Pasubio

Viale Crispi

Via Paolo Sarpi

Via Bramante

Via Melzi d'Eril

Via Bertani

Piazza Lega Lombarda

Arena

V. Bertani

Viale Malta

PARCO SEMPIONE

Via Gadio

Castello Sforzesco

Northern Station

Piazzale Cadorna

MAGENTA

Corso Magenta

Via Boccaccio

San Ambrogio

Università Cattolica

Via San Vittore

Via Carducci

Borsa (Stock Exchange)

Via Meravigli

Via Luini Cappuccio

V.S.M. Fulcorina

V.S. Orsola

Via Circo

Via C. Correnti

Via Edmondo de Amicis

Via Olona

Via Ausonio

Via Papiniano

C. di Pta. Genova

TICINESE/ NAVIGLI

Via Molino d. Armi

Corso di Pta. Ticinese

Corso Italia

Porta Garibaldi

Viale Monte Grappa

Bastioni di Pta. Nuova

Viale Monte Grappa

Corso Garibaldi

Via A. Volta

Via Solferino

Via Moscova

Pta. Nuova

BRERA

Via Fatebenefratelli

Via Mercato

Via Brera

Piazza della Scala

Foro Buonaparte

Via Broletto

Via Dante

Via Orefici

Galleria Vittorio Emanuele II

Piazza del Duomo

Il Duomo

Piazza Castello

Piazza Missori

Corso di Porta Romana

Corso di Porta Vittoria

Via Larga

Via Torino

Via Mazzini

Via Francesco Sforza

Via Lamarmora

Viale di Melchiorre Gioia

Via Fabio Filzi

Via V. Pisani

Piazza della Repubblica

Viale Vittorio Veneto

Bastioni di Porta Venezia

Via Turati

Pta. Nuova

GIARDINI PUBBLICI

Piazza Cavour

Via Palestro

Villa Reale

Via Senato

Corso Venezia

Via Monte Napoleone

Via Manzoni

C. V. Emanuele

Via V. di Modrone

V. Fil. Corridoni

Corso di Porta Vittoria

Via Verziere

V. S. Barnaba

ATTRACTIONS
Castello Sforzesco **14**
Civica Galleria d'Arte Moderna **9**
Civico Museo Archeologico **17**
Duomo **25**
Museo Civico d'Arte Contemporanea **26**
Museo del Duomo **26**
Museo Nazionale della Scienza e delle Tecnica Leonardo da Vinci **34**
Museo Poldi-Pezzoli **23**
Pinacoteca Ambrosiana **30**
Pinacoteca di Brera **13**
San Lorenzo Maggiore **36**
Sant'Ambrogio & Museo Sant'Ambrogio **33**
Santa Maria delle Grazie (The Last Supper) **16**
Santa Maria Presso di San Satiro **28**
Teatro alla Scala **22**

ACCOMMODATIONS
Antica Locanda Solferino **11**
Ariosto **15**
Doriagrand **2**
Giulio Cesare **20**
Kennedy **7**
London **19**
Paganini **4**
Promessi Sposi **8**
Rovello **18**
Santa Marta **32**
Speronari **29**
Ullrich **27**

DINING
Al Pont de Ferr **37**
Brek **5**
Da Abele **1**
Joia **6**
La Créperie **35**
La Milanese **31**
Latteria **10**
Luini **24**
Peck **21**
Pizzeria Grand'Italia **12**
Premiata Pizzeria **37**
Ristorante Versilia **3**

ⓘ Information
✉ Post Office

ITALY
Rome

Milan in a Day

For an excellent overview of the city, hop aboard vintage 1920s **tram 20,** distinguished by "Ciao Milano" emblazoned on its sides, for a tour with commentary in English and five other languages. The 1¾-hour tours are hop-on/hop-off for a full day and run daily at 11am and 1 and 3pm from Piazza Castello (Metro: Cairoli). The cost is 30,000L ($15) adults or 15,000L ($8) those under 12. For more details, call ☎ **02-805-5323.**

Among the legions of statuary saints is a gem of a painting by Jacopo Tintoretto, *Christ at the Temple,* and some riveting displays chronicling the cathedral's construction. Adjoining this is the **Museo Civico d'Arte Contemporanea,** with works by living artists and such masters as De Chirico and Modigliani.

Santa Maria delle Grazie & *The Last Supper*. Piazza Santa Maria delle Grazie. ☎ **02-498-7588** for church. Book *The Last Supper* tickets (even in winter they can be sold out days in advance) at 199-199-100 in Italy or 02-8942-1146 outside Italy. Admission *The Last Supper* 12,000L ($6) plus 2,000L ($1) booking fee; church free. *The Last Supper* Tues–Sun 8:15am–6:45pm (Sat to 11pm June–Sept), church only Mon–Sat 7:30am–noon and 3–7pm, Sun 3:30–6:30pm. Metro: Cardona or Conciliazione.

What draws so many visitors here is the ✪ *Cenacolo Vinciano* (*The Last Supper*). From 1495 to 1497, Leonardo da Vinci painted this poignant portrayal of confusion and betrayal for the far wall of the refectory when this was a Dominican convent. Aldous Huxley called this fresco the "saddest work of art in the world," a comment in part on the deterioration that set in even before the paint had dried on the moisture-ridden walls. The fresco was completely repainted in the 18th and 19th centuries, and a recent lengthy restoration has done away with these centuries of overpainting, along with clumsy patching and damage inflicted when Napoléon's troops used the wall for target practice and World War II Allied bombing tore off the room's roof, leaving the fresco exposed to the elements for 3 years. In short, *The Last Supper* is a mere shadow of what the artist intended it to be, but the work, capturing the moment Christ tells his Apostles that one of them will betray him, remains amazingly powerful and emotional nonetheless. Only 25 people are allowed to view the fresco at one time, and they must pass through a series of devices that remove pollutants from clothing. Accordingly, lines are long and tickets usually sold out days in advance.

Often overlooked are the other treasures of this late-15th-century church, foremost among them the fine **dome** and other **architectural innovations** by the one of the High Renaissance's great architects, Donato Bramante, who was also one of the first architects of St. Peter's in Rome. To one side of the apse, decorated in marble and terra cotta, is a lovely **cloister.**

Galleria Vittorio Emanuele II. Just off Piazza del Duomo and Piazza della Scala. Metro: Duomo.

Built in the late 19th century, this wonderful steel-and-glass-covered arcade shaped like a cross is the prototype of the enclosed shopping malls that became the hallmark of 20th-century consumerism. It's safe to say that none of the imitators has come close to matching the Galleria for style and flair. Alas, the designer of this urban marvel, Giuseppe Mengoni, didn't live to see the Milanese embrace his creation: He tripped and fell from a girder a few days before the Galleria opened in 1878. His shopping mall par excellence provides a lovely route between the Duomo and La Scala and is a fine locale for watching the flocks of well-dressed Milanese—you'll understand why the Galleria is called *Il Salotto di Milano* (the drawing room of Milan).

⊙ **Pinacoteca di Brera (Brera Picture Gallery).** Via Brea 28. ☎ **199-199-100** in Italy, or 02-8942-1146. Admission 8,000L ($4), sometimes 12,000L ($6) for a special show. Tues–Sun 8:30am–7:15pm (Sat to 11pm June–Sept). Metro: Lanza or Montenapoleone.

The world's finest collection of Northern Italian painting, this 17th-century palazzo houses one of Italy's finest collections of medieval and Renaissance art. The concentration of so many masterpieces is the work of Napoléon, who used the palazzo as the repository for the art he confiscated from public and private holdings throughout northern Italy; a bronze likeness of the emperor greets you in the courtyard. Three of Italy's greatest masterpieces hang in these 40 or so rooms: Andrea Mantegna's amazingly foreshortened ⊙ *Dead Christ,* Raphael's *Betrothal of the Virgin,* and Piero della Francesa's *Madonna with Saints (Montefeltro Altarpiece).* It's an indication of this museum's ability to overwhelm visitors that the last two hang near each other in a single room dedicated to works by Tuscan and Umbrian painters.

The paintings are continually being rearranged, but in the wake of a recent renovation, in the first rooms you won't encounter Napoleonic bounty but a sizable collection of 20th-century paintings. From there, you enter several galleries of sumptuous Venetian works, including Jacopo Tinteretto's *Finding of the Body of St. Mark,* in which the dead saint eerily confronts startled grave robbers who come on his corpse. Caravaggio (*Supper at Emmaus* is his masterpiece here) is surrounded by works of his followers, and just beyond is a room devoted to works by foreigners, among them Rembrandt's *Portrait of a Young Woman.* Given Napoléon's fondness for the Venetian schools, it's only fitting that the final rooms are again filled with works from that city, including Canaletto's *View of the Grand Canal.*

You can rent an **audioguide** for 7,000L ($3.50) for one person or 10,000L ($5) for two people. **Guided tours** cost 8,000L ($4) and are available Saturdays at 3 and 5pm; Sundays at 10am, noon, and 3 and 5pm; and weekdays if you arrange a time at least 2 to 3 days ahead (they'll do it even for just one person).

Castello Sforzesco. Piazza Castello. ☎ **02-6208-3940.** Admission free. Tues–Sun 9am–5:30pm. Metro: Cairoli or Lanza.

Though it's been clumsily restored many times, most recently at the end of the 19th century, this fortresslike castle continues to evoke Milan's two most powerful medieval and Renaissance families, the Viscontis and the Sforzas. The Viscontis built the castle in the 14th century and the Sforzas, who married into the Visconti clan and eclipsed them in power, reconstructed it in 1450. The most influential residents were Ludovico il Moro and Beatrice d'Este (he of the Sforza and she of the famous Este family of Ferrara). After ill-advisedly calling the French into Italy at the end of the 15th century, Ludovico died in the dungeons of a château in the Loire Valley—but not before the couple made the Castello and Milan one of Italy's great centers of the Renaissance. It was they who commissioned the works by Bramante and Leonardo da Vinci, and you can see these splendors on a stroll through the miles of salons surrounding the castello's enormous courtyard.

The salons house a series of small city-administered museums known collectively as the **Civici Musei Castello Sforzesco.** They include a **Pinacoteca (Picture Gallery)** with works by Bellini, Correggio, and Magenta and the extensive holdings of the **Museo d'Arte Antica (Museum of Ancient Art),** filled with Egyptian funerary objects, prehistoric finds from Lombardy, and the last work of 89-year-old Michelangelo, the unfinished ⊙ *Rondanini Pietà.*

San Lorenzo Maggiore. Corso di Porta Ticinese. ☎ **02-8940-4129.** Admission free. Mon–Sat 7:30am–6:45pm, Sun 10:30–11:15am and 3–5:30pm. Metro: Missori.

The oldest church in Milan attests to the days when the city was the capital of the Western Roman Empire. The 4th-century early Christian structure has been rebuilt and altered many times over the centuries (it's dome, the highest in Milan, is a 16th-century embellishment) but still retains the flavor of its roots in its octagonal floor plan and a few surviving remnants. These include fifth-century **mosaics** (one depicting a beardless Christ) in the **Cappella di Sant'Aquilino,** which you enter from the atrium. A **sarcophagus** in the chapel is said to enshrine the remains of Galla Placidia, sister of Honorius, last emperor of Rome and wife of Ataulf, king of the Visigoths. She doesn't, however, actually rest in peace here. In fact, she also has a mausoleum in Ravenna, its mosaics one of that city's masterworks, but it is most likely she's buried in Rome, where she died. You'll be rewarded with a glimpse at even earlier history if you follow the stairs from behind the altar to a crypt-like room that contains what remains of a **Roman amphitheater.**

Sant'Ambrogio & Museo Sant'Ambrogio. Piazza Sant'Ambrogio 15. ☎ **02-8645-0895.** Church free; museum 3,000L ($1.50). Church Mon–Sat 9:30am–noon and 2:30pm–6:30pm; Museum Mon, Wed–Fri 10am–noon and 3–5pm, Sat–Sun 3–5pm, Tues 10am–noon. Metro: Sant'Ambrogio.

From the basilica he constructed on this site in the 4th century—when he was bishop of Milan and the city was briefly capital of the Western Roman Empire—St. Ambrose had a profound effect on the development of the early church. Little remains of his church, but the 11th-century structure built in its place (and renovated many times since) is remarkable. It has a striking **atrium,** lined with columned porticos and opening on one side to the brick facade, with two ranks of loggias and a bell tower. Look at the door on the left, where you'll see a relief of St. Ambrose. Note the overall effect of this architectural assemblage, because the church of Sant'Ambrogio set a standard for Lombard Romanesque architecture that you'll see imitated many times on your travels through Lombardy.

On your wanderings through the three-aisled nave, you'll come on a **gold altar** from Charlemagne's days in Milan, and, in the right aisle, the all-too-scant remains of a **Tiepolo fresco cycle,** most of it blown into oblivion by World War II bombs. The little that remains of the original church is the **Sacello di San Vittore in Ciel d'Oro,** a little chapel in which the cupola glows with 5-century mosaics of saints (enter from the right aisle). The skeletal remains of Ambrose himself are on view in the **crypt.** One of the "later" additions as you leave the main church from the left aisle is another work of the great Bramante—his **Portico dell Canonica,** lined with elegant columns, some of which are sculpted to resemble tree trunks. The adjoining **Museo di Sant'Ambrogio** houses a small but riveting collection of treasures connected with the church, including some fragments of 5th-century mosaics.

Santa Maria Presso di San Satiro. Where Via Mazzini, Via Speronari, and Via Falcone meet. ☎ **02-874-683.** Admission free. Daily 9am–noon and 2:30–6pm. Metro: Duomo or Missori.

What makes this beautiful church, just south of Piazza del Duomo, so exquisite is what it doesn't have—space. Stymied by not being able to expand the T-shaped apse to classical Renaissance cross-shaped proportions, the architect Bramante created a **marvelous relief** behind the high altar. The effect of the trompe-l'oeil columns and arches isn't entirely convincing but nonetheless magical. Another gem lies to the rear of the left transept: the **Cappella della Pietà,** so called for the 15th-century terra-cotta *Pietà* it now houses, but built in the 9th century to honor St. Satiro, brother of

St. Ambrose. The namesake statue isn't the most alluring adornment in this charming structure; it's the lovely **Byzantine frescoes** and **Romanesque columns** that'll catch your eye. While more famous Milan churches now eclipse this complex, it was an important pilgrimage site in the 13th and 14th centuries, after news spread through Christendom that an image of the Madonna here shed real blood when stabbed.

Civica Galleria d'Arte Moderna (Civic Gallery of Modern Art). In the Villa Reale, Via Palestro 16. ☎ **02-7600-2819.** Admission free. Tues–Sun 9am–5:30pm. Metro: Porta Venezia.

The sumptuous palazzo, where Napoléon and his stepson, Eugene de Beauharnais, lived, houses a collection that's "modern" in the true 19th-century sense. The salons are filled with works by Lombardians and other Italian painters who embraced trends from France. You'll probably be more familiar with the works by Cézanne, Gauguin, and other non-Italian modernists also included (in a section housing the noted Grassi Collection), but it's fascinating to see the same dreamy landscapes and the flight from creeping industrialism reflected in the works of lesser-known Italians. The upper floors house the equestrian works of 20th-century sculptor Marino Marini.

Civico Museo Archeologico (Civic Archaeological Museum). Corso Magenta 15. ☎ **02-8645-0011.** Admission free. Tues–Sun 9:30am–5:30pm. Metro: Cadorna.

The most fascinating finds in this sizable repository of civilizations past are the everyday items—tools, eating utensils, and jewelry from Roman Milan. The exhibits, which seem to fill every corner of the 16th-century monastery, also include Greek, Etruscan, and Roman pieces from throughout Italy; there's also a section devoted to ancient remains from Ghandara, India. You can get a glimpse of Roman architecture in the garden, where two Roman towers and a section of a road, part of the walls enclosing the settlement of Mediolanum, once capital of the Western Roman Empire, remain in situ. This lovely patch of greenery, incidentally, is an evocative place to rest from the rigors of museum going.

Museo Nazionale della Scienza e delle Tecnica Leonardo da Vinci (Leonardo da Vinci National Museum of Science and Technology). Via San Vittore 21. ☎ **02-485-551** or 02-4801-0040. Admission 12,000L ($6) adults, 6,000L ($3) under 18 and over 60. Tues–Fri 9:30am–4:50pm, Sat–Sun 9:30am–6:20pm. Metro: Sant'Ambrogio.

The heart and soul of this engaging museum are the working **scale models** of Leonardo's submarines, airplanes, and other engineering feats that, for the most part, the master ever invented only on paper (each exhibit includes a reproduction of the master's drawings and a model of his creations). This former Benedictine monastery and its beautiful cloisters are also filled with planes, trains, carriages, sewing machines, typewriters, optical devices, and other exhibits, including some enchanting re-creations of workshops, that comprise one of the world's leading collections of mechanical and scientific wizardry.

Museo Poldi-Pezzoli. Via Manzoni 12. ☎ **02-794-889.** Admission 10,000L ($5); includes admission to Teatro alla Scala (below), so visit here first. Tues–Sun 10am–6pm; often closed Sun afternoons Apr–Sept. Metro: Duomo or Montenapoleone.

The pleasant effect of seeing the Bellinis, Bottecellis, and Tiepolos amid these salons is reminiscent of a visit to other private collections, such as the Frick Collection in New York City and the Isabella Stewart Gardner Museum in Boston. This stunning treasure trove leans a bit toward Venetian painters (such as Francesco Guardi's elegantly moody *Grey Lagoon*) but also ventures widely throughout Italian painting and into the northern and Flemish schools. It was amassed by 19th-century collector Giacomo Poldi-Pezzoli, who donated his villa and its treasures to the city in 1881.

Antonio Pollaiuolo's *Portrait of a Young Woman* is often likened to the *Mona Lisa*, in that it's a haunting image you'll recognize immediately. The collections also include porcelain, watches, jewels, and many of the palazzo's original furnishings.

Teatro alla Scala. Piazza della Scala. ☎ **02-887-9473.** lascala.milano.it. Admission to Museo Teatrale 6,000L ($3) adults, 4,000L ($2) students; or free with Museo Poldi Pezzoli ticket (see above). Daily 9am–noon and 2–5pm (closed Sun Nov–Apr). Metro: Duomo.

Built in the late 18th century on the site of a church of the same name, La Scala is hallowed ground to lovers of Giuseppe Verdi, Callas, and legions of other composers and singers who've hit the high notes of fame in the world's most revered opera house. Although it emerged from a renovation only in 1999, La Scala is set for an overhaul again, to begin at the end of the 2001–2002 season. A whiff of nostalgia for days gone by pervades the **Museo Teatrale alla Scala,** where you'll find Toscanini's baton, a strand of Mozart's hair, and a fine array of Callas postcards.

Pinacoteca Ambrosiana (Ambrosiana Picture Gallery). Piazza Pio XI 2. ☎ **02-806-921.** Admission 12,000L ($6). Tues–Sun 10am–5:30pm. Metro: Cardusio.

Much to the joy of art lovers who waited through the late 1990s for the **Pinacoteca** to reopen, this exquisite collection, focusing on treasures from the 15th to the 17th century, is housed in newly restored galleries. An *Adoration* by Titian, Raphael's cartoon for his *School of Athens* in the Vatican, Bottecelli's *Madonna and Angels,* Caravaggio's *Basket of Fruit* (his only still life), and other stunning works hang in a series of intimate rooms. Notable (or infamous) among the paintings is *Portrait of a Musician,* attributed to Leonardo but of dubious provenance; if it's indeed a Leonardo, the haunting painting is the only portrait of his to hang in an Italian museum. The adjoining **Biblioteca Ambrosiana,** open to scholars only except for special exhibits, contains a wealth of Renaissance literaria, including the letters of Lucrezia Borgia and a strand of her hair. The most notable holdings, though, are Leonardo's *Codice Atlantico,* 1,750 drawings and jottings the master did between 1478 and 1519. These and the library's other volumes, including a rich collection of **medieval manuscripts,** are frequently put on view to the public; at these times, an entrance fee of 18,000L ($9) allows entrance to both the library and the art gallery.

SHOPPING

The best **fashion** gazing is to be done along four adjoining streets north of the Duomo known as the Quadrilatero d'Oro (Golden Quadrilateral): **Via Montenapoleone, Via Spiga, Via Borgospesso,** and **Via Sant'Andrea.** (To enter this hallowed precinct, follow Via Manzoni a few blocks north of Piazza della Scala; Metro: San Babila or Montenapoleone.) If your fashion sense is greater than your credit line, don't despair: Even the most expensive clothing of the Armani ilk is usually less expensive in Italy than it is abroad, and city-wide *saldi* (sales) run from early January into early February and again in late June and July.

Even if your wallet can't afford it, stop by to browse the new **Armani Megastore,** Via Manzoni 31, near La Scala (☎ **02-7231-8630;** www.armani-viamanzoni31.com; Metro: Montenapoleone). To celebrate 25 years in business in the summer of 2000, Giorgio opened this new flagship store/offices covering 8,000 square feet with outlets for his high-fashion creations, the Emprio Armani and Armani Jeans lines, plus the new Armani Casa selection of home furnishings; flower, book, and art shops; a high-tech Sony electronics boutique/play center in the basement; and an Emporio Café and branch of New York's Nobu sushi bar.

Or, inspired by the window displays in the Quadrilatero, you can scour the racks of shops elsewhere for designer seconds, last year's fashions, imitations, and other bargains. (Unless otherwise indicated, most of these discount shops are open Monday 3:30 to 7:30pm and Tuesday to Saturday 9am to 1pm and 3:30 to 7:30pm). The place to begin is **Il Salvagente,** Via Bronzetti 16, several blocks east of the Quadrilatero off Corso XXII Marzo (☎ **02-7611-0328;** Metro: San Babila), with an enormous collection of designer clothing for men, women, and children at wholesale prices. Other havens for bargain hunters are the used high-fashion shops, where the merchandise may be secondhand but only in the sense that a model donned them briefly for a show or shoot; the tops are **L'Armadio di Laura,** Via Voghera 25 (☎ **02-836-0606;** Metro: Porta Genova), and **Mercatino Michela,** with many locations, including Corso Venezia 8 (☎ **02-7600-3205;** Metro: Palestro or Porta Venezia), Via Quadronno 34 (☎ **02-5831-4033;** Metro: Crocetta), Via della Spiga 33 (☎ **02-799-748;** Metro: Montenapoleone), Piazza de Angeli 3 (☎ **02-498-6000;** Metro: De Angeli), and Via Tazzoli 11 (☎ **02-2900-3538;** Metro: Garibaldi FS).

The other hunting ground for discount fashions is **Corso Buenos Aires,** northeast of the center and just east of Stazione Centrale (Metro stops Lima and Loreto are the gateways to this bargain stretch). **Calzaturificio di Parabiago,** Corso Buenos Aires 52 (☎ **02-2940-6851;** Metro: Lime), shods men and women fashionably at reasonable prices, with an enormous selection and a helpful staff.

For Milanese design with which to dress the bed and table and not the body, visit **Frette,** with outlets at Via Montenapoleone 21 (☎ **02-7600-3791;** Metro: San Babila), Corso Vercelli 23 (☎ **02-498-9756;** Metro: Pagano), and Via Manzoni 11 (☎ **02-864-339;** Metro: Montenapoleone). The high-fashion linen house offers some, but certainly not all, of its tablecloths, towels, robes, and bedding at substantial discounts. To complete the tabletop, make a stop at **Richard Ginori,** the renowned Florentine purveyor of fine china, at Corso Buenos Aires 1 (☎ **02-2951-6611;** Metro: Porta Venezia or Lima); the house's fine porcelain and crystal, as well as offerings from other manufacturers, are often available at discounted prices. **Bassetti,** Corso Buenos Aires 52 (☎ **02-2940-0048;** Metro: Lima), is a discount outlet of the august Bassetti line of high-quality linen, and the huge spaces offers the luxurious towels and sheets at excellent prices.

If its a bookish souvenir you're after, **Remainders',** in the Galleria Vittorio Emanuele II (☎ **02-8646-4008;** Metro: Duomo), hawks glossy coffee-table tomes and art books at half price and offers cut rates on English books on the second floor—just a few novels, plus lots of art and academic books. For more books in English, see "Fast Facts: Milan," at the beginning of this section.

ACCOMMODATIONS YOU CAN AFFORD

While you can pay more for a hotel room in Milan than you would almost anywhere else in Europe, there are also some decent accommodations at reasonable prices in good locations. It's difficult to find rooms in any price category when fashion shows and trade fairs are in full swing (often October and March). Many hotels raise their prices at these times too. August is low season, and hotels are often willing to bring prices down considerably, as they will sometimes on slow weekends. Unless otherwise indicated, price ranges below reflect a seasonal fluctuation. Always ask for the lowest possible rate when booking and be prepared to bargain.

Though they won't book a room for you, the tourist office (see above) will help you track down hotels within your budget (and, if you go to the main office in person, will even call around for you).

NEAR THE DUOMO

Santa Marta. Via Santa Marta 4, 20123 Milano. ☎ **02-804-567.** Fax 02-8645-2661. www.tema-multimedia.com/italyhotel. 15 units. A/C TV TEL. 140,000–190,000L ($70–$95) single; 230,000–320,000L ($115–$160) double; 280,000–380,000L ($140–$190) triple. Rates include continental breakfast. AE, DC, MC, V. Parking in nearby garage 30,000L ($15). Closed 15 days in Aug. Metro: Cordusio or Duomo. Tram: 1, 2, 3, 4, 12, 14, 15, 19, 20, 24, 27.

Narrow Via Santa Marta is a slice of old Milan, cobblestoned and lined with charming buildings, one of which houses the Santa Marta. It's also across from one of the city's most atmospheric restaurants (the Milanese) and a short walk from the Duomo and other sights. Recent modernizations have preserved the old-fashioned ambience while adding modern comforts like air-conditioning. The tile-floored rooms are comfortable and decorated with a matter-of-fact style, some cramped and others quite large. If they're full, they'll send you to their sibling hotel, the Rovello (below).

Speronari. Via Speronari 4, 20123 Milano. ☎ **02-8646-1125.** Fax 02-7200-3178. 33 units, 17 with bathroom. TEL. 75,000L ($38) single without bathroom, 95,000L ($48) single with bathroom; 110,000L ($55) double without bathroom, 160,000L ($80) double with bathroom; 150,000L ($75) triple without bathroom, 215,000L ($108) triple without bathroom; 240,000L ($120) quad with bathroom. MC. Metro: Duomo or Missori. Tram: 1, 2, 3, 4, 12, 14, 15, 19, 20, 24, 27.

This is a one-star hotel in a four-star location, on a tiny pedestrian side street between Via Torino and Via Mazzini across from Santa Maria presso San Satiro. The staff is earnest, and the rooms are basic but done well (cool tiles floors, functional furnishings, ceiling fans, new cot springs, and fuzzy towels in the baths). Even those without baths have sinks and bidets, and all but a few of the bathless rooms have TVs. Third- and fourth-floor rooms are brighter and those on the courtyard are a tad quieter than rooms facing the street (there are convenient trolleys a half-block in either direction, but they come with a distant but noisy rumble).

Ullrich. Corso Italia 6 (from the courtyard, turn left and go up 10 steps for the elevator to the 6th floor), 21023 Milano. ☎ **02-8645-0156.** Fax 02-804-535. 8 units, none with bathroom. TV. 80,000L ($40) single; 120,000L ($60) double; 150,000L ($75) triple. Breakfast 10,000L ($5). No credit cards. Metro: Missori. Tram/Bus: 15, 24, 65, 94.

A 10-minute walk south of the Duomo, this attractive pensione offers a lot of comfort and amenities in addition to its good location. The management is friendly, and the rooms are furnished with pleasant modern pieces and decent beds. Each has a tiny washroom with sink and bidet but no toilet; spanking-clean large baths are in the hall. Rooms on the street side open to small balconies but are noisier than those overlooking the *cortile*. One of the baths is equipped with a washing machine, and you can do a load for 15,000L ($8). The Ulrich books up quickly, so be sure to call ahead.

IN MAGENTA & BRERA

Giulio Cesare. Via Rovello 10, 20121 Milano. ☎ **02-7200-3915.** Fax 02-7200-2179. 20 units. A/C TV TEL. 150,000–165,000L ($75–$83) single; 240,000–270,000L ($120–$135) double. Rates include breakfast. AE, MC, V. Metro: Cordusio. Tram/Bus: 1, 2, 3, 4, 12, 14, 18, 19, 20, 24, 27.

A recent renovation has brought this old place thoroughly up-to-date, with a grandiose marble lobby and a handsome lounge and bar area. Upstairs, the rooms are contemporary chic but reflect the building's centuries-old heritage with tall windows and high ceilings. Some are quirkily shaped, and a few singles are cramped, but the white tile floors and minimalist furnishings are starkly modern. The new baths gleam and come with stall showers and flat towels. This is one of several similarly priced hotels on the block, a quiet street tucked away off Via Dante between the Duomo and

La Scala in one direction and the Castello in the other (see the listings for the London and Rovello, below).

London. Via Rovello 3, 20121 Milano. ☎ **02-7202-0166.** Fax 02-805-7037. www.travel europe.it/hotellondon.htm. E-mail: hotel.london@traveleurope.it. 29 units, 20 with bathroom. A/C TV TEL. 130,000L ($65) single without bathroom, 150,000L ($75) single with shower only, 160,000L ($80) single with bathroom; 210,000L ($105) double without bathroom, 230,000L ($115) double with shower only, 250,000L ($125) double with bathroom. 10% off if pay cash. Continental breakfast 10,000L ($5). MC, V. Parking 35,000L ($18). Closed Aug and Christmas. Metro: Cordusio. Tram/Bus: 1, 2, 3, 4, 12, 14, 18, 19, 20, 24, 27.

Unlike its neighbor, the Giulio Cesare, the family-run London sticks to its old-fashioned ways. The big fireplace and cozy green velvet furniture in the lobby say a lot about the comfort level and friendly atmosphere that bring many guests back time after time. Just beyond the lobby is a bar where beverages are available almost around the clock; you can get a cappuccino or a continental breakfast in the morning. Upstairs, the rooms look like they haven't been redecorated in a number of decades, but they're bright and clean, and the heavy old modular units are in excellent shape. First-floor rooms tend to be the largest, and they get smaller as you go up.

Rovello. Via Rovello 18, 20121 Milano. ☎ **02-8646-4654.** Fax 02-7202-3656. 10 units. A/C TV TEL. 220,000–290,000L ($110–$145) single; 250,000–320,000L ($125–$160) double; 350,000–390,000L ($175–$190) triple. Rates include continental breakfast. AE, DC, MC, V. Metro: Cordusio. Tram/Bus: 1, 2, 3, 4, 12, 14, 18, 19, 20, 24, 27.

The Rovello is one of three hotels I recommend on this quiet street between the Duomo and the Castello, and it has recently completed a striking renovation. The unusually large rooms occupy the first and second floors of a centuries-old building and incorporate many of the original architectural details, like exposed timbers and beamed ceilings. The handsome contemporary Italian furnishings are set on gleaming hardwood floors, and the orthopedic mattresses are covered with thick quilts for a homey feel. Many rooms have dressing areas in addition to the large new baths. A breakfast of rolls and coffee is served in a sunny room off the lobby.

Worth a Splurge

✪ **Antica Locanda Solferino.** Via Castelfidardo 2, 20121 Milano. ☎ **02-657-0129.** Fax 02-657-1361. 11 units. TV TEL. 180,000L ($90) single; 260,000–280,000L ($130–$140) double. Rates include continental breakfast. AE, MC, V. Parking 25,000–40,000L ($13–$20) in nearby garage. Closed 2–3 weeks in mid-Aug. Metro: Moscova or Repubblica. Tram/Bus: 11, 29, 30, 33, 41, 43, 94.

If this charming old hotel in the arty Brera neighborhood hadn't been discovered long ago by fashion and film stars (this was Marcello Mastroianni's preferred Milan hostelry), you'd consider it a find. The rooms have more character than modern comforts, but, to the loyal guests, the smattering of country antiques and art nouveau pieces more than compensates for the absence of minibars and air-conditioning (they're considering adding the latter). And the repeat customers don't seem to mind that some of the baths are miniscule (though modern) or that there's no lobby or breakfast room (coffee and rolls are delivered to your room). The rooms on the tiny courtyard are quieter, but those on the street have plant-filled balconies (the best is no. 10 on the corner). The reception manager, Gerardo Vitolo, is very friendly.

Ariosto. Via Ariosto 22, 20145 Milano. ☎ **02-481-7844.** Fax 02-498-0516. www. hotelariosto.com. 48 units. A/C MINIBAR TV TEL. 240,000L ($120) single; 340,000L ($170) double. Rates include breakfast. AE, DC, MC, V. Parking 35,000–50,000L ($18–$25) in garage. Closed 20 days in Aug. Metro: Conciliazione. Tram/Bus: 29, 30, 61, 67, 68.

In a residential neighborhood of apartment houses and old villas near Santa Maria della Grazie, the Ariosto is a refreshingly quiet retreat—all the more so because many of the newly refurbished rooms face a private garden and some open onto balconies overlooking it. All the rooms contain wood-and-wicker furnishings, parquet floors, and hand-painted wallpaper. Most are decently sized, but singles tend to be skinny. Many of the doubles have separate dressing areas off the tile or stone baths, which come with hairdryers and a few with Jacuzzis. There's free Internet access in the lobby, and satellite movie channels on the TV.

EAST OF THE DUOMO, NEAR STAZIONE CENTRALE & CORSO BUENOS AIRES

Kennedy. Viale Tunisia 6 (6th floor), 20124 Milano. ☎ **02-2940-0934.** Fax 02-2940-1253. E-mail: hotelkennedy@galactica.it. 12 units, 5 with bathroom. 60,000–80,000L ($30–$40) single without bathroom; 90,000–100,000L ($45–$50) double without bathroom, 130,000–150,000L ($65–$75) double with bathroom. Continental breakfast 4,000L ($2). AE, DC, MC, V. Parking 25,000–50,000L ($13–$25) in nearby garage. Metro: Porta Venezia. Tram: 5, 11.

The name reflects the English-speaking management's fondness for the late president, and the family is genuinely welcoming to the many Americans who find their way to their pensione a block off the southern end of Corso Buenos Aires. Their homey establishment on the sixth floor of an office-and-apartment building (with an elevator) is sparkling clean and offers basic accommodations in large tile-floored rooms. Room 13 has a terrace, while 15 has a small balcony that even glimpses the top spires of the Duomo. Amenities include a bar in the reception area, where coffee and soft drinks are available, as is a light breakfast of brioche and coffee that doesn't cost much more than it would in a cafe.

Paganini. Via Paganini 6, 20131 Milano. ☎ **02-204-7443.** 8 units, 1 with bathroom. 90,000–100,000L ($45–$50) single or double without bathroom; 120,000L ($60) double with bathroom. AE, DC, MC, V. Parking in garage across street 20,000–25,000L ($10–$13), or free on street. Metro: Loreto. Tram/Bus: 33, 55, 55/, 56, 56/, 90, 91, 93.

Occupying an old house on a quiet residential street off the north end of Corso Buenos Aires, the Paganini has minimal public areas (except for a reception area with a self-serve espresso machine), but the guest rooms are large, bright, and embellished with tile floors, high ceilings with elaborate moldings, solid beds, and modular furnishings of varying ages. The one room with bath is just inside the entrance, with wood floors, a stuccoed ceiling, and plenty of elbow room. The shared facilities are modern enough and kept spanking clean by the owners (one lived in Brooklyn for a number of years). The best rooms are in the rear, overlooking a huge private garden. The station is only a 10-minute walk way down Via Pergolsi.

✪ **Promessi Sposi.** Piazza Oberdan 12, 20129 Milano. ☎ **02-2951-3661.** Fax 02-2940-4182. www.milanoin.it/hotels. 31 units. A/C TEL TV. 110,000–160,000L ($55–$80) single; 150,000–240,000L ($75–$120) double; 195,000–310,000L ($98–$155) triple. 5% discount for stays of longer than 3 days (but not during trade fairs). Rates include buffet breakfast. AE, DC, MC, V. Parking 25,000–30,000L ($13–$15) in nearby garage, or free on street. Metro: Porta Venezia. Tram: 9, 20, 29, 30.

People often find their way to this rambling hotel on the recommendation of former guests, many in the fashion world, who rave about the friendly service (Jerry at the desk lived in New York City until age 10), unusually pleasant accommodations, and excellent value. The cheerful lobby/bar area overlooks Piazza Oberdan and the public gardens through large windows. The spacious rooms are outfitted with comfortable rattan furniture painted burgundy and/or cream, and the baths are spacious and nicely maintained. Rooms on the back, overlooking a drab narrow alley between buildings, are considerably quieter (but less well lit) than those on busy Corso Buenos Aires and Piazza Oberdan—double glazing helps a bit. However, I'd still ask for no. 222 or 332, which sit at the narrow end of the building and are quite large, with windows on three sides and small balconies.

Worth a Splurge

Doriagrand. Viale Andrea Doria 22, 20124 Milano. ☎ **02-6741-1411.** Fax 02-669-6669. www.doriagrandhotel.it. 118 units. A/C MINIBAR TV TEL. 190,000–590,000L ($95–$295) single or single use of double room; 250,000–530,000L ($125–$265) double; 450,000–750,000L ($225–$375) suite. Rates include buffet breakfast. AE, DC, MC, V. Parking 50,000L ($25) in garage. Metro: Loreto or Caiazzo. Tram: 1, 90, 91, 92.

This luxury hotel offers a special price (the lower rates above) that brings it within this book's splurge category and applies on weekends (Friday to Sunday nights), most of August, and the Christmas/New Year's holiday (check for exact dates before booking; never applied during trade fairs). The Doriagrand is one of the large newer hotels clustering around the station and is far more comfortable and stylish than most hotels in its class. The good-sized guest rooms are appointed with handsome wood and marble-topped furniture, rich wall coverings and draperies, and amenities like linen sheets, ISDN jacks, satellite channels and pay-per-view, and complimentary bedroom slippers and bathrobes. The marble baths are equipped with large tubs, vanities, hairdryers, and a generous selection of toiletries. A sumptuous buffet breakfast is served in a stylish room on a level above the lobby (where they also serve 55,000L/$28 fixed menus at mealtimes), and Thursday and Friday evenings the piano bar becomes a jazz club.

GREAT DEALS ON DINING

Geared to business as the city is, the Milanese are more willing than Italians elsewhere to break the sit-down-meal tradition and grab a sandwich or other light fare on the run. And with so many students and young professionals underfoot, Milan has no shortage of pizzerie and other low-cost eateries.

NEAR THE DUOMO

La Crêperie. Via C. Corenti 21. ☎ **02-839-5913.** Crêpes 3,000–6,000L ($1.50–$3). Mon–Sat 11am–1am, Sun 4pm–midnight. Metro: Sant'Ambrogio. CRÊPERIE.

About a 10-minute walk southeast of Piazza del Duomo (Via C. Corenti is an extension of Via Torino, one of the major avenues fanning out from the square), this busy crêperie is an ideal stop for a light lunch or snack while visiting the nearby Sant'Ambrogio or Museo Nazionale di Scienza e di Tecnica. The far-ranging offerings include meal crêpes like *prosciutto e formaggio* (ham and cheese) and the dessert variety (the Nutella, with the creamy chocolate spread, is highly recommended). There are a few value menus: Before 3pm, you can get one nondessert crêpe, plus one sweet one and a drink, for 10,000L ($5); until 9pm, you can get two "salty" ones, one dessert crêpe, and a drink for 15,000L ($8).

Luini. Via Santa Radegonda 16 (off Via Ragazzi del '99). ☎ **02-8646-1917.** www.luini.it. *Panzerotto* 4,000L ($2). No credit cards. Tues–Sat, 9am–6pm. Closed Aug 7–27. Metro: Duomo. SNACKS.

At this stand-up counter near the Galleria, you'll have to elbow your way through a throng of well-dressed people to purchase the house specialty: *panzerotto,* a pocket of pizza crust stuffed with cheese and tomato or prosciutto. They're so popular they've even opened up a branch in London. You'll also find many kinds of *panini.*

IN MAGENTA & BRERA

Latteria. Via San Marco 24. ☎ **02-659-7653.** Reservations not accepted (and it fills up fast). Primi 15,000–17,500L ($8–$9), secondi 13,000–28,000L ($7–$14). No credit cards. Mon–Fri 12:30–2:30pm and 7:30–9:30pm. Metro: Moscova. MILANESE.

The main business here at one time was dispensing milk and eggs to neighborhood shoppers, but now the emphasis is on serving homemade fare in rooms decorated with paintings and photographs of roses. The minestrone and other vegetable soups are delicious, as are the many variations of risotto, including some otherwise hard-to-find variations like *riso al salto,* leftover *risotto alla milanese* that's fried with butter. The menu changes daily, and the friendly staff, including owners Arturo and Maria, won't mind explaining what the dishes are or allowing you to take a look in the kitchen.

Worth a Splurge

✪ **La Milanese.** Via Santa Marta 11. ☎ **02-8645-1991.** Reservations required. Primi 14,000–16,000L ($7–$8); secondi 12,000–32,000L ($6–$16); *menù turistico* 58,000L ($29) without wine. AE, DC, MC, V. Wed–Mon noon–3pm and 7pm–1am. Metro: Cardusio. MILANESE.

Giuseppe and Antonella Villa preside over the centuries-old premises (a restaurant since 1933) tucked into a narrow lane in one of the oldest sections of Milan, just west of the Duomo. In the three-beamed dining room, Milanese families and other patrons share the long crowded tables. Giuseppe prepares some of the city's best traditional fare. The *risotto alla milanese* with saffron and beef marrow, not surprisingly, is excellent, as is a minestrone that's served hot in winter and at room temperature in summer. The *costolette alla milanese,* breaded and fried in butter, is all the better here because only the choicest veal chops are used and it's served with the bone in, and the osso buco is cooked to perfection. If you want to try their twin specialties without pigging out, the dish listed as *risotto e osso buco* buys you a half portion each of their *risotto alla milanese* and the osso buco for just 32,000L ($16). Polenta with rich Gorgonzola cheese is one of the few non-meat second courses. The attentive staff will help you choose an appropriate wine.

Peck. Via Victor Hugo 4. ☎ **02-876-774** or 02-802-3161. www.peck.it. Primi 7,000–12,000L ($3.50–$6), secondi 18,000–22,000L ($9–$11). AE, DC, MC, V. Mon–Sat 7:30am–9pm. Closed Jan 1–10 and July 1–20. Metro: Duomo. DELI.

Milan's most famous food emporium offers a wonderful selection of roast veal, risottos, porchetta, salads, aspics, cheeses, pastries, and other fare from its exquisite larder in this natty snack bar around the corner from its shop. If you choose to eat here, you'll do so at a stand-up bar where, especially around lunch, it can be hard to find room. This shouldn't discourage you, though, because the pleasure of having access to such a cornucopia of delicacies at a reasonable price is a gourmand's vision of paradise. Of course, you can also wander through Peck's food halls (a few steps away at Via Spadari 9) to equip yourself amply for a picnic or hotel-room dinner.

Pizzeria Grand'Italia. Via Palermo 5. ☎ **02-877-759.** Pizza from 7,500L ($3.75), salads from 11,000L ($6). No credit cards. Wed–Mon 12:15pm–2:45pm and 7pm–1:15am. Closed Tues (except in Aug). Metro: Moscova. PIZZA/PASTA.

One of Milan's most popular pizzerie serves a huge assortment of salads, pizzas, pastas, and *focacce farcite* (focaccia stuffed with cheese, mushrooms, and other fillings). Rather than get a whole pie, you get one thick-crusted megaslice topped however you like it. The late hours make this a prime night spot, and part of the fun is watching the chic young Milanese stopping by for a snack as they make the rounds of the nearby Brera district bars and clubs.

NEAR STAZIONE CENTRALE & CORSO BUENOS AIRES

Brek. Via Lepetit 20. ☎ **02-696-686** or 82-670-5149. Primi and pizza 6,000–10,000L ($3–$5); secondi 7,000–13,000L ($3.50–$7). AE, MC, V. Mon–Sat 11:30am–3pm and 6:30–10:30pm. Metro: Stazione Centrale. CAFETERIA.

Don't dismiss this outlet of Italy's popular cafeteria chain too quickly. Brek takes food, as well as its presentation, seriously. The pastas and risottos are made fresh; pork, veal, and chicken are roasted to order; and the large selection of cheeses would put many a formal restaurant to shame. Excellent wines and many kinds of beer are also available. The counter service is friendly and helpful, and the country-style decor is quite attractive.

Da Abele. Via Temperanza 5. ☎ **02-261-3855.** Primi 8,000–15,000L ($4–$8), secondi 14,000–22,000L ($7–$11). MC, V. Tues–Sun 7–10:30pm. Closed July 15–Sept 1. Metro: Pasteur. MILANESE

Once you get away from the city center, you'll find yourself in middle-class neighborhoods. Da Abele is in one of them, a pleasant enclave of shops and apartment houses east of Stazione Centrale and north of Corso Buenos Aires. This pleasant trattoria caters to locals (hence it's evening-only hours) and serves a nice selection of soups (like a hearty seafood *zuppa di pesce*) and many kinds of risotto, including one with *frutti di mare* (a selection of fresh seafood) and others with porcini mushrooms in season. The amiable staff doesn't mind if you venture no further into the menu, but if you do, there's a nice selection of roast meats as well.

Ristorante Versilia. Viale Andrea Doria 44. ☎ **02-670-4187.** Primi 9,000–10,000L ($4.50–$5), secondi 10,000–13,000L ($5–$7). MC, V. Mon–Sat noon–2:30pm and 7–10pm. Metro: Loreto. NORTHERN ITALIAN.

The white tiles and high-tech lighting suggest that this single room between the station and Corso Buenos Aires has more pretensions than it does. The modern environs are the result of a recent renovation to this friendly family-run eatery that serves the neighborhood with excellent food and attentive service. The *risotti* are superb, including *alla pilota* with sausage. While the menu lists a *costoletta alla milanese* and other meat dishes, daily specials often also include a wide selection of the freshest seafood.

Worth a Splurge

Joia. Via P. Castaldi 18. ☎ **02-204-9244.** www.joia.it. Reservations highly recommended. Primi 28,000–34,000L ($14–$17), secondi 34,000–36,000L ($17–$18); tasting menus 70,000–90,000L ($35–$45). AE, DC, MC, V. Mon–Fri noon–2:30pm and 7:30–11:30pm. Closed Aug. Metro: Repubblica. VEGETARIAN.

The Milanese tend to be carnivorous but have embraced this refined vegetarian restaurant just north of the public gardens with great enthusiasm. Some people may welcome the respite from northern Italy's orientation to red meat; those accustomed to smoke-free environments at home will enjoy the *non fumatore* section of Joia's blonde-wood dining rooms. The innovative vegetarian creations of Swiss chef Pietro Lemman incorporate the freshest vegetables and herbs, which appear in many traditional pasta dishes, like *lasagne con zucchine pomodoro* (layered with zucchini and fresh tomatoes and served at room temperature), *ravioli di melanzana* (stuffed with eggplant), or tagliolini with a simple tomato sauce. Any of these first courses can be ordered as a main course, and many of the main courses can be ordered as starters. These secondi include excellent fish choices, as well as elaborate vegetables-only creations like *melanzani viola al vapore con finferli* (steamed eggplant with chanterelle mushrooms). There's a wonderful assortment of cheeses and a long wine list.

IN THE NAVIGLI

Al Pont de Ferr. Ripa di Porta Ticinese 55 (on the Naviglio Grande) ☎ **02-8940-6277.** Primi 10,000L–18,000L ($5–$9), secondi 25,000L ($13). Mon–Sat 12:30–2:15pm and 8:30pm–1am. AE, MC, V. PAN-ITALIAN.

This is one of the more culinarily respectable of the dozens of restaurants around the Navigli, with tables set out on the flagstones overlooking the canal (regulars know to bring tiny cans of bug spray to battle the mosquitoes in summer). The *paste e fagioli* is livened up with bits of sausage and the ricotta-stuffed ravioli inventively sauced with a pesto of arugula and veggies. For a second course, try the *tocchetti di coniglio* (oven-roasted rabbit with potatoes), *porchetta* (pork stuffed with spices), or vegetable *cous-cous alla Trapanesi,* or just sack the whole idea of a secondo and order a *tavolozza* selection of excellent cheeses. There's a surprisingly good selection of half-bottles of wine, but most full bottles start at 30,000L ($15) and go senselessly higher. On the whole, the portions could be a whole lot larger, but you gotta love a place whose menu opens with the quip "Good cooking is the friend of living well and the enemy of a hurried life."

Premiata Pizzeria. Via Alzaia Naviglio Grande 2. ☎ **02-8940-0648.** Reservations suggested. Primi 15,000–17,000L ($8–$9); secondi 24,000–35,000L ($12–$18); pizze 9,000–20,000L ($4.50–$10). Wed–Mon noon–2:30pm and 7:30–11:30pm, Tues 7:30–11:30pm. MC, V. PIZZA/PAN-ITALIAN.

The most popular pizzeria in the Navigli stays packed from early dinnertime until the bar-hopping crowd stops by for late-night munchies. The restaurant rambles back forever, exposed copper pipes tracing across the ceilings of rooms wrapped around shaded outdoor terraces set with long raucous tables. The seating is communal and service hurried, but the wood-oven pizzas are excellent. If you're hungrier, there's a long menu of pastas and meat courses, while lighter appetites can enjoy a selection of salads.

CAFES & GELATO

Bar Zucca/Caffè Miami, at the Duomo end of the Galleria Vittorio Emanuele II (☎ **02-8646-4435;** Metro: Duomo), is best known by its original name, "the Camparino." It's the most attractive and popular of the Galleria's many bars and introduced Italy to Campari, the country's ubiquitous red cordial. You can linger at the tables set up in the Galleria or in one of the art nouveau rooms inside. You can find organic gelato at the **Gelateria Ecologica,** Corso di Porta Ticinese 40 (☎ **02-5810-1872;** Metro: Sant'Ambrogio or Missori), in the Ticinese/Navigli neighborhood. It's so popular, there's no need for a sign out front. Strollers in the atmospheric Brera neighborhood sooner or later stumble upon the **Gelateria Toldo,** Via Ponte Vetero 9 (☎ **02-8646-0863;** Metro: Cordusio or Lanza), where the gelato is wonderfully creamy and many of the sorbetto selections are so fruity and fresh they seem healthy.

The **Pasticceria Confetteria Cova,** Via Montenapoleone 8 (☎ **02-7600-0578;** Metro: Montenapoleone), is nearing its 200th year in refined surroundings near the similarly atmospheric Museo Poldi-Pezzoli. It's usually filled with shoppers making the rounds in this high-fashion district. You can enjoy a quick coffee and a brioche at the long bar or take a seat in one of the elegant adjoining rooms. The **Pasticceria March-esi,** Via Santa Maria alla Porta 13 (☎ **02-876-730;** Metro: Cardusio), is a distinguished pastry shop, with an adjoining wood-paneled tearoom. Since it's only steps from Santa Maria delle Grazie, you can enjoy the old-world ambience and a cup of excellent coffee (or one of the many teas and herbal infusions) as you dash off postcards of *The Last Supper.* Of course, you'll want to accompany your beverage with one of the elegant pastries, perhaps a slice of the panettone (cake laden with raisins and candied citron) that's a hallmark of Milan. No one prepares it better than they do at Marchesi. It's open Tuesday to Sunday 8am to 8pm.

MILAN AFTER DARK

On Wednesdays and Thursdays, Milan's newspapers tend to devote a lot of ink to club schedules and cultural events. If you don't trust your command of Italian to plan your nightlife, check out the tourist office on Piazza del Duomo—there are usually piles of fliers announcing upcoming events. The tourist office also keeps visitors up to date with *Milano: Where, When, How,* a periodical it distributes for free with schedules of events, as well as listings of bars, clubs, and restaurants.

THE PERFORMING ARTS   The ✪ **Teatro alla Scala,** Piazza della Scala (☎ **02-860-787** or 02-860-775 box office; 02-7200-3744 information line; http://lascala.milano.it; Metro: Duomo), will be closing at the end of the 2001–2002 season for a major technical renovation, but until then it's opera as usual (the season runs December 7 into July). Although tickets sell out well in advance, it's worth checking with the box office for one of the less-desirable (and more likely to be available) seats at the top of the house. The box office is open daily noon to 6pm. (For a tour of the theater, see "Seeing the Sights," above) Tickets run 30,000L to 80,000L ($15 to $40) at the **Conservatorio Giuseppe Verdi,** Via del Conservatorio 12 (☎ **02-762-1101;** Metro: San Babila), Milan's major venue for classical music. The year-round schedule brings the world's finest musicians and orchestras to the city.

BARS   A publike atmosphere, induced in part by Guinness on tap (8,000L/$4), prevails at Liberty-style **Bar Magenta,** Via Carducci 13 at Corso Magenta (☎ **02-805-3808;** Metro: Cadorna), in the neighborhood for which it takes its name. One of the more popular La Brera hangouts, with a young following, is **El Tombon de San Marc,** Via San Marco 20 at Via Montebello (☎ **02-659-9507;** Metro: Moscova), which despite its name is an English-pub style bar/restaurant.

If you're not quite young and up to partying with those who are, a pleasant alternative to is **Bar Margherita,** Via Moscova 25 in La Brera (☎ **02-659-0833;** Metro: Moscova), where there's jazz on the sound system (and sometimes live on stage) and a nice selection of wines and grappa from about 4,000L ($2), and they lay out a good selection of munchies-on-toothpicks (crostini, frittata wedges, and other canapes) around dinner time.

Among the Navigli night spots (growing in number all the time) is **El Brelin,** an intimate canal-side piano bar (Saturdays) with its own mini-canal on Vicolo della Lavandaia, off Alzaia Naviglio Grande 14 (☎ **02-5810-1351;** Metro: Genova FS). **Birreria La Fontanella,** Alzaia Navilgio Pavese 6 (☎ **02-837-2391;** Metro: Genova FS), has canal-side tables outside and the oddest-shaped beer glasses around—that half-a-barbell kind everyone seems to order is called the "Cavalliere."

DANCE CLUBS   The dance scene changes all the time in Milan, but at whatever club is popular (or in business) at the moment, expect to pay a cover of 20,000L to 30,000L ($10 to $15). Models, actors, sports stars, and the fashion set favor **Hollywood,** Corso Como 15 (☎ **02-655-5574** or 02-659-8996 or 02-679-8896 after 10:30pm; Metro: Moscova), which is small, chic, and centrally located in La Brera; the

Nightlife Tip

The Navigli/Ticinese neighborhood is currently on the ascent as Milan's prime night turf, though the Brera retains its pull with night owls as well.

25,000L ($13) cover includes a drink. **Grand Café Fashion,** Corso di Porta Ticinese 60 at Via Vetere (☎ **02-8940-0709** or 0336-347-333; Metro: Porta Genova), is a multipurpose nightspot halfway to the Navigli with a restaurant open from 9pm and a disco nightly from 11:30pm. It brings a beautiful crowd to the Ticinese neighborhood, where they dance the night away, sometimes to thematic evenings like Latino Mondays.

Milan's most venerable disco/live-music club is **Rolling Stone,** Corso XXII Marzo 32 (☎ **02-733-172;** Tram: 12, 27, 45, 60, 66, 73, 92), in business since the 1950s. Most of the performers these days are of a rock bent, and the club is as immensely popular as ever. Cover runs about 25,000L ($13), depending on who's performing, less expensive for women than for men, and more expensive on weekends than on weekdays.

GAY CLUBS   Milan's largest gay club is **Nuovo Idea,** Via de Castillia 30 (☎ **02-6900-7859;** www.dinet.it/nuovaidea; Metro: Gioia); it attracts a mostly male crowd of all ages and offers everything from disco to polkas in a huge techno room. The 15,000L ($8) cover includes a drink. **Recycle,** Via Calabria 5 (☎ **02-376-1531;** Metro: Lancetti), is a women-only club Friday to Sunday 9pm to 2am, sometimes later (mixed crowd welcome Wednesdays and Thursdays).

Via Sammartini along the train station's left flank (Metro: Central FS) is a good street to hit, with **Next Groove** at no. 23 (☎ **02-6698-0450**), a gay-and-lesbian disco/bar of the phone-on-the-table sort and thematic evenings; and **After Line Disco Pub** at no. 25 (☎ **02-669-2130**), a bar/restaurant where a giant-screen TV and strobe light switch on after dinner to turn it into a disco with a games room for lesbians Tuesday to Sunday.

DAY TRIPS FROM MILAN

PAVIA & THE CERTOSA   At one time the quiet and remarkably well-preserved little city of **Pavia,** 40km (22 mi.) south of Milan, was more powerful than Milan. It was the capital of Lombardy in the 7th and 8th centuries, and by the early Renaissance, the Viscontis and then the Sforzas, the two families who so influenced the history of Milan and all of Lombardy, were wielding their power here. It was the Viscontis who built the city's imposing **Castello,** made Pavia one of Europe's great centers of learning (when they founded the university) in 1361, began construction on the **Duomo** (with the third largest dome in Italy) in 1488, and founded the city's most important monument and the one that brings most visitors to Pavia, the Certosa.

The **Certosa** (☎ **0382-925-613**) lies 8km (5 mi.) north of Pavia. One of the most unusual buildings in Lombardy, if not in Italy, it was commissioned by Gian Galeazzo Visconti in 1396 as a Carthusian monastery and burial chapel for his family—officially as thanks for curing his second sickly wife (the first died) and granting him children and heirs. It was completed by the Sforzas. The facade of colored marbles, the frescoed interior, and the riot of funerary sculpture are evidence that these often tyrannical despots were also dedicated builders with grand schemes and large coffers. The finest and most acclaimed statuary monument here, that of Ludivico il Moro (buried in France, where he died a P.O.W.) and Beatrice d'Este (buried in Milan's Santa Maria della Grazie), sits in the left transept of the massive church, beneath lapis lazuli–rich frescoes by Bergognone. Its presence is a twist of fate—the monks at Milan's Santa Maria della Grazie (which houses *The Last Supper*) sold the tomb to the Certosa to raise funds. In the right transept is the 15th-century tomb of Gian Galeazzo Visconti. Across from the tomb is the entrance to the enormous cloister, lined with the monk's cells, each of which is actually a two-story cottage with its own garden. Most are now inhabited by a small community of Cisternian monks; you can visit their refectory and an adjoining shop, where they sell their Chartreuse liqueur and herbal soaps and scents. Admission to the Certosa is free; it's open Tuesday to Sunday 9:30am to 11:30am and 2:30 to 6pm (to 4:30pm November to February and 5pm September, October, March, and April).

Half-hourly trains from **Milan** usually stop at the station near the Certosa, just before the main Pavia station (30 min.; 4,600L/$2.30). To reach the Certosa from Pavia, take one of the half-hourly buses from the Autocorriere station (next to the train station); the trip takes about 15 minutes and costs 1,900L (95¢). By car, the Certosa is about half an hour south of Milan via A7 (follow exit signs). The **tourist office** is near the train station at Via Fabio Filzi 2 (☎ 0382-22-156), open Monday to Saturday 8:30am to 12:30pm and 2 to 6pm.

CREMONA   Violins have been drawing visitors to the little city of **Cremona** on the river Po, 103km (57 mi.) southeast of Milan, since the 17th century, when fine string instruments began emerging from the workshops of Nicolo Amati and his more-famous protégé, Antonio Stradivari. The tradition continues: Cremona's **Scuola di Luteria (Violin School)** is world renowned.

Cremona's charms extend far beyond the musical. Its central **Piazza del Comune** is one of the largest and most beautiful town squares in Italy, fronted by remarkable structures. Among these is the 12th-century **Duomo** (☎ 0372-26-707), clad in pink marble and overshadowed by Italy's tallest campanile; inside, it's covered with 16th-century frescoes (admission is free and hours are daily 7:30am to noon and 3:30 to 7pm). The **Palazzo del Comune** rises gracefully above a Gothic arcade and is embellished with terra-cotta panels. Its **Raccolta dei Violini** (☎ 0372-22-138) displays a small collection of 17th- and 18th-century violins by Amati, the Guarneri, and a Strad. The **Museo Stradivariano,** Via Palestro 17 (☎ 0372-461-886), displays the finest violins ever made, including those by Amatis, Stradivari, and Guaneri. Each museum charges 6,000L ($3) adults and 3,000L ($1.50) students and over 65; both are open Tuesday to Saturday 8:30am to 6:30pm and Sunday 10am to 6pm.

Trains arrive almost hourly from **Milan** (65 min.; 9,000L/$4.50). Hourly trains to **Brescia** (50 min.; 6,300L/$3.15) also make it possible to combine an excursion from Milan to Cremona and Brescia (below). If you're traveling by car, you can make the trip to Cremona by following A1 from Milan to Piacenza and A21 from Piacenza to Cremona. The **tourist office** is near the Duomo at Piazza del Comune 5 (☎ 0372-23-233; www.cremonaturismo.com); open Monday to Saturday 9:30am to 12:30pm and 3 to 6pm and Sunday 10am to 1pm.

2 Bergamo

47km (28 mi.) NE of Milan, 52km (31 mi.) NW of Brescia.

Bergamo is two cities. Bergamo Bassa, the lower, a mostly 19th- and 20th-century city, concerns itself with everyday business. Bergamo Alta, a beautiful medieval/Renaissance town perched on a green hill, concerns itself these days with entertaining the visitors who come to admire its piazze, palazzi, and churches; enjoy the lovely vistas from its belvederes; and soak in a hushed beauty that inspired Italian poet Gabriel d'Annunzio to call old Bergamo "a city of muteness." The distinct characters of the two parts of this city go back to its founding as a Roman settlement, when the *civitas* was on the hill and farms and suburban villas dotted the plains below.

ESSENTIALS

GETTING THERE   By Train   Trains arrive from and depart for **Milan** hourly (50 min.; 6,300L/$3.15); service to and from **Brescia** is even more frequent, with half-hourly service during peak early morning and early evening travel times (50 min.; 5,500L/$1.75). Given the frequency of train service, you can easily make a daylong sightseeing loop from Milan, arriving in Bergamo in the morning, moving on to Brescia in the afternoon, and returning to Milan from there. If you're coming from or going on to nearby **Lake Como,** there's hourly service between Bergamo and Lecco, on the southeast end of the lake (40 min.; 4,600L/$2.30).

By Bus   An extensive bus network links Bergamo with many other towns in Lombardy. There are five to six buses a day to and from **Como** (2 hr.; 8,300L/$4.15) run by SPT (☎ **031-247-247**). Service to and from **Milan** by Autostradale (☎ **02-3391-0843**) runs every half hour (1 hr.; 7,400L/$3.70). The bus station is next to the train station on Piazza Marconi.

By Car   Bergamo is linked directly to Milan via the A4, which continues east to Brescia, Verona, and Venice. The trip between Milan and Bergamo takes a little over half an hour. Parking in or near the Città Alta, most of which is closed to traffic, can be difficult. There is a parking lot on the northern end of the Città Alta near Porta Garibaldi (about 2,000L/$1 per hour) and street parking along Viale delle Mura, which loops around the outer flanks of the walls of the Città Alta.

VISITOR INFORMATION   The **Città Bassa tourist office,** Viale Vittorio Emanuele 20 (☎ **035-210-204;** fax 035-230-184; www.apt.bergamo.it), is nine long blocks straight out from the train station; it's open Monday to Friday 9am to 12:30pm and 2 to 5:30pm. The **Città Alta office,** Vicola Aquila Nera 2 (☎ **035-232-730;** fax 035-242-994), is just off Piazza Vecchia, open daily the same hours.

FESTIVALS & MARKETS   Bergamo is a cultured city, and its celebrations include the May-to-June **Festivale Piantistico,** one of the world's major piano competitions. In September, the city celebrates its native composer **Gaetano Donizetti** with performances of his works, most of them at the Teatro Donizetti in the Città Bassa (see below).

CITY LAYOUT   Piazza Vecchia, the Colleoni Chapel, and most of the other sights that bring visitors to Bergamo are in the **Città Alta**—the exception is the Accademia Carrara, which is in the Città Bassa but on the flanks of the hillside, so within easy walking distance of the upper town sights. **Via Colleoni** cuts a swath through the medieval heart of the Città Alta, beginning at **Piazza Vecchia.** To reach this lovely square from the funicular station at **Piazza Mercato delle Scarpi,** walk along **Via Gombito** for about 5 minutes. Most of the Città Alta is closed to traffic, but it's compact and easy to navigate on foot. Down below, the main square known as the **Sentierone** is the center of the **Città Bassa.** It's about a 5-minute walk from the train station north along **Viale Papa Giovanni XXIII.**

EXPLORING THE CITTÀ BASSA

Most visitors scurry through Bergamo's lower, newer town on their way to the Città Alta, but you may want to pause long enough to enjoy a coffee along the **Sentierone,** the elongated piazza/street at the center of town. This spacious square graciously combines a mishmash of architectural styles (including 16th-century **porticos** on one side, the Mussolini-era **Palazzo di Giustizia** and two **imitation Doric temples** on another). Locals sit in its gardens, lounge in its cafes, and attend classical concerts at the **Teatro Donizetti.** This 19th-century theater is the center of Bergamo's lively culture scene, with a fall opera season and a winter-to-spring season of dramatic performances; for details, check with the tourist office or call the theater at ☎ 035-416-0611 (http://teatro.gaetano-donizetti.com).

The main draw for most visitors down here, though, is the **Galleria dell'Accademia Carrara,** Piazza Carrara 82a (☎ **035-399-677**). The city's exquisite art gallery is one of the finest in Italy, founded in 1795 when Napoléon's troops were busy rounding up the art treasures of their newly occupied northern Italian states. Many of these works ended up in Bergamo under the stewardship of Count Giacomo Carrara. The collection came into its own after World War I, when a young Bernard Berenson, the 20th century's most noted art connoisseur, took stock of what was here and classified the immense holdings, making sure "every Lotto [was] a Lotto." Lorenzo Lotto (1480 to 1556) was a Venetian who fled the stupefying society of his native city and spent 1513 to 1525 in Bergamo perfecting his highly emotive portraits. Many of his works from the Accademia recently toured the United States, but they're now back in place in the salons of a neoclassical palace alongside a staggering inventory that includes paintings by Bellini, Canaletto, Carpaccio, Guardi, Mantegna, and Tiepolo. Most of these masterworks are in the 17 third-floor galleries.

It's easy to become overwhelmed here, but among the paintings you may want to view first is Lotto's *Portrait of Lucina Brembrati,* in which you'll see the immense sensitivity with which the artist was able to imbue his subjects. Look carefully at the moon in the upper-left corner—it has the letters "ci" painted into it, a playful anagram of the sitter's first name; in Italian, *moon* is *luna,* and this one has a "ci" in the middle). Botticelli's much reproduced *Portrait of Giuliano de Medici* hangs nearby, as does Raphael's sensual *St. Sebastian.* You can visit the Accademia on foot from the Città Alta by following Via Porta Dipinta halfway down the hill to the Porto Sant'Agostino and then a terraced, ramplike staircase to the doors of the museum. From the Città Bassa, the museum is about a 10-minute walk from the Sentierone—from the east end of the square, take a left on Largo Belloti, then a right on Via Giuseppe Verdi and follow that for several blocks to Via Pignolo and turn left to Via Tomaso, which takes you to Piazza Carrara (the route is well signposted). Admission is 5,000L ($2.50), free under 18 and over 60, free for all ages on Sunday. It has been open Tuesday to Sunday 9:30am to 1pm and 2:30 to 6:30pm but may start staying open through lunch starting in 2001.

Across the street is the **Galleria d'Arte Moderna e Contemporanea,** containing works by such 20th-century masters as Fattori, Boccioni, De Chirico, Morandi, and Kadinsky. Admission is free, and it's open Tuesday to Saturday 10am to 1pm and 3 to 7pm and Sunday 10am to 7pm.

EXPLORING THE CITTÀ ALTA

The higher, older part of Bergamo owes its stone palazzi, proud monuments and what remains of its extensive fortified walls to more than 3 centuries of Venetian rule, beginning in 1428, when soldiers of the Republic wrestled control of the city out of the hands of the Milan-based Viscontis. The Venetians left their mark elegantly in the town's theatrically adjoining squares, **Piazza Vecchia** and **Piazza del Duomo,** which together create one of the most beautiful outdoor assemblages in Italy—actually, French writer Stendahl went so far as to call this heart of old Bergamo the "most beautiful place on earth."

On Piazza Vecchia, you'll see traces of the Venetian presence in the 12th-century **Palazzo della Ragione (Courts of Justice),** which has been embellished with a graceful ground-floor arcade and the Lion of San Mark's, symbol of the Venetian Republic, above a 16th-century balcony reached by a covered staircase (the bells atop its adjoining tower, the **Torre Civico,** sound the hours sonorously). Across the piazza, the **Bibliotheca Civica** was modeled after the Sansovino Library in Venice. Piazza del Duomo, reached through one of the archways of the Palazzo della Ragione, is filled with an overpowering collection of religious structures that include the **Duomo** and the much more enticing **Cappella Colleoni** (see below), the **Baptistry,** and the **Basilica di Santa Maria Maggiore** (see below).

Colleoni has lent his name to the upper town's delightful main street, cobblestoned and so narrow you can just about touch the buildings on either side when standing in the center. If you follow it to its far western end, you'll emerge into **Largo Colle Aperto,** refreshingly green and open to the Città Bassa and valleys below. For better views and a short excursion into the countryside, board the **Funicolare San Vigilo** for the ascent up the San Vigilo hill; the funicular (1,600L/80¢) runs daily every 12 minutes or so between 7am and midnight. The strategic importance of these heights was not lost on Bergamo's medieval residents, who erected a summit-top **Castello** (☎ **035-236-284**), now mostly in ruin. Its keep, still surrounded by the old walls, is a park in which every bench affords a far-reaching view. It's open daily: April to September 9am to 8pm, October and March 10am to 6pm, and November to February 10am to 4pm.

The Castello is a good place to begin a trek around the flanks of the Città Alta— first back down the San Vigilo hill (or take the funicular), then back into the Città Alta through the Porta San Alessandro. For a look at the old walls and some more good views, instead of following Via Colleoni back into the center of the town, turn left on Via della Mura and follow the 16th-century bastions for about half a mile to the Porta Sant'Agostino on the other side of the town.

Cappella Colleoni. Piazza del Duomo. ☎ **035-210-061.** Admission free. Tues–Sun 9am–12:30pm and 2–6:30pm (to 4:30pm Nov–Feb).

Bartolomeo Colleoni was a Bergamese *condottiere* who fought for Venice to maintain the Venetian stronghold on the city. In return for his labors, the much-honored soldier was given Bergamo to rule for the republic. If you've already visited Venice, you may have seen Signore Colleoni astride the Verrocchio equestrian bronze in Campo Santi Giovanni e Paolo. He rests for eternity in this elaborate funerary chapel designed by Amadeo, the great sculptor from nearby Pavia (where he completed his most famous work, the Certosa; see "Day Trips from Milan," above). The pink-and-white marble exterior, laced with finely sculpted columns and loggias, is airy and almost whimsical; inside, the soldier and his favorite daughter, Medea, lie beneath a ceiling frescoed by Tiepolo and surrounded by reliefs and statuary; Colleoni appears on horseback again atop his marble tomb.

Basilica di Santa Maria Maggiore. Piazza del Duomo. ☎ **035-223-327.** Admission free. Mon–Sat 9am–noon and 3–6pm (to 4:30pm Oct–Apr), Sun 8–10:30am and 3–6pm.

Behind the plain marble facade and a portico whose columns rise out of the backs of lions lies an overly baroque gilt-covered interior hung with Renaissance tapestries. Gaetano Donizetti, the wildly popular composer of frothy operas who was born in Bergamo in 1797 (see below) and returned here to die in 1848, is entombed in a **marble sarcophagus** that's as excessive as the rest of the church's decor. The finest works are the **choir stalls,** with rich wood inlays depicting landscapes and biblical scenes; they're the creation of Lorenzo Lotto, the Venetian who worked in Bergamo in the early 16th century and whose work you'll encounter at the Accademia and elsewhere around the city. The stalls are usually kept under cloth to protect the sensitive hardwoods from light and pollutants, but they're unveiled for Lent. The octagonal

Baptistry in the piazza outside the church was originally inside but removed, reconstructed, and much embellished in the 19th century.

Museo Donizettiano. Via Arena 4. ☎ **035-399-269.** Admission free. Tues–Sat 9am–noon and 2–5pm, Sun 10am–noon and 2–4pm.

This charming little museum commemorates Gaetano Donizetti, who was born in Bergamo in 1797 and—little wonder, given the romance of his boyhood surroundings—became one of Italy's most acclaimed composers of opera. Fans can swoon over his sheet music, piano, and other memorabilia and see the deathbed where he succumbed to syphilis in 1848. Thus inspired, you can make the pilgrimage to the humble house where he claimed to have been born in a cellar, the **Casa Nateledi Gaetano Donizetti,** Via B. Canale 14 (☎ **035-399-432**), a rural street that descends the hillside from the Porta Sant'Alessandro on the western edge of the city. It's open Saturday and Sunday only 11am to 6:30pm (donations requested).

AFFORDABLE PLACES TO STAY

The charms of staying in the Città Alta are no secret. Rooms tend to fill up quickly, especially in summer and on weekends. Reserve well in advance.

Agnello d'Oro. Via Gombito 22, 24100 Bergamo. ☎ **035-249-883.** Fax 035-235-612. www.agnello.it. 20 units. TV TEL. 95,000L ($48) single; 155,000L ($78) double. Continental breakfast 10,000L ($5). AE, DC, MC, V.

In keeping with its location a few steps from Piazza Vecchia, the Agnello d'Oro looks like it's right out of an old tourist brochure extolling the quaint charms of Italy. The tall, narrow ocher-colored building, with flower boxes at each of its tall windows, overlooks a small piazzetta where a fountain splashes next to potted greenery. The wood-paneled lounge and intimate dining room add to the charm quotient, which declines somewhat as you ascend in a tiny elevator to the rooms. These lean more toward serviceable comfort than luxury, but warm color schemes and old prints help compensate for the lack of space and amenities; the baths are roomy and have been modernized. Front rooms (the ones to request) have narrow balconies overlooking the piazza. This is the most popular hostelry in the Città Alta, so reservations are mandatory.

Gourmet. Via San Vigilo 1, 24129 Bergamo. ☎ /fax **035-437-3004.** 11 units. A/C MINIBAR TV TEL. 110,000L ($55) single; 165,000L ($83) double; 330,000L ($165) apt. for 4. Continental breakfast 20,000L ($10). AE, DC, MC, V. Closed Dec 26–Jan 7.

This pleasant hotel offers the best of both worlds—it's only steps away from the Città Alta (a few hundred feet outside the Porta Sant'Agostino on the road leading up to the Castello) but on a rural hillside, giving it the air of a country retreat. The villa-style building is set behind walls in a lush garden and enjoys wonderful views. A wide terrace on two sides makes the most of these views and the song of caged canaries. Many of the very large, bright rooms look across the hillside to the heavily developed valley too. They're furnished in plain modern (or at least modern a few decades ago) fashion geared more to solid comfort than to style, with king-sized beds. The apartment is large, on two floors with a sitting area and kitchen downstairs and upstairs two bedrooms, a double and a twin, each with bath. There's a highly reputed restaurant downstairs, hence the name, with indoor and outdoor tables and mid-range prices on Bergamesco and Lombard cuisine.

San Lorenzo. Piazza Mascheroni 9A, 24129 Bergamo. ☎ **035-237-383.** Fax 035-237-958. 25 units. A/C MINIBAR TV TEL. 148,000L ($74) single; 215,000L ($108) double. Rates include buffet breakfast. AE, DC, MC, V. Parking free.

Bergamo Alta was blessed with some much needed additional hotel rooms when this stylish place opened in 1998, in a former convent building of Santa Agata. The centuries-old setting is tailor-made for this unusually pleasant inn—most of the rooms face a courtyard and open through French doors to a balcony that wraps around it; though the hotel is right in town, just a few steps off Via Colleoni, its hillside location provides views over the green slopes flowing down to the valley below. The rooms are small but comfortable, with striped silk draperies and bed coverings and cane-backed lounge chairs; the marble baths come with hand-held shower massagers and hair dryers. A sumptuous buffet breakfast is served in the breakfast room. The discovery of Roman ruins put the brakes on construction of an underground parking facility, though the hotel provides a permit allowing you to park for free in the adjoining square.

GREAT DEALS ON DINING

Your gambols through the Città Alta can be nicely interspersed with fortifying stops at the city's many pastry shops and stand-up eateries. **Forno Tresoldi,** Via Colleoni 13, sells excellent pizzas and foccacia breads topped with cheese, salami, and vegetables by the slice (from 3,000L/$1.50); it's open Tuesday to Sunday 8am to 1:30pm and 4 to 10pm.

Al Donizetti. Via Gombito 17a. ☎ **035-242-661.** www.donizetti.it. Panini 5,000–15,000L ($2.50–$8), salads and platters of cheese and/or meats 15,000–30,000L ($8–$15). MC, V. Thurs–Mon noon–3pm and 6:30–10:30pm. WINE BAR.

Bergamo's revered composer lends his name to this charming restaurant facing the upper city's old covered market, which now serves no purpose other than to look medieval and romantic. In good weather, tables are set out under the market's arcaded loggia, and meals are also served in the two small vaulted-ceilinged dining rooms. The bulk of the menu is devoted to various kinds of salami, ham, and cheeses, though many dishes also rely on fresh vegetables—perhaps a light zucchini flan or *raddichio con gorgonzola* (the bitter red greens are lightly grilled and the creamy cheese is added at the last minute). More than 360 wines are available (most by the glass, from 5,000L/$2.50) to accompany a meal, and the staff will help you choose the right one.

Antica Hosteria del Vino Buono. Via Donizetti 25. ☎ **035-247-993.** Reservations recommended. Primi 10,000–15,000L ($5–$8), secondi 15,000–22,000L ($8–$11). AE, DC, MC, V. Tues–Sun noon–2:30pm and 7:30–10:30pm. NORTHERN ITALIAN.

At this cozy restaurant tucked into smallish rooms in a corner house on Piazza Mercato delle Scarpe at the top of the funicular station, an enthusiastic young staff takes food and wine seriously. It's a pleasure to dine in the handsome surroundings of brick, tile work, and photos of old Bergamo. For an introduction to food from the region, try one of the several tasting menus. Polenta figures prominently among the primi and is served *alla bergamese* (with wild mushrooms) and sometimes with olive paste folded into it. The main courses lean toward meat. A dish like roast quail or rabbit should be accompanied by a Valcalepio Rosso, a medium-strength red from local vineyards.

Vineria Cozzi. Via Colleoni 22. ☎ **035-238-836.** Sandwiches from 7,500L ($3.75); primi 8,000–15,000L ($4–$8), secondi 13,000–20,000L ($7–$10); fixed-price menus 18,000L ($9) without wine and 23,000L ($12) with wine. MC, V. Thurs–Tues 10am–2am. NORTHERN ITALIAN.

Cozzi isn't just a wine bar but a Bergamo institution. Its cane chairs are well worn with use by Bergamese and visitors who can't resist stopping in for a glass of wine while walking down Via Colleoni. Hundreds of bottles from throughout Italy line the walls and are served by the glass (from 3,000L/$1.50). Sandwiches are always available, as are several kinds of cheese, but the changing daily offerings usually include several pasta dishes and polenta with rich cheese folded into it, perhaps a torta stuffed with fresh vegetables and a main course or two—if the duck breast stuffed with cabbage is available, order it.

CAFES

Caffè del Tasso, Piazza Vecchia 3, is a prime piece of real estate on the main square of the Città Alta. It began life as a tailor's shop 500 years ago, but it's been a bar since 1581. Legend has it that Garibaldi's Redshirts used to gather here (Bergamo was a stronghold of Italian independence, which explains why an edict from the 1850s on the wall of this cafe prohibits rebellion). While the location of **Caffè della Funicolare** in the Piazza Mercato delle Scarpe, in the upper terminal of the funicular that climbs the hill from the Città Bassa to the Città Alta, doesn't suggest a memorable dining experience, the station dates from 1887 and has enough belle époque flourishes and curlicues to make the surroundings interesting. Plus, the dining room and terrace look straight down the hill to the town and valley, providing some the best tables with a view (accompanied by low-cost fare) in the upper town. Stop in for a coffee, one of the 50 kinds of beer on tap, a sandwich, or a salad.

3 Mantua: A Gem of Lombardy

158km (95 mi.) E of Milan, 62km (37 mi.) N of Parma, 150km (90 mi.) SW of Venice.

One of Lombardy's finest cities is in the farthest reaches of the region, making it a logical addition to a trip to Venice or Parma as well as to Milan. Like its neighboring cities in Emilia-Romagna, **Mantua (Mantova)** owes its past greatness and its beautiful Renaissance monuments to one family, in this case the Gonzagas, who rose from peasant origins to conquer the city in 1328 and ruled benevolently until 1707. You'll encounter the Gonzagas—and, because they were avid collectors of art and ruled through the greatest centuries of Italian art, the treasures they collected—in the massive Palazzo Ducale that dominates much of the town center; in their refreshing suburban retreat, the Palazzo Te; and in the churches and piazze that grew up around their court.

One of Mantua's greatest charms is its location—on a meandering river, the Mincio, which widens here to envelop the city in a necklace of moodily romantic lakes. Often shrouded in mist and surrounded by flat, lonely plains, Mantua can seem almost melancholy. Aldous Huxley wrote of the city, "I have seen great cities dead or in decay—but over none, it seemed to me, did there brood so profound a melancholy as over Mantua." Since his visit in the 1930s, though, the Palazzo Ducale and other monuments have been restored, and what will probably strike you more is what a remarkable gem of a city Mantua is.

ESSENTIALS

GETTING THERE **By Train** Ten trains daily arrive from **Milan** (2 hours; 16,000L/$8). There are hourly runs from **Verona,** with connections to Venice (30–40 minutes; 4,100L/$2.05).

By Car The speediest connections from Milan are via the autostradas, the A4 to Verona and the A22 from Verona to Mantua (the trip takes less than 2 hours). From Mantua, it's also an easy drive south to Parma and other cities in Emilia-Romagna, on S420.

VISITOR INFORMATION The **tourist office** is at Piazza Mantegna 6 (☎ **0376-328-253,** fax 0376-363-292; www.aptmantova.it), open Monday to Saturday 8:30am

Mantua By Bike

Mantua is flat and much of its center is closed to traffic, making it good biking terrain. You can join the residents and get around on two wheels with a **bike rental** from La Rigola, on the lakeside on Lungolago dei Gonzaga, in front of Piazza Arche (☎ **0376-366-677** or 0335-605-4958); follow Via Accademia east to the lake from Piazza Sordello. The concession is open daily 8:30am to around 8pm, and rentals are 4,000L ($2) per hour (5,000L/$2.50 on Sunday) or 20,000L ($10) per day (25,000L/$13 on Sunday).

to 12:30pm and 3 to 6pm and Sunday 9:30am to 12:30pm (closed most Sundays in January and February).

FESTIVALS & MARKETS   Mantua enlivens its steamy summer with a **jazz festival** the third weekend (Thursday to Sunday) of July. Year-round, Piazza delle Erbe is the scene of a bustling **food market** Monday through Saturday from 8am to 1pm. On Thursday mornings, a bigger **market,** filled with clothing, housewares, and more food, spills through Piazza Magenta and adjoining streets.

CITY LAYOUT   Mantua is tucked onto a point of land surrounded on three sides by the **river Mincio,** which widens here into a series of lakes, named prosaically **Lago Superiore, Lago di Mezzo,** and **Lago Inferiore.** Most of the sights are within an easy walk of one another within the compact center, which is only a 10-minute walk from the lakeside train station. Follow **Via Solferino** to **Via Marangoni,** turn right and follow that to **Piazza Cavallotti,** where a left turn on **Corso Umberto I** will bring you to **Piazza delle Erbe,** the first of the gracious piazze that flow through the city center to the palace of the Gonzogas. You can also make the trip on the no. 2 bus (1,500L (75¢), which leaves from the front of the station.

EXPLORING THE CITY

As you wander around, you'll notice that Mantua's squares are handsomely proportioned spaces surrounded by medieval and Renaissance churches and palazzi. The piazze open one into another, creating the wonderful illusion that walkers in the city are strolling through a series of opera sets.

The northernmost of these squares, and the place to begin your explorations, is **Piazza delle Erbe (Square of the Herbs),** so named for the produce-and-food market that transpires in stalls to one side (see "Festivals & Markets," above). Mantua's civic might is clustered here in a series of late-medieval and early Renaissance structures that include the **Palazzo della Ragione (Courts of Justice)** and **Palazzo del Podestà (Mayor's Palace),** from the 12th and 13th centuries, and the **Torre dell'Orlogio,** topped with a 14th-century astrological clock. Also on this square is Mantua's earliest religious structure, the **Rotunda di San Lorenzo,** a miniature round church from the 11th century (summer hours are daily 10am to noon and 2:30 to 4:30pm and winter hours daily 11am to noon, though hours vary; admission free). The city's Renaissance masterpiece, **Sant'Andrea** (see below), is off to one side on Piazza Mantegna.

In the adjoining **Piazza Broletto** (just north as you work your way through the old city), the statue of Virgil commemorates the poet who was born near here in 70 B.C. and celebrated Mantua's river Mincio in his *Bucolics.* The next square, **Piazza Sordello** is huge, rectangular and somberly medieval, lined with crenellated palazzi. Most notably, though, the massive hulk of the **Palazzo Ducale** (see below) forms one wall of the piazza. To enjoy Manuta's soulful lakeside vistas, follow Via Accademia through Piazza Arche and the **Lungolago Gonzaga.**

Sant'Andrea. Piazza Mantegna. Admission free. Daily 7:30am–noon and 3–7pm.

A graceful Renaissance facade fronts this 15th-century church by Leon Battista Alberti, with an 18th-century dome by Juvarra. The simple arches seem to float beneath the classic pediment, and the unadorned elegance forms a sharp contrast to other Lombardy monuments, like the Duomo in Milan, the Cappella Colleoni in Bergamo, and the Certosa in Pavia. Inside, the classically proportioned vast space is centered on a single aisle. The Gonzaga court painter Mantegna is buried in the first chapel on the left. The crypt houses a reliquary containing the blood of Christ (allegedly brought here by Longinus, the Roman soldier who thrust his spear into Jesus's side), which is carried through town on March 18, the feast of Mantua's patron, Sant'Anselmo.

Palazzo d'Arco. Piazza d'Arco 1. ☎ **0376-322-242.** Admission 5,000L ($2.50). Mar–Nov 1 Tues–Sun 10am–12:30pm and 2:30–5:30pm; Nov 5–Feb Sat 10am–12:30pm and 2–5pm, Sun 10am–5pm.

Mantua's aristocratic D'Arco family lived in this elegant Renaissance palazzo until 1973, when the last member of the family donated it to the city. Though most of the extant palazzo is neoclassical (1780s), the gardens shelter a wing from the 15th century, the highlight of the rooms is the **Sala dello Zodiaco,** brilliantly frescoed with astrological signs by Giovanni Falconetto in 1520.

Palazzo Ducale. Piazza Sordello. ☎ **0376-382-150.** www.ciaoweb.net/slaves. Admission 12,000L ($6). Tues–Sun 8:45am–7:15pm.

Behind the walls of this massive fortress/palace lies the history of the Gonzagas, Mantua's most powerful family, and what remains of the treasure trove they amassed in a rule that began in 1328 and lasted into the early 18th century. Between their skills as warriors and their penchant for marrying into wealthier and more cultured houses, they managed to acquire power, money, and an artistic following that included Pisanello, Titian, and most notably Andrea Mantegna, their court painter, who spent most of his career working for his Mantua patrons. The most fortunate of these unions was that of Francesco Gonzaga to Isabelle d'Este in 1490. This well-bred daughter of Ferrara's Este clan commissioned many of the art-filled frescoed apartments you see today, including the **Camera degli Sposi** in Isabella's apartments—the masterpiece, and only remaining fresco cycle, of Mantegna. It took the artist 9 years to complete the cycle, and in it, he included many of the visitors to the court; it's a fascinating account of late-15th-century court life. Most of Mantegna's works for the palace, though, have been carted off to other collections; his famous *Parnassus,* which he painted for an intimate room known as the studiolo, is now in the Louvre, as are works that Perugino and Corregio painted for the same room (in one of the more compelling current stories from the art world, Mantua is demanding their return).

The Gonzagas expanded their palace by incorporating any structure that lay within reach, including the Duomo and the Castello di San Giorgio (1396 to 1406). As a result, it's now a small city of 500 rooms connected by a labyrinth of corridors, ramps, courtyards, and staircases, filled with Renaissance frescoes and ancient Roman sculpture. The highlights are the **Sala del Pisanello,** where frescoes of Arthurian legends (mostly Tristram and Isolde) painted by Pisanello between 1436 and 1444 were discovered beneath layers of plaster only in 1969; the **Salle degli Arazzi (Tapestry Rooms)** hung with copies—woven at the same time but by a different Flemish workshop—of the Vatican's tapestries designed by Raphael and his students (among them Giulio Romano); the **Camera degli Sposi** frescoed by Mantegna (the trompe-l'oeil oculus in the center of the ceiling is an icon of Renaissance art and a masterpiece of foreshortening); the **Galleria degli Specchi (Hall of Mirrors)**; the low-ceiling **Appartemento dei Nani (Apartments of the Dwarfs),** where a replica of the Holy Staircase in the Vatican is built to miniature scale (in keeping with noble custom of the time, dwarfs were part of Isabella's court); and the **Galleria dei Mesi (Hall of the Months).** Some of the mostly delightful chambers in the vast complex make up the **Appartimento Estivale (Summer Apartment),** which looks over a courtyard where hanging gardens provide the greenery.

Palazzo Te. Viale Te. ☎ **0376-323-266.** Admission 12,000L ($6) adults, 5,000L ($2.50) ages 12–18. Tues–Sun 9am–6pm, Mon 1–6pm.

Frederico Gonzaga, the pleasure-loving refined son of Isabella d'Este, built this splendid Mannerist palace as a retreat from court life. You'll see that the purpose of this palace was to amuse as soon as you enter the courtyard—the keystone of the monumental archway is designed to look like it's falling out of place. Throughout the lovely whimsical interior, sexually frank frescoes (by Giulio Romano, who left a scandal behind him in Rome that arose over his licentious engravings) depict Psyche and other erotically charged subject matter and make unsubtle reference to one of Frederico's favorite pastimes (horses and astrology, Frederico's other passions, also figure prominently).

The greatest and most playful achievement here, though, has to do with power: In the **Sala dei Giganti (Room of the Giants),** Titan is overthrown by the gods in a dizzying play of architectural proportion that gives the illusion that the ceiling is falling. The palazzo is a 20-minute walk from the center of town along Via Mazzini. En route, devotees of Mantua's most famous painter may choose to stop for a look at the **Casa di Mantegna.** Via Acerbi 47 (☎ **0376-360-506**); admission is free and it's open Tuesday to Sunday 10am to 12:30pm and 3 to 6pm (hours may vary).

AFFORDABLE PLACES TO STAY

If you're interested in the lowest-priced accommodations, the tourist office can provide details and make reservations for rooms at five hostel-like farmhouses in the surrounding countryside. Rates are about 30,000L ($15) per person. Since several of the properties are within a few kilometers of town, you can reach them without too much trouble by bike or combination bus ride and trek.

ABC Moderno. Piazza Don Leoni 25, 46100 Mantova. ☎ **0376-323-347.** Fax 0376-322-349. 31 units. TV TEL. 70,000–105,000L ($35–$53) single; 80,000–145,000L ($40–$73) double; 140,000–190,000L ($70–$95) triple. Rates include buffet breakfast. MC, V. Parking 10,000–20,000L ($5–$10).

The prices at this recently renovated hotel across from the train station are remarkably low, considering the pleasant surroundings and the amenities. A pleasant lounge area and breakfast room open onto a sunny terrace. Upstairs, the renovated rooms have bright tile floors, fresh plaster and paint, new modular furnishings, and modern baths. Architectural details, such as stone walls and patches of old frescoes, have been uncovered to provide decorative touches. The management is extremely helpful, and their hospitality extends to bike rentals (10,000L/$5 per day). If the Moderno is full, bypass the other nearby hotels, which tend to be dreary and overpriced.

Broletto. Via Accademia 1, 46100 Mantova. ☎ **0376-326-784.** Fax 0376-221-297. http://space.tin.it/viaggi/fsmirnov. E-mail: hotelbroletto@tin.it. 16 units. A/C MINIBAR TV TEL. 115,000L ($58) single; 180,000L ($90) double. Contenental breakfast 12,000L ($6). AE, DC, MC, V. Closed Dec 22–Jan 4.

This atmospheric old hotel is in the center of the old city, only a few steps from the lake and the castello, making it a fine base for a late-night stroll through the moonlit piazze. The rooms have contemporary furnishings that are vaguely rustic in design, with orthopedic bed frames. Bright corner room 16 has balconies and windows on two sides. The most alluring feature of the decor, though, are massive beams on the ceilings and other architectural details from the palazzo's 16th-century origins.

Mantegna. Via Fabio Filzi 10, 46100 Mantova. ☎ **0376-328-019.** Fax 0376-368-564. 40 units. A/C TV TEL. 120,000L ($60) single; 190,000L ($95) double; 230,000L ($115) suite. Buffet breakfast 15,000L ($8). AE, MC, V. Parking free in courtyard. Closed Dec 24–Jan 7.

On a quiet side street just a few steps south of the *centro storico,* the Mantegna offers solid comfort in surroundings that are thoroughly modern. The cozy narrow singles resemble ships' cabins, but the doubles are unusually roomy. All have been renovated within the past few years and have new baths; many face a sunny and quiet courtyard.

WORTH A SPLURGE

San Lorenzo. Piazza Concordia 14, 46100 Mantova. ☎ **0376-220-500.** Fax 0376-327-194. www.hotelsanlorenzo.it. 32 units. A/C MINIBAR TV TEL. 300,000L ($150) single; 360,000L ($180) double; 420,000L ($210) jr. suite. Rates include breakfast. Frequent promotions may lower the price up to 40% in slow periods (ask when you call). AE, DC, MC, V. Parking 35,000L ($18) in garage.

One of Italy's more gracious inns was fashioned out of a row of old houses just off Piazza delle Erbe. Oil paintings and oriental carpets grace the marble-floored salons. The guest rooms, no two of which are alike, are furnished with exquisite reproductions of 18th- and 19th-century antiques—plus at least one original piece in each room—and come with elegant touches like a bit of stucco work on ceilings as well as all the conveniences you'd expect from a luxury hotel. A panoramic roof terrace overlooks the towers and rooftops of the *centro storico,* and the lavish buffet breakfast is served in an elegant room overlooking the rotunda, with a series of sitting salons around a bar nearby.

GREAT DEALS ON DINING

Mantovian cuisine is quite refined—exquisite risotto dishes, an array of pastas stuffed with pumpkin and squash, and given the proximity of lakes and rivers, a fine selection of fish appears on menus.

Leoncino Rosso. Via Giustiziati 33. ☎ **0376-323-277.** Reservations recommended. Primi 8,000–12,000L ($4–$6); secondi 10,000–14,000L ($5–$7). AE, DC, MC, V. Mon–Sat, noon–3pm and 7–10pm. Closed in Aug and 3 weeks in Jan. MANTOVIAN.

This fine old restaurant with an attractive rustic dining room, just off Piazza Broletto (on a parallel street) in the center of the old city, has been serving food since 1750. This is a good place to sample Mantua's distinctive cuisine. Topping the list is *tortelli di zucca,* a large ravioli pillow stuffed with pumpkin. If you want to continue to eat as the Mantovese do, move on to *stracotto mantovano* (stewed donkey; that store next door is a horse-meat butcher). For more familiar fare from the barnyard, try the delicious *cotechino e fagioli* (pork sausage and beans). You can tell it's a local place by the TV in the corner (a bit loud, actually) that always manages to have a soccer game playing.

Ochina Bianca. Via Finzi 2. ☎ **0376-323-700.** Reservations required. Primi 12,000L ($6); secondi 18,000L ($9). MC, V. Tues 7:30–10:30pm, Wed–Sun 12:30–2:30pm and 7:30–10:30pm. MANTOVIAN.

Gilberto and Marcella Venturini serve distinctive variations on the local cuisine in these simple yet elegant dining rooms a few blocks north of the center. Many of the dishes rely on fresh fish from the Mincio, which finds it way into such creations as *peperoni ripieni di pesce di fiume* (peppers filled with smoked fish and topped with a fresh tomato sauce) and many of the risotti. Grilled or sautéed freshwater fish is also often on the menu, as are traditional meat specialties like *coniglio alla porchetta* (roasted rabbit with pork stuffing). The zucchini flowers stuffed with ricotta and parmigiano and kissed with anchovy paste are almost as good an antipasto as the tiny salmon rolls (wrapped around fat so it melts and flavors as the fish cooks) and served on a potato purée is a main course. *Torta sabbiosa* is a local dessert, a raisined plum cake soaked in Guinness, and the homemade gelato is delicious. The carefully chosen wine list is extensive.

Pescheria Lanfranchi. Via Pescherie at Via G. Matteotti. No phone. Fish specialties from 5,000L ($2.50). Tues–Sun 7:30am–1pm and 4:30–7:30pm, Mon 7:30am–1pm. SEAFOOD.

There's no end to the creatures, most of them grilled or deep-fried, at this fish stall on wheels. It's parked, appropriately enough, next to a loggia built by Giulio Romano in 1546, probably for use as a fish market south of the *centro storico* on the banks of a scenic canal. A plate of squid, octopus, or lake fish makes a fine light meal or snack. If seafood isn't your style, there's a great little nameless **rotisserie** joint almost two blocks up Via Orefici at no. 40 where freshly roasted chicken, turkey, quail, guinea hen, and other fowl starts around 5,000L ($2.50) per portion; it's open the same hours.

Trattoria due Cavallini. Via Salnitro 5. ☎ **0376-328-431.** Primi 5,000–10,000L ($2.50–$5), secondi 12,000–15,000L ($6–$8). AE, MC, V. Wed–Mon noon–3pm and 7:15pm–midnight. MANTOVIAN.

Your reward for the 10-minute walk south of the center (follow Via Trieste and its continuation, Corso Garibaldi) is a meal at one of Mantua's favorite informal trattorias, where you can eat in a shady courtyard in good weather. The menu is typically Mantovian, with excellent *tortelli di zucca* and an aromatic *stinco di miale* (roasted pork joint, infused with fresh herbs). The *torta sbrisolona*, a traditional Mantovese cake of cornmeal, almonds, and butter, is served fresh from the oven.

4 Lake Garda: Largest of the Italian Lakes

Sirmione 127km (76 mi.) E of Milan, 149km (90 mi.) W of Venice, Riva del Garda 170km (102 mi.) E of Milan, 199km (120 mi.) NW of Venice, 43km (26 mi.) S of Trent.

Poets, composers, and mere mortals have been rhapsodizing about the Italian lakes for centuries—most vocally since the 18th century, when it became de rigueur for travelers on the Grand Tour to descend through the Alps and enjoy their first days on Italian soil on the shores of the lakes.

Lake Garda (Largo di Garda), the largest and easternmost of the lakes, laps against the flat plains of Lombardy and the Veneto at its southern extremes, and in the north becomes fjordlike and moody, its deep waters backed by Alpine peaks. All around the lake, Garda's shores are green and fragrant with flowery gardens, groves of olives and lemons, and forests of pines and cypress. This pleasing, vaguely exotic landscape has attracted the likes of poet Gabriele D'Annunzio, whose villa near Gardone is one of the major attractions, and Benito Mussolini, whose Republic of Salo was headquartered here. Mussolini was also captured and executed on these shores. Long before them, the Romans discovered the hot springs that still gush forth at Sirmione, the famed resort on a spit of land at the lake's southern reaches. Today's visitors come to swim (Garda is the cleanest of the major lakes), windsurf (Riva del Garda, at the northern end of the lake, is Europe's windsurfing capital), and enjoy the easygoing ambience of Garda's many pleasant lakeside resorts.

SIRMIONE

Garda's most popular resort juts several miles into the southern waters of the lake on a narrow peninsula of cypress and olive groves. Despite an onslaught of visitors, Sirmione manages to retain its charm. Vehicular traffic is kept to a minimum (the few motorists allowed onto the marble streets of the old town are required to switch off their cars' engines at traffic lights). The emphasis is on strolling, swimming in waters that are warmed in places by underwater hot springs, and relaxing on the sunny terraces of pleasant lakeside hotels. One caveat: You may find Sirmione to be less than charming in July and August, when the crowds descend in full force.

ESSENTIALS

GETTING THERE   By Train   Connections are via nearby Desenzano (20 min. from Sirmione by half-hourly bus; 2,500L/$1.25), which is on the Milan-Venice rail lines, with trains almost every half hour in either direction, stopping in **Verona** (25 min., 4,100L/$2.05), **Brescia** (25 min., 3,800L/$1.90), **Venice** (regional: 2 hr., 14,500L/$7; High speed: 100 min., 21,700L/$11), and **Milan** (1½ hr., 12,000L/$6).

By Bus   Hourly bus service links Sirmione with **Verona** (1 hr.; 5,800L/$2.80) and **Brescia** (1 hr.; 5,800L/$2.80). For more information, contact **SAIA** buses in Brescia, ☎ **030-223-761** or **APT** in Verona ☎ **045-800-4129.** In summer, a special bus makes a 35-minute 7pm run from **Verona** Monday, Wednesday, Friday, and Saturday (24,000L/$12).

By Boat   Hydrofoils and ferries operated by **Navigazione Lago di Garda** (☎ **800-551-801** or 030-914-9511; www.navigazionelaghi.it) ply the waters of the lake. One to two hourly ferries and four daily hydrofoils connect Sirmione with **Desenzano** (20 min., 4,400L/$2.20 by ferry; 10 min., 6,900L/$3.45 by hydrofoil). Two daily ferries and three daily hydrofoils connect Sirmione with **Gardone** (70–120 min., 9,900L/$4.95 by ferry; 55 min., 14,100L/$7 by hydrofoil), **Limone** (2 daily; 3 hr., 13,900L/$7 by ferry; 1 hr. 40 min., 19,600L/$10 by hydrofoil), and **Riva** (almost 4 hr., 13,900L/$7 by ferry; 2 hr. 10 min., 19,600L/$10 by hydrofoil). Service is curtailed October to April.

By Car   Sirmione is just off the A4 between Milan and Venice. From Bologna, Florence, Rome, and other points south, take the A22 north from Modena to Verona, and from there, the A4 west to Sirmione. The trip from Venice takes about 1½ hours, and the trip from Milan a little over an hour. There's ample parking in the lakeside lots lining Viale Marconi, the broad avenue that runs down the peninsula to the entrance of the old town.

VISITOR INFORMATION   The **tourist office** is outside the old town near the castle at Viale Marconi 2 (☎ **030-916-245;** www.bresciaholiday.com). Easter to October, hours are daily 9am to 12:30pm and 3 to 6pm (though the hotel reservations people actually keep it open all day long until 9pm); November to March, hours are Monday to Friday 9am to 12:30pm and 3 to 6pm and Saturday 9am to 12:30pm. The helpful English-speaking staff dispenses a wealth of information about Sirmione and other sights on the lake and will reserve a room for you.

EXPLORING THE TOWN

In addition to its attractive though tourist-shop–ridden **old town,** Sirmione has many lakeside promenades, pleasant beaches, and even some open countryside where olive trees sway in the breeze. Anything you'll want to see can be reached easily on foot, though an open-air tram 1,500L/75¢) makes the short run out to the Roman ruins from the northern edge of the old town (but not between 12:30 and 2:30pm).

The moated and turreted **Castello Scaligero** (☎ **030-916-468**) marks the only land-side entrance to the old town. Built in the 13th century by the della Scala family, who ruled Verona and many of the lands surrounding the lake, the castle warrants a visit mainly for the views from its towers. It's open Tuesday to Sunday: April to October 9am to 8pm and October to March 9am to 1pm. Admission 8,000L ($4).

From the castle, **Via Vittorio Emanuele** leads through the center of the town and emerges after a few blocks into the greener, garden-lined lanes that wind through the tip of the peninsula to the **Grotte di Catullo** (☎ **030-916-157**). Whether or not these extensive ruins at the northern tip of the peninsula were really, as they're alleged to have been, the villa and baths of the pleasure-loving Roman poet Catullus is open to debate. Even so, their presence here, on a hilltop fragrant with wild rosemary and pines, demonstrates that Sirmione has been a deservedly popular retreat for millennia, and you can wander through the evocative remains while enjoying wonderful lake views. March to October 14, the ruins are open Tuesday to Saturday 8:30am to 7pm and Sunday 9am to 6pm; October 15 to February, hours are Tuesday to Saturday 8:30am to 4:30pm and Sunday 9am to 4:30pm (museum remains open until 7pm daily); admission is 8,000L ($4).

If you want to enjoy the clean waters of the lake, the place to head is the small **Lido delle Bionde beach** near the castle off Via Dante. In summer, the beach concession rents lounge chairs with umbrellas for 10,000L ($5) per day, as well as kayaks and pedal boats (15,000L/$8 per hour).

Affordable Places to Stay

Sirmione has many pleasant, moderately priced hotels, all of which book up quickly in July and August, when they also charge higher rates (reflected in the high end of the rates below). You aren't allowed to drive into the old town until a guard at the entrance near the castle confirms that you have a hotel reservation. The tourist office will help you find a room in your price range on the day you arrive, but they won't book ahead of time.

Eden. Piazza Carducci 17/18, 25019 Sirmione. ☎ **030-916-481.** Fax 030-916-483. www.gardalake.it/hotel-eden. 33 units. A/C MINIBAR TV TEL. 142,500–167,500L ($71–$84) single; 190,000–255,000L ($95–$128) double. Rates include breakfast. AE, DC, MC, V. Closed Nov–Easter.

American poet Ezra Pound once lived in this pink-stucco lakeside hotel, located on a quiet side street leading to the lake in the center of town. Despite its long history as a lakeside retreat, the Eden has recently been modernized with taste and an eye to comfort. You can see the lake from most of the attractive rooms, decorated in contemporary furnishings. The mirrored walls enhance the light and lake views. The large baths are new, and many have large tubs. The marble lobby opens to a delightful shaded terrace and a swimming pier that juts into the lake.

Grifone. Via Bocchio 4, 25019 Sirmione. ☎ **030-916-014.** Fax 030-916-548. 16 units. TEL. 50,000L ($25) single; 88,000L ($44) double. No credit cards. Closed Nov–Easter.

One of Sirmione's best-value lodgings is also one of its most romantic—the vine-clad stone building next to the castle enjoys a prime piece of lake property. You can enjoy this setting from a shady patio off the lobby, from a small beach, or from any of the guest rooms with a view. Brother and sister Nicola and Christina Marcolini oversee the hotel and adjoining restaurant with a great deal of graciousness, carrying on several generations of a family business. The rooms are simple but pleasant, with tile floors and plain furnishings; top-floor rooms (36 to 42) have small balconies from which to enjoy the views. The tidy baths have stall showers or curtainless tubs. The Grifone books up quickly, often with return guests, so reserve well in advance.

Olivi. Via San Pietro 5, 25019 Sirmione. ☎ **030-990-5365.** Fax 030-916-472. www.gardalake.it/hotel-olivi. 58 units. A/C MINIBAR TV TEL. 120,000–177,000L ($60–$89) single; 210,000–300,000L ($105–$150) double. Rates include breakfast. AE, MC, V. Closed Jan.

This pleasant modern hotel is my classiest choice for Sirmione, a chance to live the high life at still reasonable rates. It's not directly on the lake, which you can see from most rooms and the sunny terrace, but commands a hilltop position near the Roman ruins amid pines and olive groves. The rooms are stunningly decorated in varying schemes of bold, handsome pastels, and earth tones. They have separate dressing areas off the baths, and most have balconies. There's a pool in the garden and, to bring a lakeside feeling to the grounds, an artificial river that streams past the terrace and glass windows of the lobby and breakfast room. They're busy installing nine suites, which should be ready by mid-2001.

GREAT DEALS ON DINING

La Roccia. Via Piana 2. ☎ **030-916-392.** Primi 9,000–13,000L ($4.50–$7); secondi 14,000–25,000L ($7–$13), pizza 10,000–13,000L ($5–$7). DC, MC, V. Fri–Wed 12:30–3pm and 7–10:30pm. Closed Nov–Mar. ITALIAN/PIZZA.

This trattoria/pizza parlor caters to the flocks of tourists who stream through Sirmione, but does so with excellent food and unusually pleasant surroundings. In good weather, the best seating is in the large garden to one side of the restaurant. The menu includes over 20 excellent pizzas made in a wood-burning oven, plus plenty of traditional pastas, including lasagne and excellent cheese tortellini in cream-and-prosciutto sauce. The fish (try the trout roasted or fried in butter and sage) and meat are excellent, and the best dishes are grilled over an open fire.

Ristorante Al Progresso. Via Vittorio Emanuele 18–20. ☎ **030-916-108.** Primi 11,000–16,000L ($6–$8), secondi 15,000–30,000L ($8–$15). AE, DC, MC, V. Fri–Wed (daily in summer) noon–2:30pm and 6:30–10:30pm. Closed either Nov–Dec or Dec–Jan (depending on flow of tourism). SEAFOOD/ITALIAN.

This fan-cooled room on the main street of the old town is appealingly plain but with a touch of style. The pastas include some excellent tortellini variations, as well as some with shellfish not from the lake but from the not-too-distant Adriatic. Fresh lake trout is often on the menu—grilled or *al Sirmionese* (boiled with a house sauce of garlic, oil, capers, and anchovies)—as are some simple veal preparations, including a *vitello al limone,* made with fresh lemons that grow on the shores of the lake.

RIVA DEL GARDA

The northernmost town on the lake is not just a resort but a real town too, with medieval towers, a nice smattering of Renaissance churches and palazzi, and narrow cobblestone streets where the everyday business of a prosperous Italian town proceeds in its alluring way.

ESSENTIALS

GETTING THERE   By Train   See "Getting There: By Train," under Sirmione above for connections to Desenzano, from which you must take a bus (see below).

By Bus   Six buses a day link Riva and **Desenzano** on the southern end of the lake, about a 2-hour trip (9,500L/$4.75). You can also travel between **Sirmione** and Riva by bus, though except for a 4:30pm direct run, you must transfer at Peschiera (2 hr., 11,000L/$6). From **Limone,** there are 11 trips daily (18 min., 2,500L/$1.25). Twenty-five daily buses connect Riva and **Trento** (1 hr. 40 min., 5,500L–6,000L/ $2.75–$3). From **Verona** there are 16 a day (2 hr., 9,500L/$4.75), and from **Brescia** five daily (2 hr., 10,300L/$5).

By Boat   Navigazione Lago di Garda (see Sirmione above for information) runs the boats. Fifteen ferries and three hydrofoils per day connect Riva with **Limone** (35–45 min., 4,400L/$2.20 by ferry; 30 min., 6,900L/$3.45 by hydrofoil). Two ferries and three hydrofoils per day connect Riva with **Gardone** (2 hr. 45 min., 12,200L/$6 by ferry; 1 hr. 20 min., 17,000L/$9 by hydrofoil), **Sirmione** (almost 4 hr., 13,900L/$7 by ferry; 2 hr. 10 min., 19,600L/$10 by hydrofoil), and **Desenzano** (4 hr. 15 min., 16,600L/$8 by ferry; 2½ hr., 22,300L/$11 by hydrofoil). Schedules vary with season, with very limited service in the winter.

By Car   The fastest link between Riva and points north and south is via the A22, which shoots up the east side of the lake (exit at Mori, 13km/9 mi. east of Riva). A far more scenic drive is along the western shore, on the beautiful corniche between Riva and Salo that hugs cliffs and passes through mile after mile of tunnel. Depending on the route, by car, Riva is about an hour from Verona and about 45 minutes from Sirmione.

VISITOR INFORMATION   The **tourist office,** which supplies information on hotels, restaurants, and activities in the area, is near the lakefront Giardini di Porta Orientale 8 (☎ **0464-554-444,** fax 0464-520-308, www.garda.com or www. gardatrentino.com). June 16 to September 15, it's open Monday to Saturday 9am to noon and 3 to 6:30pm and Sunday 10am to noon and 4 to 6:30pm; April to June 15 and September 16 to October, hours are Monday to Saturday 9am to noon and 3 to 6:15pm; November to March, hours are Monday to Friday 9am to noon and 2:30 to 5:15pm.

EXPLORING THE TOWN

Riva's old town is pleasant enough, though the only historic attractions of note are the 13th-century **Torre d'Apponale** and, nearby, the moated lakeside castle, **La Rocca.** Part of the castle interior now houses an unassuming collection of local art and crafts (☎ **0464-573-869**), open Tuesday to Saturday 9:30am to 5:30pm and Sunday 9:30am to noon and 2pm to 5:30pm; admission is 4,000L ($2).

The tourist office runs a few **free guided tours** (in many languages, including English). Weekends, they do walking tours of the town itself; Tuesdays and Fridays, of a few sights in the area. You must book in advance, by 5pm the previous day, at ☎ **0464-554-444.**

The main attraction is the lake, which Riva takes advantage of with a **waterside promenade** stretching for several miles past parks and pebbly beaches. The water is warm enough for swimming May to October, and air currents fanned by the mountains make Garda popular for windsurfing year-round. A convenient point of embarkation for a lake outing is the beach next to the castle, where you can rent **rowboats** or **pedal boats** for 11,000L ($6) per hour ; March to October, the concession is open daily 8am to 8pm.

For a more adventurous outing, check out the windsurfing at the **Nautic Club Riva,** Via Roverto 44 (☎ **0464-552-453;** www.nauticclubriva.com), where you can rent equipment for 70,000L ($35) per day or 30,000L ($15) per hour; multiday and weekly packages, as well as lessons, are also available.

AFFORDABLE PLACES TO STAY
In Riva

Portici. Piazza III Novembre 19, 38066 Riva del Garda. ☎ **0464-555-400.** Fax 0464-555-453. 45 units. TEL, TV. 72,000–95,000L ($36–$48) single; 120,000–160,000L ($60–$80) double. MC, V. Closed Nov–Mar.

The management pays much more attention to their ground-floor restaurant/bar under a portico of the main square than they do to the hotel, but perhaps that's because it's mainly booked by tour groups—keeping this central and surprisingly reasonable choice off the radar of independent travelers like us. Sadly, its location in the upper leg of the piazza's L-shape deprives almost all rooms of a lake view—and they're boringly modern to boot, with a monotonous blue tone to every aspect of the functional units. But for these prices, you can easily walk to a cafe to enjoy the view.

Sole. Piazza Novembre 23, 38066 Riva del Garda. ☎ **0464-552-686.** Fax 0464-552-811. www.hotelsole.net. 52 units. MINIBAR TV TEL. 150,000–170,000L ($75–$85) single; 200,000–240,000L ($100–$120) double. AE, DC, MC, V. Parking 5,000L ($2.50). Closed Nov to mid-Mar (except at Christmastime and during frequent trade fares).

One of the finest hotels in town enjoys a wonderful location right on the lake at the main square. The attentive management lavishes a great deal of attention on the public rooms and guest rooms and charges very fairly. The lobby is filled with rare Persian carpets and abstract art. The rooms reached via a sweeping circular staircase are warm and luxurious, with tasteful furnishings and marble-trimmed baths; the best rooms have balconies hanging out over the lake. Lake-view rooms are outfitted in antique style while those overlooking the square and town are done in modern functional. Amenities include a formal restaurant, a casual cafe/bar extending onto a lakeside terrace, a rooftop solarium with sauna, and a garage.

In Limone sul Garda

Limone sul Garda is a pretty resort wedged between the lake and mountains just 10km (6 mi.) south of Riva on the lakeside corniche. For ferry connections with Riva and Sirmione, see those sections earlier in this chapter. Despite an onslaught of tourists who come down through the mountains from Austria and Germany, it's a pleasant place to spend some time and has more moderately priced lakeside hotels than Riva does. The Romans planted lemon groves here and covered them with protective structures, the ruins of which are still visible on the hills around the town. Lemons continue to thrive on every available parcel of land.

There's a small IAT **tourist info** office at Via Comboni 15 (☎ **0365-954 070;** fax 0365-954-689). March to October, it's open Monday to Saturday 9am to 12:30pm and 3:30 to 7pm and Sunday 9am to 12:30pm; November to February, hours are Monday to Saturday 9am to 12:30pm and 4:30 to 6pm. Also try the private Web sites www.limone.com and www.telmec.it.

Le Palme. Via Porto 36, 25010 Limone sul Garda. ☎ **0365-954-681** or 0365-954-612. Fax 0365-954-120. www.limone.com/splendid. 28 units. A/C TV TEL. 90,000–135,000L ($45–$68) single; 140,000–230,000L ($70–$115) double. Rates include breakfast. MC, V. Closed Nov–Easter.

This gracious hotel is one of the most pleasant places to stay on Garda. It's on the lake at one end of Limone's narrow main street and surrounded by palm trees. Downstairs, a bar and reasonably priced restaurant flow onto a flowery terrace right on the lake. Upstairs, the large pleasant rooms are furnished in Venetian-style antiques (some genuine, others reproduction), and all but a few face the lake; the three best have small balconies hanging out over the water (if your room doesn't have a balcony, you can enjoy the lake from the downstairs terrace or rooftop solarium). A small beach is just a few steps down the road, and the hotel has a small pool amid lemon-shaded terraces nearby. There's also a larger pool available at its sibling hotel, the hillside Splendid, where they'll be happy to reserve for you if Le Palme is full.

GREAT DEALS ON DINING

Birreria Spaten. Via Maffei 7. ☎ **0464-553-670.** Primi 8,000–11,500L ($4–$6), secondi 8,000–20,000L ($4–$10), pizze 7,000–13,000L ($3.50–$7). MC, V. Thurs–Tues 11am–3pm and 5:30pm–midnight. Closed Nov–Feb. ITALIAN/TYROLEAN.

This noisy indoor beer garden occupies the ground floor of an old palazzo and features a wide-ranging mix of food from the surrounding regions, so you can dine on the cuisine of Trento or Lombardy or from the other side of the Alps. Many of the German and Austrian visitors who favor Riva opt for the wide range of the schnitzel-sauerkraut-sauerbraten fare, but you can also enjoy a pasta like *strangolapreti* (spinach-and-ricotta dumplings in a butter sauce), one of 30 pizzas, or a simply grilled lake trout. if you can't decide, the *Piatto Spaten* is a 25,000L ($13) sampler of their Tyrolean specialties: *cotechino* (spicy sausage), wurstel, *canederli* (a giant bread dumpling), a ham steak, and sauerkraut.

A DAY TRIP TO GARDONE

The little resort of **Gardone,** 47km (26 mi.) south of Riva on the western shore of the lake, has two interesting attractions. Once Italy's most famous soldier/poet, Gabriele D'Annunzio is today better remembered for his adventures and grand lifestyle at **Il Vittorale** (☎ **0365-296-511;** www.vittoriale.it), a hillside estate that's one of Lake Garda's major sites, than for his lackluster verse. He bought the estate (it's also alleged that Mussolini presented it to the poet as a way to coerce his sympathies) in 1921 and died here in 1936. The claustrophobic rooms of his ornately and bizarrely decorated villa are filled with bric-a-brac and artifacts from his colorful life, including many mementos of his long affair with actress Eleanora Duse. Elsewhere on the grounds, which cascade down the hillside in a series of luxuriant gardens, are the patrol boat D'Annunzio commanded in World War I, a museum containing his biplane and photos, and his pompous hilltop tomb.

Admission is 10,000L ($5) adults and 8,000L ($4) ages 7 to 12 and over 60 to the grounds only; you pay 10,000L ($5) additional (8,000L/$4 kids and seniors) to tour the villa, which you can visit only via a 25-minute guided tour (in Italian). April to September, the grounds are open daily 8:30am to 8pm and the villa Tuesday to Sunday 10am to 6pm; October to March, the grounds are open daily 9am to 5pm and the villa Tuesday to Friday 9am to 1pm and 2 to 5pm and Saturday and Sunday 9am to 1pm and 2 to 5:30pm. The villa also hosts a **July-to-August season** of concerts and plays; call ☎ **0365-296-519;** www.vittoriale.it/teatro.

Just down the hill on Via Roma is the **Giardino Botanica Hruska** (☎ **0336-410-877**), a small but delightful bower planted a hundred years ago by the Swiss naturalist Arturo Hruska (a dentist whose clientele included European royalty). More than 2,000 species of exotic flora from around the world continue to thrive in the balmy microclimate around the lake. Admission is 9,000L ($4.50). March 15 to October 15, the garden is open daily 9am to 7pm.

For ferry connections with Riva and Sirmione, see those sections earlier in this chapter (from Limone, prices are the same as from Riva, but the trip is 30 minutes quicker by hydrofoil, 45 minutes faster by ferry). You can also **bus** here **from Riva** in 65 minutes (5,800L/$2.90). **From Sirmione,** you have to transfer at Desenzano for one of 6 daily runs (1 hr. total; 6,600L/$3.30). Hourly buses also make the 1-hour trip to and **from Brescia** (5,000L/$2.50) and two buses a day make the 3-hour trip to and **from Milan** (16,300L/$8). Gardone's **tourist office** is at Corso Repubblica 8 (☎/fax **0365-20-347**). April to October, it's open Tuesday to Saturday 9am to 12:30pm and 4 to 7pm and Sunday 9am to 12:30pm; November to March, hours are Monday to Wednesday 9am to 12:30pm and 3 to 6pm, Thursday 9am to 12:30pm, and Friday 9am to 12:30pm and 3 to 6pm.

5 Lake Como

78km (47 mi.) NE of Milan, Menaggio 35km (21 mi.) NE of Como and 85km (51 mi.) N of Milan, Varenna 50km (30 mi.) NE of Como and 80km (48 mi.) NE of Milan.

The first sight of the dramatic expanse of azure-hued **Lake Como (Lago di Como),** ringed by gardens and forests and backed by the snowcapped Alps, is likely to evoke strong emotions. Romance, soulfulness, even gentle melancholy—these are the stirrings that over the centuries Como has inspired in poets (Lord Byron), novelists (Stendhal), composers (Verdi and Rossini), and plenty of other visitors too—be they deposed queens, such as Caroline of Brunswick, whom George IV of England exiled here for her adulterous ways, or well-heeled modern travelers who glide up and down these waters in the ubiquitous lake steamers. In addition to its emotional effects, Como is also just an enjoyable place to spend time. Less than an hour from Milan by train or car, its deep waters and verdant shores provide a wonderful respite from modern life.

COMO

The largest and southernmost town on the lake isn't likely to charm you. Long a center of silk making, this city that traces its roots to the Gauls, and after them, the Romans, bustles with commerce and industry. You'll probably want to stay in one of the more peaceful settings farther up the lake, but Como amply rewards a day's visit with some fine Renaissance churches and palaces and a lovely lakefront promenade.

ESSENTIALS

GETTING THERE By Train One to three trains hourly connect **Milan** and Como's Stazione San Giovanni on Piazzale San Gottardo (regional: from Milan's Piazza Garibaldi station, 55–60 min., 5,500L/$2.75; High speed: from Milan's Stazione Centrale station, 40 min., 9,000L/$4.50).

VISITOR INFORMATION The **regional tourist office** dispenses a wealth of information on hotels, restaurants, and campgrounds around the lake from its offices at Piazza Cavour 17 (☎ **031-269-712**). It's open daily 9am to 1pm and 2:30 to 6pm (sometimes closed Sunday in winter). In May 2000, an experimental **city tourist office** opened on Piazza del Duomo (☎ **031-337-1063**), open daily 10am to 7pm, but whether it will stay open or will move (though it will likely stay near the Duomo) hasn't yet been decided.

EXPLORING COMO

Part Gothic and part Renaissance, the **Duomo,** Piazza del Duomo in the center of town just off the lake (☎ **031-265-244**), is festooned with exuberant masonry and sculpture. Statues of two of the town's famous native sons, Pliny the Elder and Pliny the Younger, flank the main entrance. Inside, beneath an 18th-century dome by Juavara—the architect who designed much of Turin—is a lavish interior hung with mostly 16th-century paintings and tapestries, with lots of helpful leaflets in English to explain the major works of art. It's open daily 7:30am to noon and 3 to 7pm. The black-and-white-striped 13th-century **Broletto (Town Hall)** abuts the Duomo's left flank, and adjoining it is the **Torre del Comune.** As a study in contrasts, the starkly modernist and aptly named **Casa del Fascio,** built in 1936 as the seat of the region's fascist government, rises just behind the Duomo.

Como's main street, **Corso Vittorio Emanuele II,** cuts through the medieval quarter, where wood-beamed houses line narrow streets; and, just two blocks south of the Duomo, the five-sided 12th-century **San Fedele** stands above a charming square of the same name; parts of the church, including the altar, date from the 6th century. It's open daily 8am to noon and 3:30 to 7pm. To see Como's most alluring church, though, it's necessary to venture into the dull outlying neighborhood southwest of the center where, just off Viale Roosevelt, you'll come to the five-aisle heavily frescoed **Basilica of Sant'Abbondio** (☎ 631-338-8111), a Romanesque masterpiece from the 11th century with great 14th-century frescoes (pay 1,000L/50¢ to illuminate them). It's open daily 8am to 6pm (unless a wedding, popular here, is on).

Lakeside life revolves around **Piazza Cavour** and the adjoining **Giardini Publici,** where the circular **Tempio Voltano** (☎ 031-574-705) houses memorabilia that'll enlighten you about the life and experiments of native son and electricity pioneer Alessandro Volta. It's open Tuesday to Sunday 10am to noon and 3 to 6pm (2 to 4pm October to March); admission is 4,000L ($2). For a quick retreat and some stunning views, take the **funicular** (☎ 031-303-608) for a 7-minute ride up to the top of **Brunate,** the forested hill above the town (it leaves from the Lungo Lario Trieste every 15 minutes or so in summer, every half hour in winter; 3,650L/$1.80 one way, 7,300L/$3.65 round-trip).

TAKING A SNACK BREAK

Pasticceria Monti. Piazza Cavour 21. ☎ **031-301-165.** Wed–Mon 7am–2am (to 1am in winter). Gelato from 1,500L (75¢) for a single scoop, pastries from 3,000L ($1.50), sandwiches from 5,000L ($2.50). MC, V. CAFE

Above all, the busy Monti on the main lakefront piazza is one of Como's favorite places to gather and watch passersby. You can enjoy some of the excellent gelato or a coffee or cocktail, plus excellent sandwiches and some other light fare, including some daily pasta dishes.

BELLAGIO & THE CENTRAL LAKE REGION

By far the loveliest spot on the lake (and where travelers should definitely set their sights) is the section known as the Centro Lago. Three towns—Bellagio, Varenna, and Mennagio—sit across the water from one another on three different shorelines.

ESSENTIALS

GETTING THERE & GETTING AROUND   By Train   The closest train station to Bellagio and the other Central Lake towns is in Como (see above); from there you can continue by bus or boat.

By Boat   From Como, boats stop first at Bellagio: by ferry 2 hr. (11,100L/$6); by hydrofoil 35–45 min. (16,100L/$8). They continue on to Menaggio: by ferry another 15 min. (from Como 11,100L/$6, from Bellagio 4,700L/$2.35); by hydrofoil, another 5 min. (from Como 16,100L/$8, from Bellagio 7,200L/$3.60). About half the boats then stop in Varenna as well (plus there are about two dozen short-haul ferries each from Bellagio and Menaggio to Varenna): by ferry another 10 min. (from Como 12,600L/$6, from Bellagio or Menaggio 4,700L/$2.35); by hydrofoil, another

5 min. (from Como 18,100L/$9, from Bellagio or Menaggio 7,200L/$3.60). You can also get **day passes** good for the whole lake for 30,500L ($15).

Many of the ferries carry cars for an additional fee. Schedules vary with season, but from Easter through September, a ferry or hydrofoil makes the trip from Como to Bellagio and other towns along the lake at least hourly. For more information contact **Navigazione Lago di Como** (☎ **800-551-801** or 031-579-211); the office is on the lakefront in Como on Lungo Lario Trieste.

By Bus   There are 1–3 **SPT buses** (☎ **031-304-744**) per hour from Como to Bellagio (about 70 min.; 4,400L/$2.20). Hourly buses to Menaggio take 65 minutes and cost 4,700L ($2.35). Buses leave Como from in front of the main train station; get tickets at the bar inside.

By Car   Bellagio is connected to Como by a picturesque lakeshore road, S583, which can be very crowded in summer. The A9 links Como with Milan in about an hour. To reach Menaggio from Como, follow route S340 along the western shore of the lake. For Varenna, follow S342 to Nibionno, a speck of a town where it intersects with S36, which runs north through industrialized Lecco and then along the lake's eastern shore. All of these roads tend to be crowded, especially on weekends and in summer, so allow at least an hour of traveling time.

VISITOR INFORMATION   The **Bellagio tourist office** is at Piazza del Chiesa 14 (☎/fax **031-950-204;** www.fromitaly.net/bellagio and www.bellagiolakecomo.com). Its hours are Monday and Wednesday to Saturday 9am to noon and 3 to 6pm and Tuesday and Sunday 10:30am to 12:30pm and 3:30 to 5:30pm.

BELLAGIO

✪ **Bellagio** is at the tip of the peninsula at a point where the lake forks into three distinct basins: One long leg sweeps north into the Alps, Como is at the southern end of the western leg, and Lecco is at the southern end of the eastern leg. Boats from Bellagio make it easy to visit the nearby shores of the Centro Lago—not that you'll be in a great hurry to leave this pretty old town, with its steep narrow streets, lakeside piazza, and beautiful gardens.

EXPLORING THE TOWN

Bellagio is often called one of the most beautiful towns in Italy. Nestled amid cypress groves and verdant gardens, its earth-toned old buildings climb from the lakefront promenade along stepped cobbled lanes. While Bellagio is a popular retreat for everyone from Milanese out for a day of relaxation to British and Americans who come to relax for a week or two, the town is for the most part unmarred by tourism.

One of Bellagio's famed gardens surrounds the **Villa Melzi** (☎ **031-950-318** or 031-950-204), built by Franceso Melzi, a friend of Napoléon and an official of his Italian Republic. The villa was later the retreat of Franz Liszt and is now the home of a distinguished Lombardian family; they allow the public to stroll through their acres of manicured lawns and fountains and visit a pavilion where a collection of Egyptian sculpture is on display. It's open March 18 to October, daily 9am to 6pm; admission is 8,000L ($4).

Bellagio's other famous gardens are those of the **Villa Serbelloni,** occupying land once owned by Pliny the Younger and now in the hands of the Rockefeller Foundation. You can visit the gardens on twice-daily guided tours (reserve ahead), about 1½ hours long, in Italian and English. April to October, tours are Tuesday to Sunday at 11am and 4pm; the tour costs 9,000L ($4.50); for more information and to book a spot on the tour, call ☎ **031-950-204.**

AFFORDABLE PLACES TO STAY

For a wider selection of moderately priced hotels, you'd do best to head across the lake from Bellagio to Mennagio or Varenna (see below).

Giardinetto. Piazza del Chiesa, 22021 Bellagio. ☎ **031-950-168.** 13 units, 11 with bathroom. 55,000L ($28) single without bathroom; 80,000L ($40) double without bathroom, 100,000L ($50) double with bathroom. Breakfast 12,000L ($6). No credit cards. Closed Nov–Apr.

The best lodging deal is at this charming little hotel at the top of town, reached from the lakefront by Bellagio's narrow stepped streets. A snug lobby, with a big fireplace, opens to a gravelly grapevine-covered terrace, where you're welcome to bring your own food for an alfresco meal. Most of the rooms also overlook the terrace (a flight and a half with no elevator). They're quite large and bright, with big windows (those on the upper floors provide nice views from balconies over the town and lake beyond, especially nos. 18 to 20) and furnishings like solid old armoires and box-spring-and-mattress beds rather than the usual cots.

Suisse. Piazza Mazzini 23, 22021 Bellagio. ☎ **031-950-335.** Fax 031-951-755. 10 units. TV. 140,000–170,000L ($70–$85) single or double; 190,000–220,000L ($95–$110) triple. AE, DC, MC, V. May close in Jan.

The simple rooms above this restaurant in a 15th-century lakeside villa on the main square are currently at one-star status, but they plan to renovate another star into them soon. The parquet floors will remain, as will the stylish solid wood furnishings—with lovely details of inlay or carving. The baths are plain, and there's no elevator, but you're right on the harbor, and the mid-priced restaurant is quite good. It offers Italian fare year-round, with an inventive fusion flair in summer; the downstairs room looks very plain (though you can also sit out front under the arcades), but the upstairs dining room is understatedly elegant, with a stuccoed ceiling and a lake-view terrace. March to November, the restaurant is open daily (closed Wednesday October to February).

Worth a Splurge

Du Lac. Piazza Mazzini 32, 22021 Bellagio. ☎ **031-950-320.** Fax 031-951-624. www. bellagiohoteldulac.com. 47 units. A/C MINIBAR TV TEL. 120,000–180,000L ($60–$90) single; 200,000–300,000L ($100–$150) double; 340,000L ($170) regular suite, 380,000L ($190) large suite. Rates include breakfast. Half-board 180,000–200,000L ($90–$100) per person; full board 200,000–220,000L ($100–$110) per person. MC, V. Closed early Nov–Easter.

The Leoni family ensures that an air of graciousness and old-fashioned comfort pervades its gracious 150-year-old hotel overlooking the lake from the main piazza. Downstairs, a bar spills onto the arcaded sidewalk in front and there are a series of pleasant sitting rooms. Meals are served in a nicely appointed dining room with panoramic views of the lake, and in the guest rooms, all of which are unique; cushy armchairs and a nice smattering of antiques and reproductions lend a great amount of charm. Many of the smallish rooms have balconies or terraces, and there's a rooftop sun terrace with sweeping lake views.

GREAT DEALS ON DINING

Bar Café Rossi. Piazza Mazzini 22/24. ☎ **031-950-196.** Fri–Wed 7:30am–10:30pm (open daily and to midnight Apr–Sept). Sandwiches 4,000–7,000L ($2–$3.50). LIGHT FARE.

One of the nicest of Bellagio's pleasant lakefront cafes is tucked under the arcades of the town's main square. You can dine at one of the few outside tables or in the delightful art nouveau dining room, with intricate tile work, carved wood cabinets, and stuccoed ceilings. Wine and the excellent house coffee are available all day, but a nice selection of pastries and sandwiches makes this a good stop for breakfast or lunch.

Ristorante Barchetta. Salita Mella 13. ☎ **031-951-389.** Reservations highly recommended. Primi 18,000–35,000L ($9–$18); secondi 30,000–35,000L ($15–$18); tasting menu for 2 only 70,000L ($35) without wine. AE, DC, MC, V. Wed–Mon noon–2:15pm and 7–10:15pm (Sat–Sun only Nov–Dec). SEAFOOD/LOMBARDA.

One of Bellagio's best restaurants specializes in fresh lake fish and other seafood. In all but the coldest weather, food is served on a bamboo-enclosed heated terrace. Most of the pastas don't use seafood but are innovative variations on traditional recipes, like *ravioli caprino* (with goat's cheese, topped with pear sauce) and savory risotto with hazelnuts and pistachios. For a main course, however, you should try one of the delicious preparations of local perch or angler fish; the meat entrees, including baby lamb chops with rosemary, are also excellent. You can enjoy a pasta dish, as well as a meat and a fish dish, on one of the set menus.

La Grotta. Salita Cernaia 14. ☎ **031-951-152.** Primi 9,000–12,000L ($4.50–$6); secondi 9,000–24,000L ($4.50–$12); pizze 9,000–18,000L ($4.50–$9). AE, DC, MC, V (only for bills over 40,000L/$20). Tues–Sun (daily Aug–Sept) noon–2:30pm and 7pm–1am. ITALIAN/ PIZZERIA.

Tucked away on a stepped street just off lakefront Piazza Manzini, this cozy informal restaurant consists of a series of vaulted-ceiling dining rooms. The service is extremely friendly, and the wide-ranging menu includes many pasta and meat dishes. Most of the regulars, though, come for the fish specials, including lake trout, or the delectable pizzas that are the best for miles around.

VARENNA

You can happily spend some time climbing up and down the steep steps that substitute for streets in this charming village (on the eastern shore of the lake about 20 minutes by ferry from Bellagio) that until not too long ago made its living by fishing. The main attractions, though, are outside of town.

The hilltop ruins of the **Castello di Vezio** (☎ **0341-831-000**) are about a 20-minute walk above the town on a gradually ascending path. The main reason for a visit is to enjoy the stunning views of the lake, its shoreline villages, and the backdrop of mountains at the northern end. March to September, the castle is open daily 10am to 10pm; admission is 2,000L ($1).

The **gardens of the Villa Monastero** (☎ **0341-830-129**) are more easily accessible at the southern edge of town, and you can reach them by following the series of lakeside promenades through the old town from the ferry landing. This villa and the terraced gardens that rise up from the lakeshore were once a not-so-Spartan monastery—until it was dissolved in the late 17th century, when the nuns in residence began bearing living proof that they were on too-friendly terms with the priests across the way. If you find it hard to tear yourself from the bowers of citrus trees and rhododendrons clinging to terraces, you'll find equally enchanting surroundings in the adjoining gardens of the **Villa Cipressi** (☎ **0341-830-113**).

Both gardens are open daily March to October: Villa Monastero 10am to 6pm and Villa Cipressi 9am to 6pm. Admission should be (they may not raise prices this much) 4,000L ($2) adults or 3,000L ($1.50) reduced for under 10 or over 60 to either garden; or 7,000L ($3.50) adults or 6,000L ($3) reduced for both. Call ☎ **0341 830-113** for more details. In season, ferries make the 20-minute run between Bellagio and Varenna about every half hour (see above).

AFFORDABLE PLACES TO STAY

○ **Milano.** Via XX Settembre 29, 23829 Varenna. ☎/fax **0341-830-298.** www.
varenna.net. 8 units. TEL. 175,000L ($88) single; 200,000L ($100) double; 270,000L ($135)
triple. Rates include buffet breakfast (ask nicely and they'll let you have the room without
breakfast, and knock 15,000L/$8 off the price). AE, DC, MC, V. Closed late Oct–Mar.

You'd have to look hard to find a more pleasant retreat by the lake. The simpatica Signora Amelia and her family run this old house hanging over Varenna's lakefront. All
of the simply furnished but comfortable rooms have balconies and views—nos. 1 and
2, which open onto a wide terrace, and nos. 5 and 6 all have full-on lake vistas, the
other half overlook the neighbor's pretty garden with askance lake views. The furnishings are a pleasant mix of old and unobtrusive modern pieces, brightened up with
small Persian rugs. Breakfast is served in an antique-filled parlor on the main floor
with a lake view (on the outdoor terrace in summer).

Villa Cipressi. Via IV Novembre 18, 22050 Varenna. ☎ **0341-830-113.** Fax 0341-830-401.
E-mail: villacipressi@libero.it. 21 units. TV TEL. 135,000L ($68) single without lake view,
150,000L ($75) single in a double room with or without lake view; 170,000L ($85) double
without lake view, 190,000L ($95) double with lake view; 210,000L ($105) suite with lake
view. Rates include buffet breakfast. AE, DC, MC, V. Usually closes late Oct–Mar, but some
years open year-round.

If you enjoyed your tour of Varenna's lush gardens (see above), there's no need to leave.
This 16th-century villa and several outbuildings were converted to a hotel in the early
1800s; it's now geared to conferences but takes other guests, space permitting. Though
the rooms have been renovated without any attempt to retain historic character,
they're extremely large and attractive. Suites take advantage of the high ceilings and
contain loft bedrooms, with sitting areas below that can easily fit a couple of single
beds for families. Although not every room gets a lake view, all, save a few small ones
on the road side, enjoy marvelous views over the gardens, which you can also enjoy on
the delightful terraces. There are plans to add air conditioning at some point.

GREAT DEALS ON DINING

Vecchia Varenna. Via Scoscesa 10. ☎ **031-830-793.** Reservations required. Primi
17,000–19,000L ($9–$10); secondi 25,000–28,000L ($13–$14). AE, MC, V. Tues–Sun
12:30–2pm and 7:30–8:30pm. Closed Jan. LOMBARD/SEAFOOD.

One of your most memorable experiences in this region could be a meal at this romantic restaurant at the water's edge in Varenna's oldest section. Dining is in a beautiful
stone-floored room with white stone walls or on a terrace on the water. The kitchen
makes the most of local herbs and vegetables and, of course, the bounty of the lake—
for starters, *quadrucci* (pasta pockets) are stuffed with trout, and one of the best of the
many risottos combines wild mushrooms and *lavarello* (a white fish from the lake).
Grilled lake trout stuffed with mountain herbs is a sublime main course, though many
other kinds of lake fish are also available.

MENNAGIO

This lively resort town hugs the western shore of the lake, across from Bellagio on its
peninsula and Varenna on the distant shore. Hikers should stop in at the **tourist office**
on Piazza Garibaldi 8 (☎/fax **0344-32-924;** www.menaggio.com), open Monday to
Saturday 9am to noon and 3 to 6pm (July and August also Sunday 7:30 to 6:30pm).
The very helpful staff distributes a booklet, **"Hiking in the Area around Mennagio,"**
with descriptions of more than a dozen walks, accompanied by maps and instructions
on what buses to take to trail heads. The town's bus stop is at Piazza Garibaldi

(Sundays on Via Mazzini); tickets are sold at Bar Centrale or the newsstand on Via Calvi at the piazza.

The major nearby attraction is about 2.5km (1.5 mi.) south of town: The **Villa Carlotta** (☎ **0344-40-405;** www.unicei.it/villacarlotta) is the most famous villa on the lake and was begun in 1643 for the Marquis Giorgio Clerici, who made his fortune supplying Napoléon's troops with uniforms; he spent much of it on his neoclassical villa and gardens. After a succession of owners, including Prussian royalty who lavished their funds and attention on the gardens, the villa is now in the hands of the Italian government. It's filled with romantic paintings, statues by Canova and his imitators, and Empire furnishings, but the gardens are the main attraction, with azaleas, orchids, banana trees, cacti, palms, and forests of ferns spreading in all directions. You can take the C10 bus (1,900L/95¢) from Menaggio or walk along the lake. The nearest ferry landing is at Cadenabbia, just north of the gardens, though ferries to Menaggio are more frequent. The villa and gardens are open daily: March 15 to March 31 and October 9 to 11:30am and 2 to 4:30pm and April to September 9am to 6pm. Admission is 12,000L ($6) adults and 6,000L ($3) students and seniors over 65.

The lido, at the north end of town, has an excellent **beach,** as well as a **pool,** and is open late June to mid-September daily 9am to 7pm. For information on waterskiing and other activities, contact **Centro Lago Service,** in the Grand Hotel Victoria along the lakeside Via Castelli (☎ **0344-320-03**).

AN AFFORDABLE PLACE TO STAY & DINE

Albergo-Ristorante Il Vapore. Piazza Grossi 3, 22017 Menaggio. ☎ **0344-32-229.** Fax 0304-34-850. www.italiaabc.com. *Hotel:* 10 units. 50,000L ($25) single; 85,000L ($43) double with lake view, 75,000L ($38) double without lake view. Breakfast 10,000L ($5). No credit cards. *Restaurant:* Thurs–Tues noon–2:30pm and 6:30–9:30pm (daily June 15–Sept 15). Primi 8,000–12,000L ($4–$6); secondi 15,000–25,000L ($8–$13). Closed 20 days in Nov and late Feb/early Mar.

This very pleasant small restaurant/hotel faces a quiet square just off the lakefront. The rooms are comfortable, with rather nice modern furnishings (plus antiques in a few) and fuzzy towels in the cramped baths. Six rooms open onto partial lake views: 21 and 22 from tall windows; 25 and 26 from small terraces; 28 and 29 (the biggest room, with windows on two sides for a breeze) from tiny balconies. They usually won't accept reservations for just one night (but you can just stop by and ask). Meals are served beneath a wisteria-shaded arbor or in an attractive pale-blue dining room with paintings by local artists. The kitchen prepares many local specialties from the nearby mountain valleys, including *sciatt* (whole- wheat pasta stuffed with cheese and fried) and *strangolepreti* (small spheres of bread, spinach, eggs, pine nuts, and raisins showered with cheese).

6 Lake Maggiore & the Borromean Islands

Stresa 80km (48 mi.) NW of Milan.

Anyone who reads Hemingway will know this lake and its forested shores from *A Farewell to Arms.* That's just the sort of place **Lake Maggiore (Lago Maggiore)** is—a pleasure ground that's steeped in associations with famous figures (Flaubert, Wagner, Goethe, and Europe's other great minds seem to have been inspired by the deep, moody waters, backed by the Alps) and not-so-famous wealthy visitors. Fortunately, you need not be famous or wealthy to enjoy Maggiore, which is on the Swiss border just a short dash east and north of Milan.

STRESA

The major town on the lake is a pretty, festive little place, with a long lakefront promenade, a lively and attractive commercial center, and a bevy of restaurants and hotels that range from the expensively splendid to the affordably comfortable.

ESSENTIALS

GETTING THERE By Train Stresa is linked with **Milan** by 20 trains a day (regional: 75 min., 7,100L/$3.55; High speed: 58 min., 12,600L/$6).

By Boat Boats arrive and depart from Piazza Marconi, connecting Stresa with the Isole Borromee and with many other lakeside spots; most boats on the lake are operated by Navigazione Sul Lago Maggiore (☎ 800-551-801 or 0322-233-200; www.navlaghi.it).

By Car A8 runs between Milan and Sesto, near the southern end of the lake; from there, Route S33 follows the western shore to Stresa. The trip takes a little over an hour.

VISITOR INFORMATION The **tourist office** is half-way between the station and the center at Via Canonica 8 (☎/fax **0323-31-308**), open Monday to Saturday (daily March to October) 10am to 12:30pm and 3 to 6:30pm. You can also get info from the private sites www.lagomaggiore.it and www.stresa.it. For hiking information, ask for the booklet **"Percorsi Verdi."**

EXPLORING STRESA & THE ISLANDS

Stresa

Strolling and relaxing seem to be the main activities in Stresa. The action is at the **lakeside promenade,** running from the center of town north past the grand lakeside hotels, including the Iles des Borromees, where Hemingway set *A Farewell to Arms.* Sooner or later, though, most visitors climb into a boat for the short ride to the famed islands themselves, the Isole Borromee.

Borromean Islands

These three islands, named for the Borromeo family, which has owned them since the 12th century, float in the misty waters off Stresa and entice visitors with their stunning beauty. Note that Isola Bella and Isola Superiore have villages you can hang out in for free, but Isola Madre consists solely of the admission-charging gardens.

Public **ferries** leave for the islands every half hour from Stresa's Piazza Marconi; a **day pass** (17,000L/$9) is the most economical way to visit all three. Buy tickets only from the public Navigazione Lago Maggiore (☎ **800-551-801** or 0322-233-200; www.navlaghi.it), in the big building with triple arches. Private boats also make the trip out to the island–at obscene rates; you'll see other ticket booths and hucksters dressed as sailors will try to lure you aboard (for large groups, the prices can be reasonable, but do your negotiating on the dock before you get on the boat).

ISOLA BELLA Isola Bella (5 minutes from Stresa, 8,800L/$4.40) remains true to its name, with splendid 17th-century gardens that ascend from the shore in 10 luxuriantly planted terraces. The Borromeo palazzo provides a chance to explore opulently decorated rooms, including the one where Napoléon and Josephine once slept. It's open daily: March 27 to September 9am to noon and 1:30 to 5:30pm and October 1–24 9am to noon and 1:30 to 5pm; admission is 15,000L ($8) adults and 6,000L ($3) ages 6 to 15; for details, call ☎ **0323-30-556.**

ISOLA SUPERIORE Most of Isola Superiore, also known as Isola Pescatore (10 minutes from Stresa and the round-trip fare is 8,800L/$4.40), is a occupied by a not-so-quaint old fishing village—every one of the tall houses on this tiny strip of land seems to harbor a souvenir shop or pizza stand, and there are hordes of visitors to keep them busy.

ISOLA MADRE   The largest and most peaceful of the islands is Isola Madre (30 minutes from Stresa, 12,400L/$6), every inch of which is covered with the exquisite flora of the 8-acre **Orto Botanico** (☎ **0323-31-261**). The botanical garden is open daily: March 27 to September 9am to noon and 1:30 to 5:30pm and October 1 to 24 9:30am to 12:30pm and 1:30 to 5pm; admission is 15,000L ($8) adults and 6,000L ($3) ages 6 to 15.

HIKING & BIKING IN THE AREA

The forested slopes above Stresa are prime hiking and mountain biking terrain. To reach a network of trails, take the funivia from the near the lakefront at the north end of town up **Monte Mottarone;** the funivia (☎ **0323-30-399;** www.paginegialle.it/funistresa) runs every 20 minutes 9:20am to noon and 1:40 to 5:20pm and the fare is 12,000L ($6) one way or 20,000L ($10) round-trip (kids 4 to 12 are 7,000L/$3.50 and 11,000L/$6, respectively). It costs 17,000L ($9) to take a bike, which you can rent at the station for 25,000L ($13) for a half day or 35,000L ($18) for a full day. The **Alpina garden** halfway up is open Tuesday to Saturday 9am to 6pm and Sunday (and July to August) 9:30am to 6:30pm.

If you don't want to venture too far from the lake, there's a nice **beach** near the station.

AFFORABLE PLACES TO STAY

Meeting. Via Bonghi 9, 28049 Stresa. ☎ **0323-32-741.** Fax 0323-33-458. www.stresa.it. 27 units. TV TEL. 100,000–130,000L ($50–$65) single; 130,000–170,000L ($65–$85) double. Rates include breakfast. AE, DC, MC, V. Parking 15,000L ($8). Closed Jan–Feb.

The name comes from the proximity of Stresa's small conference center, where a much-attended music festival is held from July to early September. Although the lakefront is a 5-minute walk away, the setting is quiet and leafy, though light sleepers on the back may notice the trains passing in the distance. The rooms, in Scandinavian modern, are big and bright, and many have terraces. There's a cozy bar and lounge downstairs, as well as a casual (but slightly impersonal) dining room. In November 2000, they overhauled the exterior, adding balconies to all rooms lacking them (they plan to add air conditioning soon as well).

Mon Toc. Via Duchessa di Genova 67–69, 28049 Stresa. ☎ **0323-30-282.** Fax 0323-933-860. TEL TV. 14 units, 12 with bathroom. 85,000L ($43) single; 140,000L ($70) double. (5,000L/$2.50 less for the two rooms that share a bathroom). Rates include breakfast. AE, DC, MC, V. Sometimes closed 2nd week Jan.

Just uphill from the train station, this family-run hotel surrounded by a big private garden and lawn is convenient to the lake and town (a 10- to 15-minute walk) but enough removed to provide an almost country-like atmosphere. With functional furniture, the rooms are unusually pleasant for a hotel in this price range and have tidy baths (though a few are of the miniscule, molded, airplane variety). The friendly owner refuses, out of honesty, to call the sliver of lake visible over the rooftops from the second-floor rooms (no elevator) a "lake view."

Primavera. Via Cavour 30, 28049 Stresa. ☎ **0323-31-286.** Fax 0323-33-458. www.stresa.it. 32 units. TV TEL. 95,000–110,000L ($48–$55) single; 150,000–170,000L ($75–$85) double. Rates include breakfast. AE, DC, MC, V. Parking 15,000L ($8) at Hotel Meeting. Closed mid-Nov to Dec 20, Jan 7–Feb.

For much of the spring and summer, the street in front of this hotel is closed to traffic and filled with flowering plants and cafe tables. The relaxed air prevails throughout this bright little hotel, a block off the lake in the town center. A tiny lounge and bar are downstairs. Upstairs, the tile-floored rooms are furnished in functional walnut veneer; you can have a minifridge on request. Many rooms have balconies, just wide enough to accommodate a pair of chairs, with flowerboxes overlooking the town. A few fourth-floor rooms get in a sliver of lake view around the apse and stone bell tower of the Duomo.

Worth a Splurge

Palma. Lungolago Umberto 133, 28049 Stresa. ☎ **0323-32-401** or 0323-933-906. Fax 0323-933-930. www.hlapalma.it. 128 units. A/C MINIBAR TV TEL. From 170,000–240,000L ($85–$120) single; 260,000–380,000L ($130–$190) double. Rates include buffet breakfast. AE, DC, MC, V. Parking free. Closed mid-Nov to mid-Mar.

The Palma is one of the nicest of Stresa's luxury hotels and, given the high-level comfort and the amenities, one of the most reasonably priced. Most of the large rooms, recently redone in rich floral fabrics and wood tones, open to balconies overlooking the lake, and 98% of the spacious marble baths have Jacuzzis. There's a rooftop sun terrace and fitness center, with hot tub and sauna, but the most pleasant places to relax are in the flowery garden in front of the hotel and the terrace surrounding the lakeside pool.

GREAT DEALS ON DINING

Hotel Ristorante Fiorentino. Via Bolongaro 9–11. ☎ **0323-30-254.** Primi 6,000–8,000L ($3–$4); secondi 11,000–18,000L ($6–$9); menù turistico 23,000L ($12) without wine. AE, DC, MC, V. Mar–Oct daily 11am–3pm and 6–10pm. Closed Nov to mid-Mar. ITALIAN.

It's hard to find friendlier service or homier trattoria-type food in Stresa, especially at these prices. Everything that comes out of the family-run kitchen is made fresh daily, including cannelloni and other pastas. You can dine in a big cozy room or on a patio out back in good weather.

Ristorante Pescatore. Vicolo del Poncivo. ☎ **0323-31-986.** Reservations recommended. Primi 15,000–34,000L ($8–$17); secondi 20,000–36,000L ($10–$18); fixed-price menu 26,000L ($13) without wine. DC, MC, V. Fri–Wed noon–4pm and 7–9:30pm. SEAFOOD.

This small dining room in the center of town is where residents of Stresa come for a fish meal. The starters include a wonderful seafood salad, an appetizer of smoked salmon or tuna, or any number of pasta dishes served with clams or squid. The main courses include a paella worthy of southern Spain (the owners and some of the cooks and waiters are Spanish) as well as zarzuela de pescada, a rich fish stew. Lake or ocean fish are always fresh and served grilled and topped with the simplest sauces.

Taverna del Pappagallo. Via Principessa Margherita 46. ☎ **0323-30-411.** Primi and pizza 7,000–14,000L ($3.50–$7); secondi 18,000–30,000L ($9–$15). No credit cards. Thurs–Mon 11:30am–2:30pm and 6:30–10:30pm (daily in summer). ITALIAN/PIZZERIA.

Most of Stresa seems to congregate in this pleasant restaurant for the most popular pizza in town. But just about all the fare, including delectable homemade gnocchi and such dishes as grilled sausage, that comes out of the family-run kitchen is delicious. Weather permitting, try to dine at one of the tables in the pleasant garden.

Piemonte & the Valle d'Aosta

by Reid Bramblett

Piemonte (Piedmont) means "at the foot of the mountains." The mountains, of course, are the Alps, which define the region and part of Italy's northern and western borders. These dramatic peaks are visible throughout the province, most of which rises and rolls over fertile foothills that produce a bounty as rich as the region is green. This is the land of cheeses, truffles, plump fruit, and, of course, wines, among them some of Italy's most delicious reds, including Barbaresco, Barbera, and Barolo—the latter considered (along with Tuscany's Brunello) to be one of Italy's top two beefy, structured reds. Rising from the vineyards are medieval and Renaissance towns and villages, many of which remain untrammeled by the modern world.

Not that all of Piemonte is rural, of course. **Turin,** an industrial capital and home to Fiat, Italy's main auto manufacturer, is the region's capital, and within the ring of sprawling suburbs lies an elegant city of mannerly squares, baroque palaces, and stunning art collections. The Turinese and their neighbors from other parts of Italy often retreat to the **Valle d'Aosta,** the smallest, northernmost, and most mountainous of Italian provinces.

1 Turin & the Mysterious Shroud

669km (401 mi.) NW of Rome, 140km (84 mi.) E of Milan.

It's often said that **Turin** is the most French city in Italy or the most Italian city in France. The reason is partly historic and partly architectural. From the late 13th century to Italy's unification in 1861 (when the city served very briefly as capital), Turin was the capital of the House of Savoy. The Savoys were as French as they were Italian, and their holdings extended well into the present-day French regions of Savoy and the Côte d'Azur. The city's Francophile 17th- and 18th-century architects, inspired by the tastes of the French court, laid out broad avenues and airy piazzas and lined them with low-slung neoclassical buildings.

Most visitors come to Turin with business in mind (often at the Fiat and Pirelli works in the sprawling industrial suburbs). Those who take the time to look around the historic center, though, will find an elegant and sophisticated city that has changed little since more gracious centuries, with some fine museum collections and the charm of a place that, for all its Francophile leanings, is quintessentially Italian and perhaps the most pleasant big city in Northern Italy.

A Taste of Piemonte & the Valle d'Aosta

Given such vast geographic diversity, it's not surprising that the region's cuisine varies according to the topography. In the southern stretches of Piemonte, the palate turns primarily to those magnificent red **wines** from the wine villages around Asti and Alba. Barbaresco, Barbera, Barolo, Dolcetto, Nebbiolo—the names are legendary, and they often appear on the table to accompany meat dishes stewed in red wine; one of the most favored of these is *brasato al barolo* (beef or veal braised in Barolo). The best dish to kick off a meal here is usually only available in winter: *bagna cauda,* literally translated as "hot bath," a plate of raw vegetables that are dipped into a steaming sauce of olive oil, garlic, and anchovies. Two pastas you will encounter on menus are *agnolotti* (a thick tube often stuffed with an infusion of cheese and meat) and *tajarin,* a flat egg noodle that may be topped with porcini mushrooms, sauces made with walnuts, or the local delicacy that is perhaps the region's greatest contribution to Italian cuisine: **white truffles.** As the land climbs higher toward the Valle d'Aosta, mountain fare takes over—*polenta* (a cornmeal mush varying from soupy-and-sticky to almost cakelike) is a popular *primo* or side to a *secondo;* stews are thick with beef and red wine (*carbonada* is the most common of these), and buttery **fontina** is the preferred cheese.

ESSENTIALS

GETTING THERE   By Plane   Domestic and international flights land at the **Caselle International Airport** (☎ 011-567-6361), 16km (9 miles) north of Turin. Buses run between the airport and the city's main bus terminal on Corso Inghilterra and Porto Nuova train station; the trip takes 30 minutes and costs 6,000L ($3).

By Train   Turin's main train station is **Stazione Porta Nuova,** just south of the center on Piazza Carlo Felice, which marks the intersection of Turin's two major thoroughfares, Corso Vittorio Emanuele and Via Roma. From this station, there are 18 trains a day to and from **Milan** (regional: 1 hr. 50 min., 14,500L/$7; High speed; 1 hr. 20 min., 21,600L/$11); 12 trains a day to and from **Venice** (two direct in 4½ hr., others via Milan in 5 hr.; 51,500L/$26); 16 trains a day to and from **Genoa** (regional: 1 hr. 40 min., 14,500L/$7.25; High speed: 1 hr. 50 min., 27,500L/$14); and 9 trains a day to and from **Rome** (5½–7 hr.; 75,200–91,700L/$37–$46). **Stazione di Porta Susa,** west of the center on Piazza XVIII Dicembre, connects Turin with many outlying Piemonte towns.

By Bus   Turin's main bus terminal is Autostazione Terminal Bus, Corso Inghilterra 3 (near Stazione di Porta Sousa) (☎ 011-433-2525). For regional bus and train info, call ☎ **800-990-097** or check on the Web at www.regione.piemonte.it/tplpiemonte. Buses connect Turin and Aosta (only 1 or 2 direct in 2 hr.; most change in Ivrea in 3 hr.; 12,500L/$6), and Milan (2 hr.; 17,200L/$9), and many smaller towns in Piemonte.

By Car   Turin is at the hub of an extensive network of autostradas. A4 connects Turin with Milan, a little over an hour away; A6 connects Turin with the Ligurian coast (and from there, with Genoa via A10, with a total travel time between the two cities of about 1½ hr.); A5 connects Turin with Aosta, about an hour away; and A21 connects Turin with Asti and Piacenza, where you can connect with the A1 for Florence (about 3½ hr. from Turin) and Rome (about 6½ hr. from Turin).

VISITOR INFORMATION   Tourist offices are at Piazza Castello 161 (☎ **011-535-181,** fax 011-530-070, www.turismotorino.org) and in the Porta Nuova train

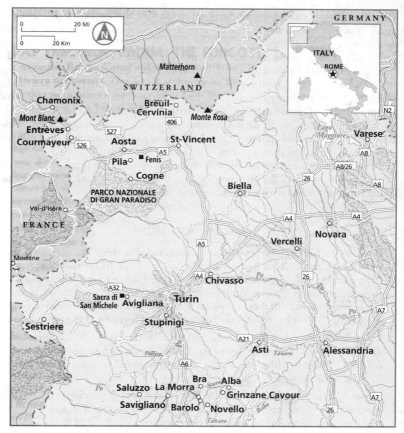

station (☎ **011-531-327**). Both are open Monday to Saturday 9:30am to 7pm and Sunday 9:30am to 3pm and will book rooms for you up to 48 hours in advance. There's also an office in the airport (☎ **011-567-8144**), open daily 8:30am to 11pm.

FESTIVALS & MARKETS Dance, opera, theater, and musical performances (mostly classical) are on the agenda in June and the first week of July, during the **Sere d'Estate** festival; companies come from around the world to perform. September is the month to enjoy more classical music—more than 60 classical concerts are held on stages around the city during the month-long **Settembre Musica** festival (☎ **011-442-4777**).

Bric-a-brac of all kinds, be it household utensils, books, or used clothing, fills the stalls of the **Mercato del Baton,** held every Saturday at Piazza della Republica. **Gran Baton** fills the piazza the second Sunday of every month and is a larger affair, with some genuine antiques and artworks included in the mix. **Mercato della Crocetta** at Largo Cassini sells clothing at very low prices. For a look at the bounty of the surrounding farmlands, wander through the extensive outdoor **food market at Porta Palazzo,** Monday to Saturday 6:30am to 1:30pm and Saturday 3:30 to 7:30pm.

CITY LAYOUT You will get a sense of Turin's refined air as soon as you step off the train into the mannerly 19th-century **Stazione Porta Nuova.** The stately arcaded **Via**

Roma, lined with shops and cafes, proceeds from the front of the station through a series of piazzas toward the **Piazza Castello** and the center of the city, about a 15-minute walk.

Directly in front of the station, the circular **Piazza Carlo Felice** is built around a garden surrounded by outdoor cafes that invite even business-minded Turinese to linger. A few steps farther along the street will lead you into the **Piazza San Carlo,** which is flanked by the twin churches of San Carlo and Santa Christina. At the end of Via Roma, the **Piazza Castello** is dominated by the Palazzo Madama, so named for its 17th-century inhabitant Marie-Christine. Just off the piazza is the Palazzo Reale, residence of the Savoys from 1646 to 1865, whose gardens now provide a pleasant respite from traffic and paving stones.

From here, a walk east toward the river along **Via Po** takes you through Turin's university district to one of Italy's largest squares, the much-elongated **Piazza Vittorio Veneto** and, at the end of this elegant expanse, the **Po River.**

Fast Facts: Turin

Bookstore **Libreria Internazionale Luxemborg,** between Piazza San Carlo and Piazza Castello at Via Accademia delle Scienze 3 (☎ **011-561-3896**), has a large selection of English-language books and a helpful staff; it is open Monday to Saturday 7am to 7:30pm. Turin has many stores specializing in rare books and old prints, and many of these shops sell their wares from the secondhand book-stalls along the Via Po, which runs between Piazza Castello and the river.

Consulates **British** subjects will find their consulate at Via Saluzzo 60 (☎ **011-650-9202**), open Monday and Thursday only 9am to noon; otherwise, call the consulate in Milan (see chapter 9). **Americans** will find their nearest consulate in Milan as well.

Crime Turin is a relatively safe city, but use the same precautions you would exercise in any large city. Specifically, avoid the riverside streets along the Po at night, when they tend to be deserted. In an emergency call ☎ **113.**

Drugstores A convenient late-night pharmacy is **Farmacia Boniscontro,** Corso Vittorio Emanuele 66 (☎ **011-541-271**); it's open most of the day and night, closing only between 12:30 and 3pm.

Emergencies The general emergency number is ☎ **113;** for an ambulance dial ☎ **118.**

Laundry **Speedy Wash,** east of the station at Via Principe Tommaso 12 (☎ **0338-589-8990**), charges 12,500L ($6.25) for a wash-and-dry (soap included) of a small load, and though it's technically do-it-yourself, the staff is always around to throw it into the dryer for you, provided you pick up your things by the end of the day. It's open daily 9am to 8:30pm, and offers do-it-yourself dry cleaning as well.

Post Office Turin's **main post office** is just west of Piazza San Carlo at Via Alfieri 10 (☎ **011-546-800**); it's open Monday to Friday 8:15am to 5:30pm and Saturday 8:15am to 1pm.

Taxis You can find taxis at cab stands; especially convenient in the central city are the stands in front of the train stations, around Piazza San Carlo and Piazza Castello. Dial ☎ **011-5737,** 011-5730, or 011-3399 for a radio taxi. The basic fare is 4,500L ($2.25) plus 1,200L (60¢) for each kilometer. There is a 4,000L ($2) night surcharge and a 2,000L ($1) surcharge on Sundays and holidays.

WHAT TO SEE & DO

The tourist office sells a **Torino Card** for 21,000L ($11), valid for one adult plus one child under 12, that grants you 48 hours of free public transport within Turin, discounts on concerts and the like, and that lets you pick two museums to enter for free, and with the rest you get a reduction (though no reduction is available at the most popular museums, including Palazzo Reale/Armeria Reale, Galleria Sabuada, and the Museo Egizio).

Cattedrale di San Giovanni. Piazza San Giovanni. ☎ **011-521-5960.** Free admission. Daily 8am–12:30pm and 3–7pm.

The controversial **Shroud of Turin (Santissima Sindone)** and the chapel in which it is sometimes enshrined, **Capella della Santa Sindone,** hold pride of place in this otherwise uninteresting, pompous 15th-century church. Even without the presence of one of Christendom's most precious relics (and it's only rarely on view in the silver casket elevated on an altar in the center of the room), the chapel is well worth a visit. Recently restored after a 1997 fire (one of many the shroud has miraculously survived, with an occasional singeing, over the centuries), the chapel is somberly clad in black marble. But, as if to suggest that better things await us in the heavens, it ascends to an airy, light-flooded six-tiered dome, one of the masterpieces of Italian baroque architecture.

The shroud, of course, is allegedly the one in which the body of Christ was wrapped when taken from the cross—and to which his image was miraculously affixed. The image is of a man 5 feet 7 inches tall, with bloodstains consistent with a crown of thorns, a cut in the ribcage, cuts in the wrists and ankles, and scourge marks on the back from flagellation. Recent carbon dating suggests that the shroud was manufactured sometime around the 13th or 14th centuries, but the mystery remains, at least in part, because no one can explain how the haunting image appeared on the cloth. Also, additional radio carbon dating has suggested that, since the shroud has been exposed to fire (thus affecting carbon readings), it could indeed date from around the time of the death of Christ. Despite scientific skepticism, the shroud continues to entice hordes of the faithful.

The shroud is usually tucked away out of sight at **Museo della Sindone (Holy Shroud Museum)** around the corner at Via San Domenico 28 (☎ **011-436-5832;** www.sindone.org), open daily 9am to noon and 3 to 7pm; admission 10,000L ($5) adults and 8,000L ($4) under 14 and over 65. The shroud was last on view during Italy's Jubilee celebrations in 2000. Technically, it shouldn't be on display again until the next Jubilee, in 25 years, but it tends to pop up every 5 to 15 years for special occasions (and rumor has it that it may go on permanent display, either in the cathedral or in its own space). Otherwise, you'll have to content yourself with a series of dramatically backlit photos of the relic near the entrance to the Capella della Santa Sindone.

In front of the cathedral stand two landmarks of Roman Turin—the remains of a **theater** and the **Porta Palatina,** flanked by twin 16-sided towers.

Mole Antonelliana & Museo Nazionale del Cinema (National Film Museum). Via Montebello 20. ☎ **011-812-5658.** Admission to museum 10,000L ($5); observation platform 6,000L ($3); both combined 13,000L ($6.50). Tues–Fri and Sun 9am–8pm, Sat to 11pm.

Turin's most peculiar building—in fact, one of the strangest structures anywhere—is comprised of a squat brick base, a steep conelike roof supporting several layers of Greek temples piled one atop the other, topped in turn by a needlelike spire, all of it rising 552 feet above the rooftops of the city center (a height that at one time made the Mole the world's tallest building). Begun in 1863 and designed as a synagogue, the Mole is now a monument to Italian unification and architectural hubris and, as of fall 2000, home to Italy's **National Film Museum.**

The museum's first section tracks the development of moving pictures from shadow puppets to kinescopes. The rest is more of a tribute to film than a true museum, offering clips and stills to illustrate some of the major aspects of movie production, from *Empire Strikes Back* storyboards to the creepy steadycam work in *The Shining*. Of memorabilia, masks from *Planet of the Apes, Satyricon,* and *Star Wars* hang together near *Lawrence of Arabia*'s robe, Chaplin's bowler, and *What Ever Happened to Baby Jane*'s dress. Curiously, most of the clips (all in Italian dubbed versions), as well as posters and other memorabilia, are heavily weighted toward American movies, with exceptions mainly for the major players of European/International cinema like Fellini, Bertolucci, Truffaut, and Wim Wenders.

Even if you skip the museum, you can still ascend to an **observation platform** at the top, an experience that affords two advantages—the view of Turin and the surrounding countryside, backed by the Alps, is stunning, and, as Guy de Maupassant once said of the Eiffel Tower, it's the only place in Turin where you won't have to look at the damned thing.

Museo dell Automobile (Automobile Museum). Corso Unita d'Italia 40. ☎ **011-677-666.** Admission 10,000L ($5) adults, 7,000L ($3.50) under 15 or over 65. Tues–Sun 10am–6:30pm.

As befits a city that is responsible for 80% of Italian car manufacturing, this shiny collection of mostly Italian automobiles, housed in a purpose-built, light-filled exhibition hall of classic 1960s design, draws car buffs from all over the world. Not too surprisingly, a century's worth of output from Fiat, which is headquartered in Turin, is well represented, and displays trace how the company influenced the 20th-century history of the city. The collection includes most of the cars that have done Italy proud over the years, including Lancias, Isotta Frashinis, and the Itala that came in first in the 1907 Peking-to-Paris rally. Oddities include a roadster, emblazoned with the initials ND, that Gloria Swanson drove for her role as faded movie queen Norma Desmond in *Sunset Boulevard.*

✪ **Museo Egizio & Galleria Sabauda.** Via Accademia delle Scienze 6. Museo Egizio: ☎ **011-561-7776;** www.multix.it/museoegizio_to. Admission 12,000L ($6) adults, free under 18 or over 60. Tues–Sat 8:30am–6:30pm (to 11pm Sat in summer), Sun 8:30am–7:30pm. Galleria Sabauda: ☎ 011-547-440. Admission 8,000L ($4) adults, 4,000L ($2) ages 18—25, free under 18 or over 65. Tues–Sun 8:30am–7:30pm (to 11pm Sat in summer). Cumulative ticket for both museums 15,000L ($8).

Turin's magnificent **Egyptian collection** is one of the world's largest. This was in fact the world's first Egyptian museum, thanks to the fact that the Savoys ardently amassed artifacts through most of their reign, and the museum continued to mount collecting expeditions throughout the early 20th century. Of the 30,000 pieces on display, some of the more captivating exhibits are in the first rooms you enter on the ground floor. These include the **Rock Temple of Ellessiya,** from the 15th century B.C., which the Egyptian government presented to the museum in gratitude for Italian efforts to save monuments threatened by the Aswan Dam. The two statuary rooms nearby are staggering in the size and drama of the objects they house, most notably two **sphinxes** and a massive, richly painted **statue of Ramses II.** Smaller objects—mummies, funerary objects, and a papyrus *Book of the Dead*—fill the galleries on the next floor; the most enchanting exhibit here is the everyday paraphernalia, including eating utensils and shriveled foodstuffs, from the tomb of the 14th-century-B.C. architect Khaie and his wife.

The Savoy's other treasure trove, a magnificent collection of **European paintings,** fills the salons of the Galleria Sabauda above the Egyptian collection. The Savoy's royal taste ran heavily to painters of the Flemish and Dutch schools, and the works by Van

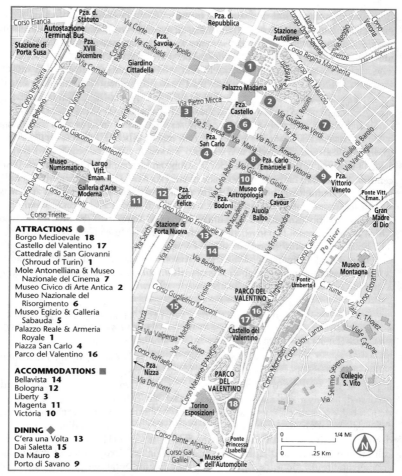

ATTRACTIONS ●

Borgo Medioevale **18**
Castello del Valentino **17**
Cattedrale di San Giovanni
(Shroud of Turin) **1**
Mole Antonelliana & Museo
Nazionale del Cinema **7**
Museo Civico di Arte Antica **2**
Museo Nazionale del
Risorgimento **6**
Museo Egizio & Galleria
Sabauda **5**
Palazzo Reale & Armeria
Royale **1**
Piazza San Carlo **4**
Parco del Valentino **16**

ACCOMMODATIONS ■

Bellavista **14**
Bologna **12**
Liberty **3**
Magenta **11**
Victoria **10**

DINING ◆

C'era una Volta **13**
Dai Saletta **15**
Da Mauro **8**
Porto di Savano **9**

Dyck, Van Eyck, Rembrandt, and Van der Weyden, among others, comprise one of Italy's largest collections of northern European paintings. In fact, two of Europe's most prized Flemish masterpieces are here, Jan van Eyck's **Stigmata of St. Francis** and Hans Memling's **Passion of Christ.** Italian artists, including those from the Piemonte, are also well represented; one of the first canvases you see upon entering the galleries is the work of a Tuscan, Fra' Angelico's sublime **Virgin and Child.**

Museo Nazionale del Risorgimento (National Museum of the Risorgimento). Via Accademia delle Scienze 5. ☎ **011-511-147.** Admission 8,000L ($4) adults, 5,000L ($2.50) ages 10–18, students under 25, seniors over 65. Tues–Sun 9am–7pm.

Much of modern Italian history has been played out in Turin and much of it, fittingly, in this palazzo that was home to the first king of a unified Italy, Vittorio Emanuele II, and the seat of its first parliament, in 1861. While any self-respecting town in Italy has a museum of the Risorgimento, the movement that launched Italian unification, this one is the best. Documents, paintings, and other paraphernalia recount the heady days when Vittorio Emanuele banded with Garibaldi and his Red Shirts to oust the

Bourbons from Sicily and the Austrians from the north to create a unified Italy. The plaques summing up each room are in English, and will finally reveal to you just who those people are after whom half the major streets and piazzas in Italy are named— including Mazzini, Vittorio Emanuele II, Massimo d'Azeglio, Cavour, and Garibaldi. The last rooms house a fascinating collection that chronicles Italian Fascism and the resistance against it, which evolved into the Partisan movement during World War II.

Museo Civico di Arte Antica (Civic Museum of Ancient Art). In the Palazzo Madama, Piazza Castello. ☎ **011-442-9911.** www.comune.torino.it/palazzomadama. *Note:* The museum is scheduled to reopen, at least partially, in spring 2001 after a decade-long restoration. Admission 8,000L ($4). Tues–Sat 9am–7pm and Sun 10am–1pm and 2–7pm. Check hours and prices with the tourist board.

Don't be misled by the baroque facade, added by architect Filippo Juvarra in the 18th century. If you walk around the exterior of the palazzo (named for its most popular resident, Madama Reale, aka Marie Christine of France), you'll discover that the massive structure incorporates a medieval castle, a Roman gate, and several Renaissance additions. Juvarra also added a monumental marble staircase to the interior, most of which is given over to the far-reaching collections of the Museo Civico di Arte Antica. The holdings focus on the medieval and Renaissance periods, shown off against the castle's unaltered, stony medieval interior. One of Italy's largest collections of ceramics is here, as well as some stunning canvases, including Anotello da Messina's *Portrait of a Man.*

Palazzo Reale (Royal Palace) & Armeria Royale (Royal Armory). Piazza Castello (Armeria entrance at no. 191). Palazzo: ☎ **011-436-1455.** Admission 8,000L ($4). Tues–Sun 8:30am–7:30pm (to 11pm Sat in summer). Armeria: ☎ **011-543-889.** Admission 8,000l ($4). Tues–Sun 8:30am–7:30pm.

The residence of the House of Savoy, begun in 1645 and designed by the Francophile count of Castellamonte, reflects the ornately baroque tastes of European ruling families of the time—a fact that will not be lost on you as you pass from one opulently decorated, heavily gilded room to the next. (The Savoys had a keener eye for painting than for decor, and most of the canvases they collected are in the nearby Galleria Sabauda). What's most notable here are some of the tapestries, including the Gobelins depicting the life of Don Quixote, in the Sala delle Virtu (Hall of Virtues), and the collection of Chinese and Japanese vases in the Sala dell'Alcova. One of the quirkier architectural innovations, an antidote to several monumental staircases, is a manually driven elevator from the 18th century.

One wing houses the **Armeria Reale,** one of the most important arms and armor collections in Europe, especially of weapons from the 16th and 17th centuries. Behind the palace, and offering a refreshing change from its frippery, are the **Giardini Reali (Royal Gardens),** laid out by Le Nôtre, more famous for the Tuileries and the gardens at Versailles.

PARKS & PIAZZAS

Piazza San Carlo, Turin's most beautiful square, is the city's outdoor living room, surrounded by arcaded sidewalks that house the terraces of the cafes for which Turin is famous (see below). In the center is an equestrian statue of Duke Emanuele Filiberto of Savoy, and facing each other at the northern end of the piazza are a pair of 17th-century churches, San Carlo and Santa Cristina. The overall effect is one of elegant harmony.

The **Parco del Valentino** (☎ **011-669-9372**), a lush sweep of greenery along the Po south of Corso Vittorio Emanuele II, provides a wonderful retreat from Turin's well-mannered streets and piazzas. It is open daily 8am to 8pm. Aside from riverfront promenades and extensive lawns and gardens, inside the park, there's a collection of enchanting buildings. The **Borgo Medioevale** (☎ 011-443-1701), built for Turin's 1884 world exposition, is a faithful reconstruction of a medieval village based on those in rural Piemonte and the Val d'Aosta, with shops, taverns, houses, churches, and even a castle—but since Italy is home to literally thousands of bona-fide medieval villages, it's hard to imagine a good reason to pony up 5,000L/$2.50 admission for a look; it's open daily 9am to 8pm.

The nearby **Castello del Valentino** is the real thing—a royal residence, begun in the 16th century but completed in the 17th century for Turin's beloved Marie Christine ("Madama Reale," wife of Savoy king Vittorio Amedeo) as a summer residence. It's a sign of Madama's Francophile leanings that, with its sloping roofs and forecourt, the castle resembles a French château. Since used as a school of veterinary medicine and a military barracks and currently as a university facility, the castello is continually undergoing renovations and much of it, including many frescoed salons, is open to the public only on special occasions.

NEARBY ATTRACTIONS

Basilica di Superga. About 4 mi. northeast of the town center in Parco Naturale della Collina di Superga. ☎ **011-898-0083.** Free admission. Apr–Sept daily 9:30am–noon and 3–6pm, Oct–Mar 10am–noon and 3–5pm. Reached by rack railway (4,000L/$2), with a terminus at Stazione Sassi on Piazza Gustavo Modena (follow Corso Casale on east side of the River Po). Tram: 15 from Via XX Settembre to Stazione Sassi.

As thanksgiving to the Virgin Mary for Turin's deliverance from the French siege of 1706, Vittorio Amadeo II commissioned Juvarra, the Sicilian architect who did his greatest work in Turin, to build this baroque basilica on a hill high above the city. The exterior, with a beautiful neoclassic porch and lofty drum dome, is far more interesting than the gloomy interior, a vast circular chamber beneath the dome with six side chapels. The church more or less serves as a pantheon for the House of Savoy, whose tombs are scattered about, many in the so-called **Crypt of Kings** beneath the main chapel. There's a fine view of the Alps from the terrace in front. The trip up to the basilica on a narrow railway through verdant parkland is a favorite Turinese outing.

Palazzina di Caccia di Stupinigi. Stupingi, 8.5km (5 mi.) southwest of the city center. ☎ **011-358-1220.** Admission 10,000L ($5) adults, 8,000L ($4) ages 6–14, 5,000L ($2.50) over 65; 23,000L ($11.50) family ticket with 1 child under 18, 30,000L ($15) family ticket with 2 children. Tues–Sun 10am–6pm (to 5pm late Oct–late Mar). Bus: 63 from Porta Nouva train station to Piazza Caio Mario; change to bus 41.

The other great work of the architect Juvarra (see the Basilica di Superga, above) is this sumptuous, lavishly decorated hunting lodge that the Savoys commissioned in 1729. The main part of the lodge, to which the members of the House of Savoy retired for hunts in the royal forests that still surround it, is shaped like a Saint Andrew's cross (the lower arms extended and curved back inwards like giant pincers), fanning out from a circular, domed pavilion topped with a large bronze stag. The lavish interior is filled with furniture, paintings, and bric-a-brac assembled from the many Savoy residences, technically comprising a **Museo d'Arte e Ammobiliamento (Museum of Art and Furniture).** Stroll through the acres of excessively decorated apartments to understand why Napoléon chose this for his brief residency in the region. Outstanding among the many, many frescoes are the scenes of a deer hunt in the King's Apartment and the *Triumph of Diana* in the grand salon. The elegant gardens and surrounding forests provide lovely terrain for a jaunt.

AFFORDABLE PLACES TO STAY

Unlike the areas around train stations in most large cities, the **Porta Nuova** neighborhood is semi-stylish and perfectly safe, and many of the city's hotels are here, just a 10-minute stroll from the center.

Bellavista. Via B. Galliari 15 (between Via Sant'Anselmo and Via Principe Tommaso), 10125 Turin. ☎ **011-669-8139.** Fax 011-668-7989. 16 units, 9 with bathroom. TV TEL. 60,000L ($30) single without bathroom, 75,000L ($38) single with bathroom; 90,000L ($45) double without bathroom, 110,000L ($55) double with bathroom; 140,000L ($70) triple with bathroom. Breakfast 8,000L ($4). No credit cards.

The neighborhood between the Porta Nuova railway station and Parco del Valentino is a pleasant enough residential area, and this pensione occupies the sixth floor of an apartment house on a quiet street. What is likely to strike you immediately is just how pleasant the surroundings are—step off the elevator and you will find yourself in a sun-filled corridor that's a garden of houseplants and opens onto a long terrace. Rooms are airy and comfortable but a little less inspiring in decor, with banal, functional modern furnishings and squishy beds. Most, though, afford pleasant views over the surrounding rooftops, some from terraces—the best outlooks in the house are across the river toward the hills. What most rooms don't have is a private bath, though the two communal ones are nice enough.

Bologna. Corso Vittorio Emanuele II 60 (at Via XX Settembre), 10121 Turin. ☎ **011-562-0290.** Fax 011-562-0193. 46 units. TV TEL. 95,000L ($47.50) single; 140,000L ($70) double; 170,000L ($85) triple. Rates include continental breakfast. AE, DC, MC, V.

This family-run hotel just across the street from the Porta Nuova train station offers location, affordable comfort, and a very attentive, English-speaking staff. Each of the rooms, spread over several floors of a gracious 18th-century apartment house, is different. Some are quite grand, incorporating frescoes, fireplaces, and other original details (of these, nos. 52, 64, and 68 are the largest and most elegant). Some rooms were very nicely renovated in 2000, with polished wood floors, spreads and drapes in matching patterns but contrasting colors, and large baths with double-sized stall showers. Others were revamped some 10 years ago, but their sleek modern style, laminated built-in cabinetry, and neutral carpeting have aged well—and a few of the baths even have Jacuzzis. Whatever the vintage, all the rooms are spotlessly clean and nicely maintained.

Liberty. Via P. Micca 15 (between Via Mercanti and Via San Francesco d'Assisi), 10121 Turin. ☎ **011-562-8801.** Fax 011-562-8163. E-mail: hotelliberty@tiscalinet.it. 35 units. TV TEL. 170,000L ($85) single; 230,000L ($115) double; 270,000L ($135) triple. Rates include continental breakfast. AE, DC, MC, V. Parking 25,000L ($13) in a few spots in courtyard (ask when booking) or 28,000L ($14) in nearby garage.

An excellent location a few blocks southeast of Piazza Castello puts the Liberty within easy walking distance of most of Turin's museums, other monuments and shops, and restaurants. What's most remarkable about this hotel, though, is its ambience. It occupies an early 20th-century mansion built in the Italian Liberty (art deco) style. Many of the original features, such as ornately carved doorway cornices and etched windows, remain, and the public rooms (there's a small bar, a restaurant, and sitting rooms off the lobby) retain a great deal of grandeur with early 1900s furnishings and polished parquet floors. The guest rooms are large and nonfussily stylish, with some period pieces augmented by comfortable newer furnishings, including firm beds. The smallish baths have been nicely brought up to date. These surroundings seem all the more pleasant with the attentive presence of the Anfossi family, who have run this charming hotel for decades and who head up a consortium of small family-run hotels in Italy.

Magenta. Corso Vittorio Emanuele II 67 (between Via Gioberti and Via Massena), 10121 Turin. ☎ **011-542-649.** Fax 011-544-755. 17 units, 9 with bathroom. TEL TV. 70,000L ($35) single without bathroom, 90,000L ($45) single with bathroom; 80,000L ($40) double without bathroom, 120,000L ($60) double with bathroom; 100,000L ($50) triple without bathroom, 150,000L ($75) triple with bathroom; 160,000L ($80) quad without bathroom but with shower; 200,000L ($100) quad without bathroom but with shower. Breakfast 10,000L ($5). AE, DC, MC, V.

This is one of the least expensive of the station-area hotels, located just west of the station along one of the arcaded sidewalks that follows busy Corso Vittorio Emanuele. The Magenta is not quite as nice as its across-the-street neighbor the Bologna (see above), but many of the original design features offer evidence that this pleasant pensione, occupying a wing of the second floor of an apartment house, has seen grander days. Ornate moldings and polished parquet floors and crystal chandeliers grace a long central hallway furnished with upholstered easy chairs. With standard-issue hotel furnishings, the guest rooms are rather less opulent but are spacious and high-ceilinged nonetheless, with orthopedic beds; some even have new baths (which can be quite cramped). In the morning, enjoy an espresso and pastry at the little bar in the lobby.

WORTH A SPLURGE

Victoria. Via Nino Costa 4 (a tiny street, unlabeled on most maps, off Via Giuseppe Pomba between Via Giolitti and Via Cavour), 10123 Turin. ☎ **011-561-1909.** Fax 011-561-1806. www.hotelvictoria-torino.com. E-mail: reservation@hotelvictoria-torino.com. 96 units. MINI-BAR TV TEL. 180,000L ($90) single, 220,000L ($110) deluxe single; 260,000L ($130) double, 290,000L ($145) deluxe double. Rates include breakfast. AE, DC, MC, V.

Step through the doors of this somewhat plain-looking building between Via Roma and the river and you'll think you're in an English country house. The lobby is decorated as a drawing room, with floral sofas, deep armchairs, and a view onto a garden; it doubles as a bar. A sumptuous buffet is served in the glass-enclosed breakfast room. The rooms are classified as deluxe or standard (about half of each), depending on size and decor. Standard rooms are on the small side but handsomely furnished in a chic style that marries contemporary and traditional, with some mahogany bedsteads and writing desks. Deluxe rooms, each with its own distinctive look, are oversize and contain carefully chosen antiques and classy wood furnishings, with such flourishes as richly covered divans or canopied beds; plus they have air-conditioning. All have sleek baths with hair dryers. By mid-2001, more than a dozen deluxe rooms will have been added in a new wing, and ongoing renovations over the next few years will turn some standards into deluxe rooms.

GREAT DEALS ON DINING

Da Mauro. Via Maria Vittoria 21 (between Via Bogino and Via San Francesco da Paola). ☎ **011-817-0604.** Primi 10,000–12,000L ($5–$6); secondi 10,000–18,000L ($5–$9). No credit cards. Tues–Sun noon–2:30pm and 7:30–10pm. Closed July. ITALIAN/TUSCAN.

These simple tile-floored rooms are more relaxed than many Turinese restaurants, and if the informal ambience and the menu remind you of regions farther south, your instincts are right. The family that owns and runs the restaurant emphasizes Tuscan dishes, though the range seems to run the gamut of Italian cooking. The menu has any number of spicy pasta dishes, including a deftly prepared cannelloni, and the meat courses are indeed similar to those you would find in Tuscany—steak, lamb, sausages, and game birds are simply grilled or roasted.

Dai Saletta. Via Belfiore 37 (just south of Via Oddino Morgari). ☎ **011-668-7867.** Primi 13,000L ($6.50); secondi 15,000L ($7.50). AE, DC, MC, V. Mon–Fri 12:30–2pm and 8pm–midnight, Sat 8pm–midnight. Closed Aug. PIEMONTESE.

One of the few kitchens in Turin that remains open into the wee hours turns out a nice selection of homey trattoria fare, served in a tiny, cramped dining room several long blocks south of the train station. Homemade pasta dishes are delicious; try the hearty *tortelloni alla salsiccia* (a large pasta shell stuffed with sausage) or *peposelle* (a thick pasta tossed with Gorgonzola and walnuts) as an appetizer or a main course. For those who want to venture on, the kitchen offers such traditional favorites as tripe.

Porto di Savano. Piazza Vittorio Veneto 2. ☎ **011-817-3500.** www.portodisavona.com. Primi 10,000–15,000L ($5–$8); secondi 10,000–26,000L ($5–$13); fixed-price *"monopiatti"* 15,000–20,000L ($8–$10) with wine. MC, V. Tues 7:30–10:30pm, Wed–Sun 12:30–2:30pm and 7:30–10:30pm. Closed Aug 15–31. PIEMONTESE.

What is probably the most popular trattoria in Turin is tucked under the arcades along the city's largest piazza. Seating is family style, at long tables that crowd a series of rooms beneath old photos and mementos, and the typically Piemontese fare never fails to please (all the more so on Sunday, when many other restaurants in central Turin are closed). Several variations of gnocchi are usually made fresh daily, as is the Piemontese flat noodle, *tajarin*, and *agnolotti al sugo d'arrosto* (cheese-stuffed pasta in a roast pork ragu). Another way to start a meal is with a *risotto ai porcini*. Follow these primi with one of the grilled meat (or trout or salmon) dishes, which are the house specialties. At lunch, you can order a *monopiatto:* one course with dessert, coffee, and wine or water.

WORTH A SPLURGE

C'era una Volta. Corso Vittorio Emanuele II 41 (between Via Goito and Via Sant'Anselmo). ☎ **011-650-4589.** Reservations recommended. Primi 12,000–16,000L ($6–$8); secondi 18,000–25,000L ($9–$13); tasting menu 45,000L ($23) without wine. AE, DC, MC, V. Mon–Sat 8–10:30pm. Closed Sun and Aug. TURINESE.

To enter Once Upon a Time, you must ring a bell at street level, then climb the stairs or take the elevator to an old-fashioned large dining room filled with heavy tables and chairs and dark credenzas. The food, delivered by a highly professional wait staff that has been here for years, is authentically Turinese and never seems to stop coming. A typical menu, which changes daily, might include crepes with ham and cheese, risotto with artichokes, *plin alla Piemontese* (tiny meat-filled ravioli in gravy), a carrot flan, rabbit stew, a slice of beef with polenta, pork chops with pomegranate, and any number of other wonderfully prepared dishes.

CAFES & DELICACY SHOPS

Cafe sitting is a centuries-old tradition in sophisticated Turin. **Via Roma** and the piazzas it widens into are lined with gracious salons that have been serving coffee to Turinese for decades, even centuries. Below are some of the city's classic cafes. While espresso and pastries are the mainstays of the menu at all of them, most also serve chocolates—including the mix of chocolate and hazelnuts known as *gianduiotti*— that are among the city's major contributions to culinary culture. Turin has a sizable sweet tooth, satisfied by any number of pastry and candy shops. Perhaps the best chocolatier north of Perugia is **Pfatisch/Peyrano,** Corso Vittorio Emanuele II 76 (☎ **011-538-765**), open Monday to Saturday 9am to 12:45pm and 4 to 7:30pm and Sunday 9am to 1pm. A wide variety of chocolates and other sweets, including sumptuous meringues, have been dispensed since 1836 at **Fratelli Stratta,** Piazza San Carlo 191 (☎ **011-547-920**), open Tuesday to Sunday 9:30am to 1pm and 3 to 7:30pm and Monday 3 to 7:30pm.

The surrounding region is known not only for its wines but also for **vermouth**—the famed Cinzano, for instance, is produced south of the city in the town of Santa Vittoria d'Alba. Come evening, a glass of vermouth is the preferred drink at many of the city's cafes. **Paissa,** at Piazza San Carlo 196 (☎ **011-562-8462**), open Monday to Saturday 9am to 1pm and 3:30 to 7:30pm (closed Wednesday afternoons), is an excellent place to purchase local vermouths by the bottle.

Caffè Confetteria al Bicerin. Piazza della Consolata 5. ☎ **011-518-794.** Mon–Tues and Thurs–Fri 8:30am–9:30pm, Sat–Sun 8:30am–12:30pm and 3:30–7:30pm. AE, DC, MC, V. CAFE.

What claims to be Turin's oldest cafe in continuous operation (since 1763) is famous for its illustrious clientele, which has included Nietszche, Dumas, and Puccini, as well as its signature drink—the Bicerin (local dialect for "something delicious"). It's a heady combination of coffee, hot chocolate, and cream—to be accompanied by one the house's exquisite pastries.

Caffè-Pasticceria Baratti e Milano. Piazza Castello 27. ☎ **011-561-3060.** Tues–Sun 8am–1am. CAFE.

No small part of the pleasure of sitting for a time in this stylish cafe, opened in 1875, is watching a clientele that includes auto executives, students from the nearby university, elegantly clad shoppers, and visitors to the nearby museums, all sipping espressos and munching on the delicious house pastries.

Caffè San Carlo. Piazza San Carlo 156. ☎ **011-532-586.** Tues–Sun 7am–1am, Mon 7am–8pm. CAFE.

One of the essential stops on any tour of Turin is this classic cafe. The San Carlo opened its doors in 1837 and ever since has been accommodating patrons beneath a huge chandelier of Murano glass in a salon that's a remarkable assemblage of gilt, mirrors, and marble. An adjoining, frescoed tearoom is quieter and only a little less grand.

TURIN AFTER DARK

Turin has a lively classical-music and opera scene, and you can get info on these and other cultural events at the **Vetrina Infocultura** office at Piazza San Carlo 159 (☎ **800-015-475**), open Monday to Saturday 11am to 7pm. Aside from the city's much attended summer festivals (see "Festivals & Markets," above), there are regular classical concerts at **Auditorium della RAI,** Via Rossini 15 (☎ **011-810-4653**). Other concerts, dance performances, and operas are staged at the city's venerable **Teatro Regio** (☎ **011-881-5241;** www.teatroregio.torino.it), in the center of the city on Piazza Castello.

A DAY TRIP FROM TURIN

Sacra di San Michele. Outside Aviglina, 15km west of Turin's ring road. ☎ **011-939-130.** www.sacradisanmichele.com. Admission 5,000L ($2.50) adults, 3,000L ($1.50) ages 6–14 and over 65 (Sun afternoon it's 7,000L/$3.50 adults, 4,000L/$2 youths and seniors, because they give tours leaving every 20 min. that cover even more of the complex). Mar 16–Oct 15 Tues–Sat 9am–12:30pm and 3–6pm, Sun 9:30am–noon and 2:40–6pm; Oct 16–Mar 17 closes 5pm.

Perched high atop Monte Pirchiriano—part of it projecting over the precipice on an elaborate support system that was one of the engineering feats of the Middle Ages—this dramatically situated abbey dedicated to St. Michael provides views and an astonishing look at medieval religious life. It may well remind you of Mont-St-Michel in France (both are laced with endless flights of stairs) or, with its dizzying views and scary drops, of the abbey in the novel and film *The Name of the Rose* (probably because author Umberto Eco based his fictional abbey on this one). (Actually, Mont-St-Michel was one of the 176 religious institutions that once fell under the jurisdiction of San Michele.) It was started in 983, but the extant church dates to the abbey's 12th-century heyday. A vast staircase hewn out of rock and clinging to the abbey's buttresses (known as Scalone dei Morti, Stairs of Death, because corpses were once laid out here) leads to the massive carved doorway depicting the signs of the zodiac and the drafty Gothic and Romanesque church, decorated only with scraps of 16th-century frescoes by Secondo del Bosco. Another stairway leads down to three tiny chapels carved into the rock and containing tombs of some of the earliest members of the House of Savoy.

On Saturday evenings (and some Fridays) from April to July and August to September, the atmospheric church hosts free concerts of everything from chant and liturgical music to Renaissance chamber pieces, gospel, and traditional Celtic airs; check the Web site for schedules.

GETTING THERE   Take one of 15 trains a day from Turin to Sant'Ambrogio Torinese (30 min.; 3,600L/$1.80); from there, it's a stiff 1½ hour trek up to the abbey. In summer only, call ahead to see about the once-daily bus that in past years has met trains from Torino at the Avigliana station (usually around 9am) to carry pilgrims up here. By car, follow the A32 from Turin's western ring highway toward Bardonecchia/Frejus. Get off at the Avigliana exit and follow brown signs to the Sacra; the trip takes about an hour.

2 The Piemonte Wine Country

Asti is 60km (36 mi.) SE of Turin, 127km (78 mi.) SW of Milan; Alba is 60km (32 mi.) S of Turin, 155km (95 mi.) SW of Milan.

South of Turin, the **Po Valley** rises into the rolling Langhe and Roero hills, flanked by orchards and vineyards. You'll recognize the region's place names from the labels of its excellent wines, among them Asti Spumanti, Barbaresco, and Barolo. Tasting these vintages at their source is one reason to visit the wine country, of course; another is to stroll through the medieval and Renaissance towns that rise from the vineyards and the picturesque villages that crown many a hilltop. Vines are not all that flourish in the fertile soil—truffles top the list of the region's gastronomic delights, which also include down-home country fare like rabbit and game dishes, excellent cheeses, and plump fruit.

ASTI

The **Asti** of sparkling-wine fame is a bustling city more concerned with everyday business than entertaining visitors, but many treasures can be found in the history-drenched old town—medieval towers (120 of them still stand), Renaissance palaces, and broad piazzas provide the perfect setting in which to sample the town's famous product.

ESSENTIALS

GETTING THERE   By Train   One to four trains an hour link Asti with **Turin** (30–60 min.; 6,000–9,400L/$3–$4.70). There are six trains daily between Asti and Alba, but you must change at Nizza Monferrato and occasionally also at Castagnole delle Lanze (1 hr. 15 min. to 2 hr.; 6,800L/$3.40).

By Bus   From Turin, Arfea (☎ **0144-322-023** or 0131-445-433) runs two buses per day, one morning and one mid-afternoon, on the hour-long ride to Asti (7,400L/$3.70). Giachino (☎ **0141-937-510**) makes the hour trip to and from Alba (5,300L/$2.65), about once per hour.

Horses & Donkeys

Asti and Alba, bitter rivals through much of the Middle Ages, each celebrate the autumnal harvest with equine celebrations that are horses of very different colors.

The **Palio,** Asti's annual horse race, is run the third Sunday of September. Like the similar but more famous horse race that the Tuscan city of Siena mounts, Asti's palio begins with a medieval pageant through the town and ends with a wild bareback ride around the Campo del Palio. The race coincides with Asti's other great revel, the **Douja d'Or,** a weeklong fair-cum-bacchanal celebrating the grape.

On the first Sunday of October, Alba pulls a spoof on Asti with the **Palio degli Asini (Race of the Asses).** The event, which coincides with Alba's annual truffle fair, is not as speedy as Asti's slicker, horseback palio, but it's a lot more fun. Good-natured as the event is, though, it is rooted in some of the darkest days of Alba's history. In the 13th century Asti, then one of the most powerful republics of Northern Italy, besieged Alba and burned the surrounding vineyards. Then, to add insult to injury, the victors held their palio in Alba, just to put the humbled citizenry further in its place. Alba then staged a palio with asses, a not-so-subtle hint of what they thought of their victors and their pompous pageantry.

By Car Asti, 73km (44 mi.) east of Turin, can be reached from Turin in less than an hour via the A21 autostrada.

VISITOR INFORMATION The **APT tourist office** is near the train station at Piazza Alfieri 34 (☎ **0141-530-357;** fax 0141-538-200; www.axt.it/atl and www.terredasti.it). March to October, hours are Monday to Saturday 9am to 7pm and Sunday 10am to 1pm; November to February, hours are Monday to Saturday 9am to 1pm and 2:30 to 6:30pm and Sunday 10am to 1pm. Among the office's offerings is a **Carta Terre e Vini d'Asti,** an annotated map that will point you to surrounding vineyards that offer wine tastings.

FESTIVALS & MARKETS In late June and early July, Asti stages **Asti Teatro,** a theater festival with performances that incorporate dance and music as well. September, though, is the town's busy cultural month, with townsfolk and horses alike donning medieval garb for its famous **Palio** on the third Sunday (see "Horses & Donkeys," above). Local wine producers converge on the town the week or so before the Palio for the **Douja d'Or,** an exhibition of local vintages accompanied by tastings (from 4,000L/$2); this is an excellent way to sample the products of the many wineries in the hills surrounding Asti and nearby Alba. On the second Sunday of September, surrounding villages mount feasts (almost always accompanied by a communal meal) known collectively as the **Pjasan.**

Agricultural center that it is, Asti has two **food markets.** The largest is held Wednesdays and Saturdays 7:30am to 1pm in the **Campo del Palio,** with stalls selling every foodstuff imaginable—seeds, herbs, flowers, farm implements, and no end of other merchandise spilling over to two adjoining piazzas, the Piazza della Liberta and Piazza Alfieri. Meanwhile, Asti's covered food market, the **Mercato Coperto,** is also located in this vicinity, on Piazza della Liberta, and is open Monday to Wednesday and Friday 8am to 1pm and 3:30 to 7:30pm, Thursday 8:30am to 1pm, and Saturday 8am to 7:30pm.

EXPLORING THE TOWN

If you take the train to Asti, you will step right into the heart of the action—the town's lively clothing-and-food **markets** occupy three adjoining piazzas just to the north of the station (Campo del Palio, Piazza Liberta, and **Piazza Alferi**). If you're driving into Asti, you're most likely to find parking in one of the lots in this area as well.

Walk through the piazzas to **Corso Alfieri;** the town's Renaissance palaces are located on or just off this major thoroughfare, usually closed to traffic. This street and Asti's grandest piazza are named for the town's most famous native son, the 18th-century poet Vittorio Alfieri. His home, on the Corso at 375, houses a small, memento-filled museum.

Second to none in Asti is San Secondo, the town's patron saint. He was imprisoned at the western end of Corso Alfieri in the **Torre Rossa**—much of which dates to the 1st century (probably part of a Roman gate) with two levels tacked on in the 11th century—then beheaded on the spot just south of Corso Alfieri where the church erected in his honor, the **Collegiata di San Secondo** (☎ 0141-530-066), now stands. Not only does this Romanesque-Gothic structure have the honor of housing the saint's remains in its eerie crypt, but it is also the permanent home of the coveted Palio Astigiano, the banner awarded to the horseman who wins the town's annual Palio (see "Horses & Donkeys," above; Secondo is the patron saint of this event). The church is open daily 10:45am to noon and 3:30 to 5:30pm (Sunday morning for mass only).

Asti's "other" church is its 14th-century, redbrick **Cattedrale** (☎ 0141-592-924), which you can reach by walking through Piazza Cairoli, at the western end of Corso Alfieri, into the nearby Piazza Cattedrale. Every inch of this brick church's cavernous interior is festooned with frescoes by late 18th-century artists, including Gandolfino d'Asti; trompe l'oeil vines climb many of the columns. The cathedral is open daily 8:30am to noon and 3 to 5:30pm.

The most notable feature of the church of **San Pietro in Consavia** (☎ 0141-353-072), at the eastern end of Corso Alfieri, is its 10th-century round baptistry; the 15th-century interior and adjoining cloisters house a one-room paleontology collection (open Tuesday to Sunday 10am to 12:30pm and 3 to 7pm).

AN AFFORDABLE PLACE TO STAY

Rainero. Via Cavour 85. ☎ **0141-353-866.** Fax 0141-594-985. 55 units A/C MINIBAR TEL TV. 95,000L ($47.50) single; 160,000L ($80) double. Added bed 35% more. Breakfast: continental 4,000L ($2), buffet 15,000L ($8). AE, DC, MC, V. Parking 15,000L ($8) in garage. Closed first week of Jan.

Occupying a centuries-old house, the Raneiro enjoys a wonderful location near the Campo del Palio and San Secondo. Not only is this setting convenient, but, since many of the surrounding streets are closed to traffic, the neighborhood is quiet. Rooms 301 to 303 have terraces (views of surrounding modern buildings), and 153 and 155 have balconies looking onto a cobbled street; there's also a large roof terrace. Despite the provenance of the structure, renovations are tasteful but lean toward a clean modern look. As result, the rooms are perfectly comfortable though a little bland. The modular furnishings vary and seem to represent each decade since the 1960s; the best have bent-tube bedsteads and granite-topped sinks with brass-plated fixtures. Rooms 157 and 158 (which families can connect) open off a hanging walkway over a pretty pair of tiny courtyards and red-tile roofs; 158 is large enough to be a quad and has a table and chairs on the walkway out front. Large room 161 gets one of those plant-filled courtyards all to itself.

GREAT DEALS ON DINING

✪ **Il Convivio.** Via G. B. Giuliani 4–6. ☎ **0141-594-188.** Reservations recommended. Primi 9,000–11,000L ($4.50–$5.50); secondi 14,000–16,000L ($7–$8). AE, DC, MC, V. Mon–Sat, 12:15–2:15pm and 8–10pm. PIEMONTESE.

The decor of this double-height pastel-colored dining room is straightforward, with a clean contemporary look. These no-nonsense surroundings reflect the fact that the main business here is to serve excellently prepared food and accompany it with the region's best, but not necessarily most expensive, wines (dispensed from an extensive cave you're welcome to visit, and you can also buy wine by the bottle or case on the premises). Only a few starters, pasta dishes, and main courses are prepared daily. They always include some wonderful fresh-made pastas, such as the lightest gnocchi in a sweet pepper sauce, a soup incorporating vegetables bought that morning from Asti's markets, and some serious meat dishes, such as a masterful *ossobucco di vitello* or *coniglio,* a rabbit that here is often sautéed with olives and white wine. Desserts, including a heavenly *panna cotta al cioccolato,* are as memorable as the rest of the dining experience.

L'Altra Campana. Via Q. Sella 2. ☎ **0141-437-083.** Reservations recommended. Primi 12,000–15,000L ($6–$8); secondi 16,000–20,000L ($8–$10). AE, MC, V. Wed–Mon noon–2pm and 7:30–10pm. PIEMONTESE.

As you pass through the large gate into the paved stone courtyard backed by this little building, you'll feel as if you've arrived at a country inn from a forgotten age—which, actually, it once was. The Natta family's medieval palazzo stood at the city walls and was used as a prison from the 16th century through 1777, at which point it was converted into La Campana Inn. Only the restaurant part of the inn is still in operation and continues to offer fantastic Piemontese food. The menu changes so frequently it's recited rather than printed up. Some delicious local dishes may include *agnolotti* in *ragu, taglierini* with truffles, *cinghiale* (stewed wild boar), *stracotta alla Barbera* (strip beef cooked in red wine), or *coniglio al vino bianco* (rabbit cooked in white wine). The wine list is extensive and well-priced, and the only real detraction here is an often-curt wait staff.

ALBA

Lovely old **Alba** retains a medieval flavor that's as mellow as the wines it produces. It's a pleasure to walk along the Via Vittorio Emanuele and the narrow streets of the Old Town, visit the 14th-century duomo, and peer into shop windows with lavish displays of Alba's wines, its other famous product, truffles, and its less noble but enticing *nocciola,* a decadent concoction of nuts and chocolate.

ESSENTIALS

GETTING THERE   By Train   Only one direct train (in the evening, after 6pm) runs between Turin and Alba (1 hr.; 6,800L/$3.40); otherwise, there's one per hour requiring a change either in Bra or Cavallarmaggiore (80–90 min.; 6,800–7,600L/ $3.40–$3.80). There are six trains daily between Alba and Asti, but you must change at Nizza Monferrato and occasionally also at Castagnole delle Lanze (1 hr. 15 min. to 2 hr.; 6,800L/$3.40).

By Bus   Alba's Autostazione bus terminal (☎ **0173-362-949**) is on Piazza Medford. Hourly Satti (☎ **800-217-216**) buses make the trip between Alba and Turin in about 1½ hours (4,800L/$2.40).

Giachino (☎ **0141-937-510**) makes the hour trip to and from Asti (5,300L/ $2.65), about once per hour.

By Car The most direct way to reach Alba from Turin is to follow A6 for 35km (21 mi.) south to the exit near Brà, and from the autostrada exit S231 east for 24km (14½ mi.) to Alba. If you want to work Alba into a trip to Asti, take A21 to Asti and from there follow S 231 southwest for 30km (18 mi.) to Alba.

VISITOR INFORMATION Alba has two **tourist offices.** The downtown branch is halfway along Corso Vittorio Emanuele at no. 19 (☎/fax **0173-362-562;** www.comune.alba.cn.it), open daily 9am to 1pm and 2 to 6pm (may close Sundays in winter). A **regional info office** is at Piazza Medford 3, across from the bus station (☎ **0173-35-833,** fax 0173-363-878; www.langheroero.it), open Monday to Friday 9am to 12:30pm and 2:30 to 6:30pm and Saturday 9am to 12:30pm (afternoons too in October).

FESTIVALS & MARKETS October is Alba's big month. Its annual **truffle festival** is held the first week, and this in turn climaxes in the **Palio degli Asini (Race of the Asses),** a humble version of neighboring Asti's equine palio (see "Donkeys & Horses," above). On Saturday and Sunday mornings from the second weekend in October through December, Alba hosts a **truffle market** where you may well be tempted to part with your hard-earned cash for one of the fragrant specimens (which could cost as much as $1,000 a pound).

EXPLORING THE TOWN

Alba's two major sights face the brick expanse of **Piazza Risogimento,** at the northern end of its major thoroughfare, **Corso Vittorio Emanuele.** The 14th-century brick **Duomo** is flanked by a 13th-century bell tower. Most of the interior and paintings hail from the late 19th century, save the two late baroque lateral chapels and the ✪ **elaborately carved and inlaid choir stalls** from 1512.

The town's two art treasures hang in the council chamber of the **Palazzo Comunale** across the square (go through the right-hand door and up to the top of the stairs)—an early 16th-century portrait of the *Virgin* by Alba's greatest painter, Macrino d'Alba, and *Concertino,* by Mattia Preti, a follower of Caravaggio. It's open only during city office hours, Tuesday to Friday 8:15am to 12:15pm, Saturday 8:15am to noon.

From here, stroll the shopping promenade **Corso Vittorio** a few blocks to enjoy the low-key pace in the traffic-free heart of the town.

AFFORDABLE PLACES TO STAY

Piemonte. Piazza Rossetti 6, 12051 Alba. ☎/fax **0173-441-354.** 11 units, 10 with bathroom. 65,000L ($32.50) single; 90,000L ($45) double without bathroom, 120,000L ($60) double with bathroom. Breakfast 10,000L ($5). AE, MC, V. Parking free in courtyard. Closed 15 days in Aug.

This homey, old-fashioned hotel is nicely tucked away on a quiet piazza across from the apse end of the Duomo, making it a fine base for strolls through Alba's medieval streets. The hotel occupies a centuries-old, though much altered, palazzo, and most of the pleasant rooms face a quiet courtyard. Even those facing the street are relatively quiet, because much of the central town is closed to traffic. The decor is modest and modern, but rooms have comfy beds and high ceilings (some cross-vaulted) and are kept in sparkling, tiptop shape.

Savona. Via Roma 1 (a block from Piazza Savona), 12051 Alba. ☎ **0173-440-440.** Fax 0173-364-312. www.hotelsavona.com. 99 units. A/C MINIBAR TEL TV. 105,000–120,000L ($53–$60) single; 160,000L ($80) double; 205,000L ($103) triple; 200,000L ($100) jr. suite. Rates include breakfast. AE, DC, MC, V. Parking 10,000L ($5) in courtyard.

Renovations have added a slick, modern look to this old hotel facing a shady little piazza at the south edge of the old town. In fact, the premises have more or less been denuded of character, but the hotel offers solid comfort and many more amenities than you would expect for the price. Downstairs are a slick breakfast room and a bar that is also popular with patrons from the town. Upstairs, the guest rooms are pleasantly decorated in pastel shades and have contemporary furnishings and shiny new baths, most with bathtubs and many with Jacuzzis, especially in the modest split-level junior suites preferred by bigwigs like Pavarotti when they stay. Many open on to small terraces; the quietest face an interior courtyard. The TVs are interactive, allowing you to call up reams of information on Alba, its wines, and the surrounding area (or watch satellite channels and pay-per-view movies). The housekeeping staff seems to work overtime to keep the premises clean and running like clockwork.

✪ **Villa La Meridiana/Az. Agrituristica Reine.** Loc. Altavilla 9, 12051 Alba. ☎/fax **0173-440-112.** 9 units. MINIBAR TV. 130,000L ($65) double with bathroom; 150,000L ($75) mini-apts. Rates include breakfast. No credit cards.

On a hillside outside Alba (about a mile from the town center), this sprawling ivy-covered villa, the home of the Pionzo family, is a pleasant retreat. Most of the public areas are outdoors and include a flower-filled patio, a covered terrace overlooking the town and countryside, a room with a billiard table and gym equipment, a patio with a barbecue and wood oven you can use, and (in summer) a pool. A breakfast of home-made cakes and jams, accompanied by cheeses from local farms, is served in a brick-vaulted dining room. You'll find an array of accommodations in the main villa and its extension, formally the stalls and peasant quarters. Some (nos. 3 and 4 or nos. 5 and 6) can be combined to create family suites, and the four mini-apartments come with kitchenettes (no. 1 has two rooms and a large terrace). All are decorated in a pleasant mix of old country furnishings that have been passed down through the family; no. 6 even has a working fireplace. All save two cozy doubles (nos. 4 and 5, which have shady groves out the windows) provide airy views over the city and the surrounding hill towns with a snowy alpine backdrop or of the family's Barbera vineyards, apricot orchard, and pine grove; some have terraces.

To get here, from the Piazza Grassi in Alba follow signs to Barbareso, which will take you into the hills on Via Nizza-Acqui; a sign to the villa is about a mile outside of Alba; turn left and follow the unpaved road to its end, where there is a gated drive onto the property.

GREAT DEALS ON DINING

✪ **Lalibera.** Via E. Pertinace 24a. ☎ **0173-293-155.** Reservations recommended. Primi 10,000–40,000L ($5–$20); secondi 17,000–30,000L ($9–$15). AE, DC, MC, V. Tues–Sat noon–2pm and 8–10pm, Mon 8–10pm. Closed 2 weeks in late Feb/early Mar and 1st 2 weeks of Sept. PIEMONTESE.

A careful eye to design permeates this stylish osteria in the center of town. The marble floors, blonde contemporary furnishings, and pale-green walls provide a restful environment in which to enjoy the variations on traditional cuisine. An *antipasto misto* (25,000L/$13) is a nice way to sample the daily specialties, which are often lighter than most of the regional cuisine—it might include *insaltina de tacchino* (a salad of fresh greens and roast turkey breast), *vitello tonato* (the traditionally warm-weather Venetian dish of veal and tuna sauce), *fiori di zucca* (zucchini flowers stuffed with a trout mouse), or another truffle season specialty, the *raviolone* (one giant ricotta-and-spinach-ravioli cupped around an egg yolk and showered with *parmigiano* and truffle shavings). Pasta dishes are equally innovative, and many of them, such as *agnolotti* (a large tubular pasta stuffed with cabbage and rice), often combine fresh vegetables.

Enoclub. Piazza Savona 4. ☎ **0173-33-984.** Primi 12,000–15,000L ($6–$8); secondi 20,000–25,000L ($10–$13); tasting menu 55,000L ($28) without wine. AE, MC, V. Tues–Sun noon–2:30pm and 7:30pm–midnight. Closed Aug. PIEMONTESE.

The evocatively chic brick-vaulted basement is devoted to fine wine coupled with solid, slightly refined Piemontese cooking. The nice variety of rich pasta dishes includes tarajin (Piemonte's answer to tagliatelle) topped with a rich lamb sauce and *fettucine di farro* (noodles made from the barley-like grain emmer rather than wheat) tossed with pesto and served with potatoes and beans. The *secondi* are meaty: veal steak with aromatic herbs, rabbit cooked in red wine, and duck breast in a black olive paste.

Up on the ground floor is the busy **Umberto Notte** bar (open evenings only), one of Alba's few late-night scenes, dispensing wines by the glass, from 2,000L ($1). This is a fine place to sample the produce of the local vineyards as well as wines from all over the world.

VISITING THE WINE VILLAGES

Just to the south of Alba lie some of the region's, and Italy's, most enchanting wine villages. As you set out to explore the wine country, consider three words: **Rent a car.** While it's quite easy to reach some of the major towns by train or bus from Turin, setting out from those centers for smaller places can be difficult (there are some buses, but they tend to be very few and far between). In Turin, contact **Avis,** Corso Turati 15 (☎ **011-500-852**), or **Hertz,** at Via Magellano 12 (☎ **011-502-080;** www.hertz.it) and at Via Ascoli 39 (☎ **011-437-8175**). Before you head out on the labyrinth of small country roads, outfit yourself with a good map and list of vineyards from the tourist office in Alba or Asti.

THE WINES While the wines of Chianti and other Tuscan regions are on the top of the list for many oenologically minded travelers, the wines of Piemonte are often less heralded among non-Italians, and unjustifiably so. Most are of exceptional quality and usually made with grapes grown only in the Piemonte and often on tiny family plots, making the region a lovely patchwork of vineyards and small farms. Here are some wines you are likely to encounter again and again as you explore the area.

Barbesco is refined, dry, and, with Barolo, one of the region's most exalted wines. **Barbera d'Alba** is smooth and rich, the product of many of the delightful villages south of Alba. **Barolo** is called the king of reds (and is considered one of Italy's top two wines), the richest and heartiest of the Piemonte wines, and the one most likely to accompany game or meat. **Dolcetto** is dry, fruity, and mellow (not sweet, as its name leads many to assume). **Nebbiolo d'Alba** is rich, full and dry (the best Nebbiolo grapes are used to make Barbaresco and Barolo).

Spumanti is the sparkling wine that has put Asti on the map for many travelers, and **Moscato d'Asti** is a floral dessert wine. You can taste and purchase these wines at cantinas and enotecas in almost all towns and villages throughout the region; several are noted below.

THE REGION The central road through the region and running between Alba and Asti is S231, a heavily trafficked and unattractive highway that links many of the region's towns and cities; turn off this road whenever possible to explore the region's more rustic backwaters.

One of the loveliest drives takes you south of Alba to a string of wine villages in what are known as the **Langhe hills** (from Corso Europa, a ring road that encircles the Old City in Alba, follow signs out of town for Barolo). After 8km (5 mi.), you'll come to the turnoff for **Grinzane di Cavour,** a hilltop village built around a castle housing an enoteca (open Wednesday to Monday 9am to noon and 2:30 to 6:30pm) where you can enjoy a fine sampling of local wines.

Continuing south another 4km (2½ mi.) you'll come for the turnoff to **La Morra,** another hilltop village that affords stunning views over the rolling, vineyard-clad countryside from its central Piazza Castello (with parking). It has several places to eat (see below) and taste the local wines. The **Cantina Comunale di La Morra** (☎ **0173-509-204**), on Piazza del Municipo, operates both as the local tourist office and as a representative for local growers, selling and offering tastings of Barolo, Nebbiolo, Barbara, and Dolcetto (1,000L–4,500L/50¢–$2.25 per glass). You can also procure a map of hikes in the local countryside, many of which take you through the vineyards to the doors of local growers. It's open Wednesday to Monday 10am to 12:30 and 2:30 to 6:30pm.

Barolo, a romantic-looking place dominated by its 12th-century castle (about 2km/1½ mi. from La Morra), is directly across the valley and enticingly in view from miles around. Here, too, are a number of restaurants (see below) and shops selling the village's rich red wines. Among these outlets is the ✪ **Castello di Barolo** itself (☎ **0173-56-277;** www.turismoinlanga.it), which houses a wine museum, enoteca, and tourist office in its cavernous cellars. It's open Friday to Wednesday 10am to 12:30pm and 3 to 6pm.

Tiny **Novello** is a hilltop village about 15km (9 mi.) south of Alba located about 3km (2 mi.) away from Barolo on well-signposted roads. It crowns the adjoining hilltop, offering some pleasant accommodations and yet more stunning views.

AFFORDABLE PLACES TO STAY

See "Visiting the Wine Villages," above, for information on how to get to the towns where the following hotels and restaurants are located.

✪ **Al Castello da Diego.** Piazza G. Marconi 4, 12060 Novello. ☎ **0173-744-011.** Fax 0173-731-250. www.areacom.it/biz/alcastello. E-mail: alcastello@areacom.it. 11 units. TV TEL. 150,000L ($75) double (also price for single, but in that case it includes breakfast), 250,000L ($125) suite for 4 (or for two, but again that includes breakfast). Buffet breakfast 15,000L ($8). AE, MC, V. Closed Jan–Feb.

Admittedly there is something forbidding about this wonderfully spooky hilltop mansion, a brick Victorian built in the early 1800s atop the ruins of a 12th-century castle. However, the family welcome is friendly, the lodgings are unusual and delightful—all narrow stained-glass windows, brick turrets and battlements, and spidery cross-vaulting—and the views from the hillside perch are memorable. Guest rooms, reached by an endlessly winding marble staircase niched with statues, are huge and filled with a pleasant mix of reproduction antiques and oversize beds. Some of the baths are circular, tucked into turrets (including room 101 and suite 210), and all save two of the doubles (those two have their own balconies) open onto an enormous terrace. Four large two-bedroom suites occupy entire wings of the house, each with late 19th-century furnishings that may include claw-footed divans and canopy beds—the one in suite 109 was the bed of Maria Allora Nigra, the artist who had this castle built and who painted the wall hangings in the Tapestry Salon. Breakfast is served in another paneled salon. A cavernous dining room seats 1,000 and is a popular place for weddings and other fetes, but for more intimate meals you would do better to drive to nearby Barolo or La Morra.

Barbabuc. Via Giordano 35, 12060 Novello. ☎ and fax **0173-731-298.** www.turismoinlanga.it. 9 units. TEL. 145,000L ($73) single; 165,000L ($83) double. Buffet breakfast 15,000–25,000L ($8–$13). AE, DC, MC, V. Closed Jan.

This charming new hotel, which wraps around a garden, lies behind the centuries-old facade of a house near the village square and is managed by the same private tourism consortium that owns nearby Barolo castle. Walls of glass brick and open terraces fill the premises with air and light. The rooms are placed on different levels of a central staircase and are simply furnished in a tasteful mix of contemporary Italian pieces and country antiques on terrazzo floors. A few even have third beds or hide-a-beds for families. The well-equipped baths have corner stall showers. A roof terrace offers countryside views; downstairs, you'll find a handsome bar area and sitting room that opens to the pretty garden, an enoteca where you can taste local wines, and an intimate dining room where a lavish buffet breakfast is served.

✪ **La Cascina del Monastero.** Fraz. Annunziata 12064 La Morra. ☎/fax **0173-509-245.** 5 units. 120,000–140,000L ($60–$70) double. Rates include breakfast. No credit cards. Closed Jan–Feb.

The main business at this delightful farm complex just minutes away from La Morra toward Barolo (4km/2½ mi.), is bottling wine and harvesting fruit. But Giuseppe and Velda di Grasso have converted part of the oldest and most character-filled building into a bed-and-breakfast. Guests relax on a large covered terrace, furnished with wicker couches and armchairs, or on the grassy shores of a pond. A sumptuous breakfast of fresh cakes, yogurt, cheese, and salami is served in a vast brick-walled reception hall. The guest rooms, reached by a series of exterior brick staircases, have been smartly done with exposed timbers, golden-hued tile floors, and attractive antique bureaus and armoires and brass beds. Baths are sparkling new and quite luxurious, with state-of-the-art stall showers and luxuriously deep basins. The higher rate is for larger rooms, including one mini-apartment with kitchenette.

GREAT DEALS ON DINING

L'Osteria del Vignaiolo. Santa Maria 12, La Morra. ☎ **0173-50-335.** Reservations recommended. Primi 10,000L ($5); secondi 18,000–20,000L ($9–$10); tasting menu 45,000L ($23). AE, DC, MC, V. Thurs 7:45–9:15pm, Fri–Tues 12:30–2pm and 7:45–9:15pm. PIEMONTESE.

Halfway up the road to hilltop La Morra in the village of Santa Maria, this stylish countryside restaurant draws a clientele from many of the surrounding villages as well as from Alba, about 8 miles away. Pale gold walls, richly hued tiled floors, and handsome furnishings achieve a sophisticated rustic ambience, and the kitchen adds flair to local favorites. Duck breast appears in a salad of fresh picked greens; wild mushrooms are served in many variations, perhaps lightly fried or grilled (porcini) and served with polenta. The *tortelli di zucca* (pumpkin-stuffed pasta pillows in a sauce of toasted hazelnuts) is flavorful and light. Veal appears thinly sliced in tagliatelle or, more traditionally, infused with herbs and simply grilled. Wines, of course, are local, many from Barolo, the lights of which you can see twinkling across the valley (especially if you snag one of the wrought-iron tables out on the flagstone terrace next to a hillside of grapevines).

La Cantinetta. Via Roma 33, Barolo. ☎ **0173-56-198.** Reservations recommended. Primi 12,000–14,000L ($6–$7); secondi 18,000L ($9); tasting menu 50,000L ($25). AE, DC, MC, V. Fri–Tues, noon–3pm and 7–10:30pm, Wed noon–3pm. PIEMONTESE.

Two brothers, Maurilo and Paolo Chiappetto, do a fine job of introducing guests to the pleasures of the Piemontese table in their cozy dining room grouped around an open hearth (in nice weather, book ahead for a table out on the tiny back terrace). A seemingly endless stream of servings, which change daily, emerge from the kitchen: a wonderful country pâté; *bagna cauda* (translated as "hot bath"), in which raw vegetables are dipped into a heated preparation of oil, anchovies, and garlic; ravioli in a truffle sauce; risotto with wild mushrooms; that funky giant egg-stuffed *raviolo* also found at Lalibera in Alba (see above); a thick slab of roast veal; a tender cut of beef; and salad made with wild herbs. The wonderful house wines come from the vines that run right up to the back door of this delightful restaurant (a bar/enoteca is up front if all you want is a glass or two).

Ristorante Belvedere. Piazza Castello 5, La Morra. ☎ **0173-50-190.** Reservations recommended. Primi 15,000L ($8); secondi 15,000–20,000L ($8–$10). AE, DC, MC, V. Tues–Sat 12:30–2pm and 7:30–9pm, Sun 12:30–2pm. Closed Jan–Feb. PIEMONTESE.

The outlook from the baronial main room, built around a large brick hearth and perched high above vineyards that roll away in all directions, is in itself a pleasure and draws many diners here. When tour buses arrive to fill the back rooms and downstairs, service can turn brusque. But while the Belvedere is no longer the welcoming rustic retreat it once was, it's moves toward refinement (classy table settings, complimentary Spumanti and crostini while you consider the menu, etc.) have been pulled off well, and the kitchen maintains the high standards that have made it one of the region's most popular restaurants. A wonderful salad of truffles and Parmesan cheese, and homemade ravioli in a mushroom sauce, are among the house specialties, which include many other pastas and risottos. Main courses lean heavily to meat, including a rich *petto di anatra* (duck breast), *coniglio farcito alle erbe aromatiche* (deboned rabbit stuffed with herbs), and *straccotto di vitello al Barolo,* a shank of veal braised with the local wine. The wine list is 83 pages long and has a table of contents, and the prices are surprisingly decent (keep in mind that this area's wines are among Italy's most expensive).

Vineria San Giorgio. Via Umberto I 1, La Morra. ☎ **0173/509-594.** Tues–Sun 11am–2am (daily in Oct). Light meals 3,000–16,000L ($1.50–$8). AE, MC, V. WINE BAR.

Not only is this friendly wine bar in the center of La Morra, at the corner of Piazza Castello, but it also serves as the village social center, and the series of attractive rooms are filled with amiable chatter throughout the day and evening. Rough stone walls and vaulted brick ceilings provide just the right ambience in which to linger and enjoy the local wines (sold by the glass from 2,000L/$1) and such regional fare as salamis and cheeses, accompanied by homemade bread. Sandwiches are also available, as are three or four special daily dishes, usually including a delicious lasagna or other pasta dish.

3 Aosta & the Valle d'Aosta

Aosta: 113km (68 mi.) NW of Turin, 184km (111 mi.) NW of Milan. Courmayeur-Entrèves: 35km (21 mi.) W of Aosta, 148km (89 mi.) NW of Turin.

Skiers, hikers, and fresh-air and scenery enthusiasts flock to this tiny mountainous region less than 2 hours by train or car north of Turin, eager to enjoy one of Italy's favorite Alpine playgrounds. At its best, the **Valle d'Aosta** fulfills its promise. Snow-capped peaks, among them the Matterhorn and Mont Blanc, rise above the valley's verdant pastures and forests; waterfalls cascade into mountain streams; romantic castles cling to wooded hillsides.

Also plentiful in the Valle d'Aosta are crowds—especially in August, when the region welcomes hordes of vacationing Italians, and January through March, the height of the winter ski season—and one too many overdeveloped tourist center to accommodate them. You would be best off coming at one of the nonpeak times, when you can enjoy the valley's beauty in relative peace and quiet.

Whenever you happen to find yourself in the Valle d'Aosta, two must-sees are the town of **Aosta** itself, with its Roman and medieval monuments set dramatically against the backdrop of the Alps (and a fine place to begin a tour of the surrounding mountains and valleys), and the natural wonders of **Parco Nazionale de Gran Paradiso.** If you are looking for drama, add to the itinerary the thrill of a cable car ride over the shoulder of Mont Blanc to France. While much of the Valle d'Aosta is accessible by train or bus, you'll probably want a car to explore the quieter reaches of the region.

Of course, recreation, not sightseeing, is what draws many people to the Valle d'Aosta. Some of the best **downhill skiing,** accompanied by the best facilities, is on the runs at Courmayeur and Brevil Cervina. The Valle D'Aosta is also excellent for **cross-country skiing** and **hiking** (see "Into the Great Outdoors," below).

AOSTA

GETTING THERE   By Train   Aosta is served by 12 trains a day to and from **Turin** (2 hr.; 12,500L/$6); there are 10 trains a day to and from **Milan** (3 hr., with a change in Chivasso; 18,600L/$9).

By Bus   Aosta's bus station, across the piazza and a bit to the right from the train station, handles about eight buses (only one or two direct; most change in Ivrea) to and from **Turin** daily; the 3-hour trip (2 hr. on the direct) costs 12,500L ($6.25). Four to five daily buses also connect Aosta and **Milan** (2½–3½ hr.; 21,500L/$10.75). Buses also connect Aosta with other popular spots in the valley, among them **Courmayeur,** where you can connect with a shuttle bus to the Palud cable car (see below) and **Cogne,** a major gateway to the Parco Nazionale de Gran Paradiso (see below). For information, call ☎ **0165-262-027.**

By Car   The A5 autostrada from Turin shoots up the length of the Valle d'Aosta en route to France and Switzerland via the Mont Blanc tunnel; there are numerous exits in the valley. The trip from Turin to Aosta normally takes about 1½ hours, but traffic can be heavy in the busy tourist months—especially in August and from January through March, the height of the ski season.

VISITOR INFORMATION   The **tourist office** in Aosta, Piazza Chanoux 8 (☎ **0165-236-627;** www.regione.vda.it/turismo), dispenses a wealth of info on hotels, restaurants, and sights throughout the region, along with listings of campgrounds, maps of hiking trails, information about ski-lift tickets and special discounted ski packages, outlets for bike rentals, and rafting trips. It's open Monday to Saturday from 9am to 1pm and 3 to 8pm (closed Sunday afternoons October to May).

FESTIVALS & MARKETS   Aosta celebrates it patron saint and warm winter days and nights with the **Fiera Sant'Orso** on the last two days of January. The festival fills the streets and involves dancing, drinking vast quantities of mulled wine, and perusing the local craft pieces, such as lovely wood carvings and woven blankets, that vendors from throughout the Valle d'Aosta offer for sale. Aosta's other major event is the **Battaille des Reines,** the Battle of the Cows, in which these mainstays of the local economy lock horns—the main event is held the third Sunday in October and preliminary heats take place throughout the year. Aosta's **weekly market** day is Tuesday, when stalls selling food, clothes, crafts and household items fill the Piazza Cavalieri di Vittorio Veneto.

EXPLORING THE AREA

This mountain town, surrounded by snow-capped peaks, is not only pleasant but it has soul—the product of a history that goes back to Roman times. While you're not going to find much in the line of pristine Alpine quaintness here in the Valle d'Aosta's busy tourist and economic center, you can spend some enjoyable time strolling past Roman ruins and medieval bell towers while checking out the chic shops that sell everything from Armani suits to locally made Fontina cheese.

The "Rome of the Alps" sits majestically within its preserved walls, and the monuments of the Empire make it easy to envision the days when Aosta was one of Rome's most important trading and military outposts. Two Roman gates arch gracefully across the Via Anselmo, Aosta's main thoroughfare: The **Porta Pretoria,** the western

Into the Great Outdoors

Recreation, of course, is what draws many people to the Valle d'Aosta. You'll find some of the best **downhill skiing** and facilities on the runs at **Courmayeur, Brevil Cervina,** and in the **Valle di Cogne.** At the first two, you can expect to pay 35,000L ($17.50) and up for daily lift passes. Cogne is a little less expensive, with daily passes running around 25,000L ($12.50). Multi-day passes, providing access to lifts and slopes of the entire valley, run about 160,000L ($80) for 3 days, 208,000L ($104) for 4 days, with per-day rates sliding down a scale to 14 days at 565,000L ($282.50). For more info, call ☎ **0165-238-871;** www. skivallee.it. Ski season starts in late November/early December and runs through April, if the snow holds out.

A money-saving option is to take one of the **"white-week" packages** that include room and board and unlimited skiing and are available at resorts throughout the Valle d'Aosta. You can expect to pay at least 500,000L ($250) at Courmayeur, and 350,000L ($125) at Cogne or one of the other less fashionable resorts. Contact the tourist board in Aosta for more information.

Cross-country skiing is superb around Cogne in the Parco Nazionale del Gran Paradiso, where there are more than 30 miles of trails.

The Valle d'Aosta is also excellent **hiking** terrain, especially in July and August. For information about hiking in Parco Nazionale del Gran Paradiso, ask at the tourist offices of Aosta and especially Cogne.

---

entrance to the Roman town, and the **Arco di Augusto** (sometimes called Arco Romano), the eastern entrance built in A.D. 25 to commemorate a Roman victory over the Celts. A **Roman bridge** spans the river Buthier; just a few steps north of the Porta Pretoria you'll find the facade of the **Teatro Romano (Roman Theater)** and the ruins of the **amphitheater,** which once accommodated 20,000 spectators; the ruins of the forum are in an adjacent park. The theater and forum are open daily, in summer 9:30am to noon and 2:30 to 6:30pm, in winter 9:30am to noon and 2 to 4:30pm); admission is free. Architectural fragments from these monuments and a sizable collection of vessels and other objects unearthed during excavations are displayed in Aosta's **Archaeological Museum** on Piazza Roncas (☎ **0165-238-680**); it's open daily from 9am to 7pm and admission is free.

Behind the banal 19th-century facade of Aosta's **Duomo,** Piazza Giovanni XXIII (☎ **0165-40-251**), lie two remarkable treasures: an ivory diptych from A.D. 406 that depicts the Roman emperor Honorius and is housed along with other precious objects in the treasury; and 12th-century mosaics on the floor of the choir and before the altar. Heavy-handed restorations cloud the fact that the church actually dates from the 10th century. It's open Monday to Saturday 8am to 12:30pm and 2:30 to 5:30pm (though I've noticed they often just stay open all day), Sunday 12:30 to 5:30pm. The treasury is open April to September Monday to Saturday 8am to 11:30am and 3 to 5:30pm, Sunday 8 to 9:30am, 10:30 to 11:30am, an 3 to 5:30pm; October to March Sunday 8 to 9:30am, 10:30 to 11:30am, and 3 to 5:30pm. Admission to the treasury is 4,000L ($2) adults, 1,500L (75¢) under age 10.

The **Collegiata dei Santi Pietro e Orso,** at the eastern edge of the old city off Via San Anselmo 9 (☎ **0165-262-026**), is a hodgepodge from the 6th through the 18th centuries. An 11th-century church was built over the original 6th-century church, and that in turn has been periodically enhanced with architectural embellishments representing every stylistic period from the Gothic through the baroque. In a room above the nave (the door on the left aisle marked "Affreschi Ottoniani"; search out sacristan or ring bell), the remains of an 11th-century fresco cycle recounts the life of Christ and the Apostles on the bits of medieval church wall above the 15th-century vaults. The frescoes are open daily: April to September 9am to 7pm and October to March 10am to 5pm. The 12th-century cloisters are a fascinating display of Romanesque storytelling—40 columns are capped with carved capitals depicting scenes from the Bible and the life of Aosta's own Saint Orso.

SIDE TRIPS FROM AOSTA

CASTLE OF FENIS   Built by the Challants, viscounts of Aosta throughout much of the Middle Ages, this castle (☎ **0165-764-263;** www.aostavalley.com), near the town of Fenis is the most impressive and best preserved of the many castles perched on the hillsides above the Valle d'Aosta. You can enjoy some fine views of the Alps and the valley below. One of the most appealing parts of a visit to Fenis is catching a glimpse into everyday life in a medieval castle—you can climb up to wooden loggias overlooking the courtyard and visit the cavernous kitchens. Alas, you can not scamper among the ramparts, turrets, towers, and dungeons, thanks to a new Italian safety law requiring that steps be short and wide, corridors wide enough, and emergency exits plentiful.

March to June and September, the castle is open daily 9am to 7pm; July and August hours are daily 9am to 8pm; October to February hours are Wednesday to Monday 10am to 5pm (to 6pm Sundays). Requisite half-hour guided tours (Italian only) leave every 30 minutes. Come early; tours tend to fill up quickly in summer and you can't book. Admission is 6,000L ($3) adults and 3,000L ($1.50) students. The castle is 30km (18 mi.) east of Aosta on route S26; there are 13 buses a day (only one, at 6:20am, on Sunday) from Aosta, 3,000L ($1.50; 30 min.).

CERVINA-BREUIL & THE MATTERHORN   You don't come to Cervina-Breuil to see the town, a banal collection of tourist facilities—the sight to see, and you can't miss it, is the ✪ **Matterhorn (Monte Cervino).** Its distinctive profile looms majestically above the valley, beckoning year-round skiers and those who simply want to savor a refreshing Alpine experience by ascending to its glaciers via cable car to the Plateau Rosa (42,000L/$21 round-trip), closed September 10 to mid-October. An excellent trail also ascends from **Cervina-Breuil** up the flank of the mountain. After a moderately strenuous uphill trek of 90 minutes you come to gorgeous ✪ **Lac du Goillet,** and from there it's another 90 minutes to the ✪ **Colle Superiore delle Cime Bianche,** a plateau with heart-stopping views.

The **tourist office,** Via Carrel 29 (☎ **0166-949-136**), can provide information on other hikes, ski packages, and serious ascents to the top of the Matterhorn. Cervina-Breuil is 54km (30 mi.) northwest of Aosta via routes A5 and S406. **From Aosta,** you can take one of the Turin-bound trains and get off at Chatillon (20 min.; 3,500L/$1.75), and continue from there on one of the seven daily buses to Cervina-Breuil (1 hr.; 4,000L/$2).

PARCO NAZIONALE DEL GRAN PARADISO   The little town of Cogne is the most convenient gateway to one of Europe's finest parcels of unspoiled nature, the former hunting grounds of King Vittorio Emanuele that now comprise this vast and lovely national park. The park encompasses five valleys and a total of 1,400 square miles of forests and pastureland where many Alpine beasts roam wild, including the ibex, a long-horned goat, and the chamois, a small antelope, both of which have hovered near extinction in recent years.

Humans can roam these wilds via a vast network of well-marked trails. Among the few places where the hand of man intrudes ever so gently on nature is in a few scattered hamlets within the park borders and in the **Giardino Alpino Paradiso** (☎ **0165-74-147**), a stunning collection of rare Alpine fauna near the village of Valnontey, just a mile south of Cogne. It's open June 10 to September daily 10am to 6:30pm (5:30pm June and September); admission is 4,000L ($2) adults, 2,000L ($1) ages 11 to 15.

Visitor Information   Cogne also offers some downhill skiing, but it is better regarded for its many cross-country skiing trails. The **tourist office** in Cogne, Piazza Chanoux 34–36 (☎ **0165-74-040**; www.cogne.org), provides a wealth of information on hiking and skiing trails and other outdoor activities in the park and elsewhere in the region; it's open Monday to Saturday 9am to 12:30pm and 3 to 6pm and Sunday 3 to 6pm. You can also get info at www.granparadiso.org. Cogne is about 18 miles south of Aosta via S35 and S507; there are also seven buses a day to and from Aosta; the 50-minute trip costs 4,000L ($2).

AFFORDABLE PLACES TO STAY

Many hotels in the Valle d'Aosta require that guests take their meals on the premises and stay 3 nights or more. However, outside of busy tourist times, hotels often have rooms to spare and are willing to be a little more liberal in their policies. Rates vary almost month by month; in general, expect to pay highest for a room in August and at Christmas and Easter, and the least for a room in the fall. For the best rates, check with the local tourist boards for information on *Settimane Bianche* (White Week) packages, all-inclusive deals that include room, board, and ski passes.

Belle Epoque. Via d'Avise 18, 11100 Aosta. ☎ and fax **0165-26-276**; www.aostashop. com. 14 units, 11 with bathroom. 45,000L ($23) single without bathroom, 55,000L ($27) single with bathroom; 80,000L ($40) double without bathroom, 90,000L ($45) double with bathroom. AE, MC, V.

The stucco exterior of this old building in a quiet corner of the historic center has a cozy Alpine look to it, but the same can't be said of the somewhat stark interior. What is appealing about this hotel is the family-run atmosphere and the price, appreciated all the more in this often-expensive resort region. Rooms are large enough but spartan, with the bare minimum of modern pieces scattered about, and some have balconies and newly installed, tidy little baths. An equally serviceable trattoria occupies most of the ground floor; you can arrange half-pensione for 65,000L ($33) per person. There's no elevator.

Bus. Via Malherbes 18, 11100 Aosta. ☎ **0165-43-645.** Fax 0165-236-962. www. netvallee.it/hotelbus. 39 units. MINIBAR TV TEL. 70,000–110,000L ($35–$55) single, 100,000–150,000L ($50–$75) double; half-board 85,000–122,000L ($43–$61) per person. Breakfast 15,000L ($8). AE, DC, MC, V.

One of the nicest things about this newer hotel is its location, on a pleasant side street just a short walk from the center of Aosta. The Roman ruins and other sights are within a 5-minute walk, yet this quiet neighborhood has an almost rural feel to it. Downstairs you'll find a contemporary-styled bar, restaurant, and breakfast area. Upstairs, the smallish guest rooms are comfortably furnished in a somewhat somber modern style that includes many wood-veneer touches and thin, worn carpeting. The baths are serviceable, but suffer from the dreaded waffle towels. Since the hotel is taller than the surrounding houses, rooms on the upper floors overlook meadows and the surrounding mountains. Except at peak times, rooms are usually available without board. Fifteen rooms have air-conditioning; if you prefer the opposite sensation, a sauna is downstairs.

Across Mont Blanc by Cable Car

One of the Valle d'Aosta's best experiences is to ride the series of cable cars from La Palud, just above Entrèves, across Mont Blanc to several ski stations in Italy and France and down into Chamonix, France. You make the trip in stages—first past two intermediate stops to the last aerie on Italian soil, **Punta Helbronner** (20 min. each way; 52,000L/$26 round-trip). At 11,000 feet, this ice-clad lookout provides stunning views of the Mont Blanc glaciers and the Matterhorn and other peaks looming in the distance. (In summer, you may want to hop off before you get to Punta Helbronner at **Pavillion Frety** and tour a pleasant botanic garden, Giardino Alpino Saussurea; open daily June 24 to September 30; admission 4,000L/$2, or 3,000L/$1.50 if you buy admission along with your cable car ticket.)

For sheer drama, continue from Punta Helbronner to **Aiguille du Midi** in France in a tiny gondola to experience the dramatic sensation of dangling more than 2,300 meters in midair as you cruise above the Géant Glacier and the Vallée Blanche (30 min. each way; tack on another 30,000L/$15—or 100 French francs–round-trip). From Aiguille du Midi you can descend over more glaciers and dramatic valleys on the French flank of Mont Blanc to the resort town of **Chamonix** (50 min. each way; tack on a further 200 French francs/$26.65 round-trip).

Hours for these cable cars vary wildly, and service can be sporadic depending on weather conditions (winds often close the gondola between Hellbronner and Aiguille du Midi), but in general they run every 20 minutes from 7:30am (8:20am in fall and spring) to 12:30pm and 2 to 5:30pm (all day long from July 22 to August 27; closed November 2 to December 10). The **Hellbronner–Aiguille du Midi gondola** is only open May to September. Note that kids aged 4 to 15 get 50% off the prices above, and seniors over 60 get a 10% discount. Hourly buses (1,500L/75¢) make the 10-minute run from Courmayeur to the cable car terminus at La Palud. For more info, call ☎ **0165-89-925;** www.montebianco.com; for a report of weather at the top and on the other side, dial ☎ 0165-89-961.

A cheaper but less dramatic way to cross the flanks of Mont Blanc is on the **Courmayeur Monte Blanc Funivia,** which leaves from a terminus in Entrèves and ascends to the Val Veny. The round-trip fare is 16,000L ($8), with 20% off over 60 and kids under 1.3 meters (4 feet, 4 inches) free. Cars depart every 20 minutes from 9am to 12:50pm and 2:15 to 5:40pm; closed September 4 to late December.

✪ **Milleluci.** In Roppoz, off Via Porossan 1km northeast of Arco di Augusto, 11100 Aosta. ☎ **0165-23-5278.** Fax 0165-235-284. www.hotelmilleluci.com. 33 units. MINIBAR TV TEL. 150,000–160,000L ($75–$80) single without balcony; 160,000–170,000L ($80–$85) single with balcony; 170,000–190,000L ($85–$95) double without balcony; 180,000–200,000L ($90–$100) double with balcony; 300,000L ($150) suite. Rates include breakfast. AE, MC, V.

From its noticeably cooler perch on a hillside just above the town, this chalet-like hotel in a breezy garden offers pleasant views. Cristina's great-grandmother converted the family farm into a hotel about 40 years ago, and it's been handed down from mother to daughter ever since. Downstairs, a large wood-beamed sitting area is grouped around an attractive hearth and woodsy bar. The spacious rooms (larger on the second floor; cozy on the first) sport some nice touches like traditional wood furnishings, beamed ceilings, canopied beds (in suites and in one double), rich fabrics, terrazzo floors, and handsome prints. All have spacious baths with heated towel racks. Two suites are tucked under the eaves; another pair is going in on the second floor. The stupendous buffet breakfast alone would be reason to stay, all homemade cakes, freshly whipped cream, *frittata* wedges (eggs from their own chickens; veggies from the garden), Alpine cheeses, and more. In nice weather, you can take breakfast on the wraparound terrace overlooking the town. Over the next 2 years, the owners will be adding a sauna, hot tub, and small workout room in the basement and a pool outside.

GREAT DEALS ON DINING

This is the land of mountain food—hams and salamis are laced with herbs from Alpine meadows; creamy cornmeal polenta accompanies meals; a rich beef stew, *carbonada,* warms winter nights; and buttery Fontina is the cheese of choice.

Grotta Azzurra. Via Croix de Ville 97. ☎ **0165-262-474.** Primi 5,000–17,000L ($2.50–$9); secondi 10,000–35,000L ($5–$18); pizze 7,500–13,000L ($3.75–$7). MC, V. Thurs–Tues noon–2:30pm and 6–10:30pm. Closed July 10–27. PIZZA/SOUTHERN ITALIAN.

The best pizzeria in town also serves, as its name suggests, a bounty of fare from southern climes, along the lines of spaghetti with clam sauce. There is a wide selection of fresh fish, which makes this somewhat worn-looking trattoria popular with a local clientele. The pizzas emerge from a wood-burning oven and are often topped with Fontina and other rich local cheeses and salamis.

Taverna da Nando. Via de Tillier 41. ☎ **0165-44-455.** Primi 11,000–28,000L ($6–$14); secondi 13,000–31,000L ($7–$16); pizze 7,000–10,000L ($3.50–$5); fixed-price menus 23,000–51,000L ($12–$26). AE, DC, MC, V. Tues–Sun noon–3pm and 7:15–10pm. Closed 15 days in late June/early July. PIZZA/VALDOSTAN.

On Aosta's main thoroughfare in the center of town, this popular basement eatery achieves a rustic ambience with stuccoed vault ceilings, traditional mountain furnishings, and warm (if excruciatingly slow) service. The kitchen, too, sticks to local traditions, serving such dishes as *fonduta* (a creamy fondue of Fontina, milk and eggs served atop polenta), *crepes à la Valdostana* (filled and topped with melted cheese), and *carbonada con polenta* (beef stew dished over polenta). There is also an excellent selection of grilled meats, pizzas, salads, and bruschette, as well as a wine list that includes many choices from the Valle d'Aosta's limited but productive vineyards and from the Piemonte.

Trattoria Praetoria. Via San Anselmo 9. ☎ **0165-44-356.** Primi 10,000–15,000L ($5–$7.50); secondi 17,000–18,000L ($8–$9); fixed-price menu 30,000L ($15). AE, MC, V. Fri–Wed, 12:15–2:30pm and 7:15–9:30pm. VALDOSTAN.

This small, woody trattoria, one of the friendliest and best-priced in Aosta, takes its name from the nearby Roman gate and its menu from the surrounding countryside. This is the place to throw concerns about cholesterol to the wind and introduce your palate to Valdostan cuisine. Begin with *fonduta* (fondue) and follow it with *boudin* (spicy sausages served with potatoes) or *carbonada* (a hearty beef stew).

COURMAYEUR-ENTRÈVES

The one-time mountain hamlet of **Courmayeur** is now the Valle d'Aosta's resort extraordinaire, a collection of traditional stone buildings, pseudo-Alpine chalets, and large hotels catering to a well-heeled international crowd of skiers. Even if you don't ski, you can happily while away the time sipping a grog while regarding the craggy bulk of Mont Blanc (Monte Bianco this side of the border), which looms over this end of the

Valle d'Aosta and forms the snowy barrier between Italy and France. The Mont Blanc tunnel—which normally makes it possible to zip into France in just 20 minutes—is still closed following a devastating March 1999 fire. It might reopen by fall 2001 at the earliest.

Entrèves, 2 miles north of Courmayeur, is the sort of place that the latter probably once was: a pleasant collection of stone houses and farm buildings surrounded by pastureland. Quaint as the village is in appearance, at its soul it is a worldly enclave with some nice hotels and restaurants catering to skiers and outdoor enthusiasts who prefer to spend time in the mountains in surroundings that are a little quieter than Courmayeur.

ESSENTIALS

GETTING THERE By Bus Thirteen daily buses connect Courmayeur with Aosta (1 hr.; 4,800L/$2.40). At least hourly buses (more in summer) run between Courmayeur's Piazzale Monte Bianco and Entrèves and La Palud (10 min.; 1,500L/75¢).

By Car The A5 autostrada from Turin to the Mont Blanc tunnel passes Courmayeur; the trip from Aosta to Courmayeur on this much-used route takes less than half an hour (lots of time in tunnels; for scenery take the parallel S26 in about 1 hr.), and total travel time from Turin is less than 2 hours.

VISITOR INFORMATION The **tourist office** in Courmayeur, Piazzale Monte Bianco 8 (☎ **0165-842-060,** 0165-842-072; www.regione.vda.it/turismo or www.courmayeur.net), provides information on hiking, skiing, and other outdoor activities in the region, as well as hotel and restaurant listings. It's open late July to late August and Christmas to January 6 daily 9am to 1pm and 2:30 to 7pm; late April to late July and late August through November Monday to Saturday 9am to 12:30 and 3 to 6:30pm, Sunday 9:30am to 12:30pm and 3 to 6pm; December 1 to 24 and January 7 to late April, Saturday and Sunday only 9am to 1pm and 2:30 to 7pm.

AFFORDABLE PLACES TO STAY

Eidelweiss. Via Marconi 42, 11013 Courmayeur. ☎ **0165-841-590.** Fax 0165-841-618. E-mail: edelweiss@courmayeur.valdigne.com. 30 units. TV TEL. 60,000–100,000L ($30–$50) single; 100,000–180,000L ($50–$90) double. Rates include breakfast. AE, DC, MC, V. Closed Oct-Nov and May.

In winter, the pine-paneled salons and cozy rooms of this chalet-style hotel near the center of town attract a friendly international set of skiers, and in summer, many Italian families spend a month or two here at a time. The Roveyaz family extends a hearty welcome to all and provides modern mountain-style accommodations. (One wonders, however, why the contemporary baths have heated towel racks but only flat towels.) Many rooms open onto terraces overlooking the mountains, and the nicest rooms are those on the top floor, tucked under the eaves. Basic, nonfussy meals are served in the cheerful main-floor dining room; you can arrange a half-board deal for 80,000L to 130,000L ($40–$65) per person, depending on season.

Drinking with the Best of Them

The **Caffè della Posta,** at Via Roma 51, Courmayeur (☎ **0165-842-272**), is Courmayeur's most popular spot for an après-ski grog. Since it opened 90 years ago, it has been welcoming the famous and not so famous into its series of cozy rooms, one of which is grouped around an open hearth.

La Grange. C.P. 75, 11013 Courmayeur-Entrèves. ☎ **0165-869-733.** Fax 0165-869-744. www.lagrange-it.com. 23 units. MINIBAR TV TEL. 150,000–250,000L ($75–$125) single or double. Rates include breakfast. AE, DC, MC, V. Closed May–June and Oct–Nov.

What may well be the most charming hotel in the Valle d'Aosta occupies a converted barn in the bucolic village of Entrèves and is ably managed by Bruna Berthold. None of the rooms are the same, though all are decorated with a pleasing smattering of antiques and rustic furnishings; some have balconies overlooking Mont Blanc, which quite literally hovers over the property. The stucco-walled, stone-floored lobby is a fine place to relax, with couches built around a corner hearth and a little bar area. A lavish buffet breakfast is served in a prettily paneled room off the lobby, and there is an exercise room and a much-used sauna.

GREAT DEALS ON DINING

Ristorante La Palud. Strada la Palud 17, Courmayeur. ☎ **0165-89-169.** Primi 12,000–15,000L ($6–$8); secondi 15,000–30,000L ($8–$15); fixed-price menus 28,000–35,000L ($14–$18; the pricier one includes wine). AE, MC, V. Thurs–Tues, noon–3:30pm and 7:30–10:30pm. SEAFOOD/VALDOSTAN.

Come to this cozy restaurant, in the little cable-car settlement just outside Entrèves in the shadows of Mont Blanc, on Friday so that you can enjoy a wide selection of fresh fish brought up from Liguria. At any time, though, a table in front of the hearth is just the place to enjoy the specialties of the Valle d'Aosta: mountain hams, creamy *polenta concia* (with Fontina cheese and butter folded into it), and *cervo* (venison) in season. There is a selection of mountain cheeses for dessert, and the wine list borrows heavily from neighboring Piemonte but also includes some local vintages.

Worth a Splurge

✪ **Maison de Filippo.** Courmayeur-Entrèves. ☎ **0165-869-797.** www.lamaison.com. Reservations required. Fixed-price menu 60,000L ($30). MC, V. Wed–Mon 12:30–2:30pm and 7:30–10:30pm. Closed June and Nov–Dec 20. VALDOSTAN.

The atmosphere at this popular and cheerful restaurant in Entrèves is delightfully country Alpine and the offerings so generous you may not be able to eat again for a week. Daily menus vary but often include an antipasto of mountain hams and salamis, a selection of pastas filled with wild mushrooms and topped with Fontina and other local cheeses, and a sampling of fresh trout and game in season. Service is casual and friendly, and in summer you can choose between a table in the delightfully converted barnlike structure or on the flowery terrace.

11

Liguria & the Italian Riviera

by Reid Bramblett

From the top of Tuscany to the French border, Italy follows a crescent-shaped strip of seacoast and mountains that comprise the region of **Liguria.** The pleasures of this region are no secret. Ever since the 19th century, world-weary travelers have been heading for Liguria's resorts to enjoy balmy weather (ensured by the protective barrier of the Alps) and turquoise seas. Beyond the beach, the stones and tiles of proud old towns and cities bake in the sun, and hillsides are fragrant with the scent of bougainvillea and pines.

Liguria is really two coasts: the beachier stretch east of Genoa is known as the **Riviera di Levante (Rising Sun),** and the rockier, more colorful fishing-village-filled stretch to the west of Genoa is known as the **Riviera di Ponente (Setting Sun).** Both are lined with fishing villages, including the remote hamlets of the Cinque Terre, and fashionable resorts, many of which, like San Remo, have seen their heydays fade but continue to entice visitors with palm-fringed promenades and gentle ways. Genoa itself, with its proud maritime history, is a world apart from the easygoing seaside places that surround it: brusque and clamorous, it is one of the more history-filled, and least visited, cities in Italy.

1 Genoa: Sophistication & Squalor

142km (85 mi.) S of Milan, 501km (300 mi.) N of Rome, 194km (116 mi.) E of Nice.

With its dizzying mix of the old and the new, of sophistication and squalor, **Genoa (Genova)** is as multilayered as the hills it clings to. It was and is, first and foremost, a port city: an important maritime center for the Roman Empire, boyhood home of Christopher Columbus (whose much restored house still stands near a section of the medieval walls), and, fueled by seafaring commerce that stretched all the way to the Middle East, one of the largest and wealthiest cities of Renaissance Europe.

It's easy to capture glimpses of these former glory days on the narrow lanes and dank alleys of Genoa's portside old town, where treasure-filled palaces and fine marble churches stand next to laundry-draped tenements. In fact, life within the old medieval walls doesn't seem to have changed since the days when Genovese ships set sail to launch raids on the Venetians, crusaders embarked for the Holy Land,

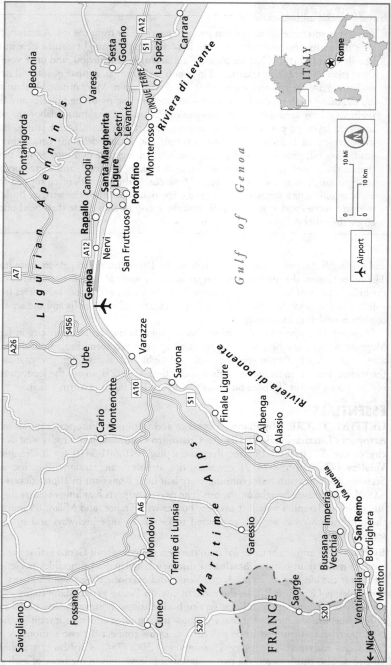

The Italian Riviera

ITALY

Rome

Carrara

A12

S1

La Spezia

Sesta
Godano

CINQUE TERRE

Varese

Bedonia

Monterosso

Riviera di Levante

Sestri
Levante

Santa Margherita
Ligure

Fontanigorda

Camogli

Rapallo

Portofino

Nervi

San Fruttuoso

A12

Genoa

Gulf of Genoa

Ligurian Apennines

A7

S456

A26

Urbe

Varazze

A10

Savona

Montenotte

Cario

Finale Ligure

S1

Albenga

Alassio

Riviera di Ponente

Maritime Alps

A6

Mondovi

Terme di Lunsia

Garessio

Via Aurelia

Imperia

Bussana
Vecchia

San Remo

Bordighera

Menton

Ventimiglia

Saorge

S20

FRANCE

Nice

Cuneo

S20

Fossano

Savigliano

Airport

10 Mi

10 Km

A Taste of Liguria

Anywhere you travel in this region you will never be far from the sea. A truism, but a bit misleading because seafood is not as plentiful as you might assume here in the heavily fished north. What are plentiful are *acciughe* (anchovies), and once you try them fresh and *marinate* (marinated in lemon) as part of an antipasto, you will never underestimate the culinary merits of this little fish again. More noticeable than fish are the many fresh vegetables that grow in patches clinging to the hillsides and find their way into tarts (the *torta pasqualina* is one of the most elaborate, with umpteen layers of pastry; some restaurants serve it year round), and sauces, none more typical of Liguria than **pesto,** a simple and simply delicious concoction of basil, olive oil, pine nuts, and parmigiano ground together in a mortar and pestle (hence the name). Ligurians are also adept at making fast food, and there's no better light lunch or snack than a piece of *focaccia,* flatbread that's often topped with herbs or olives, or a *farinata,* a chickpea crêpe that's offered by the wedges. Both are sold in bakeries and at small stands, making it easy to grab a bite then head out to enjoy the other delights of the region.

and Garibaldi shipped out to invade Sicily in the 19th-century struggle to unify Italy. The other Genoa, the modern city that stretches for miles along the coast and climbs the hills, is a city of international business, peaceful parks, and breezy belvederes from which you can enjoy fine views of this dingy-yet-colorful metropolis and the sea that continues to define its identity.

However, be prepared to deal with what is probably the seediest port city in Italy. Muggers, whores, and heroin addicts shooting up positively teem throughout the back alleys—and plenty of main streets as well—all night *and* all day long; always stick to the widest, busiest, most major roads you can find. Genoa is, to say the least, probably not going to win "favorite bit of Italy" on your list, but it is worth a visit.

ESSENTIALS

GETTING THERE **By Plane** Flights to and from most European capitals serve **Aeroporto Internazionale de Genova Cristoforo Colombo,** just 4 miles west of the city center; ☎ 010-60-151 for the central line, 010-601-5410 for information. **Volabus** (☎ 010-558-2471) connects the airport with Stazione Principe and Stazione Brignole, with buses running every half hour from 6am to 10pm; tickets are 4,000L ($2) and are bought on the bus. The nearest airports handling overseas flights are at Nice, 116 miles west just over the border with France, and Milan, 85 miles to the north; both cities are well connected to Genoa by superhighways and by train service.

By Train An important thing for train travelers to know about Genoa is that the city has two major train stations, **Stazione Principe** (designated on timetables as Genova P.P.), near the old city on Piazza Acqua Verde, and **Stazione Brignole** (designated on timetables as Genova B.R.), in the modern city on Piazza Verdi. Many trains, especially those on long-distance lines, service both stations; however, many trains stop only at one, making it essential that you know the station at which your train is scheduled to arrive and from which it will depart. Trains connect the two stations in just 5 minutes and run about every 15 minutes (1,500L/75¢). City buses numbered 40 and 37 also run between the two train stations, leaving from the front of each station about every 10 minutes (1,500L/75¢); you must allow at least 20 minutes for the connection on Genoa's crowded streets.

Genoa is the hub for trains serving the Italian Riviera, with trains arriving and departing for Ventimiglia on the French border about every half hour, and **La Spezia,** at the eastern edge of Liguria, even more frequently, as often as every 15 minutes during peak times between 7am and 7pm (regional: 105 min., 8,600L/$4.30; High speed: 1 hr., 13,000–16,600L/$7–$8). Most of these trains make local stops at the coastal resorts (for those towns covered in this chapter, see each listing for connections with Genoa). Lots of trains connect Genoa with major Italian cities: **Milan** (1 to 3 per hour; regional: 105 min., 14,500L/$7; High speed: 90 min., 24,000L/$12), **Rome** (hourly; 4½ to 5½ hr.; 59,000–62,000L/$30–$31), **Turin** (1 to 2 per hour; regional: 110 min., 14,500L/$7; High speed: 90 min., 23,500L/$12), **Florence** (hourly but always with a change, usually at Pisa; 3 hr.; 30,100L/$15), **Pisa** (hourly; regional: 3 hr., 14,500L/$7; High speed: 1½–2 hr., 27,500L/$14).

By Bus An extensive bus network connects Genoa with other parts of Liguria, as well as other Italian and European cities, from the main bus station next to Stazione Principe. While it is easiest to reach seaside resorts by the trains that run up and down the coast, buses are the only link to many small towns in the region's hilly hinterlands. For tickets and information, contact **PESCI,** Piazza della Vittoria 94r (☎ **010-564-936**).

By Car Genoa is linked to other parts of Italy and to France by a convenient network of superhighways. The A10/A12 follows the coast and passes through dozens of tunnels to link Genoa with France to the west (Nice is less than 2 hr. away) and Pisa, about 1½ hours to the southeast. The A7 links Genoa with Milan, a little over an hour to the north.

By Ferry Port that it is, Genoa is linked to several other Mediterranean ports by ferry service. Most boats leave and depart from the Stazione Marittima, which is on a waterfront roadway, Via Marina D'Italia, about a 5-minute walk south of Stazione Principe. For service to and from the **Riviera Levante,** check with **Tigullio** (☎ **800-014-808**); there's once daily service early July to late September at 19,000L to 25,000L ($10 to $13) one-way.

VISITOR INFORMATION The **main tourist office** is near the aquarium on Via al Porto Antico (☎ **010-24-871;** fax 010-246-7658; www.apt.genova.it), open daily 9:30am to 1pm and 3:30 to 6pm. The agency also has **branches** at Stazione Principe (☎ **010-246-2633**), open the same hours (but closed Sunday afternoon); and at Cristoforo Colombo airport (☎ **010-610-5247**), open Monday to Saturday 9am to 12:30pm and 3:30 to 7:30pm.

CITY LAYOUT Genoa extends for miles along the coast, with neighborhoods and suburbs tucked into valleys and climbing the city's many hills. Most sights of interest are in the **old town,** a fascinating jumble of old palazzos, laundry-festooned tenements, cramped squares, and tiny lanes and alleyways clustered on the eastern side of the old port. The city's two train stations are located on either side of the old town, known as **Caruggi;** as confusing as Genoa's topography is, wherever you are in the old

A Genoa Warning

Even locals are wary of back streets in the old city, especially after dark and in midafternoons and Sundays, when shops are closed and streets tend to be deserted. Purse snatching, jewelry theft, and armed robberies are all too common. Also, count your change here. I've never had more people consistently try to rip me off (shops, restaurants, even the public parking garages) anywhere else in Italy.

town you are only a short walk or bus or taxi ride from one of these two stations. **Stazione Principe** is the closest, just to the west; from **Piazza Aquaverde** in front of the station follow **Via Balbi** through **Piazza della Nunziata** to **Via Caroli,** which runs into Via Garibaldi (the walk will take about 15 min.). Palazzo-lined **Via Garibaldi** forms the northern flank of the old town and is the best place to begin your explorations. Many of the city's major museums and other major monuments are on and around this street, and from here you can descend into the warren of little lanes that lead through the cluttered heart of Caruggi down to the port.

From **Stazione Brignole,** follow **Via XX Settembre,** one of the city's major shopping avenues, due west for about 15 or 20 minutes to **Piazza de Ferrari,** which is on the eastern edge of the old town. From here, **Via San Lorenzo** will lead you past Genoa's cathedral and to the port, but if you want to use Via Garibaldi as your sightseeing base, continue north from the piazza on **Via XXV Aprile** to **Piazza delle Fontane Marose.** This busy square marks the eastern end of Via Garibaldi.

FESTIVALS & MARKETS   In June, an ancient tradition continues when Genoa takes to the sea in the **Regatta Storica,** competing against crews from its ancient maritime rivals, Amalfi, Pisa, and Venice. The winner of the previous year's competition hosts the event, so your chances of witnessing the regatta during a June visit to Genoa depends on the fortunes of the previous year's boatmen.

Genoa adds a touch of culture to the summer season with an **International Ballet Festival** that attracts a stellar list of performers from around the world. Performances are held in the beautiful gardens of Villa Gropallo in outlying Nervi, an early-1900s resort with lush parks and an animated seaside promenade. Contact the tourist office in Genoa for schedules and ticket information. (Frequent trains connect Genoa and Nervi in 10 min. and run about every 20 min.; fare is 2,400L/$1.20) The tourist office also keeps tabs of the summer concerts staged at venues, many of them outdoor, around the city.

The **Mercato Orientale,** Genoa's sprawling indoor food market, evokes the days when ships brought back spices and other commodities from the ends of the earth. Still a boisterous affair and an excellent place to stock up on olives, herbs, fresh fruit, and other Ligurian products, it is held Monday to Saturday 7am to 1pm and 3:30 to 7:30pm (closed Wednesday afternoons), with entrances on Via XX Settembre and Via Galata (about halfway between Piazza de Ferrari at the edge of the old city and Stazione Brignole). The district just north of the market (especially Via San Vincenzo and Via Colombo) is a gourmand's dream, with many bakeries, *pasticcerie* (pastry shops), and stores selling pasta and cheese, wine, olive oil, and other foodstuffs.

SEEING THE SIGHTS

✪ **Acquario di Genova (Aquarium of Genoa).** Ponte Spinola. ☎ **010-248-1205.** www.acquario.ge.it. Admission 22,000L ($11) adults, 13,000L ($7) ages 3–12 with 3D film; 20,000L ($10) adults, 12,000L ($6) ages 3–12 without film. Mon–Fri 9:30am–7:30pm (to 11pm Thurs), Sat–Sun 9:30am–8:30pm. July–Aug daily 9:30am–11pm. Last entry 90 min. before closing. Closed Mon Nov–Feb. Bus: 1, 2, 3, 7, 8, 54.

Europe's largest aquarium is one of Genoa's biggest draws and a must-see for travelers with children. The structure itself is remarkable, resembling a ship and built alongside a pier in the old harbor (the aquarium is about a 15-min. walk from Stazione Principe and about 10 min. from Via Garibaldi). Inside, more than 50 aquatic displays realistically recreate Red Sea coral reefs, pools in the tropical rain forests of the Amazon River basin, and other marine ecosystems. These environments provide a pleasant home for sharks, seals, and just about every other known kind of sea creature, and the displays are fun—transparent columns eerily lit and filled with jellyfish, playful seals

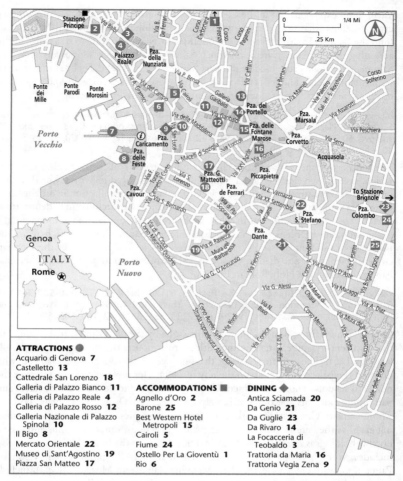

and dolphins who like to blow trick bubbles, and little rays in a shallow pool you can pet. And all the descriptions are posted in English. A popular new feature is the 10-minute 3D film on ocean life (ask for a sheet with the narration's English translation).

Cattedrale San Lorenzo. Piazza San Lorenzo. ☎ **010-311-269.** Admission to cathedral free; treasury 10,000L ($5) adults, 8,000L ($4) students and over 60, 20,000L ($10) family ticket for 2 adults & 2 children. Cathedral: Mon–Sat 8am–noon and 3–6:30pm, Sun noon–6:30pm; Treasury: by half-hour guided tour only Mon–Sat 9am–noon and 3–6pm. Bus: 17, 18, 19, 20, 30, 32, 33, 35, 37, 40, 41, 100, 605, 606, or 607.

The austerity of this black-and-white-striped 12th-century structure is enlivened ever so slightly by the fanciful French Gothic carvings around the portal and the presence of two stone lions. A later addition is the campanile, completed in the 16th century and containing at one corner a beloved Genoa artifact—a sundial known as L'Arrotino (the knife grinder) for its utilitarian appearance. In the frescoed interior, chapels house two of Genoa's most notable curiosities: beyond the first pilaster on the right is a shell fired through the roof from a British ship offshore during World War II that (*mirabile dictu*) never exploded, and in the Cappella di San Giovanni (left aisle), a 13th-century crypt contains what crusaders returning from the Holy Land claimed to be relics of John the Baptist. Fabled tableware of doubtful provenance appears to be a quirk of the adjoining treasury: The plate upon which Saint John's head was supposedly served to Salome, a bowl allegedly used at the Last Supper, and a bowl thought at one time to be the Holy Grail. The less fabled but nonetheless magnificent gold and bejeweled objects here reflect Genoa's medieval prominence as a maritime power.

Museo di Sant'Agostino (St. Augustine Museum of Ligurian Architecture and Sculpture). Piazza Sarzanno 35r. ☎ **010-251-1263.** Admission 6,000L ($3), free under 18 and over 60. Tues–Sat 9am–7pm, Sun 9am–12:30pm. Bus: 17, 18, 19, 20, 30, 32, 33, 35, 37, 40, 41, 100, 605, 606, or 607.

The cloisters of the 13th-century church and monastery of Sant'Agostino (most of which, save its two cloisters and a campanile, were destroyed in World War II bombings) are the evocative setting for an eclectic and fascinating collection of architectural fragments and sculpture. Roman columns, statuary, and architectural debris from Genoa's churches are scattered in what seems to be random fashion throughout the grassy monastery gardens and in a few bare interior spaces. The treasures here are the panels from Giovanni Pisano's *crypt for Margherita of Brabant,* wife of the German emperor Henry IV. She died in Genoa in 1312 while en route to Rome for her husband's coronation as Holy Roman Emperor.

Galleria di Palazzo Bianco (White Palace). Via Garibaldi 11. ☎ **010-557-3499** or 010-247-6377. Admission 6,000L ($3). Tues, Thurs, and Fri 9am–1pm; Wed and Sat 9am–7pm; Sun 10am–6pm. Bus: 19, 20, 30, 32, 33, 35, 36, 41, 42, 100, 605, 606.

One of Genoa's finest palaces, built of white stone by the powerful Grimaldi family in the 16th century and enlarged in the 18th century, houses the city's most notable collection of art. The paintings reflect the fine eye of the duchess of Galliera, who donated the palace and her art to the city in 1884. Her preference for painters of the northern schools, whom the affluent Genovese imported to decorate their palaces and paint their portraits, becomes strikingly obvious. Van Dyck and Rubens, both of whom came to Genoa in the early 17th century, are represented here with one painting each, as they are in the city's other major collections; one of the museum's most notable holdings is *Portrait of a Lady* by Lucas Cranach the Elder. The collection also includes works by other European and Italian masters (Filippino Lippi, Veronese, Palma il Giovanne, Caravaggio, Hans Memling, Jan Steen, Murillo, Ribera), including several Genovese masters who were the catalyst for the city's flourishing art movements—an entire room is dedicated to the works of Bernardo Strozzi, whose early-17th-century school made Genoa an important force in the baroque movement.

Galleria di Palazzo Reale (Royal Palace). Via Balbi 10. ☎ **010-271-0236.** Admission 8,000L ($4) (2,000L/$1 to visit to hanging gardens only), or 12,000L ($6) cumulative with Palazzo Spinola. Sun–Tues 9am–1:45pm; Wed–Sat 9am–7pm. Bus: 20.

The Royal Palace takes its name from its 19th- to early 20th-century tenants, the Royal House of Savoy, who greatly altered the 17th-century palace built for the Balbi

---

A Money-Saving Tip

Admission to all of Genoa's **civic museums**—Palazzo Bianco, Palazzo Rosso, Museo Sant'Agostino, and seven other minor museums around town—is free on Sunday. You can also buy a 10,000L ($5) combined ticket at any of them that's good for entry to one other.

family. The Savoys endowed the sumptuous surroundings with ostentatious frippery, most in evidence in the hall of mirrors, the ballroom, and the throne room. More aesthetically pleasing are the Van Dykes, Giordanos, and other paintings gracing many of the salons.

Galleria di Palazzo Rosso (Red Palace). Via Garibaldi 18. ☎ **010-247-6351.** Admission 6,000L ($3), 4,000L ($2) students, free under 18. Tues, Thurs, Fri 9am–1pm; Wed and Sat 9am–7pm; Sun 10am–6pm. Bus: 19, 20, 30, 32, 33, 35, 36, 41, 42, 100, 605, 606.

Another lavish 17th-century palace now houses, as does its neighbor the Palazzo Bianco, a magnificent collection of art. Many of the works—including many lavish frescoes—were commissioned or acquired by the Brignole-Sale, an aristocratic family who once lived in this red-stone palace. Van Dyck painted two members of the clan, Pauline and Anton Giulio Brignole-Sale, and their full-length portraits are among the masterpieces in the second-floor portrait galleries, whose ceilings were frescoed by Gregorio de Ferrari and Domenico Piola. *La Cuoca,* widely considered to be the finest work of Genovese master Bernardo Strozzi, and works by many other Italian and European masters—Gudio Reni, Dürer, Titian, Guercino, and Veronese among them—hang in the first-floor galleries.

Galleria Nazionale di Palazzo Spinola. Piazza Pellicceria 1. ☎ **010-270-5300.** Admission 8,000L ($4), or 12,000L ($6) cumulative with Palazzo Reale. Tues–Sat 9am–7pm, Sun 2–7pm. Bus: 1, 2, 3, 7, 8, 18, 19, 20, 30, 34, 35, 37, 39, 40, 41, 54.

Another prominent Genovese family, the Spinolas, donated their palace and magnificent art collection to the city only recently, in 1958. One of the pleasures of viewing these works is seeing them amid the frescoed splendor in which the city's merchant/banking families once lived. As in Genoa's other art collections, you will find masterworks that range far beyond native artists like Strozzi and De Ferrari. In fact, perhaps the most memorable painting here is *Ecce Homo,* by the Sicilian master Antonello da Messina. Guido Reni and Luca Giordano are also well represented, as are Van Dyck (including his fragmentary *Portrait of Ansaldo Pallavicino* and four of the *Evangelists*) and other painters of the Dutch and Flemish schools, whom Genoa's wealthy burghers were so fond of importing to paint their portraits.

HISTORIC SQUARES & STREETS

PIAZZA SAN MATTEO   This beautiful little square is the domain of the city's most acclaimed family, the seagoing Dorias, who ruled Genoa until the end of the 18th century. The church they built on the piazza in the 12th century, **San Matteo,** contains the crypt of the Dorias' most illustrious son, Andrea, and the cloisters are lined with centuries-old plaques heralding the family's many accomplishments, which included drawing up Genoa's constitution in 1529. The church is open Monday to Saturday, 8am to noon and 4 to 5pm and Sunday 4 to 5pm. The **Doria palaces** surround the church in a stunning array of loggias and black-and-white-striped marble facades denoting the homes of honored citizens—Andrea's at **no. 17,** Lamda's at **no. 15,** Branca's at **no. 14.** To get there take bus no. 18, 19, 20, 30, 32, 33, 35, 37, 40, 41, 100, 605, 606, or 607.

VIA GARIBALDI   Many of Genoa's museums and other sights are clustered on and around this street, one of the most beautiful in Italy, where Genoa's wealthy families built palaces in the 16th and 17th centuries. Aside from the art collections housed in the **Palazzo Bianco** and **Palazzo Rosso** (see above), the street contains a wealth of other treasures. The **Palazzo Podesta,** at no. 7, hides one of the city's most beautiful fountains in its courtyard, and the **Palazzo Turisi,** at no. 9, now housing the municipal offices, proudly displays artifacts of famous Genoans: letters written by Christopher Columbus and the violin of Nicolo Paganini (which is still played on special occasions). Visitors are allowed free entry to the building when the offices are open: Monday through Friday, 8:30am to noon and 1 to 4pm. To get there, take bus no. 19, 20, 30, 32, 33, 35, 36, 41, 42, 100, 605, or 606.

VIEWS & VISTAS

The **no. 33 bus** plies the scenic **Circonvallazione a Monte,** the corniche that hugs the hills and provides dizzying views over the city and the sea; you can board at Stazione Brignole or Stazione Principe.

From Piazza Portello (off the eastern end of Via Garibaldi, just before the Galleria Garibaldi tunnel), an elevator carries you up to the **Castelletto belvedere,** which offers stunning views and refreshing breezes and provides a handy break during sightseeing in the central city for 600L (30¢) each way, daily 6:40am–midnight.

A similar, view-affording climb is the one on the **Granarolo** funicular, a cog railway that leaves from Piazza del Principe, just behind the railway station of the same name, and ascends 1,000 feet to Porto Granarolo, one of the gates in the city's 17th-century walls; there's a parklike belvedere in front (1,500L/75¢ each way or you can use a bus ticket; daily every 15 minutes from 6am to 11:45pm).

An elevator lifts visitors to the top of **Il Bigo,** the modernistic, mast-like tower that is the new landmark of Genoa, built to commemorate the Columbus quincentennial celebrations in 1992. The observation platform provides an eagle's-eye view of one of Europe's busiest ports for 5,000L ($2.50) adults, 4,000L ($2) ages 3 to 12 (1,000L/50¢ off with aquarium ticket). It's open Tuesday to Friday 11:30am to 1pm and 2 to 5pm, Saturday and Sunday 11:30am to 1pm and 2 to 6pm.

Hour-long **harbor cruises** on one of the boats in the fleet of Cooperativa Battellieri dei Porto di Genova (☎ **010-265-712;** www.battellierigenova.it) provide a closer look at the bustle, along with close-up views of the **Lanterna,** the 360-foot-tall lighthouse (tallest in Europe) built in 1544 at the height of Genoa's maritime might (you can ride to the top Sunday afternoons only; visits leave from the Bigo at 2:30pm). Boats embark daily from Stazione Marittima, on the harbor, a short distance south of Stazione Principe, and the trip costs 10,000L ($5).

AFFORDABLE PLACES TO STAY

Genoa is geared more to business than to tourism, and as a result, decent inexpensive rooms are scarce. On the other hand, just about the only time the town is booked solid is during its annual boat show, the world's largest, in October. Except for the ones we include below, avoid hotels in the old city, especially around the harbor—most are unsafe and prefer to accommodate guests by the hour.

Agnello d'Oro. Via Monachette 6 (off Via Balbi), 16126 Genova. ☎ **010-246-2084.** Fax 010-246-2327. www.hotelagnellodoro.it. E-mail: hotelagnellodoro@libero.it. 25 units. TV TEL. 140,000L ($70) single; 175,000L ($88) double. Ask about lower rates on weekends and off-season. Breakfast 15,000L ($8). AE, DC, MC, V. Bus: 18, 19, 20, 30, 32, 34, 35, 37, 41, 54, 100, 605.

This converted convent enjoys a wonderful location—only a few short blocks from Stazione Principe yet on the edge of the old city. And the dead-end side street in front ensures peace and quiet. A few of the lower-floor rooms retain the building's original 16th-century character, with high (rooms numbered in teens) or vaulted (rooms numbered under 10) ceilings. Those upstairs have been completely renovated in crisp modern style, with warm-hued tile floors and mostly modular furnishings; the tiled baths are new and spotless, though many have only curtainless tubs with hand-held nozzles. Singles all come with those lovely extra-wide "French-style" beds. Some top-floor rooms come with the added charm of balconies and views over the old town and harbor (best from no. 56). The friendly proprietor dispenses wine, sightseeing tips, and breakfast in the cozy little bar off the lobby.

Barone. Via XX Settembre 2 (3rd floor), 16121 Genova. ☎ and fax **010-587-578.** 12 units, 1 with bathroom. 55,000L ($28) single without bathroom, 70,000L ($35) single with shower, 85,000L ($43) single with bathroom; 70,000L ($35) double without bathroom; 85,000L ($43) double with shower; 95,000L ($48) double with bathroom; 95,000L ($48) triple without bathroom, 105,000L ($53) triple with shower, 120,000L ($60) triple with bathroom; 120,000L ($60) quad with bathroom, 130,000L ($65) quad with shower. AE, DC, MC, V.

Near Stazione Brignole, this family-run pensione occupies the high-ceilinged large rooms of what was once a grand apartment. And, a rarity in Genoa, it offers unusually pleasant accommodations at very reasonable rates. Marco, the young proprietor, affords a gracious welcome, pointing guests to nearby restaurants, telling them what not to miss, and joining them in the communal sitting room; self-service espresso is available around the clock. The rooms are indeed baronial in size (some can be set up with extra beds for families) and are reached by elegant halls hung with gilt mirrors and paintings. While the eclectic furnishings are a bit less grand, many retain lovely touches like a stuccoed ceiling here (in most, actually) or a chandelier there. The beds are firm and comfortable, the linens are fresh, seven rooms come with TVs, and the shared facilities are spotless. Two technically bathless accommodations also have a shower in the room, but you must share the hall toilets.

Best Western Hotel Metropoli. Piazza Fontane Marose, 16123 Genova. ☎ **010-246-8888.** Fax 010-246-8686. www.bestwestern.it/metropoli_ge. 48 units. A/C MINIBAR TV TEL. 195,000L ($98) single; 295,000L ($148) double. Lower rates during slow periods. Rates include buffet breakfast. AE, DC, MC, V. Parking 32,000L ($16) in nearby garage. Bus: 19, 20, 30, 32, 33, 35, 36, 41, 42, 100, 605, 606.

Facing a lovely historic square just around the corner from the Via Garibaldi, the Metropoli brings modern amenities, combined with a gracious ambience, to the old city. No small part of the appeal of staying here is that many of the surrounding streets are open only to pedestrians, so you can step out of the hotel and avoid the onrush of traffic that plagues much of central Genoa. Guest rooms have somewhat banal and businesslike contemporary furnishings, but with double-pane windows and pleasing pastel fabrics they provide an oasis of calm in this often-unnerving city. They're renovating three or four rooms a year, and currently have the third, fourth, and fifth floors done. The style is more or less the same, but the furnishings are nicer; the biggest difference is in the newly refurbished baths, now equipped with hair dryers, heated towel racks, and double sinks with lots of marble counter space.

Cairoli. Via Cairoli 14, 16124 Genova. ☎ **010-246-1524.** Fax 010-246-7512. E-mail: htlcairoli@tin.it. 12 units. MINIBAR TV TEL. 90,000L ($45) single; 130,000L ($65) double; 160,000L ($80) triple; 180,000L ($90) quad. Breakfast 10,000L ($5). AE, DC, MC, V. Parking 25,000L ($13) in nearby garage. Bus: 18, 19, 20, 30, 34, 35, 37, 39, 40, 41.

Location is a bonus at this pleasant family-run hotel on the third floor of an old building a little ways south of Stazione Principe and near the port, the aquarium, Via Garibaldi, and the sights of the old city. The small rooms are extremely pleasant, with tasteful modern furnishings and tidy little baths; double-paned glass keeps street noise to a minimum. The friendly management leaves a little basket of snacks in your room (cookies, crackers, and Pringles) and has a soft spot for stray cats (four of them roam the place). In good weather, you can relax on a terrace covered with potted plants (compact no. 9 opens onto it). Room 14 is perfect for families, with two twin beds in the first room and a double bed in a back room separated by a curtain.

Fiume. Via Fiume 9r, 16121 Genova. ☎ **010-591-691.** Fax 010-570-2833. 20 units, 4 with bathroom. TV. 45,000L ($23) single without bathroom, 65,000L ($33) single with shower, 70,000L ($35) single with bathroom; 65,000L ($33) double with shower, 90,000L ($45) double with bathroom. AE, MC, V.

I don't include this choice as a memorable hotel experience. Rather, the Fiume is a serviceable budget option, clean, safe, and close to Stazione Brignole as well as to Genoa's intriguing Mercato Orientale food market and the profusion of food and wine shops around it. The desk staff in the brightly lit lobby can be brusquely efficient as they direct you to the rather run-down rooms, where the furnishings consist of little more than cotlike beds, tables, and functional chairs. Even so, everything—including shared facilities in the halls—is immaculate, and the travelers from around the world who stay here provide good company. This being a 19th-century palazzo, the second-floor rooms are more spacious with higher ceilings than those on the first floor (no elevator). All rooms save a few singles have a shower and sink in the room, but toilets are shared with the exception of in two doubles and two singles.

Ostello Per La Gioventù. Via Costanzi 120, 16136 Genova. ☎ and fax **010-242-2457.** E-mail: hostelge@iol.it. 213 beds. 25,000L ($13) per person in 8-bed dorm rooms; 28,000L ($14) per person in family rooms with private bathroom for 3–5; 30,000L ($15) per person in family double with private bathroom. IYH card required, or tack on extra 5,000L ($2.50) per person. Rates include breakfast. No credit cards. Closed late Dec–Jan. Check-in 3:30pm to 12:30am (curfew), though luggage drop off available 9:30–11:30am. Bus: 40.

Even if you feel you've outgrown hosteling, the quality of the accommodations and the pleasant surroundings here may convince you to take another stab at the experience. This one is new and attractive, and affords some marvelous views over the city from its hillside perch about a kilometer from the terminal of the Righi funicular (which you can take downtown to Largo Zecca every 15–20 minutes 6:40am to midnight for a regular 1,500L/75¢ bus ticket). Families make out especially well here, in rooms with private baths; other guests sleep four to eight in a room. There's a large terrace, a bar, a cafeteria where you can get a plate of pasta at dinner for 5,000L to 6,500L ($2.50 to $3.25), TV room and a laundromat (12,000L/$6 a load). Plus, though the hostel is in a safe area well above the hustle and bustle of the city, it's only about 20 minutes to Stazione Brignole on the no. 40 bus, which makes the run about every 10 minutes. (From Stazione Principe, take bus 35 to Via Napoli, where you can change for the 40.)

Rio. Via Ponte Calvi 5 (off Via Gramsci), 16124 Genova. ☎ **010-246-1594.** Fax 010-247-6871. 42 units. TV TEL. 80,000L ($40) single; 120,000L ($60) double; 140,000L ($70) triple. Rates include breakfast. AE, MC, V. Parking 25,000L ($13). Bus: 1, 2, 3, 7, 8, 54.

It's a bit of a dump, but a cheap, well-located dump at least! It's wonderfully located amid the clamor and intrigue of the old city and just a few steps from the port and aquarium. In fact, the Rio provides just about the only decent accommodations so close to the old harbor area. (You'll want to keep your wits about you, though, when coming and going late at night). The guest rooms tend to be large and are equipped with modern furnishings that do the job well enough, but baths are hurting for an overhaul. Tip: upper floors have been renovated more recently, and tend to be a bit nicer. Genoa's convention facilities are nearby, so reservations are essential at periods when the city hosts one of its trade fairs (many are held in October).

GREAT DEALS ON DINING

Da Genio. Salita San Leonardo 61r. ☎ **010-588-463.** Reservations recommended. Primi 14,000–18,000L ($7–$9); secondi 16,000–22,000L ($8–$11). AE, MC, V. Mon–Sat 12:30–3pm and 7–10pm. Closed Aug. GENOESE.

One of Genoa's most beloved trattorias, handily situated near Piazza Dante in the old quarter, Da Genio is wonderfully animated. Local artists' works brighten the cozy dining rooms, which are almost always full of Genovese businesspeople and families who have been coming here for years. The assorted antipasti provide a nice introduction to local cuisine, with such specialties as stuffed sardines and *torte di verdure* (vegetable pie). While the menu usually includes a nice selection of fresh fish and some meat dishes (including delicious tripe or steak with porcini), you can also move on to some of the homey standbys the kitchen does so well, such as *spaghetti al sugo di pesce* (topped with a fish sauce) or an amazingly fresh *insalata di mare* (seafood salad)—though almost everyone starts off with *trenette al pesto* (two-inch extra thick twisted spaghetti with pesto). The wine list includes a nice selection from Ligurian vineyards.

Da Guglie. Via San Vincenzo 64r. ☎ **010-565-765.** Primi 6,000–10,000L ($3–$5); secondi 8,000–15,000L ($4–$8). No credit cards. Daily noon–10pm. LIGURIAN.

The busy kitchen, with its open hearth, occupies a good part of this simple restaurant, which serves this neighborhood near Stazione Brignole with takeout fare from a counter and accommodates diners in a bare-bones little room off to one side. In fact, there's no attempt at all to provide a decorative ambience. The specials of the day (which often include octopus and other seafood) are displayed in the window; tell the cooks behind the counter what you want and they will bring it over to one of the oilcloth-covered tables when it's ready. Don't be shy about asking for a sampling of the reasonably priced dishes, because you can happily eat your way through Genovese cuisine here. *Farinata* (chick-pea crêpes), *focaccia* with many different toppings, gnocchi with pesto, *riso di carciofi* (rice with artichokes), and other dishes are accompanied by Ligurian wines served by the glass or carafe.

Da Rivaro. Via di Portello 16r. ☎ **010-277-0054.** Reservations recommended. Primi 12,000–18,000L ($6–$9); secondi 18,000–28,000L ($9–$14). AE, MC, V. Tues–Sat noon–3pm and 7–10pm, Mon 7–10pm. Closed Aug. LIGURIAN/ITALIAN.

Wonderfully located amid the Renaissance splendor of the nearby Via Garibaldi, this old institution does a brisk business with a loyal clientele from nearby banks and consulates, especially at lunch and in the early evening. The decor is pleasantly reminiscent of a ship's cabin, with inlaid wood panels and long wooden tables lit by brass lanterns; many of the attentive, white-jacketed waiters have worked here their entire careers. Ligurian classics such as *trenette al pesto con patate e fagiolini* (pasta with pesto, potatoes, and beans) and a *zuppa da pesce* made with local fish emerge from the kitchen, but the menu also ventures far beyond Genoa to include a wide range of pastas from other regions (many with tomato and cream sauces) and grilled meats.

Trattoria da Maria. Vico Testadoro 14r (just off Via XX Aprile). ☎ **010-581-080.** Primi 5,000–6,000L ($2.50–$3); secondi 7,000–9,000L ($3.50–$4.50); *menù turistico* 13,000L ($7) with wine. MC, V. Sun and Tues–Fri 11:45am–2:15pm and 7–9:15pm, Mon 11:45am–2:45pm. LIGURIAN.

Maria Mante is something of a local legend and for decades has turned out delicious meals from her busy kitchen, attended by relatives young and old. Her cooking and the congenial ambience of the two-floor restaurant in the old city near Piazza delle Fontane Marose draw a crowd of neighborhood residents, students, businesspeople, and tourists of all nationalities. This unlikely mix sits side by side at long tables covered with red- or blue-checked tablecloths and engages in animated conversation, while the staff hurries around them and shouts orders up and down the shaft of a dumbwaiter. Daily specials and the stupendously cheap fixed-price menu of the day—which often includes *minestrone alla genovese, risotto buonissimo alla genovese* (rice with a sauce stirred; they also feel secure labeling their creamy gelato "buonissimo"), *zuppe da pesce* (a rich fish soup you must try if it's available), and such simple main courses as a fillet of fish sautéed in white wine or grilled sausages—are listed on sheets of paper posted to the shiny pale green walls. As befits a Genovese institution like this, the pasta with pesto sauce is especially delicious, as is *pansotti,* small ravioli covered with a walnut-cream sauce.

Trattoria Vegia Zena. Vico del Serriglio 15r. ☎ **010-251-3332.** Primi 9,000–30,000L ($4.50–$15); secondi 12,000–45,000L ($6–$23). MC, V. Tues–Sat noon–2:30pm and 7:30–10pm, Mon noon–2:30pm. GENOVESE.

In the *centro storico* near the old port (on an alley across from the aquarium), this lively, white-walled and wood-paneled room lives up to its name—dialect for Old Genoa—with expertly prepared Genovese dishes. Since the restaurant is very popular with Genovese from all over the city, who consider this their favorite place to dine, you may well be asked to share one of the crowded tables with other diners. Pasta with pesto is excellent, followed by a fine selection of fresh seafood.

PASTRY & GELATO

The ✪ **Antica Pasticceria Gelateria Klainguti,** on Piazza Soziglia 98r–100r (☎ **010-247-4552**), is Genoa's best bakery as well as its oldest—it was founded in 1828 by a Swiss family. One satisfied customer was the composer Giuseppe Verdi, who said the house's Falstaff (a sweet brioche) was better than his. This and a stupefying assortment of other pastries and chocolates, as well as light snacks (including panini), are served in a pretty Rococo style room or in the piazza out front. It's open daily 8am to 7pm.

Add **Banarama,** Via San Vincenzo 65r (☎ **010-581-130**), to your explorations of the many food shops and markets in the neighborhood near Stazione Brignole. Is this the best gelato in Genoa? The jury is still out, but the creamy concoctions are indeed memorable. Just as good are the simple granites, shaved ice with fresh fruit flavorings. Open Monday to Saturday to 7:30pm. Just off the waterfront and near the

---

Fast Food Genoa Style

Fast food is a Genovese specialty, and any number of storefronts all over the city disburse *focaccia,* the heavenly Ligurian flat bread often stuffed with cheese and topped with herbs, olives, onions, vegetables, or prosciutto. A favorite place for focaccia, and so close to Stazione Principe that you can stop in for a taste of this aromatic delicacy as soon as you step off the train, is **La Focacceria di Teobaldo,** Via Balbi 115r (☎ 010-246-2294), open daily 8am to 8pm; focaccia begins at 1,000L (50¢) a slice.

Another Geonvese favorite is *farinata,* a cross between a ravioli and a crêpe made from chick-pea flour that is stuffed with spinach and ricotta, lightly fried, and often topped with a cream and walnut sauce. Locals say this delicious concoction gets no better than it is at the two outlets of **Antica Sciamada,** Via Ravecca 19r (☎ 010-280-843) and Via San Giorgio 14r, both open Monday to Saturday 9am to 7:30pm; from 3,500L ($1.75).

fairgrounds, the simple, no-frills **Cremeria Augusto,** Via Nino Bixio 5 (☎ **010-591-884**), is almost a mandatory stop when taking a stroll through this part of the city. The house makes dozens of flavors of rich, delicious gelato fresh daily and it is marvelous, but the specialty is crema, a frozen egg custard. Open Sunday to Friday to 10pm.

GENOA AFTER DARK

The harbor area, much of which is unsafe even in broad daylight, is especially unseemly at night. Confine late-hour prowls in the old city to the well-trafficked streets around Piazza Fontane Marose and Piazza delle Erbe, where many bars and clubs are located anyway.

PERFORMING ARTS   Genoa has two major venues for culture: **Teatro Carlo Felice,** Piazza de Ferrari (☎ **010-589-329;** www.carlofelice.it), is home to Genoa's opera company and hosts visiting companies as well; the new **Teatro delle Corte** (☎ **010-534-2200;** www.teatro-di-genova.it), on Piazza Borgo Pila near Stazione Brignole, hosts concerts, dance events, and other cultural programs.

BARS & CLUBS   Open all day, **Brittania** at Vico Casana (just off Piazza De Ferrari) serves pints to homesick travelers from morning to night, but caters to a largely Italian crowd at night (☎ **010-294-878**).

New Yorkers will recognize the name and chic ambience from the branch of **I Tre Merli Antica Cantina** at Vico Dietro il Coro d. Maddalena 26r. (☎ **010-247-4095;** www.itremerli.it), which does a brisk business in Manhattan with several restaurants (three in SoHo, one uptown). Here in Genoa, Ai Tre Merli operates several enotecas, and this one, with a location on a narrow street just off Via Garibaldi that makes it a safe nightspot in the old city, is delightful. A dark stone floor and walls of brick and stone provide a cozy setting, augmented by "refined country" style tables and chairs. You can sample the wide selection of wines from throughout Italy by the glass, and there is a full bar. The half-dozen each of primi and secondi are refined Ligurian, and along with the cheese and salami platters make this a good spot for a late-night meal; open Tuesday to Sunday 7pm to 1am.

Le Courbusier, Via San Donato 36 (☎ **010-246-8652**), opens early and closes late. This coffeehouse cum bar in the old quarter just west of Piazza delle Erbe is especially popular with students. The smoky room is perpetually busy, dispensing excellent coffee and sandwiches (from 5,000L/$2.50) as well as wine and spirits.

2 The Riviera di Ponente: San Remo, Bordighera & More

San Remo: 140km (81 mi.) W of Genoa, 59km (35 mi.) E of Nice. Bordighera: 155km (93 mi.) W of Genoa, 15km (9 mi.) W of San Remo, 45km (27 mi.) E of Nice.

SAN REMO

Gone are the days when Tchaikovsky and the Russian empress Maria Alexandranova joined a well-heeled mix of titled continental and British gentry in strolling along San Remo's palm-lined avenues. They left behind an onion-domed Orthodox church, a few grand hotels, and a snooty casino, but **San Remo** is a different sort of town these days. It's still the most cosmopolitan stop on the Riviera di Ponente (Setting Sun), as the stretch of coast west of Genoa is called, catering mostly to sun-seeking Italian families in the summer and elderly Romans and Milanese who come to enjoy the balmy temperatures in the winter.

In addition to the gentle ambience of days gone by, San Remo offers its visitors a long stretch of beach and a hilltop old town known as La Pigna. For cosmopolitan pleasures, the casino attracts a well-attired clientele willing to try their luck.

San Remo is an excellent base from which to explore the rocky coast and Ligurian hills. So is Bordighera, a quieter resort just up the coast. With excellent train and bus connections, both are within easy reach of a full itinerary of fascinating stops that include Giardino Hanbury, one of Europe's most exquisite gardens; the fascinating prehistoric remains at Balzi Rossi; and Docleacqua, perhaps the most enticing of all the inland Ligurian villages (for more information on these places, see below).

ESSENTIALS

GETTING THERE   By Train   There are trains almost hourly to and from **Genoa** (regional: 2½ hr., 13,500L/$6.75; High speed: 1¾ hr., 20,200L/$10). There are 2 to 3 trains per hour connecting with **Bordighera** (13 min., 2,300L/$1.15). Trains from Genoa continue west for another 20 minutes to **Ventimiglia** on the French border (2,700L/$1.35). From Ventimiglia, you can continue across the border on one of the hourly trains to **Nice,** 40 minutes west; the fare from San Remo is 17,600L ($9), from Ventimiglia 15,600L ($8).

By Bus   Riviera Trasporti buses (☎ **0184-592-706;** www3.50megs.com/rtspa) run every 15 minutes between San Remo and **Bordighera** (20 min.; 2,200L/$1.10). Almost as many buses continue on to **Ventimiglia** (40 min. from San Remo; 3,300L/$1.65).

By Car   The fastest driving route in and out of San Remo is the A10 autostrada, which follows the coast from the French border (20 min. away) to Genoa (about 45 min. away). The slower coast road, S1, cuts right through the center of town.

VISITOR INFORMATION   The **APT tourist board** is at Largo Nuvoloni 1 (☎ **0184-571-571,** fax: 0184-567-649; www.rivieratrasporti.it), at the corner with Corso Imperatrice/Corso Matteotti (exit the train station, across the street and to the left a few hundred feet). It's open Monday to Saturday 8am to 7pm and Sunday 9am to 1pm. In addition to a wealth of information on San Remo, the office also dispenses information on towns up and down the nearby coast, known as the Riviera dei Fiori.

FESTIVALS   August 15, the **Feast of the Assumption,** is celebrated with special flair in San Remo, with the festival of Nostra Signora della Costa (our Lady of the Coast). The Virgin Mary allegedly saved a local sailor from drowning, and she is honored with fireworks and a procession in medieval garb to her shrine on a hillside high above the town.

Since the 1950s, the **Sanremo Festival** (in late February or early March) has been Italy's—and one of Europe's—premier music fests. It's sort of an Italian version of the Grammys, only spread out over several days with far more live performances—by Italian pop stars, international headliners, and plenty of up-and-coming singers, songwriters, and bands. "Volare" was Sanremo's first-ever Best Recording and today most Italian CD collection contains at least a few of the yearly compilation albums. The

A Day at the Beach

Plunging into the Ligurian Sea in San Remo means spending some money. The pebbly beach below the Passaggiata dell'Imperatrice is lined with beach stations, where many visitors choose to spend their days: easy to do, since most provide showers, snack bars, and, of course, beach chairs, lounges, and umbrellas. Expect to spend at least 10,000L ($5) for a basic lounge, up to 25,000L ($13) for a more elaborate sun bed arrangement with umbrella.

festival has spawned many other contest-like celebrations of film and music (international folk to *musica lirica*) throughout the year, but this is the big one, booking hotels up and down the coast months in advance.

STROLLING AROUND TOWN

Though San Remo has a municipal bus system (fare is 1,500L/75¢), you should be able to get anywhere you want to go on foot. The train station is on the seaside and divides the commercial part of town from the resort and beach area. The tourist board is just in front of the station and just beyond that is the onion-domed **Chiesa Russa** (☎ **0184-531-807**), more formally the Chiesa di Cristo Salvatore, where the Russian nobility who once favored San Remo worshipped. You can step inside for a view of dark, icon-enriched interior; open Tuesday to Sunday 9:30am to 12:30pm and 3:30 to 6:30pm; suggested donation 1,000L (50¢).

To the left as you leave the station is the beginning of the palm-lined promenade, the **Passaggiata dell'Imperatrice,** which skirts the narrow pebbly strand between the train tracks and the busy coastal road, passing any number of cramped beach stations. One of the more pleasant stops along the way is the **Giardini Comunali Marsaglia** (signposted Auditorium Franco Alfano), a small but luxuriant hillside garden that bursts with exotic flora (open daily, dawn to dusk).

To the right of the station are the beginnings of Corso Roma and Corso Giacomo, San Remo's two main thoroughfares. Corso Giacomo will lead you past the **casino** (see below) and into the heart of the lively business district. Continue on that until it becomes Via Matteotti, which, after a block, runs into Piazza Colombo and the flower market. If you turn left (north) on Via Feraldi about midway down Corso Giacomo, you will find yourself in the charming older precincts of town. Continue through the Piazza degli Eroi Sanremesi to Piazza Mercato, where Via Monta leads into the old medieval quarter, **La Pigna.** The hill on which this fascinating district is located resembles a pine cone in its conical shape, hence the name. Aside from a few restaurants, La Pigna is today a residential quarter, with tall old houses that overshadow the narrow lanes that twist and turn up the hillside to the park-enclosed ruins of a **castle** at the top.

VISITING THE CASINO

Set intimidatingly atop a long flight of steps across from the train station—Corso degli Inglesi swoops around it off Corso Matteotti—San Remo's white palace of a casino (☎ **0184-5951**) not only lords over the center of town, it's also the hub of the local night life scene. You can't step foot inside without being properly attired (jacket for gents from October to June) and showing your passport. Monday to Thursday admission is free, but on weekends you must unburden yourself of 15,000L ($8) to get in—and that's even before you hit the tables, which attract high rollers from the length of the Riviera. Gaming rooms are open daily 2:30pm to 3am (to 4am on Sunday morning). Things are more relaxed in the rooms set aside for slot machines, where there is neither a dress code nor an entrance fee. It's open Sunday to Friday 10am to 2:30am and Saturday 2:30pm to 3am.

AFFORDABLE PLACES TO STAY

Al Dom. Corso Mombello 13, 18038 San Remo. ☎ **0184-501-460.** 15 units. TV. 60,000–80,000L ($30–$40) single; 100,000–150,000L ($50–$75) double. Half-board 60,000–85,000L ($30–$43) per person; full board 80,000–110,000L ($40–$55) per person. Breakfast included. No credit cards.

This rambling, dark, old-fashioned pensione near the casino, city center, and harbor occupies the second floor of a grand 19th-century apartment house. The rooms,

---

Is Board Necessary?

Many hotels offer room and board rates that include breakfast and lunch and dinner (full board or full-pension) or breakfast and one of these other two meals (half-board or half-pension). Only in the busy late July, early August beach season do many require you take these meals, however. If you can procure a room without the meal plan, do so—San Remo has many excellent restaurants, and this is not a place where you have to spend a lot for a good meal.

---

basically but nicely furnished with modern pieces and floral bedspreads, are carved out of former salons and tucked into the closed-off ends of ballroom-size hallways; no. 5 has a large balcony over the street. Tiny baths (some of them modular units that resemble the public facilities you find in Paris and other cities) have been appended wherever they might fit. So, be prepared for the unexpected: You may well find yourself staring up at an ornately plastered ceiling from a metal-frame bed crammed next to a marble fireplace. In short, the surroundings may not be stylish, but they are memorable, and the family that runs the pensione is friendly and always on hand to see that guests are comfortable.

Paradiso. Via Roccasterone 12, 18038 San Remo. ☎ **0184-571-211.** Fax 0184-578-176. www.paradisohotel.it. E-mail: paradisohotel@sistel.it. 41 units. MINIBAR TV TEL. 120,000–170,000L ($60–$85) single; 180,000–270,000L ($90–$135) double. Half-board, 130,000–200,000L ($65–$100) per person; full board 150,000–220,000L ($75–$110) per person. Buffet breakfast included. AE, DC, MC, V. Parking 15,000L ($8).

A former villa, set in a pretty garden above the seaside promenade, has been topped off with several extra floors of very pleasant guest rooms, many of which have flower-filled balconies overlooking the sea (rooms with balcony have a 10,000L/$5 supplement). An understated elegance characterizes these relaxing surroundings. Guest rooms are extremely well maintained but retain the sort of old-fashioned comfort that brings a loyal clientele back year after year for their month by the sea. Furnishings are a homey collection of old armoires, armchairs, and upholstered headboards, and the tiled baths, with large sinks and bathtubs, are luxuriously commodious. Cocktails are served in the comfortable, elegantly furnished salon in the evenings, or in the nicely planted garden in good weather, and guests can take meals in an airy dining room. A small pool is expected sometime in 2002 and air-conditioning should be installed by then or soon after.

Riviera. Corso degli Inglesi 86, 18038 San Remo. ☎ **0184-502-215.** Fax 0184-502-216. 14 units. TV TEL. 75,000–110,000L ($38–$55) single; 100,000–150,000L ($50–$75) double. Half-board (required at Easter, Christmas, August, and during Sanremo Festival) 85,000–120,000L ($43–$60) per person; full board 95,000–140,000L ($48–$70) per person. Breakfast 7,500L ($3.75). AE, DC, MC, V. Sometimes closed a few weeks in Nov and Mar.

While convenient to the beach and other attractions, this family-run pensione on the ground floor of a rather dire cement-cube (modern?) hillside apartment house is close to the center but just far enough off the beaten path to enjoy peace and quiet, and it often has rooms when other places in town fill up. Oriental runners and attractive slipcovered furniture lend an air of elegance to the public areas. The guest rooms, most of which overlook the sea and the old town, are spacious and modestly but attractively furnished in modern style with an eye to comfort—beds are firm, there are ample surfaces on which to spread out belongings, and most of the baths are up to date.

✪ Sole Mare. Via Carli 23, 18038 San Remo. ☎ **0184-577-105.** Fax 0184-532-778. E-mail: albergosolemare@libero.it. 21 units. MINIBAR TV TEL. 80,000L ($40) single; 130,000L ($65) double. Half-board (obligatory in Aug) 100,000L ($50) per person; full board 110,000L ($55) per person if stay at least 3 days. Continental breakfast 10,000L ($5). AE, DC, MC, V.

Don't let the location on a drab side street near the train station put you off. This cheerful pensione on the upper floors of an apartment house is a delight and offers its guests a friendly welcome along with some of the best-value lodgings in the resort area. A lounge, bar area, and dining room are airy and spacious and flooded with light, with gleaming white tile floors, blond-wood furniture, and doors leading out to a wide terrace. The large guest rooms are also cheerful and are equipped with the trappings of much more expensive hotels—pleasant modern furnishings and soothing pastel fabrics, TVs and minibars, small but modern and well-lit baths—and almost all enjoy sea views, about half from wide balconies.

Villa Maria. Corso Nuvoloni 30, 18038 San Remo. ☎ **0184-531-422.** Fax 0184-531-425. 38 units. TEL TV. 90,000–130,000L ($45–$65) single; 120,000–200,000L ($60–$100) double. Continental breakfast included. Half-board (required Easter, Christmas, and Aug 1–15) 80,000–135,000L ($40–$68) per person; full board 110,000–160,000L ($55–$80) per person. AE, DC, MC, V.

It's fairly easy to imagine San Remo's turn-of-the-century heyday in this charming hotel incorporating three villas on a flowery hillside above the casino. The promenade is only a short walk downhill, yet the hubbub of the resort seems miles away from this leafy residential district. A series of elegant salons and dining rooms with parquet floors, richly paneled ceilings, and crystal chandeliers spread across the ground floor, and many of these public rooms open to a nicely planted terrace. The bedrooms, too, retain the grandeur of the original dwellings, with silk-covered armchairs and antique beds; many have balconies facing the sea. The baths have old-fashioned details such as tubs with hand-held shower nozzles. Since rooms vary considerably in size and decor, ask to look around before you settle on one that strikes your fancy.

GREAT DEALS ON DINING

Antica Trattoria Piccolo Mondo. Via Piave 7. ☎ **0184-509-012.** Reservations recommended. Primi 9,500–12,500L ($5–$6); secondi 13,500–25,000L ($7–$13). No credit cards. Tues–Sat 12:30–1:50pm and 7:30–9:30pm. LIGURIAN.

The attentive staff will make you feel at home the moment you step into the perpetually crowded rooms of this decades-old trattoria on a narrow side street near the waterfront in the commercial district. The clientele is local, and they come here in droves to enjoy the comfortable atmosphere (which includes the furnishings installed when the restaurant opened in the 1920s) and the distinctly Ligurian fare—*verdura ripiena* (fresh vegetables stuffed with rice and seafood), fresh fish, and *polpo con patate* (octopus with potatoes). The menu changes daily to incorporate what is fresh in the markets, but also includes excellent risottos, pasta dishes, and meat dishes that are standards. (The grilled veal chop topped with fresh mushrooms is delicious.)

Cantine Sanremese. Via Palazzo 7. ☎ **0184-572-063.** Primi 6,000–10,000L ($3–$5); secondi 8,000–13,000L ($4–$7). AE, MC, V. Tues–Sun 10am–5pm. Closed July 1–15. LIGURIAN.

This cozy publike restaurant devoted to the local cuisine is firmly planted in the center of the modern town, as if to suggest that old San Remo traditions are not to be discarded. Patrons share tables as they enjoy the wide selections of wine by the glass (from 2,500L/$1.25) and sample the offerings that owner Renzo Morselli and his family prepare daily. The best way to dine here is not order a whole meal, but to sample all the dishes that tempt you. These may include *sardemaira*, the local foccacia-like bread, *torta verde* (a quiche of fresh green vegetables), and many kinds of soups, including a minestrone thick with fresh vegetables and garnished with pesto.

Ristorante L'Airone. Piazza Eroi Sanremesi 12. ☎ **0184/531-469.** Primi 11,000–18,000L ($6–$9); secondi 12,000–27,000L ($6–$14); pizze 5,000–13,000L ($2.50–$7); *menù turístico* 25,000L ($13;) without wine. DC, MC, V. Fri–Wed noon–2:30pm and 7:30–11:30pm. LIGURIAN/PIZZA.

With its pale gold walls and green-hued tables and chairs, this delightful, friendly restaurant in a pedestrian-only section of the city center looks like it's been transported over the border from Provence. The food, though, is definitely Ligurian, with a wide selection of fresh pastas, including gnocchi in pesto sauce, followed perhaps by a *grigliata mista* of fresh fish or grilled sole. For a more casual meal, light-crusted pizzas emerge from a tiled oven in the rear. In good weather, meals are served in small garden out back.

Spaghetteria Il Mulattiere. Via Palma 11. ☎ **0184-502-662.** Primi 7,000–15,000L ($3.50–$8); no secondi; *menu completo* 15,000L ($8), includes antipasto & a primo. No credit cards. Thurs–Tues noon–3pm and 7:30–10pm. LIGURIAN.

Anyone who visits San Remo should plan to visit this family-run trattoria in La Pigna, the oldest part of San Remo. Whether you come for lunch or dinner or just to enjoy a glass of wine, you'll probably first want to stroll around the surrounding quarter, an amazing warren of steep lanes clinging to the side of a hill. This two-floor eatery is as rich in character as its surroundings—the tables, covered with red-checked cloths, are overshadowed by antique farm implements (Il Mulattiere means "Mule Driver") and other rural artifacts. The menu is simple, featuring Ligurian specialties that change daily and often include delicious *crostini all'acciughe* (toasted bread topped with fresh anchovies), *zuppa al pomodoro* (a spicy soup of fresh tomatoes) or minestrone, and many fresh pastas. For a light meal, you can choose from an antipasto table laden with fresh vegetables and olives, and accompany it with a bowl of pasta.

THE CAFE & BAR SCENE

Agora Cafè, Piazza San Siro (no phone), which faces San Remo's cathedral, makes no claim other than to be a comfortable watering hole, a function it performs very well. For footsore travelers the terrace out front, facing the pretty stone piazza and cathedral of San Siro, is a welcome oasis. Sandwiches and other light fare are served late into the night, when an after-dinner crowd tends to make this one of the livelier spots in town; closed Monday.

Wanderings through the center of town should include a stop at the handsome wine bar **Enoteca Bacchus** (Via Roma 65; ☎ **0184-530-990**), open Monday to Saturday 10am to 9pm. This is where you can also stock up on olive oil and other Ligurian foodstuffs. Wine is served by the glass at a sit-down bar or one of the small tables, and you can accompany your libations with fresh focaccia, cheeses, vegetable tarts, and even such substantial fare as *buridda,* a dish of salted cod, tomatoes, and other vegetables.

BORDIGHERA

Known throughout Italy for its palm trees, **Bordighera** lays claim to the legend that the seeds of date palms carried across the sea from Egypt first took root in European soil here. To this day Bordighera has the honor of supplying its ubiquitous fronds to the Vatican for Palm Sunday services. The palm trees create a verdant canopy that extends up the hillside from the Mediterranean and the cluster of modern seaside development to the charming old town. Bordighera's other claim to fame is its enormous popularity with elderly Italian and British pensioners (its reputation as a getaway for retirees is similar to that of St. Petersburg in Florida). If you want glitter, you may be happier in San Remo; on the other hand, if you want to enjoy some peace and quiet and the same verdant vegetation that attracted Claude Monet, Bordighera may be just the stop for you.

ESSENTIALS

GETTING THERE   By Train   There are trains almost hourly to and from **Genoa** (regional: 2 hr. 20 min., 13,500L/$6.75; high speed: 2 hr., 20,200L/$10), and 2 to 3 trains per hour connecting with **San Remo** (13 min., 2,300L/$1.15).

By Bus   Riviera Trasporti buses (☎ **0184-592-706;** www.3.50megs.com/rtspa) run every 15 minutes between **San Remo** and Bordighera (20 min.; 2,200L/$1.10). Buses also run between Bordighera and **Ventimiglia;** the fare is 2,200L ($1.10).

By Car   You can take the A10 autostrada between Bordighera and San Remo, but the coast road, S1, is almost as fast. In fact, there is such a contiguous line of development along the route that you won't know where one town ends and the other begins.

VISITOR INFORMATION   The **tourist office** is at Via Vittorio Emanuele 172 (☎ **0184-262-322;** fax 0184-26-44-55). It's open Monday to Saturday 8am to 7pm and Sunday 9am to 1pm (closed Sundays October to May).

FESTIVALS & MARKETS   It's a sign of the pleasant nature of this resort that one of the major annual events is a **humor festival,** held in late August/early September. Stand-up comics perform along the streets and seaside promenade, humorous films are shown, and general merriment is presented. **Thursday morning's market** fills the Lungomare with stalls selling a bit of everything.

STROLLING AROUND TOWN

Lungomare Argentina is Bordighera's seaside promenade, and it extends for a little more than a mile along a wide **beach;** the pebbly strand is public, so you can settle down anywhere you find a spot. If you want a more civilized beach experience, you can part with 10,000L ($5) for a lounge at any number of beach stations. The promenade remains lively well past the height of the day—since it faces west toward France's Côte d'Azur—it affords spectacular sunset views that most of the town turns out to witness. The modern town, which in parts is unattractively developed, clusters around the seafront, with many businesses lining coastal route S1.

You need only head inland, though, to discover how lovely Bordighera is, with palm-fringed streets and pastel-colored villas hidden behind the walls of verdant gardens. The fortified **old town,** a picturesque cluster of ochre-colored stucco and red tile, is several hundred yards up the hillside from the sea. Aside from a few restaurants and a charming hotel (see below), there aren't specific attractions that draw visitors to town, rather it is the fusion of beauty of centuries-old architecture, charming ambience, and stunning views from the gardens that skirt the centuries-old walls.

AFFORDABLE PLACES TO STAY

Capo. Via Al Capo 3, 18012 Bordighera. ☎ **0184-261-558.** Fax 0184-262-463. 14 units, 13 with bathroom. 50,000–55,000L ($25–$28) single without bathroom, 60,000–80,000L ($30–$40) single with bathroom; 80,000–130,000L ($40–$65) double with bathroom. Breakfast 7,500L ($3.75). MC, V. Closed Nov and sometimes in Oct.

The only hotel in the old city is a delightful pinkish structure surrounded by palm trees and an inviting terrace where many guests choose to spend most of their time. The hilltop location affords stunning views over the lower town and sea below, and there always seems to be a cooling breeze. Vaulted ceilings and colorful majolica-tile floors lend almost a Moorish look to the lobby, sitting rooms, and dining area, but once upstairs the decor becomes utilitarian, though not unpleasing. Furnishings in the largish guest rooms are 1960s-style modern but unobtrusive enough not to be offensive. Baths haven't been updated for a while and tend to be small but are certainly adequate. The best features in the rooms are the shuttered doors that open to balconies and afford dazzling views up and down the coast. Take the prices above with a grain of salt, however, because the rather disagreeable owners refused to give me information or let me see the rooms to update this edition.

Palme. Via Roma 5, 18012 Bordighera. ☎ and fax **0184-261-273.** E-mail: fonando@ libero.it. 12 units, 5 with bathroom. 50,000L ($25) single without bathroom; 70,000L ($35) double without bathroom, 80,000L ($40) double with bathroom; 90,000L ($45) triple without bathroom, 100,000L ($50) triple with bathroom. Breakfast included. Full-board 70,000L ($35) without bathroom, 75,000L ($38) with bathroom. No credit cards. Closed Nov.

If you desire any degree of luxury, you would do well to look elsewhere. But if you want a decent and affordable place to lay your head, this simple pensione atop an apartment house directly across the street from the train station may fit the bill. The premises are a bit stark but the rooms are bright and sparkling clean, have old but well-maintained baths, and are just steps from the beach (and the sounds of passing trains). Many rooms (nos. 5–8, 10, 11, and 15) have balconies overlooking the pink train station and its parking lot, but also the sea beyond, plus there's a shared terrace. All of the bathless rooms have a sink and bidet, and two even have in-room showers. Add to these advantages the presence of the friendly proprietor who lived in New York for many years and enjoys speaking English.

Piccolo Lido. Lungomare Argentina 2, 18012 Bordighera. ☎ **0184-261-297.** Fax 0184-262-316. www.hplido.masterweb.it. 32 units. A/C MINIBAR TV TEL. 127,000–200,000L ($64–$100) single with or without sea view; 150,000–260,000L ($75–$130) double without sea view, 170,000–260,000L ($85–$130) double with sea view. Half– and full board available for stays of 3 days or longer. Buffet breakfast included. AE, DC, MC, V. Parking 20,000L ($10) in garage. Closed late Oct to late Dec.

This pink, sun-filled villa is at the end of the seafront promenade, with direct access to the pebble beach but far enough away from the main seafront avenue and the center of things to afford a great deal of peace and quiet. The public rooms are airy and bright, opening onto terraces like the one on the second floor scattered with deck chairs that let you soak in the sun and sounds of the surf. Upstairs, the newly renovated rooms are bright and attractive, with white tile floors, pastel area rugs, and bright contemporary furnishings that include comfortable lounge chairs and some nice extras like round tables so you can dine in your room if you choose. Baths are gleaming and modern, and nicely equipped with hair dryers and heated towel racks. The best rooms, of course, are those that open onto terraces overlooking the sea.

GREAT DEALS ON DINING

Caffè Giglio. Via Vittorio Emanuele 158. ☎ **0184-261-530.** Panini and snacks from 3,000L ($1.50). Tues–Fri 11am–3pm and 7pm–1am, Sat 11am–1am, Sun 3pm–1am. CAFE.

The most popular cafe in Bordighera seems to suit patrons of all stripes, whether they be British pensioners who sit on the terrace and sip tea, or teenagers who stop on their way to the beach for a gelato (in 30 flavors, 3,000L/$1.50 and up) or night owls looking for a place to enjoy a glass of wine (not easy to do in this sleepy town). As a result, this is almost a mandatory stop for visitors interested in checking out the local scene. The more substantial fare includes sandwiches, salads, and crepes, which depending on the filling, are served either as a meal or as a dessert.

Magiargé. Piazza G. Viale. ☎ **0184-262-946.** Reservations recommended. Primi 12,000L ($6); secondi 15,000–18,000L ($8–$9). AE, DC, MC, V. Thurs–Tues 12:30–2pm and 7:30–10pm. LIGURIAN.

Only a dozen or so tables occupy this attractive goldenrod-colored room in the old city, and the rustic cabinets that line the walls also function as display cases for the Ligurian wines and olive oils for sale. These staples are shown to their best advantage in the delicious meals that emerge from the cramped kitchen. Only three or four pastas and main courses are prepared daily and are announced on a blackboard. Pasta selections usually include trenette or another pasta with a rich pesto sauce, and there is always a selection of fresh fish and one or two meat courses, often including a game hen cooked with local olives and fresh vegetables, a house specialty.

Piemontese. Via Roseto 8. ☎ **0184-261-651.** Primi 10,000–15,000L ($5–$8); secondi 13,000–30,000L ($7–$15). AE, DC, MC, V. Wed–Mon 12:30–2:30pm and 7–10pm. Closed Nov 15–Dec 15. PIEMONTESE/SEAFOOD.

Gino and Giuliana, the husband and wife proprietors, oversee things in the kitchen and simply adorned dining room a few blocks off the seafront, serving up the cuisine of the nearby Piedmonte region. While the menu includes such classic Piemontese dishes as risotto cooked with Barolo wine and a rich *torta alla ricotta* (ricotta quiche), the offerings also suggest Liguria with their reliance on fresh seafood. Aside from simple but memorable grilled fish, there are also such delightful dishes as warm seafood salad and *tagliatelle al nero di seppia,* freshly made tagliatelle blackened with squid ink.

3 The Riviera Levante: Camogli, Santa Margherita Ligure, Portofino & Rapallo

Camogli: 26km (15 mi.) E of Genoa. Santa Margherita Ligure: 31km (19 mi.) E of Genoa. Portofino: 38km (25 mi.) E of Genoa. Rapallo: 37km (24 mi.) E of Genoa.

The coast east of Genoa, the **Riviera Levante (Shore of the Rising Sun),** is more ruggedly beautiful than the Riviera Ponente, less developed, and hugged by mountains that plunge into the sea. Four of the coast's most appealing towns are within a few miles of one another, clinging to the shores of the Monte Portofino Promontory just east of Genoa: Camogli, Santa Margherita Ligure, Rapallo, and little Portofino.

CAMOGLI

Camogli (Casa dei Mogli—House of the Wives) was named for the women who held down the fort while their husbands went to sea for years on end. The little town remains delightfully unspoiled, an authentic Ligurian fishing port with tall, ochre-painted houses fronting the harbor and a nice swath of beach. Given also its excellent accommodations and eateries, Camogli is a lovely place to base yourself while exploring the Riviera Levante. This is a restful retreat from which you can explore Genoa, which is only 20 minutes away.

ESSENTIALS

GETTING THERE   By Train   One to three trains per hour ply the coastline, connecting Camogli with **Genoa** (30–45 min., 3,600L/$1.80), **Santa Margherita** (5 min., 1,900L/95¢), and **Monterosso** (50–60 min., 6,000L/$3) and other Cinque Terre towns.

By Bus   There is at least one Tigullio (☎ **0185-288-835**) bus an hour, often more, from **Santa Margherita;** since the bus must go around and not under the Monte Portofino Promontory, the trip takes quite a bit longer, about half an hour, and costs 2,000L ($1).

By Boat   In summer, boats operated by Golfo Paradiso (☎ **0185-772-091;** www.golfoparadiso.it) sail from Camogli to **Portofino** (14,000L/$7 one way).

By Car   The fastest route into the region is the A12 autostrada from Genoa; exit at Recco for Camogli (the trip takes less than half an hour. Route S1 along the coast from Genoa is much slower but more scenic.

VISITOR INFORMATION   The **tourist office** is across from the train station at Via XX Settembre 33 (☎ and fax **0185-771-066**). It's open Monday to Saturday 8:30am to 12:30pm and 3 to 7pm and Sunday 9am to 1pm.

FESTIVALS & MARKETS   Camogli throws a much-attended annual party, the **Sagra del Pesce,** on the second Sunday of May. The town fries up thousands of sardines in a 12-foot-diameter pan and passes them around for free—a practice that is accompanied by an annual outcry in the press about health concerns and even accusations that frozen fish is used. Even so, the beloved event is much attended.

The first Sunday of August, Camogli stages the lovely **Festa della Stella Maris.** A procession of boats sails to Punta Chiappa, a point of land about a mile down the coast and releases 10,000 burning candles. Meanwhile, the same number of candles is set afloat from the Camogli beach. If currents are favorable, the burning candles will come together at sea, signifying a year of unity for couples who watch the spectacle.

EXPLORING THE TOWN

Camogli is clustered around its delightful waterfront, from which the town ascends via steep, staircased lanes to Via XX Settembre, one of the few streets in the town proper to accommodate cars (this is where the train station, tourist office, and many shops and other businesses are located). Adding to the charm of this setting is the fact that the oldest part of Camogli juts into the harbor on a little point (once an island) where ancient houses cling to the little **Castello Dragone** (now closed to the public) and the 12th-century **Basilica di Santa Maria Assunta** (☎ **0185-770-130**), with an impressively over-baroqued interior open daily 7:30am to noon and 3:30 to 7pm. Most visitors, though, seem drawn to the pleasant **seaside promenade** that runs the length of the town. You can swim from the pebbly beach below, and should you feel your towel doesn't provide enough comfort, rent a lounge from one of the few beach stations for 10,000L ($5).

AFFORDABLE PLACES TO STAY

Augusta. Via Schiaffino 100, 16032 Camogli. ☎ **0185-770-592.** E-mail: htlaugusta@yahoo.it. 14 units. TV TEL. 80,000L ($40) single; 135,000L ($68) double. Show your Frommer's guide for a discount (especially during slow periods). AE, DC, MC, V.

This is an acceptable alternative if the Camogliese (below) is full, and, more than a fallback, it's pleasant and convenient, with a handy location a short walk up a steep staircase from the harbor. The elderly couple and their son who run the pensione also operate the ground-floor trattoria, which serves as a sitting room for the guest rooms upstairs and makes it easy to enjoy a cup of coffee or glass of wine. The rooms are extremely plain, with functional furnishings and drab decor slowly being spruced up (new modular units and wood floors in 2000). But they're large and clean and have good-sized baths. You also get 15 minutes of free Internet access. Ask for a room in front—those in back face the train tracks.

✪ **La Camogliese.** Via Garibaldi 55, 16032 Camogli. ☎ **0185-771-402.** Fax 0185-774-024. 16 units. TV TEL. 70,000–90,000L ($35–$45) single; 90,000–110,000L ($45–$55) double. Breakfast 12,000L ($6). AE, DC, MC, V.

A lot of Genovese come out to spend the weekend in this friendly, attractive little hotel near the waterfront, and they appreciate it for the same simple charms that will appeal to travelers from farther afield. (In fact, given the hotel's popularity, it's always a good idea to reserve, and essential on weekends.) Proprietor Bruno and his family extend guests a warm welcome, and are happy to help them navigate the logistics of visiting the different towns on the nearby coast (which is especially easy to do from here, since the hotel is at the bottom of a staircase that leads to the train station). Rooms are large, bright, and airy, and decorated in modern furnishings that include comfortable beds; some have balconies and, while the house isn't right on the waterfront, it faces a little river and is close enough to the beach that a slight twist of the head usually affords a view of the sea (best from corner room 16B). Baths are small but adequate, and they remodeled the first floor in 2000 to add a breakfast room and overhaul the rooms on that level. The family also runs the beachfront restaurant of the same name just down the road (see below).

Worth a Splurge

✪ **Cenobio dei Dogi.** 16032 Camogli. ☎ **0185-7241.** Fax 0185-772-796. www. cenobio.it. 106 units. A/C MINIBAR TV TEL. 190,000–250,000L ($95–$125) single; 260,000–400,000L ($130–$200) double without sea view; 340,000–530,000L ($170–$265) double with sea view; 420,000–580,000L ($210–$290) jr. suite; 610,000–700,000L ($305–$350) suite. Rates include breakfast. Half-board supplement 65,000L ($33) per person, full-board supplement 130,000L ($65). AE, DC, MC, V.

This Ligurian getaway sits just above the sea at one end of town and against the forested flank of Monte Portofino. The oldest part of the hotel incorporates an aristocratic villa dating from 1565; a chapel, still occasionally used as such, dates from the 17th century. Converted to a hotel in 1956, the premises now include several wings that wrap graciously around a garden on one side and a series of terraces facing the sea on the other. There's a pool and a private beach, and several airy salons, including a lovely bar and lounge area and a glass-enclosed breakfast room that hangs over the sea. The guest rooms vary considerably in size and shape, but all are furnished with a tasteful mix of reproduction writing desks, contemporary glass-top tables, and—especially in "standard" category rooms—island-style furnishings (rattan, bent bamboo headboards, etc.). Many overlook the sea and have balconies, and a few have terraces that lead directly to the pool. In most rooms, the baths have been redone with sizeable counter space and luxurious fixtures.

GREAT DEALS ON DINING

Bar Primula. Via Garibaldi 140. ☎ **0185-770-351.** Sandwiches 6,500–7,500L ($3.25–$3.75); dishes and other light fare 12,000–16,000L ($6–$8); gelato from 3,000L ($1.50). Fri–Wed 9am–2am. AE, MC, V.

Camogli's most fashionable bar is on the waterfront, and it seems as if just about anything goes here. Drinking is taken seriously, as self-proclaimed "Capo Barman" Renato Montanari is well known in his trade. You can also enjoy a light meal (a pasta dish and seafood plate or two or are usually available, along with sandwiches, salads, and omelets), but many regulars come in for a cup of the delicious house espresso and dessert, which presents a difficult choice between the delicious ice cream and pastries (if you're torn, try the sumptuous Comogliese chocolate rumball-like concoction).

Ristorante Il Faulo. Via Garibaldi 99. ☎ **0185-772-072.** Primi, 12,000–17,000L ($6–$9); secondi 15,000–30,000L ($8–$15); fixed-price menu 35,000L ($18) without wine. AE, MC, V. Daily, noon–midnight. LIGURIAN/SEAFOOD.

This extraordinary little restaurant on the seaside consists of a small exotic-looking room with low-slung tables and divan-like chairs, and an open-air terrace over the beach and its crashing surf. You would expect the food to be Moorish, but it is strictly Ligurian, and deliciously so, with an emphasis on local seafood—*calamari ripieni* (squid stuffed with baby shrimp and vegetables), *risotto al frutti di mare* (risotto with tiny clams and other seafood) and simply grilled scampi emerge from the tiny kitchen flawlessly prepared. You can begin a seafood meal with any number of vegetarian appetizers and pastas, including a heavenly *torta di carciofi* (artichoke tart) and several kinds of pasta topped with pesto made on the premises. In order that diners may enjoy their meals fully, smoking is not permitted. Although food is always available, you can also stop in between mealtimes for drinks.

Ristorante La Camogliese. Via Garibaldi 78. ☎ **0185-771-086.** Primi 12,000–35,000L ($6–$18); secondi 20,000–36,000L ($10–$18). AE, DC, MC, V. Thurs–Tues (daily July–Sept) 12:30–2:30pm and 7:30–10:30pm. SEAFOOD.

You probably won't be surprised to find that the menu at this bright, seaside spot, perched over the beach on stilts and one of the most popular and appealing restaurants in town, leans heavily to seafood. In fact, when the weather is pleasant and the windows that surround the dining room are open, you feel you are at sea (admittedly a sea with piped-in pop music). The hearty fish soup is a meal in itself (at 35,000L/$18 it should be), as are any number of pastas topped with clam and other seafood sauces, and there is always a tempting array of fresh fish entrees, caught that day, on hand as well.

SANTA MARGHERITA LIGURE

Santa Margherita had one brief moment in the spotlight, at the beginning of this century when it was an internationally renowned retreat. Fortunately, the seaside town didn't let fame spoil its charm, and now that it's no longer as well known a destination as its glitzy neighbor Portofino, it might be the Mediterranean retreat of your dreams—a palm-lined harbor, a nice beach, and a friendly ambience make Santa Margherita a fine place to settle down for a few days of sun and relaxation.

ESSENTIALS

GETTING THERE   By Train   Between two and three coastal trains per hour connect Santa Margherita with **Genoa** (regional: 35 min., 3,600L/$1.80; High speed: 25 min., 7,500L/$3.75), **Camogli** (5 min., 1,900L/95¢), Rapallo (3 min., 1,700L/85¢), and **Monterosso** (regional: 55 min., 5,000L/$2.50; High speed: 40 min., 9,000L/$4.50) of the Cinque Terre.

By Bus   There is at least one Tigullio (☎ **0185-288-834**) bus an hour to **Camogli** (27 min., 2,000L/$1) and to **Rapallo** (10 min., 1,400L/70¢), leaving from Piazza Vittorio Veneto. Buses also ply the stunningly beautiful coast road to **Portofino,** leaving every 20 minutes from the train station and Piazza Vittorio Veneto (25 min., 1,700L/65¢).

By Boat   Tigullio ferries (☎ **0185-284-670**) make hourly trips to **Portofino** (15 min., 6,000L/$3) and **Rapallo** (15 min., 3,000L/$1.50). In summer, there is a boat about four days a week to **Vernazza** in the Cinque Terre for 25,000L ($13) one-way. Hours of service vary considerably with season; schedules are posted on the docks at Piazza Martiri della Liberta.

By Car   The fastest route into the region is the A12 autostrada from Genoa; the trip takes about half an hour. Route S1 along the coast from Genoa is much slower but more scenic.

VISITOR INFORMATION   The **tourist office** is near the harbor at Via XXV Aprile 2B (☎ **0185-287-485;** fax 0185-283-034; www.apttigullio.liguria.it). Summer hours are daily 9am to 12:30pm and 3 to 6pm; winter hours are Monday to Saturday 9am to 12:30pm and 2:30 to 5:30pm.

FESTIVALS & MARKETS   Santa Margherita's winters are delightfully mild, but even so the town rushes to usher in spring with a **Festa di Primavera,** held on moveable dates in February. Like the Sagra del Pesce in neighboring Camogli, this festival also features food—in this case, fritters are prepared on the beach and served around roaring bonfires. One of the more interesting daily spectacles in town is the **fish market** on Lungomare Marconi; this colorful event transpires from 8am to 12:30pm. On Fridays, cars are banned from Corso Matteotti, Santa Margherita's major street for food shopping, turning the area into an open-air **food market.**

EXPLORING THE TOWN

Life in Santa Margherita centers around its palm-fringed **waterfront,** a pleasant string of marinas, docks for pleasure and fishing boats, and pebbly beaches. Landlubbers congregate in the cafes that spill out into the town's two seaside squares, Piazza Martiri della Liberta and Piazza Vittorio Veneto.

The station is on a hill above the waterfront, and a staircase in front of the entrance will lead you down into the heart of town. Santa Margherita's one landmark of note is its namesake **Basilica di Santa Margherita,** just off the seafront on Piazza Caprera. The church is open daily from 8am to noon and 3 to 7pm and is well worth a visit to view the extravagant, gilded, chandeliered interior.

AFFORDABLE PLACES TO STAY

Annabella. Via Costasecca 10, 16038 Santa Margherita Ligure. ☎ **0185-286-531.** 11 units, none with bathroom. 70,000–80,000L ($35–$40) single; 120,000–130,000L ($60–$65) double. 35% more for each additional bed. Breakfast 7,500L ($3.75). No credit cards.

The nice proprietors manage to accommodate groups of just about any size in this old apartment that's been converted to an attractive pensione, with comfortable old modular furniture and whitewashed walls. Some of the rooms sleep up to four, and one family-style arrangement includes a large room with a double bed and a tiny room outfitted with bunk beds for children. None of the rooms have private baths, but the four shared facilities are ample and hot water is plentiful. Their kids run the popular Cutty Sark pub/*paninocateca* near the train station at Via Roma 35.

☼ **Fasce.** Via Luigi Bozzo 3, 16038 Santa Margherita Ligure. ☎ **0185-286-435.** Fax 0185-283-580. www.hotelfasce.it. 16 units. MINIBAR TV TEL. 148,000L ($74) single occupancy of double room; 165,000L ($83) double; 220,000L ($110) triple; 260,000L ($130) quad. Rates include breakfast. AE, DC, MC, V. Closed Dec 12–Mar 15.

Aristide, whose grandmother built this small hotel, and his British wife, Jane, take great efforts to make their guests feel at home—they do, after all, live here themselves along with his parents—and as a result they provide some of the most pleasant lodgings in Santa Margherita. Their hospitality includes the use of free bicycles, and a laundry service (30,000L/$15 for a wash and dry). If you stay three nights or longer, they'll give you a free Cinque Terre packet with train times and two free tickets to go all the way to Riomaggiore and back. The surroundings are lovely: A broad staircase leads into the flowery, courtyard like entryway, off which there's a pleasant lobby and breakfast/bar area; a roof terrace affords lovely views of the sea and town. The guest rooms are large, bright, and modern in design, with white laminate furnishings and many thoughtful touches, such as copious amounts of storage space, shelves around the beds on which to place reading matter, and safes. Four rooms have balconies, and three accommodations (the triples and a quad) have folding beds to make them perfect for families. With this many amenities at such reasonable prices, it's a good idea to reserve.

Nuova Riviera. Via Belvedere 10–2, 16038 Santa Margherita Ligure. ☎ and fax **0185-287-403.** space.tin.it/viaggi/gsabin. E-mail: gisabin@tin.it. 9 units in main house, 8 with bathroom; 4 units in B&B across the street, none with bathroom. In main house: 90,000–110,000L ($45–$55) single without bathroom, 105,000–120,000L ($53–$60) single with bathroom; 95,000–160,000L ($48–$80) double with bathroom. In B&B: 90,000–130,000L ($45–$65) double without bathroom; 120,000–175,000L ($60–$88) triple without bathroom. Rates include breakfast. MC, V (only accepted at main hotel, and there's a slight discount for paying cash).

The Sabini family acts as if its sunny, turn-of-the-century Liberty-style villa in a quiet neighborhood behind the town center is a private home and guests are old friends. Every room is different, and though eclectically furnished with pieces that look like they may have passed through a couple of generations of the family, most retain the high-ceilinged elegance of days gone by and have a great deal more character than you're used to finding in rooms at this end of the budget scale; the best have expansive bay windows. Modular furnishings mix with antiques, the beds are springy (very springy), and a few get balconies. New baths were added to all but one room in 2000. There's a pretty garden out front and a homey, light-filled dining room where Signora Sabini serves breakfast with fresh-squeezed orange juice and a home-cooked, fixed-price dinner for 35,000L ($18), or 25,000L ($13) for just homemade pasta, salad, and gelato.

Their **B&B** nearby has four very nice, simple rooms—one a large triple with balcony—which share two baths. They also rent a ground floor apartment with two double rooms, a living room, terrace, washing machine, and refrigerator for 220,000L to 300,000L ($110 to $150) for four or five people.

GREAT DEALS ON DINING

Trattoria Baicin. Via Algeria 9. ☎ **0185-286-763.** Primi 8,000–32,000L ($4–$16); secondi 16,000–32,000L ($8–$16). Fixed-price menus 28,000–30,000L ($14–$15). AE, DC, MC, V. Tue–Sun noon–3pm and 7–10:30pm. Closed Nov–Dec 15. LIGURIAN.

The husband-and-wife owners, Piero and Carmela, make everything fresh daily, from fish soup to gnocchi, and still manage to find time to greet diners at the door of their cheerful trattoria just a few steps off the harbor. You can get a glimpse of the sea if you choose to sit at one of the tables out front, and the owner/cooks are most happy preparing fish, which they buy fresh every morning at the market just around the corner; the sole, simply grilled, is especially good here, and the *fritto misto di pesce* constitutes a memorable feast. You must begin a meal with one of the pastas made that morning, especially if *trofie alla genovese* (a combination of gnocchi, potatoes, fresh vegetables and pesto) is available. By ordering the tourist menu, you can get a nice sampling of the expertly prepared dishes served here.

Trattoria da Prezzi. Via Cavour 21. ☎ **0185-285-303.** Primi 6,500–11,000L ($3.25–$6); secondi 5,000–16,000L ($2.50–$8). MC, V. Sun–Fri 11:45am–2:15pm and 6–9:15pm.

The atmosphere in this cozy little restaurant in the center of town near the market is pleasantly casual. Two whitewashed, tile-floored rooms are usually filled with local workmen and businesspeople, who invite newcomers to share a table when no other place is available. Service is minimal—the chef puts what's he's prepared for the day on a table near the front door, you tell him what you want, and one of the staff will bring it to the table when it's ready. Focaccia, *farinata* (a sort of cold pancake), and other Genovese specialties are usually on hand, as are at least one kind of soup (the minestrone is excellent), a chicken dish, and grilled fresh fish.

PORTOFINO

Portofino is almost too beautiful for its own good—in almost any season, you'll be rubbing elbows on Portofino's harborside quays with day-tripping mobs who join Italian industrialists, international celebrities, and a lot of rich but not so famous folks who consider this little town to be the epicenter of the good life. If you make an appearance in the late afternoon when the crowds have thinned out a bit, you are sure to experience what remains so appealing about this enchanting place—its untouchable beauty.

ESSENTIALS

GETTING THERE   By Train   Get off in Santa Margherita (above) and catch the bus.

By Bus   The Tigullio bus (☎ **0185-288-834**) leaves from the train station and Piazza Vittorio Veneto in **Santa Margherita** every 20 minutes and follows one of Italy's most beautiful coastal roads (25 min., 1,700L/85¢). In Santa Margherita you can change for a bus to **Rapallo** (another 15 min., 1,400L/70¢), though in summer there are also a few daily direct buses to Rapallo (3,100L/$1.60).

By Boat   The best way to arrive is to sail to Portofino on one of the Golfo Paradiso ferries (☎ **0185-772-091**) from **Camogli** (10,000L/$5) or one of the Tigullio ferries (☎ **0185-284-670**) from **Santa Margherita** (6,000L/$3) or **Rapallo** (8,000L/$4).

By Car   On a summer visit you may encounter crowds even before you get into town, since traffic on the shore hugging corniche from Santa Margherita, just a few miles down the coast of the promontory, can move at a snail's pace. In fact, given limited parking space in Portofino (visitors must pay obscene rates—7,500L/$3.75 per hour, 34,000L/$17 per day—to use the town garage) you would do well to leave your car in Santa Margherita and take the bus or boat.

VISITOR INFORMATION   Portofino's **tourist office** is at Via Roma 35 (☎/fax **0185-269-024;** www.apttigullio.liguria.it). Summer hours are daily 9:30am to 12:30pm and 2 to 7pm; winter hours are Tuesday to Sunday 9:30am to 12:30pm and 2:30 to 5:30pm.

EXPLORING THE TOWN

The one thing that's free in Portofino is its scenery, which you can enjoy on an amble around the town. Begin with a stroll around the **harbor,** which—lined with expensive boutiques and eateries as it is—is stunningly beautiful, with colorful houses lining the quay and steep green hills rising behind them. One of the most scenic walks takes you uphill for about 10 minutes along a well-signposted path from the west side of town just behind the harbor to the **Chiesa di San Giorgio** (☎ **0185-269-337**), built on the site of a sanctuary Roman soldiers dedicated to the Persian god Mithras. It's open daily 9am to 7pm.

From there you'll want to continue uphill for a few minutes more to Portofino's **Castello di San Giorgio** (☎ **0185-269-046**), built to ward off invading Turks. You can step inside the walls to enjoy a lush garden and the views of the town and harbor below; the castle is open daily from 10am to 6pm (to 5pm October to April) and admission is 3,000L ($1.50), free under 13. There are great views back over the town; for some lovely views on this stretch of coast and plenty of open sea before you, continue even higher up through lovely pine forests to the **faro** (lighthouse).

From Portofino you can also set out for a longer hike on the paths that cross the **Monte Portofino Promontory** to the Abbazia di San Fruttuoso (see the section on Camogli), about a 2-hour walk from Portofino. The tourist office provides maps.

GREAT DEALS ON DINING

Portofino's charms come at a steep price. Its few hotels are expensive enough to put them in the "trip of a lifetime" category, and the harborside restaurants can take a serious chunk out of a vacation budget. I suggest you enjoy a light snack at a bar or one of the many shops selling focaccia and wait to dine in Santa Margherita or one of the other nearby towns.

La Gritta American Bar. Calata Marconi 20. ☎ **0185-269-126.** Salads and other light fare from about 15,000L ($8). AE, MC, V. Fri–Wed 9am–3am.

James Jones called this snug little room the "nicest waterfront bar this side of Hong Kong." I'm not sure your praise will go that far, but it's very attractive, very friendly, and far enough along the harborside quay to be a little less hectic than other establishments. Most patrons stop in for a (pricey) cocktail, coffee, or other libation (the floating terrace out front is perfect for a drink at sunset), but light fare, such as omelets and salads of tomatoes and mozzarella, are also available to provide a light and relatively affordable meal.

RAPALLO

Stepping out of Rapallo's busy train station you may be put off by the traffic, blocks of banal apartment houses, and runaway development that in some places has given the resort the look of any other busy town. Keep walking, though, because at its heart Rapallo remains a gracious old seaside playground and port, and it's easy to see what drew the likes of Ezra Pound, Max Beerbohm, and D. H. Lawrence to take up residence here. Most of the town follows the sweep of a pretty harbor guarded by a medieval castle, and the gracious seafront promenade is cheerfully busy day and night.

ESSENTIALS

GETTING THERE By Train More than 30 trains a day connect Rapallo and **Genoa** (regional: 40 min., 3,600L/$1.80; high speed: 30 min., 7,500L/$3.75). The same trains connect Rapallo with **Camogli** (10 min., 1,900L/95¢), and **Santa Margherita** (3 min., 1,700L/85¢), and **Monterosso** (50 min., 5,000L/$2.50; High speed: 35 min., 9,000L/$4.50) at the north end of the Cinque Terre.

By Bus At least one bus an hour runs between Rapallo and **Santa Margherita** (about 15 min.); the fare is 1,400L (70¢).

By Boat Tigullio ferries (☎ **0185-284-670**) make hourly trips to **Portofino** (30 min.; 8,000L/$4) via **Santa Margherita** (15 min.; 3,000L/$1.50) from 9am to 4pm (hours of service varies considerably with season; schedules are posted on the docks).

By Car The A12 autostrada connects Rapallo with Genoa and takes about half an hour. Route S1 along the coast from Genoa is much slower but more scenic.

VISITOR INFORMATION The **tourist office** is at Lungomare Vittorio Veneto 7 (☎ **0185-230-346;** fax: 0185-63-051; www.apttigullio.liguria.it), open Monday to Saturday 9:30am to 12:30pm and 2:30 to 5:30pm.

FESTIVALS & MARKETS Rapallo is at its most exuberant July 1 to 3, when it celebrates the **Madonna di Montallegro,** whose hilltop sanctuary crowns the town (see below). A famous icon of the Virgin is carried through the streets and a huge fireworks display culminates in the burning of the castle (a mock event, of course). Piazza Venezia is the site of a lively outdoor **food market** on Tuesday and Thursday mornings.

EXPLORING THE TOWN

From the train station, it's a walk of only about 5 minutes to the **waterfront** (follow Corso Italia to Piazza Canessa and the adjoining Piazza Cavour, and from there Via Cairoli to the harborside Piazza IV Novembre.) Dominating this perfect half-circle of a harbor is a **castle** built on a rocky outcropping reached by a causeway; it is open only for special exhibitions but the boulders around its base are usually teeming with sunbathers. Nearby, two other buildings reflect the fact that Rapallo enjoyed a long and prosperous existence before it became known as a retreat for pleasure seekers. The **Cathedral of Santi Gervasio e Protasio,** on Via Mazzini, was founded in the 6th century, and the leper house of **San Lorenzo** across the street dates from the Middle Ages.

For striking views over the town and surrounding seacoast, make the ascent to the **Santuario di Montallegro** (☎ **0185-239-000**). You can take a bus from the train station (1,500L/75¢) or an aerial cableway (funivia) from Via Castagneto on the eastern side of town. The funivia (☎ **0185-273-444**) operates daily every 30 minutes 8am to sunset; the trip takes seven minutes and costs 7,500L ($3.75) one way or 11,000L ($6) round trip. Inside this 16th-century church are some interesting frescoes and a curious Byzantine icon of the Virgin that allegedly flew here on its own from Dalmatia. The views over the sea and surrounding valleys are the main reason to come up here, though, and they are even more so from the summit of Monte Rosa, a short uphill hike away.

AFFORDABLE PLACES TO STAY

La Vela. Via Milite Ignoto 21/7, 16035 Rapallo. ☎ and fax **0185-50-551.** 13 units, 6 with bathroom. TEL TV. 40,000–50,000L ($20–25$) single without bathroom; 50,000–60,000L ($25–$30) single with bathroom; 80,000–90,000L ($40–$45) double without bathroom; 90,000–100,000L ($45–$50) double with bathroom. AE, DC, MC, V. Closed Nov.

This friendly, family-run pensione about a block up from the seaside promenade and the center of town is one of the better bargain choices in expensive Rapallo. The old-fashioned, high-ceilinged rooms open off cozy, homey sitting rooms. Accommodations are extremely comfortable, most are spacious, and they have brand new cots, bland but serviceable modular furnishings, inlaid stone floors, and some nice practical touches like writing desks and lounge chairs. About half the rooms have private baths wedged into one corner; those that don't, have sinks and bidets and share three commodious facilities in the hallway. All baths, though, could stand an overhaul. Many of the rooms face a garden in the rear of the building, ensuring a good night's sleep, and in some rooms you can enjoy this quiet retreat from a large balcony. The hotel is connected with the excellent Ristorante Elite downstairs, where you may well want to take most of your meals. They won't take reservations for one night only, and since the phone must be manually switched over to receive faxes, please try to refrain from faxing in the morning U.S. time, which is the middle of the night in Italy!

Riviera. Piazza IV Novembre 2, 16035 Rapallo. ☎ **0185-50-248.** Fax 0185-65-668. www.hotel-riviera.it. 20 units. A/C MINIBAR TV TEL. 110,000–160,000L ($55–$80) single use of double room; 190,000–250,000L ($95–$125) double; 290,000L ($145) suite. Rates include breakfast. AE, MC, V. Closed Nov–Dec 23.

The Gambero family has run this small hotel, which occupies an old villa on the waterfront, since 1939, and it is now in the capable hands of Claudio and Silvana. They have spent the past several years improving their property, with great attention to detail, especially in the guest rooms. New hardwood floors have been laid, and handsome wood desks and shelving units have been built to match. New double-pane windows keep noise from the seaside avenue out front to a minimum, and baths have been redone with top-of-the-line fixtures. Many of the fine old touches remain, including small balconies off many of the rooms with vistas over the harbor. Three of the suites are perfect for families, consisting of two separate bedrooms and a shared bath off a hall, while the fourth is a single large corner room with three balconies, one off the double-sinked bath. A sunny terrace overlooking the sea extends from the new restaurant/breakfast room, where a generous buffet is served every morning and reasonable fixed-price menus (as well as à la carte) at mealtimes.

GREAT DEALS ON DINING

O Bansin. Via Venezia 105. ☎ **0185-231-119.** Fixed-price menu 18,000L ($9) with wine. AE, DC, MC, V. Mon noon–2:30pm, Tues–Sat noon–2:30pm and 7:30–9:30pm (to 10pm Sat), Sun 12:30–2:30pm. Closed Oct 8–20. LIGURIAN.

This colorful and boisterous restaurant has been a Rapallo institution since 1907, and even though the new young owners have moved it a few blocks away from the marketplace and spruced it up a bit, they've kept the respect for simplicity, low prices, and traditional Ligurian cuisine. Minestrone, *pasta al pesto* or *al Bansin* (with tomatoes, pesto, and cream), *polpette in umido* (stewed meatballs served with peas), and *sardine alla piastra* (roast sardines), are served without pomp and circumstance at communal tables in a plain interior room or, whenever warm enough, on the covered, semi-open deck out back. The service is as warm and friendly as the environs.

Ristorante Elite. Via Milite Ignoto 19. ☎ **0185-50-551.** Primi 6,000–16,000L ($3–$8); secondi 14,000–40,000L ($7–$20); fixed-price menu 50,000L ($25) without wine; *menù turistico* 35,000L ($180) with wine. AE, DC, MC, V. Thurs–Tues noon–2:30pm and 7:30–10pm. Closed Nov. SEAFOOD.

This popular seafood restaurant is just up a busy avenue from the harbor, and the pleasant room, hung with paintings of local scenes, is a little less formal (and less over-priced!) than the many seafood restaurants on the waterfront. The kitchen long ago won the approval of locals, who come here for the fresh fish of the day, which can follow such starters as seafood salad, a *risotto gamberetti e asparagi* (risotto with small prawns and fresh asparagus) or a *zuppe di pesce* (a hearty fish soup). Fresh fish can also be enjoyed on the fixed-price menus, veritable feasts that also include hot and cold seafood appetizers and a pasta course.

4 The Cinque Terre

Monterosso, the northernmost town of the Cinque Terre, 93km (56 mi.) E of Genoa.

Olive groves and vineyards clinging to hillsides, proud villages perched above the sea, hidden coves nestled at the foot of dramatic cliffs—the **Cinque Terre** is about as beautiful a coastline as you're likely to find in Europe, or anywhere. What's best about the Cinque Terre (named for the five neighboring towns of Monterosso, Vernazza, Corniglia, Manarola, and Riomaggiore) is what's *not* here—automobiles, large-scale development or much else by way of 20th-century interference. The pastimes in the Cinque Terre don't get much more elaborate than ✪ **walking** from one lovely village to another along trails that afford spectacular vistas; plunging into the Mediterranean or basking in the sun on your own waterside boulder; and indulging in the tasty local food and wine.

Not too surprisingly, these charms have not gone unnoticed, and American tourism especially has positively exploded in the past five years or so. Throughout summer (weekends are worst) you are likely to find yourself in a long procession of like-minded, English-speaking trekkers making their way down the coast or elbow to elbow with day-trippers from an excursion boat. Even so, the Cinque Terre still manages to escape the hubbub that afflicts so many coastlines, and even a short stay here is likely to reward you with one of the most memorable seaside visits of a lifetime.

ESSENTIALS

GETTING THERE   By Train   You often cannot coast directly into the Cinque Terre towns, as they are served only by the most local of train runs. You'll often find you must change trains in nearby **La Spezia** (1 to 2 per hour; 8 min.; 1,900L/95¢) at the coast's south tip, or in **Pisa** (about 6 daily; 75 min.; 7,700L/$3.85). This is true of the one to two trains per hour from **Rome** (total 4½ to 5 hr.; 51,500L/$26) or the hourly ones from **Florence** (2½ hr.; 14,500L/$7). There are one to two direct trains from **Genoa** (1 to 2 per hour; 1 hr. 40 min.; 8,600L/$4.30); many more from Genoa require a change in Levanto or Sestri Levanto, both a bit farther north up the coast from Monterosso.

By Car   The fastest route is via A12 autostrada from Genoa, exiting at the Corrodano exit for Monterosso. The trip from Genoa to Corrodano takes less than an hour, while the much shorter 15-mile trip from Corrodano to Monterosso (via Levanto) is made along a narrow road and can take about half that amount of time. Coming from the south or Florence, get off the A12 autostrada at La Spezia and follow "Cinque Terre" signs.

By Boat   Navagazione Golfo dei Poeti (☎ **0187-732-987** or 0187-730-336; www.navigazionegolfodeipoeti.it) runs erratic service from the **Riviera Levante towns** (but not Portovenere), as well as from **Genoa,** mid-June to mid-September, though these tend to be day cruises stopping for anywhere from one to three hours in Vernazza before returning (though you can usually talk them into not picking you up again for a day or three); they run about 20,000L to 25,000L ($10 to $13) one way, or 27,000L to 40,000L ($14 to $20) round-trip.

GETTING AROUND

By Foot   The best way to link the Cinque Terre is to devote a whole day and hoof it along the trails. See "Exploring The Cinque Terre," below for details.

By Train   Local trains make frequent runs (2 to 3 per hour) between the five towns; some stop only in Monteroso and Riomaggiore, so check the posted "Partenze" schedule at the station first to be sure you're catching a local. One-way tickets between any two towns cost between 1,500L and 1,900L (75¢ to 85¢)—the 1,900L version is good for six hours of travel in one direction, meaning you can use it to town hop—or you can buy a day ticket (5,500L/$2.75) good for unlimited trips.

By Car   A narrow, one-lane coast road hugs the mountainside above the towns, but all the centers are closed to cars; parking is difficult, and where possible, expensive.

There are public **parking** facilities as follows. Monterosso has a big open dirt lot right on the seafront that costs 2,000L ($1) per hour up to 3 hours, 12,000L ($6) anything over 3 hours up to a full day that ends at midnight—which means if you pick it up the next day, your second day already began ticking at midnight, so you owe 24,000L ($12). Practical upshot: first overnight costs 24,000L ($12), each subsequent one 12,000L ($6).

Free minibuses will carry you and your luggage from the parking facilities up above Riomaggiore and Manarola down into the respective towns. Riomaggiore has a garage at 3,500L ($1.75) per hour, 33,000L ($17) per day. Manarola has open lot for 2,500L/$1.25 per hour (hourly rate gets lower the longer you stay), 20,000L/$10 for one day, 35,000L/$18 for two days (and, again, progressively less the longer you stay).

By Boat From the port in Monterosso, Navagazione Golfo dei Poeti (☎ **0187-732-987** or 0187-730-336; www.navigazionegolfodeipoeti.it) makes 8 to 10 trips a day between Manarola and Riomaggiore (a 25-min. trip), all stopping in Vernazza and half stopping in Manarola as well. A one-way ticket is 12,000L ($6), or 8,000L ($4) just Monterosso to Vernazza; a day pass costs 20,000L ($10).

VISITOR INFORMATION The **tourist office** for the Cinque Terre is underneath the train station of Monterosso, Via Fegina 38 (☎ **0187-817-506,** fax 0187-817-825). It's open Easter to early November and again at Christmas daily 9:30 to 11:30am and 3:30 to 7:30pm. Even when it's closed or in the off-season, posted outside the office is a rather handy display of phone numbers and other useful info, from hotels to ferries.

The commune of Riomaggiore (which also covers Manarola) maintains a Web site at www.riomaggiore.net. Two other sites are www.cinqueterrenet.com and www.monterossonet.com.

EXPLORING THE CINQUE TERRE

Aside from swimming and soaking in the atmosphere of unspoiled fishing villages, the most popular activity in the Cinque Terre is ✪ **hiking from one village to the next** along centuries-old goat paths. Trails plunge through vineyards and groves of olive and lemon trees and hug seaside cliffs, affording heart-stopping views of the coast and the romantic little villages looming ahead in the distance. The well-signposted walks from village to village range in degree of difficulty and the length of time it takes to traverse them, but as a loose rule they get longer and steeper—and more rewarding—the further north you go. Depending on your pace and how long you stop in each village for a fortifying glass of *sciacchetrà,* the local sweet wine, you can make the trip between Monterosso, at the northern end of the Cinque Terre, to Riomaggiore, at the southern end, in about 5 hours.

The walk from **Monterosso to Vernazza** is the most arduous and takes 1½ hours, on a trail that makes several steep ascents and descents (on the portion outside of Monterosso, you'll pass beneath funicular-like cars that transport grapes down the steep hillsides). The leg from the **Vernazza to Corniglia** is also demanding and takes another 90 minutes, plunging into some dense forests and involving some lengthy ascents, but is among the prettiest and most rewarding stretches. Part of the path between **Corniglia and Manarola,** about 45 minutes apart, follows a level grade above a long stretch of beach, tempting you to break stride and take a dip. From **Manarola to Riomaggiore** it's easy going for about half an hour along a partially paved path known as the Via dell'Amore, so named for its romantic vistas (great to do at sunset).

Since all the villages are linked by rail, you can hike as many portions of the itinerary as you wish and take the train to your next destination. Trails also cut through the forested, hilly terrain inland from the coast, much of which is protected as a nature preserve; the tourist office in Monterosso can provide maps.

BEACHES The only sandy beach in the Cinque Terre is the crowded strand in **Monterosso,** on much of which you will be asked to pay 3,500L ($2.75) each per hour for a beach chair or umbrella, 10,000L ($5) per day for a chair, 20,000L to 25,000L ($10 to $13) per day for two chairs with umbrella, and 15,000L ($8) for an hour with a pedal boat.

Guvano Beach is a long, isolated pebbly strand that stretches just north of Corniglia and is popular with nudists (almost entirely men, many of whom are happy it's almost entirely men). You can clamber down to it from the Vernazza-Corniglia path, but the drop is steep and treacherous. A weird alternative route takes you through a unused train tunnel that you enter near the north end of Corniglia's train station. You must ring the bell at the gated entrance and wait for a custodian to arrive to unburden you of 5,000L ($2.50), which is good for passage through the dank, dimly lit mile-long gallery that emerges onto the beach at the far end.

There's also a long, rocky beach to the south of **Corniglia,** and it is easily accessible by some quick downhill scrambles from the Corniglia-Manrola path. **Riomaggiore** has a tiny crescent-shaped pebble beach reached by a series of stone steps on the south side of the harbor. Everywhere else, you're swimming off piers or rocks.

MONTEROSSO

The Cinque Terre's largest village seems incredibly busy compared to its sleepier neighbors, but it's not without its charms. Monterosso is actually two towns—a bustling, character-filled old town built behind the harbor and, separated by a rocky promontory, a relaxed resort section that stretches along the Cinque Terre's only **sand beach** and is home to the train station and the tiny regional tourist office (upon exiting the station, turn left and head through car the tunnel for the old town; turn right for the newer town and Al Gigante restaurant).

The region's most famous art treasure is here: housed in the **Convento dei Cappuccini,** perched on a hillock in the center of the old town, is a *Crucifixion* by Anthony Van Dyck, the Flemish master who worked for a time in nearby Genoa (you can visit the convent daily, 9am to noon and 4 to 7pm). While you will find the most conveniences in citified Monterosso, you'll have a more rustic experience if you stay in one of the other four villages.

AN AFFORDABLE PLACE TO STAY

Amici. Via Buranco 36, 19016 Monterosso. ☎ **0187-817-544.** Fax 0187-817-424. www.cinqueterre.it/hotel_amici. 39 units, 36 with bathroom. TV TEL. 90,000–95,000L ($45–$48) single without bathroom, 155,000L ($78) single use of double with bathroom; 170,000–200,000L ($85–$100) double with bathroom. Half-board 98,000–140,000L ($49–$70) per person; full board 105,000–155,000L ($103–$78). Breakfast included. MC, V. Closed Nov 3–Dec 22 and Jan 7–Feb 20-ish.

The aptly named Amici is unpretentious but extremely pleasant, reached by a curving marble staircase lined with flowerpots and facing a delightful garden. While the hotel isn't on the seafront, (which is only a few minutes away by foot), the garden up at the top of the property and many of the rooms overlook the town and the sea beyond, and the location on a narrow street in the old town ensures quiet. The rooms are simply but tastefully furnished in blonde-wood contemporary pieces and open to balconies through French doors. The rooms have all been equipped with air-conditioners, but the electric company has yet to provide the hotel with enough current to use them (ah, Italy)! Like most hotels in Monterosso, the Amici requires, from June 15 to September 15, that guests choose either half– or full-board. Meals, served in a cavernous dining room, are adequate, but you'd do well to opt for the half-board plan so you can sample other restaurants throughout the region.

GREAT DEALS ON DINING

✪ **Enoteca Internazionale.** Via Roma 62. ☎ **0187-817-278.** Wine from 2,500L ($1.25) a glass; bruschette 6,000–8,000L ($3–$4); cheese and cold cut platters 10,000–14,000L ($5–$7). Summer daily 8:30am–midnight; winter Wed–Mon 8:30am–8pm. Closed Jan. WINE BAR.

All the towns in the Cinque Terre have little shops like this one, where you can taste and purchase the local wines by the bottle, or simply enjoy a glass of Cinque Terre DOC (3,000L/$1.50) or *sciacchetrà* (6,000L/$3) on the premises. The selection here, in the bustling part of old Monterosso, also includes olive oil pressed just down the street and jars of homemade pesto.

Foccacerio Il Frontoio. Via Gioberti 1 (off Via Roma). ☎ **0187-818-333.** Pizza and focaccia from 1,500L (75¢). No credit cards. Fri–Wed 9am–2pm and 3:30–7pm (often afternoons only in winter). SNACKS.

Many patrons say this bustling shop, with a takeout counter and a few tables where you can dine on the premises, serves some of the best focaccia in Liguria. That's quite a claim, but suffice it to say that the freshly baked bread (especially when topped with fresh vegetables) is heavenly and provides one of the best fast meals around.

Il Gigante. Via IV Novembre 9. ☎ **0187-817-401.** Reservations recommended. Primi 10,000–20,000L ($5–$10); secondi 17,000–30,000L ($9–$15). AE, DC, MC, V. Daily noon–3pm and 6:30–10pm. Closed Nov and Tues in winter. SEAFOOD.

This friendly, simple restaurant, a block off the waterfront in the newer part of town, serves some of the freshest and best prepared seafood in the region—which is why so many residents of Genoa and nearby towns drive to Monterosso just to eat in one of the attractive rooms here. There is no set menu but the offerings vary with the local catch. Staples, though, are the *zuppe di pesce,* which is almost legendary and starts off many a meal here, often followed by a huge platter of fritto misto di pesce. Book ahead, especially to sit in the garden out back.

VERNAZZA

It's hard not to fall in love with this pretty village. Tall houses cluster around a natural harbor (where you can swim among the fishing boats) and beneath a **castle** built high atop a rocky promontory that juts into the sea (open March to October daily 10am to 6:30pm, admission 2,000L/$1). The center of town is waterside **Piazza Marconi,** itself a sea of cafe tables. The only Vernazza drawback is that too much good press has turned it into the Cinque Terre's ghetto of American tourists, in summer especially.

AFFORDABLE PLACES TO STAY

Besides the Barbara below, you can rent one of **Trattoria Gianni Franzi's** 23 rooms spread across two buildings; some come with a bath, some with excellent views up the coast, all with a steep climb up the stair-like streets of the town, then up the stairs within the building—but all are worth it. Rates are 65,000L ($33) single without bath; 95,000L ($48) double without bath, 120,000L ($60) double with bath; and 155,000L ($78) triple with bath. Call ☎ **0187-821-003** or fax 0187-812-228 to book, or stop by the trattoria's harborside bar at Piazza Marconi 5 when you arrive in town. They're closed January 8 to March 8.

Barbara. Piazza Marconi 30, 19018 Vernazza. ☎ **0187-812-398** or 0328-221-9688. 9 units, none with bathroom. 100,000L ($50) large double (nos. 8 & 9) with full sea view, 85,000L ($43) smaller room upstairs with askance sea view, 80,000L ($40) single or double without sea view; 20,000L ($10) each additional person. No credit cards. Closed late Nov to mid-Feb.

This pleasant pensione on the two upper floors of a tall old house on the waterfront is at the top of four flights of broad stone steps (63 of 'em), and from there many of the rooms are reached by an additional climb up a ladderlike spiral staircase. These efforts are rewarded, however, by an eagle's-eye view of Vernazza's harbor from almost every room. While the accommodations are basic, they are not without charm, with a pleasant smattering of homey furniture, cool tile floors, and a sink. Guests share three clean and nicely equipped baths. If no one answers the buzzer, call the second number above (a cell phone), or step across the square to Taverna del Capitano and ask about a room.

GREAT DEALS ON DINING

Gambero Rosso. P. Marconi 7. ☎ **0187-812-265.** Primi 12,000–22,000L ($6–$11); secondi 20,000–40,000L ($10–$20); tasting menu 55,000–80,000L ($28–$40). AE, DC, MC, V. Tues–Sun 12:30–4pm and 7:15–10:30pm. (sometimes open Mon in summer). Closed Dec 15–Mar 1. SEAFOOD/LIGURIAN.

It would be hard to find a more pleasant way to take in the scene on Vernazza's lively harborside square than to do so while enjoying the tasting menu on the terrace at this excellent restaurant. You will also be content ordering one or two choices from the à la carte menu—either way you can explore some hard to find dishes such as *acchiughe* (fresh anchovies) baked with onions and potatoes, ravioli di pesci (a delicate fish ravioli), and *muscoli ripieni* (*muscoli* is the Ligurian word for mussels, known as *cozze* elsewhere in Italy; here they are stuffed with fresh herbs). Another specialty, the *grigliata mista* of freshly caught fish, is excellent. Any meal should be followed by the house dessert, *sciacchetrà* (the local sweet wine) accompanied by homemade biscotti. The stone-walled, stone-floored, timbered-ceiling dining room is a pleasant alternative when the terrace is closed.

CORNIGLIA

The quietest village in the Cinque Terre is isolated by its position midway down the coast, its hilltop location high above the open sea, and its little harbor. Whether you arrive by boat, train, or trail (the last only from the south) you'll have to climb more than 300 steps to reach the village proper, which is an enticing maze of little walkways overshadowed by tall houses.

Once there, though, the views over the surrounding vineyards and up and down the coastline are stupendous—for the best outlook, walk to the end of the narrow main street to a belvedere that is perched between the sea and sky. More than these vistas, Corniglia is also the village most likely to offer you a glimpse into life in the Cinque Terre the way it was until a couple of decades ago.

AN AFFORDABLE PLACE TO STAY

✪ **Da Cecio.** 19010 Corniglia. ☎ **0187-812-043.** Fax 0187-812-138. 12 units (4 are in a *dipendenza* nearby). 90,000–100,000L ($45–$50) single or double. MC, V. Closed Nov.

Proprietors Elia and Nunzio have converted the second floor of their old stone house in the countryside just 2 minutes outside Corniglia (on the road to Vernazza) to what we consider one of the Cinque Terre's most pleasant inns. The rooms are big, bright, and stylish with dark wood veneer headboards and furnishings. Most feature great views over the sea, olive groves, and the hilltop town (nos. 2 and 6 are on a corner with those vistas out both windows), and they all have modern baths with good box showers and, in a few, marble sinks. The sun-drenched rooftop deck or flowery terrace downstairs (which at mealtimes serves as an outdoor dining room for the excellent restaurant; see below) is the perfect place to idle away an afternoon. If a room is not available here, one of the proprietors will take you down to one of their four pleasant rooms in the village. For breakfast, they'll send you to their nearby bar, which has tables set out on the village's tiny main piazza.

GREAT DEALS ON DINING

Bar Villagio Marino Europa. 19010 Corniglia. ☎ **0187-812-279.** Snacks from 1,500L (75¢); sandwiches 5,000L ($2.50). Mid-May to mid-Oct, daily 8am–midnight. Closed winter. BAR.

It would be hard to find a location more scenic than the one this simple outdoor bar enjoys, with stunning views up and down the coast from a hillside perch. Built to service guests at an attached bungalow village, the bar is also a welcome refuge for hikers on the Corniglia-Manarola path (at the Manarola end of the ramshackle tunnel of low buildings you pass through just beyond the Corniglia train station). The offerings don't get more elaborate than sodas and beer, panini, and ice cream, but you will certainly want to stop here at least once on your treks up and the down the Cinque Terre to take in the view.

✪ **De Mananan.** Via Fieschi 117, Corniglia. ☎ **0187-821-166** or 0187-812-320. Reservations recommended. Primi 8,000–16,000L ($4–$8); secondi 16,000–23,000L ($8–$12). No credit cards. Wed–Mon 12:30–3pm and 7:30–10pm. LIGURIAN.

The pleasure of being in hilltop Corniglia is well worth the trek up to town, especially if the visit includes a meal at this tiny restaurant carved into the stone cellars of an ancient house. Agostino and Marianne, the husband-and-wife owners and chefs, draw on age-old local recipes and use only the freshest ingredients in their preparations; the results, posted on a blackboard in the one handsome vaulted room furnished with granite tables, are wonderful. Fresh vegetables from gardens just outside the village are grilled and mixed with herbs and smoked mozzarella as a simple appetizer, which can be followed by any of the hand-rolled pasta topped with homemade pesto or porcini. You can continue in this meatless vein with a plate of mussels, grilled fish, or fresh anchovies stuffed with herbs, but the few meat dishes on the daily menu are also excellent—especially the *coniglio nostrano,* rabbit roasted in a white sauce. Local wines accompany the meals.

Ristorante Cecio. Corniglia. ☎ **0187-812-043.** Primi 8,000–20,000L ($4–$10); secondi 10,000–25,000L ($5–$13). Thurs–Tues (daily in summer) noon–3:30pm and 7–10pm. Closed Nov. MC, V. LIGURIAN.

Like the inn upstairs, the stone-walled, wood-beamed dining room and flower-filled terrace overlooking olive groves provide extremely pleasant surroundings. A nice selection of simple, homemade fare emerges from the family-run kitchen, including fresh pasta with a rich pesto or walnut sauce or *alla scogliera,* topped with fresh clams and mussels. Meat and fish are grilled over an open hearth. Outside of peak meals times, you can sit on the terrace and enjoy the view over a beer or glass of the house wine.

MANAROLA

Not as busy as nearby Riomaggiore or as quaint as its neighbor Corniglia, Manarola is a near-vertical cluster of tall houses that seem to rise piggyback up the hills on either side of the harbor. In fact, in this region with no shortage of heart-stopping views, one of the most amazing sights is the descent into the town of Manarola on the path from Corniglia: From this perspective, the hill-climbing houses seem to merge into one another to form a row of skyscrapers. Despite these urban associations, Manarola is a delightfully rural village where fishing and wine making are big business. The region's major **wine cooperative,** Cooperativa Agricoltura di Riomaggiore, Manarola, Corniglia, Vernazza e Monterosso, is here; call ☎ **0187-920-435** for information about tours.

AFFORDABLE PLACES TO STAY

Manarola is home to a spanking-new hostel, the **Ostello 5 Terre** (☎ **0187-920-215;** fax 0187-920-218; www.cinqueterre.net/ostello), which in addition to 25,000L to 30,000L ($13 to $15) beds in six-bed dorm rooms (4-bed family rooms with private bath also available for the same per-person rate, but you gotta rent the whole room), offers services such as kayak, bike, and snorkel rental, Internet access, and a cheap laundry. The only major drawback is the strict midnight curfew (1am in summer). It's closed January 15 to February 15.

Marina Piccola. Via Discovolo 38, 19010 Manarola. ☎ **0187-920-103.** Fax 0187-920-966. E-mail: marijes2@tin.it. 10 units. TEL TV. 115,000L ($58) single; 135,000L ($68) double. Half-board 145,000L ($73) single, 125,000L ($63) per person in double. Breakfast 20,000L ($18). AE, DC, MC, V. Closed Nov.

This cozy inn on the harbor in Manarola is a favorite with many travelers to the Cinque Terre. Part of the premises, including the glass-enclosed seafood restaurant where you may be required to take half- or full board in summer, is right on the water, and many of the guest rooms in the tall house have sea views as well. Decor is a cut above that of most inns in the region—the welcoming lobby doubles as a sitting room, with divans wrapping around a fireplace. As one of the hotel's two buildings (the one above the restaurant) is right on the port, book ahead to be sure you get one of the rooms whose windows open onto fishing boats and the rocky shoals directly below, and the Tyhrrenean Sea spread before you. As for the small but serviceable rooms, old prints, homey faded floor tiles, light pine-veneer furnishings, and white and pale blue lend a great amount of charm. Rooms in the other building (the next one up the hill, containing the hotel lobby) are done in more of a country style, with nicer heavy wooden furnishings, flower-edged wallpaper, and fancy scrolled headboards; even here about half the rooms get a sea view over, or around the side of, the pink stucco of the first building (better views as you go higher up, but no elevator). The aforementioned meals are excellent, a cut above most room and board fare. My only quibble with this otherwise pleasant hostelry is that the service can be somewhat scatterbrained and occasionally downright unfriendly.

GREAT DEALS ON DINING

Aristide. Via Discovolo 290. ☎ **0187-920-000.** Primi 8,000–12,000L ($4–$6); secondi 8,000–35,000L ($4–$18). Fixed-price fish menu 65,000L ($33) with wine. AE, DC, MC, V. Tues–Sun noon–2:30 and 7–9pm. LIGURIAN.

In this old house up the hill from the harbor (just below the train station), diners are accommodated on a couple of levels of small rooms as well as on a covered terrace across the street. Many of these patrons live in the Cinque Terre or take the train here from nearby La Spezia, because this long-standing trattoria is known for its heaping platters of grilled fish, *gamberoni* (jumbo prawns), and *frittura di mare* (a selection of fried seafood). The *antipasta di mare* includes a nice selection of octopus, clams, sardines, and other local catches and serves well as a lighter meal. The house's white wine is from the hills above the town, and if the owner is in a good mood, he may come around after your dinner proffering a complimentary glass of *sciacchetrà*, the local dessert wine.

RIOMAGGIORE

Riomaggiore clings onto the vestiges of the Cinque Terre's rustic ways while making some concessions to the modern world. The old fishing quarter has expanded in recent years and Riomaggiore now has some sections of new houses and apartment blocks. This blend of the old and new works well—Riomaggiore is bustling and prosperous and makes the most of a lovely setting, with houses that cling to the hills that drop into the sea on either side of town. Many of the lanes end in seaside belvederes.

From the parking garage, follow the main drag down; from the train station, exit and turn right to head through the tunnel for the main part of town (or, from the station, take off left up the brick stairs to walk the Via dell'Amore to Manarola).

That tunnel and the main drag meet at the base of an elevated terrace that holds the train tracks. From here, a staircase leads down to a tiny fishing harbor off the left of which heads a rambling path that, after a few hundred yards, leads to a pleasant little **beach** of large pebbles.

An Affordable Place to Stay

Villa Argentina. Via de Gaspari 187. 19017 Riomaggiore. ☎ and fax **0187-920-213.** 15 units. TV. 120,000–160,000L ($60–$80) single; 150,000–190,000L ($75–$95) double. Breakfast 13,000L ($7); lunch or dinner 38,000L ($19). No credit cards.

The only bona-fide inn in Riomaggiore is in the newer section of town, on a hillside about a 5-minute walk (up a lot of stairs) from the center. This location affords astonishing views, which you can enjoy from most of the guest rooms, and provides a nice retreat from the tourist-crowded main street and harbor. A breezy, arbor-shaded terrace and a bar area decorated by local artists off the lobby are the places to relax. And, while the tile-floored rooms upstairs will not overwhelm you with their character, they are large and pleasant, if blandly furnished, with ceiling fans and (all except room nos. 4-6 and 10) balconies featuring views over the town to the sea.

Great Deals on Dining

Riomaggiore's nightlife, such as it is, revolves around the **Bar Centrale,** smack in the middle of town at Via C. Colombo 144 (☎ **0187-920-208**), with tables set under a roofed wooden deck in the middle of the main drag, Devil's Kiss beer on tap, and a cheap ISDN Internet connection (200L/10¢ per minute; 6,000L/$3 for a half hour). It's open Tuesday to Sunday 7:30am to 1am.

La Lanterna. Riomaggiore. ☎ **0187-920-589.** Primi 9,000–11,000L ($4.50–$6); secondi 11,000–25,000L ($6–$13). AE, DC, MC, V. Daily11am–11pm. SEAFOOD/LIGURIAN.

From a table on the terrace here, perched only a few feet above Riomaggiore's snug harbor, you can hear the waves lap against the rocks and watch the local fishermen mend their nets. Seafood, of course, dominates the menu, with many unusual Ligurian-style dishes. The antipasto of shrimp, smoked tuna, and grilled swordfish is excellent and can suffice as an entree; you should, however, make room for one of the house specialties, *chiche*—homemade gnocchi filled with seafood and topped with a spicy tomato sauce.

12

Southern Italy: Campania & Apulia

by Lynn A. Levine

The province of **Campania,** rich in fertile volcanic soil deposited by the omnipotent and often menacing Mt. Vesuvius, boasts some of the most breathtaking real estate in the world. The mystery and fascination of the Bay of Naples goes back to the ancients, who claimed to have discovered the entrance to the underworld here. As a summer retreat for the wealthiest of Romans, the coastline from Naples to Sorrento was dotted with sumptuous summer villas, including those of many a retired Roman emperor. Although there's no disputing that the **Amalfi Coast** continues to captivate its visitors, this amalgam of fishing villages and holiday resorts has traded in some of its rural and pastoral charm in the name of mass tourism. Yet even at their most developed, the little towns along the formidable Amalfi Drive are an enchantment; perfect little pastel villages flowering in the limited living space between sea and cliffs. Don your Sunday best for a leisurely stroll in **Positano,** while refreshing hilltop **Ravello** requires that you simply breathe deeply. From any of the mainland towns, the islands of the Bay of Naples beckon, from the seductive vertical cliffs of **Capri,** to the rich volcanic and restorative springs of the spellbinding island of **Ischia.**

In **Naples,** you can mimic the privilege of the 18th-century court of the Bourbons in their royal palace while Caravaggio awaits in a museum. In between visits to baroque churches and Renaissance piazze, don't forget to sample a pizza in the very restaurant that invented it.

From a base amid the culture of Naples or sun-kissed **Sorrento,** you can day trip to one of the most destructive forces in western history, **Mt. Vesuvius.** A short train ride will take you to **Pompeii** and **Herculaneum,** two cities doomed to complete burial by the volcano's wrath in A.D. 79, frozen in time and offering an unparalleled glimpse into daily life almost 2,000 years ago. For even further past-life regressions, head to southern Campania, where you can wander amid the columns of some of the most intact Greek temples in the world in the forgotten 5th-century B.C. colony of **Paestum.**

To the southeast is the heel of Italy's boot, peninsular **Apulia (Puglia,** *pool*-yah**).** Nowhere else in Italy is there a more precise balance of east and west, Greek and Roman, Byzantine and Lombard, and Arab and Norman. This is the land of sunflowers and Santa Claus, olive oil and *orecchiette* pasta, Romanesque churches and Swabian castles, whitewashed villages and pearly sands. Here you'll find a cultural

---

A Taste of Campania

The world owes Naples a great debt if for no other reason than for the invention of the "plain" *pizza Margherita.* Naples had good stock to work with, as Campania is *the* center of mozzarella production in Italy, with fine *mozzarella di bufala* (buffalo-milk mozzarella) served in restaurants across the province (actually, on pizza you'll more often find *fiordilatte* cheese, which is mozzarella made with cow's milk that holds up better to the heat of cooking). Mozzarella is a key ingredient in *gnocchi alla Sorrentina* (or any other pasta thusly named), a gooey mix of pasta, tomatoes, and cheese.

But since Campania is mainly coastal, some of its best cuisine is of a fishy nature. Any pasta or risotto *alla pescatora* (fisherman's style) or *ai frutti di mare* (literally "fruits of the sea") will be infused with a selection of seafood, generally some combination of *vongole* (clams), *cozze* (mussels), *ostriche* (oysters), *calamari* (squid), *polpo* (octopus), *gamberi/gamberoni/scampi* (shrimp), *ricci di mare* (sea urchin), *aragostini* (crawfish), *aragote* (lobster), or *granchio* (crab). Any pasta cooked *al cartoccio* is basically the same sort of seafood dish, only this time all the ingredients are tossed together, wrapped in foil, and baked. Naples's most typical dish is *spaghetti con le vongole,* spaghetti tossed with the tiny, delicious clams found in the city's bay. You may find your fresh fish cooked *all'acqua pazza,* in "crazy waters" with baby tomatoes, white wine, and spices (often including capers).

Of Campanian **wines,** some of the best include *Lacryma Christi,* "Christ's Tears," grown on the slopes of Vesuvius by monks, Ravello's juicy local white, and the dry *Greco di Tufo.* In shops on Capri and along the Amalfi Coast, you'll find bottles of *limoncello,* a liqueur made with lemon zest and lots of sugar (best when drunk ice-cold).

---

melting pot unequaled in Italy, forming one of the country's most underrated, underexplored, and undiscovered regions, and full of some of the country's most hospitable residents.

The armed conflicts across the Adriatic resulted in a complete tourist vacuum in the region, so that Apuglia could easily be called Italy's "last frontier." The sweeping natural preserve of the **Gargano Peninsula,** provides the region with what little geographical variations can be found here, a rough highland that hides spectacular sea grottos and stunning bays at its base. Camouflaged in olive orchards are the whitewashed medieval walls of **Ostuni** and **Otranto,** with their swirling Baroque "new" centers and unspoiled beaches—you could travel as far as the rocky landscapes of the Salento and never once see a beach chair.

1 Naples: See It & Die

202km (125 mi.) SE of Rome, 207km (162 mi.) W of Bari.

Un gran cassino, a rather coarse expression with its roots in the whorehouse, describes a great teeming noisy mess. It also describes **Naples (Napoli)** perfectly, showcasing the quicksilver southern Italian character at its warm, friendly best and its temperamental, frenzied worst. Naples is not an easy city to love, but it's definitely worth the effort. Disregarded as seamy and squalid by northern Italians, caricatured on tile in countless American pizza parlors, Naples is generally unappreciated and undervalued. But on a sunny day, with breezes blowing off the bay and ramparts that rise high above every corner of the city, the rewards of visiting this port town are innumerable.

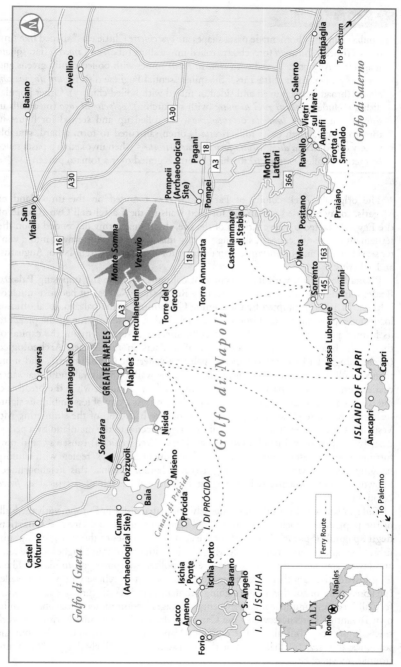

A Taste of Apulia

Apulia's trinity of homemade pasta shapes are *orecchiette* ("little ears" shaped like tiny, thick Frisbees), *cavatelli* (orecchiette rolled into a short tube), and *troccoli* (fat, square spaghetti). Any pasta served with *cime di rapa* comes with boiled turnip greens and is *very* Apulian. After "little ears," the quintessential Pugliese dish is *purè di fave con cicoria* (broad beans pureed and sided or mixed with boiled chicory). Other popular dishes include *spaghetti ricci di mare* (with sea urchin), *polpette al sugo* (meatballs in tomato sauce), and *braciola* or *involtino* (veal rolled up and stewed for hours in tomato sauce). Fresh ewe's milk *ricotta* is often salt-cured to form a hard, gratable variety called *ricotta dura, ricotta forte,* or *cacioricotta*—when invoked in a pasta sauce (sometimes called *mantecati)* the hard ricotta is grated over a tomato puree.

The original Greek colony of Parthenope was founded on the tiny island of Megaris, today enclosed within the fortified walls of the **Castel dell'Ovo (Castle of the Egg).** Attracted by the charisma of the site, the Roman army descended upon the settlement in the 4th century, shifting the city inland and transforming it into a winter seaside resort and important cultural center for the likes of Virgil, Nero, Augustus, and Tiberius.

Piazza Plebescito, with its semicircle of columns opposite the imposing **Palazzo Reale,** was the crown jewel of 18th-century Renaissance Naples but had lost much of it luster. In 1994, prompted by the coming G7 Summit at the palazzo, local officials instituted a program to clean house, which resulted in the restoration of the piazza to its former, pedestrian-only, glory. As a cultural center, Naples remains the capital of the south, boasting a superb collection of artifacts in the **Museo Archeologico (Archaeological Museum),** a superior painting gallery at **Capodimonte,** and more than a handful of museums set within the imposing walls of medieval and Renaissance **castles** and downtown palazzi. Pompeii is reachable in minutes, while the breathtaking islands of **Capri** and **Ischia** hover on the horizon. As a city of less ambitious sightseeing, Naples offers a stunning coastline below the backdrop of the simmering Mt. Vesuvius. On the waterfront, Castel dell'Ovo is connected to the mainland by a pedestrian (which, in Italy, includes two-wheeled motorized vehicles) causeway, and now fortifies a host of restaurants, cafes, and old apartment buildings, replete with laundry hanging out the windows. Enclosing a scenic harbor marina, this neighborhood, known as **Borgo Marinari,** is a magnet for those in search of a typical *al fresco* Neopolitan evening.

Today, Naples is one of the most densely populated cities in Europe, with the bulk of the population shoehorned into the tall tenements of the old city and **Quartiere degli Spagnoli (Spanish Quarter),** or the cement high-rises of the ever-growing suburbs. Unemployment is rampant, leaving Naples with one of Italy's highest crime rates and lowest standards of living. While one Neapolitan welcomes you to his city like a long-lost relative, another is reaching into your pocket to relieve you of your wallet (pickpocketing of tourists is an ongoing problem). And it's all run by a largely ineffectual, if earnest, municipal government that wages a continuous war against both its own Byzantine bureaucracy and the Camorra, the nastiest organized crime network this side of Sicily. But all of that describes Naples at its worst, and aside from the seaminess of Piazza Garibaldi outside the train station, it's unlikely that you'll run into trouble anywhere else.

Instead, this hot-blooded metropolis, enjoying the geographical advantage of a stunningly expansive bay and the double humps of Mt. Vesuvius looming above, awaits you in what has become one of the most legendary landscapes in the world.

ESSENTIALS

GETTING THERE   **By Train**   There are trains at least twice hourly **from Rome** (FS rail 1½ to 2½ hr., 18,600L/$9 or 39,500L/$20 IC/ES). If you plan on hopping directly onto a hydrofoil for Capri, or if you're staying at the Ausonia hotel (below), get off at Naples–Stazione Mergellina, otherwise stay on until Naples–Stazione Centrale/Piazza Garibaldi. For rail information call ☎ **081-553-4188.**

By Car   Follow the A1 from Rome. For parking, see "Getting Around," below.

By Plane   Naples's **Capodichino Airport** (☎ **081-789-6385**) is served extensively both nationally and internationally. Domestically, **Alitalia**'s network reaches the farthest, with daily flights arriving from Rome, Milan, Venice, Turin, Genoa, Palermo, and Catania. The privately run **Meridiana** arrives daily from Bologna, Turin, Verona, and Cagliari. From points beyond the border, **Sabena** flies direct from Brussels and Nice, **Olympic Airways** from Athens and Marseille, **Air Littoral** from Nice, **Transavia** from Amsterdam; **Lufthansa** from Munich, **Air France** from Paris; and **British Airways** from London. The airport is a 15- minute bus ride north of the center. The blue **C.L.P.** bus (☎ **081-251-4157**) shuttles passengers between the airport and Piazza Municipio via the train station in Piazza Garibaldi about every half hour (3,000L/$1.50; last departure at 11:30pm). The bus theoretically begins accepting passengers at the official *fermata* opposite the airport exit, but in actuality, it opens up its doors at the drop-off point immediately outside the airport exit to the right. Your goal is to get on the bus wherever it's parked and nab a seat, since space is first come first served.

CITY LAYOUT   Naples lies on the northern rim of the Bay of Naples, surrounded by low mountains struggling to contain the urban sprawl of the city along its slopes. You'll arrive in the dingiest corner of the city, **Piazza Garibaldi,** on the eastern edge of the center (hold your first impressions). From here, wide **Corso Umberto I** runs diagonally across the center toward **Piazza Municipio** at the main port, **Molo Beverello.**

The historic **old center** of Naples is bound by **Corso Umberto** on the south, **Piazza Cavour** on the north, **Via Duomo** on the east, and **Via Toledo** on the west. Through its heart runs **Spacca Napoli,** which translates loosely as "divide Naples in half." The name refers both to this historic district as a whole and to the arrow-straight street that runs down its center heading from east to west. The street changes names from **Via San Biagio dei Librai** to **Via Benedetto Croce** to **Via Domenico Capitelli** (it's actually the old Decumanus Maximus, or Main Street, of the Roman city).

Across Via Toledo to the west lies the checkerboard of the **Quartiere degli Spagnoli,** a grid of narrow streets laid out by the Spanish viceroys along the bottom slopes of the Vomero hill. Its tall tenements are filled with lower-income housing, and while you can see some of the most genuine Naples life in this area—ascending the winding stairs of the hill will put you practically in the living rooms of these people—be extra cautious; it is also one of the strongholds of the Camorra organized crime network. South of the Quartiere degli Spagnoli, Via Toledo spills into **Piazza Plebescito,** the heart of 18th-century Naples, with the royal palace and theater, and the docks just beyond.

West of the center is a trio of rather nice, middle-class residential neighborhoods starting with **Santa Lucia,** rising above Piazza Plebescito on the seaward slope of the Vomero. Beyond this is the long, wide harborside park of **Chiaia,** with a few blocks of buildings climbing behind it up a small ridge. At the end of Chiaia are the docks and train station of the workaday zone of **Mergellina.**

GETTING AROUND   By Metro, Bus & Funicular   Naples's **Metro** is really a commuter rail line, though it is handy for visitors to zip from Mergellina (where there are some fine hotels) into the center, or from the train station direct to Naples's top sight, the Archaeological Museum.

You'll probably be using the **bus/trolley** system more often, and **Piazza Garibaldi,** in front of the central train station, is the hub for almost every bus in Naples. The **E1 bus** circles endlessly around the heart of the historic center. **Tram 1** runs from the western edge of Piazza Garibaldi (the far side from the train station) direct to the Molo Beverello ferry docks. To get to the hilltop neighborhoods like the Vomero, Naples has built several *funiculari* (cog railways).

By Car   Only drive in Naples if you are practicing for the demolition derby. Neapolitan motorists drive twice as fast and three times as aggressively as your average Italian, and while red lights seem to be considered optional in the rest of Italy, here they're considered a nuisance and ignored entirely. No city in Europe (except for maybe Paris) is more stressful, aggravating, confusing, and downright dangerous to drive in.

Do yourself a favor and **park** as soon as you arrive in town. If you want to explore the Amalfi Coast by rental car, pick it up the day you leave Naples (or, better yet, take the train to Sorrento and pick up your car there). There are garages just south of the central train station at Via Ferraris 40 (☎ **081-264-344**); near the center at Via Shelley 11 (between Via Toledo and Piazza Municipio; ☎ **081-551-3104**); near the Molo Beverello ferry docks at Via dei Gaspari 14 (☎ **081-552-5442**); and near the Mergellina docks and Mergellina train station at Piazza Sannazaro 142 (☎ **081-681-437**). The major car rental agencies have their offices at the train station, thoughtfully located near to the entrance to the A1 (to Rome) and the A3 (to the Amalfi coast) autostradas.

By Taxi   Only use legitimate taxis, hired at the following locations, or call the Radio taxi numbers below. Taxi stands are at **Piazza Garibaldi, Piazza Municipio, Piazza Trieste e Trento, Piazza dei Martiri, Piazza Vittoria, Via Partenope, Piazza San Pasquale/Riviera di Chiaia,** and **Via Mergellina.** Naples Radio taxi numbers are ☎ **081-556-4444,** 081-556-0202, 081-551-5151, 081-552-5252 and 081-570-7070 or simply by dialing **2525.**

There are occasional reports of unscrupulous drivers trying to swindle unsuspecting tourists, so know these official rates: Rides cost an initial 4,000L ($2), plus 100L (5¢) for every 80 meters (87 yards). There are supplemental charges for Sundays (3,000L/$1.50), rides between 10pm and 7am (4,000L/$2), luggage (1,000L/50¢ per bag), small pets (2,000L/$1), calling ahead for a radio taxi (1,500L/75¢), and travel to or from the airport (5,000L/$2.50). You do not have to pay for the taxi's return trip from the airport into the city, in fact, there are fixed fares on many of Naples's main routes. Rides between the airport and any hotel on the *lungomare* or to the Mergellina docks

---

A Ticket to Ride

The *giraNapoli,* a ticket to ride any of the city's means of public transport (bus metro, funicular, or the city portions of the rail lines), is available for 1,500L (75¢) at any *tabacchi,* most newsstands, and all metro stops, funicular stations, and train stations. It's valid for 90 minutes, during which time you can transfer between as many buses as you'd like, plus once to each of the other public transport systems (metro, funicular), *but don't forget to validate it.* There's also a daily pass for 4,500L ($2.25).

The Naples daily paper *Il Mattino* has a page near the back listing the **current transportation schedules** for the entire province, including the state and private rail lines, buses, and ferries, as does the free bimonthly *Qui Napoli,* available at tourist information offices and most hotels.

---

are fixed at 30,000L ($15); from the airport to Piazza Municipio 25,000L ($13), from the train station to the Mergellina docks 20,000L ($10), from the train station to the docks at Molo Beverello 10,000L ($5).

VISITOR INFORMATION   There are a **tourist information desks** in the train station (☎ 081-268-779), the airport (☎ **081-780-5761**), the Palazzo Reale at Piazza Plebescito (☎ **081-252-5711;** fax 081-418-619), Piazza del Gesù Nuovo (☎ **081-552-3328**), and Piazza dei Martiri 58 (☎ **081-405-311**).

Fast Facts: Naples

Books   Feltrinelli (☎ **081-552-1436**) at Via Tommaso d'Aquino 70 (just off Via Torino) has travel books and novels in English (mainly Penguin classics) upstairs.

Consulates   There's a **U.S. Consulate** on Piazza della Repubblica (☎ **081-583-8111**); and a **U.K. Consulate** at Via F. Crispi 122 (☎ **081-663-511**).

Drugstores   There are **all-night pharmacies** around the **train station** (in the station itself, at Piazza Garibaldi 11, Corso Garibaldi 354); in the **city center** (at Piazza Municipio 54; Piazza Dante 71); in **Chiaia** (at Riviera di Chiaia 169, Via D. Morelli 22, Via Carducci 21); and on the **Vomero** (Via G. Merliani 27, Via Cliea 124). You can also dial ☎ **1100** (Italian operators) for the address and phone number of the three closest pharmacies open nearest to you.

Emergencies   Call ☎ **113** for any emergency. Dial ☎ **112** for the Carabinieri to get emergency aid in English, French, and Spanish; to report a fire call ☎ **115;** for an ambulance dial ☎ **081-752-0696;** for car breakdowns dial ☎ **116.**

Hospitals   Anyone can head to the *pronto soccorso* (first aid) station of the nearest *ospedale* (hospital). Near the train station, the **Ospedale Ascalesi** is at Piazza Collenda/Via Pietro Colletta just off Corso Umberto I (☎ **081-254-2111**); just south of the train station at the harbor is the **Ospedale Loreto Mare** on Via Amerigo Vespucci (☎ **081-254-2111**); in the city center there is the **Policlinico** on Piazza Miraglia/Via del Sole just above Piazza San Domenico (☎ **081-566-1111** or 081-746-1111); also in the center is the **Ospedale Vecchio Pellegrini** off Via Toledo on Via Porta Medina at the foot of the funicular up to the Vomero (☎ **081-254-2111**); and in Chiaia is the **Ospedale Loreto Crispi** where Via Francesco Crispi changes names to Via Schipa at Via A. Mirelli (☎ **081-254-7111**).

Mail & E-Mail   There are central post offices at Piazza Matteotti off Via Diaz (☎ **081-551-1456**), in the main train station, and in the Galleria Umberto I (☎ **081-552-3467**). All are open Monday to Friday 8:15am to 7:15pm and Saturday 8:15am to noon. The **Internet Café** in Piazza Garibaldi 73 (☎ **081-553-5019;** exit the station to the left), has superfast connections and 20 terminals. Their flyer, available at the nearby tourist information office, will save you 20%.

Safety   The Camorra (Neapolitan Mafia) continues to control much of the city, and petty theft is rampant—though the rate of violent crime against visitors is, as in the rest of Italy, much lower than that of any U.S. city. In recent years, Naples has made great strides in cleaning up the city, but this is not a "go ahead" to let down your guard. Clutch your camera firmly (try to keep it out of view at all times), keep a hand on your wallet, ladies should avoid carrying bags with those ineffectual magnetic closures and wear their purse straps diagonally, and proceed confidently. Be especially protective of your personal space, particularly around the train station, as pickpockets look for "accidental" body contact in order to separate you from your belongings.

The residential neighborhoods to the west—Santa Lucia, Chiaia, and Mergellina—are a bit safer, but not much so. Take comfort in knowing that even the locals are afraid to leave their cars on the street, so follow their example by parking in a garage—and don't leave anything valuable in the car.

Transportation Info   For info on city buses, metro, and funicular, call ☎ **081-562-5222** or log onto **www.connect.it/napolipass.** For further bus information, you can call ANM directly at ☎ **081-763-2177.**

EXPLORING NAPLES
IN THE CENTER

✪ **Museo Archeologico (Archaeological Museum).** Piazza Museo/Piazza Cavour (at the northern edge of the city). ☎ **081-440-166.** Admission 12,000L ($6) adults. Wed–Mon 9am–7:30pm. Bus: R1, R4, V10, 24, 42, 47, 110, and 137. Metro: Cavour.

This is one of the most significant archaeological collections in Europe (certainly southern Italy's best), the only absolutely required sight in Naples, and well worth 2 to 3 hours of your time. If you explore Pompeii without paying this museum a visit as well, you've missed out on half its riches. The best statues, mosaics, and wall paintings at Pompeii that hadn't already been carried off by looters were long ago removed from the archaeological site to be preserved here. Pompeii's artifacts, best seen *after* a visit to the site, are displayed alongside finds from across southern Italy as well as many from Rome itself (including the important and impressive statuary collected by the Farnese family). The museum is poorly labeled and in a constant state of metamorphosis, but be sure to search out these highlights throughout the collections.

The *Doriforo,* or *Policleto's Spearman* (a Pompeiian Roman copy of a 440 B.C. Greek original) is the most accurate surviving copy of a masterpiece by Policletus of Argo, one of the geniuses of Greek Golden Age sculpture. It represents Policleto's embodiment of the ideal human form, carved with exacting mathematical proportions and a perfect figurative balance. The **Pozzuoli Sarcophagus** is a well-preserved 3rd-century A.D. Roman piece with a tumultuous high relief showing a seated, contemplative Prometheus creating Man surrounded by a swirl of deities and *putti* (cherubs).

Island Hopping Made Easy

When shopping at Naples's Molo Beverello for a boat to Capri, Ischia, or Procida Island, there's no need to visit all the dock offices for the best price. **Ontano Tours** (☎ **081-580-0341**) is a central clearinghouse, located just to the left of the driveway leading into the dock area. This travel agency will book you on the next ferry or hydrofoil out, tell you which line it is, and sell you a voucher that you then carry to that line's dock office to trade in for a ticket—all at no extra cost.

Naples

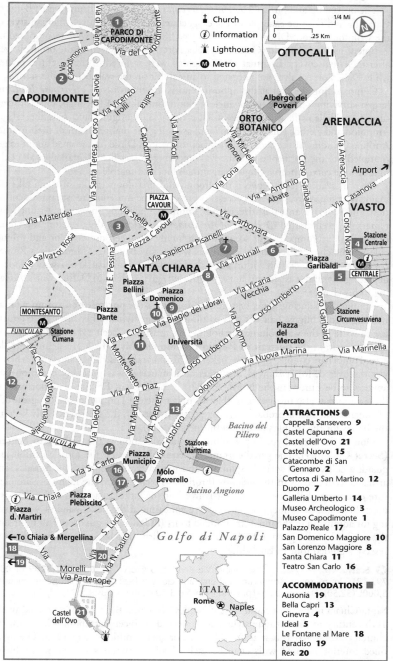

Legend:
- ✝ Church
- ⓘ Information
- ⚲ Lighthouse
- – – Ⓜ Metro

0 ___ 1/4 Mi
0 ___ .25 Km

ATTRACTIONS ●
Cappella Sansevero **9**
Castel Capunana **6**
Castel dell'Ovo **21**
Castel Nuovo **15**
Catacombe di San Gennaro **2**
Certosa di San Martino **12**
Duomo **7**
Galleria Umberto I **14**
Museo Archeologico **3**
Museo Capodimonte **1**
Palazzo Reale **17**
San Domenico Maggiore **10**
San Lorenzo Maggiore **8**
Santa Chiara **11**
Teatro San Carlo **16**

ACCOMMODATIONS ■
Ausonia **19**
Bella Capri **13**
Ginevra **4**
Ideal **5**
Le Fontane al Mare **18**
Paradiso **19**
Rex **20**

The bulked up and burly ✪ *Farnese Hercules* was excavated from Rome's Baths of Caracalla and is a fine example of the exaggerated A.D. 3rd-century Athenian style of the sculptor Glykon. Discovered without legs, the statue's limbs were recomposed by a student of Michelangelo (Guglielmo della Porta) and preferred to the originals well after their rediscovery. Eventually, the originals were restored to their rightful owner, while Della Porta's calves are relegated to an exhibit on the wall behind the statue.

Commanding the hall at the opposite end is the impressive ✪ *Farnese Bull,* the largest surviving sculpture of the ancient world. Standing 13 feet high, this 2nd-century A.D. Hellenistic work copies a 1st-century B.C. original and tells the tale of Amphion and Zethos (the two nude men) avenging the maltreatment of their mother Antiope (standing at the back) by tying her tormentor, Dirke (the woman about to get trampled), to the horns of a bull she was preparing to sacrifice. Remarkably, all of the figures were carved from a single, gargantuan block of marble.

On a mezzanine level between the ground and first floors (make sure you take the main sweeping staircase to gain access) is preserved the museum's most famous collection, the **mosaics and paintings from Pompeii,** including the slightly ruined but remarkably well-crafted ✪ *Battle of Alexander and Darius,* discovered in the House of the Faun at Pompeii. This scene, with a highly advanced use of color and minuscule mosaic chips to render the figures as well as any painting, is probably a Roman copy of an original crafted within a few decades of the actual battle of Isse of 333 B.C. depicting Alexander astride his horse (on the left) giving chase to Darius, who's retreating in his chariot.

Among the paintings here, be sure you don't miss the **portrait of a young woman** wearing a gold filigree hair net and pausing with her stylus to her lips before returning to write in the wax volume she holds. This must have been a standard pose, for it appears again in the **portrait of Paquio Proculo and his wife,** a prosperous middle-class Pompeiian couple, probably bakers. This portrait was rather shocking when it was discovered, for it showed that interracial marriage was probably common (she appears to be European, he North African) in the ancient Empire. The portrayal of these women is also intriguing in that it implies ancient Pompeii enjoyed a great deal of equality: the first is probably writing poetry (an artist), the second possibly keeping the books for the couple's bakery (a businesswoman).

One of the more hyped-up exhibits in the collection is the **Gabinetto Segreto (Secret Chamber).** The gated entrance is accessible through the mosaic exhibit and guards a collection of sexually symbolic and not so symbolic paintings, mosaics, and artifacts recovered from the *lupinare* (brothel) as well as from the many private pleasure chambers of Pompeii. The visit is free but since the capacity of the gallery is a mere 20 people at a time, you must reserve your time at the ticket window when paying for admission to the museum. Guided tours (in Italian) begin every half hour, and the exhibit is well signed in both Italian and English. (For large groups, call ahead to reserve a guided tour in English).

✪ **Santa Chiara.** Piazza Gesù Nuovo/Via Benedetto Croce. ☎ **081-552-6209** or 081-797-1256 for museum. Admission to church and cloisters free; suggested museum donation 5,000L ($2.50). Daily 9:30am–1pm and Mon–Sat 3:30–5:30pm. Bus: E1, R1, R3, R4, V10, 24.

Santa Chiara is the most rewarding of Naples' churches. Built in 1328, altered in the 18th-century to the baroque style, half-destroyed by incendiary bombs in 1943, the church was restored as best as possible to its original Gothic state in 1953. The light-filled interior is lined with chapels, each of which contains some leftover bit of sculpture or fresco from the medieval church, but the best three line the wall behind the High Altar. In the center is the towering, multilevel **tomb of Robert the Wise d'Angio,** sculpted by Giovanni and Pacio Bertini in 1343. To its right is Tino di

Camaino's **tomb of Charles, duke of Calabria;** on the left is the 1399 **monument to Mary of Durazza.** In the choir behind the altar are more salvaged medieval remnants of frescoes and statuary including bits of a Giotto *Crucifixion.*

Exit the church and walk down its left flank to enter one of Naples's top sights and the most relaxing retreat from the bustle of the city, the 14th-century ✪ **cloisters.** In 1742, Domenico Antonio Vaccaro took the courtyard of these flowering cloisters and lined the four paths to its center with arbors supported by columns, each of which is plated with colorfully painted majolica tiles, interspersed with majolica tiled benches. In the **museum** rooms off the cloisters are a scattering of Roman and medieval remains. On the piazza outside is one of Naples's several baroque spires, the **guglia dell'Immacolata,** a tall pile of statues and reliefs erected in 1750.

✪ **Cappella Sansevero (Sansevero Chapel).** Via Francesco de Sanctis 19 (near Piazza San Domenico Maggiore). ☎ **081-551-8470.** Admission 8,000L ($4) adults, 3,000L ($1.50) students. Wed–Mon 10am–8pm (to 5pm Nov–June). Bus: E1, R1, R3, R4, V10, 24, 42, 105, 105r.

If you want the best example of how baroque can be ludicrously over-the-top, hauntingly beautiful, and technically brilliant all at once, search out the nondescript entrance to one of Italy's most fanciful chapels. This 1590 chapel is a festival of marble, frescoes, and, above all, sculpture—in relief and in the round, masterfully showing off the considerable technical abilities and intricate visual storytelling of a few otherwise relatively unknown Neapolitan baroque masters. At the center is Giuseppe Sammartino's remarkable alabaster ✪ *Veiled Christ* (1753), one the most successful and convincing illusions of soft reality crafted from hard stone in the history of art, depicting the deceased Christ lying on pillows under a transparent veil.

Three ✪ **sculptures** on the walls stand out as well, including Francesco Celebrano's 1762 relief of the *Deposition* behind the altar, Antonio Corradini's allegory of *Chastity* (a marble statue of a woman whose nudity is covered only by a decidedly immodest clinging, gauzy veil), and Francesco Queirolo's virtuoso allegory of *Despair,* represented by a man struggling with a net carved in marble.

San Lorenzo Maggiore. Piazza San Gaetano 316. ☎ **081-290-580** or 081-454-948 for scavi. Admission to church free; scavi 5,000L ($2.50). Mon, Wed–Sat 9am–1pm and 4–6:30pm, Sun 9am–1:30pm. Bus: E1, 42, 105, 105r.

The greatest of Naples's layered churches was built in 1265 over a 6th-century basilica, constructed atop many ancient remains. The interior is pure Gothic, with tall pointed arches and an apse off which radiates nine chapels. Aside from some eye-popping inlaid marble baroque chapels, the highlight of the interior is Tino da Camaino's **canopy tomb of Catherine of Austria** (1323 to 1325), daughter-in-law of Robert the Wise. It was here too, in 1334, that Giovanni Boccaccio first caught sight of Robert of Anjou's daughter Maria, who inspired the "Fiammetta" in his writings.

San Lorenzo holds the best and most extensive although still largely unexcavated) **remains of the ancient Greek and Roman cities** currently open to the public. The foundations of the church are actually the walls of Neapolis' basilican law courts (this architectural type, the basilica, was adopted by the Paleochristians as a general blueprint for their first churches). In the cloisters are bits of the Roman city's treasury and marketplace. In the crypt are the rough remains of a Roman-era shop-lined street, a Greek temple, and a medieval building.

Duomo (Cathedral). Via Duomo. ☎ **081-449-097.** Admission to church free; archaeological crypt and baptistry 5,000L ($2.50); baptistry only 2,000L ($1). Daily 9am–noon and 4:30–7pm (crypt and baptistry close Sun at noon). Bus: E1, 42, 105, 105r.

The neo-Gothic facade of Naples's cathedral—built in the French Gothic style for Charles I in 1294 but rebuilt after a disastrous earthquake in 1456—was finished in

1905, but the central portal survives from the 1407 version. The 16 piers inside are made up of 110 antique columns of African and Asian granite removed from nearby pagan buildings.

The third chapel on the right is the sumptuous 17th-century **Cappella di San Gennaro,** elaborately frescoed by Domenichino and, later, Giovanni Lanfranco, who completed the concentric clouds of saints and angels spiraling up the airy dome. Also here is a painting of *San Gennaro Exiting Unharmed from the Furnace* by Giuseppe Ribera, showing a miracle by Benevento's persecuted bishop in A.D. 305, who survived both being thrown to lions and this roasting only to be done in by an axe to the neck. Among the silver reliquaries you'll see is one of *St. Irene Protecting the City,* in which the saint holds a scale model of Naples circa 1733. The most venerable item in all of Naples, however, is the silver reliquary bust that preserves the head of the city patron, St. Gennaro. Stored behind the chapel altar are two immeasurably venerated vials of his coagulated blood. The vials are taken out for the ✪ **Miracolo di San Gennaro** on the first Saturday of May, September 19, and December 16 amid much religious pomp and ceremony, whereupon they miraculously boil and liquefy again (Gennaro, incidentally, is the patron saint of blood banks). The speed with which the blood liquefies is a prediction of Naples's prosperity for the coming months and when the miracle occurs, the faithful line up to kiss the vials.

To the right of the High Altar are two chapels with staccato remnants of 13th- and 14th-century frescoes and inlaid marble floor. The **Crypt of San Gennaro** (a.k.a. Cappella Carafa) beneath the High Altar is one of the greatest examples of Renaissance design in Naples, including the Cosmatesque-style tomb of Pope Innocent IV (1315). To the left of the High Altar is a chapel containing an *Assumption* by Umbrian master painter Perugino.

Off the left aisle is the entrance to the ancient **Basilica di Santa Restituta,** a preexisting church built in the 4th century atop a Temple to Apollo, which is probably where the antique columns of the nave—rebuilt in the 14th century—come from. Luca Giordano's brush was active again here on the ceiling, but the highlight is the ✪ **baptistry** at the back. This domed cube of a room is the oldest building of its kind in Christian Europe, built in the 5th century and retaining impressive swatches of the original mosaics on the dome. From this little side church you can also descend to the basement where a few scraps of **Greek and Roman streets,** walls, and mosaics remain.

ATTRACTIONS ON THE WATERFRONT

Teatro San Carlo. Via San Carlo/Piazza Trieste e Trento. ☎ **081-797-2111.** Guided tours suspended indefinitely. Bus: R2, R3, C25, V10, 24, 105, 105r, 140.

San Carlo is one of the oldest, largest, and most respected opera houses in Italy, built (40 years before La Scala) under the auspices of Charles of Bourbon in 1737 (who didn't particularly care for opera, but cared very much about his reputation as an enlightened patron of the arts). After a fire in 1816, the theater was rebuilt by Antonio Niccolini—who, it's said, filled the walls with terra-cotta vases to help give the performance space what is still widely regarded as the best acoustics in Europe. San Carlo reopened shortly after under the musical direction of Gioacchino Rossini, opening up its sumptuous auditorium to premieres of operas by Rossini, Bellini, and Donizetti. **Tickets** (☎ 081-797-2331 or 081-797-2412) run 15,000L to 250,000L ($8 to $125), depending on the type of performance and where you sit.

Palazzo Reale (Royal Palace). Piazza Plebescito. ☎ **081-580-8326.** Admission 8,000L ($4.70), free under 18 and over 60. Tues–Thurs 9am–7pm, Sun and holidays 9am–8pm. Bus: R2, R3, C25, V10, 24, 105, 105r, 140.

This phenomenon, this "standing miracle," repeats itself on various feast days . . . except during times of strife, famine, oppression, and the election of a Communist mayor.

—On the regular liquefaction of St. Gennaro's blood,
Saints Preserve Us! (1993)

Naples's royal palace had to be restructured following Allied bomb damage in 1943, but retains some sumptuous royal apartments and, in niches along the 18th-century facade, statues of the greatest kings from the eight dynasties that have ruled Naples: Roger (Norman); Frederick II (Swabian); Charles I (Angevin); Alfonso (Aragonese); Charles V (Austrian); Charles III (Bourbon); Joachim Murat (French Napoleonic); and Vittorio Emanuele II (Savoy and ultimately Italian).

Court engineer Domenico Fontana started construction of the palazzo in 1599 under the viceroy Ruiz de Castro, who wished to create one of the most glorious palaces in the kingdom of Spain's King Philip III. The core was finished by 1616, but in 1759 Ferdinando Fuga was brought in by Ferdinand IV to amplify the palazzo, including the addition of the ornate **Teatro do Corte,** built on the occasion of the king's wedding to Maria Carolina of Hapsburg (Marie Antoinette's sister) and decorated with papier-mâché sculpture. Also here are preserved 15th-century bronze doors from the Castel Nuovo whose reliefs tell of Ferdinand of Aragon's feuds with the local barons (the cannonball jutting out of the bottom of one door is a testament to the battle waged by the French and Genoese navies in Naples' harbor). Written descriptions of each palatial room and its contents are available in English. Be sure not to miss the elaborate **Throne Room,** or Belsario Corenzio's ceiling frescoes in several chambers that depict the *Glories of the Spanish Monarchy.*

The expansive ✪ **Piazza Plebescito** in front of the royal palace is one of Naples' largest open spaces, laid out with a curving colonnade and equestrian statues of Charles III of Bourbon and Ferdinand IV in the early 18th century. At the center of the curve is the neoclassical church of **San Francesco di Paola,** modeled after Rome's Pantheon in 1817 for Ferdinand IV, who ordered it built as an offering of thanks after he retook the city from Napoleonic troops.

Castel Nuovo (New Castle) & Maschio Angioino (Angevin Fortress). Piazza Municipio. ☎ **081-795-2003.** Admission 10,000L ($5), 12,000L ($6) during some exhibitions. Mon–Sat 9am–7pm. Bus: R2, R3, C25, C82, C82b, V10, 24, 105, 105r.

Though the core Maschio Angioino was built in the 13th century, the grand ✪ **entrance arch** wedged between two massive 15th-century bastions is pure Renaissance. This unique adaptation of a triumphal arch was grafted onto the castle to commemorate Alfonso I of Aragon's arrival into the city in 1443. The highlights inside are the statues and frescoes from the 14th and 15th century in the **Cappella Palatina (Palatine Chapel);** a middling collection of paintings from the 15th to 20th centuries; and the huge **Sala dei Baroni,** the grand hall where Naples's City Council still meets.

Naples Underground. Visits are organized by both the Libera Associazione Escursionisti Sottosuoli (☎ **081-400-256;** meet at Caffè Gambrinus) and the Associazione Napoli Sotterranea (☎ **081-296-944;** meet in Piazza San Gaitano) on Sat and Sun (the latter also has a departure at 9pm Thurs).

Interred beneath the sidewalks and highways of Naples is another world, a city underground that would be impossible to explore in its entirety. During the Roman rule of

Augusto, a project for the construction of an aqueduct was completed, creating a subterranean labyrinth 170km (105.6 miles) long. Over the years, the system of aqueducts has been altered and enlarged, even functioning as air-raid shelters during WWII. The guided visit touches the surface of this complex system of tunnels, honing in on particular points of interest including **Greco-Roman remains.**

ATTRACTIONS IN THE HILLS

✪ **Museo Capodimonte.** Parco di Capodimonte, Via Capodimonte. ☎ **081-749-9111.** Admission 14,000L ($7); 12,000L/$6 after 2pm and free under 18 and over 60. Mon–Fri 10am–7pm, Sun 9am–8pm. Bus: 24, navetta, 137, 110.

Set in the green of Capodimonte Park high above the city is by far the best painting gallery in all of southern Italy. The National Picture Gallery consumes an 18th-century royal palace, and is particularly strong on works from Old Masters representing all phases of the Renaissance and baroque periods. The core of the museum's holdings is the Farnese Collection, inherited by the Bourbon dynasty, along with the historical apartments and the china and majolica collections. Among the early Renaissance paintings is a simple and beautiful 1426 *Crucifixion* by Masaccio, and one of **Giovanni Bellini's** masterpieces, his ✪ *Transfiguration* (1478 to 1479). From the great **Raphael** we have *Portrait of Cardinal Alessandro Farnese* (who became Pope Paul III; 1511), a cartoon of *Moses and the Burning Bush* (1514), and the *Eternal Father.* Representing the genius of **Michelangelo** is a cartoon of soldiers that he made as a study for his *Crucifixion of St. Peter* fresco in the Vatican.

There are High Renaissance pieces from Sebastiano del Piombo and **Correggio,** whose 1518 *Marriage of St. Catherine* is a finely studied classical work. **Titian** painted a whole gaggle of portraits of various Farnese cardinals in the 1540s, along with a provocative *Danäe* (1546) painted for Cardinal Alessandro Farnese (and probably using the cardinal's mistress as the goddess model), and the *Portrait of a Young Lady* (1546), which some scholars believe is actually a portrait of Titian's own daughter. **El Greco** contributes the haunting *El Soplón,* or *Youth Lighting a Candle with a Coal* (1575). There are many good **Mannerist** works from the brushes of Andrea del Sarto, Pontormo, Rosso Fiorentino, and Parmigianino.

After a breather of Flemish paintings (look especially for *The Misanthrope* and *The Blind Leading the Blind,* both 1568 works by **Peter Bruegel**), the baroque takes over with a survey of the **Carracci** clan, including works by Agostino, Ludovico, and especially **Annibale Carracci,** who pokes fun at his arch-competitor Caravaggio by painting that artist's leering face on his rendition of a *Satyr.* **Caravaggio** got the last laugh, though, since art history books give but a paragraph to Carracci while filling pages with homage to Caravaggio's genius for composition and dramatic use of *chiaroscuro* (strongly contrasting light and dark areas), well evident in the ✪ *Flagellation of Christ* (1609) kept here.

Early baroque's greatest (and virtually only) female artist—was **Artemisia Gentileschi,** whose rape as a teenager (and the subsequent highly public and sensational trial) may have later led her to turn her artistic lens often to the many examples throughout history, myth, and the Bible wherein women exact revenge upon men, as in this gallery's gory *Judith Beheading Holofernes.* **Luca Giordano** manages to give good compositional balance and use of light to baroque extravagance in his *Madonna del Baldacchino* (1686).

Pop into the small, excruciatingly elaborate Chinese-style **Salottino di Porcellana** for an excellent example of Italy's finest 18th-century porcelain, still being produced in a nearby factory (built in 1743) here on Capodimonte.

Catacombe di San Gennaro (Catacombs of San Gennaro). Via Capodimonte 16 (enter around the left of the Basilica del Madre di Bonconsiglio and through the gate). ☎ **081-741-1071.** Admission 5,000L ($2.50), 3,000L ($1.50) under 15. Open by guided tour only, daily at 9:30, 10:15, 11, and 11:45am (note: tours leave only if more than one person shows up). Bus: 24, 137, 110.

These wide tunnels lined with early Christian burial niches grew around the tomb of an important pagan family, but became a pilgrimage site when the bones of San Gennaro himself were transferred here in the 5th century. Along with several well-preserved 6th-century frescoes, there's a depiction of San Gennaro from the A.D. 5th century whose halo sports an alpha and omega, and a cross—symbols normally reserved exclusively for Christ's halo. The tour takes you through the upper level of tunnels, passing through several small early basilicas carved from the tufa rock. The cemetery remained active until the 11th century, but most of the bones have since been blessed and reinterred in ossuaries on the lower levels (closed to the public). The catacombs survived the centuries intact, but the precious antique frescoes suffered some damage when these tunnels served as an air raid shelter during World War II.

Certosa di San Martino. Largo San Martino/Via Tito Angelini (on the Vomero next to Castel Sant'Elmo). ☎ **081-578-1769.** Admission 6,000L ($3). Tues–Sun 9am–2pm. Funicular: Montesanto, then Bus V1 (or walk).

This 14th-century Carthusian monastery is famous for its fine church, peaceful cloisters, small painting gallery, and remarkable *presepio* collection of Christmas crèches. From here, the ✪ **views** across the city below are fantastic, and alone worth the trip up.

The marble-clad **church** has a ceiling painting of the *Ascension* by Lanfranco in the nave along with 12 *Prophets* by Giuseppe Ribera. Ribera also did the *Institution of the Eucharist* on the left wall of the choir, while Lanfranco painted the *Crucifixion* and Guido Reni the *Nativity* at the choir's back wall. In the church treasury is Luca Giordano's ceiling fresco of the *Triumph of Judith* (1704) and Ribera's masterful *Descent from the Cross.*

The vast ✪ **museum of presepi** houses dozens of Neapolitan Christmas crèches with an overall cast of thousands. These inspired peasant and holy figures have come out of the workshops of Naples's greatest artisans over the past four centuries. The modest **painting and sculpture gallery** houses 15th- to 18th-century works, including a few by Bernini, Caracciolo, and Vaccaro.

Next door to the monastery is the star-shaped **Castel Sant'Elmo** (☎ **081-578-4030**), partially carved into the tufa of this strategic position above the city. The castle was built between 1329 and 1343 by the Angevins and enlarged in the 16th century. After a walk through the dark, resonant, medieval stone halls, the castle proffers a magnificent 360° panorama of Naples and its bay. The castle is open Tuesday to Sunday 9am to 2pm; admission is 2,000L ($1).

AFFORDABLE PLACES TO STAY
NEAR THE TRAIN STATION

Ginevra. Via Genova 116, 80142 Naples. ☎ **081-283-210.** Fax 081-554-1757. www.mds.it/ginevra. E-mail: hginevra@tin.it. 14 units, 6 with shower. TV TEL. 45,000L ($23) single without shower; 70,000L ($35) double without shower; 90,000L ($45) double with shower; 100,000L ($50) triple without shower; 125,000L ($63) triple with shower. Breakfast 7,500L ($3.75). 10% discount with this book and payment in cash.

This family-run pensione three flights up in a charming palazzo offers the convenience and comfort difficult to find in this otherwise dubious neighborhood. Located two blocks from the central station, the Ginevra puts Pompeii, Herculaneum Sorrento, and Naples's historic center, only a short bus ride (or pleasantly long walk), at your fingertips. The rooms are simple, utilitarian, and clean—even cheerful now that all have been renovated—and until air-conditioning is installed, which is promised to happen in the not-too-distant future, large fans are available on request. The English-speaking receptionists (either the owner, his son, or a friend) make themselves available to their guests for reliable recommendations in town. Ask about their private guided day tours along the Amalfi coast (240,000L/$120 for up to four people).

Ideal. Piazza Garibaldi 99 (on the left side of the square as you exit the train station), 80142 Naples. ☎ **081-269-237** or 081-202-223. Fax 081-285-942. 45 units. TV TEL. 100,000L ($50) single; 150,000L ($75) double; 200,000L ($100) triple. These are special Frommer's rates, so be sure to flash this book. Rates include breakfast. AE, DC, MC, V. Nearby parking in garage 25,000L ($13). Metro: Naples Centrale. Bus: tram 1, R2, 14, 14r, 42, 110 (to Piazza Garibaldi).

The name may be a bit of wishful thinking, but this large, clean budget standby is just 200 feet from the train station (and a 10-minute tram ride from the ferry docks) and indeed ideal if you plan on lots of day trips. It's also a haven of quality and security among many seedy hotels in an often squalid area. It's been family run for 50 years and a renovation in 1998 installed baths in all rooms. Some of the tile floors are fantastically patterned, the walls decorated with simple stuccoes, and while most of the furniture is modular, some of the new units are quite stylish. Several rooms have terraces on the courtyard and are much quieter than those fronting traffic-choked Piazza Garibaldi. The student guidebooks are well aware of this place, so book in advance.

CENTRO STORICO

Bella Capri. Via Melisurgo 4 (stair B; 6th floor), 80133 Naples. ☎ **081-552-9494.** Fax 081-552-9265. www.mds.it/bellacapri. 9 units. TV TEL. 90,000L ($45) single; 120,000L ($60) double; 140,000L ($70) triple. Breakfast 5,000L ($2.50). AE, DI, DISC, EC, JCB, MC, V. From Piazza Garibaldi, take bus #152 to Molo Beverello.

The uninviting side-street entrance to this neglected residential palazzo may put you off, but once you're under the warm glow of the green neon outside this welcoming sanctuary, things can only get better. Relatively new and recently renovated, the Bella Capri provides an optimum base steps away from the historic center and the Molo Beverello ferry docks. A bayside room (2, 3, 4, and 5) includes an oversized door to a balcony overlooking the port; on warm summer mornings, breakfast will be served to you alfresco. The back rooms aren't too shabby, either, as Mt. Vesuvius hovers above. Air-conditioning should be installed by the time you get here. Best of all, Bella Capri provides free transfers from the airport. Call ahead to reserve and have a 100L coin ready to use the elevator (reimbursed).

Le Fontane al Mare. Via Niccolú Tommaseo 14 (at Via Partenope), 80121 Naples. ☎ and fax **081-764-3470.** 20 units, 7 with bathroom. Single without bathroom 80,000L ($40), single with bathroom 90,000L ($45); double without bathroom 114,000L ($57), double with bathroom 144,000L ($72); triple without bathroom 151,000L ($76), triple with bathroom 184,000L ($92). Rates include breakfast. AE, DI, MC, V. Nearby parking in garage 25,000L ($13). Bus: tram 1, R1, R3, C12, C18, C19, C24, C25, C28, 140 (to Piazza Vittoria).

Naples's best bargain in bayside hotels occupies the top floors of a 17th-century palazzo. You trade some comfort for the vistas, price, and safe neighborhood in this well-worn yet charming pensione. Although few of the rooms have private baths, most have in-room sinks along with aging tile floors and high ceilings with crown molding. There are pleasantly incongruous Asian prints on the walls, an amalgam of solid old furnishings and flea-market cast-offs, and bed springs that are rapidly losing their battle with gravity. Only the bathless rooms have sea views (except for 25, which has both), but all have balconies, resulting in plenty of cool breezes—along with traffic noise from the boulevard. The public baths are clean and large, while the private ones are showing their age. The phones aren't direct-dial (the desk will ring you through), and unless you relish a five-floor walk-up, be sure to carry 200L coins for the elevator.

Rex. Via Palepoli 12 (between Via Nazario Sauro and Via Santa Lucia), 80123 Naples. ☎ **081-764-9389.** Fax 081-764-9227. 38 units. A/C TV TEL. 150,000L ($75) single; 190,000L ($95) double; 210,000L ($105) triple. Rates include breakfast. AE, DC, MC, V. Parking 25,000–30,000L ($13–$15) in hotel garage. Bus: tram 1, R3 (to the end of Galleria d. Vittoria tunnel); C25, 140 (to Via S. Lucia).

Set back from the harbor road, the 1960s Rex is another great bargain in Naples's toniest area (it's directly behind the top hotels in town). The modular pine furnishings, wicker chairs, port-a-lamps, and brown or speckled floor tiles hint at the era in which it was built, but everything's been maintained immaculately, except for the odd plumbing glitch. Prints on the walls and the occasional painted ceiling brighten the sober decor considerably, but while most accommodations are amply sized, some don't get as much light as others. Half the rooms have balconies, but thanks to the double-paned windows, your sleep will be undisturbed.

MERGELLINA

Ausonia. Via Caracciolo 11 (at the Mergellina docks), 80122 Naples. ☎ **081-664-536.** Fax 081-682-278. 19 units. TV TEL. 125,000L ($63) single; 180,000L ($90) double; 210,000L ($105) triple. Rates include breakfast. Possible 10% discount in low season. AE, MC, V. Parking 25,000–30,000L ($13–$15). Metro: Mergellina. Bus: tram 1, R3, C16, C24, C21, 140 (to Mergellina).

In the pleasant and safe neighborhood around the hydrofoil docks, the Ausonia is convenient for boats to Capri or Ischia, but you'll have to take a bus or metro to get to the city center. Porthole mirrors, ship's helm nightstands, and polished wood surfaces create a spiffy nautical theme, making you almost feel as if you're on a cruise rather than in on land. Maritime living carries over to the curtainless showers and in spotlessly kept rooms, but happily not in the size of these relatively roomy accommodations. It's location at the back of a harborfront building means you're cheated of an ocean view, but you're spared the traffic noise of the seaside boulevard. Instead, windows open onto the courtyard or a noisier back alley, and gauzy curtains graze the marble floors in the breeze.

WORTH A SPLURGE

Paradiso. Via Catullo 11, 80122 Naples. ☎ **800-528-1234** or 081-761-4161. Fax 081-761-3449. www.bestwestern.it. 70 units. AC MINIBAR TV TEL. 180,000L ($90) single; 290,000L ($145) double; 320,000L ($160) triple. Rates include breakfast. AE, DI, JCB, MC, V. Public parking lot across the street. Metro: Mergellina then Funiculare to San Gioacchino; the hotel is around the bend to your right.

If you're looking for reliable quality and comfort and to remove yourself from the chaos of the city center, the air is noticeably cleaner up on the hilltops of Mergellina at this Best Western property. It may take some effort to get there, but a seaside room with astounding views of the Bay of Naples (and particularly from the rooftop terrace restaurant) makes the trip worth your while. The rooms are typical of what you'd expect from this modern chain: plush wall-to-wall carpeting, pleasing modular furnishings, subtly elegant bedspreads, and standard baths. Because the Paradiso is built on a hill, views from the lower rooms are obstructed by neighboring buildings; request a room on the third or fourth floor to ensure a sea view.

GREAT DEALS ON DINING

Quickie meals can be had nearest the train station (the pizza in the McDonald's dominated complex to the left is actually pretty good), or you can get all the **picnic fixings** you need in the string of little shops lining the first block of Salita Santa Anna di Palazzo, off Via Chiaia. Treat yourself to at least one sit-down Neapolitan meal, and order the antipasto of *mozzarella di bufala* every chance you get.

NEAR THE TRAIN STATION

Da Michele. Via Sersale 1 (off Corso Umberto). ☎ **081-553-9204.** Pizza 6,000–8,000 ($3–$4) No credit cards. Mon–Sat 10am–11pm.

If you don't mind the wait—and there will be one—head over to the most highly trafficked pizzeria in town. You'll be seated at a table set with paper placemats and hastily placed utensils and treated to anything but a sophisticated dining experience. Even the service will be rushed. But apparently the pizza—that's all there is—is worth the wait because Michele's clients keep coming back for a simple margherita or the marinara (with shellfish) over an authentic thick and spongy "*pasta Napolitana*" (thick crust).

Iris Caffetteria Restaurant and Pizzeria. Piazza Garibaldi 121–125. ☎ **081-269-988.** Primi: 3,000–10,000L ($2–$5); secondi: 5,800–19,000L ($3–$10). 10% discount for 2 or more with this book. AE, DC, DISC, JCB, MC, V. Open Sun–Fri, noon–midnight or 1am. Closed for 3 unpredictable days in August. NEAPOLITAN.

I can't count the number of times I found myself at the train station and in need of a meal, only to look around distrustfully at the eateries lining Piazza Garibaldi. Thank the day I fell upon the Iris! This restaurant even won an award from the *Associazione Cuochi Italiani* for "la fantasia ed esecuzione" (creativity and execution). Nobody should pass up the mozzarella di Bufala or the *polipo in cassuola* (octopus and tomato cooked in a casserole). Overcome your revulsion of the *pizza con bianchetti* (little eel-like white minnows with the eyes staring out at you)—this specialty of the house is actually pretty good.

Mimi alla Ferrovia. Via Alfonso d'Aragona 21 (off northwest corner of Piazza Garibaldi). ☎ **081-553-8525.** Reservations recommended. Primi 9,000–20,000L ($5–$10); secondi 18,000–28,000L ($9–$14). AE, MC, V. Mon–Sat noon–4pm; 7:30pm–midnight. Closed 1–2 weeks in Aug. Metro: Naples Centrale. Bus: tram 1, R2, 14, 14r, 42, 110 (to Piazza Garibaldi). NEAPOLITAN.

Ceiling frescoes and photos of celebrity patrons give a refined air, almost elegant by Neapolitan standards, to this long-respected restaurant—certainly they help it to rise above the hookers, porn cinemas, and shifty eyes you have to wade through to get here. The few tourists who brave the surrounding streets join tables full of contented local regulars to dig into antipasti of *pepperoni ripieni* (peppers stuffed with mozzarella and prosciutto) or primi like *linguine alla Mimi* (with prawns and shrimp in a scampi) and the rich pea-green *pasta e ceci* (flat pasta squares in a pasty chickpea puree). For secondo order a *bistecca di manzo ai ferri* (grilled steak) or plate-licking *polpi in cassuola* (octopus in a tomato casserole).

IN THE CENTRO STORICO

'a Taverna 'e zi Carmela. Via Nicolò Tommasea 11–12 at Via Partenope). ☎ **081-764-3581.** Primi 5,000–18,000L ($3–$9); secondi 5,000–18,000L ($3–$9). No credit cards. Open Tues–Sun 9am–3pm and 6pm–midnight. Closed for 2 unpredictable weeks in Aug. NEAPOLITAN/PIZZERIA.

This is a simple, down-to-earth, cozy family taverna conveniently located next to Le Fontane al Mare and Piazza Vittoria. The walls are covered in pictures of the family posing with the odd Italian actor who has happened by, and bottles of wine casually line the shelves. Try a plate of their *linguini alle vongole* (in a clam sauce), with or without a dusting of Naples's infamously succulent tomatoes.

✪ **Osteria al Canterbury.** Via Ascensione 6 (just up from the Riviera Chiaia, down from Piazza Amadeo). ☎ **081-411-658.** Reservations recommended. Primi 8,000–10,000L ($4–$5); secondi 9,000–16,000L ($5–$8). AE, MC, V. Sun–Fri 1–4pm, 8pm–midnight; Sat 8pm–midnight. Closed Sun June–Aug and 15 days in Aug. Bus: tram 1, R3, C12, C18, C28, 140 (to Riviera di Chiaia). NEAPOLITAN.

During their courtship, the future Rino and Lilly Adamo had one of those singularly memorable meals in a tiny, friendly, old-fashioned osteria of a dozen wooden tables with high-back straw-seated chairs set on terra-cotta floors. They decided on the spot that one day, they'd open a place of their own just like it, and thus the Canterbury was born. Its name is apt, since it's cozy in a vaguely British manner: close tables set with flowers, a modest chandelier, dark wood cupboards, little curtains. Trust your waiter's advice implicitly. Perhaps he'll suggest starting with *paccheri con coccio* (wide pasta loops in a light sauce of baby tomatoes and local fish) or *maccheroni di casa Canterbury* (pasta with tomatoes, cheese, and eggplant). Move on to no-nonsense secondi like *agnello alla brace* (grilled lamb) or *petto di pollo in vino bianco* (chicken breast cooked in white wine), and definitely cap it all off with the homemade tiramisù.

Pizzeria Brandi. Salita Sant'Anna di Palazzo 1–2 (just off Via Chiaia, 2 blocks up from Piazza Trieste e Trento). ☎ **081-416-928.** www.brandi.it. Reservations highly recommended. Primi 9,000–17,000L ($5–$9); secondi 10,000–25,000L ($5–$13); pizza 9,000–16,000L ($5–$8). AE, DC, MC, V. Daily noon–3:30pm, 7:30pm–midnight. Closed Aug 14–16. Bus: R2, R3, V10, C22, C25, 24 (to Via S. Cairo/Piazza Trieste e Trento). PIZZA/NEAPOLITAN.

Owned and operated by the same Neapolitan family for over 200 years, Pizzeria Brandi is Naples's most famous pizzeria and a local institution. Popular legend holds that it was on this very spot in 1889 that, in honor of a visit by the first queen of a newly unified Italy, the *pizzaiolo* concocted a patriotic pizza modeled after the colors in the country's new flag: white *mozzarella di bufalo,* red tomato sauce, and green basil. They named it after the queen herself and delivered it straight to the palace at Capodimonte, pioneering not only the first pizza Margherita, but also the first pizza to go. Although the hordes descend here just for the pizza (which is still actually pretty good), Brandi does offer pasta dishes like *linguine agli scampi,* and some secondi as well, such as *scaloppine al limone.* Book ahead for one of the six outside tables, or be contented watching the activity at the open wood-fired oven.

Pizzeria Port'Alba. Via Port'Alba 18 (between Piazza Bellini and Piazza Dante). ☎ **081-459-713.** Reservations not accepted. Primi 7,000–22,000L ($4–$11); secondi 9,000–25,000L ($5–$13); pizza 9,000–15,000L ($5–$8). AE, DC, MC, V. Thurs–Tues noon–2:30am. Closed 1 wk in Aug. Bus: E1, R1, R4, V10, 24, 137 (to Piazza Dante). PIZZA/NEAPOLITAN.

A Money-Saving Tip

April to October, in conjunction with the ferries and a few cooperating restaurants, **combination tickets** for day trips to the three nearby islands (Ischia, Capri, or Procida) are available for 57,000L ($29) at most hotels, travel agents and tour operators. The deal includes roundtrip transport via hydrofoil or ferry, lunch at one of six established restaurants, and the funicular (required for trips to Capri only, 500L/75¢ value). This is a good deal if you want a complete restaurant lunch included in your outing (you save $10–$15). Independently, the ferry or hydrofoil will run you 33,000L ($17) or 36,000L ($18) round trip, depending on which mode you choose, so if you're planning on eating a *panino,* you're better off going it alone.

Notwithstanding its touristy location and ability to accommodate bus groups, Port'Alba serves a most respectable pizza Margherita. Located on a pedestrian side street in the heart of old Naples (two blocks from the archaeological museum or from Santa Chiara), Port'Alba is said to be Naples' oldest pizzeria (est. 1738). You can dine in the alley under umbrellas or in the air-conditioned upstairs dining room. If the margherita doesn't grab you and you don't feel like going in for *pizza lasagna* (with ricotta) or *port'alba* (covered with shellfish), there's a substantial menu that goes well beyond pizza with entrees that include *linguine al cartoccio,* veal scallop in Marsala wine and fresh fish.

Ristorante Transatlantico. Borgo Marinari, Isola di Megaris. ☎ **081-764-8842.** Primi: 12,000–20,000L ($6–$10); secondi: 16,000–20,000L ($8–$10). Fish sold by weight. AE, DC, MC, V. Open Wed–Mon 12:00–3pm, 7:30pm–midnight or 1am.

This wonderful little harborside restaurant is a favorite among locals for its evocative location and characteristic meals, and many a visitor has discovered this spot, only to return here for an encore. Set on the edge of the marina alongside the Castel dell'Ovo, Transatlantico lets you choose between tables on the delightful laundry-draped piazza, or harborside to watch the local boys swimming or rowing around the marina. You can rely on a good pasta or pizza here, but the fish, although pricey, is excellent. Try it grilled or in their cold seafood salad accompanied by a local wine.

WORTH A SPLURGE

Ristorante Umberto. Via Alabardieri 30–31 (2 blocks behind the Chiaia park at the Santa Lucia end, near Piazza dei Martiri). ☎ **081-418-555.** Reservations recommended. Primi 6,000–18,000L ($3–$9); secondi 9,000–25,000L to 60,000L for fish ($5–$13 to $30); pizza 5,500–12,000L ($3–$6). AE, DC, MC, V. Tues–Sun noon–3:30pm, 7:00pm–1am. Closed 15 to 20 days in August. Bus: tram 1, R1, R3, C12, C18, C19, C24, C25, C28, 140 (to Piazza Vittoria). NEAPOLITAN/PIZZA.

The Umberto is a touch of class among Naples's minimalist eateries, an upscale trattoria atmosphere with waistcoated waiters bringing you tidbits to nibble along with the menu. The walls are stark white, hung with antique mirrors and pictures. Cutting through the convivial chatter of satisfied diners are the folksy strains of a guitar player who belts out Neapolitan *bel canto* all evening long (not as touristy as it sounds, the clientele here is largely Italian). Try a primo of *spaghetti alle vongole* or *pasta e lenticchie* (pasta with lentils). Among the hearty secondi are *impepata di cozze* (peppery mussel stew), fresh fish, or *involtini alla Umberto* (veal wrapped around prosciutto and provolone, then stewed in a mushroom-and-pea sauce). If you just want to pop in for a meal without much ado, there's a pizzeria connected in back.

CAFES

The grand dame of Neapolitan cafes is the 1860 ✪ **Gran Caffè Gambrinus,** Piazza Trieste e Trento (☎ **081-417-582**), where intellectuals and writers as diverse as Gabriele d'Annunzio and Oscar Wilde have gathered since 1860 under the stuccoes, silks, and frescoes of the belle époque interior. The ambience offers the perfect background for enjoying a cappuccino and *sfogliatella* (Naples's premier pastry, a cream-stuffed horn made of flaky millefeuille dough). There's an outdoor cafe with an elegant view of the Teatro San Carlo, the Royal Palace, and Piazza Plebescito, but the noise and fumes from the cars that roar down Via Toledo around the traffic circle at your back might induce you to stand (and save lire in the process) at the bar. The cafe is closed Tuesdays and in August.

The pastry shop and bar **Scaturchio,** Piazza San Domenico 19 (☎ **081-551-6944**), has also long been a favored spot to sample the rich bounty of Neapolitan pastry, though the setting is far less elegant (and prices a bit lower). You'll find the best gelato in town at **Gelateria della Scimmia,** Piazza Carità 4 (☎ **081-552-0272**), established in 1934; and the **Gran Bar Riviera,** Riviera di Chiaia 183 (no phone), which opened in 1860 and claims to have invented the tartufo ice cream ball.

2 Herculaneum: A Prelude to Pompeii

230km (143 mi) SE of Rome; 25km (16 mi) SE of Naples.

The builders of ✪ **Herculaneum (Ercolano)** were still working to repair the damage caused by an A.D. 63 earthquake when Vesuvius erupted on that fateful August day in A.D. 79, burying the town under up to 82 feet of burning mud, sand, and rocks. About one-fourth the size of Pompeii, Herculaneum didn't start to come to light again until 1709, when Prince Elbeuf launched the unfortunate fashion of tunneling through it for treasures, more intent on profiting from the sale of objets d'art than in uncovering a dead Roman town.

ESSENTIALS

GETTING THERE   The private **Circumvesuviana rail line** (☎ **081-772-2444**) services Herculaneum (from Naples 8 min; 2,200L/$1.30; from Sorrento 50 min; 8,200L/$4.10), Vesuvius (same stop), Pompeii, and Sorrento (the latter two are covered later in this chapter). It leaves from its own station in Naples on Corso Garibaldi, just south of the central station, every 20 minutes (you also catch Circumvesuviana trains underneath the main Stazione Centrale itself; follow the signs).

EXPLORING THE AREA

Pompeii gets all the press, but **Herculaneum** (☎ 081-739-0963) is just as enthralling. Unlike workaday Pompeii, this ancient Roman city was a resort and retirement town for the rich, inauspiciously set on the shore under the menacing gaze of Vesuvius. **Admission** to Herculaneum is 16,000L ($8; free for those up to 18 yrs and over 60) and the site is open daily 9am to an hour before sunset.

The archaeological site is considerably smaller than that of Pompeii. Herculaneum was around one-third the size, with about 5,000 inhabitants to Pompeii's 20,000, but the homes of the rich and famous, uncovered largely intact, were much more elaborate, extensive, and sumptuously decorated than those in its illustrious neighbor. Many still have their second stories. Floor mosaics, wall frescoes, ceiling stuccoes, and even wooden furnishings have all been preserved. Plenty of plebeian houses are mixed in as well, along with shops like the bakery with its stone grain grinders set up in the backyard.

Although all the streets and buildings of Herculaneum hold interest, some ruins merit more attention than others. The **Terme (baths)** are divided between those at the forum and the **Terme Suburbane (Suburban Baths)** on the outskirts, near the more elegant villas. The municipal baths, which segregated the sexes, are larger, but the ones at the edge of town are more lavishly adorned. The **Palestra** was a kind of sports arena, where games were staged to satisfy the spectacle-hungry denizens.

The typical plan for the average town house was to erect it around an uncovered atrium. In some areas, Herculaneum possessed the forerunner of the modern apartment house. Important private homes to seek out are the **Casa del Bicentenario (Bicentennial House), Casa a Graticcio (House of the WoodenTrellis), Casa del Tramezzo di Legno** or **Casa del Tramezzo Carbonizzato (House of the Wooden/Charred Partition),** and **Casa di Poseidon (House of Poseidon),** as well as the **Anfiteatro (Amphitheater).** The finest example of how the aristocracy lived is the **Casa dei Cervi,** named the **House of the Stags** because of the sculpture found

Herculaneum

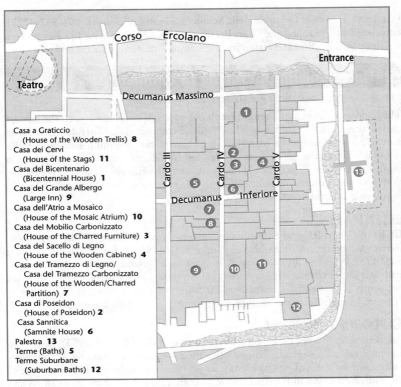

Corso Ercolano

Teatro

Entrance

Decumanus Massimo

Casa a Graticcio
(House of the Wooden Trellis) **8**
Casa dei Cervi
(House of the Stags) **11**
Casa del Bicentenario
(Bicentennial House) **1**
Casa del Grande Albergo
(Large Inn) **9**
Casa dell'Atrio a Mosaico
(House of the Mosaic Atrium) **10**
Casa del Mobilio Carbonizzato
(House of the Charred Furniture) **3**
Casa del Sacello di Legno
(House of the Wooden Cabinet) **4**
Casa del Tramezzo di Legno/
Casa del Tramezzo Carbonizzato
(House of the Wooden/Charred
Partition) **7**
Casa di Poseidon
(House of Poseidon) **2**
Casa Sannitica
(Samnite House) **6**
Palestra **13**
Terme (Baths) **5**
Terme Suburbane
(Suburban Baths) **12**

Cardo III

Cardo IV

Cardo V

Decumanus Inferiore

inside. Guides are fond of showing the males on their tours a statue of a drunken Hercules urinating. Some of the best of the houses are locked and can be seen only by permission.

For a long time, scholars believed that most of Herculaneum's elite had closed up their summer homes for the season, or that inhabitants had time to escape, since only six bodies were found in the streets and houses (this compared to the 2,000 found at Pompeii). Then in 1982, while excavating around the docks at what was the shoreline in ancient times, a worker discovered hundreds upon hundreds of bodies, scorched by volcanic gasses right down to the bone, huddled in the dock houses under 60 feet of hardened volcanic mud. They had died waiting for the boats to carry them to safety.

3 Pompeii & Its Amazing Ruins

20km (12 mi.) SE of Naples, 15km (9 mi.) SE of Herculaneum, 33km (20 mi.) NE of Sorrento.

Though the ancient Oscan city of ✪ **Pompeii,** founded before the 6th century B.C., had its ups and downs, by A.D. 1st century it was a Roman colony of 20,000 and a thriving, bustling seaport. It occupied a prime stretch of coastline southeast of *Neapolis* (Naples), just on the other side of that huge mountain called Vesuvius. After 14 years of hard work, Pompeii was just getting back on its architectural feet following the massive earthquake of A.D. 63. The columns of the forum had been re-erected, and villa owners had piled lime next to the last walls that needed replastering. They thought the worst was over.

The "I's" Have It

No, you're not seeing things. "Pompeii" (with two *i*'s) refers to the ancient city and archaeological site. "Pompei" (with one *i*) is the official name of the modern town just next door. Apparently, the second *i* got buried by Vesuvius along with everything else in A.D. 79.

At noon, August 24, A.D. 79, the peak of Mt. Vesuvius exploded, sending a mottled black-and-white mushroom cloud 12 miles into the air at twice the speed of sound, raining ash and light pumice down on the region. For 12 hours, the sheer force of the eruption kept the cloud aloft. Some Pompeiians fled. But more than 2,000 bodies have been uncovered at Pompeii—these souls probably thought the enormous cloud hanging over Vesuvius was just smoke, and saw no need to leave. When the cloud finally collapsed, the horror engulfed the city before anyone could run more than a few feet. Pompeii was buried by a pyroclastic flow, a superfast rush of hot ash and pumice with an undercurrent of rock and burning gasses, all of which came barreling down the mountain like a tidal wave, the force ripping the doors and roofs off houses, fusing metal house keys to skulls, and dismembering human bodies.

The 17-year-old Pliny the Younger was across the bay at the time, and he saw "a cloud of unusual size and appearance . . . like an umbrella pine." His uncle, the famed writer Pliny the Elder, fared worse. When he saw the volcano go, he took some boats to try to evacuate friends from a village on the shore below the mountain. The elder Pliny dictated his impressions to a scribe as they sailed, but the great author succumbed to the poisonous gasses while ashore and suffocated.

ESSENTIALS

GETTING THERE   By Train   From **Naples,** take the half-hourly private Circumvesuviana train (☎ **081-772-2444**) toward Sorrento and get off at POMPEII–VILLA DEI MISTERI (27 to 40 min; 3,200L/$2). The train passes through **Ercolano** (20 min; 2,000L/$1). (*Note:* There are four Circumvesuviana lines and a bit of confusion: One of the two lines headed to Sarno diverges just before the site and also features a stop called "Pompei," but this is for the modern town, *not* the archaeological site, so make sure you pay attention to the destination marker on the lead car as well as on the platform departures board). This half-hourly Circumvesuviana train also runs to or from **Sorrento** (20 min; 2,300L/$1).

The bar in the train station will let you **store your luggage** for 5,000L ($3) per bag for up to 12 hours. Turn right out of the station, and the entrance to the site is just a few hundred feet down on your left. A 5-minute walk past the site entrance down this road leads to modern Pompei.

By Bus   C.L.P. bus line ☎ **081-251-4157** runs direct service to the *scavi,* or archaeological site, from Naples' Capodichino Airport (30 minutes; 7,000L/$4) leaving at 9:30am, 12:45pm and 6:15pm. **SITA** buses ☎ **081-552-2176** leave from Naples' Piazza Municipio on Via Pisanelli (35 minutes; 3,200L/$2) for Pompeii, continuing on to Positano and Amalfi.

VISITOR INFORMATION   The **ticket booth** at the archaeological site will give you the free map and all the information you need to explore the excavations at Pompeii. There's also a **tourist office** in modern Pompei at Via Sacra 1 (☎ **081-850-7255;** fax 081-863-2401; www.uniplan.it/pompei/azienda), open Monday to Friday 9am to 2:30pm and Saturday and Sunday 9am to 2pm.

Mt. Vesuvius: Contents Under Pressure

Though one of the smallest and least regularly active volcanoes in the world, the infamous Mt. Vesuvius, inspiration for Dante's *Inferno,* is one of the most destructive. The only active volcano on continental Europe, the 4,214-foot-high, broad cone of Mt. Vesuvius dominates the Bay of Naples from the northeastern shore. Its unexpected eruption in A.D. 79, buried the Roman cities of Herculaneum and Pompeii in ash and mud, but its activity has been sporadic ever since—the last time it even put on any mild fireworks was back in 1944.

To visit the surprisingly calm, rather plain gravel-filled depression that is Vesuvius' crater, take the Circumvesuviana train from **Naples** or **Sorrento** to the Ercolano stop, from which there's a special bus (☎ **081-739-2833**) five times daily up to the Colle Margherita parking lot (55 min.; 3,000L/$2 each way). A guide (☎ **081-777-5720;** 5,000L/$3) will walk you the 15 minutes from here to the crater's rim, a barren landscape with unparalleled views across Campania on clear days. The last return bus to the parking lot leaves at 2:10pm, with the last bus back to Ercolano at 5:30pm.

EXPLORING THE ANCIENT CITY

Pompeii wasn't buried entirely; in fact, the top floors of many houses poked above the new ground level. But between survivors returning to dig for personal belongings, the inevitable looters, and later farmers plowing their fields over the site, these building tops where shorn off. Within a few generations, incredibly, Pompeii was forgotten. In 1594, the architect Domenico Fontana was building an aqueduct through the area when he struck the ruins of Pompeii quite by accident. Most of the excavations have been carried out since the 18th century. **Admission** to Pompeii is 16,000L ($8; free under 18 and over 60); the site is open daily 9am to an hour before sunset (as early as 3:45pm in December, 8pm June to August).

The ✪ **archaeological site** (☎ **081-861-0744;** www.uniplan.it/ruins) is now enclosed and takes a full day to explore. At the very least, it takes 4 hours to pop into the major sights. The roads are made of stone slabs, rutted deep with centuries' worth of wagon wheels. At most intersections are crosswalks of raised stepping stones—so citizens wouldn't have to step in the mucky, muddy streets. Besides the public buildings and mansions highlighted below, Pompeii is full of buildings that may be more pedestrian, but are just as fascinating for the insight they offer into daily life in an ancient Roman city. Poke around to find the shops with counters still in place and paintings describing the wares sold, bakeries with millstones and brick ovens in the backyard, even fast-food parlors with deep bowls set into the counters where prepared food was kept hot.

The ✪ **Foro (Forum),** the central square of any Roman city, sits a few blocks up from the entrance. Around the edges you'll see that there was once a two-story colonnade, its 470-foot length oriented so that, ironically, "scenic" Mt. Vesuvius serves as a natural backdrop. At the northern end of the eastern edge is a small room with a countertop embedded with bowl-shape depressions of increasing sizes. The Forum was also a central marketplace, and to forestall arguments between buyer and seller, these were used as the city's standards of measure.

Plaster casts of bodies are located just past the measuring table in an enclosed building. During the early excavations, archaeologists realized that the ash had packed

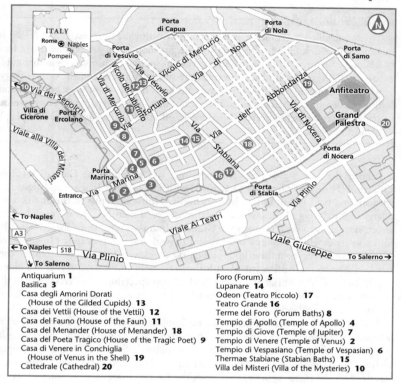

ITALY
Rome • Naples
Pompeii

Porta di Capua
Porta di Nola
Porta di Vesuvio
Porta di Samo
Via dei Sepolcri
Vicolo di Mercurio
Via di Nola
Anfiteatro
Villa di Cicerone
Porta Ercolano
Via di Mercurio
dell' Abbondanza
Via di Nocera
Grand Palestra
Viale alla Villa dei Misteri
Via Fortuna
Via Stabiana
Porta di Nocera
Porta Marina
Via Marina
Porta di Stabia
Via Plinio
Entrance
Viale Ai Teatri
To Naples
A3
To Naples
S18
Via Plinio
Viale Giuseppe
To Salerno
To Salerno

Antiquarium **1**
Basilica **3**
Casa degli Amorini Dorati
   (House of the Gilded Cupids) **13**
Casa dei Vettii (House of the Vettii) **12**
Casa del Fauno (House of the Faun) **11**
Casa del Menander (House of Menander) **18**
Casa del Poeta Tragico (House of the Tragic Poet) **9**
Casa di Venere in Conchiglia
   (House of Venus in the Shell) **19**
Cattedrale (Cathedral) **20**

Foro (Forum) **5**
Lupanare **14**
Odeon (Teatro Piccolo) **17**
Teatro Grande **16**
Terme del Foro (Forum Baths) **8**
Tempio di Apollo (Temple of Apollo) **4**
Tempio di Giove (Temple of Jupiter) **7**
Tempio di Venere (Temple of Venus) **2**
Tempio di Vespasiano (Temple of Vespasian) **6**
Thermae Stabiane (Stabian Baths) **15**
Villa dei Misteri (Villa of the Mysteries) **10**

around dying Pompeiians and hardened almost instantly. The bodies decayed, leaving just the skeletons lying in human-shaped air pockets under the ground. Holes were drilled down to a few and plaster was poured in, taking a rough cast of the moment of death. Some people writhe in agony. A dog, chained to a post, turns to bite desperately at his collar. One man sits on the ground, covering his face in grief.

Exit the Forum onto Via dell Abbondanza, detouring left down Via del Teatro to see the **Teatro Grande,** a 2nd-century B.C. theater that could seat 5,000. Under the stage lay a reservoir so that water would flood the area during mock naval battle scenes (some suggest the water also helped amplify the acoustics during performances). Nearby on Via Stabiana is the **Odeon** or **Teatro Piccolo,** a much smaller theater (seating 1,000) used mainly for concerts. The **Casa di Menander (House of Menander)** has painted scenes from the Trojan cycle in some rooms, and a floor mosaic of the Nile in the peristyle. Members of the family that lived here were all found together, huddled in one room, killed when the roof caved in on them.

Past the intersection with Via Stabiana along **Via dell Abbondanza** marks the site of the "New Excavations," undertaken since 1911. Many of the houses on both sides of this street retain their second stories. While those on the north/left side haven't been excavated much beyond the facades, those on the right have. And unlike in much of the older, more famous excavations (north of the Forum; we'll get there in a minute), many of the frescoes, mosaics, and statuary have been left in place rather than shipped off to a museum.

To get a detailed background of Pompeii, it's worthwhile to invest 16,000L ($8) in a nice guidebook full of color photos at the gift shop *before you explore.* If you have a large family or small group, you may want to splurge on hiring a registered guide for 150,000L ($75). It's hard to escape the sun at Pompeii, and the dust is every-where, so bring a hat with a brim and sunblock. If you forgot your bottled water, there's a decent cafeteria tucked at the back of the site. Be prepared for crowds, espe-cially on weekends (on average there are 4,700 visitors a day, up to 22,000 people come here on holidays).

Among the houses along this street, be sure you pop into the **Casa di Octavio Quartius (House of Octavius Quartius),** with lots of good frescoes and replanted gardens; and the **Casa di Venere in Conchiglia (House of Venus in the Shell),** with a large wall painting of the goddess stretched out on a clamshell. Near the end of the street, turn right to walk through the **Grand Palestra**—a huge open space shaded by umbrella pines where the city's youths went to work out and play sports (many came here seeking shelter from the eruption; their skeletons were found huddled in the cor-ner latrine)—to the **Anfiteatro (Amphitheater).** Built in 80 B.C., this is the oldest amphitheater in the world, and could hold 12,000 spectators who, according to the records, were just as wont to break into a brawl in the stands as watch the gladiators fighting on the field below.

Return down Via dell Abbondanza to Via Stabiana. On the northwest corner sit the **Thermae Stabiane,** a series of baths with stuccoed and painted ceilings surviving in some rooms and a few glass caskets with more twisted plaster cast bodies of Pompeii victims. Head up Vico del Lupanare on the other side of these baths to the acute inter-section with the overhanging second story, the ✪ **Lupanare.** This brothel left noth-ing to the imagination. Painted scenes above each of the little cells inside graphically showed potential clients the position in which the lady of that particular room spe-cialized. Until a few decades ago, only male tourists were allowed in to see it.

Continuing north to the heart of the Old Excavations, stop by the ✪ **Casa dei Vet-tii (House of the Vettii),** one of the most luxurious mansions in town (it belonged to two trading mogul brothers) and in a wonderful state of preservation. Behind a glass shield at the entrance is a painting of a little guy with a grotesquely oversized male member—here shown weighing the appendage on a scale. This was not meant to be lewd, but rather was a common device believed to ward off evil spirits and thoughts. Painted putti (cherubs) dance around the atrium while the rooms are filled with fres-coes of mythological scenes and characters. Don't miss the "Sala Dipinta," where a black band around the walls is painted with cherubs engaging in sports. The **Casa del Poeta Tragico (House of the Tragic Poet)** is closed, but between the bars of the gate you can still see the most famous mosaic in Pompeii: a fearsome chained dog with a spiked collar and the epithet *Cave Canem* (Beware of the Dog). The nearby **Foro Terme (Forum Baths)** retain ribbed stucco on some ceilings and a strip of tiny tela-mons along one wall.

Walk north along Via Consolare to exit the ruins (hold on to your ticket) and follow the path for 5 minutes to the suburban ✪ **Villa dei Misteri (Villa of the Mysteries),** which you get into on the same ticket. Built around the 2nd century B.C., this villa was converted into a center for the Dionysian cult, and the walls are gorgeously and skillfully painted with life-size figures engaging in the Dionysian Mysteries of an initiate (though these paintings have helped modern scholars guess at the nature of these rites, we still don't know exactly what was involved). The scenes play out against a background of such deep, intense red that the color used is still called "Pompeiian red."

AN AFFORDABLE PLACE TO STAY

Villa dei Misteri. Via Villa dei Misteri 11, 80045 Pompei (NA). ☎ **081-861-3593.** Fax 081-862-2983. www.ptn.pandora.it/hmisteri. 41 units. 70,000–90,000L ($35–$45) single or double. A/C 15,000L ($8) per day. Breakfast 8,000L or 12,000L ($4 or $6). AE, DC, MC, V. Free parking. ¼ mile from site entrance and train station; turn left upon exiting station.

This remains the bland roadside inn of choice for die-hard archaeology buffs that want to sleep a stone's throw from the excavations (the entrance is a 2-minute walk down-hill with the Circumvesuviana at the halfway mark). Once you get past the cement war casualty exterior, the amply sized rooms are pleasant enough, with balconies, shiny new tile floors, well-worn but serviceable furnishings, and recently overhauled baths. The mattresses, however, still rest on lazy-springed cots. An outdoor pool ringed with statues (open late May to October) does wonders for the hotel's appeal.

A GREAT DEAL ON DINING

Zi Caterina. Via Roma 20, about a 10- to 15-minute walk to Pompei center. ☎ **081-850-7447** or 081-863-1263. Reservations recommended. Primi 10,000–15,000L ($5–$8); secondi 12,000–28,000L ($6–$14). AE, DC, MC, V. Wed–Mon noon–11pm. CAMPANIAN.

Among the countless glorified pizza joints with polyglot menus on modern Pompei's main drag, Zi Caterina stands out for its solid cooking and reasonable prices. The cavernous single room, antiqued with lots of wood, can get noisy as with the arrival of the strolling troubadour strumming his guitar. The delicious *risotto alla pescatora* is heavily laden with shellfish, calamari, and shrimp, and the *gnocchi alla sorrentina* is also good. Secondi tend to be fishy as well, with a beach platter *sauté di frutti di mare* (clams, oysters, and mussels) or *baccalà* (dried salt cod), but landlubbers can always order *coniglio alla cacciatora* (rabbit stewed with tomatoes and mushrooms).

4 The Isle of Capri

4.8km (3 mi.) off the tip of the Sorrentine peninsula.

The isle of **Capri** (pronounce it "*cap*-ree") glitters with international polish like a fairy-tale Hollywood movie set. At once, the island packs a scenic punch: 4 square miles of sharp lava rising dramatically above the sparkling surfaces of deep blue and green waters. Most of Capri is blanketed in lush green foliage, an Eden of oleander, jasmine, and bougainvillea spilling over the walls of the white cube houses. Pedestrian alleyways branch off from Capri's main piazza, draped in high-end shops sporting price tags way beyond what the common man (read: me) can afford, winding leisurely down the cliff side toward swimming holes and luminescent grottos that pockmark the island's perimeter.

Capri's sheer physical beauty and dreamy laid-back lifestyle have attracted sun-seekers for millennia, from Roman emperors to modern-day hedonists. Homer certainly chose his spot well when he designated this island as the home of the mythical Sirens, beautiful but monstrous flesh-eating women who lived on the offshore rocks and sang an irresistible song to lure ancient sailors to their doom. Capri's allure today is still just as strong, though the only doom you're likely to face these days is the damage done to your wallet.

Most visitors pop over on the ferry in the morning, fork over the lire for a quick row through the Blue Grotto, gawk at the obscene prices in Capri boutiques, or hike out to explore the ruins of Tiberius's Villa, missing entirely the magic and mystery of the island. By day, especially in summer, Capri witnesses a tourist crush that veritably sucks the enjoyment right out of the island. If at all possible, spend the night. As the day-trippers leave on the 5pm ferry, the sounds and scents of Capri creep out of hiding and locals come together to reclaim the island. Spend the evening strolling down a quiet cobbled alleyway as the skies turn a seductive purple, and take your extra day to visit Capri's sibling village, Anacapri, hike the undeveloped side of the island, or ride the chairlift up Monte Solaro for a panoramic sweep of the bay.

ESSENTIALS

GETTING THERE By Ferry or Hydrofoil The *aliscafo* (hydrofoil) from Naples takes 40 minutes and costs 16,500L ($8).From Naples, **Caremar** (☎ **081-837-0700; www.caremar.it**) and **NLG** (☎ **081-837-0819**) hydrofoils leave from Molo Beverello dock and **SNAV** (☎ **081-837-7577**) hydrofoils leave from Mergellina docks. Both Caremar and **Linee Marittime Partenopee** (☎ **081-807-3024**) run 50-minute hydrofoils from Sorrento for 14,000L ($7).

Ferries cost half the hydrofoil rate, but take about three times as long. Caremar runs a *traghetti* (ferry) line out of **Naples's** Molo Beverello.

If you're staying in Capri, take the **funicular** ☎ **081-837-0420** (1,800L/90¢) up to the center of town, from where you'll have to walk to your hotel, since almost all of Capri is pedestrian only. The last funicular up coincides with the arrival of the last Caremar ferry from Naples, so choose your carrier wisely. Because of the effort involved in hauling your bags, most hotels provide the services of a porter at an extra charge of about 10,000L ($5) per bag.

Buses run every 15 minutes between Marina Grande (via Capri) and Anacapri; add on waiting time to actually board the bus at the ferry docks (unimaginable in July and August). The bus stop is defined by a group of hand rails at the exit of the marina (behind the taxi stand); since more than one route departs from here, be sure to get in the correct line. Luggage is looked at disapprovingly, as it takes up valuable rider space, but a simple "cosa devo fare?" ("what am I supposed to do?") should get you *and* your bags on. If you can't take the heat, go ahead and splurge for a convertible taxi cab 25,000L to 30,000L ($13 to $15) or stay at one of the hotels that provides free pickup service at the docks (don't forget to tip the guy who carries your bags).

GETTING ORIENTED Capri's transportation hub is **Marina Grande,** the busy, touristy main port sitting at the base of the island's soaring cliffs. A bus or funicular will take you up to Capri center, the main town and home to most of the boutique shopping, posh hotels, chic nightlife, and Beautiful People. The heart of Capri (the town) is **Piazza Umberto I,** called by everyone the **Piazzetta,** sprouting a handful of narrow passages and cobbled lanes away from the fray. On the other side of Capri, down the backside of the cliffs, is **Marina Piccola,** a smaller yachting port consisting of several beach establishments and restaurants. Capri and the two ports occupy the narrowest part of the island, from which a mountain rises in either direction.

Halfway up the larger of these, Monte Solaro, sits the village of **Anacapri,** Capri town's historic rival but today the cooler, calmer, cheaper, and more bucolic of the two towns. Saying that Anacapri is less crowded than Capri fails to convey the crush of Capri's piazzetta, but if any village life survives on this touristy island, it's in Anacapri.

GETTING AROUND Capri has some gorgeous walks, but most have a significant grade to them. The Greek-era Scala Fenicia connects Anacapri with Marina Grande, a half-hour hike that requires you to walk a good part of the way along the main road. If you don't mind a little vertigo, you may want to tackle the 700 steps going down, rather than up the hill. From Capri, you can easily stroll down to Marina Grande in about 15 minutes or to Marina Piccola in 20 minutes. From Anacapri, you can reach the Faro in 20 minutes or the Blue Grotto in half an hour. (The problem is getting back up.)

Capri town is completely off limits to motor vehicles (as is Anacapri's old center, but this is less of a problem, being essentially one street), and bus service is frequent and exhaustive enough to make up for the lack of independent wheels. In Capri, buses depart from the roundabout at Due Golfi; in Anacapri, you can hop on either at the main Piazza Vittoria or further down the road at Piazza Caprile. **SIPPIC** buses (☎ **081-837-0420**) provide regular service (generally every 20 minutes) between Marina Grande (via Capri) and Anacapri, Marina Grande and Marina Piccola, Marina Grande and Damecuta and Marina Piccola and Anacapri, with connections possible at the roundabout just before the entrance to Capri. **Staiano Autotrasporti** (☎ **081-837-1544**) runs service between Anacapri and the Grotta Azzurra and Anacapri and Faro di Punta Carena from Anacapri's depot on Via de Tommaso. Buy your tickets when boarding the bus or at any tabacchaio (1,800L/90¢).

For the more adventurous, attacking those mountainous roads on a 50hp scooter with nothing between you and the road but your crash helmet (required by law) is an experience to be savored. **Oasi Motor Rent at Marina Grande,** Via Cristoforo Colombo 47, up the road past Bar Corallo (☎ **081-837-7138**) or on Piazza Caprile 3A in **Anacapri,** at the very far end of town before heading out on the road to Faro (☎ **080-837-2444**) has rather high but nevertheless competitive rates for scooter rentals. Expect to pay 25,000L ($13) per hour and 90,000L ($45) for the day, gas included (instead of 125,000L/$63 per day elsewhere, gas not included).

By Taxi   Those colorful 1950s convertibles are highly seductive. You can often bargain, but to go anywhere usually costs about 25,000L ($13). There are stands in Capri on Piazza Martiri d'Ungheria, in Anacapri on Piazza Vittoria, and at the docks of Marina Grande and Marina Piccola. You can also call for one in Capri at ☎ **081-837-0543** or in Anacapri at ☎ **081-837-1175.**

VISITOR INFORMATION   There's a little **tourist office** along the right side of the ferry dock (☎ **081-837-0634**) that fills up as the ferries empty out, so you may want to take advantage of the tiny **satellite offices** in Capri, Piazza Umberto I, open Monday to Saturday 8:30am to 8:30pm and Sunday 9am to 1pm and 2:30 to 6pm (☎ **081-837-0686**); or Anacapri, Via Giuseppe Orlando 19a (just off Piazza Vittoria), open Monday to Saturday 9:45am to 1:30pm and 2 to 5:30pm (☎ **081-837-1524**). The tourist office puts out a free map of the island, which they avoid telling you about; rather, they push the more colorful and detailed one for 1,500L (75¢; recommended if you plan on taking any of the scenic hikes). Even more utilitarian is the free map printed by SIPPIC, the organization that administers the public transport on the island of Capri. Ask at the funicular ticket window, or pop into any of the travel agencies to see if the map is on display.

Capri OnLine (www.capri.it) is the best Web site for general info on Capri and its businesses and includes the official tourist office site (e-mail: touristoffice@capri.it).

FESTIVALS   The festival of Capri's patron saint, **San Costanzo,** traditionally opens with an all-out procession on May 14 behind a silver reliquary bust of the saint (people stand on their balconies and strew flower petals on the bust as it passes). The statue is carried to the church of San Costanzo in Marina Grande, until 2 days later, when the procession resumes up to Capri. The festivities continue throughout the week with community-sponsored concerts and other events. Anacapri throws its own version to honor its patron saint, **St. Antonio di Padova,** on June 13. Nonreligious events take place the 1st week of January, when **folklore groups** perform on the main piazzas of Capri and Anacapri. And on Fridays at 7:45pm from June to August, The Villa Axel Munthe (☎ **081-764-0737**) hosts free "**sunset concerts.**"

EXPLORING THE LAND OF THE SIRENS

✪ **Grotta Azzurra (Blue Grotto).** No phone. Admission 8,000L ($4), Sun and holidays 9,000 ($5); private rowboat into cave 7,500L ($4). Daily 9am–5pm. Limited hours in winter.

Capri's greatest claim to fame is this long, low sea cavern whose water glows a brilliant, awe-inspiring blue from the effect of light refracting through the entrance tunnel. Although the scandalous wallet-gouging admission only gets you a 3-minute row through, the walls echoing unromantically with a half dozen boats full of tourists with their oarsmen spewing out facts (occasionally true) or, even worse, attempting to sing, this natural phenomenon is a must-see. The oarsmen often point out a tunnel in one of the cave's walls, claiming that it is connected with the villa of Tiberius above, when in fact it is unremarkably a natural fissure that leads nowhere. The Roman villa above did however use the cave as a nymphaeum, and several statues were discovered at the bottom.

You can save about half the admission by swimming into the cave, but for obvious reasons the boatmen don't appreciate that, leaving very little room between the boats to slip through (plus, they'll scream at you, pretending it's illegal to swim in). Better to wait until the early evening hours, when it won't cost you a dime to enjoy this natural wonder as nature intended. Be extremely careful: There's a strong undertow, so wait until the waters are extraordinarily placid and absolutely, swim in pairs.

To get to the Grotta Azzurra, you can either take a local bus (15 min.) from Anacapri to the land entrance or hook up with a boat excursion from the Marina Grande docks (1 hr.; 24,500L/$12 includes admission).

✪ **Villa Jovis (Tiberius's Villa).** Follow signs from Capri's Piazzetta up Via di Botteghe (a 40-min. hike). No phone. Admission 4,000L ($2). Daily 9am to 1 hr. before sunset.

Set majestically at the top of a 977-foot sheer bluff above the sea, this is but one of 12 villas that Roman Emperor Tiberius built on his favorite island. You can clamber around the half-decayed walls that once defined the imperial apartments, baths complex, and servants' quarters, but none of it is in very good shape—come more for the romantic setting than the archaeology. Built into the ruins right on the cliff's edge at what is called the Salto di Tiberio (Tiberius' Leap) is the tiny 17th-century church of Santa Maria del Soccorso, which treats you to a great sweeping view across the Bay of Naples.

Rome's second emperor, Tiberius, rose to power as an army general. After 12 years on the throne, he got tired of the political infighting of Rome and semi-retired to his beloved Capri. A gruff, dour man, he was swift in meting out punishments, prudently modest in refusing most honors during his reign, tough to get along with, second guess, or bribe, and probably a little too fond of dallying with young boys and girls.

Tiberius spent his final 10 years throwing banquets on the island and communicating imperial decrees to the mainland by signaling with flashing lights. For centuries, we moderns have taken the famous ancient chronicler Suetonius's depiction of the emperor as gospel truth, which is why Tiberius has gone down in history as the man who, sitting in judgment at this cliff-top villa, ". . .ordered his victims, after prolonged and skillful torture, to be thrown into the sea before his very eyes. Below, a company of sailors beat them with boat hooks until the life was crushed from their bodies."

Had Suetonius lived today, he probably would have been a reporter for *Hard Copy.* There is little doubt his reports were greatly exaggerated if not outright fabricated. The

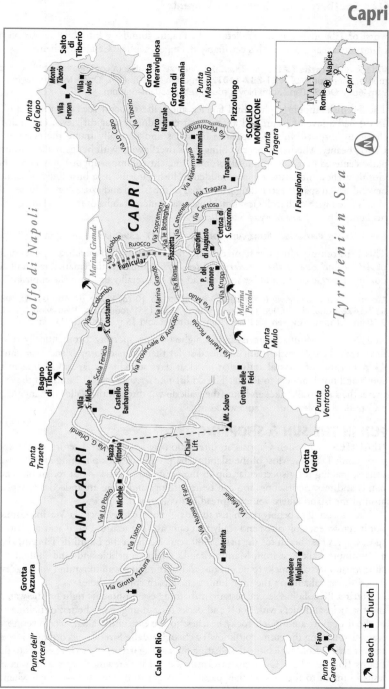

Salto di Tiberio

Monte Tiberio ▲

Villa Jovis

Villa Fersen

Punta del Capo

Grotta Meravigliosa

Grotta di Matermania

Punta Massullo

Pizzolungo

SCOGLIO MONACONE

Punta Tragera

Arco Naturale

Via Matermania

Via Matermania

Tragara

Via Tragara

Via Sopramonte

Via le Botteghe

Via Camerelle

Via Certosa

Certosa di S. Giacomo

CAPRI

Golfo di Napoli

Marina Grande

Via Lo Capo

Via Tiberio

Via Giobbe

Ruocco

Piazzetta

Funicular

Via Roma

Via Marina Grande

Giardini di Augusto

P. del Cannone

Via Krupp

Marina Piccola

Via C. Colombo

S. Coastanzo

Via Mulo

Via Provinciale di Anacapri

Via Marina Piccola

Punta Mulo

I Faraglioni

Tyrrhenian Sea

Bagno di Tiberio

Scala fenicia

Villa S. Michele

Castello Barbarossa

Grotta delle Felci

Punta Ventroso

Punta Trasete

Mt. Solaro ▲

Chair Lift

Grotta Verde

Via G. Orlandi

Piazza Vittoria

Via Lo Pozzo

San Michele

ANACAPRI

Via Tuoro

Via Migliar

Via Nuova del Faro

Materita

Belvedere Migliara

Grotta Azzurra

Via Grotta Azzurra

Punta dell' Arcera

Cala del Rio

Faro

Punta Carena

ITALY
Rome ⊛ Naples
Capri

N

↗ Beach   ✝ Church

worst of Tiberius's crimes were letting the empire founder a bit while he was on his island retreat, and naming his certifiably deranged nephew Caligula as heir.

Villa Axel Munthe (Villa San Michele). Via Axel Munthe (a continuation of Via Capodimonte), Anacapri. ☎ **081-837-1401.** Admission 8,000L ($4). Open May through Sept 9am–6pm; Oct 9:30am–5pm; Nov through Feb 10:30am–3:30pm.

The Swedish autobiographer, bird fancier, and selfless doctor Axel Munthe (1857 to 1949) had a love of Capri and an eye for tremendously magical views. He built his classically inspired villa to capitalize on vistas and naturally frame the essences of Capri's beauty, whether it be crumbling walls overflowing with bougainvillea, arbored paths centered on copies of Greek bronzes, ancient columns supporting whitewashed Gothic arches, miniature temples hidden in lush gardens, or a bust-lined balustrade beyond which span breathtaking panoramas of the island and azure waters. Inside, the villa is filled with archaeological knickknacks and memorabilia of the good doctor and his famous book, *The Story of San Michele.*

San Michele. Piazza San Nicola, Anacapri. ☎ **081-837-2396.** Daily 9am–2pm and 3–5pm.

This 18th-century church is floored with a fantastical studied majolica representation of ***Adam and Eve in the Garden of Eden*** (1761), filled with remarkable detail and dozens of exotic plants and beasts. You can get an overall view from the choir loft.

Monte Solaro. Seggovia (chairlift) at Via Caposcuro 10 (of Piazza d. Vittoria). ☎ **081-837-1428.** Chairlift 7,000L ($4) one way, 9,500L ($5) round-trip. Wed–Mon Mar–Oct 9:30am–7:15pm, Nov–Feb 10:30am–3pm; last ticket sold 15 min prior to closing.

At 1,945 feet, Monte Solaro is Capri's highest point, sporting a romantically ruined little 1806 British castle (built medieval-style) that offers dreamy island vistas and a ✪ **panorama of coastal Italy** that on clear days stretches as far as Calabria to the south and north almost to Rome. The ski lift-like *seggovia* takes 12 minutes to get up there; the steep walk takes an hour (the walk down, through the Valley of Santa Maria a Cetrella, is a pleasantly scenic workout).

FUN IN THE SUN & SHOPPING

BEACHES   Although Capri is an internationally known island resort, don't expect great sandy beaches. Most of the island is sharp volcanic rock plunging into the azure waters, making for a spectacular dip in the crystalline waters— but rough on tender hands and feet. Snorkeling, too can be rewarding, and there are indeed a few places around the island where you can spread out your towel.

There's a scrap of pebbly beach just to the right of the ferry docks at **Marina Grande,** but it's crowded, a bit dirty, and really best only as a last resort "I need a swim" bathing spot. Capri's best beach for the past 2,000 years has been the **Bagni di Tiberio,** about a 20-minute walk west from Marina Grande. There's a pebble-and-sand shore, lots of sun worshippers and rocks to lie out on, and a crumbling wall to remind you that even Tiberius, capitalizing on the spot, built a small bath complex here.

Marina Piccola has several restaurant/bathing establishments right on the water— mostly rocks and piers with pools and decks for tanning. Even better, out either side of the little port are modest rocky beaches: to the east under a Saracen tower, to the west surrounding the stony spit known as **Scoglio delle Sirene**—according to legend the very rocks from which the flesh-eating Sirens sang irresistibly to lure sailors to their deaths (Homer's hero Odysseus prudently stuffed his crewmen's ears with wax and lashed himself to the mast as they passed so as not to be tempted—though when he heard their seductive song he fell under its spell and begged to be untied so he could rush to them; lucky for him, his crewmen refused).

A bus ride or 20-minute walk from Anacapri (down Via Nuovo del Faro, off Piazza Caprile) takes you to Lido del Faro at **Punta Carena** (☎ **081-837-1798;** take the bus from Anacapri piazza direct), a lovely watering hole tucked into a rocky cove. The raw terrain is scattered with private rowboats and with your back to the hideously modern nearby lighthouse, there's a view out over rocks into azure waters. Watch where you set your feet, though, these rocks support colonies of spiny sea urchins.

Best of all are the "beaches" at **Punta Tragara,** framed by the huge *faraglioni* (rocks slicing up through the water). The boat ride here is spectacular, cutting between the faraglioni just as Odysseus did; but walking the steep path from Capri center, doable in about a half hour, is just as breathtaking.

BOAT TRIPS A cruise around the island is a splendid way to see Capri's rocky perimeter and many sea-level grottoes (the Blue Grotto is just the most famous). As of this writing, only **Gruppo Motoscafisti** ☎ **081-837-5646** (20,000L/$10 plus 1,000L/50¢ for Sunday and holidays) and **Laser Capri** ☎ **081-837-5208** (15,000L/$8) circle the island, in a 90-minute excursion that leaves you wanting more. Both run the excursion to the Grotta Azzurra by both land and sea, as well as excursions from Marina Grande to Faraglioni (12,000L/$6).

SHOPPING The most popular Capri purchase is *limoncello,* that wonderful, sugary lemon liqueur, best when consumed close to freezing in an icy shot glass. Luckily, it can also be one of the cheapest souvenirs you can buy. You pay more for the funky shape of the bottle than for the amount of booze inside, and can get sample-size gift bottles for as little as 3,000 to 5,000L ($2 to $3) but for your own consumption, you may want to shell out 15,000 to 20,000L ($8 to $10) for ¾ liter. To buy the brand tossed back by Gorky, Krupp, and Axel Munthe, head to the shop run by their supplier's grandkids, **Limoncello di Capri,** Via Roma 79 (☎ **081-837-5561**), in Anacapri at Via Capodimonte 27 (☎ **081-837-2927.**

Staying on the aromatic end of shopping, Capri is a wonderfully scented island, and the **perfumes and colognes** sold here reflect it. You can find some good bargains at the popular **Carthusia,** Via Camerelle 10 in Capri; Via Capodimonte 26 in Anacapri (☎ **081-837-0368**). The store's Aria di Capri concoction of orange, lemon, mimosa, and peach was developed in the 17th century by the monks at the nearby *certosa* (Carthusian monastery). You can also tour the store's tiny lab at Via Giacomo Matteotti 2b.

Capri's other famous product is handmade strap **sandals**—but don't try to hike the island in them. The famous, bijou-studded footwear pounded out at **Canfora,** Via Camerelle 3 in Capri (☎ **081-837-0487**), will run you a whopping 170,000L ($85). For the best bargains, head to **Vincenzo Faiella's** shop on Capri's Via Vittorio Emanuele 49 (no phone), where cloth and rope shoes and slippers start at 26,000L ($15). My favorite cobbler is old Antonio Viva, who sits outside his Anacapri shop **L'Arte del Sandolo Caprese** at Via Giuseppe Orlandi 75 (☎ **081-837-3583**) and proclaims gently through his mustache "We make these shoes the artisan's way. We make them with heart." Antonio has the widest selection of handmade slippers on Capri, and his work goes for a modest 55,000L to 90,000L ($28 to $45).

AFFORDABLE PLACES TO STAY

The isle of Capri is no secret to vacationers, so that room vacancies, especially in a more affordable price range, are rare, if not nonexistent. Book as much in advance as possible, and be prepared for rejection. Below is a longer than average list of possibilities to counter this problem. High season usually runs mid-June to September, and unless otherwise noted, this seasonal variance is reflected in the price ranges listed for hotels below.

In Capri Town

Belsito. Via Matermania 9–13, 80073 Capri (NA). ☎ **081-837-0969.** Fax 081-837-6622. www.hotelbelsito.com. E-mail: hbelsito@mbox.caprinet.it. 13 units. MINIBAR TEL. 60,000–120,000L ($30–$60) single; 140,000–240,000L ($70–$120) double. Half-pension of 30,000L ($15) required Sat–Sun, and daily in high season. Rates include breakfast. AE, DC, MC, V. Closed Nov.

This converted 18th-century house run as a hotel and restaurant by Liliana and Mario Tarantino is removed from the town bustle and very tranquil, yet still just 5 minutes from Capri's main piazza. The tile-or linoleum-floored rooms are small but bright, and the beds won't punish your spine. Rooms 22 to 27 have views over the arc of Capri, the sea, and the mass of Monte Solaro, while the balance of rooms do not have a view or indeed much light, but are cheaper. Everyone can enjoy the vistas from the roof terrace, however, and even if you don't take the half-pension deal, you still get a 10% discount at the attached and recommended restaurant/pizzeria.

La Tosca. Via Dalmazio Birago 5, 80073 Capri (NA). ☎ and fax **081-837-0989.** www. caprionline.com/latosca.. E-mail: h.tosca@capri.it. 12 units. TEL. 65,000–75,000L ($33–$38) single; 105,000–135,000L ($53–$66) double. Breakfast 12,500L ($6). MC, V. Closed late Oct to mid-Mar. From the tourist information office in the Piazzetta, go straight through the large archway (to the left of the steps) until you reach the church. Follow the narrow walkway to the right of the church, and follow signs for the hotel.

This charming villa is hidden on one of Capri's back alleys, surrounded by birdsong and seemingly a world away, yet only a 5-minute stroll from the tourist crush of the Piazzetta. Ettore Castelli and his Connecticut-born wife have been improving La Tosca since taking it over in 1997, and the investment is paying off. Most of the clean, sizable rooms have newish functional furniture and high ceilings. Only 10% of the baths still creak, as most were recently replaced. For view-value, rooms 47 through 51 are the best, with small terraces looking over the nearby monastery to the sea and the *faraglioni.* The rooms get smaller as they go up in number; after no. 49, trees begin to block much of the view. You can take breakfast privately on your own terrace or communally on the patio amid jasmine and rose bushes.

Worth a Splurge

✪ Villa Krupp. Viale Giacomo Matteotti 12, 80073 Capri (NA) (a long but pleasant path up from the main road). ☎ **081-837-0362.** Fax 081-837-6489. 12 units. A/C TEL. 135,000L ($68) single; 180,000–250,000L ($90–$125) double. Breakfast 5,000L ($3). MC, V. Closed Nov–Apr.

Villa Krupp is set like a crown jewel of old-world style atop the Giardini d'Augusto at the end of a path that winds up amid the umbrella pines. Its breezy back hill location is very quiet, but still convenient to Capri's shopping and restaurants and Marina Piccola's beach below. An old favorite of Russian intellectuals (Lenin lodged and Gorky lived here), the Krupp's rooms have period or antique-style furnishings on tile floors, brand-new baths, and firm beds. The larger and more expensive nos. 18 to 21 are the best in the house, with high ceilings, small chandeliers, hair dryers, and killer terrace views over the monastery and the wooded slopes of Monte Tuoro to *faraglioni* and the sea. Smaller, cheaper doubles look over the white-cube tumble of Capri's houses. Guests sit in the TV solarium to read and gaze out at the trees and bits of sea peeking through.

In Anacapri

Biancamaria. Via Giuseppe Orlandi 54, 80071 Anacapri (NA). ☎ **081-837-1000.** Fax 081-837-2060. 25 units. A/C TEL. 190,000L ($95) single; 220,000L ($110) double. Rates include breakfast; 20,000L ($10) supplement for A/C. AE, MC, V. Closed Nov–Mar.

The family-run Biancamaria has an old-fashioned attitude (they turn away scruffy backpackers) in this spacious and decorous hotel right in the center of town. Rooms are generally big, furnished with ultramodern veneer furnishings, contemporary tile floors, small easy chairs, and not-so-terrible floral bedspreads. Better yet are the sparkling new huge baths featuring heated towel racks and hair dryers. Rooms with the view of Monte Solaro have small terraces over the town's main drag, which *does* quiet down late at night. For even more silence, request a sea-view room with French doors opening onto a fantastic panorama of the Bay of Naples.

Il Girasole. Via Linciano 47, 80071 Anacapri (NA). ☎ **081-837-2351.** Fax 081-837-3880. www.ilgirasole.com. E-mail: ilgirasole@capri.it. 24 units. 50,000–150,000L ($25–$75) single; 120,000–220,000L ($60–$110) double. Breakfast 6,000–15,000L ($3–$8). AE, MC, V. A 5- to 10-min. walk from Anacapri. Call from Marina Grande or before your ferry departs and they'll come pick you up for 20,000L($10) for 2 people. Otherwise, ride the Anacapri bus to the end of line and follow signs along the footpath.

Nestled amid vineyards and olive groves and just a 10-minute stroll from Anacapri, the family-run Girasole has changed dramatically from the student pensione of a few years ago. Rooms are now bungalows opening up onto the terrace (nos. 8, 9, and 12) with summery accommodations of tile floors, new functional furnishings in wicker or wood, modern (if not miniscule) baths, and good beds. On lazy days, you can take a dip in the pool or lounge around the bricked terrace garden with views over the island to the Bay of Naples. Rates can fluctuate wildly (and are often spontaneous) so bargain, bargain, bargain. Internet access is available.

Loreley. Via Giuseppe Orlandi 16, 80071 Anacapri. ☎ **081-837-1440.** Fax 081-837-1399. 14 units. TEL. 60,000–120,000L ($30–$60) single; 120,000–160,000L ($60–$80) double. Rates include breakfast. No credit cards. Closed November-Easter.

Having lived in a furnished apartment in Italy, this predominantly backpacker hideaway was a little too authentic for my taste, but this family-run hotel has three very redeeming characteristics: it's centrally located, staffed by exceedingly hospitable and helpful people, and the price is right. Expect soft beds (the way I like them) and lumpy pillows, old worn leather chairs out of the 1950s, and my favorite: the shoe print on the wall left by an angry mosquito assassin. The baths are old and dilapidated, beyond salvation by any amount of cleaning, and the tile floors are waxless and slightly gritty to the touch; but on a lighter note, the bed linens are clean, and the balcony doors welcome a little fresh air at night.

San Michele. Via Giuseppe Orlandi 1/3/5, 80071 Anacapri. ☎ **081-837-1427.** Fax: 081-837-1420. E-mail: smichele@capri.it. 60 units. TV TEL. 125,000–155000L ($63–$78) single; 210,000–260,000L ($105–$130) double. Rates include breakfast. Half and full pension available. Reduced rates for stays over 10 days. AE, DISC, MC, V. Closed Nov–Easter.

Entering through the main gate and driving up to the hotel entrance, it's hard to believe that the San Michele is in your price range. Converted from a 19th-century villa, the hotel has all the trappings of aristocracy: rooms with terraces or balconies enjoying either a sea or mountain view, marble and terra-cotta surfaces, and a grand salon dressed in aging pink brocade. Rooms are amply sized but a bit dowdy. The bonus is the huge pool in the garden, sculpted into the surrounding greenery—just what the doctor ordered to wind down from a scorching day sightseeing or at the beach.

✪ **Villa Eva.** Via la Fabbrica 8, 80071 Anacapri (NA). ☎ **081-837-1549.** Fax 081-837-2040. www.caprionline.com/villaeva. 15 units. 130,000–150,000L ($65–$75) double; 55,000L ($28) per person in room for 3, 5, or 6; Rates include breakfast. AE, DI, MC, V. Closed mid-Nov to Feb. A 10- to 15-min. walk out the far end of Anacapri toward the Blue Grotto; call from Marina Grande for directions. If possible, someone will pick you up, or take the Blue Grotto bus from Anacapri and ask the driver to let you off for a 2-min. walk.

This is one of the island's best inns, an exotic tropical paradise amid lush gardens. The accommodations—small bungalows nestled in the nooks and crannies of the grounds—are a perfect getaway for the regulars who book for weeks at a time. An outdoor pool flanked by a rustic breakfast bungalow peek through the greenery, guarded by a lazy St. Bernard whose bark is worse than his bite. The place is run by the husband-and-wife team of Vincenzo and Eva Balestrieri, and most of the comfy furnishings were built by Vincenzo. If painting the decorative artwork on the walls and personalizing the structures with majolica tiles weren't enough, he also installed thoughtful touches like mosquito screens and architectural details like wood beams or tiny bifore windows.

GREAT DEALS ON DINING

Island cuisine is mostly Campanian, relying heavily on fish, but one dish deserves to be singled out. Invented here in the 1950s for calorie-counting vacationers, the *insalata caprese*—often just called the *caprese* and now served in restaurants throughout Italy—is a salad of fresh tomato slices and mozzarella topped with torn basil and some cracked black pepper. If ever the mozzarella is fresh or *di bufala* (made from buffalo milk), **order it.** You won't get anything quite this fresh or this amazingly good.

There's no lack of overpriced, poor-quality snack bars in Capri. For a good quick bite, your best bet is to pop into a local *alimentari* (grocery shop) and make your own panino or small picnic. For a treat, stop by **Sfizi di Pane,** a short stroll from the Piazzetta at Via Le Botteghe 4 (☎ **081-837-0160**), to sample some of Ottavio Serena's outstanding pastries and breads, or a slice of passable pizza (closed Sunday afternoon).

AROUND CAPRI

Al Grottino. Via Longana 27 (standing on the Piazzetta with your back to the Duomo, duck through the tunnel/alley in the center). ☎ **081-837-0584.** Reservations highly recommended. Primi 11,000–17,000L ($6–$9); secondi 11,000–29,000L ($7–$15); fixed-price lunch menu 40,000L ($20) no wine. AE, DC, MC, V. Daily noon–3pm and 7pm–midnight. Closed mid-Nov to mid-Mar and Tues in Oct. CAPRESE/ITALIAN.

The "Little Grotto" is one of our fanciest choices, the sort of place where the waiter debones your fish tableside and good Italian and French vintages supplement the local table wine. It has changed little since the days that Ted Kennedy, the Gabor sisters, and Igor Stravinsky dined in the single room of tightly spaced tables under a stuccoed, vaulted ceiling. Wine flasks, photos of famous patrons, and a rose on every table complete the decor, while a dozen foreign tongues (mixed with some local dialect) and the clamor of the adjacent kitchen set the tone. *Agnolotti al pomodoro caprese* (giant ravioli of cheese and ham topped with fresh baby tomatoes and torn basil) or *risotto alla pescatora* (rice infused with shellfish and tiny squid) make excellent first courses. For secondo, you can order *involtino alla Napoletana* (veal roll stewed in tomatoes) or *mozzarella in carrozza* (fresh mozzarella on toast fried to a golden brown). But Al Grottino's strong suit is fresh fish; try it cooked *all'acqua pazza* (with tomatoes, white wine, and spices).

Worth a Splurge

Da Luigi. Via Faraglioni 5. ☎ **081-837-0591.** Reservations recommended. Primi 9,000–20,000L ($5–$10); secondi 15,000–25,000L ($8–$13). AE, DI, MC, V. Daily noon–4pm (later June–Aug). Closed Oct–Easter. Call ahead and they'll pick you up at Marina Piccola for 10,000L ($5) a head; or walk the long stair/path to the Faraglioni in about 20–30 min. CAPRESE.

Wedged into the rocks at sea level between the cliffs of Capri proper and the *faraglioni,* sharp boulders that rise dramatically from the waters, Da Luigi is more of a state of mind than just a meal. The site is a natural wind tunnel—sometimes chilly in spring or fall, but welcome at the height of summer when the locale's beach umbrellas can no longer keep the sweat off your brow. Unfortunately, the food isn't nearly as remarkable as the setting. Best are the *spaghetti alla malafemmina* ("evil woman's" pasta, with baby tomatoes, capers, olives, basil, and hot peppers) and *ravioli alla caprese* (sauced with tomatoes and mozzarella). Afterward, try *pollo alla griglia*, a *fritto Italia* (mixed fry of julienned zucchini, ravioli, suppli rice balls, eggplant, and potato croquettes), or *zuppa di cozze* (mussel soup).

AROUND ANACAPRI

Al Nido d'Oro. Via de Tomasso 30–32. ☎ **081-837-2148.** Reservations not accepted. Primi 10,000–22,000L ($5–$11); secondi 12,000–22,000L ($6–$11). Thurs–Tues noon–3pm and 8pm–midnight (from 7pm in winter). Closed Jan 20–Feb 20. CASARECCIA CAPRESE/PIZZA.

Make no mistake: This ain't fine dining or a tourist restaurant with a view. This is one of the few places locals like to keep to themselves, with pizza take-out on one side and families crowding the eight tables of the other room in the early evening, giving way to couples and small groups after 9:30pm. Caprese dialect sets the tone while the busy chef in the kitchen whips up heaping plates of simple, filling, fragrant home cooking. The *ravioli caprese* gets you pasta pockets stuffed with ricotta and basil, while the *penne con crema di carciofi* is in a flavorful creamy artichoke sauce. Secondi are basic: *scaloppina al limone* or the overwhelmingly popular *frittura di calamari* (fried squid). You can also enjoy pizzas such as *pizza capricciosa* (topped with tomato, mozzarella, prosciutto, mushrooms, olives, capers, and Parmesan).

Il Cucciolo. Via la Fabbrica 52 (take bus to Blue Grotto and ask to be let off at the turnoff; it's another 200 yards; or a 20-min. walk from Anacapri). ☎ **081-837-1917.** Reservations recommended. Primi 10,000–18,000L ($5–$9); secondi 13,000–24,000L ($7–$12); early bird menu includes items as low as 9,500L ($5). AE, DC, MC, V. Wed–Mon noon–2:30pm and daily 7–11:30pm. Closed late Oct–Easter. CAPRESE.

Tucked away on a back path off the road to the Blue Grotto, Il Cucciolo offers abundant portions of quite excellent food on a terrace surrounded by lush greenery and views of the Bay of Naples below. The *caprese* salad is excellent, as are the *pennette alla contadina* (mini-tube pasta in a savory sauce of onions, parmesan, and lean pancetta). For secondo try *pollo marinato alla griglia* (succulent marinated and grilled chicken—ask for the special "Argentina" sauce) or fresh *pesce alla griglia*. Head over in the evening when the candlelight adds to an already romantic ambiance, and when the walk back to town will allow you to work off the guilt.

Il Solitario. Via Giuseppe Orlandi 96 (on the main road in town). ☎ **081-837-1382.** Reservations recommended. Primi 8,000–15,000L ($4.70–$9); secondi 15,000–22,000L ($9–$13); *menù turistico* 15,000L ($9) no wine. AE, DC, MC, V. Tues–Sun noon–3pm and 7:30–midnight (daily June 21–Sept 21). Closed Nov–Mar. CAPRESE.

The clientele in this garden trattoria is likely to be half regulars on a first-name basis with the chef/owner and half tourists here for the second time, fending off the insistent stares of the owner's little dog. The house dish is ravioli stuffed with fresh cheeses and is deservedly the most popular menu item. Also good are the *gnocchi alla sorrentina, tagliolini all'aragosta* (ribbons of egg pasta with tomatoes and baby lobsters), and *cannelloni caprese* (ricotta and spinach-stuffed paste tubes). For secondi, sample the simple omelet with mozzarella or *spiedini di carne mista* (shish kebabs of beef, sausage, and rabbit). Reserve ahead in nice weather for the best seating out on the back terrace, where little tile-topped tables are shaded by the vines of a low hanging arbor.

5 The Emerald Isle of Ischia

After scouring the Amalfi Coast for the unspoiled innocence described in the book, Anthony Minghella, director of *The Talented Mr. Ripley*, disqualified the real thing when he stumbled on ✪ **Ischia,** a luxurious island spa. Ischia, pleasantly devoid of the polish and glitz of the Amalfi, remains untainted by the overdevelopment that plagues the mainland coast and forgotten by visitors caught in the undertow toward Capri. Known as the **Emerald Isle,** this island is no secret—Ischia is mentioned in Homer's *Iliad* as well as Virgil's *Aeneid*—but while a good number of German and British tourists have discovered its charms, the influx hasn't been enough to spoil the forthcoming and earnest nature of the Ischians. The face of tourism is not a stranger to the island, but Ischia still retains much of its agricultural quality, boasting the production of the first D.O.C. (Denominazione di Origine Controllata—meaning it's quality controlled by the State) wine in the country. The marinas still bustle in the earliest hours of the morning, as local fishermen prepare their nets for the day's work.

The island comprises six municipalities; with the village of Ischia, sitting atop an ancient crater, serves as the capital and is home to an abundance of **curative thermal waters and mineral springs.** Beneath all of that restorative bubbly is a volcanic system whose eruption in 302 B.C. transformed the original ancient settlement into a natural lake. The lake was opened up in 1854 and transformed into a port by Ferdinand II, now enveloped by modern-day **Ischia Port,** which revolves around **Via Vittoria Colona,** a progressive avenue of cafes, smart boutiques, and beauty and thermal spas. A 15-minute walk (more, if you stop to shop) down the road will lead you to **Ischia Ponte,** named for the long pedestrian bridge connecting the mainland to the islet and the 15th century **Castello Aragonese,** built by Alfonso d'Aragona, king of Spain, on the foundations of an earlier 474 B.C. fortress.. **Mt. Epomeo** can leave you breathless, not only for the 90-minute hike uphill, but for the perfect panorama of the island that will be your reward. Or you can simply take a week or two of complete decadence and utter self-indulgence, scheduling your day around massages, mud packs, and meals—the perfect vegetative beach vacation you've always dreamed of.

ESSENTIALS

GETTING THERE & GETTING AROUND **By Ferry or Hydrofoil** The *aliscafo* (hydrofoil) from **Naples** takes 40 minutes and costs 18,000L ($9); the *traghetto* (ferry) takes about 1hour, 20 minutes and costs 9,800L ($4.95). Both **Caremar** (☎ **081-837-0700;** www.caremar.it) and **Alilauro** (☎ **081-552-7209;** www.lauro.it) run hydrofoil and ferry service from both Molo Beverello and Mergellina docks. From **Sorrento, Linee Marittime Partenopee** ☎ 081-807-3024 runs a direct hydrofoil to Ischia via **Capri** or Naples. The hydrofoil takes 1 hour and costs 20,000L ($10).

If you're heading to or from Capri or just feel like day-tripping, **Ischia So. Gen. Ma.,** ☎ 081-985-080 runs daily excursions to/from Ischia Port for 36,000L ($18) roundtrip. **Linee Marittime Partenopee** (☎ **081-991-888**) also goes once a day for slightly more (21,000L/$11 one way and 42,000L/$21 round trip); buy your tickets at the Alilauro ticket window at the port.

By Bus **SEPSA** buses (1,800L/90¢ for 70-minute pass; 5,000L/$3 day pass) circle the island clockwise and counterclockwise, departing from the terminus in Piazzale Trieste, behind the port. You can also catch a bus to specific points toward the center of the island; check with the tourist information office for schedules and destinations. Buses run every 20 minutes, but since services overlap, it's unlikely you'll have to wait very long to get where you're going.

By Taxi Those farcical three-wheeled Ape (the car marque pronounced *AH-pay*) minitrucks you may have spotted on your travels have been transformed into utilitarian public transport, but it's going to cost you. The minimum fare for stepping foot into one of these babies is 10,000L ($5), plus 2,550L ($2) per bag and 3,000L ($2) per dog, slightly less shocking than the 15,000L ($8) minimum fare for a regular taxi. Travel light or take the bus.

By Rental Car/Scooter There are dozens of auto- and scooter-rental offices on the left bank of the port (exit the ferry and continue on foot to the left). That imposter of a tourist information office across from the ferry landing also manages a scooter and auto rental service, at prices slightly above the others. Expect to pay in the area of 40,000L to 50,000L ($20 to $25) per day for a scooter and from 70,000L ($35) per day for a car (rates increase in August). Most rental agencies are closed from November through March.

By Water Taxi A **water taxi** and excursion service is run by the Cooperative Rimessaggio Barche Ischitana, Via Pontano 7 (next to the Miramare Hotel; ☎ and fax **081-984-854**). The cooperative is open 24 hours from June through August, cutting back to an 8am to 8pm schedule during the shoulder season and closing altogether in the height of winter. Prices vary according to distance, from 4,000L ($2) per person to get to Scogli di Sant'Anna up to 100,000L ($50; maximum three people) to Istmo di Sant'Angelo. A relaxing half-day *giro dell'isola* (tour of the island) will cost you 30,000L ($15) per person, allowing you swimming stops at some astoundingly beautiful spots while you circle the island. They also rent boats with or without a captain.

VISITOR INFORMATION All the services you'll need are crowded around the port. There's an **unofficial information office** with the dubious right to display the official "*i*" international symbol, located just opposite the ferry dock (open 9am to1:30pm; longer hours in July and August). They offer services like money exchange, money wire transfers, auto and scooter rentals, but you'll pay a premium for the convenience. If you continue out of the port to your left, you'll hit the **official Azienda Turismo,** next to the unmistakable hydrofoil and ferry ticket office (☎ **081-507-4211),** open daily 9am to 7pm. You can change money or withdraw cash using your ATM card at the Banco di Napoli (walk left from the ferry landing) at Via Iasolino 34.

THINGS TO SEE & DO

Castello Aragonese. Piazzale Aragonese, Ischia Ponte. ☎ **081-992-834.** 12,000L ($6). Mar–Nov and one week between Christmas and New Year's daily 9am–7pm.

The fortress occupies an exceptionally picturesque islet connected to the "mainland" by a narrow causeway. Begin your visit at the summit, reachable via elevator, and work your way down through the **terraced gardens** and medieval paths that echo with the sounds of the nearby camouflaged chicken coop. From the upper terraces (where there is also a cafe), the grounds open onto a breathtaking **view** of the Gulf of Naples. Worth seeing are the ruins of a 14th-century Romanesque **cathedral,** altered in the 18th century with the addition of baroque elements. The heavy gates and massive gratings of the **prison** detained political prisoners, particularly those martyred during the Italian *Risorgimento.* At the upper reaches of the outcropping is the **convent,** founded in the 16th century and abandoned in 1818 at the King of Naples's secularization decree. Beneath the convent is a **Cemetery of the Poor Clares,** two confined cellars lined with, well, latrines . . . upon which the corpses were seated (the holes, rather than seats, allowed the fluids to drain). This ghoulish display served as a place of meditation for those among the living, until the bones putrefied and were piled up in the charnel house.

If you've forgone the elevator either coming or going, you're bound to pass the exhibit, **Attrezzi di Torture** (5,000L/$3), a private display showing the history of torture, composed mainly of drawings illustrating the process of vertical impalement and other sick methods of torment that I really didn't need to know about (I left before seeing the whole thing).

La Mortella. Via Francesco Calise 35. ☎ **081-986-220.** www.ischia.it/mortella. Admission 12,000L ($6). Apr–Nov Tues, Thurs, Sat, and Sun 9am–7pm. Take "La Mortella" bus from Ischia Port to the "La Mortella" bus stop; entrance is about 150 yards from the turnoff.

La Mortella, home and creative refuge to the late English composer William Walton, began as a stark and arid stone quarry. While Walton toiled about in his studio, his wife, Susana, with the tireless help of renowned landscape architect Russell Page, created the lavish botanical gardens that now consists of over 1,000 Mediterranean and tropical plants enveloping the property. The gardens and studio are open to visitors now and **classical vocal recitals** are performed every Saturday and Sunday (free with park admission) in combination with a yearly workshop for singers. Susana continues her labor of love, from personally supervising the addition of rare or endangered species to the gardens, to hand-feeding the hummingbirds in the aviary. **Victoria's House,** a tropical greenhouse named after the resident giant Brazilian water lily *Victoria Ammazonica* (time your visit around the automatic sprinkler mist), was one of the exhibitions invited to the prestigious Chelsea Flower Show in 2000.

BEACHES & WATERWORKS

With 34km (21 mi.) of alternating pine woods and *spiaggie* (beaches) and a total of eight thermal springs and innumerable mineral springs, you'll be hard-pressed to find something to do that doesn't involve getting wet. Halfway between Ischia Port and Ischia Ponte beckons the **Spiaggia dei Pescatori,** littered with colorful fishing boats and buoys and with postcard views of the Castello Aragonese. On the opposite side of the island is the **Spiaggia di Citara,** spreading out under the protection of the majestic headland of Punto Imperatore. The fishing village of Sant'Angelo lies at the southern tip of the island, with the **Spiaggia dei Maronti,** extending several miles to the east. Sant'Angelo spills out into the sea by way of a narrow strip of sand flanked on both sides by the sea and ending in the great green rock of La Roia at **Punta Sant'Angelo.**

If your budget won't allow you accommodations in a hotel with its own thermal spa, you'll definitely need to sample some of the **giardini thermali (thermal gardens),** private establishments charging a basic entrance fee that'll generally include use of the thermal pool, dressing rooms, sauna, and whirlpool and access to the beach and a beach chair. The **Parco Termale Castiglione,** Via Castiglione 36, Casamicciola Terme (☎ **081-982-551**), charges 32,000L ($16) for the day and 28,000L ($14) for a half-day, with discounts for children under 14. The park, open daily April to November 9am to 7pm, also has a full-service spa, including a medical checkup (60,000L/$30), various massages (40,000L to 80,000L/$20 to $40), and decadent beauty treatments (peelings, pedicures, waxings, facial treatments). From Ischia Port bus terminal, take no. CS, or 2 to the second stop (about ½ mile). The **Giardini Poseidon Terme** in Forio (☎ **081- 907-122**) is open daily April to November 8:30am to sundown and charges an entrance fee of 40,000L ($20) for use of its 17 outdoor and 3 indoor thermal pools. You also get to wander around the peaceful and enchanting gardens, or make use of one of the many curative treatments that are available here as well.

AFFORDABLE PLACES TO STAY

✪ **Il Monastero.** Castello Aragonese 3, 80070 Ischia Ponte (NA). ☎ **081-992-435.** 21 units. 93,000L ($47) single; 166,000L ($83) double. Rates slightly lower off season and include breakfast and dinner. No credit cards. Just past castle museum entrance, turn right to access the elevator; exit to the right past the Chiesa dell'Immacolata; the hotel entrance is to the left opposite the gift shop.

Occupying the former Convent di Clausura, Il Monastero sits high atop the castle grounds, affording panoramic views over the communal terrace from every room. Accommodations are spartan, while the baths are unexpectedly modern and utilitarian. The dining room is small and cozy, much like a *trattoria* in the countryside, but still maintains the reticence of monastic living of all those years ago. To get up to the pensione, go to the castle's ticket window and have the employee call up and announce your arrival, where you will be provided with a pass.

✪ **Terme Oriente.** Via delle Terme 9/11, 80077 Ischia Porto (NA). ☎ and fax **081-991-306.** www.ischia.it/oriente. E-mail: florenzo@pointel.it. 80 units. TV TEL. 120,000L ($60) double in high season. Breakfast 5,000L ($3). 20,000L ($10) supplement for full board. Rates lower September through July. Spa packages available. AE, DI, JCB, MC, V.

Occupying a mansion in the center of Ischia Port, the Hotel Terme Oriente strikes you as elegant in a sort of colonial way. Gorgeous ceramic tile floors are everywhere, and most rooms come with a spacious balcony. The house is surrounded by porches and terraces on all sides: there's a rear garden with an outdoor thermal pool and a panoramic rooftop terrace with two iron-rich hydromassage tubs (no extra charge). You can also sign up for a regimen of curative treatments (including acupuncture, reflexology, aerosol inhalation treatments, physiotherapy) or rehabilitation services for, among other ailments, arthritic problems and spinal and back ailments. The hotel arranges musical entertainment nightly, although with its restaurant putting out food this respectable, you may not need any coaxing to dine in.

WORTH A SPLURGE

✪ **Il Moresco Grand Hotel Terme.** Via Emanuele Gianturco 16, 80077 Ischia Porto. ☎ **081-981-366.** Fax 081-992-338. E-mail: moresco@pointel.it. 70 units. A/C MINIBAR TV TEL. 250,000–350,000L ($125–$175) double; 380,000L ($190) suite. Spa packages available. Rates are for high season/Aug and include breakfast and dinner. AE, DC, DISC, JCB, MC, V. Closed Nov–Mar.

Thanks to a raging dollar, this sublime five-star hotel and thermal spa may be within reach. Il Moresco is a classical Mediterranean-designed hotel with Moorish-influenced arches and spaces that open onto terraces. The hotel surfaces shimmer with ceramic tile and terra-cotta, underpinning an eclectic decor that reflects an elegant mix of styles. Every room has a terrace or balcony overlooking the pool, the sea, or the tropical fauna, or even all three. Trickling down from the exceptionally hospitable owner, Alessandro, is a service staff trained in deluxe treatment. The baths are filled with standard goodies you'd expect in a hotel, plus towel warmers and plush bathrobes. Even the singles are graciously large. And since two of your meals are included, your self-indulgent vacation won't break the bank. Spa treatments (request price list at reception) include mud baths, connective toning massage, electrotherapy, and aerosol inhalation.

GREAT DEALS ON DINING

Coco. Piazzale Aragonese 1, Ischia Ponte. ☎ **081-981-823.** Primi 10,000–18,000: ($5–$9); secondi 10,000–15,000 ($5–$8) and up for fish. AE, DC, MC, V. Daily 12:30–3:30pm and 7:30pm–midnight. Closed Wed in winter.

It's a bit unconvincing, this ideal tourist spot in the shadow of the castle, but who'd expect the food to be so good? Another local eatery that specializes in fish, Coco puts out a fantastic *frittura mista,* with calamari and baby whiting as fresh as the day they were born. The primi are exceptional, faultlessly executed traditional recipes like

Cruising Down the Amalfi Coast

The Amalfi Coast is one of Europe's greatest scenic wonders. High on the cliff side, the ✪ **Amalfi Drive** road winds dizzily along the coast, a marvel of engineering and one of the world's best white-knuckle thrill rides outside of an amusement park. This 50km (30-mi.) stretch of crinkly coastline between Sorrento and Salerno offers breathtaking scenery as you make your tortuous, winding way from one gorgeous sea cove into the next, past craggy inlets so sheer and deep they almost qualify as minifjords. High, tree-swathed cliffs on your left plunge tumultuously into the azure waters below you. The coastline's inlets and headlands are punctuated by scraps of beaches, terraced groves of giant lemons, and some of the most inviting, relaxing, and picturesque small towns in Italy.

The bougainvillea-crowned and jasmine-scented villages of the Amalfi Coast range from pricey resort towns to old-fashioned fishing hamlets. Among the dozen or so communities strung along the coast is a trinity of required stops: posh Positano, historic Amalfi, and garden-filled Ravello. In between you'll find everything from the Emerald Grotto sea cave to the ceramics of Vietri sul Mare. Many people on a daytrip take the bus from Sorrento to Amalfi then turn around to come back, but the most spectacular, least-developed sections of the coast lie east of Amalfi en route to Salerno. Information on specific towns is detailed below. *Note:* While riding down the Amalfi Coast, fight for a seat on the right side of the vehicle. You'll get the best view—and worst case of vertigo (unless you're coming from Salerno north, in which case you'll want to sit on the left).

The **bus** ride down the Amalfi Coast is one of the world's cheapest carnival rides, and by far the one with the most stunning scenery. The skilled drivers take on the stressful job of navigating the twists and turns, leaving you free to focus your camera and gasp in awe (and a bit of terror) as each bend brings vistas even more spectacular than the last into view and the side of the giant blue bus swings out over the edge of the cliff, giving you the sensation of dangling high above the sparkling waters.

spaghetti *alle vongole* (with clam sauce), although you could easily fill up before the meal begins, on antipasti like *fiori di zucca* (fried zucchini flowers) or marinated anchovies. The nearby castle ramparts loom above, making this a scenic and extremely romantic spot.

Ristorante Il Torchio. Via Campagnano 98. Campagnano. ☎ **081-901-986.** Reservations highly recommended. Primi: 10,000–18,000L ($5–$9); secondi 14,000–35,000L ($7–$18). AE, DC, MC, V. Open noon–midnight. Closed Dec–Easter. Call ahead for free minibus transfer from Ischia.

It'll take a little extra time to get here, but it won't take a minute to be won over by this simple country restaurant. Il Torchio specializes in traditional recipes using game, like their *coniglio alla moda della nonna*, a dish so utterly ingrained in the local consciousness that it's known as *alla moda d'Ischia*. You're not in the Sahara however, so if you're not yet weary of fish, save your appetite for the primo of *fusilli ai frutti di mari*, made with fresh pasta, shellfish, and tomatoes.

Enoteca Pane & Vino. Via Porto 24. ☎ **081-991-046.** Primi 6,000–12,000L ($3–$6); Salads 12,000–15,000L ($6–$8). AE, DC, MC, V. 9am–3pm and 6pm–1am.

Unflinching **SITA** (☎ 081-552-2176) bus drivers make the drive down the Amalfi Coast from Sorrento to Amalfi. Buses leave about hourly from in front of Sorrento's train station (buy your tickets at the station newsstand outside the exit). The Amalfi Drive itself skirts above **Positano** (35 min.), with the bus stopping twice (the second stop, "Sponda," is closer to the heart of town and the beach). The bus continues on to stop above **Praiano** (another 20 min.), **Conca dei Marini** (15 min. past Praiano), and ends in the center of **Amalfi** at the port (10 min. from Conca, or 85 min. from Sorrento). It's a commuter bus, so while you can hop on and off, you must buy a new ticket for each leg (see individual sections for exact fares) From Amalfi, hourly SITA buses run through Atrani up to **Ravello** and back (25 to 30 min.; 1,800L/90¢), while other SITA buses run at least hourly through Atrani, Maiori, Minori, and **Vietri sul Mare** (1 hr. from Amalfi; 3,100L/$2), to end in **Salerno** (10 min. from Vietri, 1,700L/85¢; or 70 min from Amalfi, 3,100L/$2).

If your stomach is strong enough and you're up to the task, you can take these curves from behind the wheel of your own **car,** but concentrating on the road (and not losing your lunch) will definitely detract from the event. If you are determined to take your life into your own hands, you can drive yourself along the twisting, death-defying Amalfi Coast down the **SS163** from Sorrento to Salerno. Buses blare their horns when rounding blind, outside curves so you'll know they're coming. Be prepared for inevitable delay: when there's not enough room for the bus to pass, chaos (and congestion) ensues, with masses of gesticulating locals getting involved to figure a way out of the mess. Chances are, you'll have to back up along with everybody else. **Tra.vel.mar.** (☎ 089-873-190) services the Amalfi Coast with six or seven daily **boat** connections between Sorrento, Positano, Amalfi, and Salerno. Both **Caremar** (☎ 081-807-3077) and **Linee Marittime Partenopee** (☎ 081-807-1812) provide limited service to Capri from the Amalfi Coast (see the specific sections for time/fare listings).

An intimate wine bar on the marina, Enoteca Pane & Vino has been here in one form or another since 1888. This version is obviously more recent, a stylish spot for a light meal of the freshest typical dishes. Try the salad of arugula, buffalo mozzarella, basil, tomatoes, and pears, or an even simpler plate of thinly sliced prosciutto and melon.

Worth a Splurge

Ristorante Alberto Sul Mare. Via Cristoforo Colombo, on the opposite side of Bagno Lido. ☎ **081-981-259.** Primi 25,000–36,000 ($13–$18); secondi 33,000L ($17); fish by weight around 50,000L ($25) per person. AE, DC, MC, V. Daily noon–3pm and 7:30pm–1am. Closed Nov–March. CREATIVE ISCHIAN.

Unaware of the sublime dining experience that awaits, rarely do day-trippers make it to this side of Ischia Lido. A family-run establishment and a team effort, Ristorante Alberto combines whimsical and inventive recipes along with exuberant hospitality. In this beachside shack with walls of glass giving onto the sea, it's not surprising that fresh fish dominates the menu. If you like your fish raw, start with *the marinati misti,* a variety of raw or marinated local fish in lemon or balsamic vinegar. Or throw caution to the wind and start with the *linguini all'astice,* prepared with male lobster, said to be the tastier of the species, over a bed of pasta bought fresh daily from the *granaio.* A tasty second would be the *spigola in salsa di pere* (fish in a pear sauce). With the sun's receding rays turning Procida Island a burnt orange, you'll probably want to drag out your meal as long as possible, leaving you to indulge in the house tiramisù.

6 Sorrento: Hear the Sirens Call

48km (29 mi.) SE of Naples, 8km (4.8 miles) NE of Capri, 17km (10 mi.) W of Positano.

Those mythical femme fatale Sirens certainly made an impression, leaving their legacy in the very name Sorrentum, a modern city perched on the clifftops high above the Bay of Sorrento. The allure of the sweeping picturesque bays, the narrow alleyways of the old town, and the ancient and endless stone stairways leading down to crystal-clear waters have drawn pleasure-seekers as far back as antiquity—wealthy Romans who left a legacy of crumbling aqueducts and cisterns, along with a smattering of villas occupying the most coveted panoramic positions along the coast.

Sorrento never gained status as a major trading port, but that didn't stop the Longobards or the Normans from asserting their might here, albeit in a relatively hands-off fashion. Not so the Turks, who in 1558, sacked the town and carted much of the local population back to Constantinople as slaves. In a classic case of closing the barn door after the horse, the city walls were fortified, but Sorrento's streak of bad luck continued soon after with the arrival of a plague that swooped down and killed over 2,000 people throughout the peninsula. It wasn't until the 19th century that the city was able to regain her momentum as a tourist destination, regaining enough appeal to attract such illustrious figures as Lord Byron, John Keats, Walter Scott, Charles Dickens, Wolfgang Goethe—it was even here that Wagner met Nietzche and Ibsen completed *Peer Gynt.* Although Sorrento doesn't have the fishing-village charm (or prices) that you'll find in Positano or Amalfi, it's a good central location (with connections for major highways and transport routes) for touring the Amalfi Coast, Pompeii, and Capri.

ESSENTIALS

GETTING THERE **By Train** From Naples, the private **Circumvesuviana rail line** (☎ 081-536-8932 or 081-772-2444) runs efficiently every half hour or so from 5:09am to the last train at 10:42 pm. making stops at Hercolaneum, Pompeii, Castellammare, Vico Equense, San'Agnello and finally Sorrento (80 min; 9,800L /$5).

By Car From Naples, take route 18 to Castellammare di Stabia, where you transfer over to the SS145 to Sorrento.

By Ferry/Hydrofoil There's an **Alilauro** (☎ 081-552-2838) hydrofoil leaving seven times daily **from Naples's** Molo Beverello (35 min; 18,000L/$9) and **Tra.vel.mar.** (☎ 089-873-190) runs connections to and from Amalfi (18,000L/$9). From Capri, **Caremar** (☎ 081-807-3077) runs ferries three times a day (40 to 50 min; 10,000L/$5.00) and hydrofoils once a day (20 min; 11,000L/$6). **Linee Marittime Partenopee** (☎ 081-807-1812) runs four ferries daily from Capri (40 minutes; 10,000L/$5) and frequent hydrofoils (20 min; 14,000L/$7) in addition to running one hydrofoil daily from Ischia (60 min; 20,000L/$10).

By Bus **Autolinee Curreri Service** (☎ 081-801-5420) runs four buses daily from Napoli's Capodichino Airport (1 hour; 10,000L/$5) and two buses daily from Rome's Tiburtina Station (4 hours; 30,000L/$15). **SITA** (☎ 081-552-2176) buses run along the coastal road between Amalfi and Sorrento passing through Positano and Priano. (optimistically 85 min; 4,100L/$2.10).

GETTING AROUND **By Bus** The historic center around Piazza Tasso is walkable, but for longer stretches and to avoid the endless stairs down to the harbor—or worse, up—orange buses run from around 7am to around 11:30pm. From the station, **Bus D** runs to Piazza Tasso (city center) and Corso Italia (the main drag). **Bus A** runs from Piazza Tasso out Via Capo (where you'll find lots of hotels). **Buses B and C** run from Piazza Tasso down to Marina Piccola (ferry dock) and back again. Tickets cost 1,800L (90¢) and must be bought before boarding the bus (tickets are sold at several booths at Marina Piccola, and in *tabacchi*).

By Rental Car   Since Sorrento makes such a good base, picking up a car or scooter here (rather than fighting the traffic in Naples) can make a lot of sense. The most reputable agencies, roughly in order from cheapest to most expensive, **De Martino** (Auto Europe), Corso Italia 253 (☎ **081-878-2801**); **Sorrento Rent a Car,** Corso Italia 210A (☎ **081-878-1386**); and **Avis,** Viale Nizza 53, (☎ **081-878-2459**). All except Avis also rent scooters—as does **Jolly Rent A Scooter,** Via Fuorimura 29 (☎ **081-878-1719**)—for around 45,000 to 55,000L ($23 to $28) for 4 to 5 hours or around 95,000 ($48) per day, with discounted rates for multiple day rentals.

VISITOR INFORMATION   Sorrento's **tourist office** is inside the Circolo dei Forestieri club just down from Piazza San Antonio at Via Luigi de Maio 35 (☎ **081-807-4033;** fax 081-877-3397). It's open Monday to Saturday: 8:30am to 8pm May to September and 8:45am to 2:45pm and 3:30 to 6:30pm October to April. If you're arriving by boat, take the orange bus up to Piazza San Antonio and walk back to the gated entrance across the street on your right.

Check your e-mail at the **Internet Café** at Via Fuorimura 20D, near Piazza Tasso (☎ **081-807-4854**). It's open daily 10:30am to1:30pm and 4:30pm to 1am.

FESTIVALS   In honor of **Good Friday,** the town hosts a solemn Byzantine procession. In July and August, Sorrento hosts both a **classical music festival** in indoor and outdoor venues across town, and an **international film festival** that, although lacking the star quality of Cannes or Venice, is beginning to gain a certain following.

STROLLING AROUND SORRENTO

Sorrento's sights consist of the 14th-century **cloisters of San Francesco** (now an art school) on Via Vittorio Veneto, a former convent standing on a system of interlaced arcades typical of Sicilian Saracen architecture. A closer inspection reveals elements recycled from pagan temples.

The neighboring public gardens of the **Villa Comunale** offer great views down to the marina and up the coastline. There's also a small museum at the east end of town, the **Museo Correale di Terranova,** Via Correale 50 (☎ **081-807-4033**), open Monday and Wednesday to Friday 9am to 2pm (Saturday and Sunday to 1pm).

The collections include lots of locally inlaid wood furnishings, majolica, porcelain figurines, Neapolitan baroque paintings (plus a Rubens), marvelous views over the gardens to the Bay of Sorrento, and crumbling bits of Roman statuary to remind you of the city's venerable, if little visible, heritage. Admission is a steep 8,000L ($4) adults, 5,000L ($3) children under 12.

If you're not convinced of Sorrento's allure, some of the best sightseeing happens along the streets of the old town. Italians out for a *passeggiata* head to modern Corso Italia and the parallel and cobbled Via San Cesareo, the old Decumanus Maximus of the Roman town. While tourists and locals mill about the streets in the late afternoon, peering into shops cramped with *objets* of inlaid wood or locally fired ceramics, the town elders gather under the 15th-century loggia of the **Sedile Dominova** at the corner of Via San Cesareo and Via Giuliano to play Italian cards games under the 18th-century frescoes (be sure you filter back amid the bar umbrellas on the tiny piazza out front to glimpse the Sedile's majolica dome growing weeds).

Sorrento

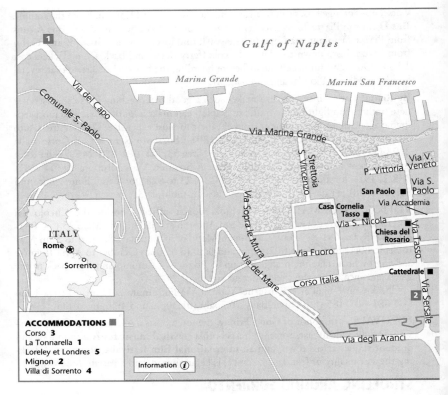

Gulf of Naples

Marina Grande

Marina San Francesco

Via del Capo

Comunale S. Paolo

Via Marina Grande

Strettoia S. Vincenzo

P. Vittoria

Via V. Veneto

San Paolo ■

Via S. Paolo

Via Accademia

Casa Cornelia Tasso ■

Via S. Nicola

Chiesa del Rosario ■

Via Sopra le Mura

Via del Mare

Via Fuoro

Corso Italia

Cattedrale ■

Via Tasso

Via Sersale

2

ITALY

Rome ✪

○ Sorrento

Via degli Aranci

ACCOMMODATIONS ■
Corso **3**
La Tonnarella **1**
Loreley et Londres **5**
Mignon **2**
Villa di Sorrento **4**

Information ⓘ

SWIMMING   Although Sorrento is a seaside town, don't come here expecting beaches. While the water's a bit cleaner than along most of the bay, swimming is mainly off piers jutting out over the rocks plus a few tiny pebble beaches that charge admission. An elevator ride down from the town (look for these elevators along Via Marina Grande) will take you down near the water's edge.

AFFORDABLE PLACES TO STAY

It's certainly possible to find accommodations in one of the budget hotels that line Corso Italia from the train station to the town center. But you can get significantly better quality at competitive rates if you make the effort and walk a little further. You can also find a number of cheaper hotels along **Via Capo,** the ultra-scenic clifftop road leading out the far end of town.

Corso. Corso Italia 134 (½ block beyond Piazza Tasso), 80067 Sorrento (NA). ☎ **081-807-1016.** Fax 081-807-3157. www.hoteldelcorso.com. 21 units. TV TEL. 130,000L ($60) single; 160,000L ($80) double; 220,000L ($110) triple. Rates include breakfast. AE, DC, MC, V. Parking 16,000–25,000L ($8–$13) in nearby garage or lot. Closed Dec–Jan.

Located in the fringes of the historic center, the family-run Corso is probably the best bargain hotel along the car-trafficked main drag of Via del Corso. The plain accommodations feature exceedingly firm beds, the usual modular furnishings, and are of generous proportions, though the overall effect can be a bit bland. Its biggest selling point is also its greatest drawback: Sorrentine life passes below your streetside window, well into the wee hours of the morning (adolescents poke holes in the

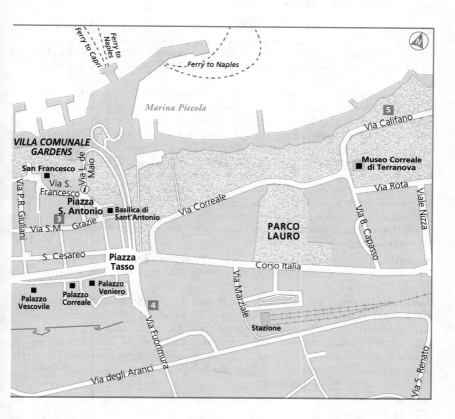

mufflers of the scooters to make them go faster!). Rooms 52 through 55 have tiny mostly-for-show balconies that hang over quiet, pedestrianized Via San Cesareo, but if you can't score one of these, go for nos. 62 to 65 deprived of the view, but still on the building's quieter back side.

✪ **La Tonnarella.** Via Capo 31, 80067 Sorrento (NA). ☎ **081-878-1153.** Fax 081-878-2169. 21 units. A/C TV TEL. 200,000–240,000L ($100–$120) double with breakfast. Half-pension 266,000–300,000L ($133–$150); full-pension 280,000–320,000L ($140–$160). AE, MC, V. Free parking. Closed Jan–Feb. Bus: A from Piazza Tasso.

Rising cliffside high above Sorrento Bay, the vista-blessed Tonnarella gives the coastal road to Amalfi an auspicious beginning. Sharing the grounds with gardens of citrus, the hotel is the best of Via Capo's inns, offering first-class amenities and decor at criminally low prices. Persian runners spill down over the rich parquet floors, antiques fill the halls, and though it's only a 10- to 15-minute walk from town, you'll feel like a tourism fugitive in a coastal hideaway. The brightly tiled rooms sport an odd mix of 19th-century chairs and modern built-in headboards. Some of the baths are getting on in years, but many are *modernissimo,* with hyperspray showers and heated towel racks. There's a pleasing abundance of pine-shaded terra-cotta terraces—some public, others attached to rooms such as nos. 1 to 4, whose windows take in the full sweep of the bay (book ahead for a room with view). The picture-window restaurant, with open balconies, could almost be recommended separately for its plump ravioli and fresh fish. There's an elevator (or stairs through a verdant gorge) down to a little private pebble beach, open May to September.

✪ **Loreley et Londres.** Via Califano 2, 80067 Sorrento (NA). ☎ and fax **081-807-3187.** 28 units. Single or double 150,000L ($75); triple 190,000L ($95); quad 220,000L ($110). Rates include breakfast. 50,000L ($25) supplement for half-pension. DC, MC, V. Parking free behind hotel. Closed Nov–Easter. (It's a long walk from Piazza Tasso or the station; no bus makes the trip regularly.)

This hospitable 100-year-old pensione is the most popular of Sorrento's budget hotels, despite the 10- to 15-minute walk from town and lack of phones or air-conditioning. The hotel, well covered by the guidebook industry and word-of-mouth, sits on the cliff's edge. Accommodations are very well worn, with mismatched functional furniture and a few near-antiques, featuring tile floors (some with painted designs), baths with curtainless showers, cool breezes, and medium-soft beds. Most have at least a balcony, and in the case of no. 14, which has its own wraparound patio, the terrace is almost as large as the room. Most rooms (the best are nos. 11 to 13) get at least part of the remarkable view sweeping from Sorrento and its marina around the bay to Vesuvius, but a few are on the road. Everyone enjoys the panorama from the bamboo-shaded terrace where you take meals in high season, and an elevator takes you down to a little bar and private swimming pier.

Mignon. Via Sersale 9, 80067 Sorrento (NA). ☎ **081-807-3824.** Fax 081-532-9001. 23 units. A/C TV TEL. 120,000L ($60) double; 180,000L ($90) triple. Rates include breakfast. MC, V.

Located under a stone arch in one of the older back streets in Sorrento, Mignon picks up the overflow from the Loreley, which is owned and operated by the same local family. The hotel, convenient to the station and located just off the main drag, makes up for its lack of a view with reasonable prices and sensible decor. Late risers should request rooms at the back, which face the garden and courtyard, because rooms on the street facing the Chiesa del Cattedrale get the full force of the ringing church bells. Book early; rooms fill up in summer.

Villa di Sorrento. Via Fuorimura 6 (½ block north of Piazza Tasso.), 80067 Sorrento (NA). ☎ **081-878-1068.** Fax 081-807-2679. 21 units. A/C TV TEL. 100,000–110,000L ($50–$55) single; 160,000–190,000L ($80–$95) double. Breakfast 20,000L ($10). AE, DC, MC, V. Parking 20,000L ($10) in nearby lot.

The comfortably sober Villa di Sorrento is excellently located just half a block up a tree-lined street from Piazza Tasso. As befits an upscale inn, the wood-framed beds are large and firm and the baths are modern. Some rooms are smallish, but the air-conditioning and other amenities more than make up for it. Paintings or prints decorate the walls and a few near-antiques give most rooms a touch of class. Nos. 41 and 42 have terraces with the best views over red-tiled roofs. If you splurge by opting for the breakfast—not bad, but not worth 20,000L ($10) either—you'll enjoy the vaulted dining room beyond a sofa scattered sitting room.

GREAT DEALS ON DINING

If you're suffering from carb overload, head over to **Angelina Lauro** a self-serve cafeteria and bar in Piazza Angelina Lauro 39-40. (☎ **081-807-4097**), where you can fuel up on a refreshing selection of alternatives that will get you through the meal without even one slice of bread. Expect to spend 6,000L ($3) on a vegetarian casserole of escarole, currants, pignoli nuts, and mozzarella cheese, and up to 15,000L ($8) for pork chops. Angelina Lauro is open Wednesday through Monday 8am to midnight. Worth a mention also is **Da Franco,** a homey *panetteria* and pizzeria at Corso Italia 265 (between Piazza Tasso and Piazza Angelina Lauro; ☎ **081-877-2066**), with masses of hanging prosciutto beckoning the passers-by.

Da Gigino. Via degli Aranci 15 (just down from Corso Italia). ☎ **081-878-1927.** Reservations recommended. Primi 10,000–18,000L ($5–$9); secondi 12,000–30,000L ($6–$15); pizza 9,000–15,000L ($4.50–$8); all-seafood *menù turistico* 50,000L ($25). AE, MC, V. Daily noon–3pm and 7–11pm. Closed Tues Sept–June. SORRENTINA/PIZZA.

Although all of Sorrento's restaurants cater to tourists, this one has a loyal local following as well; the TV in the corner adds a neighborhood-joint touch. Most opt to sit outside on the cobbles of the tiny side street, enjoying a pizza from the wood-burning oven or a primo such as *scialatielli ai frutti di mare* (homemade pasta with seafood), *gnocchi verdi provola e gamberi* (potato-and-spinach dumplings tossed with provolone cheese and shrimp), or, as always, *gnocchi alla Sorrentina* (a rich, gooey casserole of gnocchi baked with tomatoes under a lid of mozzarella and Parmesan). The primi shine here, but the straightforward secondi don't disappoint, including the *grigliata di pesce* (mixed fish grill) and *pollo arrosto con patate* (roast chicken sided with bland potatoes you could just as well do without).

Ristorante della Favorita O'Parrucchiano. Corso Italia 71–73. ☎ **081-878-1321.** Reservations recommended. Primi 10–14,000L ($5–$7); secondi 10,000–18,000L ($5–$9) and up for fish. MC, V. Thurs–Tues noon–4pm and 7–midnight (daily May–Nov 15).Closed Jan–Feb. SORRENTINA.

Under a thicket of vines and lemon and orange trees, in botanical gardens with greenhouse-like terraces, you won't even notice the tour groups dining beside you. Founded as "*la Favorita*" in the late 19th century by a seminarian snatched from the fold by the love of a young girl ("o'parrucchiano" is Neapolitan dialect for "parish priest" and was added later by local regulars), the restaurant has remained family managed ever since. While the place can boast celebrities like Sophia Loren, Andy Warhol, and Vittorio de Sica as former patrons, its vast popularity has neither led to price gouging nor compromised quality. Most seafood dishes, since they change with daily availability, are printed on the "chef recommends" menu. Look for *scialatielli ai frutti di mare* (pasta with seafood) and *involtini di pesce spada* (swordfish roll-ups). Otherwise, try *cannelloni "Favorita"* (pasta leaves wrapped around meat fillings and baked) followed by a *scaloppina di vitello alla Sorrentina* (veal scallops under tomato sauce and slices of mozzarella) or a *filetto al pepe rosa* (beef fillet with pink peppercorns).

7 Positano: A Posh Resort

56km (35 mi.) SE of Naples, 16.1km (10 mi.) E of Sorrento, 266km (165 mi.) SE of Rome.

Positano grips onto the cleavage of two intersecting mountainsides, its white and pastel buildings crowned by the green and yellow majolica-tiled cupola of the Duomo, and dripping off the cliff face like the jewels around the necks of Academy Award hopefuls. But whether you're celebrity-spotting or poking your nose around the boutiques along public passageways draped in bougainvillea, an extended layover in Positano is an absolute must. A tony resort with fine beaches, swanky shops laden with seaside fashions and languorous, terraced cafes, Positano's popularity among trendsetters has introduced several fashions to the world, including the bikini (polka-dot, in 1959). Not bad for a humble fishing village of coarse volcanic origins. Risen from the ashes after several centuries, Positano continues to serve as a jet-set playground—everyone from Picasso and Stravinsky to John Steinbeck, Liz Taylor, and Sir Laurence Olivier have vacationed here. Director Franco Zefferelli is among the many notables to keep a summer villa in town, and even Rudolf Nureyev bought up the entire **Li Galli** islets you'll see offshore on your way into town (once thought to be the home of Homer's Sirens).

ESSENTIALS

GETTING THERE   Once you've arrived in town, be it by bus, car, or ferry, you're still only halfway there, as arriving at any hotel will most likely involve some trek up a hill or an endless set of stairs. If you're willing to drop 7,000L ($4) per bag, all you have to do is yell "**Porter!**" and a handsome man with a mechanical trolley will come to the rescue (**Carovana Facchini,** Piazza dei Mulini; ☎ 089-875-310).

By Bus   SITA (☎ 081-552-2176) buses run up and down the coastal road between Naples and Salerno, offering one of the best, if not torturous, hair-raisingly scenic rides in Italy. There's more than one stop in Positano along the highway so if you're headed to the beach or the center of town, get off at the stop marked "**Sponda,** " but take the "**Chiesa Nuova,**" stop if you're staying at Hotel Casa Albertina or Casa Guadagno. The fare from Naples (leaving from Via Pisanelli near Piazza Municipio) is 6,100 ($3); from Amalfi 1,800L (90¢); and from Sorrento 2,300L ($1).

The orange "Interno Positano" minibus will run you from Chiesa Nuova down the wide, looping Viale Pasitea to Piazza dei Mulini at the heart of town (1,500L/75¢, paid on the bus), leaving half-hourly from 9am to midnight (one earlier bus leaves at 7:50am). The bus makes its way down and around through the more reasonable heights of Positano, a welcome respite to the traveler weary of lugging baggage up and down narrow steps.

By Car   From the north, take the Autostrada del Sole to Naples, then follow signs for the Salerno-Reggio Calabria highway. Exit at Castellammare di Stabia, then follow signs for Positano. If you'll be arriving by car, my best advice is to leave your car in the first lot available, and expect to pay anywhere from 30,000 to 50,000L per day ($15 to $25) depending on the size of your car. There's limited street parking along the road that winds down into Piazza dei Mulini, but you can only park for up to 3 hours at a time (1,000L/50¢ for the first hour; 3,000L/$2 for 2 hours; 6,000L/$3 for 3 hours).

By Ferry   **Tra.vel.mar.** (☎ 089-873-190) runs seven daily ferries to Positano from Amalfi (25 min; 7,000L/$4) and six daily from Salerno (70 min; 9,000L/$5). **Linee Marittime Partenopee** (☎ 081-807-3024) runs service from Capri (50 min; 20,000/ $10). There's also a **transportation cooperative** at the docks (☎ 089-811-986) offering comprehensive service along the coast.

VISITOR INFORMATION   There's a small **tourist office** at Via Saracino 4, in front of the Duomo at the heart of town (☎ 089-875-067; fax 089-875-760), open Monday to Friday 8:30am to 2pm and Saturday 8:30am to noon (8am to 8pm Monday to Saturday in summer). More than just a repository for brochures, the office is staffed with people ready to give advice—they'll also help you find a room in town if you're having trouble.

EXPLORING THE AREA

Once you've seen the baroque majolica-tiled dome of the 13th-century **Santa Maria Assunta** church, you've finished with the historic sights of Positano. But the real sight-seeing here is wandering the twisting and scenic alleyways near the port, window shopping at the boutiques, and sipping aperitifs at one of the beachside bars while scoping out celebrities.

BEACHES   Unmistakably at the heart of town is the **Spiaggia Grande.** Much of the beach is taken up by bathing establishments' chair and umbrella rental: 14,000L/$7 for the day) and boat-rental agencies, but about half of the beach is free of charge. From the dock next to Spiaggia Grande, Via Positanesi d'America wraps around the headland to Positano's quieter half above **Fornillo Beach.** It's calmer and less trendy than Spiaggia

Grande, but you'll get unspoiled beauty in exchange for the pebbles. Again, the far right end is free, otherwise an umbrella and chair will cost you 14,000L ($7).

BOAT EXCURSIONS   You can rent boats from **Noleggio Barche Lucibello** (☎ **089-875-032**) right on the beach: canoes cost 10,000 to 15,000L ($5 to $8) per hour; rowboats and paddleboats cost 20,000L ($10) per hour, 80,000L ($40) per day; motorboats 50,000 to 60,000L ($25 to $30) per hour, 180,000L ($90) per day (discounts apply for multiple hours). This outfitter also runs an all-day **tour to Capri** (32,000 to 40,000L/$16 to $20 per person), a 2-hour tour to the **Emerald Grotto** (25,000L/$13; info below), and a half-day trip to the Emerald Grotto along with a swim at **Li Galli** islets (35,000L/$18). Entrance fees to the Emerald Grotto (or the Blue Grotto on Capri) are not included. Night excursions are also available.

AFFORDABLE PLACES TO STAY

California. Via Cristoforo Colombo 141, 84017 Positano (SA). ☎ **089-875-382.** Fax 089-812-154. 15 units. TEL. 200,000–250,000L ($100–$125) double. Rates include breakfast. AE, DC, MC, V. Parking free. Closed mid-Nov to Feb.

Run by an exceedingly friendly local couple, the California is installed in a 17th-century palazzo just 5 minutes from the beach, poised above street level with a wide terrace trailing with vines where guests read and take their drinks in the cool breezes with a sweeping maritime vista. Most of the rooms sport balconies with a sea view, and four have high frescoed ceilings. Rear rooms have only small windows up high for light, so while you save some money you lose much atmosphere (use this as a bargaining chip when making a reservation). If you're happiest with fresh tile floors and newer baths, check into one of the rooms in the modern wing. The proprietors have begun adding TVs to the rooms, and until they arrive in every room, there's a common TV lounge to pick up the slack.

La Bougainville. Via Cristoforo Colombo, 25, 84017 Positano. ☎ **089-875-047.** Fax 089-811-150. www.argosid.it/aziende/bougan. E-mail: bougan@positano.argosid.it. 14 units. TEL. 80,000L ($40) single; 100,000–130,000L ($50–$65) double; 20,000L ($10) supplement for view. 10,000L ($5) breakfast. AE, DC, MC, V. Closed Nov–Mar 15.

Centrally located on the hill just above Piazza dei Mulini, the Bougainville offers clean, friendly accommodations and gracious common areas at just the right price. Rooms at the front have panoramic views of the sea, while rooms at the back tend to be dark and a bit claustrophobic due to the high placement of the window. Room 10 has a large terrace overlooking a garden, and no. 12 lacks the sea view but is a bit larger and is graced with a window overlooking an inner courtyard. The hotel is one flight up (with rooms up another flight) and there's no elevator, so pack light and bring a bag with straps.

✪ Villa Rosa. Via C. Colombo 127, 84017 Positano (SA). ☎ and fax **089-811-955.** 12 units. A/C MINIBAR TV TEL. 190,000–210,000L ($95–$105) double. Rates include breakfast. AE, DC, MC, V. Parking 30,000 ($15) in garage. Closed Nov–Feb. Get off SITA bus at "la Sponda" and walk down hill. From the port, head up to Piazza dei Mulini and turn uphill; the hotel is on the left.

Across the street from famous Hotel Le Sireneuse and up an endless flight of steps lined with bougainvillea, Villa Rosa offers twice the view at one quarter the price. The large, high vaulted square rooms are quiet (no. 11 even has frescoes) and all are graced with large terraces draped in vine-strewn arbors. There are postcard views of Positano, bits of the harbor and sea while the mattresses are orthopedic, furnishings peasant style, and baths functional yet modest. My favorite feature (next to breakfast being served on your private terrace) is the decorative tile ceramic floors, polished to a glistening white and a pure delight for bare feet. Owners see an elevator in the hotel's future, but for now, you'll have to be in good cardiac shape. If there's no room at the inn, the owners can offer the same hospitality and identical decor close to the beach at their *dipendenza*, **La Tartana** at Via della Tartana 5 ☎ **089-875-645** or 089-812-193 (12 units; A/C TV TEL; same rates).

WORTH A SPLURGE

Casa Albertina. Via Tavolozza 3 (a staircase tucked into a bend of Viale Pasitea), 84017 Positano (SA). ☎ **089-875-143.** Fax 089-811-540. E-mail: info@casalbertina.it. 19 units. A/C MINIBAR TEL. 260,000–290,000L ($130–$145) single; 340,000–380,000L ($170–$190) double. Rates include breakfast and dinner (ask for rates without half pension Nov–Mar). AE, DC, MC, V. Parking 35,000L ($15) with valet service. SITA coastal bus to first Positano stop, then walk down Viale Pasitea to the Hotel San Pietro—the white main hotel, not its yellow "residence" branch up the road—and take the stairs down just to the hotel's left; coming from Positano's center, take the stairs up between Bar Ciro and Trattoria da Vincenzo.

Rather hard to find and up a prodigious number of stairs from the beach, but definitely in a class by itself. Many of the rooms were recently renovated and, while small, have built-in closets and small terraces to make up for it. Most are done in Mediterranean blue and white, with padded headboards, marble-top sinks in modern baths, and cool tile floors. The outrageous 100% increase in price since last year is supposedly justified by the addition of Jacuzzis in half of the rooms, or maybe it's the daily Baci chocolates left on your pillow. . . . What you really come for is the perfect panorama over the Spiaggia Grande, Positano's posh other half, its majolica church dome and the stunning, undulating coastline beyond. Way up here, you're anything but stranded—you can head a few dozen steps down to Bar Ciro, with tables set on a panoramic curve of Viale Pasitea and often a guitar or mandolin player entertaining evening customers.

GREAT DEALS ON DINING

✪ **Donna Rosa.** Via Montepertuso 97–99 (a village in the hills above Positano). ☎ **089-811-806.** Reservations recommended. Primi 12,000–35,000L ($6–$18); secondi 10,000L and up to 50,000L for lobster ($5–$25). DC, MC, V. July–Sept daily 7pm–1am and Wed–Sun 12:30–3pm. Closed Tues in Winter and Jan–Feb. Bus: bus to Montepertuso every 2 hr from Via Colombo; for lunch take the 10:20am or schoolchildren-packed 12:20pm. If you reserve ahead, they might be able to pick you up in Positano. INVENTIVE CAMPANIAN.

The food at this countryside trattoria located high above Positano blows away the competition down in town. Attention to detail, from using the freshest of ingredients and making pastas and desserts by hand to a thoughtful presentation on your plate, is impeccable. Open with the *ravioli ripieni di arragosta* for delicately flavored dumplings stuffed with lobster. To sample a variety of the kitchen's bounty, order a *trittico* for primo, a trio of pastas perhaps including *pappardelle funghi porcini e gamberi* (wide noodles with porcini mushrooms and shrimp), or *ravioli del Marchese* (stuffed with pumpkin in a sauce of fused butter, crisped sage, and Parmesan). Fresh fish is an excellent choice for a secondo, accompanied by a perfectly refreshing house white wine. The kitchen is open to view—always a sign of honest cooking—and although it's almost deserted at lunch when everyone's down at the beach (but you can be up here in the cool breezes), nighttime packs it full until long after midnight. Definitely worth the journey.

Lo Guarracino. Via Positanesi d'America 12 (from the port, follow stairs up and around "La Saracena" towards Fornillo Beach). ☎ **089-875-794.** Reservations recommended. Primi 10,000–18,000L ($5–$9); secondi 15,000–28,000L ($8–$14); pizza 10,000–15,000L ($5–$8). AE, MC, V. Wed–Mon noon–3pm and 7:30–11pm. Open Tues July–Aug. Closed Nov–Easter. POSITANO/PIZZA.

A quiet cliff-hugging path wraps around the fortress towers to this seaside trattoria/pizzeria in a scenic 5-minute stroll, and you'll know you've arrived by the bougainvillea-shrouded entrance unobtrusively to the right. The food is genuinely tasty, even more so tucked into a table at the edge of the terrace, where the sound of the crashing sea and the dreamy views of the Galli islets beyond, with ranks of floating fishing boats, will tweak your appetite. Surprisingly, Lo Guarracino has resisted the temptation to keep up with local inflation, and maybe we have this isolation to thank. The pizzas are quite good if you want something light and quick, or go local with linguine *ai ricci di mare* (sea urchin) or homemade gnocchi sorrentina. Unless you opt for something basic like a scaloppina al limone, the proximity of the sea guarantees you'll be following up with something fishy like *pesce spada* (grilled swordfish steak) or *zuppa di cozze* (mussel soup).

WORTH A SPLURGE

Buca di Bacco. Via Rampa Teglia 4. ☎ **089-875-699.** www.starnet.it/buca. Reservations required. Primi 12,000–28,000L ($6–$14); secondi 12,000–40,000L ($6–$20). AE, DC, MC, V. Daily noon–3:30pm and 7–11:30pm. Closed Nov–Easter. POSITANO/SEAFOOD.

Buca di Bacco (not to be confused with the beach-level fast-food joint below) offers the best value among the see-and-be-seen spots at the center of town. Even if it's only to rehydrate after a sizzling afternoon under the sun, definitely stop by to hobnob with the occasional celebrity. Head upstairs to the arbor-covered terrace and reserve well ahead of time for a table along the railing with the sea below. There's also an ample wine list to satisfy the demanding palate of the international set.

POSITANO AFTER DARK

At the far end of Spiaggia Grande is the dance club **Music on the Rocks** (☎ 089-875-874), carved into the cliff side and overlooking its own section of beach. Catch a boat with the Beautiful People to nearby Praiano and the hot club of the coast, **Africana** (☎ 089-874-042), another sea-level grotto, this one with watery sinkholes in the dance floor (which fishermen sometimes come to dredge while the party's going on). You must book ahead at **Agenzia Viaggi Positour** (☎ 089-875-555) or **Music Station Quicksilver** (☎ 089-811-963) for the boat (15,000L/$9 round-trip) that leaves at 11:30pm from the Pontile Lucibello dock at Spiaggia Grande, to return at 3am. Both clubs open nightly June to August, weekends in May and September, and close the rest of the year.

EN ROUTE TO AMALFI

About 3km (2 mi.) beyond Positano is its sister hamlet of **Praiano,** also a trendy resort (only much smaller and still little known) with a majolica-domed church. If you're making the trip by sea, keep your eyes peeled for the *Madonna Col Bambino di Praiano,* a particular rock formation rising from the cliff face that mimics the image of the Madonna and Child, and another that resembles a great pharaoh.

Past the village of Furore the bus pops out of a tunnel to ride a bridge across one of the coast's most dramatic gorges, the **Vallone del Furore.** At kilometer marker 24, outside the fishing community of Conca dei Marini, are the stairs (or elevator) down to the **Grotta dello Smeraldo (Emerald Grotto).** This cavern was originally formed above sea level by the volcanic activity that affected the whole region (notice the stalactites and stalagmites, which can't form in sea grottoes). Mysteriously sunken deep in the water is a ceramic crèche, on which the effect of light refracting an emerald green is unusually mystical. Admission is 5,000L ($3; plus the cost of the excursion boat to get there; see individual sections for info) and it's open daily 9:30am to 3:30pm.

8 Amalfi: A Modest Seaside Village

61km (38 mi.) SE of Naples, 18km (11 mi.) E of Positano, 34km (21 mi.) W of Salerno, 272km (169 mi.) SE of Rome.

The modest seaside village of **Amalfi,** tacked tastefully onto the cliffside, will surprise you initially because of its lack of pretentiousness and abundance of charm. Long a legendary tourist destination and home of movie stars (Sophia Loren kept a home on the hill), you'd expect something at least *bigger*. But not even the decades-long tourist crush has turned this once-great maritime port sour; rather, hospitality is clearly alive and well in Amalfi.

The whitewashed streets of Amalfi are full of history, recalling a time in the Middle Ages when it rivaled Genoa, Pisa, and Venice as a trading behemoth. Amalfi's connections with the Orient (mainly Constantinople) led it to introduce to Europe such novelties as paper, carpets, and the compass—though Amalfi holds that they themselves invented the latter, having gone so far as to erect a statue in the middle of the piazza in honor of hometown boy Flavio Gioia (who more than likely just perfected it).

At its height in the 11th century, Amalfi had a population of 70,000 and dominated the Tyrrhenian Sea. But the Normans moved in in 1131, and soon after, Pisa swept in not once but twice to trounce its rival. The final blow came in 1343, when a one-two punch of tidal waves and earthquakes slumped much of the grand city into the sea. Amalfi is now a much-reduced little resort town of 6,000 inhabitants, but left over from its glory days are a spectacular Duomo and the Tavole Amalfitane, the western world's first maritime code, a set of laws that continued to rule trade and the sea until 1570.

ESSENTIALS

GETTING THERE   SITA buses run frequently and efficiently (except for the inevitable road blockage at those tight curves) up and down the Amalfi coast, from **Sorrento** (4,100L/$2) to **Salerno** (3,200L/$2). Piazza Flavio Gioia is the hub for all buses, including those for excursions to **Ravello** (1,800L/90¢) and **Positano** (2,300L/$15). SITA buses also run to **Napoli** (6,100L/$3) via the autostrada. Tickets can be purchased in a number of establishments around the terminus, just look for the blue SITA insignia.

Ferries arrive and depart regularly to and from **Sorrento** (18,000L/$9), **Positano** (7,000L/$4), and **Salerno** (6,000L/$3). For information and reservations call **Tra.vel.mar** at ☎ **089-873-190,** but it's just as easy pick up the tickets at the dock.

If you've come by **car,** you'll just be carrying around dead weight, because local traffic laws prohibit the circulation of vehicles during specified times daily, effectively closing the town (for those compliant) to traffic for extended periods daily. Die-hard drivers can park at the lot in town for 3,000L ($2) per hour, but most hotels offer parking either free or in conjunction with a nearby lot for around 25,000L ($13) per day.

VISITOR INFORMATION The **tourist office** (☎ **089-871-107;** fax 089-872-619) is hidden at the back-left corner of a lovely little courtyard inside Corso Roma 19, up the slope past Piazza Gioia.

AMBLING THROUGH AMALFI

The star of Amalfi is the 13th-century ✪ **Duomo,** on Piazza del Duomo, its magnificent Lombard-Norman facade of striped arches, Gothic tracery, interlocking arches and glittering mosaics rising majestically at the top of a mighty set of 62 stairs.

Towering over it on the left is a 13th-century bell tower with a majolica-tiled drum surrounded by four smaller drums. Simeon of Syria crafted the cathedral's massive bronze doors (whose panels feature crosses and saints inlaid with silver) in Constantinople in 1066. Like other great maritime powers, Amalfi stole itself a saint from the Holy Land in the 12th century. This is why the body of St. Andrew the Apostle lies under the altar and why 30 days prior to the sacred "feasts" of 27 June (patron festivities for St. Andrew) and Christmas, the venerable saint's head is exposed in a glass reliquary atop the tomb. A side entrance to the left of the main entrance gives access (for 3,000L/$2; open daily 9am to 5pm) to the crypt via the Chiostro del Paradiso (Cloisters of Paradise), tiny Saracen-style cloisters from 1263 composed of interlocking and superimposed pointed arches forming a complex pattern above the colonnade.

Off Corso delle Repubbliche Marinare (the road east along the harbor), upstairs in the municipal buildings that surround a small piazza, is a tiny **Museo Civico** (free), which preserves the original *Tavole Amalfitane* outlining the oldest maritime code in the world.

Up the main road past the Monastery of St. Basilio, Via Pietro Capuano becomes Via Marino del Giudice and finally Via delle Cartiere, where you'll find some of the oldest paper mills in Europe. Today the mills form a center for the production of **local traditional paper** and stationery, some crafted by descendents of the original artisans.

HITTING THE BEACH & A BOAT EXCURSION   Amalfi's **beach,** right in the center of the port off Piazza Flavio Gioia, isn't much to write home about, but it is convenient, the pastels of Amalfi are at its back and the water is exceptionally clear. A lounge chair and umbrella will cost you a sizable 20,000L ($10) per day, but considering the alternative of unforgiving pebbles, the expense is well worth the trouble. You can rent a canoe on the beach closest to the parking lot at **Andrea Beach** (☎ **089-872-956**) for only 10,000L ($5) per hour. Jolly Signor Rosa at **Da Rosa** (at the far end of the port; ☎ **089-872-147**) rents **rowboats** (15,000L/$$8 per hour; 50,000L/$25 per day) and **motorboats** (from 60,000L/$30 for 2 hours to 200,000L/$100 for 7 hours, depending on the horsepower; rates include gas); boats have a capacity of up to four people.

From the docks, excursion boats leave hourly between 9am and 3pm for **trips to the Grotta dello Smeraldo** (see above) for 10,000L ($5) not including the admission fee. The round-trip jaunt lasts about 1 hour. By land, **SITA** runs service from Piazza Gioia to Conca dei Marini, 24 torturous kilometers away, where you can get an elevator down to the cave. Once you've exhausted the modest sites and sounds in town, consider hopping over to **Capri** (21,000L/$11) or evading the coastal road by cruising to nearby **Positano** (7,000L/$4) or **Sorrento** (18,000L/$9).

AFFORDABLE PLACES TO STAY

The Papal Jubilee sent prices sky high, even for the lower end hotels, with no relief in sight. Luckily, the increases for the most part have been accompanied by renovations, so in Amalfi, as in life, you get what you pay for. If you have no luck finding a spare room and you're willing to wing it, **Divina Costiera Travel** across from the SITA depot (☎ **089-872/467**) will find you a place to stay for a service charge of 5,000L ($2.50). But don't try this in July and August, when any hotel within driving distance of the beach won't even be able to offer you floor space for a sleeping bag. High season in Amalfi usually runs June to September.

Amalfi. Via dei Pastai 3 (about halfway up the main road in town, look for a sign pointing up a stair/street off to the left), 84011 Amalfi (SA). ☎ **089-872-440.** Fax 089-872-250. www.starnet.it/hamalfi. E-mail: hamalfi@starnet.it. 40 units. TV TEL. 70,000–135,000L

($35–$68) single; 90,000–180,000L ($45–$90) double. Rates include breakfast; you may request a room without breakfast for a savings of 10,000L/$5 per person. 25,000–30,000L ($13–$15) half-pension supplement preferred in June–Aug. AE, MC, V. Parking 20,000–25,000L ($10–$13).

Located in a back corner of whitewashed streets just off the main drag, the Amalfi is a hands-on enterprise, managed by a capable team of seven siblings, along with their husbands and wives. The hotel itself is basic, with spare and functional light-toned wood furnishings on broad tile floors. Some rooms overlook the narrow white alleys surrounding the hotel, (no. 406 has a view of the dome's drum) while others face the pretty gardens whose orange trees provide the fruit for your breakfast juice. There's a pretty good **restaurant** on the roof terrace with views of the historic center and a shaded garden patio perfect for reading a book as the sun dips in the sky.

☼ Cappuccini Convento. Via Annunziatella 46, 84011 Amalfi (SA). ☎ **089-871-877.** Fax 089-871-886. www.amalfinet.it/cappuccini. E-mail: Cappuccini@amalfinet.it. 54 units. 150,000–200,000L ($75–$100) single; 260,000–320,000 ($130–$160) double. Rates include breakfast. 30,000L ($15) supplement for A/C. AE, DC, MC, V. Parking in garage 30,000L ($15) per day.

Don't expect sharp angles and pristine paint in this 13th-century monastery built around the still existing chapel of San Pietro and its Arabic-style Norman cloisters. Instead, this Member of Historic Places offers character to spare in rooms combined from units of two monastic cells each. All rooms are the same (except for no.138, a breathtaking suite with a sunken stone tub, Gothic arches, and a terrace for 80,000L to 100,000L/$40 to $50 more)—worn but clean spaces with long narrow solariums overlooking the bay. The baths are unrenovated, more utilitarian than anything. What's superior about the monastery is its spectacular clifftop position, spread out along endless terraces wrapped in vines and lemon trees. The grounds were designed to have nooks for introspection, turned into a sundeck here or a garden cafe there. The private beach is free to guests, with all the amenities you can imagine available on request. Note that late-night arrivals have to call up to the reception from the phone below to request that the elevator be turned on.

Residence. Via delle Reppubliche Marinare 9, 84011 Amalfi (SA). ☎ **089-872-229.** Fax 089-873-070. 27 units. TV TEL. 140,000–170,000L ($70–$85) single; 180,000–220,000L ($90–$110) double. Rates include breakfast. AE, MC, V. Parking 25,000L ($13) in nearby garage. Closed mid-Oct to Easter (but open all year if demand exists).

The faded, harbor-front facade doesn't bode well, but upstairs in the guest quarters, the Residence is decidedly more upscale than one might expect. A large vaulted dining room has a shaded terrace overlooking the beach, there are statues in niches, and a swirling central wrought iron staircase. The rooms, all with balconies, are nicer than the price would suggest, and two of them even have Jacuzzis. Many have patterned tile floors, new bath fixtures, oils on the walls, and pleasantly unobtrusive furniture mixed with some antiques. Rooms on the front are filled with the traffic sounds of the Amalfi Drive below by day (and Vespa-mounted teens by night), but they also have a great view of the beach and port for people-watching. Side rooms overlook the slightly quieter road leading into Piazza del Duomo.

Worth a Splurge

Marina Riviera. Via Pantaleone Comite 9, 84011 Amalfi (SA). ☎ **089-871-104.** Fax 089-871-351. 22 units. A/C MINIBAR TV TEL. 190,000–220,000L ($95–$110) tiny single; 230,000–290,000L ($115–$145) double used as single; 250,000–300,000L ($125–$150) double. Rates include breakfast. AE, DC, MC, V. Parking 25,000L ($13) in garage with valet.

Partly carved into the rock on an outward curve of the Amalfi Drive leading east out of town, the Marina Riviera overlooks Amalfi's beach side, with the Duomo a 4-minute stroll away. It's run by the hospitable Gargano family, which also owns the Amalfi Coast's premier Santa Caterina as well as the Residence (above). The rooms are big and airy and done with Mediterranean simplicity: whitewashed walls, clean tile floors, and firm beds. The spacious baths were recently redone, loaded with useful amenities you probably forgot, and well stocked with fabulously plush towels. All the rooms are spacious, with double-glazed balcony doors that provide front-row seats to the morning spectacle of light over the bay. An ample breakfast, enhanced by stunning views, is served on the terrace overlooking the water.

GREAT DEALS ON DINING

Don't come to Amalfi looking for bargains, and be prepared to eat a lot of pasta and pizza. Several beachfront establishments offer the added pleasure of the sound of the lapping waves, but the hard-to-find trattorias are bound to be more characteristic of the countryside. For a quick bite, grab a warm shrimp salad panino (they have other standards like prosciutto and mozzarella) at **Lo Spuntino di Cecilia** in the courtyard on Corso Repubbliche Marinare east of Piazza Flavio Gioia (sandwiches for under 6,000L/$3). The ladies behind the counter can get you discounts on beach lounges and scooter rentals (just ask). Another quick and hearty bite can be had at **Porto Salvo** off of Piazza del Duomo (under the arch to the port ☎ **089-872-445**), where an enormous slice of potato pizza or a panino goes for 6,000 to 8,000L ($3 to$4).

✪ Da Barraca. Piazza degli Dogi (off the left of Piazza del Duomo, duck under the arched street and bear right). ☎ **089-871-285.** Reservations recommended. Primi 10,000–14,000L ($5–$7); secondi 10,000–30,000L ($5–$15; fixed-price menu 25,000L ($13) without wine. AE, MC, V. Thurs–Tues noon–3pm and 7pm–midnight. CAMPANIAN/SEAFOOD.

A real bargain gem, this restaurant is the only one on a truly typical piazza in Amalfi, surrounded by the fruit stands, butcher shops, and *alimentari* (neighborhood grocery stores) that ensure your food will be fresh. In cooler weather, you can sit under the fishing nets of the glassed-in veranda listening to records of Neapolitan guitar music. The meat-stuffed cannelloni are hearty, with cracked pepper for a spicy edge, while the perfectly cooked gnocchi alla sorrentina and *farfalle vongole e rughetta* (bow-tie pasta with clams and rughetta) are also worthy. Secondi include scaloppine al Marsala, an omelet with mozzarella, or roasted fresh fish. The waiters are perennially harried, but give them time and while you wait for the bill, enjoy a *profitterole al limone* (pastry stuffed with lemon cream).

Il Tarì. Via Pietro Capuano 9–11 (a continuation of Via Cavour, the main road into town). ☎ **089-871-832.** Reservations recommended. Primi 9,000–15,000L ($5–$8); secondi 15,000–27,000L ($8–$14); pizza 4,000–16,000L ($2–$8); *menù turistico* 30,000L ($15) without wine. AE, MC, V. Tues–Sun 11:30am–3pm and 7–11pm. AMALFITANA/PIZZA.

Il Tarì's two packed rooms on Amalfi's main street are separated by low arches that do nothing to stem the flow of humanity drawn by the friendly atmosphere and reasonable prices. It's a bit cozier than Da Maria down the block, despite the noisy babble in a half dozen tourist tongues that keeps the atmosphere lively. The pizza has excellent crust—try it topped *à la Tarì*, with mozzarella, prosciutto, Parmesan shavings, and arugula. If you'd prefer pasta, dig into local specialty *scialatielli*, either *con frutti di mare* (seafood) or *con pomodoro, melanzane, e mozzarella* (a rich gooey mix of tomatoes, eggplant, and mozzarella). Secondi are less exciting, with a list of the same old *scaloppine* (veal cooked with herbs), *calamari in umido* (stewed octopus), or the somewhat more successful *pesce al cartoccio* (fish baked in foil).

La Taverna del Duca. Piazza Spirito Santo 26 (at the end of the main shopping drag). ☎ **089-872-755.** Primi 12,000–22,000L ($6–$11); secondi 15,000–32,000L ($8–$16). AE, MC, V. Fri–Wed noon–3pm and 7–10:30pm. Closed Nov– Dec.

Just as the crowds thin out on the main drag and you thought it was time to turn back, a handful of checked tablecloths appear, sharing the Piazza Spirito Santo with crowds of locals, holding their children's hands in one hand and dinner's *pagnotta* (bread loaf) in the other. With only ten tables snugly placed under brick arches, Taverna del Duca fulfills exactly your expectation of a local Italian *cantina*, with the outdoor tables on the small piazza picking up the slack in warm weather. The portly chef sits outside between meals, studiously streamlining the upcoming menu. Expect simple high-quality local cuisine like the omnipresent *spaghetti alle vongole* (with mussels), or the fresh catch of the day prepared with olives.

WORTH A SPLURGE

Eolo. Via. Pantaleone Comite 3 (on the left up the hill after leaving Piazza Flavio Gioia. ☎ **089-871-241.** Reservations suggested. Primi 18,000L–25,000L ($9–$13); secondi with *contorno* (side dish) 22,000–35,000L ($11–$18). AE, DC, MC, V. Daily 12:30–2:30pm and 7:30pm–midnight. Closed Tues in winter and one month in winter. SICILIAN.

The Gargano family (of the Marina Riviera, among other hotel establishments in town) taught their family well, and the proof is in the pudding, or shall we say, pasta. Schooled in the art of international cuisine, daughter Catherina also fills the roles of chef, sommelier, and manager, bringing dining in Amalfi to a new level. The menu changes daily and according to the season, but you can always count on the finest quality produce, fresh pasta, desserts made on the premises, and a decadent rotation of homemade breads (if you get olive bread, it's your lucky night). Eolo also boasts a superior selection of regional Italian wines.

9 Ravello: A Retreat for Celebrities

275km (171 mi.) SE of Rome, 66km (41 mi.) SE of Naples, 29km (18 mi.) W of Salerno.

Poised between sea and sky, the mountain retreat of ✪ **Ravello,** 6km (3½ mi.) from Amalfi and 1,155 feet up in the hills, peeks through the stunning natural beauty of its surroundings with sculpted gardens, luxuriant villas, and medieval churches. A tiny town of profuse flowering vines and sweet-scented landscapes bursting in color, Ravello makes a marvelous escape from the tourist crush of the sun-worshiping towns down on the coast, and has long been a favorite among celebrities like Matt Dillon, Susan Saran-don, Tim Robbins, and Sean Connery looking for a quiet retreat. Gore Vidal maintains a villa here, and D. H. Lawrence and Greta Garbo both spent time unwinding in Rav-ello, a lofty Garden of Eden along the already enchanting Amalfi Coast.

Almost every bend in the narrow alleys and stone steps opens up to another eye-popping vista down into the **Valle del Dragone (Valley of the Dragon),** a deep and lush terraced ravine strewn with white houses and small hamlets or over the distant eastern stretch of the Amalfi Coast. Crumbling villas whose grounds and lush pleasure gardens have become public parks provide most of the attractions, leaving you to do little more than relax and smell the freshly scented air.

While exploring the coast from Ravello will require a trip into Amalfi (for bus trans-fers or ferry excursions), the indulgent absolute relaxation of Ravello will certainly make the added effort worth your while.

ESSENTIALS

GETTING THERE   SITA minibuses run hourly from Amalfi's Piazza Flavio Gioia to Ravello (1,800L/90¢). Ideally, the trip takes under 15 minutes, but during rush hour, expect unparalleled gridlock at the coastal road turnoff. The bus lets you off just outside the tunnel-like gate into town.

VISITOR INFORMATION   There's a **tourist office** at the unmistakable Piazza del Duomo under the left side of the cathedral (☎ **089-857-096;** fax 089-857-977). The office is open Monday to Saturday 8am to 8pm (7pm October to March) and administers a technically challenged billboard outside with a list of the hotels in town.

WHAT TO SEE & DO

A constant assault of natural perfumes of lily, lemons, bougainvillea, and pine fabricate the perfect settings for the **series of chamber music,** orchestra, and soloist concerts that run throughout the year. In July, the music of Richard Wagner (another Ravellophile) is celebrated with performances by the likes of Plácido Domingo, conducted by Zubin Mehta and backed by world-class orchestras from Israel, London, Moscow, and so on. The Villa Rufolo (see below) sponsors a series of outdoor concerts, but seating for 2,700 still can't support the demand for the annual sunrise concerts that take place on August 10 and 11 (for info contact the **Ravello Concert Society** ☎ **089-858-149;** www.rcs.amalficoast.it).

Duomo. Piazza del Duomo. Admission to church free, museum entrance 2,000L ($1). Daily 9:30am–1pm and 3–7pm.

Ravello's Romanesque cathedral was built in 1076. The central bronze doors were cast in 1099 in Constantinople and feature disarmingly simple low-relief panels of archers, warriors, and Bible scenes. Inside are a pair of gorgeous 12th-century pulpits, carved of marble and carried on the backs of lions. The panels of the pulpits are inlaid with mosaics of swirling designs, Christian symbols (look for the whale swallowing Jonah), and fantastic mythical beasts. The small museum displays Renaissance busts, late Imperial cinerary urns, and more medieval carvings and bits of mosaic.

✪ **Villa Cimbrone.** At the end of Via Santa Chiara (take Via San Francesco out of Piazza del Duomo). No phone. Admission 8,000L ($4) adults, 5,000L ($3) under 12. Daily 9am–7:30pm.

Getting to Villa Cimbrone is half the fun, down a stepped alley open to the verdant valley below. The parts of the 1904 villa you can explore are full of crypt-like nooks and cloistered crannies. The grounds are a huge playground of palms, magnificently spreading umbrella pines, ivy-clad walls, hidden flower gardens guarded by statues, panoramic terraces lined with busts, and vertigo-inducing cliff-top vistas from tiny temple-like gazebos.

✪ **Villa Rufolo.** Piazza Duomo. ☎ **089-857-657.** Admission 5,000L ($3) adults, 3,000L ($2) under 12 and over 65. Daily 9am to 8pm (some days it closes at 4pm).

The villa itself was started by the powerful Rufolo family in the 11th century and served as a residence for several popes. The Saracen and Norman motifs were added in later generations—take a moment to enjoy the Moorish cloisters with their sharply pointed arches and interlacing patterns. The rooms of the restructured central villa are now used for art exhibits, and the surrounding grounds—filled with intimate flowering gardens set into the extensive villa ruins above a spectacular view down the eastern Amalfi Coast—are the backdrop for excellent outdoor concerts. This is only appropriate, since upon seeing this tropical paradise in 1880, composer Richard Wagner exclaimed, "The magical garden of Klingsor has been found!" and, inspired, went on to complete his *Parsifal.*

AFFORDABLE PLACES TO STAY

Villa Amore. Via dei Fusco 5 (a cross street of Via Santa Chiara), 84010 Ravello (SA) ☎/fax **089-857-135.** 16 units. TEL. 65,000–75,000L ($33–$38) single; 110,000–120,000L ($55–$60) double. Rates include breakfast. MC, V.

This gorgeous spot on the hilltop has a spectacular view of the valley and mountains— but you'll have to get there first. Run by a pair of kindly ladies, Villa Amore is quite a climb above the main piazza, but that only makes it feel more like a hidden retreat. The old-lady bedspreads are a little soft and the phones aren't direct dial, but most baths are fairly new, the tile floors are scattered with rugs, it's heated in winter, and there are abundant breezes to part the curtains in summer. All rooms have small terraces; from second-floor rooms this vista is unobstructed, but downstairs you have to peek past a little flowering garden. The setting is quiet as can be, and breakfast is served on the panoramic terrace. If you simply can't bear the thought of hauling your luggage up and down stepped alleyways, head over for lunch or dinner on the terrace restaurant.

✪ **Villa Maria.** Via San Chiara 2 (follow Via San Francesco toward the Villa Cimbrone), 84010 Ravello (SA). ☎ **089-857-255.** Fax 089-857-071. 26 units. A/C MINIBAR TV TEL. 250,000–290,000L ($125–$145) single; 300,000–380,000L ($150–$190) double; 600,000–680,000L ($300–$340) suite. Rates include breakfast. AE, DC, MC, V. Free parking at nearby sister hotel.

Sight unseen, Villa Maria is the type of place you book for your 2 nights in Ravello, but once arrived, enchants you into extending your stay. Converted from a 1935 private home, this hotel offers a taste of the refined elegance that Ravello enjoyed in past centuries. The tone is set by an old-fashioned salon off the entrance, where a grand chandelier hangs over an antique silver tea setting. Floor tiles in the rooms are richly patterned, the walls are hung with quality prints and oils, and the period furnishings mix with the odd futon couch. Firm mattresses rest on genuine box springs backed by antique wooden or brass headboards, and many of the ample baths feature Jacuzzi tubs and multiple-jet showers. Almost all of the rooms enjoy some type of outdoor access or view, enhancing the luxurious tone of this spectacular location. Villa Maria's garden restaurant, recommended below, is one of the town's best. For an afternoon in the quiet refuge of little Villa Eva across the way, pop across the way to the owners' little Villa Eva park; in the summer, an outdoor pizzeria and bar set the mood (ask for key at reception).

GREAT DEALS ON DINING

La Colonna. Via Roma 22. ☎ **089-857-411.** Reservations recommended. Primi 12,000– 18,000L ($6–$9); secondi 12,000–25,000L ($6–$13); pizza 8,000–15,000L ($4–$8). AE, DC, MC, V. Daily noon–3pm and 7–midnight; Closed Wed Nov–Easter. CAMPANIAN.

Call ahead for one of the few tables set in the ancient flower-filled courtyard, or sit under the Gothic ceilings of the long main room that hint at the building's origins 800 years ago as stables for the palazzo above. Ask about the fresh pasta of the day, which may be *tagliatelle* (thick, flat pasta ribbons) with frutti di mare or in a creamy tomato sauce studded with eggplant, or *agnolotti* (like ravioli) stuffed with seafood in a zucchini sauce. In the secondi department, the restaurant's specialty is fish. If you're looking for something light, try the baked tomatoes stuffed with rice.

✪ **Cumpá Cosimo.** Via Roma 44–46. ☎ **089-857-156.** Reservations highly recommended. Primi 10,000–25,000L ($5–$13); secondi 15,000–40,000L ($8–$20); pizza 8,000–15,000L ($4–$8). AE, MC, V. Daily 12:15–3:30pm and 6:30pm–midnight. Closed Mon Nov–Dec 10 and Jan 8–Feb. Left at Duomo, hidden behind hanging beads on your right immediately after arch. CAMPANIAN.

Beloved culinary matriarch Netta Buttone presides over these wood-beamed dining rooms, effusively displaying her joys of cooking and providing her guests with a memorable evening. Cumpá Cosimo has been a Ravello institution for more than 70 years—Bogie and Jackie O were once customers, and Gore Vidal is something of a regular. Ingredients come from the family farm, concocted into the likes of *gnocchi alla sorrentina*, marvelous *crespolini alla Cumpá Cosimo* (pasta crepes layered with prosciutto and cheese then rolled and baked), *fusilli al ragout*, and cheesy *maccheroni al forno*. The best way to sample the bounty is the *piatto misto della casa*, seven sampler-sized portions of Netta's primi, each better than the last. Secondi include *coniglio alla cacciatore* (rabbit with tomatoes and olives), *agnello scottaditto* (delicious lamb chops), and fresh fish. For dessert, try one of Netta's storied soufflés, or a peach or fig from the family orchards.

WORTH A SPLURGE

Villa Maria. Via Santa Chiara 2. ☎ **089-857-255.** Reservations highly recommended. Primi 11,000–22,000L ($7–$13); secondi 13,000–28,000L ($8–$17). AE, DC, MC, V. Daily 12:30–3pm and 7:30–10:30pm. Closed Tues Oct–Easter. CAMPANIAN.

Villa Maria scores twice, with both the best splurge hotel and the finest restaurant in town. The dining terrace, which overlooks the hamlets of the Dragone Valley, is shaded by spreading tree branches and filled with the strains of classical music from hidden speakers. The waiter will suggest the specialties of the day, but if you can't choose from among the mouth-watering array of primi, order the *trittico*, a sampler of the chef's proudest recipes. If you're lucky, this may include *soffiatini* (crepes with local cheese and spinach) or *ravioli del pescatore* (seafood stuffed ravioli in a red clam sauce). The menu changes daily according to seasonal availability of ingredients. Up in the mountains and this close to the sea, you can bet on fresh fish and local game. The extremely versatile owner, Vincenzo Palumbo, sponsors cooking courses, headed by the highly respected chef, Goffredo Mansi, who occasionally leads training sessions for the American chain, the Olive Garden.

10 Paestum & Its Greek Temples

42km (26 mi.) S of Salerno, 100km (62 mi.) SE of Naples, 304km (189 mi.) SE of Rome.

Poseidonia, or the City of Poseidon, was founded in the 6th century B.C. by Greek colonists from Sybaris. It went about its business unremarkably as the Roman colony of **Paestum** from 273 B.C. until around 79 B.C., when a series of eruptions from Mt. Vesuvius resulted in the silting up of the city's river. These swamplands brought about a malarial plague that decimated the population, and in the midst of a decline during the 9th century, the citizens of Paestum didn't know whether to flee to the hills from the brutal Saracen invaders or the mosquitoes.

Despite legends of a lost city, Paestum was all but forgotten until the 18th century, when a bunch of local farmers, working to build a road through the area, stumbled across three incredible ✪ **Greek temples** jutting out of the landscape, surrounded by blue-gray mountains. The rest is bureaucratic history.

You'll need about 2 hours for a leisurely visit of the archaeological area, but gauge another hour for a visit to the museum. Although the site is doable as a day-trip from Naples or the Amalfi Coast, it'll be best enjoyed at sunset or during the magical morning hours before the day-trippers arrive and there's still time before the site gets overrun to stop and smell the infamously enormous roses (which continue to bloom twice a year in gardens around the site).

ESSENTIALS

GETTING THERE   By Train   Only local trains (*diretto* or *regionale*) stop at Paestum. **From Naples,** there are eight daily runs (90 min; 8,500L/$4). **From Salerno,** nine daily trains headed to the "Paola" stop at Paestum (35 min; 4,900L/$3).

By Bus   SCAT buses (☎ **0974/838-415**) from **Salerno** (☎ **089-226-604**) are more frequent than trains (four per day; none on Sundays) and let you off right at the museum in front of the archaeological site (50 min; 4,900L/$3). They leave Salerno from Piazza della Concordia at the waterfront, a few blocks down from the train station (and a few blocks over from where the Amalfi Coast SITA buses stop).

By Car   From Naples, follow the A3 to the Battipaglia exit and follow the S18 to Paestum. From Salerno, take provincial road 175 south.

GETTING AROUND   Paestum is in the middle of nowhere in mozzarella country, and the only signs of civilization are the postcard stands, hotels, and restaurants that a tourist site draws. From the train station, you can bargain with a taxi driver for the trip to your hotel (don't go over 20,000L/$10). Otherwise, head out of the station and continue straight under the arch at the intersection. After a 15-minute, 1km (½-mi.) stroll, the road ends at the archaeological site and Albergo delle Rose. For the museum, main site entrance, and a dinky tourist office, turn right. For the Hotel Helios, Nettuno restaurant, Porta della Giustizia site entrance (and, eventually, the beach): turn left, then right, for another 5-minute walk.

VISITOR INFORMATION   There's a **tourist office** near the museum at Via Magna Grecia 155 (☎ **0828-811-016;** fax 0828-722-322;). It's open Monday to Saturday 8am to 2pm.

EXPLORING ANCIENT GREECE IN CAMPANIA

Scavi (Archaeological Site). Via Magna Grecia. ☎ **0828-811-023.** Combo ticket with museum: 12,000L ($6); 8,000L($4) independently. Daily 9am–an hour before sunset (as early as 3:30pm in late Nov, 7:30pm June–July). Closed first and third Mon of every month, May 1, Dec 25, and New Year's Day.

Amid the grasses stained with poppies and crisscrossed by the low stone walls that outline the remains of the ancient city rise three mighty temples, all of which still go by their erroneous old names. The modestly sized **Basilica** was actually a **Temple of Hera,** built in 530 B.C. and the oldest temple at Paestum. Next door is the enormous and strikingly well-preserved ✪ **Temple of Neptune,** in reality, probably dedicated to Apollo or Zeus, built in 450 B.C. and one of the three most complete Greek temples in the world. Its pediments and entablature are virtually intact atop fourteen 30-foot-high fluted columns down each side, six each across the front and back, and a cella in the center divided by two more rows of smaller columns. Farther off in the site is the **Temple of Ceres,** more likely a temple to Athena, and the midget of the bunch, built around 500 B.C. and preserving, along with all 34 of its columns, some architrave and large chunks of its pediments. The temples of Hera and Neptune have been swathed in scaffolding for restoration work, and there's no word as yet on when they'll be unveiled.

Museo Nazionale (National Museum). Via Magna Grecia. ☎ **0828-811-023.** Combo ticket with archaeological site: 12,000L ($6); 8,000L ($4) independently. Daily 9am–6:30pm. Closed first and third Monday of every month, May 1, Dec 25, and New Year's Day.

Along with archaic Greek sculpture and vases, this museum preserves a great series of **metopes** (carved reliefs) from a nearby sanctuary of Hera, which depict scenes from Homeric myth and women dancing to honor the goddess. The museum's ✪ **Tomb of the Diver** paintings from 480 B.C., are the only surviving examples of ancient

Greek painting in the world. Aside from their namesake image of a bronzed youth diving into a blue sea (a symbol of the journey to the afterlife), these paintings focus on a homoerotic banquet scene in which the revelers play at games and musical instruments (and at flirting) while reclining on couches.

A GREAT DEAL ON DINING

Ristorante Nettuno. Via Principe di Piemonte (in the archaeological zone). ☎ **0828-811-028.** Reservations recommended. Primi 8,000–16,000L ($4–$8); secondi 12,000–24,000L ($6–$12). AE, DC, MC, V. Tues–Sun 12:30–3pm. July–Aug sometimes open evenings and on Mon. ITALIAN.

Paestum's best, and certainly most scenic, lunch remains at this 18th-century country villa, converted to a restaurant in 1920s and often taken over by entire busloads of tourists. It's wedged between the parking lot and archaeological site entrance, with a glassed-in patio a scant 500 feet from the temples. Arrive or book early to get that prime view of the ruins, but if you find the crowds milling about the souvenir stands and into the site distracting, you can retreat to the grandly arched interior. The house dish is *crespolini* (baked pasta crepes wrapped around fresh mozzarella studded with prosciutto), or start with *stracciatella* (egg-drop soup with Parmesan) before sampling their *cotoletta alla milanese* (breaded veal cutlet) or *pollo al forno* (oven-roasted chicken).

11 The Gargano Peninsula & Tremiti Islands

237km (142 mi.) NE of Naples, 39km (23.4 mi.) NE of Foggia.

Originally an island, the **Gargano Peninsula,** a rugged and surging landmass forming a spur above the heel of Apuglia, was connected to the mainland by deposits carried down from the Apennines. The resulting formations are mountainous steppes that descend dramatically into the sea, perforated by glittering caves of emerald and blue, and largely accessible only by boat. Ancient fishing villages have grown into resort towns like **Vieste,** with its long beaches and a 13th-century cathedral dominating a whitewashed historic center, and **Mattinata,** a simple agricultural town surrounded by miles and miles of olive groves. In the center of the promontory is the **Foresta Umbra,** the largest leafy forest in Europe and a cool shaded retreat protecting a host of endangered species.

   The Tremiti Islands comprise an archipelago of mini islands, including the isle-mountain of San Nicola (capped by the 11th century, half-ruined abbey of Santa Maria a Mare) and the pine-forested **San Domino,** where Roman Emperor Augustus' granddaughter Julia died in exile. The surrounding waters have been declared a marine preserve—good news for fish and scuba enthusiasts, with dives up to 150 feet in lukewarm waters amidst swarms of fish and spectacular red and yellow corals thriving offshore.

   As a primarily industrial port town, **Manfredonia's** only redeeming factor is that it hasn't yet succumbed to an overwhelming tourist influence, not that that would do it any harm. The city's main monument is its 13th- to 16th-century **Castello Svevo-Aragonese,** undergoing restorations as of this writing and housing a ✪ **museum** (☎ **0884-587-838**) that boasts a fantastic collection of funerary steles whose carvings reflect the whim of the day. The museum is open daily 8:30am to 1pm and 3:30 to 7pm (in summer the museum adds Saturday evenings 8:30 to 11:30pm) and is closed the first and last Monday of the month. Admission is 4,000L ($2) and half price for all under 18 or over 65.

   The Gargano has also long been a destination of religious pilgrimages, turning formerly forgotten towns into Las Vegas look-alikes, especially on religious holidays.

Monte Sant'Angelo manages to maintain its dignity in and around the **Basilica San-Michele Arcangelo** ☎ **0884-561-150,** a church assembled over the centuries atop a grotto where St. Michael the Archangel miraculously appeared to a local bishop in A.D. 490. This consecrated spot was once so important as to be an obligatory stop on the road to the Holy Land. Notice the ✪ **marble statue of the saint** carved by the hands of Andrea Sansovino in the 16th century. Entrance to the cave/basilica is free, but there is a fee of 5,000L ($3) to visit the crypt, during which a minimum of five people must be accompanied by a (non-English speaking) guide. If you (and four friends) ask the custodian (seated at the desk near the entrance) nicely, she'll take you down and charge you only 3,000L ($2) for a quick look.

Nearby is the 9th- to 15th-century **castello** (☎ **0884-565-444**), restored and embellished by Frederick II, who lived here with Bianca Lancia, mother of Manfredi and Enzo, his two illegitimate sons. Your kids might be creeped out but delighted by the fly-infested dungeons, making the admission of 3,000L ($2) worth your while. The castle can be visited daily from 8am to 7pm in summer, 9am to noon in winter.

Ultimately, the Gargano offers an undisturbed and always scenic escape from life, and most visitors head straight for the crystal clear waters along one of the numerous and painfully lovely rocky coves. If you're planning to drive the coast in search of a refreshing swim, be aware that you'll have to pay, and possibly lunch, in one of the dozens of campsites signposted along the roadside. While you're sweating, keep in mind that 40km (about 20 miles) can take 2 to 3 hours, and that much of the road rides the upper reaches of the cliffs and sadly out of the line of sight of the coastline. Plan your trip for the spring or early fall, for landscapes of irises in bloom and wondrous wild orchids of purple and green.

ESSENTIALS

GETTING THERE   Unless you're already in Apuglia and approaching from the direction of Bari, the unexciting provincial capital of **Foggia** will most likely be your gateway into the Gargano region. There are five **Eurostar trains** daily from **Rome** (3½ hours; 55,000L/$28) or if you're counting every lira, one Intercity night train (5 hours; 39,900L/$20). From **Bari,** you can either hop on one of the half-hourly trains (90 minutes; 12,000L/$6) or on the ultra comfortable Eurostar, which stops in Foggia on the way to Rome (1 hour; 25,100L/$13). If you're coming from **Napoli** Central, you'll have to change in Caserta for a Eurostar or Intercity train to Foggia (33,500L/$17); depending on how good your connections are, total travel time can vary from 2 hours and 20 minutes to 5½ hours. Less of a hassle and equally comfortable is the bus service run by **C.L.P. Bus** Line right from the middle of **Naples's** Piazza Garibaldi   ☎ 081-269-966 to Foggia's train station/transport hub (2 hours; 17,000/$9) leaving seven times a day, four on Sundays.

Ferrovie del Gargano, which runs both bus and train service, as well as SITA, run frequent daily connections (service is drastically reduced on Sundays) from **Foggia's** train station to **Manfredonia** (45 min.; 3,500L/$2), the logical gateway into the Gargano. A few buses continue up the coast to Vieste (another 85 minutes; 5,500L/$3).

GETTING AROUND   In addition to connecting Manfredonia to Vieste, Ferrovie del Gargano (☎ **167-296-247** toll-free, or 0881-772-491) and SITA (☎ **0881-773-117**), make frequent connections to Monte Sant'Angelo (40 to 60 minutes; 3,500L/$2), San Giovanni di Rotondo (40to 60 minutes; 3,500L/$2) and Mattinata (40 minutes; 2,000L/$1). Remember that service is greatly reduced (or nonexistent) on Sundays.

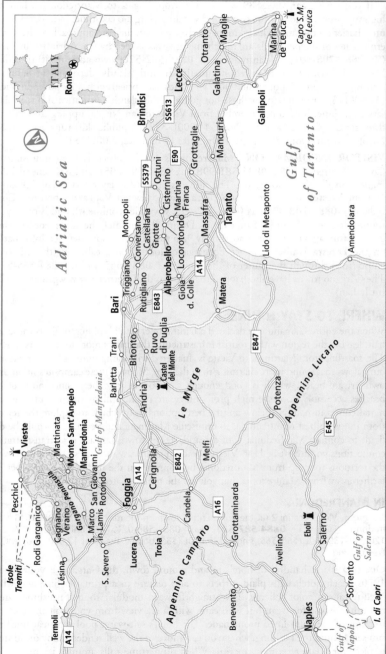

If you have a **car,** the SS89 will get you from Foggia to Manfredonia, where the highway begins to follow the scenic and winding Gargano coastline, in under 30 minutes. Easier on the stomach and more captivating than the land approach to the northern reaches of the peninsula are the changing vistas as seen by sea. **Adriatica** in Vieste (☎ **0884-708-501;** in Manfredonia ☎ **0884-582-520;** www.adriatica.it) runs daily hydrofoil service from Manfredonia to the Tremiti Islands, departing at 8am and returning at 5pm (2 hours; 68,000L/$34; kids half price) with a stopover in Vieste (34,000L/$17 round-trip for those not going to the islands). Adriatica also runs daily service in June, July, and September from Vieste to San Nicola, upping frequency to three times a day in August (1 hour; 44,000L/$22). A public skiff runs between San Nicola and San Domenico every 10 minutes (5 minutes; 2,000L/$1).

VISITOR INFORMATION   Manfredonia's tourist office is located upstairs at Corso Manfredi 26 (☎ **0884-581-998,** fax 0884-583-295), and has general information on the Gargano region. The office is open Monday to Saturday 8:30am to 1:30pm. **Vieste's** tourist office is on Piazza Kennedy, where Via Fazzini becomes Corso Italia (☎ **0884-708-806,** fax 0884-707-495, www.viesteonline.it). and is open year-round Monday to Saturday 8am to 2pm. During the summer, the office reopens Monday to Saturday 4 to 9:30pm and Sunday 9am to 1pm. For more-detailed information on the **Foresta Umbra,** contact Ecogargano, located in a cabin on the otherwise empty road through the center of the forest (☎ **0884-565-444** or 0884-565-579). The Gargano towns have also banded together on the Internet at www.gargano.it/citta (in Italian).

WHERE TO STAY & DINE

When the entire Gargano was declared a natural reserve, all building projects came to a halt, leaving the region with a tourist infrastructure that caters more to travelers in RVs. The coastline from Mattinata to Vieste is smattered with campgrounds with or without bungalows that sound more charming than they are. Many of these campsites sit on their own private beach, which is good enough a reason to stay there, since none of the beaches accessible from the high promontory are public (this is where a private boat rental comes in handy). Below are the best options from which to explore the region, from industrialized Manfredonia, to miniscule Mattinata and beyond. It would be difficult to confuse Manfredonia with a seaside resort town, but as far as transportation connections go, it can't be beat. Vieste comes in at an easy second, since you can avoid the tortuous road up from Manfredonia by hopping on the hydrofoil. Remember the farther away from Manfredonia that you go, the more isolated you will be.

IN MANFREDONIA

Gargano. Vle. Beccarini 2 (at the north end of town on the main shore drive), 71043 Manfredonia (FG). ☎ **0884-587-621.** Fax 0884-586-021. 46 units. A/C TV TEL. 120,000–130,000L ($60–$65) single; 170,000L ($85) double. Breakfast 12,000L ($6). MC, V. Free parking.

One of a sparse handful of hotels in and around town, the Gargano is your typical 1970s beach hotel, with plaid carpets to add texture to a primarily blue and white Mediterranean color scheme. The straightforward modular room furnishings aren't too much worse for wear, but who cares with a sea view from your balcony over the treetops of the palm-lined promenade? The hotel's salt-water pool is a treat until the sun sets behind the building, when you can move to the well-tended lobby or outdoor terraces for a late afternoon aperitif. When dinnertime rolls around, it's only a 10-minute seaside stroll to the castle and main drag on Corso Manfredi, but don't turn your nose up at the hotel restaurant; this is the best meal you'll get in town.

IN MATTINATA

Baia delle Zagare. 71030 Mattinata (11km/7 mi. north of Mattinata on the road to Vieste).
☎ **0884-550-155.** Fax 0884-550-884. 150 units. A/C MINIBAR TV TEL. 90,000–
110,000($45–$55) per person. Rates include breakfast. Half or full pension obligatory in Aug.
AE, DI, MC, V. Free parking. Closed Sept 22–May 26.

Located on one of the more scenic bays along the Mattinata-Vieste coastline, this bay
is featured in all the marketing brochures of the region. Horse-shaped "faraglione" and
"piramide" rock formations slice through the surface of the water, and there are
enough nearby marine caves to keep you occupied for some time. The resort is sensitively tucked amidst the pines high above the private beach, which is accessible via
either an elevator down through the rock or for the heartier, by stairs. Mediterranean
cottages dot the landscape, and the result is a welcoming, well-tended and rustic getaway. The only down side is that getting here without a car is nearly impossible. Book
early, because the convention center serves to fill up beds fairly regularly.

IN VIESTE

Hotel Seggio. Via Vieste 7/Piazza Seggio, 71019 Vieste (FG). ☎ **0884-708-123.** Fax
0884-708-727. E-mail: hotel.seggio@tiscalinet.it. 28 units. A/C TV TEL. Apr 1–July 27 and
Aug 25–Nov 31: 90,000–140,000L ($45–$70) single; 110,000–160,000L ($55–$80) double;
Half-pension required July 28–Aug 24: 145,000L ($73) per person. Rates include breakfast. AE,
DC, MC, V. Limited free parking; additional parking 10,000L ($5) per day. Closed Dec–Mar.

Vieste's 17th-century town hall, tucked halfway up the hill of the old quarter, is now
home to the Hotel Seggio. Although rooms vary greatly, most have functional furnishings, and sadly, time-weary beds. Some are low ceilinged and poorly lit, but almost
all accommodations are fairly large, and about half have water views. The choice room,
no. 104, has windows on two sides, a high wooden ceiling, and a terrace overlooking
both the sea and the postcard-size square below. The stone-walled restaurant has a
medieval flair and Pugliese menu. There's a sofa-filled bar area for piano music after
dinner some nights, and set into the cliffs below is a tiny pool and cement pier over
the shallow, sandy waters, accessible via a brand new elevator from the hotel down to
the beach.

A CASTLE EN ROUTE TO BARI

Frederick II's 1240 masterpiece of octagonal proportions, the ✪ **Castel del Monte**
(☎ **0883/569-848** or 0883/290-286), commands a 1780-foot hilltop in the solitude
of the Pugliese countryside, rising above wheat fields and olive groves in its pale
honey-gray stone and geometric perfection. No documentation survives to tell us the
history of the castle, but its unique design and location rule out such possibilities as
fortress or hunting lodge. The best supported hypothesis is that the castle served as
some type of astronomical observatory; in fact, when the sun is at its zenith, the shadows projected on the walls correspond to the changing signs of the zodiac, as well as
to the measurements of the castle. Corroborating this is Frederick II's affinity to
cultures of the East, including the *infidels,* who were intellectually light years ahead of
the West in terms of science (another revolutionary feature of the castle is the existence
of baths and toilets). Later used as a prison, the castle was left to decay until the end
of the 19th century, when the locality of Andria sold it to the State for the bargain
price of 25,000L ($13 in today's dollars). Private guides through the castle are pro-
vided free of charge (plus a donation at your discretion) by the City of Andria; look
for the kiosk near the entrance to the site marked "Comune di Andria."

Admission is 6,000L ($3); free for kids under 18. It's open daily 10:00am to
1:30pm and 2:30 to 7pm, ticket window closes a half-hour before; closed Christmas
and New Year's Day.

The castle sits along the **SS170bis** 20km (12 mi.) from the town of **Andria** (tourist info: ☎ **0883-592-283**). With or without a car, you'll have to pass through the town of Andria, where public transportation to the castle outside of the summer months is nonexistent. But even in the height of summer, bus service from Andria is kept to a minimum (25 min.; 2,000L/$1). For those throwing caution to the wind, a taxi will run a whopping 50,000L ($25) round-trip.

To get to Andria, take a twice hourly train **from Bari,** a **Ferrotranvia** bus from Bari Nord (60 to 90 min.; 10,200L/$5), or 1 of 23 (nine Sunday) SITA buses **from Trani** (25 min.; 2,500L/$1).

12   Bari

138km (83 mi.) SE of Foggia and the Gargano.

If the fact that Princess Cruises has added **Bari** as a port of call is any measure of the city's status, Bari is back. The second-largest city in southern Italy, Bari was founded even before the Greeks landed in Apuglia, and has been an industrial and commercial powerhouse ever since. The city earned itself a bad rap due to a high rate of petty crime, but if you lived this close to your neighbors, you'd probably raise some hell too. The ✪ **Città Vecchia (Old City)** is the medieval heart of Bari, characterized by excruciatingly narrow alleyways and people's lives separated literally by thin curtains. Tables and chairs are set out on the street until the early hours of the morning, as people chat and smoke, or gather around an open grill for a triangle of moist fried polenta. Local entrepreneurs are taking advantage too, by opening stylish bars and eateries in archaeologically outstanding spaces. Bari is also the home of Santa Claus—or rather, the bones of St. Nicholas. Stolen from their penultimate resting place in the Bishop's hometown of Myra in Asia Minor, the Saint's bones are sheltered in Apulia's first grand Romanesque church here in Bari.

The refreshing thing about Bari is that it doesn't pander to tourism, inviting the visitor instead to experience the city as a viable and livable center. In spite of the action being a world away, the war in the Balkans handicapped the region quite a bit, creating panic in an entire industry unwilling to come anywhere near the Adriatic. This unwanted breathing space gave the city the opportunity to regroup, and today the city is reaping the rewards of an ongoing facelift. Piazza Mercantile is under construction, injecting new life into an important historic, social, and commercial space. There are even the rumblings of a new airport under construction. With time to spare, Bari also harbors some of the best shopping I encountered in all of the south, with a surprising concentration of decorative boutiques for the home, as well as bargain basement ready-to-wear along Corso Vittorio Emmanuel and Via del Corso. At night, the castle ramparts light up with activity, when the large piazzas with views of the marina fill up with the overflow from the crowded bars and cafes.

GETTING THERE   By Train   Daily trains run twice an hour from **Foggia** (67 to 100 min.; 12,00L/$6 or 25,100L/$13 for the Eurostar). There are also six daily trains (that pass through Foggia) from **Rome** (4½ hr.; 42,000L/$25).

The **Bari Centrale station** (☎ **080-524-0148**) is on Piazza Aldo Moro, in the middle of the modern city and only a 5- to 10-minute walk to the *Città Vecchia*. This station is serviced by national FS trains (from points north you'll be passing through Foggia) plus several private lines, including the **Ferrovia Bari Nord** (ticket office on the left of Piazza Aldo Moro as you exit the main rail station; ☎ **080-521-3577**). The private **Ferrovia del Sud-Est** (☎ **080-546-2111**), services Alberobello and the Valle D'Itria (see "Alberobello & the Land of the Trulli," below) as well as Lecce.

A Travel Tip

In the old section of Bari, streets laid with black stones indicate a thoroughfare, while those paved in white stones are dead ends.

By Bus   There are only two daily SITA buses from **Manfredonia** (2 hr. 15 min.; 12,000L/$6; none on Sunday) and four Maco buses daily from Napoli's Piazza Garibaldi (2 to 3 hrs.; 34,000L/$17). In Bari, buses stop at the back of the train station on Via Giuseppe Capruzzi where you may or may not find an off-duty taxi willing to give you a ride (insist on running the meter *before* you get in the car). Otherwise, you'll have to tackle a whole lot of station stairs to get to the main entrance on Piazza Aldo Moro or to walk to the old city.

The SITA office is at the edge of town, Via Bruno Buozzi 35 (☎ **080-574-1800**), but you can get tickets and info at the Marozzi office (☎ **06-407-6140 in Rome** or **080-574-1800 in Bari**), a division of SITA, at Corso Italia 3 (at the corner of Piazza Aldo Moro). **Marozzi** runs service daily from Rome's Stazione Tiburtina departing at 10am, 11am, 3:30pm and midnight (2½ to 3 hrs; 62,000L/$31), stopping in Bari before continuing on to Brindisi and Lecce.

By Car   Bari is on the SS116 from Trani and Barletta and the A14 highway from Foggia. From Manfredonia, just follow the coastal road until it merges with the SS116.

VISITOR INFORMATION   The tourist information office is at Piazza Aldo Moro 32 (☎ **080-524-2244** or 080-524-2361) on the right side of the square as you exit the train station. There's also an office inside the station (☎ **080-558-0817**) open Monday to Friday 8:30am to 7pm, Saturday 8:30am to noon, and one on Corso Vittorio Emanuele 68 (☎ **080-523-5186**).

SEEING THE SIGHTS

✪ **San Nicola.** Piazza San Nicola. ☎ **080-521-1205.** Admission free. Daily 7am–noon and 4:30–7pm.

Bari built the first great Norman Romanesque church in Apulia in 1087 to house the earthly remains of St. Nicholas, today mythologized as Santa Claus, but originally a 4th-century Turkish bishop renowned for his piety, kindness, and miracles, including the re-memberment and resurrection of three children after they had been chopped up with a butcher's knife and pickled in brine. St. Nick's tomb is in the **crypt below** the main altar, where a service is most likely in progress (and where here, at least, the Saint is depicted with dark skin). It's best not to circulate during prayer, but you can find a vacant corner from which to examine the Byzantine and Romanesque capitals carved with lions, griffins, and peacocks. Near the right entrance is a **pillar** said to have miraculous healing powers, unfortunately enclosed within an iron grating. The legend goes that after having been found floating in the Tiber, the Bishop of Myra had the pillar sent to his church on the Mediterranean, where it stood for 7 centuries. The column miraculously appeared in Bari in 1098, and was finally erected in the crypt, where it is still a magnet for hopeful pilgrims.

The church's **central portal** is an especially fine marriage of Arab, Byzantine, and native styles, with carved decorations and a griffin-crowned gable whose columns are supported by two worn bulls. Inside the apse sits the **Bishop's throne,** crafted in 1098 with telamones supporting the legs.

Cattedrale (Cathedral). Piazza dell'Odegitria. No phone. Admission free. Daily 7am–noon and 4:30–7pm.

Built about a century after the church of San Nicola, the cathedral is a striking Romanesque edifice, with a tall bell tower and an octagonal drum. The **facade** has some more recent embellishments, including baroque canopies over the doors and a modern rose window. The **pulpit** is a curious cobbling together of 13th-century fragments. Bits of **mosaic** flooring from an earlier, 8th-century church survive in the transept alongside some medieval **frescoes.** In the sacristy is a precious **Byzantine scroll** in typical medieval Beneventan script. The illustrations are upside down so that they would be visible to the congregation as the scroll was unrolled.

Museo del Castello Svevo & Gypsoteca. Piazza Frederico II di Svevia. ☎ **080-528-6111.** Admission 4,000L ($2). Free guided tours with admission at 10am. Tues–Sun 9am–1pm and 3:30–7:30pm.

The massive bastion standing today takes on the name of its builder, Frederick II of Swabia, and was instrumental in re-establishing Bari's fortunes as an independent and thriving cultural and trade center in the 13th century. In the 16th century the castle was expanded by the Aragonese, when Isabella of Aragon and her daughter, Bona Sforza, took up residence here and transformed it into a Renaissance showpiece fit for a king. Under the Bourbons, the castle was neglected, serving once again as a fortress, a prison, and an army barracks, until its final tour of duty during the French revolution.

The structure alone is interesting enough, if not a bit barren. In the "minors" tower, so-called because of its use as a prison for juveniles in the mid-19th century, is a 13th century Gothic portal decorated with a magnificently engraved lunette arch. The Renaissance (inner) courtyard has an interesting double-arched loggia whose columns support capitals decorated with sculptures of eagles and acanthus leaves. The castle houses the **Gypsoteca,** a collection of plaster casts and architectural remnants taken from ancient Apulian monuments, in addition to a small permanent collection that includes some good 15th-century frescos and what was probably a portrait in stone of Frederick II. The castle also occasionally hosts temporary exhibitions; check with the tourist information office or keep an eye out for billboard advertisements.

Pinacoteca Provinciale (Provincial Picture Gallery). Via Spalato 19 (off Lungomare N. Suaro). ☎ **080-541-2421.** Admission 5,000L ($3), 1,000L (50¢) students. Tues–Sat 9am–1pm and 4–7pm, Sun 10am–1pm.

This small collection is marked by some good pictures by medieval and baroque Pugliese painters, the Neapolitan school (including several by Luca Giordano), Venetian works by Bellini, Paolo Veronese, and Tintoretto, and some fine folk art (ceramics, presepio figurines) and canvases by local 19th-century artists.

AFFORDABLE PLACES TO STAY

Bari is a business town, leaving very little choice for the middle-of-the-road budget traveler. Stick to the choices below, since most of the budget inns are dives. If you're having trouble lining up a room, stop at the train station **tourist office.**

Moderno. Via Crisenzio 60, 70122 Bari. ☎ **080-521-3313.** Fax 080-521-4718. 34 apts. A/C TV TEL. 70,000L ($35) single; 115,000L ($58) double. MC, V. Parking 25,000L ($13) overnight (extra charge for daytime).

Probably the best value in Bari, the Moderno is more of a residence than a hotel, the result being that the rooms are cleaned twice a week rather than daily (plus, of course, before a new customer moves in). Accommodations are all mini-apartments featuring modern baths and kitchenettes; even the singles are spacious. The furniture is standardized, the beds predictably saggy, but the prices are excellent, and it's convenient for day-tripping (the train station is just around the corner).

WORTH A SPLURGE

Boston. Via Piccinni 155, 70122 Bari. ☎ **080-521-6633.** Fax 080-524-6802. www.inmedia.it/boston. 69 units. A/C MINIBAR TV TEL. 140,000L ($70) single; 210,000L ($105) double. Rates include breakfast. AE, DC, MC, V. Parking 25,000L ($13).

You pay for the level of comfort at this businessperson's hotel, located halfway between the train station and historic district. Most rooms are cut to a modest size, and the comfort level is everything an executive might require. The well-built modular furnishings have suede accents, and while windows are fairly soundproof, you may want to request a room on the back *cortile* (courtyard) to escape the bus and traffic noise. Ask for lower rates on weekends and in August.

GREAT DEALS ON DINING

Abusuan. Strada Vallisa 67/68, in the Città Vecchia. ☎ **080-528-3361.** Primi 7,000–10,000L ($4–$5); secondi 10,000–15,000L ($5–$8). No credit cards. Daily noon–late. With your back to the Palazzo del Senile, turn left onto Strada Vallisa; the restaurant is on your right. ECLECTIC.

Actually a stylish intercultural center, Abusuan extends the international theme into the kitchen, serving an ever-changing and eclectic menu that reflects the cuisine of Palestine, Eritrea, or any number of international culinary traditions (expect something like couscous, or rice with peanuts). Not to exclude its main customer, there's pasta on every menu, but rather than a ragu, expect something a bit more exotic like spaghetti in a sauce of mussels and coconut milk. The restaurant/center occupies a church dating to the 5th century, and if you sneak past the baths you may get a glimpse of the cloisters through the half-moon window, discovered during renovations behind a solid stone wall.

La Credenze. Via Verrone 25. ☎ **080-524-4747.** Reservations suggested. Primi 8,000–12,000L ($4–$6); secondi 10,000–20,000L ($5–$10). AE, DC, MC, V. Thurs–Tues 1–3pm and 8:30pm–midnight. Closed June–Aug. BARESE.

Although La Credenze has an attractive and ample menu, customers come here to entrust themselves to the discretion of Cosimo, the affable optometrist-cum-restaurateur. With the wave a hand, your table will be buried under a parade of antipasti, including *cozze ripieni* (stuffed mussels), *panzelottini* (wonderful little fried cheese triangles), and a variety of fish proudly served *crudo* (raw). Not for the faint of heart is the *braciola*, in Bari, a thick slice of horsemeat stuffed with garlic, cheese, and cubes of lard, once a recipe for the poor, and now enjoying a renaissance as a Saturday night treat. It's still possible to order from the menu, while a full meal (including two pasta dishes) will cost a mere 40,000L($20) or 50,000L ($25) for a fish-based *secondo*, wine included.

Manfredi. Via Re Manfredi 19. ☎ **080-523-6499.** Reservations suggested. Primi 12,000–15,000L ($6–$8); secondi 15,000–20,000L ($8–$10). AE, DI, MC, V. Daily 1–3pm and 8pm–midnight. From Piazza Mercantile, follow the street directly behind the statue of the lion; the restaurant is on your left. BARESE/PUGLIESE.

Here just over a year, this trattoria occupies an old stone building in the Città Vecchia, a smart yet typical barrel arched dining room that even spills its candlelight out onto the street during the warmer months. The chef was hard pressed to single out one outstanding dish, but we can recommend the *risotto tartufato con asparagi* (prepared with butter, truffle essence, and asparagus) or the *tagliolini con gamberetti e limone* (pasta with shrimp and lemon) for starters. The *tagliata*, a mouth-watering dish of sliced beef served with arugula, is a flavorful and light option for a secondo, even if the dish has roots in the Tuscan rather than the Pugliese kitchen.

Taverna Verde. Largo Adua 19 (on Lungomare Nazario Sauro). ☎ **080-554-0870.** Reservations recommended. Primi 8,000L ($4); secondi 9,000–16,000L ($5–$8); pizza 5,000–10,000L ($3–$5). AE, DC, MC, V. Mon–Sat noon–3pm and 7:30pm–midnight. Closed Aug 14–24 and Dec 24–Jan 6. BARESE/PUGLIESE.

It pays to book ahead here since Bari families treat it as sort of a dining room away from home, filling the tables with three generations and lots of noisy chatter. Although there's a good selection of regional and national wines, a giant beer is the beverage of choice to accompany *papardelle alla taverna verde* (wide noodles with tomatoes, mushrooms, and prosciutto), *spaghetti alle cozze* (with mussels), or *orecchiette alla barese* (in a ragu with turnip greens). As a nice change of pace, there are several light secondi such as an *omletta al prosciutto* or *crostino di mozzarella al prosciutto* (a log of alternating mozzarella and bread slices, toasted and topped with prosciutto). More substantial fare includes *filetto di manzo al pepe verde* (beef filet with green peppercorns) or the ever-popular *frittura di pesce mista* (mixed fried fish).

13 Alberobello & the Land of the Trulli

63km (38 mi.) SE of Bari.

Hidden in plain sight is the fairy-tale village of ✪ **Alberobello,** an otherworldly cityscape of cone-shaped houses called trulli, where, at any moment, you may be greeted by a mob of pointy-eared elves in green shoes. Well, not exactly.

Concentrated on a pair of low hills are two sizable neighborhoods composed of some 1,000 trulli—ancient mysterious dwellings forming a vision so unique and well preserved that the entire town has been declared a national monument. For this reason, Alberobello has become the defacto capital of the region, even if it's not the largest town among those in the magical landscape of the Itria Valley.

Italy's oddest example of idiosyncratic vernacular architecture, a *trullo* is a single-room, whitewashed cylindrical structure with a conical roof made of dark, flat rocks fixed—without mortar—into a dry roof made of piled up stone refuse. No one is sure where the trulli came from, though there are plenty of theories. One novel idea is that, during the Aragonese rule, the locals used them to avoid taxation; when they saw King Ferdinand's tax man coming, they'd just collapse the roof, rendering the structure "unfinished," and hence untaxable. Plausible, but questions remain as to why similar ancient structures appear in eastern Turkey and in Syria.

As one might expect, Alberobello sees its share of tour buses whose arrival encourages the manufacture of tacky back-lit plaster trulli and other useless memorabilia. Many are seduced into purchasing a tablecloth or set of hand towels typical of the exquisite hand-woven textiles (at extortionist prices) produced in the region.

The crowds tend to swarm around the boutiques, leaving these marvelous cobbled lanes empty once the sun goes down, and allowing the local elderly to emerge from their own private trulli for a bit of fresh air and late-night chatter.

ESSENTIALS

GETTING THERE   The **Ferrovia del Sud-Est** private rail line (☎ **080-546-2111**) from **Bari** to Taranto services the Itria Valley Monday through Saturday, with 14 to 16 trains daily stopping at the Grotte di Castellana (1 hr.; 4,700L/$2), **Alberobello** (95 min.; 5,900L/$3), Locorotondo (104 min.; 6,700L/$3), and Martina Franca (110 min.; 6,700L/$3).There are no trains on Sundays, and only limited bus service into and out of the secondary provincial hub of Martina Franco.

By Car   From Bari or Brindisi, take State Highway 16 to Monopoli, passing through Fasano on the way to Alberobello (once arrived, follow yellow signs for *"zona trulli."*

VISITOR INFORMATION   Alberobello's tourist office is in the *Casa d'Amore* trullo at Piazza Ferdinando IV (☎ **080-432-5171;** fax 080-932-5706; www.traveleurope. it/trulli.htm). The office is open Monday to Friday 9am to 1pm and 3 to 8pm, Saturday and Sunday 9am to 8pm (possibly shorter hours in winter).

WHAT TO SEE & DO

Alberobello is rather touristy, but with two swatches of the whitewashed townscape made almost entirely of cone-topped dwellings, the roofs dotted and topped with ancient, symbolic "knobs," it is a sight to behold, lost in the low-lying olive groves of the Itria Valley.

Don't be put off by the town's central parking lot: bordering this access area is the slope known as **Rione Monti,** the larger of the two trullo zones, with blindingly white stone pedestrian streets and character to spare. Although most of Rione Monti's trulli now house souvenir or craft stands, the character of the zone is not compromised. But if you want to see a more genuinely residential trullo zone, head across the parking area, behind Piazza XXVII Maggio through Piazza Plebescito for the **Aia Piccola** district.

The 18th-century **Trullo Sovrano,** on Piazza Sacramento, was the only trullo built with two stories. Originally a seminary, it was bought by a local family who returned from America with modest riches and set it up as a house. The admission of 2,500L ($1), 1,000L (50¢) under 12, includes a free guided tour through rooms decked out as they would have been two generations ago. It's open daily 10am to 1pm (9am in August) and 3 to 7pm.

A CAVERN EN ROUTE TO ALBEROBELLO

The **Grotte di Castellana** (☎ **080-496-5511** or 080-499-8211; www.grottedicastellana. it) is one of Italy's most spectacular cave systems, glittering with crystals and filled with wondrous rock formations spread throughout a series of massive caverns and long narrow tunnels formed by an ancient underground torrent. The first great chamber is almost 200 feet deep, with a naturally formed oculus at the top open to the sunlight and rimmed with streamers of vegetation.

Throughout the underground system are groupings of colossal stalagmites, formations in the shapes of a wolf, a camel, an owl, a serpent and (of course) a Madonna in miniature, near a rocky congregation of faithful kneeling in prayer.

The short, 1-hour, 1km (½-mi.) tour gives you a taste for this underworld, but it's worthwhile to take the 2 hour, 3km (2-mi.) tour that includes the most stunning sight of the caverns, the fabulous "Grotta Bianca" where the calciferous water seeping through has so few impurities that the crystalline stalactites and stalagmites it has formed shine a brilliant white.

The longer tour (in English) costs 25,000L ($14) for adults and 20,000L ($10) for ages 6 to 14, currently leaves at 11am and 4pm; the shorter English-language tours, which costs 15,000L ($8) for adults and 12,000L ($6) for kids 6 to 14, leaves at 1pm and 6:30pm. If your schedule doesn't coincide with these times, you can catch one of the long (hourly on the hour from 9am to noon and 3 to 5pm; 6pm in summer) or short (hourly on the half hour) tours, guided in Italian. The caves are open daily 8:30am to 7pm. The drop in temperature is sudden and drastic, getting as low as 48°F in the main cave, so bring a sweater.

To get there by car from Bari, take the SS16 to the Conversano Cozze exit and follow signs; from Taranto take the A14 to Gioia del Colle, then follow signs for Putignano and finally for Castellana, or take the FSE train to the site entrance.

Ferries to Greece

Throughout the centuries, the shores of Apulia have launched more ships than Helen of Troy, who'd blanch today if she were forced to embark at Brindisi, where almost every doorway in town that isn't a pizza joint is a smarmy travel agency. Not actually hailed as a tourist destination, Brindisi acts as a magnet for voyagers on their way to or from Greece; and those transients not necessarily interested in the city's paltry (but lovely, if not for their location) medieval monuments. Few are aware that ferries to Greece also depart from infinitely more inviting Bari, a city that is equally, if not more easily, reachable, and without a doubt, better smelling.

Superfast Ferries (☎ **080-521-1416;** www.ferries.gr/sff) on Corso Antonio De Tullio, leave from **Bari** four to six times daily to both **Igoumenitsa** (9 hrs.) and **Patras** (15 hrs). The price for both runs is the same, although at 74,000L to 89,000L ($37 to $45), the same chilly bench on the deck might be more sufferable on the shorter haul. A reclining airplane-style chair runs from 91,000 to 110,000L ($46 to $55), while a cabin, depending on the services you ask for, will set you back from 108,000L ($54) all the way up to 414,000L ($207) for a first-class cabin.

Otherwise, both Strintzis Lines' **Blue Star Ferries** at Corso Garibaldi 65 (☎ **0831-562-200;** http://www.ferries.gr/strintzis) and **Hellenic Mediterranean Lines** (☎ **0831-528-531;** www.ferries.gr/hml) down the street at Corso Garibaldi 8, depart from **Brindisi** for **Patras.** A spot on the deck runs between 52,000 to 70,000L ($26 to $35); a reclining seat costs 64,000 to 86,000L ($32 to $43), and a cabin for four costs from 124,000 ($62) per person up to 340,000L ($170). **Hellenic Mediterranean Lines** also makes the trip from **Brindisi to Corfu** (8 hrs.) and to **Igoumenitsa** (10 hrs.) Depending on the season, a ticket will cost anywhere from 46,000L ($23) for a spot on the deck to a maximum of 202,000L ($101) for a cabin.

Purchase your tickets at any reputable travel agency, or better yet, from the ferry companies themselves, which are conveniently situated near the harbor port. Some rail passes like Eurail get you the travel free *but you must still reserve and pay for a cabin or deck chair.* Pick up *Frommer's Greece from $50 a Day* for more information on these and other destinations.

AN AFFORDABLE PLACE TO STAY & DINE

✪ **Trullidea.** Via Monte Nero 18, 70011 Alberobello (BA). ☎/fax **080-432-3860.** www.trullidea.com. E-mail: info@trullidea.com. 10 trulli apts (sleep 2–6 each). 120,000L ($60) double, rates 20% higher in Aug. Lower weekly rates available. Rates include breakfast. No credit cards.

The difference between a good hotel and a great one, regardless of star-ratings, is that great ones become destinations in themselves. Trullidea is just this type of place, a preserved and restored group of abandoned trulli transformed into atmospheric miniapartments by the exceptionally warm and accessible Dino and Antonella. The accommodations are terribly atmospheric, with their stone floors, wood beams crossing the inside of the conical roofs, sturdy peasant-style furnishings, kitchenettes and courtyards (great for hanging out wash). Baths are basic and clean, and space heaters and fireplaces are provided for added warmth, though trulli are naturally cool in summer and warm in winter. Dino and Antonella recently took their idea one step further with **L'Aratro,** an elegant and atmospheric restaurant on an adjoining lane (☎ **080-432-2789;** Via Monte San. Michele 25/29). The restaurant serves local specialties in a trullo at affordable prices, and I recommend the *arrosto misto,* a mouthwatering assortment of meats roasted over an olive wood fire.

A GREAT DEAL ON DINING

Ristorante Trullo d'Oro. Via Felice Cavallotti 29. ☎ **080-432-1820.** Reservations recommended. Primi 9,000–15,000L ($5–$8); secondi 15,000–30,000L ($8–$15). AE, DC, MC, V. Tues–Sat noon–3pm and 8–11pm; Sun noon–3pm. Closed Jan. PUGLIESE/ITALIAN.

One of the more highly recommended favorites in town, Trullo d'Oro takes up a complex of trulli providing not only killer atmosphere, but good food as well. You can sample three of the most traditional primi with the *assaggini dello chef,* perhaps including *spaghetti al trullo* (with fresh tomatoes, arugula, and Parmesan), *orecchiette alberobellesi* (in ragu with savory bread balls on top), and *purè di fave con cicoria* (fava puree with chicory). If the huge portions of assaggini were almost too much, go easy with *melanzane ripiene* (stuffed eggplant); otherwise dine on *capretto ai carboni* (kid cooked over coals), or the regionally popular *arrosto misto* (mixed meat roast).

14 Ostuni

75 km (47 mi) SE of Bari; 35 km (22mi) NW of Brindisi.

The attraction of ✪ **Ostuni** is in its whitewashed medieval alleys and the unexpected appearance of sand-toned and isolated baroque portals within its labyrinth. Dubbed the **Città Bianca (White City),** Ostuni boasts a medieval center that receives a fresh coat of whitewash every year. A handful of unblemished **sandy coves** only 3km (2 mi) through silvery olive groves only help to boost the magnetism of this very special place.

Inserted like a puzzle into the structures at the top of the hill is the 15th-century **cathedral,** whose facade gracefully marries Romanesque, Gothic, and Venetian elements. The huge Goldomagno/Baroque **archway** in front of the cathedral is so artfully crafted that you might easily be deceived into thinking that you're at the Bridge of Sighs in Venice. The large medieval cobblestones have been polished smooth by time, so avoid Ostuni in icy or wet weather, and wear rubber-soled shoes.

Not to be outdone by Venice, Ostuni has a tradition of hand-painted glass, so that you may want to check out the lamps and aperitif sets at **Eleonora Ruggero,** Via Cattedrale 11/13 (☎ **0368-779-3296**) who was busy filling an order for wedding party favors when I stopped in. (If you plan on taking any of this home, pack bubble wrap in your suitcase.)

On the way up to the cathedral, you'll pass the **Museo della Civiltà Preclassica (Museum of Preclassical Civilizations),** open Tuesday, Wednesday, Saturday 8:30am to 1pm, Thursday and Friday 8am to 1pm; Sunday 10am to12:30pm; Thursday, Friday, Sunday 3:30 to 7pm from April through September; admission is 3,000L ($2). Located in a deconsecrated church, much of the exhibit is of interest to scientists, with explanations exclusively in Italian, although you may just want to stop in to see the 25,500-year-old **skeleton** of a woman found in the Santa Maria D'Agnano cave in 1991.

ESSENTIALS

GETTING THERE   By Train   Trains run at least hourly from Bari (about 1 hr.; 7,000L/$4; 19,200L/$10 IC) and Lecce 40 to 65 min.; 7,000L/$4; 19,200L/$10

Intercity www.fs-on-line.com). The station is located about 3km outside the historic center, so you'll have to take one of the local orange buses to Piazza Libertà (about every ½ hour; 1,000L/50¢) to begin your *passeggiata* around the old city.

By Bus   If you're arriving from Rome, hop on one of the three Marozzi buses from Rome (☎ **06-407-6140 in Rome** or **080-574-1800 in Bari**), bound for Bari and continuing on to Brindisi and Lecce.

By Car   Take the Ostuni exit of the Bari-Brindisi state highway. From Alberobello, follow the two-lane road following signs first to Locorotondo, then Cisternino, and finally Ostuni.

GETTING AROUND   There's only one intra-urban bus, running a circular route from Ostuni's station to Piazza Libertà in the town center. If you're headed to the beach, take the bus marked Villanova (1,500L/75¢) from Piazza Libertà (the one with the column near the hugely Baroque Palazzo di Città).

VISITOR INFORMATION   Finally, a tourist office staffed with people who like what they do! This exceedingly helpful tourist office is located steps from Piazza Libertà behind the Palazzo di Città on Corso Vittorio Emanuele 39 ☎ (**0831-307-219;** e-mail: comuneostuniturismo@mail.clio.it). The tourist information office puts out a useful map of the old city (Città Vecchia) showing color-coded walking tours into medieval streets according to historic, architectural, or scenic interest.

AFFORDABLE PLACES TO STAY

Tre Torre. Corso Vittorio Emanuele 298, Ostuni 72017. ☎ **0831-331-114.** 15 units, most with bathroom. 63,000L ($33) single without bathroom; 70,000L ($35) single with bathroom; 85,000L ($43) double without bathroom; 95,000L ($48) double with bathroom. AE, MC, V. Free parking in garage.

Located on the road out of Ostuni toward the beach, this hotel, run by three women, is the only reasonable option if you're on a budget but still want to stay in town. Although the hotel is about 40 years old, recent renovations guarantee a level of cleanliness without having sacrificed any of its old-world charm. Rooms are simple yet comfortable with tile floors and area rugs, which get rolled up around beach season to keep them sand-free. As of this writing, not all of the rooms had been redone, so you may want to confirm the state of the baths to avoid the one whose shower resembles a kitchen sink sunken into the floor. Otherwise, the baths are in good shape, and 9 of the 15 rooms that have a bath also come with a TV and a mini-fridge (empty).

GREAT DEALS ON DINING

Wednesday was my unlucky day, because before the commencement of the crushing summer tourist influx, restaurants can still afford the luxury of closing during the day. The other problem you're up against is that the ones that do stay open for lunch generally close in the heat of the summer, when most people are grabbing a sandwich on the beach. Nevertheless, Ostuni is a gourmand's paradise, with wonderfully typical Ostunese trattorias like the **Restaurant Club Spessite** (Via Brancasi 43 ☎ **0831-302-866,** open Thursday through Tuesday, 6pm to1am), a teeny venue for local fare like *orecchiette,* fava puree and chicory at more than fair prices. You'll wind up paying a bit more at **Porta Nova** (Via Gaspare Petrarolo 38 ☎ **0831-338-983;** open Thursday to Tuesday 1 to 3pm and 8pm to midnight), whose panoramic terrace and *cucina casereccia* attract a stream of famed Italian actors and singers. Located behind the cathedral, **Osteria del Tempo Perso** (Via Tanzarella Vitale 47 ☎ **0831-303-320,** open daily 5:30–12:30am) serves up good quality at fair prices.

15 Lecce: The Florence of the Baroque

143km (86 mi.) SE of Bari, 85km (51 mi.) E of Taranto.

Not unlike the rich pedigree of most of Italy's lower boot, ✪ **Lecce's** ancestry dates back to a prehistoric settlement and runs the gamut through the Greeks, the Romans, Byzantines, Normans, and Bourbons. Thanks to an early leaning toward scholarship, Lecce earned itself the title of the Athens of Apuglia (it's still home to one of Apulia's two universities). But the name that stuck still defines the city's artistic heritage, the Florence of the Baroque; the swirls and cornucopias of this late Renaissance style are reflected in Lecce's basilicas, churches, and chapels, but also in the massively decorated portals to the old city and various private residences. Lecce's historic center is crowded with a legacy of these ecclesiastical excesses, as much of the creative impulses would have remained unexpressed were it not for the benefaction of the Church. The municipality has done its homework, as many of the major baroque attractions have explanatory plaques (in Italian and English) out front. You can visit them at night, when the best sights are floodlit and the piazzas come alive with people out for their evening *passeggiata* or to enjoy one of the city's free summer concerts.

ESSENTIALS

GETTING THERE   There are twice-hourly **trains** from **Bari** (2 hr.; 13,100L/$7 FS; 20,600L/$10 ES or IC) that pass through **Brindisi** (23 to 43 min.; 4,500L/$2; 15,800L/$8 ES or IC) and six daily trains from **Rome** (6½ to 9½ hrs.; 56,600L/$28; 79,500L/$40 ES or IC), passing through Bari and Brindisi as well. The train station is within easy walking distance to the main baroque sites of the old city.

  Marozzi (☎ **06-407-6140** or 0832-303-016), a division of SITA, runs service daily from Rome's Stazione Tiburtina (departures at 10 and 11am, 3:30pm, and midnight), stopping at **Bari's Estramurale Capruzzi** (2½ to 3 hrs; 6:15am, 4:30pm, 9pm) and **Brindisi's Viale Regina Margherita,** 8/9 (30 min.; 8am, 6:30pm, 11pm). The price is 62,000L ($31) for all or a portion of the journey. Marozzi also makes the 13½ hour trip from **Pisa** (7:30pm; 106,000L/$53), passing through **Florence** (8:15pm; 96,000L/$48; leaving from the SITA bus station) and **Siena** (9:30pm; 89,000L/$45, leaving from the train station). If you're driving, Lecce is on the fast moving **SS613** from Brindisi.

VISITOR INFORMATION   The **main tourist office** is at Via Monte San. Michele 20 (☎ **0832/314-117;** fax 0832/310-238), but the central information office is near the Duomo on Via Vittorio Emanuele, open Monday to Friday 9am to 1pm and 5 to 7pm, Saturday 9am to 1pm. Their map of the old city is especially useful in identifying the old city gates and other sites of major importance.

SEEING THE SIGHTS

Lecce's center revolves around broad **Piazza Sant'Oronzo,** which preserves the lower levels of a 1st-century B.C. **Anfiteatro Romano (Roman Amphitheater),** much of which is still buried under Santa Maria delle Grazie at the piazza's southeastern end. At the square's center is an **ancient Roman column,** topped by a copper statue of the patron, St. Oronzo, which was cast in Venice. The column's original home was Brindisi, where, as one of a pair, it marked the end of this stretch of the Appian Way. In fulfillment of a promise made during the plague of 1656 (aided no doubt by the fact that lightning had recently felled the thing), the column was brought to Lecce by its citizens. Nearby is the **Sedile,** serving as the town hall when it was built in 1592 until 1851.

The greatest of Lecce's baroque facades, ✪ **Santa Croce,** on Via Umberto, was built between 1549 and 1679, a time span that explains the relative sobriety of the facade's lower half compared to the top-heavy and fantastic exuberance of Giuseppe Zimbalo's work above. The balustrade is supported by a series of telamons, each representing a symbol of paganism. Notice the figure of the "infidel Turk," against which the Papacy and the Empire combined forces in an unprecedented union at the victorious Battle of Lepanto. Supported by the balustrade are cherubs, which expand on this theme of triumph over evil. Next door is the long and only slightly more subdued facade of the **Palazzo del Governo** (1659 to 1595), formerly a Celestine convent.

Hiding off Via Vittorio Emanuele is one of Lecce's other gorgeous baroque corners, the enclosed L-shaped ✪ **Piazza del Duomo.** This piazza, intentionally designed with only one way in as a defensive measure, wows the visitor as much for its starkness (especially on a lonely summer Sunday,) as for its grandeur. Giuseppe Zimbalo rebuilt the 12th-century **Duomo** in 1570, giving it a 225-foot bell tower and two facades: on the main entrance and around on the right transept, tucked into the other half of the piazza's "L" where it faces down the **Palazzo Vescovile** (1420 to 1632). Adjoining the cathedral is the Palazzo del Seminario, designed by Giuseppe Cino, who also built the piazza's picturesque central well.

The **Museo Sigismundo Castromediano,** Viale Gallipoli at Viale F. Lo Re (☎ **0832-247-025**) and its collection of Stone Age tools, "Venus" figurines, painted pottery, and terra-cottas are currently under wraps, as the museum is closed for renovations.

SHOPPING

The province of Lecce has been a *cartapesta* (papier-mâché) center since at least the 17th century, so if you're looking for artistically crafted additions to your crèche, here's the place to stock up. Perhaps the best artisan studio is that of **Claudio Riso** and his brothers at Via del Tufo 16 (off Via Federico d'Aragona; ☎ **0832-242-362**). They produce remarkably detailed figures (starting at 60,000L/$30) of everyday, 18th-century Lecce life that have won them international prestige. Another noteworthy *bottega* is that of **Maurizio Ciafano,** Via Carlo Russi 10 (☎ **0360-740-906**), where three young men work hard in their tiny space to create peasant figures carrying bundles of twigs or wine jugs for 25,000 to 30,000L ($13 to $15) a figure. If you're looking for more variety, check out the **Mostra Permanente dell'Artigianato Salentino,** Via Rubichi 21 (☎ **0832-246-758**), where you can peruse traditional crafts from across the province: small-town ceramics, cast iron, Lecce-made stone carving, and papier-mâché.

GREAT DEALS ON DINING

✪ **Guido e Figli.** Via XXV Luglio 14. ☎ **0832-305-868.** Reservations recommended. Primi 9,000–14,000L ($5–$7); secondi 8,000–12,000L ($4–$6); pizza 6,000–12,000L ($3–$6). AE, DC, MC, V. Tues–Sun noon–3pm and 7:30pm–1am. Open daily in Aug. Closed July 1–15. PUGLIESE/ITALIAN/PIZZA.

The low stone vaulting is atmospheric enough, but most patrons head straight back to the self-service area, where neighborhood regulars, the Sunday paper in hand, partake of the same items as the main restaurant at half the prices. The *orecchiette alla Guido* (Lecce's large whole wheat orecchiette in a tomato sauce with mini meatballs, eggplant, and Parmesan) isn't bad, nor are the *fusili gran gusto* (pasta spirals with shrimp and salmon) or *parmigiana di melanzane* (a tomato, eggplant, and cheese casserole). Secondi include *polpette e messicane* (two types of meatballs), *pollo al forno con patate* (oven-roasted chicken with roast potatoes), or *lumache* (snails) cooked however you like them (assuming you like them). Service is friendly, but can drag, another reason to head straight to the back. Their popular **tavola calda** branch (a cafeteria sort of place) around the corner at Via San Trinchese 10 (☎ **0832-300-802**) also has outdoor tables on a pedestrian street off the main Piazza Sant'Oronzo.

Villa della Monica. Via S. S. Giacomo e Filippo, 40. ☎ **0832-458-432.** Reservations suggested. Primi 5,000–10,000L ($3–$5); secondi 10,000–18,000L ($5–$9). AE, MC, V. Thurs–Tues noon–midnight (or later). Closed Dec 24–Jan 6. (From Giardini Publici, walk up Via Imperatore Adriano and veer left. The restaurant is down on the left.) PUGLIESE.

Set in a grand 15th-century Renaissance villa, della Monica is the place of choice for extended Italian families celebrating baptisms, communions, and weddings. In warmer weather, tables are moved to a vast marble and tile inlay courtyard, whose fountain and wide open space provide hours of delight for small energetic children. You may want to avoid heading over here on Sundays, when the banquets are booked through the afternoon and evening, especially in spring and summer, and when service becomes excruciatingly unhurried. Come with time to spare, and expect your check to be shockingly low. The menu alters somewhat on a daily basis, so that the waiters are more accustomed to reciting the daily dishes *a voce.* The *orecchiette di grano della casa* (homemade ear-shaped pasta) is a simple yet classic primo in a light and flavorful tomato sauce, or if you hit the season right, you may luck out with the risotto con vongole e asparagi (clams and asparagus risotto). What's even better (and surprising) is that della Monica stays open throughout the day, accommodating those who like a late afternoon lunch.

13 Sicily

by Lynn A. Levine

My first impressions of Sicily were of car bombs and surprise Mafia hits in reruns of *The Godfather* and its sequels, with pastoral hills and wrinkled peasants in the background to add local "texture." If anything in these movies' depictions of this terrible triangle is accurate, it's in the extremes. Everything about Sicily is intense and complex (from the pungent juice of its lemons to the layers of its antiquities covered by pale dirt to the fiery disposition of its natives). Even the island's historic icons are radical: Phalaris, the tyrant of Agrigento, was notorious for his cruelty and not above dining on infants to make his point. But under the surface lies an intangible familiarity, the result of an economic depression in the 1920s and 1950s that resulted in a mass exodus of Sicilians to America.

Well off the coast of Italy's mainland (and only nominally considered part of the country), Sicily is the largest island in the Mediterranean, enjoying the benefits of a whopping average of 2,500 hours of sunlight per year. Sicily alone could easily fill a guidebook, but here, I barely have space to cover the highlights. If you try to see everything, you'll see nothing, so pace yourself well—and don't forget to stop and smell the flowers. An archaeological tour of the island will take you to some of the ancient world's most spectacularly sited temples (Agrigento, Selinute, Segesta) and theaters (Siracusa, Taormina, Segesta), remnants of powerful **Greek** outposts in the Mediterranean. You can see the **Roman** legacy in the sumptuous mosaics of Agrigento's Piazza Armerina and Taormina's Greco-Roman Theater, and the **Arabic Saracens'** founding of their capital at Palermo in the 9th century left regal pointed arches and graceful domes. The **Normans** came along in the early 11th century and set up a highly advanced monarchy incorporating the best of Greek, Arabic, Roman, and Celtic fashions. Under such enlightened rulers as **Roger II** and the Hohenstaufen emperor **Frederick II,** Sicilian literature came into its own a full 200 years before Dante, laying a linguistic minefield for territorial disputes between Sicilians and Florentines for having founded the Italian language. Frederick II was such a wise ruler and committed patron of the arts that he earned the nickname *Stupor Mundi* ("Wonder of the World") for ushering in an era of artistic, scientific, cultural, and intellectual prosperity. The Normans left the northern coast (Cefalù, Palermo, Monreale) scattered with perfectly balanced Norman cathedrals and Arab-style palaces filled with some of Europe's most gorgeous mosaic cycles. The marriage of **Ferdinand of Aragona** to

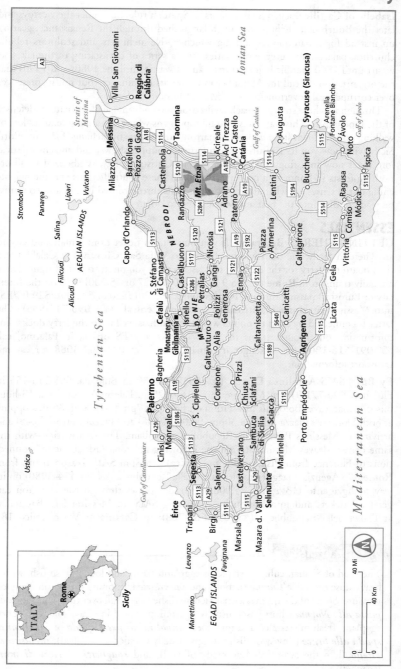

Isabelle of Castille opened Sicily's doors to **Spanish** rule, but under the viceroys and later the **Bourbons,** Sicily pretty much languished through the Renaissance, gearing up instead for a baroque fest during which native architects and sculptors rebuilt churches, palaces, and even entire cities after a series of devastating earthquakes. It wasn't until 1860 that Sicily joined Italy, and it wasn't until the 1980s and 1990s that the organization we call the Mafia began to lose its dominance (but not its presence) over corrupt local governments (see "Men of Honor," below).

Throughout these struggles, each civilization took advantage of the natural defenses of the topography. This translates into hilltop towns where sightseeing requires lots of walking up and down steep inclines or narrow stone stairs. In exchange for your effort, Sicily will show you its treasures: pagan festivals, puppet shows, and ancient mystical lore that's now indistinguishable from fervent Christian piety, symbolized in all-or-nothing feasts in honor of a city's patron saint. These contradictions and the heightening of the senses are what attract visitors to this three-pointed island, and you must be ready to dive into the best and worst it has to offer.

ESSENTIALS
GETTING THERE   By Train   If you buy a train ticket from a mainland city to anywhere in Sicily, the train will head south to **Villa San Giovanni** in Calabria and then board the ferry for the crossing to Messina with you on it, so just sit tight. There are daily trains from **Rome** (7½ to 9 hr.; 54,600L/$27 or 75,200L/$38 on the Intercity or Eurostar) passing through **Naples** (6 hr.; 39,700L/$20 or 57,200L/$29 IC/ES) into Messina's **Stazione Marittima** or **Stazione Centrale** (☎ **090-714-935**). The latter is connected by train to points west and south as well as to the ferry docks. For information on through trains to Sicily, contact any **FS office;** in Palermo, call ☎ **091-616-1806** for passenger information and ☎ **091-603-3088** for car rail transport information.

By Bus   SAIS Autolinea Diretta (☎ **051-242-150** in Bologna, 055-215-155 in Florence, 090-771-914 in Messina, 091-616-6028 in Palermo) provides a 13-hour bus ride that leaves Bologna's bus station on Friday at 7pm (106,000L/$53), stopping at both Florence's Piazza Adua (8:30pm; 96,000L/$48) and Piazza Certosa (8:45) and arriving in Messina's Piazza della Repubblica at 8:30am. The return trip—with the same driver—leaves Messina at 7am the following morning (ask about the connections to Florence from **Pisa, Siena,** and **Lucca**). An 8pm **SAIS Trasporti** bus from **Rome** (c/o Agenzia Viaggi Eurojet, Piazza della Repubblica; ☎ **06-474-3980**) on its way to **Agrigento** (13½ hrs.; 75,000L/$38) also passes through Messina. You can get local tickets and information by contacting SAIS: in **Messina** (c/o Bar Italia) at Piazza della Repubblicca (☎ **090-661-768**); in **Catania** at Via d'Amico 181

A Taste of Sicily

The triad of Sicilian culinary staples is eggplant, pasta, and lots of fresh fish, with a heavy dose of native *limone* (lemon) and *mandorle* (almonds) thrown in for good measure. Some of the quintessential Sicilian dishes served all over the islands include *pasta alla Norma* (short pasta, usually rigatoni, prepared in a casserole with cubed eggplant, fresh mozzarella, and tomatoes), *involtini di pesce spada* or *involtini di spada alle brace* (tiny swordfish roll-ups, usually breaded and grilled), *involtini di vitello* (like the swordfish but made of veal), and *spaghetti ai ricci di mare* (spaghetti with sea urchins).

Men of Honor

In Sicily, they don't call it the Mafia (from the Arabic *mu'afah* or "protection"); they call it Cosa Nostra (literally "our thing," but more accurately "this thing we have"). Its origins are debated, but the world's most famed criminal organization seemed to grow out of the convergence of local agricultural overseers working for absentee Bourbon landowners—hired thugs, from the peasant workers' point of view.

Members of the Sicilian Mafia—or "Men of Honor" as they like to be called—traditionally operated as a network of regional bosses who controlled individual towns by setting up puppet regimes of thoroughly corrupt officials. It was a sort of devil's bargain with the national Christian Democrat party, which controlled Italy's government from World War II until 1993 and, despite its law-and-order rhetoric, tacitly left Cosa Nostra alone so long as the bosses got out the party vote.

Men of honor trafficked in illegal goods, of course, but until the 1960s and 1970s, their income was derived mostly from funneling state money into their own pockets, low-level protection rackets, and ensuring that public contracts were granted to fellow *mafiosi* (all reasons why Sicily has experienced grotesque unchecked industrialization and modern growth at the expense of its heritage, invaluable real estate, and the good of its communities). But the younger generation of Mafia underbosses got into the highly lucrative heroin and cocaine trades in the 1970s, transforming the Sicilian Mafia into a major player on the international drug-trafficking circuit—and raking in the dough. This ignited a clandestine Mafia war that, throughout the late 1970s and 1980s, generated lurid headlines of bloody Mafia hits. The new generation was wiping out the old and turning the balance of power in their favor.

This situation gave rise to the first Mafia turncoats, disgruntled ex-bosses, and rank-and-file stoolies who opened up and told their stories, first to police prefect Gen. Alberto Dalla Chiesa (assassinated 1982) and later to crusading magistrates Giovanni Falcone (slaughtered 1992) and Paolo Borsellino (murdered 1992), who staged the "maxitrials" of *mafiosi* that sent hundreds to jail. The magistrates' murders, especially, garnered public attention to—and, perhaps for the first time, true shame regarding—the *dis*honorable methods that defined the new Mafia.

On a much broader, and in many ways culturally important, scale it's these young *mafiosi,* without a moral center or check on their powers, that have driven many Sicilians to at least secretly break the unwritten code of *omertà,* which translates as "homage" but means "silence," when faced with harboring or even tolerating a man of honor. The Mafia still controls much of Palermo, the small towns south of it, and the provincial capitals of Catania, Trapani, and Agrigento. Throughout the rest of Sicily, though, its power has been slipping, notwithstanding the indelible print left on the island's citizens that leaves them suspicious and closemouthed about even the most innocuous subjects. But the heroin trade is a far cry from construction schemes and protection money, and the Mafia is swiftly outliving its usefulness *and* its welcome.

Separated at Birth

Recently, the bus company SAIS split into two unrelated entities, **SAIS Autolinea Diretta** and **SAIS Trasporti.** Since these companies generally provide nonoverlapping service, I've referred to them in this chapter as simply SAIS. I've attempted to provide separate and accurate contact information wherever possible (don't underestimate this feat!).

(☎ **095-536-201**); in **Caltanissetta** on Via Collajanni (☎ **0934-564-072**); and in **Agrigento** at Via Ragazzi del '99 (☎ **0922-595-933**).

Reservations are required for seats on **Interbus,** making the trip daily at 7:30am from **Rome** (c/o Tiburviaggi, Piazzale FS Tiburtina; ☎ **06-4429-0091**) to **Messina** (9½ hrs.; 55,000L/$28; Piazza della Repubblica 6; ☎ **090-661-754**), on its way to **Taormina** (10 hrs.; 58,000L/$29; ☎ **0942-625-301**), **Catania** (11½ hrs.; 62,000L/$31; for transfers to Piazza Armerina and so on) and **Siracusa** (12½ hrs.; 67,000L/$34; Via Trieste 28; ☎ **0931-66-710**). There's a 10,000L ($5) discount on the price of all tickets for travelers under 25 or over 65.

By Car Ferry   The car ferry from Villa San Giovanni in Calabria to Messina on Sicily runs like clockwork. When you exit the highway, just follow the lanes indicated by the pictogram of a boat with a car in it. When you see everyone parking haphazardly in an open lot to hop out and run into a little building, that's your cue to do the same to buy your ticket (take your car-rental form in with you; they'll need documentation of the license plate). The ferry runs every 20 minutes or so and costs 28,000L to 36,000L ($14 to $28), depending on the size of your car. The crossing takes 25 minutes. Foot passengers pay a mere 1,700L (85¢). For car ferry information, contact **Tourist Ferry Boat s.p.a.**in Messina (☎ **090-3718510**) or in Villa San Giovanni (☎ **0965-751-413**).

VISITOR INFORMATION   The **main tourist office** in Palermo (see below) has information on the entire island. The island's official Web site is **www.sicily.infcom.it**; two other good sites are **Etna Decade Volcano** (www.geo.mtu.edu/~boris/ETNA.html), where you can learn all you want to know about one of the world's most active volcanoes, and the **Palermo Page** (www.comune.palermo.it), the official site of Sicily's capital.

1 Passing Through Messina

237km (142 mi.) E of Palermo, 683km (410 mi.) SE of Rome, 469km (281 mi.) S of Naples.

Sicily's primary port and third-largest city doesn't offer many attractions aside from swordfish dinners and a pair of Caravaggios in the **Museo Regionale,** Via della Libertà 465 (☎ **090-361-292;** Bus: 76 or 81; admission 8,000L/$4); but unless you fly or ferry straight to Palermo, Messina will be your introduction to the island. There's a **provincial tourist office** outside the **Stazione Marittima** (Port) at Via Calabria 36 (☎ **090-675-353** or 090-675-675), open Monday to Thursday 8am to 1:30pm and 3 to 6pm and Friday and Saturday 8am to 1:30pm.

In case you get stuck overnight, try the simple and reliable modern **Nuovo Albergo Monza,** Viale San Martino 63 (☎ and fax **090-673-755**). It has 59 units; 49 with bath and all with phones, air-conditioning, and TVs. Doubles without bath go for 116,000L ($58); those with bath are 140,000L ($70). For a dining experience where you'll be the only nonregular, head just below Via La Farina for ultra-Messinese cuisine at **Trattoria Al Padrino,** Via Santa Cecilia 54 (☎ **090-292-1000**), open Monday to Saturday 12:30 to 2:30pm and 8 to 10:30pm).

2 Cefalù

165km (99 mi.) W of Messina, 70km (42 mi.) E of Palermo.

At first sight, **Cefalù** (*chay*-fa-loo) can be a bit discouraging: modern concrete apartments with red rooftops sandwiched between the foothills of a towering mountain and a naturally sheltered bay. But the pearl is hidden deep within, easily overlooked at the base of an irregularly formed rocky promontory that served as an effective defense against potential invaders during the 11th and 12th centuries. The *centro storico* (historic center) is tidily laid out on the tip of a small cape, protected by a medieval system of construction employing tight alleys that provided little access from the sea. The sweeping curve of the sandy beach extends southwest, giving way in both directions to secluded rocky coves and picturesque *faraglioni* (cliffs).

The 5th-century B.C. Greeks left a few vases for the museum, and Roger II gave the town a mighty Norman cathedral whose authority over the main piazza gives you a viable excuse for cooling your heels here for a day or two, but unless you've decided to base yourself here for excursions to nearby Palermo, Mt. Etna, or Agrigento (anything else is a bit far), you'll probably get bored by the third day.

ESSENTIALS

GETTING THERE   By Train   There are 10 trains daily from **Rome** (10½ to 12 hr.; 66,000L/$33 or 89,100L/$45 on the Intercity) from **Naples** (8½ to 11½ hr.; 50,500L/$25 or 70,100L/$35 IC); be sure to check your departure location, as some trains leave from Rome's Tiburtina Station and from Naples's Campo Flegrei Station rather than from Roma Centrale/Napoli Centrale.

There are at least hourly trains from **Palermo** (45 to 75 min.; 7,000L/$3.50; 4,000L/$2 supplement for the IC or ES train) and 10 to 12 trains daily from **Messina** (2½ to 4 hr.; 14,500L/$7 or 20,300L/$10 IC/ES). For local train information, contact the train station at ☎ **0921-421-169.**

By Car   Construction of the A20 highway from Messina ran out of funding years ago, making the 46km (28-mi.) stretch between Sant'Agata to Castelbuono a much longer drive than it needs to be. If you're driving from Messina, you'll have to drop to the parallel old coastal SS113 (expect traffic); coming from the other direction **(Palermo),** though, the A20 *is* complete. The *centro storico* is closed to traffic during business hours, so once you arrive, you may want to look for a parking spot along the lungomare (ocean drive) or in the often fully occupied Piazza Cristoforo Colombo adjacent to the historic quarter.

VISITOR INFORMATION   The **tourist office** (☎ **0921-21050;** fax 0921-22-386), is in the old city across from the medieval **Osteria Magna (Great Guesthouse),** where King Roger himself stayed during his visits. It's open Monday to Saturday 8am to 2:30pm and 3:30 to 7:00pm. There are information booths at the train station and on Piazza Garibaldi, open Monday to Saturday 9am to 1pm and 5:30 to 9pm (in winter, the hours may be shorter or it may close altogether).

A Money-Saving Tip

Pick up a copy of **"Cefalù Consiglia"** at any local travel agency. This advertising booklet contains some incentive discounts for frequenting some area restaurants, consisting of coupons that are generally 3,000L ($1.50) off of a daily rental of beach lounges and umbrellas at cooperating establishments.

STROLLING THE TOWN & CLIMBING THE MOUNTAIN

Corso Ruggiero is the quaint and lively pedestrianized main drag of Cefalù, lined with shops and modest medieval palazzi and prime real estate for the evening *passegiata*. A leisurely stroll leads to **Piazza del Duomo,** a palm-shaded, cafe-lined square serving as a stage for the monumental twin-towered facade of the ✪ **Duomo** (☎ **0921-922-021**), a Norman architectural masterpiece magnificently set against the foot of the towering cliffs. Roger II built this first of Sicily's western-style cathedrals in 1131, supposedly in thanks after his ship found shelter here during a violent storm. By 1166, they'd put the finishing touches on the altar mosaics, fantastic Greek-Byzantine creations featuring a mighty *Christ Pancrator* in the curve of the apse with outstretched hands. Local lore says that although nine workers had been hired for the creation of the mosaic, ten men were present during the actual inlaying, so the face of Jesus, whose eyes follow you from any point within the church, is said to have been done by an angel. The cathedral is open daily 8am to noon and 3:15 to 7:30pm (later in summer).

From the edge of the Duomo square, Via Mandralisca leads down to the **Museo Mandralisca** at no. 13 (☎ **0921-421-547**). Be sure to take a look at the family's restored glass-enclosed **oil warehouse** on your way into the small museum whose sparse treasures include a 4th-century B.C. vase showing a tuna vendor and customer haggling, and ✪ **Antonella da Messina's** smirking *Portrait of a Man* (1460s). Admission is 8,000L ($4); it's open daily 9am to 1pm and 3 to 7pm (in summer 9am to 7pm or later).

Continue down Via Mandralisca to Via Vittorio Emanuele, turn left, and head to the large opened wrought-iron gate marked **Discesa Fiume,** leading right down to the **Lavatorio** (washroom). This small enclosed courtyard was used as a Laundromat during the Arab époque and takes advantage of a natural freshwater spring. The washroom is complete with stone basins and wedge-shaped scrubbing slabs. Head the other way down Via Vittorio Emanuele to glimpse into the dock-front rooms on the left where fishermen mend their nets, and finally turn left into the little **fishing wharf** itself, where the pebbly beach is filled with sun-bleached wooden boats and (in summer) suntanned swimmers. The uneven row of waterfront boathouses with their yawning Gothic arches was used for scenes in the Oscar-winning film *Cinema Paradiso,* and the washed-out colors of the ancient facades are as poetic as ever.

If you have a hankering for a steep climb, you can tackle the hearty 917-foot hike up the **Rocca** (wear shoes with good treads for the slippery walk down). An hour should provide plenty of time for a brisk walk straight up and down, but allow enough time to enjoy the sunset from the **panoramic position** above Cefalù Bay. To get there, follow the yellow sign from Corso Ruggiero through the alleyway and up a set of iron stairs, continuing up until you spot the railed stairway on the left. About halfway (at the outer fortress wall), the path splits. Steps to the right lead the long way up to the overgrown foundations of a 13th-century **Byzantine fortress** at the very top of the mountain. The path to the left leads past ancient cisterns and remnants of medieval houses (and a long picturesquely crenellated wall), to the **Tempio di Diana (Temple of Diana),** a tiny chapel of a monument, one of the oldest structures left standing in Sicily. Left neglected and overgrown and in dire need of a pooper-scooping, this Greek-era temple rests on foundations from the 9th-century B.C. The temple, made of huge stones fitted together, is hauntingly isolated, with just of a few of its doorways surviving. A path to the right above the temple leads steeply to the mountaintop fortress.

AFFORDABLE PLACES TO STAY

Cefalù is a compact and picturesque town on the beach. Even so, as a pool rather than a beach person, I preferred secluded accommodations on the outskirts, even when the train tracks passed just beyond my door. No matter where you choose to stay, be prepared for funny-tasting tap water that never truly gets hot.

✪ **Baia del Capitano.** 90015 Contrada Mazzaforno/Cefalù. ☎ **0921-420-003.** Fax 0921-420-163. E-mail: seac@kefa.it. 29 units. AC TV TEL. 95,000–130,000L ($48–$65) single; 160,000–210,000L ($80–$105) double. A/C 20,000L ($10) per day. Rates include breakfast (less 15,000L/$8 without breakfast) and reflect seasonal fluctuations. Special rates for families and newlyweds. AE, MC, V. Free parking. Exit the state hwy to the right, then immediate left, follow signs. From train station, a taxi costs 20,000L ($10).

Isolated from Cefalù's modern center, the Baia del Capitano provides a piece of paradise for those seeking solitude. The location also offers a bit of rural charm, as you have to pass through a slightly overgrown gravel road to access the eye-catching rocky beach below (at press time, a safety warning had been placed at the top of the steps to the rocks, but people in these parts don't pay attention to minor impediments). There's also foot access to a pebble beach 10 minutes away. Without sacrificing charm, the rooms are noticeably more welcoming than those at most of the other places in town, with the additional pleasure of a small terrace overlooking the pool. There's bus service (2,500L/$1.25) about every 2 hours between the hotel and Cefalù's center, and in summer, an outdoor garden becomes a barbecue and Sicilian folklore show.

La Giara. Via Veterani 40 (between the Duomo and the harbor), 90015 Cefalù (PA). ☎ **0921-421-562.** Fax 0921-422-518. www.move.to/la_giara. E-mail: la_giara@freemail.it. 24 units. TEL. 58,000–100,000L ($29–$50) single; 100,000–160,000L ($50–$80) double. July 15–Sept 15 required half-pension supplement 25,000L ($13) per person. Rates include breakfast. AE, MC, V.

The only hotel in the historic center is the sort of place where repeat guests hug the owners good-bye when checking out. An elevator scoots you up to the pleasantly functional midsize rooms with wood-plated furnishings and well-worn cots. The units on the street are a bit noisier, but most rooms overlook tiny Arab courtyards and narrow Saracen alleys. The roof terrace gets lots of sun and views of the city roof tiles, with the top half of the Duomo rising under the Rocca a few hundred feet away. The owners are very proud of the city and its history and traditions, especially in the kitchen, and will be unhappy if you don't indulge in the half-pension in their adjunct restaurant.

Le Calette. Via Vincenzo Cavallaro 12, 90015, Cefalù (PA). ☎ **0921-424-144.** Fax 0921-423-688. 50 units. AC TV TEL. 75,000–150,000L ($38–$75) single; 100,000–200,000L ($50–$100) double. Rates include breakfast. AE, DC, MC, V. Free parking. Closed Nov–Easter. Follow Via Roma to the end; turn right at the "T" onto Via Gibbilmanna; turn left immediately after tunnel; follow the road around ¾ mile; turn left at stop sign and left again following signs to the hotel entrance. A taxi from the train station will run around 10,000L/$5.

The rooms commune with nature in this rustic-style motel a few kilometers east of the *centro storico*. Even though Le Calette is sandwiched between the cliff's edge and the train tracks, I chose this spot over the Baia del Capitano for the second-floor balcony overlooking the pool area and small cement marina. The rooms are a bit bland, but the baths are roomy and well kept, and wood-shuttered doors opening onto the terrace (ground-floor rooms open onto the pool patio) make you feel more connected with the outdoors. An inner door separates the sleeping area from the entryway and bath, effectively muffling the commotion from frequent train runs. For those doubtful of the train, the neighboring and slightly more upscale and modern (if not a bit sterile) **Kalura Hotel** (☎**0921-421-354,** fax 0921-423-122, www.kefa.it/kalura;

e-mail: kalurakef@pn.itnet.it) is better positioned away from the tracks and enjoys an unspoiled beach location below the cliffs. Singles run 115,000L ($58) and doubles 210,000L ($105).

GREAT DEALS ON DINING

Considering that historic Cefalù occupies such a small area, there are certainly plenty of places to eat. If you're absolutely set on sticking to your budget, skip dinner on the bayside terraces and walk to the fringes along the beach. But even here along the *lungomare*, don't be so smug and convince yourself that you've exited the tourist trap. Even oceanside trattorias need to unload yesterday's fish, so if you'd like to avoid food poisoning, stick to the old reliable pastas and pizzas.

La Brace. Via 25 Novembre 10 (off Corso Ruggero). ☎ **0921-423-570.** Reservations required for dinner. Primi 9,000–10,000L ($4.50–$5); secondi 12,000–24,000L ($6–$12); fixed-price menus 30,000L ($15;) with wine but no *primo* or 50,000L ($25) with everything but wine. AE, DC, MC, V. Tues–Sun 1–2:30pm and 7–11pm. Closed Dec 15–Jan 15. INNOVATIVE SICILIAN.

The service can be interminably slow and the owner slightly overwhelmed by the flow of people at the oldest restaurant in town, but Le Brace remains popular among locals as well as visitors. Co-owner Dietmar Beckers' Dutch influence must be in the more creative dishes, such as *involtini di melanzane* (eggplant wrapped around tagliatelle and ricotta, then baked under tomatoes and parmesan) and roast beef over ricotta with balsamic vinegar, though the eggplant rolls would've been better served hot and the roast beef would've been tastier as a carpaccio. Perhaps these innovations are a bit of a stretch for these Italian cooks, so it's advisable to stick to sure bets like *spaghetti alla crudaiola* (with garlic, capers, tomatoes, and basil), *spaghetti con gamberi e pesce spada* (with shrimp and swordfish), or *tagliatelle con funghi porcini.* Prices include the usual *pane, coperto,* and *servizio* (bread, cover, and service), leaving you to splurge on that *banana Le Brace,* a banana doused with orange liqueur, baked in foil, and topped with whipped cream.

L'Antica Corte. Cortile Pepe 7 (near the end of Corso Ruggero). ☎ **0921-423-228.** Reservations recommended. Primi 7,500–15,000L ($3.75–$8); secondi 9,000–22,000L ($4.50–$11); pizza 6,500–14,000L ($3.25–$7); *menù turistico* 23,000L ($12) with wine. AE, MC, V. Fri–Wed noon–3pm and 7pm–midnight (daily June 15–Sept 15 and Sat–Sun only in Nov). SICILIAN.

It's a bit schlocky, with waiters wearing red bandannas around their necks and pirate sashes, but fun nonetheless, especially if you booked ahead for one of the few tables set under grape vines in the tiny Arab courtyard. The pizzas are reliably good, as are the primi; try the *casarecci all'arrabbiata* (homemade pasta in spicy red sauce) or *agli antichi sapori* (homemade pasta with baby shrimp, limoncello liqueur, and mushrooms) or *pasta con sarde* (with sardines, raisins, pine nuts, fennel, and tomatoes). Secondi include the ubiquitous *couscous di pesce* and a *fileto bisanzio* (a pepper steak under a rich gravy with peppers and mushrooms). When the heat gets unbearable, you'll welcome the long rooms of the air-conditioned interior.

✪ **Vecchia Marina.** Via Vittorio Emanuele 73–75 (near Piazza Cristoforo Colombo). ☎ **0921-420-388.** Reservations suggested for dinner. Primi 8,000–10,000L ($4–$5); secondi 14,000–22,000L ($7–$11); *menù* 30,000L ($15). AE, MC, V. Daily noon–3pm and 7–11:30pm. Closed Tues Nov–Easter. SICILIAN.

Popular among locals and a magnet for visitors in the know, Vecchia Marina boasts a romantic location and an outstanding execution of typical Sicilian cuisine. But if you arrive late and find all the waterside tables occupied, the not-so-shabby consolation prize is a narrow dining room elegantly framed under a single-vaulted ceiling. Fresh pasta is featured in the *pasta fresca con sarde fresche,* a local favorite with an intense flavor. Another typical local dish is the appetizer of *bottarga di tonno,* salty smoked tuna roe mashed and formed into rolls that are sliced and served with lemon and toast. The mixed grilled fish tastes like it just landed in the boat, except that the fishermen actually delivered it live to the dining room's centerpiece holding tank. Oysters, clams, and mussels are alive in tanks, and with all this bounty, it'll be hard to leave room for the *cassata,* a sweet pie of creamy ricotta topped with white frosting.

3 Palermo: Sicily's Capital

70km (42 mi.) W of Cefalù, 237km (142 mi.) W of Messina.

"You ain't seen Italy until you've seen Palermo" was Charlie's mantra at Zito's Bakery on New York's Bleecker Street, and though there's no debating the grandeur of the country's sites and there's no doubt to his prejudice, I must say I agree. Sicily's capital is a city of sensory overload, a city that comes to life with the opening of the busy fish markets that burst with life and color, well before the piazzas fill with schoolchildren procrastinating till the last minute, and *cornetti* (croissant) shops clog with the steady flow of laborers ready for their morning shot of caffè.

Founded by the Phoenicians, conquered by the Romans, briefly absorbed by Byzantium, and later made the Saracen capital, **Palermo** lived its "Golden Age" under Norman and Swabian rule. Roger II, along with Frederick II and successive kings, succeeded in blending the city's heritage of architectural styles, resulting in richly ornamented basilicas, stuccoed oratories, luxuriant gardens, and eastern-style arches and arcades. Other layers were added by later empires: the Hohenstaufen and Angevin kings brought the Gothic to Palermo, while the Bourbons of Naples gave Palermo a definite baroque tradition, even if, during 6 centuries of Spanish and Bourbon rule, only one king, Charles V, ever set foot on Sicily. (This hands-off approach effectively dropped Palermo into the clutches of the Mafia, creating problems that have plagued the city ever since.)

Aside from harboring some of Sicily's greatest palaces, churches, and art museums, Palermo retains a decidedly local flavor, with its puppet theaters, local markets, and those infuriating street CD vendors blasting popular selections.

To see Palermo's highlights—the churches, markets, and art museums of the Old Center, the Cappella Palatina, and a day trip to nearby Monreale—plan 2 to 3 days.

ESSENTIALS

GETTING THERE   By Train   There are eight "diretta" trains daily from **Rome** (about 13 hr.; 73,200L/$37) only 90 minutes slower and about 25,000L ($13) cheaper than the first-class Intercity trains (11 hr. 15 min). Three trains daily make the trip from **Naples** (about 10 hr.; 58,200L/$29 or 79,900L/$40 IC); 13 to 16 trains daily from **Messina's Stazione Marittima** (about 4 hr.; 19,500L/$10); and at least hourly trains from **Cefalù** (50 to 75 min.; 7,000L/$3.50). Almost all trains pull into the **Stazione Centrale** (☎ **091-616-7514** or 091-616-806) at the foot of Via Roma (***don't*** get off at the suburban Stazione Notarbartolo).

By Bus   SAIS lines, Via P. Balsamo 16 at Piazza Stazione (☎ **091-616-6028**) runs six buses daily (four on Sunday) from **Messina's** Piazza della Repubblica (3 hr. 15 min; 24,000L/$12); and hourly buses from **Catania** (☎ **095-536-201** or 095-536-168; 2 hr. 40 min.; 22,500L/$11), leaving from both the airport and the Via d'Amico 181 in Piazza Stazione. **Interbus** (☎ **091-616-7919**) also services the Catania-Palermo road with one daily departure (2½ hr.; 22,500L/$11). **Cuffaro lines,** Via P. Balsamo 13 (☎ **091-616-1510**), runs seven buses daily from **Agrigento** (2 hr.; 13,000L/$7). **Segesta lines,** Via Paolo Balsamo 26 (☎ **091-616-7919**), runs every half hour (13 times on Sunday) from **Trapani** (1 hr. 45 min.; 12,000L/$6). From **Rome's** Tiburtina station, there's a daily 9:30pm **Segesta** lines bus (☎ **091-616-7919**; 12 hr.; 65,000L/$33 one-way; 110,000L/$55 round-trip).

By Car   Palermo lies on the coastal A20 autostrada that travels the 237km (147 mi.) from **Messina** through **Cefalù** (though you'll have to detour part of the way onto the old SS113 road due to an unfinished stretch in the superhighway). From Catania, much of the A19 autostrada cuts through the center of Sicily, but it'll be a relatively quick 208km (129 mi). There are **parking** garages at the train station at Piazza Giulio Cesare 43 (☎ **091-616-8297**); near the port at Via Guardione 81 (☎ **091-322-649**); and a 24-hour garage in the new city (between the Politeama theater and Ucciardone prison) at Via Archimede 88 (☎ **091-581-658**).

By Ferry   SNAV (☎ **081-761-2348** in Naples, or 091-611-8525 in Palermo) runs a 4-hour hydrofoil from **Naples** daily at 5:30pm (120,000L/$60) but only from June 26 to September 14. The return to Naples leaves Palermo at 9am. Year-round, **Tirrenia** (68,100L/$34 deck; 77,100L/$39 recliner in high season; see a travel agent for information or consult their Italian-language Web site at www.tirrenia.com) makes the 11-hour trip nightly, departing Naples at 8pm and arriving promptly in Palermo at 7am. A shared cuccette in 2nd class costs around 90,500L ($45), a 1st-class share costs 132,000L ($66), and singles are 50% more. A bench on deck will keep you within your budget, but does not include trips to the chiropractor; airline-type reclining seats are available as a happy medium.

By Plane   Palermo's **Aeroporto Falcone-Borsellino** (☎ **147-865-643** toll free or 091-702-0313 for information), also called Punta Raisi, is 30km (18 mi.) west of the city center on A29. There are daily direct flights in from all of Italy's major cities and from London, Barcelona, and Frankfurt. The **Prestia & Comandè bus** (☎ **091-580-457**) heads to central Palermo every 30 minutes from 5am until the arrival of the last scheduled flight, and costs 6,500L ($3.25), making stops at Piazza Ruggero Settimo and Hotel Elena at the train station. If you're laden with luggage, you can catch a taxi for 60,000L ($30) (that's the regular fare plus an obligatory and totally legal 15,000L/$8 supplement; add 3,000L/$1.50 for nights plus 500L/25¢ per bag).

CITY LAYOUT   Central Palermo is divided into a **Centro Storico (Old City)** to the south and a **Città Moderna (New City)** to the north by **Via Cavour.** There are two main north-south roads. **Via Maqueda/Via Ruggero Settimo** starts just left of the train station and crosses Via Cavour at the central **Piazza Verdi,** also called **Teatro Massimo** after the theater at its center. Roughly parallel to Via Maqueda to the east is **Via Roma,** a busier and more commercialized boulevard that starts directly across from the train station.

Old Center   **Corso Vittorio Emanuele** runs east-west through the heart of this area. It crosses Via Maqueda at the **Quattro Canti (Four Corners),** neatly dividing the Old Center into traditional quadrants. To the southeast of this intersection lies **La Kalsa,** once the Saracen Emir's walled quarter for his and other Arab nobles' palaces. These were later replaced with medieval *palazzi* and baroque oratories, but the neighborhood was badly bombed during World War II and is still partly in ruins. Though many of Palermo's central sights are here, it's one of the more dangerous areas after dark and probably not the best place to base yourself. To the southwest of Quattro Canti lies the residential **Alberghiera,** home to the vast Ballarò market and more bombed-out

A Surrey Without the Fringe

On Sundays, when the historic center is closed to traffic, it's the perfect time to take advantage of the romance of the 19th century in **pedal carriages** for two or four people (5,000L/$2.50 and 10,000L/$5 per hour, respectively). Organized by **Cici Time** (☎ **0347-666-3269**), the carriages are available on weekends year-round and daily in summer.

zones, and also less than safe after dark. The center's northwest quadrant is **Sincaldi,** and aside from the Capo market holds relatively little of specific interest to the visitor. Finally, the northeast **Amalfitani** district is the smallest of the quarters (La Cala harbor intrudes to fill half of it), home to the Vucciria fish market. It's so small that the Via Roma division down its middle helps keep the zone less mazelike, a bit brighter, and more commercially oriented.

New City   The center of this grid of easily navigable, broad roads is **Piazza Castelnuovo/Politeama,** where Via Maqueda (now called **Via Ruggero Settimo**) crosses **Via** Emerico **Amari.** We're most interested in the hotel-, bar-, and restaurant-filled southern half of the New City—centered on such streets as the wide **Via Mariano Stabile** to the port and the pedestrian-only **Via Principe di Belmonte**—than the sprawling urban residential section to the north.

GETTING AROUND   By Bus   Palermo's bus system is modern and efficient, with the **major central lines** routed down Via Roma, Via Maqueda, and Corso Vittorio Emanuele. The most useful **hubs** are at the Stazione Centrale/Piazza Giulio Cesare (the train station), Piazza Indipendenza (behind the royal Palazzo dei Normanni at the end of Corso Vittorio Emanuele), Piazza Verdi/Teatro Massimo, and Piazza Castelnuovo/Politeama. A **bus ticket,** available at most newsstands and *tabacchi* (tobacconists) costs 1,500L (75¢) and is valid for 60 minutes; an all-day pass is 5,000L ($2.50).

By Metro   Mostly a commuter railway, Palermo's metro (☎ **091-616-1806**) basically doesn't go near the major tourist sites Take the bus.

By Taxi   To call a taxi, dial ☎ **091-513-311,** 091-513-374, 091-225-455 or 091-225-460. There are taxi stands at the train stations as well as at Piazza Verdi (Teatro Massimo), Piazza Ruggero Settimo (Teatro Politeama), and Piazza Indipendenza. Taxis cost 6,000L($3), plus 4,000L($2) for the first kilometer and 1,300L (65¢) per kilometer after that. Make sure the meter is always on and running.

VISITOR INFORMATION   There's a **tourist office** in the main train station (☎ **091-616-5914;** www.aapit.pa.it) open Monday to Friday 8:30am to 2pm and 3 to 6pm and Saturday 8:30am to 2pm (Saturday evening and Sunday hours may be added; call ahead). Besides the city map, make sure you ask for a copy of *Palermo & Provincia Live,* a bimonthly publication with lots of handy tourist information plus an events calendar. The main office, at Piazza Castelnuovo 34 (☎ **091-583-847;** fax 091-586-338), is a little less harried and has a few more pamphlets, as well as lots more information on not only the province and day-tripping possibilities but all of Sicily. There's a branch at the airport as well (☎ **091-591-698**).

A FESTIVAL   Palermo's blowout festival, U Fistinu, the **feast of patroness St. Rosalia,** takes place on July 14 and is celebrated with costumed processions and a fantastic fireworks display over the harbor.

FAST FACTS: Palermo

American Express   The local AMEX representative is at **Giovanni Ruggieri e Figli,** Via Emerico Amari 40 at the corner of Via La Masa (☎ **091-587-144**). It's open Monday to Friday 9am to 1pm and 4 to 7pm and Saturday 9am to 1pm. To report a lost card, dial ☎ **167-018-839.**

Bookstores   By far the best selection of books in English is at **Feltrinelli,** Via Maqueda 395 (☎ **091-587-785**). For the best music books and recordings head to **Ricordi** at Via Cavour 133.

Consulates   The **U.S. Consulate** is at Via Vaccarini 1 (☎ **091-305-857**). The **U.K. Consular representative** is at Via Cavour 117 (☎ **091- 326-412**).

Emergencies   For general emergencies, call the Carabinieri at ☎ **112.** For the city **police,** dial ☎ **113;** for an **ambulance,** ☎ **118** or 091-306-644; for **fires,** ☎ **115;** for **road assistance,** ☎ **116.**

Hospitals   The emergency room closest to the center is at the **Ospedale Civico** (☎ **091-606-2207**), off Via Carmelo Lazzaro (in the upper left-hand corner of the tourist office map). Take bus 108 from Politeama or Piazza Indipendenza or bus 246 from the train station. *Warning:* It's not the most modernized hospital, out in no-man's land beyond empty lots and dirt roads. The people at the main emergency desk are the ones who can help you, despite the sign that tells tourists to go to some other office down around the corner (they'll just send you back to the main desk). For an ambulance, dial ☎ **118** or 091-306-644.

Police   Dial ☎ **113** for the Carabinieri (national police force), **112** for the city police.

Mail & E-Mail   The **main post office** (with fax service) is at Via Roma 322 (☎ **091-321-507**), open Monday to Friday 8:15am to 6:30pm, Saturday 8:30am to 1:30pm. There are branches at the **train station** (no phone), open Monday to Saturday 8:30am to 1pm; and the **airport** (☎ **091-651-9239**), open Monday to Saturday 8:10am to 1:20pm. There's **an Internet cafe, Internett@mente,** at Via Sammartino 3A, near Piazza Amendola and the Politeama Theater (☎ **091-612-1174**), open Monday 2 to 8pm and Tuesday to Saturday 10am to 8pm. **Safety**   Palermo is not the safest of Italian cities, with the crime problems of both a big city and a port town, but it isn't much more dangerous than Big Town, USA, either. Yes, there's a strong Mafia presence, but despite splashy headlines and Hollywood imaginations, you're not going to be caught in some kind of good-fellas crossfire. You should be more worried about common thievery and **rampant pickpocketing;** take the necessary common-sense precautions, don't flash valuables, and keep your camera inconspicuous and firmly in hand. Most of the Old Center is a bit dicey, especially after dark—steer clear particularly of the southern half of the Old Center: La Kalsa, the Alberghiera, and around the train station. Stick to Via Roma and Corso Vittorio Emanuele at night. Most of the New City is as safe as any Italian city.

Transit Information   The city bus company is **AMAT** (toll-free ☎ **167-018-378** or 091-690-2690).

A Sightseeing Tip

August sees many Palermo sights locked up and the custodians of smaller churches and stuccoed chapels ordered to hang up their keys for a month. However, some of the major sights actually go on longer hours, re-opening 8:30 to 11pm or so; ask the tourist office for a list.

A Money-Saving Tip

The city's experimental closing of the *centro storico* to traffic on the first Sunday of every month was so successful that they've extended it to every Sunday, freeing the entire zone of exhaust fumes and noise pollution. Making the event even more attractive to visitors, admission is free on the first Sunday of every month to the following museums: Galleria Regionale Siciliana, Museo Archaeologico Salinas, Palazzo Mirto, and San Giovanni degli Eremiti.

SEEING THE SIGHTS

✪ Galleria Regionale di Palazzo Abatellis. Via Alloro 4. ☎ **091-623-0011.** Admission 8,000L ($4). Mon–Sat 9am–1pm; Sun 9am–12:30pm and Tues, Thurs 3–7:30pm. Bus: 103, 105, 139, 225, 824.

This is one of the best art museums in Sicily, well worth an hour or two of your time. The ground floor of this 15th-century, Catalan-Gothic-meets-Renaissance palazzo contains the sculpture collection, including one room devoted to Francesco Laurana (look for his bust of Eleonora of Aragon) and another room to a passel of Madonnas by the Gagini clan. Also down here is the 1449 fresco of the ✪ *Triumph of Death,* by an unknown but clearly warped hand (possibly Flemish or from the school of Pisanello). The skeleton of death rides an emaciated horse, felling with his arrows an undue number of bishops and popes.

Upstairs is the painting gallery, starring works by Sicily's greatest Renaissance master, Antonella da Messina, including his signature masterpiece, the ✪ *Madonna Annunziata.* This is an "Annunciation" scene from the angel Gabriel's point of view, wherein a quiet, delicately featured Mary interrupted at her reading stretches out her hand to us from under the voluminous pyramid of an intensely blue shawl. Also be on the lookout for the incredibly detailed 16th-cenutry *Malvagna Triptych* by Mabuse, Pietro Novelli's early-17th-century Mannerist *Madonna and Child in Glory,* and Francesco Solimena's *Return of Joseph's Brothers.*

Palazzo Mirto. Via Merlo 2 (off Piazza Marina). ☎ **091-616-4751.** Admission 4,000L ($2) adults, free under 18 and over 60. Mon–Sat 9am–7pm; Sun and holidays 9am–12:30pm. (Also open some evenings in summer). Bus: 103, 105, 139, 225, 824.

Most of Palermo's glorious and famed 18th- and 19th-century palazzi are rotting behind their massive doors, but this one is open to the public for a glimpse into the lifestyle of Palermo's wealthy caste of centuries past. The noble Filangeri-Lanza family lived in this palace from the 17th century until 1982, and it's furnished exactly as it was in the 19th century, which included many 17th- and 18th-century pieces. Don't miss the tiny Chinese-style room with its remarkable trompe l'oeil ceiling.

✪ Museo Internazionale delle Marionette (International Museum of Marionettes). Via Butera 1 (off Piazza Marina). ☎ **091-328-060.** 5,000L ($2.50) adults, 3,000L ($1.50) under 18, over 60, and students. Mon–Fri 9am–1pm, 4–7pm, Sat 9am–1pm. Bus: 103, 105, 139, 225, 824.

This is one of the world's largest collections of puppets, inventively documenting a cultural and artistic craft heritage that spans the globe from Javanese stick puppets, Indonesian silhouettes, the Turkish "shadow play," and Chinese dolls to Neapolitan *Pulcinella* (Punch and Judy) hand puppets and, of course, Sicilian marionettes—many displayed against original stages and backgrounds.

Marionette shows were Sicily's poor man's theater over the past few centuries, telling tales of Charlemagne and the adventures of his knights, as well as swashbuckling

Saracen pirate stories and even opera. No visit to Sicily is complete without attending a show, and on Fridays at 5:30pm (10,000L/$5; 2,000L/$1 last Friday of the month) the lights dim and these artistic creatures come to life as warriors in battle or fire-eating dragons. For other puppet plays, see "Palermo After Dark," below.

Quattro Canti (Four Corners) & Piazza Pretoria. The intersection of Corso Vittorio Emanuele and Via Maqueda. Bus: 101, 102, 105.

Quattro Canti is the nickname for old Palermo's dead-center intersection. Each of the four corners of the intersection are sculpted into elaborate concave corner facades, each containing three sculptural levels stacked atop fountains. The lower level symbolizes the seasons, the middle level contains statues of the four Spanish kings of Sicily, and the upper section is adorned with statues of the patronesses of the city: Santa Cristina, Sant'Oliva, Sant'Agata, and Santa Ninfa. Today, the site is choked by heavy traffic and its facades are blackened by pollution, but a recent cleaning has uncovered a glimmer of the grandeur the Quattro Canti must have enjoyed during Palermo's theatrical 17th century.

Just south of this intersection, off Via Maqueda, is the raised pedestrian **Piazza Pretoria,** centered on a Mannerist **fountain** sculpted for a Florentine villa in the 1550s but rejected by its commissioners. Palermo bought the thing and set it, piece by piece (644 in all), proudly at city center, though the local populace, scandalized by the racy nude figures and lewd glances these statues were throwing each other across the water jets, promptly renamed it the **Fontana della Vergogna (Fountain of Shame).** This hasn't stopped them from making it a 24-hour sight, dramatically floodlit at night. Alas, the circular fountain is currently visible only through a disappointing peephole, as it's completely encased in a huge wooden barrel for restorations.

Clearly, Palermo didn't make the Jubilee deadline for restoration, so if, by divine providence, the church of **Santa Caterina** capping the piazza's east end has finally reopened when you visit, pop inside for one of the most elaborate baroque marble-and-stucco interiors in Palermo. If it's still closed, content yourself with the grand baroque interior of **San Giuseppe dei Teatini,** on the southwest corner of the Quattro Canti (enter from the front on Corso Vittorio Emanuele or the side on Via Maqueda). Aside from the dome frescoes by Borremans, there's not much to single out inside, but the scale and richness of the decorations make it stand out.

✪ La Martorana (aka Santa Maria dell'Ammiraglio) & San Cataldo. Piazza Bellini 3 (next door to Piazza Pretoria). ☎ **091-616-1692.** Admission free. La Martorana open Mon–Sat 8:30am–1pm, 3:30–7:00pm, Sun 8:30am–1pm; San Cataldo open Mon–Fri 9am–3:30pm, Sat, Sun 9am–1pm. Bus: 101, 102.

La Martorana may have submitted to a number of disfiguring modifications, but this mosaic church and its next-door neighbor San Cataldo—that of the little dark pink domes—are still some of the finest works of Sicilian architecture. Enter **La Martorana** under the surviving 12th-century bell tower of lithe columns and corrugated archways where you can still make out the original Greek cross layout. Aside from some

---

A Money-Saving Tip

The purchase of a 2-day combination ticket will gain you access to the Archaeological Museum, the Palazzo Mirto, and the Palazzo Abatellis for 15,000L ($8), a savings of 22,000L ($11). Two alternative combinations allow for visits to the Archaeological Museum and Palazzo Abatellis (12,000L/$6) or just the two palazzi (10,000L/$5). Tickets are available at the ticket windows of any of the three sites.

Palermo

ATTRACTIONS ●

Catacombe del Convento
  dei Cappuccini **5**
Cattedrale **8**
Galleria Regionale di Palazzo
  Abatellis **22**
La Martorana & San Cataldo **11**
Museo Archeologico Regionale **3**
Museo Internazionale delle
  Marionette **20**
Palazzo dei Normanni **6**
Palazzo Mirto **18**
San Giovanni degli Eremiti **7**
Santa Caterina **13**

ACCOMMODATIONS ■

Casa Giuditta **21**
Centrale Palace Hotel **9**
Gardenia **2**
Moderno **14**
Posta **4**
Sausele **24**
Sole **10**
Villa Archirafi **23**

DINING ◆

Antica Focacceria San Francesco **17**
Bellini **12**
Casa del Brodo **16**
Hosteria Al Duar **1**
La Cambusa **19**
Santandrea **15**

minimal baroque redecoration and 1717 frescoes by Borremans, the interior is pure glittering gold-back mosaic, done between 1140 and 1155 by the finest artists imported from Constantinople. Notice the dedicatory mosaic of George of Anti-ochia—whose generous donation made the church possible—at the feet of the Virgin Mary, and the symbolic crowning of Christ by Roger II.

In sharp contrast, the only thing the little Arab/Byzantine church of **San Cataldo** got for decorations are those pink, mosquelike domelets and some crenellations ringing the top. Although San Cataldo served for a time as a post office in the 18th century, today the interior has been stripped wonderfully bare again, a quiet stony vault whose trio each of aisles, apses, and domes are lit through the traditionally Islamic stone latticework of the small windows.

Cattedrale (Cathedral). Corso Vittorio Emanuele. ☎ **091-334-376.** Admission to church free; crypt 1,000L (50¢); treasury 1,000L (50¢). Church Mon–Sat 7am–9pm, Sun 8am–1:30pm and 4–7pm; treasury Mon–Sat 9:30am–5:30pm. Bus: 104, 105.

Palermo's cathedral is not the city's greatest church, rather it's a hodgepodge of styles uncomfortably knitted together. The original 1185 Norman structure (visible in the towers and apses at the east end), was constructed on the oldest and most sacred part of Palermo, replacing a Muslim mosque. Over time, additions and restorations modified the original structure, from the 15th-century Catalan-Gothic overhaul, to the incongruous 1801 baroque dome inflicted upon it by Ferdinando Fuga (who also revamped the interior).

The entrance is partway down the right aisle, through the well-crafted **Catalan-Gothic porch,** with 15th-century wooden doors and a column on the far left, salvaged from the 9th-century mosque that once stood here (carved with a worn Arabic inscription from the Koran). Once inside, to your left are the dark, gated-off chapels containing a block party of **Norman royal tombs,** housing the mortal remains of, among others, **Emperor Frederick II** in the left-front sarcophagus, and, partially obstructed, the mosaicked canopy tomb of **Roger II** behind him.

The **former High Altar** sculptural ensemble by Antonello Gagini has since been dismantled and dispersed throughout the church. Its statues line the nave, a bit still serves as the main altar, and three reliefs and an *Assumption* reside in the second chapel of the left aisle, while in the Santa Rosalia chapel in a 17th-century silver urn are the **ashes of the patron saint** of Palermo. The seventh chapel on the left has a nice *Madonna* statue by Francesco Laurana.

One of the most interesting things about the interior is the **meridian** line transecting the floor of the nave near the altar, central to a system of time-telling instituted in 1794 by astronomer Giuseppe Piazzi in order to bring Sicily up to European standards. The meridian is made up of an opening in the roof of a lateral cupola, and a long line of brass, bordered by the symbols of the zodiac.

Don't bother paying to visit the boring collection of tombs in the **crypt,** but the **treasury** is worthwhile for the nifty, 12th-century bejeweled caplike crown that Frederick II's wife, Constance of Aragon, was wearing when her tomb was opened in the 18th century.

✪ Palazzo dei Normanni (Palace of the Normans) & Capella Palatina (Palatine Chapel). Piazza Indipendenza. ☎ **091-705-4317** palazzo, 091-705-4879 Cappella Palatina. Admission free. Palazzo open Mon, Fri, Sat 9am–noon; Capella Palatina open Mon–Fri 9–11:45am and 3–4:45pm, Sun 9–10am and noon–1pm. Bus: 104, 105, 108, 109, 110, 118, 304, 305, 309, 318, 327, 339, 364, 365, 368, 380, 389.

Most of the royal palace itself—built by the Saracens and enlarged by the Normans (Roger II and Frederick II both held court here) and again later by the Aragonese—

The Wheel Deal

In an effort to make Palermo more tourist-friendly, foreigners get **free bike rentals,** while Italians still have to cough up the lire). The principal (and most central) location is Piazza Castelnuovo at Politeama, open every day from 9am to 6pm (longer hours in summer); with future sites planned for Stazione Notarbartolo and on the beach at Mondello. Call ☎ **091-322-425** for bike rental information.

---

has been closed for years. Among the visitable sections are the **royal apartments**—little to write home about—and the not-to-be-missed mosaicked **Sala di Re Ruggero,** one of the few rooms retaining its original Norman look and swathed in details of stylized beasts.

Even with the palace closed, the tour buses still line up, bringing visitors to file into Palermo's most stunning sight, the Byzantine Greek mosaics of the ✪ **Cappella Palatina,** built by Roger II in the 1130s. It takes the form of a tiny basilica, every inch covered in rich religious mosaics symbolically glorifying the enlightened reign of Roger II. The craftsmanship is exquisite, using not only gold-backed tessere but also silver mosaic tiles to cause the softly lit surfaces to sparkle and gleam in a kaleidoscope of saints and Old Testament characters. The mosaics on the nave walls date from a bit later (1150s) and exhibit a more Roman styling, while the mosaicked *Christ with Sts. Peter and Paul* above the Norman throne are 15th century. The unexpected *muqarna* design—a traditionally Islamic motif—on the ceiling, carved in Lebanese cedar, is surprising considering its placement in a church, but indicative of the multiplicity of character of not only Palermo, but all of Sicily.

San Giovanni degli Eremiti. Via dei Benedettini (at Via Antonio Mongitore). ☎ **091-651-5019.** Admission 4,000L ($2). Mon–Sat 9am–7pm; Sun 9am–12:30pm. Sometimes closed Sun in winter. Bus: 109, 108, 305, 318, 368.

One of the city's most romantic spots is this ruined 12th-century church and monastery complex on the Albergheria's western edge, whose five unmistakable Arabo-Norman red domes are often used as a symbol of the city. The simple church is set amid luxuriant gardens of palm, Indian fig cacti, and citrus and pomegranate trees, where little paths lead to the evocative remains of 13th-century cloisters and into a small rectangular building that was once a mosque.

✪ **Catacombe del Convento dei Cappuccini (Capuchin Catacombs & Convent).** Via Cappuccini 1 (many blocks up from Piazza Indipendenza). ☎ **091-212-117.** Obligatory "donation" 2,500L ($1.25). Daily 9am–noon, 3–5pm. Bus: 327 from Piazza Independenza.

This is one of the most macabre yet fascinating sights in Italy, a subterranean house of the dead for only those entitled (read: rich) enough to afford such an extravagant "burial." The monks began preserving their dead here in 1599, but it soon became fashionable, and sections were created for the wealthy (men and women separate), priests, professors, and children. The plaster-walled network of high, lit tunnels is crammed with the fully dressed, mummified bodies of some 8,000 dead Palermitani dangling from hooks, some preserved in lime or arsenic, but most simply dried out by the naturally controlled climate. The last entombment was in 1920, when 2-year-old Rosalia Lombardo was mummified using a secret chemical injection method that has kept her so remarkably preserved (if a little sallow) she's dubbed the "Sleeping Beauty." But even in death, gravity takes its toll, and many of these aristocrats have simply lost their heads over it.

Museo Archeologico Regionale (Regional Archaeological Museum). Via Bara all'O-livella 24 (between Piazza Verdi and Via Roma). ☎ **091-611-6805** or 091-662-0220. Admission 8,000L ($4). Daily 9am–1:45pm and Tues, Wed, Fri 3–6:45pm. Bus: 101, 102, 103, 104, 107, 122, 124.

Palermo's archaeology museum gathers artifacts from across Sicily, from prehistoric times through the Romans, including one of the most comprehensive collections of Etruscan artifacts in the world. It's not a sizeable collection, but it is rich, and worth at least an hour of your time. The highlights are the ✪ **metopes of Selinunte,** a series of decorative friezes—the only ones in Sicily decorated with sculpture—that show a development from the 6th-century B.C. archaic style to the more classically inspired 5th-century B.C. metopes from Temple E (see Selinunte, below). Among the rest of the collections, look for the 6th-century B.C. **oinochoe vase** from the Etruscan town of Chiusi (Tuscany), one of the most elaborate pieces of Etruscan *bucchero* (blackened earthenware) in existence. Among the Roman bronzes are a 3rd century B.C. **ram** and a **Heracles fighting a stag** that may have served as the centerpiece for a Pompeiian villa's fountain.

Sanctuario di Santa Rosalia & Monte Pellegrino. Via Pietro Bonanno (14km/9miles north of the city center). ☎ **091-540-326.** Admission free. Daily 7:45am–6pm (you have to pop in between frequent masses). Bus: 812. The road to the sanctuary is temporarily closed for construction, so you'll have to hike the old pilgrimage foot path up the hill for 458m (1,500 ft).

Looming impressively over north Palermo and thankfully protected as parkland, the sheer cliffs and green cradles of trees covering the 2,000-foot **Monte Pellegrino** headland make it look more like it belongs at Yosemite or in some Japanese silk painting than in Sicily. This mountain has seen Paleolithic cave art (casts of which are in the archaeology museum), a 3-year battle during the first Punic War between Rome and Carthage, and hordes of Christian pilgrims for the past 4 centuries.

Santa Rosalia, a niece of William II, lived and died as a religious hermit here on the mountain. In 1624, during a vicious plague, she appeared in a vision to a man and showed him the cave where her remains lay unburied. Palermitani carried these relics through the town to give them a consecrated burial, whereupon the plague stopped and Rosalia was swiftly granted patron-saint status. Her cave was outfitted with pews and a baroque foyer to become the popular pilgrimage chapel **Sanctuario di Santa Rosalia,** where the holy water flows from plastic cooler jugs and all the merchandise in the gift shop has been blessed for your convenience. In the cave sanctuary itself, thin spikes of flattened steel cobweb hang from the ceiling like some conceptual modern sculpture—they're to channel the watery mineral drippings from would-be stalactites away from the heads of the devout and collect them as a holy, miraculous liquid.

AFFORDABLE PLACES TO STAY

While most of the hotels listed below are on the fringes of the historic quarter, you can get a taste of the days of yore at the newly renovated **Casa Giuditta,** Via Savona 10 (☎ **328-225-0788;** fax 02-7004-01920; e-mail casagiuditta@yahoo.com), a four-star hotel/residence at two-star prices. Apartments (with clothes washers!) are located in the admittedly dubious but ornate neighborhood of La Kalsa and are available for one to six people (more on request) at prices beginning at 80,000L ($40) per person. Rates go down the longer you stay.

✪ **Gardenia.** Via Mariano Stabile 136, 90139 Palermo. ☎ **091-322-761.** Fax 091-333-732. www.gardeniahotel.com. E-mail: gardenia@gardeniahotel.com. 16 units. A/C TV TEL. 100,000L ($50) single; 140,000L ($70) double; 35,000L ($18) supplement for extra bed. Breakfast 10,000L ($5). MC, V. Parking 25,000L ($14). Bus: 101, 102, 103, 104, 107, 122, 124.

Street Markets—The Best Free Sightseeing in Town

Markets are an integral part of Palermo life and a colorful sight not to be missed. Vendors hawk potbellied silvery fish, next to Levi's jeans, spiny sea urchins, bootleg CDs, olives from barrels, and succulent fruits and vegetables picked directly from the vine. Bring your camera (but little else) and guard it well. There are close to a dozen markets in town; here are the best.

Even if you're in town for just a day, the **Vucciria** should be on your list of top sites. Originally a meat market (the name is a bastardization of the French "boucherie"), today you're just as likely to see dozens of fish stalls and vegetable stands, or rub elbows with unshaven regulars at an enoteca for a 500L (25¢) glass of wine. The market is sunk below the surrounding streets (head down the stairs just up Via Roma from its intersection with Corso Vittorio Emanuele), and there are some good old-fashioned trattorie hidden here that serve the freshest fish in town (see "Shanghai," under "Great Deals on Dining," below). This most famous of Palermo's markets has gotten a bit touristy in recent years, but the Vucciria is still a sight to behold.

More ebullient these days is the sprawling **Ballarò,** in the Albergheria quadrant, spreading roughly from Piazza Carmine to Piazza Casa Professa and Piazza Santa Chiara. It, too, is mainly a food market, but with a better balance of veggies, meat, cheese, and dry goods mixed in among the fish stalls, plus a section selling cut-price clothing and toys.

The **Capo** market has two parts: a long line of mainly **clothing** stalls snaking down the middle and sides of Via Bandiera/Via Sant'Agostino in the city center; and the Via Porta Carini/Via Beati Paoli **food** section off Via Volturno, where many of the streets have been reduced to dirt roads between the buildings and awnings, and sometimes it's hard to tell whether you're indeed in a major European city or a North African Casbah. Lastly, a treasure trove of **antiques** stalls await in the short, shady **Piazza Peranni,** behind the bishop's palace off Corso Vittorio Emanuele, but this last breaks down and locks up in the early afternoon.

Salvatore Genduso is proud of the renovations in his hotel, especially of the fact that the Gardenia is now completely up to fire code in anticipation of three-star status. What was formerly a worn but comfortable pensione has been transformed into a crisp and spacious collection of rooms sporting brand new modular wooden furniture, bedspreads, bed linens embroidered with hotel initials, and parquet floors contrasting with Persian-style area rugs. The baths are all freshly renovated, though the removal of safety mats in the shower stalls means you'll have to be extra careful not to slip. The upper-floor rooms share a wraparound terrace that has been sectioned off to provide some privacy, with the rooms furthest away from the reception enjoying a glorious view of the mountain. Book well in advance, as Gardenia had few vacancies even prior to the upgrade.

Moderno. Via Roma 276 (at Via Napoli), 90133 Palermo. ☎ **091-588-260.** Fax 091-588-683. 38 units. AC TV TEL. 80,000L ($40) single; 110,000L ($55) double; 145,000L ($73) triple. Breakfast 4,000L ($2). AE, DC, MC, V. Bus: 101, 107.

Signore Consalez has been running his tight ship for 40 years and attributes his success to a rigid no-nonsense policy: If he doesn't like the looks of you—even with a reservation—he'll send you and your grubby attire off packing to sleep on a bench at the train station. If approved, you get to stay in immaculate, modestly sized rooms with shower stalls that glisten and smell faintly of pine. The fourth floor (there's an elevator) has two lucky rooms with a sea view, and if you've booked for an extended stay, you may get breakfast throw in for free.

Posta. Via A. Gagini 77 (parallel to Via Roma, between Piazza San Domenico and Via Cavour), 90133 Palermo. ☎ **091-587-338.** Fax 091-587-347. 27 units, 22 with bathroom. TV TEL. 120,000L ($60) single; 140,000L ($70) double. Rates include breakfast. AE, DC, MC, V. Parking 15,000L ($8); reservations required. Bus: 101, 102, 103, 104, 107, 122.

Posta has been family-run since 1921, and despite its lackluster decor, has been a favorite of Italian actors and writers (including Nobel prizewinner Dario Fo) for years. Everything was redone in 1998, from the modern wood veneer to the white lacquer furniture, so in exchange for the dreariness you get sparkling white tile floors, comfortably large rooms, and a central location. The downsides to this excellent central choice are that the paint and lacquer is chipping in spots, and with the city's major thoroughfare just a narrow block away there is some background traffic noise mixed with those Palermo sirens—but at least it isn't right under your balcony. Air-conditioning is planned for the near future, but for the time being, fans are available to help combat the summer heat.

Sausele. Via Vincenzo Errante 12, 90127 Palermo (exiting the train station, turn left, then left again onto Via Oreto, then right). ☎ **091-616-1308.** Fax 091-616-7525. E-mail: htlsausele@tin.it. 36 units. A/C TEL. 80,000L ($40) single, 125,000L ($63) double. Breakfast 10,000L ($5). AE, DC, MC, V. Parking 15,000L ($9). Bus: Any to Stazione Centrale.

This family-run inn would stand out anywhere in Palermo, let alone in this wasteland of an area behind the train station. You'll be greeted at the reception desk by an amicable staff and their very protective but benign German shepherd, both of whom will escort you past a collection of tchotchkes brought back by the late Signore Sausele on his travels through Asia and Africa. The rooms come with newish wood modular furnishings, high ceilings, and strikingly clean linoleum or tile floors; while those on the street can be a bit noisy, rooms overlooking the courtyard are blissfully quiet. There's a living room-style TV lounge with antiques and white doilies, plus a rustically cozy breakfast room.

Sole. Corso Vittorio Emanuele 219, 90133 Palermo. ☎ **091-581-811.** Fax 091-611-0182. 150 units. A/C TV TEL. 150,000L ($75) single, 200,000L ($100) double. Breakfast included. AE, DC, MC, V. Parking 10,000L ($5). Bus: 101, 102, 104, 105.

Located practically on top of Piazza Pretoria, the Sole is hidden in plain sight smack-dab in the center of town behind an ugly cement facade, steps away from its fancier neighbor the Centrale Palace (below). The hotel is unexceptional in appearance, but the staff is friendly and courteous, the prices and location are a dream, and it's so huge that there are usually plenty of rooms available. Accommodations differ greatly, though—most are furnished with standard built-in units, but the gems are the ones with the sleigh beds, period armoires, and comfy chairs. While rooms right on the Corso are noticeably noisier, some provide a partial view of the Fontana Pretoria across the street. There's also a panoramic roof terrace—360° of downtown Palermo rooftops, domes, the fountain and Quattro Canti below, and beyond, the mountains that ring the city.

Villa Archirafi. Via Lincoln 30, 90133 Palermo. ☎ **091-616-8827.** Fax 091-616-8631. 33 units. TV TEL. 90,000–120,000L ($45–$60) single; 125,000–150,000L ($63–$75) double. Breakfast 10,000L ($5). MC, V. Free parking. Turn right outside of the train station and walk five blocks.

Villa Archirafi is yet another dull exterior that hides the bright decor within. Located near the train station but not *too* near, the hotel borders *centro storico* and sits only blocks away from the botanical gardens (Orto Botanico). The hotel underwent a complete renovation in 1999, and the lobby was transformed into the only Liberty style salon in town. The ground floor opens onto a flowery terra-cotta patio, and a narrow inside staircase leads up to the guest quarters. Rooms are cheerfully decorated with yellow, blue, and red plaid bedspreads covering firm beds, and the baths sport shiny new fixtures. Almost all of the rooms have air-conditioning, and some of the upper rooms have views of the botanical gardens.

WORTH A SPLURGE

✪ **Centrale Palace Hotel.** Corso Vittorio Emanuele 357 (a few steps west of the Quattro Canti), 90134 Palermo. ☎ **800-528-1234** in the U.S., or 091-336-666. Fax 091-334-881. E-mail: centrale@palermo.pandora.it. 63 units. A/C MINIBAR TV TEL. 265,000L ($133) single; 380,000L ($190) double; 490,000L ($245) suite. Rates include breakfast. AE, CB, DC, MC, V. Parking onsite. Bus: 101, 102, 104, 105.

Palermo's best splurge is also one of its most central inns, an elegant 17th-century palazzo converted to a hotel in 1892 and recently modernized by Best Western. The furnishings are discreet in mild yet aristocratic tones of gold, both functional and modern, with a few period or Empire antiques and oriental rugs. Most doubles are medium-sized, while the spacious suites come with contemporary wood furnishings and fainting couches. All the baths are new, with built-in hair dryers and embroidered linen towels. The quietest rooms are on the *cortile* or side streets, but the double-glazing on the front windows block traffic noise fairly efficiently, plus on the first and second floor these Corso-side rooms have balconies with askance views of the Quattro Canti. The top-floor breakfast room has a sublime vista over Palermo rooftops to Monte Pellegrino and, most impressively, the personnel couldn't be more gracious.

GREAT DEALS ON DINING

Thanks to centuries of cross-cultural invasions, Palermo offers a variety of restaurants from Tunisian to African to Arabic. Naturally, there's plenty of pasta and fish on the menu, but when you simply can't stomach another sit-down meal, head over to the **Mercato Vucceria** (see above) for an impromptu meal. Hidden behind hanging beads or set out on the table, these "ad hoc" eateries do look somewhat intimidating, and you're sure to pay more than your wine-swigging neighbor, but you won't get much more authentic than this. For those unwilling to brave this level of authenticity, the streets across from the Teatro Massimo, especially along **Via Bara all'Olivetta** and **Via dell'Orologio,** are good for bars, trattorias, or pizzerias.

✪ **Antica Focacceria San Francesco.** Via Allesandro Paternostro 58 (on Piazza San Francesco d'Assisi). ☎ **091-320-264.** Panini & primi 3,000–7,500L ($1.50–$3.75). No credit cards. Daily 10am–midnight. Bus: 103, 105, 225. SANDWICHES/POOR MAN'S FARE.

This Palermitano institution has been stuffing customers with stuffed focaccia sandwiches and other cheap eats since 1834 in a high-ceilinged space that resembles nothing so much as an old-fashioned train-station waiting room. A huge central counter proudly displays trays of deep-dish *focaccie* fresh from the oven and a bubbling cauldron of steaming *milza* (spleen). Regulars usually order a beer and two dishes each, the most popular being *arancie* (giant fried rice balls filled with ragout, peas, and cheese) and split, stuffed *focaccie,* best served *maritata* (with spleen, heart, ricotta, and hard caciocavallo cheese); the squeamish can order the *schietta* (with ricotta and hard caciocavallo cheese only) or *con panelle* (with chickpea fritters).

Bellini. Piazza Bellini 6 (off Via Maqueda). ☎ **091-616-5691.** Reservations recommended. Primi 10,000–16,000L ($5–$8); secondi 16,000–18,000L ($8–$9) and up for specials; pizze 6,000–15,000L ($3–$8). MC, V. Wed–Mon noon–3:30pm and 7pm–midnight (daily June–Sept). Bus: 101, 102, 104, 105. SICILIAN/PIZZA.

Spread on the piazza in front of the floodlit domes of La Martorana, Bellini has one of the choicest settings in Palermo. It's set into the entryway of the recently revived Bellini theater, and is undoubtedly more popular for its outdoor cafe than its menu. The pizza is reliable, although there are more substantial selections on the menu, and there's live keyboard music on summer evenings.

✪ **Casa del Brodo.** Corso Vittorio Emanuele 175. ☎ **091-321-655.** Reservations highly recommended. Primi 8,000–15,000L ($4–$8); secondi 10,000–20,000L ($5–$10). AE, DI, MC, V. Thurs–Tues 1–3pm and 7:30pm–midnight. SICILIAN.

Recommended by countless barmen, trashed by a family of visiting Americans, and confused with a similarly named neighboring establishment by a British guidebook, the verdict is finally in: *"si mangia veramente bene"* (the food's great!). Affectionately named "Brodino" by the Palermitani and a favorite hangout for post-theater actors and artists, Casa del Brodo began as a simple workingman's stop for ample bowls of boiled meats. Over a hundred years later (and still a father-son business), the restaurant has evolved into an elegant yet unpretentious Sicilian dining experience, although if you're truly adventurous, you can still order the *lingua in salse varie* (cow's tongue). The antipasto spread is difficult to resist and easily a meal in itself (don't pass up the little fried sardine balls), while the seafood risotto is best described as an abundant cornucopia of shellfish over a few (exceptionally tasty) grains of rice. Get there close to opening time, otherwise forget about getting a table.

Hosteria Al Duar. Via Ammiraglio Gravina 31–33 (between Via Principe di Scordia and Via La Masa; don't confuse with Via Benedetto Gravina). No phone. Primi 6,000–9,000L ($3–$5); secondi 3,000–16,000L ($2–$8); completo Tunisiano 18,000L ($9) with wine. MC, V. Tues–Sun noon–3pm, 7pm–midnight. Open Mon in summer. Bus: 101, 102, 103, 104, 106, 107, 108, 124, 134, 164, 806, 812, 824, 833, 837. TUNISIAN/ITALIAN.

Homesick Tunisians and hungry Palermitani come for one thing only—the gut-busting *completo tunisiano,* perhaps Palermo's best dining deal. The full menu is a conga line of North African specialty stews and couscous dishes, attracting regulars with a hankering for a taste of the *merghes* (veal sausage with Tunisian spices) or the *sceptie* (vegetable balls of potato, eggs and greens). Julietta and Simone have created a comfy home away from home in this long, air-conditioned room hung with battered pots and pans and brightened by handpainted Tunisian plates. There will surely be no room left for the cream pudding, but order it anyway, as it's made with warm milk straight from the cow. If you're not in a Tunisian mood, there's plenty of standard Italian fare as well.

La Cambusa. Piazza Marina 16. ☎ **091-584-574.** Primi 8,000–13,000L ($4–$7); secondi 12,000–15,000L ($6–$8); antipasto buffet 15,000L ($8). AE, MC, V. Tues–Sun 1–3pm and 8–11pm. SICILIAN.

Set near the shadows of the immense rubber trees of the Garibaldi Gardens, La Cambusa provides the perfect "getaway" to a vast yet quiet corner of the city. Although the menu is limited, it's sufficient enough to have a loyal following among regulars who fill up the tables by 1:30pm. This close to the marina, you'd be wise to order fish, with your pick of the catch of the day in the cold display, but if you don't want a full meal, you can pretend to eat a light meal at the ample antipasto buffet.

⭐ **Santandrea.** Piazza Sant'Andrea 4 (south of Piazza San Domenico). ☎ **091-334-999.** Reservations highly recommended. Primi 12,000–16,000L ($6–8); secondi 16,000–27,000L ($8–$14). AE, DC, MC, V. Wed–Mon 1–3pm, 8pm–midnight. Closed Jan. Bus: 101, 102, 103, 104, 107, 122. INNOVATIVE SICILIAN/SEAFOOD.

Family-run and casually classy, Santandrea is all about candlelit tables on a small Palermo piazza of half-decayed buildings and a forgotten church facade (in winter, they retreat under terra-cotta ceilings). Instead of a menu, waiters recite in delicious detail the daily offerings based on the freshest ingredients from the market. The excellent *antipasto misto* is heavy on the seafood. The *spaghetti con bottarga e aragosta* (lobster and dried, grated fish roe) is excellent, as are the fresh tagliatelle with mullet, shrimp, capers, and black olives or in a pesto of zucchini leaves, toasted pine nuts, and sun-dried tomatoes. Roasted or grilled fish is the most popular main course, like the *tonno all'agredolce* (sweet-and-sour tuna with mint and onions) or the *spigola con asparagi selvatici* (with wild asparagus grown on the premises), though a mix of grilled meats is also tempting. The desserts are all made in-house. Still little known among foreigners, this place is popular with Palermitani, so book ahead, especially in summer.

⭐ **Shanghai.** Vicola Mezzani 34 (on Piazza Caracciolo). ☎ **091-589-702.** Reservations not accepted. Primi 4,000–6,000L ($2–$3); secondi 6,000–12,000L ($3–$6). No credit cards. Mon–Sat noon–3pm, 6:30–10:30pm. Bus: 101, 102, 103, 104, 105, 107, 122, 225. PALERMITANO.

A bit of a shabby Palermo institution, this terrace trattoria overlooking the Vucciria market serves mediocre but dirt-cheap food in a fun tumultuous setting. The name supposedly comes from the sea of stall awnings below, reminiscent of Shanghai. The entry is basically someone's living room, with platters of fish displayed on a table, beyond which locals at a long central table wolf down plates of spaghetti and drink wine straight from the bottle. The terrace is reserved for the tourists, most of whom get intimidated into springing for the *misto di golfo* (mixed fish fry). Although I've heard rumors that you can pick a fish from the stalls below, I've only seen the restaurant cook what's on the menu: *pasta con broccoli integrame* (with broccoli and saffron), or steaks of *tonno naturale* (tuna) or *pesce spada* (swordfish) garnished with shrimp.

WINE & DESSERTS

Palermo is still filled with old-fashioned **wine shops.** The market areas are great places to seek out these joints. A favorite watering hole for many an arid throat is in the Vucciria, the **Taverna Azzurra,** Via Maccheroni 9 (no phone), where Nino will hook you up with a 500L (25¢) shot of wine or a 66-centiliter bottle of hearty, frosty Forst beer for 2,000L ($1).

You can find great Sicilian **pastries**—including the rich Sicilian candied fruit *cassata* cake and treats made of *marzipan* almond paste that for centuries has been artistically shaped to mimic fruits, vegetables, and other foods (sometimes even whole plates of spaghetti) in miniature—at **Peccatucci di Mamma Andrea,** Via Principe di Scordia 67 (☎ **091-334-835**), or **Spinnato il Golosone,** Piazza Castelnuovo 16 (☎ **091-329-220**). On All Soul's Day, sweet shops flood with *pupi a cera* (delicious marzipan figures of knights and ladies). For ice cream, head to a legendary favorite in the city wall across from the harborfront turned fun park, **Gelateria Ilardo,** Via Foro Italico 11/12 (no phone).

PALERMO AFTER DARK

Extremely proud of having checked the advance of the local Mafia, Palermitani are quick to say how far their city has come with regard to safety. But the truth is, you just won't want to be hanging around after dark in many parts of Palermo. You can consider most of the narrow streets of the old center off limits at night, especially to women, but even men will find themselves fending off advances from prostitutes (both male and female) in the Kalsa, the Alberghiera, and around the train station or first few blocks of Via Roma. Stick to the New City, which is perfectly safe, and Piazza Verdi and Piazza Castelnuovo, which are both generally full of people.

Palermo's selection of classical arts makes it a city to rival any major European city. The newly restored **Teatro Massimo,** Piazza Verdi (☎ 091-605-3315), takes its rightful position as presenter of the official season of **theater, music, opera,** and **dance** in an historic venue. From November to May, the **Politeama Garibaldi,** Piazza Ruggero Settimo (☎ 091-605-3315) stages concerts and ballets, while at the **concert** hall of the Sicilian Symphonic Orchestra in **Teatro Golden,** Via Terrasanta 60 (☎ 091-305-217), internationally acclaimed soloists team up with leading conductors. The tourist office has detailed schedules of everything going on in town (pick up the *Palermo & Provincia Live* pamphlet here), including lists of restaurants and cafes presenting live music in the summer.

For an early evening of traditional fun for all ages, hunt down a *teatro dei pupi* (marionette theater) to watch professional puppeteers stage elaborate stories from the Charlemagne/Orlando sagas or tales of Saracen warriors. For a long time, this was the poor Sicilian's version of theater—colorful and rousing enough to have survived and established itself as a cultural institution. The **Museo delle Marionette** (see "Seeing the Sights," above) puts on shows every Friday at 5pm, September to July. Otherwise, the Cuticchio siblings are the only artists currently really active in Palermo; Mimmo puts on 5:30pm shows Saturday and Sunday on **Via Bara all'Olivella 95** (☎ 091-323-400), while over at the Palazzo Asmundo, on Via Pietro Novelli (across from the Duomo) the **Opera dei Pupi** (☎ 091-611-3680) puts on scheduled performances.

Also check with the **Teatro Bradamente,** Via Lombardi 25 (☎ 091-625-9233), to see if the free 10pm Friday performances are still on.

If all you want to do is kick back with a beer or sink a spoon into a gelato, head to **Via Principe di Belmonte** (between Via Ruggero Settimo and Via Roma), a pedestrian strip lined with **bars and cafes,** many of which have outdoor seating in nice weather, a few with live pianists.

A SIDE TRIP TO MONREALE'S MONASTERY

Perched majestically on the hillside 8km (5 mi.) south of Palermo is the home to Europe's greatest medieval mosaic cycle: ✪ **Monreale,** the last and greatest of Sicily's Norman cathedrals in the town of the same name. The polychrome scenes on a shimmering gold background literally carpet the walls, arches, and apses. When Palermo's British bishop Walter of the Mill started building the downtown cathedral, young William II decided in 1174 to exert his independence from that ecclesiastical potentate by raising his own cathedral outside the city. His intention was to surpass the Duomo in Cefalù, and at least match the splendor of Constantinople's Santa Sophia on Norman land. His efforts proved more than adequate, in one of the most visually sumptuous day trips you can take anywhere in Italy. Even if you have only one day in Palermo, spend half of it here; nothing in town can compare.

Few people don't gasp in awe when they enter this cathedral, swathed with 68,472 square feet (6,430 square meters) of luminous ✪ **mosaics** consisting of 130 panels plus an innumerable collection of isolated series. The glittering interior competes with

St. Mark's of Venice as the most mosaicked church in Christendom—only less well lit, since few visitors arrive with sufficient coins to feed the eleven 2,000L ($1) light boxes. Many panels do stand out, like the old and new testament scenes of the central nave, but none more magnificently than the 66-foot-high, all-embracing *Christ Pantocrater* in the main apse, whose gaze, thanks to an optical illusion, appears to follow yours from anywhere in the church. The two side apses are dedicated to St. Paul (left) and St. Peter (right) respectively. The restored **wood ceiling** of the nave is gorgeous, too, as is the marble inlay work on the **floor,** but don't forget to admire the sculpture work   especially noteworthy are the Corinthian capitols depicting heads of the pagans that were converted (notice the cross on the capitol above the heads).On the way out, take a closer look at the main portal, framing a splendid 12th-century **bronze door** crafted by Bonanno Pisano.

The attached monastery preserves the beautiful and serene ✪ **cloisters,** an Islamic and Byzantine festival of pointed arches supported by twin columns, each pair different from the last: some carved or twisted, some plain, and many inlaid with colored marble and gold mosaic chips in geometric patterns. Every column capital, too, is unique, carved in a beautifully symbolic medieval style with mythological figures and religious scenes. Even with the bused-in tour groups, these cloisters manage to retain a relaxed, contemplative air, helping make this day trip a double escape from the urban chaos of Palermo.

The **Duomo** itself (☎ **091-640-4413**) is free, and open daily 8am to noon and 3:30 to 6:30pm. The **Tesoro del Duomo (Treasury)** is hidden behind a red velvet curtain to the left of the altar; admission is 4,000L ($2) and it's open daily from 9:30 to 11:45am and 3:30 to 5:45pm. You can get a view of the cloisters backed by a panorama of the Conca d'Oro (Golden Basin, referring to the Gulf of Palermo) from the terrace through a door at the back of the nave (terrace admission: 3,000L/$1.50) but you may prefer instead to empty your wallet in the actual cloisters (☎ **091-640-4403**), open Monday to Saturday 9am to 6:30pm and Sundays and holidays 9am to 1pm. Admission is 4,000L ($2).

For ridiculously huge portions of home cooking at remarkably low prices, the huge **La Fattoria** restaurant, just below town on the main road from Palermo at Via Circonvallazione di Monreale 26 (☎ **091-640-1134**), serves up an excellent *cannelloni alla casalinga* (homemade pasta leaves wrapped with meat and ricotta, topped with tomatoes and cheese, then baked) and tasty *pollo al forno* (oven-roasted chicken). They also serve pizza, and stay open Tuesday to Sunday noon to 1am (daily in July and August). Credit cards are not accepted.

GETTING THERE   Take **bus 389** from Palermo's Piazza Indipendenza right to the cathedral. Monreale has a **tourist office** to the left of the cloisters entrance on Piazza V. Emanuele (☎ **091-646-6070**), open Monday to Saturday 9am to 1pm, and Tuesday and Thursday again from 3:30 to 5:30pm, but you're better off stocking up on printed material over at the tourist office in Palermo (although the Monreale office can provide you with a detail-rich map of the mosaics).

THE GREEK RUINS OF SEGESTA EN ROUTE TO ERICE

The temple and theater of ancient Egesta (not a typo) are two of the most beautifully sited classical monuments in the world, set in the middle of nowhere on the rolling hills of the Sicilian countryside. Settled by the Elymi, a people said to have come from Troy, Segesta exhibits quintessentially classical features in its 5th-century B.C. ✪ **Doric temple,** perched at the lip of a wide ravine surrounded by a high natural amphitheater of verdant hills. Of the main cities settled by the Elymi, Egesta, rival city of Selinus (Selinunte; see below), was the most powerful, exerting its influence over its sister cities, Erice and Entella, probably in no small part due to the commercial and spiritual implications of its sulfur springs. The city was probably destroyed by Saracen invaders (note the excavations of what may have been the first mosque in Sicily, on the summit of Mount Barbaro, above the theater).

The nearby theater is chipped out of a mountaintop with a sweeping vista across the lush landscape to the Gulf of Castellammare. Undergoing restoration since October 1999, the theater is roped off and only accessible from one restricted platform, making the hike up hardly worth the effort. Completion of the project is slated for October 2001 (check before you go), when once again it will serve as the stage for **classical plays** (for tickets and information call ☎ **0924-951-131**). But even with the tour-bus crowds and modern highways nearby, Segesta remains one of the most magical corners of Italy.

Admission to the site is 4,000L ($2) and it's open 9am to an hour before sunset; in summer, until 6pm on show days. The site is wedged between the A29 autostrada from Palermo to Trapani and the old SS113 road (exits from both). There's limited service into Segesta. Trains from **Palermo** (four morning departures daily; 2 hr.; 9,500L/$4.75) stop at the train station Segesta Tempio, about a 1km (½-mi.) walk from the site. **Tarantola** (☎ **0924-31-020**) runs bus service direct to the site entrance from both **Palermo** (75 min.; 10,000L/$5) and **Trapani** (60 min.; 6,000L/$3), but don't assume regular daily service; hours are ever-changing so check the schedule at least two days ahead of time.

If after the short hike up to the temple you're too pooped to make it the 1km (½ mi.) up the hill to the theater, there's a shuttle outside the cafe/ticket office/souvenir stand (☎ **0924-952-356**) leaving every half-hour. Tickets for the shuttle are on sale in the cafe and must be purchased in advance; they're good for the ride up and back, so don't hike up without a ticket expecting to hitch a free ride down.

4 Erice

112km (67 mi.) W of Palermo.

Located atop a headland that rises almost vertically above the Trapani plain, ✪ **Erice** is an enchanting medieval city of narrow and labyrinthine cobbled streets, rich in mythology, splendid landscapes, and romance. The protection provided by this dramatic and solitary hilltop was a natural magnet for the Elymi, who, after migrating to nearby Segesta, established their spiritual center on the foundations of this native Sicani city. The city is laid out along the lines of a mystical triangle, punctuated by the 13th-century **Norman castle,** constructed on the remains of an ancient temple dedicated to the supreme mother goddess, known as Astarte by the Carthaginians, Aphrodite by the Greeks, and Venus Erycina by the Romans.

This thrilling mountaintop setting 2,478 feet up, conceals flowering courtyards, dozens of medieval structures, and views of majestic Monte Cofano rivaling anything you'd see in Capri. Nevertheless, that exhilarating and windy ride up will set you back at least 30 minutes, making this anything but a convenient base for day trips off the mountaintop. Undeterred by either the effort to arrive or the tourist-gouging prices (equaling prices in Taormina), tourists and honeymooners swarm to this landlocked promontory to steep in an environment little changed over the centuries. Adding to the mystique are the clouds that frequently rise (yes, rise) to an altitude great enough to allow them to "descend" upon the narrow cobbled streets, or when the only sound is the clip-clop of your soles on the ancient stones. Stay at least one night, when, devoid of raucous groups and schoolkids, Erice is at its most enchanting.

FESTIVALS   On Good Friday, there's a street ❂ **procession of the *misteri,*** a parade of sculpted scenes (some are papier mâché) of the Passion. From late July to early September, the churches around town host a **festival of medieval and Renaissance music,** and in December a Sicilian **folk music festival** comes to town.

ESSENTIALS

GETTING THERE   By Train or Bus   To get to Erice by public transportation, you must pass through the hideous provincial capital of Trapani 14km (8½ mi.) below Erice on the coast. There are eight to nine trains daily from **Palermo** (2 to 4 hr.; 17,000L/$9) to Trapani. By bus from **Palermo,** Segesta (☎ **0923-20-066**) runs half-hourly (105 min.; 12,000L/$6) in addition to their twice-daily service (none on Sundays) from the airport (75 min; 9,000L/$4.50). **Lumia** (☎ **0922-596-490**) runs four buses (two Sunday) from **Agrigento** (3 to 4 hr.; 17,400L/$9). From Trapani, the **AST** bus (☎ **0923-21-021**) to Erice makes 10 runs daily on weekdays and four on weekends (40 min.; 3,500L/$1.75).

By Car   Follow A29dir from Palermo or Segesta to the first Trapani exit, then continue up along the signposted switchback road up the mountain. If you're arriving by car and staying at the Edelweiss or Moderno, it's best if you park in the parking lot along the road up to Erice (free, in spite of the "attendant") as you'll surely crash your car if you attempt to navigate the windy narrow medieval streets (forget about the car; I scraped a 1,000-year-old building!).

VISITOR INFORMATION   The **tourist office** at Viale Conte A. Pepoli 11 (☎ **0923-869-388;** fax 0923-869-544), is open Monday to Friday 8am to 2:30pm.

STROLLING THROUGH ERICE

Erice has plenty of medieval hill town character, and the best way to enjoy it is simply to wander the back streets. If you need an agenda, the tourist information office (or your hotel) can provide you with a brochure listing the numerous historic churches you will encounter as you amble through alleys set with strategically placed flowering vines and pots, baroque balconies, and medieval shop fronts (today, private home entrances).

One excellent church is the ❂ **Duomo (Chiesa Matrice)**, built in 1314 with a fine Gothic porch. The neo-Gothic interior, open 8am to noon and 4 to 7pm, has a Domenico Gagini *Madonna* on the right aisle. The 15th-century **bell tower** sometimes opens its staircase for 1,000L (50¢); at the top, you get a great view over the town in one direction and a panorama across the gulf of Trapani and the Egadi Islands on the other.

Make sure you head to the southwest corner of town where you'll find the **Villa Balio gardens**—shaded by thick shrubbery laid out in the 19th century when Count Agostino Pepoli reconstructed the Norman castle in their midst. Beyond the gardens, a path is slung along the cliff edge to lead up to Erice's highest point, the ❂ **Castello di Venere,** today little more than crumbling Norman-era walls surrounding the sacred site where the Temple to Venus once stood. Piercing the walls are several windows and doorways with spectacular views across the countryside.

AFFORDABLE PLACES TO STAY

Edelweiss. Cortile Padres Vincenzo, 91016 Erice. ☎ **0923-869-420.** Fax 0923-869-158. TV TEL. 15 units. 100,000L ($50) single; 130,000L ($65) double. For stays of longer than 1 day in Aug, obligatory half-pension runs 120,000L ($60) per person. Rates include breakfast. MC, V.

Comfortable, friendly, and family-run, this pensione is tucked away in a quiet corner of town off Piazza San Domenico. It's a simple place whose large rooms have patterned rugs on tile floors and sometimes a few choice architectural elements like a column-flanked archway (room 106). The beds aren't the firmest but will do. Some accommodations come with an adjacent room for a third bed—great for families. Six rooms have sea views, four from balconies (though the vista itself is best from the top-floor rooms 115 and 118). If business is slow, they'll let the half-pension requirement slide.

○ La Pinetta. Viale Nunzio Nasi, 91016 Erice. ☎**0923-869-783.** Fax 0923-869-788. www.comeg.it/LaPineta. E-mail: LaPineta@Comeg.it. 23 cottages. MINBAR TV TEL. 85,000–115,000L ($43–58) single; 160,000–200,000L ($80–$100) double. Half-pension 115,000–135,000L ($58–68) per person, with a 30,000L ($15) supplement for singles in high season. Rates include breakfast. AE, DI, MC, V. Free parking. Follow signs for "Quartiere Spagnolo," then for La Pinetta. In July and August, the road becomes one way; instead: from the main parking area on Piazza Grammatica, follow Viale Conte Pepolo, turn left after Via Anchise, right onto Via San Francesco, left on Via. Cusenza, right after Piazza San Giovanni, and left onto Via Nunzio Nasi to the entrance).

After 20 minutes of ascending the hilltop past jaw-dropping views, it seems a shame to have to cloister yourself behind narrow alleys when La Pinetta offers the tranquillity of shady pines and private cottages. The best value in Erice by a long shot, each cottage has its own patio, some with death-defying drops below, and interiors offer the simplicity of white stuccoed walls, ceramic tile floors, and the odd Persian rug. All the baths are spacious and functional, with amenities like shower caps, hairdryers, and nice big towels. The bonus: They'll pick you up at Trapani train station on request.

GREAT DEALS ON DINING

Almonds feature prominently in Erice cooking, which is otherwise dominated by Trapanese cuisine like couscous covered with a fish stew.

Monte San Giuliano. Vicolo San Rocco 7 (off Corso Vittorio Emanuele). ☎ **0923-869-595.** Reservations highly recommended. Primi 10,000-13,000L ($5–$7); secondi 13,000–18,000L ($7–$9). AE, DC, MC, V. Tues–Sun 12:30–3pm and 7:30–11pm. Open daily July–Aug. Closed Nov 3–16 and Jan 7–16. TRAPANESE/SEAFOOD.

Tucked away in a stone courtyard beyond a medieval double gate is Monte San Giuliano, serving some of the best food in Erice. Its fair prices and terrace setting make it stand out, so you may want to book ahead for a seat on the walled flagstone terrace. Try the pungent *pasta con sarde,* the savory *busiati San Giuliano* (in an almond pesto with tomatoes, eggplant, and pecorino added), or the ubiquitous *cuscus alla Trapanese* (doused in fish broth and ladled with the meat of various white fish). Follow it up with *pescespada al salmorgiano* (swordfish with marjoram), or a *zainetto dello chef* (beef rolled around tomatoes, mozzarella, and eggplant then roasted). The desserts here are divine.

Osteria di Venere. Via Roma 6 (at Piazza San Giuliano). ☎ **0923-869-362.** Reservations recommended. Primi 10,000–14,000L ($5–$7); secondi 11,000–21,000L ($7–$12). MC, V. Thurs–Tues 12:30–3pm and 8–11pm. SICILIAN/TRAPANESE.

Having never before noticed a "guarantee of hygiene" sticker on a restaurant's storefront, I wasn't sure whether I should feel secure to dine here or dubious about all the other places I've eaten. Nevertheless, this one-room restaurant has a touch of refinement that makes it popular with locals who turn out for the finely observed Sicilian recipes. Luckily, you can dabble in much of it via the *tris di primi,* a trio of pastas that may include papardelle with shrimp and tuna, ravioli in cream sauce, or *casarecce* prepared *all'Ericino* (an almond/tomato pesto) or *alla venere* (with eggplant, tomatoes, swordfish, and mint). Secondi run from the expected *involtini alla siciliana* (veal rolls) and fresh fish to more inventive dishes like *calamari ripieni* (stuffed squid).

Pastries & Rugs

Erice is renowned for two products: pastries and hand-woven rugs. The former is a craft developed and refined by various orders of nuns based in Erice from the 14th to 18th century. The tradition is carried on by the *pasticceria* founded by **Maria Grammatica** in 1950 at Via Vittorio Emanuele 14 near Piazza Umberto (☎ **0923-869-390**), where you'll find various sugary almond treats kissed with lemon or citrus juices and made famous by *Bitter Almonds,* the cultural cookbook she co-wrote with Mary Taylor Simetti.

Local **rugs,** about 2 feet wide with colorful basic geometric designs in zigzags and diamonds, were traditionally woven from textile leftovers. The best weavers still use scraps on their hand-worked looms, although they also turn their artisans' hands to more innovative designs using first-rate threads and a wide range of dyes. These woven rugs sell for between 100,000L and 250,000L ($50 and $125).

5 Selinunte & Its Temple Ruins

120km (72 mi.) S of Palermo, 98km (59 mi.) SE of Erice, 90km (54 mi.) NW of Agrigento, 88km (55 mi.) SE of Trapani.

The westernmost outpost of Greek territories in Sicily, **Selinunte** was founded in the 7th century B.C., enjoying a brilliant if short-lived existence as an important and powerful capital. Selinunte got rich quick, built a series of outstanding temples to prove it, and then was defeated by Carthage not once but twice, definitively in 250 B.C., only to fade into malaria-borne obscurity until the 16th century.

One of the most striking things about this archaeological site is the sheer quantity of ruins, stretched out over 709 acres wedged between the impossible blue of the Mediterranean and a natural plain of hills covered in wildflowers, bundles of low bushes, and the odd lone tree. For the most part uninhabited until the 16th century, the ancient capital city remains uncorrupted by modernity—a few re-erected rows of columns standing on two plateaus backdropped by the wild celery (*selinon*) for which the city is named.

Selinunte's modern support town is **Marinella,** a fishing village turned modest beach resort that has in the past decade boomed from a single road with a few hotels to a thriving little town flanking the eastern edge of the site.

ESSENTIALS

GETTING THERE **Getting to Castelvetrano by Train or Bus** The gateway to Selinunte is Castelvetrano, a city undistinguished except for the magnificent **Ephebe of Selinunte**, a 460 B.C. bronze tomb statuette, moved here in 1997 from Palermo's Museo Archeologico Regionale. Located about 23km (14 mi.) inland from the ruins, Castelvetrano receives 13 trains daily (7 on Sunday) from **Trapani** (68 to 83 min.;

Selinunte Tips

You'll need the better part of a day to visit the archaeological site of Selinunte, much of it spent in solitary walks along the picturesque glades. If you're short on time or physically unable to cover the territory, you can save the hike between the East Hill and the Acropolis by driving to the entrances   both zones are served by a parking lot. Be sure to avail yourself of the toilets *outside the main gate,* fill up on carbohydrates before you go, wear a hat and sunscreen, and carry enough water to withstand the relentless rays of the sun.

8,000L/$4); and five to seven trains daily (one direct, the others entailing an iffy change at "Alcamo Diramazione" with just a 3-minute window to transfer; 2 hr. 45 min.; 11,000L/$6) from Palermo.

To **bus** it, contact **AST** (☎ **0924-47-392** in Castelvetrano), which runs four daily buses from **Trapani** (95 min.; 10,000L/$5) through Castelvetrano on the way to Agrigento. **Lumia** lines (☎ **0922-596-490**) will also carry you here from **Agrigento** three times daily (2 to 2½ hr.; 13,000L/$7) and lets you off near the hospital on Via Marinella (wait for the local bus to the ruins across from the "Bar Selinus"). **Salemi** (☎ **091-617-5411**) has a direct bus from **Palermo** to Castelvetrano eight times Monday to Saturday, two on Sunday (2 hr.; 12,000L/$6).

Getting to the Site   From Castelvetrano's train station, the linea urbano **bus** makes the 20-minute run to Marinella/Selinunte only five times daily (four on Sunday), dropping you off across from the site entrance. Purchase tickets (1,500L/75¢) either on the bus or at the **Bar Selinus** across from the hospital (near the train station). The last departure back to Castelvetrano currently leaves at 6:40pm; check with the friendly tourist information office at the entrance to the site for schedule changes before you find yourself stranded. In July and August, there is an infrequent shuttle bus from outside the archaeological site that winds through Marinella. By **car**, the roads are well marked from SS115; from Castelvetrano, just take Via Marinella out of town, which becomes SS115, branching left into SS115d.

VISITOR INFORMATION   The **tourist office** at the parking lot/site entrance (☎/fax **0924-46-251**) is staffed by knowledgeable, helpful, and jolly Italians. It hands out an indispensable site plan and is open Monday to Saturday 8am to 8pm and Sunday 9am to noon and 3 to 6pm. If you're short on cash, don't put your money on finding a cash machine—the only place you can fill up is at the **money exchange** arm of the post office in Marinella.

A FESTIVAL   In summer (when there's sufficient funding), there's a series of **nighttime performances amid the ruins,** usually at Temple E. These can range from classical plays like *Oedipus Rex* to southern U.S. gospel, and productions of *A Chorus Line* to modern dance. Call the **Agenzia Mondo Servizi** in Castelvetrano ☎ **0924-904-555** for information and tickets.

EXPLORING THE TEMPLES

Selinunte's archaeological site (☎ **0924-46-277**) is split between two zones: the **East Hill** temples right behind the ticket office and arrival center—nearest to Marinella and boasting the largest temples—and the **West Hill/Acropolis,** picturesquely sited overlooking the sea. Admission is 8,000L ($4); hold on to your ticket to get into the separately fenced West Hill. Selinunte is open daily 9am to one hour before sunset.

Selinunte's temples lie in scattered ruins, the honey-colored stones littering the ground as if an earthquake had struck (as one did in ancient times). Some columns and fragments of temples are still standing, with great columns pointing to the sky. Parts of the zone have been partially excavated and reconstructed, as much as is possible with the bits and fragments remaining. All the temples are known simply by letters, since no one is certain to which god any one was dedicated. All have descriptive plaques to provide background; most date from the 6th and 5th centuries B.C.

Near the entrance, the Doric **Temple E** contains fragments of an inner temple. Standing on its ruins before the sun goes down, you can look across the water that washes up on the shores of Africa, from which the Carthaginian fleet emerged to destroy the city. **Temple G,** in scattered ruins north of Temple E, was one of the largest erected in Sicily and also built in the Doric style. The ruins of the less impressive **Temple F** lie between Temples E and G. Not much remains of Temple F and little is known about what it was.

After viewing Temples G, F, and E, all near the parking lot at the entrance, you can get in your car and drive along the Strada dei Templi west to the Acropolis. You can also walk there in about 20 minutes. The site of the western temples was the **Acropolis,** which was enclosed within defensive walls and built from the 6th to the 5th century B.C.

The most impressive site here is **Temple C,** which towers over the other ruins and gives a good impression of what all the temples might have looked like at one time. In 1925, 14 of the 17 columns of the temple were re-erected, and today, behind scaffolding, efforts have been set into motion to reconstruct even more of the temple. This is the earliest surviving temple at ancient Selinus, having been built in the 6th century B.C. and probably dedicated to Hercules or Apollo. The pediment, ornamented with a clay Gorgon's head, lies broken on the ground. Also here is **Temple A,** which, like the others, remains in scattered ruins. The streets of the Acropoli were laid out by Hippodamus of Miletus along classical lines, with a trio of principal arteries bisected at right angles by a grid of less important streets. The Acropoli was the site of the town's most important public and religious buildings, and it was also the residence of the town's aristocrats. If you look down below, you can see the site of the town's harbor, now an arid stretch of beachfront property. After all this earthquake damage, you can only imagine the full glory of this place in its golden era.

AN AFFORDABLE PLACE TO STAY & DINE

Lido Azzurro. Via Marco Polo 98, 91020 Marinella (TP). ☎ /fax **0924-46256.** 14 units. TEL. July–Aug 65,000L ($33) single, 95,000L ($48) double; Sept–June 60,000L ($30) single, 85,000L ($43) double. Breakfast 5,000L ($2.50). AE, DC, MC, V. Street parking.

This beachside crash-pad sits at the heart of Marinella's miniscule main drag, across from its own beach and newly reopened restaurant. The management makes up for the scarcity of amenities with good old friendliness, *plus* the bulk of the rooms have balconies with views of the Mediterranean. It's kept tolerably clean, the beds aren't *too* soft, the modular furnishings aren't too worn, and the prices are still reasonable. The management may want to pour some baking soda down the bath drains though. In 1999, TVs were installed in some of the rooms. The ✪ **restaurant** is definitely worth a stop; having upgraded both ambiance and quality from its previous incarnation as a pizzeria. Expect the most velvety of olive oils (made from their own orchard), delectable antipasti, and fresh fish.

6 Agrigento & the Valley of the Temples

129km (80 mi.) S of Palermo, 175km (109 mi.) SE of Trapani, 90km (54 mi.) SE of Selinute, 256km (154 mi.) W of Siracusa.

"The most beautiful city of mortals," said the poet Pindar when describing the great city of **Akragas (Agrigento).** These words ring true as you cross the Morandi Viaduct into the **Valle dei Templi (Valley of the Temples),** over an open expanse of flowering fertile hills and the pale peach tones of the imperial ✪ **Templo della Concordia (Temple of Concord)** crowning the highland in the distance. Of the original 10 **Doric temples** built on the ridge below the new city line, parts of 9 are still visible in various states of ruin, except for the Temple of Concord—one of the best-preserved Greek temples in the world.

Agrigento produced another famed son in Luigi Pirandello, winner of the Nobel Prize in 1934 and author of the play *Six Characters In Search Of An Author.*

The ancient Greek colony of Akragas was founded around 581 B.C. and flexed its muscle around 570 B.C. under the leadership of one of the cruelest despots of them all, the tyrant Phalaris. Born locally, Phalaris is remembered more for his barbarism notably his taste for babies and the invention of the bronze grated bull, a means of torture in which his victims were slowly roasted over an open flame than for his contribution to the city's fortunes. Under the tyrant Theron, the city continued to prosper, attracting the greatest artistic and cultural minds of the day. Subsequent years saw Agrigento submitting to the humiliation of numerous invasions, from recurrent Carthaginian sackings, to defeat by the mighty Roman Empire in 210 B.C. Renewed prosperity during the Imperial Age relied heavily on the production of wine and grain, making use of its bustling port (now San Leone), and transforming a beaten Agrigento once again into a destination for the likes of Strabo, Ptolemy, and Pliny. Agrigento now makes headlines thanks to an ongoing State war against the Mafia, concentrated around these parts.

The best way to approach a visit to the area is to plan a bridge of 2 days. This will allow you to devise a plan of attack that will maximize time away from the blight of tour buses and still allow you time to witness one of the most breathtaking and romantic sunsets you will ever see. To beat the crowds, visit the upper temples near sundown, when the grounds once again become a solitary sight and the floodlights flicker on to bathe the temples in a golden glow. Save the lower temples (the area with the entrance fee) for the following morning, but get there before 10:30am, because the tour groups will by then have completed the first half of their visit, which began at the upper gate. Plan a full day for a visit to the Archaeological Museum, the Insula Romana, and the Valley of the Temples, and be prepared to cover expansive distances on foot (again). If your time is limited, just hit the temples. With any spare time, head up to the modern city (notwithstanding the eyesore of 600 concrete condominium monstrosities illegally erected by the overwhelming presence of the Mafia) to take in a leisurely itinerary of Norman, Gothic, and Arab sites and for a few hours of shopping and dining.

ESSENTIALS

GETTING THERE   By Train   There are five trains daily including Sunday) from **Palermo** (2 hr.; 12,500L/$6); and five to eight trains from **Catania,** direct or with a transfer at Caltanissetta Xirbi (3½ to 4½ hr.; 17,000L/$9). The **Agrigento Centrale station** (☎ 0922-26-669) is on Piazza Marconi, just down the steps from Agrigento's central Piazzale Aldo Moro. Don't get off at the suburban station *Agrigento Bassa.*

By Bus   Buses arrive into Agrigento's depot at Piazzale Rosseli just steps away from Piazza Vittorio Emanuele, where you can also pick up a local bus (see "Seeing the Valley of Temples," below) to the archaeological zone. **Lumia** lines (☎ 0922-596-490) runs Monday to Saturday three times a day from **Castelvetrano** (the **Selinunte** stop; 2¼ hr.; 12,500L/$6) and a local bus from Trapani (4¼ hrs.; 18,000L/$9). **Cuffaro** (☎ 091-616-1510) runs seven daily buses from **Palermo** (2 hr.; 13,000L/$7). The Agrigento-based **Camilleri-Lattuca & Argento** (☎ 0922-471-886) runs four times a day from **Palermo** (2 hr.; 13,000L/$7), with its first departure at 1:30pm. **Autolinea Licata** (☎ 0922-401-360) runs two buses from Palermo's airport; **SAIS** ☎0922-595-933 has 11 runs (6 on Sunday) between 11am and 9pm from both

Catania's airport and train station (2½ hrs.; 19,000L/$10); their office is behind the booth on Via Ragazzi del 99 (☎ **0922-595-933**). **SAIS Trasporti** makes the long trip down from **Rome** once a day (10 hr.; 57,000L/$29).

Buses 1, 2, and 3 run from in front of the train station down Via dei Templi into the Valley of the Temples. You can get off at the Museum/Insula Romana or stay on all the way to the Posto di Ristoro (a.k.a. Piazzale dei Templi), a pricey cafe/souvenir stand at the entrances to the two temple zones. Stops along this route are not obligatory, so remember to alert the bus driver when you want to get off.

By Car   Agrigento lies on the coastal SS115, which you can follow from Castelvetrano near Selinunte or from Siracusa (the latter drive is interminable, passing by industrial panoramas worthy of the New Jersey Turnpike). From Palermo, take the SS121/SS189.

VISITOR INFORMATION   In Agrigento, there are five unrelated local offices dealing with provincial, local, municipal, and regional information. You'll find the best information on the site, or at least the most willing staff, at the little Posto Ristoro **booth** (☎ **0922-26-191**) in the parking lot near the entrance to the archaeological site, opened daily 8:30am to 7pm (shorter hours in winter; expect the booth to be closed for "coffee breaks"). There's also an adjacent **money change** booth. If you need help with accommodations in town, there's an **Ufficio Informazioni Turistiche** (☎/fax **0922-20-454**) above the train station just behind Piazzale Aldo Moro at Via Cesare Battisti 15, your first left off Via Atenea. For a **taxi**, call ☎ **0922-26-670** or 0922-21-899.

A FESTIVAL   The temple zone is even more lovely than usual in early February during the **Festival of Almond Blossoms,** a folkloric harvest celebration with music, flag-tossing, and traditional foods.

SEEING THE VALLEY OF THE TEMPLES

MUSEO ARCHEOLOGICO REGIONALE (REGIONAL ARCHAEOLOGICAL MUSEUM)   The rich collection of temple leftovers, pottery fragments, and even prehistoric findings in this museum (☎ **0922-497-111**) makes this one of the most important archaeological museums in all Sicily. The entrance is past the little garden of the San Nicola (see below), along a catwalk over the Roman **Comitium,** a 4th-century B.C. assembly arena (originally a Greek Ekklesiasterion) and past the **Oratorio di Falaride (Oratory of Phalaris),** a funerary monument said to have been built above the first tyrant's palace. Among the painstakingly classified and labeled items are an outstanding collection of superbly painted vases spanning the 6th to 3rd centuries B.C. in room 3. Room 6 is devoted to the Temple of the Olympian Zeus (see below), along with the museum's most striking exhibit, a reconstituted 25-foot giant ✪ *telamon—* sculpted male figure—stacked up against one wall in its original position as a supporting column. In the rest of the museum, look for the 2nd-century B.C. alabaster sarcophagus of a child, carved with happy childhood moments and a touching death scene; the 5th-century B.C. **Efebo (Ephebe),** a masterpiece of masculine features and feminine lines; and the 5th-century B.C. painted krater from Gela showing a battle with the Amazons. Admission is 8,000L ($4). It's open daily 9am to 1:30pm and Wednesday to Saturday 2 to 6pm (last ticket sold ½ hour before closing).

Next to the entrance to the museum is **San Nicola,** a small Norman church built on the foundation of Greco-Roman ruins. Admission of 3,000L ($1.50) includes a guided visit in English upon request and will get you a look at the **Sarcofago di Phaedra (Sarcophagus of Phaedra),** a Roman-era work dating to the 2nd or 3rd century, and an enamel-on-wood **Crucifix** above the altar. The church, recently reopened to the public, is open from 10am to 2pm Monday to Saturday, September to June.

INSULA ROMANA (ROMAN QUARTER) Across from the museum is the Roman-Hellenistic Quarter, over 10,000 square meters of excavated urban living, inhabited as far back as the 2nd century B.C. and covered by some wonderful 4th-century Roman polychrome floor mosaics. You can see some terra-cotta storage vases still stuck in the mortar, and it's worth a walk through the grid for a look under those glass huts at mosaic floors laid out as rhomboids, magical symbols, and gazelles. Admission is free; it's open daily 9am to 1 hour before sunset and is across the street from the Museo Archeologico Regionale (through a less than obvious gate; bring a picnic lunch).

✪ **TEMPLES** Down the road, you'll arrive at the main attraction of Agrigento—a series of 5th-century B.C. Doric wonders surrounded by olive and almond trees (☎ **0922-20-014**). To the right of the road, past the ticket booth, are the massive, jumbled remains of the **Tempio di Zeus Olimpio (Temple of Olympian Zeus),** or **Olympieion.** At 363 by 174 feet, this is the largest Doric temple ever attempted, begun in 480 B.C. but left unfinished when the Carthaginians invaded in 409. Earthquakes and wars brought some of it down, but sadly, most of the stones were carted off as building materials for the construction of the nearby wharf of Porto Empedocle.

It's hard to fathom the sheer size of the thing—little remains other than a weedy mound of ancient cut rubble—but here are some ciphers to help. Each column was over 55 feet high and 13 feet thick at the base—there's half of one capital sitting near the top of the rubble pile. Lying in the dust nearby is a worn replica of one of the *tela-mones,* or columns carved as a man (the original's in the museum up the road). This 25-foot giant took up less than half the height of the columns (never mind adding in the steps, pediment, and roof). Beyond is a pile of cut blocks with U-shaped grooves, which were used to help haul them into place.

Surging above the far end of the sacred hill are the four remaining columns of the **Tempio di Dioscuri (Temple of the Dioscuri).** Probably dedicated to the earth gods Demeter and Persephone, the temple dominates an area dating to the first generation of settlers, pockmarked with the remains of round altars, *bothroi* (sacred wells used for sacrifice and libations) and an agora.

THE TRIO OF TEMPLES The postcard trio of temples are up off the east/left side of Via dei Templi, balancing atop a wide ridge with a wash of olive groves spilling down on the Agrigento side, and a partially man-made cliff falling off toward the sea on the other. Rather than follow the paved ramp into the site, clamber up into the area on some steps chipped out of the stone, up to the ruins of the **Tempio di Ercole (Temple of Hercules),** the oldest shrine here (500 B.C.). Most of it is in piles, but eight, 33-foot-high columns have been re-erected and you can scramble about the remains of the cella.

Just up the road, past a **paleo-Christian necropolis** (closed to visitors as of this writing) with tombs honeycombed into the rocky ground and tunnels under the road,

---

The Valley's Hours & Admission

Oddly enough, you have to pony up 4,000L ($2) to get into the least interesting section—the ruinous Temple of Olympian Zeus—but the rest of the valley's temples are free and gateless. The free areas are open daily, 8:30am to 1 hour before sunset. With this inconsistency in mind, officials are talking about instituting a combination admission ticket good for the archaeological zone; check in with the tourist information office near the entrance to the site for an update.

is the spectacular ✪ **Tempio della Concordia (Temple of Concord).** Raised in 430 B.C., this is the best-preserved and most complete temple in the Greek world outside the Theseion in Athens and the Temple of Hera at Paestum. In the days when pagan temples were being burned and razed, this temple survives mostly intact because Agrigento's bishop converted it into a church in the 6th century. Thanks to classically minded 18th-century purists, the temple was restored to its original state, although it was probably at this point that the name "Concord," taken off an unrelated inscription on one of the stones, stuck. The cella and 34 Doric columns all still stand, supporting an architrave and miraculously complete entablatures on both ends. The temple's in such good shape, they've fenced it off to keep us from stomping all over it.

The road continues to slope up, past ancient city walls on the right perforated with some Byzantine tombs, to the broken-toothed **Tempio di Hera (Temple of Hera),** also incorrectly called the Temple of Juno. It was built around 450 B.C. at the very edge of the cliff, probably as a mirror image to the one just below. Twenty-five of its 34 columns remain standing, with bits of the entablature intact on one end, while the blackened walls of the cell stand as a reminder to the temples destruction by fire at the hands of the Carthaginians. The temple is partially disfigured by scaffolding, and remains closed indefinitely for fear of another landslide at its edge like they had in 1976. A low, stepped wall on the far side makes (wind notwithstanding) an ideal spot to picnic with the panorama of temples before you.

AFFORDABLE PLACES TO STAY

✪ **Concordia.** Piazza San Francesco 11, 92100 Agrigento. ☎/fax **0922-596-266.** 30 units. TV TEL. 40,000L ($20) single; 80,000L ($40) double. Breakfast: 5,000L ($2.50) . AE, DC, MC, V. Take Via Pirandello (left parallel to Via Atenea), which becomes Via San Francesco; the hotel's about 500 feet down on the left.

If you aren't forking over the dough for the Villa Athena (below), call here first. The Concordia is an eternally Agrigento favorite, an inexpensive family-run inn with by far the warmest reception in town. Although the cots are lazy-springed and the baths cramped, the modestly sized rooms are kept clean, the modular veneer furnishings nice enough, and the stuccoed walls repainted regularly; some rooms have air-conditioning. Best of all, you get to take advantage of the terrific lunch menu at their trattoria La Forchetta (see below).

WORTH A SPLURGE

✪ **Villa Athena.** Via dei Templi 9, 92100 Agrigento. ☎ **0922-596-288.** Fax 0922-402-180. 40 units. A/C MINIBAR TV TEL. 210,000L ($105) single; 250,000L ($125) double. Rates include breakfast. AE, DC, MC, V. Free parking. Take Via Petrarca (or bus 1, 2, or 3), following signs into the archaeological zone; it's a private drive off to the left after the museum (ask bus driver to let you off).

This 18th-century villa is a steal at any price. It just may have the most fantastic location of any hotel in Italy: right inside the archaeological zone of and across an olive grove from the Temple of Concord, whose practically perfect Doric profile is framed by the windows of half the rooms (best from rooms 302 to 304 or 202 to 206). If you can tear your eyes off the ancient splendor, you'll see the carpeted rooms are smallish but comfortable, with genuine beds and mattresses and nice functional pieces. There are several restaurant and bar spaces set into terraced gardens that look over the temple, plus a pool at the base for washing off the dust of a day. Book far in advance for this romance, especially during summer.

GREAT DEALS ON DINING

If you're planning on a day at the temples, pack a lunch, because there's nothing worth eating at the sandwich bar at the site anyway, and whatever is leftover by the bus crowds is ridiculously expensive. Most of the hotels near the archaeological zone have first-class restaurants, but even these cater to the demands of an international clientele with international wallets. For *nonna's* cooking, you'll have to head to Agrigento's *centro*.

ARCHAEOLOGICAL ZONE

Le Caprice. Via Panoramica dei Templi 25 (a road leading around the east side of the archaeological zone, south of town). ☎ **0922-26-462.** Reservations recommended. Primi 10,000L ($6); secondi 15,000–25,000L ($8–$13) and up. AE, DC, MC, V. Sat–Thurs 12:30–3pm and 7:30–11pm. Closed July 1–15. SEAFOOD/SICILIAN.

It seems pastoral enough, on the panoramic road down to the temples, although the corner floodlights and the rushing traffic below your feet may distract from the idyllic scene. You can enjoy that view *and* a full meal for under 40,000L ($20) alongside regulars so long as you don't do anything foolish like order the 7,000L ($4.10) green salad or the waiter-recited "*bella frittura mista,*" a mixed fish fry that'll run you close to 25,000L ($13) per plate. The menu is limited (be sure you get one), with local basics like risotto with seafood to *cavatelli della casa* (macaroni mixed with fried eggplant, tomato, ricotta, mozzarella, and basil, then baked in foil). If you prefer a meaty secondo, try the tasty *involtini all siciliana* or simply opt out for a heaping plate filled off the ample antipasto spread.

AGRIGENTO CENTRO

✪ **La Forchetta.** Piazza San Francesco 11. ☎ **0922-596-266.** Reservations recommended. Primi 10,000–12,000L ($5–$6); secondi 10,000L ($5). MC, V. Mon–Sat noon–3pm and 7–11pm. In summer, also Sun 7–11pm. AGRIGENTESE/SICILIAN.

La Forchetta has grown from its humble osteria roots, but one thing hasn't changed: It still serves the best food in town at prices that can't be beat. Gone is the bare room where locals filed in and grabbed their own bread from the kitchen. Now we get bonafide ambiance (seven tables amid pine paneling and historic photos) to go with our meal, and tourists have become the major clients, at least in summer. The prices, however, have stayed low, and if anything, the food's improved. The judiciously spicy *penne pirandello* (tomatoes, sausage, pepperoncino, and cream) is delicious, as is the *pasta del giorno* (pasta of the day), which is usually made with fish or eggplant. Secondi are simple, be it a *panata siciliana* (breaded steak) or a *cotolette di agnello arrosto* (roast lamb chop).

La Corte degli Sfizi. Cortile Contarini 4 (perpendicular to Via Atenea, near the end). ☎ **0922-20052.** Primi 8,000–12,000L ($4–$6); secondi 8,000–12,000L ($4–$6); fish dishes 13,000–20,000L ($7–$10). Open Fri–Wed noon–3pm and 7–10:30pm; open daily in July and August. AE, DI, MC, V. SICILIAN.

Still in its infancy, La Corte degli Sfizi occupies both an indoor cantina space and a peaceful garden courtyard in the palazzo opposite the entrance with a wooden deck and hanging lights for meals alfresco. To get business off the ground, the amiable owner instituted a tourist menu offering the works, drinks included, for a meager 26,000L ($13). But as a work-in-progress, the menu was slated to undergo some major overhauls. Expect a wide array of local dishes, fresh antipasti, and regular dishes like *cavatelli alla Norma.*

EN ROUTE TO SIRACUSA: THE MAGNIFICENT MOSAICS OF PIAZZA ARMERINA

In the hamlet of Casale outside the small city of Piazza Armerina lies the ✪ **Villa Romana del Casale** (☎ **0935-680-036**), a 4th-century villa carpeted in some 37,800 square feet of the most extensive, intact, and colorful ancient mosaics in western Europe, and certainly in all of the Roman world. Situated on the heights of inland Sicily's hills, Piazza Armerina rose out of its medieval ashes—it was destroyed by William I for treasonous hospitality given to rebel barons—and built a patrimony of 12th-century churches and baroque palaces. While most visitors make a beeline from the train station to the mosaics on the fringes of town, the "modern" Piazza Armerina, with its narrow and winding cobbled lanes and a concentration of Baroque monuments in the *centro storico*, is charming enough to hold your interest for at least an afternoon.

ESSENTIALS

GETTING THERE   No matter where you're coming from, you'll have to change buses in Enna. **SAIS** (☎ **0935-500-902**) handles the connections from Enna to Piazza Armerina (40 min.; 5,000L/$2.50) nine times daily, as well as connections into Enna from Palermo (90 min.; 15,000L/$8) and Catania (100 min.; 11,500L/$7). It gets a little complicated from Agrigento because of an additional connection in Caltanisetta, and is practically undoable from Siracusa, requiring two bus companies and as many transfers. In these last two cases, it'll be worth your time and money to rent a car for the day or make it an overnight trip.

Once in Piazza Armerina, the B bus (1,200L/60¢) makes the 15-minute run out to the Villa Imperiale at Casale hourly (look for buses marked "Piazza Armerina/Mosaici Servizio Urbano") from 9 to 11am and 4pm to 6pm (return trips hourly 9:30 to 11:30am and 4:30 to 6:30pm).

VISITOR INFORMATION   Piazza Armerina has a friendly **tourist office** inside the palazzo at the top of Via Cavour (☎ **0935-680-201;** fax 0935-684-565), open Monday to Saturday 8am to 2pm.

SEEING THE MOSAICS

✪ **Villa Romana del Casale.** ☎ **0935-680-036.** Admission 4,000L ($2). Open 8am to 30 minutes before sunset (ticket office closes between 1 and 3pm). By car from the city center, follow Viale Libertà (which becomes Via Manzoni, then SS 117bis) to the intersection of the Ristorante da Battiato (mentioned above). Turn left and follow the signs for *i mosaici.*

Still shrouded in mystery is the identity of the wealthy patrician and patron of this vast country villa and surrounding complex. Experts cite clues, and lots of 'em, suggesting that this was the hunting lodge of Maximanus, Diocletian's co-emperor. Beginning with the former grand entrance, the faint remains of a main triumphal arch and dual troughs for horses intimates the stature of the head of the household. Also look for the recurring **heart-shaped emblem**—often resembling Mickey Mouse ears and symbolic of Hercules—and the **"coat of arms"** for the emperor, a.k.a. Massimiliano Hercoleo.

More interesting than the clues is the notion that the villa's 40 sumptuously decorated rooms represent less than 50% of the area yet to be excavated, with the kitchens and stables still buried under the now-hardened mud deposits left by a disastrous 12th-century flood. Ironically, it was this very event that has allowed these remarkable mosaics to survive in such a state of preservation, blanketed as they were for centuries in a moist protective layer.

The current visit begins with an overview of the extensive system of heating and water supply for the baths. Notice the craftsmanship of the pavements inside the bath's tiled rooms, probably attributable to North Africans artisans, and exhibiting early attempts at perspective, seen in the use of darkened areas around the feet to represent shadows. This being a hunting lodge, many of the scenes involve big-game hunting and other sports, no more spectacularly than in the **Great Hunt,** a mosaic scene undulating for 200 feet in a catalogue of animals found throughout the ancient empire. Most are shown being captured alive and herded onto the ships that'll carry them to Rome to be sacrificed in stadium spectacles (look for the North African lion, rendered extinct by such Roman excesses). Note that the sunken areas of the corridor, caused by the flood mentioned earlier, resulted in an area of mosaics rendered even more vivid than in adjacent areas. In the nearby *palestra* (gym), you'll see a **Chariot Race** held at Rome's Circus Maximus (another clue to the ownership of the villa), complete with cheering fans. But the most famous scene is hands-down the **Ten Bikini Girls,** a lineup of female athletes either working out at the gymnasium or competing in various events and clad in strapless bikinis. Part of an earlier layer of geometric flooring, dating to the Byzantine era, is left exposed in the corner. At this point, the catwalk leads outside to an elliptical peristyle and into the **triclinium,** a three-apsed dining room decorated with the **Twelve Trials of Hercules** (two more clues: the shape of the building and the decorative theme). The peristyle featured a central basin indispensable during these extended gluttonous food orgies—often lasting for days —when Roman high society would make room for the constant supply of delicacies by regurgitating the last course.

The path back into the private apartments leads first to the children's rooms, especially amusing for their pint-size versions of the main halls' majestic scenes and a red disc **alphabet** translated into both Greek and Roman. Finally, be on the lookout for the mosaic ✪ **erotic couple** stealing a kiss in one side room. This is where the master of the house would sneak away for illicit rendezvous, but by the pristine state of preservation of the entire series, this room apparently didn't see much action.

A GREAT DEAL ON DINING

Pepito. Via Roma 140 (near the corner of Via Sturzo). ☎ **0935-685-737.** Primi 8,000–12,000L ($4–$6); secondi 10,000–15,000L ($5–$8). AE, DI, CB, MC, V. Wed–Mon 9am–midnight. RUSTIC SICILIAN.

It's amazing what table linens and cloth napkins can do. Pepito is simple without being bare, but even neighborhood trattorie are expected to display a minimum amount of propriety, after all. It's welcoming without being overbearing, and there's an upstairs dining area for those looking for a more elegant setting. Expect hearty mountain dishes like the tasty *coniglio alla cacciatore* (rabbit with artichokes and olives in a sauce of tomatoes and white wine), and a small but pleasingly fresh "Wendy's Fixins"–type table for the antipasto spread. This far inland, you'll need to give a bit of advanced notice for the Paella alla Valençiana—well worth the planning.

7 Siracusa & Ortigia

256km (154 mi.) E of Agrigento, 87km (52 mi.) S of Catania, 330km (198) miles SE of Palermo, 182km (110 mi.) S of Messina.

One of the most influential, powerful, and culturally rich cities in Magna Graecia, **Siracusa (Syracuse),** some 2,700 years later, is the heir to an incredible artistic and archaeological patrimony. Siracusa was settled by Greeks from Corinth in 733 B.C.

and almost immediately began a systematic suppression of and expansion to neighboring territories. Eventually falling under tyrant rule, by 480 B.C. Siracusa had become the most important center in Sicily and a major political and military player among the most powerful civilizations in the Mediterranean, to the great displeasure of Athens and Carthage. At its height, Siracusa welcomed such greats as Archemides, whose mathematic genius ultimately led to the city's defeat at the hand of the Romans in 212 B.C.

The effect of the tyrants still lies just below the surface: This is *cosa nostra* territory, a tangible presence probably behind the destruction of the "aesthetically inferior" Spanish Gate and the construction of that inappropriate cement eyesore of a parking lot on Ortigia Island. In spite of the warm welcome you won't receive (modern Siracusa suffers from a glaring deficiency in basic hospitality), the city benefits from a perfect seaside location, a thriving trading port and some fantastic ruins—including one of the world's largest intact Greek theaters. If you can actually find a vacant room—preferably on charming and historic Ortigia, a zone of baroque monuments that supports a wonderful array of cafes, seaside strolls, and alfresco restaurants—an overnight visit to Siracusa will allow you to take advantage of the city's top-notch sights with enough spare time to wander amidst the mythical bounty of the morning market.

FESTIVALS & MARKETS   Siracusans parade a statue of their patron **Santa Lucia,** an opulent figure of solid silver, around with pomp and ceremony on December 13 and again the first two Sundays in May. The city also sponsors summertime **performances in the ancient Greek theater** (even years only). These tend to be of classical plays translated into Italian (some of which even premiered in this very theater 2,500 years ago). The next repertory will be in 2002; tickets can be purchased at the theater, or call toll free within Italy ☎ **800-907-080.** There's also an Internet site for information: www.chartanet.it. Tickets in the general seating area cost 50,000L ($25); seats go for 75,000L ($37.50) to 155,000L ($77) depending on the performance and location. Check with the box office for deep discounts on seats for weekday performances.

ESSENTIALS

GETTING THERE   By Train   You can get here by train from **Agrigento,** but take my word for it, you don't want to: Take one of nine daily trains to Canicatti (45 to 60 min.; 5,500L/$2.75), where you transfer for one of four trains (two on Sunday) to Siracusa, usually changing trains again in Gela, Modica, or Catania, and sometimes in two out of three (4½ hr., not including transfer; 22,000L/$11 total). From **Palermo,** you can take one of five daily trains through **Catania** (3½ to 4 hr.; 20,500L/$11), from which there are at least hourly runs (85 min.; 8,500L/$4.25) on to Siracusa or through **Messina** (about 4 hr.; 19,500L/$10), from which there are at least hourly runs (3 to 4 hr.; 16,000L/$8 or 23,000L/$12 IC). If you buy a "through ticket from Palermo, you'll save around $3–$4). **Siracusa's station** (☎ **0931-67-964** or 0931-66-640) is on the mainland, west of Ortigia and south of the archaeological zone.

By Bus   Three lines currently service Siracusa, so if you're arriving from a provincial town, you'll have to change to one of these services in one of the major cities listed here. **AST** (☎ **0931-462-711**) runs buses (originating in Palermo) about twice an hour (60 to 75 min.; 8,000L/$3.80) from **Catania. Interbus,** Via Trieste 28, Siracusa (☎ **0931-66-710** in Siracusa or 095-532-716 in Catania) runs the same route, with five or six buses departing daily from both the Catania's airport and train station (1¼ hrs.; 8,000L/$4).You can also hop on **Interbus** (☎ **0935-503-141**) in **Rome's** Piazza

---

Navigating No-Traffic Zones By Bike

Thanks to a local socially conscious cooperative, bike rentals are now available to ease both your stay in town and alleviate local levels of pollution. Bikes are set up on Ortigia in Largo XXV Luglio on the little island across from the Temple of Apollo Tuesday through Sunday from 9am to 7pm. Hourly rates start at 4,000L ($2) for the first hour and go up to 15,000L ($8) for a full day. For information call ☎ **0931-32887.**

---

della Repubblica for a 7:30am departure that will get you into Siracusa at 10pm that night (14½ hrs.; 67,000L/$34). If you can get to Gela, (☎ **0931-462-711**) you can either change for one of the four to five direct daily trains (3½ hr.; 16,000L/$8) or take one of two **AST** buses (6:25am or 3:20pm) directly into Siracusa (90 min.; 13,000L/$7).

By Car   From **Piazza Armerina,** follow the scenic, twisty, fragrant SS124 through the mountains. From **Agrigento,** take this hideous stretch of SS115 all the way. From **Palermo,** take the A20 autostrada east toward Cefalù, exiting onto the A19 through Enna and the interior to where it hits the SS114 just south of Catania and follow that into Siracusa. From **Messina,** you can follow the coastal SS114 all the way through **Taormina** and **Catania** to Siracusa.

GETTING AROUND   City **buses** cost 1,500L (75¢) and make circular routes. Most start and end at Piazza della Posta just over the bridge on Ortigia. Although lines 21 to 23 stop at the train station and continue to Ortigia, these run infrequently; you're better off turning left out of the station and walking a few blocks to Piazza Marconi (a.k.a. Foro Siracusiano), where just about every line passes. From here, it's an easy 5-minute walk down Corso Umberto to Ortigia. For a **taxi,** dial ☎ **0931-69-722,** 0931-60-980, or 0931-64-323.

VISITOR INFORMATION   There's a **tourist office** on Ortigia at Via Maestranza 33 (☎ **0931-464-255;** fax 0931-60-204); they don't seem to appreciate disruptions, so keep it simple with questions for maps and materials. It's open Tuesday to Friday 8:30am to 1pm and 4:30 to 7pm and Monday and Saturday 8:30am to 2pm. There's also an office in modern Siracusa at Via San Sebastiano 45 (☎ **0931-67-710** for the desk, 0931-482-100 for the main office; fax 0931-67-803) across from the San Giovanni catacombs; June to September hours are Monday to Saturday 8am to 7pm and Sunday 9am to 1pm and October-to-May hours Monday to Saturday 8am to 2pm and 3 to 6pm. Finally, there's an **info kiosk** at the entrance to the archaeological zone at **Largo Anfiteatro** (☎ **0931-60-510**), open daily 8:30am to 7pm (they may close during *riposo* in winter).

SEEING THE ARCHAEOLOGICAL ZONE ON THE MAINLAND

✪ **Archaeological Park of Neapolis.** Largo Anfiteatro, off Corso Gelone/Viale Teracrati. ☎ **0931-66-206.** Admission 8,000L ($4). Daily 9am–2 hours before sunset (site closes at 5pm when there are performances). Bus: there 1, 4, 8, 11, 12, 15, 21, 22, 23, 25; back 2, 3, 8, 11, 12, 14, 26.

This vast archaeological park contains Siracusa's greatest concentration of ruins. It's divided into three main sections: the *latomie* (stone quarries), the Greek theater, and the Roman amphitheater, all of which you can see in about 2 hours. The first two are together beyond the main gate. Hold on to your ticket, for upon exiting the Greek theater/*latomie* area you backtrack up the souvenir stand–lined road to enter the amphitheater area, where you must again present your ticket.

Along the entry path past the Roman amphitheater area (see it on the way out), you'll be on your left the few columns still standing and the long stone base of the 3rd-century B.C. **Altar of Hieron II.** At 653 by 75 feet, it's the longest altar ever built and was used for sacrifices of entire herds of cows. Veer right onto the path down to the **Latomia del Paradiso (Paradise Quarry),** an ancient quarry now overgrown with a jungle of orange and lemon trees. Along the back wall is a narrow cavern 76 feet high, 214 feet deep, and only about 25 feet wide. Used as a prison for the survivors of the Athenian army after their defeat in 413 B.C., the cave was later dubbed by Caravaggio as the "Ear of Dionysius"—either due to its pointy shape, like the ear on a satyr, or its remarkable acoustics, which amplify even the quietest whisper. According to local legend, these remarkable acoustics allowed the tyrant Dionysius to spy on his captives by listening in through a crack in the cave's roof (further conjecture theorizes the space as a former cistern).

Next door to the "ear" is the cordoned off **Grotta dei Cordari (Ropemaker's Cave),** a wide quarry fissure romantically filled with water and maidenhead ferns; its preservation is in a precarious state, so it is closed to visitors.

Return to the ticket office and take the left path, which leads to the stark white curve of the ✪ **Teatro Greco (Greek theater),** whose 455-foot diameter makes it one of the largest in the world. Built in the 5th century B.C. and later expanded, its 42 rows of seats were hewn directly out of the living rock, and probably saw the first productions of some of Aeschylus' plays. The Romans, who felt serious drama was to be taken only in moderation, adapted the theater so they could occasionally flood the stage and stage tiny mock sea battles.

Summer productions (mostly classical plays) are still staged at the theater—great if you can attend one, but don't be crushed if you can't: during the 2 months of performances, the theater is blanketed in steel railings and gray wooden planks, diminishing significantly the impact of the site, naturally backed by a scrim of pine trees and azure sea. At the top of the *cavea* are niches that once contained little votive altars, plus a little niched pond that collects the cold water flowing from an ancient aqueduct—temporarily boarded up during show season because the actors complain of the distraction created by the running water.

On your way out of the site, stop into the A.D. 1st-century ✪ **Anfiteatro Romano (Roman Amphitheater),** where Siracusans once held bloody gladiator fights and the like when they tired of the plays at the Greek theater. It, too, is used today for productions (mainly musicals) in the summer, when bright red poppies bloom against the green wash of the overgrown seating sections.

✪ **Museo Archaeologico Paolo Orsi (Archaeological Museum).** Viale Teocrito 66. ☎ **0931-464-022.** Admission 8,000L ($4.70). June–Aug Mon 3:30–7:30pm, Tues–Wed 9am–7:30pm, Thurs–Sat 9am–11pm, 1st and 3rd Sun of month 9am–1pm; Sept–May Tues–Sat 9am–2pm, 1st and 3rd Sun of month 9am–1pm. Bus: there 1, 4, 8, 11, 12, 15, 21, 22, 23, 25; back 2, 3, 8, 11, 12, 14, 26.

This fantastic museum is one of Italy's top archaeological collections, and by far the best in Sicily. It'd be a worthwhile stop simply for the aesthetic beauty of many pieces, but the well-documented exhibits make it invaluable for understanding the Greek and other cultures of ancient Sicily.

A Money-Saving Tip

A combo ticket that includes entrance to the Museo Archeologico Paolo Orsi and the Teatro Greco, normally 8,000L ($4) apiece, costs 12,000L ($6) for a savings of $2. The ticket can be purchased at either museum.

Section A covers the island's southeastern corner during prehistoric times, kicking off with a pair of articulated dwarf elephant skeletons found in nearby caves. A closer look at the skulls and it's easy to see why many academics believe that their odd shape and large central nasal passage led the local ancients—who surely stumbled across them—to invent the myth of the one-eyed, cave-dwelling giant called Cyclopes. But the best part of the prehistoric section is the remains left by humans, a collection of tools, ceramics, and sculptures that open a window onto the richness of Sicily's Stone and Bronze Age cultures.

Section B covers Siracusa and its province in all its ancient Greek glory. The highlights include a terra-cotta statue of a goddess nursing twins (550 B.C.); the headless *Venus Landolina,* an Imperial Roman copy of a 2nd-century B.C. statue that's a lesson in both anatomy and aesthetics; the museum's mischievous mascot of a 6th-century B.C. terra-cotta Gorgon, grinning and sticking his tongue out; and cases full of 5th- and 4th-century B.C. votive statuettes dedicated to Demeter/Ceres and Kore/Persephone, to whom there was apparently a temple across the street (workers breaking ground for the huge Sanctuary of the Madonna discovered it a few decades back).

Section C contains the best remains from Magna Graecia settlements across eastern Sicily, including decorated vases from Gela spanning the 6th and 5th centuries B.C.; an enthroned goddess from 6th-century B.C. Grammichele; and a trio of rare 7th-century B.C. wooden statues found near Agrigento. Lookout for the spectacularly carved 4th-century sarcophagus from the Catacombe di San Giovanni (San Giovanni catacombs).

Catacombe di San Giovanni (Catacombs of San Giovanni). Via San Giovanni alle Catacombe (between the archaeological park and museum). ☎ **0931-67-955.** 4,000L ($2) adults, 1,000L (50¢) under 10. Wed–Mon 9am–12:30pm (Apr–Oct 4:30–5:30pm). Bus: there 1, 4, 8, 11, 12, 15, 21, 22, 23, 25; back 2, 3, 8, 11, 12, 14, 26.

What is now the ruined church of San Giovanni was a potters' cave in Greek times, but once St. Paul came here to preach it became serious holy ground, topped by a 6th-century basilica until it was knocked down by the Saracens. The church was rebuilt by the Normans in the 12th century and once again ruined when a 1693 earthquake shook it to the ground, but undissuaded, locals grafted a baroque structure onto the ruins. The Siracusans gave up after a 1908 earthquake destroyed it once and for all, leaving the roofless Norman walls and half an apse as they were, romantically sprouting flowers and weeds. It's still consecrated, and marriages and summer Sunday services take place around a sarcophaguslike altar.

A guide will whisk you through the original 6th-century Greek-cross crypt, with remnants of frescoes and capitals from the Byzantine and Norman eras, including the purported column where Siracusa's first bishop, San Marziano, was flogged to death. But the real treat is the catacombs, the only set of Siracusa's many early Christian subterranean burial grounds currently open to the public. There are some 20,000 tombs down here, niched into tunnels that honeycomb the earth connecting former Greek cisterns (recycled by early Christians into chapels). Along with cornrows of graves that once housed extended families, you'll see a few faded frescoes and early Christian symbols etched into stone slabs.

EXPLORING ORTIGIA

Just across the Ponte Umbertino bridge to **Ortigia** is the long, shaded Piazza Panciale, the end of which opens up into Piazza XXV Luglio, a traffic circle bounded on the east by a sunken archaeological zone that sprouts a few Doric column stumps, a long low set of stairs, half a wall, lots of weeds, and a few palm trees. This is what remains of the early 6th-century B.C. **Temple of Apollo,** the first Doric temple in Sicily.

If you manage to find yourself here during the morning hours, follow the white cloth awnings of the local market to Piazza Pancali for a look at what Mother Nature is capable of. Carry lots of 1,000L and 2,000L notes and brace yourself to choose among an abundance of **local produce** the likes of which you've never seen: enormous lemons, nuclear-sized zucchinis, strawberries the size of racquet balls, succulent cherry tomatoes and stacks of mussels garnished in lemon halves and girthy local tuna.

Make your way to the oblong, cafe-lined Piazza del Duomo at Ortigia's center to the ✪ **Duomo** (open 8am to noon and 4 to 7pm), adapted by the Byzantines and then the Normans from a 5th-century B.C. **Temple to Athena.** The interior is marvelously simple, a honey-colored world of sacred quiet that feels about as close as stepping back in time and into an ancient temple as you're ever going to find. To convert the Greek temple to a church wasn't hard: They just punched archways through the *cella* (the sacred central chamber of the temple) to make it into a nave, and filled in the spaces between the 19 giant Doric columns from the temple's peristyle (all a bit askew from a 1542 earthquake) to make the outer walls of the aisle. Aside from Andrea Palma's 1728 to 1754 baroque facade, the cathedral remains essentially medieval and plain (Baroque additions in the interior were stripped away in the 1920s). Look in the first chapel on the right for a baptismal font recycled from an ancient marble font resting on 13th-century bronze lions. Along the left aisle there are four statues by the **Gagini** (three in between the second to fifth columns and a *Madonna della Neve* up near the end of the aisle) and a painting on wood with gold background of *St. Cosimo* attributed to **Antonella da Messina.**

Just down Via Picherali from the south end of the piazza you'll find the harborside Largo Aretusa, whose centerpiece is the lovely little sunken pond containing the **Fonte Aretusa,** Siracusa's most famous mythological site. Half a dozen Greek poets wrote the tale of the nymph Aretusa, who was bathing in the Alpheus River in Greece one day when the god of that river took a liking to her. She begged for deliverance from his persistent amorous advances, and Artemis in pity turned the nymph into a spring, allowing her to escape underground. She traveled under the sea to emerge here in Siracusa, but Alpheus, was hot on her heels and came gushing out in the same spot, mingling his waters with hers for eternity. They used to say you could toss a goblet into a spring at Arcadia in Greece and it would pop up here. Today, the font still flows softly from its grotto into the pond, planted with puffy-headed, willowy papyrus (supposedly a gift from Egyptian ruler Ptolemy II) and swimming with fish and ducks. Shops selling sheets of papyrus "paper" can be found in the surrounding streets, especially Via Capodieci.

The **Palazzo Bellomo,** just up Via Capodieci at Via Roma, was built between the 13th and 15th centuries. It features a Catalan-Gothic staircase and courtyard, and is home to the **Museo Regionale di Arte Mediovale e Moderna (Regional Museum of Medieval and Modern Art)** (☎ **0931-69-617**). Its two stellar works are Antonello da Messina's highly ruinous but still exquisitely painted *Annunciation* (1474), and Caravaggio's moody *Deposition of Santa Lucia* (1608). Other standouts include medieval and Renaissance sculptures on the ground floor—among which a *Madonna* by Domenico Gagini—and a comical early 17th-century painting of angels ferrying the Madonna's house across the sea to Loreto with baby Jesus perched on the roof. The collections are rounded out by 18th- and 19th-century carriages, livery, furnishings, and ceramics, including a 15th-century Spanish/Moorish faience plate patterned in metallic reddish gold. Admission is 8,000L ($4.70). It's open Monday to Saturday 9am to 1:30pm and Sundays and holidays 9am to 12:30pm. Check for expanded afternoon and evening hours in July and August.

AFFORDABLE PLACES TO STAY

This is certainly a wonderful place to pass some time, to while away the hours at a streetside cafe, in a local trattoria, or along the *lungomare*. Siracusans love to have you (and your money), but the truth is, *they don't need you,* and it doesn't take long to feel superfluous, especially if you've tried to book a room for the night. Modern-day tyrants prefer to take care of repeat customers who take precedence over us pitiable stragglers looking for an honest place to stay. (I experienced this firsthand, after having been booted unceremoniously out of a pensione I had booked only to have the room given over to someone else *after* I had shown up with my passport as a deposit. This is illegal; if this happens to you, immediately notify the local *carabinieri,* and avoid the Palazzo Gargalo Pensione.) The establishments listed below are the exceptions to the rule in that they're straight-shooting and reliable, the only problem being that you have to book decades in advance. My advice? Make Siracusa a day trip (see "Getting There," above).

✪ **Gran Bretagna.** Via Savoia 21 (on Ortigia, near Piazza XXV Luglio), 96100 Siracusa. ☎ **0931-68-765.** Fax 0931-462-169. E-mail: mcapill@tin.it. 12 units, 4 with bathroom. 52,000L ($26) single without bathroom, 62,000L ($31) single with bathroom; 88,000L ($44) double without bathroom, 100,000L ($50) double with bathroom. Rates include breakfast. AE, DC, MC, V. Closed mid-Nov to early Dec.

This is not only the most reasonably priced hotel on Ortigia itself, run by a family that keeps it immaculate, it's also the most welcoming. In spite of these appealing traits, plans are under way to renovate the entire operation (call to check the status), with seven additional units and a private bath in each room. For now, first-floor rooms are older and bathless but gracious in size, with big carved wooden furnishings and high vaulted ceilings. A few even have frescoes—nos. 2 and 3 just around the light fixture, but in huge, family-perfect no. 7, the whole ceiling is painted. Upstairs rooms were more recently redone and most have baths, but they're cramped with less attractive modular furnishings. The best is no. 8, with a spiral staircase up to a little terrace from which you can see the sea in both directions.

WORTH A SPLURGE

Domus Mariae. Via Vittorio Veneto 76 (on the east side of Oritiga, just below Via Mirabella), 96100 Siracusa. ☎ and fax **0931-24-858.** 12 units. A/C MINIBAR TV TEL. 170,000L ($85) single; 200,000–230,000L ($100–$115) double. 30,000L ($15) supplement per person for half board (minimum 3 days).Breakfast included. AE, DC, MC, V.

In 1995, the Suore Orsoline turned part of their old convent into a quietly stylish, modern hotel, located on the quiet coastal road on the far side of Ortigia. Half the room's balconies front the sea and a few feature fold-out couches that make them great for families. Rooms are large—even the singles are spacious—with built-in units and patterned rugs on tile floors. Baths are modern and like new, with pristine finishes and marble-top sinks. Those sea-view rooms, kindly reception, and all these comforts make this upscale nunnery worth the splurge.

GREAT DEALS ON DINING

The restaurants along the *lungomare* are expectedly posh, with white tablecloths, candles, and prices commensurate with the views. A good place to seek out a down and dirty characteristic *taverna* is along Via Cavour and its arteries, where the tables fill up with big appetites for fresh pasta and typical casereccia meals.

○ **Il Cedro.** Via Capodieci 49, summer entrance also around the corner on Via Maniace 3 (off of Largo Aretusa). ☎ **0931-465-860.** Primi 9,000–14,000L ($4.50–$7); secondi 9,000–18,000L ($4.50–$9). AE, DI, MC, V. Thurs–Tues noon–3pm and 7:30pm–1 or 2am. TRATTORIA/PIZZERIA.

You wouldn't expect such a reasonably priced outstanding meal this close to the "uptown" crowd along the *lungomare*, but it's always refreshing when a meal exceeds your expectations. The courtyard tables are shaded by huge canvas umbrellas, and there's a cozy dining room for cooler weather. The quality of the shellfish is irreproachable, making the delicate flavors of the *antipasto cedro* (mixed seafood salad) or the smoked swordfish come to life. The *linguine ai frutti di mare* in a slightly tomato-based garlic sauce is divine, but if you've had enough fish, try Cedro's impossibly delicious invention of *garganelli con panna e mandorle* (screw-shaped pasta in a light cream-and-almond sauce). Finish the meal with their exceptional homemade *limoncello*, which is neither too sweet nor too syrupy.

Il Cenacolo. Via dei Consiglio Regionale/Corte degli Avolio 9–10 (just north of Piazza Duomo). ☎ **0931-65-099.** Reservations recommended. Primi 8,000–18,000L ($4–$9); secondi 8,000–18,000L ($4–$9); pizze 5,000–20,000L ($2.50–$10). AE, MC, V. Thurs–Tues noon–3pm and 7pm–1am. SICILIAN/PIZZA.

The real attraction of this restaurant—not that we're overlooking the menu or the cozy vaulted dining room covered in local historical photos—is the relaxed setting under dwarf palms tucked into a pocket-sized piazza hidden at the very heart of Ortigia. Although the prices may seem slightly overblown, the *pane e coperto* ("bread and cover" charge) is included in the prices, making the price of a meal at "The Last Supper" pretty competitive. Of course there's the amusing theological exercise of matching the pizzas' biblical names with their toppings (the "Lazarus" comes with the mushrooms of decay, "Judas" with the sting of hot peppers). There's also the standard array of Sicilian dishes like spaghetti alla bolognese or *ai ricci di mare* (with a sauce of sea urchins), *zuppa di cozze e vongole verace* (steamed mussels and littleneck clams), *bistecca alla pizzaiola* (steak covered in pizza sauce and mozzarella), but you can also "discover the pleasure of variety" by calling ahead and ordering something special like *paella valenciana* (a Spanish rice dish rich with seafood) or couscous (with meat or fish).

WORTH A SPLURGE

Jonico-'A Rutta 'E Ciàuli. Riviera Dionisio Il Grande 194 (just down from Largo Latomie). ☎ **0931-65-540.** Reservations highly recommended. Primi 9,000–14,000L ($4.50–$7); secondi 15,000–32,000L ($8–$16); pizze 7,000–12,000L ($3.50–$6). AE, DC, MC, V. Wed–Mon noon–3pm, 5pm–2am. Bus: 3, 7. SIRACUSAN.

This splurge is one of Sicily's best restaurants, certainly Siracusa's finest, and so staunchly traditional that the menu's written entirely in dialect. The setting is especially romantic: on a curving terrace lined with blown-glass lamps 50 feet above the soft surf lapping against the rocks with a sweeping vista of the Ionian sea and Ortigia. Try the traditional Siracusan *spaghetti c'a muddica e anciovi* (with grated bread and anchovies) or the specialty *spaghetti co tunnu friscu* (with fresh tuna, tomatoes, and capers). The kitchen's best secondi are *bistecca a siciliana* (steak smothered with tuna, onion, and cheese) and *orata 'c'aranciu* (gilt-head bream cooked with orange juice, orange zest, and white wine). Meat eaters may prefer the *custati ri agneddu panate* (breaded mutton chops). A less formal pizzeria is on the open-air roof.

8 Mt. Etna: The Forge of Vulcan

Mt. Etna is the biggest, baddest volcano in Europe and one of the largest in the world, 10,990 feet of massive molten energy that dominates all of eastern Sicily with a menacing unpredictability. Etna's active crater is constantly blowing a thin yet steady trail of smoke, as if relishing a quality Cuban cigar. You know her temper is flaring by the white mushroom cloud that emerges, inevitably turning an ominous black before blowing its top in bright red jet streams of molten lava and ash (when you see that black smoke, high-tail it outta there; you've only got about 20 or 30 minutes to get to safe ground). Etna's show of fireworks plays to an appreciative audience about every 10 days or so, depositing its lava flows harmlessly into an enormous and isolated crater. But every few years it goes into a dangerously violent volcanic fit. In 1989, at the summit, a new crater grew over 330 feet in just a month. From 1991 to 1993, it erupted almost continuously, and in 1998, 8 months of violent activity culminated in an eruption on July 12 that spewed ash almost a mile into the air, closing Catania's airport and covering the mountain with a fresh layer of pumice and lava. Etna's lava flows have threatened, and occasionally actually swallowed, several of the small towns that brave the danger to take agricultural advantage of the rich volcanic soil, making the locals rather nervous.

The most popular arrival point by car is the **Rifugio Sapienza,** a base station at the 6,300-foot mark more than slightly disfigured by the infestation of souvenir shops, postcard stands, and snack bars. There's a tourist information office at the far end of the parking lot to the right (☎ **095-911-505**).

The **Rifugio** (☎/fax **095-911-062**) providing the only guest accommodations on the mountain, allows for a solitary and more in-depth exploration of the nearby extinct craters. The hotel is closed for renovations until May or June 2001, as it's undergoing a complete overhaul, with the intention of offering three-star service at rates above those of its former and spartan incarnations. Rates are yet to be fixed; call for information.

GETTING TO THE VOLCANO

From almost any major town in Sicily, you can count on the local travel agencies offering day excursions to Mt. Etna. Prices vary according to the jumping-off city; just check around town for these tour offerings, or ask your hotel concierge for information.

BY CAR   Take the Catania-Messina **A18** Autostrada to the **Giarre** exit and follow signs for **Santa Venerina,** then **Zafferana Etnea** and **Etna Sud.** You'll be rewarded by a fertile and verdant path that winds up the mountain (an **alternative** approach via **Nicolosi** will take you through an entirely different landscape—a monotone and barren terrain of dark volcanic detritus). Driving north on Catania's Tangenziale highway, take the exit for Gravina di Catania heading in the direction of Nicolosi–Etna Sud.

BY BUS   You can catch an early morning **AST** bus (☎ **095-723-0511**) from Catania (2½ hr.; 9,000L/$4.50 round-trip), currently leaving at 8:15am Monday to Saturday; the return bus leaves the Rifugio at 4:15pm. On Sundays, the bus departs Catania at 8:30am and returns from the *Rifugio* at 4:30pm.

GETTING TO THE CRATER

At the Rifigio, **Funivia dell'Etna** (☎ **095-911-158**) administers the cable car (9am to 4:30pm daily and until 6pm July through mid-September) and visits up to one, two or all three stages up to the top. The *funivia* cable car to the Torre dell Filosofo stops at 8200 feet. Thirty-five thousand lire ($18) round-trip will get you an espresso and sweeping views of the gravelly moonscape. For the full excursion (68,000L/$34), you

A Travel Tip

Nothing's going to stop you from hiking up the volcano or camping along an active vapor vent—nothing, that is, except prudence. You can buy a ticket on the cable car (departures every 15 minutes, much like an amusement park ride) and decide to walk all or part of the way up or down. If you've opted out of the excursion in favor of unfettered exploration, wear sturdy shoes you don't love, and bring a substantial jacket. Boots, parkas and even socks are available for rental up at the arrival point for the cable car (2,000L/$1 each).

get a ride on an off-road Mercedes or IVECO turbo minibus from here to the second stage at 9,580 feet (or as close as conditions will allow); you've also bought yourself a guide who'll walk you as close to the top as conditions will allow. On a clear day, the vistas from up here encompass all of Sicily, but most certainly you'll be eyeing up the spectacular former active crater of the **Valle delle Bove,** an enormous yawning cleft measuring 11 miles around and almost 4,000 extremely steep feet down, scooped out of the southeast slope. Much of the lava flows this century have found their way safely into this channel, away from inhabited soil.

ADVENTUROUS EXCURSIONS UP THE MOUNTAIN

Just beneath the dusty earth-toned gravel is snow—meters and meters of it, camouflaged in layers like the icing on a seven-layer cake. It snows and it blows, and the cycle simply repeats itself. It's not beautiful, this barren lunar landscape. But it's there, and that seems to be enough for adventurers in search of offbeat amusement. In winter, the Rifugio Sapienza becomes the springboard point for **skiing** on Mt. Etna, weather and volcanic conditions permitting, naturally. The **Funivia dell'Etna** (☎ 095-911-158) runs four lifts continuously from 9am until the last ride up at 3:30pm; a one-day lift ticket costs 27,000L ($14) weekdays and 36,000L ($18) weekends and holidays. Skis, poles, and boots are also available for rental for 24,000L ($14) per day. With advanced notice, they will also arrange cross-country excursions for up to ten people (with English speaking guide) for 250,000L ($125).

    Biosport Management (☎ 090-640-9800 or 091-545-623) organizes **trekking** excursions up the slope of Mt. Etna on Saturdays and Sundays. Off-road transport is provided from Provenzano (located at the 1,800-meter mark) to Pizzi Deneri on the NE slope, where you continue on foot along the canyons and up to some of the largest temporary cones. The trip takes about 3 to 5 hours and costs 130,000L ($65).

    In conjunction with the Scuola Nazionale Maestri di MTB in Messina, **Etna Trekking Bike** (☎ 0942—36-267) gets you up to Etna, provides you with a bike, helmet, and guide (in English on request). The price, including transfers to the mountain, is 60,000L ($30).

9 Taormina

134km (80 mi.) N of Siracusa, 48km (29 mi.) S of Messina.

Dominating the surrounding headland from atop a richly fragrant and flowering hilltop, **Taormina,** together with its sibling resort, Giardini-Naxos, accommodates over 50% of all Sicily's tourism. In spite of the hoards clamoring for their share of paradise, Taormina remains a spot of extraordinary beauty, with its narrow hidden staircases (some as narrow as 100cm!), characteristic homes that blend into the rock face, and its large concentration of hotels, one more gracious than the next, all clinging to the promontory with terrifically terraces facing mighty Etna and the sea.

At the base of the mountain at the southern point of the pleasure-seeking seaside resort of Giardini-Naxos is the sweeping Bay of Schisò, the original landing place of Greek settlers blown here by an unexpected crosswind as early as the 8th century B.C. The site was eventually built up into the thriving center of Naxos, an orderly city of gridded streets doomed to annihilation at the hands of the terrible tyrant Dionysius in 403 B.C. Those citizens not massacred or sold as slaves managed to escape up the hill, founding a colony along the steep and impregnable hill now known as Taormina. Centuries later, the medieval palazzi, tiny churches, breathtaking panorama, and ✪ **Teatro Greco-Romano (Greco-Roman Theater)** serve as a backdrop to the hedonistic tendencies of mass tourism and Hollywood glitterati alike. Taormina has been a favorite over the years of everyone from Greta Garbo, who returned every spring for 30 years, to D. H. Lawrence, whose inspiration for his feverishly sensual *Lady Chatterly's Lover* was, according to local rumor, based on his own wife's dalliances with a Sicilian mule driver.

ESSENTIALS

GETTING THERE   By Train   There are 12 to 13 trains daily from **Siracusa** (2 to 3½ hr.; 12,500L/$6 or 17,700L/$9 IC), and hourly ones from **Catania** (45 to 50 min.; 5,500L/$2.75 or 7,900L/$3.95 IC) and from **Messina** (35 to 65 min.; 5,500L/$2.75). There are also three daily trains from **Rome** (8½ to 10 hrs.; 58,200L/$29 or 79,900L/$40 IC) that pass through **Naples** (6½ to 8 hrs.; 43,300L/$22 or 61,300L/$31 IC). The train **station, Taormina-Giardini** (☎ **0942-51-026** or 0942-51-511), is down on the SS114 coastal road. A local bus makes the 15-minute trip up to Taormina twice an hour between 7am and 12:30am for 2,500L ($1.25).

By Bus   Interbus (☎ **0935-503-141**) has daily departures to Giardini-Naxos and Taormina from Rome (58,000L/$29).They also make the trip about hourly (60 to 90 min.) to Taormina from **Catania** (☎ **095-532-716**), beginning at the airport and making stops in the city before continuing on to Giardini-Naxos and then Taormina. Bus service runs just about every hour (less frequently on Sundays) and costs 8,000L ($4). You'll have to change buses in Catania if you're headed in from **Siracusa** (2 hrs. 45 min. total; 8,000L/$4 not including fare after transfer) or from points beyond.

There's an Interbus ticket booth at the bus station just outside the town gate on Via Pirandello (☎ **0942-625-301**), and one down at the Taormina-Giardini train station.

By Car   Taormina is above the coastal A18 autostrada (and its parallel, SS114) from Messina to Catania and Siracusa.

VISITOR INFORMATION   The **tourist office** is in the Palazzo Corvaja on Largo Santa Caterina (☎ **0942-23-243;** fax 0942-24-941; www.taormina-ol.it). If you're lucky, they won't have run out of the handy and colorful local map that clearly highlights a series of walks in and around the town. Otherwise, you'll have to be satisfied with the basic map and a steely smile. Useful however is that all of the train and bus schedules in and out of town are posted on the wall.

There's an **Internet Café** keeping shop hours across from the Municipio on Corso Umberto 214 (☎ **0942-628-839**).

FESTIVALS & MARKETS   In May, there's a festival to show off **traditional Sicilian carts and costumes.** There are **concerts and performances in the Greek theater** and churches around town from June to September. And in July and August, Taormina hosts an **international film festival.** There's a daily morning **market** in Via Cappuccini.

PASSEGGIATA DESTINATIONS

The single most popular activity in Taormina is simply strolling along the main drag, **Corso Umberto,** window-shopping, people watching, and occasionally getting caught amidst a marching-band parade. The east end of Corso Umberto is anchored by Largo SantaCaterina, home to **Palazzo Corvaja,** a fine 14th-century example of local masonry style, which highlights gray limestone walls with black and white lava trim. The staircase in the pretty little courtyard leads up to the **Museo Siciliano d'Arte e Tradizioni Popolari (Sicilian Museum of Art and Popular Traditions),** a small collection of Sicilian folk art and crafts. Admission is 5,000L ($2.50) and it's open Tuesday to Sunday 9am to 1pm and 4 to 8pm.

Via Teatro Greco leads to Taormina's only required sight, the 3rd-century B.C. ✪ **Teatro Greco-Romano (Greco-Roman Theater)** (☎ 0942-23-220), a drama in and of itself. Carved into the mountainside in the traditional Greek style, the *cavea* (the curved seating) enjoys sweeping vistas of the coastline, the mountains of Calabria across the straight and mighty Mt. Etna in the near distance. Why the Romans thought they could improve on the majesty of Mother Nature is beyond me, but in the 2nd century A.D., they were compelled to brick up the back wall, creating a system of claustrophobic underground passageways with low barrel vaults constructed of local stones. The view of the sea would have been completely eliminated but for a millennium of seismic activity, which has opened up a cragged window in the *scena* that once again allows for a magnificent sea view. Admission is double what it was last year at 8,000L ($4); it's open from 9am until an hour before sunset.

Walk back to Largo Santa Caterina and around the right side of its eponymous church to see a section of curving seats belonging to the **Odeon,** a modest Roman-era theater currently growing weeds. Continuing up Corso Umberto, turn left down Via Numachie to see the **Naumachie,** a 400-foot brick wall of 16-foot-high niches that formed a wall between an Imperial Roman gymnasium and an ancient cistern. A bit farther up the Corso is the town center, **Piazza IX Aprile,** a communal living room built as a terrace with a view over the Ionian Sea from the railing bounding one side. Lined with pricey cafes and brimming with visitors and caricature artists, it's the best place to sit back with a cappuccino and enjoy the relaxed resortlike ambience of Taormina.

Pass under the 12th-century **clock tower** and you'll be in the medieval section of town, where Corso Umberto eventually spills into **Piazza del Duomo.** The battlemented Duomo sports six huge antique pink marble columns inside and free concerts many summer evenings. The square's centerpiece is a fantastical 1635 fountain atop which perches a copy of the odd two-legged female centaur, a Greek mythological creature whose meaning or function no one quite seems to understand—ironically, Taormina made it the town mascot.

With a bit of enthusiasm and a lot of energy, head up the hillside staircase for increasingly unobscured panoramas and ultimately the sanctuary of the **Madonna della Rocca,** a tiny 17th-century church carved into and built onto an outcropping.

HITTING THE BEACH

Sitting unceremoniously at the base of the cliffs is **Mazzarò,** the seaside beach resort also known as Taormina Bassa. A *funivia* (cable car; ☎ 0942-23-906) links Mazzarò with Taormina Alta (entrance at Via Pirandello, between the bus depot and the gate into town) and runs every 15 minutes (3,000L/$1.75).

At the bottom and exiting the funivia to the right past the Capo Sant'Andrea headland, is the region's prettiest cove, where twin crescents of beach sweep from a sand spit out to the minuscule ✪ **Isola Bella** islet. Locals say that Isola Bella once was the home of an Italian Principessa who had her home built over the remains of ancient rock dwellings. Hidden in this scenic islet are over 40 rooms and two swimming pools, both fed with sea water by way of a pump located in a stone well on the southern side of the sandbar. Owing to the pebbles, this beach may be slightly unkind to your delicate little feet, but what a small price to pay for crystalline water and this level of natural beauty. You can either set yourself up at one of the beach establishments, or lay out a towel along the sandbar.

If instead you turn left out of the funivia, duck into one of those narrow stone staircases that will lead you over the train tracks and down to the beach to **Lido Il Delfino** (☎ **0942-24528**). Here an umbrella and chair run 10,000L to 15,000L ($5 to $8) per day and paddle boats rent for 15,000L ($8) an hour—great for a mini-excursion around Capo Sant'Andrea, passing by a few grottoes with excellent light effects on the seaward side towards Isola Bella. Show them this book and they'll give you a 20% discount. To the right of Il Delfino is **Lido La Pigna** (☎ **0942-24464**) a much posher beach establishment owing to gracious service, including towels and free minibus service to the beach. Lounges and umbrellas go for 15,000L ($8); the attendants will bring you as many coffees as you like and run a tab for the day (a nice tip will get you a front row seat for the next day). Check for their business card at local hotels for a 20% discount.

North of Mazzarò are the scenic rock fortress of **Spisone** (frequented by gays but popular in general), long, wide beaches, and **Letojanni.** There's a local bus that leaves Taormina for Mazzarò, Spisone, and Letojanni, and another that heads down the opposite coast to Giardini. No matter where you lay your towel, you'll have the chance to hop on one of the many **roving fishing boats** that near the shoreline, shaded by a romantically utilitarian sun-umbrella that advertises minitours of the area waters. They'll take you to some of the area's most infamous caves (if you see unmanned paddle boats near a cave's entrance, you'd be prudent to knock before entering), and as far south as Punto Capo Taormina for a sweeping view of Punto Schisò and the built-up resort of Giardini-Naxos. The boat ride lasts about 40 minutes and costs (25,000L/$13).

AFFORDABLE PLACES TO STAY

It's hard to believe a town so obscenely crammed with hotels can fill up, but in summer it does, even down below at Mazzarò and at nearby and sprawling Giardini-Naxos. Obviously, the high demand keeps prices high, but so does the quaintness quotient, especially up in Taormina proper. Book well in advance, and don't show up here looking for vacancies at the last minute.

TAORMINA ALTA

Villa Gaia. Via Fazzello 34/Piazza Carmine 6 (turn up Salita Badia Vecchia staircase from Piazza del Duomo), 98039 Taormina (ME). ☎/fax **0942-23-185.** 8 units. A/C TV TEL. 45,000–60,000L ($23–$30) single; 80,000–120,000L ($40–$60) double. Rates include breakfast in Aug; otherwise 5,000L ($2.50). Reduced rates off-season. AE.

Staying at this cozy little hotel in the heart of town is like moving in with a local family—or like moving into the kid's room for a night. The entire pensione was renovated in 2000, giving a fresh look to the mix of florals, statues, and mismatched furniture. The beds are a little soft but not bad, and almost all rooms have a terrace or balcony: The view from no. 5 gets in a bit of the sea and Etna, while the long terrace shared by nos. 1 through 4 will soon be divided so each room has a private one. Breakfast is served in a small garden shaded by mandarin orange and grapefruit trees. The renovations should boot Villa Gaia up to two-star status, so book early—these prices are hard to beat.

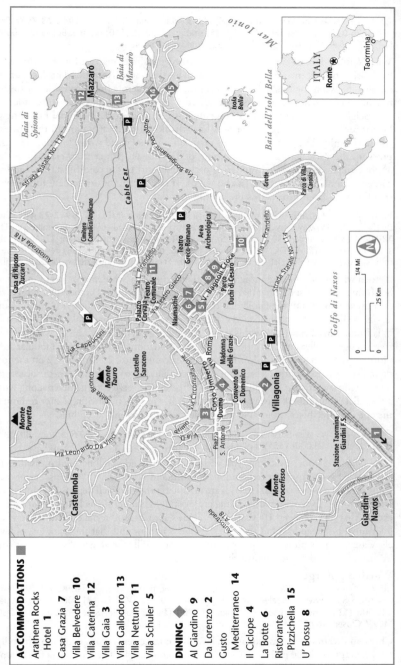

Taormina

Mar Ionio

Baia di Spisone

Baia di Mazzarò

Mazzarò

12 **13** **14** **15**

Isola Bella

Baia dell'Isola Bella

ITALY

Rome ✪

Taormina

Cable Car

Via Pirandello

Cimitero Cattolico/Anglicano

Casa di Riposo Zuccaro

Strada Statale No. 114

Autostrada A18

Teatro Greco-Romano

Area Archeologica

10

Via Prandello

11

Naumachie

Via Teatro Greco

Palazzo Corvaja

Teatro Comunale

6 **7**

5 **V. Bagnoli Croce** **8** **9**

Parco Duchi di Cesaro

Via Cappuccini

Via Bronco

Monte Tauro

Castello Saraceno

Via Circonvallazione

Madonna delle Grazie

Corso Umberto Roma

Convento di S. Domenico

4

2

Villagonia

Strada Statale No. 114

Via Prandello

Grotte

Parco di Villa Caronia

Golfo di Naxos

¼ Mi

25 Km

Monte Puretta

Castelmola

Via Leonardo Da Vinci

Primo

V & D

3

Duomo

Piazza S. Antonio

Autostrada A18

Monte Crocefisso

Stazione Taormina Giardini F.S.

Torrente Sirina

Giardini-Naxos

1

○ **Villa Nettuno.** Via Pirandello 33, 98039 Taormina (ME). ☎ **0942-23-797.** Fax 0942-626-035. 13 units. TEL. 70,000 ($35) single; 120,000L ($60) double. Breakfast 8,000L ($4). MC, V. Parking 10,000L ($5). Closed some weekdays in Jan.

Villa Nettuno is a gracious family house turned pensione, managed with loving care by Maria and Vicenzo Sciglio and assisted by their son, Antonio. The location is handy—between the bus stop and town gate and just across from the cable car to the beach, while perched high enough to afford a sea view from all except three rooms. The Sciglios are in the process of upgrading, in fact, rooms L and B are brand new, but since they insist on keeping prices low (thank the no-agency policy), the process may be lengthy. The remaining rooms may be a bit creaky and worn, but the Nettuno picks up the slack with a healthy amount of Taormina's 19th-century class, from the antique-filled salon and the wandering paths and stairs of the colorful statue-studded gardens. Climb to the peaceful gazebo temple at the summit of the gardens for an outstanding vista from Etna across the sea to Calabria.

Villa Schuler. Piazzetta Bastione/Via Roma, 98039 Taormina (ME). ☎ **0942-23-481.** Fax 0942-23-522. www.infoservizi.it/hotels/taormina.htm. E-mail: schuler@tao.it. 26 units. TV TEL. 180,000L ($90) double; 230,000L ($115) junior suite. 20% discount from Mar 11–Apr 1; July 1–29 and Nov 2–12. AE, DC, MC, V. Limited parking; reserve for 16,000L ($8) per day. Closed mid-Nov to mid-Mar. Turn left off Corso Umberto on Scesa Morgana just before Piazza IV Aprile.

Nestled within its own fragrant terraced gardens, the Villa Schuler looks over the Ionian Sea from a premier site below Piazza IV Aprile. Gerardo Schuler's grandfather built it to be a private home, but the family has run it as a hotel since 1905. Sea-view rooms look across the flowery and palm-shaded gravel terrace where most guests take their breakfast. (Via Roma runs directly below this terrace, meaning garden-view rooms are slightly quieter, though smaller and less attractive.) Accommodations are fitted with modular furniture mixed with antiques. Most rooms have balconies; nos. 29 through 32 on the top floor share a terrace with a vista from the Greek Theater to the coast. There's access to nearby tennis courts for 10,000L ($5) and a free shuttle service to the beach along with a free chair and umbrella (May to November). If you plan on sticking closer to home, they provide free bikes for tooling up and down the sometimes steep hills.

Casa Grazia. Via Iallia Bassia 20. 98039 Taormina (ME). ☎ **0942-24776.** 5 units. 80,000L ($40) double; 110,000L ($55) triple. No credit cards.

Casa Grazia's Signora welcomes you with open arms, and you'll be hard pressed tearing yourself away from her tremendous warmth and hospitality. The house, unobtrusively located down a central street, is small, but as crisp and well kept as any three-star establishment. Even the marble baths are pristine, glimmering as if freshly installed, except that they're over 10 years old. There's also a roof terrace with views over Taormina, but keep in mind that the staircase is narrow and that there are lots of levels. Casa Grazia is no secret, and with so few rooms, it'll take an act of God to get you in there, but it's definitely worth the try.

Worth a Splurge

Villa Belvedere. Via Bagnoli Croci 79, 98039 Taormina (ME). ☎ **0942-23-791.** Fax 0942-625-830. www.villabelvedere.it. E-mail: . 47 units. TV TEL. 171,000L ($86) single; 240,000 ($120) double used as single; 272,000 ($136) double. Rates include breakfast. MC, V. Closed Nov 15–Mar 13 (sometimes open Dec 18–Jan 10).

Christian Pécaut's hotel has remained a favorite for three generations thanks to a friendly reception, professional maintenance, and old-fashioned style. The terra-cotta floors support firm beds and a variety of furnishings, all functional but with a touch of class. Most rooms have slivers of balconies to enjoy views over the neighboring public gardens to the sea. The top-floor rooms have small terraces from which you can glimpse Mt. Etna (these are also air-conditioned, as are rooms on the back, which have double-paned windows to block noise from the street). The flowering property is terraced down the hillside, with the pool at the lowest level sprouting a palm tree from its center.

TAORMINA MARE/MAZZARÒ

✪ **Villa Gallodoro.** Via Nazionale 151(next to the Sea Palace), 98039 Mazzarò (ME). ☎/fax **0942-23-860.** 15 units. 80,000L ($40) single; 110,000L ($55) double. V. Closed Nov–Easter. Free parking.

Kudos to the Gallodoro for providing the best balance of quality for price in a characteristic 1920s house that's practically on the beach. The recently renovated rooms are in pristine condition, as are the baths, where tiled shower partitions gleam with bright white grout. And for the reasonable price of 140,000L ($70), you can book one of the few rooms with air-conditioning, minibars, and TVs. Newly installed double-glazed windows and doors block out the noise from the train below, but keep in mind that anywhere in Mazzarò you're going to hear some engine noise. The original stone arches provide a contrast to the pink stucco of the exterior, which is flanked on two sides by sun terraces and on the third by a lovely overgrown garden cafe. Book early for this gem.

Villa Caterina. Via Nazionale 155, 98039 Mazzarò (ME). ☎ **0942-24-709.** 9 units. 125,000L ($63) double. No singles. Rates include breakfast. No credit cards. Closed Nov–Easter. Free parking in small lot. (Turn left out of the funicular; the pensione is up the road on your right. If you're arriving by Interbus, get off at the Sea Palace and continue up the road for about 100 yards.)

You can tell by the pristine Mediterranean garden and flawless terra-cotta patio that this is actually somebody's home, but more than that, it is a verdant oasis sunken into the hill and surrounded by trees. The yellow tile floor and brown bath tile recall the 1950s, with a local *artigianato* wrought iron headboard thrown in for good grace. The location is convenient to (but not immediately on top of) the beach as well as the cable car to Taormina Alta, and after a day in the sun, what better to do than to write postcards under the lemon tree?

GIARDINI-NAXOS

✪ **Arathena Rocks Hotel.** Via Calcide Eubea 55, 98035 Giardini-Naxos. ☎ **0942-51-349.** Fax 0942-51690. 49 units. TEL. 105,000–115,000L ($55–$58) per person. Half board obligatory. From the train station a taxi will run around 20,000L ($10)

Arathena Rocks Hotel takes full advantage of its secluded position on the furthermost tip of Punto Schisò, overlooking the black lava rock formations that constitute essentially the hotel's "beach." But above the salt water is a gracious sun terrace laid with lava stone featuring a refreshing outdoor pool, which shares the hotel's grounds with a garden fit for nobility, bursting with the scent of freshly cut grass and flowers. The accommodations are no less gracious, with handpainted Venetian-style pieces interspersed with tasteful antiques and oriental rugs. Rooms off the garden and parking lot have air-conditioning. A shuttle runs twice daily between the hotel and Taormina Alta.

GREAT DEALS ON DINING
TAORMINA ALTA

Al Giardino. Via Bagnoli Croci 84. ☎ **0942-23-453.** Reservations recommended. Primi 10,000–15,000L ($5–$8); secondi 14,000–22,000L ($7–$11). AE, MC, V. June–Sept daily noon–2:30pm and 7:30–11pm; Oct–May Fri–Wed noon–2:30pm and 7:30–11pm. Closed Nov. SICILIAN/ITALIAN.

Friendly Sebatiano Puglia really cares about his simple, tasty dishes. There are only a dozen small tables scattered on the patio out front, shaded by an awning dripping with flowers, so call ahead if you want one. The only drawback is the occasional car that whizzes by (but other than that, the sole sound is birdsong from the public gardens across the street). His *spaghetti alla carbonara* is great, as is the *paglia e feino alla bolognese* (strands of green and yellow pasta tossed with a meat sauce). For a secondo, try the *omlette al prosciutto* or the *involtini alla rusticana* (veal rolls stuffed with cheese and skewered with lemon slices and Sicilian sausages before being grilled).

Il Ciclope. Piazzetta San Leone 1 (on Corso Umberto). ☎ **0942-23-263.** Reservations recommended. Primi 7,000–14,000L ($4–$9); secondi 12,000–20,000L ($7–$12). DC, MC, V. Daily 11:15am–3pm and 7–10:30pm. Closed Wed in winter. SICILIAN/ITALIAN.

Although it looks awful touristy, with its shaded terrace fronting the main drag in the medieval part of town, Il Ciclope is actually quite good. Salvatore Sturiale's restaurant serves simple-looking dishes bursting with flavor, like the *rigatoni alla ciclope* (just spicy enough with ham, tomatoes, hot and black peppers, and oil), *fettucine con pescespada* (with swordfish, olives, and pistachios), *cuscinotto alla polifemo* (veal rolled with mozzarella, prosciutto, and mushrooms, breaded, and coated with an herbed cream sauce), and *bocconcini di vitellina alla turiddu* (almost a veal stew, with olives, tomatoes, pancetta, onions, pepperoncino, and basil). Call ahead for a streetside table or take your chances.

La Botte. Piazza Santa Domenica 3 (not Piazza San Domenico; this square's near the Greek Theater). ☎ **0942-24-198.** Reservations recommended. Primi 10,000–20,000L ($5–$10); secondi 14,000–28,000L ($7–$14); pizze 11,000–18,000L ($6–$9). AE, DC, MC, V. Daily noon–3:30pm and 7pm–1am. Closed Mon Jan–May. From the east end of Piazza Santa Caterina, take the little street parallel to and sunk below the right of the road to the Greek theater. SICILIAN/PIZZA.

La Botte is a bit more expensive than it should be, probably owing to its setting, which is terrific. It sits on a quiet, breezy little piazza off Taormina's beaten passeggiata path, made even more welcoming by the umbrellas shading the outdoor section. Inside are stuccoed rooms lined with photos of noted patrons who come here for a good pizza to be washed down with Messina beer. The antipasto buffet, a prodigious spread, is one of La Botte's main draws; follow up with the *pasta fresca al cuore di carciofo* (homemade pasta with artichoke hearts), *maccheroni alla Norma* (with tomatoes, eggplant, basil, and ricotta),or *zuppa di cozze* (steamed mussels).

✪ **U' Bossu.** Via Bagnoli Croci 50. ☎ **0942-23-311.** Reservations recommended. Primi 9,000–13,000L ($4.50–$7); secondi 15,000–18,000L ($8–$9). DC, MC, V. Tues–Sun noon–3pm and 7:30–11:30pm. Closed Nov 15–Dec 20, Jan 10–Mar 20. Open Mon evenings mid-June to Aug. SICILIAN.

Historic opera recordings mix with Mariah Carey in this superlative hole-in-the-wall—why Enzo's place isn't more well known is beyond me. It has killer prices (especially for Taormina), a friendly staff, an almost excruciatingly quaint trattoria decor (plants, garlic ropes, and bunches of peppers hanging from wood beams in a candlelit room), and rather excellent food. Still, the tourists manage to find it, so either go early or book ahead for one of the nine tables arranged around a great antipasto buffet. The primi are flavorful works of art, from the *spaghetti alla mafiosa* (with tuna and tomatoes) to the *casareccia alla turiddu* (homemade pasta with tomatoes, cream, capers, olives, baked ricotta, and eggplant). The best secondo is *involtini "U' Bossu"* (veal rolls), though the swordfish *alla Messinese* with olives, capers in a tomato broth is great too. By all means, don't miss Enzo's terrific homemade pepperoncino liqueur.

Worth a Splurge

✪ **Da Lorenzo.** Via Roma 12 (near the San Domenico Hotel). ☎ **0942-23-480.** Primi: 8,000–16,000L ($4–$8); secondi 18,000L ($9) and up for chateaubriand and fish by weight. AE, DC, MC, V. Thurs–Tues 12:30–2:30pm and 7:30–midnight. Closed a month in winter. SICILIAN.

Forget about slipping on your swimsuit after a meal at Da Lorenzo, where you'll fight to clear you plate of what is essentially food of *Travel & Leisure* caliber. And with any luck, you'll have arrived at the corner table on the terrace in time for an unexpected light show over at nearby Etna. For starters, dig into a plate of varied smoked fish and carpaccio (on request there are also individual selections like octopus and tuna). My favorite primi are the *gamberoni al curry con riso* (curried prawns and rice) and the flavorful and not overly rich *ravioli ai carciofi* (in a delicate artichoke-cream sauce). The *cordon bleu al gorgonzola* (a good-quality steak with blue cheese) seems to be a house classic, but expect to be stuffed well before the arrival of the *secondo.* Try to leave room for one of their homemade desserts and a refreshing finisher of mandarin liqueur. Da Lorenzo also has the best selection of Italian wines in all of Taormina.

TAORMINA MARE/MAZZARÒ

Gusto Mediterraneo. Mazzarò (up the hill toward Isola Bella). No phone. Salads and sandwiches 5,000L and 6,000L ($2.50 and $3). No credit cards. Daily 10am–9pm. Closed Tues in May and Nov–Easter.

This little take-away spot is just a short walk from the Lidos to the left of the funivia and Isola Bella, perfectly positioned as it is for when those lazy beach munchies get a hold of you. If you've timed it so that none of the local shopkeepers are taking up the lone two tables (rigged from wine barrels and boxes of timber) you'll be able to eat the hot dishes hot. The food is outstanding—exactly what you'd have prepared in your own kitchen—from stuffed focaccia to *insalata riso* to a simple and healthy grilled chicken sandwich.

Ristorante Pizzichello. Spiaggia Isola Bella (next to the boats). No phone. Primi: 8,000–12,000L ($4–$6); secondi 10,000L–16,000L ($5–$8). No credit cards. Daily 12:30–3pm.

I guess this is what would be considered your local "dive," although this crooked old shack keeps a respectable face with great food and white tablecloths. The ceiling is hung with crab traps and netting, a nod to their working fisherman clientele. Have a plate of their *frittura mista* (mixed fried shrimp, calamari, and whatever else is available) with a cold beer, or the *zuppa di cozze e vongole,* (mussel-and-clam "soup"), then sit back and enjoy the incomparably fabulous views of Isola Bella and Taormina Alta.

TAORMINA AFTER DARK

Corso Umberto never seems to quiet down, as the day's passeggiata simply blends into the starlight. **Piazza IX Aprile** is no less popular by night, where the town's salon continues to serve caffè) and gelato into the wee hours. In a hidden garden below Corso Umberto (turn down stairs at Il Ciclope) is **Café Marrakech,** Piazza Garibaldi 2 (☎ 0942-625-692), an Arab/Moroccan-themed bar/cafe serving mixed drinks, light snacks, and exotic teas imported from North Africa. It's open daily 6pm to 2 or 3am, with a belly-dancing show on Thursdays 10:30pm to midnight; closed Mondays in winter.

The locals and Italians on vacation seem to go nuts for late-night discos, the most popular being **La Giara,** Via La Floresta off Corso Umberto (☎ 094-223-360), which doubles as a piano bar (they also serve dinner). **Tiffany Club,** Via San Pancrazio 5 (☎ 0942-625-430), is a smaller version of the same beast, while **Septimo,** 50 Via San Pancrazio (☎ 0942-625-522), is somewhat more appealing (and enormous) because of the large garden. Add to the list the slightly wilder **Tout Va,** outside town along Via Pirandello 70 (☎ 094-223-824; linea urbano no. 4), open summers only.

Appendix: Italy in Depth

by Reid Bramblett

Lord Byron called Italy his magnet; Robert Browning said Italy was engraved on his heart. Being poets, these fellows might have been given to hyperbole, but Italy does have a remarkably strong, and usually favorable, effect on visitors.

Part of the draw is Italy's cultural legacy—the country, after all, was the cradle of both ancient Rome and the Renaissance, two of the highest points of Western civilization. It's blessed with an endlessly varied and seductive scenery of azure seas, silvery olive groves, stony hill towns, snow-capped mountains, and colorful fishing villages. The cuisine only seems to get better from region to region, and an enormous emphasis is placed on hospitality. Most appealing of all is the emphasis Italians place on enjoying life—from strolling through town on the evening *passaggiata* to lingering over a 3-hour dinner—and they seem determined to ensure their visitors do the same.

But Italy isn't just a postcard: It has suffered its share of social and economic woes and has been riddled with political scandal. If you care to look, you'll find poverty, crime, unchecked urban development, and social injustice, just as there is in any other industrialized Western nation. But Italy offsets these realities with more grace notes than most other places manage, and in so doing rewards the traveler with a remarkable and enduring experience.

1 History 101: Italy Past & Present

In its 3,000 years of history, Italy has endured emperors and kings, duchies and despots, fools and knaves, popes and presidents. Italy has been a definer of democracy, has fallen prey to dictators, and has sagged into anarchy. Italy knows triumph, and it knows loss, but above all, it knows how to survive.

PREHISTORY TO MAGNA GRAECIA

Findings in caves around Isneria in the Abruzzi suggest that humans settled in Italy about a million years ago. Neanderthal man made a brief appearance, and Cro-Magnon, who knew how to fish and domesticate animals, showed up about 18,000 years ago.

Magna Graecia, "Greater Greece," describes Greek colonies established beginning in the 8th century B.C. in Sicily and on the mainland from Apulia northwest to Naples. The coastal land, never tilled, quickly turned out bumper crops. Abundant timber and wool production underpinned highly profitable trading. But these successful colonies fell to warring amongst themselves, and by the 4th century B.C., Greece was a fading influence in southern Italy. The best evidence of Magna Graecia exists in the temples at Paestum (in Campania); in those at Agrigento, Segesta, and Selinute (all in Sicily); and amid the artifacts at the archaeological museums of Paestum and Siracusa (both in Sicily) and Crotone and Reggio di Calabria (both in Calabria).

THE ETRUSCAN ENIGMA

The Etruscans were an innovative and influential people who settled primarily in what is today Tuscany, Umbria, and northern Lazio. Despite the great deal of excavated physical evidence we have, little is known about their origins. The great Roman historian Herodotus (corroborated by most modern-day researchers) wrote that the Etruscans filtered into the Italian peninsula, probably from Asia Minor, as early as the 12th century B.C. By the 8th century, there was a clearly delineated Etruscan culture; it reached a peak of power and wealth in the 6th century B.C. with the Tarquin dynasty, which ruled Rome itself (later to be ejected). Savaged by the Gauls (Celtic peoples from present-day France), the Etruscans began to lose power. Their cities were slowly defeated and absorbed into the growing Roman Republic during the 1st century B.C.

The Etruscan political hegemony extended over Etruria (a loose association of city-states connected along religious rather than political lines). Key centers were such modern-day locations as Chiusi and Cortona in Tuscany, Cerveteri and Tarquinia north of Rome, Veio near Rome, and Orvieto and Perugia in Umbria. Etruscan artifacts are displayed in museums in Chiusi, Volterra, Florence, and Cortona; tombs at Tarquinia, Cerveteri, Veio, Cortona, and Chiusi; and the Etruscan walls and gateways preserved at Volterra and Perugia.

The Etruscans were highly skilled artisans who worked not only iron but also bronze, silver, copper, and gold. Etruscan potters threw handsome black *bucchero* vases with bas-relief figures and later adopted Greek fashions to produce fine painted vessels. They were adept engineers, constructing walled cities astride hilltops and sophisticated canal systems that drained the enormous swampy lowlands of southern

Dateline

- **Prehistory.** Neanderthal humans roam Italy; around 10,000 B.C., Cro-Magnon shows up.
- **1200 B.C.** Etruscans begin to emigrate from Asia Minor, settling in Tuscany.
- **800 B.C.** Greeks colonize Sicily and the peninsula's boot (collectively "Magna Graecia").
- **753 B.C.** Romulus, says legend, founds Rome. In fact, Rome grows out of a strategically located shepherd village.
- **700 B.C.** Etruscans rise in power, peaking in the 6th century and make Rome their capital.
- **509 B.C.** Republic of Rome is founded; power is shared by two consuls.
- **494–450 B.C.** Office of the Tribune established to defend plebeian rights. The Twelve Tablets stating basic rights are carved, the foundation of Roman law.
- **279 B.C.** Romans now rule all of the Italian peninsula.
- **146 B.C.** Rome defeats Tunisian power in Carthage; the Republic now controls Sicily, North Africa, Spain, Sardinia, Greece, and Macedonia.
- **100 B.C.** Julius Caesar born.
- **60 B.C.** Caesar, Pompey, and Crassus share power in the First Triumvirate.
- **51 B.C.** Caesar triumphs over Gaul (France).
- **44 B.C.** March 15, Caesar assassinated, leaving all to his nephew and heir, Octavian.
- **27 B.C.** Octavian, now Augustus, is declared emperor, beginning Roman Empire and 200 years of peace and prosperity.

continues

continues

- **A.D. 29 (or 33)** Jesus is crucified in Roman province of Judea.
- **64–100** Nero persecutes Christians; a succession of military commanders restore order; Trajan expands the empire.
- **200** Goths invade from the north; the empire begins to decline.
- **313** With the Edict of Milan, Emperor Constantine I declares Christianity the official religion and establishes Constantinople as eastern capital, splitting the empire in half.
- **476** Fall of the Roman Empire; the Dark Ages begin.
- **Late 6th century** Lombards sweep through much of Italy.
- **600–675** Church asserts political control as Pope Gregory I brings some stability to the peninsula.
- **774–800** Frankish king Charlemagne invades Italy and is crowned emperor by Pope Leo III. Upon his death, Italy dissolves into a series of small warring kingdoms.
- **962** Holy Roman Empire founded under Otto I, king of Saxony; serves as the temporal arm of the church's spiritual power.
- **11th century** Normans conquer southern Italy and introduce feudalism. The first Crusades are launched.
- **1309–77** Papacy abandons Rome for Avignon, France.
- **1350** The Black Death decimates Europe, reducing Italy's population by a third.
- **1450** City-states hold power; Venice controls much of the eastern Mediterranean. The Humanist movement rediscovers the art and philosophy of ancient Greece and gives rise to the artistic Renaissance.

Tuscany and turned them into a breadbasket. The Etruscans also introduced that eventual favored vehicle of Ben-Hur, the chariot.

THE RISE OF ROME

Leaving aside the famous legend of a she-wolf nursing the abandoned twins Romulus and Remus (the former kills his brother and founds a village called Rome) and Virgil's *Aeneid* (Aeneas of Troy flees the burning city at the end of the Trojan War, makes his way to Romulus's little village, and turns it into an ancient superpower), Rome probably began as a collection of Latin and Sabine villages in the Tiber Valley. It was originally a kingdom ruled by the Etruscan Tarquin dynasty. In 509 B.C., the last Tarquin king raped the daughter of a powerful Roman. After the girl committed suicide, infuriated Romans ejected the king and established a republic ruled by two consuls (chosen from among the patrician elite) whose power was balanced by tribunes elected from among the plebian masses.

The young Roman Republic sent its military throughout the peninsula and by 279 B.C. ruled all of Italy. Rome's armies trampled Grecian colonies throughout the Mediterranean, and after a series of brutal wars defeated Carthage (present-day Tunisia), a rival sea power and once Rome's archenemy. By 146 B.C., Rome controlled not only all of the Italian peninsula and Sicily but also North Africa, Spain, Sardinia, Greece, and Macedonia.

Still, Rome wanted more. It invaded Gaulish lands to the north and added what we now call France and Belgium to its realm. Rome even crossed the English Channel and conquered Britain all the way up to the Scottish Lowlands (Hadrian's Wall still stands as a testament to how far north the Roman army got). However, so much military success so distant from Rome itself resulted in a severely weakened homefront. With war booty filling the coffers, Rome ended taxation on its citizens. So much grain poured in from North Africa that the Roman farmer couldn't find a market for his wheat and simply stopped growing it. The booty had an additional price tag: corruption. Senators advanced their own lots rather than the provinces ostensibly under their care. Plebeians clamored for a bigger share, and the slaves revolted repeatedly. More reforms appeased the plebes while the slaves were put down with horrific barbarity.

HAIL CAESAR!

At the end of the 2nd century B.C., the Republic, sped along by a corrupt Senate, was corroding into near-collapse. Julius Caesar—successful general, skilled orator, and shrewd politician—stepped in to help maintain control over Rome's vast territories, but from the day Caesar declared himself "dictator for life," Rome, as a Republic, was finished. After sharing governmental power with others in a series of Triumvirates, Caesar became the sole Consul in 44 B.C.

Caesar rose in popular influence partly by endearing himself to the lower classes through a lifelong fight against the corrupt Senate. As his power crested, he forced many immoral senators to flee Rome, introduced social reforms, inaugurated the first of many new public building programs in the center of Rome (still visible as the Forum of Caesar), and added Gaul (France) to the dying Republic. But Caesar's emphasis on the plebeians and their concerns (as well as his own thirst for power) did little to endear him to the old guard of patricians and senators. On March 15, 44 B.C., Caesar strolled out of the Baths of Pompey to meet Brutus, Cassius, and other "friends" who lay in wait with daggers hidden beneath their togas.

Caesar left everything to his nephew and heir, the 18-year-old Octavian. From the increasingly irrelevant Senate, Octavian eventually received the title Augustus, and from the people, lifetime tribuneship. And so Octavian became Emperor Augustus, sole ruler of Rome and most of the Western world.

THE EMPIRE

Augustus's long reign ushered in Pax Romana, 200 years of peace under Roman rule. The new emperor, who preferred to be called "First Citizen," reorganized the military and the provincial governments and reinstituted constitutional rule. Succeeding emperors weren't so virtuous: Deranged Tiberius and Caligula, henpecked Claudius I, and Nero, who in A.D. 64 persecuted the Christians of Rome with a viciousness easily equal to the earlier slave repressions. Several of the military commanders who became emperors were exceptions to the tyrant mold. Late in the 1st century, Trajan expanded the empire's eastern boundaries and constructed great public works, including a vast series of markets (recently reopened to visitors in Rome).

- **1500** Peak of the High Renaissance. Brunelleschi's dome caps Florence's Duomo. Leonardo da Vinci completes *The Last Supper.* Lorenzo "the Magnificent" de' Medici (1449–92) of Florence becomes patron of artists like Michelangelo.
- **1508** Michelangelo begins the Sistine Chapel ceiling.
- **1550** Carlos I of Spain is crowned Holy Roman Emperor as Charles V; wages war against pope and Italian princes and city-states, occupying nearly all of Italy.
- **18th century** Italy's darkest hour: brigands control the countryside, the Austrians and Spanish everything else.
- **1784** The French Revolution sparks Italian nationalism.
- **1796–1814** Napoléon sweeps through Italy, installing friends and relatives as rulers.
- **1814** Napoléon's defeat at Waterloo.
- **1830** Beginning of the Risorgimento national political movement and a new renaissance of literature and music.
- **1861** Kingdom of Italy is created under Vittorio Emmanuele II, Savoy king of Piemonte, and united through the military campaign of General Garibaldi. Turin and Florence both serve as interim capitals.
- **1870** Rome, last papal stronghold, falls to Garibaldi, and the city is declared Italy's capital.
- **Late 19th century** Mass emigration to America and other foreign shores, mostly from the impoverished, agricultural south.
- **1915** Italy enters World War I on Allied side.
- **1922** Mussolini marches on Rome and puts his

continues

Fascist Blackshirts in charge of the country, declaring himself prime minister.

- **1935** Mussolini defeats and annexes Ethiopia.
- **1939** Italy enters the war by signing an alliance with Nazi Germany.
- **1943** Italy switches sides as Allied troops push Nazis north up peninsula; by 1945, Mussolini and mistress executed by partisans.
- **1946** A national referendum narrowly establishes the Republic of Italy.
- **1950–93** Fifty changes of government but also the "economic miracle" that has made Italy the world's fifth leading economy.
- **1993–2000** Italy's Christian Democrat–controlled government dissolves amid corruption allegations. Silvio Berlusconi's right-wing coalition holds power for a few months, followed by center–left wing coalitions that introduce the most stable governments in decades under Prime Ministers Romano Prodi, then Massimo d'Alema, and Giuliano Amato.
- **1993–97** Series of disasters rock Italy's cultural roots: 1993 Mafia bombing of Uffizi Galleries, January 1996 fire at Venice's La Fenice opera house; April 1997 conflagration in Turin's cathedral; September 1997 earthquakes in Umbria, which destroyed priceless frescoes in Assisi.
- **2000** Some 30 million visitors and pilgrims head to Rome for a Holy Year Jubilee. They found not only papal indulgences by passing through St. Peter's Holy Door but also a city freshly scrubbed and restored for the occasion. Over the previous 2 years, several major new sights and

continues

At this peak, Rome knew amenities not to be enjoyed again in Europe until the 18th century. Citizens were privileged to have police protection, fire fighting, libraries, sanitation, huge public baths such as the Caracalla by the Appian Way, and even central heating and running water—if they could afford them.

The empire's decline began around A.D. 200. After sacking the city several times, Goths and other Germanic tribes set up their own leaders as emperors and were more interested in the spoils of an empire than in actually running one. And while Gibbon's famous opus *The Decline and Fall of the Roman Empire* takes up an entire bookshelf to explain Rome's downfall, in the end it all boils down to the fact that the empire had gotten just too big to manage.

After embracing Christianity in his famous 313 Edict of Milan, Emperor Constantine I tried to resolve the problem by moving the capital of the empire from Rome to the city of Byzantium (later renamed Constantinople and today known as Istanbul). The Roman empire was irrevocably split in half: a western Roman Empire comprising most of Europe and North Africa, and an eastern Roman Empire filling southeast Europe and the Near East.

CURTAIN GOING DOWN: THE DARK AGES

In 476, the last emperor (ironically, named Romulus) fell from power and the Roman Empire collapsed. It would be 1,500 years before Rome and Italy were once again united as capital and nation. As the 6th century opened, Italy was in chaos. Waves of barbarians from the north poured in while provincial nobles engaged in petty bickering and Rome became the personal fiefdom of the papacy. The Goths continued to rule nominally from Ravenna but were soon driven out by Constantinople.

It was the Roman Catholic church, beginning with Pope Gregory I late in the 6th century, that finally provided some stability. In 731, Pope Gregory II renounced Rome's nominal dependence on Constantinople and reoriented the Roman Catholic church firmly toward Europe—in the process finalizing the empire's division into east and west.

During the Middle Ages, northern Italy fragmented into a collection of city-states. The papacy's temporal power shrunk considerably (mainly encompassing only Rome and its province), and its political concerns turned to arguing with the German (Gothic) emperors over the increasingly irrelevant office of Holy Roman Emperor. The southern half of the country went a different road when, in the 11th century, the Normans invaded southern Italy, wresting control from the local strongmen and, in Sicily, the Muslim Saracens who had occupied the region throughout the dark ages. To the south, the Normans introduced feudalism, a repressive social system that discouraged individual economic initiative, and the legacy of which accounts in large part for the social and economic differences between north and south that have continued into the 21st century.

In the mid-14th century, the Black Death ravaged Europe, killing a third of Italy's population. Despite such setbacks, northern Italian cities grew wealthy from Crusade booty, trade with one another and with the Middle East, and banking. These wealthy principalities and pseudorepublics ruled by the merchant elite flexed their muscles in the absence of a strong central authority.

museums had opened and old favorites—including the Capitoline Museums, Coloseum, Trajan's Markets, and Baths of Diocletian—were overhauled and expanded. Sadly, with the Holy Year came a price-inflation that didn't end with the closing of the Holy Doors in early 2001.

- **2001** The first cases of BSE ("Mad Cow Disease") in Italy are confirmed; beef consumption plummets over 70%, and the government considers banning such institutions as the famed *Bistecca Fiorentina*.

CURTAIN GOING UP: THE RENAISSANCE

The Renaissance peaked in the 15th century as northern cities bullied their way to city-state status. Even while warring constantly with one another to extend their territories, such ruling families as the Medicis in Florence, the Estes in Ferrara, and the Gonzagas in Milan grew incredibly rich and powerful.

The princes, popes, and merchant princes who ruled Italy's city-states, spurred on by the Humanist philosophical movement, collectively bankrolled the explosion of poetic and artistic expression we now call the Renaissance (see the section on art and architecture below). But with no clear political authority or unified military, Italy was easy pickings and by the mid-16th century, Spain, courtesy of Charles V, occupied nearly all of the country.

THE SECOND FALL

From the mid-16th century until the end of the 18th century, Italy suffered economic depression and foreign domination. As emphasis on world trade shifted away from the Mediterranean, Italy's influence diminished. Within Italy itself, Spanish Bourbons controlled the duchies of the south, while Austria ruled those of the north. These foreign overlords kept raising taxes, farming declined, the birthrate sank, and bandits proliferated. The 18th century is viewed as Italy's nadir. In fact, only Europe's eager ear for Italian music and eye for art and architecture kept the Italian profile haughty and its cultural patrimony resplendent.

It was the late-18th-century French Revolution and the arrival of Napoléon that lit Italy's nationalistic fire, although it would be the mid–19th century before the *Risorgimento* movement and a new king could spread the flame.

THE SECOND RISE: THE 19TH CENTURY

Italians initially gave Napoléon an exultant *ciao* when he swept through the peninsula and swept out Italy's 18th-century political disasters (along with the Austrian army). But Napoléon, in the end, neither united Italy nor provided it with self-government—he merely set up his own friends and relatives as new princes and dukes. Many Italians, however, were fired up by the Napoleonic revolutionary rhetoric. The Risorgimento ("resurgence") nationalist movement—an odd amalgam of radicals, moderate liberals, and Roman Catholic conservatives—struggled for 30 years to create a single, united Italy under a constitutional monarchy.

You'll find Risorgimento heroes' names recalled in streets and piazze throughout Italy: Giuseppe Mazzini provided the intellectual rigor for the movement; the political genius of noble-born Camillo Cavour engineered the underpinnings of the new nation; and Gen. Giusseppe Garibaldi and his "Redshirt" soldiers did the legwork by conquering reluctant or foreign-controlled territories. In 1861, Vittorio Emanuele II, of the Piedmont House of Savoy, became the first King of Italy. By 1871, Garibaldi finally defeated the papal holdout of Rome and the great city once again became capital of a unified Italy.

FINALLY, A NATION UNITED

A united nation? On paper, yes, but the old sectional differences remained. While there was rapid industrialization in the north, the south labored under the repressive neofeudal agricultural ways of the late 19th century. Many southerners escaped economic hardship and political powerlessness by emigrating to the industrialized north, or to greener pastures abroad in America, South America, or northern Europe.

Italy entered World War I on the Allied side in exchange for territorial demands, and to vanquish that old foe, Austria. In the end the Austro-Hungarian Empire was defeated, but at the Paris Peace Conference, Italy was granted much less territory than had been promised (though it did receive Trieste), which compounded the country's problems. As southerners abandoned the country in droves, the economy stagnated, and what remained of Italy's world importance seemed to be fading rapidly, along came Benito Mussolini, promising to restore national pride and bring order out of the chaos.

FASCISM REIGNS

Mussolini marched on Rome in 1922, forced the king to make him premier, nicknamed himself Il Duce (The Duke), and quickly repressed all other political factions. He put his Fascists "Blackshirts" in charge of the entire country: schools, the press, industry, and labor. Seeking, as Italian despot-hopefuls throughout history have done, to endear himself to the general populace, Mussolini instituted a vast public works program, most of which eventually failed. Mussolini fancied himself a second Caesar and spent some time excavating the archaeological remains of ancient Rome—not always with the most stringent scientific methods—to help glorify his reign and lend it authority. The Great Depression of the 1930s made life considerably more difficult for Italians, and, to divert attention from his shortcomings as a ruler, Mussolini turned to foreign adventures, defeating and annexing Ethiopia in 1935.

Mussolini entered Italy into World War II as an Axis ally of the Nazis, but the Italian heart was not really in the war, and most Italians had little wish to pursue Hitler's anti-Semitic policies. Armed partisan resistance to the official government forces and to the Nazis remained strong. By 1945, the Italian people had had enough. They rose against Mussolini and the Axis, and the Fascists were disbanded. King Victor Emmanuele III, who had collaborated with the Fascists without much enthusiasm during the past 2 decades, appointed a new premier. At the end of the war, Mussolini and his mistress were pictured in the world press hanging by their heels at a Milanese gas station after being shot by partisans.

DEMOCRACY AT LAST

After the war, Italians narrowly voted to become a republic, and in 1946, a new republican constitution went into effect. Various permutations of the center-right Christian Democrat party ruled in a succession of more than 50 governments until 1993, when the entire government dissolved in a flurry of corruption and graft. The country's leaders were prosecuted (and many jailed) by what became known as the "Clean Hands" judges of Milan. The two main parties, the Christian Democrats and the Communists, both splintered in the aftermath, giving rise to some 16 major political parties and countless minor ones. The parties formed various coalitions, leading to such strange political bedfellows as the Forza Italia alliance, headed by media mogul Silvio Berlusconi, which filled the national power vacuum during 1994. It included both the nationalist Alleanza Nazionale party (the modern incarnation of the Fascist party) and the Lega del Nord, the separatist "Northern League," which wants to split Italy in half, making Milan capital of a new country in the north called "Padania" and leaving Rome to govern the poor south. (In 2000, the Lega changed its tune and is now calling for a far more decentralized government, with more power going to individual regions—though their true goal, as always, is to ensure that tax lire stay within the region that generated them, keeping the wealth of the industrialized north from being shunted to government programs to help the relatively poorer south.)

In 1994, the center-left Olive Tree coalition swept the national elections and Italy enjoyed a novelty: 3 years of stable rule under the government of Prime Minister Romano Prodi, recently replaced by a center-left government of Massimo D'Alema. Interestingly, given the stereotype among fellow Europeans of Italy as a nation prone to graft and political chaos, Prodi—an economist before becoming prime minister and the man who reigned in Italy's debt to qualify the country for the European Union—was later named to head the European Commission.

In April 2000, as regional elections revealed popular opinion, D'Alema stepped down and place-holder Giuliano Amato took over as Prime Minister pending new elections in April 2001 (just after this book goes to print). That election pits right-wing opposition leader Silvio Berlusconi (recently "cleared" of numerous corruption charges) against charismatic and effective seven-year mayor of Rome, Francesco Rutelli.

Politically, though, some things never change in Italy. The same mistrust among factions continues: Cities are still paranoid about their individuality and their rights, and the division between north and south is as sharp as ever. The Mafia had, by the late 19th century, become a kind of shadow government in the south, and to this day, controls a staggering number of politicians, national officials, and even judges, providing one scandal after another. Even powerful Christian Democrat and senator-for-life Giulio Andreotti, who served seven terms as prime minister, was sentenced to 12 years in prison for corruption and Mafia collusion as this book went to press (though, given Italy's odd laws that exempt government officials from serving jail terms, it's unlikely Andreotti will ever actually end up behind bars).

Economically, it's a different story. The "economic miracle" of the north has worked around the political chaos (and often has even taken advantage of it) to make Italy the world's fifth largest economy. Even the south, while continuing to lag behind, isn't in the desperate straits it once was. The outsider looks and wonders how the country keeps going amid the political chaos, Byzantine bureaucracy, and deep regional differences. The Italian just shrugs and rolls his eyes. Italians have always excelled at getting by under difficult circumstances and making the most of any situation. If nothing else, they're masters at survival.

2 Italy's Artistic Heritage

When you mention art in Italy, most people's thoughts fly first to the Renaissance, to Giotto, Donatello, Michelangelo, Raphael, and Leonardo. But Italy's artistic heritage actually goes back at least 2,500 years.

ART & ARCHITECTURE

THE GREEKS, ETRUSCANS & EARLY ROMANS   Today all, or almost all, design roads lead to Milan. In the beginning, though, all roads led from Athens. What the **Greeks** identified early on that captured the hearts and minds of so many others was classical rendering of form. To the ancients, *classic* or *classical* simply meant perfection—of proportion, balance, harmony, and form. To the Greeks, man was the measure of perfection, an attitude lost in the Middle Ages and not rediscovered until the dawn of the Renaissance.

Although those early tourists to the Italian peninsula the **Etruscans** arrived with their own styles, by the 6th century B.C. they were borrowing heavily from the Greeks in their sculpture (and importing thousands of Attic painted vases). The **Romans,** in turn, made use of certain Greek innovations, particularly architectural ideas. The first to be adopted was post-and-lintel construction—essentially, a weight-bearing frame, like a door. Later came adaptation of Greek columns for supporting buildings, following the classical orders of Doric column capitals (the plain ones) on the ground floor, Ionic capitals (with the scrolls on either end) on the next level, and Corinthian capitals (flowering with acanthus leaves) on the top.

Romans thrived on huge complex problems for which they could produce organized, well-crafted solutions. Roman builders became inventive engineers, developing hoisting mechanisms and a specially trained workforce. They designed towns, built civic centers, raised grand temples and public baths, and developed the basilica, a rectangle supported by arches atop columns along both sides of the interior and with an apse at one or both ends. Basilicas were used for courts of justice, banking, and other commercial structures. The design was repeated all over the Roman world, beginning around the 1st century A.D. Later, early Christians adapted the architectural style for the first grand churches, still called basilicas.

Although marble is traditionally associated with Roman architecture, Roman engineers could also do wonders with bricks or even prosaic concrete, as still evident in Rome at the public baths of Caracalla, the Pantheon, and the Basilica of Maxentius. Concrete seating made possible such enormous theaters as Rome's 6-acre, 45,000-seat Colosseum.

Although painting got rather short shrift in ancient Rome (it was used primarily for decorative purposes), bucolic frescoes, the technique of painting on wet plaster, adorned the walls of the wealthy in Rome. Some of the best preserved of these frescoes are now on display in the Museo Nazionale Romano (Palazzo Massimo in Rome) and at Pompeii (in the Villa dei Misteri).

Sculpture, so much more useful for aggrandizing, is another story. Regrettably, the Roman aesthetic was quite unadventurous, happily adapting Greek styles into original designs but also setting up sculpture factories that churned out endless clones of Grecian classics. Bronze portraiture, a technique with Greek and Etruscan roots, was polished to photographic perfection; the majestic, gilded equestrian statue of Marcus Aurelius in Rome's Capitoline Museums is a late but excellent example.

ROMANESQUE, BYZANTINE & GOTHIC When Pope Gregory the Great's strong hand brought some stability to Italy late in the 6th century, the rise of Catholicism created a demand for construction of new churches and cathedrals. The builders turned to the basilican form and the resultant style, called Romanesque, recalled the ancient building style of Rome. The word describes an architecture heavy and solid, with rounded arches—as opposed to the Gothic style whose spires would later thrust dramatically into the skies of France and Germany (and in Milan's Duomo). For an example of northern, or Tuscan, Romanesque, visit Pisa's cathedral buildings, with their stacked arcades of mismatched columns in the cathedral's facade and wrapping around the famous leaning cylindrical bell tower.

During the Dark Ages and early Middle Ages, painting languished under eastern, Byzantine traditions, which reproduced stylized Madonna and Child and Crucifixion paintings that remained eerily unchanged for centuries. In sculpture, the idiosyncratic Byzantine style gave way to the emotive Gothic carvings exemplified by the **Pisano** clan and their pulpits in Siena and Pisa cathedrals (and in the latter city's baptistry as well).

THE RENAISSANCE From the 14th to the 16th century, the popularity of the Humanist movement in philosophy prompted princes and powerful prelates to patronize a generation of innovative young artists. These painters, sculptors, and architects experimented with new modes in art and broke with static medieval traditions to pursue a greater degree of expressiveness and naturalism. The term *Renaissance* was only later applied to this period in Florence (from which the movement spread to the rest of Italy and Europe).

The Renaissance also inspired a rediscovery and renewal of classical Greek and Latin literature and art and a revitalized interest in exploring man's capabilities. To most of us since then, *Renaissance* has become a label for an era of explosion in science (Galileo), exploration (Columbus, among many others), politics (Machiavelli), religion (the growth of monastic orders in Italy and the Protestants in northern countries), and, most vividly, the arts.

Giotto, in the 1290s and early 1300s, charted a radical course change in Italian, and indeed all, painting when he insisted on rendering the human figure and face with life and warmth in his frescoes in Assisi's Basilica of San Francesco and Padua's Scrovegni Chapel. It was probably an architect, **Filippo Brunelleschi,** in the early 1400s, who first truly grasped the concept of perspective and provided artists with ground rules for creating the illusion of three dimensions on a flat surface. Brunelleschi built Florence's Pazzi Chapel and the church of Santo Spirito and, most famously, raised the dome over Florence's Duomo. His theories helped his contemporaries **Donatello** and **Ghiberti.** These sculptors achieved wonderful effects by using the nascent rules of perspective to produce evocative low reliefs. **Massacio,** who died at 27, drew upon Brunelleschi's findings to produce the first example of painted perspective in his *Trinità* fresco in Florence's Santa Maria Novella, as well as the famous fresco cycle in the Brancacci Chapel of Florence's Santa Maria della Carmine.

The High Renaissance of the late 15th and the early 16th century lasted for only about 25 years. It was driven and dominated by the triumvirate of Michelangelo, Leonardo da Vinci, and Raphael, as each tried to outdo the other (Michelangelo claiming the other two were stealing his ideas, which in the case of the older Leonardo was a bit silly, but in the case of young Raphael probably wasn't far-fetched). **Raphael,** considered Western art's greatest draftsman, produced in his 37 short years a body of work that ignited European painters for generations to come. **Leonardo da Vinci** was a true "Renaissance Man," dabbling his genius in a bit of everything from art to philosophy to science (on paper, he even designed machine guns and rudimentary helicopters). Little of his remarkable painting survives, however, as he often experimented with new pigment mixes that proved to lack the staying power of traditional materials. Leonardo invented such painterly effects as the fine haze of *sfumato,* "a moisture-laden atmosphere that delicately veils . . . forms." Alas, the best example of this effect, his fresco of *The Last Supper* in Milan, is sadly deteriorated, and even the multi-decade restoration saved but a shadow of the fresco's glory. See his early *Annunciation* in Florence's Uffizi Gallery for a better-preserved example.

Pope Julius II both funded **Michelangelo** and drove him to despair. Michelangelo's artistic focus was on the human figure, and he devoutly believed sculpture was the only true expression of that belief, as he showed in his 13-foot *David* in Florence. Though he originally trained as a frescoist before turning to the chisel and marble, he tried everything to void the contract when Julius II ordered him to decorate the Sistine Chapel with paintings. Luckily for us, Michelangelo decided to give the commission his best, and the product influenced an entire generation of painters, inspiring Raphael to new heights and giving rise to the hyperstylized mannerist movement.

The peculiar coincidence of circumstances of the High Renaissance in Italy—the combined force of available money, a philosophy that stated that certain artists had a God-granted genius, and, of course, the spectacular talents of those geniuses—were never to be repeated. The next couple of hundred years brought little but variations on Renaissance themes. The late-16th-century *chiaroscuro* style of **Caravaggio** differed mainly in his insistence on working in a more realistic mode. His paintings reflect, with their renderings of the common man in dramatic contrasts of dark and light, his street-fighter origins.

By the mid-16th century, Charles V of Spain occupied much of Italy. The Spanish laid the Inquisition on full bore and decreed that art was to serve the church alone. While there were indeed talented baroque artists, their heavy religious themes dominate any minor innovations they might have introduced to Italian art.

ON TO THE 20TH CENTURY   By the early 17th century, baroque (one definition says *baroque* is derived from the Portuguese word for "irregular, oversized pearl") influence was creeping in. Baroque architects, including **Bernini** and **Maderno** (who completed St. Peter's) were the pathfinders in European architecture for the next 150 years.

Except for a few rococo (baroque gone awry) architectural designs—**de Sanctis'** Spanish Steps (1726), and **Salvi's** Trevi Fountain (1762)—the 18th to the 20th centuries comprised one long decline in Italian painting, sculpture, and architecture. By the 19th century, Italy had become a learning facility for eager students from all over the world who wanted to learn from the great masters, but Italy made few artistic innovations. In the early 20th century, Italian futurism, in its brief life, directly influenced cubism. Painters **Modigliani** and

De Chirico drew international attention. Modigliani painted undulating, languorous figures, while Giorgio De Chirico, who called his work "metaphysical painting," inspired the early surrealists. In recent years, architect **Pier Luigi Nervi** has designed significant buildings, including his Exhibition Hall in Turin.

Today the Italian eye focuses, profitably for sure, on high fashion (Gucci, Armani, Versace, Ferragamo, Valentino), graphics, and industrial design (from Ferraris to whimsical Alessi coffee pots).

3 From the *Cucina Italiana:* Food & Wine

For Italians, eating is not just something to do for sustenance three times a day. Food is an essential ingredient of the Italian spirit, practically an art form in a place that knows a lot about art. Even when Italy was a poor nation it was said that poor Italians ate better than rich Germans or English or Americans.

Italians pay careful attention to the basics in both shopping and preparation. They know, for instance, which region produces the best onions or choicest peppers and when is the prime time of year to order porcini mushrooms, asparagus, truffles, or wild boar. If they're dining out, Italians expect the same care and pride they put into home cooking—and they get it. There are a lot of wonderful places to eat in Italy, from fancy *ristoranti* to neighborhood *trattorie.*

MEALS

Breakfast is treated lightly—a cappuccino and *cornetto* (croissant) at the corner bar. There are exceptions: many hotels, tired of hearing foreign guests grouse about the paltry morning offerings, have taken to serving sumptuous buffets like those offered in the United States and north of the Alps, complete with ham, cheese, and eggs.

At the big meal of the day (be it **lunch** or **dinner**) portions on a plate may be smaller than visitors are accustomed to, but a traditional meal gets you four full courses: *antipasto, primo, secondo,* and *contorno.* The *antipasto* (appetizer) is often a platter of *salumi* (cold cuts), *bruschette,* or *crostini* (toasted or grilled bread topped with pâté or tomatoes) and/or vegetables prepared in oil or vinegar or perhaps melon and prosciutto. Next is the *primo* (first course), which may be a *zuppa* (soup), *polenta* (a cornmeal mush), *risotto* (a rice dish), or pasta. The *secondo* (entree) may include meat, fish, seafood, chicken, or game, and to accompany it you order a *contorno* (side dish) of vegetables or a salad.

Coffee All Day Long

Italians drink coffee throughout the day, but only a little at a time and often while standing in a bar—and a "bar" in Italy is a place that serves coffee. There's usually liquor available too, but it's the caffeine that draws the customers.

Five types of coffee are popular in Italy. **Demitasse caffè** is straight espresso, downed in one gulp. **Cappuccino** is espresso with an overlay of foamy steamed milk, usually sipped for breakfast with a pastry and never as an after-dinner drink. **Caffè macchiato** is espresso with a wee drop of steamed milk, while **latte macchiato** is a glass of hot milk "stained" with a shot of espresso. **Caffè coretto** is espresso "corrected" with a shot of liquor. **Caffè hag** is decaf. Most Italians hold in disdain the murky watered-down coffee that percolates in offices and kitchens across America, but if you want a big mug like the stuff at home, you'll have to order **caffè Americano.**

At the end of the meal, dig into a *dolce* (dessert)—fruit, gelato (ice cream), tiramisù (sweet cream atop espresso-soaked lady fingers), or *formaggio* (cheese) are traditionally offered.

Meals are usually accompanied by **wine** and a bottle of mineral water (*con gas* or *senza gas*/fizzy or still), and followed by an espresso. (One sure way to alienate an Italian waiter is to order cappuccino after dinner—it's usually drunk only in the morning.) Espresso is often followed by *grappa,* a fiery *digestivo* liqueur made from what's left over after the wine-making process.

Traditionally, a *ristorante* (restaurant) is a bit formal and more expensive than a family-run *trattoria* or *osteria,* but the names are used almost interchangeably these days (trendy, expensive eateries often call themselves *osterie,* and little local joints may aggrandize themselves with the term *ristorante*). Snacks, perhaps a small plate of pasta, can be found in various *tavola calda* (literally "hot table," a kind of tiny cafeteria where prepared hot dishes are sold by weight), *rosticcerie* (a tavola calda with chickens in roasting the window), and some trendy *enoteche* (wine bars).

PASTA

Aside from pizza, pasta is probably Italy's best-known export. It comes in two basic forms: *pastaciutta* (dry pasta), the kind most of us buy at the grocery store, and *pasta fresca* (fresh pasta), the kind that most self-respecting establishments in Italy, even those of the most humble ilk, will probably serve.

Pastaciutta comes in long strands including *spaghetti, linguine, trenette;* and in tubular *maccheroni* (macaroni) forms such as *penne* (pointed pasta quills) or *rigatoni* (fluted tubes), to name only a few. Pasta fresca is made in broad sheets, then cut into shapes used in lasagna, cannelloni, and the stuffed pastas tortelloni and ravioli or into noodles ranging from wide papparedelle to narrow fettuccine. If you sense that this isn't even a dent in the world of pasta, you're right: There are more than 600 pasta shapes in Italy.

WINE

Italy, with the right kind of terrain and the perfect amounts of sun and rainfall, happens to be ideal for growing grapes. Centuries ago, the Etruscans had a hearty wine industry, and the ancient Greeks bolstered it by transplanting their vine cuttings to Italy's southlands. And it was Italy, under the Romans, that first introduced the vine and its possibilities to France and Germany. Today, Italy exports more wine to the rest of the world than any other country. But there's plenty left at home from which to choose—more than 2,000 wines are produced in Italy.

The DOC/DOCG/IGT System

More than 30 years ago, the Italian government instituted Denominazione di Origine Controllata, or **DOC,** a system that is akin to the French Appellation Controlée and certifies a wine's quality and place of origin. Some years later, a second, higher category was ordained, Denominazione di Origine Controllata e Garantita, or **DOCG,** to denote wines of particularly high quality. Recently **IGT** (Indicazione Geografica Tipica) was introduced so that modest local wines would be labeled as such. This leaves the title **vino da tavola** (table wine) to be used as it has for years—on bottles of superior "super" wines, often made using foreign grape varietals like merlot, cabernet, and chardonnay. Although highly complex and structured wines, these *supervini* fell outside the strict traditional DOC or DOCG categories.

Wines of the north are generally drier than those of the south, which are usually sweeter and often quite a bit higher in alcohol volume (more sun equals more sugar). Each region has different growing conditions, and so each has its own special wines. **Piemonte** is known for its heavy reds, including Barolo, Barbaresco, Barbera, and Grignolino, as well as sparkling white Asti Spumante; the **Veneto,** for Valpolicella and Bardolino reds and, among whites, Pinot Grigio and Soave; **Emilia-Romagna,** for white Albano and red Lambrusco.

Tuscany is one of Italy's most important wine producers, with reds like Chianti Classico, powerful Brunello di Montalcino, and refined Vino Nobile di Montepulciano (along with the famed white Vernaccia di San Gimignano); **Umbria** weighs in with Orvieto white and Montefiascone red; the **Marches** produce a compelling white called Verdicchio.

Montefiascone and Frascati, both whites, come from the vines that flourish on the hills around **Rome;** Ischia and Lacryma Christi have a delicate, somewhat sulfurous taste, due to the volcanic soil of **Campania; Apulia** is home to both white and red Locorotondo and the earthy red Salice Salentino. **Sicily** is known for its sweet Marsala, an aperitif, as well as Corvo whites and reds.

Throughout Italy, and especially in Tuscany, you're likely to encounter **Vin Santo (sacred wine),** made from grapes that are partly dried on the vine, then dried on racks before being pressed and aged in tiny oak *barriques.* This sweet wine may be drunk alone, but more often, it's used for dunking hard almond cookies called *biscotti* as a dessert. **Grappa,** made from the skins, seeds, vines, and other remnants at the bottom of the pressing barrel, is a fiery digestivo drunk at the end of a meal. An **amaro** is a bitter liqueur drunk in midafternoon or before or after a meal.

Italy in Depth

Index

General Index

FROMMER'S® COMPLETE TRAVEL GUIDES

Alaska
Amsterdam
Argentina & Chile
Arizona
Atlanta
Australia
Austria
Bahamas
Barcelona, Madrid & Seville
Beijing
Belgium, Holland &
  Luxembourg
Bermuda
Boston
British Columbia & the
  Canadian Rockies
Budapest & the Best of Hungary
California
Canada
Cancún, Cozumel & the
  Yucatán
Cape Cod, Nantucket &
  Martha's Vineyard
Caribbean
Caribbean Cruises & Ports
  of Call
Caribbean Ports of Call
Carolinas & Georgia
Chicago
China
Colorado
Costa Rica
Denmark
Denver, Boulder & Colorado
  Springs
England
Europe

European Cruises & Ports of Call
Florida
France
Germany
Greece
Greek Islands
Hawaii
Hong Kong
Honolulu, Waikiki & Oahu
Ireland
Israel
Italy
Jamaica
Japan
Las Vegas
London
Los Angeles
Maryland & Delaware
Maui
Mexico
Montana & Wyoming
Montréal & Québec City
Munich & the Bavarian Alps
Nashville & Memphis
Nepal
New England
New Mexico
New Orleans
New York City
New Zealand
Nova Scotia, New Brunswick &
  Prince Edward Island
Oregon
Paris
Philadelphia & the Amish
  Country
Portugal

Prague & the Best of the Czech
  Republic
Provence & the Riviera
Puerto Rico
Rome
San Antonio & Austin
San Diego
San Francisco
Santa Fe, Taos & Albuquerque
Scandinavia
Scotland
Seattle & Portland
Shanghai
Singapore & Malaysia
South Africa
Southeast Asia
South Florida
South Pacific
Spain
Sweden
Switzerland
Texas
Thailand
Tokyo
Toronto
Tuscany & Umbria
USA
Utah
Vancouver & Victoria
Vermont, New Hampshire
  & Maine
Vienna & the Danube Valley
Virgin Islands
Virginia
Walt Disney World & Orlando
Washington, D.C.
Washington State

FROMMER'S® DOLLAR-A-DAY GUIDES

Australia from $50 a Day
California from $70 a Day
Caribbean from $70 a Day
England from $70 a Day
Europe from $70 a Day

Florida from $70 a Day
Hawaii from $70 a Day
Ireland from $60 a Day
Italy from $70 a Day
London from $85 a Day

New York from $80 a Day
Paris from $80 a Day
San Francisco from $60 a Day
Washington, D.C.,
  from $70 a Day

FROMMER'S® PORTABLE GUIDES

Acapulco, Ixtapa &
  Zihuatanejo
Alaska Cruises & Ports
  of Call
Amsterdam
Australia's Great Barrier Reef
Bahamas
Baja & Los Cabos
Berlin
Boston
California Wine Country
Charleston & Savannah
Chicago

Dublin
Hawaii: The Big Island
Hong Kong
Houston
Las Vegas
London
Los Angeles
Maine Coast
Maui
Miami
New Orleans
New York City
Paris

Phoenix & Scottsdale
Portland
Puerto Rico
Puerto Vallarta, Manzanillo &
  Guadalajara
San Diego
San Francisco
Seattle
Sydney
Tampa & St. Petersburg
Vancouver
Venice
Washington, D.C.

FROMMER'S® NATIONAL PARK GUIDES

Family Vacations in the
  National Parks
Grand Canyon

National Parks of the American
  West
Rocky Mountain
Yellowstone & Grand Teton

Yosemite & Sequoia/
  Kings Canyon
Zion & Bryce Canyon

FROMMER'S® MEMORABLE WALKS

Chicago
London

New York
Paris

San Francisco
Washington, D.C.

FROMMER'S® GREAT OUTDOOR GUIDES

Arizona & New Mexico
New England

Northern California
Southern California & Baja

Southern New England
Vermont & New Hampshire

FROMMER'S® BORN TO SHOP GUIDES

Born to Shop: France
Born to Shop: Hong Kong,
   Shanghai & Beijing

Born to Shop: Italy
Born to Shop: London

Born to Shop: New York
Born to Shop: Paris

FROMMER'S® IRREVERENT GUIDES

Amsterdam
Boston
Chicago
Las Vegas
London

Los Angeles
Manhattan
New Orleans
Paris
San Francisco

Seattle & Portland
Vancouver
Walt Disney World
Washington, D.C.

FROMMER'S® BEST-LOVED DRIVING TOURS

America
Britain
California
Florida

France
Germany
Ireland
Italy

New England
Scotland
Spain
Western Europe

THE UNOFFICIAL GUIDES®

Bed & Breakfasts in California
Bed & Breakfasts in
   New England
Bed & Breakfasts in the
   Northwest
Bed & Breakfasts in Southeast
Beyond Disney
Branson, Missouri
California with Kids
Chicago
Cruises
Disneyland
Florida with Kids

Golf Vacations in the
   Eastern U.S.
The Great Smoky &
   Blue Ridge Mountains
Inside Disney
Hawaii
Las Vegas
London
Mid-Atlantic with Kids
Mini Las Vegas
Mini-Mickey
New England with Kids

New Orleans
New York City
Paris
San Francisco
Skiing in the West
Southeast with Kids
Walt Disney World
Walt Disney World for
   Grown-ups
Walt Disney World for Kids
Washington, D.C.
World's Best Diving Vacations

SPECIAL-INTEREST TITLES

Frommer's Britain's Best Bed & Breakfasts and
   Country Inns
Frommer's France's Best Bed & Breakfasts and
   Country Inns
Frommer's Italy's Best Bed & Breakfasts and
   Country Inns
Frommer's Caribbean Hideaways
Frommer's Adventure Guide to Australia &
   New Zealand
Frommer's Adventure Guide to Central America
Frommer's Adventure Guide to India & Pakistan
Frommer's Adventure Guide to South America
Frommer's Adventure Guide to Southeast Asia
Frommer's Adventure Guide to Southern Africa
Frommer's Gay & Lesbian Europe
Frommer's Exploring America by RV
Hanging Out in England

Hanging Out in Europe
Hanging Out in France
Hanging Out in Ireland
Hanging Out in Italy
Hanging Out in Spain
Israel Past & Present
Frommer's The Moon
Frommer's New York City with Kids
The New York Times' Guide to Unforgettable
   Weekends
Places Rated Almanac
Retirement Places Rated
Frommer's Road Atlas Britain
Frommer's Road Atlas Europe
Frommer's Washington, D.C., with Kids
Frommer's What the Airlines Never Tell You